7.18.78

THE MUSIC LOCATOR

Edited by *v. 1*
W. Patrick Cunningham
with introductory chapters by
W. Patrick Cunningham
Eileen E. Freeman
William Burns
Cover design by
George F. Collopy

© Copyright 1976 by Resource Publications
P.O. Box 444, Saratoga, CA 95070. All rights reserved. 78 8359 7

Library of Congress Catalog Card Number 76-24220
ISBN 0-89390-001-X

Preface

Worship in the Judaeo-Christian tradition is songful prayer in common. Probably no other world religious tradition has such a rich variety of textual and musical art, expressive of the many moods of people in adoration of God. Awe, repentance, exultation, and every other human emotion are lifted to God in song.

Since there are well over 12,500 currently published titles of religious music, we see the typical parish or prayer community settling on a fairly small number of compositions (one to three hundred) which they learn well and use regularly in worship. Sources for the selection of these titles are numerous, and vary with the creativity, time, energy, and general resourcefulness of those charged with leading the music program.

In the past, the chore of researching available music for a particular theme was virtually impossible to do thoroughly. Even so, many skilled and energetic musicians have done superb jobs of following the efforts of well over one hundred publishers of religious music, and have more than met the needs of the parishes they serve.

It is the purpose of this book to make this research effort easier, and to give the typical music person the full range of available titles to choose from when searching for music to fill out a particular music program. This publication is a unique source of information of great value to those who need and use music. The presence of a conventional alphabetic listing of song titles in these pages can deceive readers about the true value of this book. As with any other reference book, the alphabetical listing can help trace music about which something is already known. In many cases, illegal and incomplete reproductions of musical compositions have left only a title or perhaps the text of a song, with no reference to the composer or publisher, and often not even the melody or appropriate chord notations. The alphabetical section of this book can help resolve this kind of dilemma. It can help to re-establish the connection between title, composer, and publisher of a song.

But the true value of this book is the revolutionary power it gives to those who choose music for worship. In the past, normal limits of human consciousness have restricted choices to those titles with which individual musicians were familiar. Even for musicians who vigorously researched available titles, much of the familiarity was the result of random promotional efforts by publishers, the "inertia" of local traditions, their own original work, or other subjective factors. The Music Locator removes these limitations. Now a musician may select from virtually every published composition available which fits the theme or desired use. The Music Locator breaks down over 12,500 compositions into manageable chunks as it sorts the titles into musical style, and then again into thirty-six common thematic or use categories.

The Music Locator is a novel application of modern computers to the unlikely field of music ministry. Just as computers extended the capability of scientists and engineers so that they could travel to the moon and beyond, so The Music Locator extends the capability of ministers of music to cover the full range of music available for their use.

Given the infinite variety of parish music situations which occur, it will not be long until a reader encounters a need for a song and finds that no category exists which clearly points out songs for that situation. Such a discovery does not mean that the book is useless, nor even that it is useless for the problem at hand. The Music Locator begins with a series of chapters of introductory material which will help readers to use the book for all religious music situations. Thus, when you grab for The Music Locator, flip through it for a few minutes, and fail to find it of any value; do not cast it aside. Instead, take a few more moments and read through the section entitled "Introduction". It will give you some fresh ideas. 2019369

The entire introductory section contains valuable information, and a few moments invested in reading it will be amply repaid in efficient use of the book for its intended purposes.

A Living Resource The Music Locator is as much a concept as it is a product. This book is incomplete. There are titles that are not included. There are several reasons for this. First of all, music is a living art form. New songs are being written, recorded, and published every day. In fact, before the first copies of this book are opened, its publisher will have released, or approved for release, several titles which are not listed here. Also, we have intentionally omitted music over 56 years old, since most such music is in the public domain. Another problem is the coordination of information from, and participation of, over a hundred publishers of various sizes from all over the country. A third problem is the human factor in the editorial process. All of these problems can be overcome, but it takes time. Thus, we have decided to present what we have gathered over the past eighteen months, and allow the omissions to be released in a supplement along with new titles, at a later time.

WHAT TO DO IF THE TITLE YOU SEEK IS NOT LISTED
If you are chasing down a song and you do not find it in the alphabetical listing in this book, please send us as much information as you have available: title, composer (if possible), and where you obtained knowledge of the song. We will continue the research and will include the title in the next supplement produced. Include a stamped, self-addressed envelope and $1.00 per title if you wish an individual reply.

Biographies

W. Patrick Cunningham is director of music at Blessed Sacrament parish in San Antonio, Texas. He is also chairman of the Archdiocesan Music Commission for the Archdiocese of San Antonio. Mr. Cunningham teaches at Central Catholic High School in San Antonio. He is both a composer of liturgical music and a writer on contemporary religious problems. His writings have appeared in several religious periodicals.

Eileen E. Freeman is a scripture scholar, musician, and liturgist. She is employed by the Diocese of Fort Wayne — South Bend, Indiana where she works with parish musicians, and simultaneously studies for her PhD in Scripture at Notre Dame, and for her MA in Music at St. Joseph's College, Rensselaer, Indiana.

William Burns is the editor and publisher of MODERN LITURGY magazine, a periodical which provides music, visual arts, example services, and creative resources for worship. He has worked with Resource Publications since 1973, and has been involved with parish music programs and religious education for over fifteen years.

Table of Contents

Preface 3
Introduction 7
Music and Liturgy 13
Planning Music for the Liturgy of the Word 18
Planning Music for the Liturgy of the Eucharist 21
Planning Music for Other Celebrations 23
A Copyright Primer 26
Categorized Index of Titles 31
   Music for Formal Liturgy 31
   Seasonal Music 38
   Thematic Music 55
Alphabetical Index of Titles (With Category Codes) . 99
Composer Index 143
Publishers of Religious Music 186

Introduction

The use of sacred music in the liturgy of any community helps to give variety to the celebration. It is often said that the psalms are the "lifeblood" of the Book of Leviticus. The same can be said for the music in any rite. Music adds the dimension of purposeful, ordered variety to the sometimes stark forms of ritual. One might say that music is to rite as the charismatic is to the institutional life of a church. Neither is quite adequate by itself. Together, music and ritual form a powerful dyad that makes worship a "humanly attractive experience". Together, they symbolize the everlasting liturgy of the kindgom of God, and can even be said to prepare the worshiper for this liturgy.

Worship patterns in many congregations have changed, sometimes dramatically, in the past twenty years. The human environments themselves have changed; so that human concerns, which show up in worship, may be quite different today from their counterparts of even ten years ago. Long ago, for instance, there was not much praying for clean air and water. Today these problems may be addressed in worship. New emphases in theology, perhaps on the liberation of the human spirit or on the transformed humanity of Christ, may change approaches to worship. Changed rites themselves create new needs, for instance, for the responsorial psalms or litanies of petition.

As a result, the planning team of any church is now challenged to expand the musical repertoire of choir and congregation. This is not done out of an unconditional love for novelty, but out of a desire to meet the worship needs of the praying congregation. Perhaps the most balanced approach to this need is to maintain strong links with the living traditions of the church, while introducing tasteful and theologically sound new music in reasonable quantity.

This index offers users a unique opportunity to do both. New arrangements of familiar hymns may be found by title or category. Traditional music is distinguished by style (not copyright date) from contemporary liturgical pieces. The availability of recordings is indicated; these can speed up the learning of music.

The introduction of popular and folk styles into the liturgies of mainstream denominations has created particular repertoire problems. In the beginning, the small number of publishers and titles in this field created a situation where boredom was always a danger. Today, there are thousands of "folk" titles, making it possible to change music too quickly, or even to be totally ignorant of much good music.

This index gives the musical planner much flexibility in this new area of folk music. Varying liturgical seasons can now be filled with many different good songs, either commercially purchased or legally reprinted. "Old" and recent folk music can be located with equal ease. Publishers can now be contacted for both permissions and new products with little trouble.

The Overall Structure of The Music Locator The next chapter surveys the liturgical music field, and provides the background information necessary for sound planning of music for worship.

The following chapter presents essential information on the concept of copyright law and the responsibilities which rest on those who use creative works. Since the reference information in this book virtually eliminates ignorance of ownership as an excuse for illegal use of religious music, this section is offered as a source of information on how to proceed to set things right between your prayer community and the composers and publishers of sacred music.

The rest of the volume is made up of song titles, composers, publishers, and availability and category information on each title. Each song title is listed precisely three times in this book, once in the alphabetical listing, once in the composer listing, and once again in the particular category and style section in which it has been placed. The major indexes are:

1. The Categorized Index. This is the heart of *The Music Locator,* and is actually a collection of about 180 sub-listings, based on the liturgical use of each song, and on the musical style of the piece. Since the greatest value of the book is in this section, all available information about each title is listed with the title here.

2. The Alphabetical Listing. This index is a straightforward listing of every title in alphabetical order. Along with the title are codes which identify the publisher, song style, and primary use category. Other information on each title can then be found in the Categorical Index.

3. The Composer Index. This section lists each composer and each title alphabetically by composer name. The titles may then be looked up in the other sections for more information.

4. The Publisher Index. Each title listed in *The Music Locator* is accompanied by a three letter identification for the publisher of the song. The publisher index lists each publisher twice. One time the publisher is listed in a section with the identification codes in alphabetical order, and the other listing gives the publisher alphabetically by publisher name.

Finding a Song in The Music Locator

1. If you know the title of the song, look it up in the Alphabetical Index. If you find the title listed, turn to the style/category listing indicated with the title to find the complete listing for the song. In the case of songs with many arrangements or composers (such as Psalm 150), the publisher code or song style may help locate the exact version you have in mind. If the song title begins the "The" or "A", you may find it alphabetically under T or A, or perhaps listed alphabetically by the second word in the title. If, after checking this listing, you do not find the title you seek, and you are relatively sure you have the correct title of the song, then please send us the title, composer (if possible), and explain where you discovered the song. We will continue the search and will include such titles in the next supplement issued. For a personal reply enclose $1.00 per title and a stamped, self-addressed envelope.

2. If you know the composer of a song, and would recognize the title you wish if you saw it, then look up the composer's name, alphabetically, in the Composer Index. The composer's name is listed here, once for each title in the book. Be sure to check for different spellings or forms of a composer's name. Upon finding the title you seek, look that up in the alphabetical listing to find the song style and category. Finally, look up the title again in the categorized listing to find the complete listing. No inconvenience is intended here. It was necessary to compromise between small print, multiple listings, and more pages.

3. If you do not know the title or the composer, but you know some of the words of the song; or if you know the general theme of the song, or the primary use to which it would be put in worship; then check the categorized listing in the style you need, to see if one of the titles listed is the one you seek. For example, "We Are One in the Spirit" is a line from Peter Scholtes's hymn entitled *They'll Know We Are Christians*. Check for this song in the categorical listing under category TR or TU, or *hymns to the Spirit* (category SS).

Finding Songs in The Music Locator *The Music Locator* is of greatest value as a planning tool. Thus, the greatest value is derived not so much from looking up songs with which you are already familiar as it is from looking up song use and style categories to discover new or different titles which you can investigate for use in your music program. It is in this way that you put our computer to work for you in sorting through thousands of published titles to obtain the most objective list of candidate songs to meet your particular needs. Five song style categories have been assigned, as listed below.

Song Style Category	Code
Children's Music	C
Folk	F
Gospel	G
Contemporary Liturgical Music	L
Traditional Sacred Music	T

If you seek music which may cross these style lines, you may wish to check several style listings. After all, you may think of a song as being in the "folk" style, while the composer may wish it categorized as "contemporary liturgical music", or "Gospel".

In general, these categories were supplied by music publishers. There are nearly 300 children's songs listed here (style C). The folk style (F) includes blues, pop, rock, jazz, and country western music as well — over 1500 titles. Gospel style music (G) was abundant enough to rate a category of its own, with over 1500 titles listed.

Most publishers chose to classify their music as either contemporary liturgical music (L), or as traditional religious music (T). These two categories divide equally over 9000 titles. Much of the music listed as "L" is suitable for guitar and small group use, so folk musicians should check both "C" and "L" categories, in addition to "F".

The categorized listing of titles has been organized into four major sections to facilitate its use in planning music:

Music for Liturgy	(L)
Seasonal Music	(S)
Thematic Music	(T)
Collections and instrumental Music	(Z)

Within these major sections, the songs have been further separated into sub-categories which follow a logical, chronological, or alphabetic sequence.

The category code is made up of two characters. The first (left) character classifies the title into a general group (L, S, T, or Z), while the second character further classifies the title in logical sequence within the larger grouping.

Music for Liturgy (L)
This category includes music for each part of a formal Roman liturgy, but much of the music in this section may be used in other situations. The sub-categories and codes are listed below:

Category	Code
Entrance Processional Songs	LA
Petitions (Lord Have Mercy)	LB
Glorias	LC
Responsorial Psalms	LD
Acclamations (General)	LE
Gospel Acclamations (Alleluia)	LF
Gospel Acclamations (Lenten)	LG
Litanies for the Prayer of the Faithful	LH
Acclamations (Holy)	LI
Memorial Acclamations	LJ
Acclamations (Great Amen)	LK
Lord's Prayers (Our Father)	LL
Petitions (Lamb of God)	LM
Communion Processional Songs	LN
Communion and Eucharistic Hymns	LO
General Processional Songs	LP

Seasonal Hymns (S)

Music in this section is appropriate for use at its logical time in the cycle of the liturgical year. The sub-categories are:

Category	Code
Advent Hymns, Anthems, Songs	SA
Christmas Hymns and Carols	SC
Lenten Hymns and Songs	SL
Easter Hymns (Hymns of Resurrection)	SR
Pentecostal and Holy Spirit Songs	SS

Thematic Music (T)

The music in this section is the most abundant, and at the same time the most difficult to classify. Twelve sub-categories were assigned; and music which came in uncategorized, or which was not readily categorizable by title alone, was assigned to the "General" sub-category — listed at the end of the section (category TX). The full group of categories is given below (note that the second letter of the code can be associated with the first letter of a word in the name for the category):

Category	Code
Music for Baptisms	TB
Music for Confirmation or Religious Commitment	TC
Music for Funerals	TF
Hymns for or about Jesus Christ	TJ
Hymns about the Kingship of God	TK
Hymns about Mary the Mother of Jesus	TM
Hymns of Offering	TO
Patriotic Hymns	TP
Hymns of Peace and Reconciliation	TR
Hymns of Praise and Thanksgiving	TT
Prayers for Unity	TU
Music for Weddings	TW
General Topical Songs	TX

Collections and Instrumental Music (Z)

This section lists two sub-categories:

Category	Code
Collections of Hymns	ZA
Instrumental Music (collected and otherwise)	ZB

To further enhance the usability of this categorized index, the titles in each sub-category are broken into the five song style categories listed above (C, F, G, L, or T).

The categorized listing also contains other information which may prove valuable in tracking down music. The year of copyright is listed (when available) to help distinguish between versions with the same title. Also, availability information is listed for the titles:

M — indicates availability of sheet music

B — indicates a booklet is available

R — indicates the song is available on a recording

L — indicates that reprint permission may be arranged for by writing the publisher

These codes are transcribed from information made available by individual publishers; and this information is incorrect in some cases, but we felt it to be worth including as a guide. Since publishers often license other firms to make and sell recordings of their music, many songs may be available on records, even if the listing does not so indicate.

A final aid to selecting music is the brief comment off to the side of each listing. Comments made here indicate the complexity of the song, the version which is available, and multiple parts (when available). Also, after the titles to many pieces, a parenthetical remark has been added to describe the piece in some way, or to indicate the level of difficulty or the instrumentation. The abbreviations used throughout are usually clear from their context. A list of abbreviations appears below.

Abbreviations used in this index

A CAP = a capella number: choir or congregation without accompaniment

brs, brass = brass choir, usually 2 trumpets, horn and trombone

bs = string bass required

cant = cantor required for performance

d = difficult number; not to be attempted without good choir

des or ds = descant, either optional or required

e = easy number; usually no polyphony, straightforward

fl = flute accompaniment or descant; usually oboe can substitute

full = compulsory divisi passages (eg. SSAATB or SATTBB) or double choir required for performance

guit = guitar accompaniment required or optional; this is assumed on most folk-style songs

ICET = text from the International Committee on English in the Liturgy. Especially for Mass parts, this can be important. Usually copyrights after 1969 have this translation.

m or md = moderately difficult music; experienced choirs have no trouble

me = moderately easy music

2mel = two melodies in the piece

ob = oboe accompaniment or descant; flute or recorder substitutes

org = compulsory organ accompaniment (piano can sometimes substitute); organ solo

perc = percussion (bells, timpani, drums)

pian or pi = compulsory piano accompaniment (substitute an organ with discretion). Harpsichord can substitute in baroque music (before 1800)

2pt, 3pt = equal voices, usually either SSA or TTB

round = song can be executed as a round or canon, the melody being repeated after a given number of melodies by a second or third group within the choir or congregation.

SAB = mixed chorus of three parts; good when there are few men

SATB = mixed chorus of four parts

SSAA = full female chorus of four parts

solo = solo voice needed. Usually indicated by part what the range required is (S, A, T, or B)

tmb = trombone

tpt(s) = trumpet(s)

trad = traditional arrangement

U or UNIS = unison chorus or congregational song

USATB = congregation or youth choir and SATB choir

VAR = various arrangements available (eg. SATB and SAB); write publisher or see a music dealer if in doubt. Usually anthems are availabe in SATB, and other arrangements

viol(s) = violin(s) needed. Since the violin is a C instrument, it *may* be possible to substitute it for a flute or oboe, or vice-versa

+ = additional accompaniment (organ, piano, guitar are usually indicated in the title) is needed

These simplified abbreviations are intended to help the user to find the kinds of songs he or she needs more quickly.

Many assumptions were made in the editorial process, and we can not be responsible for mistaken categorization or availability information. For example, it was assumed that psalms submitted were numbered according to the Hebrew Psalter, as is the case with all modern translations of the Scriptures. If the Vulgate numbering was followed by a publisher and not so noted, then a mistake in category may have resulted.

SOME SUGGESTIONS AND EXAMPLES The following examples give the flavor of *The Music Locator* and show how it can be used to search for appropriate music for several situations. Give it a try yourself. You will find that it gives you a powerful handle on religious music.

Theme	References
Ascension	See Hymns of Praise and Thanksgiving (TT) and Easter Hymns (Hymns of Resurrection) (SR)
Bishops	Entrance Songs (LA), or Hymns of Commitment (TC)
Candlemas (Purification)	See Christmas music (SC), Songs of Peace and Reconciliation (TR), Music for Baptism (TB)
Catechetical Songs	Check all children's songs and category TX for possibilities. See also the specific Seasonal and Thematic Categories for suggestions.
Church Hymns	Any of the Songs of Peace and Reconciliation (TR), Hymns of the Spirit (SS), or Hymns of the Resurrection (SR)
Coming of Christ	See Resurrection Songs (SR), Kingship of God (TK), also Psalms in Category TR and Advent Hymns (SA)
Confirmation	See Hymns of Religious Commitment (TC), Songs of the Holy Spirit (SS), Baptismal Hymns (TB), Hymns of Praise and Thanksgiving (TT)

Evensong (Vespers)	See Hymns of Reconciliation (TR); also since this is a night prayer, some music from TF may be appropriate
Holy Orders	Hymns of Religious Commitment (TC), Hymns of Peace and Reconciliation (TR), Entrance Processional Hymns (LA) and Responsorial Psalms (LD)
Morning Praise	See General Topical Hymns (TX), Hymns of Praise and Thanksgiving (TT), Hymns of Commitment (TC), Songs for Advent (SA) and other seasonal hymns
Mother's Day	See Hymns about Mary the Mother of Jesus (TM) and also General Topical Hymns (TX)
New Year	See Christmas Songs (SC), General Topical Songs (TX), Hymns of Commitment (TC), and Hymns of Praise and Thanksgiving (TT)
Penance	Any Hymn of Peace and Reconciliation (TR) or Psalms from LD. See also Hymns of Praise and Thanksgiving (TT)
Recessional	See General Processional Hymns (LP), Hymns of Praise and Thanksgiving (TT), and Hymns of Religious Commitment (TC)
Reformation Sunday	Hymns of Peace and Reconciliation (TR), Hymns of Praise and Thanksgiving (TT), Songs of Religious Commitment (TC) (*A Mighty Fortress* is in Category TR)
Saints' Feasts	See General Topical Hymns (TX)

Other Sources *The Music Locator* will meet uniquely the needs of many musicians in churches throughout English-speaking countries. There are other publications and indexes available, but they are the more conventional reference-style indexes. One source of valuable reference information to supplement this volume is the publisher catalog that each publisher makes available.

Organ Plus, edited by Leslie P. Spelman, indexes about 700 compositions for organ and various instruments. It is available from the American Guild of Organists at $2.00 per copy. Many of these compositions are also indexed in *The Music Locator.*

Music in Print contains an alphabetical listing of sacred choral music and organ music currently in print. It is very thorough and very expensive, but will have some reference value to religious musicians. A good library will have this publication.

The Index to Song Books was compiled by Robert Leigh, and published in 1964. It is available from P.O. Box 4054, Stockton, CA 95204, but your library should have a copy. It contains secular and religious song titles which appear published in well known collections or songbooks.

Songs In Collections: An Index was published in 1966 by Desiree de Charms and Paul F. Breed, of 1435-37 Randolph, Detroit, MI 48226. This is another index of collected songs, newer and much more complete than Leigh's collection, but international in scope. It contains a special section on carols. Again, check your library for this since its primary value is reference.

The Popular Song Index, by Patricia Pate Havlice, was published in 1975 by The Scarecrow Press, Inc., of Metuchen, NJ. This is the newest and most complete index we could find and its purpose is to provide a tool for finding the words to pop tunes, spirituals, etc. It indexes 301 collections published between 1940 and 1972.

The Song Index (1926), and *Song Index Supplement* (1934), by Minnie Earl Scars and Phyllis Crawford, are other standard references. These are now very old volumes, but they are not without value for those tracking down older songs.

Several older indexes exist which list exhaustively traditional hymns from published hymnals. No attempt has been made to include such music in this book unless a special arrangement or revised text has brought it back out of the public domain.

A good reference work to consult, one available at most record stores for in-store work, is the Schwann catalog. An up-dated listing of recorded classical music by composer can be found there, along with the companies that record the same.

Acknowledgements A publication of this magnitude is not possible without the cooperation and support of large numbers of people.

All of the music publishers listed in this book have shown a remarkable spirit of cooperation and have provided much assistance in gathering and editing the material.

The editor wishes to acknowledge Donald W. Miller, Elaine Meffin, John Van der Borght, Robert C. Kelleher, Ina R. Belochi and Clifford Defayette who, as data processing students at DeAnza College, Cupertino, California, devoted a great deal of energy to the development of computer programs with which the song data in these pages was processed. I am grateful to Central Catholic High School, San Antonio, Texas for use of some of their facilities during the editing of this volume.

Special thanks are due Regina Whitney for editorial assistance on the introductory chapters, Eileen E. Freeman for her critical suggestions and for contributing the chapter entitled *Planning Liturgical Music,* and also to William Burns for the chapter entitled *A Copyright Primer,* and for his cooperation, support, and assistance in the preparation of this volume for publication. The assistance, patience, and broad knowledge of music of my wife, Carolyn, has been invaluable in the proofing and revising of this work.

W. Patrick Cunningham
San Antonio, Texas
July 1976

Music and Liturgy

I Some Notions of Liturgy Liturgy is the means of worship with which a group of people officially identify themselves. The term derives from two Greek words: *laios*, meaning *people*, and *orge*, meaning *work*. The *laios* of ancient Greece were ordinary people rather than aristocracy. The family of words which derives from *orge* has such diverse meanings as manual labor, working tools, musical or surgical instruments, natural impulse, secret rites or mysteries. Lit-urgy is both means and end, in a way. The means are the natural impulses, the tools one uses such as art and music, and the actual form or rite. The end is the common worship of men and women which draws them together and to God.

Liturgy cannot exist in a vacuum or impersonally. One cannot study the "liturgy" of a group of people; for, in the academic dis-section, one discovers that what he or she is studying is not the liturgy, but merely the ritual, the words and thoughts which liturgy uses. It could even be said that one could not take part in a liturgy not one's "own" and understand it, unless one were able to participate fully. A Roman Catholic congregation would not be doing liturgy if the form they were using were, for example, the Methodist communion service. This does not mean that the Methodist service is bad liturgy, merely that it is not the way of worship with which Catholics identify themselves. For Catholics, the Methodist service is not liturgy, just as for Methodists, the Catholic service is not liturgy. One ought not to separate liturgy from its context in life.

Similarly, one cannot participate in a liturgy by one's self alone. By nature, liturgy is a communal event, just as *laios* is a collective noun. Private prayer is not liturgy, although it may use many of the same means to an end that liturgy uses: ritual symbols and instruments. A person who prays by himself or herself the ritual used in liturgical celebrations is only doing liturgy in a very metaphysical and derived sense. It is exceedingly difficult to celebrate Mass with only the (absent) church universal and the "choirs of heaven" for company! Morning and evening praise liturgies are hollow and empty if only the minister is there to pray.

Liturgy, then, is a word that can only be used correctly in the actual context of worship. A ritual, or service, only becomes liturgy when it is being celebrated by people. Rather than existing as a dissectable entity, static, which one could preserve in a bottle forever, liturgy is by nature always alive, always changing, always whole. As the people who celebrate vary, so does their liturgy within the limits which they set for it.

II Ecumenical Implications Today we speak of some churches as "liturgical" churches and others as non-liturgical churches. In the former we have various Catholic and Orthodox groups, as well as Episcopalian and Lutheran. In the latter group are placed most all of the other Protestant denominations as well as the third stream of Christianity, the Pentecostal churches. This labeling seems to be quite a misnomer. What it does is to ignore the fact that the worship of the "non-liturgical" churches is most always true liturgy. It is their official ways of worshiping as a people. The definition of liturgy in this context would imply that liturgy means a particular type of ritual and symbols used to celebrate the Eucharist. In the Catholic, Orthodox, Episcopalian, and Lutheran traditions, the Eucharistic celebration is the norm around which people gather to worship. Moreover these traditions make use of symbols, of gestures, of postures, of art, etc., which are found less frequently in other traditions where the service of the Word (in myriad forms) is the nucleus around which people liturgize. To misuse the term liturgy by identifying it with the rituals used to celebrate it may be a good example of short-cut jargon, but it is inaccurate.

Liturgy encompasses ritual, but it cannot be identified with it. Perhaps it is cumbersome to make the distinction (if it needs to be made at all) between "churches where the Eucharistic celebration is normative" and "churches where the Word service is normative" — yet this is the case. In this preface, where the term liturgy is used, it refers to the act of worship of a group of people. *Ritual* refers to the actual words of the service which is being celebrated by the liturgical community. *Media* designates the audio-visual and tactile stimuli used when a community liturgizes. *Symbol* refers to ritual and media when they have other layers of meaning below their surfaces.

Planning Liturgical Music

I Introduction Music alone, out of all those many elements that go into liturgy, is or can be, ritual, media and symbol. Art may be both media and symbol, but it is not ritual. Ritual, since it was traditionally an oral form, may share in media. The feel or texture of a vestment or of bread is certainly part of media, but not often of symbol, and never of ritual.

Perhaps it is the universality of music that makes it such an integral part of a worshiping community. Sacred music is not primarily a solo activity done in the privacy of one's room. For some people, of course, music does form a real part of personal prayer. Individuals do not usually sing the same type of songs as they do when at liturgy. The priest who celebrates a "private" Mass hardly ever sings the Eucharist, and never adds hymns and canticles. This seems to indicate that the "private" Mass tends away from liturgy as it was defined here. The minister who holds a weekday service to which no one comes will probably not sing the hymns he or she has put up on the hymn board. Sacred music is by nature a communal means of liturgizing.

Sacred music in the context of liturgy involves many different groupings of people (*laios*). In any society there are different roles and parts for people to play: this is also true of liturgical music.

II Responsorial Singing The most ancient type of participation is one in which the assembly sings a response to lines or stanzas sung by an individual or small group. This is called responsorial singing. Until modern times no civilization or group based its celebration of liturgy on books which all held in their hands, and out of which they followed the ritual that they were liturgizing. Perhaps the celebrant or president of the assembly had something written down, but even this did not come until just a few thousand years ago. Societies which are not dependent on print for daily life usually possess tremendous memories and are capable of remembering hundreds, even thousands of musical selections collectively and individually. The monks of Christian Egypt were required to have memorized the entire Psalter and the Gospels — and there were thousands of monks! Since their daily celebrations emphasized the psalms, they needed to know them. Books were scarce, and in any case, one could not read a book at midnight or two a.m. when services often began.

We have largely lost the feel of oral liturgy today. When a hymn is announced, we turn to it mechanically in our hymnals, even if we have sung it a thousand times. Yet if we are asked to learn a very simple musical refrain orally, by hearing it sung and repeating it, we are sometimes helpless. This is because we no longer are used to learning by hearing. College teachers have found that students often have difficulty following the train of their lectures and learning from them; even following simple oral directions has become difficult. Why should we expect anything different in church?

Does this mean that for most Americans at liturgy, responsorial and other forms of orally learned singing are inappropriate and outdated? By no means. Rather it is an idea to strive to reintroduce, as is already being done in many Roman Catholic churches. The benefit of singing responses is tremendous. First, it forces one to turn outward and to pay attention to the person who is teaching the music and who is singing the solo part. To an extent, what should be a communal celebration reaching up and out can become a personal devotion between "me and Jesus". Responsorial singing wakes a person up to the fact that his or her prayer is ultimately tied up with that of a neighbor's. Second, oral singing frees the hands and eyes for better things. Our hymn books have become millstones around our necks. When Catholics give the kiss of peace, they often have to shift books to do so. When they receive the Eucharist, the same hymnal comes between the hands that hold the bread and cup and is an awkward nuisance. In any church, it is next to impossible to hold a baby, pass the collection plate or wave palm branches while juggling a blasted hymnal! Unless told to do so, most people would rather not carry a hymn book when they are processing in the church. Yet they are unused to singing orally from memory. The tension inherent in all this is obvious.

Moreover, to have one's nose glued to a page limits the eyes. Just as our hands bring the tactile medium into range, our eyes should be open to all around us at liturgy, especially to our brothers and sisters around us, their faces and expressions. We all know of at least one church where the whole congregation reads the ritual out of pew books. They follow every word carefully. Just getting eye contact with them is a major hurdle. Sometimes when the response varies from that in their books, they go on reading exactly what is in front of their eyes. The Cantor will teach them the response with only a word or two changed, and will explain the change carefully — and then when the time comes they will sing the words that they see rather than those they heard! One wonders, too, how much visual media is simply never noticed, when people keep their hymnbooks open and look in them all the time. Liturgy is a visible thing, its symbols and media are often visual ones. For it to reach its goal successfully, we must allow the means it uses to touch us.

A third reason why responsorial singing is valuable is that it provides for more flexibility in celebrating the liturgy. Instead of being tied down to what is available in the hymnal, a congregation can use new resources steadily. Only the cantor or schola need learn new music continually — this is his or her function.

In practice we find that responsorial singing is most common in Catholic, Orthodox (and Jewish!) communities. Lutheran, Episcopalian (Eucharist-centered), and Protestant and Pentecostal (Word-centered) groups make more use of hymnody, antiphonal and anthem-type singing. This can be limiting in some cases. For example, in the Eucharistic celebrations of Lutheran and Episcopalian groups, what to sing at Communion is sometimes a problem. If a hymn is scheduled at this time, people must drag their books with them, put them down at the Communion rail, pick them up, and get back to the pews, dodging steps, pews and people. The limited options are memorizing the whole hymn or not singing. Very often the assembly will know the first verse but not the rest. After all, how many of us know the second and third verses of the National Anthem? The singing is therefore much more spotty and sloppy than when the whole community is standing in order, singing the "Old One Hundredth". Often the music director, knowing this, will schedule a choir anthem at this time, and wait until all are in the pews to do a thanksgiving hymn *after* Communion. Too often what could be a fine way for a whole body to give thanks becomes a "me-and-Jesus" affair, because with our eyes on the hymnal, we tend to forget those around us with whom we are giving thanks. Also, the Communion procession itself is of such importance to making liturgy that the people should sing. Responsorial singing solves all these problems. First, all would be able to sing, while the choir, an important group in many churches, could still play an important role. Second, juggling hymnals or weak singing would be eliminated. Third, the tendency to ignore others would be minimized.

It takes patience and practice to accustom a congregation to singing refrains from memory. A congregation will learn better if the person who is teaching them can draw their attention to the words and music of the refrain rather than to that person. The cantor should be imposing enough to command attention, but transparent enough not to block the light of the music. This technique seems to be a personal one. A shadow of it can be acquired through study and practice, but in the end, the most successful teachers have a ministerial charism for it. Some people communicate very well orally. These people include tellers of fairy tales and myths, the aged, and friends whose lengthy family geneology has been passed down for 400 years by word of mouth. The best of these had a gift for telling or singing a tale and making you hear it without getting in the way themselves. They could unconsciously exploit the natural rhythm of words and syllables and so facilitate the learning of what they said. For example

Once upon a time there was a...
rather than
There once used to be a...

The first example has a natural cadence, the second does not. People who always use a lot of fillers in their conversations such as "yeah", "huh", "ya'know", "well", "see", rarely are good natural teachers of music to a congregation. They can discipline themselves to avoid such expressions like the plague, but it is hard work. Such trite language actually prevents people from learning orally. Ask someone who uses fillers to say something and see if you can memorize it complete with fillers. It is very difficult, because we know that fillers mean nothing.

The good teacher always exudes a confident, optimistic air with which a congregation can unconsciously identify. Yet the teacher rarely mentions it. A sentence like, "I'm sure that, well, you can learn this, ah, refrain, because the melody is quite simple, you know." is deadly! A successful cantor *under*whelms an assembly.

More people are writing responsorial music today. When choosing among responsorial type pieces, one must keep certain things in mind. If possible, have someone sing the congregational refrain to you before you learn it yourself. Do the words have a natural rhythm? Does the music fit the natural rhythm of the words? Are the words short enough to be easily memorized? A refrain like:

Glory to God in the highest

is more easily learned than

"Your magnificence is beyond our understanding,
O king of all nations."

Notice that the second example is much longer, contains more difficult words and has no natural rhythm. While the words are acceptable, the music alone will have to bear the burden of rhythm. This will make it more difficult for the less musically gifted to learn. If the cantor cannot learn the refrain after two hearings, a congregation cannot be expected to.

What one group can learn easily, another cannot. Moreover, there are still differences of terminology among different religious bodies. Even if one could find a Presbyterian congregation agreeable enough to try a Marian hymn, the refrain of *Salve Regina*, because of its language and use of Latin would be difficult to teach. So in trying to find good responsorial music for use at liturgy, one should select music that fits not only the occasion, but also the congregation.

III Antiphonal Singing Antiphonal singing involves alternating groups singing parts of a hymn. In the ancient church, the alternation of choirs and/or congregation in singing psalms and hymns was widespread. Today it is rarely practiced in Eucharistic celebrations. However, in liturgies of the Word it does occur and can be used in the Eucharist, too.

The Catholic and Orthodox churches have a definitely liturgical Word service which is celebrated by itself apart from the Eucharist. It is called the Liturgy of the Hours in the Roman tradition, and part of it has endured as Morning Praise and Evensong in other traditions. It is based on the psalms, on hymns, and prayers. As a rule the two halves of the congregation, sometimes assisted by two choirs, alternate in singing verses of a hymn or psalm. The Episcopalian psalm chant makes use of this form of singing. In the Catholic Eucharist, the Word service which precedes it could make use of this technique as an alternative to the responsorial psalm, or as a way to sing psalms.

Advantages to antiphonal singing are numerous. It is not for use as an orally learned method. However, this form does not keep one's eyes buried in a hymnal with the same finality that a six verse hymn does. After every other verse, one's eyes are freed to see; one's mind is freed to focus on the symbols, and one's ears are attuned to what the other choir is singing.

The disadvantage is that since antiphonal singing was originally oral (remember the monks had the psalms memorized) it will only achieve its full potential as a liturgy-facilitator if it is allowed to be oral today. If people are reading their verse, they will unconsciously follow along and read silently what the other choir is singing, rather than *listen* and *hear* what they are singing. This is inimical to really moving antiphonal singing, which is too sophisticated a musical form for most liturgical bodies to practice well. It can, however, be done successfully by using a text that the group knows, like *The Shepherd Psalm* or the *Magnificat*. Since psalm/hymn tunes are repetitive, they are easy to learn if the words are allowed to fall naturally into rhythm. A compromise solution is to print cards for each side, printing only what that half is to sing. This will help them to pay attention to their brothers and sisters in the other choir.

A very simple form of antiphonal singing is one in which the second choir gives back exactly what the first choir or cantor has sung, like an echo, but carried all the way through the piece. This has appeared, not surprisingly, in many folk pieces for worship, designed to be accompanied on guitar or piano. Folk music is essentially oral; once written down it petrifies. Some Black and

Pentecostal types of music also fall into this category. *Oh Happy Day* is a good example. No congregation can learn this very simple piece while looking in a hymn book. It *must* be oral or it dies.

Echo-antiphonal singing can have a sort of snowball effect and should never be done when there is time for only a verse or two. It needs time to get rolling, since it usually starts out slowly and builds. Once people "throw the book away", they get involved with the repetitiveness which is the virtue of this genre (not a negative feature!). It can even have a mesmerizing quality; people begin to pick up emotions and feelings from those around them. I have been to some Pentecostal liturgies in which this type of singing went on non-stop for hours. It was rather reminiscent of the early Church described by St. Ambrose. The Christians barricaded themselves in their churches and sang antiphonal hymns for days and prayed to be delivered from their enemies.

Echo-antiphonal singing can obviously become boring and deadly dull if the lyrics are not sound. Each set is sung twice, so they must have enough content to keep people thinking for two rounds. The music must have a clear rhythm and a good tempo. *The Missa Luba* is one of the best examples of this type of music. Written by and for tribal Africans, it combines insistent rhythm, lively tempo, and the Mass text. One must keep in mind that the *Kyrie Eleison, Gloria, Sanctus* and *Agnus Dei* are antiphonal pieces, and that the first/last are also of the echo type. These are texts well known to Eucharist-oriented groups and can be ideal situations in which to use antiphonal singing.

In teaching antiphonal singing it is necessary to have at least one person to lead each group. They should stand close to the side they lead. The chief of them will introduce the text or if the text is familiar, will teach the music. Unless the congregation is skilled at this type, two leaders are essential to give the congregation security. As in all cases, these cantors must be placed so they can not only be heard, but seen by all. One difficulty in teaching music in churches with a rear or side placed choir is their practical invisibility. One never leads, whether it be a congregation, an orchestra, or a flock of sheep, from behind. Try putting the celebrant in the rear of the church — the response will be minimal. The visual medium is important in sacred music, a fact we too often ignore. It is useless to rebuild the organ if the congregation has no effective musical director that it can see.

Good antiphonal music is not melismatic. It rarely has any long stanzas or lines. It never drags. All of these things destroy the undulating rhythm that flows between the choirs. The above faults are like offshore reefs which break up the waves as they roll ashore and slow their return to the sea. Good antiphonal music creates a sense of unity in diversity and helps ritual, media and symbol to become liturgy.

IV Hymnody The piece of music which is sung in its entirety by a congregation is called a hymn. For centuries this type of music existed side by side with responsorial singing and antiphonal singing. The reformation churches did not invent, but rather popularized the hymn sung by all. In the Roman tradition, liturgical hymns were usually sung by alternating choirs. Hymn singing was designed to bring singing back to the people and away from the professional choirs. In time hymn singing became the dominant type of church music outside of the Catholic tradition.

Within the past century, Catholicism has turned increasingly to hymn singing. Popular hymns used for centuries at various non-liturgical or para-liturgical services were used at the Eucharistic celebrations. Within the past two decades, hymns from the Protestant Eucharistic traditions have been added. A reverse process has also gone on, although to a limited degree, since Catholic hymns were often more clearly denominational than their Protestant counterparts, and were never as numerous.

Hymns are supposed to be the easiest type of sacred music for a congregation, outside of the choir solo. In reality, responsorial or echo-antiphonal singing is easier to learn. What is easy about hymn singing is that when everyone sings together the massed effect is tremendous. Of course it also obviates the difficulty one encounters in antiphonal singing when the two groups are too small to carry the singing and the product is thin. Hymns, however, require a congregation to learn as many as six or seven lines of music, and to read a many-versed text. In our society it dooms those with learning disabilities or functional illiterates to non-participation. It is not that they could not learn the hymn. Children with reading handicaps routinely memorize prodigious amounts of material. It is just that we do not gear hymn teaching to anyone with less than a eighth grade reading ability. Furthermore, having lost the technique of the orally learned hymn, some modern composers have relied less on the natural rhythm of words than on catchy melodies (or even dull melodies with elaborate accompaniments). This makes hymns even harder to learn.

Thousands of hymns exist, some written by masters of the art; most, however, have been written by dabblers in doggerel and rhyming jargonese. Not everything in hymnal or octavo form is good, so one must be very selective. Many hymns easily become trite and syrupy; they have gut appeal but nothing else. These hymns are fatal to a congregation. They provide no nourishment, rather like junk food. In the end, a community fed only with this stuff will become stunted and retarded by malnutrition. However, if they are given substantial hymns to worship with, they can stand a few of the other type, which are frequently among their sentimental favorites. One should never introduce a congregation to a new hymn of dubious value.

V Solo/Choir Pieces Hymnody, responsories, and antiphons are styles of singing. Choirs may sing in all of them, as well as forms like canons, which are echo-antiphons sung at intervals. The uniqueness of the choir is that it often sings in parts, and it is rehearsed, hence, complex but error-free music. Depending on its skill, a choir may do music that the congregation might never even understand, let alone sing.

In most churches, while the choir does, to some extent, support and sustain congregational singing, in reality it is a unique group. It sings many pieces which the congregation is only supposed to listen to and pray with. In this sense it fills some of the vacuum left when the bards and saga-singers vanished from our religious heritage. Rarely, however, is this value of the choir noticed at all. In many churches the choir's anthem is listened with as little care as the sermon. To an outsider not part of that liturgy, it seems as though the choir is performing for an impassive uninvolved audience. It seems that music divides rather than unites. But to the initiate the truth appears: the choir and congregation are intimately co-operating in legitimate musical liturgy. The impassive "audience" is really taking everything in and responding to the choir as did the ancient tribes to their bards. A close bond is formed, not broken, between choir and people. Therefore I say that it is good and valuable for the choir to make their own and unique contribution to liturgy.

Of course the ideal is not always the actual, and the choir has, on any number of occasions, overstepped its role. This is true in Protestant churches and in Catholicism where the choir at one time took over the entire singing function of the Mass. After the Second Vatican Coucil, it seemed for a while as though the trained choir would disappear from Catholicism. The choir had been downgraded to the role of supporting the congregational hymns and singing. Many of them disbanded. Happily, things are returning to an even balance in which the choir can once again sing as a unit in addition to helping the congregation.

The dichotomy that sometimes exists between choir and congregation is not initially caused by too many choir pieces, but by the wrong ones, or anthems sung poorly. They may be tired of hearing the *Hallelujah Chorus* for the twentieth year in a row. They may not understand an anthem sung in another language, or if the words are so poorly articulated as to be unintelligible. A sensitive music minister with a pastoral concern for the congregation can avoid most of the above problems. Of course, the last named flaw can only be corrected by a choir director who knows choral techniques well.

If the above problems are not corrected, the congregation will cease to listen to the choir. In time congregational singing declines and the director, seeing it but not knowing why, decides to do another anthem rather than hear the discouraging sound coming from the pews. Soon the choir is dominating the music and the congregation is reduced to spectator. Generally they turn to a private devotion to try to recover the kinship of spirit they once shared quite naturally with each other in song.

The other extreme is the lazy congregation that has a top-notch choir. Very often they are content to let the choir do everything, and the choir director winds up leading musical performances while the people in the pews watch. The only way to stop this is to limit the choir role until the congregation's role is built up again.

Thousands of the entries in *The Music Locator* are choir pieces. One must be sensitive in choosing them, especially when they are in a foreign language. The choir role is an oral one. To perform their role successfully, they must communicate. To communicate, they must speak in a language the congregation understands. Even English can be a barrier if the idiom is strange. Some religious language is untranslatable between denominations and probably ought to be left alone. The phrase "covered by the Blood" is as hard to explain to a Catholic as "the Sacred Heart of Jesus" is to a Pentecostal, yet neither term represents a theology alien to Catholic or Pentecostal Christianity. Remember that for a song to be in a comprehensive index does not imply anything as to its musical, textual, theological, pastoral or ritual value. That judgement can only be made by the community planning to use it.

Planning Music for the Celebration of the Eucharist

I Introduction What this section will do is sketch the different parts within the Eucharistic liturgy from the point of view of music. The form for the celebration of the Eucharist is relatively stable among those churches which use the Eucharistic liturgy as the norm. Some of what follows may also be useful in para-liturgical services and in Liturgies of the Word. The order of celebration in the Latin Rite of the Roman Catholic Church will be used.

The ritual which is used to celebrate the Eucharist in the Latin Rite and in the Lutheran and Episcopalian churches is divided into two sections. The first section proclaims the Word of God and prays for the needs of the worshiping group. The second section celebrates the Eucharist and culminates in the reception of Communion. This arrangement of things is quite ancient and with certain variations can be traced back to the second century A.D. The Liturgy of the Word was loosely based on the synagogue service in the time of Jesus and has developed from it. Those churches whose liturgical norm is the Word service based on scripture, sermon, and song, are in this stream of tradition. The liturgy of the Eucharist has certain similarities to the Jewish Passover Seder. Most churches that are Word-oriented still celebrate a Eucharistic Memorial occasionally in remembrance of the first Eucharist.

II Beginning at the Beginning
1. Entrance Procession
It is probably tautological to say that every Eucharist must have a beginning. But from the number of liturgies we have all seen in which the celebrant sneaks out into the church to one quick verse of a hymn, the point needs to be made. A liturgy is only as good as its beginning. Generally the time is too short to start off slowly and build. Whatever is important in a liturgy ought to be emphasized in the beginning. In the Latin and other rites a scripture verse called the Introit is appointed for the beginning to set the tone of the liturgy. However, this is omitted often when an entrance hymn is sung; and, instead of reading the Introit, a commentator will read a prosy introduction.

The Entrance Rite is a processional one. It involves movement by its nature. It is important not to truncate it. Unfortunately in Catholicism the Entrance Rite is often looked upon merely as the way the priest gets to the altar. Entrance music is just music to cover shuffling feet and noise. What a tragedy! Processions are important parts of the liturgy. They symbolize the coming, the moving together of the whole body to worship. They have a positive value. Liturgies in which the celebrant slips in from the side are not beginning with a procession at all.

Musically the Entrance Procession should involve the whole congregation. Most often this is done through a hymn. Hymns of gathering, of worship and praise, hymns about the Body of Christ are all appropriate. During the seasons of the church year, hymns appropriate to Advent, Lent, Easter, etc. may be more obvious choices. But hymns are not the only type of congregational singing. They can alternate verses with the choir. They can do a response to choir-led verses. This author has observed that the cantor plus the congregation does not usally have the same effect here as choir plus congregation. The single voice of the cantor does not have the same massiveness of a choir. Another alternative, particularly during Advent and Lent, is to use a solemn instrumental and have the congregation tune in to the whole visual aspect of the Entrance Procession. A choir piece at this time is usually poor planning, since a congregation generally has difficulty in watching a procession and listening to words at the same time. But this is not an absolute. If the procession is being emphasized with media: dance, banners, books, people, etc., let the people focus on the visual rather than ask them to sing. Mixing a brightly visible procession with an unfamiliar congregational hymn loses emphasis on both sides. After all, at how many weddings does the congregation sing while the bride comes down the aisle? They would rather watch, so let them.

It is not necessary to cut off a hymn just because the procession has arrived at the front and taken their places. Most hymns have verses that develop themes and to end them early emasculates the hymn and leaves people with an unfinished feeling. If the hymn is short and the procession long, use an interlude at the end. The important thing to remember is that entrance music is not filler music to cover up a movement and keep people from being "distracted" from prayer. It is music to accompany and enhance that very important rite called the Entrance Procession.

2. Secondary Entrance Rites
During the course of time, various other prayers and songs have been tacked on to the entrance procession and finally sewn permanently into the cloth. Among these are the Confession, Kyrie, and Gloria.

The Confession has several forms in the Latin Rite. When used together with the Kyrie, it can be sung; but usually it is not sung. The most ancient tradition puts the Confession/Reconciliation immediately before Communion. However, in penitential seasons, an instrumental entrance procession followed by a sung penitential rite can be effective. In the Latin Rite, this Confession can be totally omitted and a sprinkling with water substituted. This is always useful and especially appropriate in Advent, Lent, Easter, at Baptisms, whenever the idea of cleansing or washing is important to the liturgy. Try doing the water blessing at the back of the church and combine the procession with the sprinkling, using an appropriate hymn or singing the Gloria.

The Kyrie, whether placed at the beginning of the Eucharistic liturgy or elsewhere, is an echo-antiphonal prayer made up of short invocations. In the Latin Rite, long and elaborate musical settings of it are out of place since they give undue importance to the litany. Good melodies for the Kyrie are short and direct. The Kyrie is like a "cry for help": "Lord, have mercy". If a congregation cannot learn the melody to the Kyrie in only one hearing, the setting may be too elaborate, except on those few days when the liturgy emphasizes repentance.

The Gloria has shifted its position several times over the centuries. In the Latin Rite it is part of the Entrance Procession and preliminary prayers. In other churches it is a thanksgiving hymn after Communion. Both uses have venerable traditions. The Gloria is a hymn, but because of repetitive phrases, it has an antiphonal quality that could be used effectively. A number of responsorial Glorias have been written; this approach works well in many places. In the Latin Rite, the Gloria was originally *the* processional hymn *par excellence*. As time went on it was tacked on permanently to festal Masses outside of Advent and Lent. This means that liturgically the Latin Rite now often has two entrance hymns; a problem of repetition seen elsewhere in the ritual. When feasible, the Gloria makes an excellent hymn for the Entrance Procession.

Many composers have given different interpretations to the Gloria. It can be florid, simple, light, heavy, etc. Many older settings were written for choir alone. Today, the Gloria is part of the congregation's role, and the best settings for choirs will actively involve the congregation. Singing the Gloria at every Eucharist is not wise if the Gloria is normally used at the beginning, since it heavily overloads the opening ceremonies and takes away from the procession and liturgy of the Word. If, however, the Gloria is normally used as a thanksgiving hymn after Communion, it is quite appropriate to sing it often, since song serves to dramatize the community's giving of thanks. The Gloria ought not be recited, since it is first and foremost a hymn.

III Proclamation of the Word
1. Responsorial Psalm
After the opening prayer the readings from scripture begin. These are not normally sung, although in some Eastern liturgies and in the liturgy of the Council of Trent they could be or can be chanted on great feast days.

Between the readings various types of biblical canticles and psalms are usually sung. In the Latin Rite a psalm is sung responsorially by cantor or choir and congregation. There are many varieties to this type of song, but one should keep in mind that the norm of the ritual emphasizes that the text be a psalm or canticle sung responsorially.

It is important to sing the psalm rather than recite it. For one thing the singing gives people a chance to rest their ears from listening to the reading. It is a change of medium. It saves people from having to concentrate so long. Also, singing the psalm gives people a chance to respond positively to the reading. The third reason, and an important one, is that the psalms were composed to be sung responsorially or antiphonally. They were never recited. (After all, can you imagine attending a baseball game and *reciting* the National Anthem?)

Directives for singing the responsorial psalm in the Latin Rite leave many options. The Lectionary text need not be followed slavishly, since different composers will have different texts. A music-poor congregation can learn seasonal responses. If necessary the psalm verses can be read expressively with an instrumental accompaniment.

Psalms may even be substituted for each other, provided the minister of music knows how to do it. The Psalms may be divided into a number of categories; praise, thanksgiving, petition, lament, grief, repentance, etc. Very often if no setting of the appointed psalm for the day will work, a similar psalm with a suitable setting can be found. But one must substitute carefully. Often the appointed psalm is chosen because it reflects a theme or is quoted in one of the readings.

One must be choosy in deciding on settings for responsorial psalms. The principal purpose of these texts is to provide opportunities for meditation. Thus ornate or distracting settings are out of place here.

Once in a great while it is possible to do something entirely different from the psalm. A short dance, mime, reflective solo, or meditative anthem may be done. When and how and what to do are best decided by a competent liturgist.

In Catholic para-liturgy as well as Morning and Evening Praise there may be more than one psalm or canticle sung. Music directors generally try to balance these so they are in harmony with each other.

2. Gospel Acclamation

Good things come in small packages, I have often heard, good things like rings or photographs or snowflakes. Such things can easily be hidden at the toe of a stocking or under a pillow, or with billions of other snowflakes in a snowdrift. Their ability to be concealed so easily only adds to the fun of discovering and opening them, and marveling at their contents.

Liturgically speaking, the Alleluia and Verse before the Gospel is such a surprise package. Time and again it gets ignored, if not completely omitted, in favor of more "showy" acclamations like the Holy. I honestly don't think that most people have ever really looked inside the Alleluia and discovered its riches. What I propose to do is to cut the ribbons on this small package and open the box a little.

We call the Alleluia an acclamation, and there are several others in the Liturgy: the Holy, the Memorial acclamation and the Great Amen. If you think of the Mass as a drama, these acclamations are part of the peoples' role; their "lines", as it were. But when you look closely at the actual words involved in the acclamations, it is easy to see that almost none of them are addressed directly to God. How strange that during our most important act of worship together, our most important speaking parts are not spoken to God as "You" but as "He"! Actually, the reason for this is not all that obscure. An acclamation is something that is cried out or shouted, something that is proclaimed. It is analogous to an enthusiastic football cheer (which is not usually addressed directly to the team on the field). It is, in a sense, "cheering" for God and his love.

I have been wondering why it is that we so often ignore the Alleluia and Verse before the Gospel. I have come into many churches only to find that they have no tradition at all of singing this particular acclamation. Perhaps much of it is due to so many Sundays of hearing a commentator recite tonelessly, "alley-loo-yuh, alley-loo-yuh, alley-loo-yuh," and responding (under our breaths) "Alley-loo-yuh." Often the Gospel acclamation is just omitted.

What exactly does the Alleluia proclaim? In order to see its function, we need to look at its place in the Liturgy of the Word. Although it may seem to be a response to the second reading on Sundays, in reality it comes before the Gospel. We do not sit when we sing the Alleluia; we stand, a posture of energy, of readiness, of acclamation. In singing the Alleluia, we proclaim our faith in everything Jesus said and did. We cry out, "Thank God for the Good News of salvation!" "Hallelujah" is a word that goes back at least 3000 years to ancient Israel. It was the Jews' acclamation, "Praise God!" to a God who had brought them through the Red Sea into the Promised Land.

The Alleluia that we, their descendants, sing at Mass is very similar to the Jews' cry of praise. Normally a cantor sings "Alleluia" three times and the congregation repeats it. Then the cantor sings a verse, a one-line commentary that echoes the Gospel in a way, and the congregation repeats the Alleluia. On many Sundays, when there is no special Verse, the cantor is given a choice of several more general verses of praise. This is the suggested way of doing things. The importance of singing the Alleluia is evidenced by the fact that the rubrics suggest that it be omitted entirely if it is not going to be sung.

How can we make the Alleluia a joyful chorus of praise to the Lord?

Let's look first at the majority of our Masses, which are accompanied with organ music. For these celebrations, finding good ways of singing the Alleluia is fairly easy. In fact, only two things are necessary; the organist to play the organ, and a cantor to lead the congregation. The easiest solution is to use a "psalm-tone", a simple musical line with predictable changes in pitch, based on the old plainchant. A number of missalettes use this approach. It would be worth the price of two or three subscriptions to have this music available for use.

A second approach is to use a piece such as Deiss' *Wonderful and Great,* which has an "alleluia" refrain. The verses are short and lend themselves to this purpose, but because they are more general in tone, fall a little flat during the Church's Seasons, when special verses are provided. The missalette approach provides music for every verse.

A final approach to singing the Alleluia is to use some familiar alleluia melody and to recite the verse, preferably with some appropriate chording in the background. One might use Deiss, or *O Sons And Daughters,* or Vermulst's *Psalm 150,* for example. This approach brings the Alleluia within reach of parishes which have no cantors or song leaders to sing solo on the verses.

Masses at which the music is accompanied by guitar have some different options or approaches for singing the Alleluia. I have often noticed that even in places where guitar music is well established, the Gospel acclamation is not done. This is a situation that can easily be avoided, if one is willing to use a little ingenuity.

The missalette approach will not work as satisfactorily with guitars, as it does with organ accompaniment. For some reason, the first mode, to which many psalm-tones are adapted, sounds forced when done with guitar. Unfortunately, no one to my knowledge has written music for the different Gospel verses for guitar accompaniment. However, a number of composers have written Alleluias with more general verses which are suitable at many celebrations: Wise, Szigray, Quinlan, etc. These acclamations can be used as written, which makes them ideal for guitar groups that are still "new" to the folk Mass.

A second approach for guitarists is one which requires some discretion and some liturgical sensitivity, but which is worth the effort. This is to take the refrain and a verse of some appropriate guitar hymn and use it as the acclamation and verse. Most hymns

do not adapt to use as Gospel acclamations. They may have refrains or verses that are too long. They may be too slow or sad to be really acclamatory in tone. One example of a successful adaptation is *Alleluia #1* by Donald Fishel. Here is the refrain and verse one:

Alleluia, alleluia, give thanks to the risen Lord,
Alleluia, alleluia, give thanks to his Name.

Jesus is Lord of all the earth, He is the King of creation. One can do the same thing to such songs as *Allelu* and the *Song of Good News.* The Rivers piece, *Glory to God, Glory,* is another example.

A third way of singing the Gospel acclamation using guitar accompaniment is to sing the refrain of a hymn that is acclamatory in nature and recite the verse, using appropriate chording in the background. This approach benefits congregations with a limited repertoire and groups which have no members able or willing to sing alone on the verses. Paul Quinlan has written a number of "alleluia" refrains to psalms which are not otherwise suitable for Gospel acclamations.

Like all other acclamations in the Mass, the musical versions we choose can be used for quite a while before being replaced. If we begin now to sing the Alleluia, then in a couple of months we will be acclimated to doing it regularly and will be ready to try other versions as the need arises.

Let's open up the wrappings around the Alleluia and let our congregations see the beauty inside!

3. Profession of Faith
On Sundays and major feasts the Nicene or Apostles' Creed is recited by the congregation. In antiquity this profession had great importance. Those who had not yet been baptized were asked to leave after the sermon, and were not permitted to profess publicly their faith during liturgy until their Baptism. The Creed was a solemn recital of awesome mysteries.

Today, the Creed has become less important to many people who regard it as a long and cumbersome prayer. It is hard to know what to do for the Creed. Because it is a long statement, of irregular and unrhythmic phrases, it is difficult, often impossible, to sing. Occasions for singing it are quite rare, but it is possible to sing the Creed, and an inspired singing will be more effective than a dry recitation. Many of the older settings for the Eucharist contain long and elaborate settings for the Creed. These are designed to be sung by choirs. As a rule, These settings should be saved for concerts and performances, since their use at Mass generally is distracting, not to say time consuming. A responsorial or antiphonal treatment of the Creed, with a refrain such as "This we believe, increase our faith O Lord", and simple cantor or choral verses, can be most effective.

4. General Intercessions
Before the table is set for the Eucharistic celebration, minister and congregation share in solemn prayers for all needs and people. In the Eastern liturgies these are regularly chanted. Here in the West we, too, can make good use of music at this time on solemn

occasions. In the Latin Rite, the Solemn Prayers of the Faithful on Good Friday are supposed to be sung.

There seems to be a trend in Eucharistic-oriented churches away from rigid and unchanging intercessory prayer to more flexible intercessions with which the congregation can relate.

IV Preparation for the Eucharistic Liturgy Many people, in planning liturgies, come to the time after the prayers of the faithful and stop dead, thinking, "What are we going to do here?". That spot between the intercessions and the preface is one of our best examples of liturgical limbo. Generally, this time has been called the "Offertory". The problem arises when one considers things like: what is being "offered"? who is doing the "offering"? why? The general result is that either the congregation is asked to sing an "offering" sort of hymn, or the planner gives up in confusion and has the choir fill in the space with an anthem or something, anything, as long as it has an "offertory" theme. They have not yet heard that there is no such thing as an "Offertory" at Mass any more. As a result, they are trying to make songs fit molds they were never intended to fill.

What is this time after the Universal Prayer? At present it is called the Presentation of the Gifts. It is the time when the gifts, the bread and wine, are brought forward and presented. In fact, it amounts to little more than setting the table for the banquet to come. The bread and wine are offered during the Eucharistic prayer, not at this time. The presentation of the gifts and their preparation is a sort of breathing space for the congregation, a time when they can reflect a little on the liturgy of the Word and the Eucharistic liturgy to follow. The priests' prayers at this time are almost private prayers, and may be said silently, even if there is no music during this time. These prayers are modeled on Jewish blessings and are called *berakoth*. They are said because it was and is a Jewish custom to begin any meal with a blessing, just as we say a grace.

To use music during this time, which is always of a Eucharistic or an offering nature, is to mistake completely what the presentation of gifts means. This is not to say that Eucharistic music is *ipso facto* to be avoided, but that we should eliminate a dependence on it. We should not get tied down to a thematic "mania", here or at any place in the Mass. The purpose of the Mass is to celebrate Christ among us in his Body, not to catechize, to teach or inform people about different parts of the Mass.

How, then do we help people to use the time of the presentation of the gifts to celebrate Christ's presence in our midst? First, we should keep this time from becoming a catchall. Very often there still is a procession with the gifts, some announcements, the taking up of the collection, etc., during the interim. This is terribly distracting, and often can quite effectively prevent people from praying. We should concentrate on one kind of symbol or another.

Processions and collections are visual, tactile sorts of things. They are things that people *watch*. If this is what is being emphasized, then don't ask people to *sing* as well. Singing is an oral-aural symbol; the combined voices emphasize our unity in Christ, so don't plan elaborate processions if what you're concentrating on is a song. This is true whether the song is con-

gregational, antiphonal, responsorial, or simply a choir piece. Use the organ or guitars to provide suitable instrumental music, and let the people watch the symbols of their life being brought forward, Continue the music until the "Pray, brethren..." prayer. If there is no procession, or if that is not emphasized, use a hymn. This is a time when a straight hymn will often work well, particularly a hymn of praise or a hymn which emphasizes the theme of the liturgy.

What is the place of choir pieces or solos at this time? Generally, since this has been a catchall, the time of the presentation of gifts has been used for music in which the congregation has no vocal part. However, we must be careful; this is still an important part of the liturgy. There is obviously no room in the liturgy for "show-off" music, but it can be quite effective to use a choir piece that celebrates in some way what we are doing at the Mass. Choir pieces must be sung with crystal clear diction on the part of all the singers. If the congregation can't understand the words, they will not be able to pray with the song. And that is the only reason to have an anthem at this or any time, namely, to facilitate and support the congregation's prayer. In fact, if a choir is not experienced enough to sing clearly, they should not sing anthems, since the whole point of them will be lost. A choir director ought to have someone listen to the choir, someone who doesn't know the piece being sung, to test the diction.

What kind of music ought we to sing during the presentation of the gifts? Generally, any music that calls us to celebrate God-with-us is good music, provided the melody and arrangement are of good quality. Certainly we should get out of the "offertory" rut. If we have gotten into a "four-hymn syndrome", i.e., hymnody at the entrance, presentation, communion and recessional, we need to get out of it. Very often, music which captures a little of the spirit of a particular liturgy is most effective. This does not necessarily mean the theme of a particular liturgy. What it does mean is that feeling one gets after studying the readings and feast, of whether a Mass is likely to get people excited or calm, ebullient or reflective, gay or chastened, etc. This is a matter of careful preparation on the part of the choir director.

The transition from "offertory" to "presentation" is one that will come hard to many parishes, but it's one they respond well to. Very often they have been looking for a few moments at Mass to catch their (spiritual) breaths for the real Offering of the Body and Blood of Christ during the Eucharistic liturgy. As liturgists, it's our responsibility to respond to that need. If we orient our music in this way, we will all pray better together as we celebrate Christ the Lord who has brought us into life by his death and resurrection.

V Liturgy of the Eucharist This is the most solemn part of the whole liturgy, the central action and mystery of the Christian life, Christ-among-us. It is possible on many occasions to solemnize the whole Eucharistic Prayer in song. From the introductory prayer to the Communion rite itself, music can and should be done in whatever way is pastorally most appropriate.

At this point most Eucharist-centered churches differ most noticeably. Episcopalian, Lutheran, Catholic, etc. Eucharistic Prayers are not usually interchangeable. There are some small textual differences among forms of the Sanctus as well. However, the basic structure is the same.

In the Latin Rite the people have three acclamations which they profess during the Eucharistic Prayer: The Sanctus, Memorial Acclamation, and Great Amen. These acclamations are as ancient as Christianity and in some cases ante-date it. These are the people's parts and are *never* in the Latin Rite to be usurped by the choir.

As with the Gospel Acclamation, musical settings for these texts ought to have some life to them. Reflective, meditative, quiet settings are a little too tame for the texts. Some good settings of the acclamations have the choir sing part of the acclamation with the people answering antiphonally. If the choir does not dominate, this can be an especially festive way of singing the acclamations.

In children's worship, the length of the Eucharistic Prayer and its difficult language can present a problem. The new children's prayers can be interspersed with more frequent acclamations in order to help the children pray.

Chants for the celebrant's parts are being written, though not all have been yet set to music. Ministers of music need to be sensitive here to the key in which the celebrant sings, and, if possible, harmonize it with the key of the peoples' acclamations. The flow of language is broken up all too often by the celebrant singing in one key and the congregation responding in another.

VI The Communion After the *Amen*, preparations for Communion begin. There are many important musical possibilities and options here.

1. Our Father
In the most ancient liturgies of the church, the Our Father is appointed to be prayed right before Communion. The point of the Our Father, the Greeting of Peace, even the Agnus Dei, is to awaken us to the necessity of being reconciled with our brothers and sisters before coming to the Lord's table. Singing the Our Father may be done on any occasion, whenever it is desirable to emphasize especially the prayer of Jesus. More than any other prayer, the Our Father is *our* prayer, Christian prayer. It links together the whole Body of Christ, stretched out through time and space. Because it is *our* prayer, it ought never to be sung by a choir alone or a soloist, no matter how beautiful or traditional the setting may be. Such settings should be used in sacred concerts or elsewhere.

Good settings of the Our Father will respect the basic text and will not be so drawn out or complicated that the natural flow of the words is distorted. They will be such that a congregation can learn to sing them easily.

2. Greeting of Peace
During this point in the Eucharistic liturgy, the congregation is invited to exercise its sense of touch in embracing each other in some way. To touch someone in our society implies a certain familiarity or relationship. Many people are afraid of this, unfortunately, so the Greeting of Peace is still quite stilted in many places.

If the greeting is an important or extended part of a particular liturgy, there is occasionally room for the choir or soloist to do a simple and very short meditation on a suitable theme. An in-

strumental, as long as it is more meaningful than merely "busy" music to cover noise, is also quite suitable.

3. Lamb of God
In the early days of the church, the consecrated loaves of bread were broken at this time for distribution to the congregation. As time went on, this took more and more time. To help keep peoples' attention focused on the Lord during this period, litanical and antiphonal singing was used. Eventually this solidified into the Lamb of God with its triple invocation. The Lamb of God is not a repentant prayer for forgiveness. Rather, it is a triumphant invocation of the victorious Lamb whose mercy extends throughout the world.

Unfortunately in most places the Bread is no longer truly broken. Instead a single cracker is snapped in two. The need for singing to occupy time prayerfully is not there.

When can the Lamb of God be sung most effectively? If bread is broken, if various preparations and movements are going on, then the "Lamb" ought to be sung. Some liturgies emphasize Christ as Lamb: These can be further occasions.

In the Latin Rite the traditional form of the Lamb of God is not obligatory. New texts of an antiphonal, litanical nature can be used and indeed, a few have been written. Sometimes the melodies used for the Penitential Rite can be used here as well. The "Lamb" can be sung by the choir and congregation alternating.

4. Communion
The reception of Communion involves a procession of the community together. Communion song of some kind is important, since it concretizes the tremendous unity we share. Responsorial singing is often the easiest to do, since it does not require the congregation to carry any hymnals. A familiar hymn will also work, as will antiphonal singing between choir and congregation.

If Communion takes a while, it is often better to use two musical selections than one, which can become repetitious. The choir could do one of these pieces and so give the congregation's voices a rest.

Choir pieces at communion need to be sensitive to the demands of the Communion rite. Music done at this time ought to help the congregation to pray and should emphasize, by words and/or music, the unity shared by all in the Eucharist. Choir pieces should be specifically prepared for a particular Sunday, not trotted out casually from a stock repertoire to have some religious filler music.

In many places and churches it is customary for choir or congregation to sing a meditation or thanksgiving song. A straight hymn works very well here; the sound of everyone singing together is a powerful sign of unity at this time. A hymn used here should be a community-oriented one, rather than one that emphasizes private or sentimental feelings that foster a "me and Jesus" attitude.

VII Dismissal After the thanksgiving there is a simple prayer, blessing and dismissal. Usually a final hymn is sung. In the Latin

Planning Music for Other Celebrations

Rite the final hymn is not of great liturgical importance. It can easily be omitted, and the ministers can leave quietly or to instrumental music. In actual practice a congregational hymn is most frequently used. Since this is the last thing in the liturgy, the final words the congregation will take home with them, the lyrics should have some depth, something rememberable about them.

I Introduction In some churches, the celebration of the Eucharist is the most frequent liturgical event, perhaps constituting a majority of community worship. In these churches, especially the Catholic church, however, there is currently a movement toward celebrations of other kinds, especially toward a more solemn celebration of baptisms, weddings, and funerals. At the same time, as noted earlier, some churches celebrate Holy Communion only infrequently. *The Music Locator* provides a valuable resource for these churches for use in planning the celebration of the Word.

Some general principles should always be kept in mind: the use of music is a valuable part of worship, and therefore must be directed toward prayer. Specifically, it should facilitate *common* prayer. Sometimes this will mean that all will sing together. At other times responsorial psalmody will be called for. And there are times when choral singing will express the common prayer of all in the worshipping community. Music is not to be so ornate that it becomes an end unto itself. Nor should it be so simple-minded as to be boring. The person or group responsible for planning liturgical music must always ask the question: does this piece of music fulfill its *function* in our worship? Does it do what it should be doing?

II Celebrations of the Word of God Worship in many churches can be characterized as celebrations of the *Word of God*. We might reflect briefly on the meaning of this phrase. The Word of God is first of all a personal Word, the second Person of the Godhead, Jesus the Messiah. In Jesus of Nazareth, the divine Word shed the glorious form of God (the "emptying" St. Paul describes in Philippians 2) and became human. By becoming human, the Word could take on all of mankind's weakness and sinfulness (without sinning Himself) and redeem mankind through suffering and death and Resurrection. By appropriating this Redemption, men and women "lock into" this mystery of grace and have the hope of being transformed into images of God.

Different Christian traditions have different ways of describing the Redemption, and the appropriation by the new Christian of the grace of Redemption. Hence, as a first corollary to this study, the musician must be sensitive to language in selecting music. Some hymns or translations are not compatible with the religious expressions of particular churches. Other hymns and songs should be used there.

The Word of God is expressed in a particular way today in the proclamation and interpretation of Sacred Scripture. The "Word service" is normative for many churches whose celebration of Holy Communion is reserved for special occasions. Music plays a special part in these services, and it is easy to see why. First, music is a way of dressing up words, and of making them say what they mean, without merely saying them. Music is, in a sense, dramatized speech. A common example from the literature is Handel's *All We like Sheep Have Gone Astray* from *The Messiah*. The choral rendition of the word "astray" is an interweaving of meandering melodies that aurally depict the visual scene of scattered sheep. Without becoming technically impossible, congregational music can serve to carry the text and underline its meaning. We can accept this as a second corollary of music selection.

The second reason for the importance of music in "Word services" is that music making involves more of the person than many other ways of participation. To sing, the churchgoer makes use of his head, eyes, ears, his entire respiratory system, including vocal cords, teeth and nose, and indirectly the rest of his body. There is mental, physical and spiritual involvement in song. There is also symbolic commitment to the Word being heard or expressed.

Lastly, and perhaps most importantly for a theologian, to sing the Word or about the Word is to treat it with the expected flourish. Our worship is, after all, a reflection of the "liturgy" of heaven, the unending celebration and drama that Revelations assigns much singing to. Many of the books of Sacred Scripture were designed for singing, expecially Psalms and the Song of Songs. Nearly every book of Sacred Scripture, both Hebrew and Christian Scriptures, has at least one song in it. Singing, then, is a biblical medium, and in the strict sense is a godly activity (Zephaniah 3: 17).

In every celebration of the Word special place should be given to the singing of the psalms and canticles of Scripture. Why is this? In the reading of Scripture we listen to God speak to us through a reader. Some churches have one reading, while others have two or three in a service. Vigils may have as many as ten readings. If we respond with a hymn, even a good one, we are at best singing our words to God. If on the other hand, our response to the Word of God is a psalm, then the response to the Word is itself the Word, and it will have a special impact on the growth of the individual Christian and the community. For the Word of God has power of itself to change and to give life, and its action always bears fruit (cf. Isaiah 55: 10-11, Matthew 13: 4-9). By using the Scriptural songs as our own song, we are providing the Word of God with an additional opportunity to take root in the human heart and bear fruit. Our third corollary, then, for hymn or response selection is that the texts used should "be drawn chiefly from Scripture".

With this in mind, we cannot be surprised to realize that the most popular of hymns in all the churches usually are metrical psalms or canticles from Scripture. A short list will suffice to illustrate this fact: "A Mighty Fortress is our God" (Psalm 18); "The King of Love my Shepherd Is" (Psalm 23); "O God Our Help in Ages Past" (Psalm 91); "All People That on Earth Do Dwell" (Psalm 100); "Praise the Lord Ye Heavens" (Psalm 148). Metrical adaptations of the psalms formed the basis for the original French hymnbook, the *Genevan Psalter*.

Now that several churches have adopted a similar three-year lectionary, with three readings on Sundays and important feasts, it is obvious to all that back-to-back readings, one each from the Hebrew Scriptures, Epistles and Gospels, are not conducive to really taking root in the Word of God. Supposing we can assume that those who come to a Sunday service really want to be there, we can take our time in planning an attractive liturgy that will help them to assimilate the Word into their lives.

III A Service of the Word In a typical service of the Word, be it a Methodist Sunday service or Catholic Bible Vigil, the proclamation of the Word itself takes a central place. There should be preparation before the reading: an entrance rite with song and

prayer. Perhaps a profession of faith (not necessarily the Nicene or Apostles Creed) would be appropriate to set the tone for hearing the Word of God.

The reading from the Hebrew Scriptures is appropriately followed by a psalm. A responsorial psalm is ideal — a brief refrain can be quickly and easily learned (hopefully *before* the service). Music actually helps the congregation to learn the words, and so a sung refrain is more easily participated in than a recited one. Either a choir or a cantor can sing the verses (at least three, to allow for prayerful reflection by the people), as long as they are intelligible. It is best to allow a minute of silence between the first reading and the sung psalm.

The reading from the New Testament letters may be followed by silence and either an acclamation or a New Testament canticle. Responsorial music is best in this place, but a familiar hymn (one or two verses) that fits the message of the lesson or Gospel might be appropriate as well. Traditionally, before the Gospel the refrain "alleluia" is sung to an easily learned melody.

It is sometimes objected that singing between the lessons will draw out the readings and make it necessary to shorten the sermon. This may be true. But it has been found that the congregation that has sung along with the Word before the sermon will get more out of the sermon.

The reading of the Gospel is the high point of the service of the Word. The Gospels proclaim the life of Jesus, the very Word of God made flesh. Hence they have a particular relevance for modern men and women who are themselves imitating Jesus. The song before the Gospel has led to the Gospel. It would be appropriate to sing again after the Gospel — perhaps the same refrain that was used before it.

Modern culture, especially Western culture, is much too wordy. The modern brain is assailed by entirely too much verbal input. An overflow response is generated in which the person simply refuses to accept any more words. We minimize the risk of being wordy when we separate the various proclamations of the Word by song and other media.

After the sermon, or homily on the Word, a period of silence can be effective. A meditative organ solo (quietly) can accompany the prayer. Or a word of "testimony," spontaneous or prearranged, could be spoken by a member of the congregation. Whether the service of the Word ends at this point, or continues through a collection, recitation of the Lord's Prayer, or suitable action, music should fit the mood and theme of the celebration, and summon forth prayer from the assembly.

IV Celebrations of the Sacraments In the Catholic, Lutheran, Episcopal and Orthodox churches there are a number of sacraments that are celebrated communally. There is room for song in all of them, from Baptism to Holy Orders. *The Music Locator* provides categories for listing pertinent music for these rites. Many of the observations made in the preceding pages will follow for the celebration of the sacraments, but some additional ones should be made as well:

First, it is realized that in the churches mentioned, the prime

24

In Conclusion

sacrament, the sacrament of the Lord's presence, is the Eucharist. It is common for the sacraments to be celebrated at a Eucharist, usually around the time of the homily. Baptism, Confirmation and the other sacraments are not isolated actions, but in some way can be said to derive from the Eucharist. Even outside the celebration of the Lord's Supper, their unity with that sacrament should be understood and made obvious.

Second, whether or not each sacrament is celebrated within a Eucharist, there is first a "Liturgy of the Word." Especially when the Eucharistic liturgy does not follow, the Word service should be highlighted with song.

Lastly, it is wise in choosing music for the sacraments to highlight the symbolism of the sacraments. In Baptism, the principal symbol is water: both death-dealing and life-giving. In Confirmation, it is oil: an anointing for strength and spiritual warfare. In the sacrament of Reconciliation (Penance), repentance and sorrow for sins, as well as healing (through the imposition of hands) is signed. Likewise, in the Anointing of the Sick the healing of the whole person is emphasized, through anointing and imposition of hands. Holy Orders carries with it a rich symbolism of power and service, including anointing, a prayer with laying on of hands, and acceptance by the congregation of the spiritual headship of the ordinand (perhaps by an appropriate acclamation). The symbolism of marriage is profuse, but focuses on commitment and the union of two lives into one. Music and text for each of these ceremonies will be special, and must be planned with great care so that it is both prayerful (God-centered) and relevant (meaningful to those worshipping).

V The Liturgy of the Hours A rediscovery of the beauty and relevance of daily common prayer is a characteristic of our age. In a number of churches, Christians are coming together daily to pray, formally and informally. The formal prayer of the Church is called the Liturgy of the Hours, and the two principal times of prayer are early morning (Morning Praise or Lauds) and late evening (Evensong or Vespers). The very names of these "offices" suggests that they are to be sung.

In the past, the psalms of the hours have been chanted to simple plainsong melodies. As appropriate as this was when many psalms had to be learned and sung, it may not be adequate in the contemporary situation. There are a number of metrical psalm versions with interesting melodies available, and these can be adopted. Reflective silence, testimony, solo music or dance may be appropriate between the psalms. The psalms themselves should be sung antiphonally (explained earlier) or responsorially (especially when done with a larger congregation). Occasionally a familiar psalm-type hymn could be sung by the entire body.

Morning Praise and Evensong can be a valuable liturgical event for a community. Song should be considered an important part of this event, one that should work in conjunction with other media and symbols and rites to establish and promote a prayerful atmosphere. An often-given example is the singing of the antiphon "Let my evening prayer come like incense before you, Lord" with psalm 40, 134, or 141 and the incensation of the people. The symbolism of the fragrant prayers of God's people rising to Him can be powerful indeed. Likewise the singing of the hymn "When Morning Gilds the Skies," or "Morning Has Broken" as the first rays of dawn break into a chapel can be a moving experience.

Planning liturgical music requires that those who plan it be persons of faith, understanding, and musical skill, who are knowledgeable about the liturgy and who care for and about the people with whom they celebrate. Only faith and understanding can tell a music director whether or not a musical selection expresses something the worshiping community can or should believe. Understanding of scripture can enable one to choose alternate psalms, for instance, and to see the biblical Word as the underpinning of liturgy.

Some liturgical knowledge is essential for music directors. This chapter has been designed as a very brief introduction to liturgical rationale. Each church has its own forms of liturgy, and each congregation or assembly within that church has its own variants of those liturgies. Often, the people who attend one liturgy at a parish have a variant liturgy from those people who worship at another service. Awareness of ritual and liturgy sensitizes one to these subtleties and enables one to highlight them so that all may pray.

A musician with some specific knowledge of the art can make fullest use of *The Music Locator*. It takes a musician to decide among ten settings of a single text which one fits the resources available to him or her.

Finally a music director needs also to be a minister of music. A pastoral concern for the worshiping community will be motivation in selecting not only prayerful music, but the particular type of musical prayer that is needed.

Liturgical music must be:

1. musically aesthetic

2. clear and faith-oriented in its lyrics

3. suited to the part of the liturgy in which it is used

4. suited to the pastoral needs of the celebrating assembly

If these basic criteria are fulfilled, then liturgical music will best be able to achieve its purpose among the people of God at liturgy.

Eileen E. Freeman
South Bend, Indiana
July 1976

25

A Copyright Primer

The increase of congregational participation in liturgical music has brought with it some serious problems with copyright abuse in American churches. The problems are almost always caused by a misunderstanding or, more frequently, a complete ignorance of the concept of copyright protection for creative works. The following discussion is offered as a source of basic information to those who wish to use creative works which belong to others.

Who has the right to use a published song?

The answer to this question depends on the wishes of the composer, the policies of the publisher, and the eligibility of the individual who wishes to use the song. The specific way in which a song is to be used is an important factor, too. In general, the answer is: only the composer, and those who derive rights from the composer by explicit agreement, have the right to use any creative work.

When a composer completes a musical composition, the law of the United States (Title 17, U.S. Code) grants to the composer several exclusive rights to his or her work.[1] Some of the rights the composer has are:

1. The right to print, reprint, and copy the work.

2. The right to sell or distribute copies of the work.

3. The right to transform or revise the work by means of dramatization, translation, or musical arrangement.

4. The right to perform the work.

5. The right to record the work.

But when I go out and purchase a published copy of a song, don't I pay for all of the rights to the song I purchase?

The answer is almost always "No, you do not!" In fact, the mere purchase of a published copy of a song does not imply transfer of *any* of these rights as a result of the purchase. The only right that comes with such purchase is the right to *perform* the song privately, and the right to *perform* it publicly in a non-profit manner.

Some Background A composer with a musical composition, or a collection of musical compositions, will often enter into an agreement with a publisher. The details of the business agreement will vary, depending on the unique situation in each case, but what will often occur is a transfer of rights. The composer agrees to transfer all of his exclusive rights to the composition to the publisher. The publisher, in turn, agrees to invest time, money, and energy in the composer's work.

The number of possible variations in such agreements is large, but very seldom (if ever) does the agreement provide for the transfer of any of the exclusive rights to an individual who purchases one copy of the song. In fact, the law specifically states that these rights are available only to the composer and to those who specifically derive rights from the composer by a written agreement or explicit permission.

Thus, when a choir, cantor, or soloist purchases one or more copies of a published composition, rehearses the music, and performs the music in a worship situation, no rights are violated. The congregation listens to the performance. Even if a person hums along and eventually learns to sing the song with the choir, no rights are violated.

Congregational participation in musical prayer has been increasing since the second Roman Catholic Vatican Council. The many changes in contemporary worship have included more active roles for the individuals in the pew, including musical roles. To have the typical member of the congregation participate in song requires aids, especially printed copies or projected images of the songs to be sung, so that large numbers of people can perform the music together. This is where the rights of the composer are often violated. The right to reproduce copyrighted music in any way (except via performance or recording, as explained earlier), is forbidden by law without explicit permission from the copyright holder. Such permission does not transfer when a published copy is purchased.

Limitations of Copyright Law Copyright law explicitly restricts printing, reprinting, copying, selling, distributing copies, or transforming a work. These restrictions may be interpreted to the letter of the law. There is no loophole by which a person is exempt from the law for these activities. Therefore any reproduction of a piece of music requires explicit permission from the holder of the copyright for the piece of music. Music copied for any purpose (even for non-profit worship) is illegal unless permission is obtained first.

There are some limitations to copyright protection for the composer. For example, once a song has been recorded and release of the recording has been authorized by the copyright owner, anyone who wishes to record the song may do so, according to what is called the "cumpulsory license" provision of the copyright law, provided the copyright holder is correctly credited on the label, and provided certain royalties are paid. This means that the copyright holder may not refuse permission to anyone who wishes to make a recording of the song, provided proper conditions are met.

Another limitation is one of time. The law provides these exclusive rights to the composer for only 28 years. It allows for a renewal for a second 28 year period. After 56 years, the copyright protection is removed and the work is placed in the "public domain". No one has exclusive rights to a song, once it is in the "public domain". However, recent acts of Congress have extended some renewal (second term) copyrights which would have expired on or after September 19, 1962, so it would be wise to check with an attorney if a question exists about this matter.

A further limitation refers to the performance of music. When you purchase a copy of a song, you do have the right to play and sing the song privately, for yourself or for a private gathering of people. You may also perform the song at a public gathering, as long as no profit is involved. Commercial performance uses of musical compositions are often organized around performing rights agencies such as ASCAP, BMI, SESAC, or a number of smaller agencies. Commercial users of music pay a license fee to these agencies. The fee they pay is then distributed to those who hold the performing rights to the composition.

Since the liturgical situation is public, but not "for profit", there is no inherent restriction of the right to "perform" music in any educational or liturgical situation. But, notice the emphasis on the word "perform". Performance does not include the preparation of copies, or the projection of text on a screen, or any other act which violates the exclusive rights listed previously.

Proper Markings People who produce hymnals (or any form of participation aid) have both a moral and legal responsibility to educate themselves as to the vital importance of proper copyright markings on the creative works of others.

The copyright law is a fragile one; one which is dependent on the composer/publisher boldly marking each copy with the copyright symbol ©, or the word COPYRIGHT, or the abbreviation COPYR., and the year of copyright, along with the name of the copyright holder. Each song must also carry the title, composer's name, and any explicit reservation or permission.

An example of the detail required for proper compliance with the law is clearly shown by this specific case; "Where do you put the legal copyright marks for a song which requires more than one page? Does it go at the end of the song, or at the bottom of the first page?" The answer is: It should go on the bottom of the first page, so that the title, composer's name, and correct copyright information are all on the same page. The typical untrained individual is not likely to realize this and could quite possibly choose the incorrect location.

Early post-Vatican II parish hymnals often omitted all of this information with the possible exception of the song title. The omission is understandable, since the information to be copied was often in "fine print", and the impact on the holder of the rights was not understood by those who put the hymnal together.

Human nature makes it very difficult for people to care about "fine print" unless there are personal, immediate, and well-understood repercussions for those who break the law.

What is the impact on the composer/publisher when a published song is put into a publication and distributed by the hundreds with improper copyright markings?

For the people who break the law and fail to include this information, there has been little penalty in times past; and there is a limit to the legal penalty allowed. If a copyright holder discovers an offense, brings suit against the offender, and wins in a court of law, damages can be awarded up to $5,000. Note that this could happen even to an individual who has obtained permission in writing, and who has paid money for the right to make copies of the song. Such permission does not remove the heavy burden of properly marking each song copied; and, as we shall see, the impact of a badly marked copy is devastating to the holder of the rights. Therefore, it is not surprising to see growing numbers of lawsuits against church groups on this subject.

For the composer/publisher whose song was distributed without proper markings, the penalty is extremely harsh. The composer/publisher can lose *all* rights to such music (in a court of law) even

though they have carefully marked each copy they printed and sold. When music is printed and distributed without proper copyright markings, even at a parish or confined local level, such music is said to be "in the public domain" because hundreds of copies exist without proper markings. This is true even if the copies are illegally produced. This makes it impossible to prosecute those who would make further copies from one of the mismarked copies. They could argue that when they saw a copy without proper markings, they assumed the song to be in the public domain.

Some reflection on these consequences should clarify the urgent concern that publishers have for proper markings. It also explains why several publishers flatly refuse permission to parishes which wish to make copies of their music. They are not so much opposed to religious use as they are afraid that the music will be mismarked, and that their rights will be jeopardized.

Religious users of creative works are in a special situation. They must care not only about the legal aspects of copyright law; they must also resolve their moral obligation to the composer/publisher of music for worship. This obligation consists of first, obtaining proper permission before using copyrighted works; second, preserving the correct legal markings so that the composer/publisher does not lose rights to his or her music; and third, complying with whatever terms and conditions the copyright holder extends in exchange for permission.

Participation Aids Participation aids are natural requirements if members of church congregations are going to sing songs together, or take active roles in other liturgical activities. The experimentation and development of new material is occurring at such a pace that the problem of providing lasting participation aids has no solution which will easily satisfy all concerned.

Publishers would generally prefer that parishes purchase copies of songs from them so that they may ensure proper marking, and so they may earn their deserved royalty on the songs they make available. This is a possible solution; and it would really be the simplest, if parishes would accept a limited number of variations in size and format of the reprints.

It is too early to tell what the final answer will be. The wide variety of programs made available by publishers, combined with the growing independence of parish musicians, makes it unlikely that a uniformly satisfactory solution will be reached in the near future.

Parishes exert a heavy financial pressure on publishers; and if they were to begin ordering 300, or 800, or more copies of a song to fit an 8½" x 11" collection, or a 5½" x 8½" collection, most publishers would be happy to fill the order. This would be the ideal way for parishes to take advantage of the best music from each of many publishers, while minimizing the chance of injustice to the composers and publishers. This approach would also minimize the red tape which is necessarily associated with licensing programs and other permission policies.

In the absence of any imposed standard, many parishes have been putting together their own collections of published music, often illegally, in a variety of mediums. Some of the most common aids are discussed briefly below.

The Parish Hymnal (Homemade) One of the most fascinating rewards of music publishing is seeing the enormous amount of creative energy which springs forth spontaneously and regularly in our contemporary churches. There is increased effort in production of creative works, and also in the special new field of providing participation aids for congregational singing.

In one sense it is frustrating for a publisher to receive so many requests to do so many different things, for it is not easy to dream up new ways to provide universal aids when such diverse and creative aids are being developed in parishes everywhere.

Every publisher secretly wishes he could come up with a "perfect" hymnal, one which could satisfy the needs and tastes of every parish. This same instinctive wish may be at the root of all the different hymnals which are compiled each year in parishes around the country. Some parishes prefer to present the song text only; others prefer to present text and guitar chords; others present text, melody, and guitar chords; while still others opt for text, melody, guitar chords, and keyboard accompaniment. Some type the text; others arrange for hand script; still others pay for professional engraving and typography. A growing number of them order copies of printed music from the publisher rather than prepare their own. They have discovered that it takes plenty of time and money to do the job right.

This whole area is a very positive symptom of creative expression. We have many example parish hymnals of all shapes and sizes and degrees of legality, which have been sent from parishes everywhere. (In fact, if you are preparing a hymnal, we would appreciate a complimentary copy. When we get a thousand different hymnals. We will set up an exhibit for interested people to review. Mail the copies to *The Music Locator*, P.O. Box 444, Saratoga, CA 95070.)

One major problem in parish hymnal publication is that no one in the parish is specifically and directly involved with the rights to the individual songs included. This often results in less attention being paid to copyright markings than should be, and the result is that three out of four hymnals we receive contain improper notation for copyright on at least a few songs. (Don't let that stop you from sending us a copy!).[2]

The Sunday Program Many parishes have a practice of preparing a special program for each liturgy to be distributed to each individual who attends the service. These programs often incorporate the music for the liturgy with special prayers, art work, and other elements to yield a valuable aid for the liturgy of the day. Each week new programs must be made. The talent and energy for such work is rare, but many parishes find programs to be a superior solution.

While all the problems of permissions and proper copyright markings persist, the program offers a high degree of flexibility to the ministers of music, in that new material can be incorporated as it is produced. Often a hymnal is too expensive an endeavor to change frequently or discard easily.

Custom programs are common at weddings, funerals, and even baptisms; but they do not seem to be as popular as the hymnal or songbook, in spite of their flexibility. It would seem that such programs could be put together very hastily at times; thus the danger of having music mismarked is higher with these temporary publications than with any other form of participation aid.

Projected Images This form of participation aid is growing steadily and may some day replace the booklets and programs described above. Projecting songs provides the most flexible of participation aids. New songs can be added regularly and substitutions can be made at the last minute without complication. When a song is projected on a screen or wall, the copyright information must be projected also, so that there is no chance that someone who views the projection will assume that a song is in the public domain when it is not.

It is interesting to note that the projected image participation aid is less expensive for parishes than either hymnal or program, even if a special screen is purchased and installed in a tasteful location.

Other There are many other participation aids, including professionally published worship books, hymnals, and missalettes; but since use of these aids does not normally require copyright markings or permission requirements, they are not discussed here.

Your Friendly Publisher Many publishers have permission plans, licenses, or special programs available which grant organizations the right to reporduce copies as participation aids, provided certain conditions are met. There are almost as many programs as there are publishers, and we will not attempt to state the policies of each publisher in this book.[3]

From the point of view of one who seeks permission to make or obtain participation aids, music publishers seem to fall into one of the following categories.

1. Popular music publishers: These people devote their energies to making a commercial success of a musical work. They frequently shun permission-seekers from the religious music field, and some have policies which absolutely refuse to grant reproduction rights under any terms. The few dollars they would earn from an occasional religious user would not justify the office work such a program would generate or the high risk that a poorly done copying job could cost them their rights to a popular song.

2. Publishers of choral music for worship: These publishers specialize in arrangements of hymns for use by choirs and more traditional users of music. By design, their music is not intended for full congregational participation; it is difficult enough that each choir member is usually given a purchased copy of the music. Therefore, these publishers are not very active with licensing programs.

3. Publishers of contemporary music for worship: The publishers in category 2 also publish music which is contemporary and there is substantial overlap between the previous category and this one. However, this third category consists of those publishers who emphasize the kind of music which is designed for congregational participation. These publishers actively seek ways to involve parishes in developing legal participa-

tion aids. Each one has a unique policy. Each one would prefer that parishes order music from them rather than requesting reprint permission. All of these publishers will, however, grant permission to produce participation aids, subject to a set of terms and conditions.

4. Special publishers: Since the publishing field is open to any individual or organization, it encompasses many non-profit organizations which have become involved in publishing religious music, either as a side venture, or as a main activity. Often an individual composer who is not satisfied with an agreeement offered to him (or her) by an established publisher will make the music available to the public himself (or herself).

It is these last two categories of publishers who will be most cooperative and interested in your parish music program, especially in providing participation aids.

Since no single publisher has succeeded in creating the one perfect participation aid, parishes are for the foreseeable future going to have the problem, but also the privilege, of shopping among the various publishers for aids which are useful in their particular situations. This should result in stimulating and creative liturgies, planned in each parish by people who are closest to the needs and situations of their own congregations.

William Burns
San Jose, California
September, 1976

Notes:
1. Write for Circular 1, *General Information On Copyright*, Copyright Office, Library of Congress, Washington, D.C. 20402. This publication is slanted toward the procedure that a composer/publisher would follow when filing for copyright protection, but it explains the concept of copyright nicely in its first sections. It also gives clear instructions on how the markings should appear. Free.

Circular 50, *Copyright For Musical Compositions*, is available from the same address. It provides a more specific discussion of the problems of music copyrights. Free.

If you really get interested in copyright law, write the Library of Congress for Circular 2, *Publications Of The Copyright Office*. Free.

2. For a further discussion of the parish hymnal, the article, *Making A Parish Songbook*, is available in Volume 3 Number 6 of MODERN LITURGY magazine, (special music ministry issue) P.O. Box 444, Saratoga, CA 95070, $2.00. Also, *How To Produce A Songbook* is a free publication of the Word of God Music, Ann Arbor, MI.

3. Folk Liturgies Unlimited has a collection of the policies of major music publishers, with regard to permission for reprinting or reproducing participation aids. Policies change rapidly, and music publishers come and go; but as of mid-1976, this report could be of interest to parishes. (Folk Liturgies Unlimited, 48 S. 14th St., Pittsburgh, PA 15203)

MUSIC FOR FORMAL LITURGY

This first major category lists 16 sub categories which closely follow the structure of a roman liturgy. The categories, sub-categories, and various codes gived here are explained in the introduction to THE MUSIC LOCATOR. The sub categories, and their codes are repeated here for easy reference.

CODE – CATEGORY
LA–Entrance Processional Songs
LB–Acclamations(Lord Have Mercy)
LC–Glorias
LD–Responsorial Psalms
LE–Acclamations(General)
LF–Gospel Acclamations(Alleluia)
LG–Gospel Acclamations(Lenten)
LH–Litanies for the Prayer of the Faithful
LI–Acclamations(Holy)
LJ–Memorial Acclamations
LK–Acclamations(Great Amen)
LL–Lord's Prayers(Our Father)
LM–Acclamations(Lamb Of God)
LN–Communion Processional Songs
LO–Communion and Eucharistic Hymns
LP–General Processional Hymns

Entrance Processional Songs

These are processional hymns which may be selected for the entrance procession for a liturgy, or for general processional use. Note that the titles in all sub categories are further divided by song style, and then listed alphabetically. First are children's songs, code (C), then folk style music (F) which includes blues, jazz, pop, rock, and country-western. This is followed by Gospel (G), then by contemporary liturgical music (L), and finally by traditional style music (T). Look for these codes (C, F, G, L, or T) just to the left of the major category code.

Come And Go With Me	Landry, Carey (Rev.)	75 Nal	B R C La
Come Out	Miffleton, Jack	71 Wlp	B R C La
Hi God!	Landry, Carey (Rev.)	73 Nal	B R C La
I've Got A Light	Mcgrath, Roberta	75 Rpb	M B R L C La
Run, Come, See(1)	Blue, Robert	66 Fel	B R C La
Run, Come, See(2)	Blue, Robert	66 Fel	B R C La
A People Marching To Freedom (Opt Brs)	Montague, George T.	72 Mcc	B R L F La Unis+
A Voice Cries Out In The Wilderness	Berlucchi, James	74 Wgm	B R L F La
And I Will Follow (Psalm 23)	Repp, Ray	66 Fel	B R F La
Children Gather Round	Williams, J.	76 Sil	F La
Come On In	Lewis, E.	74 Sil	L F La
Come To Jerusalem	Ste. Marie, Patricia	74 Sha	M B R L F La
Come To The Lord	Hunkele	67 Wlp	B R F La
Come To The Lord (4-Part Arr.)	Cirou, Joseph	73 Acp	L F La
Come, Let Us Sing To The Lord	Wyrtzen, Don	75 Zon	M F La Satb
Coming Together	Shaw, Jim	73 Fel	B F La
Enter And Sing To The Lord	Gerrish, James	76 Rpb	M B R L F La
Gathering Song	Davis, Bob	73 Fcc	B R L F La
He Is Here Among Us	Tucciarone, Angel	73 Wlp	B R F La
Here We Are	Repp, Ray	66 Fel	B R F La
I Will Arise (So Early)	Farra, Mimi A.	72 Gia	M B R L F La Var+
In Your Holy Place (4-Part Arr)	Silvia, Helen	70 Acp	L F La
It's A Sign Of Love	Repp, Ray	68 Fel	B R F La
Let Us Make Music For God	Shaltz, Gregory	74 Sms	M R L F La
Light Of Christ	Kohl, Jon	73 Fel	B F La
People Everywhere Are Gathered	Williams, J.	76 Sil	F La
Psalm 100	Blake, Kevin	Na Zon	M F La 2-Pt-Sa
Psalm 100 The Lord Be With You	Quinlan, Paul	66 Fel	B F La
Psalm 11 Run Like A Deer	Quinlan, Paul	66 Fel	B R F La
Rejoice Always	Gryniewicz, Tom & Elle	74 Wgm	B L F La
Rejoice, My Friends	Caesar, Paul	73 Fcc	B R L F La
The Lord Is Here	St. Benedict's Farm	75 Sbf	B R I F La
The Lord Is Present In His Sanctuary	Cole, Gail	75 Chm	B F La See Wgm
The Love Of Christ	Repp, Ray	66 Fel	B R F La
We Come Praising God	Yantis, David	Na Yan	B F La
We Go Into The House Of The Lord	Schaffer, Robert J.	67 Wlp	M B R F La
We're Gonna March Down	Blue, Robert	66 Fel	B F La
Where Two Or Three	Reilly, Cyril A.	66 Fel	B F La
Where Two Or Three Are Gathered	Temple, Sebastian	71 Gia	B R L F La Var+
Come Thou Almighty	Newbury, Kent A.	75 Wrd	M G La Satb+
Come Unto Me	Gaither/Gaither, G.	63 Gmc	M B G La Satb
Shall We Gather At The River	Lowry/Decou	Na Zon	M G La Satb
A Song For The Sabbath	Mueller, Luise	76 Abi	M L La Satb
Arise, Come Sing In The Morning	Zsigray, Joe	73 Nal	B R L La
As We Gather	Patenaude, Andre, M.	71 Nal	B R L La
Awake, Awake, Good People (Solo)	Cassler, G. W.	67 Aug	M L La
Awake, My Soul!	Martin	Na Lor	M L La
Behold A Great Priest	Cunningham, Patrick	74 Gra	M R L L La Satb
Behold A Great Priest	Murphy, J A	Na Gia	L La
Behold The Great Priest	Stadler, M	68 Gia	M L La Var+
Behold The High Priest	Fitzpatrick, Dennis	65 Fel	B L La
Behold The Priest Of The Lord	Fitzpatrick, Dennis	65 Fel	B L La
Boldly Let Us Come With Confidence	Fitzpatrick, Dennis	65 Fel	B L La
Christmas Introit	Starks	Na Lor	M L La
Come All You People	Lynch, Michael B.	75 Rav	B R L L La
Come And Sing	Fabing, Bob	74 Ahc	B R L L La
Come Let Us Join In Prayer Today	Richo	68 Wlp	B L La
Come My Friend	Page, Paul F.	75 Rpb	M B R L L La
Come You Faithful	Neale, John M.	70 Acp	L L La
Come You Faithful (4-Part Arr)	Roh, Johann	73 Acp	L L La
Come, All Ye Saints	Telemann	75 Her	M L La Satb
Come, Let Us Bow Down	Wapen, Francis A	70 Gia	M L La 2pt
Come, Ye Faithful	Denton	Na Lor	M L La Satb
Come, Ye Thankful People	Thompson	Na Lor	M L La Satb
Come, Ye That Love The Lord	Young, Gordon	75 Sac	M L La Satb
Come, Ye That Serve (Me) W/2 Tpts	Englert, Eugene	Na Gia	M L L La Satb+
Easter Introit, An	Slater	75 Sac	M L La Satb
Enter O People Of God	Strahan-Cross, R.	70 Wlp	B L La
Entrance Song For Christmas	Cunningham, Patrick	72 Gra	B R L L La U+Brs
Fanfare & Choral Procession (W/Brass)	Moe, Daniel	71 Aug	M L La Satb+
Father, Eternal, Ruler Of Creation	Pelz, W.	73 Aug	M L La Satb+
Festival Introits	Couper, Alinda B.	Na Abi	M L La Satb
Gather 'round	Page, Paul F.	74 Rpb	M B R L L La
Gathering Song (W/ Org, Perc)	Peloquin, C Alexander	76 Gia	M L L La Unis
God Is In This Holy Place	Peloquin, C Alexander	75 Gia	M L La Satbu+
Here Is A Great Priest	Roff, Joseph	67 Gia	M L La Var+
Holy, Holy, Holy	Collins, Ray	62 Gam	M L La Satb
How I Rejoiced	Quinlan, Paul	68 Nal	B R L La
How I Rejoiced When I Heard Them Say	Fitzpatrick, Dennis	65 Fel	B L La
I Come With Joy	Lovelace, Austin C.	74 Aug	M L La U+Ds
I Will Go To The Altar Of God	Cunningham, Patrick	76 Gra	B R L L La Satb
I Will Go To The Altar Of God	Fitzpatrick, Dennis	65 Fel	B L La
In Love We Gather	Schaffer, Robert J.	67 Wlp	B L La
In The Presence Of God	Landry, Carey (Rev)	Na Nal	M L La
Introductory Rite	Zsigray, Joe	73 Nal	B R L La
Introits For Lent And Easter	Nelson, Ronald A.	Na Abi	M L La Sab
Jesus Wher'e'er Thy People Meet	Ford, Virgil	Na Gsc	B L La Satb
Let Us Enter The House Of The Lord	Hughes, Howard	72 Gia	M L La Usatb+
Let Us Stand In Prayer	Schroth, G	70 Gia	M L La U+2pt
Lift Up Your Heads, O Ye Gates	Ratzlaff, Paul	Na Zon	L La Satb
Lift Up Your Heads, O Ye Gates	Thompson, Robert B.	Na Zon	L La Satb
Lift Up Your Heads, Ye Gates Of Brass	Leupold	57 Aug	M L La Sab
Lift Up, O Gates	Fitzpatrick, Dennis	65 Fel	B L La
Listen To The Word	Ellis, Ron	76 Rav	B R L L La
Lo! God Is Here	Hughes, Robert J.	Na Lor	M L La Satb
Now We Are Met	Goodban-Hardwicke	76 Pro	M L La 2pt+
O Come Let Us Sing	Butler	75 Sac	M L La Satb
O Come, All Ye Children	Bender, Jan	63 Aug	M L La Unis
O Come, Let Us Sing	Black	75 Sac	M L La Satb
O Come, Let Us Sing To The Lord	Track, Gerhard	72 Gia	M L La Satb+
O Come, Let Us Sing Unto The Lord	Harries, David	Na Oxf	M L La Satb
O Lord, How Good It Is To Be Here	Fitzpatrick, Dennis	65 Fel	B L La
Only In The Midst Of The World	Schneider, Kent E.	75 Ccc	B L La
Open The Gates Of Justice	Fitzpatrick, Dennis	65 Fel	B L La
Praise Song	Lynch, Michael B.	76 Rav	B R L L La
Priest And Bishop	Roff, Joseph	67 Gia	M L La Var+
Processional "Let There Be Light"	Ives, Charles E.	55 Pic	M L La
Processional Psalm	Proulx, Richard	72 Gia	M L La Var+
Psalm 100	Garlick, Antony	Na See	M L La
Psalm 100	Zimmermann	70 Aug	M L La Satb+
Psalm 100 (99)	Somerville, S. 1	60 Wlp	B L La
Psalm 121 (Unacc)	Copes, V. Earle	Na Abi	M L La Satb
Psalm 122: Hail Jerusalem!	Catalanello, Michael	75 Str	M L La
Psalm 127 (126)	Westendorf/Picca	64 Wlp	B L La
Psalm 24 (Lift Up Your Heads)	Nelson, Ronald A.	66 Aug	M L La Satb
Psalm 98	Proulx, Richard	72 Cfc	M L L La
Rejoice In Hope	Peloquin, C Alexander	72 Gia	M L La Satbu+
Send Forth Your Light And Your Truth	Fitzpatrick, Dennis	65 Fel	B L La
Sing Out Use Your Voice Now	Isele, David C.	74 Gia	B L L La Var+
Stand Up And Bless The Lord	George	66 Aug	M L La Sa
Stand Up And Bless The Lord	Peterson, John W.	Na Zon	L La Satb
The Lord Is In This Place (W/Brs)	Pfautsch, Lloyd	75 Abi	M L La Satb
The Love Of Christ Has Joined	Nachtwey, Roger	65 Fel	B R L La
We Gather At Your Table, Lord	Ehret, Walter	76 Sac	L La Sab+
We Gather Together	Lisicky, Paul	76 Rpb	M B R L L La
We Gather Together (4-Part Arr)	Cirou, Joseph Et Al	73 Acp	L L La
We Shall Enter Your Courts	Fitzpatrick, Dennis	65 Fel	B L La
We're Gathered Together	Lisicky, Paul	76 Rpb	M B R L L La
Welcome, Lord (W/Guitar)	Temple, Sebastian	71 Gia	B R L L La Satb+
Well, It's A New Day	Miffleton, Jack	69 Wlp	B R L La
Where Charity And Love Are	Roff, Joseph	65 Lit	B L La
Where Two Or Three Are Gathered	Deiss, Lucien	70 Wlp	B R L La
Whereever Faithful Men Assemble	Fitzpatrick, Dennis	65 Fel	B L La
With Gladness And Rejoicing	Fitzpatrick, Dennis	65 Fel	B L La
A Mighty Fortress (Inst. Optional)	Luther, M.-Johnson	65 Aug	M T La Var
Awake, My Soul	Nelson, Ronald A.	73 Aug	M T La Sab
Awake, Psaltry And Harp	Young	68 Aug	M T La Satb
Brethren, We Have Met To Worship	Traditional/Johnson	Na Zon	T La Ssatb
Come Unto Me	Roberts, Ricky	74 Fis	M T La
Come With Rejoicing	Leaf, Robert	70 Aug	M T La Unis
Come, Let Us Worship	Carroll, J. R.	Na Gia	T La
Come, Ye That Love The Lord	Williams/Decou	Na Zon	T La Satb
Come, Ye Thankful People, Come	Nelson, Ronald A.	68 Aug	M T La Satb+
Entrata Festiva	Peeters, Flor	75 Cfp	M T La
Father, Once More Within	Matthews, H A	Na Gsc	B T La Full
Festival Anthem On Crown Him	Proulx, Richard	70 Aug	M T La Satb+
God Is Here-Let's Celebrate	Leaf, Robert	70 Aug	M T La Satb
God Is My Strong Salvation	Ford	Na Wbp	T La
God's Holy Mountain We Ascend	Westendorf, Omer	64 Wlp	B T-La
Great Shepherd Of A Loyal Flock	Westendorf, Omer	64 Wlp	B T La
Hail To The Lord's Anointed	Traditional/Johnson	Na Zon	T La Satb
He Is Here	Owens, Jimmy	72 Lex	M T La
I Was Glad (Ps 122)	Slack, Roy	Na Oxf	M T La Satb
In Ecclesiis	Gabrieli, G	Na Gsc	B T La 8mix
Introit For The New Year (M)	Cabena, Barrie	Na Oxf	M T La Satb
Lift Up Your Hands, O Ye Gates	Handel, G. F.	Na Gsc	B T La Ssatb+
Lift Up Your Heads, O Ye Gates	Handel, G. F.	Na Gsc	M T La 5pt
Lo! God Is Here!	Burroughs	75 Maf	M T La Satb
Lo, God Is Here	Rosley, John M.	Na Zon	T La Satb
Lo, God Is Here!	Mueller, Carl F	Na Gsc	B T La 8mix

Lord God We Worship Thee	Bach, J.S./Ed Lee	73 Gia	B R L T La Satb+
Lord We Gather At Your Altar	Westendorf, Omer	64 Wlp	B T La
Morning Has Broken	Martin, Gilbert M	Na Lor	M T La Satb
O Come, Let Us Worship	Mendelssohn, F.	Na Gsc	B T La Satb+
O God Our Help In Ages Past	Christiansen, P.	58 Aug	M T La Satb
O God, Our Help In Ages Past	Cassler, G. W.	70 Aug	M T La Satb+
O God, Our Help In Ages Past (Brass)	Pasquet, Jean (Arr)	72 Elv	M T La Satb+
One Hundredth Psalm, The	Beverst	75 Sac	M T La Satb
Open Now Thy Gates Of Beauty	Peninger	75 Sac	M T La Satb
Open The Gates Of The Temple	Knapp/Johnson	Na Zon	M T La Satb
Psalm 95	Berger, Jean	57 Bbl	M T La Satb
Sing To The Lord	Goemanne, Noel	71 Sms	M R L T La
Surely God Is In This Place	Price	Na Lor	M T La Satb
Surely God Is In This Place	Rasley	Na Lor	M T La Satb
This Is The Day (M)	Copley, R. Evan	75 Abi	M T La Satb
To Come, O Lord, To Thee	Stickles, William	Na Gsc	B T La Satb+
Trust God And Come Before Him	Mischke/Vermulst	61 Wlp	B T La
Unfold Ye Portals (The Redemption)	Gounod, Charles	Na Gsc	B T La Full+
Unfold, Ye Portals	Gounod, Charles	Na Lor	M T La Satb
We Come To Praise His Name (Jud Mac)	Handel, G. F. (Wiley)	73 Pro	M T La Sab
We Gather Together	Westendorf, Omer	70 Wlp	B T La
When Morning Gilds The Skies	Denton	Na Lor	M T La
When Morning Gilds The Skies	Hughes, Robert J.	Na Lor	M T La

Acclamations(Lord Have Mercy)

The ancient Greek "Kyrie Eleison" is a song of repentence to the risen Christ. Additional material for this category can be found under Masses in category za (collections).

Kyrie (Mass For Schools)	Kostos, Patti	66 Fel	B C Lb
Kyrie (Mariachi Mass)	Lojewski, Harry V.	69 Fel	B R F Lb
Kyrie (Mass Of The Western Tribes)	Indian Melodies	66 Fel	B F Lb
Lord Have Mercy	Davis, Bob	73 Fcc	B R L F Lb
Lord Have Mercy	Yantis, David	Na Yan	B F Lb
Lord Have Mercy (Kyrie)	Scholtes, Peter	68 Fel	B R F Lb
Lord Have Mercy (Kyrie)	Scholtes, Peter	66 Fel	B R F Lb
Lord Have Mercy (Kyrie)(Funeral Folk)	Mitchell, Ian	67 Fel	B R F Lb
Lord Have Mercy (Kyrie)(Jazz–Rock)	Mitchell, Ian	68 Fel	B R F Lb
Lord Have Mercy (Icet)	Schaffer, Robert J.	69 Wlp	B F Lb
Lord Have Mercy (Icet)	Wise, Joe	69 Wlp	B F Lb
Lord Have Mercy (Upon Me)	Farra, Mimi A.	73 Gia	M B R L F Lb Var+
Lord Have Mercy (1964 Text)	Winter, Miriam T.	66 Van	B R F Lb
Lord Have Mercy (3 Fold)	Markaitis, Bruno	67 Van	B R F Lb
Prayer For Mercy (First Mass)	Repp, Ray	66 Fel	B R F Lb
Prayer For Mercy (Second Mass)	Repp, Ray	66 Fel	B R F Lb
Prayer Of Petition (Kyrie)	Blue, Robert	66 Fel	B F Lb
Kyrie	Zsigray, Joe	75 Nal	B R L Lb
Kyrie (Eng Mass)	Goemanne, Noel	70 Gia	B L L Lb 2pt+
Kyrie (Eng, Icet Pen Rite C)	Cunningham, Patrick	74 Gra	M R L L Lb Var
Kyrie (Lord, Have Mercy)	Moultry, Prince Joseph	74 Nal	B R L Lb
Kyrie (Mass For New Rite)	Hampton, Calvin	76 Gia	B L L Lb Satb+
Kyrie (Sung Mass No.2)	Fitzpatrick, Dennis	63 Fel	B L Lb
Kyrie (Thomas More Mass)	Reilly, Cyril A.	66 Fel	B L Lb
Kyrie (With Narrator)	Christiansen, P.	71 Aug	M L Lb Satb+
Kyrie (3fold) Mass For King	Pulkingham, Betty C.	73 Gia	B R L L Lb Satb+
Kyrie (6fold) Mass For King	Pulkingham, Betty C.	73 Gia	B R L L Lb Satb+
Kyrie (9fold) Mass For King	Pulkingham, Betty C.	73 Gia	B R L L Lb Satb+
Kyrie Eleison	Deiss, Lucien	70 Wlp	B R L Lb Var
Kyrie I (Notre Dame Mass)	Isele, David C.	74 Gia	B L L Lb Satb+
Kyrie I (Rite A)	Goemanne, Noel	73 Gia	B L L Lb 2pt+
Kyrie ii (Notre Dame Mass)	Isele, David C.	74 Gia	B L L Lb Satb+
Kyrie ii (Rite C)	Goemanne, Noel	73 Gia	B L L Lb 2pt+
Lord Have Mercy	Davis, Paulette	76 Rpb	M B R L L Lb
Lord Have Mercy	Gentemann, Sr Elaine	70 Gia	B L L Lb Satb+
Lord Have Mercy	Gentemann, Sr Elaine	75 Gia	B L L Lb Sa+
Lord Have Mercy	Mahoney, Patrick	74 Rpb	M B R L L Lb
Lord Have Mercy	Nix, Donna	74 Nal	B L Lb
Lord Have Mercy	Page, Paul F.	76 Rpb	M B R L L Lb
Lord Have Mercy	Page, Paul F.	73 Rpb	M B R L L Lb
Lord Have Mercy	Patterson, Keith	74 Rpb	M B R L L Lb
Lord Have Mercy	Proulx, Richard	71 Gia	B L L Lb Satb+
Lord Have Mercy	Schneider, Kent E.	75 Ccc	B L Lb
Lord Have Mercy	Schutte, Dan, S. J.	73 Nal	B R L Lb
Lord Have Mercy	Smith, Roger	75 Nal	B R L Lb
Lord Have Mercy	St. Benedict's Farm	72 Sbf	B R L L Lb
Lord Have Mercy	Sylvester, Erich	74 Nal	B R L Lb
Lord Have Mercy (Kyrie)	Fitzpatrick, Dennis	63 Fel	B L Lb
Lord Have Mercy (Kyrie)(Chardin Mass)	Rudcki, Stanly	66 Fel	B L Lb
Lord Have Mercy (Kyrie)(Folk Mass #4)	Quinlan, Paul	66 Fel	B L Lb
Lord Have Mercy On Us	Gilligan, Michael	67 Acp	L L Lb
Lord Have Mercy (Cel Of Unity)	Hebble, Robert	72 Gia	B L L Lb Satb+
Lord Have Mercy (Child Mass)	Andrews, Carroll T.	70 Gia	B L L Lb Satb+
Lord Have Mercy (Community Mass)	Lee, John	71 Gia	B L L Lb U+Org
Lord Have Mercy (Danish Amen)	Kraehenbuehl/Frischman	73 Jsp	B L Lb +Org
Lord Have Mercy (Icet)	Kraehenbuehl, David	67 Jsp	B L Lb +Org
Lord Have Mercy (Icet)	Kreutz, Robert	69 Wlp	B L Lb
Lord Have Mercy (Icet)	Lojewski	69 Wlp	B L Lb
Lord Have Mercy (Icet)	Picca, Angelo Della	69 Wlp	B L Lb
Lord Have Mercy (Icet)	Vermulst, Jan	69 Wlp	B L Lb
Lord Have Mercy (Lyric Mass)	Andrews, Carroll T.	70 Gia	B L L Lb 2pt+
Lord Have Mercy (Mass For All Seasons)	Andrews, Carroll T.	73 Gia	B L L Lb Var+
Lord Have Mercy (New Mass)	Andrews, Carroll T.	70 Gia	B L L Lb Unis+
Lord Have Mercy (Short Mass)	Lee, John	69 Gia	M B L L Lb Satb+
Lord Have Mercy (Threefold)	Deiss, Lucien	70 Wlp	B L Lb
Lord Have Mercy (Twofold)	Deiss, Lucien	70 Wlp	B L Lb
Lord Have Mercy (W/Cantor)(Dominic)	Goemanne, Noel	71 Gia	B L L Lb Satb+
Lord Have Mercy – 2nd Version	Patterson, Keith	74 Rpb	M B R L L Lb
Lord Have Mercy On Us (2–Part Arr)	Cirou, Joseph/Oconnell	73 Acp	L L Lb
Lord Have Mercy On Us All	Gutfreund, Ed (Rev.)	74 Nal	B R L Lb
Lord Have Mercy 2	Moultry, Prince Joseph	74 Nal	B R L Lb
Lord Have Mercy (Opt Brs/Timp)	Goemanne, Noel	70 Gia	B L L Lb Sab+
Lord Have Mercy (Vianney Mass)	Andrews, Carroll T.	75 Gia	B L L Lb Var+
Two–Fold Kyrie	Carroll, J. R.	71 Gia	B L L Lb 3pt+
Kyrie	Durante, Francesco	Na Gsc	B T Lb Satb
Kyrie	Haydn, Joseph	Na Gsc	B T Lb Satb+
Kyrie	Mendelssohn, F.	Na Oxf	B T Lb Satb
Kyrie	Mozart, Wolfgang A	75 Her	M T Lb Satb
Kyrie	Pergolesi, G B	Na Gsc	B T Lb 5mix+
Kyrie	Schubert, Franz J.	Na Gsc	B T Lb Ssaa+
Kyrie (Missa Brevis)	Lotti, A & Weber, R.	66 Fel	B T Lb
Kyrie Eleison	Chihara	75 Her	M T Lb Satb
Kyrie Eleison	De Victoria	75 Sac	M T Lb Satb
Kyrie Eleison	Haydn, Joseph	75 Her	M T Lb Satb
Kyrie Eleison	Haydn/Hirt	Na Wbp	T Lb
Kyrie From "Missa Secunda"	Hassler	75 Her	M T Lb Satb
Kyrie From Missa Super L'homme Arme	Des Pres, Josquin	75 Bbl	M T Lb Satb
Kyrie In D Minor	Mendelssohn, F.	Na Gsc	B T Lb Satb+
Lord Have Mercy	Bixel, James W.	74 Flp	M T Lb
Lord Have Mercy	Haydn, J. – Ehret	73 Aug	M T Lb Satb
Lord Have Mercy (Kyrie)(Hymn Tune)	Traditional	65 Fel	B T Lb
Lord Have Mercy (4 Voices)	Lant's Roll/Tortolano	75 Gia	B L T Lb Round
Missa Super L'homme Arme Kyrie Ii	Dufay, Guillaume	73 Bbl	M T Lb Satb

Glorias

"Glory to God in the Highest" is an ancient hymn to Christ. These opening words are attributed to Christmas angels.

Gloria (Mass For Schools)	Kostos, Patti	66 Fel	B C Lc
Gloria (Mariachi Mass)	Lojewski, Harry V	69 Fel	B R F Lc
Gloria (Mass For King Of Glory) Org/Gui	Pulkingham, Betty C.	73 Gia	B L F Lc Satb+
Gloria A La Samba (W/Org, Bongos)	Peloquin, C Alexander	70 Gia	B L F Lc Var+
Glory	Yantis, David	Na Yan	B F Lc
Glory Be To God On High (Jazz–Rock)	Mitchell, Ian	68 Fel	B R F Lc
Glory To God	Yantis, David	Na Yan	B F Lc
Glory To God (Folk Mass No.4)	Quinlan, Paul	66 Fel	B F Lc
Glory To God (Missa Bossa Nova)	Scholtes, Peter	66 Fel	B R F Lc
Glory To God (1964 Text)	Winter, Miriam T.	66 Van	B R F Lc
Glory To God (64 Text)	Markaitis, Bruno	67 Van	B R F Lc
Hymn Of Praise (First Mass)	Repp, Ray	66 Fel	B R F Lc
Hymn Of Praise (Second Mass)	Repp, Ray	66 Fel	B R F Lc
Gloria	Carroll, J. R.	71 Gia	B L L Lc 3pt+
Gloria	Gentemann, Sr Elaine	70 Gia	B L L Lc Satb+
Gloria	Zsigray, Joe	73 Nal	B R L Lc
Gloria	Zsigray, Joe	75 Nal	B R L Lc
Gloria (A Cappella, Long)	Rickard	71 Aug	M L Lc
Gloria (Eng Mass)	Goemanne, Noel	70 Gia	B L L Lc 2pt+
Gloria (Eng, Icet) Opt Brass	Cunningham, Patrick	74 Gra	M R L L Lc Chcor
Gloria (From Celebration)	Peloquin, C Alexander	75 Gia	B L L Lc Satb+
Gloria (Icet) From Community Mass	Lee, John	71 Gia	B L L Lc 2pt+
Gloria (Liturgy Of Joy)	Blue, Robert	66 Fel	B L Lc
Gloria (Lyric Liturgy)	Peloquin, C Alexander	74 Gia	B L L Lc Satbu
Gloria (Mass For New Rite)	Hampton, Calvin	76 Gia	B L L Lc Satb+
Gloria (Notre Dame Mass)	Isele, David C.	74 Gia	B L L Lc Satb+
Gloria (Sung Mass No.2)	Fitzpatrick, Dennis	63 Fel	B L Lc
Gloria (Thomas More Mass)	Reilly, Cyril A.	66 Fel	B L Lc
Gloria (W/Fl, Cello)	Goemanne, Noel	73 Gia	B L L Lc 2pt+
Gloria A Dios (Chant)	Lee, John	70 Gia	B L L Lc Uspar
Gloria And Alleluia	Lekberg, Sven	Na Gsc	B L Lc Satb
Gloria And Sanctus/Benedictus	Arnatt, Ronald	75 Gia	B L L Lc Satbu
Gloria Of The Bells Icet	Peloquin, C Alexander	72 Gia	B L L Lc Satb+
Gloria Tibi (From Mass)	Bernstein, Leonard	Na Gsc	B L Lc 2pt+
Glory To God	Batozynski, Lawrence	74 Cfc	M L L Lc
Glory To God	Gentemann, Sr Elaine	75 Gia	B L L Lc Sa+
Glory To God	Hytrek, S. Theophane	74 Cfc	M L L Lc
Glory To God	Marier, Theodore	74 Cfc	M L L Lc
Glory To God	Schneider, Kent E.	75 Ccc	B L Lc
Glory To God	Schutte, Dan, S. J.	70 Nal	B R L Lc
Glory To God	Shelley, Tom	75 Ahc	B R L L Lc
Glory To God	St. Benedict's Farm	72 Sbf	B R L L Lc
Glory To God	Sylvester, Erich	71 Nal	B R L Lc
Glory To God	Vickers, Wendy	75 Nal	B R L Lc
Glory To God (American Saint)(Icet)	Kreutz, Robert	69 Wlp	B L Lc Satb
Glory To God (Angelic Hymn)	Proulx, Richard	71 Gia	B L L Lc Satb+
Glory To God (Bcl)	Schaffer, Robert J.	67 Wlp	B L Lc
Glory To God (Cel Of Unity)	Hebble, Robert	72 Gia	B L L Lc Satb-
Glory To God (Chardin Mass)	Rudcki, Stanley	66 Fel	B L Lc
Glory To God (Child Mass)	Andrews, Carroll T.	70 Gia	B L L Lc Satb-
Glory To God (Choir Alone) (M)	Fitch, Donald	75 Wlp	M L Lc Sab+
Glory To God (Community Mass)	Lee, John	71 Gia	B L L Lc U+Or
Glory To God (Danish Amen Mass)	Kraehenbuehl/Frischman	73 Jsp	B L Lc +Org
Glory To God (Icet)	Deiss, Lucien	69 Wlp	B L Lc
Glory To God (Icet)	Kraehenbuehl, David	67 Jsp	B L Lc +Org
Glory To God (Icet)(Mass Of Hope) M	Picca, Angelo Della	70 Wlp	B L Lc Var
Glory To God (Lyric Mass)	Andrews, Carroll T.	70 Gia	B L L Lc 2pt+
Glory To God (Mass Assembly)(Icet)	Lojewski	69 Wlp	B L Lc Satb
Glory To God (Opt Brs/Timp)	Goemanne, Noel	70 Gia	B L L Lc Sab+
Glory To God (People's Mass)(Icet)	Vermulst, Jan	70 Wlp	B L Lc Satb
Glory To God (Sung Mass No.1)	Fitzpatrick, Dennis	63 Fel	B L Lc
Glory To God (W/Cantor) Dominic Mass	Goemanne, Noel	71 Gia	B L L Lc Satb+
Glory To God (Icet)(Holy Spirit Mass)	Deiss, Lucien	75 Wlp	B L Lc
Glory To God (Mass For All Seasons)	Andrews, Carroll T.	73 Gia	B L L Lc Var+
Glory To God (New Mass)	Andrews, Carroll T.	70 Gia	B L L Lc Unis+

CATEGORIZED INDEX

Glory To God(Vianney Mass)	Andrews, Carroll T.	75 Gia	B L L Lc Var+
Gloria	Burroughs	71 Aug	M T Lc Unis
Gloria	Carter	74 Aug	M T Lc Ssatb
Gloria	Hassler, H L	Na Gsc	B T Lc Satb+
Gloria	Hoag, Charles K	Na Gsc	B T Lc Ssaa+
Gloria	Pergolesi, G B	Na Gsc	B T Lc 5mix
Gloria	Rutter, John	Na Oxf	M T Lc Satb
Gloria	Vivaldi, A.	Na Kal	B T Lc Satb
Gloria	Walton, William	Na Oxf	B T Lc Satb
Gloria (D)	Power, Leonel	Na Oxf	M T Lc Ttbb
Gloria (From The Twelfth Mass)	Mozart, Wolfgang A	Na Lor	M T Lc Satb
Gloria (Latin)	Brown, Christopher	Na Oxf	B T Lc Full
Gloria (Md)	Mathias, William	Na Oxf	M T Lc Ttbb
Gloria (Missa Brevis)	Lotti, A.	66 Fel	B T Lc
Gloria From Messa A 4 Voci Da Cappella	Monteverdi, Claudio	Na Gia	T Lc
Gloria In Excelsis	Cockshott, Gerald R.	57 Ron	M T Lc Ssaatte
Gloria In Excelsis	Mozart, Wolfgang A	Na Gsc	B T Lc Var
Gloria In Excelsis	Sprague, Richard L	Na Gsc	B T Lc Satb
Gloria In Excelsis	Vivaldi, Antonio	75 Maf	M R T Lc Satb
Gloria In Excelsis ("12th Mass")	Mozart, Wolfgang A	Cfs	M T Lc Satb
Gloria In Excelsis (Md)	Weelkes, Thomas	Na Oxf	M T Lc Full
Gloria In Excelsis Deo	Gounod, Charles	Na Gsc	B T Lc Satb
Gloria In Excelsis Deo	Lorenz	Na Lor	M T Lc Satb
Gloria Patri	Pergolesi, G B	Na Gsc	B T Lc Satb+
Gloria(Mass In B Flat)	Farmer, H	Na Gsc	B T Lc Satb+
Glory Be To God	Bruckner, Anton	67 Gia	M T Lc Satb+
Glory To God	Schutz, Heinrich	Na Abi	M T Lc Full
Glory To God In The Highest	Haydn–Coggin	75 Wlp	M T Lc Var
Glory To God In The Highest	Kennedy	75 Maf	M T Lc Satb
Glory To God In The Highest	Pergolesi	Na Lor	M T Lc Var
Glory To God In The Highest	Pergolesi, G B	Na Gsc	B T Lc Satb+
Glory To God In The Highest	Pergolesi, G. B.	50 Pro	M L T Lc Satb
Glory To God In The Highest	Track, Gerhard	Na Gsc	B T Lc Satb
Glory To God In The Highest, Glory	White, Edward L	75 Maf	M T Lc Full
Glory To God On High	Milgrove–Riedel	57 Aug	M T Lc Sab

Responsorial Psalms

Individual psalms and some collections appear here. See also category ZA.

Believe	Mcgrath, Roberta	74 Rpb	M B R L C Ld Respons
My God, My God	Kostos, Patti	66 Fel	B C Ld
Psalm 103	Mcgrath, Roberta	74 Rpb	M B R L C Ld Resp
Psalm 33	Murphy, Angela	75 Rpb	M B R L C Ld Resp
The Lord Is My Shepherd(1)	Blue, Robert	66 Fel	B R C Ld

Epistle (Response)	Meltz, Ken	72 Wlp	B F Ld
Let The Heavens Be Glad (Ccd)	Wise, Joe	68 Wlp	B R F Ld
Lord Be Not Far From Me	Shaltz, Gregory	74 Sms	M R L F Ld
Lord Make Me Know Your Ways	Ste. Marie, Patricia	74 Sha	B R L F Ld
Lord, Send Out Your Spirit	Cunningham, Patrick	70 Gra	B R L F Ld Satb
Lord, Whom Need I Fear	Aridas, Chris	73 Fel	B F Ld
Lord's My Shepherd (Ps 23)Opt Guit	Wyatt 1	76 Pro	M F Ld 2pt+
Lowly People You Save (Ps 18)	Cunningham, Patrick	68 Gra	B R L F Ld
My Soul Thirsts For The Lord	Quinlan, Paul	65 Wlp	B R F Ld
Peace I Leave With You (Ps 23)	Cunningham, Patrick	68 Gra	B R L F Ld
Pray For The Peace Of Jerusalem	Cunningham, Patrick	68 Gra	B R L F Ld
Pray For The Peace Of Jerusalem	Johnson, Gary L.	74 Bfi	B L F Ld
Psalm 148 (From Come Follow)	Kramper, Jerry	69 Gia	B R L F Ld
Psalm 30 I Praise You, O Lord	Zunic, Sr. Mary Grace	66 Fel	B F Ld
Psalm 65 (From Come Follow)	Kramper, Jerry	69 Gia	B R L F Ld
Psalm 84 (How Lovely)	Toolan, Sr Suzanne	71 Gia	B R L F Ld Ar+
Steadfast In Your Paths (Ps 17)	Cunningham, Patrick	68 Gra	B R L F Ld
The Lord Has Set His Throne	Cunningham, Patrick	70 Gra	B R L F Ld
Twenty–Third Psalm	Edwin, Robert	67 Van	B R F Ld
Who Will Dwell On God's Mountain?	Quinlan, Paul	65 Wlp	B R F Ld

Psalm 40	Crouch, Andrae	67 Man	R G Ld

All The Ends Of The Earth (Icet)	Picca, Angelo Della	70 Wlp	B L Ld
All You Peoples, Clap Your Hands	Roff, Joseph	71 Gia	M L Ld Unis+
Antiphons	Page, Paul F.	74 Rpb	M B R L L Ld
As The Hills Are Round About Jerusalem	Gilsdorf, Sr. Helen	74 Rpb	M B R L L Ld Ps 124
At All Times I Will Bless (Ps 34)	Cunningham, Patrick	75 Gra	B R L L Ld Unis
Be Glad, Be Happy	Gilsdorf, Sr. Helen	74 Rpb	M B R L L Ld Respons
Be Merciful O Lord (Icet)	Picca, Angelo Della	70 Wlp	B L Ld
Be With Me Lord (Icet)	Picca, Angelo Della	70 Wlp	B L Ld
Christmas Psalm (Today Is Born)	Cunningham, Patrick	70 Gra	B R L L Ld Satbu
Christmas Vigil Psalm (Icet)	Picca, Angelo Della	69 Wlp	B L Ld
Clean Heart(Ps 51)	Ellis, Ron	73 Rav	B L L Ld
Common Of Doctors (Icet) Psalm	Schaffer, Robert J.	69 Wlp	B L Ld
Common Of Martyrs Psalm (Icet)	Schaffer, Robert J.	69 Wlp	B L Ld
Common Of Pastors (Icet) Psalm	Smith	69 Wlp	B L Ld
Common Of Saints (Icet)	Picca, Angelo Della	69 Wlp	B L Ld
Common Of Saints Psalm (2cet)	Burns, James	69 Wlp	B L Ld
Common Of Virgins (Icet) Psalm	Kreutz, Robert	69 Wlp	B L Ld
Common Responses (Icet)	Picca, Angelo Della	70 Wlp	B L Ld
Create In Me	Johnson, Gary L.	75 Bfi	B R L Ld
Cry Out To God(Ps 66)	Ellis, Ron	75 Rav	B R L L Ld
Cry Out With Joy! (1s 12:1–6)	Cunningham, Patrick	76 Gra	B L L Ld Unis+
Every Day I Will Praise You (Ps 145)	Gilsdorf, Sr. Helen	75 Rpb	M B R L L Ld
Father, I Put My Life In Your Hands	Schaffer, Robert J.	73 Cfc	M R L L Ld
Fill Us With Your Love (Ps 90)	Cunningham, Patrick	70 Gra	B R L L Ld Satbu
Forever I Will Sing(Ps 89)	Ellis, Ron	73 Rav	B L L Ld
Forever I Will Sing(Ps 89)	Lynch, Michael B.	73 Rav	B L L Ld
Give Thanks To The Lord (Ps107)	Cunningham, Patrick	76 Gra	B L L Ld Satbu+
Give The Lord Glory(Ps 96)	Lynch, Michael B.	73 Rav	B L L Ld
God Mounts His Throne (Icet)	Picca, Angelo Della	69 Wlp	B L Ld
God Mounts His Throne (Ps47)	Cunningham, Patrick	76 Gra	B L L Ld Satb+
Halay, When To God I Send A Plea	Quinlan, Paul	68 Fel	L Ld
Happy Is He Who Regards (Ps 41)	Cunningham, Patrick	76 Gra	B R L L Ld
Happy Is He Whose Fault Is Taken	Cunningham, Patrick	76 Gra	B R L L Ld 2ptan
Harden Not Your Hearts(Ps 95)	Ellis, Ron	73 Rav	B R L L Ld
Have Mercy On Me	Peloquin, C Alexander	71 Gia	M L Ld Satb
He Heals The Broken Hearted (Ps147)	Cunningham, Patrick	76 Gra	B L L Ld Unis+
He Who Does Justice (Ps 15)	Cunningham, Patrick	76 Gra	B L L Ld Unis+
Hear O Israel	Husted, Richard S.	76 Chh	B L L Ld
Here Am I Oh Lord(Ps 40)	Lynch, Michael B.	73 Rav	B L L Ld
His Love Is Everlasting (Icet)	Picca, Angelo Della	69 Wlp	B L Ld
His Saving Power Revealed (Ps98)	Cunningham, Patrick	76 Gra	B L L Ld Unis+
I Believe That I Shall See(Ps 27)	Lynch, Michael B.	76 Rav	B R L L Ld
I Have Waited For The Lord (Ps 40)	Cunningham, Patrick	75 Gra	B R L L Ld
I Love You Lord My Strength (Ps 18)	Cunningham, Patrick	75 Gra	B R L L Ld Satbu
I Rejoiced (Psalms 121 & 122)	Malone, Miriam	76 Rpb	M B R L L Ld Resp
I Will Praise You Lord (Ps 22 End)	Cunningham, Patrick	76 Gra	B L L Ld Satb+
I Will Walk In God's Presence	Cunningham, Patrick	70 Gra	B R L L Ld Satbu
Icet Responsorial Antiphons	Cunningham, Patrick	74 Gra	B R L L Ld Satb
If Today You Hear His Voice (Icet)	Picca, Angelo Della	69 Wlp	B L Ld
In Manibus Tuis (Eng) Ps 31	Cunningham, Patrick	76 Gra	B L L Ld Satb
In The Presence (Ps 116)	Ellis, Ron & Ellis, Rob	73 Rav	B L L Ld
Israel, Rely On Yahweh	Fitzgerald, Michael	74 Wgm	B L L Ld
It Is Good To Give Thanks To You	Cunningham, Patrick	76 Gra	B L L Ld Unis+
Keep Me Safe (Psalm 16)	Monday, Robert	76 Rpb	M B R L L Ld Resp
Keep Me Safe O God (Ps 16)	Cunningham, Patrick	76 Gra	B L L Ld Unis+
Let My Tongue Be Silenced (Ps137)	Cunningham, Patrick	76 Gra	B L L Ld Satbu+
Let My Tongue Be Silenced(Ps 137)	Ellis, Ron	73 Rav	B L L Ld
Let Us Go Rejoicing (Icet)	Picca, Angelo Della	69 Wlp	B L Ld
Look Toward Me (Psalm 25)	Lisicky, Paul	76 Rpb	M B R L L Ld Resp
Lord Every Nation (Icet)	Picca, Angelo Della	69 Wlp	B L Ld
Lord Every Nation(Ps 72)	Ellis, Ron	73 Rav	B L L Ld
Lord Has Done Great Things(Ps 126)	Lynch, Michael B.	75 Rav	B R L L Ld
Lord Is My Shepherd (Ps 23)	Lynch, Michael B.	73 Rav	B L L Ld
Lord Let Us See Your Kindness (Icet)	Picca, Angelo Della	69 Wlp	M B L Ld
Lord Send Out Your Spirit (Icet)	Picca, Angelo Della	69 Wlp	B L Ld
Lord Send Out Your Spirit(Ps 104)	Ellis, Ron & Lynch, M.	75 Rav	B R L L Ld
Lord You Are Good And Forgiving	Cunningham, Patrick	75 Gra	B R L L Ld
Lord You Have The Word (Icet)	Picca, Angelo Della	69 Wlp	B L Ld
Lord, Let Your Face Shine (Ps 4)	Cunningham, Patrick	76 Gra	B L L Ld Unis+
Lord, Send Out Your Spirit	Peloquin, C Alexander	70 Gia	B L Ld
Lord, You Have The Words	Peloquin, C Alexander	71 Gia	M L Ld Var+
Lord, You Have The Words	Proulx, Richard	Na Gia	L Ld
Lord, You Have The Words (Ps 19)	Cunningham, Patrick	76 Gra	B L L Ld Unis+
Lord, Your Love Is Eternal	Cunningham, Patrick	75 Gra	B R L L Ld Unis
May God Have Pity On Us	Schoen, F	71 Gia	M L Ld Unis+
May The Lord Bless Us (Ps 126)	Cunningham, Patrick	70 Gra	B R L L Ld Satbu
My God, My God	Peloquin, C Alexander	71 Gia	M L Ld Satb
My God, My God (Icet)	Picca, Angelo Della	69 Wlp	B L Ld
My God, My God (Ps 22)	Cunningham, Patrick	76 Gra	B L L Ld Satb+
My Light And Salvation (Ps27)	Cunningham, Patrick	76 Gra	B L L Ld Satb
My Soul Is Thirsting (Ps 63)	Ellis, Ron	75 Rav	B R L L Ld
My Soul Is Thirsting For You (Icet)	Picca, Angelo Della	69 Wlp	B L Ld
O Bless The Lord (Ps 103)	Cunningham, Patrick	75 Gra	B R L L Ld Unis
O God, Pity Us (Ps67)	Cunningham, Patrick	76 Gra	B L L Ld Unis+
O God, Save Me With Your Name	Cunningham, Patrick	70 Gra	B R L L Ld Unis
Peace To His People (Ps85)	Cunningham, Patrick	76 Gra	B L L Ld Var+
Praise The Lord For He Is Good	Cunningham, Patrick	76 Gra	B R L L Ld Unis
Praise The Lord My Soul (Ps146)	Cunningham, Patrick	76 Gra	B L L Ld Unis+
Praise The Lord Who Heals(Ps 147)	Lynch, Michael B.	73 Rav	B L L Ld
Psalm For Epiphany	Peloquin, C Alexander	71 Gia	B L Ld Satbu+
Psalm 103	Lynch, Michael B.	76 Rav	B R L L Ld
Psalm 104	Monday, Robert	76 Rpb	M B R L L Ld Resp
Psalm 121: Let Us Go To God's House	Verdi, Ralph C.	73 Gia	M L Ld Cantu+
Psalm 150	Gilsdorf, Sr. Helen	73 Rpb	M B R L L Ld Resp
Psalm 33	Theophane, Sr. M	71 Gia	M L Ld Var+
Psalm 41	Schmidt, Jackie	76 Rpb	M B R L L Ld Resp
Psalm 51	Lynch, Michael B.	75 Rav	B R L L Ld
Psalm 98	Schneider, Kent E.	75 Ccc	M B L L Ld
Psalms For Advent	Hughes, Howard	74 Gia	B L Ld Cantu+
Remember Your Mercies O Lord (Ps 25)	Cunningham, Patrick	75 Gra	B R L L Ld
Response To The First Reading	Page, Paul F.	73 Rpb	M B R L L Ld
Responsorial Psalm For Christmas	Cunningham, Patrick	72 Gra	B R L L Ld Var
Responsorial Psalms Ritual Masses	Picca, Angelo Della	70 Wlp	B L Ld
Resurrection Psalm	Peloquin, C Alexander	71 Gia	B L Ld Satbu+
Sing Joyfully To The Lord	Roff, Joseph	71 Gia	M L Ld Unis+
Sing To The Lord A New Song	Cunningham, Patrick	74 Gra	M R L L Ld Satb
Sing With Joy To God (Ps81)	Cunningham, Patrick	76 Gra	B L L Ld Unis+
Song Of The Three Young Men	Proulx, Richard	74 Gia	M L Ld Var+
Soundings For New Beginnings	Schneider, Kent E.	69 Ccc	M B R L Ld
Springs Of Water (Icet)	Picca, Angelo Della	69 Wlp	B L Ld
Taste And See	Peloquin, C Alexander	71 Gia	M L Ld Uvar+
Taste And See (Icet)	Picca, Angelo Della	71 Wlp	B L Ld
Taste And See (Ps 34)	Ellis, Ron	74 Rav	B R L L Ld
Teach Me Your Ways (Ps 25)	Lynch, Michael B.	73 Rav	B R L L Ld
The Glorious Deeds Of The Lord (Ps78)	Cunningham, Patrick	76 Gra	B L L Ld Unis+
The Hand Of The Lord Feeds Us	Cunningham, Patrick	75 Gra	B R L L Ld Unis
The Law Of God Is Perfect	Cunningham, Patrick	71 Gra	B R L L Ld Satbu
The Lord Has Done Great Things	Cunningham, Patrick	70 Gra	B R L L Ld Saabu
The Lord Is King (Psalm 93) W/Brs	Cunningham, Patrick	74 Gra	B R L L Ld
The Seed That Falls (Psalm 65)	Lisicky, Paul	76 Rpb	M B R L L Ld Resp
The Vineyard Of The Lord (Ps 80)	Cunningham, Patrick	72 Gra	B R L L Ld
This Is The Day	Peloquin, C Alexander	71 Gia	B L Ld Satbu+
This Is The Day (W/ Perc, Bells, Org)	Proulx, R.; Gelineau	75 Gia	M L L Ld
This Is The Day The Lord Has Made	Deiss, Lucien	70 Wlp	M B L Ld
This Is The Day The Lord Has Made	Picca, Angelo Della	70 Wlp	B L Ld
To You, O Lord (Icet)	Picca, Angelo Della	69 Wlp	B L Ld
Triumph Of The Cross (Psalm) (Icet)	Burns, James	69 Wlp	B L Ld
Upright Is The Word	Cunningham, Patrick	71 Gra	B R L L Ld Satbu
Vigil Assumption–Psalm (Icet)	Schaffer, Robert J.	69 Wlp	B L Ld

CATEGORIZED INDEX

Title	Composer	Pub	Codes
Vigil Pentecost Psalm (Icet)	Picca, Angelo Della	69 Wlp	B L Ld
Vigil Peter & Paul Psalm (Icet)	Phillip	69 Wlp	B L Ld
Vineyard Of The Lord (Ps 80)	Lynch, Michael B.	73 Rav	B L Ld
We Are His People	Peloquin, C Alexander	71 Gia	M L Ld Uvar+
Whom Shall I Fear (Ps 27)	Lynch, Michael B.	69 Rav	B R L L Ld
With The Lord There Is Mercy (Icet)	Picca, Angelo Della	69 Wlp	B L Ld
You Drew Me Clear (Ps30)	Cunningham, Patrick	76 Gra	B L L Ld Satb
You Knew Me Before I Was Born (Ps 139)	Ellis,Ron&Lynch,M.	75 Rav	B R L L Ld

General Acclamations

Acclamations which do not fit any of the other categories are listed here, including Hosannas and Doxologies.

Title	Composer	Pub	Codes
Rejoice In The Lord Always	Unknown	73 Nal	B R C Le
Stand Up	Miffleton, Jack	73 Wlp	B R C Le
A Shelter For Me	Johnson, Gary L.	75 Bfi	B R F Le
Centurion's Song	Rowe, D.	76 Sil	R F Le
David's Song	Barker, Sherrell	72 Fis	M L F Le
Emmanuel	Eimer	67 Wlp	B F Le
Hosanna In The Highest	Tucciarone, Angel	73 Wlp	B R F Le
Jesus Song	Kohl, Jon	73 Fel	B F Le
Sorsum Corda (English)	Pulkingham, Betty C.	73 Gia	B R L F Le
We Will Hear Your Word	Wise, Joe	67 Wlp	B R F Le
Bless The Lord	Rivers, Clarence	64 Wlp	B G Le
Glory, Glory (A Capella)	Montague, George T.	72 Mcc	B R L G Le 2pt
Hallelujah, I Want To Sing	Turner, Roy	67 Cam	M L G Le
The Word Of God Endureth	Mier, Audrey	65 Man	B G Le
Thou Art There	Johnson, Gary L.	75 Bfi	B R G Le
Acclamations From Sacred Scripture	Blattert, Cloutier	73 Cfc	M L L Le
Christ Our Passover (Mass For N.Rite)	Hampton, Calvin	76 Gia	B L L Le Satb+
Christ Our Passover (Notre Dame Mass)	Isele, David C.	74 Gia	B L L Le Satb+
Christ Our Passover (Org,Guit)	Pulkingham, Betty C.	73 Gia	B R L L Le Satb+
Doxology	Creed, Dan	73 Nal	B R L Le
Doxology	Dufford, Bob, S. J.	73 Nal	B R L Le
Doxology To The Lord's Prayer	Fitzpatrick, Dennis	69 Fel	B L Le
Emmanuel Come Save Your People	Deiss, Lucien	70 Wlp	B R L Le
Hosanna	Christiansen, F. M.	68 Aug	M L Le Satb
Hosanna	Fetler, Paul	71 Aug	M L Le Satb
Hosanna	Medling, Rebecca	76 Rpb	M B R L L Le
Hosanna	Nelson, Ronald A.	67 Aug	M L Le Full
Hosanna	Pooler, Marie	62 Aug	M L Sa:
Hosanna	Ugartechea, Michael	72 Mar	B L L Le
Hosanna For Joy	Smith, Roger	75 Nal	B R L Le
Hosanna!	Zsigray, Joe	72 Nal	B R L Le
Hosanna! O Blessed Is He	Nelson, Ronald A.	68 Aug	M L Le Unis
Hosanna, Blessed Is He	Nystedt, Knut	64 Aug	M L Le Sab
Hosanna, Hosanna, Hosanna	Deiss, Lucien	70 Wlp	B R L Le
Hosanna, Son Of David	Sateren, Leland B.	48 Aug	M L Le Satb
Introduction To Canon Acclamation	Page, Paul F.	76 Rpb	M B R L L Le
Liturgy Of The Word (Icet)	Deiss, Lucien	70 Wlp	B L Le
Music For Eucharistic Prayer	Somary, Johannes	73 Gia	B L L Le Satb+
Pen. Rite And Lit. Of Word	Peloquin, C Alexander	74 Gia	B L Le Satb
Prayer Intonations	Goode, Jack	Na Abi	M L Le Satb
Preface & Eucharistic Acclamations	Cirou, Joseph	73 Acp	L L Le
Preface, Sanctus, Benedictus	Pulkingham, Betty C.	73 Gia	B R L L Le Satb+
Sing Hosanna (W/Org, Opt 3 Tpts)	Armitage	70 Aug	M L Le Sabu
The Lord Bless You And Keep You	Lutkin, Peter	Na Gsc	B L Le Var+
Trisagion (Mass For New Rite)	Hampton, Calvin	76 Gia	B L L Le Satb+
Trisagion (Notre Dame Mass)	Isele, David C.	74 Gia	B L L Le Satb+
Your Words, O Lord	Deiss, Lucien	70 Wlp	B R L Le
Hail Festal Day	Grieb, Herbert	Na Gsc	B T Le Var+
Hosanna	Beck, John Ness	Na Gsc	B T Le Full
Missa Super L'homme Arme Kyrie	Des Pres, Josquin	75 Bbl	M T Le Satb
The Lord Bless You And Keep You	Mueller, Carl F	Na Gsc	B T Le Satb

Gospel Acclamations (Alleluia)

The Hebrew word "Alleluia" means "Praise Yah(weh)".

Title	Composer	Pub	Codes
Gospel Halleluia	Blue, Robert	66 Fel	B C Lf
Scripture Response, Alleluia	Miffleton, Jack	69 Wlp	B R F Lf
Amens	Wilson, Roger C.	76 Lor	G Lf Satb+
Alle, Alle, Alleluia (Gospel Accl.)	Landry, Carey (Rev.)	75 Nal	B R L Lf
Alleluia	Creed, Dan	73 Nal	B R L L Lf
Alleluia	Horn, Richard	74 Rpb	M B R L L Lf
Alleluia	Korhonen, J	72 Gia	M L Lf Ssa(A)
Alleluia	Lisicky, Paul	76 Rpb	M B R L L Lf
Alleluia	Lynch, Michael B.	73 Rav	B L L Lf
Alleluia	Olivier, John H.	74 Rpb	M B R L L Lf
Alleluia	Page, Paul F.	75 Nal	M B R L L Lf
Alleluia	Page, Paul F.	73 Rpb	M B R L L Lf
Alleluia	Sylvester, Erich	71 Nal	B R L L Lf
Alleluia	Wise, Joe	75 Nal	B R L L Lf
Alleluia	Wood, Mike	76 Rpb	M B R L L Lf
Alleluia	Zsigray, Joe	74 Nal	B R L L Lf
Alleluia (Icet)	Picca, Angelo Della	58 Gia	B L Lf
Alleluia (Icet)	Twynham, R. F.	58 Wlp	B L Lf
Alleluia (Notre Dame Mass)	Isele, David C.	74 Gia	B L L Lf Satb+
Alleluia (8x)	Sinclair, Jerry	72 Din	M L L Lf Var
Alleluia From Brazilian Psalm	Berger, Jean	Na Gsc	B L Lf Var
Alleluia No. 1	Fishel, Donald	73 Wgm	B R L L L Lf
Alleluia Verse (Christmas Vigil)(Icet)	Smith	69 Wlp	B L Lf
Alleluia(A Maj)	Ellis, Ron	73 Rav	B L L Lf
Alleluia(F Maj)	Ellis, Ron	73 Rav	B L L Lf
Alleluia! Alleluia! Alleluia!	Smith, Roger	74 Nal	B R L Lf
Alleluia—Amen	Theobald, James	Na See	M L Lf
Alleluia/Amen	Page, Paul F.	76 Rpb	M B R L L Lf
Alleluia, Alleluia (Tone Special 148)	Fitzpatrick, Dennis	65 Fel	B R L Lf
Alleluia, Alleluia Your Words O Lord	Deiss, Lucien	70 Wlp	B R L Lf
Alleluia, Alleluia, Alleluia	Deiss, Lucien	70 Wlp	B R L Lf
Alleluia, Alleluia, Alleluia	Fitzpatrick, Dennis	67 Fel	B L Lf
Alleluias (Accompaniment)	Pross, Daniel J.	71 Gia	B L L L Lf Org
Alleluias (Sixteen)	Creed, Dan	73 Nal	B R L Lf
At The Gospel	Hampton, Calvin	76 Gia	B L Lf Satb
Common Blessed Virgin Alleluia (Icet)	Kreutz, Robert	69 Wlp	B L Lf
Common Of Doctors Alleluia (Icet)	Schaffer, Robert J.	69 Wlp	B L Lf
Common Of Virgins Alleluia Verse(Icet)	Kreutz, Robert	69 Wlp	B L Lf
Echo Alleluia	Young, Gordon	75 Sac	M L Lf Full
Echoing Alleluia	James, Allen	Na Abi	M L Lf Satb
Eight Alleluias, Gospel Acclamations	Marier, Theodore	71 Cfc	M R L L Lf
Gospel Acclamation In A Maj	Lynch, Michael B.	73 Rav	M L L Lf
Gospel Acclamation Verses A,B,C	Pross, Daniel J.	71 Gia	B L L L Lf Satb+
Gospel Acclamations	Arnatt, Ronald	74 Cfc	M L L Lf
Gospel Acclamations, Bvm	Blanchard, R. I.	73 Cfc	M R L L Lf
Gospel Acclamations, Confirmation, Etc	Hughes, Howard (Bro.)	73 Cfc	M R L L Lf
Gospel Acclamations, Holy Orders	Proulx, Richard	74 Cfc	M L L Lf
Gradual And Alleluia	Toolan, Sr Suzanne	75 Rpb	M B R L L Lf
Psalm 150	Vermulst, Jan	64 Wlp	M L Lf Var+
Psalm 150 (Alleluia)	Westendorf/Vermulst	64 Wlp	B R L Lf
Psalm 150 (W/Triple Alleluia)	Picca, Angelo Della	70 Wlp	B L Lf
Responses 87—88 Gospel Acclamation	Picca, Angelo Della	70 Wlp	B L Lf
Roger's Alleluia (Gospel Acclamation)	Smith, Roger	75 Nal	B R L Lf
Serene Alleluias	Ferris, W	70 Gia	M L Lf Sa+
Triumph Of The Cross Alleluia (Icet)	Burns, James	69 Wlp	B L Lf
Vigil Assumption—Alleluia (Vv)(Icet)	Schaffer, Robert J.	69 Wlp	B L Lf
Vigil Pentecost Alleluia (Vv)(Icet)	Picca, Angelo Della	69 Wlp	B L Lf
Vigil Peter & Paul Alleluia (Vv)(Icet)	Kreutz, Robert	69 Wlp	B L Lf
Yes, Lord, Alleluia	Gilsdorf, Sr. Helen	75 Rpb	M B R L L Lf
Alleluia	Muczynski, R	Na Gsc	B T Lf Satb
Alleluia (A Cap)	Pergolesi, Giovanni B.	Na Abi	M T Lf Ssatb
Alleluia (From Coronation Anthem No.2)	Handel, G.F.	Na Gsc	B T Lf Satb+
Alleluia (3 Voices)	Boyce,W./Tortolano Ed	70 Gia	B L T Lf Round
Alleluia (3 Voices)	Unknown/Tortolano Ed	70 Gia	B L T Lf Round
Alleluia And Psalm For Easter(E)	Proulx, Richard	75 Gia	M L T Lf
Alleluia	Pergolesi, G B	Na Gsc	B T Lf Ssatb+
Alleluia From Motet Exultate	Mozart, Wolfgang	Na Gsc	B T Lf Var+
Hallelujah Chorus ("Messiah")	Handel, G. F.	Cfs	M T Lf Satb
Responsorium	Schutz, Heinrich	Na Gsc	B T Lf Satb

Gospel Acclamations (Lenten)

Title	Composer	Pub	Codes
Praise Him (From Come Follow)	Murphy, Charles	69 Gia	B R L G Lg Acap
A Great Sign Appeared In Heaven	Fitzpatrick, Dennis	65 Fel	B L Lg
Christ Became Obedient (E) (Holy Wk)	Cunningham, Patrick	76 Gra	B L L Lg Satb
Glory And Praise To You	Deiss, Lucien	65 Wlp	B R L Lg
Glory And Praise To You	Regan, Joe	75 Nal	B R L Lg
Glory And Praise To You (Icet)	Picca, Angelo Della	70 Wlp	B L Lg
Glory To You	Lisicky, Paul	76 Rpb	M B R L L Lg Gospel
Glory To You, Word Of God(Icet)	Picca, Angelo Della	69 Wlp	B L Lg
Gospel Acclamation (Notre Dame Mass)	Isele, David C.	74 Gia	B L L Lg Satb+
Gospel Acclamations, Good Friday, Etc.	Biggs, John	72 Cfc	M R L L Lg
Praise And Honor	Wood, Mike	76 Rpb	M B R L L Lg
Praise And Honor To You (Icet)	Picca, Angelo Della	69 Wlp	B L Lg
Praise To You Lord Jesus Christ Icet	Picca, Angelo Della	69 Wlp	B L Lg

Litanies for the Prayer of the Faithful

Title	Composer	Pub	Codes
God The Father	Repp, Ray	66 Fel	B R F Lh
General Intercessions	Deiss, Lucien	70 Wlp	B L Lh
General Intercessions	Frischman/Deiss	74 Wlp	B L Lh
General Intercessions (Notre Dame Mass)	Isele, David C.	74 Gia	B L L Lh Satb+
Intercession Prayer For Cath. Church	Deiss, Lucien	65 Wlp	B L Lh
Litany	Landry, Carey (Rev.)	68 Nal	B R L Lh
Litany	Peloquin, C Alexander	Na Gia	L Lh
Petitions For Help	Hoffman	70 Aug	M L Lh Satb
Prayer Of The Faithful	Fitzpatrick, Dennis	65 Fel	B L Lh
Prayer Of The Faithful (Response)	Deiss, Lucien	70 Wlp	B L Lh
Prayer Of The Faithful For Advent	Cirou, Joseph	73 Acp	L L Lh
Prayer Of The Faithful For Advent	Gilligan, Michael	67 Acp	L L Lh
Prayer Of The Faithful For Christmas	Gilligan, Michael	67 Acp	L L Lh
Prayer Of The Faithful For Christmas	Silvia, Helen	73 Acp	L L Lh
Prayer Of The Faithful For Easter	Gilligan, Michael	67 Acp	L L Lh
Prayer Of The Faithful For Easter	Silvia, Helen	73 Acp	L L Lh
Prayer Of The Faithful For Lent	Gilligan, Michael	67 Acp	L L Lh
Prayer Of The Faithful For Lent (4pt)	Silvia, Helen	73 Acp	L L Lh
Prayer Of The Faithful For Ordinary	Silvia, Helen	73 Acp	L L Lh
Prayer Of The Faithful For Ordinary Tm	Gilligan, Michael	67 Acp	L L Lh
Prayer Of The Faithful For Pentecost	Gilligan, Michael	67 Acp	L L Lh
Prayer Of The Faithful For Pentecost	Silvia, Helen	73 Acp	L L Lh
Litania K 243	Mozart, Wolfgang A	Na Kal	B T Lh Satb
Litaniae Lauretanae K 195	Mozart, Wolfgang A	Na Kal	B T Lh Satb

Acclamations (Holy)

The "Holy, Holy" is an acclamation of praise borrowed from Isaiah 6:3

Title	Composer	Pub	Codes
Holy, Holy, Holy (W/Rhythm)	Hager	71 Aug	M C Li Unis

Sanctus (Mass Of Schools)	Kostos, Patti	66 Fel	B C Li	
Angelic Song (First Mass)	Repp, Ray	66 Fel	B R F Li	
Angelic Song (Second Mass)	Repp, Ray	66 Fel	B R F Li	
Holy Holy Lord	Leyko, Patricia J.	76 Chh	B R L F Li	
Holy, Holy, Holy	Davis, Bob	73 Fcc	B R L F Li	
Holy, Holy, Holy	Miffleton, Jack	68 Acp	L F Li	
Holy, Holy, Holy	Wise, Joe	67 Wlp	B R F Li	
Holy, Holy, Holy	Yantis, David	Na Yan	B F Li	
Holy, Holy, Holy (Celebration Lit)	Yantis, David	Na Yan	B F Li	
Holy, Holy, Holy (Folk Mass No. 4)	Quinlan, Paul	66 Fel	B F Li	
Holy, Holy, Holy (Funeral Folk Mass)	Mitchell, Ian	67 Fel	B R F Li	
Holy, Holy, Holy (Jazz–Rock Mass)	Mitchell, Ian	68 Fel	B R F Li	
Holy, Holy, Holy (Lord God Sabaoth)	Farra, Mimi A.	73 Gia	M B R L F Li	Var+
Holy, Holy, Holy (Missa Bossa Nova)	Scholtes, Peter	66 Fel	B R F Li	
Holy, Holy, Holy (1964 Text)	Winter, Miriam T.	66 Van	B R F Li	
Holy, Holy, Holy (64 Text)	Markaitis, Bruno	67 Van	B R F Li	
Holy, Holy, Holy (67th Street Mass)	Scholtes, Peter	68 Fel	B R F Li	
Hosanna	Webber/Rice	70 Lds	F Li	
Hosanna (Folk Communion Service)	Johnson, D.	74 Aug	M F Li	
Hosanna In The Highest	Leyko, Patricia J.	76 Chh	B R L F Li	
Sanctus (Mariachi Mass)	Lojewski, Harry V	69 Fel	B R F Li	
Sanctus (Mass Of The Western Tribes)	Indian Melodies	66 Fel	B F Li	
Alleluia Alleluia	Prichard/Decou	Na Zon	M G Li	Satb
Acclamation	Monday, Robert	76 Rpb	M B R L L Li	
Acclamation	Page, Paul F.	75 Rpb	M B R L L Li	
Acclamation	Page, Paul F.	73 Rpb	M B R L L Li	
Acclamation	Purri, Ralph	76 Rpb	M B R L L Li	
Acclamation	Toolan, Sr Suzanne	74 Rpb	M B R L L Li	
Acclamation	Unknown	74 Rpb	M B R L L Li	
Acclamation	Wood, Mike	76 Rpb	M B R L L Li	
Acclamation (C)	Johnson, Paul	75 Rpb	M B R L L Li	
Acclamations	Deiss, Lucien	70 Wlp	B R L Li	
Acclamations	O'connell, Timothy	70 Acp	L L Li	
Acclamations (Icet)	Bottenberg	68 Wlp	B L Li	
Acclamations (Icet)	Englert, Eugene	69 Wlp	B L Li	
Choral Fanfare On "Holy, Holy, Holy"	Rasley	Na Lor	M L Li	Satb
Echo Holy Holy	Landry, Carey (Rev.)	75 Nal	B R L Li	
Holy	Dufford, Bob, S. J.	73 Nal	B R L Li	
Holy	Foley, John, S. J.	70 Nal	B R L Li	
Holy	Schutte, Dan, S. J.	71 Nal	B R L Li	
Holy	Sylvester, Erich	71 Nal	B R L Li	
Holy Holy (Icet)	Kraehenbuehl/Frischman	70 Jsp	B L Li	+Org
Holy, Holy	Collard, Terry	71 Nal	B R L Li	
Holy, Holy	Creed, Dan	73 Nal	B R L Li	
Holy, Holy	Vickers, Wendy	75 Nal	B R L Li	
Holy, Holy	Zsigray, Joe	74 Nal	B R L Li	
Holy, Holy (Icet)	Kraehenbuehl, David	67 Jsp	B L Li	+Org
Holy, Holy (Opt Brs/Timp)	Goemanne, Noel	70 Gia	B L L Li	Sab+
Holy, Holy !	Wise, Joe	73 Nal	B R L Li	
Holy, Holy, God Of Hosts	Greif, Jean A	66 Vrn	M L L Li	
Holy, Holy, Holy	Davis, Paulette	76 Rpb	M B R L L Li	
Holy, Holy, Holy	Gentemann, Sr Elaine	70 Gia	B L L Li	Satb+
Holy, Holy, Holy	Johnson, Jeff	75 Rpb	M B R L L Li	
Holy, Holy, Holy	Landry, Carey (Rev.)	68 Nal	B L Li	
Holy, Holy, Holy	Landry, Carey (Rev.)	75 Nal	B R L Li	
Holy, Holy, Holy	Lisicky, Paul	76 Rpb	M B R L L Li	
Holy, Holy, Holy	Lynch, Michael B.	73 Rav	B L L Li	
Holy, Holy, Holy	Lynch, Michael B.	75 Rav	M B R L L Li	
Holy, Holy, Holy	Mcgrath, Roberta	74 Rpb	M B R L L Li	
Holy, Holy, Holy	Moultry, Prince Joseph	74 Nal	B R L Li	
Holy, Holy, Holy	Page, Paul F.	76 Rpb	M B R L L Li	
Holy, Holy, Holy	Page, Paul F.	73 Rpb	M B R L L Li	
Holy, Holy, Holy	Proulx, Richard	71 Gia	B L L Li	Satb+
Holy, Holy, Holy	Schneider, Kent E.	75 Ccc	B L Li	
Holy, Holy, Holy	St. Benedict's Farm	72 Sbf	B R L L Li	
Holy, Holy, Holy (Cel Of Unity)	Hebble, Robert	72 Gia	B L L Li	Satb+
Holy, Holy, Holy (Chardin Mass)	Rudcki, Stanley	66 Fel	B L Li	
Holy, Holy, Holy (Child Mass)	Andrews, Carroll T.	70 Gia	B L L Li	Satb+
Holy, Holy, Holy (Community Mass)	Lee, John	71 Gia	B L L Li	U+Org
Holy, Holy, Holy (Hymn Tune Mass)	F.E.L.	65 Fel	B L Li	
Holy, Holy, Holy (Icet)	Goemanne, Noel	69 Wlp	B L Li	
Holy, Holy, Holy (Icet)	Kreutz, Robert	69 Wlp	B L Li	
Holy, Holy, Holy (Icet)	Lojewski	69 Wlp	B L Li	
Holy, Holy, Holy (Icet)	Picca, Angelo Della	69 Wlp	B L Li	Var
Holy, Holy, Holy (Icet)	Schaffer, Robert J.	67 Wlp	B L Li	
Holy, Holy, Holy (Icet)	Vermulst, Jan	69 Wlp	B L Li	
Holy, Holy, Holy (Lyric Mass)	Andrews, Carroll T.	70 Gia	B L L Li	2pt+
Holy, Holy, Holy (Short Mass)	Lee, John	69 Gia	B L L Li	Satb+
Holy, Holy, Holy (Sung Mass No. 1)	Fitzpatrick, Dennis	63 Fel	B L Li	
Holy, Holy, Holy (W/Cantor)(Dominic)	Goemanne, Noel	71 Gia	B L L Li	Satb+
Holy, Holy, Holy (3pt Rhythm)	Ehret, Walter	76 Pro	M L Li	Satb+
Holy, Holy, Holy (4–Part Arr)	Dykes, John B.	73 Acp	L L Li	
Holy, Holy, Holy (4–Part Arr)	Silvia, Helen	70 Acp	L L Li	
Holy, Holy, Holy Lord	Gentemann, Sr Elaine	75 Gia	B L L Li	Sa+
Holy, Holy, Holy Lord (Vianney Mass)	Andrews, Carroll T.	75 Gia	B L L Li	Var+
Holy, Holy, Holy (Mass For All S.)	Andrews, Carroll T.	73 Gia	B L L Li	Var+
Holy, Holy, Holy (New Mass)	Andrews, Carroll T.	70 Gia	B L L Li	Unis+
Holy, Holy, Holy, Lord God	Heber, Reginald	70 Acp	L L Li	
Sanctus	Carroll, J. R.	71 Gia	B L L Li	3pt+
Sanctus	Zsigray, Joe	75 Nal	B R L Li	
Sanctus (Eng Mass)	Goemanne, Noel	70 Gia	B L L Li	2pt+
Sanctus (Eng, Icet)	Cunningham, Patrick	74 Gra	M R L L Li	Var
Sanctus (Mass For New Rite)	Hampton, Calvin	76 Gia	B L L Li	Satb+
Sanctus (Mus For Euch Prayer Acc)	Hughes, Howard	72 Gia	B L L Li	Var+
Sanctus (Notre Dame Mass)	Isele, David C.	74 Gia	B L L Li	Satb+
Sanctus (Sung Mass No. 2)	Fitzpatrick, Dennis	63 Fel	B L Li	
Sanctus (Thomas More Mass)	Reilly, Cyril A.	66 Fel	B L Li	
Sanctus (W/Fl, Cello)	Goemanne, Noel	73 Gia	B L L Li	2pt+
Sanctus (From Mass)	Bernstein, Leonard	Na Gsc	B L Li	Full+
Sanctus, The	Dietterich, Philip	Na Abi	M L Li	Satb
Santo, Santo, Santo	Lee, John	70 Gia	B L L Li	Uspan
Benedictus	Gabrieli, G	Na Gsc	B T Li	12mix
Benedictus	Palestrina, Giovanni P	Na Gsc	B T Li	Ssaa
Benedictus And Sanctus	Gounod, Charles	Na Gsc	B T Li	Var+
Blessed Is He Who Cometh	Gounod, Charles	Na Gsc	B T Li	Satb+
Heilig	Mendelssohn, F.	Na Gsc	B T Li	8mix
Holy, Holy, Holy	Monteverdi, Claudio	Na Gsc	B T Li	Satb+
Holy, Holy, Holy	Rasley	Na Lor	M T Li	Satb
Holy, Holy, Holy	Spicker, M	Na Gsc	B T Li	Full+
Holy, Holy, Holy (Cong+Choir)	Cassler, G. W.	Na Abi	M T Li	Satb
Holy, Holy, Holy (Me)	Handel, G. F.	Na Oxf	M T Li	Satb
Holy, Holy, Holy Lord God Almighty	Stewart, H J	Na Gsc	B T Li	Satb+
Holy, Holy, Holy!	Johnson, Norman	Na Zon	T Li	Satb
Hosanna	Newbury, Kent A.	Na Gsc	B T Li	Satb+
Lord Hosanna In The Highest	Glarum, L Stanley	Na Gsc	B T Li	Var
Sanctus	Gounod, Charles	Na Aug	M T Li	Satb
Sanctus	Gounod, Charles	Na Lor	M T Li	Satb
Sanctus	Haydn, Joseph	Na Gsc	B T Li	Satb+
Sanctus	Mendelssohn, F.	Na Gsc	B T Li	Satb+
Sanctus	Palestrina, Giovanni P	Na Gsc	B T Li	Ssaa
Sanctus	Power, Leonel	Na Gsc	B T Li	3pt+
Sanctus	Scarlatti, Alessandro	Na Gsc	B T Li	5mix
Sanctus (B Minor Mass)	Bach, J. S.	Na Gsc	B T Li	Full
Sanctus (From Missa Brevis In G Maj)	Mozart, Wolfgang A	75 Pro	M T Li	Satb+
Sanctus (Holy, Holy, Holy)	Na	Na Gsc	B T Li	3eq
Sanctus (Mass In Bm)	Bach, J. S.	Cfs	M T Li	Full
Sanctus (Missa Brevis)	Lotti, A & Weber, R.	66 Fel	B T Li	
Sanctus & Benedictus (St Cec Mass)	Gounod, Charles	Cfs	M T Li	Satb
Sanctus And Benedictus (St. Cec)	Gounod, Charles	Na Gsc	M T Li	Full+
Sanctus And Hosanna	Mendelssohn, F.	Na Gsc	B T Li	Satb+
Sanctus In D	Bach, J. S.	Na Oxf	B T Li	Satb

Memorial Acclamations

Christ Has Died (1 & 2)	Miffleton, Jack	75 Wlp	B F Lj	
Christ Has Died #1	Leyko, Patricia J.	76 Chh	B R L F Lj	
Christ Has Died #2	Leyko, Patricia J.	76 Chh	B R L F Lj	
Lord By Your Cross	Miffleton, Jack	75 Wlp	B F Lj	
When We Eat This Bread	Miffleton, Jack	75 Wlp	B R F Lj	
When We Eat This Bread	Tucciarone, Angel	73 Wlp	B R F Lj	
When We Eat This Bread	Wise, Joe	61 Wlp	B R F Lj	
Acclamaciones (Memorial)	Lee, John	70 Gia	B L L Lj	Uspan
Acclamation	Patterson, Keith	76 Rpb	M B R L L Lj	
Acclamation (A)	Lynch, Michael B.	75 Rav	M L L Lj	
Acclamation (B)	Lynch, Michael B.	75 Rav	M B R L L Lj	
Acclamation (C)	Lynch, Michael B.	75 Rav	M L L Lj	
Acclamation (D)	Lynch, Michael B.	75 Rav	M B R L L Lj	
Acclamation (D)	Page, Paul F.	76 Rpb	M B R L L Lj	
Christ Has Died	Cunningham, Patrick	76 Gra	M L L Lj	
Christ Has Died	Wojcik, Richard J.	70 Acp	L L Lj	
Christ Has Died (Acclamation)	Landry, Carey (Rev.)	75 Nal	B R L Lj	
Christ Has Died (Acclamation)	Zsigray, Joe	73 Nal	B R L Lj	
Christ Has Died (Icet)	Bottenberg	69 Wlp	B L Lj	
Christ Has Died (Icet)	Deiss, Lucien	71 Wlp	B L Lj	
Christ Has Died (Icet)	Englert, Eugene	68 Wlp	B L Lj	
Christ Has Died (Icet) Ascap	Wise, Joe	69 Wlp	B R L Lj	
Christ Our Lord Has Died (Acclamation)	Smith, Roger (Adpt.)	75 Nal	B R L Lj	
Dying You Destroyed Our Death	Cunningham, Patrick	76 Gra	M L L Lj	
Dying You Destroyed Our Death	Englert, Eugene	69 Wlp	B L Lj	
Dying You Destroyed Our Death	Sylvester, Erich	71 Nal	B R L Lj	
Dying You Destroyed Our Death	Wise, Joe	72 Nal	B R L Lj	
Dying You Destroyed Our Death	Zsigray, Joe	73 Nal	B R L Lj	
Eucharistic Acclamation (Simple)	Deiss, Lucien	65 Wlp	B L Lj	
Eucharistic Acclamation (Solemn)	Deiss, Lucien	65 Wlp	B L Lj	
Keep In Mind	Schneider, Kent E.	75 Ccc	B L Lj	
Lord By Your Cross	Moultry, Prince Joseph	74 Nal	B R L Lj	
Lord By Your Cross	Wise, Joe	73 Nal	B R L Lj	
Lord By Your Cross	Zsigray, Joe	74 Nal	B R L Lj	
Lord By Your Cross (Icet)	Englert, Eugene	69 Wlp	B L Lj	
Lord By Your Cross And Resurrection	Cunningham, Patrick	76 Gra	M L L Lj	
Lord, By Your Cross And Resurrection	Zsigray, Joe	72 Nal	B R L Lj	
Memorial Acclamation	Hilf, Robert	74 Rpb	M B R L L Lj	
Memorial Acclamation	Patterson, Keith	76 Rpb	M B R L L Lj	
Memorial Acclamation	Romfh, Paul	74 Rpb	M B R L L Lj	
Memorial Acclamation (Christ Has Died)	Hampton, Calvin	76 Gia	B L L Lj	Satb+
Memorial Acclamation (Christ Has Died)	Isele, David C.	74 Gia	B L L Lj	Satb+
Memorial Acclamation 1	Fitzpatrick, Dennis	69 Fel	B L Lj	
Memorial Acclamation 1	Udulutsch, Irvin	69 Fel	B L Lj	
Memorial Acclamation 2	Fitzpatrick, Dennis	69 Fel	B L Lj	
Memorial Acclamation 2	Nachtwey, Roger	69 Fel	B L Lj	
Memorial Acclamation 3	Fitzpatrick, Dennis	69 Fel	B L Lj	
Memorial Acclamation 3	Mcguire, Thomas	69 Fel	B L Lj	
Memorial Acclamation 4	Fitzpatrick, Dennis	69 Fel	B L Lj	
Memorial Acclamation 4	Nachtwey, Roger	69 Fel	B L Lj	
Memorial Acclamation (Christ Has Died)	Hughes, Howard	72 Gia	B L L Lj	Satb+
Memorial Acclamations	Cirou, Joseph	70 Acp	L L Lj	
Memorial Acclamations (Icet)	Hooper	69 Wlp	B L Lj	
Memorial Acclamations I–Iv	Roff, Joseph	70 Gia	B L L Lj	Satb+
Syriac Acclamation	Cunningham, Patrick	76 Gra	M L L Lj	Satb+
The Acclamations (Christ Has Died)	Pulkingham, Betty C.	73 Gia	B R L L Lj	Satb+
When We Eat This Bread	Landry, Carey (Rev.)	75 Nal	B R L Lj	
When We Eat This Bread	Moultry, Prince Joseph	74 Nal	B R L Lj	
When We Eat This Bread	Zsigray, Joe	75 Nal	B R L Lj	
When We Eat This Bread	Zsigray, Joe	72 Nal	B R L Lj	
When We Eat This Bread (Icet)	Englert, Eugene	69 Wlp	B L Lj	

Acclamations (Great Amen)

Title	Composer	Pub	Codes	Voicing
Amen •	Yantis, David	Na Yan	B F Lk	
Great Amen •	Leyko, Patricia J.	76 Chh	B R L F Lk	
Great Amen •	Miffleton, Jack	68 Acp	L F Lk	
The New Amen Song	Yantis, David	Na Yan	B F Lk	
Yes, Amen	Blue, Robert	66 Fel	B R F Lk	
Amen	Deiss, Lucien	66 Wlp	B R L Lk	
Amen	Goldsmith, J.	63 Snm	L Lk	
Amen	Medling, Rebecca	76 Rpb	M B R L L Lk	
Amen	Moultry, Prince Joseph	74 Nal	B R L Lk	
Amen	Sylvester, Erich	71 Nal	B R L Lk	
Amen	Wise, Joe	75 Nal	B R L Lk	
Amen! (4-Part Arrangement)	Silvia, Helen	73 Acp	L L Lk	
Amen, Alleluia!	Zsigray, Joe	72 Nal	B R L Lk	
Amen, Lord	Landry, Carey (Rev.)	69 Nal	B R L Lk	
Doxology	Husted, Richard S.	76 Chh	B L L Lk	
Doxology And "Amen"	Zsigray, Joe	72 Nal	B R L Lk	
Doxology And Amen (I)	Landry, Carey (Rev.)	75 Nal	B R L Lk	
Doxology And Amen (Ii)	Landry, Carey (Rev.)	75 Nal	B R L Lk	
Doxology And Great Amen	Zsigray, Joe	75 Nal	B R L Lk	
Doxology--Amen	Wise, Joe	72 Nal	B R L Lk	
Final Doxology	Isele, David C.	74 Gia	B L L Lk	Satb+
Great Amen	Dresden	66 Wlp	B L Lk	
Great Amen	Fitzpatrick, Dennis	69 Fel	B L Lk	
Great Amen	Goemanne, Noel	66 Wlp	B L Lk	
Great Amen	Hooper	75 Wlp	B L Lk	
Great Amen	Page, Paul F.	73 Rpb	M B R L L Lk	
Great Amen (Icet)	Deiss, Lucien	68 Wlp	B L Lk	
Great Amen (Mus For Euch Prayer Acc)	Hughes, Howard	72 Gia	B L L Lk	Satb+
Great Amen (4-Part Arr)	Silvia, Helen	70 Acp	L L Lk	
Great Amen For Advent	Gilligan, Michael	67 Acp	L L Lk	
Great Amen For Advent (4-Part Arr)	Cirou, Joseph	73 Acp	L L Lk	
Great Amen For Christmas And Epiphany	Cirou, Joseph	73 Acp	L L Lk	
Great Amen For Christmas And Epiphany	Gilligan, Michael	67 Acp	L L Lk	
Great Amen For Easter	Gilligan, Michael	70 Acp	L L Lk	
Great Amen For Easter (4-Part Arr)	Cirou, Joseph	73 Acp	L L Lk	
Great Amen For Pentecost	Gilligan, Michael	67 Acp	L L Lk	
Great Amen For Pentecost (4-Part Arr)	Cirou, Joseph	73 Acp	L L Lk	
Great Amen's Through The Year	Gilligan, Michael	67 Acp	L L Lk	
Great Amens Through The Year (4-Part)	Cirou, Joseph/Silvia,H	73 Acp	L L Lk	
The Sevenfold Amen	Stainer, Sir John	Na Gsc	B T Lk	Satb
Twelve Benediction Amens (E-Md)	Cabena, Barrie	Na Oxf	M T Lk	2-8pt

Lord's Prayers (Our Father)

Title	Composer	Pub	Codes	Voicing
The Lord's Prayer	Hamblen Suzy	Na Ham	M C Ll	
The Lord's Prayer (Liturgy Of Joy)	Blue, Robert	66 Fel	B R C Ll	
Lord's Prayer	Davis, Bob	73 Fcc	B R L F Ll	
Lord's Prayer, The	Cunningham, Patrick	76 Gra	B L F Ll	
Our Father	Meltz, Ken	72 Wlp	B R F Ll	
Our Father	Parker, Tom	68 Wlp	B R F Ll	
Our Father	Winter, Miriam T.	66 Van	B R F Ll	
Our Father	Winter, Miriam T.	67 Van	B R F Ll	
Our Father	Wise, Joe	67 Wlp	B R F Ll	
Our Father	Yantis, David	Na Yan	B F Ll	
The Lord's Prayer	Fischer, John	69 Fel	B R F Ll	
The Lord's Prayer	Yantis, David	Na Yan	B F Ll	
The Lord's Prayer (First Mass)	Repp, Ray	66 Fel	B R F Ll	
The Lord's Prayer (Jazz-Rock Mass)	Mitchell, Ian	68 Fel	B F Ll	
The Lord's Prayer (Missa Bossa Nova)	Scholtes, Peter	66 Fel	B R F Ll	
The Lord's Prayer (Second Mass)	Repp, Ray	66 Fel	B R F Ll	
The Lords Prayer (Spiritual)	Pont, Kenneth (Arr)	Na Oxf	M G Ll	Unis
For Theirs Is The Kingdom Of Heaven	Nelson, Paul	Na Gsc	B L Ll	Ssa
Lord's Prayer	Schneider, Kent E.	69 Ccc	M B R L L Ll	
Lord's Prayer (Mass For New Rite)	Hampton, Calvin	76 Gia	B L L Ll	Satb+
Lord's Prayer (Notre Dame Mass)	Isele, David C.	74 Gia	B L L Ll	Satb+
Lord's Prayer (Org Or Guitar)	Johnson, D.	76 Aug	L Ll	Solo+
Lord's Prayer For Hours	Kelly, Columba (Rev.)	72 Cfc	M L L Ll	
Lord's Prayer For Mass (Icet)	Englert, Eugene	73 Cfc	M R L L Ll	
Lord's Prayer Icet	Hampton, Calvin	76 Gia	B L L Ll	Satb+
Lord's Prayer, The	Christiansen, P.	71 Aug	M L L Ll	Satb+
Lord's Prayer, The	Sylvester, Erich	71 Nal	B R L Ll	
Our Father	Dailey, Joe	75 Ahc	B R L L Ll	
Our Father	Deiss, Lucien	65 Wlp	B L Ll	
Our Father	Derosa, Judy	76 Rpb	M B R L L Ll	
Our Father	Ford, Paul	72 Fel	M B L Ll	
Our Father	Garza, Juliana, S. P.	73 Nal	B R L Ll	
Our Father	Gough, Nancy	73 Nal	B R L Ll	
Our Father	Kranz, James R.	70 Acp	L L Ll	
Our Father	Kush, Joseph	70 Acp	L L Ll	
Our Father	Mahoney, Patrick	74 Rpb	M B R L L Ll	
Our Father	Page, Paul F.	73 Rpb	M B R L L Ll	
Our Father	Riegel, Bob	73 Nal	B R L Ll	
Our Father	Shaw, Jim	75 Fel	B R L L Ll	
Our Father	Shelley, Tom	72 Ahc	B R L L Ll	
Our Father	St. Benedict's Farm	75 Sbf	B R L L Ll	
Our Father	Zsigray, Joe	72 Nal	B R L Ll	
Our Father (Icet)	Deiss, Lucien	69 Wlp	B L Ll	
Our Father (Organ + Guitar)	Pulkingham, Betty C.	73 Gia	B R L L Ll	Satb+
Our Father (Unison Or Choral)	Fitzpatrick, Dennis	63 Fel	B L Ll	
Our Father In Heaven	White, Jack Noble	76 Rpb	M B R L L Ll	
Our Father (D Maj)	Lynch, Michael B.	73 Rav	B R L L Ll	
Our Father (E Maj)	Ellis, Ron	73 Rav	B L L Ll	
Our Father, The Lords Prayer	Shelley, Tom	71 Ahc	B R L L Ll	
Padre Nuestro	Lee, John	70 Gia	B L L Ll	Uspan
The Lord's Prayer	Fitzpatrick, Dennis	63 Fel	B L Ll	
The Lord's Prayer	Peloquin, C Alexander	Na Gia	L Ll	
The Lord's Prayer	Phillips, J. Gerald	71 Cfc	M R L L Ll	
The Lord's Prayer (E)	Clements, John	Na Oxf	M L Ll	Unis
The Lord's Prayer (Merbecke)	Hilty, Everett J.	Na Oxf	M L Ll	Unis
They Kingdom Come	Berger, Jean	Na Gsc	B L Ll	Satb+
Thy Will Be Done	Ford, Virgil	Na Gsc	B L Ll	Satb
Lord's Prayer	Zaumeyer, John	73 Hal	T Ll	Full
Lord's Prayer 1	Picca, Angelo Della	69 Wlp	B T Ll	
Lord's Prayer 2	Picca, Angelo Della	69 Wlp	B T Ll	
Lord's Prayer, The	Kennerly	Na Lor	M T Ll	Satb
Lord's Prayer, The	Schutz, Heinrich	67 Bbl	M T Ll	Satb
Our Father	Tchaikovsky, P. I.	Na Gsc	B T Ll	Satb
Our Father Thou In Heaven Above	Franck, Melchior	Na Gsc	B T Ll	Satb
Our Father's Care	Ball	Na Lor	M T Ll	Satb
Pater Noster	Verdi, Giuseppe	Na Gsc	B T Ll	5mix
The Lord's Prayer	Forsyth, J	Na Gsc	T Ll	Var+
The Lord's Prayer	Malotte, A H	Na Gsc	T Ll	Solo+
The Lord's Prayer	Mueller, Carl F	Na Gsc	B T Ll	Satb+
The Lord's Prayer	Proulx, Richard	Na Gia	T Ll	Solo+
The Lord's Prayer (Bcp) Adapted	Farmer, John	Na Oxf	M T Ll	Ssaa
The Lord's Prayer (E)	Stone, Robert	Na Oxf	M T Ll	Satb
Thy Will Be Done	Foster, Will	Na Gsc	B T Ll	Satb+
Vaterunser, Das	Schutz, Heinrich	67 Bbl	M T Ll	T

Acclamations (Lamb Of God)

Title	Composer	Pub	Codes	Voicing
Agnus Dei (Mass For Schools)	Kostos, Patti	66 Fel	B C Lm	
Agnus Dei (Mariachi Mass)	Lojewski, Harry V	69 Fel	B F Lm	
Agnus Dei (Mass Of The Western Tribes)	Indian Melodies	66 Fel	B F Lm	
Lamb Of God	Davis, Bob	73 Fcc	B R L F Lm	
Lamb Of God	Mitchell, Ian	67 Fel	B R F Lm	
Lamb Of God	Wise, Joe	67 Wlp	B R F Lm	
Lamb Of God (Folk Mass No.4)	Quinlan, Paul	66 Fel	B F Lm	
Lamb Of God (Icet)	Schaffer, Robert J.	69 Wlp	B F Lm	
Lamb Of God (Liturgy Of Joy)	Blue, Robert	66 Fel	B F Lm	
Lamb Of God (Missa Bossa Nova)	Scholtes, Peter	66 Fel	B R F Lm	
Lamb Of God (1964 Text)	Winter, Miriam T.	66 Van	B R F Lm	
Lamb Of God (64 Text)	Markaitis, Bruno	67 Van	B R F Lm	
Lamb Of God (67th Street Mass)	Scholtes, Peter	68 Fel	B R F Lm	
O Lamb Of God	Farra, Mimi A.	73 Gia	M B R L F LmVar+	
O Lamb Of God	Yantis, David	Na Yan	B F Lm	
Song To The Lamb Of God (First Mass)	Repp, Ray	66 Fel	B R F Lm	
Song To The Lamb Of God (Second Mass)	Repp, Ray	66 Fel	B R F Lm	
Agnus Dei	Carroll, J. R.	71 Gia	B L L Lm3pt+	
Agnus Dei (Eng Mass)	Goemanne, Noel	70 Gia	B L L Lm2pt+	
Agnus Dei (Eng, Icet)	Cunningham, Patrick	74 Gra	M R L L LmChcon	
Agnus Dei (Mass For New Rite)	Hampton, Calvin	76 Gia	B L L LmSatb+	
Agnus Dei (Sung Mass No. 2)	Fitzpatrick, Dennis	63 Fel	B L Lm	
Agnus Dei (Thomas More Mass)	Reilly, Cyril A.	66 Fel	B L Lm	
Cordero De Dios	Lee, John	70 Gia	B L L LmUspan	
Dona Nobis Pacem (Round)	Foster, Anthony	Na Oxf	M L Lm3pt	
Lamb Of God	Christiansen, F. M.	33 Aug	M L LmSatb	
Lamb Of God	Collard, Terry	71 Nal	B R L Lm	
Lamb Of God	Davis, Paulette	76 Rpb	M B R L L Lm	
Lamb Of God	Foley, John, S. J.	70 Nal	B R L Lm	
Lamb Of God	Gentemann, Sr Elaine	75 Gia	B L L LmSa+	
Lamb Of God	Gentemann, Sr Elaine	70 Gia	B L L LmSatb+	
Lamb Of God	Goemanne, Noel	73 Gia	B L L Lm2pt+	
Lamb Of God	Medling, Rebecca	75 Rpb	M B R L L Lm	
Lamb Of God	Moultry, Prince Joseph	74 Nal	B R L Lm	
Lamb Of God	Page, Paul F.	73 Rpb	M B R L L Lm	
Lamb Of God	Page, Paul F.	76 Rpb	M B R L L Lm	
Lamb Of God	Proulx, Richard	71 Gia	B L L LmSatb+	
Lamb Of God	Schneider, Kent E.	75 Ccc	B L Lm	
Lamb Of God	St. Benedict's Farm	72 Sbf	B R L L Lm	
Lamb Of God	Sylvester, Erich	71 Nal	B R L Lm	
Lamb Of God	Wood, Mike	76 Rpb	M B R L L Lm	
Lamb Of God	Zsigray, Joe	75 Nal	B R L Lm	
Lamb Of God	Zsigray, Joe	72 Nal	B R L Lm	
Lamb Of God (Agnus Dei) (Sung Mass No 1	Fitzpatrick, Dennis	63 Fel	B L Lm	
Lamb Of God (Cel Of Unity)	Hebble, Robert	72 Gia	B L L LmSatb+	
Lamb Of God (Chardin Mass)	Rudcki, Stanley	66 Fel	B L Lm	
Lamb Of God (Child Mass)	Andrews, Carroll T.	70 Gia	B L L LmSatb+	
Lamb Of God (Community Mass)	Lee, John	71 Gia	B L L LmU+Org	
Lamb Of God (Icet)	Deiss, Lucien	70 Wlp	B R L Lm	
Lamb Of God (Icet)	Kraehenbuehl/Frischman	71 Jsp	B L Lm+Org	
Lamb Of God (Icet)	Kreutz, Robert	69 Wlp	B L Lm	
Lamb Of God (Icet)	Lojewski	69 Wlp	B L Lm	
Lamb Of God (Icet)	Vermulst, Jan	69 Wlp	B L Lm	
Lamb Of God (Icet) (Me)	Picca, Angelo Della	69 Wlp	B L LmVar	
Lamb Of God (Lyric Mass)	Andrews, Carroll T.	73 Gia	B L L Lm2pt+	
Lamb Of God (Mass For All Seasons)	Andrews, Carroll T.	70 Gia	B L L LmVar+	
Lamb Of God (New Mass)	Andrews, Carroll T.	70 Gia	B L L LmUnis+	
Lamb Of God (Notre Dame Mass)	Isele, David C.	74 Gia	B L L LmSatb+	
Lamb Of God (Opt Brs/Timp)	Goemanne, Noel	70 Gia	B L L LmSab+	
Lamb Of God (Short Mass)	Lee, John	69 Gia	B L L LmSatb+	
Lamb Of God (Vianney Mass)	Andrews, Carroll T.	75 Gia	B L L LmVar+	
Lamb Of God (W/Cantor)Dominic Mass	Goemanne, Noel	71 Gia	B L L LmSatb+	
Lamb Of God (With Rhythm Inst)	Hager	71 Aug	M L LmUnis	
Senor, Ten Piedad	Lee, John	70 Gia	B L L LmUspan	
Whatsoever Things	Curry, R D	Na Gia	L Lm	

Agnus Dei	Barber, Samuel	Na Gsc	B T Lm Satb+
Agnus Dei	Christiansen, P.	68 Aug	M T Lm Satb
Agnus Dei	Haydn, Joseph	Na Gsc	B T Lm Satb+
Agnus Dei	Victoria, Tomas Luis	Na Gsc	B T Lm 6mix
Agnus Dei (Missa Brevis)	Weber, Richard F	66 Fel	B T Lm
Angus Dei (Lamb Of God) (Deis)	Bizet, G	Na Gsc	B T Lm Satb
Dona Nobis Pacem (In 19 Rounds)	Latin–Tortolano Ed	75 Gia	B L T Lm 3pt
Lamb Of God	Barber, Samuel	Na Gsc	B T Lm Satb+
Lamb Of God	Decius–Pooler	62 Aug	M T Lm Var
Lamb Of God	Monteverdi, Claudio	Na Gsc	B T Lm Satb+
Lamb Of God	Monteverdi, Claudio	66 Som	M T Lm
O Lamb Of God	Newbury, Kent A.	Na Gsc	B T Lm Satb
O Lamb Of God	Stainer, Sir John	Na Gsc	B T Lm Satb+
O Lamb Of God (Agnus Dei)	Traditional	65 Fel	B T Lm

Communion Hymns(Processional)
See also category LO.

Come Along With Me To Jesus	Landry, Carey (Rev.)	75 Nal	B R C Ln
Come, Lord Jesus	Landry, Carey (Rev.)	75 Nal	B R C Ln
Let Us Break Bread Together	Blue, Robert	66 Fel	B R C Ln
We Come To Your Table	Landry, Carey (Rev.)	75 Nal	B R C Ln
Behold I Stand At The Door	Toolan, Sr Suzanne	71 Gia	B R L F Ln Ar+
God And Man At Table	Stamps, Robert J.	72 Sta	M R L F Ln
I Am The Bread Of Life	Toolan, Sr Suzanne	71 Gia	B R L F Ln Ar+
I Am The Resurrection	Repp, Ray	67 Fel	B R F Ln
Sons Of God	Thiem, James	66 Fel	B R F Ln
Taste And See (Ps 34)	Cunningham, Patrick	76 Gra	B R L F Ln
We All Stand At Your Table	Wise, Joe	71 Wlp	B R F Ln
We Come To Join In Your Banquet	Parker, Tom	69 Wlp	B R F Ln
We Gather Together	Scholtes, Peter	68 Fel	B R F Ln
Fill My Cup, Lord	Blanchard, Richard	59 Wrd	M R G Ln
God Is Love	Rivers, Clarence Jos.	64 Sti	M R G Ln
Come To My Table	Vickers, Wendy	75 Nal	B R L Ln
Come To The Table Of The Lord	Tracy, Shawn (Rev.)	72 Nal	B R L Ln
Come, Rich And Poor	Gilligan, M. (Text)	70 Acp	L L Ln
Communion Song (O Taste And See)	Isele, David C.	74 Gia	B L L Ln Satb+
Do This In Remembrance Of Me	Fortunate, Lou	72 Jsp	B L Ln Unis
Give The Bread Of Life	Deiss, Lucien	70 Wlp	B R L Ln
He Feeds Us With The Finest Of Wheat	Fitzpatrick, Dennis	65 Fel	B L Ln
He Gives Us Bread Which Comes	Fitzpatrick, Dennis	65 Fel	B L Ln
I Am The Living Bread	Fitzpatrick, Dennis	65 Fel	B L Ln
I Am The True Vine	Fitzpatrick, Dennis	65 Fel	B R L Ln
Let All Mortal Flesh Keep Silence	Proskinisomen, D	71 Gia	M L Ln Satb+
May We All One Bread, One Body Be	Fitzpatrick, Dennis	65 Fel	B L Ln
O Bread Of Life	Christiansen, F. M.	25 Aug	M L Ln Satb
Psalm 34	Blanchard, R. I.	72 Cfc	M L L Ln
Taste And See How Good The Lord Is	Fitzpatrick, Dennis	65 Fel	B L Ln
Thanks Be To Christ (Your Body)	Weber, R/Bradbury, W.	70 Jsp	B L Ln Satb
This Is My Body	Anon/Kraehenbuehl	68 Jsp	B L Ln Unis
To Your Table	Shelley, Tom	72 Ahc	B R L L Ln
We Come To Your Table	Garza, Juliana, S. P.	73 Nal	B R L Ln
You I Carry, O Lord (Ancient Text)	Deiss, Lucien	70 Wlp	B R L Ln Var
Come To Me	Hughes, Dvorak	Na Lor	M T Ln Satb
Come To The Banquet (Chant)	Nolan, J. & Huck, G.	65 Lit	B T Ln
He Is Lord (Verses)	Cunningham, Patrick	75 Gra	B R L T Ln Satb
How Sacred A Feast	Remondi/Andrews	70 Gia	B L T Ln Var
Jesu, The Very Thought Of Thee (Me)	Devictoria, Tomas L.	Na Oxf	M T Ln Satb
Let Us Break Bread Together	Rogers	75 Maf	M T Ln Sab
Let Us Break Bread Together	Sateren, Leland B.	55 Aug	M T Ln Satb
My God, And Is Thy Table Spread (Me)	Vanderhoek, Bert	Na Oxf	M T Ln Satb
O Food We Pilgrims Pray For	Isaak/Andrews	70 Gia	B L T Ln Var
O Taste And See (Ps 34)	Williams, Vaughan R.	Na Oxf	M T Ln Var

Communion Hymns(General)
These songs include metrical hymns and anthems as well as full communion services.

Give Me Your Hand	Blue, Robert	66 Fel	B R C Lo
I'll Fashion Me A People	Temple, Sebastian	69 Fcc	R L C Lo
We Are The Body Of Christ	Landry, Carey (Rev.)	75 Nal	B R C Lo
What Makes Love Grow?	Landry, Carey (Rev.)	73 Nal	B R C Lo
Abba, Father	Vissing, Sr. Rosalie	74 Sha	B R L F Lo
As We Grow	Eldridge, R.	75 Sil	L F Lo
Be Still	Leyko, Patricia J.	76 Chh	B R L F Lo
Blessed Sacrament, The	Temple, Sebastian	67 Fcc	B R F Lo Gia
Bread You Have Given Us	Wise, Joe	68 Wlp	B F Lo
Come Before The Table Of The Lord	Parker, Tom	67 Wlp	B R F Lo
Come Together	Yantis, David	Na Yan	B F Lo
Daily Bread	Wood, Mike/Randall, Win	76 Rpb	M B R L F Lo
I Am The Living Bread	Miffleton, Jack	69 Wlp	B R F Lo
In Remembrance Of Me	Johnson, Gary L.	74 Bfi	B L F Lo
In The Lord We Will Live	Radice, John	70 Acp	L F Lo
Kum Ba Yah	Traditional/Mayfield	Na Zon	M F Lo Var
Let Us Break Bread Together	Armstrong, M	Na Gia	F Lo
Let Us Break Bread Together	Goemanne, Noel	72 Gia	M F Lo Satb+
Let Us Break Bread Together	Mayhew, K. (Arr)	69 Van	B R F Lo
Let Us Break Bread Together	Mitchell, Ian	66 Fel	B F Lo
Let Us Break Bread Together	Silvia, Helen	73 Acp	L F Lo
Let Us Break Bread Together (Arr)	Farra, Mimi A.	72 Gia	M B R L F Lo Var+
Pass My Love Around	Yantis, David	Na Yan	B F Lo
Remain In Me	Vissing, Sr. Rosalie	74 Sha	B R L F Lo
Said The Lord	Temple, Sebastian	67 Fcc	B R L F Lo Gia
Sign Of Total Giving	Ault, Gary	70 Fel	B R F Lo
The Banquet Of The Lord	Hurd, Bob	73 Fel	B R F Lo
The Body Of Christ	Yantis, David	Na Yan	B F Lo
They'll Know We Are Christians	Scholtes, Peter	66 Fel	B R F Lo
To Be Your Body	Wise, Joe	68 Wlp	B R F Lo
Unites Us All Together As One	Tucciarone, Angel	74 Wlp	B R F Lo
We Are One	Temple, Sebastian	67 Fcc	B R L F Lo Gia
Whatsoever You Do	Jabusch, Willard F.	67 Acf	M R F Lo
You Are With Me	Whitemore, Joan M.	74 Sms	M R L F Lo
Beyond This Place	Mieir, Audrey	72 Man	B R G Lo
Fellowship Divine	Rogers	Na Zon	M G Lo
He Comes To Me	Mieir, Audrey	62 Man	B G Lo
In Christ There Is No East Or West	Traditional/Johnson	75 Zon	G Lo Satb
Let Us Break Bread Together	Myers, Gordon	Na Abi	M G Lo Satb
Let Us Break Bread Together	Na	Na Gsc	B G Lo Ttbb
Let Us Break Bread Together	Na	Na Lor	M G Lo Var
Litany Of The Eucharist.	Greif, Jean A	65 Vrn	M L G Lo
Love All The Brethren	Gaither/Gaither B/G	75 Gmc	M B R G Lo
One Bread, One Body Are We.	Greif, Jean A	66 Vrn	M L G Lo
Plenty Of Room In The Family	Gaither/Gaither B/G	74 Gmc	M B R G Lo Satb
The Family Of God	Gaither/Gaither B/G	70 Gmc	M B R G Lo Var
A Banquet Is Prepared	Kavanaugh, John, S. J.	73 Nal	B R L Lo
Almighty God, Unto Whom All Hearts	Mcafee, Don	Na Abi	M L Lo Satb
Amazing Grace	Mcbride, James	75 Ccc	M B R L L Lo
An Anthem For Communion	Martin, Gilbert M	Na Lor	M L Lo Satb
Are Not Our Hearts?	Landry, Carey (Rev.)	73 Nal	M B R L Lo
At That First Eucharist	Turton, William, Alt.	70 Acp	L L Lo
At That First Eucharist (4part Arr.)	Silvia, Helen	73 Acp	L L Lo
Become To Us The Living Bread	Drury, M/Kraehenbuehl	76 Jsp	B L Lo Satb
Before Us, Lord, The Sacrament	Macroberts	Na Lor	M L Lo
Beneath The Forms Of Outward Rite	Lovelace, Austin C.	Na Abi	M L Lo Satb
Bread Of Heaven	Rasley	Na Lor	M L Lo Satb
Bread Of Life	Russell	Na Lor	M L Lo Satb
Bread Of Life, The	Young, Carlton R.	Na Abi	M L Lo Sa–Tb
Bread Of Presence	Schneider, Kent E.	73 Ccc	M B R L L Lo
Bread Of The World	Horder, Mervyn	Na Abi	M L Lo Satb
Bread Of The World	Schmutz, Albert C.	Na Abi	M L Lo Satb
Bread To The Hungry	Page, Paul F.	76 Rpb	M B R L L Lo
Come, Live In Us	Price, William (Text)	70 Acp	L L Lo
Come, Live In Us (4–Part Arr.)	Cirou, Joseph	73 Acp	L L Lo
Come, The Lord Is Waiting For Us	Greif, Jean A	66 Vrn	M L L Lo
Communion Anthem	Mcafee, Don	75 Maf	M L Lo Satb+
Communion Hymn	Hopson, Hal	Na Abi	M L Lo Satb
Communion Hymn Sequence For Choir	James	Na Lor	M L Lo Satb
Communion Hymn (Bread Of The World)	Buck	Na Gsc	M L Lo Satb
Communion Muse	Garza, Juliana, S. P.	73 Nal	B R L Lo
Communion Rite (Lyric Liturgy)	Peloquin, C Alexander	74 Gia	B L L Lo Satb+
Corpus Christi Carol (Me)	Britten, Benjamin	Na Oxf	M L Lo Unis
Cup Of Blessing That We Share	Mischke/Papale	66 Wlp	B L Lo
Depth Of Mercy	Mueller, Luise	Na Abi	M L Lo Satb
Do This In Remembrance Of Me	Fitzpatrick, Dennis	65 Fel	B L Lo
Eucharist, Most Holy.	Greif, Jean A	76 Vrn	M L L Lo
Face To Face (Psalm 42–43)	Hillebrand, Frank	75 Ahc	B R L L Lo
Father While This Bread Is Readied	Farrell, Melvin/Goeman	62 Wlp	B L Lo
Fold To Thy Heart Thy Brother	Hovdesven, E A	Na Gsc	B L Lo Satb
For The Bread	Copes, V. Earle	Na Abi	M L Lo Satb
Gentle Rains	Ellis, Ron	76 Rav	B R L L Lo
He Fed Them With Most Precious Wheat	Ty, C	66 Gia	M L Lo Satb
He Who Eats My Flesh	Fitzpatrick, Dennis	65 Fel	B L Lo
Here At The Table Of The Lord	Temple, Sebastian	71 Gia	B R L L Lo Satb+
Holy, Holy, Holy	Walter, Samuel	Na Abi	M L Lo Satb
I Am The Bread Of Life	Roff, Joseph	75 Sac	M L Lo Satb
I Am The Vine	Morgan	75 Sac	M L Lo Satb
I Am With You	Roff, Joseph	Na Zon	M L Lo Satb
I'm Feasting On The Living Bread	Unknown	73 Mar	B L L Lo
If Anyone Thirst	Fitzpatrick, Dennis	65 Fel	B L Lo
In Christ There Is No East Or West	Couper	75 Sac	M L Lo Sa+
In Memory Of The Savior's Love	Burroughs, Bob	Na Abi	M L Lo Satb
In Remembrance Of Me	Parks, J.	75 Zon	L Lo Satb
In This Bread (We Share The Cross)	Temple, Sebastian	71 Gia	B R L L Lo Satb+
Is Not The Cup That We Bless	Fitzpatrick, Dennis	65 Fel	B L Lo
Jesu Dulcis Memoria (E & Lat)	Drayton, Paul	Na Oxf	M L Lo Ssattb
Jesus	Catalanello, Michael	72 Str	M L Lo
Jesus, Come To Us.	Greif, Jean A	66 Vrn	M L L Lo
Let All Mortal Flesh Keep Silence	Christiansen, F.M. & P	56 Aug	M L Lo Satb
Let All Mortal Flesh Keep Silence	Moultrie, Gerard	70 Acp	L L Lo
Let All Mortal Flesh Keep Silence	Silvia, Helen	73 Acp	L L Lo
Let Us Break Bread	Schneider, Kent E. (Arr)	76 Ccc	M B L L Lo
Litany For Breaking Bread	Freeman, Eileen	76 Rpb	M B R L L Lo
Liturgy Of Eucharist (Lyric Liturgy)	Peloquin, C Alexander	74 Gia	B L L Lo Satb+
Lord, Have Mercy Upon Us	Walter, Samuel	Na Abi	M L Lo Satb
Lord, Surround Us With Holy Symbols	Wetzler, Robert	72 Aug	M L Lo Satb
Lord's Supper, The	Burroughs	75 Maf	M L Lo Satb
Love	Goeboro, Jean	74 Wgm	B R L L Lo
Many Are We Yet One We Are	Zsigray, Joe	75 Nal	B R L Lo
Members Of One Mystic Body	Westendorf/Picca	61 Wlp	B L Lo
Moist With One Drop Of Thy Blood	Young, Gordon	Na Abi	M L Lo Satb
Music For The Lord's Supper	Dean, T. W.	61 Gam	B L Lo Satb
My Flesh Is Food	Fitzpatrick, Dennis	65 Fel	B L Lo
No Man Is An Island	Berry, Wallace	68 Som	M L Lo
O Come And Dwell In Me	Ford, Virgil	Na Gsc	B L Lo Satb
O Food Of Men Wayfaring	Harris	75 Pro	M L Lo Satb+
O Holy Banquet	Theophane, Sr. M	Na Gia	L Lo
O Lamb Of God	Walter, Samuel	Na Abi	M L Lo Satb
O Lord, I Am Unworthy	Fitzpatrick, Dennis	65 Fel	B L Lo
O Taste And See	Williams	Na Lor	M L Lo Satb
O Taste And See (From 5 Anthems)	Ferris, William	69 Gia	B L L Lo 2pt

CATEGORIZED INDEX

Title	Composer/Author	Codes
One O'er All The Earth	Lorenz, Ellen Jane	Na Abi M L Lo Satb
Panis Angelicus	Franck, Cesar	72 Gia M L Lo Solo+
Psalm 34	Smith, P.	76 Sil R L L Lo
Receive Ye The Body Of Christ	Roff, J/Bobak, J	Na Gia R L L Lo
Sign Of His Life In The World, The	Hubert, Yvon	72 Fcc R L L L Lo
Sweet Sweet Sound	Welch, Phil	72 Rav B R L L L Lo
Sweet Wine	St. Benedict's Farm	75 Sbf B R L L L Lo
Taste And See	Hughes, Howard	76 Rpb M B R L L L Lo
The Bread Is One	Peloquin, C Alexander	65 Gia L Lo Satbu+
They Ate And Were	Fitzpatrick, Dennis	65 Fel B L Lo
This Bread Commits Us To Christ	Fitzpatrick, Dennis	65 Fel B L Lo
This Is My Body	Foley, John, S.J.	70 Nal B R L Lo
This Is The Covenant	Berger, Jean	73 Aug M L Lo Satb
This, The Bread I Give You	Fitzpatrick, Dennis	65 Fel L Lo
We Are Hungry	Shaw, Jim	73 Fel B R L L Lo
We Long For You, O Lord	Reilly, Cyril A.	66 Fel B R L Lo
We Stand In Need	Lynch, Michael B.	73 Rav B R L L Lo
Where Two Or Three	Landry, Carey (Rev.)	68 Nal B R L Lo
While I Sup With Thee	Haxby, Wm. G.	76 Lor L Lo Unis+
Whoever Eats This Bread	Fitzpatrick, Dennis	65 Fel B L Lo
With God On Our Side	Lynch, Michael B.	76 Rav B R L L Lo
Words Of Institution	Zsigray, Joe	74 Nal B R L Lo
You Give Us Bread, O Lord	Fitzpatrick, Dennis	65 Fel L Lo
Angelic Bread Of Heaven	Cui, C	74 Gia M T Lo Satb
Anthem For Communion, An	Martin	Na Lor M T Lo Satb
Ave Verum	Mozart, Wolfgang A	Na Gia T Lo
Ave Verum	Mozart, Wolfgang A	70 Gia B L T Lo Var
Ave Verum	Saint–Saens, Camille	Na Gsc T Lo Satb+
Ave Verum (Hail, True Body)	Des Pres, Josquin	70 Gia B T Lo Sab
Ave Verum (Me)	Mozart, Wolfgang A	Na Oxf T Lo 2pt
Ave Verum Corpus	Mozart, Wolfgang A	Na Gsc B T Lo Satb+
Ave Verum Corpus	Mozart, Wolfgang A	52 Bbl M T Lo Satb&Or
Ave Verum Corpus K 618	Mozart, Wolfgang A	Na Kal T Lo Satb
Ave Verum (Jesu Word Of God Incarnate)	Gounod, Charles	Na Gsc B T Lo Satb
Blessed Are The Faithful	Graun, K. H.	69 Smc M T Lo Satb
Break Thou The Bread Of Life	Lockwood, Normand	56 Smc M T Lo Satb
Christ's Body, Given Up For Us	Shaltz, Gregory	74 Sms M R L T Lo
Coenam Cum Discipulis	Gumpelzhaimer, Adam	Na Gsc T Lo Var+
Come Together	Owens, Jimmy & Carol	72 Lex M T Lo
Communion From Four Folk–Hymns	Robison	75 Bbl B T Lo Sb+
Communion Hymn	Buck, Dudley	Na Gsc B T Lo Satb+
Communion Hymn	Opie, M P	Na Gsc B T Lo Satb+
Communion Meditations	Carlson	74 Aug M T Lo Satb
Communion Service	White, L. J.	Na Oxf M T Lo Unis
Communion Service	Willan, Healey	Na Oxf M T Lo Unis
Communion Service (Alt Series 2)	Ridout, Alan	Na Oxf M T Lo Unis
Communion Service (Mass Of Quiet Hour)	Oldroyd, George	Na Oxf M T Lo Satb
Communion Service E.E. Series 3 (Md)	Jackson, Francis	Na Oxf M T Lo Satb
Communion Service In A Minor (M)	Darke, Harold	Na Oxf M T Lo Unis
Communion Service In C (Me)	Mathias, William	Na Oxf M T Lo Unis
Communion Service In D (E)	Leighton, Kenneth	Na Oxf M T Lo Usatb
Communion Service In D Minor	Statham, Heathcote	Na Oxf M T Lo Satbu
Communion Service In D Minor	Williams, Vaughan R.	Na Oxf M T Lo Satb
Communion Service In E (Md)	Darke, Harold	Na Oxf M T Lo Satb
Communion Service In E Flat	Bairstow, Edward C.	Na Oxf M T Lo Unis
Communion Service In F With Kyrie	Darke, Harold	Na Oxf M T Lo Satb
Communion Service In F (Md)	Jackson, Francis	Na Oxf M T Lo Satb
Communion Service, Series 3 (E)	Rutter, John	Na Oxf M T Lo Satbu
Communion Service, Series 3 (M)	Dearnley, C. & Wicks A	Na Oxf M T Lo Unis
Communion Service, Series 3 (M)	Kelly, Bryan	Na Oxf M T Lo Satb
Devoutly I Adore Thee	Creston, Paul	Na Gsc B T Lo Ttbb+
Domine Non Sum Dignus (E & L)(Md)	Vittoria, T. L. Da	75 Gia M L T Lo Satb
Ego Sum Panis Vitae	Back, Sven–Erik	Na Gsc B T Lo Satb
Ego Sum Panis Vivus	Palestrina, Giovanni P	Na Gia T Lo
Father Most Merciful	Franck, Cesar	Na Gsc B T Lo Var+
Father, God Of All Things Living	Farrell, Melvin/Burns	63 Wlp B T Lo
Feed Us Now, O Son Of God	Allen, Peter (Swenson)	74 Gal M T Lo
Fill My House	Kearney, Peter	66 Jas M R T Lo
Hail, Noble Flesh	Ferris, W	Na Gia T Lo
Hail, O Hail True Body	Viadana, Lodovico	66 Som M T Lo
Hail, O Hail True Body (Md)	Byrd, William	Na Oxf M T Lo Satb
Hail, True Body Born Of Mary	Des Pres, Josquin	Na Gsc B T Lo Sab
Holy Manna	Rogers, Lee (Arr.)	76 Lor T Lo Satb+
Humbly Let Us Voice Our Homage	Farrell, Melvin	64 Wlp B T Lo
Humbly We Adore Thee	Farrell, Melvin	55 Wlp B T Lo
Humbly We Adore You	Nachtwey, Roger;Harm.,	65 Fel B T Lo
I Am The Bread Of Life	Schiavone, J.	74 Gia M T Lo Sa
Jesu, The Very Thought Of Thee (M)	Bairstow, E.C.	Na Oxf M T Lo Satb
Jesu, Word Of God Incarnate	Mozart, Wolfgang A	Na Gsc B T Lo Satb+
Jesus, Let Our Souls Be Fed	Sateren, Leland B.	54 Aug M T Lo Satb
Just As A Heart	Palestrina, Giovanni P	75 Bbl M T Lo Satb
Last Supper	Carter, J.	76 Bec M T Lo
Lauda, Sion, Salvatorem	Nachtwey – Fitzpatrick	65 Fel M T Lo
Let All Mortal Flesh Keep Silence	Butler	75 Sac M T Lo Satb
Let All Mortal Flesh Keep Silence	Denton	Na Lor M T Lo Satb
Let All Mortal Flesh Keep Silence	Diggle, R	Na Gsc B T Lo Satb+
Let All Mortal Flesh Keep Silence	Track, Gerhard	72 Gia M T Lo Sab+
Let Us Break Bread Together	Lojeski, Ed (Arr)	76 Hal T Lo Var
Lo, Angels Bread (Eng Only)	Casciolini, C./Ed Lee	70 Gia B L T Lo Satb
Lo, Angels' Bread	Casciolini, C.	73 Gia M T Lo 2pt
Lord In Thy Presence Lead Us	Huerter, C.	Na Gsc B T Lo Satb+
O Bread Of Angels	Gannon, Michael	63 Wlp B T Lo
O Bread Of Angels	Lambillotte/Andrews	70 Gia B L T Lo Var
O Bread Of Life	Gannon, Michael	55 Wlp B T Lo
O Lamb Of God	Eccard, Johannes	Na Abi M T Lo Satt
O Lord With Wondrous Mystery	Gannon, Michael	55 Wlp B T Lo
O Sacrament Most Holy (Music)	Dejong	61 Wlp B T Lo
O Sacred Feast (Eng Only)	Farrant, R./Ed Lee	70 Gia B L T Lo Satb
O Sacrum Convivium	Lallouette, J F	75 Maf M T Lo 2pt
O Sacrum Convivium (Md)	Tallis, Thomas	Na Oxf M T Lo Saatb
O Sacrum Convivium (Me)	Devictoria, Tomas L.	Na Oxf M T Lo Ttbb
O Salutaris Hostia	Rossini, Gioacchino	54 Bbl M T Lo Satb
O Salutaris Hostia (Md)	Mathias, William	Na Oxf M T Lo Ttbb
O Taste And See	Rogers, J H	Na Gsc B T Lo Satb+
Of The Glorious Body Telling	Devictoria, Tomas L.	Na Oxf B T Lo Satb+
Of The Glorious Body Telling	Vittoria–Sateren, L.	55 Aug M T Lo Satb
Pange Lingua, Eucharistic Hymn(Lat)	Bruckner, Anton	Cfp R T Lo Satb+
Panis Angelicus (E&L) (Md)	Palestrina, Giovanni P	76 Gia M L T Lo Satb
Panis Angelicus (Prayer For Peace)	Franck, C. (Hoffman)	Hof M T Lo
Praise We Christ's Immortal Body	Farrell, Melvin	64 Wlp B T Lo
Prepare Now Your Finest Chamber	Scarlatti, Alessandro	74 Bbl M T Lo Satb
Quotiescumque	Fitzpatrick, Dennis	63 Fel B T Lo
Receive Now The Body Of Christ	Carroll, J. R.	72 Gia M T Lo Satb
Shepherd Of Souls In Love Come Feed	Westendorf, Omer	64 Wlp B T Lo
Short Communion Service W/Congregation	Hall, Alan	Na Oxf M T Lo Usatb
Short Communion Service: Kyrie Etc	Batten, Adrian	Na Oxf M T Lo Satb
Sicut Cervus	Palestrina, Giovanni P	75 Bbl M T Lo Satb
Tantum Ergo	Faure	Na Kal B T Lo Satb
Tantum Ergo	Schubert, Franz J.	Na Gsc B T Lo Satb+
Tantum Ergo	Vittoria, T L	Na Gia T Lo
Tantum Ergo, Opus 65, No. 2	Faure, Gabriel	54 Bbl M T Lo Ssa+
Verily, Verily, I Say Unto You	Tallis, Thomas	Na Oxf M T Lo Satb

Processional Hymns(General)

Listed here are processional songs which did not fit in any of the other categories.

Title	Composer/Author	Codes
The Rock Holler	Blue, Robert	66 Fel B R C Lp
Come To The Lord	Radice, John	70 Acp L F Lp
God Gives His People Strength	Winter, Miriam T.	66 Van B R F Lp
Mass Is Ended, The	Temple, Sebastian	67 Fcc B R L F Lp Gia
Morning Has Broken	Lojeski, Ed	74 Hal F Lp Satb
To The Mountain Lord!	Cunningham, Patrick	76 Gra B R L F Lp Var+
Walk On	Sullivan, Sr.Mary Hope	74 Sha B R L F Lp
Climbin' Jacob's Ladder (P.D.)	Akers, Doris (Arr.)	60 Man M R G Lp
Come To My House	Culverwell, Andrew	73 Man B R G Lp
Come Unto Me	Hamblen Suzy	Na Ham M G Lp
Come With Me	Mieir, Audrey	68 Man B G Lp
He Who Believes In Me.	Greif, Jean A	66 Vrn M L G Lp
I Will Arise And Go To Jesus	Traditional/Mickelson	Na Zon M G Lp Satb
I'll Go Now	Peterson, John W.	Na Zon M G Lp Var
Let's Join In Songs Of Love	Hendrix, James	Na Gmp M L G Lp Satb
Marching To Zion	Slauson, Loyal	Na Zon M G Lp Satb
Oh, Let Me Walk With Thee	Chitwood, Joe	58 Man M B G Lp
Psalm 100 (Spoken/Song)	Allen, Lanny	76 Wrd M G Lp Satb+
We Are The Light Of The World.	Greif, Jean A	66 Vrn M L G Lp
We're Marching To Zion	Lowry/Ayers	Na Zon M G Lp Satb
Blessed Is The Man	Trombley, Richard	75 Wgm B R L L Lp
Call To Worship (No 5027)	Johnson, Norman	Na Zon B L Lp
Come By Here	Gilligan, Michael	67 Acp L L L Lp
Come, Christians, Join To Sing	Engler, Eugene	73 Gia M L Lp Satb+
Come, Faithful People, Come Away	Peek, Richard	Na Abi M L Lp 2pt
Come, Let Us Join	Darst, S. Glen	66 Som M L Lp
Glory Be To The Father	Greif, Jean A	65 Vrn M L Lp
Good Shepherd, We Love You (Org,Flute)	Cunningham, Patrick	76 Gra B R L L Lp Satb+
Hail Thee Festival Day (W/Org,Perc)	Hampton, Calvin	76 Gia M L Lp Satbu+
I Come, O Lord, Unto Thee	Sateren, Leland B.	75 Sac M L Lp Satb
I Will Go To The Mountain	Wortley, Howard S.	Mem M L Lp
Isaiah 43	Zawacki, Cathy	75 Wgm B R L L Lp
Jesus Went With Them	Fitzpatrick, Dennis	65 Fel B L Lp
Light Has Come	Ellis, Ron	73 Rav B R L L Lp
Lord, Inspire Our Worship	Schneider, Kent E.	75 Ccc M B L Lp
On The Way To The Mountain	Hubert, Yvon	72 Fcc R L L Lp
Psalm 121	Korgstad, Bob	75 Zon L Lp Satb
Sunday Carol (A Cap)	Kirk, Theron	76 Pro M L Lp Satb
This Is The Lord's Own Day	Kreutzer, Conradin	Na Gsc L Lp Var+
Welcome In	Wise, Joe	73 Nal B R L Lp
Come Unto Me	Fischer, Irwin	76 Cob M T Lp
Come Unto Me And Rest	Nathan/Mcgranahan	Na Gph M T Lp
Come, Ye Thankful People, Come	Williamson, Malcolm	Na Gsc T Lp Satb+
How Godly Is The House Of God	Meyerowitz, Jan	59 Pon T Lp Satb
Immanuel	Johnson, Gary L.	75 Bfi B R T Lp
O Day Of Rest And Gladness	Traditional/Decou	Na Zon T Lp Satb
Processional & Alleluia(Xmas & Easter)	Rockwood, Gay Hylander	Na Oxf M T Lp Eatb
With The Blessing Of God	Husted, Richard S.	76 Chh B L T Lp
Ye Servants Of God	Smith, Lani	76 Lor T Lp Satb+

SEASONAL HYMNS

This section lists music for celebrating the seasons of the liturgical year. The sections are divided into sub-categories as follows.

CODE – CATEGORY
SA–*Advent Hymns, Anthems, and Songs*
SC–*Christmas Hymns and Carols*
SL–*Lenten Hymns and Psalms*
SE–*Easter Hymns*
SS–*Pentecostal Music*

Advent Hymns, Anthems, and Songs

CATEGORIZED INDEX

Alabanzas Del Adviento	Santa Cruz, Domingo	62 Pic	M C Sa
Chariots Of Clouds	Fabing, Bob	74 Ahc	B R L C Sa

A Promise Has Been Made	Ahearn, Dennis	70 Fel	B R F Sa
Advent Glad Song (Heartily Rejoice)	Toolan, Sr Suzanne	71 Gia	B R L F Sa Ar+
Come Down, Lord	Winter, Miriam T.	66 Van	B R F Sa
Come Lord Jesus	Vissing, Sr. Rosalie	74 Sha	B R L F Sa
Come, Lord Jesus (The Night)	Winter, Miriam T.	67 Van	B R F Sa
Get Up, Jerusalem	Mudd, C. P.	68 Wlp	B R F Sa
He Comes	Winter, Miriam T.	72 Van	B R F Sa
How Long, O Lord	Repp, Ray	67 Fel	B R F Sa
Jesus We're Waiting For You	Temple, Sebastian	71 Gia	B R L F Sa Ar+
John	Winter, Miriam T.	68 Van	B R F Sa
John The Baptist	Hurd, Bob	73 Fel	B R F Sa
John The Baptizer	Ylvisaker, J & A.	69 Van	B R F Sa
Joy Is Like The Rain	Winter, Miriam T.	66 Van	B R F Sa
Joyous Coming Of Our Lord	Schaffer, Robert J.	69 Wlp	B R F Sa
Look Up	Corda, M. And Flint, J.	76 Cor	M F Sa
Lord Make Us Ready	Parker, Tom	68 Wlp	B F Sa
Marana-Tha	Gilligan, Michael	67 Acp	L F Sa
Maranatha	Meltz, Ken	72 Wlp	B R F Sa
My Lord Will Come Again	Wise, Joe	67 Wlp	B R F Sa
Prepare For The Coming	Risewick, Jack M.	73 Fel	B F Sa
Prepare Ye The Way Of The Lord	Schwartz, Stephen	71 Val	B R F Sa
Prepare You For The Day	Montague, George T.	68 Fel	B R F Sa
Preparing Now	Schaffer, Robert J.	67 Wlp	B R F Sa
Promise Of Salvation	Tucciarone, Angel	73 Wlp	B R F Sa
Psalm 19 Drop Down Dew	O'sheil, Judy	66 Fel	B F Sa
Rejoice, The Messiah Is Coming	Miller, Dan	73 Fel	B F Sa
Seasons Of Rapture	Wyrtzen, Don	Na Zon	M F Sa Satb
See How The Virgin Waits	Jabusch, Willard F.	75 Rpb	M B R L F Sa
The Coming Of Christ (3 Pts)	Summerlin, E., Miller, W.	69 Van	B R F Sa
The Day Of The Lord	Cunningham, Patrick	68 Fel	B R F Sa
The Judgement Day	Williams, J.	76 Sil	F Sa
The Race That Long In Darkness Pined	Peek	76 Abi	M F Sa Sab+
The Time Has Come	Meltz, Ken	72 Wlp	B R F Sa
Waiting	Thiem, James	66 Fel	B F Sa
Why Did Jesus Come To Earth	Finley, Ken	73 Fel	B F Sa
Will You Be Ready?	Peterson/Wyrtzen	Na Zon	M F Sa Satb

Christ Returneth	Mcgranahan/Mickelson	Na Zon	M G Sa Satb
Even So, Lord Jesus, Come	Gaither/Gaither B/G	63 Gmc	M B R G Sa Var
Even So, Lord Jesus, Come	Gaither, William J	Na Lor	M G Sa Satb
He Had It Planned Long Ago	Culverwell, Andrew	74 Man	B R G Sa
He Is Coming Again	Mieir, Audrey	64 Man	B G Sa
He'll Break Through The Blue	Wyrtzen, Don	Na Zon	M G Sa Satb
How Long Will It Be?	Peterson, John W.	Na Zon	M G Sa Satb
I Will Come Again (Cantata)	Corss/Rasley	Na Zon	B G Sa
I'm Coming	Gaither/Gaither B/G	64 Gmc	B R G Sa Satb
It May Be Today	Bixler/Mickelson	Na Zon	M G Sa Satb
It Won't Be Long (We'll Be Goin')	Crouch, A./Floria, C.	72 Wrd	B R G Sa Satb+
It's So Nice To Have Jesus	Billman, M./Brown, C.	74 Wrd	B R G Sa "2pt+
Jesus Is Coming (Musical)	Peterson, John W.	Na Zon	B R G Sa
Jesus Is Coming (Theme Ii)	Peterson, John W.	75 Zon	M G Sa Satb
Jesus Is Coming Again	Peterson/Decou	Na Zon	M G Sa Satb
Jesus Is Coming Again	Peterson/Mickelson	Na Zon	M G Sa Satb
Someday My Lord Will Come	Purifoy, John	75 Wrd	M G Sa Satb+
Somewhere In Heaven	Na	Na Zon	M G Sa
The King Is Coming	Gaither/Gaither B/G	70 Gmc	M B R G Sa Var
The Times And The Seasons (No 5668)	Wyrtzen, Don	Na Zon	G Sa Solo
These Times Must Come	Akers, Doris	73 Man	B R G Sa
This Could Be The Dawning Of That Day	Gaither/Gaither B/G	71 Gmc	M B R G Sa Var
Until The Day Breaks	Gaither/Gaither B/G	67 Gmc	B R G Sa Satb
When Earth's Last Picture Is Painted	Hamblen Stuart	Na Ham	M G Sa
When Jesus Breaks The Morning	Gaither/Gaither	61 Gmc	M B R G Sa Satb
Will It Be Soon?	Johnson, Norman	Na Zon	M G Sa Full
Yes I'll Know Him	Redd, Gc/H. Hubbard	Na Sav	M G Sa

A Light Shall Shine Upon Us	Fitzpatrick, Dennis	65 Fel	B L Sa
A Message Came To A Maiden Young	Held, Wilbur C	69 Aug	M L Sa Unis
Advent Service	Held, Wilbur C	71 Aug	M L Sa Satb+
All Men Shall See The Salvation	Fitzpatrick, Dennis	65 Fel	B L Sa
An Age Had Passed	Gilligan, M. (Text)	67 Acp	L L Sa
Are You Ready?	Kerner, Debby Melle	72 Mar	R L L Sa
Because You Were Good	Fitzpatrick, Dennis	65 Fel	B L Sa
Behold, The Lord Shall Come	Fitzpatrick, Dennis	65 Fel	B L Sa
By The Shores Of The Jordan	Engel, J.	62 Som	M L Sa
Christ Our Prophet	Gilligan, Michael	70 Acp	L L Sa
Christ Our Prophet (4-Part Arr.)	Kocher, Conrad, Alt.	73 Acp	L L Sa
Come Heavenly Child	Burke, John	Na Abi	M L Sa Full
Come Jesus Christ	Deiss, Lucien	70 Wlp	B R L Sa
Come O Lord, O Come For Our Saving	Deiss, Lucien	65 Wlp	B R L Sa
Come Thou Long-Expected Jesus	Darst, S. Glen	66 Som	M L Sa
Come, O Come	Hughes, Robert J.	Na Lor	M L Sa Satb
Come, O Come, Lord Jesus, Come	Fitzpatrick, Dennis	65 Fel	B L Sa
Come, O Long Awaited Savior	Korhonen, J	72 Gia	M L Sa Var
Come, Redeemer Of Mankind	Fitzpatrick, Dennis	65 Fel	B L Sa
Come, Shake The Mountains	Gilligan, M. (Text)	70 Acp	L L Sa
Come, Thou Long-Expected Jesus	Lewis, John Leo	Na Gsc	B L Sa Satb+
Coming Of Our Lord, The	Zsigray, Joe	68 Nal	B R L Sa
Daughter Of Zion	Denton, James	Na Lor	M L Sa Satb
Daystar	Fryxell, Regina	Na Abi	M L Sa Satb
Desert Shall Rejoice, The	Wilson	Na Lor	M L Sa Satb
Drop Down Ye Heavens	Ferris, William	69 Gia	B L L Sa 2pt
Ecce Dominus Veniet (E,L)(Md)	Herter, J. (Ed)	76 Gia	M L L Sa Satb
Even So Lord Jesus Quickly Come	Cunningham, Patrick	76 Gra	M L L Sa Sab+
Even So, Lord Jesus	Narum And Preus	64 Aug	M L Sa
Every Valley	Dufford, Bob, S. J.	70 Nal	B R L Sa
For As The Rain Cometh Down	Lekberg, Sven	Na Gsc	B L Sa Satb
He Came Among Us W/Solo	Carlson, G.	76 Aug	L Sa Satb(B)
He Shall Come Down	Ortlund, A.	Na Zon	L Sa Ssatb
Heavens Drop Dew From Above	Deiss, Lucien	65 Wlp	B R L Sa
Herald Of Good Tiding (W/Tpts)	Titcomb, Everett	64 Cfp	M L Sa Satb
I Wait For The Lord	Slates, Philip	Na Abi	M L Sa Sa-Tb
In Ages Now Long Past	Gilligan, Michael	70 Acp	L L Sa
John The Baptist	Gilsdorf, Sr. Helen	75 Rpb	M B R L L Sa
Joseph, Take Mary As Your Wife	Fitzpatrick, Dennis	65 Fel	B L Sa
Keep Christ In Christmas	Hughes, Robert J.	Na Lor	M L Sa Satb
Lord Is Drawing Near, The	Gilligan, Michael	73 Acp	L L Sa
Lord Is Drawing Near, The (4-Part Arr)	Woodward, George R.	67 Acp	L L Sa
Lord Is Nigh, The	Mcafee, Don	75 Sac	M L Sa Satb
Maranatha	Deiss, Lucien	65 Wlp	B R L Sa
My Soul Doth Magnify	Gore Richard	76 Abi	M L Sa Satb+
My Soul Is Waiting For The Lord	Deiss, Lucien	65 Wlp	B R L Sa
O Antiphons	Deiss, Lucien	65 Wlp	B L Sa
O Antiphons	Gilsdorf, Sr. Helen	74 Rpb	M B R L L Sa
O Christ Your Church Is Waiting Still	Gilligan, Michael	70 Acp	L L Sa
O Christ Your Church Is Waiting Still	Liturgical Press	73 Acp	L L Sa
O Come, Emmanuel (E)	Hilty, Everett J.	Na Oxf	M L Sa U2pt
O Come, O Come Emmanuel	Neale, John M.	67 Acp	L L Sa
O Come, O Come Emmanuel	Silvia, Helen	73 Acp	L L Sa
O How Shall I Receive Thee	Ehret, Walter	74 Gia	M L Sa Satb+
On Jordan's Stormy Banks	Smith	Na Lor	M L Sa Satb
Prepare Ye The Way	Johnson, Jeff	75 Rpb	M B R L L Sa
Prepare Ye The Way	Warren, William	75 Gia	M L Sa Satb+
Prepare! The Lord Is Near	Amann, M. Angelita	74 Rpb	M B R L L Sa
Proper Offertories Of The Sundays	Hegedus, A	Na Gia	L Sa
Psalm For Advent, To You, O Lord	Peloquin, C Alexander	Na Gia	L Sa
Psalm 98 (D)	Crawford, John	Na Oxf	M L Sa Ttbb
Rejoice Believers (M)	Brosseau, Jean	76 Gia	M L L Sa Satb+
Rise Up	Gilligan, Michael	67 Acp	R L L Sa
Savior Of The Nations, Come	Krapf, Gerhard	65 Aug	M L Sa Satb+
See, Your King Shall Come	Fitzpatrick, Dennis	65 Fel	B L Sa
Send Out Thy Light (Short Anthem)	Lenzo, Joseph	74 Smc	M L Sa Ttb
Shout For Joy, For He Comes	Fitzpatrick, Dennis	65 Fel	B L Sa
Someday	Hurd, Bob	75 Fel	B R L L Sa
Song Of Watchfulness	Ellis, Ron	75 Rav	B R L L Sa
The Earth Shall Be Filled	Roff, Joseph	70 Gia	M L Sa Satb+
The Holy City (From Revelations)	Montague, George T.	76 Gra	B R L L Sa 2pt+
The Last Day (We're A Pilgrim)	Temple, Sebastian	71 Gia	B R L L Sa Satb+
The Lord Is Near To All	Fitzpatrick, Dennis	65 Fel	B L Sa
The Redeemer Shall Come	Hegarty, David H	Na Lor	M L Sa Satb
There's A Voice In The Wilderness	Lovelace, Austin C.	75 Sac	M L Sa Sab
Up, O Jerusalem	Fitzpatrick, Dennis	65 Fel	B L Sa
Wait For The Lord With Courage	Fitzpatrick, Dennis	65 Fel	B L Sa
Wake Awake	Gilligan, Michael	67 Acp	L L Sa
When He Shall Come	Pearce/Johnson	Na Zon	L Sa Satb
Wonder When He's Coming	Hughes, Miki	Na Lor	M L Sa 2pt
You Are Near	Schutte, Dan, S. J.	71 Nal	B R L Sa
You, O Lord, Are Near	Fitzpatrick, Dennis	65 Fel	B L Sa
Zion Sing	Deiss, Lucien	65 Wlp	B R L Sa

Advent Anthem	Proulx, Richard	69 Aug	M T Sa Satb
Advent Carol	Brandon, George	72 Gia	M T Sa
Advent Chorale, The (C)	Mendelssohn, F.	Na Lor	M T Sa Satb
Advent Song Op 84	Schumann, Robert	Na Kal	B T Sa Satb
Almighty Word (As By R.V. Williams)	Tallis, Thomas	Na Oxf	M T Sa Satb
And The Glory Of The Lord	Handel, G. F.	Na Aug	M T Sa Satb
Audivi, Media Nocte (Md)	Tallis, Thomas	Na Oxf	M T Sa Satb
Be Glad Ye Heavens (Md)	Byrd, William	Na Oxf	M T Sa Satbb
Behold A Virgin Bearing Him	Gannon, Michael	55 Wlp.	B T Sa
Behold, I Stand At The Door	Newbury, Kent A.	Na Gsc	B T Sa Satb
Behold, Your God Will Come	Newbury, Kent A.	Na Gsc	B T Sa Satb
Cantata #140 Sleepers Awake (E & Ger)	Bach, J. S.	Na Kal	B T Sa Satb
Cantata #61 Nun Komm (E & Germ)	Bach, J. S.	Na Kal	B T Sa Satb
Come Beloved Monarch	Naggin, Elwood	Na Gsc	B T Sa Var
Come Down, O Love Divine	Dietterich, Philip	Na Abi	M T Sa Satb
Come, Jesu, Come (Motet 5)	Bach, J. S.	Na Kal	B T Sa Satb
Come, Lord Jesus	Arceneaux, Tommy	Pd Arc	T Sa
Come, Thou Almighty King	Burroughs	75 Maf	M T Sa Satb
Come, Thou Fount Of Every Blessing	Peek, Richard	Na Abi	M T Sa Satb
Come, Thou Long Expected Jesus	Lovelace, Austin C.	Na Abi	M T Sa Satb
Come, Thou Long Expected Jesus	Tyler, Don	Na Abi	M T Sa Satb
Come, Thou Long Expected Jesus (Me)	Ley, Henry G.	Na Oxf	M T Sa Satb
Come, Thou Long-Expected Jesus	Pooler, Marie	62 Aug	M T Sa Var
Come, Thou Long-Expected Jesus	Rameau (Nelson)	67 Aug	M T Sa Unis
Come, Thou Long-Expected Jesus	Sateren, Leland B.	59 Aug	M T Sa Satb
Darkness Concealed The Earth	Haydn, Joseph	Na Lor	M T Sa Satb
Drop Down, Ye Heavens From Above	Cassler, G. W.	63 Aug	M T Sa Satb
Emmanuel	Batozynski	73 Aug	M T Sa Satb
From Isaiah (In Three Parts)	Berger, Jean	65 Aug	M T Sa Satb
God So Loved The World	Goss, John	Na Gsc	B T Sa Sab
Hark, The Glad Sound	Wilson, Roger C.	76 Lor	T Sa Satb+
Haste Thee O Lord (In 19 Rounds)	Ford, T/Tortonalo	75 Gia	B L T Sa 3pt
He Sha l Come Down Like Rain	Buck, Dudley	Na Gsc	B T Sa Satb+
How Beauteous Are Their Feet	Thiman, Eric H.	Na Gsc	B T Sa Satb+
How Lovely Are The Messengers	Mendelssohn, F.	Na Gsc	M T Sa Satb+
I Am Alpha And Omega	Stainer, Sir John	Na Gsc	B T Sa Satb+
I Long For Thy Salvation	Newbury, Kent A.	Na Gsc	B T Sa Satb
I Waited For The Lord	Mendelssohn, F.	Na Gsc	B T Sa Var+
I Will Be As The Dew	Nystedt, Knut	60 Aug	M T Sa Satb
If The Christ Should Come To Me	Wilson	Na Lor	M T Sa Satb
Let Mount Zion Rejoice	Herbert	Na Lor	M T Sa Satb
Lift Up Your Heads	Ashford	Na Lor	M T Sa Var
Lift Up Your Heads	Emerson	Na Lor	M T Sa Satb
Lift Up Your Heads	Hopkins, John L	Na Gsc	B T Sa 2pt+
Lo! He Comes In Clouds Descending	Holyoke, Samuel	76 Bbl	M T Sa Atb
Lo, I Am The Voice Of One Crying	Schutz, Heinrich	Na Gsc	B T Sa 6mix
Lord Have Mercy Upon Us	Lalande, Michael R.	Na Gsc	B T Sa 3mix+

Lovely Appear(The Redemption)	Gounod, Charles	Na Gsc	B	T Sa	Full+
Nox Praecessit	Back, Sven-Erik	Na Gsc	B	T Sa	Satb
O Come Emmanuel	Na	Na Gsc	B	T Sa	Satb+
O Come, Emmanuel (Ancient Hymn)	Na	Na Lor	M	T Sa	Var
O Come, O Come Emmanuel	Christiansen, P.	50 Aug	M	T Sa	Satb
O Come, O Come Emmanuel	Demone, Richard	75 Maf	M	T Sa	Var
O Come, O Come Immanuel	Traditional/Johnson	Na Zon	M	T Sa	Satb
O Thou That Tellest	Handel, G. F.	Na Gsc	B	T Sa	Satb+
O Welcome Light (Cantata)	Bach, J. S.	75 Lps	B R	T Sa	Satb
Prepare The Way Of The Lord	Newbury, Kent A.	Na Gsc	B	T Sa	Satb+
Prepare Ye (Cantata)	Bach, J. S.	75 Lps	B R	T Sa	Satb
Prepare Ye The Way Of The Lord	Garrett, G M	Na Gsc	B	T Sa	Satb+
Prope Est Dominus	Haydn, Michael	75 Bbl	M	T Sa	Satb+
Redeemer Of The Nations	Quinn, M.	61 Wlp	B	T Sa	
Savior Of The Nations, Come	Melby	72 Aug	M	T Sa	Unis
See What Love Hath The Father	Mendelssohn, F.	Na Gsc	B	T Sa	Satb
Sing, Heaven Imperial (Md)	Byrd, William	Na Oxf	M	T Sa	Saatb
Sleepers Wake From Cantata 140	Bach, J. S.	Na Gsc	B	T Sa	Var+
Sleepers, Wake, A Voice Is Calling	Mendelssohn, F.	Na Gsc	B	T Sa	Satb+
Teach Me, O Lord (Ps 119 Me)	Byrd, William	Na Oxf	M	T Sa	Ssatb
Tenebrae Factae Sunt	Ingegneri, Marc A	Na Gsc	B	T Sa	Satb
The Great Day Of The Lord Is Near	Martin, G C	Na Gsc	B	T Sa	Satb+
There Shall Be Star Come Out Of Jacob	Mendelssohn, F.	Na Gsc	B	T Sa	Satb+
This Is Our Accepted Time	Gannon, Michael	55 Wlp	B	T Sa	
This Is The Record Of John (M)	Gibbons, Orlando	Na Oxf	M	T Sa	Saatb
Wake Awake The Night Is Dying	Farrell, Melvin	61 Wlp	B	T Sa	
We Believe That Thou Shalt Come	Handel, G. F.	Na Gsc	B	T Sa	Var+
We Wait For The Coming Of Jesus	Denton, James	76 Lor		T Sa	Satb+
Welcome Welcome Dear Redeemer	Franck, Cesar	Na Gsc	B	T Sa	Satb+
When The Son Of Man Shall Come (D)	Locke, Matthew	Na Oxf	M	T Sa	Full
You Heavens Open From Above	Farrell, Melvin	61 Wlp	B	T Sa	

Christmas Hymns and Carols

Most available Christmas music is listed here, but also see collections (ZA), hymns about Jesus Christ (TJ), and hymns about Mary the mother of Jesus (TM).

And The Word Was Made Flesh	Curzio, Elaine	70 Van	B R	C Sc	
And This Shall Be A Sign	Benedict, Em	74 Man	B R	C Sc	
Christ Is Born	Boalt	Na Lor	M B	C Sc	Sa
Christmas	Benedict, Em & Ford, Ol	74 Man	B R	C Sc	
Christmas Bells	Benedict, Em	74 Man	B R	C Sc	
Christmas Carols For Children (No 5805	Peterson, John W.	Na Zon		C Sc	
Christmas Story, The	Graham, Robert	Na Abi	M	C Sc	
Christmas/Folk Style	Hadler	Na Lor	M B	C Sc	Sa
Colored Christmas Lights	Spencer, Hal	70 Man	R	C Sc	
Happy Birthday, Merry Christmas	Benedict, Em	74 Man	B R	C Sc	
Jesse Tree Song	Miffleton, Jack	71 Wlp	B R	C Sc	
Jesus Is Born	Benedict, Em	74 Man	B R	C Sc	
Littlest Christmas Tree	Pickell	76 Pro	M	C Sc	U/2pt
Merry Merry Christmas	Spencer, Hal	70 Man	R	C Sc	
Shepherd Boy	Benedict, Em And Ford	74 Man	B R	C Sc	
Shepherds' Carol, The	Emig	Na Lor	M B	C Sc	Sa
Song Of Bethlehem, A	Emig	Na Lor	M B	C Sc	Sa
The Birthday Of The King (No 5524)	Habecker, Marilyn P.	Na Zon		C Sc	
The Little King Of The World	Pooler, Marie	61 Aug	M	C Sc	Unis
The Miracle	Benedict, Em	74 Man	B R	C Sc	
There Never Was A Christmas Day	Benedict, Em	74 Man	B R	C Sc	
Two Anthems For Children's Voices	Caperton, Florence	Na Abi	M	C Sc	Sa
Violet In The Snow	Landry, Carey (Rev.)	75 Nal	B R	C Sc	
Visit, The	Wise, Joe	74 Nal	B R	C Sc	
Walk In Sunlight (Cantata)	Wright, Alberta C.	73 Wrd	B R	C Sc	Unis+
You Ask Me Why	Benedict, Em	74 Man	B R	C Sc	

All Things New	Meyer, Ron	73 Fel	B	F Sc	
Behold The Lord (From Come Follow)	Murphy, Charles	69 Gia	B R L	F Sc	
Break Open (A Choir In The Dawn)	Belt, Thomas/Batastini	72 Gia	B R L	F Sc	Var+
Child Of Morning	Winter, Miriam T.	72 Van	B R	F Sc	
Christmas Ballad	Winter, Miriam T.	72 Van	B R	F Sc	
Down In Yon Forest	Na	Na Gsc	B	F Sc	Satb
Gatatumba (Andalusian Carol)	Na	Na Gsc	B	F Sc	Var+
Gentle Mary	Harris (Arr)	75 Pro	M	F Sc	Satb+
Glory Be To Israel	Scholtes, Peter	66 Fel	B R	F Sc	
Great Day In Bethlehem	Hershberg, Sarah	70 Fcc	R L	F Sc	
Great Day In Bethlehem (Cantata)	Temple, S./Hershberg, S	73 Gia	B R L	F Sc	U+
Happy Xmas	Ono/Lennon	Na Mcl		F Sc	
In Holy Splendor (Ccd)	Miffleton, Jack	68 Wlp	B R	F Sc	
In The Beginning	Winter, Miriam T.	72 Van	B R	F Sc	
In The Month Of December	Repp, Ray	69 Fel	B R	F Sc	
It's The Lord's Thing.	Smith, Lani	Na Lor	M B	F Sc	
Jesus The Christ Is Born	Niles (Warrell)	35 Gsc	M	F Sc	Satb
Jesus, Jesus Rest Your Head	Niles (Warrell)	38 Gsc	M	F Sc	Satb
Joy To The World	Silvia, Helen	73 Acp	L	F Sc	
Joy To The World	Watts, Isaac	67 Acp	L	F Sc	
Light	Fischer, John	70 Fel	B R	F Sc	
Love Divine (God Incarnate)	Belt, Thomas	70 Gia	B R L	F Sc	Var+
Mary Had A Baby Boy (E)	Pickell, Ed	73 Pro	M	F Sc	Satb+
Mary's Boy Child	Hairston/Lojeski(Arr)	76 Hal		F Sc	Satb
Mary's Little Boy Child	Hairston, Jester	56 Sch	M R	F Sc	Var
My Cactus Christmas Tree	Harper/Barnett	Na Zon	M	F Sc	
No Longer Alone	Winter, Miriam T.	72 Van	B R	F Sc	
No Vacancy	Fischer, John	69 Fel	B R	F Sc	
Now He Is Born	Mccarthy, John	70 Van	B R	F Sc	
O Come, All Ye Faithful	Oakeley, Frederick	67 Acp	L	F Sc	
O Come, All Ye Faithful (4 Part Arr)	Wade, John F.	73 Acp	L	F Sc	
O Listen, Brother	Davis F. Clark	76 Abi	M	F Sc	2pt++
O What A Happening	Winter, Miriam T.	72 Van	B R	F Sc	
One Small Child	Smith, Lani	Na Lor	M B	F Sc	Satb
Open Up Your Heart(W/Guitar)	Belt, Thomas	71 Gia	B R L	F Sc	Var+
Peace Upon Earth	Winter, Miriam T.	72 Van	B R	F Sc	
Prince Of Peace (Born In Bethlehem)	Farra, Mimi A.	73 Gia	M B R L	F Sc	Var+
See Jesus The Savior	Niles	38 Gsc	M	F Sc	Satb
Silent The Night	Winter, Miriam T.	72 Van	B R	F Sc	
Simple Christmas Song	Ellis, Ron	74 Rav	B L	F Sc	
Sing Of Birth	Winter, Miriam T.	72 Van	B R	F Sc	
Sleep Celestial Infant (Mex–Am Carol)	Workentin	76 Pro	M	F Sc	Satb
Song Of Glory	Winter, Miriam T.	72 Van	B R	F Sc	
Song Of The Stable Boy	Ylvisaker, J & A.	69 Van	B R	F Sc	
Streams In The Desert	Belt, Thomas	70 Gia	B R L	F Sc	Var+
Take Courage	Winter, Miriam T.	72 Van	B R	F Sc	
The Birth	Ylvisaker, J & A.	69 Van	B R	F Sc	
The Cherry–Tree Carol	Na	Na Gsc	B	F Sc	Full
The Little Drummer Boy	Simeone/Davis/Onorati	Na Bel		F Sc	
The Lord Is Come (W/Guitar)	Belt, Thomas	70 Gia	B R L	F Sc	Var+
The Lord Said To Me (Ccd)	Wise, Joe	68 Wlp	B R	F Sc	
The Three Kings Of Orient (Opt Perc)	Forcucci, Samuel (Arr)	73 Pro	M	F Sc	Sab
The Visitor.	Smith, Lani	Na Lor	M B	F Sc	
This Little Babe (W/Guitar)	Wetzler, Robert	70 Aug	M	F Sc	Satb
Tis Christmas This Night	Mccarthy, John	70 Van	B R	F Sc	
Wasn't That A Mighty Day!	Thygerson, Robert W	75 Her	M	F Sc	Satb
Yours Is Princely Power (Ccd)	Wise, Joe	68 Wlp	B R	F Sc	

A Christmas Folk Song	Byles, B D	Na Gsc	B	G Sc	Satb
A Song Was Born Cantata (No 4455)	Parks, Joe	75 Zon	R	G Sc	Satb
And Holy Is His Name	Harmon, P.	76 Sil		G Sc	
Bethlehem Isn't Very Far	Lee, Johnnie	73 Mmc	M	G Sc	
Birth Of The King	Hubbard, H.	Na Sav	M	G Sc	
Christmas Cantata In Spanish	Peterson, John W.	Na Zon		G Sc	Spa
Christmas Morn (Spiritual)	Pickell	76 Pro	M	G Sc	Var+
Down From His Glory	Clibborn	Na Zon	M	G Sc	
Go Tell It On The Mountain	Stevens (Arr)	57 Pro	M L	G Sc	Satb
Go Tell It On The Mountain	Traditional/Decou	Na Zon	M	G Sc	Satb
Go, Tell It On The Mountain	Broughton	Na Lor	M	G Sc	Satb
God's Great Love Came Down At Xmas	Lee, Johnnie	74 Mmc	M	G Sc	
Gospel Song Of Christmas, The	Lorenz	Na Lor	M B	G Sc	Satb
Happy Birthday, Gentle Saviour	Rogers	Na Zon	M	G Sc	
Hey, Manger Child	Smith	Na Lor	M	G Sc	Sab
I'll Keep Christmas In My Heart Always	Brock	Na Zon	M	G Sc	
In The Stillness Of The Night	Lee, Danny	72 Man	B	G Sc	
It's Christmas	Llord, J./Dejesus, G.	67 Csm	M B R L	G Sc	
Jesus Is Born Today	Akers, Doris	55 Man		G Sc	
Love Came Down At Christmas	Rossetti Young	75 Wrd	M	G Sc	Satb
Love Came Down(Musical)	Salsbury, Sonny	75 Wrd	B R	G Sc	Satb
Mary Had A Baby	Na	Na Gsc	B	G Sc	Ttbb
Roun' De Glory Manger	Na	Na Gsc	B	G Sc	6mi
Something To Remember At Xmas	Butler, Dorothy	74 Pmp	M B L	G Sc	
Sweet Little Jesus Baby	Ehret, Walter	75 Maf	M	G Sc	Satb
The Star	Stevens, Sammy	Na Sav	M	G Sc	
What Did You Say Was The Baby's Name?	Gaither/Gaither	71 Gmc	M B R	G Sc	Satb

A Carol For Christmas Morn (5 Carols)	La Berge, Nellie J.	74 Gia	B L	L Sc	Satb
A Child Is Born	Deiss, Lucien	65 Wlp	B R	L Sc	
A Child Is Born To Us	Fitzpatrick, Dennis	65 Fel	B	L Sc	
A Christmas Cantata	Dean, T. W.	63 Gam	B	L Sc	Full
A Christmas Carol	Bacon, Ernst	56 Pic	M	L Sc	
A Christmas Carol (In 5 Carols) E	La Berge, Nellie J.	74 Gia	B L	L Sc	Satb
A Christmas Fantasy	Wade, Walter	Na Abi	M	L Sc	Ttbb
A Song Unending (No 5953)	Peterson, John W.	Na Zon		L Sc	
A Song Unending (No 5961)	Peterson, John W.	Na Zon		L Sc	
A Song Unending (No 5979)	Peterson, John W.	Na Zon		L Sc	
A Star In The Sky	Johnson, D.	76 Aug		L Sc	Solo
A Thousand Stars (Opt Perc)	Cavalieri, Angelo	73 Pro	M	L Sc	2pt
A Time For Joy! (W/Piano)	Besig, Don	73 Pro	M	L Sc	Satb
A Winter Carol	Mcafee, Don	66 Pic	M	L Sc	
Ah, Dearest Jesus(A Cap)	Harris	75 Pro	M	L Sc	Satb
All From Saba Shall Come	Schroth, G	69 Gia	M	L Sc	Var+
All Kings Shall Pay Him Homage	Fitzpatrick, Dennis	65 Fel	B	L Sc	
All Men Seek God	Track, Gerhard	72 Gia	B	L Sc	Var+
All The Ends Of The Earth	Fitzpatrick, Dennis	65 Fel	B	L Sc	
All The Nations Shall Come	Fitzpatrick, Dennis	65 Fel	B	L Sc	
Alleluia	Eilers, Joyce	76 Hal		L Sc	3–P
An Angel Speaks To The Shepherds	Rorem, Ned	56 Som	M	L Sc	
And One Bright Star	Martin	75 Her	M	L Sc	Satb
And There Were Shepherds	Wilson, I	Na Lor	M	L Sc	Satb
Angels We Have Heard On High	Gilligan, Michael	67 Acp	L	L Sc	
Angels We Have Heard On High	Silvia, Helen	73 Acp	L	L Sc	
Anointed Of God	Powell	76 Abi	B	L Sc	Satb
Arise, Shine!	Martin	Na Lor	M B	L Sc	Satb
As I Sat Under A Holly Tree	Holst, Imogen	Na Gsc	B	L Sc	3pt
Babe In A Manger	Brandt Dorothea	76 Abi	M	L Sc	U2p
Balulalow	Aston, Peter	Na Gsc	B	L Sc	Satb
Behold The Star!	Peery	Na Lor	M B	L Sc	Satb
Behold, A Simple Tender Babe	Lee, John	71 Gia	M	L Sc	Var
Behold, The Lord, The Ruler	Fitzpatrick, Dennis	65 Fel	B	L Sc	
Bells Ring Out Joyfully	Auerbach	75 Her	M	L Sc	Ssa
Bethlehem Star, The	Kenney	Na Lor	M B	L Sc	Satb
Bethlehem Town	Lipscomb, Helen	Na Gsc	B	L Sc	2eq
Born A King	Goode	76 Abi	B	L Sc	Satb
Born A King (Cantata)	Peterson, John W.	Na Zon		L Sc	Var
Born In A Manger	Hughes, Robert J.	Na Lor	M	L Sc	Satb
Born In A Stable	Thygerson, Robert W	75 Sac	M	L Sc	Satb
Born Today	Sweelinck	Na Lor	M	L Sc	2me
Break Forth Into Joy	Simper	Na Lor	M	L Sc	Satb
Burst Of Christ	Schneider, Kent E.	75 Ccc	B	L Sc	
By The Manger	Rodgers, David	37 Tcp	M	L Sc	
Call His Name Jesus	Moffatt	Na Lor	M B	L Sc	Satb
Canticles Of Christmas (Cantata)	Dean, T. W.	61 Gam	B	L Sc	Treb
Carol For Children, A	Pfautsch, Lloyd	75 Her	M	L Sc	Satb
Carol For The Christ–Child, A	Rasley	Na Lor	M	L Sc	Satb

Carol Of Christmas (No 5969)	Peterson, John W.	Na Zon		L Sc Var
Carol Of Christmas (No 5999)	Peterson, John W.	Na Zon		L Sc Var
Carol Of Christmas (No 6011)	Peterson, John W.	Na Zon		L Sc Var
Carol Of The Bells	Rogers	Na Lor	M B	L Sc Satb
Carol Of The Gifts (In 5 Carols) E	Laberge, Nellie J.	74 Gia	B	L L Sc Sab+
Carol Of The Questioning Ch ld	Kountz, Richard	Na Gsc	B	L Sc Var+
Carol Of The Roses	Kountz, Richard	Na Gsc	B	L Sc Satb+
Carol Of The Tree	Hovdesven	Na Lor	M	L Sc Satb
Carol Of The Trees	Wetherill	75 Sac	M	L Sc Satb
Carol Ye	Wilson	Na Lor	M	L Sc Satb
Carols For Christmastide	Brown, J/Descroquettes	Gia		L Sc
Carols Of Christmas	Lorenz	Na Lor	M B	L Sc Satb
Celestial Visitor The	Cain	Na Lor	M B	L Sc Satb
Cherry Tree Carol (Drama)	Berger, Jean	75 Aug	M	L Sc Satb+
Child Of Bethlehem, The	Candlyn, T. Fred	Na Abi	M	L Sc
Child Of Bethlehem, The	Walter	Na Lor	M B	L Sc Satb
Child Of Heaven	Wilson	Na Lor	M B	L Sc Satb
Child Of Hope, A	Smith	Na Lor	M	L Sc Satb+
Child This Day Is Born, A	Hughes, Robert J.	Na Lor	M	L Sc Satb
Child Was Born, A	Gilligan, Michael	67 Acp		L L Sc
Child Was Born, A	Silvia, Helen	73 Acp		L L Sc
Chimes Of The Holy Night	Holton	Na Lor	M B	L Sc Satb
Choir Of Bethlehem, The	Benson	Na Lor	M B	L Sc Satb
Chorus In The Skies, The	Holton	Na Lor	M B	L Sc Satb
Christ Child Is Born (Opt Orch Bells)	Pickell	76 Pro	M	L Sc 2pt+
Christ Is Born	Newbury, Kent A.	75 Her	M	L Sc Satb
Christ Is Born	Richolson	Na Lor	M	L Sc
Christ Is Born (No 4451)	Peterson, John W.	75 Zon	R	L Sc Var
Christ Is Born!	Wilson	Na Lor	M	L Sc
Christ The Lord Is Born	Smith	Na Lor	M	L Sc
Christ The Lord Is Born	Walter	Na Lor	M	L Sc
Christmas Acclamation	Davis, Paulette	74 Rpb	M B R L	L Sc
Christmas At The Cloisters	Corigliano, John	Na Gsc	B	L Sc Satb
Christmas Ballad	Patenaude, Andre, M.	71 Nal	B R	L Sc
Christmas Bells	Sevitzky, Fabien	66 Tcp	M	L Sc
Christmas Candlelight Procession	Orland, Henry	Na See	M	L Sc
Christmas Carol	Kay, Ulysses	57 Pic	M	L Sc
Christmas Carol	Smit, Leo	50 Pic	M	L Sc
Christmas Chimes	Malloch, David J.	Na Abi	M	L Sc Satb
Christmas Concertato	Bender, Jan	68 Aug	M	L Sc Full+
Christmas Day In The Morning	Foster	Na Lor	M	L Sc
Christmas Ensemble Ssa And Ttbb 5764	Collected	Na Zon		L Sc
Christmas Exultation, A	Ferguson	75 Sac	M	L Sc Satb
Christmas Fanfare	Burnham	75 Her	M	L Sc Satb
Christmas Gloria, A	Johnston	Na Lor	M	L Sc
Christmas In The Western World	Still, William Grant	67 Som	M	L Sc
Christmas Invitation, The	Lorenz	Na Lor	M	L Sc
Christmas Is A Beautiful Word	Rawls, Kathryn	Na Abi	M	L Sc Uorsa
Christmas Joy	Couper, Alinda B.	Na Abi	M	L Sc Sa
Christmas Legend, A	Orland, Henry	Na See	M	L Sc
Christmas Lullaby	Lapo, Cecil E.	Na Abi	M	L Sc Satb
Christmas Lullaby From China, A	Graham	75 Sac	M	L Sc 2mel
Christmas Meditation	Sullivan/Denton	Na Lor	M	L Sc
Christmas Prayer	Mead, Edward G.	65 Som	M	L Sc
Christmas Processional	Proulx, Richard	72 Gia	M	L Sc 2pt
Christmas Season	Lohr, Al	55 Pic	M	L Sc
Christmas Song Of Songs The	Wilson, I	Na Lor	M B	L Sc Satb
Christmas Story	Decou, Harold	75 Zon	M	L Sc Satb
Come And Gather, Little Children	Wihtol, A. A.	Na Zon	M	L Sc Ssa
Come To Bethlehem	Emig	Na Lor	M B	L Sc Satb
Concertato On "Adeste Fideles"	Lovelace, Austin C.	76 Aug		L Sc Satb+
Concierto De Navidad	Csonka, Paul	58 Pic	M	L Sc
Could This Be A Special Night?	Martin	75 Her	M	L Sc Satb
Coverdale's Carol	Pfautsch, Lloyd	Na Abi	M	L Sc Tbb
Cradled All Lowly	Cassler, G. W.	Na Abi	M	L Sc Sa
Dawn Of Christmas, The	Nolte	Na Lor	M B	L Sc Satb
Dear Jesus Boy	Wehr, David A.	Na Abi	M	L Sc U
Dear Little Jesus (Unison) (C)	Farner	Na Lor	M	L Sc Satb
Each Winter As The Year Grows Older	Gay, Wm. & A.	69 Ucp	M B	L L Sc
Echo Of Christmas The	Lorenz	Na Lor	M B	L Sc Satb
Epiphany Adoration (Solo)	Seagard	75 Aug	M	L Sc
Epiphany Prayer, An	Martin	75 Sac	M	L Sc Satb
Everlasting Joy	Bach–Lorenz	Na Lor	M B	L Sc Satb
Festival Of Christmas	Wilson	Na Lor	M B	L Sc Satb
Festival Of Lessons And Carols	Wilson	Na Lor	M B	L Sc Satb
Fill The World With Light (Epiphany)	Brandon, George	76 Pro	M	L Sc Var+
First Noel, The	Silvia, Helen	73 Acp		L L Sc
For The Christ Child	Champagne, Claude	66 Pic	M	L Sc
Four Canticles For Christmas	Moore	75 Sac	M	L Sc Satb
Four Carols	Stevens, Halsey	54 Pic	M	L Sc
From East To West	Lovelace, Austin C.	75 Sac	M	L Sc Sab
From Heaven Above	Krapf, Gerhard	Na Abi	M	L Sc
From The Rising Of The Sun	Powell, Robert J.	Na Abi	M	L Sc Satb
Gloria In Excelsis	Mendelssohn, F.	Na Lor	M B	L Sc Satb
Gloria In Excelsis Deo	Beverst	75 Sac	M	L Sc Satb
Glorious Message, The	Krieger, Jacob	Na Lor	M B	L Sc Satb
Glory Of The Star The	Landon	Na Lor	M B	L Sc Satb
Glory To God	Gounod, Charles	Na Lor	M B	L Sc Satb
Glory To God	Rogers	Na Lor	M	L Sc Var
Glory To Thee (Me) 1	Gilbert, Norman	Na Oxf	M	L Sc Satb
God In A Star	Denton	Na Lor	M B	L Sc Satb
God With Us (Opt Brs)	Pfautsch, Lloyd	Na Abi	M	L Sc
God/Man (Satb) (No 4520) Cantata	Wyrtzen, Don	Na Zon		L Sc
God's Love Gift (No 4369) Cantata	Decou, Harold	Na Zon		L Sc Satb+
Golden Slumbers Carol	Fiske, Milton	60 Som	M	L Sc
Good Folk On Earth Below	Reeve	Hof	M	L Sc Sab
Good Tidings	Wetzler, Robert	74 Aug	M	L Sc Solo
Good Tidings Of Joy	Walter	Na Lor	M B	L Sc Satb
Hark! The Glad Sound	Korgstad, Bob	75 Zon	M	L Sc Ssatbb
He's For Real	Cooper, Ken	73 Pro	M	L Sc Satb
Hear The Bells! See The Star!	Ehret, Walter	75 Maf	M	L Sc 2pt
Hear The Glad Tidings	Kirk, Theron	Na Her	M	L Sc Satb
Hodie	Goossen, Frederic	72 Pic	M	L Sc
Holiday And Holy Day	Ehret, Walter	75 Her	M	L Sc Sa
Holy Infant Of Bethlehem	Mcafee, Don	75 Sac	M	L Sc Satb
Holy Night!	Schroth	75 Sac	M	L Sc Full
How Dark Was The Stable?	Mayhew, Kevin & Singers	75 Ahc	M B R	L Sc
How Far Is It To Bethlehem?	Nelson, Ronald A.	65 Aug	M	L Sc
How Many Miles Must We Go?	Thygerson, Robert W.	Na Her	M	L Sc Satb+
Hush, My Babe	Thygerson	75 Sac	M	L Sc Satb
Hymn Of Nativity	Serly, Tibor	49 Som	M	L Sc
I Am So Glad Each Christmas Eve	Wood	69 Aug	M	L Sc Sab
I Will Give My Baby	Mayhew, Kevin & Singers	75 Ahc	M B R	L Sc
I Wonder As I Wander	Van	76 Aug		L Sc U+Guit
Infant Christus W/Solo	Cassler, G. W.	76 Aug		L Sc (S)Satb
Infant Jesus	Cassler, G. W.	Na Abi	M	L Sc Ttbb
Innkeeper, The	Lewis	75 Sac	M	L Sc Var
It's A Glorious Alleluia!	Hughes, Robert J.	Na Lor	M B	L Sc Satb
Jesu, My Little One (In 5 Carols) E	Laberge, Nellie J.	74 Gia	B	L L Sc Satb+
Jesus Is Born The King!	Denton	Na Lor	M B	L Sc Satb
Jesus, Of A Maid Thou Wouldst Be Born	Brown, Charles	Na Abi	M	L Sc Satb
Joseph Dearest, Joseph Mine	Lapo, Cecil E.	Na Abi	M	L Sc Usatb
Joy To All People!	Denton	Na Lor	M B	L Sc Satb
Joy To The World (No 5944)	Peterson, John W.	Na Zon		L Sc Var
Joy To The World (No 5945)	Peterson, John W.	Na Zon		L Sc Var
Joy To The World (No 6012)	Peterson, John W.	Na Zon		L Sc Var
Joyous Christmas Carol	Brahms, J./Goldman	76 Pro	M	L Sc Satb+
Joyous Christmas Song	Christiansen, P.	51 Aug	M	L Sc Var
Keep Christ In Christmas	Jones/Decou	Na Zon	M	L Sc Satb
King All–Glorious	Nolte	Na Lor	M B	L Sc Satb
King Forever	Denton	Na Lor	M B	L Sc Satb
King In The Stable, The	Johnston	Na Lor	M B	L Sc Satb
King Indeed, A (Easy)	Parks, Joe E.	Na Zon	M	L Sc Sa(Tb)
King Of Glory, The	Glarum, L Stanley	Na Abi	M	L Sc Satb
King Of Kings (No 4294)	Peterson, John W.	Na Zon		L Sc Var
Knight Of Bethlehem, The	Burroughs	75 Maf	M	L Sc Satb
Let All On Earth	Dosogne, R	70 Gia	M	L Sc Satb
Let The Heavens Be Glad	Roff, Joseph	Na Gia		L Sc
Like Dew Before The Daystar	Fitzpatrick, Dennis	65 Fel	B	L Sc
Little Child Sleeping Boy (E)	Heckel, M.P. & Carroll, J	75 Gia	M	L L Sc Satb+
Long Ago In Bethlehem	Thygerson	75 Her	M	L Sc Satb
Long Time Ago	Sleeth	75 Sac	M	L Sc 2pt
Long Years Ago	Ford, Virgil	Na Gsc	B	L Sc Satb
Love Came Down At Christmas	Jennings, K.	75 Aug	M	L Sc Ssaa
Love Came Down At Christmas	Wetzler, Robert	73 Aug	M	L Sc Satb
Love Came Down At Christmas (W/Inst)	Mitchell	74 Aug	M	L Sc Satb+
Love Gift, The	Martin	Na Lor	M	L Sc Unis
Love Transcending (No 5954)	Peterson, John W.	Na Zon		L Sc Var
Love Transcending (No 5974)	Peterson, John W.	Na Zon		L Sc Var
Love Transcending (No 5975)	Peterson, John W.	Na Zon		L Sc Var
Lovely Child, Holy Child	Johnson, D.	66 Aug	M	L Sc Var
Lullaby At Christmas	Lapo, Cecil E.	Na Abi	M	L Sc Satb
Lullaby On Christmas Eve	Christiansen, P.	33 Aug	M	L Sc Var
Manger And Star	Brandt Dorothea	76 Abi	M	L Sc Satb+
Manger King, The	Johnston	Na Lor	M B	L Sc Satb
March Of The Three Kings	Ramsfield (Arr)	76 Pro	M	L Sc Sab
Mary, Mary	Pfautsch, Lloyd	Na Abi	M	L Sc Satb
Mary's Gift (A Christmas Carol)	Bales, Richard	52 Pic	M	L Sc
Mary's Lullaby	Lee, John	71 Gia	M	L Sc Var
Mary's Lullaby	Young, Carolyn K.	67 Man	M B	L Sc
Memories Of The Manger	Nolte	Na Lor	M B	L Sc Satb
Men Of Old	Ford, Virgil	Na Gsc	B	L Sc Satb
Mexican Christmas Procession	Christiansen, P.	75 Aug	M	L Sc Satb
Midnight, Sleeping Bethlehem	Staton	74 Aug	M	L Sc 2pt
Midst The Deep Silence (Handbells)	Hunnicutt, J.	72 Aug	M	L Sc Usatb
Miracle Of Bethlehem, The	Rasley	Na Lor	M B	L Sc Satb
Miracle Of Love, The	Moffatt	Na Lor	M B	L Sc Stab
Music Filled The Sky (E)	Englert, Eugene	76 Gia	M	L L Sc Satb+
Music Of Bethlehem, The	Holton	Na Lor	M B	L Sc Stab
Music Of Christmas, The	Wilson, I	Na Lor	M B	L Sc Stab
My Christmas Prayer	Carleton	Na Lor	M	L Sc Satb
My Heart Is A Manger	Hovdesven, E A	Na Gsc	B	L Sc Satb+
My Little Lamb	Lewis, John Leo	Na Abi	M	L Sc Satb
Nativity, The	Wilson	Na Lor	M B	L Sc Stab
Newborn Baby	Van Horn	Na Lor	M	L Sc Unis
Night Of Holy Memories	Wilson, I	Na Lor	M B	L Sc Stab
Night Of Miracles (No 5976)	Peterson, John W.	Na Zon	R	L Sc Var
Night Of Miracles Spanish Edition	Peterson, John W.	Na Zon		L Sc Var
Night Of Miracles–Dramatization (5921)	Peterson, John W.	Na Zon		L Sc Var
Night Of The Star	Carleton	Na Lor	M B	L Sc Satb
Night So Dark And Hour So Late	Wihtol, A. A.	Na Zon	M	L Sc Ssa
Nightingale Carol	Hovdesven, E A	Na Gsc	B	L Sc Satb+
No Cradle Song	Hughes, Robert J.	Na Lor	M	L Sc Var
No Room In The Inn	Thygerson	Na Lor	M	L Sc Satb
Noel	Gilligan, Michael	67 Acp		L L Sc
Noel	Landon, Stewart	Na Lor	B	L Sc Satb
Noel	Silvia, Helen	73 Acp		L L Sc
Noel, A	Fletcher	75 Her	M	L Sc Satb
Now It Is Christmas Time	Pooler, Marie	55 Aug	M	L Sc Var
Now Proclaim His Birth In Song	Preuss, Arthur	75 Sac	M	L Sc Satb
Now Sing We All Noel	Young, Gordon	75 Sac	M	L Sc Satb
O Christ, Why Should A Manger Be?	Denton	Na Lor	M	L Sc Satb
O Come Let Us Adore Him (Chil Choir)	Pooler, Marie	60 Aug	M	L Sc
O Glorious Night	Andrews, Carroll T.	70 Gia	M T	L Sc Satb+
O God, Who By The Leading Of A Star	Attwood, Thomas	Na Oxf	M	L Sc Satb
O Holy Child	Grauert	71 Aug	M	L Sc Sa
O I Would Sing Of Mary's Child	Lovelace, Austin C.	59 Aug	M	L Sc Unis
O Man, Rejoice	Burns, William K.	Na Abi	M	L Sc Satb
O Newborn Child	Powell, Robert J.	Na Abi	M	L Sc Satb
O Shepherds	Beuerle	68 Aug	M	L Sc Ssa

CATEGORIZED INDEX

O Sleep, My Fairest One	Wilson	Na Lor	M	L Sc Satb
O Star Of Bethlehem	Kathe Willis/Eielrs	75 Hal		L Sc Satb
O Wonder Of This Christman Night	Lekberg, Sven	Na Gsc	B	L Sc Satb
Olive Tree Lullaby	Hovdesven, E A	Na Gsc	B	L Sc Satb
On A Day When Men Were Counted	Lovelace, Austin C.	75 Sac	M	L Sc Satb
On Christmas Night	Merritt, Charles	Na Abi	M	L Sc Satb
Once In Royal David's City	Proulx, Richard	76 Aug		L Sc Satb+
Out Of Your Sleep Arise And Wake	Holst, Imogen	Na Gsc	B	L Sc Ssattb
Peace Of Lord	Slates, Philip M.	Na Abi	M	L Sc Satb
Prayer On Christmas Eve	Peeters, Flor	56 Aug	M	L Sc Satb
Prepare Him Room	Hadler	Na Lor	M B	L Sc Satb
Prince Of Peace (Cantata)	Innes, John	Na Zon		L Sc Satb
Prince Of Peace, The	Holton	Na Lor	M	L Sc
Prince Of Peace, The	Hughes, Robert J.	Na Lor	M B	L Sc Satb
Promised One, The	Smith	Na Lor	M	L Sc
Promised One, The	Sydow	Na Lor	M B	L Sc Satb
Psalm 98	Stevens, Halsey	68 Pic	M	L Sc
Puer Nobis	Pfautsch, Lloyd	Na Abi	M	L Sc Satb
Quietly He Came	Davis, Paulette	74 Rpb	M B R L	L Sc
Rejoice Today With One Accord	Brandon, George	76 Aug		L Sc U/2pt
Rejoice! Rejoice!	Zimmerman, James	75 Maf	M	L Sc Satb
Ring, Christmas Bells	Jordan	75 Sac	M	L Sc Unis
Ring, Ye Bells	Williams	75 Sac	M	L Sc Unis
Rose Of Christmas, The	Thompson	Na Lor	M B	L Sc Satb
Shepherd's Alleluia	Landry, Carey (Rev.)	68 Nal	B R	L Sc
Shepherds Come A-Running	Wetzler, Robert	74 Aug	M	L Sc Var
Shepherds Went Their Hasty Way, The	Williams, David	Na Abi	M	L Sc Satb
Sing And Rejoice	Thygerson	75 Sac	M	L Sc Satb
Sing Joy, Sing Love	Hunnicutt, J.	75 Gia	M	L Sc Unis+
Sing Softly	Hoag, Charles K	Na Gsc	B	L Sc 2pt+
Sing We Noel	Young	75 Her	M	L Sc Satb
Sing, O Sing	Hegenbart, Alex F	Na Gsc	B	L Sc 8mix
Singers, Sing	Price, William	70 Acp		L L Sc
Sleep Of The Child Jesus	Howell, Richard D.	Na Abi	M	L Sc Satb
Slumber, O Holy Jesu (Christmas)	Wood, Dale	Na Abi	M	L Sc Solo
So Dark The Night	Emery, Dorothy R.	Na Abi	M	L Sc Full
So Great A Gift (No 5985) Cantata	Thomas, Daniel B.	Na Zon		L Sc Satb
Something New For Christmas (No 5594)	Peterson, John W.	Na Zon		L Sc
Son, Why Have You Treated Us So	Fitzpatrick, Dennis	65 Fel	B	L Sc
Song Of The Angels, The	Thompson	Na Lor	M B	L Sc Satb
Song Of The Crib	Christiansen, P.	52 Aug	M	L Sc Satb
Song Of The Holy Night	Wilson	Na Lor	M B	L Sc Satb
Song Of The Shepherd Boy	Hughes/Thygerson	75 Sac	M	L Sc Satb
Song Of The Shepherds, The	Marshall, Paul A.	Na Zon	M	L Sc Satb
Songs Of Praise The Angels Sang	Fiske, Milton	60 Som	M	L Sc
Star In The Sky, A	Carleton	Na Lor	M B	L Sc Satb
Star Of The Silent Night	Nolte	Na Lor	M B	L Sc Satb
Still, Still, Still	Eilers (Adapted)	75 Hal		L Sc Ssa
Story Of Love, The	Hughes, Robert J.	Na Lor	M B	L Sc Satb
Sweet Was The Song The Virgin Sang	Johnson, D.	69 Aug	M	L Sc Solo
Take The Child And His Mother	Fitzpatrick, Dennis	65 Fel	B	L Sc
Tell The Blessed Tidings	Vick, B.	76 Aug		L Sc 2-Pt+
That One Bright Star	Hughes, Robert J.	76 Lor		L Sc Satb+
The Bagpiper's Carol (Arr)	Track, Gerhard	70 Gia	M	L Sc Var+
The Blessing-Song Cycle	Bucky, Frida Sarsen	51 Som	M	L Sc
The Christ-Child Lay On May's Lap	Lee, John	68 Gia	M	L Sc Var
The Christmas Choir No 1 (No 5949)	Peterson, John W.	Na Zon	B	L Sc
The Christmas Choir No 2 (No 5890)	Rasley, John M.	Na Zon	B	L Sc
The Darkest Night (E) W/Keyboard	Heckel, M.P.&Carroll, J	75 Gia	M	L L Sc Satb+
The Embodied Word (Nar, Flute, Perc)	Pelz, W.	73 Aug	M	L Sc Full
The Glory Of The Lord (Md) W/Brs	Warren, William	75 Gia	M	L L Sc Satb+
The Heavens Rejoiced	Andrews, Carroll T.	68 Gia	M	L Sc Var
The Incarnation (No 5952) Cantata	Larowe, Jane	Na Zon		L Sc Satb
The Joyous News Of Christmas (No 5055)	Parks, Joe	Na Zon		L Sc Satb
The Light Has Come (Service)	Narum & Jennings	75 Aug	M	L Sc Treb+
The Little Saviour	Ager, Laurence	Na Gsc	B	L Sc Satb+
The Lord Has Made Known	Fitzpatrick, Dennis	65 Fel	B	L Sc
The Lord Has Sworn	Fitzpatrick, Dennis	65 Fel	B	L Sc
The Lord Said To Me (Icet)	Ferris, William	76 Gia	M	L L Sc Satb+
The Night The Angels Sang (No 5986)	Peterson, John W.	Na Zon		L Sc
The Shepherd's Vigil (W/C Inst)	Beuerle	69 Aug	M	L Sc Unis
The Shepherds' Adoration	Seagard	75 Aug	M	L Sc Satb
The Sounding Skies W/Organ Or Piano	Brandon, George	Na Gsc	B	L Sc 2mix+
The Story Of Christmas (No 5881)	Peterson, John W.	Na Zon		L Sc
The Story Of Christmas (No 5882)	Peterson, John W.	Na Zon		L Sc Var+
The Story Of Christmas (No 5943)	Peterson, John W.	Na Zon		L Sc
The Three Gifts (W/Keyboard)	Heckel, M.P.&Carroll, J	75 Gia	M	L L Sc Satb+
The Voices Of Christmas	Graham, Robert	65 Som	M	L Sc
The Wonder Of Christmas (No 5967)	Peterson, John W.	Na Zon		L Sc
The Wonder Of Christmas (No 5970)	Peterson, John W.	Na Zon		L Sc
The Wonder Of Christmas (No 5973)	Peterson, John W.	Na Zon		L Sc
The Word Of God (Opt Insts)	Berger, Jean	69 Aug	M	L Sc Satb+
The Word Was Made Flesh	Fitzpatrick, Dennis	65 Fel	B	L Sc
There Came A Star (W/Solos, Trios)	Fox, Luacine Clark	Na Lor	B R	L Sc Satb+
There Is Rachel Weeping	Fitzpatrick, Dennis	65 Fel	B	L Sc
There Might Have Been A Stranger	Lewis, John Leo	Na Abi	M	L Sc Satb
There'll Always Be A Christmas (4291)	Rasley, John M.	Na Zon		L Sc Satb
They Came From Sheba	Fitzpatrick, Dennis	65 Fel	B	L Sc
They Took Him Up To Jerusalem	Fitzpatrick, Dennis	65 Fel	B	L Sc
This Day A Rose Of Judah	Gilligan, Michael	67 Acp		L L Sc
This Day A Rose Of Judah	Silvia, Helen	73 Acp		L L Sc
This Day Our Lord Is Born (Piano/Cinst)	Ehret, Walter	73 Aug	M	L Sc Sa+
This Is The Lord	Binckes	75 Sac	M	L Sc Satb
This Night	Christiansen, F. M.	34 Aug	M	L Sc Satb+
This Night Did God Become A Child	Leaf, Robert	73 Aug	M	L Sc Satb+
Three Carols For Christmas Nad New Yr	Davies, Westbrook, Frost	Na Abi	M	L Sc Satb
Three Christmas Anthems For Sa Voices	Powell, Robert J.	Na Abi	M	L Sc Sa
Three Christmas Carols	Brown, J/Descroquettes	Gia		L Sc
Three Original Carols For Junior Choir	Baker	75 Sac	M	L Sc Satb
Three Riders, The	Grieb	75 Sac	M	L Sc Satb

Three Wise Kings (E)	Cooke, Arnold	Na Oxf	M	L Sc Unis
Through The Eyes Of A Child	Pickell	76 Pro	M	L Sc Satb
Tidings Of Comfort And Joy	Porter	Na Lor	M B	L Sc Satb
Time For Joy	Besig	76 Pro	M	L Sc Var
To Greet The Babe So Holy	Kinsman, Elmer F.	Na Abi	M	L Sc Sa
Today In Bethlehem	Powell, Robert J.	Na Abi	M	L Sc Satb
Today The World Is Filled	Gilligan, Michael	70 Acp		L L Sc
Twelve Days Of Christmas, The	James, Allen	Na Abi	M	L Sc Satb
Two Christmas Carols	Mcafee, Don	Na Abi	M	L Sc Satbe
Unto Us A Boy Is Born	Goemanne, Noel	72 Gia	M	L Sc Satb+
Unto Us A Child Is Born	Cantata	75 Maf	M	L Sc Satb+
Unto Us A Child Is Born	Deiss, Lucien	65 Wlp	B R	L Sc
We Have Seen His Star In The East	Fitzpatrick, Dennis	65 Fel	B	L Sc
We Have Seen His Star In The East	Lipscomb, Helen	Na Gsc	B	L Sc Sab+
We Sing Now At Christmas	Graves-Track, G.	74 Aug	M	L Sc Satb+
We Three Kings	Schneider, Kent E. (Arr)	75 Ccc	M B	L Sc
What Kind Of King?	Boeringer, James	Na Abi	M	L Sc Satb
When Jesus Left His Father's Throne 1	Johnson, D.	67 Aug	M	L Sc Solo
When Lights Are Lit On Christmas Eve	Knudsen/Johnson	Na Zon	M	L Sc Satb
When Love Came Down	Thompson	Na Lor	M B	L Sc Satb
When Love Was Born	Thompson	Na Lor	M B	L Sc Satb
Where Is He?	Peterson, John W.	Na Zon	M	L Sc Sa
Where Shall I Find The Christ Child?	Exner, Max	Na Abi	M	L Sc Satbm
Where Were You, O Shepherd?	Burke, John T.	Na Abi	M	L Sc Satb
While Shepherds Watched Their Flocks	Belcher, Supply	Na Abi	M	L Sc Solo
Why Do The Nations Rage?	Diercks, John H.	Na Abi	M	L Sc Unis
Why Thus Cradled Here?	Lynn, George	Na Abi	M	L Sc Satb
Winter Song	Huijbers & Oosterhuis	76 Nal	M	L L Sc
Wise Men From The East (Guit, Trio)	Walker, Jack	73 Pro	M	L Sc Satb+
With All My Heart	Ellis, Ron	75 Rav	B R L	L Sc
Wonder Of The Star, The	Carleton	Na Lor	M B	L Sc Satb
World's Redeemer, The	Holton	Na Lor	M B	L Sc Satb
Ye Folk Afar	Ream, Albert	Na Abi	M	L Sc Satb
You Are My Son	Fitzpatrick, Dennis	65 Fel	B	L Sc
Your Light Has Come, O Jerusalem	Fitzpatrick, Dennis	65 Fel	B	L Sc
Yours Are The Heavens	Lee, John	Na Gia		L Sc
Yours Are The Heavens	Roff, Joseph	Na Gia		L Sc
Yours Is Princely Power	Schroth, G	70 Gia	M	L Sc Satb+
Yuletide Memories	Wilson, I	Na Lor	M B	L Sc Satb
A Carol (Mary, The Mother, Song To Her)	Byles, B D	Na Gsc	B	T Sc Var+
A Child Is Born In Bethlehem	Pooler, Marie	58 Aug	M	T Sc Var
A Child Is Born In Bethlehem	Schalk	74 Aug	M	T Sc Satb
A Child This Day Is Born	Herrmann, William	Na Gsc	B	T Sc Satb
A Child To Us Is Born	Schutz, Heinrich	Na Gsc	B	T Sc Satb+
A Child's Noel	Beck, John Ness	Na Gsc	B	T Sc 2chor
A Child's Present To His Savior	Byles, B D	Na Gsc	B	T Sc Var+
A Christmas Concert	Wilson, Roger C	Na Lor	B R	T Sc Satb
A Christmas Folk Song	Gardner, Don	Na Gsc	B	T Sc Ssa
A Christmas Lullaby	Grieb, Herbert	Na Gsc	B	T Sc Satb
A Christmas Mosaic	Lamb, Richard	76 Her	M	T Sc Satb+
A Cradle Hymn	Christiansen, F. M.	38 Aug	M	T Sc Satb
A Flemish Carol	Christiansen, P.	50 Aug	M	T Sc Satb
A Great And Mighty Wonder	Fetler, Paul	67 Aug	M	T Sc Satb
A Great And Mighty Wonder	Soteren, Leland B.	Na Gsc	B	T Sc Full
A La Venue De Noel	Five French Noels	Na Gsc	B	T Sc Satb
A Little Christmas Cantata	Serly, Tibor	Na Gsc	B	T Sc Unis+
A Little Hymn To Mary	Searle, Humphrey	Na Gsc	B	T Sc Satb
A Long, Long Time Ago	Na	Na Gsc	B	T Sc Satb
A Minuet Fut Fait Un Reveil	Five French Noels	Na Gsc	B	T Sc Ssatt
A Son Is Born Of Mary	Wetzler, Robert	64 Aug	M	T Sc Satb
A Song Of Mary & Jesus (W/Fl)	Slater, Richard W.	75 Wlp	M	T Sc Satb-
A Star	Track, Gerhard	72 Gia	M	T Sc Var+
A Symbol Is This Child (Cantata)	Bach, J. S.	75 Lps	B R	T Sc Satb
A Very Merry Christmas	Robinson, G W	Na Gsc	B	T Sc Var+
A Virgin Most Pure	Na	Na Gsc	B	T Sc Unis+
A Virgin Pure And Fair (W/Flute)(E)	Ehret, Walter (Arr)	75 Gia	M	L T Sc Satb-
A Wealden Trio. Song Of The Women	Britten, Benjamin	Na Gsc	B	T Sc Ssa
Adeste Fideles	Na	Na Gsc	B	T Sc Var
Adeste Fideles (W/Tpts, Org, Cong)	Wolf, S.D.	75 Con	B	T Sc Satb
Adeste Fideles (With Brass)	Cassler, G. W.	65 Aug	M	T Sc Satb
Adoration, The	Russell (Arr)	65 Pro	M	L T Sc Satb
Against The Morn Is Come A King	Curry, W Lawrence	Na Gsc	B	T Sc Satb
Ah Dearest Jesus	Bach, J. S.	Na Gsc	B	T Sc Satb
Ah, Dearest Jesu, Holy Child	Wetzler, Robert	61 Aug	M	T Sc Satb
All My Heart This Night	Ebeling-Beckhard	62 Pro	M	L T Sc Satb
All My Heart This Night Rejoices	Mueller, Carl F	Na Gsc	B	T Sc Satb
All My Heart This Night Rejoices	Roff, Joseph	68 Gia	M	T Sc Var
All They From Saba Shall Come	Bach, J. S.	Na Gsc	B	T Sc Satb
Allelu! Rejoice And Sing!	Wilhelm	75 Her	M	T Sc Satb
Alleluia (From "For Us A Child")	Bach, J. S. (Kirk)	64 Pro	M	L T Sc Satb
Alleluia Noel	Ball, Albert C	Na Gsc	B	T Sc Satb
Alleluia! Christ Is Born	Mccabe, Michael	76 Sac		T Sc Unis
Alleluia! O Praise Ye The Lord	Bach/Black	75 Sac	M	T Sc Satb
Alleluia, For Christmas From Cantata	Bach, J. S.	Na Gsc	B	T Sc Satb
Allons, Gay Bergeres	Costeley, Guillaume	Na Gsc	B	T Sc Satb
Almighty God, Why By The Leading	Bull, John	Na Oxf	M	T Sc Full
An Early American Christmas Triptych	Read, Holden & Law	75 Aug	M	T Sc Satb
And Lo, The Star	Petzold	68 Aug	M	T Sc Satb
And Rejoice!	Polistina/Hebble	75 Her	M	T Sc Satb
And The Glory Of The Lord	Handel, G. F.	Cfs	M	T Sc Satb
And The Glory Of The Lord	Handel, G. F.	Na Gsc	M	T Sc Satb
And The Glory Of The Lord	Handel, G. F.	Na Lor	M	T Sc Satb
And The Glory Of The Lord	Handel, G. F.	50 Pro	M	L T Sc Satb
Angel And The Shepherds, The	Trusler, Ivan	Na Abi	M	T Sc Satb
Angels And Shepherds	Traditional/Decou	Na Zon	M	T Sc Satb
Angels Are Singing	Coggin (Arr)	72 Pro	M	L T Sc Satb
Angels From The Realms Of Glory	Ehret, Walter	74 Gia	M	T Sc Sab-
Angels From The Realms Of Glory	Pooler, Marie	58 Aug	M	T Sc Satb
Angels From The Realms Of Glory-	Montgomery-Scott	Cfs	M	T Sc Satb

CATEGORIZED INDEX

Angels Song That Christmas Morn	Cockshott, Gerald R.	59 Ron	M		T	Sc	Satb
Angels We Have Heard On High	Christiansen, P.	55 Aug	M		T	Sc	Satb+
Angels We Have Heard On High	Hughes, Robert J.	76 Lor			T	Sc	Satb+
Angels We Have Heard On High	Na	Na Gsc	B		T	Sc	Full
Angels We Have Heard On High	Stone (Arr)	52 Pro	M	L	T	Sc	Satb
Angels We Have Heard On High	Traditional/Peterson	Na Zon	M		T	Sc	Satb
Angels, From The Realms Of Glory	Smart/Decou	Na Zon	M		T	Sc	Satb
Angelus Ad Pastores Ait	Hassler, H L	Na Gsc	B		T	Sc	Satb+
Angelus Ad Pastores Ait	Monteverdi, Claudio	Na Gsc	B		T	Sc	Var 1
Antiphonal Carol	Manz, Paul	58 Aug	M		T	Sc	Unis
Arise, O Ye Servants	Sweelinck, J. P.	Na Gsc	B		T	Sc	6mix
Arise, Shine	Maker, F C	Na Gsc	B		T	Sc	Satb+
Arise, Shine, For Thy Light	Elvey	56 Pro	M	L	T	Sc	Satb
Arise, Shine, For Thy Light Has Come	Jennings, K.	67 Aug	M		T	Sc	Satb
As I Watched Beside My Sheep	Fuller (Arr)	50 Pro	M	L	T	Sc	Satb
As Lately We Watched	Pooler, Marie	60 Aug	M		T	Sc	Satb
As With Gladness Men Of Old	Hokanson, Margrethe	Na Abi	M		T	Sc	Satb
As With Gladness Men Of Old	Kocher/Johnson	Na Zon	M		T	Sc	Ssatb
At Last We're In The Town	Na	Na Gsc	B		T	Sc	Satb+
At The Cradle	Franck, Cesar	Na Lor	M		T	Sc	Sa
Austrian Shepherd's Carol	Wood	68 Aug	M		T	Sc	Var
Awake The Trumpet's Lofty Sound	Handel, G. F.	Na Gsc	B		T	Sc	Satb+
Away In A Manger	Kirkpatrick/Decou	Na Zon	M		T	Sc	Satb
Away In A Manger	Luther, M. (Swift)	49 Pro	M	L	T	Sc	Satb
Away In A Manger	Pooler, Marie	63 Aug	M		T	Sc	U+Ds
Away In A Manger	Spilman	Na Lor	M		T	Sc	
Away In A Manger	Van Dyke, Paul C.	Na Gsc	B		T	Sc	Satb+
Babe In Bethlehem's Manger Laid	Collins (Arr)	55 Pro	M	L	T	Sc	Satb
Babe Is Born, A	Diemer	75 Sac	M		T	Sc	Satb
Babe Is Born, A	Forsblad (Arr)	58 Pro	M	L	T	Sc	Satb
Baby In The Cradle Lies (Opt A Cap)	Coggin (Arr)	75 Pro	M		T	Sc	Satb+
Baby Jesu	Crow	59 Pro	M	L	T	Sc	Satb
Beat The Drum	Peloquin, C Alexander	Na Gia			T	Sc	
Before The Paling Of The Stars	Byles, B D	Na Gsc	B		T	Sc	Satb+
Behold A Mystical Rose	Cross, Richart (Alt)	63 Wlp	B		T	Sc	
Behold, The Star!	Hedges, H	Na Gsc	B		T	Sc	Satb+
Bells Are Ringing (Perc)	Kirk, Theron (Arr)	73 Pro	M		T	Sc	Satb+
Bells At Christmas (A Cap)	Pohlmann	Hof	M		T	Sc	Satb
Bells Of Paradise	Nyquist, R.	55 Pro	M	L	T	Sc	Satb
Bells On Christmas Day, The	Wilson	Na Lor	M		T	Sc	
Bethlehem	Billings, William	Cfp	R		T	Sc	Saatb
Bethlehem	Gounod, Charles	Na Lor	M		T	Sc	Sab
Bethlehem Carol	Brandt	69 Pro	M	L	T	Sc	Satb
Bethlehem Road	Byles, B D	Na Gsc	B		T	Sc	Ssa+
Bethlehem Star, The	Wilhelm	72 Pro	M	L	T	Sc	Satb
Birthday Of A King, The	Neidlinger	Na Lor	M		T	Sc	Satb
Birthday Of The King, The	Neidinger/Johnson	Na Zon	M		T	Sc	Satb
Blow, Winds, O Softly Blow (Trad)	Na	Na Gsc	B		T	Sc	Var+
Blow, Ye Winds, Softly	Kennerly	Na Lor	M		T	Sc	Satb
Born A King	Peterson, John W.	Na Zon	M		T	Sc	Satb
Born In A Manger (Gaelic Melody)	Hughes, Robert J.	Na Lor	B		T	Sc	Satb
Born King Of Kings (E & Lat) (A Cap)	Handel, G. F./Hardwick	76 Pro	M		T	Sc	Satb
Born Today	Marenzio, Luca	66 Som	M		T	Sc	
Branch Of Promise, The	Brandon, George	69 Pro	M	L	T	Sc	Satb
Break Forth Into Joy	Simper, C	Na Gsc	B		T	Sc	Sab+
Break Forth O Beauteous Heavenly Light	Bach, J. S.	Na Gsc	B		T	Sc	Satb
Break Forth O Beauteous Heavenly Light	Bach, J. S.	Na Aug	M		T	Sc	Satb
Bright & Joyful Is The Morn (Opt 2 Tpt	Milgrove/Douglas (Arr)	75 Pro	M		T	Sc	Satb+
Brightest And Best	Coombe, C W	Na Gsc	B		T	Sc	Satb+
Brightest And Best	Wesley, C. (Stone)	62 Pro	M	L	T	Sc	Satb
Bring A Torch, Jeannette	Stone (Arr)	59 Pro	M	L	T	Sc	Satb
Bring A Torch, Jeannette Isabella	Bitgood, Roberta	75 Sac	M		T	Sc	Sa+
Bring A Torch, Jeannette...Acap	Boyd, Jack (Arr)	75 Wlp	M		T	Sc	Ssa
Bring Your Torches	Na	Na Gsc	B		T	Sc	Var+
Calm On The List'ning Ear Of Night	Harker, F F	Na Gsc	B		T	Sc	Var+
Calm On The Listening Ear	Kinsman (Arr)	60 Pro	M	L	T	Sc	Satb
Cantata #106 God's Time Is Best (E&G)	Bach, J. S.	Na Kal	B		T	Sc	Satb
Cantata #142 To Us A Child Is Born	Bach, J. S.	Na Kal	B		T	Sc	Satb
Canticle Of Christmas	Mahler, Gustov	Na Her	M		T	Sc	Usatb+
Cantique De Noel	Adam, Adolphe	Na Lor	M		T	Sc	Satb
Cantique De Noel	Gevaert, F A	Na Gsc	B		T	Sc	Satb
Cantique De Noel (O Holy Night)	Adam, Ad	Na Gsc	B		T	Sc	Var+
Carol Fantasy	Bish, D.	76 Bec	M		T	Sc	
Carol For Epiphany	Hunnicutt, J.	71 Aug	M		T	Sc	Sa
Carol Of A Rose	Daniels, Mabel	Na Gsc	B		T	Sc	Ssa
Carol Of Joy (Aleria)	Zgodava	74 Aug	M		T	Sc	Satb+
Carol Of Polish Grenadiers	Niles-Horton	Cfs	M		T	Sc	Satb
Carol Of Praise, A	Rasley, John M.	Na Zon	M		T	Sc	Satb
Carol Of The Advent	Dietterich, Philip	Na Abi	M		T	Sc	Satb
Carol Of The Angels (Sop Soli)	Wyatt (Arr)	76 Pro	M		T	Sc	Satb+
Carol Of The Bagpipers	Traditional/Rasley	Na Zon	M		T	Sc	Satb
Carol Of The Bells	Burns	Na Lor	M		T	Sc	Ssa
Carol Of The Bells (A Capella)	Leontovich-Wilhousky	Cfs	M		T	Sc	Satb
Carol Of The Birds	Shaw-Parker	Na Gsc	B		T	Sc	Full
Carol Of The Russian Children	Na	Na Gsc	B		T	Sc	Var
Carol Of The Three Kings	Gesangbuch (Canavati)	60 Pro	M	L	T	Sc	Satb
Carol Of The Visitation	Brandon, George	72 Gia			T	Sc	Satb+
Carol-Noel (A Capella)	Wilhousky (Arr)	Cfs	M		T	Sc	Satb
Carols And Songs For Christmas	Verrall, John Ed	50 Bos	B		T	Sc	Satb
Carols For Christmas (Ssa)	Strickling, George F.	Na Abi	M		T	Sc	Ssa
Carols From Many Lands	Na	Na Lor	M		T	Sc	Satb
Chanson Des Anges	Vidal, Paul	Na Gsc	B		T	Sc	Ssa
Chanson Joyeuse Do Noel	Gevaert, F A	Na Gsc	B		T	Sc	Satb
Child Of Bethlehem, The	Hankinson	75 Maf	M		T	Sc	Satb
Chorales From The Christmas Oratorio	Bach, J. S.	Na Gsc	B		T	Sc	Satb
Chorus Of The Angels	Schutz, Heinrich	Na Gsc	B		T	Sc	Satb+
Christ Is Born	Ebeling (Kirk Arr)	60 Pro	M	L	T	Sc	Satb
Christ Is Born Of Maiden Fair	Matthews, David	Na Gsc	B		T	Sc	Satb
Christ The King Now Is Born	Rimsky-Korsakoff (Kirk)	66 Pro	M	L	T	Sc	Satb
Christ The Lord In Silence Coming	Hughes, H/Wilson, P	72 Gia	M		T	Sc	Satb
Christ Was Born On Christmas Day	Kirk, Theron	73 Pro	M		T	Sc	Satb
Christ Was Born On Christmas Day	Na	Na Gsc	B		T	Sc	Satb
Christ Was Born On Christmas Day	Roff, Joseph	68 Gia	M		T	Sc	2pt
Christmas	Holden, Oliver	76 Bbl	M		T	Sc	Satb
Christmas (From Holiday Motets)	Krenek, Ernst	67 Ron	B		T	Sc	Ssaa
Christmas Alleluia	Elliott	Hof	M		T	Sc	Var
Christmas Bells	Elliott	Hof	M		T	Sc	Var
Christmas Bells With Joy Are Ringing	Hopson, Hal H.	76 Sac			T	Sc	Satb+
Christmas Bells, The	Talmadge	75 Sac	M		T	Sc	Satb
Christmas Carols From The Masters	Na	Na Lor	M		T	Sc	
Christmas Comes Anew	Ehret, Walter	73 Gia	M		T	Sc	Sab+
Christmas Dawn	Wetzler, Robert	76 Sac			T	Sc	Satb+
Christmas Ensemble S.S.A. & T.T.B.B.	Decou/Johnson	Na Zon	B		T	Sc	
Christmas Eve Is Here	Sarner, Richard	Na Gsc	B		T	Sc	Tb+
Christmas Hymn (While By My Sheep)	Na	Na Gsc	B		T	Sc	Var
Christmas In Bethlehem	Beckhard	65 Pro	M	L	T	Sc	Satb
Christmas Is Coming	Milkey, E T	Na Gsc	B		T	Sc	Ssa+
Christmas Jubilate (Russian Melody)	Na	Na Lor	M		T	Sc	
Christmas Long Ago	Swanson/Drevits	Na Zon	M		T	Sc	Satb
Christmas Lullabies	Bishop, M. & Weatherly	45 Smc	M		T	Sc	Unis
Christmas Mosaic, A	Lamb	75 Maf	M		T	Sc	Satb+
Christmas Motet	Paminger, Leonhard	Na Gsc	B		T	Sc	Sattb
Christmas Night	Raph, Alan	Na Gsc	B		T	Sc	Satb+
Christmas Night	Wolf, Hugo	52 Bbl	M		T	Sc	Full+
Christmas Night (Stille Nacht)	Na	Na Gsc	B		T	Sc	Full+
Christmas Oratorio	Bach, J. S.	Na Gsc	B		T	Sc	Var+
Christmas Oratorio	Bach, J. S.	Na Kal	B		T	Sc	Satb
Christmas Oratorio	Saint-Saens, Camille	Na Kal	B		T	Sc	Satb
Christmas Oratorio	Schutz, Heinrich	Na Kal	B		T	Sc	Satb
Christmas Oratorio (Ger)	Bach, J. S.	Cfp	R		T	Sc	Satb+
Christmas Rose, A	Burroughs	75 Maf	M		T	Sc	Satb+
Christmas So Wonderful Fair	Czajanek, Victor	Na Gsc	B		T	Sc	Satb
Christmas Song	Cornelius, Peter	Na Gsc	B		T	Sc	Full
Christmas Song	Herzogenberg	Na Gsc	B		T	Sc	Satb
Christmas Song, The	Adam, Adolphe	Na Lor	M		T	Sc	
Come And Adore Him	Rasley	Na Lor	M		T	Sc	Satb
Come And Thank Him (Me)	Bach, J. S.	Na Oxf	M		T	Sc	Sa
Come Hasten Ye Shepherds (Traditional)	Na	Na Gsc	B		T	Sc	Var+
Come To The Manger	Gresens	71 Aug	M		T	Sc	Satb
Come To The Stable With Jesus	O'hara, Geoffrey	Na Gsc	B		T	Sc	Var
Come Ye Lofty, Come Ye Lowly	Gurney-Douglas	62 Pro	M	L	T	Sc	Satb
Come, All Ye Faithful	Lorenz	Na Lor	M		T	Sc	
Command Thine Angel That He Come	Buxtehude, D.	52 Bbl	B		T	Sc	Satb+
Coventry Carol	Currie, Randolph	74 Bec	M		T	Sc	
Coventry Carol	Nasteley, Guillaume	Na Gsc	B		T	Sc	Satb
Coventry Carol	Stone (Arr)	52 Pro	M	L	T	Sc	Satb
Cradle Song Of The Virgin	Brahms, Johannes	Na Gsc	B		T	Sc	Ssa+
Cradle Song Of The Virgin (E&Ger)	Brahms, J. (Deis)	38 Gsc	M		T	Sc	Satb+
Dearest Jesu, Holy Child	Kirk, Theron	66 Pro	M	L	T	Sc	Satb
Deck The Halls	Na	Na Gsc	B		T	Sc	Satb
Deep Was The Silence	Traditional/Rasley	Na Zon	M		T	Sc	Satb
Dies Sanctificatus	Byrd, William (Ehret)	65 Pro	M	L	T	Sc	Satb
Ding Dong Merrilly On High	Na	Na Gsc	B		T	Sc	Satb
Do You Know?	Purcell, Henry	Na Gsc	B		T	Sc	Satb+
Dost Thou In A Manger Lie	Held, Wilbur C	68 Aug	M		T	Sc	Unis
Dost Thou In A Manger Lie?	Van Dyke, Paul C.	Na Gsc	B		T	Sc	Satb+
Echo Carol, The	Thompson	Na Lor	M		T	Sc	
El Nino Perdido	Nin-Culmell, Joaquin	55 Ron	M		T	Sc	Satb
Epiphany (From Holiday Motets)	Krenek, Ernst	67 Ron	B		T	Sc	Ssa
Epiphany Carol (E)	Merrick, Frank	Na Oxf	M		T	Sc	Satb
Et Verbum Caro Factum Est	Back, Sven-Erik	Na Gsc	B		T	Sc	Satb
Favorite Christmas Carols	Selner, J	Na Gia			T	Sc	
First Noel, The	Traditional English	70 Acp		L	T	Sc	
First Noel, The (C)	Denton	Na Lor	M		T	Sc	
Flee Into Egypt Land (Christmas)	Hendrix, James	73 Jhe	M R	L	T	Sc	
Flower Of Jesse	Niles, John Jacob	Na Gsc	B		T	Sc	Ssa
For God So Loved The World	Prather, Lillian	70 Lym	R		T	Sc	
For Unto Us A Child Is Born	Handel, G. F.	Na Lor	M		T	Sc	
For Unto Us A Child Is Born	Handel, G. F.	52 Pro	M	L	T	Sc	Satb
For Unto Us A Child Is Born	Handel, G. F.	Na Gsc	B		T	Sc	Sab+
For We Have Seen His Star	Newbury, Kent A.	Na Gsc	B		T	Sc	Satb
For You Shall Go Out In Joy	Newbury, Kent A.	Na Gsc	B		T	Sc	Satb+
For Your Light Has Come	Nelson, Ronald A.	72 Aug	M		T	Sc	Var
Four Carols For A Holy Night	Lekberg, Sven	Na Gsc	B		T	Sc	Satb
Friendly Beasts, The (C)	French, Carol	Na Lor	M		T	Sc	
From Heaven An Angel (Hungarian Carol)	Na	Na Gsc	B		T	Sc	Satb+
From Heaven On High	Praetorius, M	Na Gsc	B		T	Sc	Satb
Fum, Fum, Fum	Na	Na Gsc	B		T	Sc	Var+
Gabriel's Message	Niles, John Jacob	Na Gsc	B		T	Sc	Satb+
Gentle Jesus	Moats	Na Lor	M		T	Sc	Satb
Gentle Mary Catalan Folk-Song	Mcfeeters Arr	Na Gsc	B		T	Sc	Ssa+
Gift Of Light	Wescott	73 Aug	M		T	Sc	Satb
Gift Of Love	Hughes, Miki	76 Lor			T	Sc	Sab+
Gifts We Shall Bring	Ehret, Walter	73 Gia	M		T	Sc	Sab+
Give Praise Unto The Lord (A Cap)	Pitoni-Douglas (Arr)	76 Pro	M		T	Sc	Satb
Glad Tidings Of Great Joy	Wiley	Na Pro	M	L	T	Sc	Satb
Gloria	Newbury, Kent A.	Na Gsc	B		T	Sc	Satb+
Gloria In Excelsis Deo	Krenek, Ernst	67 Ron	B		T	Sc	Ssaa
Gloria To God On High	Thygerson	75 Her	M		T	Sc	Satb
Glorious Song, The	Harris, Kent	58 Pro	M	L	T	Sc	Satb
Glorious Star Is Beaming	Hardwicke (Arr)	75 Pro	M		T	Sc	Satb+
Glorious The Day When Christ Was Born	Green, F.P.	Na Oxf	B	L	T	Sc	
Glory To God	Handel	Na Lor	M		T	Sc	Satb
Glory To God ("Messiah")	Handel, G. F.	50 Pro	M	L	T	Sc	Satb
Glory To God We Sing	Skoog/Johnson	Na Zon	M		T	Sc	Satb
God Give Ye Merry Christmastide	Beckhard (Arr)	62 Pro	M	L	T	Sc	Satb
God Rest Ye Merry, Gentlemen	Elliot	Na Lor	M		T	Sc	Sab
God Rest You Merrie Gentlemen	Na	Na Gsc	B		T	Sc	Men+
God Rest You Merry Gentlemen	Stevens (Arr)	53 Pro	M	L	T	Sc	Satb
God Rest You Merry Gentlemen	Traditional/Decou	Na Zon	M		T	Sc	Satb

CATEGORIZED INDEX

God's Gift Of Love	Chopin	Na Lor	M		T Sc	Satb
God's Infant Son	Praetorius, M	Na Gsc	B		T Sc	Satb
Golden Harps Are Sounding	Sullivan-Handley	58 Pro	M	L	T Sc	Satb
Good Christian Men Rejoice	Na	Na Gsc	B		T Sc	Full
Good Christian Men, Rejoice	Johnson (Traditional)	Na Zon	M		T Sc	Satb
Good Christian Men, Rejoice	Lorenz	Na Lor	M		T Sc	Unis
Good Christian Men, Rejoice	Nyquist, R.	52 Pro	M	L	T Sc	Full
Good Christian Men, Rejoice	Nystedt, Knut	64 Aug	M		T Sc	Satb+
Good King Wenceslas	Na	Na Gsc	B		T Sc	Full
Great Day (A Cap)	King (Arr)	76 Pro	M		T Sc	Satb
Hacia Belen Va Un Borrico	Na	Na Gsc	B		T Sc	Satb
Haec Dies (From Holiday Motets)	Krenek, Ernst	67 Ron	B		T Sc	Ssa
Hail The Long Expected Star (Me)	Brandon, George (Arr)	76 Gia	M	L	T Sc	Sab+
Hail, All Hail The Glorious Morn	Na	Na Gsc	B		T Sc	Full
Hark The Glad Sound	Thiman, Eric H.	Na Gsc	B		T Sc	Satb+
Hark The Herald Angels Sing	Dare, Elkanah K	75 Bbl	M		T Sc	Satb
Hark The Herald Angels Sing	Mendelssohn, F.	51 Pro	M	L	T Sc	Satb
Hark Ye! What News The Angels Bring	Follett (Arr)	76 Pro	M		T Sc	Satb+
Hark! A Thrilling Voice	Butler, Eugene	Na Abi	M		T Sc	Satb
Hark! The Herald Angels Sing	Smith	Na Lor	M		T Sc	Satb
Hark, Angel Carols	Lovelace, Austin C.	70 Aug	M		T Sc	Unis
Hark, The Herald Angels Sing	Decou, Harold	Na Zon	M		T Sc	Satb
He Is Born	Wetzler, Robert	50 Aug	M		T Sc	Var
He Is Born (W/ Finger Cymbals)	Kirk, Theron (Arr)	74 Pro	M	L	T Sc	Satb
He Is Born, Christ Is Born Today	De Clerambault	75 Sac	M		T Sc	Var
He Shall Feed His Flock	Handel, G. F.	53 Pro	M	L	T Sc	Satb
He Whom Joyous Shepherds Praised	Anderson	73 Aug	M		T Sc	Satb
Hear Oh Hear	Gadwood, Gary	Na Gsc	B		T Sc	Satb
Heart's Adoration	Marcello, Benedetto	Na Oxf	M		T Sc	2pt
Here, Mid The Ass And Oxen Mild	Na	Na Gsc	B		T Sc	Full
Heute Ist Christus Der Herr Geboren	Schutz, Heinrich	Na Gsc	B		T Sc	Var+
Hodie Apparuit	Lasso, Orlando Di	Na Gsc	B		T Sc	3eq+
Hodie Christus	Palestrina, Giovanni P	Na Gsc	B		T Sc	8mix
Hodie Christus Natus Est	Gabrieli, G	Na Gsc	B		T Sc	8mix
Hodie Christus Natus Est	Monteverdi, Claudio	Na Gsc	B		T Sc	Var
Hodie Christus Natus Est	Palestrina, Giovanni P	65 Bbl	M		T Sc	Ssaa
Holy Child, The (W/ Opt Flute)	Hruby (Arr)	75 Pro	M		T Sc	Var+
How Far Is It To Bethlehem?	Burroughs	75 Sac	M		T Sc	Var
How Far Is It To Bethlehem?	Na	Na Gsc	B		T Sc	Var+
How Far Is It To Bethlehem?	Pooler, Marie	63 Aug	M		T Sc	Var
How Great The Name Of Christ Our Lord	Pekiel, B/Herter, J	73 Gia	M		T Sc	Satb
How Shall I Fitly Meet Thee	Bach, J. S.	Na Gsc	B		T Sc	Satb+
How Still And Tiny	Peloquin, C Alexander	Na Gia			T Sc	
How Unto Bethlehem	Na	Na Gsc	B		T Sc	Full
Huron Indian Carol	Lee	75 Sac	M		T Sc	Unis
Hush My Dear	Graham, Robert	Na Abi	M		T Sc	Satb
Hushing Carol	Kountz, Richard	Na Gsc	B		T Sc	Var
I Am So Glad	Jothen, M.	76 Bec	M		T Sc	
I Come To Thee Jesus (Opt Bel, Ob, Perc)	Follett (Arr)	75 Pro	M		T Sc	2pt+
I Saw A Stranger Yester'en	Avshalomov Jacob	75 Gal	M		T Sc	Satb
I Saw Three Ships	Van Dyke, Paul C.	Na Gsc	B		T Sc	Satb+
I Sing Of A Maiden	Maconchy, Elizabeth	Na Gsc	B		T Sc	Sab
I Wonder As I Wander	Na	Na Gsc	B		T Sc	Var
In A Cave (W/Opt Flute)	Franklin/Decou	Na Zon	M		T Sc	Satb
In A Manger He Is Sleeping	Landon	Na Lor	M		T Sc	Satb
In Bethlehem	Johnston	Na Lor	M		T Sc	Satb
In Bethlehem Is Born A King 1	Ehret, Walter	74 Aug	M		T Sc	Sab
In Bethlehem That Fair City	Niles, John Jacob	Na Gsc	B		T Sc	Var+
In Dulci Jubilo	Najera, Edmund	Na Gsc	B		T Sc	Satb
In Excelsis Gloria	Peeters, Flor	57 Aug	M		T Sc	Satb
In Festo Purificationis	Byrd, William	Na Kal	B		T Sc	Satb
In Night's Deep Silence	Herter, J	74 Gia	M		T Sc	Satb+
In That Lovely Far-Off City	Niles, John Jacob	Na Gsc	B		T Sc	Ssa
In The Bleak Mid-Winter	Bonta, Stephen	Na Gsc	B		T Sc	Ttbb
In The Stillness	Marth, Helen J	Na Gsc	B		T Sc	3eq+
In The Stillness Of The Night	Peery	Na Lor	M		T Sc	Satb
Incarnatio (Dum Medium Silentium)	Johnson, Robert S.	Na Oxf	M		T Sc	Ssatb
Infant Holy	Na	Na Gsc	B		T Sc	Ssaa
Innocentes Pro Christo	Palestrina, Giovanni P	Na Gsc	B		T Sc	Ssaa
It Came Upon The Midnight Clear	Sullivan	Na Gsc	M		T Sc	Full
It Fell Upon A Winter's Day	Ehret, Walter (Arr)	73 Pro	M		T Sc	Sab+
Jesus Christ Is Born	Na	Na Gsc	B		T Sc	Satb+
Jesus Is Born	Brebeuf, St Jean De	Na Gsc	B		T Sc	Satb
Jesus The Christ Is Born	Niles, John Jacob	Na Gsc	B		T Sc	Var
Jesus, Bright And Morning Star	Sowerby, Leo	76 Sac			T Sc	Satb+
Jesus, Jesus, Rest Your Head	Hegarty, David H	Na Lor	M		T Sc	Satb
Jesus, Our Lord, We Adore Thee	James, W.	39 Gsc	M		T Sc	Full
Joseph Est Bien Marie	Five French Noels	Na Gsc	B		T Sc	Satb
Joy To The World	Broughton, Edward	76 Lor			T Sc	Sab+
Joy To The World	Eilers, Joyce	76 Her	M		T Sc	Satb+
Joy To The World	Martin	Na Lor	M		T Sc	Satb
Joy To The World	Mason/Johnson	Na Zon	M		T Sc	Satb
Joyous Carol (Divided Parts)	Wells-Williamson	Cfs	M		T Sc	Satb
Kedron	Na	Na Gsc	B		T Sc	Var+
Kings Of The Orient Three	Grieb, Herbert	Na Gsc	B		T Sc	Var+
Kneel At The Manger	Carmony	Na Lor	M		T Sc	Satb
La Nana	Na	Na Gsc	B		T Sc	Satb+
La Virgin Lava Panales	Na	Na Gsc	B		T Sc	Satb
Lambs Also Love Thee, The	Ream	75 Her	M		T Sc	Satb
Lay Down Your Staffs, O Shepherds	Na	Na Gsc	B		T Sc	Satb
Le Message Des Anges	Gevaert, F A	Na Gsc	B		T Sc	Satb
Let All Men Sing God's Praises	Na	Na Gsc	B		T Sc	Satb
Let All Mortal Flesh Keep Silence	Traditional/Rasley	Na Zon	M		T Sc	Ssatb
Let All Together Praise Our God	Smith	Na Lor	M		T Sc	Satb
Let Earth Receive Her King	Wilson	Na Lor	M		T Sc	Satb
Let Our Gladness Know No End	Pooler, Marie	66 Aug	M		T Sc	Sa
Let The Earth Resound	Pekiel, B/Herter, J	73 Gia	M		T Sc	Satb
Lippai, Wake Up!	Na	Na Gsc	B		T Sc	Satb+
Little Brother Jesus	Niles	70 Gsc	M		T Sc	Satb
Little Lord Jesus	Smith, Lani	76 Lor			T Sc	Satb+
Little White Dove	Grieb, Herbert	Na Gsc	B		T Sc	Satb
Lo The Angel Said To The Shepherds	Gabrieli, Andrea	Na Gsc	B		T Sc	7mix
Lo! Star-Led Chiefs (Me)	Crotch, William (Arr)	Na Oxf	M		T Sc	2pt
Lo, A Child Is Born	Morales, Cristobal De	67 Bbl	M		T Sc	Sab
Lo, How A Rose	Bish, D.	76 Bec	M		T Sc	
Lo, How A Rose	Praetorius/Christiansn	37 Aug	M		T Sc	Satb
Lo, How A Rose (4 Voices)	Praetorius/Vulpius	70 Gia	B	L	T Sc	Round
Lo, How A Rose E'er Blooming	Caldwell, M	75 Sac	M		T Sc	Satb
Lo, How A Rose E'er Blooming	Praetorius, M	Na Gsc	B		T Sc	Var
Lo, How A Rose E'er Blooming	Praetorius, M. (Cain)	Hof	M		T Sc	Satb
Lo, How A Rose E'er Blooming (E)	Jergenson, Dale (Arr)	76 Gia	M	L	T Sc	Sab+
Lo, How A Rose Ere Blooming	Praetorius, M.-Overby	46 Aug	M		T Sc	Satb
Lo, The Angel Said To The Shepherds	Schutz, Heinrich	Na Gsc	B		T Sc	7mix
Long Ago In Bethlehem	Graham	75 Sac	M		T Sc	Mel
Long Time Ago	Denton	Na Lor	M		T Sc	Var
Lord Christ, When First Thou Cam'st	Johnson, D.	67 Aug	M		T Sc	Sab
Lord, When The Wise Men Came	Spedding, Frank	Na Oxf	M		T Sc	Satb
Love Came Down At Christmas	Greestone	75 Sac	M		T Sc	Satb
Love Came Down At Christmas	Lovelace, Austin C.	75 Sac	M		T Sc	Satb
Love Came Down At Christmas	Martin, Gilbert M	75 Sac	M		T Sc	Satb
Love Came Down At Christmas	Preus	64 Aug	M		T Sc	Sab
Love Came Down At Christmas	Thiman, Eric H.	Na Gsc	B		T Sc	Unis+
Lullaby For Jesus	Peloquin, C Alexander	Na Gia			T Sc	
Lullaby, Jesus Dear	Na	Na Gsc	B		T Sc	Satb+
Make We Joy Now In This Feast	Emery, John	Na Gsc	B		T Sc	Satb
Man's Redemption	Headington, C.	Na Gsc	B		T Sc	Satb
Manger Carol, A	Burnham	Na Lor	M		T Sc	Sab
Many Shall Come From The East And West	Schutz, Heinrich	Na Gsc	B		T Sc	Sattb+
March Of The Kings	Cain, Nobie	Na Gsc	B		T Sc	Satb+
March Of The Kings	Na	Na Gsc	B		T Sc	Var
Mary Laid Her Child	Mccabe, John	Na Gsc	B		T Sc	Satb
Mary's Lullaby	Boozer	75 Maf	M		T Sc	Satb
Mary's Manger Song	Salter, S	Na Gsc	B		T Sc	Satb+
Mary's Nowell	Thiman, Eric H.	Na Gsc	B		T Sc	Satb
Mary's Soliloquy (From The Cantata)	Effinger, C	Na Gsc	B		T Sc	Satb+
Marys Little Baby	David, Elmer L	Na Gsc	B		T Sc	Satb
Masters In This Hall (In 19 Rounds)	French/Tortolano Ed	75 Gia	B	L	T Sc	4pt
Memories Of Christmas	Carleton	Na Lor	M		T Sc	Satb
Merrily On High	Hadler	Na Lor	M		T Sc	Satb
Merrily On High	Traditional/Rasley	Na Zon	M		T Sc	Ssatb
Merry Christmas	Johnston/Lebar	75 Zon	M		T Sc	Satb
Miles Coverdale's Carol	Paget, Michael	Na Gsc	B		T Sc	Satb
Minor Carol, The	Gunter/Johnson	Na Zon	M		T Sc	Satb
Missa Puer Qui Natus Est Nobis	Guerrero, Francisco	Na Kal	B		T Sc	Satb
Missas Est Gabriel	Morales, Cristobal De	Na Gsc	B		T Sc	Ssaa
Mistletoe And Holly Bright	Bach, J. S.	Na Gsc	B		T Sc	Ssa+
Morning-Song For The Christ Child	Sculthorpe, Peter	Na Gsc	B		T Sc	Satb
Music For Christmas	Meyerowitz, Jan	52 Bbl	B		T Sc	Var
Nazareth	Gounod, Charles	Na Gsc	B		T Sc	Full+
Never Was A Child So Lovely	Niles, John Jacob	Na Gsc	B		T Sc	Var
New Coventry	Na	Na Gsc	B		T Sc	Satb+
Newborn, The	Martin	75 Sac	M		T Sc	Satb
No Room In The Inn	Grieb, Herbert	Na Gsc	B		T Sc	Satb+
No Room In The Inn	Traditional/Johnson	Na Zon	M		T Sc	Satb
Noel (Ox And Donkey's Carol) W/Inst	Fetler, Paul	69 Aug	M		T Sc	Unis
Noel Noel	Chenoweth, Wilbur	Na Gsc	B		T Sc	Ssa+
Noel Noel A Saviour Is Born	Chaplin, M W	Na Gsc	B		T Sc	Satb+
Noel Noel Bells Are Ringing	Chenoweth, Wilbur	Na Gsc	B		T Sc	Var+
Noel Nouvelet	Zgodava	66 Aug	M		T Sc	Satb
Noel!	Landon	Na Lor	M		T Sc	Satb
Norwegian Christmas Carol, A	Wilson (Arr)	Na Lor	M		T Sc	Satb
Now Every Child That Dwells	Farjeon, E/Sowerby	27 Gia	B	L	T Sc	
Now, Arise Ye Shepherds Mild	Costeley, Guillaume	Na Gsc	B		T Sc	Satb
O Come All Ye Faithful (W/Org, Tpt)	Nystedt, Knut	64 Aug	M		T Sc	Satb+
O Come To My Heart (No 6010) Cantata	Liljestrand, Paul	Na Zon			T Sc	
O Come, All Ye Faithful	Frazier, M. (Arr)	76 Bec	M		T Sc	
O Come, All Ye Faithful	Moffatt	Na Lor	M		T Sc	Satb
O Come, All Ye Faithful	Na	Na Gsc	B		T Sc	2chor
O Come, All Ye Faithful	Smith	Na Lor	M		T Sc	Satb
O Come, All Ye Faithful	Wade/Peterson	Na Zon	M		T Sc	Satb
O Joyful Day! (Christmas Motet)	Haydn, Michael	Na Gsc	B		T Sc	Satb+
O Little One Sweet	Leist, Warren C	Na Gsc	B		T Sc	Satb
O Little Town Of Bethlehem	Neidlinger	22 Gsc	M		T Sc	Satb+
O Little Town Of Bethlehem	Redner/Hess	Na Zon	M		T Sc	Ssaattb
O Little Town Of Bethlehem	Smith	Na Lor	M		T Sc	Satb
O Little Town Of Bethlehem (Easy)	Redner/Decou	Na Zon	M		T Sc	Sa(Tb)
O Lovely Son Of God	Moore, D	Na Gsc	B		T Sc	Satb+
O Magnum Mysterium	Morales, Cristobal De	Na Gsc	B		T Sc	Ssaa
O Magnum Mysterium	Na	Na Gsc	B		T Sc	Satb
O Nata Lux De Lumine	Tallis, Thomas	Na Gsc	B		T Sc	Sattb+
O Nata Lux De Lumine (Lat & Eng)	Tallis, T. (Arr Lynn)	Na Gsc	M		T Sc	5pt+
O Night Of Holy Memory	Wilson, I	Na Lor	M		T Sc	Satb
O Rejoice Ye Christians Loudly	Bach, J. S.	Na Gsc	B		T Sc	Satb
O Tannenbaum	Na	Na Gsc	B		T Sc	Ttbb
O Thou That Tellest Good Tidings	Handel, G. F.	Na Lor	M		T Sc	Satb
O'er Bethlehem A Star (Polish Carol)	Follett, Charles (Arr)	73 Pro	M		T Sc	2pt+
Of The Father's Love Begotten	Ashfield, Robert	Na Gsc	B		T Sc	Satb+
Of The Father's Love Begotten	Beck, J. (Arr)	76 Bec	M		T Sc	
Oh, Little Child Of Bethlehem	White, Michael	Na Gsc	B		T Sc	Satb
Omnes De Saba Venient	Handl, Jacob	Na Oxf	M		T Sc	Satb
On A Morning Long Ago	Na	Na Gsc	B		T Sc	2eq+
On A Pallet Of Straw	Meyerowitz, Jan	54 Ron	M		T Sc	Ssaa
On Christmas Night, We Laud & Sing	Brahms, J./Goldman (Arr)	76 Pro	M		T Sc	Satb+
On The Way To Bethlehem	Beck, J N	75 Sac	M		T Sc	Sa
On This Fair Night The Angels Sing (Me)	Mendelssohn, F.	75 Gia	M	L	T Sc	Satb
Once A Fair Maiden	Niles, John Jacob	Na Gsc	B		T Sc	Satb+
Once In Royal David's City	Beck, John Ness	75 Sac	M		T Sc	Satb
Once In Royal David's City	Hughes, Robert J.	Na Lor	M		T Sc	Satb
Once In Royal David's City	Na	Na Gsc	B		T Sc	2chor+
One Night So Long Ago	Ehret, Walter	75 Maf	M		T Sc	2pt

CATEGORIZED INDEX

One Star	Weaver	Na Lor	M	T Sc	Satb
Ou Sen Vont Ces Gais Bergers	Five French Noels	Na Gsc	B	T Sc	Satb
Pastores A Belen	Na	Na Gsc	B	T Sc	Satb+
Pastores, Dicite, Quidnam Vidistis?	Morales, Cristobal De	Na Gsc	B	T Sc	Satb
Peaceful Eve So Still & Holy (E)	Andrews, Carroll T.	76 Gia	M	L T Sc	2pt+
Planets, Stars And Airs Of Space	Bach, J. S.	Na Gsc	B	T Sc	Satb+
Praise And Elation	Scott, T. (Arr)	76 Bec	M	T Sc	
Prelude On Psalms	Bach, J. S.	Na Gsc	B	T Sc	Full
Prince Of Peace Is Born Today	Auerbach	75 Her	M	T Sc	Ssa
Pro Adventus & Post Nativitatem Dom	Byrd, William	Na Kal	B	T Sc	Satb
Pro Nobis Puer Natus Est	Jones	75 Sac	M	T Sc	Satb
Promise Fulfilled, The	Carter, J. (Arr)	76 Bec	M	T Sc	
Puer Natus Est Nobis	Morales, Cristobal De	67 Bbl	M	T Sc	Sab
Puer Nobis Nascitur (In 19 Rounds)	Massie–Tortolano	75 Gia	B	L T Sc	2pt
Pueri Concinite	Gallus, J/Jacob, H	Na Gsc	B	T Sc	Ssaa
Qonswe Od Qonswea	Peterson, John W.	Na Zon	M	T Sc	Satb
Quem Vidistis, Pastores?	Na	Na Gsc	B	T Sc	6mix
Quiet Carol, The (German)	Na	Na Lor	M	T Sc	
Redeemer Shall Come, The	Hegarty, David H	Na Lor	M	T Sc	
Rejoice And Sing	Bach, J. S.	Na Gsc	B	T Sc	Satb+
Rejoice, For Christ Is Born!	Martin	Na Lor	M	T Sc	
Rejoice, Give Thanks And Sing	Jothen, M.	76 Bec	M	T Sc	
Rejoice, Our Lord Is Born	Okolo/Kulaks, A	Na Lor	M	T Sc	
Rejoice, The Lord Is King	Wilson	Na Lor	M	T Sc	
Ring Out Wild Bells	Gounod, Charles	Na Gsc	B	T Sc	Full+
Ring The Bells	Bollbach/Decou	Na Zon	M	T Sc	Satb
Ring The Bells (East)	Bollbach/Rasley	Na Zon	M	T Sc	Sa(Tb)
Ring, Bells, O Ring	Snogren/Johnson	Na Zon	M	T Sc	Satb
Rise Up, Shepherd	Kennedy	75 Maf	M	T Sc	Satb
Rise Up, Shepherd, And Follow	Hughes, Robert J.	Na Lor	M	T Sc	
Russian Christmas Hymn	Ippolitov–Ivanov, M	Na Gsc	B	T Sc	Full
See That Babe In The Lowly Manger	Ryder, Noah F	Na Gsc	B	T Sc	Ttbb
Seven French Noels	Carroll, J. R.	72 Gia	B	T Sc	Var+
Shadow Scenes Of The Saviour's Birth	Rains, Dorothy Best	Na Zon		T Sc	
Shepherd, Hark	Takacs, Jeno	Na Gsc	B	T Sc	Satb
Shepherd's Nativity Song, The	Shenk	75 Maf	M	T Sc	Satb
Shepherds In The Field	Obenshain	Na Lor	M	T Sc	Satb
Shepherds Tell Your Wondrous Story	Graham	76 Abi	M	T Sc	Sab
Shepherds' Carol, The	Pugh	Na Lor	M	T Sc	Satb
Silent Night	Baker	75 Sac	M	T Sc	Satb
Silent Night	Filers, Joyce	75 Maf	M	T Sc	Satb
Silent Night	Gruber/Gruber	Na Lor	M	T Sc	Var
Silent Night (Full, Original Arr)	Gruber, F.–Track, G.	73 Aug	M	T Sc	
Silent Night (4–Part Arr)	Cirou, Joseph Et Al	73 Acp		L T Sc	
Silent Night Holy Night	Gruber/Decou	Na Zon	M	T Sc	Satb
Silesian Lullaby	Meyerowitz, Jan (Ed)	57 Ron	M	T Sc	Satb
Sing A Song Of Christmas	Henson, Jack E.	70 Dis	M	R L T Sc	
Sing Alleluiah Christ Is Born	Dretke, Leora	Na Gsc	B	T Sc	Var
Sing Glory Hallelujah	Lona	Na Lor	M	T Sc	
Sing Joy!	Graham, Robert	75 Sac	M	T Sc	Sa
Sing Noel, Merry Noel	Stainer, Sir John	Na Gsc	B	T Sc	Satb
Sing Praises To Our King	Morgan	Na Lor	M	T Sc	
Sing We All Noel	Strickling	76 Abi	B	T Sc	+Bell
Sing We Now Of Christmas	Wilson	Na Lor	M	T Sc	Sa
Sing We The Virgin Mary	Niles, John Jacob	Na Gsc	B	T Sc	Satb
Sing We To Christ The King	Chaplin, M W	Na Gsc	B	T Sc	Satb+
Sing With Wonder And Delight	Graham	Na Lor	M	T Sc	
Sing Ye Nowell!	Jothen, M.	75 Bec	M	T Sc	
Sing, O Heavens	Tours, B.	Na Gsc	B	T Sc	Satb
Sing, Sing For Christmas	Miller	Na Lor	M	T Sc	
Sing, This Blessed Morn.	Van Dyke, Paul C.	Na Gsc	B	T Sc	Satb+
Sir Christmas	Bonta, Stephen	Na Gsc	B	T Sc	Ttbb+
Sleep In Peace, O Heavenly Child	Haydn, Michael	Na Gsc	B	T Sc	Satb+
Sleep My Little One	Lynn, George	55 Smc	M	T Sc	Satb
Sleep Of The Child Jesus	Gevaert, F A	Na Lor	M	T Sc	
Sleep Well, Thou Lovely Heavenly Babe	Ehret, Walter	73 Gia	M	T Sc	Sa+
Sleep, Holy Babe	Matthews, H A	Na Gsc	B	T Sc	Var+
Sleep, Little Jesus	Blanchard	75 Sac	M	T Sc	Satb
Sleep, Little Lord	White, Michael	Na Gsc	B	T Sc	2eq
Sleep, My Jesus, Sleep	Coggin (Arr)	75 Pro	M	T Sc	Satb+
Sleep, My Savior, Sleep	Traditional/Rasley	Na Zon	M	T Sc	Satb
Slumber, O Holy Jesu	Wood, Dale	76 Sac		T Sc	Satbu+
Snow Lay On The Ground, The	Na	Na Lor	M	T Sc	
Softly The Winds Blew (Polish Carol)	Coggin, Elwood (Arr)	73 Pro	M	T Sc	Sab
Song From St. Matthew	Kettering, E L	Na Gsc	B	T Sc	2pt
Song Of The Angels	Denton	Na Lor	M	T Sc	
Song Of The Angels, The	Hughes, Robert J.	Na Lor	M	T Sc	
Song That The Angels Sang, The	Soechtig	Na Lor	M	T Sc	Sab
Star In The East	Niles, John Jacob	Na Gsc	B	T Sc	3pt
Star In The Night, A	Martens	Na Lor	M	T Sc	Satb
Star Of Bethlehem, Op 164 Eng	Rheinberger	Na Kal	B	T Sc	Satb
Star Of The East	Kennedy	Na Lor	M	T Sc	Satb
Star Of The Orient	Shelley, H R	Na Gsc	B	T Sc	Satb+
Star, A Shepherd, A Lamb, A	Shure	Na Lor	M	T Sc	Satb
Stars Shone Bright, The (Norwegian)	Na	Na Lor	M	T Sc	Unis
Stephen Was A Stable–Boy	Na	Na Gsc	B	T Sc	Unis+
Still, Still (Arr)	Track, Gerhard	69 Gia	M	T Sc	Var+
Sweet Little Boy Jesus	Niles, John Jacob	Na Gsc	B	T Sc	Var
Sweet Marie And Her Baby	Niles, John Jacob	Na Gsc	B	T Sc	Var
Sweet Was The Song	Britten, Benjamin	Na Gsc	B	T Sc	Ssaa
Sweet Was The Song (W/Solo)	Jankins	Cfs	M	T Sc	Satb
Symphonia Sacra: Mein Sohn, Warum	Schutz, Heinrich	Na Oxf	B	T Sc	Satb
That Beautiful Name	Camp/Decou	Na Zon	M	T Sc	Satb
That Holy Night	Hughes, Robert J.	Na Lor	M	T Sc	Satb
The Angel's Carol	Billings, William	Cfp		R T Sc	Satbb
The Angel's Song	Cornell	73 Aug	M	T Sc	Sa
The Angels And The Shepherds	Howorth, Wayne	Na Her	M	T Sc	Satb
The Angels And The Shepherds	Riedel	Na Gsc	B	T Sc	Full
The Angels Song	Grieb	Na Gsc	B	T Sc	Satb+
The Babe	Wasner	Na Gsc	B	T Sc	Satb

The Bells Of Heaven	Niles, John Jacob	Na Gsc	B	T Sc	Satb
The Bells Ring Out For Christmas	Sacco, John	Na Gsc	B	T Sc	Var+
The Birth Of Our Lord And Saviour	Schutz, Heinrich	Na Gsc	B	T Sc	Satb+
The Birthday Of A King	Neidlinger, W H	Na Gsc	B	T Sc	Var+
The Blessed Bird	Niles, John Jacob	Na Gsc	B	T Sc	Var+
The Boys' Carol	Na	Na Gsc	B	T Sc	Unis+
The Carol Of The Angels	Niles, John Jacob	Na Gsc	B	T Sc	Var
The Carol Of The Birds	Niles, John Jacob	Na Gsc	B	T Sc	Var
The Child Of Love	Grimm, Johann D.	72 Aug	M	T Sc	Satb
The Christ–Childs Lullaby	Na	Na Gsc	B	T Sc	Satb+
The Christmas Nightingale	Wasner, Franz	Na Gsc	B	T Sc	Ssa+
The Christmas Symbol	Christiansen, F. M.	47 Aug	M	T Sc	Satb
The Cradle	Christiansen, P.	50 Aug	M	T Sc	Satb
The Cuckoo Carol	Na	Na Gsc	B	T Sc	Ssaa
The Dove	Licht, Myrtha B	Na Gsc	B	T Sc	2eq+
The Eastern Heavens Are All Aglow	Edwards, Clara	Na Gsc	B	T Sc	Var
The First Christmas	Dougherty, Celius	Na Gsc	B	T Sc	Ttbb
The First Christmas Morn	Mozart, Wolfgang A	Na Gsc	B	T Sc	2eq+
The First Noel	Na	Na Gsc	B	T Sc	Ttbb
The Friendly Beasts (Arr)	Ehret, Walter	74 Gia	M	T Sc	Sa+
The Friendly Beasts (Trad Old English)	Na	Na Gsc	B	T Sc	Satb
The Gift Of Christmas	Schirmer, Rudolph	Na Gsc	B	T Sc	Satb+
The Gift Of Christmas Morn	Miller, John	Na Gsc	B	T Sc	Satb+
The Halo	Licht, Myrtha B	Na Gsc	B	T Sc	2eq+
The Holly And The Ivy	Thomson, Virgil	Na Gsc	B	T Sc	Satb
The Holly Carol	Anderson, Ruth	Na Gsc	B	T Sc	Satb
The Holy Child	Brown, E Bouldin	Na Gsc	B	T Sc	Ssa+
The Icy December (Arr)	Track, Gerhard	69 Gia	M	T Sc	Var+
The Infant Christ	Cornelius, Peter	Na Gsc	B	T Sc	Ttbb+
The Innkeeper's Carol	Na	Na Gsc	B	T Sc	Full
The Light Of Bethlehem	Mueller, Carl F	Na Gsc	B	T Sc	Satb+
The Little King	Corbeil, Pierre De	Na Gsc	B	T Sc	Satb
The Lord Said You Are My Son	Scheidt/Tortolano Ed	70 Gia	B	L T Sc	Canon
The Lute–Book Lullaby	Martin, Gilbert M.	76 Sac		T Sc	Satb+
The Magic Morning	White, Michael	Na Gsc	B	T Sc	Satb
The Morning Star	Praetorius, M	Na Gsc	B	T Sc	Var
The Nativity	Niles, John Jacob	Na Gsc	B	T Sc	Var+
The Newborn Babe	Buxtehude, D.	Na Kal	B	T Sc	Satb
The Oxen. A Carol	Britten, Benjamin	Na Gsc	B	T Sc	Sa+
The Shepherd On The Hill	Niles, John Jacob	Na Gsc	B	T Sc	Satb+
The Shepherds Saw A Star	Pasquet, Jean	Na Gsc	B	T Sc	2eq+
The Shepherds' Chorus	Menotti, Gian Carlo	Na Gsc	B	T Sc	Var+
The Shepherds' Farewell	Berlioz, Hector	Na Gsc	B	T Sc	Var+
The Silver Bells	White, Michael	Na Gsc	B	T Sc	Satb
The Snow Lay On The Ground	Wetzler, Robert	68 Aug	M	T Sc	Satb
The Snow Lay On The Ground (Me)	Andrews, Carroll T.	76 Gia	M	L T Sc	Satb+
The Song Of The Birds	Millet Arr	Na Gsc	B	T Sc	Ttbb
The Spelling Of Christmas	Sacco, John	Na Gsc	B	T Sc	Var+
The Star Road	O'hara, Geoffrey	Na Gsc	B	T Sc	Satb+
The Sussex Carol	Nasanni	Na Gsc	B	T Sc	Unis+
The Sycamore Tree	Britten, Benjamin	Na Gsc	B	T Sc	Satb
The Three Kings	Cornelius, Peter (Arr)	Na Oxf	M	T Sc	Var
The Three Kings	Na	Na Gsc	B	T Sc	Satb
The Three Kings	Willan, Healey	Na Oxf	M	T Sc	Var
The Three Part Christmas Choir (5932)	Peterson, John W.	Na Zon	B	T Sc	Sab
There Is A Child	Na	Na Gsc	B	T Sc	Satb
There Was A Pig	Na	Na Gsc	B	T Sc	3pt
There Were Shepherds	Vincent, Chas.	Na Gsc	B	T Sc	Satb+
There Were Three Lights	Blake	Na Lor	M	T Sc	Satb
There's A Song In The Air	Harrington/Johnson	Na Zon	M	T Sc	Satb
They Sang That Night In Bethlehem	Schubert, Franz J.	Na Gsc	B	T Sc	Var+
This Christmastide	Snyder	Na Lor	M	T Sc	Satb
This Day	Maconchy, Elizabeth	Na Gsc	B	T Sc	2eq
This Day We Welcome A Little Child	Ehret, Walter	73 Gia	M	T Sc	Sa+
This Glorious Christmas Night	Yes, Huai–Deh	Na Gsc	B	T Sc	Satb
This Holy Day	Grieu, Herbert	Na Gsc	B	T Sc	Satb+
This Is The Birthday Of The Lord	Douglas (Arr)	75 Pro	M	T Sc	Ssa+
This Is The Day When Christ Was Born	Andrews, Carroll T.	68 Gia	M	T Sc	Var+
Three Bell Carols For Junior Choirs	Hadler	Na Lor	M	T Sc	Unis
Three Early American Christmas Carols	Owens, Barbara	Na Abi	M	T Sc	Satb
Three Kings	Barnes, E S	Na Gsc	B	T Sc	Satb+
Through Midnite Silence (Opt Oboe)	Hardwicke (Arr)	75 Pro	M	T Sc	Sab+
Thy Little Ones Dear Lord Are We	Track, Gerhard	70 Gia	M	T Sc	Var+
Tis Noel Again!	Follett (Arr)	76 Pro	M	T Sc	Ssa
To The Town Of Bethlehem	Peloquin, C Alexander	Na Gia		T Sc	
To Us A Child Is Given (Cantata)	Bach, J. S.	75 Lps	B R	T Sc	Satb
To Us Is Born (W/Bells)	Praetorius	Na Abi	M	T Sc	Sab
To Us Is Born Immanuel	Praetorius, M	Na Gsc	B	T Sc	Satb
Tous Les Bourgeois De Chastres	Five French Noels	Na Gsc	B	T Sc	Satb
Traditional German Carol	Susanni	Na Gsc	B	T Sc	Satb
Twas In The Moon Of Wintertime	Ehret, Walter	74 Gia	M	T Sc	Sab+
Two Carols	Miller, M R	Na Gia		T Sc	
Two Motets From Kancjonaxy	Herter, J	74 Gia	M	T Sc	Satb
Ukrainian Bell Carol	Leontovich, M	Na Lor	M	T Sc	Var
Unto Us A Boy Is Born	Na	Na Gsc	B	T Sc	Satb+
Vamos Al Portal	Guerrero, Francisco	Na Gsc	B	T Sc	Ssatb
Venite Adoremus	Young, Gordon	75 Sac	M	T Sc	
Verbum Caro Factum Est	Hassler, H L	Na Gsc	B	T Sc	6mix
Verbum Patris Humanatur	Na	Na Gsc	B	T Sc	Var
Videntes Stellam (Md)	Palestrina, Giovanni P	Na Oxf	M	T Sc	Full
Vidimus Stellam	Krenek, Ernst	67 Ron	B	T Sc	Ssa
Virga Jesse Floruit (Lat)	Bruckner, Anton	Cfp	R	T Sc	Satb+
Voices Of The Sky	Matthews, H A	Na Gsc	B	T Sc	Ssa+
Von Himmel Hoch (In 5 Carols) Me	Bainton–Luther–Laberge	74 Gia	B	L T Sc	Satb+
Vox In Rama (E & L) (M)	Zielenski, Mikolaj	Na Gia	M	L T Sc	Lsatb
Wake Awake For Night Is Flying	Buxtehude, D.	67 Aug	M	T Sc	Sab+
Wake, Awake	Nicolai–Christiansen	25 Aug	M	T Sc	Satb
Wake, Awake (W/Str Bass)	Carlson	74 Aug	M	T Sc	Satb+
Wake, O Shepherds (W/Violin)	Rameau–Nelson	67 Aug	M	T Sc	Unis+
Wake, O Wake (Wachet Auf) (Me)	Bach, J.S. (Arr)	Na Oxf	M	T Sc	Satb

CATEGORIZED INDEX

Wake, Ye Shepherds	Na	Na Gsc	B	T Sc	Satb+
Waken, Little Shepherd	Niles, John Jacob	Na Gsc	B	T Sc	Satb
We Have Been A-Rambling	Na	Na Gsc	B	T Sc	Ssa
We Sing In Celebration	Cornell, G.	76 Bec	M	T Sc	
We Three Kings	Tower, A Wesley	Na Abi	M	T Sc	Full
We Three Kings Of Orient Are	Hopkins-Nightingale	Cfs	M	T Sc	Satb
Welcome Son Of Mary	Gannon, Michael	61 Wlp	B	T Sc	
Westminster Carol	Wilson	Na Lor	M	T Sc	
What Can I Give Him?	Emery	Na Lor	M	T Sc	
What Can I Give Him?	Rasley	Na Lor	M	T Sc	
What Child Is This?	English	Na Lor	M	T Sc	
What Child Is This?	Fenstermaker, John	75 Maf	M	T Sc	Satb
What Child Is This?	Hughes, Robert J.	Na Lor	M	T Sc	
What Child Is This?	Na	Na Gsc	B	T Sc	Full
What Child Is This?	Ruggles	71 Aug	M	T Sc	Satb+
What Child Is This?	Traditional/Johnson	Na Zon	M	T Sc	Satb
What Child Is This?	Wilson	Na Lor	M	T Sc	
What Child Is This? (W/Perc)	Young, C.	75 Aug	M	T Sc	Satb+
What Is This Pleasant Fragrance?	Na	Na Gsc	B	T Sc	Satb
What Shall We Give	Na	Na Gsc	B	T Sc	Satb
What Songs Were Sung	Niles, John Jacob	Na Gsc	B	T Sc	Satb
What Star Is This?	Traditional/Johnson	Na Zon	M	T Sc	Satb
What You Gonna Call Yo Pretty Little	Ryder, Noah F	Na Gsc	B	T Sc	Ttbb
When Christ Was Born Of Mary Free	Na	Na Gsc	B	T Sc	Var
When Christmas Morn Is Dawning	Luvas	52 Aug	M	T Sc	Satb
When Jesus Left His Father's Throne	Johnson, D.	65 Aug	M	T Sc	Ssa
When Jesus Lived In Galilee	Niles, John Jacob	Na Gsc	B	T Sc	3eq
When Love Was Born	Traditional/Rasley	Na Zon	M	T Sc	Satb
When The Lord Was Born	Peloquin, C Alexander	Na Gia	·	T Sc	
Whence Art Thou My Maiden? (Arr)	Track, Gerhard	72 Gia	M	T Sc	Var+
While Angels Sing	Christiansen, P.	55 Aug	M	T Sc	Satb
While By My Sheep	Cassler, G. W.	60 Aug	M	T Sc	Sa
While By My Sheep	Na	Na Gsc	B	T Sc	Satb
While By Our Sheep	Traditional/Johnson	Na Zon	M	T Sc	Satb
While I Did Watch My Sheep	Christy (Arr)	39 Gsc	M	T Sc	Full
While Shepherds Watch'd Their Flocks	Read, Daniel	76 Bbl	M	T Sc	Satb
While Shepherds Watched	Lockwood, Normand(Arr)	55 Smc	M	T Sc	Satb
While Shepherds Watched Their Flocks	Praetorius, M	Na Gsc	B	T Sc	Ttbb
Who Will Come To Bethlehem?	Na	Na Gsc	B	T Sc	Var+
Why Rage Fiercely The Heathen	Mendelssohn, F.	Na Aug	M	T Sc	Full
Winds Through The Olive Trees	Rees	Na Lor	M	T Sc	
Wise Men Still Seek Him	Peterson, John W.	Na Zon	M	T Sc	Satb
Wonder Of The Ages, The	Hughes, Robert J.	Na Lor	M	T Sc	
Wondrous Cross, The	Lorenz	Na Lor	M	T Sc	
Worship The Christ-Child	Ball	Na Lor	M	T Sc	
Ya Viene La Vieja	Na	Na Gsc	B	T Sc	Satb
Ye Shepherds, Ye Wise Men! (Opt Flute)	Hardwicke (Arr)	75 Pro	M	T Sc	Ssa+

Lenten Hymns and Psalms

The lenten music listed here includes penitential psalms, psalms of sorrow and repentence, and music for Passiontide (Holy Week). Churches that do not celebrate the days before Easter Sunday will also find hymns about the Crucifixion in this section. See also Hymns of Peace and Reconciliation (TR).

Devil, Devil Go Away	Spencer, Hal	70 Man	R	C Sl	
Fifty Just Men	Temple, Sebastian	69 Fcc	R L	C Sl	
Forbidden Fruit	Temple, Sebastian	69 Fcc	R L	C Sl	
Little Black Sheep	Hamblen Stuart	Na Ham		C Sl	
Rainy Day Song	Comeau, Bill	67 Van	B R	C Sl	
A Lenten Folk Song	Yantis, David	Na Yan	B	F Sl	
A Sky Without Sunlight	Thiem, James	66 Fel	B	F Sl	
All My Trials	Lojeski, Ed (Arr.)	74 Hal		F Sl	Satb
American Genesis (Reconciliation)	Montague, George T.	72 Mcc	B R L	F Sl	+Pian
Ballad Of The Prodigal Son	Winter, Miriam T.	67 Van	B R	F Sl	
Ballad Of The Women	Winter, Miriam T.	71 Van	B R	F Sl	
Be Consoled My People	Parker, Tom	66 Wlp	B	F Sl	
Believe And Repent	Meltz, Ken	72 Wlp	B	F Sl	
Born To Die	Fischer, John	69 Fel	B R	F Sl	
Bring On	Miffleton, Jack	71 Wlp	B	F Sl	
But As For Me, God Forbid (Gal 6:14)	Murphy, Charles	69 Gia	B R L	F Sl	
By The Streams Of Babylon	Cunningham, Patrick	69 Gia	B R L	F Sl	Mcc
By The Streams Of Babylon	Hurd, Bob	73 Fel	B R	F Sl	
Come And Rescue Me	Cunningham, Patrick	68 Fel	B R	F Sl	
Complete Love	Yantis, David	Na Yan	B	F Sl	
Create In Me A Clean Heart Willing	Yantis, David	Na Yan	B	F Sl	
Dark/Light	Wyrtzen, Don	Na Zon	M	F Sl	Satb
Death In The City	Fischer, John	69 Fel	B R	F Sl	
Ezekiel	Montague, George T.	68 Fel	B R	F Sl	
Faithful Cross	Mitchell, Ian	65 Fel	B R	F Sl	
Father, Thy Will Be Done	Winter, Miriam T.	68 Van	B R	F Sl	
Go To Dark Gethsemane	Johnson, Gary L.	74 Bfi	B L	F Sl	
Handful Of Clay	Wilkey, Terrence	73 Fel	B	F Sl	
Hard Time Smiling	Bisignano/Furman	71 Wlp	B R	F Sl	
Hear My Call	Winter, Miriam T.	71 Van	B R	F Sl	
Hear, O Lord	Repp, Ray	66 Fel	B R	F Sl	
Help Me Know The Way	Quinlan, Paul	65 Wlp	B R	F Sl	
How I Have Longed	Winter, Miriam T.	66 Van	B R	F Sl	
How Long O Lord	Quinlan, Paul	65 Wlp	B R	F Sl	
Howl My Soul	Winter, Miriam T.	66 Van	B R	F Sl	
I Am The Way (4-Part Arr)	Silvia, Helen	73 Acp	L	F Sl	
I Built A Garden	Winter, Miriam T.	68 Van	B R	F Sl	
If Only You'll Answer Me	Montague, George T.	68 Fel	B R	F Sl	
Into Your Hands	Repp, Ray	67 Fel	B R	F Sl	
It Is Not Too Late	Mccarthy, John	70 Van	B R	F Sl	
Jerusalem	Germaine	66 Fel	B R	F Sl	
Jerusalem	Stewart, Malcolm	69 Van	B R	F Sl	
Jesus Took My Sins Away	Adams/Krogstad	75 Zon	M	F Sl	2-Pt

Job's Story	Johnson, Gary L.	75 Bfi	B R	F Sl	
Judas Iscariot	Ylvisaker, J. & A.	69 Van	B R	F Sl	
Judas, Why?	Mccarthy, John	70 Van	B R	F Sl	
Lament	Mudd, C. P.	70 Wlp	B R	F Sl	
Lamentations	Hurd, Bob	73 Fel	B R	F Sl	
Lamentations	Thiem, James	66 Fel	B	F Sl	
Leaves A-Fallin' (Good Friday)	Belt, Thomas/Batastini	72 Gia	B R L	F Sl	Var+
Lonely Days	Wood, Mike/Zettler, M.	76 Rpb	M B R L	F Sl	
Look At Jesus	Temple, Sebastian	71 Gia	B R L	F Sl	Ar+
Lord Give Me A Heart Of Flesh	Wise, Joe	71 Wlp	B R	F Sl	
Lost-But Still He Loves You	Peterson/Wyrtzen	Na Zon	M	F Sl	Satb
Love Is Almost Worth The Dying	Balhoff, Mike & Ducote	70 Fel	B R	F Sl	
Lower Your Eyes	Cockett, M/Mayhew, K.	69 Van	B R	F Sl	
Many Times I Have Turned	Jabusch, Willard F.	75 Rpb	M B R L	F Sl	
Morning, Mourning	Miller, Dan	73 Fel	B	F Sl	
On The Mount Of Olive Groves	Mccarthy, John	70 Van	B R	F Sl	
On The Willows	Schwartz, Stephen	71 Val	B R	F Sl	
Out Of The Depths (From Come Follow)	Cunningham, Patrick	69 Gia	B R L	F Sl	
Palm Sunday	Ylvisaker, John	69 Van	B R	F Sl	
Pardon Peace	Hunkele	67 Wlp	B	F Sl	
Psalm 130 From The Depths	Quinlan, Paul	66 Fel	B	F Sl	
Psalm 39 When My Heart Was Burning	Quinlan, Paul	66 Fel	B	F Sl	
Psalm 51 Have Mercy, Lord	Quinlan, Paul	66 Fel	B	F Sl	
Recreation (Sin & Penance)	Montague, George T.	72 Mcc	B R L	F Sl	Unis
Rise, O Lord! (From Come Follow)	Murphy, Charles	69 Gia	B R L	F Sl	
Sadness Song	Miller, Dan	73 Fel	B	F Sl	
Save Me	Quinlan, Paul	65 Wlp	B R	F Sl	
Save Me My God	Parker, Tom	68 Wlp	B R	F Sl	
Sometimes	Miller, Dan	72 Fel	B R	F Sl	
Song Of The Thankful (Come Follow)	Kramper, Jerry	69 Gia	B R L	F Sl	
Sons Of Cain	Fischer, John	70 Fel	B R	F Sl	
Teach Me To Die	Edwards, Deanna	74 Fcc	R L	F Sl	
The Dream Of God	Cunningham, Patrick	68 Fel	B R	F Sl	
The Father Had But One Son	Germaine	66 Fel	B R	F Sl	
The Lord Of The Dance	Carter	63 Gal		F Sl	
The Reproaches (Prophecy)	Cunningham, Patrick	72 Gra	B R L	F Sl	Solo
The Road I'm On	Kostos, Patti	66 Fel	B	F Sl	
The Stones Will Shout Out	Meyer, Ron	73 Fel	B	F Sl	
There Once Was A Man	Anderson, Clyde	68 Fel	B R	F Sl	
Three Men Died On A Hillside	Mitchell, Ian	66 Fel	B R	F Sl	
Trouble, Lord	Belt, Thomas/Batastini	72 Gia	B R L	F Sl	Var+
Turn Back, O Man	Schwartz, Stephen	71 Val	B R	F Sl	
Up To Jerusalem (Lk 18:3)	Miffleton, Jack	69 Wlp	B R	F Sl	
Way Of All Flesh	Fischer, John	70 Fel	B R	F Sl	
Weep, Little Children, Weep	Hershberg, Sarah	71 Fcc	R L	F Sl	
What Can A Man Say?	Montague, George T.	68 Fel	B R	F Sl	
What Do You Do	Montague, George T.	68 Fel	B R	F Sl	
What Love Have We Denied To The Lord	Gilligan, Michael	67 Acp	L	F Sl	
What Love Have We Denied To The Lord	Silvia, Helen	73 Acp	L	F Sl	
What Then Of Your Soul?	Yantis, David	Na Yan	B	F Sl	
When I Walk Through The Valley	Parker, Tom	68 Wlp	B R	F Sl	
Why Have You Forsaken Me	Finley, Ken	73 Fel	B	F Sl	
Willow Tree	Hershberg, Sarah	71 Fcc	R L	F Sl	
Wondering Why	Furman	71 Wlp	B R	F Sl	
Yet I Believe	Winter, Miriam T.	67 Van	B R	F Sl	

After The Storm	Hendrix, James	Na Gmp	M L	G Sl	Solo
All Things Work Together For Good	Vibbert-Eastman/Estma	69 Gmc	M	G Sl	
And Can It Be?	Barnett	Na Zon	M	G Sl	
At Calvary	Towner/Peterson	Na Zon	M	G Sl	Satb
At The Foot Of The Cross	Oldham/Gaither	64 Gmc	M R	G Sl	
Behind The Shadows	Owens, J & Hopkins, Mrs.	60 Man	M	G Sl	
Between The Cross And Heaven	Gaither/Gaither B/G	75 Gmc	M R	G Sl	
Beyond The Cross	Mieir, Audrey	58 Man	M B	G Sl	
Blessed Calvary	Latham/Decou	Na Zon	M	G Sl	Satb
Blood Upon Your Hands	Hamblen Stuart	Na Ham	M	G Sl	
Burdens Are Lifted At Calvary	Moore/Decou	Na Zon	M	G Sl	Satb
But For The Grace Of God	Hamblen Stuart	Na Ham	M	G Sl	
By Grace	Mieir, Audrey	59 Man	M B	G Sl	
Calvary	Culross, David	75 Zon	M	G Sl	Satb
Calvary	Gaither/Gaither	63 Gmc	B	G Sl	Satb
Calvary	Shaw, Robert Arr	Na Gsc	B	G Sl	Satb
Calvary Love	Hughes/Decou	Na Zon	M	G Sl	Satb
Christians Tribulation	Redd/Hubbard/Merriwea	Na Sav	M	G Sl	
Condemned	Mieir, Audrey	58 Man	M	G Sl	
Do You Care?	Lucht	Na Zon	M	G Sl	
Forever Gone	Mieir, Audrey	72 Man	B	G Sl	
Forgive My Lord	Floria, C.	74 Wrd	B	G Sl	Satb+
Get On The Right Road	Ohler, Susan	73 Pmp	M B R L	G Sl	
Hallelujah For The Cross	Mcgranahan/Johnson	Na Zon	M	G Sl	Ssatb
Hallelujah I Love Him (W/Piano)	Angell, W.M.	76 Wrd	M	G Sl	Satb+
Have You Had A Gethsemane?	Gaither-R.Allen	62 Gmc	M B R	G Sl	Satb
He Bought My Soul At Calvary	Hamblen Stuart	Na Ham	M	G Sl	
He Brought Me Out	Gilmour/Kirk	Na Zon	M	G Sl	Satb
He Didn't Have To Do It	Na	Na Gmc	R	G Sl	
He Never Said A Mumblin' Word	Smith	Na Lor	M	G Sl	Satb
He Said He Would Deliver Me	Redd, Gc/R.Merriw.	Na Sav	M	G Sl	
Help Me Speedily	Mieir, Audrey	72 Man	B R	G Sl	
Here Comes Jesus	Salisbury, Sonny	71 Wrd	M R	G Sl	
His Hands	Hamblen Stuart	Na Ham	M	G Sl	
His Nail-Pierced Hands	Hatfield, Steve & Mcnee	74 Man	R	G Sl	
Holy Hands	Farrer, Carl	50 Man	M	G Sl	
How Much He Cared	Mieir, Audrey	65 Man	B	G Sl	
How Much He Cares	Calkin, Ruth H.	64 Man	M	G Sl	
I Believe In A Hill Called Mt. Calvary	Gaither, D.Oldham	68 Gmc	M B R	G Sl	Var
I Believe That Jesus Died For Me	Dunlop, Merrill	Na Zon	M	G Sl	Satb
I Find No Fault In Him	Crouch, Andrae	66 Man	M B R	G Sl	
I Know, They're Gone	Newman/Huntley	Na Zon	M	G Sl	
I Wish That I Had Been There	Redd, G.C./H. Hubbard	Na Sav	M	G Sl	
I Wonder How It Felt	Gaither/Gaither B/G	74 Gmc	M B R	G Sl	Var

CATEGORIZED INDEX

Title	Composer	Yr Pub	Codes	Voicing
I'll Never Be Lonely	Mieir, Audrey	57 Man	M B R G SI	
I've Been To Calvary	Gaither/Gaither	60 Gmc	M B R G SI	Satb
It Is Finished	Gaither/Gaither B/G	76 Gmc	M R G SI	
Jesus Died	Hubbard, H./G.C. Redd	Na Sav	M G SI	
Jesus Prayed As They Slept	Hendrix, James	Na Gmp	M R L G SI	
Joy Of A Sinner Set Free, The	Rogers/Harper	Na Zon	M G SI	
Just A Wayward Lamb	Rramon/Decou	Na Zon	M G SI	Satb
Keep Me At The Foot Of The Cross	Mieir, Audrey	68 Man	B G SI	
Known Only To Him	Hamblen Stuart	Na Ham	M G SI	
Lay Your Burden Down	Girard, Chuck	74 Wrd	B R G SI	Unis+
Let My Heart Be Broken	Mieir, Audrey	72 Man	B R G SI	
Lift Up Jesus	Gaither/Gaither B/G	76 Gmc	M R G SI	
Linger A Little Longer	Mieir, Audrey	64 Man	B G SI	
Lone Calvary	Myring, Charles	72 Jhm	M L G SI	
Lonely	Smith, Gloria Jean	75 Man	R G SI	
Look To The Lamb Of God	Black/Mercer	Na Zon	M G SI	Satb
Lost In The Night	Peterson, John W.	Na Zon	M G SI	Satb
My Sins Are Blotted Out, I Know	Dunlop/Carmichael	Na Zon	M G SI	Satb
My Sins Are Blotted Out, I Know	Dunlop/Ferrin	Na Zon	M G SI	Satb
My Sins Are Gone	Vandall/Decou	Na Zon	M G SI	Sab
Never In A Million Years	Peterson, John W.	Na Zon	M G SI	Satb
No Dark Valleys	Chitwood, Joe	70 Man	M G SI	
Not All Of Those Who Say Lord, Lord	Greif, Jean A	76 Vrn	M L G SI	
Oh, He's A Wonderful Savior	Peterson/Carmichael	Na Zon	M G SI	Satb
Old Book And The Old Faith, The	Carr/Decou	Na Zon	M G SI	Satb
On The Cross	Carlson	Na Zon	M G SI	
Overshadowed (A Cap)	Ironside/Schuler/Carmi	35 Wrd	B R G SI	Full
Part The Waters (W/Piano)	Brown, C.F.	75 Wrd	M G SI	Satb+
Precious Crimson Fountain	Cram, Fisk	73 Mam	R L G SI	
Pretty Me Up On The Inside Lord	Androzzo A Bazel	Na Ham	M G SI	
Rally Round The Cross	Harper, Redd	Na Zon	M G SI	
Redeemed	Herring, J.	76 Sil	R G SI	
Redeemed	Kirkpatrick/Mercer	Na Zon	M G SI	Satb
Redeeming Love	Gaither/Gaither, G.	63 Gmc	M B R G SI	Var
Redeeming Love	Gaither, William J	Na Lor	M G SI	Satb
Return Again	Mieir, Audrey	75 Man	B G SI	
Saved, Saved	Scholfield/Carmichael	Na Zon	M G SI	Satb
Sin's Darkest Valley	Butler, Dorothy	68 Pmp	M B R L G SI	
Sometimes	Smith/Harper	Na Zon	M G SI	
Song Of Job (From Come Follow)	Murphy, Charles	69 Gia	B R L G SI	
Song Of The Prodigal	Spencer, Glenn	56 Man	M B G SI	
Sunday School Sinner	Laney E, C. Angus Beth	74 Jhm	R L G SI	
Teach Me, Lord, To Wait	Hamblen Stuart	Na Ham	M G SI	
Temptation	Mieir, Audrey	72 Man	B R G SI	
Thanks To Calvary	Gaither/Gaither B/G	69 Gmc	M B R G SI	Satb
That Lonesome Valley	Hamblen Stuart	Na Ham	M G SI	
The Broken Vessel	Crouch, Andrae	68 Man	M B R G SI	
The Christ Of Every Crisis	Gaither/Gaither B/G	62 Gmc	M B R G SI	Satb
The Old Rugged Cross Made	Gaither/Gaither B/G	70 Gmc	M B R G SI	Satb
The Via Dolorosa	Lee, Johnnie	71 Mmc	M R G SI	
There Is No Future In Gaining	Overstreet, Rev. L.	69 Sto	G SI	
There Is No Greater Love	Peterson/Draper	Na Zon	M G SI	Sab
They That Sow In Tears	Gaither/Gaither B/G	64 Gmc	M B R G SI	Satb
They That Sow In Tears	Gaither, William J	Na Lor	M G SI	Satb
Tho' Autumn's Coming On	Hamblen Stuart	Na Ham	M G SI	
Through My Tears	Gaither/Gaither B/G	64 Gmc	B R G SI	Satb
Thy Cross	Childs	Na Zon	M G SI	
Time Stood Still On Calvary's Hill	Mieir, Audrey	75 Man	B G SI	
Trouble	Akers, Doris	58 Man	M B R G SI	
Wayfaring Stranger, The	Traditional/Johnson	Na Zon	M G SI	Satb
Were You There	Gentemann, Sr. Elaine	48 Smc	M G SI	Ssa
Were You There?	Goodell (Arr)	Hof	M G SI	Sab
Were You There?	Spiritual/Decou	Na Zon	G SI	Satb
Were You There? (No 4014)	Grant, Don	Na Zon	G SI	Satb+
Were You There? (Spiritual)	Na	Na Lor	M G SI	Var
What Makes A Man Turn His Back On God	Crouch, Andrae	68 Man	B R G SI	
When I Think Of Calvary	Gaither/Gaither	62 Gmc	M B R G SI	Satb
Where Were You Going	Redd, Gc/H.Hubbard	Na Sav	M G SI	
Whispering Hope (A Cap)	Hawthorne, Alice	75 Wrd	M G SI	Full
Will I Have To Pay	Powers James	73 Jhm	L G SI	
Yes, He Did	Spiritual/Decou	Na Zon	M G SI	Sab
You Ought To Walk Right	Duncan, Leo	56 Man	B G SI	

Title	Composer	Yr Pub	Codes	Voicing
A Prayer Of Supplication (Me)	Noble, J. & Hopson, H.	75 Gia	M L L SI	Satb
A Service Of Shadows	Smith, Lani	75 Sac	M B L SI	Satb+
Above My Adversaries	Fitzpatrick, Dennis	65 Fel	B L SI	
Adoramus Te, Christe (A Cap)	Di Lasso, Orlano	Na Abi	M L SI	Ssa
Alas! And Did My Savior Bleed (Me)	Ehret, Walter	76 Gia	M L L SI	Satb+
Alas, And Did My Savior Bleed	Hughes, Robert J.	Na Lor	M L SI	Satb
All Alone	Butler, Charles Franci	75 Mar	R L L SI	
All My Enemies Shall Fall Back	Fitzpatrick, Dennis	65 Fel	B L SI	
All The Way Down (Jonah 2)	Merton, T./Peloquin C A	68 Gia	B L L SI	Satb+
Alone In The Garden	Wilson, I	Na Lor	M L SI	Ssa
And Did'st Thou Love The Race (Me)	Brown, Allanson G. Y.	Na Oxf	M L SI	Unis
Antiphons For Holy Week	Twynham, R. F.	65 Lit	B L SI	
Arise, O Lord, And Defend Me	Fitzpatrick, Dennis	65 Fel	B L SI	
Arise, O Lord, And Help Us	Fitzpatrick, Dennis	65 Fel	B L SI	
Away They Went With Weeping	Cavnar, James	74 Wgm	B L L SI	
Be Not Far From Me	Zingarelli, N	Na Lor	M L SI	
Behold The Crucified!	Carmony	Na Lor	M L SI	
Behold The Savior Of Mankind	Gibbs	Na Abi	M L SI	
Behold The Sorrow Of The Lord	Graham, Robert	Na Abi	M L SI	Satb
Beneath The Cross Of Jesus	Rasley	Na Lor	M L SI	
Beneath The Cross Of Jesus	Wilson	Na Lor	M L SI	Satb
Big City Blues	Stipe, Thomas Richard	73 Mar	R L L SI	
Blessed Is He That Comes	Cram	75 Sac	M L SI	Satb
Blessed Is The Man Who Has Endured	Fitzpatrick, Dennis	65 Fel	B L SI	
Bow My Head, O Lord	Lekberg, Sven	Na Gsc	B L SI	Full
By The Babylonian Rivers	Bash/Laycock	71 Gsc	M B L L SI	
By The Rivers Of Babylon	Fitzpatrick, Dennis	65 Fel	B L SI	
By The Streams Of Babylon	Hughes, Howard	75 Wlp	M L SI	Satb+
By The Waters Of Babylon (Piano)	Fletcher, Grant	75 Wlp	M L SI	Ssa+
By The Wood Of The Cross	Fitzpatrick, Dennis	65 Fel	B L SI	
Can't Work Your Way To Heaven	Fong, Preston Bing	75 Mar	R L L SI	
Cantata De Semana Santa	Csonka, Paul	70 Pic	M L SI	
Christ Died For Our Sins	Zsigray, Joe	72 Nal	B R L SI	
Christ, For Our Sake	Fitzpatrick, Dennis	65 Fel	B L SI	
Cinco Invocaciones Al Crucificado	Montsalvatge, Xavier	72 Som	M L SI	
Come Save Me, Lord	Gilligan, Michael	67 Acp	L L SI	
Complete Holy Week Services (Chant)	Bauman/Batastini	71 Gia	B L L SI	Var+
Consider, Lord	Thomson, Virgil	62 Som	M L SI	
Cross Was His Own, The	Heller	Na Lor	M L SI	Satb
Crucifixion (Long)	Zimmermann	69 Aug	M L SI	
Darkness Was Over All	Vittoria, Tomas L. De	66 Som	M L SI	
Deep In The Boding Night	Ferguson	75 Sac	M L SI	Satb
Defend My Cause, My God	Fitzpatrick, Dennis	65 Fel	B L SI	
Deliver Me, Lord, From Evil Men	Fitzpatrick, Dennis	65 Fel	B L SI	
Did Jesus Weep For Me?	Wilson	Na Lor	M L SI	Satb
Do Not Forsake Me, O Lord	Fitzpatrick, Dennis	65 Fel	B L SI	
Do Not Give Me Up, O Lord	Fitzpatrick, Dennis	65 Fel	B L SI	
Do You Feel The Change	Angle, Dana P	75 Mar	R L L SI	
Dried Up Well	Fong, Preston Bing	75 Mar	R L L SI	
Drop, Drop Slow Tears (A Cap)	Green, Russell	74 Hwg	M L SI	Satb
Drop, Drop, Slow Tears	Lapo, Cecil E.	Na Abi	M L SI	Unis
Earthen Vessels	Foley, John, S. J.	75 Nal	B R L SI	
Earthquake (Isaiah 52)	Merton, T./Peloquin C A	68 Gia	B L L SI	Satb+
Even Though I Am Tormented	Fitzpatrick, Dennis	65 Fel	B L SI	
Father, If This Cup	Fitzpatrick, Dennis	65 Fel	B L SI	
Father, O Hear Me	Strickling, George F.	Na Abi	M L SI	Satb
Forget The Sins Of Our Past	Fitzpatrick, Dennis	65 Fel	B L SI	
Forgive Our Sins As We Forgive	Herklots/Lowens	Na Gia	M B L L SI	
From Despair To Hope	Tucciarone, Angel	75 Rpb	M B R L L SI	
From My Distress	Fitzpatrick, Dennis	65 Fel	B L SI	
From The Depths	Gilligan, Michael	67 Acp	L L SI	
From The Depths	Quinlan, Paul	67 Fel	B L L SI	
From The Depths (4-Part Arr.)	Herbst, Martin	73 Acp	L L SI	
From The Depths Do I Cry	Deiss, Lucien	65 Wlp	B R L SI	
From Wanton Sin	Fitzpatrick, Dennis	65 Fel	B L SI	
Gather Us From Among The Nations	Fitzpatrick, Dennis	65 Fel	B L SI	
Give Light To My Eyes	Fitzpatrick, Dennis	65 Fel	B L SI	
Give Me Justice, O God	Fitzpatrick, Dennis	65 Fel	B L SI	
Give To The Winds Thy Fears (Opt Acc)	Marshall, Jane	Na Abi	M L SI	Satb
God Forbid That I Should Boast	Shafer, William	70 Acp	L L SI	
God Forbid That I Should Boast (4pt)	Cirou, Joseph	73 Acp	L L SI	
God So Loved The World	Fitzpatrick, Dennis	65 Fel	B L SI	
God, Hear Me Calling (Psalm 55)	Gilsdorf, Sr. Helen	76 Rpb	M B R L L SI	
Grant To Us (A Heart Renewed)	Deiss, Lucien	65 Wlp	B R L SI	
Greater Love Than This	Fitzpatrick, Dennis	65 Fel	B L SI	
Have Mercy O Lord, Have Mercy	Deiss, Lucien	65 Wlp	B R L SI	
Have Mercy On Us, O Lord	Deiss, Lucien	65 Wlp	B R L SI	
Have Mercy Upon Us	Lekberg, Sven	Na Gsc	B L SI	Satb
Have Mercy, Lord, On Me	Fitzpatrick, Dennis	67 Fel	B L SI	
Have Pity On Me, O Lord	Fitzpatrick, Dennis	65 Fel	B L SI	
He Has Borne Our Woes	Schroth, G	69 Gia	M L SI	Satb
He Heard My Voice	Fitzpatrick, Dennis	65 Fel	B L SI	
Hear My Cry	Moore	75 Her	M L SI	Satb
Help Us, O God, Our Savior	Fitzpatrick, Dennis	65 Fel	B L SI	
Hide Not Thou Thy Face	Farrant, Richard	Na Oxf	M L SI	Satb
Hide Not Your Face From Me	Fitzpatrick, Dennis	65 Fel	B L SI	
His Yoke Is Easy	Hudson/Decou	Na Zon	L SI	Satb
Hosanna Be The Children's Song	Rawls	75 Sac	M L SI	Sa
Hosanna To The Son Of David	Fitzpatrick, Dennis	65 Fel	B L SI	
Hosanna To The Son Of David	Nelson, Ronald A.	59 Aug	M L SI	Sab
Hosanna, Loud Hosanna	Ferguson	75 Sac	M L SI	Full
How Can You Really Care? (Ps. 6)	Quinlan, Paul	68 Nal	B R L SI	
How Long, O Lord	Fitzpatrick, Dennis	65 Fel	B L SI	
I Call On You, O God	Fitzpatrick, Dennis	65 Fel	B L SI	
I Caused Thy Grief	Manz, Paul	56 Aug	M L SI	Satb
I Go To The Father	Fitzpatrick, Dennis	65 Fel	B L SI	
I Have Given You An Example	Fitzpatrick, Dennis	65 Fel	B L SI	
I Looked For Someone	Fitzpatrick, Dennis	65 Fel	B L SI	
I Mingle My Drink With Tears	Fitzpatrick, Dennis	65 Fel	B L SI	
I Will Lift Up My Eyes	Sowerby, Leo	20 Bos	M L L SI	Stab
If I, The Lord And Master	Fitzpatrick, Dennis	65 Fel	B R L SI	
If You Keep Our Transgressions	Deiss, Lucien	65 Wlp	B R L SI	
Immortal Love	Darst	75 Sac	M L SI	Satb
In Memory Of The Savior's Love	Peninger	75 Sac	M L SI	Satb
In This Season Of Lent	Greif, Jean A	76 Vrn	M L L SI	
In Your Kindness Save Me, Lord	Fitzpatrick, Dennis	65 Fel	B L SI	
Insult Has Broken My Heart	Fitzpatrick, Dennis	65 Fel	B L SI	
Into Your Hands	Deiss, Lucien	65 Wlp	B R L SI	
Into Your Hands, O Lord	Fitzpatrick, Dennis	65 Fel	B L SI	
Jeremiah Sings The Blues	Hurd, Bob	75 Fel	B R L L SI	
Jerusalem	Gilsdorf, Sr. Helen	75 Rpb	M B R L L SI	
Jerusalem	Parker, Henry	Na Gsc	B L SI	Var
Jesus Gave His Life Away	Hurd, Bob	75 Fel	B R L L SI	
Jesus Paid It All	Grape/Rasley	75 Zon	L SI	Satb
Jesus Remember Me	Ellis, Ron	75 Rav	B R L L SI	
Jesus Said To His Mother	Fitzpatrick, Dennis	65 Fel	B L SI	
Judge Us With Mercy, Lord	Fitzpatrick, Dennis	65 Fel	B L SI	
Lamb, The	Wood, Dale	Na Abi	M L SI	Full
Lamentations	Michaelides, Peter	Na See	M L SI	
Lamentations	Schoenbachler, Tim	75 Nal	B R L SI	
Land Without Water (Psalm 63)	Hillebrand, Frank	75 Ahc	B R L L SI	
Last Trip To Jerusalem	Wilson	74 Aug	M L SI	Satb+
Lenten Holy	Regan, Joe	74 Nal	B R L SI	
Lenten Invocation	Ellis, Ron	73 Rav	B L L SI	
Lenten Invocation	Ellis, Ron & Ellis, Rob	73 Rav	B L L SI	
Lenten Invocation	Lynch, Michael B.	73 Rav	B L L SI	
Let My Prayer Come Before You	Fitzpatrick, Dennis	65 Fel	B L SI	

CATEGORIZED INDEX

Let The Old Man Die	Butler, Charles F.	75 Mar	R L L Sl	
Let Us Only Glory	Fitzpatrick, Dennis	65 Fel	B L Sl	
Let Your Eye Be To The Lord	Moe, Daniel	73 Aug	M L Sl	Satb
Life Without You	Hubert, Yvon	72 Fcc	R L L Sl	
Lighter Side Of Darkness	Fong, Preston Bing	75 Mar	R L L Sl	
Listen To My Words, Lord	Adler	74 Aug	M L Sl	2pt
Listen To Their Sighs	Fitzpatrick, Dennis	65 Fel	B L Sl	
Living Water (Lenten Invocation)	Lynch, Michael B.	75 Rav	B R L L Sl	
Look On Me, O Lord	Fitzpatrick, Dennis	65 Fel	B L Sl	
Lord, Do Not Forget Forever	Fitzpatrick, Dennis	65 Fel	B L Sl	
Lord, From Your Cross, Look Upon Us	Englert, Eugene	74 Gia	M L Sl	
Lord, I Am Not Worthy	Shelley, Tom	71 Ahc	B R L L Sl	
Lord, I Cry Unto Thee	Diercks, John H.	Na Abi	M L Sl	Satb
Lord, If You Remember Sins	Fitzpatrick, Dennis	65 Fel	B L Sl	
Lost In The Night	Christiansen, F. M.	32 Aug	M L Sl	Satb
Love In Grief	Christiansen, F. M.	36 Aug	M L Sl	Satb
Man Of Sorrows	Pooler, Marie	50 Aug	M L Sl	U+Tb
Man On The Cross, The	Martin	75 Sac	M L Sl	Satb
Mary's Song	Schneider, Kent E.	75 Ccc	B L Sl	
Meditation On "Passion Chorale"	Bock	75 Sac	M L Sl	Satb
Miserere: Psalm 51 (Eng)	Catalanello, Michael	76 Str	M L Sl	
Moses Pleaded With God	Fitzpatrick, Dennis	65 Fel	B L Sl	
Must Jesus Bear The Cross Alone?	Lynn, George	Na Abi	M L Sl	Satb
My God, My God, Why Have You	Fitzpatrick, Dennis	65 Fel	B L Sl	
My God, My God, Why Have You Abandoned	Jones, G. Thaddeus	73 Cfc	M R L L Sl	
My House Shall Be Called	Fitzpatrick, Dennis	65 Fel	B L Sl	
My People	Dufford, Bob, S. J.	68 Nal	B R L Sl	
My People	Lisicky, Paul	76 Rpb	M B R L L Sl	
My Soul Longs For Your Salvation	Fitzpatrick, Dennis	65 Fel	B L Sl	
Never Knew The Day	Golden, James Reed	73 Mar	R L L Sl	
Never Shall A Man	Foley, John, S. J.	70 Nal	B R L Sl	
No Help	Wilson, Janet	Na Abi	M L Sl	Satb
None Other Lamb	Burroughs	67 Aug	M L Sl	Satb
None Other Lamb	Lovelace, Austin C.	75 Sac	M L Sl	Satb
Not On Bread Alone	Fitzpatrick, Dennis	65 Fel	B L Sl	
O Come And Mourn	Lipscomb, Helen	Na Gsc	B L Sl	Sab+
O Dearest Lord	Lovelace, Austin C.	Na Abi	M L Sl	Satb
O Faithful Cross	Predmore, G	71 Gia	M L Sl	Var
O God, Have Mercy And Bless Us	Fitzpatrick, Dennis	65 Fel	B L Sl	
O God, Hear My Prayer, Deliver Me	Fitzpatrick, Dennis	65 Fel	B L Sl	
O God, Please Rescue Me	Fitzpatrick, Dennis	65 Fel	B L Sl	
O God, You Have Rejected Us	Fitzpatrick, Dennis	65 Fel	B L Sl	
O Lord Be Not Mindful	Deiss, Lucien	65 Wlp	B L Sl	
O Lord Have Mercy	Deiss, Lucien	70 Wlp	B L Sl	
O Lord, Do Not Be Far From Me	Fitzpatrick, Dennis	65 Fel	B L Sl	
O Lord, Do Not Deal With Us	Fitzpatrick, Dennis	65 Fel	B L Sl	
O Lord, Let My Enemies See	Fitzpatrick, Dennis	65 Fel	B L Sl	
O Love That Triumphs Over Loss (A Cap)	Dietterich, Philip	Na Abi	M L Sl	Sab
O Thou To Whose All-Searching Sight	Powell, Robert J.	Na Abi	M L Sl	Satb
Often They Fought Me	Fitzpatrick, Dennis	65 Fel	B L Sl	
Oh, That Out Of Zion	Fitzpatrick, Dennis	65 Fel	B L Sl	
One Of The Soldiers	Fitzpatrick, Dennis	65 Fel	B L Sl	
Our Eyes Are On You, O Lord	Fitzpatrick, Dennis	65 Fel	B L Sl	
Our Soul Has Been Resuced	Fitzpatrick, Dennis	65 Fel	B L Sl	
Out Of The Deep (D)	Hoddinott, Alun	Na Oxf	M L Sl	Satb
Out Of The Depths	Butler	75 Sac	M L Sl	Satb
Out Of The Depths	Cirou, Joseph	73 Acp	L L Sl	
Out Of The Depths	Gilligan, Michael	70 Acp	L L Sl	
Out Of The Depths I Cry To You	Fitzpatrick, Dennis	65 Fel	B L Sl	
Palm Sunday Processional	Zsigray, Joe	75 Nal	B R L Sl	
Penitential Song	Hurd, Bob	75 Fel	B R L L Sl	
Pickin' Up The Pieces	Nelson, Erick Martin	74 Mar	R L L Sl	
Protect Me From Those Who Do Evil	Fitzpatrick, Dennis	65 Fel	B L Sl	
Psalm 13	Baksa, Robert	71 Som	M L Sl	
Psalm 130	Peek, Richard	Na Abi	M L Sl	Satb
Psalm 130	Wyton	75 Aug	M L Sl	Satb+
Psalm 51 (50)	Westendorf/Takass	63 Wlp	B L Sl	
Put To Shame And Confusion	Fitzpatrick, Dennis	65 Fel	B L Sl	
Redeem Me, O Lord; Give Me Life	Fitzpatrick, Dennis	65 Fel	B L Sl	
Redeem Me, O Lord, And Have Pity	Fitzpatrick, Dennis	65 Fel	B L Sl	
Remember Me	St. Benedict's Farm	75 Sbf	B R L L Sl	2 Pt
Remember Me, Lord, When You Come	Fitzpatrick, Dennis	65 Fel	B L Sl	
Remember Us O Lord	Deiss, Lucien	70 Wlp	B R L Sl	
Remember, Man, That You Are Dust	Fitzpatrick, Dennis	65 Fel	B L Sl	
Reproaches, The	Cirou, Joseph	73 Acp	L L Sl	
Reproaches, The	Shafer, William	70 Acp	L L Sl	
Rescue Me From My Enemies	Foley, John, S. J.	70 Nal	B R L Sl	
Response: Stations Of The Cross	Page, Paul F.	76 Rpb	M B R L L Sl	
Restore Us	Gilsdorf, Sr. Helen	75 Rpb	M B R L L Sl	
Return To Your People, O Lord	Dufford, Bob, S. J.	68 Nal	B R L Sl	
Return, O Lord, And Save My Life	Fitzpatrick, Dennis	65 Fel	B L Sl	
Salvation Belongeth Unto The Lord	Copley, R. Evan	Na Abi	M L Sl	Satb
Save Me, O God, By Thy Name	Lewis, John Leo	Na Gsc	B L Sl	Satb+
Save Me, O Lord!	Trued, S. Clarence	66 Som	M L Sl	
Save Me, O Lord, And Rescue Me	Fitzpatrick, Dennis	65 Fel	B L Sl	
Save Me, O Lord, From The Hands	Fitzpatrick, Dennis	65 Fel	B L Sl	
Save Us, O Lord, Our God	Fitzpatrick, Dennis	65 Fel	B L Sl	
See The Land	Jordan, Alice	Na Abi	M L Sl	Satb
Seven Words From The Cross	Nystedt, Knut	61 Aug	M L Sl	Satb
Show Us Your Mercy, Lord	Fitzpatrick, Dennis	65 Fel	B L Sl	
Simon The Cyrenean Speaks	Roff, Joseph	75 Sac	M L Sl	Satb
Sing We A Song Of High Revolt	Kaan/Kraehenbuehl	76 Jsp	B L Sl	Satb
Sing We Now Hosanna	Graham	75 Sac	M L Sl	2mel
So Lonely	Repp, Ray	69 Fel	M R L Sl	
So Lowly Doth The Savior Ride	Ream	75 Sac	M L Sl	Satb
Sometimes, O Lord	Page, Paul F.	76 Rpb	M B R L L Sl	
Son Come Out	Angle, D P	73 Mar	R L L Sl	
Song Of The Wounded	Wise, Joe	75 Nal	B R L Sl	
Sorrowful Road, The	Soteren, Leland B.	Na Abi	M L Sl	Satb
Streams Of Babylon (Psalm 137)	Hillebrand, Frank	75 Ahc	B R L L Sl	
Sundown (Bar Solo, Orch Or Piano)	Merton, T./Peloquin C A	68 Gia	B L L Sl	Satb+
Surely He Has Borne Our Griefs	Hunnicutt, J.	71 Aug	M L Sl	Sab
Tear Down The Walls	Strange, J D	75 Mar	R L L Sl	
Temptation Of Christ, The	Pfautsch, Lloyd	Na Abi	M L Sl	Satb
The Bell Doth Toll	Thomson, Virgil	62 Som	M L Sl	
The Bones You Have Crushed	Fitzpatrick, Dennis	65 Fel	B L Sl	
The Children Of The Hebrews	Fitzpatrick, Dennis	65 Fel	B L Sl	
The Crucifixion	Jacobs, Peter	73 Chd	B R L L Sl	
The Death Of God (W/Narrator)	Holloway, Robin	Na Oxf	B L Sl	
The Dirge Of David	Thiem, James	66 Fel	B L Sl	
The Hebrew Children Spread	Fitzpatrick, Dennis	65 Fel	B L Sl	
The Last Supper	Donato, Anthony	58 Som	M L Sl	
The Lord Is Good (Ps 71)	Merton, T./Peloquin C A	68 Gia	B L L Sl	Satb+
The Lord Is My Light	Dean, T. W.	63 Gam	M L Sl	Satb
The Passion According To St. Mark	Nelson, Ronald	62 Aug	M L Sl	Satb+
The Reproaches	Page, Paul F.	76 Rpb	M B R L L Sl	
The Shepherd Boy Sings In The Valley	Diamond, David	49 Som	M L Sl	
The Sorrows Of My Heart Are Enlarged	Ferris, William	69 Gia	B L L Sl	2pt
The Words From The Cross	Fetler, Paul	72 Aug	M L Sl	Satb+
There Is No Room	Peterson, John W.	75 Zon	M L Sl	Satb
They Cried To The Lord	Fitzpatrick, Dennis	65 Fel	B L Sl	
They Divide My Garments	Fitzpatrick, Dennis	65 Fel	B L Sl	
They Gossip About Me	Fitzpatrick, Dennis	65 Fel	B L Sl	
Those Who Sow In Tears	Fitzpatrick, Dennis	65 Fel	B L Sl	
Though I Walk Amid Distress	Fitzpatrick, Dennis	65 Fel	B L Sl	
Throned Upon The Awful Tree	Lovelace, Austin C.	75 Sac	M L Sl	Sab
Throughout These Days	Cirou, Joseph	73 Acp	L L Sl	
Throughout These Days	Hernaman, Claudia F.	67 Acp	L L Sl	
Thy Will Be Done	Eilers, Joyce E	75 Her	M L Sl	Satb+
Tis Midnight	Ford, Virgil	Na Abi	M L Sl	Satb
To You I Cry, O Lord	Fitzpatrick, Dennis	65 Fel	B L Sl	
Travelin' 40 Days	Schneider, Kent E.	76 Ccc	M B R L Sl	
True Fasting	Brandon, George	Na Abi	M L Sl	Satb
Up The Hill Of Calvary With Love	Fox, Baynard (Keene)	75 Elv	M L Sl	Satb+
We Adore You, O Christ	Fitzpatrick, Dennis	65 Fel	B L Sl	
We Give Thanks To Thee, O Lord	Palestrina, Giovanni P	Na Abi	M L Sl	Satb
Were You There?	Hamill, Paul	Na Abi	M L Sl	Satb
Were You There?	Vickers, Wendy (Arr.)	75 Nal	B R L Sl	
What Wondrous Love	Wade, Walter	Na Abi	M L Sl	Satb+
Whatcha Gonna Do	Culverwell, Andrew	73 Man	B R L Sl	
When From Our Exile	Huijbers & Oosterhuis	74 Nal	M B R L Sl	
When I Had Fallen Low Indeed	Gilligan, Michael	70 Acp	L L Sl	
When I Had Fallen Low Indeed	Liturgical Press	73 Acp	L L Sl	
When Jesus Wept (Med Voice)	Billings, William	Na Abi	M L Sl	Solo
When My Weak Eyes Can See That Cross	Cirou, Joseph Et Al	73 Acp	L L Sl	
When My Weak Eyes Can See That Cross	Watts, Isaac	70 Acp	L L Sl	
When We In Spirit View Thy Passion	Freydt (Ed Nolte)	Na Abi	M L Sl	Ssab
When, His Salvation Bringing	Baumgartner, H. Leroy	Na Abi	M L Sl	Satb
Who Passes Yonder Through The Throng?	Williams, David H.	74 Hwg	M L Sl	Satb+
Who Will Deliver Me?	Hubert, Yvon	72 Fcc	R L L Sl	
Wilt Not Thou Turn Again?	Dietterich, Philip	Na Abi	M L Sl	Satb
With These Our Lenten Prayers	Quinn, M.	65 Wlp	B L Sl	
Without Clouds	Ducote, Darryl	71 Fel	B R L Sl	
Woe Is Me (Me)	Amner, John	Na Oxf	M L Sl	Satb
Wondrous Love (A Cap)	Van Iderstine, A. P.	Na Abi	M L Sl	Satb
Words From The Cross, The	Schaffer, Jeanne E.	Na Abi	M L Sl	
Words Of Jesus (Cantata)	Dean, T. W.	62 Gam	B L Sl	Full
Yes I Shall Arise	Deiss, Lucien	65 Wlp	B R L Sl	
Yes, Lord (I Heard You Calling)	Temple, Sebastian	71 Gia	B R L Sl	Satb+
You Have Mercy On All	Fitzpatrick, Dennis	65 Fel	B L Sl	
You Were There	Gulliksen, Kenn	75 Mar	R L L Sl	
Your Holy Cross	Hruby, Dolores	74 Gia	M L Sl	Satb+
Your Holy Death	Deiss, Lucien	65 Wlp	B R L Sl	
A Litany (M)	Walton, William	Na Oxf	M T Sl	Satb
A New Heart Will I Give You	Beck, John Ness	Na Gsc	B T Sl	Var+
Ach, Arme Welt (Alas, Poor World)	Brahms, Johannes	Na Gsc	B T Sl	Satb
Ad Flumina Babylonis	Najera, Edmund	Na Gsc	B T Sl	2chor
Adoramus	Palestrina, Giovanni P	Na Gsc	B T Sl	Satb
Adoramus Te	Dilasso, O. Arr Avalos	76 Pro	M T Sl	3pt+
Adoramus Te	Perti, G A	Na Gsc	B T Sl	Satb
Adoramus Te	Rossello, Francesco	Na Gsc	B T Sl	Satb
Adoramus Te (Lat & Eng)	Palestrina, Giovanni P	49 Hof	M T Sl	Satb
Adoramus Te (We Adore Thee)	Gasparini, Quirino	Na Gsc	B T Sl	Satb
Adoramus Te (We Adore Thee)	Rossello (Ar Beveridge)	Na Gsc	M T Sl	Satb+
Adoramus Te Christe	Dubois, T	Na Gsc	B T Sl	Satb+
Adoramus Te Christe	Parthun	69 Aug	M T Sl	Satb
Adoramus Te Christe (Md)	Lasso, Orlando Di	Na Oxf	M T Sl	2pt
Adoramus Te, Christe	Lasso, Orlando Di	Na Gsc	B T Sl	3eq
Ah Lord Thy Dear Sweet Angels Send	Bach, J. S.	Na Gsc	B T Sl	Satb
Air	Bach, J. C.	52 Bbl	B T Sl	Satb+
All Flesh Is Grass	Monaco, Richard	Na Gsc	B T Sl	Satb+
All My Friends Have Forsaken Me	Palestrina, Giovanni P	75 Elv	M T Sl	Satb
All We Like Sheep Have Gone	Handel, G. F.	Cfs	M T Sl	Satb
All Ye That Pass By	Farmer, Floyd	Na Abi	M T Sl	Satb
Almighty Lord And God Of Love (Me)	Giles, Nathaniel	Na Oxf	M T Sl	Satb
Am I A Soldier Of The Cross?	Thompson	Na Lor	M T Sl	Satb
Amazing Grace	Lee, Anthony	75 Maf	M T Sl	Satb
Amazing Grace	Lynn, George	Na Abi	M T Sl	Satb
Amazing Grace!	Martin	75 Sac	M T Sl	2mel
And Can It Be?	Campbell/Johnson	Na Zon	T Sl	Ssatb
And Can It Be?	Lynn, George	Na Abi	M T Sl	Satb
And With His Stripes	Handel, G. F.	Cfs	M T Sl	Satb
Arise, O Lord	Hoffmeister, L A	Na Gsc	B T Sl	Satb+
As A Rose Among Thorns	Lasso, Orlando Di	67 Fel	B T Sl	
As By The Streams Of Babylon	Dett, R N	Na Gsc	B T Sl	Satb+
As By The Streams Of Babylon (Acap)	Campian, T	Na Gsc	B T Sl	Satb
Aus Meiner Suden Tiefe	Lasso, Orlando Di	Na Gsc	B T Sl	Satb
Awake! Do Not Cast Us Off (Ps 44)	Adler, Samuel	Na Oxf	M T Sl	Satb
Babylonian Captivity	Dare, Elkanah K	75 Bbl	B T Sl	Satb

CATEGORIZED INDEX

Title	Composer	Pub		Voicing
Be Merciful Unto Me (Md)	Blow, John	Na Oxf	M	T SI Satb
Be Merciful Unto Me, O God	Glarum	55 Aug	M	T SI Satb
Before The Crucifix	La Forge, F	Na Gsc	B	T SI Satb+
Behold He Bore Our Infirmities	Buxtehude, D.(D1707)	Na Kal	B	T SI Satb+
Behold The Lamb Of God	Handel, G. F.	Na Gsc	B	T SI Satb+
Behold The Royal Cross On High	Quinn, M.	63 Wlp	B	T SI
Behold This Child Is Set For The Fall	Schutz, Heinrich	Cfp	R	T SI Satb
Blessed Is He That Cometh	Brown, Leon F.	55 Smc	M	T SI Satb
Boundless Mercy Traditional (Acap)	Na	Na Gsc	B	T SI Satb
Bow Down Thine Ear, O Lord (Md)	Hayes, William	Na Oxf	M	T SI Satb
Bow Thine Ear, O Lord (Md)	Byrd, William	Na Oxf	M	T SI Sattb
Bread Of Tears	Christiansen, P.	48 Aug	M	T SI Satb
By Babylon's Wave	Gounod, Charles	Na Gsc	B	T SI Full+
By The River Of Babylon (E & L)	Lasso, Orlando Di	69 Gia	B	L T SI Satb+
By The Waters Of Babylon	Bach, J. C.	52 Bbl	M	T SI Satb
By The Waters Of Babylon	Boyce, William	75 Bbl	M	T SI Satb
By The Waters Of Babylon (3voices)	Nares/Tortolano Ed	70 Gia	B	L T SI Round
Caligarerunt Oculi Mei	Ingegneri, Marc A	Na Oxf	M	T SI Satb+
Call To Remembrance (Md)	Hilton, John	Na Oxf	M	T SI Full
Calvary	Rodney	Na Lor	M	T SI Var
Calvary	Rodney, Paul	Na Gsc	B	T SI Satb+
Calvary's Mountain	Pooler, Marie	53 Aug	M	T SI Satb
Cantata #12 Weping (Eng/Germ)	Bach, J. S.	Na Kal	B	T SI Satb
Cantata #26 Ach Wie Flueschtig	Bach, J. S.	Na Kal	B	T SI
Cantata #4 Christ Lag (Eng/Germ)	Bach, J. S.	Na Kal	B	T SI Satb
Cantiones Sacrae: Heu Mihi Domine	Schutz, Heinrich	Na Kal	B	T SI
Careworn Muther Stood Attending	Mckenna/Traditional	61 Gia	M B	L T SI
Chandos Anthem 3 (Have Mercy On Me)	Handel, G. F.	Na Oxf	M	T SI Satb
Choral Var On "Ah Holy Jesus" (Cruger)	Petrich, Roger T.	Na Oxf	M	T SI
Christ Became Obedient (Me)	Anerio, F./Ehret(Ed)	75 Gia	B	L T SI Satb
Christ Became Obedient For Us	Lee, John	70 Gia	B	L T SI Satb+
Christ On The Mount Of Olives (Germ)	Beethoven, L	Na Kal	B	T SI Satb
Christ Our Blessed Savior	Praetorius–Scholk	70 Aug	M	T SI Full
Christ, Our Blessed Savior	Schutz, Heinrich	Na Gsc	B	T SI Satb
Christe, Adoramus Te	Lat, E	76 Abi	M	T SI Satb+
Christus Factus Est	Anerio, Felice	Na Gsc	B	T SI Satb
Christus Factus Est	Bruckner, Anton	Na Gsc	B	T SI Satb
Christus Factus Est	Sartori, Baldasaro	Na Gsc	B	T SI Satb
Christus Factus Est (E & L) (Me)	Leo, Leonardo	Na Gia	M	L T SI Sa+
Christus Factus Est Pro Nobis Obediens	Bruckner, Anton	Cfp	R	T SI Satb+
Christus Factus Est (Lat,Eng)	Sartori (Beveridge)	39 Gsc	B	T SI Satb
Columbia From Two Songs Of Mourning	Ingalls, Jeremiah	75 Bbl	B	T SI 3pt
Come, Ye Disconsolate	Webbe/Decou	Na Zon		T SI Satb
Comfort, O Lord (E)	Crotch, William (Arr)	Na Oxf	M	T SI Sa
Confitemini (From Holiday Motets)	Krenek, Ernst	67 Ron	B	T SI Ssa
Conserva Me And Lamentationes	Parsley, Osbert(D1585)	Na Kal	B	T SI Satb
Create In Me A Clean Heart	Pasquet, Jean	68 Aug	M	T SI Sab
Create In Me A Clean Heart, O God	Mueller, Carl F	Na Gsc	B	T SI Var+
Create In Me O God	Brahms, Johannes	Na Gsc	B	T SI Sattb
Creator Of The Earth And Skies	Hughes, D/Trad	Na Gia	M B	L T SI
Crucifixus	Lotti, A	Na Gsc	B	T SI Var+
Crucifixus	Palestrina, Giovanni P	Na Gsc	B	T SI Ssaa
Crucifixus	Vivaldi, A. Arr Ehret	71 Aug	M	T SI Satb
Crucifixus (From The Mass In B Minor)	Bach, J. S.	Na Gsc	B	T SI Satb+
Crux Fidelis (E & L) (Me)	John Iv (Ed Tortolano)	Na Gia	M	L T SI Satb
Darkly Rose The Guilty Morning S	Buck, Dudley	Na Gsc	B	T SI Satb+
Darkness Was Over All	Haydn, Michael	Na Gsc	B	T SI Ssa+
David's Lamentation	Billings, William	Na Cac	B	T SI Satb
David's Lamentation	Billings, William	Cfp	R	T SI Sattb
Davide Penitente	Mozart, Wolfgang A	52 Dbl	B	T SI Snth+
Davide Penitente K 469 (Eng/It/Germ)	Mozart, Wolfgang A	Na Kal	B	T SI Satb
Day Of Sorrow	Haydn, Michael(Ehret)	75 Elv	M	T SI Satb+
De Profundis	Mozart, Wolfgang A	Na Kal	B	T SI Satb+
De Profundis (Out Of The Depths)	Chorbajian, John	Na Gsc	B	T SI Full
De Profundis K 93	Mozart, Wolfgang A	Na Kal	B	T SI Satb
De Propundis (From Holiday Motets)	Krenek, Ernst	67 Ron	B	T SI Ssa
Deep Were His Wounds	Sateren, Leland B.	65 Aug	M	T SI Satb
Deliver Us, Good Lord (Me)	Tye, Christopher	Na Oxf	M	I SI Satb
Deliver Us, O Lord (Me)	Batten, Adrian	Na Oxf	M	T SI Satb
Deus, Misereatur Nostri	Schutz, Heinrich	Na Gsc	B	T SI Satb
Did They Crucify My Lord?	Davidson	Na Lor	M	T SI Satb
Didst Thou Suffer Shame?	Telemann	75 Her	M	T SI Satb
Domine Memento Mei Jesu Think Of Me	Back, Sven–Erik	Na Gsc	B	T SI Satb
Doth Not Wisdom Cry	Rogers, J H	Na Gsc	B	T SI Satb+
Draw Near O Lord	Farrell, Melvin	61 Wlp	B	T SI
Drop, Drop Slow Tears	Bullock, Ernest	Na Oxf	M	T SI
Drop, Drop, Slow Tears	Burroughs	75 Sac	M	T SI Satb
Drop, Drop, Slow Tears	Powell	75 Sac	M	T SI Satb
Drop, Slow Tears	Kechley, Gerald	73 Gal	M	T SI Satb
Early, O Lord, My Fainting Soul	Purcell, Henry	Na Gsc	B	T SI Satb+
Ecce Ascendimus Jerusolym	Back, Sven–Erik	Na Gsc	B	T SI Satb
Ecce Nunc Tempus	Guerrero, Francisco	Na Gsc	B	T SI Satb
Ecce Quomodo Moritur Justus (Me)	Handl, Jacob	Na Oxf	M	T SI Satb
Es Ist Nun Aus	Bach, J. C.	52 Bbl	B	T SI Satb+
Faithful Cross	Fitzpatrick, Dennis	65 Fel	B	T SI
Father, Forgive Them	Lynn, George	55 Smc	M	T SI Satb
Father, I Will Obey	Andrews, Carroll T.	70 Gia	B	L T SI Var
Father, If This Cup (Choral)	Fitzpatrick, Dennis	65 Fel	B	T SI
Fierce Was The Wild Billow	Hewlett, W H	Na Gsc	B	T SI Satb+
Fling Wide The Gates	Stainer, Sir John	Cfs	M	T SI Satb
Fling Wide The Gates	Stainer, Sir John	Na Gsc	B	T SI Satb+
For He Shall Give His Angels Charge	Jennings, K.	67 Aug	M	T SI Satb+
For Thy Great Mercy(Double Chorus)	Durante, Francesco	Na Gsc	B	T SI Full
Forty Days To Easter	Wilson, R C	Na Lor	M	T SI
From The Deep, Lord (Cantata)	Bach, J. S.	75 Lps	B R	T SI Satb
Give Unto The Humble	Cherubini, L	Na Gsc	B	T SI Satb+
Go To Dark Gethsemane	Landon (Arr)	Na Lor	M	T SI Satb
Go To Dark Gethsemane	Ritter	Na Lor	M	T SI Satb
God Be Merciful	Moe, Daniel	56 Aug	M	T SI Satb
God Be Merciful Unto Us	Hovhaness, Alan S.	74 Ron	M	T SI Satb+
God Is Merciful	Haydn, Michael	Na Gsc	B	T SI Satb+
God Of All Grace	Van Dyke, Paul C.	Na Gsc	B	T SI Satb
God Our Father	Eberlin, Ernst	Na Gsc	B	T SI Satb
God So Loved The World	Bruckner, A./Ed Klein	67 Gia	B	L T SI Satb+
God So Loved The World	Stainer, Sir John	Cfs	M	T SI Satb
God So Loved The World	Stainer, Sir John	Na Aug	M	T SI Satb
God So Loved The World	Stainer, Sir John	Na Gsc	M	T SI Satb+
God So Loved The World	Stainer, Sir John	Na Lor	M	T SI Var
Good Friday Meditation	King	Na Lor	M	T SI Satb
Grief Is In My Heart	Eberlin, Ernst	Na Gsc	B	T SI Satb
Hammering	Ferguson	75 Sac	M	T SI Satb
Hamshire, (Good Friday) W/Viol,Cello	Read, Daniel	76 Bbl	M	T SI Satb
Haste Thee, O God (Me)	Batten, Adrian	Na Oxf	M	T SI Satb
Haste Thee, O God (Me)	Shepherd, John	Na Oxf	M	T SI Satb
Have Mercy On Me	Tompkins, Thomas	74 Gia	M	T SI Sab
Have Mercy Upon Me, O God (M)	Tompkins, Thomas	Na Gsc	M	T SI Satb
Have Thine Own Way, Lord	Smith	Na Lor	M	T SI Satb
Have Thine Own Way, Lord	Stebbins/Landon	Na Lor	M	T SI Satb
He Endured The Cross	Graun–Wetzler	63 Aug	M	T SI Satb
He Was Despised	Graun, Karl H	Na Gsc	B	T SI Satb+
He Was Despised	Johnston	Na Lor	M	T SI Satb
He Was Silent (Choral)	Fitzpatrick, Dennis	65 Fel	B	T SI
He Was Wounded For Our Transgressions	Dunlop/Meckelson	Na Zon		T SI
He Who With Weeping Soweth	Schutz, Heinrich	Na Gsc	B	T SI Ssatb
Healing Of The Nations	Sheehan, Ann Marie	Na Ams	M	T SI
Hear Me, O Lord	Foster, Will	53 Smc	M	T SI Satb
Hear Now Our Cry	Keel, Richard	Na Gsc	B	T SI Satb+
Hear Us, O Father	Nystedt, Knut	66 Aug	M	T SI Satb
Hear Us, O Lord	Obrecht, J	Na Gia		T SI
Hear, O Heavens (Is 1, M)	Humfrey, Pelham	Na Oxf	M	T SI Satb
Helas! Mon Dieu.	Lejeune, Claude	Na Oxf	M	T SI Ssatb
Help Us, O Lord, Deliver Us	Haydn, Michael	Na Gsc	B	T SI Satb+
Here Yet Awhile	Bach, J. S.	Na Gsc	B	T SI Full+
Here Yet Awhile (St Mt Passion)	Bach, J. S.	Cfs	M	T SI Full
Holy Redeemer! Be Thy Rest	Latrobe	Na Abi	M	T SI Satb
Hosanna	Gregor	Na Lor	M	T SI Var
Hosanna Filio David (Choral)	Fitzpatrick, Dennis	65 Fel	B	T SI
Hosanna In The Highest!	Martin	Na Lor	M	T SI Satb
Hosanna To The King	Emig	Na Lor	M	T SI Satb
Hosanna To The Son Of David	Weelkes, Thomas	Na Oxf	M	T SI Full
Hosanna We Sing	Dykes	Na Lor	M	T SI Unis
Hosanna! Blessed Is He!	Sydow	Na Lor	M	T SI Satb
Hosanna! Hosanna!	Robers	Na Lor	M	T SI Satb
Hosanna, Loud Hosanna	Smith	Na Lor	M	T SI Satb
Hosanna, Loud Hosanna!	Hadle	Na Lor	M	T SI Satb
Hosannah To The Son Of David (Md)	Gibbons, Orlando	Na Oxf	M	T SI Full
How Can Sinner Know	Ford, Virgil	Na Gsc	B	T SI Satb
How Long Wilt Thou Forget Me	Battishill, Jonathan	Na Gsc	B	T SI Unis+
How Long Wilt Thou Forget Me	Brahms, Johannes	Na Gsc	B	T SI Ssa+
How Long Wilt Thou Forget Me?	Pflueger	Na Lor	M	T SI Satb
How Still The Garden Of Gethsemane	Graham, Robert	Na Abi	M	T SI Satb
I Cried To God In Tribulation	Haydn, Michael	Na Gsc	B	T SI Satb+
I Saw The Cross Of Jesus	Denton	Na Lor	M	T SI Satb
Ich Aber Bin Eland(Lord, God I Am Wear	Brahms, Johannes	Na Gsc	B	T SI Full
If With All Your Hearts	Mendelssohn, F.	Na Aug	M	T SI Satb
If With All Your Hearts	Mendelssohn, F.	Na Gsc	R	T SI Satb+
If With All Your Hearts	Mendelssohn, F.	Na Lor	M	T SI Satb
Improperium	De Lussus, O	75 Maf	M	T SI Satb
In Tears Of Grief (St.Matt Pass) (Md)	Bach, J.S. (Arr Dawes)	Na Oxf	M	T SI Satb
In The Cross Of Christ I Glory	Conkey/Burkwall	75 Zon		I SI Satb
Ingrediente (Choral)	Fitzpatrick, Dennis	65 Fel	B	T SI
Is It Nothing (O Vos Omnes)	Vittoria, T.L./Klein	69 Gia	B	L T SI Satb+
Is It Nothing All Of You Who Pass By	Croce, Giovanni	Na Gsc	B	T SI Satb
Is It Nothing To You	Pedrette, Edward A	Na Gsc	B	T SI Satb
Il Was For You	Daniels, E.	70 Sil		L T SI
Jerusalem	Parker	Na Lor	M	T SI Var
Jerusalem O Turn Thee To The Lord	Gounod, Charles	Na Gsc	B	T SI Var+
Jerusalem, Jerusalem (+Ps 130)	Gregorian Mel/Lee(Arr)	70 Gia	B	L T SI Satb+
Jesu, Grant Me This I Pray	Kitson, C. H.	Na Oxf	M	T SI Satb
Jesu, Grant Me This I Pray (Md)	Whitlock, Percy	Na Oxf	M	T SI Satb
Jesus Died On Calvary's Mountain	Hughes, Robert J.	Na Lor	M	T SI Satb
Jesus Speaks From The Cross	Carmony	Na Lor	M	T SI Satb
Jesus, By Thy Cross (Cantata)	Bach, J. S.	75 Lps	B R	T SI Satb
Jesus, In Thy Dying Woes	Sateren, Leland B.	56 Aug	M	T SI Satb
Jesus, Our Savior	Bruckner, Anton	Cfp	R	T SI Full+
Jesus, Thy Blood And Righteousness	Gardiner/Carmichael	Na Zon		T SI Satb
Judas, Mercator Pessimus	Na	Na Gsc	B	T SI Satb
Judge Me O God	Barbee, N	Na Lor	M	T SI Satb
Judge Me, O God (W/Sop Solo)	Mueller, Carl F	39 Gsc	M	T SI 8pt
Lacrymosa	Mendelssohn, F.	Na Gsc	B	T SI Satb+
Lamb Of Calvary	Reske	75 Sac	M	T SI Satb
Lamb Of God, For Sinners Slain	Cherubini, L	74 Gia	M	T SI Satb+
Lamentation	Anonymous	75 Bbl	M	T SI Satb
Lamentation Over Boston	Ingalls, Jeremiah	75 Bbl	M	T SI Ttb
Lamentations For 5 & 6 Voices	Billings, William	Cfp	R	T SI Satb
Last Words Of Christ	White, Robert (1574)	Na Kal	B	T SI Satb
Lead Me To Calvary	Kirkpatrick/Wilson	Na Lor	M	T SI Satb
Leave, Then, Thy Foolish Ranges	Street, Tilson	Na Gsc	B	T SI Full
Lent (From Holiday Motets)	Krenek, Ernst	67 Ron	B	T SI Ssa
Let My Complaint Come Before Thee	Batten, Adrian	Na Oxf	M	T SI Satb
Let Thy Mercy, O Lord, Be Upon Us	Roff, Joseph	Na Gia		T SI
Libera Me (Choral)	Fitzpatrick, Dennis	65 Fel	B	T SI
Libera Me (Unison)	Fitzpatrick, Dennis	65 Fel	B	T SI
Lift Up Your Heads, O Ye Gates	Schutz, Heinrich	Cfp	R	T SI Satb+
Lonesome Valley	Wilson	Na Lor	M	T SI Var
Lord For Thy Tender Mercies Sake	Farmer, H	Na Gsc	B	T SI Satb+

CATEGORIZED INDEX

Lord Jesus By Thy Passion	Christiansen, P.	71 Aug	M	T Sl	Satb
Lord Jesus On The Cross Was Hung	Schutz, Heinrich	Na Gsc	B	T Sl	Satb
Lord Jesus, Think On Me	Freestone G. S.	Na Abi	M	T Sl	Satb
Lord To Thee I Make My Moan (M)	Weelkes, Thomas	Na Oxf	M	T Sl	Saatb
Lord, Create In Me A Clean Heart	Schutz, Heinrich	75 Maf	M	T Sl	2pt
Lord, For Thy Tender Mercies	Rogers, J H	Na Gsc	B	T Sl	Satb+
Lord, For Thy Tender Mercy's Sake (E)	Hilton, John	Na Oxf	M	T Sl	Satb
Lord, I Can Suffer	Purcell, Henry	Na Gsc	B	T Sl	4mix+
Lord, I Trust Thee (From Passion)	Handel, G. F.	Na Oxf	M	T Sl	Satb
Lord, If I But Thee May Have	Schutz, Heinrich	Na Gsc	B	T Sl	8mix
Lord, Redeemer Of All Who Know Thee	Schutz, Heinrich	Na Gsc	B	T Sl	Satb
Lord, Remember Us	Wetzler, Robert	72 Aug	M	T Sl	Satb
Lord, Thou Hast Been Our Dwelling	Monaco, Richard	Na Gsc	B	T Sl	Satb+
Lord, We Beseech Thee (Me)	Batten, Adrian	Na Oxf	M	T Sl	Satb
Meditabor	Biggs, John	Na Gsc	B	T Sl	Full
Mensch, Vom Weibe Geboren, Der	Bach, J. C.	52 Bbl	B	T Sl	Satb+
Miserere Mei (Ps 51)	Byrd, William	Na Oxf	M	T Sl	Satbb
Miserere Mei Deus	Allegri, G	Na Gsc	B	T Sl	Full
Misericordia Dominis K 222	Mozart, Wolfgang A	Na Kal	B	T Sl	Satb
Mit Weinen Hebt Sichs An	Bach, J. C.	52 Bbl	B	T Sl	Satb
Mount Calvery	Wright	Na Lor	M	T Sl	Satb
Music For Palm Sunday	Diemente, E	Na Gia		T Sl	
Must Jesus Bear Another Cross?	O'hara, Geoffrey	Na Gsc	B	T Sl	Satb+
My Days Are Gone Like A Shadow (Md)	Blow, John	Na Oxf	M	T Sl	Satb
My Friend Of Calvary	Faure, Gabriel	Na Lor	M	T Sl	Unis
My God Shall Raise Me Up	Noble, Harold	Na Gsc	B	T Sl	Satb
My Heart Sings Hosanna	Johnson/Drevits	Na Zon	M	T Sl	Ssatb
My Lord, My Love, Is Crucified!	Burroughs	Na Lor	M	T Sl	
My Soul Is Exceeding Sorrowful	Neff	64 Aug	M	T Sl	2pt
Night In The Desert	Jenkins, Cyril	Na Gsc	B	T Sl	Ssa+
Nolo Mortem Peccatoris (M)	Morley, Thomas	Na Oxf	M	T Sl	Satb
Nos Qui Sumus In Hoc Mundo	Lasso, Orlando Di	Na Gsc	B	T Sl	Satb
Now Quit Your Care	Ripper, Theodore W.	Na Abi	M	T Sl	Satb
O Cast Me Not Away (2nd Mov't)	Brahms, Johannes	Na Gsc	B	T Sl	Satb
O Christ, Who Art The Light & Day (M)	Byrd, William	Na Oxf	M	T Sl	Satbb
O Come And Mourn	Smith, Harold	71 Smc	M	T Sl	Satb
O Come And Mourn With Me	Burroughs	Na Lor	M	T Sl	Satb
O Come And Mourn With Me Awhile	Pergolesi, G-Riedel	62 Aug	M	T Sl	Satb
O Come Ye To The Cross	Carissimi, Giacomo	Na Abi	M	T Sl	Ssaatb
O Cross Thou Only Hope	Morales, Cristobal De	67 Bbl	M	T Sl	Sattb
O Crux Ave	Victoria, Tomas Luis	75 Bbl	M	T Sl	Satb
O Crux Ave, Spes Unica	Morales, Cristobal De	67 Bbl	M	T Sl	Sattb
O Dearest Lord, Thy Sacred Head	Johnson, D.	70 Aug	M	T Sl	Satb
O Deepest Woe	Peninger	75 Sac	M	T Sl	Satb
O Faithful Cross (A Cap) (E)	Englert, Eugene	76 Gia	M	L T Sl	Satb
O For The Wings Of A Dove	Mendelssohn, F.	Na Gsc	B	T Sl	Satb+
O God Who Called The Hebrews	Farrell, Melvin/Picca	61 Wlp	B	T Sl	
O Hail Sacred Cross	Victoria, Tomas Luis	75 Bbl	M	T Sl	Satb
O Jesu, Look	Kirby, George	Na Oxf	M	T Sl	Ssatb
O Let Me Tread In The Right Path (Me)	Walton, William	Na Oxf	M	T Sl	Satb
O Look To Golgotha	Mason-Riedel	57 Aug	M	T Sl	Satb
O Lord God Of My Salvation	Schubert, F (Arr Hines)	70 Gsc	M	T Sl	Satb+
O Lord In Thy Wrath (Md)	Gibbons, Orlando	Na Oxf	M	T Sl	Full
O Lord You Know Our Weakness	Westendorf, Omer	64 Wlp	B	T Sl	
O Lord, How Numerous Are My Foes	Jeppesen, Knud	75 Bbl	M	T Sl	Satb
O Lord, My Trust Is In Thy Mercy	Hall, King	Na Gsc	B	T Sl	Satb+
O Loving Jesus	Andrews, Carroll T.	70 Gia	B	L T Sl	Var
O Sacred Head	Hassler-Christiansen	57 Aug	M	T Sl	Satb
O Sacred Head	Hassler/Bach	Na Lor	M	T Sl	Satb
O Sacred Head Now Wounded	Bach, J. S.	Na Gsc	B	T Sl	Satb
O Sacred Head Surrounded	Farrell, Melvin	61 Wlp	B	T Sl	
O Sacred Head, Now Wounded	Hassler/Peterson	Na Zon	M	T Sl	Satb
O Savior Our Refuge	Eberlin, Ernst	Na Gsc	B	T Sl	Satb
O Spotless Lamb	Bach, J.S.-Thoburn	55 Aug	M	T Sl	Satb
O To Be Like Thee	Landon, Stewart	Na Lor	M	T Sl	Satb
O Vos Omnes	Esquivel, Juan De	Na Gsc	B	T Sl	Satb
O Vos Omnes	Palestrina, Giovanni P	Na Gsc	B	T Sl	Satb
O Vos Omnes	Perti, G A	Na Gsc	B	T Sl	Satb
O Vos Omnes (Accompanied)	Couperin, F. (Hines)	75 Elv	M	T Sl	Sa+
O Vos Omnes (Come Ye People)	Perti (Arr Beveridge)	39 Gsc	M	T Sl	Satb
O Vos Omnes (Lam 1, V. 12) (Md)	Wickens, Dennis	Na Oxf	M	T Sl	Satb
O Vos Omnes (M)	Correa, Carlos	Na Oxf	M	T Sl	Satb
Oh Come And Mourn With Us	Faber-Mathews	Na Wbp		T Sl	
Old Rugged Cross, The	Bennard/Wilson	Na Lor	M	T Sl	Satb
Omnes Amici Mei Dereliquerunt Me	Haydn, Michael	Na Gsc	B	T Sl	Satb
On A Rugged Hill	Whitford/Decou	Na Zon	M	T Sl	Satb
On Calvary's Hill	Wetzler, Robert	68 Aug	M	T Sl	Var
On The Mount Of Olives (E & Lat)	Bruckner, A./Ed Klein	67 Gia	B	L T Sl	Satb+
On The Way To Jerusalem	Maunder	Na Lor	M	T Sl	Satb
On The Way To Jerusalem	Maunder, J H	Na Gsc	B	T Sl	Satb+
On The Wood His Arms Are Stretched	Sateren, Leland B.	68 Aug	M	T Sl	Satb
One There Is Above All Others	Lynn, George	56 Smc	M	T Sl	Full
Os Justi (The Just Mouth)	Bruckner, Anton	Na Gsc	B	T Sl	Full
Our Days Are As A Shadow	Bach, Johann (1604)	Na Kal	B	T Sl	Satb
Our Lord Did Suffer Death	Schutz/Ehret	75 Sac	M	T Sl	Satb
Out Of Darkness (Cantata On Ps 130)	Gounod, Charles	Na Kal	B	T Sl	Satb
Out Of The Deep (M)	Morley, Thomas	Na Oxf	M	T Sl	Full
Out Of The Depths	Silver	75 Maf	M	T Sl	2pt
Out Of The Depths (A Cap)	Track, Gerhard	75 Hal		T Sl	Satb
Out Of The Depths (2 Voices)	Unknown/Tortolano Ed	70 Gia	B	L T Sl	Round
Out Of The Depths I Cry (Ps 129)	Cunningham/Quinn	65 Wlp	B	T Sl	
Out Of The Depths I Cry To Thee	Bach, J. S.	Na Gsc	B	T Sl	Satb+
Out Of The Depths I Cry To Thee	Franck, Melchior	Na Gsc	B	T Sl	Satb
Out Of The Depths We Cry, Lord	Schutz, Heinrich	69 Aug	M	T Sl	Satb
Palm Sunday Procession	Newbury, Kent A.	Na Gsc	B	T Sl	Satb+
Palms, The	Faure, Gabriel	Na Lor	M	T Sl	Var
Parce Mihi Domini (Job's Complaint)	Franco, Fernando	52 Pic	M	T Sl	
Passion Chorale	Bach, J. S.	Na Gsc	B	T Sl	Satb+
Passion Chorale, The	Martin	Na Lor	M	T Sl	Sab
Penitential Psalms (3)	Lasso, Orlando Di	Na Kal	B	T Sl	Satb
Penitential Tears Of St. Peter (3 Vol)	Lasso, Orlando Di	Na Kal	B	T Sl	Satb
Perfect Through Suffering	Bingham	75 Cfp	M	T Sl	Satb+
Planctus Mariae (Latin & English)	Smoldon, W. L. Ed	Na Oxf	B	T Sl	Satb
Popule Meus	Palestrina, Giovanni P	Na Gsc	B	T Sl	8mix
Prayer To Jesus (Me)	Oldroyd, George	Na Oxf	M	T Sl	Satb
Prepare The Way O Zion	Traditional/Johnson	Na Zon	M	T Sl	Satb
Prevent Us, O Lord, In All Our Doings	Byrd, William	Na Oxf	M	T Sl	Satb
Proba Me Deus	Lasso, Orlando Di	Na Gsc	B	T Sl	Satb
Processional Psalm For Lent (E)	Proulx, Richard	75 Gia	M	L T Sl	2pt+
Psalm 102 (Becker Psalter) Eng	Schutz, H./Ed Reuning	74 Gia	B	L T Sl	Satb
Psalm 13	Martin, Warren	55 Ron	M	T Sl	Satb
Psalm 13 Lord How Long	Liszt, Franz	Na Kal	B	T Sl	Satb
Psalm 13 Lord, How Long Wilt Thou	Brahms, Johannes	Na Gsc	B	T Sl	Ssa+
Psalm 130 (Becker Psalter) Eng	Schutz, H./Ed Reuning	74 Gia	B	L T Sl	Satb
Psalm 143 (Becker Psalter) Eng	Schutz, H./Ed Reuning	74 Gia	B	L T Sl	Satb
Psalm 32 (Becker Psalter) Eng	Schutz, H./Ed Reuning	74 Gia	B	L T Sl	Satb
Psalm 34	Goudimel, C W	Na Gsc	B	T Sl	Satb+
Psalm 38 (Becker Psalter) Eng	Schutz, H./Ed Reuning	74 Gia	B	L T Sl	Satb
Psalm 40 (M)	Adler, Samuel	Na Oxf	M	T Sl	Satb
Psalm 51	Mcafee, Don	75 Maf	M	T Sl	
Psalm 51 (Becker Psalter) Eng	Schutz, H./Ed Reuning	74 Gia	B	L T Sl	Satb
Psalm 6 (Becker Psalter) Eng	Schutz, H./Ed Reuning	74 Gia	B	L T Sl	Satb
Purge Me, O Lord (Me)	Tallis, Thomas	Na Oxf	M	T Sl	Satb
Quoniam Ad Te Clamabo, Domine	Schutz, Heinrich	Na Gsc	B	T Sl	Satb
Remember, O Thou Man	Sheppard, J Stanley	Na Gsc	B	T Sl	Satb+
Renew A Right Spirit Within Me	Davis, K K	Na Gsc	B	T Sl	Sa+
Saint Matthew Passion	Bach, J. S.	52 Bbl	B	T Sl	Satb
Saints & Sinners (Cantata)	Bach, J. S.	75 Lps	B R	T Sl	Satb
Salvation Is Created	Tschesnokoff, P.	Na Gsc	B	T Sl	Satb
Salvation Is For All	Ford	Na Lor	M	T Sl	Satb
Salvator Mundi (Md)	Tallis, Thomas	Na Oxf	M	T Sl	Satb
Save Us, O Lord	Newbury, Kent A.	Na Gsc	B	T Sl	Satb
Saw Ye My Savior? (W/Flute)	Johnson, D.	68 Aug	M	T Sl	Satb+
Search Le, O Lord	Nordman	Na Lor	M	T Sl	Satb
Search Me, O God	Mueller, Carl F	Na Gsc	B	T Sl	Satb
Search Me, O God	Smith	Na Lor	M	T Sl	Satb
See What Love	Mendelssohn, F.	Na Aug	M	T Sl	Satb
Seek Ye The Lord	Roberts	46 Aug	M	T Sl	Satb
Seek Ye The Lord	Roberts	Na Lor	M	T Sl	Satb
Seek Ye The Lord	Roberts, J V	Na Gsc	B	T Sl	Satb+
Seek Ye The Lord	Southbridge, James	Na Lor	M	T Sl	Satb
Seven Last Words	Dubois, Theodore (D1924)	Na Kal	B	T Sl	Satb
Seven Last Words	Schutz, Heinrich	Na Kal	B	T Sl	Satb
Seven Last Words, The	Ritter	Na Lor	M	T Sl	Satb
Seven Sayings From The Cross	Lorenz, E J	Na Lor	M	T Sl	
Seven Words From The Cross	Powell, Robert J.	Na Abi	M	T Sl	
Seven Words Of Love	Pfautsch, Lloyd	Na Abi	M	T Sl	
Shall I Crucify Him?	Ellis	Na Lor	M	T Sl	Satb
Shall I Crucify My Savior?	London	Na Lor	M	T Sl	Satb
Show Me The Way	Price	Na Lor	M	T Sl	
Sic Deus Dilexit Mundum	Scheidt, S	74 Gia	M	T Sl	Satb+
Sing, My Tongue (Choral)	Fitzpatrick, Dennis	65 Fel	B	T Sl	
Solus Ad Victimam (Me)	Leighton, Kenneth	Na Oxf	M	T Sl	Satb
Sometimes I Feel Like A Motherless Ch.	Na	Na Gsc	B	T Sl	Ttbb+
Sorrow And Grief	Kuhnau, Johann	75 Bbl	M	T Sl	Ssatb
Sorrow's Tear (From Three Songs)	Jenks, Stephen	76 Bbl	M	T Sl	Ssb
Sorrowful Now Is My Soul	Lasso, Orlando Di	66 Som	M	T Sl	
St John Passion, The	Handel, George F.	Na Abi	M	T Sl	
St. John Passion (Germ/Eng)	Bach, J. S.	Na Kal	B	T Sl	Satb
St. John Passion (Ger)	Bach, J. S.	Cfp	R	T Sl	Satb+
St. John's Passion	Harzer, B. Resinerius	Na Kal	B	T Sl	Satb
St. Mark Passion (W/Soli)	Pinkham	75 Cfp	M	T Sl	Satb
St. Matthew Passion (Eng)	Bach, J. S.	Na Kal	B	T Sl	1satb
St. Matthew Passion (Ger)	Bach, J. S.	Cfp	R	T Sl	Satb+
Stabat Mater	Dvorak, A. (D1904)	Na Kal	B R	T Sl	Satb
Stabat Mater	Haydn, Joseph	Na Kal	B	T Sl	Satb
Stabat Mater	Pergolesi, G. B.	Na Oxf	B	T Sl	Sastr
Stabat Mater	Rossini, G.A. (D1868)	Na Kal	B	T Sl	Satb
Stabat Mater	Schubert, Franz J.	Na Kal	B	T Sl	Satb
Stabat Mater (Unfinished)	Pergolesi, G.B. (D1736)	Na Kal	B	T Sl	Satb
Stabat Mater (W/Sop Solo)	Pinkham	75 Cfp	M	T Sl	Satb
Stabat Mater 1	Verdi, Giuseppe	Na Kal	B	T Sl	Satb
Standin' In The Need O' Prayer	Na	Na Gsc	B	T Sl	Ttbb
Super Flumina Babylonis	De Lassus, O	75 Maf	M	T Sl	Satb
Surely He Hath Borne Our Griefs	Handel, G. F.	Na Gsc	B	Sl	Satb+
Surely He Hath Borne Our Griefs	Handel, G. F.	Cfs	M	T Sl	Satb
Surely He Hath Borne Our Griefs	Roff, Joseph	75 Sac	M	T Sl	Satb
Surely He Hath Borne Our Griefs	Salathiel, L	Na Gsc	B	T Sl	Satb+
Sweet Is Thy Mercy	Barnby, Jos	Na Gsc	B	T Sl	Satb+
Take Up Thy Cross	Price, Benton	Na Lor	M	T Sl	Satb
Take Us, O Lord	Andrews, Carroll T.	70 Gia	B	L T Sl	Var
Teach Me O Lord	Attwood, Thos	Na Gsc	B	T Sl	Var+
Teach Me Thy Way	Wilson	Na Lor	M	T Sl	Satb
Teach Me To Love Thee More	Tarner	Na Lor	M	T Sl	Satb
Teach Me To Pray	Mcphail	Na Lor	M	T Sl	Satb
Tenebrae Factae Sunt	Biber, C H	Na Gsc	B	T Sl	Satb
The "Leroy" Kyrie	Taverner, John	Na Oxf	M	T Sl	Satb
The Appeal Of The Crucified	Stainer, Sir John	Na Gsc	B	T Sl	Satb+
The Cliff Barrows Choir (No 5843)	Barrows, Cliff	Na Zon	B	T Sl	
The Crucifixion (No 5808)	Stainer, Sir John	Na Zon		T Sl	
The Donkey	Purdie, Hunter	Na Gsc	B	T Sl	Satb
The Head That Once Was Crowned	Brandon, George	73 Gia	M	T Sl	So(T)B
The Lamb	Chorbajian, John	Na Gsc	B	T Sl	Full
The Lament Of Job	Jergenson, Dale	Na Gsc	B	T Sl	Full
The Lamentations Of Jeremiah (Lat & E)	Tallis, Thomas	Na Oxf	M	T Sl	Sattb
The Passion According To St John	Schutz, Heinrich	Na Oxf	B	T Sl	Satb
The Passion According To St Luke	Schutz, Heinrich	Na Oxf	B	T Sl	Satb
The Passion According To St Matthew	Schutz, Heinrich	Na Oxf	B	T Sl	Satb
The Passion Of Christ (1716)	Handel, G. F.	Na Oxf	B	T Sl	Satb
The Past Is Dark	Na	Na Gsc	B	T Sl	Satb+

CATEGORIZED INDEX

The Seven Last Words From The Cross	Schutz, Heinrich	Na Oxf	B T Sl	Satb
The Shadows Of The Cross (Tenebrae)	Green, James R.	75 Abi	M T Sl	
The Sorrows Of My Heart (Ps 25) (E)	Bowie, William	Na Oxf	M T Sl	Ss
The Sufferings Of The Present	Franck-Ehret	76 Abi	M T Sl	Satb+
The Sufferings Of The Present (Me)	Kinsman, Franklin	75 Abi	M T Sl	Satb
Thee We Adore (A Cap)	Warland, Dale	Na Abi	M T Sl	Satb
There's Room At The Cross For You	Stanphill	Na Lor	M T Sl	Satb
These Forty Days Of Lent	Westendorf/Hern	70 Wlp	B T Sl	
Thou Knowest Lord, The Secrets	Morley, Thomas	Na Gsc	B T Sl	Satb
Thou Wilt Keep Him In Perfect Peace	Fryxell, Regina	Na Abi	M T Sl	Satb
Though Deep Has Been My Falling	Lasso, Orlando Di	41 Gsc	M T Sl	Satb
Through Bitter Tribulation	Bach, J. S.	75 Lps	B R T Sl	Satb
Tis Finished	Na	Na Gsc	B T Sl	Satb
Tis Finished! So The Savior Cried	Sateren, Leland B.	63 Aug	M T Sl	Satb
To God Almighty We Confess	Farrell, Melvin	55 Wlp	B T Sl	
To Zion Jesus Came	Smith	Na Lor	M T Sl	Satb
Tristis Est Anima Mea	Haydn, Michael	Na Gsc	B T Sl	Satb
Tristis Est Anima Mea	Kuhnau, Johann	75 Bbl	M T Sl	Ssatb
Tristis Est Anima Mea	Lasso, Orlando Di	Na Kal	B T Sl	Satb
Trust In The Lord	Eberlin, Ernst	Na Gsc	B T Sl	Satb
Turn Thy Face From My Sins (M)	Locke, Matthew	Na Oxf	M T Sl	Ssatb
Turn Ye Even To Me	Harker, F F	Na Gsc	B T Sl	Satb+
Ubi Caritas Et Amor (Eng & Lt)(M)	Proulx, Richard	76 Gia	M L T Sl	Satb+
Unto Thee Will I Cry (Ps 28)	Barnes, Charles	Na Oxf	M T Sl	Full
Venite Ad Me Omnes	Lasso, Orlando Di	Na Gsc	B T Sl	5mix
Vere Languores Nostros	Na	Na Gsc	B T Sl	Satb
Via Crucis	Liszt, Franz	Na Kal	B T Sl	Satb
Vigilate	Byrd, Wm/Kendall	75 Aug	M T Sl	Satbb
Walpole (From Two Plain-Tunes)	Wood, Abraham	76 Bbl	M T Sl	Satb
Watch Ye, Pray Ye (Cantata)	Bach, J. S.	75 Lps	B R T Sl	Satb
Wayfaring Stranger	Niles, John Jacob	Na Gsc	B T Sl	Full
We Adore Thee	Ayers, Jacob S.	Na Zon	M T Sl	Full
We Adore You (E & Lat)	Berti, G./Ed. Klein	69 Gia	B L T Sl	Satb+
We Adore You (E & Lat)	Gasparini, Q./Ed Klein	67 Gia	B L T Sl	Satb+
We Adore You, Jesus Christ	Andrews, Carroll T.	70 Gia	B L T Sl	Var
We Adore You, O Lord Jesus Christ	Remondi/Lee	70 Gia	B L T Sl	Satb
Weary Marching Up The Calvary Road	Colom/Johnson	Na Zon	M T Sl	Satb
Weeping Nature (From Three Songs)	Jenks, Stephen	76 Bbl	M T Sl	Satb
Were You There	Lojeski/Ed(Arr)	76 Hal	T Sl	Satb
What Is It Troubles Thee (Cantata)	Bach, J. S.	75 Lps	B R T Sl	Satb
What Pain Our Master Did'st Endure	Schutz, Heinrich	67 Aug	M T Sl	Satb
What Wondrous Love Is This	Denton	Na Lor	M T Sl	
When David Heard	Chorbajian, John	Na Gsc	B T Sl	Full
When His Salvation Bringing	Traditional/Peterson	Na Zon	M T Sl	Sa
When I Remember	Peterson/Decou	Na Zon	M T Sl	Satb
When I Stood At Calvary	Mccluskey	Na Lor	M T Sl	
When I Survey The Wondrous Cross	Copes, V Earle	Na Gsc	B T Sl	Satb+
When I Survey The Wondrous Cross	Lovelace, Austin C.	75 Sac	M T Sl	
When I Survey The Wondrous Cross	Peninger	75 Sac	M T Sl	
When I Was Sinkin' Down	Na	Na Gsc	B T Sl	Satb
When Jesus In The Garden	Wasner, Franz	Na Gsc	B T Sl	Sab
When Jesus Wept	Billings, William	Na Gsc	B T Sl	Round
When Jesus Wept (In 19 Rounds)	Billings, W./Tortolano	75 Gia	B L T Sl	4pt
When Wilt Thou Save The People?	Mueller, Carl F	Na Gsc	B T Sl	Satb+
When Woe Assails Us Through And Throug	Brahms, Johannes	Na Gsc	B T Sl	Full
Where Have You Gone, My Lonely Lord?	Shea	Na Lor	M T Sl	
Where There Is Charity And Love	Nachtwey, Roger	65 Fel	B R T Sl	
While Standing At The Cross	Carrier	Na Lor	M T Sl	
Who Can Behold	Lovelace, Austin C.	74 Aug	M T Sl	2pt
Why Art Thou So Heavy, O My Soul (M)	Loosemore, Henry	Na Oxf	M T Sl	Satb
Why Should He Love Me So?	Wilson	Na Lor	M T Sl	
With Broken Heart And Contrite Sigh	Slater	75 Sac	M T Sl	
With Weeping Life Begins	Bach, J. C.	52 Bbl	B T Sl	Satb+
Wondrous Love	London	Na Lor	M T Sl	
Wounded For Me	Ovens/Decou	Na Zon	M T Sl	Satb
Ye Who Pass By	Lotti, Antonio	66 Som	M T Sl	
You Got To Cross That Lonesome Valley	Niles, John Jacob	Na Gsc	B T Sl	3eq+

Easter Hymns(Hymns of Resurrection)

This category lists hymns for Easter and Ascensiontide, as well as hymns which celebrate the resurrection of the dead.

A Child's Message Of Easter (Cantata)	Rains, Dorothy Best	Na Zon	C Sr	Ussa
Butterfly Song	Walker, Mary Lou	73 Pnp	B R C Sr	
Oh, Yes, Lord Jesus Lives	Landry, Carey (Rev.)	75 Nal	B R C Sr	
On That First Bright Easter Day	Lang, C Tilghman	Na Gsc	B C Sr	Unis+
Resurrection	Curzio, Elaine	70 Van	B R C Sr	
This Is The Day	Landry, Carey (Rev.)	75 Nal	B R C Sr	

Allelu	Repp, Ray	66 Fel	B R F Sr	
Alleluia (Easter Day)	Fischer, John	69 Fel	B R F Sr	
Alleluia, Praise His Name	Greif, Jean A	66 Vrn	M L F Sr	
Ascension Song	O'sheil, Judy	66 Fel	B F Sr	
Beautiful City	Lojeski, Ed	74 Hal	F Sr	Var
But Then Comes The Morning	Miffleton, Jack Et Al	69 Wlp	B F Sr	
Canticle Of The Gift (4-Part Arr.)	Cirou, Joseph	73 Acp	L F Sr	
Christ Is Risen 1	Coppock, Doug	69 Fis	M L F Sr	
Christ, Our Passover	Mitchell, Ian	68 Fel	B R F Sr	
Clap Your Hands (Ascension)	Graap, Augustine	66 Car	M R L F Sr	2mel
Come Away	Repp, Ray	66 Fel	B R F Sr	
Come In, Pilgrim	Ault, Gary	71 Fel	B R F Sr	
Dogwood Cross, The	London	Na Lor	M F Sr	Satb
Early American Tune	Salem	Na Gsc	B F Sr	Satb+
Easter Song	Winter, Miriam T.	67 Van	B R F Sr	
Forever Together With Him	Peterson/Wyrtzen	Na Zon	M F Sr	Satb
Glory Bound (From Psalm 29)	Quinlan, Paul	65 Wlp	B R F Sr	
Glory Land	Ault, Gary	71 Fel	B R F Sr	
Glory To The Risen Lord	Cockett, M./Pearson, J.	69 Van	B R F Sr	
Goin' Home	Welz, Joey-Wray, Link	71 Urs	M B R F Sr	
Golden Morning	Ault, Gary	71 Fel	B R F Sr	
Greet The Risen Lord With Joy	Miffleton, Jack	68 Acp	L F Sr	
Greet The Risen Lord With Joy 4-Part	Silvia, Helen	70 Acp	L F Sr	
Have You Ever Been	Ault, Gary	70 Fel	B R F Sr	
He Has Life Restored	Meltz, Ken	72 Wlp	B R F Sr	
I Saw The Holy City	Blue, Robert	66 Fel	B F Sr	
I'll Raise You Up (Calypso)	Temple, Sebastian	71 Gia	B R L F Sr	Var+
I'm Living, I'm Living	Sweeney	71 Wlp	B R F Sr	
It Is A Great Day Of Joy	Mccarthy, John	70 Van	B R F Sr	
It's A Brand New Day	Quinlan, Paul	67 Van	B R F Sr	Bro?
Jesus Has Come	Ault, Gary	70 Fel	B R F Sr	
Jesus My Lord	Fischer, John	70 Fel	B R F Sr	
Jubilation!	Smith, Lani	Na Lor	M B F Sr	Satb
Kingdom Song	O'sheil, Judy	66 Fel	B F Sr	
Let Trumpets Sound	Cockett, M/Mayhew, K.	69 Van	B R F Sr	
Look Around	Meyer, Ron	73 Fel	B F Sr	
Lord Has Risen In Glory, The	Silvia, Helen	73 Acp	L F Sr	
New Day Dawning	Hunkele	67 Wlp	B F Sr	
New Life	Jacobs, Peter	71 Chd	B R L F Sr	
New Tomorrow, A	Marsh, Donald T.	Na Zon	M F Sr	Ssatb
Peter & The Angel	Ylvisaker, J. & A.	69 Van	B R F Sr	
Planted Wheat (Trad Hb Mel)	Cothran, Jeff(Wds, Arr)	72 Gia	M B R L F Sr	Var+
Psalm 96 This Is The Day	Blue, Robert	66 Fel	B F Sr	
Redemption Song (Exodus)	Cunningham, Patrick	76 Gra	B R L F Sr	
Resurrection	Germaine	66 Fel	B R F Sr	
Resurrection (Life W/New Direction)	Belt, Thomas	72 Gia	B R L F Sr	Var+
Right Hand Of The Lord, The	Shafer, William	70 Acp	L F Sr	
Right Hand Of The Lord, The (4-Part Arr)	Cirou, Joseph/Silvia H	73 Acp	L F Sr	
Roll That Stone Away	Connaughton/O'riordan	69 Van	B R F Sr	
Rolled Away (Revisited)	Traditional/Wyrtzen	Na Zon	M F Sr	2-Pt
Russian Alleluia (Victimae)	Graap, Augustine	66 Car	M R L F Sr	3pt
Salvation Song	Fischer, John	70 Fel	B R F Sr	
Sing, Christians, Sing	St. Benedict's Farm	75 Sbf	B R L F Sr	
The Butterfly Song	Howard, Brian	73 Fis	M L F Sr	
The Lord Is Risen	Mudd, C. P.	67 Wlp	B R F Sr	
The Lord Is Takin' Us Home	Montague, George T.	68 Fel	B R F Sr	
The New Creation	Ault, Gary	70 Fel	B R F Sr	
The New Morn (The Sun Came Over)	Belt, Thomas/Batastini	72 Gia	B R L F Sr	Var+
The Tree Of Life	Thiem, James	66 Fel	B F Sr	
The Victory Dance	Ylvisaker, J. & A.	69 Van	B R F Sr	
This Is The Day	Meltz, Ken	72 Wlp	B R F Sr	
This Is The Day	Reilly, Cyril A.	66 Fel	B F Sr	
This Is The Day	Repp, Ray	66 Fel	B R F Sr	
This Is The Day That The Lord	Repp, Ray	67 Fel	B R F Sr	
To Be Redeemed	Bowers, Jane	Na Gia	B R L F Sr	
To Rise Again	Schaffer, Robert J.	69 Wlp	B F Sr	
When The Morning Comes	Ducote, Darryl	70 Fel	B R F Sr	

Away Over In The Gloryland	Parks, Joe E.	Na Zon	M G Sr	Satb
Because He Lives	Gaither/Gaither B/G	71 Gmc	M B R G Sr	Var
Beulah Land	Sweney/Mclellan	Na Zon	M G Sr	Ssatb
Beyond Tomorrow	Huntley/Campbell	Na Zon	M G Sr	
Bound For Canaan	Traditional/Rasley	Na Zon	M G Sr	Satb
Chariot Of Clouds	Peterson, John W.	75 Zon	M G Sr	Satb
Christ Arose (W/Piano)	Johnson, P. (Arr)	74 Wrd	M G Sr	Satb+
Deep River	Na	Na Gsc	B G Sr	Var
Easter Cantata In Spanish	Peterson, John W.	Na Zon	G Sr	Span
Face To Face	Hamblen Stuart	Na Ham	M G Sr	
Faith, Tears And Resurrection Cantata	Fasig, Bill	Na Zon	G Sr	
Five Minutes More	Harper, Redd	Na Zon	M G Sr	
Going To That Holy Land	Amason, B.	75 Sil	L G Sr	
Gonna Ride That Heavenly Train	Young	75 Her	M G Sr	Satb
Hallelujah! We Shall Rise	Thomas/Decou	Na Zon	M G Sr	Satb
Hammering (Spiritual)	Na	Na Lor	M G Sr	Sab
He Really Has Set Me Free	Culverwell, Andrew	74 Man	B R G Sr	
He Satisfied That Longing In My Soul	Owens, Jimmie	53 Man	M G Sr	
He'll Make My Dream Come True	Farrer, C And Miller, C.	74 Man	B G Sr	
Heaven	Mcspadden, Boyd & Helen	48 Man	M B G Sr	
Heaven's Lights Ahead	Hall J. Barnett	74 Jhm	R L G Sr	
Homecoming In Glory	Butler, Dorothy	67 Pmp	M B R L G Sr	
I Believe Heaven's God's Will	Dan Reta, Laney E.C.	74 Jhm	R L G Sr	
I Found Joy (W/Piano)	Grundy, S.K.	75 Wrd	M G Sr	Satb+
I Know The Story	Akers, Doris	54 Man	M B G Sr	
I Remember The Time	Chitwood, Joe	70 Man	M G Sr	
I Want To Be There	Hamblen Stuart	Na Ham	M G Sr	
I Want To Be There	Peterson, John W.	Na Zon	M G Sr	Satb
I Want To Go To Heaven	Coakley J. Blevins D.	74 Jhm	R L G Sr	
I'll Wear A New White Robe	Stacy M. Laney E.C.	74 Jhm	R L G Sr	
I'm A-Goin To Glory	Stanphill/Ferrin	75 Zon	M G Sr	Satb
I'm Almost Home	Gaither/Gaither B/G	66 Gmc	M B R G Sr	Satb
I'm Glad To Know There's A Heaven	Akers, Doris	67 Man	M B G Sr	
I'm Going To Fly Away To Heaven	Coakley J. Blevins D.	74 Jhm	R L G Sr	
I'm Going To Make It Through	Coakley J. Blevins D.	74 Jhm	R L G Sr	
I'm Gonna Ride That Train To Heaven	Sizemore, G/Hall, T	44 Kmp	M B L G Sr	
I'm Gonna' Take A Trip	Barry, Jody	74 Man	R G Sr	
I'm Watching For His Coming	Coakley J. Blevins D.	74 Jhm	R L G Sr	
I've Got So Many Million Years	Hamblen Stuart	Na Ham	M G Sr	
If I Should Go To Heaven	Carey, T/Mel, L./Kelly	75 Kmp	M B R L G Sr	
In God's Tomorrow	Gaither/Gaither	63 Gmc	M B R G Sr	Sato
It Will Be Worth It All	Gaither/Gaither	66 Gmc	M B R G Sr	Satb
It's Gonna' Be A Morning To Remember	Barry, Jody	74 Man	R G Sr	
It's Just Like Moses On The Mountain	Cunningham, Patrick	76 Gra	B R L G Sr	
Jesus, I Heard You Had A Big House	Gaither/Gaither B/G	74 Gmc	M B R G Sr	Var
Keep This In Mind	Hamblen Stuart	Na Ham	M G Sr	
Life Eternal	Akers, Doris	55 Man	M B G Sr	
Lord, I Want A Diadem	Dunlop/Johnson	Na Zon	M G Sr	Sab
Meet Me In Heaven	Akers, Doris	58 Man	M B R G Sr	
My Melody Of Longing	Bystrom	Na Zon	M G Sr	
New Day	Dodd/Johnson	Na Zon	M G Sr	Satb
No More Death	Peterson, John W.	Na Zon	M G Sr	Satb

CATEGORIZED INDEX

No More Sorrow Over There	Brock, Linda	74 Mam R L G Sr
No Tears Tomorrow	Decou, Harold	75 Zon M G Sr Satb
One Day Nearer Home	Hamblen Stuart	Na Ham M G Sr
One Step Beyond	Butler, Dorothy	74 Pmp M B L G Sr
Paradise	Childs	Na Zon M G Sr
Proclaim His Great Love	King, Lew	75 Wrd M G Sr Satb+
Promises Of God (W/Piano)	Lanier, Gary	76 Wrd M G Sr Satb+
Reaching For My Crown	Overstreet, Rev. L.	68 Sto G Sr
Shall We Gather At The River?	Martin	Na Lor M G Sr Satb
Some Beautiful Morning	Lee, Johnnie	72 Mmc M G Sr
Someday I'll See His Face	Crouch, Andrae	67 Man B R G Sr
Somewhere Beyond The Sun	Hamblen Stuart	Na Ham M G Sr
Soon I'll See His Face	Spencer, Hal	74 Man B G Sr
Swing Low Sweet Chariot	Foley Et Al (Arr)	67 Pmp M B R L G Sr
Thank God For The Promise Of Spring	Gaither/Gaither B/G	73 Gmc M B R G Sr Satb
The Blood Will Never Lose It's Power	Crouch, Andrae	66 Man M B R G Sr
The Church Triumphant	Gaither/Gaither B/G	73 Gmc M B R G Sr Satb
The Resurrection Morn	Gaither/Gaither B/G	72 Gmc M B R G Sr Var
There's Glory In My Soul	Cram, W. Francis	74 Mam M R L G Sr
This Is The Day The Lord Hath Made	Gaither/Gaither B/G	75 Gmc M B R G Sr Var
This Ole House	Hamblen Stuart	Na Ham M G Sr
Time Is Short; Eternity's Long	Ohler, Susan	73 Pmp M B R L G Sr
Treasure Of Heaven, The	Rogers	Na Zon M G Sr
Trying To Make Heaven My Home	Peninger, David	75 Her M G Sr Sab
Victory Ahead	Grum/Smith	Na Zon M G Sr Satb
Wanna Go To Heaven?	Akers, Doris	64 Man B G Sr
We Don't Have Much Farther To Go	Irwin	Na Zon M G Sr
When God Calls Us Home	Ohler, Susan	74 Pmp M B R L G Sr
When I Climb Them Golden Stairs	Petty Doug	71 Jhm L G Sr
When We See Christ	Rusthoi/Mickelson	Na Zon M G Sr Satb
Where The Seasons Never Change	Hamblen Stuart	Na Ham M G Sr
Will You Be There	Butler, Dorothy	68 Pmp M B R L G Sr
Your Shining Hour	Mieir, Audrey	66 Man M G Sr

A Brand New Promised Land	Fabing, Bob	70 Ahc B R L L Sr
A Prayer For Eastertide	Barry, Rev. John	75 Rpb M B R L L Sr
A Song To The Lamb (W/Brass, Tim)	Hancock, Gerre	74 Hwg M L Sr Satb+
Alleluia	Young, Gordon	75 Sac M L Sr Satb
Alleluia! Alleluia!	Ehret, Walter	74 Gia M L Sr Satb+
Alleluia! Christ Has Risen	Gilligan, M. (Text)	67 Acp L L Sr
Alleluia! Christ Has Risen(4-Part Arr)	Nardella, Faith	73 Acp L L Sr
Alleluia! He Has Risen	Ford	Na Lor M L Sr Var
Alleluia! Let The Song Of Glory Rise	Gilligan, M. (Text)	70 Acp L L Sr
Alleluia! Let The Song Of Glory Rise	Terry, Richard, Silvia,	73 Acp L L Sr
Alone (E)	Moffatt	Na Lor M L Sr Satb
An Easter Processional	Near, Gerald	74 Hwg M L Sr
And Peace Shall Reign Again	Mabry	Na Lor M L Sr Satb
At The Lamb's High Feast We Sing	Bach, J. S. Alt.	73 Acp L L Sr Satb
At The Lamb's High Feast We Sing	Campbell, Robert, Alt.	67 Acp L L Sr
Before The Dawn	Sibelius	Na Lor M L Sr Unis
Behold Your King Cantata	Peterson, John W.	Na Zon L Sr Var
Bells Of Easter, The	Mcafee, D	75 Maf M L Sr Unis
Best Is Yet To Come, The	Sylvester, Erich	71 Nal B R L Sr
Blessed Be The Day	Kerner, Debby Melle	72 Mar R L L Sr
Bright & Glorious Is The Sky	Melby, J.	76 Aug L Sr U+ Org
But Now Is Christ Risen	Peterson, John W.	Na Zon M L Sr Satb
Cantares De Pascua	Santa Cruz, Domingo	52 Pic M L Sr
Canticle For Easter, A	Young, Gordon	75 Sac M L Sr Satb
Celestial Country	Ives, Charles E.	71 Pic M L Sr
Children Of The Eighth Day	Mudd, C. P.	72 Nal B R L Sr
Children's Hosanna, The	Emig	Na Lor M L Sr Satb
Christ Arose (Easy)	Lowry/Johnson	Na Zon M L Sr Sa(Tb)
Christ Arose!	Hughes, Robert J.	Na Lor M L Sr
Christ Being Raised From The Dead	Cook, E. T.	Na Oxf M L Sr Satb
Christ Has Risen	Gilligan, M. (Text)	67 Acp L L Sr
Christ Has Risen From The Dead	Cirou, Joseph	73 Acp L L Sr Satb
Christ Has Risen From The Dead	Gilligan, M. (Text)	67 Acp L L Sr
Christ Hath Triumphed, Alleluia!	Hughes, Robert J.	Na Lor M L Sr
Christ Is Risen	Emerson	Na Lor M L Sr
Christ Is Risen	Goemanne, Noel	Na Gia L Sr
Christ Is Risen!	Lovelace, Austin C.	75 Sac M L Sr Sab
Christ Is Risen!	Perry	Na Lor M L Sr
Christ Is Risen, Alleluia!	Silson	Na Lor M L Sr
Christ Our Passover (M)	Gibbs, Alan	Na Oxf M L Sr Satb
Christ Our Passover (Md)	Powers, George	75 Abi M L Sr Satb
Christ Rose From Death	Fitzpatrick, Dennis	65 Fel B L Sr
Christ The Lord Is Risen Again(Org,Br)	Pelz, W.	72 Aug M L Sr Satb
Christ The Lord Is Risen Today	Denton	Na Lor M L Sr
Christ The Lord Is Risen Today	Ehret, Walter	Na Lor M L Sr
Christ The Lord Is Risen Today	Fiske, Milton	60 Som M L Sr
Christ The Lord Is Risen Today	Wilson	Na Lor M L Sr
Christ The Lord Is Risen! (E)	Gilbert, Norman	Na Oxf M L Sr Satb
Christ The Lord Today Has Risen	Cirou, Joseph, Lyrica	73 Acp L L Sr Satb
Christ The Lord Today Has Risen	Gilligan, M. (Text)	70 Acp L L Sr
Christ The Lord, Our Risen King	Nachtwey, Roger	65 Fel B L Sr
Christ Walked This Way Before	Norman	Na Lor M L Sr
Christ Who Has Risen From The Dead	Deiss, Lucien	70 Wlp B R L Sr
Christ, Our Lamb	Fitzpatrick, Dennis	65 Fel B L Sr
Christ, Our Paschal Lamb	Roff, Joseph	70 Gia M L Sr Satb+
Christians, Sing Joyfully	Emig	Na Lor M L Sr
Come Alive	St. Benedict's Farm	75 Sbf B R L L Sr 2 Pt
Come To The Tomb	Lovelace, Austin C.	Na Abi M L Sr Satb
Come Ye Faithful, Raise The Strain	Ayers, Jacob S.	Na Zon M L Sr Satb
Come Ye Faithful, Raise The Strain	Darst, W. Glen	74 Hwg M L Sr Satb+
Cross Was Not The End, The	Johnson	Na Lor M L Sr Satb
Cross, The	Buettell	Na Lor M L Sr Satb
Darkness Now Has Taken Flight, The	Lovelace, Austin C.	Na Abi M L Sr U-Sa
Day Of Celebration, The	Hubert, Yvon	72 Fcc R L L Sr
Death Shall No Longer Have	Fitzpatrick, Dennis	65 Fel B L Sr
Early In The Morning	Grimes, Travis	75 Sac M B L Sr Sa
Early Spring, The	Eliot	Na Lor M L Sr
Easter	Champagne, Claude	66 Pic M L Sr
Easter Bell Carol	Pfautsch, Lloyd	Na Abi M L Sr Satb
Easter Bells (Opt Group Lection)	Durocher	Hof M L Sr Var
Easter Carol	Rasley	Na Lor M L Sr
Easter Celebration Cantata	Decou, Harold	Na Zon R L Sr
Easter Dawn	Hine	Na Lor M L Sr
Easter Day (A Cap)	Drayton, Paul	75 Hwg M L L Sr Full
Easter Fanfare	Peninger	75 Sac M L Sr Full
Easter Hallelujah, The	Lorenz	Na Lor M L Sr
Easter Hymn Of Praise (Opt Acc)	Lapo, Cecil E.	Na Abi M L Sr Satb
Easter Praise (E)	Martin	Na Lor M L Sr
Easter Song	Dowdy	75 Sac M L Sr Satb
Easter Song	Ellis, Ron	76 Rav B R L L Sr
Easter Song! (Cantata)	Peterson, John W.	Na Zon L Sr Var+
Emmaus Road	Smith	Na Lor M L Sr Sb
Even For One	Smith	Na Lor M L Sr
Exultet (Easter Proclamation)	Ellis, Ron	75 Rav B R L L Sr
Eye Hasn't Seen	Wise, Joe	73 Nal B R L Sr
Feel The Place Of The Nails	Fitzpatrick, Dennis	65 Fel B L Sr
Festal Alleluia, A	Lorenz	Na Lor M L Sr
Forgive Me (E)	Townsend	Na Lor M L Sr
Gates Of Heaven Are Open	Youse	Hof M L Sr Var
Glory To Our Risen King	Butler	75 Sac M L Sr Satb
Glory To The Lamb (Cantata) (No 4269)	Johnson, Norman	Na Zon L Sr Satb+
God Ascends Amid Shouts Of Joy	Fitzpatrick, Dennis	65 Fel B L Sr
God Gave Him Life Again!	Wilhelm	75 Sac M L Sr Satb
God Mounts His Throne	Peloquin, C Alexander	71 Gia B L Sr Satbu+
God Reigns	Deiss, Lucien	65 Wlp B R L Sr
Hail, Glorious King (No 5964)	Peterson, John W.	Na Zon L Sr
Hail, Thou Once-Despised Jesus	Peterson, John W.	Na Zon L Sr Satb
Hallelujah For The Cross (No 5959)	Peterson, John W.	Na Zon L Sr
Hallelujah! What A Savior! (No 5978)	Peterson, John W.	Na Zon B L Sr
Hallelujah, Hallelujah, Jesus Christ	Kerner, Debby Melle	72 Mar R L L Sr
He Has Risen As He Said	Fitzpatrick, Dennis	65 Fel B L Sr
He Is Lord	Unknown	73 Mar B L L Sr
He Is Risen	Jennings, K.	76 Aug L Sr Var+
He Is Risen	Moultry, Prince Joseph	74 Nal B R L Sr
He Is Risen	Patenaude, A. & Charbo	71 Nal B R L Sr
He Is Risen (E)	Cope, Cecil	Na Oxf M L Sr 2-4pt
He Is Risen, Alleluia (Opt Brass)	Diercks, John H.	Na Abi M L Sr Satb+
He Is Risen, Alleluia (W/Org)	Englert, Eugene	Na Gia M L L Sr 2pt
He Lives	Nelson, Erick Martin	72 Mar R L L Sr
He Saved Me Because He Loves Me	Fitzpatrick, Dennis	65 Fel B L Sr
He Shall Return As He Has Left	Fitzpatrick, Dennis	65 Fel B L Sr
He Shall Rule From Sea To Sea	Schroth, G	69 Gia M L Sr Var+
He's Alive	Unknown	73 Mar B L L Sr
He's Back In The Land Of The Living	Kaan, Fred/Metcalf	68 Gal B L L Sr
He's Risen	Collard, Terry	71 Nal B R L Sr
He's Risen, Christ Jesus The Lord	Pelz, W.	63 Aug M L Sr Satb
Heaven Haven	Flanagan, William	52 Pic M L Sr
Heaven My Home	Burroughs, Bob	Na Abi M L Sr Satb
I Am The Resurrection	Fitzpatrick, Dennis	65 Fel B L Sr
I Am The Resurrection And The Life	Williams	75 Sac M L Sr Satb
I Believe That My Redeemer Lives	Fitzpatrick, Dennis	65 Fel B L Sr
I Believe That My Redeemer Lives	Peloquin, C Alexander	73 Gia M L Sr Var+
I Have Arisen And Am With You	Fitzpatrick, Dennis	65 Fel B L Sr
I've Been Sealed	Angle, Dana P	75 Mar R L L Sr
In Honour Of A King	Ager, Laurence	Na Gsc B L Sr Sa+
In Praise Of Easter (5 Movements)	Locklair	75 Jfs B L Sr
It Is The Joyful Eastertime	George	65 Aug M L Sr Sa
Jerusalem, My Happy Home	Walter	75 Sac M L Sr Satb
Jesu, Jesu, Why Did You Die?	Lipscomb, Helen	Na Gsc B L Sr Sab+
Jesus, Our Lord, Is Risen Today!	Young, Gordon	75 Sac M L Sr Satb
Joy Dawned Again On Easter Day	Rogers	75 Sac M L Sr Sa
Jubilate Deo (W/Brs)	Sleeth, Natalie	Na Abi M L Sr Satb
Keep In Mind	Deiss, Lucien	65 Wlp B R L Sr Var
King Of Glory Cantata (No 5990)	La Rowe, Jane	Na Zon L Sr Satb+
Litany For Easter (A Cap)	Young, Gordon	Na Abi M L Sr Full
Long Live The Lord	Deiss, Lucien	70 Wlp B R L Sr
Lord, You Live	Landry, Carey (Rev.)	68 Nal B R L Sr
Love Your Brother	Hughes, Robert J.	Na Lor M L Sr Satb
Loving Shepherd Of Thy Sheep (E)	Cabena, Barrie	Na Oxf M L Sr Unis
Meditation	Hegenbart, Alex F.	Na Abi M L Sr Satb
My Song Is Love Unknown	Peninger	75 Sac M L Sr Satb
My Soul, There Is A Country	Drayton, Paul	Na Oxf M L Sr
No Greater Love	Brumbaugh, Harley	76 Lor L Sr Unis+
No Greater Love (No 5977)	Peterson, John W.	Na Zon B L Sr
No Greater Love (No 5984)	Peterson, John W.	Na Zon B L Sr
No Greater Love (No 5992)	Peterson, John W.	Na Zon B L Sr
Nothin' Left To Fear	Schneider, Kent E.	75 Ccc B L Sr
Now Is Christ Risen (W/Instruments)	Nystedt, Ronald	65 Aug M L Sr Satb+
Now Is Christ Risen Cantata	Rasley/Cross	Na Zon R L Sr
Now Tell Us, Gentle Mary (Instruments)	Hunnicutt, J.	72 Aug M L Sr Unis
O Glorious Resurrection Day	Peterson, John W.	Na Zon M L Sr Satb
O God, Thou Hast The Dawn Of Life	Denton	Na Lor M L Sr Satb
O Where Are Kings And Empires Now	Strickler, David	Na Abi M L Sr Satb
On This Blessed Easter Day	Hughes, Robert J.	Na Lor M L Sr Sab
Our Lord Is Risen	Powell	75 Sac M L Sr Satb
Pasch Of The New Law	Deiss, Lucien	65 Wlp B L Sr Var
Pearly Mansions	Butler, Charles F.	74 Mar R L L Sr
Praise The Savior	Cassler, G. W.	Na Abi M L Sr Satb
Praises For The Risen Christ	Martin	75 Sac M L Sr Satb+
Psalm 118 (W/Brs)	Corina, John	Na Abi M L Sr Satb
Rejoice! For We Are Saved	Taranto	75 Pro M L Sr Satb+
Rejoice, Rejoice This Glad Easter Day	Leaf, Robert	69 Aug M L Sr Satb+
Rejoice, Rejoice.	Greif, Jean A	66 Vrn M L L Sr
Rejoice, You Pure In Heart	Engler, Eugene	73 Gia M L Sr Satb+
Ring Ye Joy Bells	Durocher	Hof M L Sr Sa
Risen Christ!	Caldwell, M	75 Sac M L Sr Var

CATEGORIZED INDEX

Saw Ye My Savior	Johnson, D.	76 Aug		L Sr	Unison+
Sing Alleluia, Jesus Lives	Sateren, Leland B.	75 Sac	M	L Sr	Satb
Sing To The Lord (Ascension)	Fitzpatrick, Dennis	65 Fel	B	L Sr	
Sing, Soul Of Mine! The Lord Is Risen	Clothier	66 Aug	M	L Sr	Satb
Song Of Deliverance, A	Mccormick	75 Sac	M	L Sr	Satb
Song Of Hope	Goemanne, Noel	72 Gia	M	L Sr	W/Inst
Song Of Tears And Triumph	Winston, Colleen, Osb	73 Nal	B	L Sr	
Swing Low, Sweet Chariot	Westbrook, Francis B.	Na Abi	M	L Sr	Satb
Taken Up In Glory	Roff, Joseph	75 Gia	M	L Sr	Sa(T)B+
That Easter Day	Neale, John N.	70 Acp	L	L Sr	
That Easter Day	Silvia, Helen	73 Acp	L	L Sr	
That Glorious Day	Eddins, Martha A.	75 Pdm		L Sr	
That I May Too Arise	Patterson	Na Lor	M	L Sr	Satb
That The World Might Be Renewed	Isele, Bill	71 Nal	B	L Sr	
The Day Of Resurrection	Brandon, George	74 Gia	M	L Sr	Satb+
The Earth Feared	Mcgrath, J J	Na Gia		L Sr	
The Earth Feared And Was Silent	Roff, Joseph	74 Gia	M	L Sr	
The Earth Was Fearful And Silent	Fitzpatrick, Dennis	65 Fel	B	L Sr	
The Easter Song	Repp, Ray	67 Fel	B R L	L Sr	
The Empty Cave	Neff	73 Aug	M	L Sr	Full
The Glory Of Easter (No 5983)	Peterson, John W.	Na Zon		L Sr	Var
The Horsemen	Kerner, Debby Melle	72 Mar	R L	L Sr	
The Lord Ascendeth Up On High	Sowerby, Leo	76 Sac		L Sr	Satb+
The Lord Has Risen	Fitzpatrick, Dennis	65 Fel	B	L Sr	
The Miracle (No 4312)	Mickelson, Paul	75 Zon	R	L Sr	
The Resurrection	Rorem, Ned	56 Som	M	L Sr	
The Resurrection (W/Insts)	Wilson	74 Aug	M	L Sr	Satb
The Saints You Gave	Fitzpatrick, Dennis	65 Fel	B	L Sr	
The Salvation Of The Just	Fitzpatrick, Dennis	65 Fel	B	L Sr	
The Word (Though The Rivers)	Temple, Sebastian	71 Gia	B R L	L Sr	Satb+
There Is A Land	Lewis, John Leo	Na Gsc	B	L Sr	Satb
There'll Be Bread	Culverwell, Andrew	73 Man	B R	L Sr	
This Day God Made	Creed, Dan (Arr.)	73 Nal	B R	L Sr	
This Day God Made	Westendorf, Omer	70 Wlp	B	L Sr	
This Is The Day	Mcbride, James	75 Ccc	M B	L Sr	
This Is The Day	Moultry, Prince Joseph	74 Nal	B R	L Sr	
This Is The Day	Potenaude, Andre, M. S	71 Nal	B R	L Sr	
This Is The Day	Schroth, G	71 Gia	M	L Sr	Ssatb+
This Is The Day	Toolan, Sr Suzanne	74 Rpb	M B R L	L Sr	
This Is The Day	Unknown	73 Mar	B L	L Sr	
This Is The Day The Lord Has Made	Lee, John	71 Gia	M	L Sr	Var+
This Is The Day The Lord Hath Made	Near, Gerald	71 Aug	M	L Sr	Sab
This Is The Day The Lord Hath Made	Peterson, John W.	Na Zon		L Sr	Satb
This Is The Day Which The Lord	Fitzpatrick, Dennis	65 Fel	B R	L Sr	
This Is The Day Which The Lord Hath	Ford, Virgil	Na Gsc	B	L Sr	Var
This Is The Day Which The Lord Hath	Peeters, Flor	59 Aug	M	L Sr	Satb
Today Is The Crown Of Creation	Sylvester, Erich	71 Nal	B R	L Sr	
Truly, We Shall Be In Paradise	Neumann, Alfred	Na Gsc	B	L Sr	Satb+
Two Junior Choir Anthems	White	75 Sac	M	L Sr	
Upon Easter Day	Roff, Joseph	74 Gia	M	L Sr	Satb+
What The Future Hath W/Organ Acc	Brandon, George	Na Gsc	B	L Sr	3mix+
When I Get To Heaven	Unknown	73 Mar	B L	L Sr	
When Israel	Huijbers & Oosterhuis	74 Nal	M B R	L Sr	
Who Is He That Stands Triumphant?	De Vere, Aubrey	70 Acp	L	L Sr	
Ye Sons And Daughters	Track, Gerhard	67 Gia	M	L Sr	Satb+
You Broke The Reign Of Death	Deiss, Lucien	65 Wlp	B R	L Sr	
You Have Crowned Him With Glory	Fitzpatrick, Dennis	65 Fel	B	L Sr	
You Have Set On His Head	Fitzpatrick, Dennis	65 Fel	B	L Sr	
You Shall Make Them Princes	Fitzpatrick, Dennis	65 Fel	B	L Sr	
You Will Show Me The Path To Life	Zsigray, Joe	72 Nal	B R	L Sr	
A Hymn To The Risen Christ	Curry, W Lawrence	Na Gsc	B	T Sr	Satb+
Abroad The Regal Banners Fly	Pergolesi (Ed Agey)	Na Abi	M	T Sr	Satb
Alleluia (Hearts And Voices)	Lockwood, Normand	56 Smc	M	T Sr	Satb
Alleluia Haec Dies	Donati, Ignazio	Na Gsc	B	T Sr	Satb+
Alleluia! Hearts To Heaven (E)	Stanton, W. K.	Na Oxf	M	T Sr	2pt
Alleluia! Let The Holy Anthem Rise!	Englert, Eugene	72 Aug	M	T Sr	Satb
Alleluia! Tulerunt Dominum	Palestrina, Giovanni P	Na Gsc	B	T Sr	Sattb
Alleluia, Christ Is Risen	Lockwood, Normand	74 Bbl	M	T Sr	Satb
Alleluia, Jesus Lives	Lindeman–Leupold	57 Aug	M	T Sr	Sab
An Easter Carillon (E)	Beck, W. Leonard	Na Oxf	M	T Sr	Unis
An Easter Dialogue (W/Brass, Org)	Hammerschmidt	75 Cfp	M	T Sr	Full
An Easter Sequence (Eng, Lat)	Leighton, Kenneth	Na Oxf	B	T Sr	Ssaa
And God Shall Wipe Away All Tears	Coombe, C W	Na Gsc	B	T Sr	Satb+
And He Showed Me A Pure River	Dalby, Martin	Na Gsc	B	T Sr	Satb+
And Then Shall Your Light	Mendelssohn, F.	Na Gsc	B	T Sr	Satb+
As It Began To Dawn	Foster, M B	Na Gsc	B	T Sr	Satb+
As It Began To Dawn	Harker, F F	Na Gsc	B	T Sr	Var+
As It Began To Dawn (W/Bar Solo)	Coombs, C W	Na Gsc	M	T Sr	Full+
Ascendit, Deus (Md)	Philips, Peter 1	Na Oxf	M	T Sr	Satb
At Calvery	Wilson	Na Lor	M	T Sr	Satb
Awake Arise	Edwards, Clara	Na Gsc	B	T Sr	Satb+
Awake My Heart With Gladness (E)	Bach, J. S.	Na Oxf	M	T Sr	Satb
Awake Up My Glory	Barnby, Jos	Na Gsc	B	T Sr	Satb+
Away The Gloom	Holman, Derek	Na Gsc	B	T Sr	Satb
Bell Carol (Jr + Sr Choirs)	Wichmann, Russell	Na Oxf	M	T Sr	Satb
Blessing For Easter Morning, A	Ferguson	75 Sac	M	T Sr	Satb
Cantata For Easter	Gardner, John	Na Oxf	B	T Sr	Satb
Canticum Gaudii (W/Brass, Org)	Peeters, Flor	75 Cfp	M	T Sr	Satb+
Carol For Eastertide, A	Rasley	Na Lor	M	T Sr	Satb
Chorus Of Angels	Schubert, Franz J.	Na Gsc	B	T Sr	Satb
Christ Has Risen (Choral)	Fitzpatrick, Dennis	65 Fel	B	T Sr	
Christ Hath Arisen	Lasso, Orlando Di	Na Gsc	B	T Sr	Satb
Christ Is Arisen	Eccard, J	Na Gsc	B	T Sr	Ssatb
Christ Is Arisen (E & Ger)	Hassler, H.L./Ed Klein	69 Gia	B L	T Sr	Satb+
Christ Is Arisen!	Pfautsch, Lloyd	Na Abi	M	T Sr	Satb
Christ Is Risen	Neander/Rasley	75 Zon	M	T Sr	Satb
Christ Is Risen	Williams/Johnson	Na Zon	M	T Sr	Satb
Christ Is Risen (Bohemian Melody)	Na	Na Gsc	B	T Sr	Satb+
Christ Is Risen From The Dead	Dunlop/Decou	Na Zon	M	T Sr	Satb
Christ Is Risen Indeed	Hampton, Calvin	75 Maf	M	T Sr	Satb
Christ Is Risen!	Mueller, Carl F	Na Gsc	B	T Sr	2chor
Christ Is Risen, Alleluia	Maker–Wetgzler	61 Aug	M	T Sr	Satb+
Christ Rising Again (M)	Tye, Christopher	Na Oxf	M	T Sr	Satb
Christ Rising Again (Md)	Amner, John	Na Oxf	M	T Sr	Satb
Christ The Lord Hath Risen	Na	Na Gsc	B	T Sr	Tb
Christ The Lord Is Ris'n (A Cap)	Rorem	75 Cfp	M	T Sr	Satb
Christ The Lord Is Risen	Johnson, D.	64 Aug	M	T Sr	Satb
Christ The Lord Is Risen	Pelz, W.	66 Aug	M	T Sr	Satb
Christ The Lord Is Risen (W/Brs)	Titcomb, Everett	75 Cfp	M	T Sr	Satb
Christ The Lord Is Risen Again	Carter, J. (Arr)	76 Bec	M	T Sr	
Christ The Lord Is Risen Again	Proulx, Richard	72 Gia		T Sr	Satb+
Christ The Lord Is Risen Again	Rutter, John	Na Oxf	M	T Sr	Satb
Christ The Lord Is Risen Again	Williams	59 Aug	M	T Sr	Satb+
Christ The Lord Is Risen Today	Hallstrom, Henry	Na Abi	M	T Sr	Satb
Christ The Lord Is Risen Today	Hughes, Robert J.	Na Lor	M	T Sr	
Christ The Lord Is Risen Today	Na	Na Gsc	B	T Sr	Satb+
Christ The Lord Is Risen Today	Rogers	Na Lor	M	T Sr	
Christ The Lord Is Risen Today	Weber, Dennis	Na Zon	M	T Sr	Satb
Christ The Lord Is Risen Today (Easy)	Traditional/Decou	75 Zon	M	T Sr	Sa(Tb)
Christ The Lord Is Risen Today (W/Opt	Traditional/Peterson	Na Zon	M	T Sr	Ssatb
Christ The Lord, Is Risen Again	Powell, Robert J.	Na Gsc	B	T Sr	Satb
Christ Whose Glory Fills The Skies	Lovelace, Austin C.	Na Abi	M	T Sr	Sab
Christ, Be Thine The Glory	Schutz, Heinrich	Na Gsc	B	T Sr	Satb
Christus Resurgens (D)	Johnson, Robert S.	Na Oxf	M	T Sr	Satb
Come Ye Faithful, Raise The Strain	Traditional/Rasley	Na Zon	M	T Sr	Satb
Come, O Blessed	Bixel, James W.	74 Flp	M	T Sr	
Come, Risen Lord	Near, Gerald	70 Aug	M	T Sr	Satb
Come, Ye Blessed	Scott, J P	Na Gsc	B	T Sr	Var
Day Of Resurrection, The	Haydn/Yungton	75 Zon	M	T Sr	Satb
Did Not Our Heart Burn Within Us	Salathiel, L	Na Gsc	B	T Sr	Satb+
Early Easter Morning	Grieb, Herbert	Na Gsc	B	T Sr	Satb+
Easter (From Holiday Motets)	Krenek, Ernst	67 Ron	B	T Sr	Ssa
Easter (Most Glorious Lord)	Gibbs, C. Armstrong	Na Oxf	M	T Sr	Satb
Easter Alleluia, An	Peterson, John W.	75 Zon	M	T Sr	Satb
Easter Anthem (Shaw)	Billings, William	Na Gsc	B	T Sr	Satb
Easter Cantata (W/Brass, Perc)	Pinkham	75 Cfp	M	T Sr	Satb
Easter Carol	Byles, B D	Na Gsc	B	T Sr	Sa+
Easter Carol	Williamson, Malcolm	Na Gsc	B	T Sr	Satb+
Easter Chorale	Barber, Samuel	Na Gsc	B	T Sr	Satb+
Easter Dawning	Wetzler, Robert	60 Aug	M	T Sr	Satb
Easter Fanfare: Christ The Lord	Fetler, Paul	70 Aug	M	T Sr	Satb
Easter Glory	Lindeman–Cassler	73 Aug	M	T Sr	Satb+
Easter Hymn	Rasley, John M.	75 Zon	M	T Sr	Satb
Easter Morning	Christiansen, P.	48 Aug	M	T Sr	Satb
Easter Oratorio	Bach, J. S.	75 Lps	B R	T Sr	Satb
Easter Oratorio (Eng)	Bach, J. S.	Na Kal	B	T Sr	Satb
Eye Has Not Seen	Lasso, Orlando Di	67 Fel	B	T Sr	
Eye Hath Not Seen	Matthews, H A	Na Gsc	B	T Sr	Satb
Fair Easter	Licht, Myrtha B	Na Gsc	B	T Sr	Var+
Gates Of Jerusalem, The	Mcafee, Don	75 Maf	M	T Sr	Var
Gates Of Jerusalem, The	Moussorgsky, Modest	Na Lor	M	T Sr	Satb
Glorification	Christiansen, F. M.	60 Aug	M	T Sr	Satb
Glory And Triumph	Hammerschmidt/Pooler	75 Sac	M	T Sr	Satb
Glory Around His Head, The	Handel, G. F.	53 Bbl	B	T Sr	Satb+
Glory Hallelujah To The Lamb	Jones/Johnson	75 Zon	M	T Sr	Satb
God Shall Wipe Away All Tears	Sullivan, Arthur	Na Gsc	B	T Sr	Sba+
Goin' Home On A Cloud	White, Michael	Na Gsc	B	T Sr	Satb
Good Christian Men Rejoice & Sing (E)	Bullock, Ernest	Na Oxf	M	T Sr	Satb
Great Is Thy Reward	Raymond, Joseph	Na Gsc	B	T Sr	Satb+
Haec Dies (Md)	Palestrina, Giovanni P	Na Oxf	M R	T Sr	Full
Hail The Day	Monk, William Henry	Na Gsc	B	T Sr	Sab+
Hail To The King	Peterson, John W.	75 Zon	M	T Sr	Satb
Hail To Thee, Glad Day	Lockwood, Normand	56 Smc	M	T Sr	Satb
Hallelujah! Christ Is Risen (Brs)	Mcgranahan, J. (Field)	75 Elv	M	T Sr	Satb+
Hallelujah, What A Savior	Bliss/Wyrtzen	Na Zon	M	T Sr	Satb
Halleluyah, Christ Is Risen	Wihtol, A. A.	Na Zon	M	T Sr	Satb
He Has Made A Special Place For Me	Waterman, Frances	76 Lor		T Sr	Unis+
He Is Risen	Mueller, Carl F	Na Gsc	B	T Sr	2chor
He Is Risen	Pelz, W.	63 Aug	M	T Sr	Unis
He Is Risen	Peterson, John W.	Na Zon	M	T Sr	Satb
He Lives	Hughes, Robert J.	Na Lor	M	T Sr	Satb
He Was Wounded For Our Transgressions	Peterson, John W.	75 Zon	M	T Sr	Satb
He'll Understand, And Say, "Well Done"	Campbell	Na Lor	M	T Sr	Satb
Head That Once Was Crowned With Thorns	Thomas, Paul	Na Abi	M	T Sr	Satb
Hearts To Heaven And Voices Raise	Walter, Samuel	Na Abi	M	T Sr	Satb
Hilariter	Na	Na Gsc	B	T Sr	Satb
Holy City, The	Gaul, Harvey(D1945)	Na Kal	B	T Sr	Satb
Holy Easter Morning	Mcfarland	Na Lor	M	T Sr	Unis
Hosanna	Grainer, J	Na Gsc	B	T Sr	Var+
Hosanna	Lockwood, Normand	Na Gsc	B	T Sr	Satb
Hosanna (Lat)	Lockwood, Normand	40 Gsc	M	T Sr	Satb
How Calm And Beautiful The Morn	Grieb, Herbert	Na Gsc	B	T Sr	Satb+
How Lovely Are Those Dwellings	Mendelssohn, F.	Na Zon		T Sr	Satb
Hymn For Ascensiontide (E)	Purcell, Henry	Na Oxf	M	T Sr	Satb
I Am The Resurrection And The Life	Gibbons, Orlando	Na Oxf	M	T Sr	Sattb
I Am The Resurrection And The Life	Peterson, John W.	Na Zon	M	T Sr	Satb
I Am The Resurrection And The Life	Schutz, Heinrich	Cfp	R	T Sr	Satb+
I Know That My Redeemer (W/Org)	Peeters, Flor	75 Cfp	M	T Sr	Satb
I Know That My Redeemer Lives	Schutz, Heinrich	Na Gsc	B	T Sr	Full+
I Know That My Redeemer Lives	Traditional/Decou	Na Zon		T Sr	Unison
I Know That My Redeemer Lives (M)	Bach, J. S.	Na Oxf	M	T Sr	Satbb
I Know That My Redeemer Liveth	Handel, G. F.	35 Aug	M	T Sr	Satb
I Know That My Redeemer Liveth	Handel, G. F.	Na Lor	M	T Sr	Var
I Longed To Find The Risen Lord	Lynn, George	56 Smc	M	T Sr	Satb
I Want To Be Ready	Denton	Na Lor	M	T Sr	Satb
I Will Lift Mine Eyes	Edwards, Clara	Na Gsc	B	T Sr	Satb+
If Ye Then Be Risen (Opt Acc)	Powell, Robert J.	Na Abi	M	T Sr	Ssatb
In My Father's House	Pasquet, Jean	Na Gsc	B	T Sr	Satb
In Resurrectione Domini	Wellesz, Egon	61 Bbl	M	T Sr	

CATEGORIZED INDEX

In The End Of The Sabbath	Speaks, Oley	Na Gsc	B T Sr Var+
Introit For Easter	Nelson, Ronald A.	Na Abi	M T Sr Satb
Ivory Palaces	Barraclough/Mccluskey	Na Lor	M T Sr Satb
Ivory Places	Barraclough/Wilson	Na Lor	M T Sr Satb
Jerusalem The Golden	Na	Na Gsc	B T Sr 2chor
Jesus Christ Is Risen Today (+ Tpts)	Pelz, W.	65 Aug	M T Sr Satb
Jesus Christ Is Risen Today (W/Inst)	Copley, R. Evan	Na Abi	M T Sr Var
Jesus, Come Abide With Me	Johnston	Na Lor	M T Sr Satb
King All—Glorious	Vail	Na Lor	M T Sr Var
King Is Riding By, The	Price	Na Lor	M T Sr Satb
Leoni	Goemanne, Noel	Na Gia	T Sr
Let All The Earth Rejoice & Sing	Farrell, Melvin	55 Wlp	B T Sr
Let Hymns Of Joy	Fitzpatrick, Dennis	65 Fel	B T Sr
Let Hymns Of Joy Of Grief Succeed	Lee, John	73 Gia	M T Sr
Let's Celebrate Easter	Wyrtzen, Don	Na Zon	M T Sr Satb
Lift Up Your Heads (Ps 24)	Gibbons, Orlando	Na Oxf	M T Sr Full
Lilies (Mumma)	Na	Na Lor	M T Sr Unis
Llanfair	Goemanne, Noel	73 Gia	M T Sr Satb
Lo The Tomb Is Empty	Broome, Ed	Na Gsc	B T Sr Satb+
Lo, Round The Throne A Glorious Band	Powell, Robert J.	Na Gsc	B T Sr Satb+
Look Ye Saints, The Sight Is Glorious	Wetzler, Robert	68 Aug	M T Sr Sab
Lord Christ, When First Thou Cam'st	Na	Na Gsc	B T Sr Full
Lord In Thy Resurrection	Gallus,J/Jacob,H	Na Gsc	B T Sr 8mix
Lord Is Merciful, The	Kortkamp	Na Lor	M T Sr Satb
Lord Is Risen Today, The	Vail	Na Lor	M T Sr Sab
Lord, Build Me A Cabin In Glory	Stewart, Curtis	47 Ivm	M B R L T Sr
Love Is Come Again	Na	Na Gsc	B T Sr Satb
Love Not The World	Gaul, A R	Na Gsc	B T Sr Satb+
Magdalen, Cease From Sobs And Sighs	Hurford, Peter	Na Oxf	M T Sr Satb
Magdalena Op 22 No 6	Brahms, Johannes	Na Gsc	B T Sr Satb
Maria Magdalene Et Altera Maria	Gabrieli, Andrea	74 Bbl	M T Sr Satb
Maria Magdalene Et Altera Maria	Schein, Johann H	74 Bbl	M T Sr Ssatb
Message Of The Bells	Pohlmann (Durocher)	Hof	M T Sr Ssa
Most Glorious Lord Of Life (Md)	Milner, Anthony	Na Oxf	M T Sr Satb
Most Glorious Lord Of Life!	Lord, David	Na Oxf	M T Sr Satb
My Lord Has Set Me Free	Grieg	Na Lor	M T Sr Sab
My Lord, What A Morning	Wilson	Na Lor	M T Sr Sab
My Redeemer Liveth	Loucks	Na Lor	M T Sr Satb
No Shadows Yonder (From Holy City)	Gaul, Harvey	Cfs	M T Sr Satb
None Other Lamb (No 4271)	Ayers, Jacob	Na Zon	T Sr Satb+
Now April Has Come	Na	Na Gsc	B T Sr Satb
Now If Christ Be Preached	Rogers, J H	Na Gsc	B T Sr Satb+
Now Is Christ Risen	Johnson, Norman	75 Zon	M T Sr Ssatbb
Now Sing, All Saints	Peterson, John W.	Na Zon	M T Sr Satb
Now The Green Blade Riseth (Arr)	Strickler, David	Na Oxf	M T Sr Satb
O Clap Your Hands (Ps 47)	Rutter, John	Na Oxf	M T Sr Satb
O Clap Your Hands (Ps 47)	Young, Gordon	Na Oxf	M T Sr Satb
O Clap Your Hands (With Doxology) (Md)	Gibbons, Orlando	Na Oxf	M T Sr Full
O Joyful Day Of Our Salvation (Cant)	Bach, J. S.	75 Lps	B R T Sr Satb
O Sons And Daughters	Na	Na Gsc	B T Sr Satb
On Easter Morn	Na	Na Gsc	B T Sr Satb
On This Day Of Glory (W/3 Tpts)	Leaf, Robert	74 Aug	M T Sr Satb+
Open The Gates Of The Temple	Knapp	Na Lor	M T Sr Var
Paradise	Na	Na Gsc	B T Sr Satb
Passiontide Carol	Anderson, Ruth	Na Gsc	B T Sr Satb
Peregrinus (Acting Version)	Smoldon, W.L. (Ed)	Na Oxf	B T Sr Satb
Praise Our God	Denton	Na Lor	M T Sr Satb
Procession Of Palms	Williamson, Malcolm	Na Gsc	B T Sr Satb+
Promised Land	Carter, J.	76 Bec	M T Sr
Psalm 47 (O Clap Your Hands) W/Brass	King	69 Aug	M T Sr Satb+
Purge Ut Therefore The Old Leaven	Schutz, Heinrich	Cfp	R T Sr Satb+
Redemption Anthem	Benham, Asahel	75 Bbl	M T Sr Satb
Resurrection Alleluia	Traditional/Decou	Na Zon	M T Sr Satb
Resurrection Morn	Van Woert	Na Lor	M T Sr
Revelation Motet	Franck, Melchior	54 Bbl	M T Sr Satb
Ride On King Jesus!	Southbridge	Na Lor	M T Sr Sab
Ride On!	Broughton	Na Lor	M T Sr
Ride On, King Jesus	Traditional/Johnson	Na Zon	M T Sr Satb
Ride On, Ride On In Majesty	Hughes, Robert J.	Na Lor	M T Sr
Ride On, Ride On In Majesty	Mcafee, Don	75 Sac	M T Sr Var
Rise Up My Love (From Sg)	Bruckner, A./Ed Klein	67 Gia	B L T Sr Satb+
Rise Up, My Love	Bruckner, Anton	Na Gia	T Sr
Risen Christ, The	Smith	Na Lor	M T Sr
Risen Today	Hughes, Robert J.	Na Lor	M T Sr
Shall We Gather At The River	Lynn, George (Arr)	56 Smc	M T Sr Satb
Since By Man Came Death	Handel, G. F.	Na Gsc	B T Sr Satb+
Sing Hallelujah, Praise The Lord	Mueller, Carl F	Na Gsc	B T Sr Var+
Sing To The Lord (3 Voices)	Telemann,G./Tortolano	70 Gia	B L T Sr Round
Sing Up All Now Alleluia	Ehret, Walter	75 Gia	M T Sr Satb+
Sleepers Awake (Cantata)	Bach, J. S.	75 Lps	B R T Sr Satb
So Let Me Live	Wyrtzen, Don	Na Lor	M T Sr Var
Song Of Deliverance	James	Na Lor	M T Sr
Souls Of The Righteous	Johnson, D.	74 Aug	M T Sr Satb
Sound The Trumpet (2 Pt Acc)	Purcell, Henry (Ehret)	75 Elv	M T Sr Satb
Strife Is O'er, The	Palestrina, Giovanni P	Na Zon	M T Sr Satb
Sunrise On A Hill	Lorenz	Na Lor	M T Sr Satb
Surrexit Dominus	Handl, Jacob	Na Gia	T Sr
Surrexit Pastor Bonus	Lasso, Orlando Di	Na Gsc	B T Sr 5mix
Sweet Music	Wilson	Na Lor	M T Sr Satb
Ten Thousand Angels	Overholt	Na Lor	M T Sr Satb
That Easter Day With Joy Was Bright	Pooler, Marie	62 Aug	M T Sr Var
That Easter Day With Joy Was Bright	Wood	69 Aug	M T Sr U+Ds
That Easter Morn At Break Of Day (Tpt)	Leaf, Robert	74 Aug	M T Sr Satb
That God Doth Love The World We Know	Wadely, F. W.	Na Oxf	M T Sr Sab
That Virgin's Child	Tallis, Thomas	Na Gsc	B T Sr Satb
The Blessed Christ Is Risen Today	Lee, John	73 Gia	M T Sr 2eq+
The Desert Shall Blossom	Christiansen, P.	54 Aug	M T Sr Satb
The Earth Feared	Andrews, Carroll T.	70 Gia	M T Sr 2pt+
The Earth Feared And Was Silent	Albrecht, K	Na Gia	T Sr
The Easter Anthems	Shaw, Martin	Na Oxf	M T Sr Full
The Easter Choir (No 5330)	Rasley, John M.	Na Zon	B T Sr
The Glory Of This Day	Moe, Daniel	73 Aug	M T Sr Satb
The King Of Love My Shepherd Is (Me)	Bairstow, E. C.	Na Oxf	M T Sr Satb
The Little Family	Niles, John Jacob	Na Gsc	B T Sr Var
The Lord Is Ris'n Indeed	Billings, William	Cfp	R T Sr Satb
The Lord Is Ris'n Indeed (A Cap)	Billings (Ed. Daniel)	75 Cfp	M T Sr Satb
The May Carol	Niles, John Jacob	Na Gsc	B T Sr Satb+
The Morning Of The Day Of Days	Williamson, Malcolm	Na Gsc	B T Sr Satb+
The Resurrection	Curran, P G	Na Gsc	B T Sr Satb+
The Resurrection	Shelley, H R	Na Gsc	B T Sr Satb+
The Resurrection According To St Mat	Keel, Richard	Na Gsc	B T Sr Satb+
The Right Hand Of The Lord (Canon)	Scheidt,S./Tortolano	70 Gia	B L T Sr 2f1
The Robin And The Thorn	Niles, John Jacob	Na Gsc	B T Sr Var+
The Strife Is O'er	Palestrina, Giovanni P	Na Gsc	B T Sr Satb
The Sun Shall Be No More Thy Light	Woodward, H. H.	Na Gsc	B T Sr Satb+
The Three Lilies	Gaul, Harvey	Na Gsc	B T Sr Full+
The Triumph—Song	Mueller, Carl F	Na Gsc	B T Sr Satb+
Then Round About The Starry Throne	Handel, G.F.(Christy)	39 Gsc	M T Sr Full
Then Shall The King Say Unto Them	Pasquet, Jean	Na Gsc	B T Sr Satb+
They Have Taken Away My Lord	Stainer, Sir John	Na Gsc	B T Sr Satb+
Thine Accounting (Cantata)	Bach, J. S.	75 Lps	B R T Sr Satb
Thine Is The Glory (Easy)	Handel/Montgomery	Na Zon	M T Sr Sa(Tb)
This Glad Day (Md)	Byrd, William	Na Oxf	M T Sr Ssattb
This Is The Day	Hampton, Calvin	75 Maf	M T Sr Satb
This Is The Day	Handl, Jacob	66 Som	M T Sr
This Is The Day (Ps 118) (Me)	Anonymous	Na Oxf	M T Sr Satb
This Is The Day (W/Flute)	Johnson, D.	73 Aug	M T Sr Satb
This Is The Day The Lord Has Made	Proulx, Richard	68 Aug	M T Sr Ssa
This Joyful Eastertide	Na	Na Gsc	B T Sr Satb
This Most Glorious Day	Track, Gerhard	74 Hal	T Sr Satb
Thou Art The Living Christ	Wilson, I	Na Lor	M T Sr
Tis Well (Cantata)	Bach, J. S.	75 Lps	B R T Sr Satb
Today There Is Ringing	Christiansen, F. M.	56 Aug	M T Sr Satb
Triumph	White	75 Bbl	M T Sr Tb
Twas On One Sunday Morning	Price	Na Lor	M T Sr Var
Two Easter Anthems	Billings, William	Cfp	R T Sr Satb
Two Easter Anthems (A Cap)	Billings (Ed. Daniel)	75 Cfp	M T Sr Satb
Unto Christ The Victim (Victimae)	Byrd, William	Na Oxf	M T Sr Ssatb
Upper Room, The	Wilson	Na Lor	M T Sr Satb
Vexilla Regis Prodeunt (Lat)	Bruckner, Anton	Cfp	R T Sr Satb+
Victimae Paschali Laudes	Fitzpatrick, Dennis	63 Fel	B T Sr
Victimae Paschali Laudes	Victoria, Tomas Luis	74 Gia	M T Sr Satb+
Visitatio Sepulchri (Acting Version)	Smoldon, W. L. Ed	Na Oxf	B T Sr Sol/Un
We Know That Christ Is Raised (W/Perc)	Nelson, Ronald A.	74 Aug	M T Sr Unis
We Welcome Glad Easter	Southbridge	Na Lor	M T Sr Unis
Welcome Happy Morning	Matthews, H A	Na Gsc	B T Sr Satb+
Welcome Happy Morning (Md)	Bowie, William	Na Oxf	M T Sr Satb
Welcome, Happy Morning	Havergal/Decou	Na Zon	M T Sr Satb
What Think Ye Of Christ?	Rasley	Na Lor	M T Sr
When Mary Magdalene	Schein, Johann H	74 Bbl	M T Sr Ssatb
When Mary Through The Garden Went (Me)	Judd, Percy	Na Oxf	M T Sr Ssa
When The Lord Turned Again (Me)	Batten, Adrian	Na Oxf	M T Sr Satb
Who Is This That Comes In Glory?	Young, Gordon	75 Sac	M T Sr
With Joyful Voice (Opt Tpts)	Neander, J. (Carlton)	75 Elv	M T Sr Satb+
Wondrous Is The Life In Heaven	Schutz, Heinrich	Na Gsc	B T Sr 6mix
Ye Sons And Daughters (Choral)	Fitzpatrick, Dennis	63 Fel	B T Sr
Ye Watchers And Ye Holy Ones (Me)	Oldroyd, George	Na Oxf	M T Sr Satb

Pentecost(Hymns of the Holy Spirit)

This section lists songs celebrating the presence of God through His Holy Spirit. Hymns about the gifts of God are included here, as are "Pentecostal" hymns. See also category TC.

Where The Spirit Leads	Curzio, Elaine	70 Van	B R C Ss
A New Song (Joy, Joy, Joy Is)	Belt, Thomas	70 Gia	B R L F Ss Var+
Blow, Wind (W/Guitar)	Belt, Thomas	70 Gia	B R L F Ss Var+
Come Holy Spirit	Belt, Thomas/Batastini	72 Gia	B R L F Ss Var+
Come Holy Spirit Come (Fire Of Love)	Temple, Sebastian	71 Gia	B R L F Ss Var+
Come To The Running River	Silvia, Helen	73 Acp	L F Ss
Come, Holy Spirit	Cunningham, Patrick	73 Gra	B R L F Ss Satb
Drink Deep Of The Fountain	Cunningham, Patrick	76 Gra	B R L F Ss
Fill Me, Holy Spirit	Yantis, David	Na Yan	B F Ss
Flies The Dove (From Young Carpenter)	Miffleton, Jack	71 Wlp	B R F Ss
Flowing Free (Love Is Flowing)	Farra, Mimi A.	73 Gia	M B R L F Ss Var+
Ho! Everyone That Thirsteth	Pulkingham, Betty C.	72 Gia	M B R L F Ss Var+
Holy Spirit	Williams, J.	76 Sil	F Ss
Holy Spirit Song	Jacobs, Peter	74 Chd	R L F Ss
I Would Renew The Whole World	Cunningham, Patrick	72 Gra	B R L F Ss Solo
If I Had All The World's Money	Farra, Mimi A.	72 Gia	M B R L F Ss Var+
It's Yours For The Asking	Holiday/Johnson	Na Zon	M F Ss Ssab
Knock, Knock	Winter, Miriam T.	68 Van	B R F Ss
Litany Of The Spirit	Winberry, Mary & Malate	73 Fel	B F Ss
Living Spirit (Blessed Be The God)	Toolan, Sr Suzanne	71 Gia	B R L F Ss Ar+
Living Water	Kirschke/Krogstad	Na Zon	M F Ss Satb
Lullaby Of The Spirit	Silvia, Ray	73 Fel	B F Ss
O Living Water	Vissing, Sr. Rosalie	74 Sha	B R L F Ss
Peacebird	Edwards, Deanna	74 Fcc	R L F Ss
Pentecost Day	Winberry, Mary & Malat	73 Fel	B F Ss
Spirit Move	Ault, Gary	73 Fcc	B R L F Ss
Spirit Of Action	Miffleton, Jack	68 Acp	L F Ss
Spirit Of God	Winter, Miriam T.	66 Van	B R F Ss
Spirit Of The Lord	Winter, Miriam T.	71 Van	B R F Ss
Sweet Jesus (Your Spirit)	Krag, Lynch	74 Fis	M L F Ss
Tell The World	Ault, Gary	69 Fel	B R F Ss
The Gifts Of God	Corda, M And Lenke, W	61 Cor	M R F Ss
The Spirit And The Bride	Christmas, Charles	75 Wgm	B L F Ss
The Spirit And The Bride	Montague, George T.	72 Mcc	B R L F Ss 2pt
The Spirit Of The Lord	Ault, Gary	69 Fel	B R F Ss

CATEGORIZED INDEX

The Spirit Of The Lord	Montague, George T.	72 Mcc	B R L F Ss 2pt
The Spirit Of The Lord	Yantis, David	76 Yan	B F Ss
The Spirit Of The Lord (Hath Set Me)	Farra, Mimi A.	73 Gia	M B R L F Ss Var+
The Spirit Of The Lord (W/Guit,Fl)	Sittler	72 Aug	M F Ss Unis+
The Wind Blows	Miffleton, Jack	69 Wlp	B R F Ss
There Is A New Wind Blowin'	Yantis, David	Na Yan	B F Ss
They'll Know We Are Christians	Scholtes/Krogstad	Na Zon	M F Ss Satb
When The Spirit Moves You	Fitzgerald, Michael	74 Wgm	B L F Ss
You Fill The Day	Wise, Joe	68 Wlp	B R F Ss
By The Witness Of The Spirit	Gaither/Gaither B/G	74 Gmc	M R G Ss
Come Down O Love (W/Piano)	Hooper, W.L.	76 Wrd	M G Ss Satb+
Come To The Spirit (W/Piano)	Brooks/Dailey	75 Wrd	M G Ss Satb+
Come, Holy Spirit	Gaither/Gaither B/G	64 Gmc	M B R G Ss Satb
Come, Holy Spirit	Gaither, William J	Na Lor	M G Ss Satb
Come, Holy Spirit	Peterson, John W.	Na Zon	M G Ss Satb
Every Time I Feel The Spirit	Traditional/Johnson	Na Zon	M G Ss Satb
God Gave (Me) The Song	Gaither/Gaither B/G	73 Gmc	M B R G Ss Var
Heaven In My Heart	Parsons/Johnson	Na Zon	M G Ss Satb
Ho! Everyone That Is Thirsty	Meyer/Johnson	75 Zon	M G Ss Ssatb
Holy Spirit	Eldridge, R.	76 Sil	G Ss
Holy Spirit	Lee, Danny	75 Man	M R G Ss
I Know A Fount' So Wondrous Blest	Andreasen, Bodil	63 Man	M G Ss
I Was There When The Spirit Came	Akers, Doris	49 Man	M B R G Ss
I Wonder If It's Happened Yet To You	Wyrtzen, Don	Na Zon	M G Ss Satb
I'm A Promise	Gaither/Gaither B/G	75 Gmc	M B R G Ss Var
I'm Free	Gaither/Gaither B/G	68 Gmc	M B R G Ss Satb
I've Got It	Crouch, Andrae	71 Man	M B R G Ss
Jesus Will Move Every	Redd, Gc/H.Hubbard	Na Sav	M G Ss
Lord Don't Lift Your Spirit From Me	Crouch, Andrae	67 Man	B R G Ss
Springs Of Living Water	Peterson/Decou	Na Zon	M G Ss Satb
Sweet, Sweet Spirit	Akers, Doris	63 Man	M B R G Ss
The Breath Of God	Booth-Clibborn, W.E.	25 Wbc	M L G Ss
The Dancing Heart	Turner, Roy	67 Cam	M L G Ss
The Moving Of The Breath Of God	Mieir, Audrey	72 Man	B G Ss
The Spirit Of Jesus Is In This Place	Gaither/Gaither B/G	72 Gmc	M B R G Ss Var
There Is A Fountain	Mason/Decou	Na Zon	M G Ss Satb
There's A Power Working In My Life	Hendrix, James	Na Gmp	M R L G Ss
There's A River Of Life (Vv)	Pulkingham, Betty C.	71 Fis	M L G Ss
There's Nothing Like The Holy Ghost	Hubbard, H./G.C. Redd	Na Sav	M G Ss
Be Filled With The Spirit	Schaefer, T. & Ripelli	75 Nal	B R L Ss
Come And Pray In Us, Spirit Of The Lord	Deiss, Lucien	70 Wlp	B R L Ss
Come Creator Spirit	Gerrish, James	69 Jsp	B L Ss +Guit
Come Down, O Love Divine	Schroth, G	69 Gia	M L Ss Satb+
Come Thou Holy Spirit Come	Zsigray, Joe	74 Nal	B R L Ss
Come Walk With Me In The Spirit	Kerner, Debby Melle	72 Mar	R L L Ss
Come, Holy Ghost, Draw Near Us	Sowerby, Leo	76 Sac	L Ss Satb+
Come, Holy Spirit	Gilligan, M. (Text)	67 Acp	L L Ss
Come, Holy Spirit	Mueller, Luise	Na Abi	M L Ss Satb
Come, Holy Spirit	Silvia, Helen	73 Acp	L L Ss
Come, O Holy Spirit	Landry, Carey (Rev.)	68 Nal	B R L Ss
Come, Spirit, Come	Shelley, Tom	75 Ahc	B R L L Ss
Create In Me	Powers, George	Na Abi	M L Ss Solo
Day Of Pentecost	Sateren, Leland B.	76 Aug	L Ss Full
Descend O Spirit, Purging Flame	Brenner/Kraehenbuehl	76 Jsp	B L Ss
Earth Is Full Of The Goodness, The	Zsigray, Joe	74 Nal	B R L Ss
Fire Of Love	Collard, Terry	71 Nal	B R L Ss
Give Me More Of Thee	Unknown	73 Mar	B L L Ss
Gracious Spirit, Love Divine	Young, Gordon	Na Lor	M L Ss Satb
He Who Drinks Of The Water	Fitzpatrick, Dennis	65 Fel	B L Ss
Holy Spirit, Hear Us	Roff, Joseph	Na Lor	M L Ss 2mel
Holy Spirit, Now Outpoured	Peterson/Decou	Na Zon	L Ss Satb
Holy Spirit, Truth Divine	Mcguire, Thomas	65 Fel	B L Ss
I Have Come To Set Fire	Fitzpatrick, Dennis	65 Fel	B L Ss
I Will Breathe Into You	Fitzpatrick, Dennis	65 Fel	B L Ss
I Will Not Leave You Friendless	Fitzpatrick, Dennis	65 Fel	B L Ss
If I Wanted To Hide	St. Benedict's Farm	75 Sbf	B R L L Ss
Into Our Hearts, O Spirit Come	Gannon, Michael	61 Wlp	B L Ss
Litany Of The Holy Spirit.	Greif, Jean A	65 Vrn	M L L Ss
Living Spirit	Toolan, Sr Suzanne	Na Gia	L Ss
Living Spirit, The	Neumann, D. & Tlucek,	75 Nal	B R L Ss
Lord, By Whose Breath	Nystedt, Ronald	70 Aug	M L Ss Sab
O Holy Spirit Of God	Davidson, Ray	Na Abi	M L Ss Satb
O Holy Spirit Sent From Heaven	Lipscomb, Helen	Na Gsc	B L Ss 2eq+
O Holy Spirit, Come To Us	Fitzpatrick, Dennis	65 Fel	B L Ss
O Spirit, Who From Jesus Came	Havey, Marguerite	Na Gsc	B L Ss Satb+
Pentecost	Isele, Bill	71 Nal	B L Ss
Put Forth, O God, Thy Spirit's Might	Wehr, David A.	Na Abi	M L Ss Sab
Receive The Holy Spirit	Peloquin, C Alexander	74 Gia	M L Ss
Romans 8:14,15	Rios, David	73 Mar	B L L Ss
Send Forth Your Life-Giving Spirit	Fitzpatrick, Dennis	65 Fel	B L Ss
Send Forth Your Spirit, O Lord	Deiss, Lucien	65 Wlp	B L Ss
Send Thy Holy Breath	Peterson, John W.	Na Zon	L Ss Satb
Sing With The Spirit	Hall, Arthur	Na Abi	M L Ss Satb
Song Of The Holy Spirit	Huijbers & Oosterhuis	74 Nal	M B L Ss
Spirit Boundless	Ramseth, B.	76 Aug	L Ss U+Fl
Spirit Comes, The	Collard, Terry	71 Nal	B R L Ss
Spirit Is A-Movin', The	Landry, Carey (Rev.)	68 Nal	M B R L Ss
Spirit Of Action 4-Part Arr	Cirou, Joseph	70 Acp	L L Ss
Spirit Of Life	Landry, Carey (Rev.)	74 Nal	B R L Ss
Spirit Of Life (Violin)	Dressler, John	Na Abi	M L Ss Satb
Spirit Of Light And Life	Gilsdorf, Sr. Helen	76 Rpb	M B R L L Ss
Spirit Of Strength	Gilligan, Michael	70 Acp	L L Ss
Spirit Of Strength	Silvia, Helen	73 Acp	L L Ss
Spirit Of The Lord, The (Unacc)	Titcomb, Everett	Na Abi	M L Ss Ttbb
Stand On His Promise	Miffleton, Jack	73 Wlp	B R L Ss
Streams Of Life	Burgin, D	73 Mar	B L L Ss
Strengthen, O God	Roff, Joseph	67 Gia	M L Ss Ssa
Strengthen, O God, What You	Fitzpatrick, Dennis	65 Fel	B L Ss

Sweet Summer Rain	Lafferty, Karen Louise	75 Mar	R L L Ss
The Fire Of Love	Chardin	74 Gia	M L Ss Satb+
The Spirit Breathes Where He Will	Fitzpatrick, Dennis	65 Fel	B L Ss
The Spirit Came One Morn'	Shelley, Tom	75 Ahc	B R L L Ss
The Spirit Of God Rests Upon Me	Deiss, Lucien	70 Wlp	B R L Ss
The Spirit Of The Lord Fills	Fitzpatrick, Dennis	65 Fel	B L Ss
The Spirit Of The Lord Is Upon Me	Fitzpatrick, Dennis	65 Fel	B R L Ss
The Spirit Will Come To Guide You	Fitzpatrick, Dennis	65 Fel	B L Ss
The Spirit Will Teach You All Things	Fitzpatrick, Dennis	65 Fel	B L Ss
These Things I Have Spoken Unto You	Chew, D	73 Mar	B R L L Ss
They Were Filled With The Holy	Fitzpatrick, Dennis	65 Fel	B L Ss
Vital Spark Of Heav'nly Flame (A Cap)	Read, Gardner	Na Abi	M L Ss Satb
Whither Shall I Go	Von Kreisler, Alex	69 Smc	M L Ss Satb
Wondrous Spirit	Patenaude, Andre, M. S	71 Nal	B R L Ss
All My Heart Inflamed And Burning	Dvorak, A	Na Gsc	B T Ss Satb+
At Pentecost	Ortlip, Stephen	Na Gsc	B T Ss Satb+
Be Filled With The Spirit	Nankivell, Louise	57 Gph	M T Ss
Be Filled With The Spirit	Nelson, Ronald A.	75 Aug	M T Ss 2pt
Breath Of God	Sateren, Leland B.	47 Aug	M T Ss Satb
Breathe On Me Breath Of God	Smith, Lani	76 Lor	T Ss Sab+
Breathe On Me, Breath Of God	Rees/Morgan	Na Wbp	T Ss
Carol For Pentecost	Hunnicutt, J.	73 Aug	M T Ss Unis+
Come Down, O Love Divine	Currie, Randolph	76 Her	M T Ss Satb+
Come Gracious Spirit	Wood	69 Aug	M T Ss Satb
Come Holy Ghost	Goemanne, Noel	Na Gia	T Ss
Come Holy Ghost	Walther, J	74 Gia	M T Ss Satb
Come Holy Spirit	Brahms, J. & Klein, M.	67 Gia	B L T Ss Satb+
Come Holy Spirit, God And Lord	Zachau-Pasquet, J.	61 Aug	M T Ss Unis
Come Thou Holy Spirit Come	Caswell/Hampton	Na Gia	M B L T Ss
Come, Holy Ghost	Palestrina, Giovanni P	Na Gsc	B T Ss Satb
Come, Holy Ghost, Creator Blest	Droste, Doreen	Na Abi	M T Ss Satb
Come, Holy Ghost, In Love	Sateren, Leland B.	61 Aug	M T Ss Satb
Come, Holy Spirit	Brahms, Johannes	67 Gia	M T Ss
Come, Holy Spirit	Gibbons, Orlando	70 Gia	M T Ss
Come, Holy Spirit	Street, Tilson	Na Gsc	B T Ss Full
Come, Spirit Of The Living God	Speaks, Oley	Na Gsc	B T Ss Satb+
Come, Thou Fount	Wyeth/Decou	Na Zon	T Ss Satb
Come, Thou Holy Spirit, Come	Twynham, R. F.	65 Lit	B T Ss
Come, Thou Holy Spirit, Come (Md)	Palestrina, Giovanni P	Na Oxf	M T Ss Full
Come, Thou Spirit Everlasting	Vivaldi	75 Sac	M T Ss Satb
Diffusa Est Gratia	Gallus, J/Jacob, H	Na Gsc	B T Ss 5mix
Emitte Spiritum Tuum (Lat, Eng)	Schuetky/Howorth	Hof	M T Ss Ssa
Gentle Holy Spirit	Johnson, Gary L.	75 Bfi	B R T Ss
God Is In His Holy Temple	Mueller, Carl F	Na Gsc	B T Ss Satb
Gracious Spirit, Holy Ghost	Darst	75 Sac	M T Ss Satb
Grant Us Thy Spirit	Wallace, George	49 Smc	M T Ss Satb
Grieve Not The Holy Spirit	Stainer, Sir John	Na Gsc	B T Ss Satb+
Hail Thee, Spirit, Lord Eternal	Wetzler, Robert	62 Aug	M T Ss 2pt
I Will Give You A New Commandment (Me)	Tallis, Thomas	Na Oxf	M T Ss Ttbb
I Will Pour Out My Spirit	Leaf, Robert	72 Aug	M T Ss Satb+
If Ye Love Me (Me)	Tallis, Thomas	Na Oxf	M T Ss Satb
Komm, Heiliger Geist, Herre Gott	Osiander, Lucas	Na Gsc	B T Ss Satb+
Like A River Glorious	Mountain/Decou	Na Zon	T Ss Satb
Litany To The Holy Spirit (E)	Hurford, Peter	Na Oxf	M T Ss Unis
O Breath Of Life	Franck, Cesaril	Na Zon	T Ss Ssatb
O Come, Holy Spirit (W/Contin & Violin)	Telemann-Nelson	70 Aug	M T Ss Unis
O Holy Spirit Come To Us	Farrell, Melvin	55 Wlp	B T Ss
O Lord, Give Thy Holy Spirit (Me)	Tallis, Thomas	Na Oxf	M T Ss Satb
On All The Earth Thy Spirit Pour	Brandon, George	75 Gia	M T Ss Satb
Put Forth, O God, Thy Spirit's Might	Martin, Gilbert M.	76 Lor	T Ss Satb+
Send Forth Thy Spirit	Schuetky, Fr Jos	Na Gsc	B T Ss Var
Send Forth Thy Spirit, O Lord	Newbury, Kent A.	Na Gsc	B T Ss Satb+
Service And Strength	Naylor, Bernard	Na Gsc	B T Ss Satb+
Spirit Divine	Lovelace, Austin C	75 Sac	M T Ss Sab
Spirit Of God	Lewis, Jesse D	Na Gsc	B T Ss Satb+
Spirit Of God	Smith	Na Lor	M T Ss Satb
Spirit Of God, This Very Hour	Blakley	Na Lor	M T Ss Satb
Spirit Of The Lord, The	Wilson	Na Lor	M T Ss Satb
Sweet Rivers	Na	Na Gsc	B T Ss Satb
Sweet Spirit, Comfort Me	Noble, Harold	Na Gsc	B T Ss
The Spirit Also Helpeth (Motet 2)	Bach, J. S.	Na Kal	B T Ss Satb
Thou Sanctified Fire	Bach, J. S.	Na Gsc	B T Ss Satb
Thy Giving Power	Goodenough, Forrest	51 Smc	M T Ss Satb
To Thee The Holy Ghost, We Now Pray	Na	Na Gsc	B T Ss Satb
Veni, Sancte Spiritus	Fitzpatrick, Dennis	65 Fel	B T Ss

THEMATIC MUSIC

This section is divided into the following categories.
Code – Category
TB–Music for Baptism
TC–Hymns of Commitment
TF–Music for Funerals
TJ–Hymns about Jesus Christ
TK–Hymns about the Kingship of God
TM–Hymns about Mary the mother of Jesus
TO–Hymns and Psalms of Offering
TP–Patriotic Hymns
TR–Hymns of Peace and Reconciliation
TT–Hymns of Praise and Thanksgiving
TU–Hymns about unity and Ecumenism
TW–Music for Weddings
TX–General Topical Hymns

Music for Baptism
Also see categories SR and SS. Many songs having to do

with water are listed in this section also.

Title	Composer	Source	Codes
Baptismal Acclamation	Husted, Richard S.	76 Chh	B L C Tb
As A Doe (Ps 42)	Fitzgerald, M/Farra, M.	73 Gia	M B R L F Tb Var+
Born Again	Culverwell, Andrew	74 Man	B R F Tb
Born Again	Fortunate, Lou	72 Jsp	B F Tb Desc
Born Again	Schaffer, Robert J.	69 Wlp	B F Tb
Come To The Running River	Gilligan, M. (Text)	70 Acp	R L F Tb
Come To The Springs Of Living Water	Winter, Miriam T.	67 Van	B R F Tb
Fill The Pots With Water	Cockett, M/Pearson, J.	69 Van	B R F Tb
I Will Be Like A Father & Mother	Cunningham, Patrick	75 Gra	B R L F Tb
I'll Never Be The Same Again	Wyrtzen, Don	Na Zon	M F Tb Unis
It's Gotta Happen Within	Boud, Ron	75 Zon	M F Tb 2-Pt
Let The Little Children Come	Cunningham, Patrick	72 Gra	B R L F Tb
Lord, Bless This Little Child	Johnson, Gary L.	75 Bfi	B R F Tb
Pilgrimage	Winberry, Mary & Malat	73 Fel	B F Tb
Wade In The Water	Ylvisaker, J. (Arr)	69 Van	B R F Tb
Water Of Life	Ylvisaker, J. & A.	69 Van	B R F Tb
As Flows The River	Gaither/Gaither	62 Gmc	M R G Tb
Cleansing Wave, The	Knapp/Decou	Na Zon	M G Tb Satb
Good Life, The	Peterson, John W.	Na Zon	M G Tb Satb
I Found Life In Christ	Gonzalo, Carrie	69 Man	B G Tb
I Just Got Religion	Akers, Doris	61 Man	M B R G Tb
I Stopped Dying And Started Living	Akers, Doris	73 Man	B R G Tb
I've Been Born Again	Peck, Barry	74 Mam	R L G Tb
I've Found Something	Akers, Doris	54 Man	B R G Tb
It Happened	Gaither/Gaither B/G	70 Gmc	B G Tb Satb
Let Me Bathe In The Water	Boyd/Wall	75 Bri	M R G Tb
Look And Live	Ogden/Peterson	Na Zon	M G Tb Satb
O Happy Day	Rimbault/Decou	Na Zon	M G Tb Satb
Reborn	Peck, Barry	74 Mam	R L G Tb
Rejoice, You're A Child Of The King	Gaither/Gaither B/G	73 Gmc	M B R G Tb Var
Room At The Cross For You	Stanphill/Decou	Na Zon	M G Tb Satb
Run Deep On Well Of Mercy	Osborne/Dailey	75 Wrd	M G Tb Satb+
The Magic Touch	Pieters, Jenny & Delores	66 Man	G Tb
The Waters Are Troubled	Gaither/Gaither B/G	74 Gmc	M B R G Tb Satb
Walk In The Sunshine	Akers, Doris	73 Man	B R G Tb
You Must Be Born Again	Hamblen Stuart	Na Ham	M G Tb
All Were Saved By This Water	Fitzpatrick, Dennis	65 Fel	B L Tb
All You Who Thirst	Fitzpatrick, Dennis	65 Fel	B L Tb
As The Heart Panteth	Young, Gordon	75 Sac	M L Tb Satb
Awake Sleeper	Cunningham, Patrick	73 Gra	B R L L Tb Satb+
Baptism Prayer	Schoenbachler, Tim	75 Nal	B R L Tb
Baptized Into Union With Him	Fitzpatrick, Dennis	65 Fel	B L Tb
By Springs Of Water	Effinger, C	76 Aug	L Tb Satb+
By This We Died With Christ	Fitzpatrick, Dennis	65 Fel	B L Tb
Child Of God	Emig	Na Lor	M L Tb 2mel
Child, The	Schneider, Kent E.	73 Ccc	M B R L L Tb
Come To The Water	Gilsdorf, Sr. Helen	74 Rpb	M B R L L Tb
Crave, As Newborn Babes	Fitzpatrick, Dennis	65 Fel	B L Tb
Deer Is Panting For The Stream, The	Thompson	75 Sac	M L Tb Satb
Father Of The Human Family	Farquharson	67 Jsp	B L Tb
God Will Come Into Your Heart	Lee, Danny	71 Man	B L Tb
I Will Pour Clean Water On You	Fitzpatrick, Dennis	65 Fel	B L Tb
If You Have Risen With Christ	Fitzpatrick, Dennis	65 Fel	B L Tb
Initiation Prayer	Page, Paul F.	76 Rpb	M B R L L Tb
Moment Of Birth	Isele, Bill	71 Nal	B L Tb
My Soul Is Athirst	Fitzpatrick, Dennis	65 Fel	B L Tb
My Soul Thirsts For God (Ps 42)	Shipp, Clifford M.	62 Gam	M L Tb Satb
New Life	Dailey, Joe	75 Ahc	B R L L Tb
New Life	Landry, Carey (Rev.)	74 Nal	B R L Tb
New Life	Malone, Miriam	76 Rpb	M B R L L Tb
New Life, The	Riese	Na Lor	M L Tb Sab
Now In The Name Of Him	Kaan/Kraehenbuehl	76 Jsp	B L Tb
O Come, Good Spirit	Twynham, R. F.	65 Lit	B L Tb
O Lord Of Life (Who Wills New Life)	Dickin, M/Kraehenbuehl	76 Jsp	B L Tb
Psalm 42	Woodham, Steven Ross	73 Mar	R L L Tb
Psalm 42 (41)	Westendorf/Picca	63 Wlp	B L Tb
Regeneration	Christiansen, F. M.	32 Aug	M L Tb Satb
Song Of Baptism	Landry, Carey (Rev.)	73 Nal	M B R L Tb
Song Of New Life	Isele, Bill	71 Nal	B L Tb
Sprinkle, Me, Lord	Fitzpatrick, Dennis	65 Fel	B L Tb
The Baptism Song	Shelley, Tom	71 Ahc	B R L L Tb
The Water That I Shall Give You	Fitzpatrick, Dennis	65 Fel	B L Tb
The Water That I Will Give You	Fitzpatrick, Dennis	65 Fel	B L Tb
There Is One Lord	Deiss, Lucien	65 Wlp	B R L Tb
Thou, Who Hast Loved The Little Child	Baumgartner, Leroy	Na Abi	M L Tb Solo
Titus 3:5	Unknown	73 Mar	B L L Tb
Unless A Man Be Born Again	Fitzpatrick, Dennis	65 Fel	B L Tb
Vidi Aquam	Christiansen, P.	70 Aug	M L Tb Satb
We Have All Been To The Water	Johnson, Jeff	75 Rpb	M B R L L Tb
Welcome To The Family	Cull, Robert	74 Man	M R L Tb
As A Heart (Ps 42) (Sic)	Lockwood, Normand	56 Smc	M T Tb Satb
As A Heart Longs (3 Voices) (Sic)	Boyce, W./Tortolano	70 Gia	B L T Tb Round
As Pants The Hart	Spohr, L	Na Gsc	B T Tb 5mix
As The Rain	Beck, J.	76 Bec	M T Tb
Awake, Thou That Sleepest	Newbury, Kent A.	75 Sac	M T Tb Satb
Birth (From 'he Lived The Good Life')	Wilson	74 Aug	M T Tb 2pt
Born Again	Beethoven/Glazer	Na Wbp	T Tb
Christian, The Morn Breaks Sweetly	Shelley, H R	Na Gsc	B T Tb Satb+
From Egypt's Bondage Come	Page, Arthur	Na Gsc	B T Tb Satb+
God's Son Has Made Me Free	Grieg-Overby	45 Aug	M T Tb Satb
Ho, Every One That Thirsteth	Macfarlane, W C	Na Gsc	B T Tb Var+
Hymn Of The Initiants	Pasquet, Jean	Na Gsc	B T Tb Satb+
My Soul Thirsteth For God	James	Na Lor	M T Tb Satb
My Spirit Thirsts	Palestrina, Giovanni P	75 Bbl	M T Tb Satb
New Creation, A	Ball	Na Lor	M T Tb Satb
O God, Thou Art My God	Rhea, Raymond	48 Smc	M T Tb Satb
Open My Eyes	Lorenz	Na Lor	M T Tb Satb
Open My Eyes	Scott/Johnston	Na Lor	M T Tb Satb
Open My Eyes, That I May See	Hughes, Robert J.	Na Lor	M T Tb Satb
Psalm 42 As A Heart	Mendelssohn, F.	Na Kal	B T Tb Satb
Pure As Crystal Water	Clatterback, R.	76 Sil	T Tb
Send Out Thy Light	Gounod, Charles	Na Lor	M T Tb Satb
Sicut Cervus	Palestrina, Giovanni P	Na Gsc	B T Tb Satb
Sitivit Anima Mea	Palestrina, Giovanni P	Bbl	M K R T Tb Satb
Waters Of Love (God's Power)	Weber, R/Sibelius, J.	76 Jsp	B T Tb
We Praise You Lord For Jesus	O'neill, J/Kraehenbuehl	76 Jsp	B T Tb
Wherefore Hath The Light Been Granted	Brahms, Johannes	Na Gsc	B T Tb Ssatbb

Hymns of Commitment

See also category TR and category SS.

Title	Composer	Source	Codes
I Believe In You	Wise, Joe	74 Nal	B R C Tc
I Want To Walk	Landry, Carey (Rev.)	75 Nal	B R C Tc
It's Up To Us	Blunt, Neil	71 Wlp	B R C Tc
Lord Is Counting On You, The	Hamblen Stuart	Na Ham	M C Tc
What Shall I Do?	Landry, Carey (Rev.)	75 Nal	B R C Tc
Yes To You, My Lord	Wise, Joe	74 Nal	B R C Tc
Yes, Lord, Yes	Landry, Carey (Rev.)	75 Nal	B R C Tc
A Little Further On The Way	Quinlan, Paul	65 Wlp	B R F Tc
A Tool In The Hands Of God	Yantis, David	Na Yan	B F Tc
Be Aware	Tucciarone, Angel	74 Wlp	B F Tc
Break On Through	Miffleton, Jack	71 Wlp	B F Tc
By Their Fruit Shall Ye Know	Temple, Sebastian	71 Gia	B R L F Tc Ar+
Cast Into The Deep	Cunningham, Pat, Carol	72 Gra	B R L F Tc
Come Follow	Kramper, Jerry	69 Gia	B R L F Tc
Come Follow Me	Cadwallader, Ann	72 Gia	M B R L F Tc Var+
Come, Follow Me	Miller, Dan	72 Fel	B R F Tc
Destiny	Parks/Johnson	Na Zon	M F Tc Satb
Dusty Road, The	Klevdal/Blake	Na Zon	M F Tc Satb
Fisherman	Belt, Thomas/Batastini	72 Gia	B R L F Tc Var+
Follow Christ	Temple, Sebastian	69 Fcc	B R L F Tc Gia
Follow Me	Ylvisaker, J. & A.	69 Van	B R F Tc
Give Your Heart To Jesus (Rock)	Curry, S./Brown, C.	76 Wrd	B R F Tc Satb+
Go Forth	Yantis, David	Na Yan	B F Tc
Go Tell Everyone	Dale, A./Richards, H.	69 Van	B R F Tc Oxfrd
God Has Called You	Davis, Diane	71 Fis	M L F Tc
God Loves A Cheerful Giver	Winter, Miriam T.	67 Van	B R F Tc
God Who By Your Holy Spirit	Gemignani, Michael	71 Jsp	B F Tc +Guit
Good Lady Poverty	Temple, Sebastian	67 Fcc	B R L F Tc Gia
Happy Are They	Miller, Dan	72 Fel	B R F Tc
Happy The Man (Ps 1) W/Guitar	Wittig, Evan	76 Gra	B R L F Tc Var+
He Bought The Whole Field	Winter, Miriam T.	67 Van	B R F Tc
Headin Down The Trail	Keene	Na Zon	M F Tc
I Am Your Light (Opt Brass)	Cunningham, Patrick	76 Gra	B R L F Tc
I Believe	Johnson, Gary L.	74 Bfi	B L F Tc
I Know Where I'm Goin	Holiday/Johnson	Na Zon	M F Tc Sab-Sat
I Know Where I'm Going	Moffatt, James	Na Lor	M F Tc Sab
I Know Where I'm Going	Traditional/Wyrtzen	Na Zon	M F Tc Satb
I Want To Walk As A Child	Thomerson, Kathleen	70 Fis	M B L F Tc
I Will Go Forward And Walk	Cunningham, Patrick	73 Gra	B R L F Tc
I'll Trust And Never Be Afraid	Price/Johnson	75 Zon	M F Tc Satb
I'm Following The Son	Lewis, E.	74 Sil	L F Tc
I'm Ready To Follow	Miffleton, Jack	69 Wlp	B R F Tc
In My Name	Ducote, Darryl	71 Fel	B R F Tc
It's But A Road	Yantis, David	Na Yan	B F Tc
Jesus I Am Yours	Leyko, Patricia J.	76 Chh	B R L F Tc
Light Of The World	Schwartz, Stephen	71 Val	B R F Tc
Light Of The World (No 4292)	Parks, Joe	Na Zon	B F Tc
Live In The Light	Gilligan, Michael	70 Acp	L F Tc
Look To The Rock (From Isaiah)	Montague, George T.	72 Mcc	B R L F Tc Solo
Lord Let Me Walk	Miffleton, Jack	75 Wlp	B R F Tc
Master's Pace, The (Opt Guitar)	Kirby	75 Pro	M F Tc Satb+
My Heart Stands Ready	Vissing, Sr. Rosalie	74 Sha	B R L F Tc
My Lord Said (Come With Me)	Farra, Mimi A.	73 Gia	M B R L F Tc Var+
O Give Me A Soapbox	Wyrtzen, Don	Na Zon	M F Tc Unis
People Of Praise (New Year)	Cunningham, Patrick	75 Gra	B R L F Tc
Pilgrim's Song	Wood, Mike	76 Rpb	M B R L F Tc
Pure Light (Of The Son Of God)	Farra, Mimi A.	73 Gia	M B R L F Tc Var+
Run, Christian, Run	Shafer, William	70 Acp	L F Tc
See, The Fields Are White	Cunningham, Patrick	76 Gra	B R L F Tc
Seek First The Kingdom	Winter, Miriam T.	68 Van	B R F Tc
Shout The Good News	Winter, Miriam T.	71 Van	B R F Tc
Sing Freedom (Christ Calls)	Belt, Thomas	70 Gia	B R L F Tc Var+
Take My Life And Let It Be	Peterson, John W.	Na Zon	M F Tc Var
Tell It Out (All Creation Has Ears)	Toolan, S. & O'sullivan R	71 Gia	B R L F Tc Ar+
The Call (How Brightly Deep)	Toolan, S. & O'sullivan R	71 Gia	B R L F Tc Ar+
The God Of Abraham	Montague, George T.	72 Mcc	B R L F Tc Unis
The Rest Of Our Lives	Sabatini, Leo	74 Wgm	B L F Tc
The Song Of Joshua	Cunningham, Patrick	71 Gra	B R L F Tc
The Sower	Winter, Miriam T.	68 Van	B R F Tc
The Wedding Banquet (I Cannot Come)	Winter, Miriam T.	66 Van	B R F Tc
The Whole Armor (Spir, War)	Brown, Shirley L.	71 Fis	M L F Tc
They Cast Their Nets	Mccarthy, John	70 Van	B R F Tc
To Be What You Want Me To Be	Wyrtzen, Don	Na Zon	M F Tc Satb
Why Not Now?	Wyrtzen, Don	Na Zon	M F Tc Unis
Witness Song	Blue, Robert	66 Fel	B R F Tc
Ye Were Sometimes Darkness (Eph4)	Farra, Mimi A.	72 Gia	M B R L F Tc Var+
Yes To You, My Lord	Wise, Joe	68 Wlp	B R F Tc
Yes, Lord	Ducote, Darryl	70 Fel	B R F Tc
A Christ Centered Life	Gonzalo, Carrie	69 Man	B G Tc
All The Way	Culverwell, Andrew	74 Man	B R G Tc

CATEGORIZED INDEX

All You Need	Akers, Doris	61 Man	B G Tc
Are You Willing?	Harper, Redd	Na Zon	M G Tc
Arise And Follow Me	Hendrix, James	73 Jhe	M R L G Tc
Army Of The Lord, The	Hamblen Stuart	Na Ham	M G Tc
Believe In Your Heart	Floria, Cam	73 Wrd	B R G Tc Satb+
Branded By Jesus	Burns, R. H.	Na Gmp	M L G Tc Satb
Bringing In The Sheaves	Minor/Johnson	Na Zon	M G Tc Satb
Can't Find The Time	Sherberg/Shippy/Bolte	75 Wrd	B R G Tc Unis+
Certainly	Mieir, Audrey	72 Man	B G Tc
Child Of The King, A	Sumner/Yungton	Na Zon	M G Tc Satb
Consume Me	Mieir, Audrey	58 Man	M B R G Tc
Dare To Believe	Mieir, Audrey	64 Man	B G Tc
Deeper In The Lord	Akers, Doris	58 Man	M B R G Tc
Divine Priority, The	Wyrtzen, Don	75 Zon	M G Tc Satb
Don't Spare Me	Mieir, Audrey	59 Man	M B G Tc
Don't Stop Using Me	Akers, Doris	58 Man	M B R G Tc
Don't Waste Your Precious Years	Gonzalo, Carrie	69 Man	B G Tc
Drifting	Stanphill/Ferrin	Na Zon	M G Tc Satb
Each Step Of The Way	Harper, Redd	Na Zon	M G Tc
Fight Is On, The (W/Opt Trumpet Trio)	Morris/Mayfield	Na Zon	M G Tc Satb
Fix Me, Jesus	Na	Na Gsc	B G Tc Full
Follow All The Way	Mieir, Audrey	69 Man	B G Tc
Follow On	Litherland, Donna	Na Lor	M G Tc Sa
Follow On	Lowry/Decou	Na Zon	M G Tc Satb
Follow, I Will Follow Thee	Brown/Rasley	Na Zon	M G Tc Satb
Galilee (Jesus Took A Walk)	Girard, Chuck	74 Wrd	B R G Tc Unis+
Go Tell The Untold Millions	Peterson/Carmichael	Na Zon	M G Tc Satb
Going His Way	Haag, Preston	56 Man	M G Tc
Grow Closer	Akers, Doris	55 Man	M B R G Tc
Growing For Jesus	Ohler, Susan	74 Pmp	M B R L G Tc
Guide My Head	Na	Na Gsc	B G Tc Ttbb
Have I Done My Best For Jesus	Storrs/Decou	Na Zon	M G Tc Satb
He Changed My Life	Smith/Harper	Na Zon	M G Tc
He's Filling Up Heaven With Sinners	Peterson, John W.	Na Zon	M G Tc Satb
Here Is All Of Me	Cull, Robert	74 Man	M G Tc Choral
Higher Road, The	Warner/Gotrich	Na Zon	M G Tc
Hold Out Your Light	Spiritual/Johnson	Na Zon	M G Tc Satb
I Am Determined	Mieir, Audrey	65 Man	B G Tc
I Am Persuaded	Hamblen Stuart	Na Ham	M G Tc
I Am Resolved	Fillmore/Johnson	Na Zon	M G Tc Satb
I Am Thine	Hubbard/G.C.Redd/Merr.	Na Sav	M G Tc
I Am Willing, Lord (W/Piano)	Kaiser,K./Brown,C.	76 Wrd	B R G Tc Satb+
I Am...Because	Gaither/Gaither B/G	75 Gmc	M R G Tc
I Belong To Jesus	Gonzalo, Carrie	69 Man	B G Tc
I Could Hardly See The Road	Gaither/Gaither B/G	72 Gmc	M B R G Tc Satb
I Gave My Life To Jesus	Irwin	Na Zon	M G Tc
I Give My All To Thee (W/Piano)	Robinson,E./Brown,C.	74 Wrd	B R G Tc Satb+
I Have Decided To Follow Jesus	Traditional/Decou	Na Zon	M G Tc Satb
I Just Love My Jesus	Crouch, Andrae	71 Man	B R G Tc
I Know The Lord's Laid His Hand On Me	Spiritual	76 Lor	G Tc Satb+
I Lost It All To Find Everthing	Gaither/Gaither B/G	76 Gmc	M R G Tc
I Must Go On	Hendrix, James	Na Gmp	M L G Tc Satb
I Shall Never Let Go His Hand	Crouch, Andrae	67 Man	B R G Tc
I Walk Along With Jesus	Schmidt/Heflin	Na Zon	M G Tc
I Walk The Glory Road	Harper, Redd	Na Zon	M G Tc
I Will Serve Thee	Gaither/Gaither B/G	69 Gmc	M B R G Tc Var
I Will Serve Thee	Gaither, William J	Na Lor	M G Tc Satb
I Won't Move Unless He Tells Me	Akers, Doris	73 Man	B R G Tc
I'd Do It All Over Again	Gaither/Gaither	69 Gmc	M B R G Tc Satb
I'd Like To Walk Around	Bowers, Julia	75 Sem	R G Tc
I'll Go	Cockerham, J Barber, F	75 Sem	R G Tc
I'll Keep On Serving	Cockerham, James	75 Sem	R G Tc
I'll Live For Jesus	Schultz	Na Zon	M G Tc
I'll Walk Into That Sunset	Gaither/Gaither	66 Gmc	B R G Tc Satb
I'm A Soldier	Peterson/Mayfield	Na Zon	M G Tc Satb
I'm Gonna Keep On	Gaither/Gaither	74 Gmc	M R G Tc Satb
I'm Here To Stay	Mieir, Audrey	59 Man	M B G Tc
I'm His To Command	Kerr	Na Zon	M G Tc
I'm Not Satisfied Yet	Akers, Doris	63 Man	M B R G Tc
If It Keeps Gettin' Better	Gaither/Gaither	70 Gmc	M B R G Tc Satb
In These Times	Cockerham/Barber/Robi	75 Sem	R G Tc
In Times Like These	Jones/Anthony	Na Zon	M G Tc Satb
Is He Satisfied With Me	Hamblen Stuart	Na Ham	M G Tc
It's A Brand New Day	Hamblen Stuart	Na Ham	M G Tc
It's Not An Easy Road	Peterson/Decou	Na Zon	M G Tc Satb
Jesus Led Me All The Way	Peterson/Yungton/Decou	Na Zon	M G Tc Satb
Just A Closer Walk With Thee	Lojeski, Ed	75 Hal	G Tc Var
Keep On Holding On	Lee, Danny	71 Man	M B G Tc
Keep On Holding On	Lewis, E.	76 Sil	G Tc
Lead Me, O Lead Me	Peterson, John W.	75 Zon	M G Tc Satb
Lead On, Lord Jesus	Akers, Doris	58 Man	M B G Tc
Lead The Way (W/Piano)	Medema,K./Brown,C.	75 Wrd	B R G Tc Satb+
Lengthen The Cords And Strengthen The	Peterson, John W.	Na Zon	M G Tc Satb
Let God Take Over	Hendrix, James	Na Gmp	M R L G Tc
Live In Me	Blades, Jack	74 Man	R G Tc
Lord Send Me	Clarkson/Fischer	Na Zon	M G Tc
Lord Speak To Me	Curry, Sheldon	Wrd	M G Tc 2pt+
Lord, Keep Me Thine Own	Bennard, Mrs. George	60 Man	M G Tc
Lord, Keep My Mind On Thee	Akers, Doris	63 Man	M B R G Tc
Lost Millions Still Untold	Martin, Bruce	Na Zon	M G Tc Satb
Lovest Thou Me?	Gaither/Gaither	60 Gmc	M B R G Tc Var
Lovest Thou Me?	Gaither, William J	Na Lor	M G Tc Satb
My Heart Is Fixed	Gaither/Gaither B/G	62 Gmc	B G Tc Satb
My Own Way	Floria,C./Sherberg,J.	75 Wrd	B R G Tc Satb+
My Testimony Song	Harper, Redd	Na Zon	M G Tc
My Total Life	Androzzo A Bazel	Na Ham	M G Tc
Narrow Way, The	Irwin	Na Zon	M G Tc
New Way Of Life, A	Redd/Hubbard/Merriw.	Na Sav	M G Tc
No One But You	Mieir, Audrey	60 Man	B G Tc
O, To Be Like Thee	Gaither/Gaither	63 Gmc	M B R G Tc Satb

On And On	Mieir, Audrey	65 Man	B G Tc
Only One Life	Mcgill	Na Zon	M G Tc
Partners With The Lord	Hamblen Stuart	Na Ham	M G Tc
Promises To Keep	Baxter, D./Hamblen, S	Na Ham	M G Tc
Ready	Mieir, Audrey	68 Man	B R G Tc
Rescue The Perishing	Doane/Mayfield	Na Zon	M G Tc Satb
Rock & Roll Preacher	Girard, Chuck	74 Wrd	B R G Tc Unis+
See Me Through	Mieir, Audrey	68 Man	B R G Tc
Send The Light Gabriel	Decou, Harold	Na Zon	M G Tc Var
Shine Shine Shine	Harper, Redd	Na Zon	M G Tc
Show A Little Love	Silva	Na Zon	M G Tc
Show Me The Way	Harper, Redd	Na Zon	M G Tc
Since God Came Into My Heart	Cockerham, James	75 Sem	R G Tc
Since I Found My Life In Him	Young, Carolyn K.	64 Man	M G Tc
So Send I You (No 6002)	Collected	Na Zon	B G Tc Var+
So Send I You (With Brass)	Peterson, John W.	Na Zon	M G Tc Satb
Sold Out To Jesus	Butler, Dorothy	74 Pmp	M B L G Tc
Something Worth Living For	Oldham, D/Gaither	67 Gmc	M B R G Tc Var
Spread The Word	Tashlin/Kenner	Na Zon	M G Tc
Stand Up For Jesus (W/Opt Trumpet Trio)	Slauson, Lloyd N.	Na Zon	M G Tc Satb
Surrender	Mieir, Audrey	72 Man	B G Tc
Take My Life Precious Jesus	Brown, Charles	75 Wrd	B G Tc 2pt+
Take Up Your Cross And Follow Me	Peterson, John W.	Na Zon	M G Tc Satb
Tell The Good News	Peterson, John W.	Na Zon	M G Tc Ssatb
The Joy In Serving The Lord	Gaither/Gaither	60 Gmc	M B R G Tc Satb
The Longer I Serve Him	Gaither/Gaither	65 Gmc	M B R G Tc Var
The Right Choice	Pettis, Audrey E.	69 Sto	G Tc
The Savior Is Waiting (A Cap)	Carmichael, Ralph	58 Wrd	B R G Tc Full
Then The Lord Stood By Me	Peterson, John W.	75 Zon	M G Tc Satb
They Shall Be Mine	Hubbard, H/R.Merriw.	Na Sav	M G Tc
This Is Why I Want To Go	York/Decou	Na Zon	M G Tc Satb
This Ship Of Mine	Hamblen Stuart	Na Ham	M G Tc
Throw Out The Lifeline	Ufford/Mickelson	Na Zon	M G Tc Satb
Till He Comes	Wyrtzen, Don	Na Zon	M G Tc Satb
To Be Used Of God	Mieir, Audrey	64 Man	M B R G Tc
To The Work	Doane/Heacock	Na Zon	M G Tc Satb
Today Is The First Day	Mieir, Audrey	72 Man	B R G Tc
Traveling On	Chavira, Eli	67 Man	B G Tc
Untold Millions, Still Untold	Mieir, Audrey	67 Man	M B G Tc
Up, Up And Away	Peck, Judy	72 Man	B G Tc
Walk On The Pathway	Hubbard, H/G.C.Redd	Na Sav	M G Tc
Walkin' Down The Line	Hatfield, Steve	74 Man	R G Tc
Walking On Higher Ground	Lewis, E./Taylor, R.	76 Sil	R G Tc
We've A Story To Tell To The Nations	Nishol/Leader/Decou	Na Zon	M G Tc Satb
What A Wonderful Way To Go	Spencer, Hal	69 Man	B G Tc
Where Are You Going	Lee, Danny	71 Man	B G Tc
Where Do I Go From Here	Mieir, Audrey	58 Man	M G Tc
Where He Leads I'll Follow	Ogden/Decou	Na Zon	M G Tc Satb
Who's Goin To Walk That Road With Me?	Peterson, John W.	Na Zon	M G Tc Satb
Why Do I Sing?	Wyrtzen, Don	75 Zon	M G Tc Satb
Willing To Go	Mieir, Audrey	64 Man	B G Tc
Work Through Me	Mieir, Audrey	64 Man	B G Tc
You Have To Rise And Go	Mieir, Audrey	65 Man	B G Tc
A Prayer Of Dedication	Frederick, Donald	66 Som	M L Tc
Ain't Gonna Lay My Armor Down	Unknown	73 Mar	B L L Tc
All God's People (Me) (Evangelical)	Hughes, Robert J Et Al	Na Lor	B R L Tc Satb+
Amazing Day	Patenaude, Andre, M. S	71 Nal	B R L Tc
Be Not Wise In Your Own Eyes	Ford, Virgil	Na Abi	M L Tc Satb
Be Thou My Vision	Cannon, Jack D.	Na Abi	M L Tc Satb
Behold, I Stand At The Door And Knock	Kerner, Debby Melle	72 Mar	R L L Tc
Bid Me Come	St. Benedict's Farm	75 Sbf	B R L L Tc 2pt
Blest Are The Pure In Heart	Martin, Gilbert M.	76 Lor	L Tc Satb+
Born To Live And Die	Landry, Carey (Rev.)	68 Nal	B R L Tc
Burst My Dreams	Fabing, Bob	70 Ahc	B R L L Tc
Call, The	Whitecotton	75 Sac	M L Tc Var
Called	Isele, Bill	71 Nal	B L Tc
Cause Me To Come	Unknown	73 Mar	B R L L Tc
Church Of The Living God	Hughes, Robert J.	Na Lor	M L Tc Satb
Come Follow Me	Landry, Carey (Rev.)	68 Nal	B R L Tc
Come On Down	Arthur, Gary & Angle,	72 Mar	R L L Tc
Come With Me Into The Fields	Schutte, Dan, S. J.	71 Nal	B R L Tc
Come, Follow Me	Fitzpatrick, Dennis	65 Fel	B L Tc
Come, O Bride Of Christ	Fitzpatrick, Dennis	65 Fel	B L Tc
Committment Song	Dailey, Joe	75 Ahc	B R L L Tc
Decision	Eckler, Greg	74 Man	R L Tc
Dedication	Reske	Na Lor	M L Tc Satb
Die With Us	Wise, Joe	75 Nal	B R L Tc
Do What He Wants You To Do	Martin	Na Lor	M L Tc Satb
Doer Of The Lord	Rettino, Ernest W.	74 Mar	R L L Tc
Every Man's Work Shall Be Made	Hoddinott, Alun	Na Oxf	M L Tc Satb
Feed My Lambs	Collard, Terry	71 Nal	B R L Tc
Fight The Good Fight	George, Graham	Na Abi	M L Tc Satb
Fishers Of Men	Moore	75 Sac	M L Tc Satb
Follow Me	Wilson	Na Lor	M L Tc
Follow Me (Cantata) (No 4275)	Liljestrand, Paul	Na Zon	B R L Tc Satb
Follow The Road	Patterson	Na Lor	M L Tc
Follow You	Nelson, Erick Martin	75 Mar	R L L Tc
Footsteps Of Jesus	Landon	Na Lor	M L Tc
For A Pearl Of Great Price	Fitzpatrick, Dennis	65 Fel	B L Tc
Forth In Thy Name, O Lord	Butler, Eugene	Na Abi	M L Tc Satb
Forth In Thy Name, O Lord	Hughes, Robert J.	Na Lor	M L Tc
Forward Into Light	Ives, Charles E.	53 Pic	M L Tc
Get On Board	Vickers, Wendy	75 Nal	B R L Tc
Go Forth (Mission Song)	Fortunate, Lou	72 Jsp	B L Tc
Go Out To The Whole World	Gilsdorf, Sr. Helen	74 Rpb	M B R L L Tc
Go Ye Therefore	Mcafee, Don	75 Sac	M L Tc Satb
Go You Also Into My Vineyard	Fitzpatrick, Dennis	65 Fel	B L Tc
Go, Make All Nations	Fitzpatrick, Dennis	65 Fel	B L Tc
God Is In His Holy Temple	Lovelace, Austin C.	75 Sac	M L Tc Sab

CATEGORIZED INDEX

Title	Composer	Year / Publisher	Codes	Voicing
God Is In This Place	Davis	75 Sac	M L Tc	Satb
God's Place	Verai, Ralph C.	76 Rpb	M B R L L Tc	
Great Commission, The	Wiant, Bliss	Na Abi	M L Tc	Solo
Great Things Happen!	Landry, Carey (Rev.)	71 Nal	M B R L Tc	
Happiness (Musical)	Korgstad/Kirschke	Na Zon	B R L Tc	
Harvest Time	Herring, Bruce & Angie	72 Mar	R L L Tc	
He Called Me From Birth	Fitzpatrick, Dennis	65 Fel	B L Tc	
He Leadeth Me	Wilson	Na Lor	M L Tc	Satb
He Who Follows Me	Fitzpatrick, Dennis	65 Fel	B L Tc	
He Who Follows Me	Roff, Joseph	67 Gia	M L Tc	Var+
He Will Receive The Blessing	Roff, Joseph	67 Gia	M L Tc	Var
He's The Reason To Go On	Herring, Bruce	73 Mar	R L L Tc	
Hear Ye Him	Hughes, Robert J.	Na Lor	M L Tc	Satb
Heralds Of Christ	Johnson, Norman	Na Zon	L Tc	Satb
Here Is My Life	Wise, Joe	75 Nal	B R L Tc	
How Amiable Are Thy Tabernacles	Berger, Jean	Na Abi	M L Tc	Satb
I Bind Unto Myself Today	Suitor, Lee	Na Abi	M L Tc	Satb
I Have Faith	Patenaude, Andre, M. S	71 Nal	B R L Tc	
I Heard The Voice	Ford, Virgil	Na Abi	M L Tc	Satb
I Hold The Kingdom	Postel, C M	Na Gia	L Tc	
I Know Not Where The Road May Lead	Williams, David	Na Abi	M L Tc	Satb
I Make My Vows To The Lord	Fitzpatrick, Dennis	65 Fel	B L Tc	
I Met My Master	Wilson, Roger C	Na Lor	M L Tc	Satb
I Renew My Vows To You, Lord	Fitzpatrick, Dennis	65 Fel	B L Tc	
I Want Jesus To Walk With Me	Wehr, David A.	Na Abi	M L Tc	Satb
I Want To Serve The Lord	Low, James L	Na Lor	M L Tc	Sa
I Will Bear Witness, O Lord	Fitzpatrick, Dennis	65 Fel	B R L Tc	
I Would Be True	Peek/Decou	75 Zon	L Tc	Sa
I'll Live For Him	Lanier	75 Sac	M L Tc	Satb
I'll Never Leave You	Rettino, Ernest W.	73 Mar	R L L Tc	
I've Got Jesus	Smith, Lani	Na Lor	M L Tc	Satb
If Any Man Come After Me	Coelho, Terrye	73 Mar	R L L Tc	
If Anyone Serves Me	Fitzpatrick, Dennis	65 Fel	B L Tc	
If Anyone Wishes To Come After Me	Roff, Joseph	67 Gia	M L Tc	Var
If The Lord Does Not Build	Schutte, Dan, S. J.	75 Nal	B R L Tc	
If You Would Come After Me	Fitzpatrick, Dennis	65 Fel	B L Tc	
If You Would Serve God	Fitzpatrick, Dennis	65 Fel	B L Tc	
It Is You, O Lord	Roff, Joseph	67 Gia	M L Tc	Var
Keep The Faith On Movin'	Vickers, Wendy	75 Nal	B R L Tc	
Knight Without A Sword	Pfautsch, Lloyd	Na Abi	M L Tc	Satb
Lead Us On, O Lord	Landry, Carey (Rev.)	71 Nal	B R L Tc	
Let Go	Fong, Preston Bing	75 Mar	R L L Tc	
Let Me Walk	Stahl, Denny	72 Mar	B L L Tc	
Let The Earth Hear His Voice Cantata	Clark, Eugene L.	Na Zon	B L Tc	Satb
Let Us Serve The Lord	Fitzpatrick, Dennis	65 Fel	B L Tc	
Let's Keep Growing	Cull, Robert	74 Man	M R L Tc	
Lord Most High (Opt Brs)	Marshall, Jane	Na Abi	M L Tc	Satb
Lord, May We Follow	Bitgood, Roberta	75 Maf	M L Tc	Satb
Lord, Open Thou Our Eyes	Sullivan	Na Lor	M L Tc	Satb
Lose Yourself In Me	Landry, Carey (Rev.)	74 Nal	B R L Tc	
Make Up Your Mind	Eckler, Greg	74 Man	R L Tc	
Man Of The Lord	Gulliksen, Kenn	75 Mar	R L L Tc	
May Your Priests Be Clothed	Fitzpatrick, Dennis	65 Fel	B L Tc	
Men Of Faith	Landry, Carey (Rev.)	68 Nal	B R L Tc	
Music For Reception Ceremonies	Gentemann, Sr. Elaine	Na Gia	L Tc	
My God, Accept My Heart	Vick, Beryl Jr	Na Abi	M L Tc	Satb
My Lord, My God, My All	Rasley, John M.	Na Zon	L Tc	Satb
My Task	Ashford	Na Lor	M L Tc	Var
My Truth And My Mercy Go With Him	Fitzpatrick, Dennis	65 Fel	B L Tc	
Narrow Road	Hughes, Robert J.	76 Lor	L Tc	Sab+
No Longer Will I Call You Servants	Roff, Joseph	67 Gia	M L Tc	Var
No Turning Back	Hughes, Robert J.	Na Lor	M L Tc	Satb
Not To The Hills	Peterson, John W.	Na Zon	L Tc	Satb
Now I Belong To Jesus	Clayton	Na Lor	M L Tc	Satb
O How Blessed Is This Place	Leaf, Robert	70 Aug	M L Tc	Satb
O Lord Amen	Gulliksen, Kenn	73 Mar	R L L Tc	
O Lord, Thou Hast Searched Me	Slater, Richard W.	Na Abi	M L Tc	Satb
One Thing I Ask Of The Lord	Fitzpatrick, Dennis	65 Fel	B L Tc	
Pass It On	Kaiser, Kurt	69 Lex	M R L Tc	
Prayer (From Celebration)	Peloquin, C Alexander	75 Gia	M L Tc	Satb+
Priestly People	Deiss, Lucien	65 Wlp	B R L Tc	
Proclaim To The World	Gilligan, Michael	70 Acp	R L L Tc	
Proclaim To The World (4-Part Arr)	Wurttemberg Gesangbuch	73 Acp	L L Tc	
Psalm 139	Mcafee, Don	Na Abi	M L Tc	Solo
Recessional	Young	75 Sac	M L Tc	Satb
Right On With Number One!	Thygerson	Na Lor	M L Tc	
Rise Up, O Men Of God!	Gumma	Na Lor	M L Tc	
Save The Mission	Shaw, Jim	73 Fel	B R L L Tc	
See Your People (Ministry)	Twynham, R. F.	65 Lit	B L Tc	
Servant Of All	Floyd, Phillip	74 Mar	R L L Tc	
Show Me The Way To Thee	Ellsworth, Eugene	Na Abi	M L Tc	Satb
Soldiers Of Christ, Arise	Lewis, John Leo	Na Gsc	B L Tc	Satb+
Soldiers Of Christ, Arise!	Warner, Richard	Na Abi	M L Tc	Sa-Sab
Someone's Callin'	Butler, Charles F.	75 Mar	R L L Tc	
Something More	Burgin, D & Rios, D	71 Mar	R L L Tc	
Song Of Christian Men	Landry, Carey (Rev.)	68 Nal	B R L Tc	
Song Of Commitment	Blunt, Neil	70 Wlp	B R L Tc	
Song Of Covenant	Toolan, Sr Suzanne	75 Rpb	M B R L L Tc	
Surely The Lord Is In This Place	Moyer, J. Edward	Na Abi	M L Tc	Ttbb
Surely The Lord Is In This Place	Powell	75 Sac	M L Tc	Satb
Surely, God Is In This Holy Place	Young, Robert H.	62 Gam	M L Tc	Satb
Take Thou Our Minds, Dear Lord	Darst	75 Sac	M L Tc	Satb
Teach All Nations	Thygerson	75 Sac	M L Tc	Satb
Teach Me, Fill Me, Use Me, Lord	Ford	Na Lor	M L Tc	Satb
Thanksgiving To God For His House, A	Burnham	75 Her	M L Tc	Ttbb
The Greatest Story Yet Untold (Cantata)	Clark, Eugene L.	Na Zon	B R L Tc	Satb
The House Of Our Lord	Gustafson, Dwight	75 Sac	M L Tc	Satb
The Last Commandment (Cantata)	Clark, Eugene L.	Na Zon	B L Tc	Satb
The Lord Has Chosen Him	Theophane, Sr. M	Na Gia	L Tc	
The Lord Has Sworn	Roff, Joseph	67 Gia	M L Tc	Var
The Lord Is My Portion	Roff, Joseph	67 Gia	M L Tc	Ssa
The Prayer To St. Ignatius	Fabing, Bob	74 Ahc	B R L L Tc	
The Road Of Christ	Shelley, Tom	71 Ahc	B R L L Tc	
Their Message Goes Forth	Fitzpatrick, Dennis	65 Fel	B L Tc	
There Is A River	Lewis	75 Sac	M L Tc	Satb
There's No Sitting On The Fence	Culverwell, Andrew	74 Man	B R L Tc	
They Follow Me	Sateren, Leland B.	62 Aug	M L Tc	Satb
They Shall Walk	Bitgood, Roberta	75 Sac	M L Tc	Satb
Thine Forever	Evenson	73 Aug	M L Tc	Satb
Travelin' Road (Cantata)	Wyrtzen/Walvoord	Na Zon	B R L Tc	
Two Roads	Stipe, T R & Butler, C	71 Mar	R L L Tc	
Vow Song	Hillebrand, Frank	75 Ahc	B R L L Tc	
Walk In The Light	Lekberg, Sven	Na Gsc	B L Tc	Satb
Walk With The Years	Evelyn F Tarner	76 Lor	L Tc	Satb+
We Belong To You O Risen Lord	Cunningham, Patrick	76 Gra	B R L L Tc	Var
We Have A Strong City (Is 26)	Gardner, John	Na Oxf	M L Tc	Satb
We Have Come	Gulliksen, Kenn	75 Mar	R L L Tc	
We're Called To Be That City	Miffleton, Jack	71 Wlp	B R L Tc	
What Can Keep Us?	Mudd, C. P.	72 Nal	B R L Tc	
What Return Shall I Make To The Lord?	Roff, Joseph	67 Gia	M L Tc	Var
What Would You Have Us Do?	Landry, Carey (Rev.)	68 Nal	B R L Tc	
What You Hear In The Dark	Schutte, Dan, S. J.	75 Nal	B R L Tc	
Where Do You Want Me	Fabing, Bob	70 Ahc	B R L L Tc	
With An Everlasting Love	Roff, Joseph	Na Gia	L Tc	
With My Holy Oil	Fitzpatrick, Dennis	65 Fel	B L Tc	
Witness (Md) Spiritual	Fissinger, Edwin (Arr)	75 Wlp	M L Tc	Satb
Yes, Lord, Amen	Schoenbachler, Tim	75 Nal	B R L Tc	
Yesterday	St. Benedict's Farm	75 Sbf	B R L L Tc	
You Are A Priest Forever	Smith, Roger & Regan,	75 Nal	B R L Tc	
You Gotta Walk	Culverwell, Andrew	74 Man	B R L Tc	
You Who Have Followed Me	Fitzpatrick, Dennis	65 Fel	B L Tc	
You, Lord Are The Way	Deiss, Lucien	70 Wlp	B R L Tc	
A Dedicatory Anthem	Martin, G M	75 Sac	M T Tc	Satb
A Nun Takes The Veil	Barber, Samuel	Na Gsc	B T Tc	Var
All He Wants Is You	Mieir, Audrey	67 Man	M B R T Tc	
Am I A Soldier Of The Cross?	Arnel/Decou	Na Zon	T Tc	Satb
Am I A Soldier Of The Cross?	Arnel/Peterson	Na Zon	T Tc	Satb
As Children Walk Ye In God's Love	Dett, R N	Na Gsc	B T Tc	Satb
As For Me And My House	Peterson, John W.	Na Zon	T Tc	Full
Ave Vera Virginitas	Des Pres, Josquin	Na Gia	T Tc	
Be Thou Faithful Unto Death	Richter, Willy	Na Gsc	B T Tc	Satb+
Be Thou My Vision	Traditional/Johnson	Na Zon	T Tc	Satb
Be Ye Therefore Followers Of God	Rogers, J H	Na Gsc	B T Tc	Satb+
Beatus Vir	Carissimi, Giacomo	Na Oxf	M T Tc	
Blest Is The Man Who In Wisdom Shall	Lasso, Orlando Di	67 Fel	B T Tc	
Breast The Wave, Christian	Shelley, H R	Na Gsc	B T Tc	Satb+
Built On The Rock (E)	Hilty, Everett J.	Na Oxf	M T Tc	Unis
By Their Fruits Ye Shall Know Them	Wilkes, Jon	70 Gia	M T Tc	
Come Take My Yoke	Wetzler, Robert	72 Aug	M T Tc	Satb
Come Unto Me	Bach/Rasley	75 Zon	T Tc	Satb
Commitment (Flute Optional)	Pfautsch, Lloyd	70 Aug	M T Tc	Satb
Dedication	Edwards, Clara	Na Gsc	B T Tc	Satb+
Deeper And Deeper	Smith/Bolks	Na Zon	T Tc	Satb
Ecce Sacerdos Magnus	Vittoria, T L	Na Gia	T Tc	
Estote Fortes In Bello	Na	Na Gsc	B T Tc	Satb
Fight The Good Fight	Johnson, Norman	Na Zon	T Tc	Satb
Forth In Thy Name	Broughton, Edward	76 Lor	T Tc	Satb+
Go Forth, People Of God	Amann, M. Angelita	74 Rpb	M B R L T Tc	
Go Make Of All Disciples	Adkins/Opel	53 Abi	B L T Tc	
Go Ye And Teach All Nations	Thompson	Na Lor	M T Tc	Satb
Go Ye Into All The World	Wetzler, Robert	62 Aug	M T Tc	2pt
God Has My Heart (Cantata)	Bach, J. S.	75 Lps	B R T Tc	Satb
He That Shall Endure	Mendelssohn, F.	Na Gsc	B T Tc	Satb+
How Lovely Are The Messengers	Mendelssohn, F.	Na Gsc	B T Tc	Var+
Hymn Of Consecration	Currie, Randolph	75 Maf	M T Tc	Satb
I Bind My Heart	Proulx, Richard	75 Gia	M T Tc	2mix+
I Got My Religion In Time	White	75 Her	M T Tc	Satb
I'm Gonna Let My Love Shine	Roesch	Na Lor	M T Tc	Sb
If God Be For Us, Who Shall Be Against	Schutz, Heinrich	Na Gsc	B T Tc	Satb+
Jesus Calls Us	Macfarlane, W C	Na Gsc	B T Tc	Satb+
Jesus Calls Us	Sanders, Robert	67 Bbl	M T Tc	Satb
Jesus Calls Us	Wilson	Na Lor	M T Tc	Satb
Jesus Calls Us (W/Bass Solo)	Macfarlane	39 Gsc	M T Tc	Satb+
Jesus, I Come	Rasley	Na Lor	M T Tc	Satb
Jesus, Lead Us	Darst	75 Sac	M T Tc	Satb
Jesus, Still Lead On	Drese/Rasley	Na Zon	T Tc	Satb
John Wesley Covenant Service, The	Canning, Thomas	Na Abi	M T Tc	
Just For You	Wilson	Na Lor	M T Tc	Satb
Just One Day At A Time	Orton, Irv	Na Gsc	B T Tc	Var+
Justum Deduxit Dominus	Mozart, Wolfgang A	Na Gsc	B T Tc	Satb+
Lead Me, Lord	Wesley, S. S.	Na Gsc	B T Tc	Var+
Lead On, O King Eternal	Johnson	Na Lor	M T Tc	Satb
Lead On, O King Eternal	Rasley	Na Lor	M T Tc	Satb
Lead On, O King Eternal	Thompson	Na Lor	M T Tc	Satb
Let Him Who Would Come After Me	Lasso, Orlando Di	67 Fel	B T Tc	
Live Your Life For Him Always (E)	Bach, J. S.	Na Oxf	M T Tc	Satb
Living For Jesus	Lowden/Wilson	Na Lor	M T Tc	Satb
Locus Este A Deo Factus Est (Lat)	Bruckner, Anton	Cfp	R T Tc	Satb+
Lord I Love The Habitation	Graun-Wienandt, Karl H	63 Gam	M T Tc	Satb
Lord Take Our Lives	Lewis, E.	74 Sil	L T Tc	
Lord, Take My Heart	Hovdesven	68 Aug	M T Tc	Satb
Lord, We Are Not The Same	Johnson, Gary L.	74 Bfi	B L T Tc	
March On With Christ	Hughes, Robert J.	Na Lor	M T Tc	Satb
Master Hath Called Us, The	Hughes, Robert J.	Na Lor	M T Tc	Satb
Master Of Eager Youth	Cram	75 Maf	M T Tc	Satb+
Master, What Shall I Do?	Surovchak	Na Lor	M T Tc	Satb
Mein Herz Ist Bereit	Harrer, Johann G	75 Bbl	M T Tc	Satb
Men For The Crisis Hour	Smith	Na Lor	M T Tc	Satb
My Heart Ever Faithful	Bach, J. S.	Na Lor	M T Tc	Sa

PAGE 58

CATEGORIZED INDEX

My Heart Ever Faithful(From Cantata 6)	Bach, J.S. (Arr)	Na Oxf	M T Tc	Unis
O How Amiable (Me)	Williams, Vaughan R.	Na Oxf	M T Tc	Satb
O How Amiable (Ps 84)	Weelkes, Thomas	Na Oxf	M T Tc	Saatb
O How Happy Are They Who The Savior	Hughes, Robert J.	76 Lor	T Tc	Satb+
O Master, Let Me Walk With Thee	Hughes, Robert J.	Na Lor	M T Tc	Satb
O Master, Let Me Walk With Thee	Speaks, Oley	Na Gsc	B T Tc	Satb+
O, How Amiable	West, J. E.	Na Gsc	B T Tc	Satb
Onward, Christian Soldiers	Hughes, Robert J.	Na Lor	M T Tc	Satb
Onward, Christian Soldiers	Rasley	Na Lor	M T Tc	Satb
Onward, Christian Soldiers	Sullivan/Wilson	Na Lor	M T Tc	Satb
Onward, Christian Soldiers	Thompson	Na Lor	M T Tc	Satb
Onward, Christian Soldiers	Sullivan/Decou	75 Zon	T Tc	Satb
Our Church Proclaims God's Love And	Ellsworth Eugene	76 Abi	M T Tc	Satb+
Pilgrim's Journey (Cantata)	Williams, Vaughan R.	Na Oxf	B T Tc	Satb
Savior, Lead Me	Hughes, Robert J.	Na Lor	M T Tc	Satb
Saviour, Like A Shepherd Lead Us	Macfarlane, W C	Na Gsc	B T Tc	Sab+
Sent Forth By God's Blessing	Westendorf, Omer	64 Wlp	B T Tc	
Soldiers Of Christ, Arise	Price	Na Lor	M T Tc	
Something For Jesus	Smith, Lani	76 Lor	T Tc	Satb+
Spread Thou Mighty Word (Hymn)	Frischmann, C. G.	76 Jsp	B T Tc	Satb
Stand Up For Jesus	Hughes, Robert J.	Na Lor	M T Tc	Satb
Stand Up For Jesus	Thompson	Na Lor	M T Tc	Satb
Stand Up, Stand Up For Jesus	Young, Gordon	75 Sac	M T Tc	Satb
Take My Life And Let It Be	Hughes, Robert J.	Na Lor	M T Tc	Satb
Take My Life And Let It Be	Malan/Johnson	Na Zon	T Tc	Sab
Take Up Thy Cross	Hughes, Robert J.	Na Lor	M T Tc	Satb
Take Up Thy Cross	Wilson	Na Lor	M T Tc	Satb
The Temple Of God (E)	Bancroft, H. Hugh	Na Oxf	M T Tc	Satb
Thy Way, Not Mine, O Lord	Tenney, Mildred	Na Gsc	B T Tc	Satb+
Unfold, Unfold! Take In His Light	Powell, Robert J.	Na Gsc	B T Tc	Satb
Walk With Your God	Bell	Na Lor	M T Tc	Satb
Walk Worthy	Grieb, Herbert	Na Gsc	B T Tc	Satb+
Way Of Christ, The	Blake	Na Lor	M T Tc	Satb
We Love The Place, O God	Talmadge, C. L.	Na Gsc	B T Tc	Satb+
We Wait For Thy Loving Kindness (M)	Mckie, William	Na Oxf	M T Tc	Satb
Where Does The Uttered Music Go?	Walton, William	Na Oxf	M T Tc	Satb
Where Our Lord May Go	Heins/Lorenz	Na Zon	T Tc	Satb
Wherever He Leads I'll Go	Mckinney/Wilson	Na Lor	M T Tc	
Who Follows Me	Lasso, Orlando Di	67 Fel	B T Tc	
Who Is On The Lord's Side?	Goss/Peterson	Na Zon	T Tc	Satb
Who Is On The Lord's Side?	Traditional/Johnson	Na Zon	T Tc	Sab
Who Will Bow And Bend	Na	Na Gsc	B T Tc	2boy
Whom Shall I Send?	Berger, Jean	68 Aug	M T Tc	Satb
Ye Servants Of God	Newbury, Kent A.	75 Maf	M T Tc	Satb
You Are The Light Of The World	Newbury, Kent A.	Na Gsc	B T Tc	Satb+

Music for Funerals

With the new emphasis on Christian hope in funeral liturgies of most denominations, some of this music may no longer be appropriate for funerals. For additional music see category SR.

I'm Not Afraid Of The Dark Any More	Hamblen Stuart	Na Ham	M C Tf	
Both Sides Now	Mitchell	67 Siq	F Tf	
Eternal Rest (Introit)(Funeral—Folk)	Mitchell, Ian	67 Fel	B R F Tf	
Jerusalem, My Happy Home	Buchanan, Annabel M.	70 Acp	L F Tf	
May Light Eternal (Funeral Folk Mass)	Mitchell, Ian	67 Fel	B R F Tf	
Thine Be The Glory (W/Piano)	Lee, John	74 Wrd	B R F Tf	Solo+
Time To Die	Wise, Joe	71 Wlp	B R F Tf	
Ain't Got Time To Die	Johnson, Hall	Na Gsc	B G Tf	Satb
Come On Home	Gaither/Gaither B/G	68 Gmc	B R G Tf	Satb
Eyes Have Not Seen	Greif, Jean A	65 Vrn	M L G Tf	
Forever With Jesus	Gaither/Gaither B/G	63 Gmc	B G Tf	Satb
Free To Go Home	Gaither/Gaither B/G	74 Gmc	M G Tf	
Gathering Home	Hamblen Stuart	Na Ham	M G Tf	
God's Final Call	Peterson/Anthony	Na Zon	M G Tf	Satb
Going Home	Gaither/Gaither B/G	67 Gmc	M B R G Tf	Satb
Gone, Buried, Lost	Mieir, Audrey	64 Man	B G Tf	
He That Endureth	Crouch, Andrae	68 Man	B G Tf	
He That Overcomes	Floria, C./Holben, L.	72 Wrd	B R G Tf	Satb+
He The Pearly Gates Will Open	Ahlwen/Johnson	Na Zon	M G Tf	Satb
Heaven Will Be My Home	Hubbard, H./G.C. Redd	Na Sav	M G Tf	
I Done Got Over	Hubbard, H./S. Stevens	Na Sav	M G Tf	
Long Black Train A-Comin'	Baldwin, Bonnie	73 Pmp	M B R L G Tf	
Loved Ones Are Waiting	Hubbard, H/G.C.Redd	Na Sav	M G Tf	
Move To A Better Home	Ramey, Troy	75 Sem	R G Tf	
My Reward	Hendrix, James	Na Gmp	M R L G Tf	
Not Here For Long	Mieir, Audrey	64 Man	B G Tf	
Obituary Of Mrs. Prayer Meeting	Moye, Claud	67 Pmp	M B R L G Tf	
Over The Sunset Mountains	Peterson, John W.	Na Zon	M G Tf	Satb
Po' Mo'ner Got A Home At Las'	Johnson, Hall	Na Gsc	B G Tf	Satb
So Soon It Is Over	Mieir, Audrey	67 Man	M B R G Tf	
Well Done, Come Home	Hamblen Stuart	Na Ham	M G Tf	
When I've Changed My Address To Heaven	Smith/Huntley	Na Zon	M G Tf	
When The Roll Is Called Up Yonder	Black/Décou	Na Zon	M G Tf	Satb
Awake And Live, O You Who Sleep	Deiss, Lucien	70 Wlp	B L Tf	
Come And Let Us Drink Of That New Rivr	Neale/Smith, K.	71 Gsc	M B L L Tf	
Come, Enter My Father's House	Fitzpatrick, Dennis	65 Fel	B L Tf	
Dead, Mass Of, (Icet) Response	Picca, Angelo Della	68 Wlp	B L Tf	
Death, Be Not Proud	Goossen, Frederic	73 Pic	M L Tf	
Enlighten Mine Eyes	Ferris, William	69 Gia	B L L Tf	2pt
Eye Hath Not Seen (A Cap)	Wade, Walter	Na Abi	M L Tf	Satb
Give Them Rest	Fitzpatrick, Dennis	67 Fel	B L Tf	
Goin' Home To The Master	Stipe, Thomas	72 Mar	B L L Tf	
Going Home	Nelson, Erick Martin	75 Mar	R L L Tf	
He Asked Life Of You	Fitzpatrick, Dennis	65 Fel	B L Tf	
I Believe That My Redeemer Lives	Page, Paul F.	75 Rpb	M B R L L Tf	
I Shall Not Die, But Live	Fitzpatrick, Dennis	65 Fel	B L Tf	
I'm But A Stranger Here	Martin, Gilbert M.	76 Lor	L Tf	Satb+
In Memoriam	Manton, Robert	58 Tcp	M L Tf	
In My Old Age, O God	Fitzpatrick, Dennis	65 Fel	B L Tf	
In The End You Will Receive Me	Fitzpatrick, Dennis	65 Fel	B L Tf	
Let Us Now Praise Famous Men	Dean, T. W.	64 Gam	M L Tf	Full
Life Is A Circle	Schneider, Kent E.	75 Ccc	B L Tf	
Lighten Mine Eyes	Roff, Joseph	76 Abi	M L Tf	Satb+
Lord Jesus, Receive My Spirit	Fitzpatrick, Dennis	65 Fel	B L Tf	
Mass Of Resurrection	Peloquin, C Alexander	72 Gia	B L L Tf	Usatb+
May Choirs Of Angels Bring You	Fitzpatrick, Dennis	65 Fel	B L Tf	
May Eternal Light Shine	Fitzpatrick, Dennis	65 Fel	B L Tf	
May The Angels	Schutte, Dan, S. J.	70 Nal	B R L Tf	
May The Angels	Zsigray, Joe	74 Nal	B R L Tf	
My Lord Is Alive	Toolan, Sr Suzanne	75 Rpb	M B R L L Tf	
My Shepherd Is The Lord	Deiss, Lucien	65 Wlp	B R L Tf	
My Spirit Will Not Haunt The Mound	Diamond, David	52 Som	M L Tf	
Nunc Dimittis	Holt, Evelyn	51 Tcp	M L Tf	
O Death, Rock Me Asleep	Edmunds, John	55 Som	M L Tf	
O Lord, Give Him Eternal Life	Fitzpatrick, Dennis	65 Fel	B L Tf	
On The Day When The Radiant Star	Deiss, Lucien	70 Wlp	B R L Tf	
Psalm 13	Powell	75 Sac	M L Tf	Satb
Requiem	Rorem, Ned	50 Som	M L Tf	
Selected Music For Funerals	Roff, Joseph	72 Gia	B L L Tf	U+Org
Swing Down Sweet Chariot	Unknown	73 Mar	B L L Tf	
The Just Shall Always Be Remembered	Fitzpatrick, Dennis	65 Fel	B L Tf	
The Souls Of The Just	Fitzpatrick, Dennis	65 Fel	B L Tf	
Their Bodies Lie In Peace	Fitzpatrick, Dennis	65 Fel	B L Tf	
Well Done, Good And Faithful	Fitzpatrick, Dennis	65 Fel	B L Tf	
Yes I Will Arise	Toolan, Sr Suzanne	75 Rpb	M B R L L Tf	
Air Of Death	Bach, J. C.	52 Bbl	B T Tf	
Amanda	Morgan, Justin	75 Bbl	B T Tf	Satb
Blessed Rest (Cantata)	Bach, J. S.	75 Lps	B R T Tf	Satb
Brevity	Wood, Abraham	76 Bbl	M T Tf	Satb
Cantata #151 Suesser Tod (Eng & Germ)	Bach, J. S.	Na Kal	B T Tf	Satb
Come Soothing Death	Bach, J. S.	Na Gsc	B T Tf	Var
Come Sweet Death (Cantata)	Bach, J. S.	75 Lps	B R T Tf	Satb
Come, Soothing Death	Bach, J. S.	48 Aug	M T Tf	Satb
Death I Do Not Fear Thee	Bach, J. S.	Na Gsc	B T Tf	5mix
Ecce Quomodo Moritur	Gallus, J/Jacob, H	Na Gsc	B T Tf	Satb
Ecce! Quomodo Moritur Justus	Haydn, Michael	Na Gsc	B T Tf	Satb
Ecce, Quomodo (Lo Now, So Is)	Handl, J. (Gieringer)	39 Gsc	M T Tf	Satb
Elegy	Beethoven, L	Na Gsc	B T Tf	Satb+
Enter With The Blest (Tannhauser)	Wagner, R. (Arr Mayer)	68 Smc	M T Tf	Satb
Exit	Sherman, P	75 Bbl	B T Tf	Satb
Funeral Anthem For Queen Caroline	Handel, G. F.	Na Kal	B T Tf	Satb
Funeral Anthem On The Death	Handel, G. F.	52 Bbl	B T Tf	Satb+
Funeral Hymn	Holden, Oliver	76 Bbl	M T Tf	Satb
German Requiem (Eng & Ger)	Brahms, Johannes	Cfp	R T Tf	Satb+
Give Them Rest (Choral)	Fitzpatrick, Dennis	65 Fel	B T Tf	
Great Peace Have They	Rogers, J H	Na Gsc	B T Tf	Satb+
How Lovely Is Thy Dwelling Place	Brahms, Johannes	Na Gsc	B T Tf	Satb+
In Paradisum	Fitzpatrick, Dennis	65 Fel	B T Tf	
In Paradisum	Krenek, Ernst	66 Ron	M T Tf	Ssa
Komm Susser Tod!	Bach, J.S.—Christensen	48 Aug	M T Tf	Satb
Mortality	Read, Daniel	75 Bbl	B T Tf	Satb
My Time Is Come	Bach, J. C.	52 Bbl	B T Tf	Satb
Nearer, My God, To Thee	Wehr, David A.	75 Sac	M T Tf	Satb
No Shadows Yonder	Gaul, A R	Na Gsc	B T Tf	Satb+
Nunc Dimittis	Sluss, Robert	74 Hal	T Tf	Full
O Rest In The Lord	Macfarlane, W C	Na Gsc	B T Tf	Satb+
O Savior, Throw The Heavens Wide	Brahms, Johannes	Na Gsc	B T Tf	Satb
O Welt, Ich Muss Dich Lassen	Isaac, Heinrich	Na Gsc	B T Tf	Satb
O World I Must Be Parting (E&Ger)	Isaac, Henricus	41 Gsc	M T Tf	Satb
On The Other Side Of Time	Johnston	Na Lor	M T Tf	Satb
Pilgrim's Farewell	Anonymous	75 Bbl	M T Tf	Ttb
Requiem	Berlioz, Hector	Na Kal	B R T Tf	Satb
Requiem	Dvorak, A.	Na Kal	B R T Tf	Satb
Requiem	Faure, Gabriel(D1924)	Na Kal	B T Tf	Satb
Requiem	Verdi, Giuseppe	Na Kal	B T Tf	Satb
Requiem (Eng Or Germ)	Brahms, Johannes	Na Kal	B R T Tf	Satb
Requiem Aeternam—Christe Eleison	Mozart, Wolfgang A	Cfs	M T Tf	Satb
Requiem In D Minor	Bruckner, Anton	Na Kal	B R T Tf	Full
Requiem In D Minor (Male)	Cherubini, M.L.(D1842)	Na Kal	B T Tf	
Requiem Mass (Latin)	Mozart, Wolfgang A	Na Kal	B T Tf	Satb
Requiem(Latin)	Mozart, Wolfgang A	Cfp	R T Tf	Satb+
Sonnet (On Hearing The Dies Irae Sung)	Williamson, Malcolm	Na Gsc	B T Tf	Satb
Soul, Array Thyself	Handel, G. F.	Na Gsc	B T Tf	Tabb+
Subvenite (Choral)	Fitzpatrick, Dennis	65 Fel	B T Tf	
The Pilgrim Way	Chapman, Marie B.	48 Smc	M T Tf	Satb
They That Sow In Tears	Gaul, A R	Na Gsc	B T Tf	Satb+
Thou Knowest, Lord, The Secrets	Purcell, Henry	Na Oxf	M T Tf	Ss/Sa
Thou Wilt Keep Him In Perfect Peace	Coggin, Elwood	Na Gsc	B T Tf	Satb+
Turn Your Thoughts To Those Who	Schubert, Franz J.	52 Bbl	M T Tf	Satb+
Well Done, Good And Faithful	Welch, James	67 Fel	B T Tf	
What Wondrous Love	Goemanne, Noel	75 Gia	M T Tf	Satb+
When I Can Read My Title Clear	Lowry/Decou	Na Zon	T Tf	Satb

Hymns about Jesus Christ

These include praise hymns, catechetical songs, and other general music about Jesus. Several spirituals are included here.

Brother Jesus, I Am Small	Reilly, Cyril A.	66 Fel	B C Tj	
Jesus Loves Me As I Am	Mierzwa, Ronald	75 Rpb	M B R L C Tj	
Jesus, Jesus	Landry, Carey (Rev.)	75 Nal	B R C Tj	
Jesus, You Have The Power To Heal	Landry, Carey (Rev.)	75 Nal	B R C Tj	
Little Lost Sheep	Hamblen Stuart	Na Ham	M C Tj	
Oh, How I Love Jesus	Landry, Carey (Rev.)	73 Nal	B R C Tj	

CATEGORIZED INDEX

Psalm 27 Christ-Light	Blue, Robert	66 Fel	B R C Tj	
The Story-Tellin' Man (Musical)	Medema, Ken	75 Wrd	B R C Tj	2pt+
All Our Hope Of Salvation	Wojcik, Richard J.	70 Acp	L F Tj	
All Our Hope Of Salvation (4-Part Arr)	Silvia, Helen	73 Acp	L F Tj	
Alleluia! Sing To Jesus	Mitchell, Ian	66 Fel	B R F Tj	
Ask Not What I Can Do	Finley, Ken	73 Fel	B F Tj	
Call His Name	Kittrell, Christine	Na Sav	F Tj	
Can You Feel Him	Jacobs, Hanneke	75 Chd	R L F Tj	
Canticle Of The Gift (Version 1)	Uhl, Pat&Gilligan, M.	67 Acp	L F Tj	
Canticle Of The Gift (Version 2)	Uhl, Pat&Gilligan, M.	70 Acp	M L F Tj	
Capernaum Comes Alive	Stearnman, Dave	75 Fis	M L F Tj	
Christ Is My Rock	Winter, Miriam T.	67 Van	B R F Tj	
Come And Bless Us	Aridas, Chris	73 Fel	B F Tj	
Come To Me	Norbet, Gregory	71 Wes	M B R L F Tj	
Come, My Brothers	Repp, Ray	66 Fel	B R F Tj	
Cosmic Christ (You Are The Staff)	Temple, Sebastian	69 Gia	B R L F Tj	Uguit
Death Is Swallowed Up	Fischer, John	70 Fel	B R F Tj	
Ephesians Hymn (Blessed Be)	Toolan, Sr Suzanne	71 Gia	B R L F Tj	Ar+
Ephesians Hymn Ii (May Christ)	Toolan, Sr Suzanne	71 Gia	B R L F Tj	Ar+
Exciting Savior	Fiscus, Donna	76 Lor	F Tj	Sab+
Father, Bless This Work	Quinlan, Paul	66 Fel	B R F Tj	
Glorious In Majesty (Trad Jewish)	Cothran, Jeff (Arr)	73 Gia	M B R L F Tj	Var+
Go Tell Your People (4-Part Arr)	Silvia, Helen	70 Acp	L F Tj	
Have You Ever Thought (About Jesus)	Farra, Mimi A.	73 Gia	M B R L F Tj	Var+
Have You Seen Him	Ketchum, Teri	74 Msm	M R L F Tj	
He Said (God Is My Father)	Comeau, Josephine	69 Jsp	B F Tj	+Guit
He'll Help You Out (If You Just Don't)	Amason, B.	75 Sil	R L F Tj	
He's Standing At The Door	Berlucchi, James	74 Wgm	B R L F Tj	
Here Comes Jesus	Traditional/Mayfield	75 Zon	M F Tj	Ssatb
His Light Still Shines	Lewis, E.	74 Sil	R L F Tj	
Hope Is Finding Him	Furman	71 Wlp	B R F Tj	
I Am The Good Shepherd	Miffleton, Jack	69 Wlp	B R F Tj	
I Am The Way	Wynne, Mike	70 Acp	L F Tj	
I Am The Way (From No Time Like...)	Cooney	70 Wlp	B R F Tj	
I Found The Lord	Amason, B.	74 Sil	L F Tj	
I Heard The Lord	Krieger, Jacob	73 Wgm	B R L F Tj	
I Know Jesus	Briggs, S.	76 Sil	F Tj	
I've Been Touched By His Hand	Yantis, David	Na Yan	B F Tj	
If You'll Take My Hand	Jacobs, Peter	73 Chd	B R L F Tj	
Jesus Christ Is The Same Today	Amason, B.	74 Sil	L F Tj	
Jesus Has Something For You	Yantis, David	Na Yan	B F Tj	
Jesus Is A Loving Lord	Campbell, Helen; Goebo	74 Wgm	B L F Tj	
Jesus Is My Song	Fischer, John	70 Fel	B R F Tj	
Jesus Is The One Who Saves	Berlucchi, James	74 Wgm	B R L F Tj	
Jesus Will Come Thru	Miller, Dan	72 Fel	B F Tj	
Jesus You Are Here	Wise, Joe	67 Wlp	B R F Tj	
Jesus, I Love You	Thomerson, Kathleen	71 Fis	M L F Tj	
Just A Closer Walk With Thee	Na	Na Lor	M F Tj	Satb
Look Up And See Jesus	Wyrtzen, Don	Na Zon	M F Tj	Satb
Lord Of The Dance	Unknown/Arr Carter	67 Van	B R F Tj	
Lord Rabboni	Hunkele	67 Wlp	B R F Tj	
Love	Linder, Kristina & F.	70 Fel	B R F Tj	
Master's Touch, The	Wyrtzen, Don	Na Zon	M F Tj	Satb
My Lord Jesus	Mcguire, D./Mcguire, W.	76 Sil	R F Tj	
My Lover & My Master	Cadwallader, Ann	72 Gia	M B R L F Tj	Var+
My Sweet Lord	Harrison	71 Mcl	F Tj	
O Sweet Jesus	Christmas, Charles	74 Wgm	M R L F Tj	
O, Let Him In	Hurd, Bob	73 Fel	B R F Tj	
Ride On (He Came Riding)	Belt, Thomas/Batastini	71 Gia	B R L F Tj	Var+
Sandals	Wyrtzen, Don	Na Zon	M F Tj	Satb
Sing The Praise Of Jesus	Temple, Sebastian	71 Gia	B R L F Tj	Var+
Some Young Carpenter	Miffleton, Jack	71 Wlp	B R F Tj	
Son Come Down (Guitar Or Piano)	Belt, Thomas/Batastini	71 Gia	B R L F Tj	Var+
Stand By Me, Jesus	Young, R. Otha	75 Ste	M R L F Tj	
Teilhard's Vision	Temple, Sebastian	69 Gia	B R L F Tj	Uguit
The Man Next Door	St. Benedict's Farm	75 Sbf	B R L F Tj	
The Word Is The Life	King, Charleen	72 Fel	B R F Tj	
Turn It Over To Jesus	Yantis, David	Na Yan	B F Tj	
Water Pot (John 2)	Montague, George T.	72 Mcc	B R L F Tj	2pt
Where Else Would I Go	Stevens, Marsha J.	75 Chd	R L F Tj	
Who Is This Man	Germaine	66 Fel	B R F Tj	
Wondrous Is Your Presence	Temple, Sebastian	69 Gia	B R L F Tj	Uguit
Yesterday, Today & Tomorrow (Hb 13:8)	Miffleton, Jack	69 Wlp	B R F Tj	
You Are The Answer	Temple, Sebastian	67 Fcc	B R L F Tj	Gia
You Are The Light Of The World	Miffleton, Jack	69 Acp	L F Tj	
You Can't Buy A Savior	Salisbury Jr, Wallace	73 Fel	B F Tj	
A Few Words About Jesus	Haney, J/Thompson, S.	Na Sav	M G Tj	
A Glimpse Of The Master	Gaither/Gaither	63 Gmc	B G Tj	Satb
A Man Called Jesus	Gaither/Gaither, G.	63 Gmc	B G Tj	Satb
A Prayer To Jesus	Blevins D. Coakley J.	74 Jhm	R L G Tj	
Beholding Thee, Lord Jesus	Rasley, John M.	Na Zon	M G Tj	Satb
Bethlehem, Galilee, Gethsemane	Gaither/Gaither B/G	70 Gmc	M B R G Tj	Var
Blessed Assurance	Knapp/Decou	Na Zon	M G Tj	Satb
Blessed Jesus	Gaither/Gaither B/G	72 Gmc	M B R G Tj	Satb
Blessed Redeemer	Childs	Na Zon	M G Tj	
Born To Be Crucified	Gaither/Gaither	67 Gmc	M G Tj	Var
Call On Jesus	Cockerham, J	75 Sem	R G Tj	
Choral Stylings (No Zd-5473)	Schrader, Jack	Na Zon	B G Tj	
Christ Is The Rock	Edwards	Na Zon	M G Tj	
Close To Thee	Gaither/Gaither B/G	64 Gmc	B G Tj	Satb
Color Him Love (No 5019)	Mckay, John (Ed)	Na Zon	G Tj	Solo
Daddy, Sing For Jesus	Taylor, R.	75 Sil	M R L G Tj	
Do You Know Jesus?	Hamblen Stuart	Na Ham	M G Tj	
Does Jesus Care	Hughes, Robert J.	76 Lor	G Tj	Satb+
Every Knee Shall Bow	Floria, C.	75 Wrd	B R G Tj	Satb+
Every Time I Think About Jesus	Fleming (Arr)	73 Aug	M G Tj	Satb
Feeling At Home In The Presence	Gaither/Gaither B/G	75 Gmc	M R G Tj	
For Those Tears I Died	Stevens, Marsha J.	69 Chd	M B R L G Tj	

Give Me Jesus (Spiritual)	Fleming (Arr)	73 Aug	M G Tj	Sat
Glimpse Of Jesus	Haag, Preston	55 Man	M G Tj	
He Touched Me	Gaither/Gaither	63 Gmc	M B R G Tj	Sat
He Was More Then Just A Man	Aderholt, Norman	71 Man	B R G Tj	
He Was There	Dodd Jimmie	Na Ham	M G Tj	
He's All I Need	Brock, Linda	74 Mam	R L G Tj	
Hiding In The Arms Of Jesus	Casteel, K./Roth, P.	73 Csm	M B R L G Tj	
His Name Is The Sweetest I Know	Mathis, Ola	Na Gmp	M R L G Tj	
I Am One For Whom You Died	Cram, Wilbur & Francis	73 Mam	R L G Tj	
I Belong To Jesus	Sadler, Rebecca	74 Jhm	R L G Tj	
I Found My Life In Jesus	Ellis, Ron	73 Rav	B L G Tj	
I Hear Jesus Calling My Name	Coakley J. Blevins D.	74 Jhm	R L G Tj	
I Know He's Mine	Culverwell, Andrew	73 Man	B R G Tj	
I Know My Friend Jesus Is Piloting Me	Cram, Wilbur	73 Mam	R L G Tj	
I Love Him	Brock, Linda	74 Mam	R L G Tj	
I Love To Take A Walk	Unknown	73 Mar	B L G Tj	
I Want Jesus To Walk With Me	Spiritual	Na Lor	M G Tj	Sat
I Wish You Jesus	Androzzo A Bazel	Na Ham	M G Tj	
I've Got Jesus	Crouch, Andrae	68 Man	B G Tj	
I've Just Seen Jesus	Gaither/Gaither	64 Gmc	M B R G Tj	Sat
If I Had Not Jesus	Mieir, Audrey	68 Man	B R G Tj	
If Thou Be Jesus	Butler, Dorothy	68 Pmp	M B R L G Tj	
If You Know Christ	Finch, John D.	63 Man	M G Tj	
In Jesus' Name	Mieir, Audrey	64 Man	M B G Tj	
In This Old Troubled World	Peterson, John W.	Na Zon	M G Tj	Sat
Isn't The Love Of Jesus Something	Peterson/Parks	Na Zon	M G Tj	Sat
It Is Jesus	Akers, Doris	68 Man	B G Tj	
It Was Jesus	Irwin	Na Zon	M G Tj	
It's Just Like My Lord	Gaither/Gaither B/G	67 Gmc	M B R G Tj	Sat
It's No Wonder	Milhuff/Gaither	69 Gmc	M B R G Tj	Sat
Jesus	Gaither/Gaither	66 Gmc	M B R G Tj	Sat
Jesus And Me	Stanphill/Decou	Na Zon	M G Tj	Sat
Jesus Cares	Smith/Harper	Na Zon	M G Tj	
Jesus Descended From Majesty Glorious	Cram, Wilbur & Francis	73 Mam	R L G Tj	
Jesus Is A Friend Of Mine	Forsythe, Kenneth	Na Cpc	M G Tj	
Jesus Is A Precious Name	Peterson, John W.	Na Zon	M G Tj	Sat
Jesus Is A Wonderful Landlord	Eddins, Martha A.	75 Pdm	G Tj	
Jesus Is Everything	Cockerham, J Robinson, G	75 Sem	R G Tj	
Jesus Is Knocking	Coakley J. Blevins D.	74 Jhm	R L G Tj	
Jesus Is The Answer	Crouch, A&S/Floria, C.	73 Wrd	B R G Tj	Sat
Jesus Is The Friend Of Sinners	Peterson, John W.	Na Zon	M G Tj	Sat
Jesus Is The Name	Akers, Doris	48 Man	B G Tj	
Jesus Is Waiting	Huntley/Newman	Na Zon	M G Tj	
Jesus Knows	Pace	Na Zon	M G Tj	
Jesus My Lord	Peck, Barry	74 Mam	R L G Tj	
Jesus Paid It All	Lewis, E.	74 Sil	L G Tj	
Jesus Pleases	Shimmons, C	74 Csm	M B L G Tj	
Jesus Prayed	Butler, Dorothy	68 Pmp	M B R L G Tj	
Jesus Precious Savior	Gibson, S./Brown, C.	71 Wrd	B R G Tj	Sat
Jesus Saves	Denton, James	Na Lor	M G Tj	Sat
Jesus Sends His Sunlight	Cole Ann. Myring Charl	71 Jhm	L G Tj	
Jesus The Very Thought Of Thee	Bernard/Dykes/Carmicha	67 Wrd	B R L G Tj	Full
Jesus Told Me So	Harper, Redd	Na Zon	M G Tj	
Jesus Will Come	Fischer	Na Zon	M G Tj	
Jesus Will Fix It After Awhile	Smith, John Z.	69 Sto	G Tj	
Jesus, How Dear You Are	Lucht	Na Zon	M G Tj	
Jesus, I Believe What You Said	Gaither/Gaither B/G	66 Gmc	M B R G Tj	Var
Jesus, Jesus	Mieir, Audrey	58 Man	B G Tj	
Jesus, Let Your Light Shine	Lewis, E.	76 Sil	G Tj	
Jesus, Wonderful Lord	White/Rasley	75 Zon	M G Tj	Sat
Just A Closer Walk With Thee	Traditional/Rasley	75 Zon	M G Tj	Ssa
Lead By The Master's Hand	Hanchett, Inez; Laney	74 Jhm	R L G Tj	
Lightshine (Musical)	Hawthorne/Red, Buryl	72 Wrd	B R G Tj	Sat
Lily Of The Valley, The	Hays/Mickelson	Na Zon	M G Tj	Sat
Looking Reaching For My Lord	Sewell Homer	70 Oak	G Tj	
Love Found A Way	Loes/Decou	Na Zon	M G Tj	Sat
Mary Had A Baby	Landon	Na Lor	M G Tj	Var
My Heart Would Sing Of Jesus	Smith/Harper	Na Zon	M G Tj	
My Wonderful Jesus	Hatfield, Steve	74 Man	R G Tj	
Name Of Jesus, The	Lorenz/Rasley	Na Zon	M G Tj	Sat
No One Can Ever Be Equal To Jesus	Stone, Walter C.	68 Sto	G Tj	
O How I Love Jesus	Traditional/Rasley	75 Zon	M G Tj	Ssa
O Wondrous Life	Smith/Childs	Na Zon	M G Tj	
One Way	Crouch, Andrae	71 Man	B R G Tj	
One Way	Lee, Danny	71 Man	M B G Tj	
Put Your Hand In The Hand	Maclellan (Arr)	75 Her	M G Tj	Sat
Savior Of The World	Stevens, Sammy	Na Sav	M G Tj	
Since Jesus Passed By	Gaither/Gaither	65 Gmc	M B R G Tj	Var
Sing My Song To Jesus	Peck, Barry	74 Mam	R L G Tj	
Something Beautiful	Gaither/Gaither, G.	71 Gmc	M B R G Tj	Var
Stay With Me Jesus	Ramey, Troy	75 Sem	R G Tj	
Suffer The Children	Holben, Larry/Tewson, B.	75 Wrd	B R G Tj	Full
Sweet Jesus	Akers, Doris	58 Man	M B R G Tj	
Sweeter Than The Day Before	Trad.-Gaither/Gaither	63 Gmc	M B R G Tj	Sat
Tell Me That Name Again	Gaither/Gaither	68 Gmc	B R G Tj	Sat
That's What Jesus Means To Me	Gaither/Gaither	70 Gmc	M B R G Tj	Var
The Greatest Wonder (W/Piano)	Gaddy, Carol	76 Wrd	M G Tj	Sat
The Lily Of The Valley	Smith, Lani	Na Lor	M G Tj	Sat
The Lord Came Down	Brock, Linda	74 Mam	R L G Tj	
The Lord Is Still Around	Cross, Danny	74 Mam	R L G Tj	
The Man Of Galilee	Culverwell, Andrew	73 Man	B R G Tj	
The Power Of Jesus	Crouch, Andrae	67 Man	R G Tj	
The Smile On His Face	Akers, Doris	58 Man	M B R G Tj	
The Touch Of His Hand	Peck, Barry	74 Mam	R L G Tj	
There Is A Name	Crouch, Andrae	71 Man	B R G Tj	
There Is No One Like Jesus	Landgrave, P.	76 Wrd	M G Tj	Sat
There's Something About That Name	Gaither/Gaither B/G	70 Gmc	M B R G Tj	Var
Today I Followed Jesus	Lewis, E.	75 Sil	R L G Tj	
Today I Walked In His Footsteps	Lewis, E.	74 Sil	L G Tj	
Touch Me Savior	Farrer, Carl	67 Man	M G Tj	

rusting Jesus	Sankey/Bunzel	Na Zon	M G Tj	Satb
ry Jesus	Hatfield, Steve	74 Man	R G Tj	
ry Jesus	Nicholson	Na Zon	M G Tj	
urn Your Eyes Upon Jesus	Lemmel/Johnson	Na Zon	M G Tj	Satb
/alkin' And Talkin' With Jesus	Harper, Redd	50 Man	M G Tj	
/hat A Friend We Have In Jesus (Arr.)	Williams, G.	76 Sil	R G Tj	
/hat Would I Do Without Jesus?	Harper, Redd	Na Zon	M G Tj	
/hen I Met My Savior	Allem/Carmichael	Na Zon	M G Tj	Satb
/here Was Jesus	Petty Doug	71 Jhm	L G Tj	
'hisper One Name	Meir, Audrey	76 Man	B G Tj	
ho Do You Say That I Am	Culverwell, Andrew	73 Man	B R G Tj	
hy I Love Jesus	Knepp, David Lee	74 Pmp	M B R L G Tj	
ill He Know Me	Meir, Audrey	67 Man	M B R G Tj	
onderful Guest	Lehman, Louis P.	55 Man	M B G Tj	
onderful Wonderful Jesus (A Cap)	Russell-Sellers	75 Wrd	M G Tj	Full
esterday's Gone	Stanphill/Johnson	Na Zon	M G Tj	Satb
ou Got To Have Jesus In Your Heart	Wrightman, N.	68 Csm	M B R L G Tj	
Light Will Shine	Dailey, Joe	75 Ahc	B R L L Tj	
l For Jesus	Moffatt	Na Lor	M L Tj	Satb
l Marveled At The Words	Fitzpatrick, Dennis	65 Fel	B L Tj	
leluia! Sing To Jesus	Hughes, Robert J.	Na Lor	M L Tj	
leluia, Sing To Jesus	Goemanne, Noel	72 Gia	M L Tj	Satb+
The Name Of Jesus	Hughes, Robert J.	Na Lor	M L Tj	
e Strong For Me	Page, Paul F.	76 Rpb	M B R L L Tj	
earded Young Man	Angle, Dana P	75 Mar	R L L Tj	
ehold Among Men	Deiss, Lucien	65 Wlp	B L Tj	
ehold Him, The Name Of Whose	Fitzpatrick, Dennis	65 Fel	B L Tj	
ehold! I Stand At The Door And Knock	Burns, William K.	Na Abi	M L Tj	Satb
ehold, I Stand At The Door	Schmidt	Na Lor	M L Tj	
hold, The Bridegroom Comes	Fitzpatrick, Dennis	65 Fel	B L Tj	
other Jesus	Landry, Carey (Rev.)	74 Nal	B R L Tj	
Your Blood You Redeemed Us	Fitzpatrick, Dennis	65 Fel	B L Tj	
rist In Me	Rettino, Ernest W.	73 Mar	B L L Tj	
rist Is Our Leader (4-Part Arr.)	Cirou, Joseph	73 Acp	L L Tj	
rist Is The World's Redeemer	Lovelace, Austin C.	75 Sac	M L Tj	Satb
rist Is The World's True Light	Walter, Samuel	Na Abi	M L Tj	Sab
rist Our Light	Zsigray, Joe	75 Nal	B R L Tj	
rist Our Lord And Brother	Gilligan, M. (Text)	70 Acp	R L L Tj	
rist Our Lord And Brother (4-Part Ar)	Silvia, Helen	73 Acp	L L Tj	
rist The Light	Peloquin, C Alexander	68 Gia	B L Tj	Var+
rist Will Come Again	Sylvester, Erich	74 Nal	B R L Tj	
rist-Light	Blue, Robert	68 Fel	B R L L Tj	
rist, The Light Of The Nations	Peloquin, C Alexander	Na Gia	L Tj	
rist, We Adore Thee	Dubois	Na Lor	M L Tj	
me To Me, I've Come To You	Tracy, Shawn (Rev.)	72 Nal	B R L Tj	
me To Me, Jesus	Collard, Terry	71 Nal	B R L Tj	
st, The Last, The	Dressler, John	Na Abi	M L Tj	Satb
m Where Is His Wisdom	Fitzpatrick, Dennis	65 Fel	B L Tj	
'ations 2:20	Unknown	73 Mar	B L L Tj	
ttin' It Together In Jesus	Lewis, E.	74 Sil	L L Tj	
d So Loved (No 4278) (Musical)	Burroughs, Bob	Na Zon	B R L Tj	
od Shepherd, The	Pooler, Marie	Na Abi	M L Tj	
ding Christ Our Shepherd, The	Pfautsch, Lloyd	Na Abi	M L Tj	Satb
l, Alpha And Omega	Elmore	75 Sac	M L Tj	Satb
Come	Tracy, Shawn (Rev.)	72 Nal	B R L Tj	
Came	Winston, Colleen, Osb	73 Nal	B L Tj	
Says He Is God	Huijbers & Oosterhuis	74 Nal	M B L Tj	
art Of Christ	Elbert, Edwin	71 Jsp	B L Tj	+Guit
nn To The Saviour	Kremser, E	Na Gsc	B L Tj	Satb+
The Door	Lewis	75 Sac	M L Tj	Satb
The Good Shepherd	Fitzpatrick, Dennis	65 Fel	B R L Tj	
The Light Of The World	Darst	75 Sac	M L Tj	Satb
The Way, The Truth, And The Life	Young, Gordon	75 Sac	M L Tj	Satb
ve Him (With All My Heart)	Hale, S.	75 Sil	R L L Tj	
nt More Of Jesus	Unknown	73 Mar	B L L Tj	
hrist The Prince Of Peace	Singenberger, Otto	70 Acp	L L Tj	
hrist The Prince Of Peace (4-Part	Wojcik, Richard J.	73 Acp	L L Tj	
esus Name	Young, C & Strange, J	73 Mar	R L L Tj	
u, Creator Of The World	Bloom, C G L	Na Gia	L Tj	
u, Friend Of My Delight	Caldwell, M	75 Sac	M L Tj	Unis+
u, Our Blessed Hope Of Heaven	Young, Gordon	69 Aug	M L Tj	Satb
u, The Very Thought Is Sweet	Boeringer	75 Sac	M L Tj	Satb
us	Kerner, Debby Melle	72 Mar	R L L Tj	
us	Peter Jacobs	71 Chd	B R L L Tj	
us Can	Lewis, E.	74 Sil	R L L Tj	
us Christ	Butler, Charles F.	73 Mar	B L L Tj	
us Christ Our Lord & God (Hymn)	Sr. Margarita	76 Jsp	B L Tj	Satb
us Christ The Faithful Witness	Deiss, Lucien	70 Wlp	B R L Tj	
us In The Mornin'	Shelley, Tom	72 Ahc	B R L L Tj	
us Is All That We Need	Arthur, Gary	72 Mar	R L L Tj	
us Is All The World To Me	Lorenz	Na Lor	M L Tj	Satb
us Is Mine	Moultry, Prince Joseph	74 Nal	B R L Tj	
us Is Our Prayer	Ellis, Ron	75 Rav	M B R L L Tj	
us Is Standing Here	Coomes, Thomas William	74 Mar	R L L Tj	
us Is The Morning	Stahl, Denny	73 Mar	B L L Tj	
us Is The One	Herring, Bruce	72 Mar	R L L Tj	
us Joy	Lafferty, Karen Louise	72 Mar	B L L Tj	
us Loves Me (Arrangement)	Hale, S.	75 Sil	R L L Tj	
us! Name Of Wondrous Love	Powell, Robert J.	Na Abi	M L Tj	Satb
us, Be My Friend	Welz, Joey-Wray, Link	71 Urs	M B R L Tj	
us, Come Our Way	Hubert, Yvon	72 Fcc	R L L Tj	
us, I Need You	Creed, Dan & Fletcher,	73 Nal	B R L Tj	
us, In Our Hands	Wise, Joe	72 Nal	B R L Tj	
s, Jesus, Rock Of Ages	Lee, Danny	71 Man	B L Tj	
s, Lead The Way	Proulx, Richard	72 Gia	M L Tj	Satb
s, Thou Blessed Name Of Mercy	Young, Gordon	75 Sac	M L Tj	Satb
Giving Light	Deiss, Lucien	65 Wlp	B R L Tj	
b Of God! Thou Shalt Remain Forever	Grimm, Johann D.	Na Abi	M L Tj	Solo
b Of God, I Took To Thee	Lewis, John Leo	Na Gsc	B L Tj	2pt+

Life In Jesus	Stipe, Thomas	73 Mar	B L L Tj	
Listen To Him	Fitzpatrick, Dennis	65 Fel	B L Tj	
Living Christ, The	Elmore	75 Sac	M L Tj	Satb
Lord Jesus Come From "Lyric Liturgy"	Peloquin, C Alexander	74 Gia	M L Tj	Satbu+
Lord Jesus, Think On Me	Lewis, John Leo	Na Gsc	B L Tj	Satb
Lord Jesus, Think On Me (High Voice)	Owens, Sam Batt	Na Abi	M L Tj	Solo
Love Walks The World In Flesh	Soteren, Leland B.	70 Aug	M L Tj	Satb
Many Signs Jesus Worked	Fitzpatrick, Dennis	65 Fel	B L Tj	
No One Understands Like Jesus	Peterson, John W.	Na Lor	M L Tj	Satb
Now The Morning Son Is Here	Cirou, Joseph Et Al	67 Acp	L L Tj	
O Christ, Eternal King	Mytych, J F	Na Gia	L Tj	
O Christ, I Look To Thee	Burroughs	75 Sac	M L Tj	Sa
O Christ, Our Hope	Distler	Na Aug	M L Tj	Ssa
O Jesus, Thou Art Standing	Hughes, Robert J.	Na Lor	M L Tj	2mel
O Savior, Precious Savior	Smith, Harold	69 Smc	M L Tj	Satb
O The Deep, Deep Love Of Jesus	Hughes, Robert J.	Na Lor	M L Tj	Satb
O Virgin's Son	Nachtwey, Roger	65 Fel	B L Tj	
One, Two, Three, Jesus Loves Me	Jones, Barry	73 Mar	B L L Tj	
Only Begotten, Word Of God Eternal	Lovelace, Austin C.	57 Aug	M L Tj	Unis
Savior Of My Soul	Unknown	73 Mar	B L L Tj	
Servant Song	Schutte, Dan, S. J.	71 Nal	B R L Tj	
Servant-King, The	Gilligan, Michael	67 Acp	L L Tj	
Servant-King, The	Nardella, Faith	73 Acp	L L Tj	
Show Yourself In Me	Lewis, E.	74 Sil	R L L Tj	
Since I Met Jesus	Sprouse, W	74 Mar	R L L Tj	
Son Of God	Gilligan, Michael	67 Acp	L L Tj	
Son Of God	Silvia, Helen	73 Acp	L L Tj	
Son Of God!	Isele, Bill	71 Nal	B L Tj	
Song Of Jesus Christ	Landry, Carey (Rev.)	74 Nal	B R L Tj	
Sonshine	Mccusker, M & Ugartech	72 Mar	B L L Tj	
Strong Son Of God, Immortal Love	Darst, S. Glen	67 Som	M L Tj	
Suffering Servant Song, The	Chaumont, James	75 Nal	B R L Tj	
Sweet Jesus Morning	Fong, P B	75 Mar	R L L Tj	
Sweetest Name I Know	Unknown	72 Mar	B L L Tj	
Thank You, Jesus	Hubert, Yvon	72 Fcc	R L L Tj	
Thank You, Jesus, You're My Friend	Eldridge, R.	75 Sil	R L L Tj	
The Carpenter	Mayhew, Kevin & Singers	75 Ahc	M B R L Tj	
The Christ Hymn	Dailey, Joe	75 Ahc	B R L L Tj	
The First Of His Signs	Fitzpatrick, Dennis	65 Fel	B L Tj	
The Good Shepherd (Me)	Kaan, Fred/Peloquin A.	76 Gia	M L L Tj	U2pt+
The Light Of Christ	Fishel, Donald	74 Wgm	B R L L Tj	
The Morning Son	Enlow, H.	74 Sil	R L L Tj	
The Name Of Jesus	St. Benedict's Farm	75 Sbf	B R L L Tj	
The Son In My Life	Stahl, D	73 Mar	R L L Tj	
Thou Art The Kindler	Hubert, Yvon	72 Fcc	R L L Tj	
To Christ, Glory & Power	Deiss, Lucien	70 Wlp	B R L Tj	
We See You O Lord	Landry, Carey (Rev.)	68 Nal	B L Tj	
When Jesus Knelt	Leaf, Robert	76 Aug	L Tj	Uahs+
When The Lord Of Love Was Here	Martin, Gilbert M.	76 Lor	L Tj	Satb+
With Jesus, Our Brother	Shelley, Tom	71 Ahc	B R L L Tj	
Wonderful Is Jesus	Peterson, John W.	Na Zon	M L Tj	Satb
Word Was God, The	Lanier	75 Sac	M L Tj	
Word Who Is Life, The	Landry, Carey (Rev.)	74 Nal	B R L Tj	
You Are My Son	Miffleton, Jack	71 Wlp	B R L Tj	
You Are The Only Son	Cirou, J & O'connell	70 Acp	L L Tj	
You Are The Only Son (4-Part Arr)	Cirou, Joseph Et Al	73 Acp	L L Tj	
You Are The Way	Wise, Joe	72 Nal	B R L Tj	
You Gave Us Lord Your Sacred Heart	Weber/Elbert	71 Jsp	B L Tj	Satb
You're Enough	Cull, Robert	74 Mar	R L L Tj	
A Child Was Born	Na	Na Gsc	B T Tj	Unis+
Adoramus Te, Christe	Corsi, J	Na Gia	T Tj	
Adoramus Te, No. 1	Lotti, Antonio	74 Bbl	M T Tj	Satb
Adoramus Te, No. 2	Lotti, Antonio	74 Bbl	M T Tj	Satb
Ah, Holy Jesus	Cruger, J.	67 Aug	M T Tj	Var
Ah, Jesus Lord, Thy Love To Me	Johnson	65 Aug	M T Tj	Var
All Hail The Power (Tune "Miles Lane")	Williams, Vaughan R.	Na Oxf	M T Tj	Satb
All Hail The Power Of Jesus' Name	Darst	75 Sac	M T Tj	Satb
All Hail The Power Of Jesus' Name	Holden/Decou	Na Zon	T Tj	Satb
All Hail The Power Of Jesus' Name	Holden/Jess	Na Zon	T Tj	Ssatb
All Hail The Power Of Jesus' Name	Hughes, Robert J.	Na Lor	M T Tj	Satb
All Hail The Power Of Jesus' Name	Johnston	Na Lor	M T Tj	Satb
All Hail The Power Of Jesus' Name	Thompson	Na Lor	M T Tj	Satb
All Hail The Power Of Jesus' Name	Wilson	Na Lor	M T Tj	Satb
Alleluia! Sing To Jesus	Shea (Arr)	Na Lor	M T Tj	2mel.
Art Thou The Christ	O'hara, Geoffrey	Na Gsc	B T Tj	Satb+
At Jesus' Name	Johnson, Gary L.	74 Bfi	B L T Tj	
At The Feet Of Jesus	Ferguson	75 Her	M T Tj	Satb
At The Name Of Jesus	Williams/Johnson	Na Zon	T Tj	Satb
At The Name Of Jesus	Williams, Vaughan R.	Na Oxf	M T Tj	Satb
Beautiful Savior	Christiansen, F. M.	55 Aug	M T Tj	Var
Beautiful Savior	Hughes, Robert J.	Na Lor	M T Tj	
Beautiful Savior	Nachtwey, Roger (Arr.)	65 Fel	B T Tj	
Beautiful Savior	Perry	Na Lor	M T Tj	
Because He Touched Me	Mieir, Audrey	66 Man	M B R T Tj	
Behold The Lamb Of God	Handel/Ed Johnson	Na Zon	T Tj	Satb
Behold, The Grace Appears	Holden, Oliver	76 Bbl	M T Tj	Satb
Blessed Assurance	Hughes, Robert J.	Na Lor	M T Tj	Satb
Blessed Assurance	Wolf	Na Lor	M T Tj	Satb
Blessed Assurance (Arrangement O.)	Cato, Jim & Esther	75 Mam	R L T Tj	
Blessed Assurance, Jesus Is Mine	Wilson	Na Lor	M T Tj	Satb
Blessed Jesus	Dvorak, A	Na Gsc	B T Tj	Satb+
Blessed Jesus, At Thy Word	Bach, J.S./Ed Lee	73 Gia	B R L T Tj	Satb+
Blessed Redeemer	Wilson	Na Lor	M T Tj	Satb
Blessed Saviour, Our Lord Jesus	Hassler, H L	Na Gsc	B T Tj	Satb
Cantata #118 O Jesus Christ (E & Germ)	Bach, J. S.	Na Kal	B T Tj	Satb
Cantata #41 Jesu Nun (Eng/Germ)	Bach, J. S.	Na Kal	B T Tj	Satb
Cantata #81 Jesus Schlaeft (E & Ger)	Bach, J. S.	Na Kal	B T Tj	Satb
Childhood Of Christ (Germ, Eng, Fr)	Berlioz, Hector	Na Kal	B T Tj	Satb
Christ Hath A Garden	Holman, Derek	Na Gsc	B T Tj	Satb

Christ Is Made The Sure Foundation	Englert, Eugene	61 Aug	M T Tj	Satb
Christ Is Made The Sure Foundation	Neale/Wood, D.	Na Abi	M B L T Tj	
Christ Is Made The Sure Foundation	Owens, Dewey	Na Gsc	B T Tj	Satb+
Christ Is The World's True Light 1	Stanton, W.K.	Na Oxf	M T Tj	2pt
Christ The Sure Foundation	Sateren, Leland B.	58 Aug	M T Tj	Satb
Christ Who Knows All His Sheep	Thiman, Eric H.	Na Gsc	B T Tj	Satb
Christ, My Beloved	Holman, Derek	Na Gsc	B T Tj	Satb
Christ, Whose Glory Fills The Skies	Thiman, Eric H.	Na Gsc	B T Tj	Satb+
Christe Jesu, Gaude Plurimum, Mater	Taverner, John	Na Kal	B T Tj	Satb
Christe Jesu, Pastor Bone	Taverner, John	Na Oxf	M T Tj	Satb
Christe, Qui Lux Es Et Dies (Md)	White, Robert	Na Oxf	M T Tj	Var
Christians Sound The Name That Saved	Farrell, Melvin	61 Wlp	B T Tj	
Christus	Mendelssohn, F.	Na Kal	B T Tj	Satb
Come, My Way, My Truth, My Life (Me)	Tomblings, Philip	Na Oxf	M T Tj	Satb
Cor Jesu	Gounod, Charles	Na Gsc	B T Tj	Satb+
Crown Him With Many Crowns	Goemanne, Noel	74 Gia	M T Tj	Sab+
Crusade Choir (No Zd-5474)	Reese, Jim	Na Zon	B T Tj	
Dulcissime Et Benignissime Christe	Schutz, Heinrich	Na Kal	B T Tj	Satb
Fairest Lord Jesus	Landon	Na Lor	M T Tj	
Fairest Lord Jesus	Traditional/Rosley	Na Zon	T Tj	Satb
Garden Hymn	Na	Na Gsc	B T Tj	Satb+
Gentle Jesus, Meek And Mild	Brown, Charles	76 Abi	M T Tj	U+
Gentle Savior, Hold My Hand	Lynn, George	56 Smc	M T Tj	Satb
Give Me Jesus	Na	Na Lor	M T Tj	Satb
Guide Me Jesus	Lewis, E.	74 Sil	L T Tj	
Hallelujah! What A Savior!	Wilson	Na Lor	M T Tj	Satb
Have You Any Room For Jesus?	Williams	Na Lor	M T Tj	Satb
He Is All I Need	Buckhaus	Na Lor	M T Tj	Satb
He Smiled On Me	O'hara, Geoffrey	Na Gsc	B T Tj	Satb+
He Was Alone	Paxson, Theodore	Na Gsc	B T Tj	Satb+
Hear Ye Jesus Is The Lamb Of God	Homilius, Gottfried	75 Bbl	M T Tj	Satb
Heart Divine	Dvorak, Anton	Na Lor	M T Tj	Satb
Heart Of Christ	Farrell, Melvin	55 Wlp	B T Tj	
Homo Natus De Muliere	Wilbye, John(Ed Brown)	Na Oxf	M T Tj	Satb
Hope Of The World	Brandon, George	76 Abi	M T Tj	Satb+
How Sweet The Name	Johnson, Gary L.	74 Bfi	B L T Tj	
How Sweet The Name Of Jesus Sounds(P.D	Elrich, Dwight (Arr.)	74 Man	M T Tj	Choral
I Am	Infante, Guy	74 Sms	M R L T Tj	
I Am The Alpha And The Omega	Moe, Daniel	67 Aug	M T Tj	Satb
I Am The Light	Johnson, D.	73 Aug	M T Tj	Satb
I Am The Rose Of Sharon	Billings, William	75 Bbl	M T Tj	Satb
I Am The Rose Of Sharon	Billings, William	Na Gsc	B T Tj	Satb
I Don't Deserve His Love	Meador, C.	74 Sil	L T Tj	
I Don't Know Why Jesus Loved Me	Crouch, Andrae	71 Lex	M R T Tj	
I Heard The Voice Of Jesus Say	Thompson	Na Lor	M T Tj	Satb
I Hide Me Jesus In Thy Name	Ford, Virgil	Na Gsc	B T Tj	Satb
I Must Tell Jesus	Hughes, Robert J.	Na Lor	M T Tj	Satb
I Walked Today Where Jesus Walked	O'hara, Geoffrey	39 Gsc	B T Tj	Var+
I Will Sing Of My Redeemer	Moffatt	Na Lor	M T Tj	Satb
If I Have My Jesus(From Two Litanies)	Meyerowitz, Jan	53 Bbl	B T Tj	Satb+
In Jesus	Hughes, Robert J.	Na Lor	M T Tj	Satb
In My Heart There Rings A Melody	Roth/Landon	Na Lor	M T Tj	Satb
In Nomine Jesu	Handl, Jacob	74 Gia	M T Tj	Satb
In Nomine Jesu(At Jesus' Holy Name)	Handl, Jacob	Na Gia	T Tj	
In The Night Christ Came Walking(Acap)	Cain, Noble	Na Gsc	B T Tj	Full
Into The Woods My Master Went	Lutkin	Na Lor	M T Tj	Satb
Jesu By Thee I Would Be Blessed	Franck, Melchior	Na Gsc	B T Tj	Satb
Jesu Dulcis Memoria	Na	Na Gsc	B T Tj	Satb
Jesu Dulcis Memoria	Victoria, Tomas Luis	65 Bbl	M T Tj	Satb
Jesu Joy Of Man's Desiring	Bach, J.S.	Na Gsc	B T Tj	Var+
Jesu Priceless Treasure	Bach, J.S.	Na Gsc	B T Tj	Satb
Jesu Word Of God Incarnate(Ave Verum)	Gounod, Charles	Na Gsc	B T Tj	Satb+
Jesu, Gentlest Saviour	Saint-Saens, Camille	Na Gsc	B T Tj	2pt
Jesu, Jesu, Dulcissime	Reutter, Johann	75 Bbl	M T Tj	Satb
Jesu, Joy And Treasure(Eng)	Buxtehude, D.	Cfp	R T Tj	Solo+
Jesu, Joy Of Man's Desiring	Bach, J.S.	Na Lor	M T Tj	Var
Jesu, Joy Of Man's Desiring	Bach, J.S.(Treharne)	39 Gsc	M R T Tj	Satb+
Jesu, Joy Of Man's Desiring (E)	Bach, J.S.	Na Oxf	M T Tj	Satb
Jesu, Joy Of Man's Desiring (E)	Bach, J.S.	70 Gia	B R L T Tj	Satb+
Jesu, Lover Of My Soul (E)	Coleman, Henry	Na Oxf	M T Tj	Satb
Jesu, My Heart's Treasure	Buxtehude, D.	Na Kal	B T Tj	Satb+
Jesu, Priceless Treasure	Bach, J.S.	Na Aug	M T Tj	Satb
Jesu, Priceless Treasure (Motet 3)	Bach, J.S.	Na Kal	B T Tj	Satb
Jesu, The Very Thought Of Thee (Me)	Lang, C.S.	Na Oxf	M T Tj	2pt
Jesu, Thou My Heart's Delight	Bach, J.S.-Sateren	59 Aug	M T Tj	Satb
Jesus Joy Of Loving Hearts	Peninger, David	Na Gsc	B T Tj	Satb+
Jesus Said Unto The People	Stainer, Sir John	Na Gsc	B T Tj	Satb+
Jesus Saves	Denton	Na Lor	M T Tj	Satb
Jesus Walked	Perrin	Na Lor	M T Tj	Unis
Jesus-My Joy	Wyrtzen, Don	75 Zon	T Tj	Satb
Jesus, I Love Thee	Smith/Williams	75 Zon	T Tj	Satb
Jesus, Jesus My Lord	Krieger, Jacob	74 Krg	M T Tj	
Jesus, Lover Of My Soul	Smith	Na Lor	M T Tj	Satb
Jesus, Lover Of My Soul	Wilson	Na Lor	M T Tj	Satb
Jesus, My Lord, My God, My All	Powell	75 Sac	M T Tj	Satb
Jesus, My Saviour, Look On Me	Nevin, Geo B	Na Gsc	B T Tj	Var+
Jesus, Name All Names Above	Schop-Pooler, M.	62 Aug	M T Tj	Sa
Jesus, Name Of Wondrous Love	Butler, Eugene	75 Sac	M T Tj	Satb
Jesus, O Precious Name (New Year)	Lockwood, Normand	55 Smc	M T Tj	Satb
Jesus, Priceless Treasure	Bach, J.S./Ed Lee	73 Gia	B R L T Tj	Satb+
Jesus, Priceless Treasure	Fitzpatrick, Dennis	65 Fel	B T Tj	
Jesus, Refuge Of The Weary	Carlson	74 Aug	M T Tj	Satb
Jesus, Son Of God	Sanford	Na Lor	M T Tj	Satb
Jesus, The Very Thought Of Thee	Rasley, John M.	Na Zon	T Tj	Satb
Jesus, Thou Joy Of Loving Hearts	Baker/Decou	Na Zon	T Tj	Satb
Jesus, Thou Joy Of Loving Hearts	Darst	Na Lor	M T Tj	Satb
Jesus, Thou Joy Of Loving Hearts	Neff	66 Aug	M T Tj	Ss+N
Jesus, Thy Boundless Love To Me	Vick	75 Sac	M T Tj	Satb
Jesus, We Look To Thee	Ford	Na Lor	M T Tj	Satb
Lead Me, Savior	Wilson	Na Lor	M T Tj	Satb
Let The Savior In (Old Dutch Melody)	Na	Na Lor	M T Tj	Unis
Lily Of The Valley, The	Smith	Na Lor	M T Tj	Satb
Lo, Our Savior King Is Here	Farrell, Melvin	63 Wlp	B T Tj	
Lord Jesus Christ In Thee Alone	Franck, Melchior	Na Gsc	B T Tj	Satb
Lord Jesus Think On Me	Talmadge, Charles	72 Gal	M T Tj	
Lord Jesus, Think On Me	Hughes, Robert J.	Na Lor	M T Tj	Satb
Lord Jesus, Think On Me	Na	Na Gsc	B T Tj	2chor
Lord Jesus, Think On Me	Smith, Lani	76 Lor	T Tj	Satb+
Love Of Jesus, All Divine	Blake, George	Na Gsc	B T Tj	Satb+
Man Born Of A Woman, A	Bach, J.C.	52 Bbl	B T Tj	Satb
Messiah-Singspiration's Abridged Ed.	Handel/Johnson	Na Zon	B T Tj	Satb
My Blessed Savior (Cantata)	Bach, J.S.	75 Lps	B R T Tj	Satb
My Faith Looks Up To Thee	Conley, David	62 Gam	M T Tj	Satb
My Jesus	Bach/Christiansen	53 Aug	M T Tj	Satb
My Jesus, I Love Thee	Smith, Lani	Na Lor	M T Tj	Satb
My Master Was So Very Poor	Graham	Na Lor	M T Tj	Sa
My Redeemer	Martin	Na Lor	M T Tj	Satb
Name Of Jesus, The	Beck, J.	76 Bec	M T Tj	
Now Praise We Christ, The Holy One	Hooper	63 Aug	M T Tj	Satb
O Blessed Jesus	Brahms, Johannes	54 Bbl	B T Tj	Ssaa
O Blessed Jesus	Pierluigi, Giovanni	66 Som	M T Tj	
O Bone Jesu	Brahms, Johannes	54 Bbl	B T Tj	Ssaa
O Bone Jesu	Palestrina, Giovanni P	Na Gsc	B T Tj	Satb
O Bone Jesu (Oh Loving Jesus)	Brahms, Johannes	Na Gsc	B T Tj	Ssaa
O Christ Who Holds The Open Gate	Shaw, Martin	Na Gsc	B T Tj	Satb+
O Divine Redeemer	Gounod, Charles	Na Gsc	M T Tj	Full
O Divine Redeemer	Gounod, Charles	Na Lor	M T Tj	Satb
O Domine Jesu Christe	Des Pres, Josquin	Na Gsc	B T Tj	Ttbb
O Heart Of Christ	Farrell, Melvin	63 Wlp	B T Tj	
O Holy Jesu	Lvoff, A Von	Na Gsc	B T Tj	Satb
O Holy Savior	Traditional/Wyrtzen	Na Zon	T Tj	Satb
O Jesu Mi Dulcissime	Gabrieli, G	Na Gsc	B T Tj	8mix
O Jesus Christ, To Thee May Hymns	Moe, Daniel	57 Aug	M T Tj	Satb
O Jesus, King Of Gentleness	Ford	70 Gsc	M T Tj	Satb
O Jesus, Thou Are Standing	Shepard, T G	Na Gsc	B T Tj	Satb+
O Jesus, Thou Son Of God	Schutz, Heinrich	75 Maf	M T Tj	2pt
O Lamb Of God Most Holy	Eccard, J	Na Gsc	B T Tj	Ssatb
O Lord Who Drew From Jesus' Side	Goemanne, Noel	61 Wlp	B T Tj	
O Lord, Jesus Christ	Berchem, Jachet	66 Som	M T Tj	
O Master Let Me Walk With Thee	Bodycombe, Aneurin	Na Gsc	B T Tj	Satb+
O Redeemer Divine	Faure, Gabriel	52 Bbl	M T Tj	Satb+
O Saviour Of The World(A Cap)	Goss, John	Na Gsc	B T Tj	Var
O Thou That Art The Light Eternal	Webber, Lloyd	Na Gsc	B T Tj	Satb+
One Way	Hughes, Robert J.	Na Lor	M T Tj	Satb
Our Blest Redeemer (Trad Irish Tune)	Fraser, Jeffrey D.	Na Oxf	M T Tj	Satb
Pie Jesu(God Of Mercy)	Cherubini, L	Na Gsc	B T Tj	Satb+
Ride On, Ride On In Majesty(Opt Tpt)	Johnson, D.	70 Aug	M T Tj	Sab
Savior, I Long To Be	Hughes, Robert J.	Na Lor	M T Tj	Satb
Savior, Teach Me Day By Day (M)	Lewis, John Leo	75 Abi	M T Tj	Satb
Son Of God	Haydn, Michael	Na Gsc	B T Tj	Satb
Son Of God, Eternal Savior	Blake	Na Lor	M T Tj	
Song Of The Passion (M)	Oldroyd, George	Na Oxf	M T Tj	Satb
Soul Of My Savior	Roff, Joseph	70 Gia	M T Tj	Var+
Sweet Jesu, King Of Bliss (E)	Archer, Violet	Na Oxf	M T Tj	Sa
Sweet Jesus	Bolz, Hariett	74 Bec	M T Tj	
Take It To Jesus	Smith	Na Lor	M T Tj	Satb
The King Of Love My Shepherd Is	Englert, Eugene	73 Gia	M T Tj	Satb+
The Lamb	Goodhall, Clare	Na Gsc	B T Tj	Sa+
The Lord Into His Garden (Md)	Russell, Olive (Arr)	73 Pro	M T Tj	Satb+
The Name Of Jesus (Arrangement)	Jansen, Geneva	74 Tal	R L T Tj	
This Is His Promise	Lewis, E.	74 Sil	L T Tj	
This Is Jesus	Price (Arr)	Na Lor	M T Tj	Var
Thou Art Jesus, Savior And Lord	Schutz, Heinrich	66 Aug	M T Tj	Satb
Thou Art The Way	Talmadge, C.L.	Na Gsc	B T Tj	Satb
Thus Said The Lord	Bernardi, Steffano	Na Gsc	B T Tj	Satb+
To Jesus Holy	Gannon, Michael	61 Wlp	B T Tj	
Trusting Jesus	Benton Price	76 Lor	T Tj	Satb+
Trusting Jesus A	Ortlund	Na Zon	T Tj	Satb
Verbum Caro In A Minor	Vittoria, T L Da	Na Gia	T Tj	
Verbum Caro In G	Vittoria, T L Da	Na Gia	T Tj	
Walk With Me	Emig	Na Lor	M T Tj	Var
Walk With Us, Lord	Lokey	Na Lor	M T Tj	Satb
We Adore You	Gasparini, Q	Na Gia	T Tj	
We Adore You	Perti, G A	69 Gia	M T Tj	Satb+
We Adore You, O Christ	Palestrina, Giovanni P	66 Gia	T Tj	Var
We Hasten, O Jesu (From Cantata 78)	Bach, J.S.(Arr Davies)	Na Oxf	M T Tj	2pts
What A Friend	Rasley	Na Lor	M T Tj	
What A Wonderful Savior!	Hoffman/Decou	Na Zon	T Tj	Satb
Who At My Door Is Standing?	Moffatt	Na Lor	M T Tj	
Who Is This Man?	Burnham	75 Sac	M T Tj	

Hymns about the Kingship of God
these are hymns to God as King, and Christ as King. Also here are a number of triumphal hymns alluding to the "second coming". Songs that refer to Jesus as "Lord" may also be found here.

Children Of The King	Young, Robert H.	63 Gam	M C Tk	Unis
Alleluia, Jesus Is King	Barry, John	76 Rpb	M B R L F Tk	
Christ Is King	Winter, Miriam T.	68 Van	B R F Tk	
Christ Is Lord	Miffleton, Jack	70 Acp	L F Tk	
Christ Our Leader	Gilligan, M. (Text)	.70 Acp	L F Tk	
Christ The King	Yantis, David	Na Yan	B F Tk	
Clap Your Hands	Quinlan, Paul	66 Fel	B R F Tk	
Come, Lord Jesus	Habjan, Germaine	66 Fel	B R F Tk	
God Arises	Quinlan, Paul	67 Fel	B R F Tk	
Hallelujah, Jesus Is Lord!	Farra, Mimi A.	72 Gia	B R L F Tk	Var+
Honor And Praise (From Come Follow)	Kramper, Jerry	69 Gia	B R L F Tk	
Hymn Of The Universe	Fitzgerald, Michael &	74 Wgm	B R L F Tk	

CATEGORIZED INDEX

I Will Come Again	Johnson, Gary L.	74 Bfi	B L F Tk
It's A Brand-New World	Edwards, Deanna	74 Fcc	R L F Tk
Jesus Christ Is Lord	Temple, Sebastian	71 Gia	B R L F Tk Var+
Jesus Christ, King Of Kings	Ste. Marie, Patricia	74 Sha	B R L F Tk
Jesus Christ, Our King	Temple, Sebastian	71 Gia	B R L F Tk Ar+
Jesus Is A-Drivin' Out Satan	Ackroyd, Mary	75 Fis	M L F Tk
Jesus Is Lord	Vissing, Sr. Rosalie	74 Sha	B R L F Tk
Jesus Is Soon Coming	Coppock, Doug	Fis	M L F Tk
King Of Creation	Christmas, Charles	74 Wgm	M R L F Tk
King Of Glory, The	Jabusch, Willard F.	67 Acf	M R F Tk
King Of Kings	Christmas, Charles	74 Wgm	B R L F Tk
King's Highway	Christmas, Charles	74 Wgm	M R L F Tk
Litany For The Lord's Coming	Stamps, Robert J.	74 Sta	M R L F Tk
Lord Have Your Way With Me	Hatfield, Steve	74 Man	R F Tk
Marana-Tha	Silvia, Helen	73 Acp	L F Tk
My Lord Is Long A Comin'	Germaine	66 Fel	B R F Tk
Parousia Song	Thiem, James	66 Fel	B F Tk
Psalm 80 Maranatha	O'sheil, Judy	66 Fel	B F Tk
Sing, Sing Alleluia	Carr, Nancy	73 Gia	M B R L F Tk Var+
The Kingdom Of God	Ste. Marie, Patricia	74 Sha	B R L F Tk
The Kingdom Of Jesus	Daingerfield Richard	76 Chh	B R L F Tk
The Lion And The Lamb	Hershberg, Sarah	68 Fel	B R F Tk
The Lord Is A Great & Mighty King	Davis, Diane	73 Gia	M B R L F Tk Var+
The Lord Of Evolution	Temple, Sebastian	69 Gia	B R L F Tk Uguit
We Have A King	Jabusch, Willard F.	75 Rpb	M B R L F Tk
Yours Is The Kingdom	Miffleton, Jack	69 Wlp	B R F Tk

As Only God Above Can Do	Lile, Bobby	56 Man	M G Tk
Bring Back The King	Mieir, Audrey	74 Man	B G Tk
Bringing Back The King	Mcgranahan/Decou	Na Zon	M G Tk Satb
Didn't My Lord Deliver Daniel	Na	Na Gsc	B G Tk Satb
Hallelujah To The King	Collins, David	72 Man	M G Tk
He's Still The King Of Kings	Gaither/Gaither B/G	71 Gmc	M B R G Tk Var
I Got Shoes	Na	Na Gsc	B G Tk Full
In That Great Gettin' Up Mornin'	Zimmermann	69 Aug	M G Tk
Jesus Is Lord Of All	Gaither/Gaither B/G	73 Gmc	M B R G Tk Var
Jesus Is Lord Of All	Gaither, William J	Na Lor	M G Tk Satb
Jesus, My Wonderful Lord	Gonzalo, Carrie	69 Man	B G Tk
King Of All Kings	Hamblen Stuart	Na Ham	M G Tk
Like In Noah's Days	Borg Paula	74 Jhm	R L G Tk
My Lord Is Mighty	Hamblen Stuart	Na Ham	M G Tk
Revelation Six Six Six	Laney E.C. Drake R.	74 Jhm	R L G Tk
Ride On, King Jesus (Spiritual)	Fleming (Arr)	73 Aug	M G Tk Satb+
Seek Ye First	Childs	Na Zon	M G Tk
Some Day	Myring Charles	72 Jhm	M L G Tk
The Great Judgment Day	Ohler, Susan	74 Pmp	M B R L G Tk
The King Of Love	Page, Paul F.	76 Rpb	M B R L G Tk
The Seven Seals Revealed	Ohler, Susan	74 Pmp	M B R L G Tk
The Wedding In The Sky	Butler, Dorothy	74 Pmp	M B L G Tk
Visions Of Eternity	Butler, Dorothy	68 Pmp	M B R L G Tk
What If Christ Came Tonight	Butler, Dorothy	74 Pmp	M B L G Tk
When The Great Trumpet Sound	Hendrix, James	65 Jhe	M R L G Tk
When This World Ends	Sewell Homer	70 Oak	G Tk

All Glory, Praise, And Honor	Gilligan, Michael	67 Acp	L L Tk
All Glory, Praise, And Honor	Liturgical Press, Alt.	73 Acp	L L Tk Satb
Alleluia To Our King	Graham	Na Lor	M L Tk Satb
Alleluia! Jesus Is Lord	Gilligan, M. (Text)	70 Acp	L L Tk
Alleluia! Jesus Is Lord (4-Part Arr.)	Monk, William H. Alt.	73 Acp	L L Tk
At The Lamb's High Feast (Long) (Brass)	Pelz, W.	69 Aug	M L Tk Satb
Behold Now, The House Of God	Proulx, Richard	69 Aug	M L Tk Satb
Blessings On The King	Lynch, Michael B.	76 Rav	B R L L Tk
Blessings On The King	Manion, Tim, S. J.	72 Nal	B R L Tk
Christ Is Our Leader	Gilligan, Michael	70 Acp	L L Tk
Christ Our Leader (4-Part Arr.)	Nardella, Faith	73 Acp	L L Tk
Christ Our Leader (4-Part Arr.)	Piae Cantiones, Silvia	73 Acp	L L Tk
Christ Will Appear Again	Fitzpatrick, Dennis	65 Fel	B L Tk
Come Quickly Jesus	Stipe, Thomas Richard	73 Mar	R L L Tk
Come, Shake The Mountains	Silvia, Helen	73 Acp	L L Tk
Crown Him Lord Of All	Thygerson	Na Lor	M L Tk Satb
Crown Him Lord Of All!	Rasley	Na Lor	M L Tk Satb
Crown Him The King Of Kings	Elvey, George J.	73 Acp	L L Tk Satb
Crown Him The King Of Kings	Williams, Ralph V.	67 Acp	L L Tk
Crown Him With Many Crowns (Tpts, Org)	Pelz, W.	63 Aug	M L Tk Satb
Dies Irae, Dies Illa	Fitzpatrick, Dennis	65 Fel	B L Tk
Earth Is The Lord's, The	Kirkpatrick	Na Lor	M L Tk
Eternal God, Whose Power Upholds	Tweedy/Warrack	Na Gia	M B L L Tk
Give The King Your Final Judgment	Gilligan, Michael	70 Acp	L L Tk
Give The King Your Final Judgment	Lorenz, Matthias	70 Acp	L L Tk
Give The King Your Final Judgment (4pt)	Silvia, Helen	73 Acp	L L Tk
Give The King Your Final Judgment (4pt)	Witt, Christian F.	73 Acp	L L Tk
Glory To The King Of Kings	Thompson	Na Lor	M L Tk Var
God Is Not Dead	Roff, Joseph	75 Sac	M L Tk Satb
He That Descended (Md)	Amner, John	Na Oxf	M L Tk Satb
I Love Thy Kingdom, Lord	Young, Gordon	75 Sac	M L Tk Satb
In The Day Of The Lord	Gutfreund, Ed (Rev.)	74 Nal	B R L Tk
It's A Brand New Day	Quinlan, Paul	68 Nal	B R L Tk
Jesus The King Passes By	Peterson, John W.	Na Zon	M L Tk Satb
King Of Kings, Lord Of Lords	Catalanello, Michael	76 Str	M L Tk
King Shall Come When Morning Dawns, The	Lovelace, Austin C.	75 Sac	M L Tk Sab
Kingdom Of Children	Smith, Randy	72 Mar	R L L Tk
Lead On, O King Eternal	Johnson, D.	70 Aug	M L Tk Satb
Lord Doth Reign, The (Opt Acc)	Lynn, George	Na Abi	M L Tk Satb
Lord Is King, The	Brandon, George	Na Abi	M L Tk Satb
Lord Of All	Gilliam, R L	Na Gsc	B L Tk Ttbb+
Lord Reigneth, The	Walter, Samuel	Na Abi	M L Tk Sa-Satb
Lord Reigns, The	Butler	75 Sac	M L Tk Satb
O Christ Our King	Price, William (Text)	70 Acp	L L Tk
O Christ Our King (4-Part Arr)	Silvia, Helen	73 Acp	L L Tk
O Jesus King Of Gentleness	Ford, Virgil	Na Gsc	B L Tk Satb

O Thou Eternal Christ, Ride On!	Lovelace, Austin C.	Na Abi	M L Tk Satb
Praise The Lord Who Reigns Above (Acap)	Lovelace, Austin C.	Na Abi	M L Tk Satb
Psalm 24	Bevans, William	Na Abi	M L Tk Satb
Redeemer King	Gilligan, Michael	67 Acp	L L Tk
Redeemer King	Silvia, Helen	73 Acp	L L Tk
Reign, Master Jesus	Rigby, John	73 Fel	B R L L Tk
Remember Us	Page, Paul F.	76 Rpb	M B R L L Tk
Ride On In Majesty	Pooler, Marie	51 Aug	M L Tk Satb+
Ride On, Eternal King	Leaf, Robert	69 Aug	M L Tk Sa
Royal Banners Forward Go, The	Peek, Richard	Na Abi	M L Tk Satb
Rule Over My Soul	Unknown	73 Mar	L L Tk
Seek Ye First	Lafferty, Karen Louise	73 Mar	M R L L Tk
Show Forth, O God, Your Power	Fitzpatrick, Dennis	65 Fel	B L Tk
The Faithful Shall Rejoice In Glory	Fitzpatrick, Dennis	65 Fel	B L Tk
The King Of Love My Shepherd Is	Johnson, D.	67 Aug	M L Tk Sab
The Lord Has Brought Us	Fitzpatrick, Dennis	65 Fel	B L Tk
The Lord Has Delivered	Fitzpatrick, Dennis	65 Fel	B L Tk
The Lord Is God	Fitzpatrick, Dennis	65 Fel	B L Tk
The Lord Is King	Fitzpatrick, Dennis	65 Fel	B L Tk
The Lord Led Forth His People In Joy	Fitzpatrick, Dennis	65 Fel	B L Tk
The Lord Our God Is King Of Kings	Leaf, Robert	70 Aug	M L Tk Sa
The Lord Reigneth	Manz, Paul	61 Aug	M L Tk Satb
The Lord Thundered	Fitzpatrick, Dennis	65 Fel	B L Tk
The Meek Shall Possess The Land	Fitzpatrick, Dennis	65 Fel	B L Tk
This Is The Feast Of Victory (Opt Tpt)	Nelson, Ronald A.	72 Aug	M L Tk Satb
Thou Art Worthy	Pooler, Marie	57 Aug	M L Tk Satb
Thy Kingdom Come (Opt Tpt)	Johnson, D.	67 Aug	M L Tk Sab
Thy Kingdom Come On Earth	Christiansen, P.	72 Aug	M L Tk Satbb
Thy Kingdom Come, O Lord	Christiansen, F. M.	43 Aug	M L Tk Satb
Thy Kingdom Come, O Lord	Wehr, David A.	Na Abi	M L Tk Unis
To Christ The King	Prendergast, Richard	67 Acp	L L Tk
To Christ The King (4-Part Arr)	Cirou, Joseph Et. Al	73 Acp	L L Tk
To Jesus Christ Our Sovereign King	Hellriegel, Martin	67 Acp	L L Tk
To Jesus Christ Our Sovereign King	Silvia, Helen	73 Acp	L Tk
To Our King Immortal	Leaf, Robert	71 Aug	M L Tk Satb+
To The Lamb Who Was Slain	Fitzpatrick, Dennis	65 Fel	B L Tk
Tomorrow Christ Is Coming	Lovelace, Austin C.	72 Aug	M L Tk 2pt
Universal Lord, The	Lovelace, Austin C.	75 Sac	M L Tk
Who Is He That Stands Triumphant	Silvia, Helen	73 Acp	L L Tk
Yours Are The Heavens	Fitzpatrick, Dennis	65 Fel	B L Tk
But Our God Abideth In Heaven	Mendelssohn, F.	Na Gsc	B T Tk Smix+
Cantata #112 Der Herr (E & Germ)	Bach, J. S.	Na Kal	B T Tk Satb
Cantata #180 Schmuecke Dich (Eng & Ger)	Bach, J. S.	Na Kal	B T Tk Satb
Christ, Whose Glory Fills The Skies	Armstrong, Thomas	Na Oxf	M T Tk Satb
Come Let Us Tune Our Loftiest Song	Wyatt, Van	73 Pro	M T Tk Satb
Crown Him Lord Of All	Wetzler, Robert	62 Aug	M T Tk Satb
Crown Him With Many Crowns	Elvey/Wyrtzen	75 Zon	M T Tk Satb
Crown Him With Many Crowns	Farrell, Melvin	55 Wlp	B T Tk
Crown Him With Many Crowns	Johnson, D.	67 Aug	M T Tk Sab
Crown Him With Many Crowns	Thygerson	75 Sac	M T Tk Satb+
E'en So, Lord Jesus, Quickly Come	Manz, Paul	Na Con	B T Tk Var
Earth To Ashes	Cassler, G. W	74 Aug	M T Tk Satb
Hail Christ, Our Royal Priest & King	Westendorf, Omer	64 Wlp	B T Tk
Hail His Coming, King Of Glory	Davis	Na Wbp	T Tk
He Is Able	Paino, Paul	58 Zon	M T Tk
He Shall Reign Forever	Simper	Na Lor	M T Tk Satb
Holy City, The	Adams, Harvey	Na Lor	M T Tk Var
I Love Thy Kingdom, Lord	Na	Na Gsc	B T Tk 2chor
I Love Thy Kingdom, Lord	Williams/Peterson	Na Zon	T Tk Satb
Jerusalem, My Happy Home	Sateren, Leland B.	62 Aug	M T Tk Satb
Jesus Shall Reign	Hatton/Williams	Na Zon	M T Tk Satb
Jesus Shall Reign	Hughes, Robert J.	Na Lor	M T Tk Satb
Jesus Shall Reign	Vick	75 Sac	M T Tk Satb
Jesus, Admired And Noble King	Palestrina, Giovanni P	70 Gia	B L T Tk Var
Judgment Anthem	Morgan, Justin	75 Bbl	M T Tk Satb
King All Glorious	Barnby, Jos	Na Gsc	B T Tk Satb+
King Of Glory, King Of Peace (Me)	Bach, J.S. (Arr)	Na Oxf	M T Tk S1tb
King Of Glory, The	Emig	Na Lor	M T Tk Satb
King Of Kings	Simper	Na Lor	M T Tk Satb
King Of Kings	Simper, C	Na Gsc	B T Tk Var+
King Of Love, The	Wilson	Na Lor	M T Tk Satb
King, All Glorious (W/Solos)	Barnby (Arr Squires)	Na Gsc	M T Tk Satb+
Lead On, O King Eternal	Smart/Rasley	Na Zon	T Tk Ssatb
Lead On, O King Eternal	Smart, H	Na Gsc	B T Tk Satb+
Lift Up Your Eyes	Billings-Wienandt	69 Smc	M T Tk Satb
Lord Is King, The	Severson, Roland	Na Abi	M T Tk Satb
Lord Is King, The	Traditional/Johnson	Na Zon	T Tk Full
Lord Of The Years	Charles, Earnest	Na Gsc	B T Tk Satb+
O Day Of God, Draw Nigh	Butler	75 Sac	M T Tk Satb
O Gracious King	Thompson	Na Lor	M T Tk Var
O Jesus, King Most Wonderful	Wetzler, Robert	65 Aug	M T Tk Satb
O Lord Our Governor	Gadsby, H	Na Gsc	B T Tk Satb+
O Lord, Thou Art My God And King	Sateren, Leland B.	64 Aug	M T Tk Satb
O Quam Gloriosum Est Regnum	Vittoria, Ludovica De	Na Kal	B T Tk Satb
O Rex Gloriae	Marenzio, Luca	Na Oxf	M T Tk
O Worship The King (Me)	Lewis, John Leo	75 Abi	M T Tk Satb
Rejoice! The Lord Is King!	Darwall/Berntsen	Na Zon	T Tk Ssatb
Rejoice, The Lord Is King	Goemanne, Noel	73 Gia	M T Tk Satb+
Rejoice, The Lord Is King	Jordan	75 Sac	M T Tk Var
Ride On, Ride On In Majesty	Na	Na Gsc	B T Tk Satb
Seek Ye First The Kingdom Of God	Bruckner, A./Ed Klein	69 Gia	B R L T Tk Satb+
Sponsus (The Bridegroom) Acting Version	Smoldon, W. L. Ed	Na Oxf	B T Tk Sol/Un
The Earth Is The Lord's	Lang, C Tilghman	Na Gsc	B T Tk Satb+
The Glory Of Our King	Wood	69 Aug	M T Tk Unis
The King Shall Rejoice	Handel, G. F.	Na Kal	B T Tk Satb
Thine Is The Kingdom (Holy City)	Gaul, Harvey	Cfs	M T Tk Satb
Thy Kingdom Come	Hopkins-Cassler	59 Aug	M T Tk Satb
To Jesus Christ Our Sovereign King	Goemanne, Noel	74 Gia	M T Tk Sab+
Trumpet Of God	Barraclough	Na Lor	M T Tk Satb

CATEGORIZED INDEX

Unfold Ye Portals ("Redemption")	Gounod, Charles	Cfs	M T Tk Satb

Hymns about Mary the Mother of Jesus

Hail Mary	Landry, Carey (Rev.)	75 Nal	B R C Tm
A Virgin	Winter, Miriam T.	67 Van	B R F Tm
Mary	Hunkele	68 Wlp	B F Tm
Mary, Mother Of The Word	Cunningham, Patrick	76 Gra	B R L F Tm
Song Of Mary	Russ, Bob	67 Van	B R F Tm
The Baker Woman	Noel, M–C, Richards H.	69 Van	B R F Tm
The Mother Of Jesus Was There	Cunningham, Patrick	76 Gra	B R L F Tm Satb
O Mary Don't You Weep	Farra, Mimi A.	73 Gia	M B R L G Tm Var+
A Child, O Virgin, You Bore	Fitzpatrick, Dennis	65 Fel	B L Tm
All Glorious Is The King's Daughter	Fitzpatrick, Dennis	65 Fel	B L Tm
All The Bright Morning Stars	Deiss, Lucien	65 Wlp	B R L Tm
Alma Redemptoris Mater	Harrison, Lou	62 Pic	M L Tm
An Angel Came To Nazareth	Gilligan, M. (Text)	67 Acp	L L Tm
An Angel Came To Nazareth	Silvia, Helen	73 Acp	L L Tm
And The Waters Keep On Running	Temple, Sebastian	71 Gia	B R L L Tm Satb+
Ave Maria	Eulalia, Sister	47 Tcp	M L Tm
Ave Maria	Gilligan, Michael	70 Acp	L L Tm
Ave Maria	Lynch, Michael B.	73 Rav	B L L Tm
Ave Maria	Parente, Sr. Elizabeth	Na Gsc	B L Tm Ssa
Ave Maria	Zsigray, Joe	73 Nal	B R L Tm
Ave Maria (4--Part Arr.)	Silvia, Helen	73 Acp	L L Tm
Behold The Handmaid Of The Lord	Fitzpatrick, Dennis	65 Fel	B L Tm
Biblical Litany To Our Lady	Deiss, Lucien	70 Wlp	B L Tm
Blessed Are You Among Women	Fitzpatrick, Dennis	65 Fel	B L Tm
Blessed Is She Who Has Believed	Fitzpatrick, Dennis	65 Fel	B L Tm
Come Nearer	Peloquin, C Alexander	72 Gia	M L Tm Uvar+
Filhas De Maria	Villa–Lobos, Hector	56 Som	M L Tm
Hail Holy Queen	Deiss, Lucien	65 Wlp	B L Tm
Hail Holy Queen Enthroned (Vv)	Farrell, Melvin	55 Wlp	B L Tm
Hail Mary	Andrews, Carroll T.	Na Gia	L Tm
Hail Mary	Fitzpatrick, Dennis	65 Fel	B L Tm
Hail Mary	Roff, Joseph	Na Gia	L Tm
Hail Mary	Temple	73 Eph	L Tm
Hail Mary, Gentle Woman	Landry, Carey (Rev.)	74 Nal	B R L Tm
Hail, Holy Mother	Fitzpatrick, Dennis	65 Fel	B L Tm
Hail, True Virginity	Roff, Joseph	67 Gia	M L Tm Ssa
Holy Mary, Now We Crown You	Farrell, Melvin	55 Wlp	B L Tm
Holy Mother Of God, Intercede	Fitzpatrick, Dennis	65 Fel	B L Tm
Holy Mother Of Our Redeemer	Deiss, Lucien	65 Wlp	B R L Tm
Hymn To Mary	Ellis, Ron	73 Rav	B R L L Tm
I Saw The New Jerusalem	Deiss, Lucien	65 Wlp	B R L Tm
I Will Put Enmity	Fitzpatrick, Dennis	65 Fel	B L Tm
Joy To You O Virgin Mary	Deiss, Lucien	70 Wlp	B R L Tm
Litany Of The Blessed Virgin	Fitzpatrick, Dennis	65 Fel	B L Tm
Madonna	Haubiel, Charles	41 Tcp	M L Tm
Magnificat	Blue, Robert	66 Fel	B R L Tm
Magnificat	Foley, John, S. J.	70 Nal	B R L Tm
Magnificat (Luke), The	Quinlan, Paul	68 Nal	B R L Tm
Mary	Collard, Terry	71 Nal	B R L Tm
Mary (Optional Instruments)	Wetzler, Robert	73 Aug	M L Tm Satb
Mary The Dawn	Gilligan, Michael	67 Acp	L L Tm
Mary The Dawn (4–Part Arr)	Cirou, Joseph/Silvia H	73 Acp	L L Tm
Mary, Filled With Grace	Gilligan, Michael	70 Acp	R L L Tm
Mary, Filled With Grace	Silvia, Helen	73 Acp	L L Tm
Mary, Your Child Is God	Shelley, Tom	71 Ahc	B R L L Tm
Mary's Lament	Carlson	70 Aug	M L Tm Unis
Mary's Song	Fabing, Bob	74 Ahc	B R L L Tm
May The God Of Israel Join You	Fitzpatrick, Dennis	65 Fel	B L Tm
Mother Of Holy Hope	Deiss, Lucien	65 Wlp	B R L Tm
O Ever Radiant Virgin	Deiss, Lucien	65 Wlp	B R L Tm
O Virgin Mother, He Whom The World	Fitzpatrick, Dennis	65 Fel	B L Tm
Queen Of Heaven (Regina Caeli) Eng	Deiss, Lucien	65 Wlp	B R L Tm
Rejoice O Virgin Mary	Deiss, Lucien	65 Wlp	B L Tm
Sancta Maria	Cooper, David S.	53 Pic	M L Tm
Sing Of Mary	Gilligan, Michael	67 Acp	L L Tm
Sing Of Mary	Silvia, Helen	73 Acp	L Tm
Song Of Mary	Nachtwey, Roger	65 Fel	B L Tm
Song Of Mary (W/Insts)	Sinzheimer	72 Aug	M L Tm Unis
Splendor Of Creation	Deiss, Lucien	65 Wlp	B R L Tm
Stabat Mater	Perry, Julia	54 Som	M L Tm
The Daughters Of Kings	Fitzpatrick, Dennis	65 Fel	B L Tm
The Memorare	Kreutz, Robert	75 Gia	M L Tm Solo+
The Song Of Mary	Sinzheimer	69 Aug	M L Tm Solo
We Greet You (Litany Of Bvm)	Deiss, Lucien	65 Wlp	B L Tm
We Place Our Selves (Sub Tuum)	Deiss, Lucien	65 Wlp	B R L Tm
You Are All Beautiful	Deiss, Lucien	70 Wlp	B R L Tm
You Are Blessed, O Virgin Mary	Fitzpatrick, Dennis	65 Fel	B L Tm
You Are The Honor	Deiss, Lucien	65 Wlp	B R L Tm
Alma Redemptoris Mater	Palestrina, Giovanni P	Na Gsc	B T Tm Satb
An Angel Came In Unto Mary (Me)	Kellam, Iam	Na Oxf	M T Tm Satb
As The Lily Shines	Lasso, Orlando Di	67 Fel	B T Tm
Assumpta Est Maria	Aichinger, G	Na Gsc	B T Tm Var+
Assumpta Est Maria	Palestrina, Giovanni P	Na Kal	B T Tm Satb
Ave Maria	Arcadelt, J	Na Gsc	B T Tm Var
Ave Maria	Brahms, Johannes	Na Gsc	B T Tm Ssaa+
Ave Maria	Mouton, Jean	Na Gsc	B T Tm Satb
Ave Maria	Palestrina, Giovanni P	Na Gia	T Tm
Ave Maria	Palestrina, Giovanni P	Na Gsc	B T Tm Ssaa
Ave Maria	Schubert, Franz J.	Na Gsc	B T Tm Var+
Ave Maria	Smith, Gregg	Na Gsc	B T Tm Satb+
Ave Maria	Victoria/Krone	Na Wbp	T Tm
Ave Maria	Vittoria, T L	Na Gia	T Tm
Ave Maria (In 19 Rounds)	Mozart, W.A./Tortolano	75 Gia	B L T Tm 3pt
Ave Maria (Lat & Eng)	Pohlmann	Hof	M T Tm Ssa
Ave Maria (Lat Only)(M)	Gorczycki, G.G.	75 Gia	M L T Tm Ttbb
Ave Maria (Lat) A Cap	Verdonck, C. Ed Herter	76 Gia	M L T Tm Satb
Ave Maria (Md)	Parsons, Robert	Na Oxf	M T Tm Full
Ave Maria, Father To Thee We Pray	Gounod, Charles	Na Gsc	B T Tm Ssa+
Ave Maria, Full Of Grace	Meyerowitz, Jan	54 Bbl	M T Tm Satb
Ave Maria, Gratia Plena	Meyerowitz, Jan	52 Bbl	M T Tm
Ave Maria, Op. 12 (Eng–Lat)	Brahms, Johannes	Cfp	R T Tm Ssaa
Ave Maria, Opus 12 (Female)	Brahms, Johannes	Na Kal	B T Tm
Ave Maris Stella	Anerio, G	Na Gia	T Tm
Ave Maris Stella	Meyerowitz, Jan	54 Ron	M T Tm Ttbb
Ave Maris Stella	Palestrina, Giovanni P	Na Gia	T Tm
Ave Maris Stella	Williams, Grace	Na Oxf	M T Tm Ttbb
Ave Regina Coelorum (E & L) (Me)	Soriano, F. (Ed Lee)	76 Gia	M L T Tm Satb
Beata Es Virgo	Gabrieli, G.	Na Gsc	B T Tm 6mix+
Drop Down, Ye Heaven (Is 45)	Statham, Heathcote	Na Oxf	M T Tm Ss
Ecce Virgo Concipiet	Morales, Cristobal De	Na Gsc	B T Tm Satb
Gabriel Angelus	Tombelle, F De La	Na Gia	T Tm
Gaude Maria	Lotti, A	Na Gia	T Tm
German Magnificat	Schutz, Heinrich	Na Oxf	B T Tm Satb
Glorious Mysteries	Dejong (Music)	63 Wlp	B T Tm
Graduale: Sancta Maria, K. 273	Mozart, Wolfgang A	52 Bbl	M T Tm Satb+
Hail Blessed Lady	Westendorf, Omer	63 Wlp	B T Tm
Hail Maiden Mary	Westendorf, Omer	63 Wlp	B T Tm
Hail Mary	Arcadelt, J	69 Gia	M T Tm Satb
Hail Mary (E & Lat)	Arcadelt, J./Ed Klein	69 Gia	B R L T Tm Satb+
Hail Mary Full Of Grace	Snow, Robert J.	63 Wlp	B T Tm
Hail Mary.	Greif, Jean A	65 Vrn	M L T Tm
Hail, Dear Virgin (W/Organ)	Reutter, Johann	76 Bbl	M T Tm Satb
Hail, Holy Queen	Creston, Paul	Na Gsc	B T Tm Ttbb+
Hail, Mary (Unison Or Choral)	Fitzpatrick, Dennis	63 Fel	B T Tm
Hail, Queen Of Heaven, Be Joyful	Soriano, Francisco	66 Som	M T Tm
Hail, Queen Of Heaven, Rejoice	Lotti, A	74 Gia	M T Tm Sa
Hail, Virgin Mary	Victoria, Tomas Luis	67 Bbl	M T Tm Satb
Immaculate Mary (Modern Text)	Foley, Brian	71 Gsc	B L T Tm
In Assumptione B. Mariae & In Festo	Byrd, William	Na Kal	B T Tm Satb
In Nativitate Mariae Virginis	Byrd, William	Na Kal	B T Tm Satb
In Venisti Enim Gratiam	Na	Na Gsc	B T Tm Satb
Joyful Mysteries	Gannon, Michael	63 Wlp	B T Tm
Magnificat	Williams, Vaughan R.	Na Oxf	B T Tm Ssa
Magnificat (Long)	Pinelli, G B	74 Gia	M T Tm Satb
Magnificat In D	Bach, J. S.	75 Lps	B R T Tm Satb
Magnificat No. 1	Lopez, Francisco	68 Pic	M T Tm
Mary, We Must Go	Na	Na Gsc	B T Tm Satb
Mary's Salutation (E & Germ)	Eccard, Johann	Na Oxf	M T Tm Ssatb
Mater Patris Et Filia	Brumel, Antoine	Na Gsc	B T Tm Tbb
May Magnificat	Paynter, J. (Text Hopk)	Na Oxf	B T Tm Acap
Monstra Te Esse Matrem	Del Castillo, Fructos	52 Pic	M T Tm
Motet Super Dixit Maria	Hassler, H.L. (D1612)	Na Kal	B T Tm Satb
Mother Of God (W/Org)	Dreisoerner, Charles	37 Mcc	M L T Tm Men+
Mysteries Of The Rosary	Gannon, Michael	63 Wlp	B T Tm
O Hail, Mary	Fux, Johann J	74 Bbl	M T Tm Satb
O Maria Mater Gratiae	Crivelli, Giovanni	Na Gsc	B T Tm Sattb+
O Mary Of All Women	Gannon, Michael	55 Wlp	B T Tm
O Quam Gloriosum	Esquivel, Juan De	Na Gsc	B T Tm Satb
O Queen Of Heaven	Brahms, Johannes	52 Bbl	B T Tm Ssaa
O Queen Of Heaven	Farrell, Melvin	61 Wlp	B T Tm
O Sanctissima	Na	Na Gsc	B T Tm Satb
Offertorium, Salve Regina	Schubert, Franz J.	Na Kal	B T Tm Satb
Oh, Senora (Blessed Lady)	Franco, Fernando	52 Pic	M T Tm
Ora Pro Nobis	Isaac, Heinrich	73 Bbl	M T Tm Sattb
Over The Hills (Uber's Gebirg)	Eccard, J.	41 Gsc	M T Tm Satb
Over The Hills Maria Went	Eccard, J	Na Gsc	B T Tm Ssatb
Plegaria A La Virgen	Franco, Fernando	52 Pic	M T Tm
Post Septuagesima & In Annuntiatione	Byrd, William	Na Kal	B T Tm Satb
Queen Of Heaven	Lotti, A	Na Gia	T Tm
Queen Of Heaven (E & Lat)	Lotti, A./Ed Klein	69 Gia	B L T Tm Satb+
Regina Coeli	Brahms, Johannes	54 Bbl	M T Tm Ssaa
Regina Coeli	Mascagni, Pietro	Na Gsc	B T Tm 12mix+
Regina Coeli K 276	Mozart, Wolfgang A	Na Kal	B T Tm Satb
Regina, Coeli	Anonymous 16th Century	Na Gia	T Tm
Rejoice, O Queen Of Heaven	Andrews, Carroll T.	70 Gia	M T Tm 2pt
Rejoice, Queen Of Heaven	Gentemann, Sr. Elaine	72 Gia	M T Tm Ssa+
Salve Regina	Cavalli, Francesco	Na Gsc	B T Tm Attb
Sancta Maria Graduale	Mozart, Wolfgang A	52 Bbl	M T Tm Satb+
Sancta Maria Mater Dei K 273	Mozart, Wolfgang A	Na Kal	B T Tm Satb
Sancta Maria, Mater Dei	Mendelssohn, F.	Na Gsc	B T Tm Satb+
Sing To Mary, Mother Most Merciful	Westendorf	64 Wlp	B T Tm
Sorrowful Mysteries	Gannon, Michael	61 Wlp	B T Tm
Stabat Mater	Caldara, Antonio	54 Bbl	B T Tm Satb
Stabat Mater	Lewkovitch, Bernhard	Na Gsc	B T Tm Full+
Stabat Mater Dolorosa	Fitzpatrick, Dennis	65 Fel	B T Tm
Star Upon The Ocean	Gannon, Michael	55 Wlp	B R T Tm
The God Whom Earth & Sea & Sky	Bach, J.S./Ed Lee	73 Gia	B R L T Tm Satb+
The God Whom Earth & Sea & Sky	Neale	61 Wlp	B T Tm
The Song Of Mary	Fischer, C A	Na Gsc	B T Tm Var
The Sorrows Of Mary (M)	Bennett, Richard R.	Na Oxf	M T Tm Satb
To A Virgin, Meek And Mild	Johnson, D.	67 Aug	M T Tm Sab
Veni, Virgo Sacrata	Reutter, Johann Georg	76 Bbl	M T Tm Satb
Virgen Lava Panales, La	Nin–Culmell, Joaquin	58 Ron	M T Tm Satb
Virgin Full Of Grace	Farrell, Melvin	55 Wlp	B T Tm
Virgin Mother	Roff, J/Bobak, J	Na Gia	T Tm

Hymns and Psalms of Offering

See also category TC.

Busy Day	Comeau, Bill	67 Van	B R C To

CATEGORIZED INDEX

Silver And Gold Have I None	Landry, Carey (Rev.)	75 Nal	B R C To
Simple Gifts	Page, Paul F.	73 Rpb	M B R L C To
You Can't Love Without Giving	Hamblen Stuart	Na Ham	M C To
Accept O Lord	Schaffer, Robert J.	67 Wlp	B F To
All I Am, I Give To You	Wise, Joe	71 Wlp	B R F To
All Our Joy	Ducote, Darryl	70 Fel	B R F To
All That I Am	Temple, Sebastian	67 Fcc	B R L F To Gia
All That We Have	Ault, Gary	69 Fel	B R F To
All These Things	Miffleton, Jack	75 Wlp	B F To
Bring To The Lord	Miffleton, Jack	68 Acp	L F To
Bring To The Lord (4-Part Arr.)	Silvia, Helen	70 Acp	L F To
Gift Of Joy	Summerlin, E., Miller, W.	69 Van	B R F To
Gifts Of Bread And Wine	Hanson, Mike	70 Fel	B R F To
God Gives Freely	Wood, Mike	76 Rpb	M B R L F To
I Lift My Soul	Buck, Daniel	67 Acp	R L F To
I Lift My Soul (4-Part Arr)	Wojcik, Richard J.	73 Acp	L F To
I Will Offer Sacrifice (Ps 27)	Cunningham, Patrick	68 Gra	B R L F To
Joy (Love Is All Around)	Belt, Thomas	70 Gia	B R L F To Var+
Listen To My Words	Haubrick & Wagner	72 Sms	M R L F To
Lord, Jesus Christ (Offertory) (Funeral)	Mitchell, Ian	67 Fel	B R F To
My Gift For You	Shaltz, Gregory	74 Sms	M R L F To
Of My Hands	Repp, Ray	66 Fel	B R F To
Offer To God Praise As Your Sacrifice	Fitzpatrick, Dennis	65 Fel	B F To
Please Accept Our Gifts	O'sheil, Judy	66 Fel	B F To
Psalm 109 O Lord God	Grace, Sister Mary	66 Fel	B F To
Simple Joys	Leyko, Patricia J.	76 Chh	B R L F To
Take My Hands	Temple, Sebastian	67 Fcc	B R L F To Gia
Take My Life	Johnson, Gary L.	74 Bfi	B L F To
Take Our Bread	Wise, Joe	67 Wlp	B R F To
Take Our Gifts	Hunkele	67 Wlp	B R F To
Teilhard's Offering	Temple, Sebastian	69 Gia	B R L F To Uguit
We Are Your Bread	Wise, Joe	67 Wlp	B R F To
We Beseech Thee	Schwartz, Stephen	71 Val	B R F To
What Have You Given	Sweeney	71 Wlp	B R F To
What Shall We Give	Hanson, Mike	70 Fel	B R F To
Yahweh, Our God	Aridas, Chris	73 Fel	B F To
All That I Am	Lewis, E.	75 Sil	L G To
Bread That's Cast Upon The Water	Akers, Doris	59 Man	M B R G To
Don't Forget To Pray	Ohler, Susan	74 Pmp	M B R L G To
Go Little Prayer, Go	Hopper, E./Dell, V.	69 Csm	M B R L G To
I Want To Do What He Commands	Brock, E C	65 Pmp	M R L G To
I'm Thankful	Oakes, Henry	75 Hhh	M G To
Lord, Make Be A Better Man Today	Allen/Pallardy	75 Bri	M R G To
Lord, Make Me Your Vessel	Lee, Danny	75 Man	M R G To Choral
Our Sacrifice Of Praise	Wyrtzen, Don	Na Zon	M G To Satb
Something To Be Thankful For	Herbert, Oscar A.	56 Man	M G To
You Can't Beat God Giving	Akers, Doris	58 Man	M B R G To
A Gift	Fabing, Bob	70 Ahc	B R L L To
Accept These Gifts, O Lord	Fitzpatrick, Dennis	65 Fel	B L To
All Good Gifts Around Us	Southbridge	Na Lor	M L To Satb
All Things Are Thine	Jordan, Alice	60 Tcp	M L To
Bless Us Mighty Father	Greif, Jean A	66 Vrn	M L L To
Create In Me	Schneider, Kent E.	75 Ccc	M B L To
Every Good & Perfect Gift (M)	Sisler, Hampson	75 Wlp	M L To 2pt
Father, Hear Us Pray	Darst, W. Glen	68 Som	M L To
Freely Will I Offer	Fitzpatrick, Dennis	65 Fel	B L To
Gifts	Isele, Bill	71 Nal	B L To
God Of The Earth	Young, P	75 Sac	M L To Satb
I Bring Gifts To You, Lord	Fitzpatrick, Dennis	65 Fel	B L To
I Will Offer A Heart	Fitzpatrick, Dennis	65 Fel	B L To
I Will Offer In His House	Fitzpatrick, Dennis	65 Fel	B L To
I Will Offer Joyful Sacrifice	Fitzpatrick, Dennis	65 Fel	B L To
I Will Offer Sacrifice	Fitzpatrick, Dennis	65 Fel	B L To
If You Bring Your Gift To The Altar	Deiss, Lucien	70 Wlp	B R L To
If You Give Of Your Bread	Hubert, Yvon	72 Fcc	R L L To
Let The Thought Of My Heart	Fitzpatrick, Dennis	65 Fel	B L To
Look At My Gifts	Lynch, Michael & Blanc, M.	73 Rav	B R L L To
Look To The Skies Above	Hughes, Miki	Na Lor	M L To Sab
Love Is A Gift	Humber, Yvon	72 Fcc	R L L To
Make Me Your Own (I Give You)	Temple, Sebastian	71 Gia	B R L L To Satb+
Make Of Us O Lord A New People	Landry, Carey (Rev.)	69 Nal	B L To
May This Sacrifice Of Ours	Fitzpatrick, Dennis	65 Fel	B L To
Moses Offered Sacrifice	Fitzpatrick, Dennis	65 Fel	B L To
O God Of Earth And Altar	Chesterton, Gilbert K.	70 Acp	L L To
O God Of Earth And Altar (4 Part Arr)	Cirou, Joseph Et Al	73 Acp	L L To
Offer Unto God	Christiansen, F. M.	Na Aug	M L To Satb
Offering	Page, Paul F.	76 Rpb	M B R L L To
Simple Gifts	Merritt, Charles	Na Abi	M L To Satb
Simple Gifts	Sylvester, Erich (Arr.	74 Nal	B R L To
Steward's Prayer, The	Schoenfeld, William C.	Na Abi	M L To Rsatb
Take Our Hands	Goeboro, Jean	74 Wgm	B L L To
Take, Lord, Receive	Foley, John, S. J.	75 Nal	B R L To
The Waiting Soul	Ives, Charles E.	54 Pic	M L To
This Is What We Bring	Radice, John	70 Acp	L L To
This Is What We Bring (4-Part Arr)	Cirou, Joseph/Silvia H	73 Acp	L L To
To The Lord I Cry	Track, G/ Burke, H C	Na Gia	L To
To You Will I Offer	Fitzpatrick, Dennis	65 Fel	B L To
To You, O Lord, I Lift My Soul	Kreutz, Robert	74 Gia	M L To Satb+
We Give An Offering To Jesus	Collard, Terry	71 Nal	B R L To
We Offer Bread And Wine	Shelley, Tim	71 Ahc	B R L L To
We Offer You Our Gifts.	Greif, Jean A	65 Vrn	M L L To
We Offer You The Prayer	Fitzpatrick, Dennis	65 Fel	B L To
What Has God Given Me?	Blunt, Neil	72 Nal	B R L To
What Shall I Render	Wetzler, Robert	Na Abi	M L To Satb
What You Gave Us	Silvia, Helen	73 Acp	L L To
With Awe And Confidence	Brandon, George	74 Gia	M L To Satb+
With Gifts We Enter Your Courts	Fitzpatrick, Dennis	65 Fel	B L To
With Honest Heart	Fitzpatrick, Dennis	65 Fel	B L To
World Is The Gift	Hubert, Yvon	72 Fcc	R L L To
Accept, O Father In Thy Love	Evers, J. Clifford	Na Wlp	B T To
As Men Of Old Their First Fruits	Sateren, Leland B.	61 Aug	M T To Satb
Ask And It Shall Be Given You	Glarum, L Stanley	Na Gsc	B T To Var
Behold O God This Lowly Bread	Farrell, M. & Van Hulse,	63 Wlp	B T To
Bring Costly Offerings	Saint-Saens, Camille	Na Gsc	B T To Satb
Earth Is The Lord's, The	Bixel, James W.	74 Flp	M T To
Gift Of Wheat From Thy Teeming Fields	Schaffer, Robert J.	63 Wlp	B T To
Give Unto The Lord	Wilson, James R.	Na Gsc	B T To Satb
Hear Our Prayer	Rubinstein	Na Lor	M T To Satb
Hence With Earthly Treasure	Bach, J. S.	Na Gsc	B T To Satb
O King Of Might & Splendor	Gregory, D.	55 Wlp	B T To
O King Of Might & Splendor	Murray/Lee, John	70 Gia	B L T To Satb
O King Of Might And Splendor	Lee, John	73 Gia	M T To Sa+
O Lord Most High, With All My Heart	Mozart, Wolfgang A	Na Gia	T To
Praises To The Giver	Lorenz	Na Lor	M T To
Simple Gifts	Martin	Na Lor	M T To
Take From Us, Lord	Berger, Jean	60 Bbl	M T To Satb
Then Did Priests Make Offering (M)	Byrd, William	Na Oxf	M T To Satb
To Thee, O Lord, Our Hearts We Raise	Hughes, Robert J.	Na Lor	M T To Sa
We Would Offer Thee This Day	Marshall	75 Sac	M T To

Patriotic Hymns

I Like The Sound Of America	Price, Flo	74 Wrd	B C Tp Unis+
Save The People	Schwartz, Stephen	71 Val	B R F Tp
Wings Over America	Wright, E/Strickling,	45 Kmp	M L F Tp
America The Beautiful	Ward/Johnson	75 Zon	M G Tp Satb
Battle Hymn Of The Republic	Howe-Steefe	70 Wrd	M G Tp Satb+
Flag To Follow, A (W/Opt Brs & Percuss	Peterson, John W.	Na Zon	M G Tp Satb
If My People (Musical)	Owens, Jimmy & Carol	74 Wrd	B R G Tp Var+
In The Home Where They Love To Pray	Benedetti, Quint	75 Mdm	M R G Tp
Is This America	Sewell Homer	71 Oak	G Tp
Let Us Pray For The Usa	Butler, Dorothy	67 Pmp	M B R L G Tp
Lord Achieve Your Purpose (Org)	Owens, J&C	74 Wrd	M G Tp Satb+
Turn Back To God, America	Harper, Redd	Na Zon	M G Tp
What Can I Do For My Country?	Hamblen Stuart	Na Ham	M G Tp
A Prayer For Us (W/Bell, Timp, Brs)	Peloquin, C Alexander	75 Gia	B L L Tp Satb+
American Meditations	Goossen, Frederic	74 Pic	M L Tp
Battle Hymn Of The Republic	Silvia, Helen	73 Acp	L L Tp
Blessed Is The Nation	Fitzpatrick, Dennis	65 Fel	B L Tp
For Spacious Skies	Peery	Na Lor	M L Tp
God Bless Our Land	Kountz, Richard	Na Gsc	B L Tp Var+
God Of Our Fathers	Nardella, Faith	73 Acp	L L Tp
God Of Our Fathers	Wojcik, Richard J.	67 Acp	R L L Tp
God Of Our Fathers (4-Part Arr)	Wojcik, Richard J.	73 Acp	L L Tp
His Are The Thousand Sparkling Rills	Held, Wilbur C	75 Aug	M L Tp Satb
I Love America (Musical)	Peterson/Wyrtzen	75 Zon	B R L Tp
If My People	Vanderslice, Ellen	75 Zon	L Tp Satb
Naught That Country Needeth	Ives, Charles E.	55 Pic	M L Tp
Protect Our Country, O Lord	Fitzpatrick, Dennis	65 Fel	B L Tp
She Was America	Lewis, E./Malool, G.	74 Sil	R L L Tp
The Four Freedoms (Musical)	Cole, Bill/Mann, Johnny	75 Wrd	B R L Tp Satb+
To The Name That Guides Our Nation	Cirou, Joseph Et Al	73 Acp	L L Tp
To The Name That Guides Our Nation	Gilligan, Michael	67 Acp	L L Tp
A National Hymn Of Victory	Niles, John Jacob	Na Gsc	B T Tp 2pt+
America The Beautiful	Cunningham, Patrick	74 Gra	M R L T Tp Satb
America The Beautiful	Jordan	75 Her	M T Tp Satb
America The Beautiful	Ward/Decou	Na Zon	T Tp Sa
America, Your Torch Burns Yet	Rhea, Raymond	48 Smc	M T Tp Satb
American's Creed, The	Young, Gordon	75 Her	M T Tp Satb
At Length There Dawns The Glorious	Cutler-Lynn	56 Smc	M T Tp Satb
Battle Hymn Of The Republic	Steffe-Wilson	Na Lor	M T Tp
Battle Hymn Of The Republic	Wilson	Na Lor	M T Tp
Early American Hymnal	Kellenbenz, Eugene (Ed)	70 Gia	B L T Tp Satb
Foundation	Clapp Donald C.	76 Abi	M T Tp 2pt+
God Bless Our Native Land	Mueller, Carl F	Na Gsc	B T Tp Sab+
God Of Our Fathers	Currie, R. (Arr)	75 Bec	M T Tp
God Of Our Fathers	Warren/Johnson	Na Zon	T Tp Satb
God Of Our Fathers	Wilson	Na Lor	M T Tp Satb
God Of Our Fathers (4-Part Arr)	Warren, George	73 Acp	L T Tp
Great God Of Nations	Curry, W Lawrence	Na Gsc	B T Tp Satb+
Land Of Our Loyalty	Rogers, Lee	Na Lor	M T Tp Satb
Let Us Now Praise Famous Men (A Cap)	Wells, Dana F.	Na Abi	M T Tp Satb
Lord Of All, You Gave Us This	David N. Johnson	Na Her	M T Tp Satb+
March Of Freedom	Myrow, Gerald	56 Smc	M T Tp Satb
My Country, Tis Of Thee	Traditional/Krogstad	75 Zon	T Tp Ssattbb
Now Praise We Great And Famous Men	Young, Gordon	75 Sac	M T Tp Satb
O Brother Man	Whittier/Englert, E.	76 Wlp	M T Tp Satb+
O God Upholding These U.S.	Farrell, Melvin	55 Wlp	B T Tp
Once To Every Man And Nation	Mueller, Carl F	Na Gsc	B T Tp Satb+
Prayer For Our Country, A	Rogers	Na Lor	M T Tp
Six Early American Anthems	Collected	76 Wlp	M T Tp Sab+
This Is The Land I Love	Hughes, Robert J.	Na Lor	M T Tp
Two Hymns For The Bicentennial	Bacon/Emerson/Williams	76 Wlp	M T Tp Satb+
War Requiem (Russian-English)	Kabalewsky	Na Kal	B T Tp Satb
Washington	Anonymous	75 Bbl	B T Tp Tb
We Thank Thee	Christie-Hoffman	Hof	M T Tp Sab

Hymns of Peace and Reconciliation

This section also includes songs on Christian life and church.

CATEGORIZED INDEX

A Child's Prayer	Klemm, G	Na Gsc	B	C	Tr	Ssa+
All Things Bright And Beautiful	Alexander/Shaw	Na Gsc	M B L	C	Tr	
All Your Gifts Of Life	Landry, Carey (Rev.)	75 Nal	B R	C	Tr	
Be Happy Today	Hamblen Suzy	Na Ham	M	C	Tr	
Bright 'n' Shiny	Coburn Bill	Na Ham	M	C	Tr	
British Children's Prayer	Wolfe, Jacques	Na Gsc	B	C	Tr	Satb
Brotherhood	Mcgrath, Roberta	74 Rpb	M B R L	C	Tr	
Brothers All	Temple, Sebastian	69 Fcc	R L	C	Tr	
Celebrate God	Landry, Carey (Rev.)	73 Nal	B R	C	Tr	
Celebrate Life	Curzio, Elaine	70 Van	B R	C	Tr	
Child's Evening Prayer (M)	Coulthard, Jean	Na Oxf	M	C	Tr	U/2pt
Children Of The Lord	Landry, Carey (Rev.)	75 Nal	B R	C	Tr	
Children's Blessing	Wasner, Franz	Na Gsc	B	C	Tr	Full
Children's Prayer	Besig, Don	73 Pro	M	C	Tr	Var
Children's Prayer	Leaf, Robert	69 Aug	M	C	Tr	Unis
Close Your Eyes	Wise, Joe	74 Nal	B R	C	Tr	
Community Song	Blue, Robert	66 Fel	B R	C	Tr	
Do You Really Love Me?	Landry, Carey (Rev.)	73 Nal	B R	C	Tr	
Evening Prayer	Sylvester, Erich (Arr.	74 Nal	B R	C	Tr	
Fill It With Sunshine	Wise, Joe	74 Nal	B R	C	Tr	
Friend Song	O'sheil, Judy	66 Fel	B	C	Tr	
Friends Are Like Flowers	Landry, Carey (Rev.)	75 Nal	B R	C	Tr	
Friends, Friends	Landry, Carey (Rev.)	75 Nal	B R	C	Tr	
Giant Love Ball Song	Landry, Carey (Rev.)	73 Nal	B R	C	Tr	
God Is Alive	Curzio, Elaine	70 Van	B R	C	Tr	
God Is Building A House	Landry, Carey (Rev.)	75 Nal	B R	C	Tr	
God Is Our Father	Landry, Carey (Rev.)	73 Nal	B R	C	Tr	
Got To Get In Touch	Landry, Carey (Rev.)	73 Nal	B R	C	Tr	
Green Growing Plants	Miffleton, Jack	75 Rpb	M B R L	C	Tr	
Handful Of Sunshine, A.	Hamblen Stuart	Na Ham	M	C	Tr	
Happy The Heart	Mcguire, Margie, Ccw	73 Nal	B R	C	Tr	
Hey God!	Curzio, Elaine	70 Van	B R	C	Tr	
His Banner Over Me Is Love	Landry, Carey (Rev.)	73 Nal	B R	C	Tr	
I Believe In The Sun	Landry, Carey (Rev.)	73 Nal	B R	C	Tr	
I Like God's Love	Landry, Carey (Rev.)	73 Nal	B R	C	Tr	
It's Easy When You Rhyme With Dove	Miffleton, Jack	73 Wlp	B R	C	Tr	
Joy Of The Lord, The	Landry, Carey (Rev.)	73 Nal	B R	C	Tr	
New Hope	Landry, Carey (Rev.)	75 Nal	B R	C	Tr	
Our God Is A God Of Love	Landry, Carey (Rev.)	75 Nal	B R	C	Tr	
Peace	Blunt, Neil	71 Wlp	B	C	Tr	
Peace Song	O'sheil, Judy	66 Fel	B	C	Tr	
Peace Time	Landry, Carey (Rev.)	73 Nal	B R	C	Tr	
Reach Out!	Landry, Carey (Rev.)	73 Nal	B R	C	Tr	
Sing A Simple Song	Landry, Carey (Rev.)	75 Nal	B R	C	Tr	
Song Of The Loving Father	Landry, Carey (Rev.)	75 Nal	B R	C	Tr	
There's A Place In God's Heart	Hamblen Suzy	Na Ham	M	C	Tr	
This Is My Commandment	Landry, Carey (Rev.)	75 Nal	B R	C	Tr	
Thy Little Ones, Dear Lord, Are We	Wetzler, Robert	70 Aug	M	C	Tr	Unis
To Be A Friend	Miffleton, Jack	71 Wlp	B R	C	Tr	
A Blessing From Aaron	Miffleton, Jack	75 Wlp	B	F	Tr	
A New Commandment	Wise, Joe	68 Wlp	B	F	Tr	
A Peace For All Mankind	Risewick, Jack M.	73 Fel	B	F	Tr	
A Prayer Song	Yantis, David	Na Yan	B	F	Tr	
A Song Of Freedom	Meltz, Ken	72 Wlp	B	F	Tr	
A Time Of Joy	Yantis, David	Na Yan	B	F	Tr	
Abba, Father (Rom 8:15–16)	Robin, Bob	71 Mel	M	F	Tr	
Alleluia (Human Hands Cannot)	Belt, Thomas	71 Gia	B R L	F	Tr	Var+
And He Is Mine	Hatfield, & Mcnees, L.	74 Man	R	F	Tr	
As Ye Sow	Johnson,B/Johnson,M.	76 Sil	R	F	Tr	
Ask, And It Shall Be Given You	Pulkingham, Betty C.	71 Fis	M L	F	Tr	
Be A New Man	Wise, Joe	71 Wlp	B	F	Tr	
Be Ye Still	Wendy Fremin	73 Chd	B R L	F	Tr	
Beatitudes	Ducote, Daryll	73 Fcc	B R L	F	Tr	
Beatitudes	Miffleton, Jack	68 Wlp	B	F	Tr	
Beatitudes	Winter, Miriam T.	71 Van	B R	F	Tr	
Beauty Is	Sweeney	71 Wlp	B	F	Tr	
Believing	Yantis, David	Na Yan	B	F	Tr	
Beloved	Hale, S.	76 Sil	R	F	Tr	
Blessed Are Those	Wise, Joe	68 Wlp	B	F	Tr	
Blessed Be These Moments	Yantis, David	76 Yan	B	F	Tr	
Blessed Quietness	Boalt/Wyrtzen	Na Zon	M	F	Tr	Satb
Blessing Of St. Francis	Temple, Sebastian	67 Fcc	B R L	F	Tr	Gia
Break Loose (W/Guitar)	Belt, Thomas	70 Gia	B R L	F	Tr	Var+
Brother, Brother Mine	Davis, Bob	73 Fcc	B R L	F	Tr	
By The Grace Of God	Welz, Joey	72 Urs	B R	F	Tr	
Care Is All It Takes	Miffleton, Jack	73 Wlp	B	F	Tr	
Celebration (Timmy's Song)	Wood, Mike	76 Rpb	M B R L	F	Tr	
Children Of Light	Blunt, Neil	71 Wlp	B	F	Tr	
Christ Is Near	Meyer, Ron	70 Fel	B R	F	Tr	
Church Is Where Men Are, The	Temple, Sebastian	67 Fcc	B R L	F	Tr	Gia
Come As A Child	Yantis, David	Na Yan	B	F	Tr	
Come Lord	Leyko, Patricia J.	76 Chh	B R L	F	Tr	
Come To Me	Johnson, Gary L.	74 Bfi	B L	F	Tr	
Come To Me	Wise, Joe	71 Wlp	B R	F	Tr	
Come To The Mountain	Meltz, Ken	75 Wlp	B	F	Tr	
Day By Day	Schwartz, Stephen	71 Val	B R	F	Tr	
Dearest Father, You Are Good	Reilly, Cyril A.	66 Fel	B	F	Tr	
Do It With Your Love	Yantis, David	Na Yan	B	F	Tr	
Do You Want To Be Free	Belt, Thomas	71 Gia	B R L	F	Tr	Var+
Don't Worry (About Food)	Winter, Miriam T.	67 Van	B R	F	Tr	
Evening Song	Traditional	74 Rpb	M B R L	F	Tr	
Everybody's Got To Grow	Miffleton, Jack	73 Wlp	B	F	Tr	
Faith, Hope And Charity	Temple, Sebastian	67 Fcc	B R L	F	Tr	Gia
Father	Brown, Sally	74 Wgm	M R L	F	Tr	
Fear Not	Germaine	66 Fel	B R	F	Tr	
Fear Not, Little Flock	Grace, Sister Mary	66 Fel	B	F	Tr	
For We Are One	O'sheil, Judy	66 Fel	B	F	Tr	
Forever	Sweeney	71 Wlp	B R	F	Tr	
Free Child	Baumer/Blunt	69 Wlp	B R	F	Tr	
Free Me	Yantis, David	Na Yan	B	F	Tr	
Friendship Hymn (I Shall Not Call)	Toolan, Sr Suzanne	71 Gia	B R L	F	Tr	Ar+
Getting High On Love	Belt, Thomas/Batastini	72 Gia	B R L	F	Tr	Var+
Gift Of Peace	Germaine	66 Fel	B	F	Tr	
Give Peace, O Lord (Ps 122)	Cunningham, Patrick	68 Gra	B R L	F	Tr	
Glory Hosanna	Gilligan, Michael (Tex	67 Acp	R L	F	Tr	
Go In Joy	Johnson, Gary L.	75 Bfi	B R	F	Tr	
Go In Peace	Yantis, David	Na Yan	B	F	Tr	
God Dwells In The Hearts	Jabusch, Willard F.	74 Rpb	M B R L	F	Tr	
God Has Made Us One In His Love	Ste. Marie, Patricia	74 Sha	B R L	F	Tr	
God Is Alive	Sweeney	71 Wlp	B R	F	Tr	
God Is My Life	Wise, Joe	67 Wlp	B	F	Tr	
God Unlimited (Smile On Me)	Belt, Thomas	70 Gia	B R L	F	Tr	Var+
Guide Us	Risewick, Jack	73 Fel	B	F	Tr	
Happy Am I	Holiday, Mickey	Na Zon	M	F	Tr	Ssatb
Happy Lord	Hunkele	67 Wlp	B R	F	Tr	
Have A Nice Day	Hatfield, S & Mcnees, L	74 Man	R	F	Tr	
He Is Your Brother	Edwards, Deanna	74 Fcc	R L	F	Tr	
He Loves You, My Friend	Wyrtzen, Don	Na Zon	M	F	Tr	Satb
He Who Abides In Me	Grace, Sister Mary	66 Fel	B	F	Tr	
He's Got The Whole World In His Hands	Martin, Gilbert M	Na Lor	M	F	Tr	Sab
He's Got The Whole World In His Hands	Silvia, Helen	73 Acp	B L	F	Tr	
He's Got The Whole World In His Hands	Traditional/Mickelson	Na Zon		F	Tr	Satb
Heart Of Love, A	Wyrtzen, Don	Na Zon	M	F	Tr	Satb
Help My Unbelief	Winter, Miriam T.	71 Van	B R	F	Tr	
Hey Joy	Miffleton, Jack	71 Wlp	B R	F	Tr	
His Love Is Endless	Jones R.	Na Zon	M	F	Tr	2–Pt
His Name Is Love	Sergisson, Carol	75 Zon	M	F	Tr	Satb
Honey In That Rock	Akers, Doris	60 Man	M	F	Tr	
How Can I Be A Friend?	Fortunate, Lou	72 Jsp	B	F	Tr	+Guit
How Good, How Delightful It Is	Fitzgerald, Michael	74 Wgm	B L	F	Tr	
How Lovely Is Your Dwelling Place	Ste. Marie, Patricia	74 Sha	B R L	F	Tr	
Hymn Of Joy (Let Us Live In Christ)	Toolan, Sr Suzanne	71 Gia	B R L	F	Tr	Ar+
I Am The Handmaid Of The Lord	Dehan, Sheila	74 Sha	B R L	F	Tr	
I Am The Vine	Miffleton, Jack	75 Wlp	B R	F	Tr	
I Call You Friends	Shaltz, Gregory	74 Sms	M B R L	F	Tr	+Des
I Know The Father Loves Me	Ault, Gary	73 Fcc	B R L	F	Tr	
I Lift Up My Eyes	Repp, Ray	66 Fel	B R	F	Tr	
I Look To God	Quinlan, Paul	67 Van	B R	F	Tr	
I Trust In You	Miffleton, Jack	71 Wlp	B R	F	Tr	
I'd Like To Teach The World To Sing	Backer/Davis/Cook/Gwy	71 Cke		F	Tr	
I'll Never Contented Be	Germaine	66 Fel	B R	F	Tr	
I'm Not Afraid	Repp, Ray	66 Fel	B R	F	Tr	
I'm Not Alone	Davis, Diane	71 Fis	M L	F	Tr	
If You Love Me, Keep My Word	Fortunate, Lou	72 Jsp	B	F	Tr	+Guit
In The Arms Of My Brothers	Aguilera, Irene	73 Fel	B	F	Tr	
In The Glow Of His Love	Corda, Mike (Lyrics)	74 Cor	M R	F	Tr	
In You Do I Find My Reward	Meltz, Ken	72 Wlp	B R	F	Tr	
It Is My Faith	Miffleton, Jack	69 Wlp	B R	F	Tr	
It's A Young World	Eneberg, Gale	Na Zon	M	F	Tr	2–Pt
Jesus In Me	Fischer, John	70 Fel	B R	F	Tr	
Joy In The Morning	Ketchum, Teri	75 Msm	M R L	F	Tr	
Joy Joy Joy	Unknown	73 Mar	R L	F	Tr	
Knock, Knock	Pulkingham, Betty C.	71 Fis	M L	F	Tr	
Kum–Bah–Yah	Martin	Na Lor	M	F	Tr	Sab
Leaning On The Everlasting Arms	Showalter/Hess	Na Zon	M	F	Tr	Ssatb
Leave It In The Hands Of The Lord	Temple, Sebastian	68 Fcc	R L	F	Tr	
Let Me Introduce You	Butler/Krogstad	Na Zon	M	F	Tr	Satb
Let Me Sow Love	Yantis, David	Na Yan	B	F	Tr	
Let There Be Peace	Winter, Miriam T.	71 Van	B R	F	Tr	
Let There Be Peace On Earth	Miller/Jackson	55 Jan		F	Tr	
Let Us Pray	Jones, Richmond	Na Zon	M	F	Tr	2–Pt
Let's Get Together	Powers, Chet	63 Irv		F	Tr	
Let's Make Peace	Temple, Sebastian	67 Fcc	B R L	F	Tr	Gia
Lift Up Your Hearts	Winter, Miriam T.	71 Van	B R	F	Tr	
Like A Father	Miffleton, Jack	75 Wlp	B R	F	Tr	
Listen And Hear	Leyko, Patricia J.	76 Chh	B R L	F	Tr	
Listen Lord	Hunkele	67 Wlp	B R	F	Tr	
Listen To The Silence	Meyer, Ron	70 Fel	B R	F	Tr	
Live In The Light (4–Part Arr)	Silvia, Helen	73 Acp	L	F	Tr	
Live With The Lord	Salisbury Jr, Wallace	73 Fel	B	F	Tr	
Living Words (Mary, Simon, Etc)	Page, Jodi	73 Gia	M B R L	F	Tr	Var+
Look Behind You	Harmon, P.	76 Sil		F	Tr	
Look For Him	Marsh, Donald T.	Na Zon	M	F	Tr	Satb
Look To The Mountains	Quinlan, Paul	67 Van	B R	F	Tr	
Look Up To The Lord	Caesar, Paul (Buddy)	71 Fel	B R	F	Tr	
Look Within	Yantis, David	Na Yan	B	F	Tr	
Lord I've Come To Your Garden	Miffleton, Jack	69 Wlp	B R	F	Tr	
Lord Is My Shepherd, The	Wyrtzen, Don	75 Zon	M	F	Tr	Satb
Lord Makes Me Happy! The	Butterworth/Krogstad	75 Zon	M	F	Tr	Ssatbb
Lord You Have Blessed Us	Farra, Mimi A.	73 Gia	M B R L	F	Tr	Var+
Lord, Have Mercy; Save My Soul	Salisbury, Wallace	73 Fel	B	F	Tr	
Lord, You See Me	Quinlan, Paul	67 Fel	B R	F	Tr	
Love	Johnson, Gary L.	74 Bfi	B L	F	Tr	
Love For Life	Eneberg/Johnson	Na Zon	M	F	Tr	Sab
Love Is Like A Circle	Wood, Mike	76 Rpb	M B R L	F	Tr	
Love Is Patient	Baker, Dave	71 Fel	B R	F	Tr	
Love Is The Way	Mckenzie, Louis A	70 Acp	L	F	Tr	
Love Is The Way (4–Part Arr)	Cirou, Joseph	73 Acp	L	F	Tr	
Love Knows No Season	Belt, Thomas/Batastini	72 Gia	B R L	F	Tr	Var+
Love That Never Fades Away	Joiner, W./Clement, D	74 Sil	R L	F	Tr	
Love Was When	Wyrtzen, Don	Na Zon	M	F	Tr	Satb
Love Your Brother	Winter, Miriam T.	71 Van	B R	F	Tr	
Loved By The Lord	Winter, Miriam T.	71 Van	B R	F	Tr	
Make Me A Channel Of Your Peace	Temple, Sebastian	67 Fcc	B R L	F	Tr	Gia
May The Lord Bless & Keep You	Meltz, Ken	72 Wlp	B R	F	Tr	
May The Roads Rise Up	Toolan, Sr Suzanne	75 Rpb	M B R L	F	Tr	
My Beloved Spoke (Sg 2:10–14)	Cadwallader, Ann	72 Gia	M B R L	F	Tr	Var+
My God Is A Rock	Silvia, Helen	73 Acp		F	Tr	
My God Is A Rock	Wojcik, Richard J.	70 Acp	L	F	Tr	

CATEGORIZED INDEX

My Hope And Trust	Glees, Robert	70 Acp	L F Tr
My Shepherd	Martin/Blake	Na Zon	M F Tr Satb
New	Martin, Bruce	Na Zon	M F Tr Sab
Not A Sparrow Falleth (Mat 10)	Farra, Mimi A.	73 Gia	M B R L F Tr Var+
Number One (Prophecy)	Montague, George T.	72 Mcc	B R L F Tr 2pt
O Lord	Tucciarone, Angel	73 Wlp	B R F Tr
O Lord Give Us Light	Mcalister	70 Wlp	B F Tr
O Man, You Have Been Told	Montague, George T.	68 Fel	B R F Tr
O My Lord	Finley, Ken	73 Fel	B F Tr
O My Lord	Schaffer, Robert J.	69 Wlp	B F Tr
Of Your Love	Yantis, David	Na Yan	B F Tr
Oh Lord, I Long To See Your Face	Shaltz, Gregory	74 Sms	M R L F Tr
On Belief	Wyrtzen, Don	Na Zon	M F Tr Sab
Peace	Farra, Mimi A.	73 Gia	M B R L F Tr Var+
Peace Give I To Thee	Houser, Vic	72 Mar	M R F Tr
Peace Hymn (Truly I Assure You)	Toolan, Sr Suzanne	71 Gia	B R L F Tr Ar+
Peace In Your World	Eneberg, Gale	Na Zon	M F Tr 2-Pt
Peace Of The Lord (Reigns On High)	Barbeau, Dennis	71 Jsp	B F Tr +Guit
Peace To All	Tucciarone, Angel	73 Wlp	B R F Tr
Peace To You	Miller, Dan	73 Fel	B F Tr
Peace We Share	Aridas, Chris	73 Fel	B F Tr
Peace, Joy, Happiness	Wise, Joe	68 Wlp	B R F Tr
Peace, My Friends	Repp, Ray	67 Fel	B R F Tr
Pilgrim Song	Winter, Miriam T.	66 Van	B R F Tr
Place Your Hope In Me	Dehan, Christopher	74 Sha	B R L F Tr
Prayer For Peace	Temple, Sebastian	67 Fcc	B R L F Tr Gia
Prayer Of St. Francis	Dumin, Frank	70 Van	B R F Tr
Prayer Of St. Francis	Temple, Sebastian	68 Fcc	R L F Tr
Prayer To Our Father	Tucciarone, Angel	73 Wlp	B R F Tr
Psalm 1 He Is Like A Tree	Grace, Sister Mary	66 Fel	B F Tr
Psalm 131 Like A Child	Liberstein, Jerry	66 Fel	B F Tr
Psalm 23 The Lord Is My Shepherd	Quinlan, Paul	66 Fel	B R F Tr
Psalm 23 The Lord Is My Shepherd (2)	Blue, Robert	66 Fel	B F Tr
Psalm 34 I Looked To God	Quinlan, Paul	66 Fel	B F Tr
Psalm 63 You Are The God	O'sheil, Judy	66 Fel	B F Tr
Psalm 84 (O How Amiable)	Pulkingham, Betty C.	74 Fis	M L F Tr
Psalm 84 O Lord Of Hosts	Quinlan, Paul	66 Fel	B F Tr
Reaching Out	Yantis, David	76 Yan	B F Tr
Really Live	Peterson, John W.	Na Zon	M F Tr 2-Pt
Receive In Your Heart	Defalco, Elinor	71 Jsp	B F Tr +Guit
Rejoice	Yantis, David	Na Yan	B F Tr
Restore My Church	Temple, Sebastian	67 Fcc	B R L F Tr Gia
Seek First His Kingdom	Johnson, Gary L.	75 Bfi	B R F Tr
Sermon On The Mount	Quinlan, Paul	66 Fel	B F Tr
Serve Each Other In Loving Kindness	Fitzpatrick, Dennis	65 Fel	B F Tr
Serve The Lord With Fear	Fitzpatrick, Dennis	65 Fel	B F Tr
Seven Times	Winter, Miriam T.	71 Van	B R F Tr
Shalom	Hunkele	67 Wlp	B R F Tr
Shalom	Silvia, Helen	73 Acp	L F Tr
Shalom	Traditional Hebrew	67 Acp	L F Tr
Sing A New Song (Gonna Love)	Belt, Thomas/Batastini	72 Gia	B R L F Tr Var+
Smile Song	Yantis, David	Na Yan	B F Tr
So Full Of Song	Winter, Miriam T.	71 Van	B R F Tr
Solid Rock, The	Peterson, John W.	Na Zon	M F Tr 2-Pt
Song Of God's Kingdom (From St. Paul)	Kramper, Jerry	69 Gia	B R L F Tr
Song Of Love, Hope & Good Cheer	Yantis, David	Na Yan	B F Tr
Song Of Loveliness	Winter, Miriam T.	68 Van	B R F Tr
Song Of Repentance	Miles, Gary	74 Fis	M L F Tr
Song Of Trust	Germaine	66 Fel	B R F Tr
St. Francis Prayer	Blunt, Neil	67 Wlp	B F Tr
Take My Hand	Edwards, Deanna	74 Fcc	R L F Tr
Take My Hand	Hayes, Twila	68 Fel	B R F Tr
The Beatitudes	Wagner, Lavern J.	74 Sms	M R L F Tr
The Beatitudes (From Come Follow)	Kramper, Jerry	69 Gia	B R L F Tr Easy
The Body Song	Pulkingham, Betty C.	71 Fis	M L F Tr
The Canticle Of Canticles	Blue, Robert	66 Fel	B F Tr
The Door You Try To Open	Yantis, David	Na Yan	B F Tr
The Earth Is Filled	Wood, Mike	76 Rpb	M B R L F Tr
The Face Of God	Benedetti/Devore	76 Mdm	M F Tr
The Fire Of Love	Temple, Sebastian	69 Gia	B R L F Tr Uguit
The Foot Washing Song (Chant)	Brown, Shirley L.	72 Gia	M B R L F Tr Var+
The Joy Song	Yantis, David	Na Yan	B F Tr
The Lord Bless You	Scholtes, Peter	68 Fel	B R F Tr
The Lord Is My Shepherd	Quinlan, Paul	67 Fel	B L F Tr
The Lord Is My Shepherd	Quinlan, Paul	65 Wlp	B R F Tr
The Love Of God Will Rise	Ault, Gary	70 Fel	B R F Tr
The Peace Of Christ Be With You	Yantis, David	Na Yan	B F Tr
The Word	Fischer, John	70 Fel	B R F Tr
The Word (In The Beginning)	Toolan, Sr Suzanne	71 Gia	B R L F Tr Ar+
There Are But Three Things That Last	Miffleton, Jack	69 Wlp	B R F Tr
There's A Wideness	Mitchell, Ian	65 Fel	B R F Tr
This Is Real	Yantis, David	Na Yan	B F Tr
Tis A Gift To Be Simple (4-Part Arr)	Silvia, Helen	73 Acp	L F Tr
Together Again(Scotty's Song)	Wood, Mike	76 Rpb	M B R L F Tr
Touch Them With Love	Welz, Joey	70 Urs	M B R F Tr
Trust And Obey	Fischer, John	70 Fel	B R F Tr
Trust In The Lord	Farra, Mimi A.	70 Fis	M L F Tr
Trust In The Lord (Prov 3)	Farra, Mimi A.	73 Gia	M B R L F Tr Var+
Unbounded Grace	Wyrtzen, Don	Na Zon	M F Tr 2-Pt
Unconditional Love	Yantis, David	Na Yan	B F Tr
Under The Shadow (Of My Wing)	Jacobs, Peter	73 Chd	B R L F Tr
Walk In Light (God Is Light)	Toolan, Sr Suzanne	71 Gia	B R L F Tr Ar+
We Are All Held In His Hand	Quinlan, Paul	65 Wlp	B R F Tr
We Come And Go	Rowe, D.	76 Sil	R F Tr
We Reach Out For Love	Wood, Mike	76 Rpb	M B R L F Tr
We Shall Overcome	Cirou, J & Silvia, H	73 Acp	L F Tr
What A Great Thing It Is	Repp, Ray	66 Fel	B R F Tr
What Could Be Better	Howard, Brian	74 Fis	M L F Tr
Where Is Love Today?	Meilstrup/Johnson	Na Zon	M F Tr Sa(Tb)
Whoever Would Be Great Among You(Guit)	Nelson, Ronald A.	71 Aug	M F Tr Sab+
Why Limit God?	Yantis, David	Na Yan	B F Tr
Wondrous Love	Demone, Richard	75 Maf	M F Tr Satb
Word Of Light	Wilkey, Terrence	73 Fel	B F Tr
Written In The Book Of Love	Kirschkel/Krogstad	Na Zon	M F Tr Satb
You Are Loved	Ault, Gary	71 Fel	B R F Tr
You Are My People	Germaine	66 Fel	B R F Tr
You Are Shepherd	Reilly, Cyril A.	66 Fel	B F Tr
You Are The Joy Of Jesus	Leyko, Patricia J.	76 Chh	B R L F Tr
You're Always At Home	Leyko, Patricia J.	76 Chh	B R L F Tr
Your Will Be Done	Aguilera, Irene	73 Fel	B F Tr
Your Will Be Done	Temple, Sebastian	67 Fcc	B R L F Tr Gia
A Family That Prays Together	Twomey/Wise/Weisman	52 Ivm	M B R L G Tr
A Friend Of Mine	Cockerham, J/Robinson, G	75 Sem	R G Tr
A Little Bit Of Sunshine	Gaither/Gaither B/G	70 Gmc	B R G Tr Satb
A Song In Your Heart	Mieir, Audrey	64 Man	B G Tr
A World Of Love	Oakes, Henry	75 Hhh	M G Tr
All I Need Is You	Cull, Robert	74 Man	M R G Tr Choral
All My Hopes	Gaither/Gaither	70 Gmc	B R G Tr Satb
Amazing Grace	Traditional/Decou	Na Zon	M G Tr Satb
Amazing Grace	Traditional/Mickelson	Na Zon	M G Tr Satb
Angels Shall Keep Thee	Kaiser, Kurt	76 Wrd	M G Tr Satb+
Ask What You Will	Akers, Doris	59 Man	M B R G Tr
Be Anxious Over Nothing	Mieir, Audrey	72 Man	B G Tr
Be Still My Heart	Bougher	Na Zon	M G Tr
Because Of Love (W/Piano)	Davis, M.J.	76 Wrd	M G Tr Satb+
Beside The Still Waters	Silva	Na Zon	M G Tr
By Faith We Can Know	Duncan, Leo L.	66 Man	M G Tr
Calm Assurance	Gaither/Gaither B/G	75 Gmc	M B R G Tr
Christ Lives Through Me	Peterson, John W.	Na Zon	M G Tr Satb
Christ Liveth In Me	Mcgranahan/Johnson	Na Zon	M G Tr Satb
Church In The Home	Edwards	Na Zon	M G Tr
Close To Thee	Vail/Mickelson	Na Zon	M G Tr Satb
Come Closer Lord	Greene C & M Renfro	71 Jhm	R L G Tr
Come Rest A Little While	Smith, John Z.	69 Sto	G Tr
Come See Me	Gaither/Gaither B/G	73 Gmc	M G Tr
Come To Me All Who Labor	Purifoy, John	75 Wrd	M G Tr Satb+
Come With Your Heartache	Smith/Harper	Na Zon	M G Tr
Contented	Gaither/Gaither B/G	73 Gmc	M B R G Tr Satb
Contentment In His Love	Dunlop/Decou	Na Zon	M G Tr Satb
Count Your Blessings	Duncan, Leo L.	65 Man	M G Tr
Created In His Image	Gaither D, Sickal	69 Gmc	M B R G Tr Satb
Dear Lord	Lee, Johnnie	59 Mmc	M G Tr Satb
Dear Lord, Be My Shepherd	Hamblen Stuart	Na Ham	M G Tr
Discovery	Wyrtzen, Don	Na Zon	M G Tr Satb
Do You Want Peace?	Matthews/Decou	75 Zon	M G Tr Satb
Down Deep In My Heart	Hope, Johnnie/Lambert, O	54 Man	M R G Tr
Everlasting Mercy	Lovelace, Linda	74 Mam	R L G Tr
Evermore (I Love The Feelin')	Girard, Chuck	74 Wrd	B R G Tr Unis+
Everything Will Be All Right	Hubbard, H./G.C. Redd	Na Sav	M G Tr
Fear Thou Not	Mieir, Audrey	68 Man	B R G Tr
Friends I Know	Hamblen Stuart	Na Ham	M G Tr
From My Heart	Childs	Na Zon	M G Tr
Gentle Shepherd	Gaither/Gaither B/G	74 Gmc	M B R G Tr Satb
Gentle Shepherd (Narration)	Gaither, William J	Na Lor	M G Tr Satb
Getting Used To The Family Of God	Gaither/Gaither B/G	74 Gmc	M R G Tr
Give God A Chance And Be Made Glad	Smith, John Z.	65 Sto	G Tr
Glorious Church, A	Hudson/Decou	Na Zon	M G Tr Satb
God Don't Care Who You Are	Ugartechea, Ruth	73 Mar	R L G Tr
God Doth Not Slumber Nor Sleep	Rasley, John M.	Na Zon	M G Tr Satb
God Has Been Good To Me	Kenhow, Beulah	73 Bul	R G Tr
God Has Blessings Of All Kind	Overstreet, Rev. L.	69 Sto	G Tr
God Is Everywhere	Day	Na Zon	M G Tr
God Is Our Saviour	Coakley J. Blevins D.	74 Jhm	R L G Tr
God Is So Good	Unknown	73 Mar	B L G Tr
God Knows All About Tomorrow	Peterson, John W.	Na Zon	M G Tr Satb
God Loves To Talk To Boys While	Gaither/Gaither B/G	75 Gmc	M B R G Tr Satb
God Loves You	Oakes, Henry	75 Hhh	M G Tr
God Put His Hand On My Shoulder	Peterson, John W.	Na Zon	M G Tr Satb
God Reveals Himself To Me	Ulrich, Lorraine	67 Man	M G Tr
God Supplies What I Need	Taylor, W./Hendrix, J.	Na Gmp	M R L G Tr
God Who Made Earth (W/Piano)	Allen, Lanny	75 Wrd	M G Tr 2pt+
God's Afterglow	Mieir, Audrey	58 Man	M B G Tr
God's Been Good To Me	Ruby, Lyndal	72 Tal	L G Tr
God's Great Love	Mieir, Audrey	58 Man	M B G Tr
God's Love For Me	Chitwood, Joe	62 Man	B G Tr
God's Love Is Sucn A Beautiful Thing	Smith, Gloria Jean	75 Man	R G Tr
God's Love Is The Love For Me	Smith, John Z.	67 Sto	G Tr
Great Joy	Merriweather, Roy	Na Sav	M G Tr
Happiness	Gaither/Gaither	67 Gmc	M B R G Tr Var
Happiness Is The Lord	Stanphill, Ira F.	Na Zon	M G Tr Satb
Have A Little Talk With The Lord	Peterson/Erb	Na Zon	M G Tr Satb
Have Faith	Oakes, Henry	75 Hhh	M G Tr
Have Faith In God	Mieir, Audrey	64 Man	B G Tr
Have Faith In God	Peterson, John W.	Na Zon	M G Tr Satb
Have Faith, Don't Cry	Hamblen Stuart	Na Ham	M G Tr
He Belongs To Me	Mieir, Audrey	62 Man	M B G Tr
He Cared For Me	Logan	Na Zon	M G Tr
He Filled My Life With Ecstasy	Gaither/Gaither	62 Gmc	B R G Tr Satb
He Knoweth	Mieir, Audrey	65 Man	B G Tr
He Knows And He Cares	Akers, Doris	58 Man	M B R G Tr
He Knows What He's Doin All The Time	Stanphill/Decou	Na Zon	M G Tr Satb
He Lifted Me (P.D.)	Elrich, Dwight(Arr.)	74 Man	M G Tr Choral
He Loves Me	Mieir, Audrey	58 Man	M B G Tr
He Lovingly Guards Every Footstep	Peterson, John W.	Na Zon	M G Tr Satb
He Will Heal	Smith-Childs	Na Zon	M G Tr
He'll Make A Way	Irwin	Na Zon	M G Tr
He'll Never Fail	Mieir, Audrey	58 Man	M B G Tr
He'll Never Leave Me	Gonzalo, Carrie	69 Man	B G Tr
He's A Light Unto My Pathway	Akers, Doris	58 Man	M B R G Tr

CATEGORIZED INDEX

He's Everywhere	Akers, Doris	54 Man	B	G Tr	
He's My Friend	Rasley	Na Lor	M	G Tr	Satb
He's Willing	Mieir, Audrey	58 Man	B	G Tr	
Healer, The	Irwin	Na Zon	M	G Tr	
Healing Love Of Jesus, The	Peterson, John W.	Na Zon	M	G Tr	Satb
Heaven Came Down	Peterson/Decou	Na Zon	M	G Tr	Satb
Heaven Is Way Out There	Hale, Leonard	75 Sem	R	G Tr	
Help Me To Light A Candle	Lee, Johnnie	73 Mmc	M	G Tr	
Help Thou My Unbelief	Hamblen Suzy	Na Ham	M	G Tr	
His Love Is Wonderful To Me	White/Johnson	Na Zon	M	G Tr	Satb
His Sovereign Love	Brusseau	Na Zon	M	G Tr	
His Will	Milhuff/Gaither	68 Gmc	M B R	G Tr	Satb
Hold My Hand, Dear Lord	Sawyers	Na Zon	M	G Tr	
Honey In The Rock	Unknown	73 Mar	B L	G Tr	
How Big Is God	Hamblen Stuart	Na Ham	M	G Tr	
How Sweet It Is	Crouch, Andrae	73 Man	B R	G Tr	
I Am In His Hands	Mieir, Audrey	65 Man	B	G Tr	
I Am Persuaded	Mieir, Audrey	58 Man	M B	G Tr	
I Ask God	Hendrix, James	Na Gmp	M L	G Tr	
I Believe In Miracles	Peterson/Anthony	Na Zon	M	G Tr	Satb
I Believe It	Gaither/Gaither	70 Gmc	B R	G Tr	Satb
I Believe What The Bible Says	Toney/Toney, B.	68 Gmc	M B R	G Tr	Satb
I Believe, Help Thou My Belief	Gaither/Gaither B/G	75 Gmc	M R	G Tr	
I Cannot Fail The Lord	Akers, Doris	58 Man	M B R	G Tr	
I Could Never Outlove The Lord	Gaither/Gaither B/G	72 Gmc	M B R	G Tr	Satb
I Depend Upon My God	Liddell	Na Zon	M	G Tr	
I Found The Truth	Culverwell, Andrew	73 Man	B R	G Tr	
I Guess God Thought Of Everything	Gaither B/G, R. Powell	74 Gmc	M B R	G Tr	Var
I Have A Father Who Can	Hendrix, James	Na Gmp	M R L	G Tr	
I Have A Friend	Pettis, Audrey E.	70 Sto		G Tr	
I Heard God Today	Mieir, Audrey	58 Man	M B	G Tr	
I Know He Cares	Mieir, Audrey	58 Man	M B	G Tr	
I Know He Holdeth Me	Parks, Joe E.	Na Zon	M	G Tr	Satb
I Long To Find Perfect Peace	Mieir, Audrey	64 Man	B	G Tr	
I Love Him Because He First Loved Me	Crouch, Andrae	68 Man	B	G Tr	
I Sought The Lord	Gaither/Gaither B/G	63 Gmc	B	G Tr	Satb
I Sure Do Love The Lord	Akers, Doris	60 Man	M B R	G Tr	
I Was Hungry, And You Fed Me.	Greif, Jean A	75 Vrn	M L	G Tr	
I Will Not Question	Mieir, Audrey	58 Man	M B	G Tr	
I'll Never Forget	Crouch, Andrae	68 Man	B R	G Tr	
I'll Trust And Never Be Afraid	Van Der Puy/Ferrin	Na Zon	M	G Tr	Satb
I'll Understand	Mieir, Audrey	58 Man	M B	G Tr	
I'm A Happy, Happy Christian	Harper, Redd	Na Zon	M	G Tr	
I'm Going About My Father's Business	Eckler, Greg & Felex, J	74 Man	R	G Tr	
I'm Not Afraid Anymore	Rogers	Na Zon	M	G Tr	
I'm Not Alone	Peterson/Decou	Na Zon	M	G Tr	Satb
I'm On My Way To Heaven Anyhow	Ramey, Troy	75 Sem	R	G Tr	
I'm Sheltered In His Arms	Hubbard/Redd/Merriw.	Na Sav	M	G Tr	
I'm So Glad I Found An Altar Of Prayer	Gaither/Gaither B/G	66 Gmc	M B R	G Tr	Satb
I'm So Happy	Gavitt/Johnson	Na Zon	M	G Tr	Sa(Tb)2
I'm Still Growing	Hendrix, James	Na Gmp	M R L	G Tr	
I've Been On The Mountain	Gaither/Gaither B/G	69 Gmc	M B R	G Tr	Satb
I've Just Come From The Place	Gaither/Gaither	64 Gmc	B R	G Tr	Satb
If My People	Swanson, Darlene J.	64 Man	M	G Tr	
If You Abide (W/Piano)	Lanier, Gary	75 Wrd	M	G Tr	Satb+
If You Really Love Him	Mieir, Audrey	64 Man	B	G Tr	
In His Presence	Gottschalk	Na Zon	M	G Tr	
In Love With The Lover Of My Soul	Kerr/Boersma	Na Zon	M	G Tr	Satb
In Pleasant Places	Peterson, John W.	Na Zon	M	G Tr	Satb
In The Image Of God	Peterson/Mickelson	Na Zon	M	G Tr	Ssattbb
In The Presence Of The Master	Gaither/Gaither B/G	64 Gmc	B	G Tr	Satb
In The Upper Room	Gaither/Gaither	62 Gmc	M B R	G Tr	Var
In The Upper Room	Gaither, William J	Na Lor	M	G Tr	Satb
Is There Any Peace Anywhere	Akers, Doris	64 Man	B	G Tr	
Is There Room In Your Heart?	Gaither/Gaither	63 Gmc	B R	G Tr	Var
It Is Glory Just To Walk With Him	Lillenas/Johnson	Na Zon	M	G Tr	Satb
It Is Well With My Soul	Bliss/Rasley	Na Zon	M	G Tr	Satb
It Matters To Him	Mieir, Audrey	59 Man	M B R	G Tr	
It's A Wonderful, Wonderful Life	Peterson, John W.	Na Zon	M	G Tr	Satb
Jesus Loves Me	Bradbury/Wyrtzen	Na Zon	M	G Tr	Satb
Jesus, My Comforter	Gonzalo, Carrie	69 Man	B	G Tr	
Joy In The Camp	Gaither/Gaither	64 Gmc	M B R	G Tr	Sab
Joy, Real Joy	Gaither/Gaither B/G	66 Gmc	M B R	G Tr	Var
Just A Closer Walk	Mieir, Audrey (Arr.)	62 Man	M B	G Tr	Choral
Just Take His Hand Again	Mieir, Audrey	64 Man	M B	G Tr	
Just Trust And Obey	Mieir, Audrey	65 Man	B	G Tr	
Leaning On The Everlasting Arms	Showalter/Drevits	Na Zon	M	G Tr	Satb
Let God Tune Your Heartstrings	Day	Na Zon	M	G Tr	
Little Hands	Oakes, Henry	75 Hhh	M	G Tr	
Look For Me	Miles/Mclellan	Na Zon	M	G Tr	Ssatb
Lord Keep Me In The Holy Band	Smith, John Z.	69 Sto		G Tr	
Lord, Don't Move That Mountain	Akers, D And Jackson, M	58 Man	M B R	G Tr	
Lord, I Pray	Hamblen Stuart	Na Ham	M	G Tr	
Love Is God's Answer	Hale, S.	76 Sil	R	G Tr	
May God Bless You And Keep You	Decou, Harold	Na Zon	M	G Tr	Satb
May God Grant Us Peace	Ohler, Susan	74 Pmp	M B R L	G Tr	
More Love To Thee	Doane/Rasley	Na Zon	M	G Tr	Satb
Mustard Seed Faith	Haag	Na Zon	M	G Tr	
My Faith Still Holds	Gaither/Gaither B/G	72 Gmc	M B R	G Tr	Var
My Father	Hamblen Stuart	Na Ham	M	G Tr	
My Friend And I	Carmichael, R./Florio, C	59 Wrd	B R	G Tr	Satb+
My God Is Standing Over Me	Tricamo/Pallardy	75 Bri	M R	G Tr	
My God Is There	Lee, Johnnie	72 Mmc	M	G Tr	
My God Shall Supply	Mieir, Audrey	64 Man	B	G Tr	
My Heart Is Filled With Jesus' Love	Akers, Doris	68 Man	M B R	G Tr	
My Religion's Not Old-Fashioned	Hamblen Stuart	Na Ham	M	G Tr	
My Song Of Assurance	Akers, Doris	64 Man	B	G Tr	
Near To The Heart Of God (A Cap)	Mcafee/Carmichael	67 Wrd	B R	G Tr	Full
No End To God's Love	Gaither/Gaither	64 Gmc	B	G Tr	Satb
No Greater Love	Gaither/Gaither	74 Gmc	M R	G Tr	
No One But The Lord	Akers, Doris	59 Man	M	G Tr	
Nothing Between	Tindley/Shepard	Na Zon	M	G Tr	Satb
O Brother Man	Wilson	Na Lor	M	G Tr	Var
O Brother Man!	Denton	Na Lor	M	G Tr	Satb
O Glorious Love	Peterson, John W.	Na Zon	M	G Tr	Satb
Oh How He Loves You And Me	Kaiser, Kurt	75 Wrd	M	G Tr	Satb+
Oh That I Knew	Mieir, Audrey	58 Man	M B R	G Tr	
Old-Time Religion, The	Traditional/Shepard	Na Zon	M	G Tr	Satb
One Tender Moment	Mieir, Audrey	67 Man	B	G Tr	
Only God	Robinson, Eddie	75 Man	M	G Tr	Choral
Only Trust Him	Stockton/Rasley	Na Zon	M	G Tr	Ssatb
Peace Like A River	Moffatt, James	Na Lor	M	G Tr	Satb
Peace Within	Brock, Linda	74 Mam	R L	G Tr	
Prayer Is A Part Of Man	Ramey, Troy	75 Sem	R	G Tr	
Promises Of Love	Mieir, Audrey	75 Man	B	G Tr	
Quiet Hour (When The Day Is Done)	Girard, Chuck	74 Wrd	B R	G Tr	Unis+
Quiet Time (W/Piano)	English, Tina	72 Wrd	M	G Tr	Satb+
Quiet Time, A	Harper, Redd	Na Zon	M	G Tr	
Real Peace	Mieir, Audrey	59 Man	M B	G Tr	
Rejoice You're Free	Huntley/Newman	Na Zon	M	G Tr	
Safe In His Precious Arms	Duncan, Leo	71 Man	M	G Tr	
See What God Can Do	Harper, Redd	Na Zon	M	G Tr	
Shelter Of Your Arms	Brock, Linda	74 Mam	R L	G Tr	
Shepherd Of Love	Peterson, John W.	Na Zon	M	G Tr	Satb
Show A Little Bit Of Love And Kindness	Peterson, John W.	Na Zon	B	G Tr	
Since The Savior Found Me	Haskins/Decou	Na Zon	M	G Tr	Satb
Since We All Believe In Jesus	Peterson, John W.	75 Zon	M	G Tr	Satb
Sing Hosanna	Brock, Linda	74 Mam	R L	G Tr	
Slow Down (In The Midst...)	Girard, Chuck	74 Wrd	B R	G Tr	Unis+
Smile, Jesus Loves You	Hatfield, Steve	74 Man	R	G Tr	
Somebody Heard My Prayer	Iwin	Na Zon	M	G Tr	
Somebody Loves You	Lee, Danny	71 Man	B	G Tr	
Someone Watches Over Me	Wright, Russell	74 Sem	R	G Tr	
Speak, Lord	Gaither/Gaither	62 Gmc	M B R	G Tr	Satb
Spread A Little Love Around	Lee, Danny	72 Man	M B R	G Tr	
Steal Away	Peterson, John W.	Na Zon	M	G Tr	Satb
Sun Of My Soul (A Cap)	Ritter, P./Carmichael	67 Wrd	B R	G Tr	Full
Sunlight	Weeden/Decou	Na Zon	M	G Tr	Satb
Sunshine In My Soul	Sweney/Mayfield	Na Zon	M	G Tr	Satb
Surely Goodness And Mercy	Peterson/Smith/Carmich	Na Zon	M	G Tr	Var
Surely Goodness And Mercy (Crusade Ed)	Peterson/Smith	Na Zon	M	G Tr	Satb
Surely I Can Believe	Spencer, Glenn	61 Man	M B R	G Tr	
Sweet Peace	Akers, Doris	67 Man	B	G Tr	
Take Time To Pray	Peterson, John W.	Na Zon	M	G Tr	Satb
Tenderly	Rusthoi	Na Zon	M	G Tr	
That's How Real God Can Be	Taylor, R.	76 Sil	R	G Tr	
The Everlasting Arms Of God	Chitwood, Joe	71 Man	B	G Tr	
The First And Great Commandment	Lee, Johnnie	73 Mmc	M	G Tr	
The Garden Of My Heart	Lillenas/Carmichael(Ar	75 Wrd	B R	G Tr	Full+
The Lord Is My Light	Akers, Doris	73 Man	B R	G Tr	
The Lord Is My Shepherd	Cram, Wilbur, Fisk	73 Mam	R L	G Tr	
The One I Love	Mieir, Audrey	65 Man	B	G Tr	
The Peace That Jesus Gives (A Cap)	Lillenas/Carmichael	30 Wrd	B R	G Tr	Full
The Perfect Will	Mieir, Audrey	59 Man	B	G Tr	
The Rock Of My Salvation	Hale, S.	75 Sil	R L	G Tr	
The Sweetest Peace Of Mind	Lee, Johnnie	73 Mmc	M	G Tr	
Their Sweetest Hour	Copeland	Na Zon	M	G Tr	
There Is No Need To Walk Alone	Smith, John Z.	69 Sto		G Tr	
There Shall Be Showers Of Blessing	Mcgranahan/Decou	Na Zon	M	G Tr	Satb
There Were Ninety And Nine	Lane	Na Lor	M	G Tr	Satb
There's Something About God	Kenhow, Beulah	73 Bul	R	G Tr	
Things I Have Left Undone, The	Day	Na Zon	M	G Tr	
Think Of God	Nelson/Ogilvy	Na Zon	M	G Tr	
Think Of The Goodness Of God	Redd, Gc/H. Hubbard	Na Sav	M	G Tr	
Through It All	Crouch, Andrae	71 Man	M B R	G Tr	
Thy Will Be Done	Lewis, E.	76 Sil		G Tr	
Tis So Sweet To Trust In Jesus	Kirkpatrick/Bolkds	Na Zon	M	G Tr	Satb
To Be At Peace With God	Hendrix, James	Na Gmp	M R L	G Tr	
Touch Me Just Now	Mieir, Audrey	67 Man	B	G Tr	
Touch Of His Hand, The	Kerr	Na Zon	M	G Tr	
Truly Trust	Mieir, Audrey	72 Man	B R	G Tr	
Trust In Him	Brock, Linda	74 Mam	R L	G Tr	
Trust In Me	Culverwell, Andrew	74 Man	B R	G Tr	
Until We Meet Again (I'll Pray For You)	Haper	Na Zon	M	G Tr	
Walk On The Water	Gaither/Gaither B/G	73 Gmc	M B R	G Tr	Satb
We Have An Anchor	Kirkpatrick/Yungton	Na Zon	M	G Tr	Satb
We'll Talk It Over	Stanphill/Johnson	Na Zon	M	G Tr	Satb
What Grace Is This	Peterson/Mickelson	Na Zon	M	G Tr	Satb
When God Seems So Near	Gaither/Gaither B/G	66 Gmc	M B R	G Tr	Satb
When I Prayed Through	Gaither/Gaither	65 Gmc	M B R	G Tr	Satb
When Love Shines In	Kirkpatrick/Decou	Na Zon	M	G Tr	Satb
When My Lord Picks Up The Phone	Hamblen Stuart	Na Ham	M	G Tr	
When You Pray	Mieir, Audrey	59 Man	M B	G Tr	
Why Should I Worry Or Fret?	Gaither/Gaither	68 Gmc	M B R	G Tr	Var
Wings Of Prayer	Peterson/Decou	Na Zon	M	G Tr	Satb
Wonderful Blessing, A	Erickson/Gotrich	Na Zon	M	G Tr	
You Ask My Why (I Keep Smilin')	Girard, Chuck	74 Wrd	B R	G Tr	Unis+
You're Something Special	Gaither/Gaither B/G	74 Gmc	M B R	G Tr	Var
A Canticle Of Care	Fabing, Bob	74 Anc	B R L	L Tr	
A Family Benediction	Ellsworth, A. Eugene	Na Abi	M	L Tr	Sab
A Holy Stillness	Ream, Albert	Na Abi	M	L Tr	Satb
A New Commandment I Give You	Fitzpatrick, Dennis	65 Fel	B	L Tr	
A Pastoral Prayer	Lipscomb, Helen	Na Gsc	B	L Tr	3mix+
A Prayer For Families	Lovelace, Austin C.	Na Abi	M	L Tr	Satb
Abba, Father	Esserwein, Philip	70 Acp	B L	L Tr	
Abba, Father	Gilsdorf, Sr. Helen	75 Rpb	M B R L	L Tr	
Abba, Father (4-Part Arrangement)	Silvia, Helen	73 Acp	B L	L Tr	
Abide With Me	Ives, Charles E.	58 Pic	M	L Tr	
Agree With God And Be At Peace	Ford, Virgil	Na Gsc	B	L Tr	Satb

CATEGORIZED INDEX

All As God Wills (A Cap)	Ford, Virgil	Na Gsc	B L Tr Satb
All I Know	Fong, Preston Bing	74 Mar	R L L Tr
All Of Seeing	Fr. M.J., Alt–Gilligan	Na Acp	B L L Tr
All Of Seeing (4–Part Arr.)	Cirou, Joseph Fr. M.J.	73 Acp	B L L Tr
All Praise To Our Redeeming Lord	Wyatt, Van	73 Pro	M L Tr Satb+
All That's Good And Great And True	Vick	75 Sac	M L Tr Sa
All The Ways Of A Man (Long)	Nystedt, Knut	71 Aug	M L Tr
All Things Bright And Beautiful	Ferguson	75 Sac	M L Tr Var
All Things Depend On You, O Lord	Fitzpatrick, Dennis	65 Fel	B L Tr
Almighty And Everlasting God	Ford, Virgil	Na Gsc	B L Tr Satb
Almighty And Everlasting God	Young, Gordon	75 Sac	M L Tr Satb
Almighty Father (From "Mass") (A Cap)	Bernstein, Leonard	Na Gsc	B L Tr Var
Amazing Grace	Sylvester, Erich (Arr)	74 Nal	B R L Tr
Amen, I Say To You	Fitzpatrick, Dennis	65 Fel	B L Tr
Announce His Salvation Day After Day	Fitzpatrick, Dennis	65 Fel	B L Tr
Another Love Song	Cull, Robert	74 Mar	R L L Tr
As A Child	Jacobs, Peter	71 Chd	B R L L Tr
As A Family	Page, Paul F.	74 Rpb	M B R L L Tr
As A Husband	Gulliksen, Kenn	75 Mar	R L L Tr
As The Deer	Huijbers & Oosterhuis	74 Nal	M B R L Tr
As We Pray	Lynch, Michael B.	76 Rav	B R L L Tr
As We Wait The Lord (Antiphon)	Deiss, Lucien	65 Wlp	B L Tr
Ask And It Shall Be Given You	Fitzpatrick, Dennis	65 Fel	B L Tr
At Thy Feet Our God And Father	Ford, Virgil	Na Gsc	B L Tr Satb
Banner Of The Lord	Unknown	73 Mar	B L L Tr
Be Consoled, I Am Near	Wise, Joe	75 Nal	B R L Tr
Be Not Afraid	Dufford, Bob, S. J.	75 Nal	B R L Tr
Be Of One Mind	Fitzpatrick, Dennis	65 Fel	B L Tr
Be Still And Know	Byles, B D	Na Lor	M L Tr
Be Strong And Do Not Fear	Fitzpatrick, Dennis	65 Fel	B L Tr
Be Ye Joyful	Sateren, Leland B.	76 Aug	L Tr Satb
Beatitudes	Page, Paul F.	75 Rpb	M B R L L Tr
Beatitudes, The	Buettell	Na Lor	M L Tr
Beatitudes, The	Jordan, Alice	Na Abi	M L Tr Satb
Beatitudes, The	Martin	Na Lor	M L Tr
Beatitudes, The	Peterson, John W.	Na Zon	L Tr Satb
Beautiful Garden Of Prayer, The	Fillmore/Wilson	Na Lor	M L Tr
Because Of Your Kindness	Fitzpatrick, Dennis	65 Fel	B L Tr
Behold How Good And How Pleasant	Fitzpatrick, Dennis	65 Fel	B L Tr
Behold, God Is My Salvation	Butler, Eugene	75 Hal	L Tr Satb
Beloved, Let Us Love (Solo)	Proulx, Richard	70 Aug	M L Tr
Beloved, Let Us Love One Another	Peterson, John W.	Na Zon	L Tr Satb
Beside The Still Waters	Shields	Na Lor	M L Tr Satb
Bless The Lord, O My Soul	Peterson, John W.	Na Zon	L Tr Satb
Bless Us, God Of Loving (Solo)	Wetzler, Robert	66 Aug	M L Tr
Blessed Are The Pure In Heart (Unacc)	Walter, Samuel	Na Abi	M L Tr Satb
Blessed Are They Who Hear	Fitzpatrick, Dennis	65 Fel	B L Tr
Blessed Hope, The	Peterson, John W.	75 Zon	L Tr Satb
Blessed Is The Man	Marshall, Jane	Na Abi	M L Tr Satb
Blessed Is The Woman Who Fears	Fitzpatrick, Dennis	65 Fel	B L Tr
Blest By The Hand Of The Lord	Page, Paul F.	75 Rpb	M B R L L Tr
Blow Ye The Trumpet Blow	Frohbieter	Na Abi	M L Tr Satb
Brother, Brother	Landry, Carey (Rev.)	68 Nal	B R L Tr
Brother, Watch The Light	Eldridge, R.	75 Sil	R L L Tr
Build Up The City Of Man	Landry, Carey (Rev.)	68 Nal	B R L Tr
Built On A Rock (W/Brass, Org)	Cassler, G. W.	62 Aug	M L Tr Satb+
Built On A Rock The Church Doth Stand	Cassler, G. W.	70 Aug	M L Tr Satb+
Built On The Rock	Mcafee, Don	Na Abi	M L Tr Satb
But I, When They Were Ill	Fitzpatrick, Dennis	65 Fel	B L Tr
By This Shall All Men Know	Fitzpatrick, Dennis	65 Fel	B L Tr
Call Upon The Name	Unknown	73 Mar	B R L L Tr
Cantata Of Peace W/Tpt	Moe, Daniel	Na Abi	M L Tr Satb
Carry Me Along	Nelson, Erick Martin	75 Mar	R L L Tr
Cast Your Care Upon The Lord	Fitzpatrick, Dennis	65 Fel	B L Tr
Celebrate	Garza, Juliana, S. P.	73 Nal	B R L Tr
Change It	Williams, Charles	74 Man	R L Tr
Charity	Gulliksen, Kenn	71 Mar	M R L L Tr
Children Of Sunlight	Gutfreund, Ed (Rev.)	74 Nal	B R L Tr
Choose Life	Landry, Carey (Rev.)	68 Nal	B R L Tr
Christ Is Our Peace (Hymn)	Boccardi, Donald	68 Jsp	B L Tr Satb
Christ Loves Us	Shelley, Tom	71 Ahc	B R L L Tr
Christian Fellowship	James	Na Lor	M L Tr
Church Within Us	Schneider, Kent E.	75 Ccc	M B R L L Tr
Church, O Lord, Is Thine, The	Johnson, Norman	75 Zon	L Tr Satb
Church's One Foundation, The	Cirou, Joseph, Wesley,	73 Acp	B L L Tr Satb
Church's One Foundation, The	Gilligan, M. (Text)	70 Acp	B L L Tr
Church's One Foundation, The	Lorenz	Na Lor	M L Tr
Citizens Of Heaven	Deiss, Lucien	65 Wlp	B R L Tr
Closer To God	Arthur, Gary	73 Mar	R L L Tr
Come By Here	Silvia, Helen	73 Acp	B L L Tr
Come Home To God	Pollock	Na Lor	M L Tr Satb
Come O Thou God Of Grace	Ford, Virgil	Na Gsc	B L Tr Var
Come Save Me, Lord	Cirou, Joseph	73 Acp	B L L Tr
Come To Me All Who Are Weary	Schutte, Dan, S. J.	71 Nal	B R L Tr
Come To Me, All You Who Labor	Fitzpatrick, Dennis	65 Fel	B L Tr
Come Ye Unto Me	Danielsen	Na Lor	M L Tr Satb
Come, Let Us Use The Grace Divine	Lynn, George	Na Abi	M L Tr Satb
Come, Lord	Page, Paul F.	76 Rpb	M B R L L Tr
Come, Peace Of God	Butler	75 Sac	M L Tr Var
Come, Ye Sinners, Poor And Needy	Mccluskey	Na Lor	M L Tr Satb
Come, Ye Sinners, Poor And Needy	Young, Gordon	75 Sac	M L Tr Satb
Come, You Have My Father's Blessing	Pelz, W.	76 Aug	L Tr Sab+
Communion With God	Cain	Na Lor	M L Tr Satb
Consider The Lilies	Goeboro, Jean	74 Wgm	B R L L Tr
Consider The Lilies	Thygerson	75 Her	M L Tr Ssa
Corinthians On Love	Mcafee, D	75 Maf	M L Tr Satb
Covenant Prayer	Ellis, Ron & Lynch, M.	76 Rav	B R L L Tr
Crown With Thy Benediction	Cassler, G. W.	61 Aug	M L Tr Solo
Day By Day	Ahnfelt/Johnson	Na Zon	L Tr Satb
Day By Day	Smith	Na Lor	M L Tr Satb
Day Of Brotherhood, The	Smith	Na Lor	M L Tr Satb
Day Of Dawning Brotherhood	Ream	75 Sac	M L Tr Satb
De Spei	Polin, Claire	Na See	M L Tr
Dear Lord And Father Of Mankind	Lovelace, Austin C.	Na Abi	M L Tr Satb
Deliver Us, O God Of Israel	Foley, John, S. J.	70 Nal	B R L Tr
Desert Highways Of The Night, The	Landry, Carey (Rev.)	68 Nal	B L Tr
Do Not Be Afraid Of Those	Fitzpatrick, Dennis	65 Fel	B L Tr
Do Not Be Anxious	Fitzpatrick, Dennis	65 Fel	B L Tr
Do You Have An Empty Heart?	Fiscus	Na Lor	M L Tr Satb
Does Jesus Care?	Wilson	Na Lor	M L Tr Satb
Dream Of Shalom	Fetler, Paul	76 Aug	L Tr Satb+
Each Man's Joy	Page, Paul F.	75 Rpb	M B R L L Tr
Earth Is The Lord's The	Mcafee, Don	75 Sac	M L Tr Satb
Enduring Faith	Brandt, Dorothea	Na Abi	M L Tr Satb
Eternal God	Copes, C. Earle	Na Abi	M L Tr Sattbb
Eternal God (W/Choral Spking)	Copes, V. Earle	Na Abi	M L Tr Satb
Eternal God, Whose Power Upholds	Agey, C. Buell	Na Abi	M L Tr Sa
Eternal Hope	Ferguson	75 Sac	M L Tr Satb
Even Then	Huijbers & Oosterhuis	74 Nal	M B R L Tr
Every Person Is Gift	Landry, Carey (Rev.)	75 Nal	B R L Tr
Except The Lord Build The House	Gilchrist, W W	Na Gsc	B L Tr Satb+
Faith (Hb 11:1–3,6)	Newbury, Kent A.	75 Wlp	M L Tr Satb
Faith Of Our Fathers	Faber, Frederick	70 Acp	B L L Tr
Faith Of Our Fathers (4–Part Arr.)	Hemy, Henri	73 Acp	B L L Tr
Faith, Hope And Love (Lyric Liturgy)	Peloquin, C Alexander	74 Gia	B L L Tr Satb+
Father In Heaven	Meltz, Ken	72 Wlp	B L Tr
Father Lead Me Day By Day	Schroeder, John	Na Abi	M L Tr Sa
Father Of Peace	Lynch, Michael B.	76 Rav	M B R L L Tr
Father, Bless Our Homes (Hymn)	Farquharson	76 Jsp	B L Tr Satb
Father, Keep Them Holy	Fitzpatrick, Dennis	65 Fel	B L Tr
Father, May They Be One	Fitzpatrick, Dennis	65 Fel	B L Tr
Father, May We Be One In Christ	Fitzpatrick, Dennis	65 Fel	B L Tr
Father, Mercy	Dufford, Bob, S. J.	72 Nal	B R L Tr
Fear Not; The Lord Will Protect	Fitzpatrick, Dennis	65 Fel	B L Tr
Feast Of Joy	Pelz, W.	76 Aug	L Tr Satb+
For By Grace	Wyrtzen, Don	Na Zon	L Tr Satb
For His Mercy Will Never End	Fitzpatrick, Dennis	65 Fel	B L Tr
For The Healing Of The Nations	Kaan/Kraehenbuehl	76 Jsp	B L Tr Unis
For The Healing Of The Nations	Kaan, Fred	68 Gal	M B L L Tr
For The People Of God	Schroth, G	69 Gia	M L Tr Usatb
For With Time Our Father Has Brought	Kerner, Debby Melle	72 Mar	R L L Tr
For You Are My God	Foley, John, S. J.	70 Nal	B R L Tr
Forming God's People	Meyer, Ron	70 Fel	B R L Tr
Free From Fear	Shaw, Jim	75 Fel	B R L L Tr
Friends	Butler, Charles F.	75 Mar	R L L Tr
Friends	Kerner, Debby Melle	74 Mar	R L L Tr
From An Indirect Love	Gutfreund, Ed (Rev.)	74 Nal	B R L Tr
Full Stature	Pyle, Francis J.	Na Abi	M L Tr Satb
Garden	Lafferty, Karen Louise	75 Mar	R L L Tr
Garden Hymn, The	Thompson	75 Sac	M L Tr Satb
Gentle Love Song, A	Wise, Joe	75 Nal	B R L Tr
Get Up And Live	Meyer, Ron	79 Fel	B R L Tr
Get Yourself Together	Eckler, Greg	74 Man	R L Tr
Gift Of Love, The	Hughes, Robert J.	Na Lor	M L Tr Var
Give Ear, O Lord	Trued, S. Clarence	67 Som	M L Tr
Give It Life	Page, Paul F.	74 Rpb	M B R L L Tr
Give Me An Answer (Psalm 4)	Hillebrand, Frank	75 Ahc	B R L L Tr
Give Peace, O Lord	Fitzpatrick, Dennis	65 Fel	B L Tr
Go In Peace	Vickers, Wendy	75 Nal	B R L Tr
Go In Peace And Love (W/Guitar)	Temple, Sebastian	71 Gia	B R L L Tr Satb+
Go Now In Peace	Wise, Joe	72 Nal	B R L Tr
Go Tell It In The City	Copes, V. Earle	Na Abi	M L Tr Satb
God Be In My Head	Bentel, Franklin	Na Abi	M L Tr Satb
God Be In My Head (A Cap)	Ellsworth, A. Eugene	Na Abi	M L Tr Satb
God Be Merciful Unto Us	Staley, F. Broadus	Na Abi	M L Tr Satb
God Has Blessed You Forever	Fitzpatrick, Dennis	65 Fel	B L Tr
God Has Ears To Listen	Lewis	75 Sac	M L Tr Unis
God Himself Is With Us	Bottenberg	Na Lor	M L Tr Satb
God Is Before Me	Blakley	Na Lor	M L Tr Satb
God Is Everywhere	Hughes, Robert J.	Na Lor	M L Tr Var
God Is Love	Dailey, Joe	75 Ahc	B R L L Tr
God Is Love	Deiss, Lucien	70 Wlp	B L Tr Var
God Is Love	Hutson, Joan	74 Rpb	M B R L L Tr
God Is Love	Kavanaugh, John, S. J.	73 Nal	B R L Tr
God Is Love	Ramseth	74 Aug	M L Tr Sa+
God Is Love	Thompson	Na Lor	M L Tr Satb
God Is Love	Ugartechea, Michael	73 Mar	B L L Tr
God Is My Strong Salvation (A Cap)	Pfautsch, Lloyd	Na Abi	M L Tr Ttbb
God Is Our Refuge	Huijbers & Oosterhuis	74 Nal	B L Tr
God Is Our Refuge And Strength	Newbury, Kent A.	75 Sac	M L Tr Satb
God Is Unique And One	Kaan, Fred/Shaw	68 Gal	B L L Tr
God Is Working His Purpose Out	Lovelace, Austin C.	Na Abi	M L Tr Satb
God Of Love, King Of Peace	Leaf	75 Sac	M L Tr Satb
God Of The Earth	Mead, Edward	Na Abi	M L Tr Satb
God Will Take Care Of You	London	Na Lor	M L Tr Satb
God's House	Loucks	Na Lor	M L Tr Var
Good Lord, Shall I Ever Be The One	Papp, Akos G.	Na Abi	M L Tr Sab
Good To Me	Hadler	Na Lor	M L Tr Unis
Gospel Trumpet, The	Cassler, G. W.	Na Abi	M L Tr Satb
Grace And Peace	Gilsdorf, Sr. Helen	76 Rpb	M B R L L Tr
Gracious Love	Parker, Jerry	59 Med	M R L Tr
Grant Us Peace	Ehret, Walter	75 Her	M L Tr Satb
Grant Us Peace	Gilligan, Michael	70 Acp	B L L Tr
Grant Us Peace (4–Part Arr)	Wojcik, Richard J.	73 Acp	B L L Tr
Grant We Beseech Thee Merciful Lord	Davis, Katherine	Na Abi	M L Tr Satb
Great King Of Peace	Roff, Joseph	64 Lit	B L Tr Malc
Grow In Love	Artman (Arr)	76 Hal	L Tr Satb
Guide Me	Huijbers & Oosterhuis	74 Nal	M B R L Tr
Guiding Light	Unknown	73 Mar	B L L Tr
Happy Are The Children Of The Lord	Dailey, Joe	75 Ahc	B R L L Tr

CATEGORIZED INDEX

Happy Are They Who Hope In The Lord	Zsigray, Joe	72 Nal	B R L Tr	
Happy In Jesus	Fong, Preston Bing	73 Mar	R L L Tr	
Happy In The Lord	Unknown	73 Mar	B L L Tr	
Happy Is The Man	Huijbers & Oosterhuis	74 Nal	M B R L Tr	
Happy Is The Man	Schutte, Dan, S. J.	73 Nal	B R L Tr	
Happy The Man	Proulx, Richard	69 Aug	M L Tr	Ss+
Happy The Man Who Delights	Fitzpatrick, Dennis	65 Fel	B L Tr	
Happy The Man Who Fears	Fitzpatrick, Dennis	65 Fel	B L Tr	
Happy, Happy	Unknown	73 Mar	B L L Tr	
Have Faith In God	Roff, Joseph	Na Abi	M L Tr	Satb
Have Mercy Upon Me, O Lord (Ps. 31)	Starer, Robert	64 Som	M L Tr	
He Is Everywhere (God Is Love)	Lohr, Al	59 Pic	M L Tr	
He Laid His Hand On Me	Hughes, Robert J.	Na Lor	M L Tr	Satb
He Lifted Me	Denton	Na Lor	M L Tr	Satb
He Shall Call On Me	Fitzpatrick, Dennis	65 Fel	B L Tr	
He That Is Down Needs Fear No Fall (E)	Harris, William H.	Na Oxf	M L Tr	Ssa
He That Would Love Life	Corina, John	Na Abi	M L Tr	Satb
He Who Abides In Me	Fitzpatrick, Dennis	65 Fel	B L Tr	
He Who Believes In Me	Fitzpatrick, Dennis	65 Fel	B L Tr	
He Who Believes In Me, From Within	Fitzpatrick, Dennis	65 Fel	B L Tr	
He Who Would Valiant Be	Marshall, Jane	Na Abi	M L Tr	Satb
Heal Your People	Landry, Carey (Rev.)	68 Nal	B R L Tr	
Hear Me	Marian, Sister	66 Fel	B L Tr	
Hear Us As We Pray	Smith, Henry C	Na Gsc	B L Tr	Satb
Hear Us, Our Father	Caldwell, M	75 Sac	M L Tr	Unis
Hear, O Lord (Ps 30) (Md)	Amner, John	Na Oxf	M L Tr	Satb
Heavenly Father Hear Us	Zsigray, Joe	75 Nal	B R L Tr	
Heed My Call For Help	Foley, John, S. J.	70 Nal	B R L Tr	
Help Us, O Lord, To See	Hubert, Yvon	72 Fcc	R L L Tr	
His Angels Will Protect You	Fitzpatrick, Dennis	65 Fel	B L Tr	
His Delight Is In The Law Of The Lord	Baumgartner, H. Leroy	Na Abi	M L Tr	Satb
His Love Is All Around	Wilson	Na Lor	M L Tr	Var
His Peace We Share	Ellis, Ron	75 Rav	M R L L Tr	
Holy, Holy, Holy	Deiss, Lucien	70 Wlp	B R L Tr	
Hope Of Our Days	Dougherty, Mary/S/A	75 Rpb	M B R L L Tr	
Hope Of The World	Copes, V. Earle	Na Abi	M L Tr	Sab
Hope Of.Life	Page, Paul F.	75 Rpb	M B R L L Tr	
Hope Thou In God	Benton Price	76 Lor	L Tr	Satb+
How Blessed Are They Who Hear God's Wd	Brun, Johann N.	70 Acp	B L L Tr	
How Blest Are They	Proulx, Richard	73 Aug	M L Tr	Uorfl
How Brightly Shines The Morning Star	Gilligan, Michael	70 Acp	B R L L Tr	
How Brightly Shines The Morning Star	Nicolai, Philip	73 Acp	B L L Tr	
How Faithful God	Huijbers & Oosterhuis	74 Nal	M B R L Tr	
How Firm A Foundation	Walter, Samuel	Na Abi	M L Tr	Sab
How Good Is The Lord	Landry, Carey (Rev.)	74 Nal	B R L Tr	
How Great The Sign Of God's Love	Cromie, Marguerite Big	74 Cfc	M L L Tr	
How Lovely Is Thy Dwelling Place	Somary, J	Na Gia	L Tr	
How Lovely Is Your Dwelling Place	Fitzpatrick, Dennis	65 Fel	B L Tr	
How Sweet Is The Voice Of My Lord	Follett (Arr)	76 Pro	M L Tr	Satb+
I Am At Peace With My Neighbor	Fitzpatrick, Dennis	65 Fel	B L Tr	
I Am My Brother's Brother	Wood, Mike	75 Fel	B R L L Tr	
I Am The Good Shepherd	Caldwell, M	75 Sac	M L Tr	Satb
I Am The Salvation Of My People	Fitzpatrick, Dennis	65 Fel	B L Tr	
I Can Know	Meilstrup, David G.	Na Zon	L Tr	Satb
I Give Myself Unto Prayer	Young, Gordon	75 Sac	M L Tr	Satb
I Have A Dream	Exner, Max	Na Abi	M L Tr	Satb
I In Them	Gilsdorf, Sr. Helen	74 Rpb	M B R L L Tr	
I Lift My Eyes To The Mt (Psalm 121)	Hillebrand, Frank	75 Ahc	B R L L Tr	
I Lift Up My Eyes To The Hills	Jennings, K	67 Aug	M L Tr	Solo
I Look Up To Thee	Durocher	Hof	M L Tr	Sa
I Love You, O Lord, My Strength	Fitzpatrick, Dennis	65 Fel	B L Tr	
I Place All My Trust	Patenaude, Andre, M. S	71 Nal	B R L Tr	
I Pray To You, O Lord	Fitzpatrick, Dennis	65 Fel	B L Tr	
I See Your Face	Culverwell, Andrew	73 Man	B R L Tr	
I Shall Be Content	Fitzpatrick, Dennis	65 Fel	B L Tr	
I Sought My God	Landry, Carey (Rev.)	71 Nal	B R L Tr	
I Sought The Lord	Davis, Katherine	Na Abi	M L Tr	Satb
I Trust In You, O God	Fitzpatrick, Dennis	65 Fel	B L Tr	
I Waited And Waited For The Lord	Fitzpatrick, Dennis	65 Fel	B L Tr	
I Want To Be Your Friend	Blunt, Neil	72 Nal	B R L Tr	
I Will Call Upon The Lord	Fitzpatrick, Dennis	65 Fel	B L Tr	
I Will Hope In God	Fitzpatrick, Dennis	65 Fel	B L Tr	
I Will Lift Up Mine Eyes	Butler	75 Sac	M L Tr	Satb
I Will Lift Up Mine Eyes	Mcafee, D	75 Maf	M L Tr	Unis+
I Will Lift Up Mine Eyes	Pfautsch, Lloyd	Na Abi	M L Tr	Satb
I Will Lift Up Mine Eyes (Ps 121)	Henderson & Stoutamire	76 Pro	M L Tr	Satb+
I Will Lift Up Mine Eyes Unto The Hill	Gardner, John	Na Oxf	M L Tr	Ssa
I Will Sing Of The Mercies Of The Lord	Powell	75 Sac	M L Tr	Satb
I'll Be There	Wise, Joe	73 Nal	B R L Tr	
I'll Never Be Lonely	Golden, James Reed	73 Mar	R L L Tr	
I've Got The Liberty	Unknown	73 Mar	B L L Tr	
If God Is For Us	Foley, John, S. J.	75 Nal	B R L Tr	
If I Created You	Culverwell, Andrew	74 Man	B R L Tr	
If I Speak With The Tongues Of Men	Leonard, Clair	43 Tcp	M L Tr	
If One Member Suffers	Fitzpatrick, Dennis	65 Fel	B L Tr	
If The Lord Wills	Ford, Virgil	Na Gsc	B L Tr	Satb
If The World Could Only Be Happy	Besig	76 Pro	M L Tr	Satb+
If We Are Humble	Fitzpatrick, Dennis	65 Fel	B L Tr	
If We Have One Another	Zsigray, Joe	71 Nal	B R L Tr	
If You Receive My Words	Nystedt, Knut	73 Aug	M L Tr	
If You Will Believe	Arthur, Gary & Angie	71 Mar	R L L Tr	
Immortal Love	Christiansen, F. M.	38 Aug	M L Tr	Satb
Immortal Love	Dietterich, Philip	Na Abi	M L Tr	Sab
In Adam We Have All Been One	Franzmann/Kraehenbuehl	76 Jsp	B L Tr	Satb
In Christ There Is No East Or West	Curry, Lawrence	Na Abi	M L Tr	Satb
In Him Who Strengthens Me	Fabing, Bob	70 Ahc	B R L L Tr	
In His Care	Sateren, Leland B.	69 Aug	M L Tr	Solo
In My Garden	Young, Gordon	75 Sac	M L Tr	Sa
In Peace & Joy	Fritschel	76 Aug	L Tr	Full
In The Lord We Will Live (4-Part Arr)	Silvia, Helen	73 Acp	B L L Tr	

In The Midst Of The Assembly	Fitzpatrick, Dennis	65 Fel	B L Tr	
In The Peace Of Christ	Deiss, Lucien	70 Wlp	B R L Tr	
In Thee O Lord Have I Put My Trust	Ferris, William	69 Gia	B L L Tr	2pt
In Thee, O Lord, Do I Put My Trust	Bender, Jan	64 Aug	M L Tr	Unis
In Your Great Mercy	Fitzpatrick, Dennis	65 Fel	B L Tr	
Instrument Of Thy Peace, An	Marshall	75 Sac	M L Tr	Satb
Isaiah 40:31	Unknown	73 Mar	B L L Tr	
It Is A Thing Most Wonderful	Coggin	75 Sac	M L Tr	Unis
It's All Right	Garza, Juliana, S. P.	73 Nal	B R L Tr	
Jeremiah 31:12	Unknown	73 Mar	B L L Tr	
Jesus Heal Us	Ellis, Ron	74 Rav	B R L L Tr	
Joy Is The Spirit Of Love	Hughes, Miki	76 Lor	L Tr	Sab+
Joy, Joy, Joy	Landry, Carey (Rev.) V	73 Nal	B R L Tr	
Joyous Celebration	Wortley, Howard S.	73 Mem	M L Tr	
Judge Eternal, Throned	Holland/Kraehenbuehl	76 Jsp	B L Tr	U+Org
Keep Alive (Psalm 128)	Hillebrand, Frank	75 Ahc	B R L L Tr	
Know That I Am God	Winberry, Mary & Malate	73 Fel	B L Tr	
Let Me Do It With Love	Vickers, Wendy	75 Nal	B R L Tr	
Let Me Lord	Page, Paul F.	76 Rpb	M B R L L Tr	
Let My Prayer Come Like Incense	Kreutz, Robert	75 Wlp	M L Tr	2pt
Let Nothing Disturb Thee	Freestone	75 Sac	M L Tr	Satb
Let The Light Of Thy Countenance	Roff, Joseph	Na Gia	L Tr	
Let The Peace Of God	Roff, Joseph	75 Wlp	M L Tr	Satb+
Let This Mind Be In You (Me)	Holman, Derek	Na Oxf	M L Tr	Satb
Let Thy Love Flow Down	Powell	75 Sac	M L Tr	Sab
Let Thy Merciful Ears, O Lord, Be Open	Davis, Katherine K.	Na Abi	M L Tr	Satb
Let Us Be Happy (Opttri) Org	Leaf, Robert	76 Aug	L Tr	Sab+
Let Us Keep Silence	Martin	75 Sac	M L Tr	Satb
Let Us Look Up And Live (Opt Tpts)	Leaf, Robert	73 Aug	M L Tr	Satb+
Lift Up Your Heads (Ps 24) (Md)	Amner, John	Na Oxf	M L Tr	Satb
Like A Deer In Winter (Ps. 41)	Quinlan, Paul	68 Nal	B R L Tr	
Like Cedars They Shall Stand	Schutte, Dan	72 Nal	B R L Tr	
Like Olive Branches	Deiss, Lucien	65 Wlp	B R L Tr	Var'
Litany Of Comfort	Pellegrini, Francis	68 Jsp	B L Tr	
Live With Us	Isele, Bill	71 Nal	B L Tr	
Lo, I Am With You Always	Peek, Richard	Na Abi	M L Tr	Satb
Long Way Home (Psalm 126)	Hillebrand, Frank	75 Ahc	B R L L Tr	
Longing For God	Deiss, Lucien	65 Wlp	B R L Tr	
Look For Me In Lowly Men	Proulx, Richard	74 Cfc	M L L Tr	
Look To The Lord	Fitzpatrick, Dennis	65 Fel	B L Tr	
Look To The Lord And Be Strengthened	Fitzpatrick, Dennis	65 Fel	B L Tr	
Look Toward Me	Foley, John, S. J.	70 Nal	B R L Tr	
Lord Be With Us	Zsigray, Joe	72 Nal	B R L Tr	
Lord In Your Tenderness	Deiss, Lucien	70 Wlp	B R L Tr	Var
Lord Is Compassionate, The	Zsigray, Joe	73 Nal	B R L Tr	
Lord Is Good, The	Butler	75 Sac	M L Tr	Satb
Lord Is My Hope, The	Schoenbachler, Tim	75 Nal	B R L Tr	
Lord Is My Light And My Salvation, The	Zsigray, Joe	73 Nal	B R L Tr	
Lord Is My Light, The	Allitsen	Na Lor	M L Tr	Satb
Lord Is My Light, The	James	Na Lor	M L Tr	Satb
Lord Is My Light, The	Pfautsch, Lloyd	75 Sac	M L Tr	Satb
Lord Is My Shepherd, The	Foley, John, S. J.	70 Nal	B R L Tr	
Lord Is My Shepherd, The	Hughes, Robert J.	Na Lor	M L Tr	Satb
Lord Is My Shepherd, The	Lovelace, Austin C.	75 Sac	M L Tr	Satb
Lord Is My Shepherd, The	Zsigray, Joe	73 Nal	B R L Tr	
Lord Is My Strength, The	Moe, Daniel	75 Sac	M L Tr	Satb
Lord Is Thy Keeper, The	Sateren, Leland B.	75 Sac	M L Tr	Satb
Lord Is With Us, The	Kirk, Theron	75 Sac	M L Tr	Satb
Lord Of All Being	Hegenbart, Alex	Na Abi	M L Tr	Satb
Lord Of All Nations	Spannaus/Kraehenbuehl	76 Jsp	B L Tr	Satb
Lord Of Glory Is My Light, The	Curphey, Geraldine	Na Abi	M L Tr	Sa-Tb
Lord Of Our Life	Ford, Virgil	Na Gsc	B L Tr	Satb
Lord Will Give Us Peace, The	Humber, Yvon	72 Fcc	B R L L Tr	
Lord You Are My Refuge	Zsigray, Joe	73 Nal	B R L Tr	
Lord, Behold Us (E)	Drayton, Paul	Na Oxf	M L Tr	Unis
Lord, Give Us Strength	Isele, Bill	71 Nal	B L Tr	
Lord, I Love Your Law	Fitzpatrick, Dennis	65 Fel	B L Tr	
Lord, Make Me An Instrument	Frank, Marcel	66 Som	M L Tr	
Lord, Make Me An Instrument	Wetzler, Robert	68 Aug	M L Tr	Satb
Lord, Speak To Me	Hampton, Calvin	75 Maf	M L Tr	Satb
Lord, Speak To Me	Rickard, Jeffrey H.	76 Sac	L Tr	Satb
Lord, Speak To Me That I May Speak	Bristol, Lee	Na Abi	M L Tr	Satb
Lord, We Are Glad For Those Who Laugh	Wetzler, Robert	72 Aug	M L Tr	Unis
Lord, Will You Come To Us	Fitzpatrick, Dennis	65 Fel	B L Tr	
Lord's My Shepherd, The	Young, Gordon	75 Sac	M L Tr	Satb
Love Divine, All Loves Excelling	Cassler, G. W.	Na Aug	M L Tr	Ttbb
Love Must Rule In Man's Heart	Williams	Na Lor	M L Tr	Satb
Love Of My Lord To Me, The	Hughes, Robert J.	Na Lor	M L Tr	Satb
Love Of The Lord	Humber, Yvon	72 Fcc	R L L Tr	
Love One Another	Catalanello, Michael	76 Str	M L Tr	
Love One Another	Detweiler, Janice	73 Mar	R L L Tr	
Love That Wilt Not Let Me Go	Peace/Lorenz	Na Lor	M L Tr	Satb
Love The Lord With All Your Heart	Fitzpatrick, Dennis	65 Fel	B L Tr	
Love, Love	Unknown	73 Mar	B L L Tr	
Love, Love, Love	Brokering	70 Aug	M L Tr	Unis
Loving Shepherd Of Thy Sheep	Cooke, Arnold	Na Oxf	M L Tr	Ssatb
Make Known Your Way	Schoenbachler, Tim	75 Nal	B R L Tr	
Master, Speak! Thy Servant Heareth	Glarum, L Stanley	Na Abi	M L Tr	Satb
May God Have Mercy Upon Us	Hoag, Charles K	Na Gsc	B L Tr	Satb+
May I Be Firm In Keeping Your Law	Fitzpatrick, Dennis	65 Fel	B L Tr	
May The Lord Bless Us With Peace	Fitzpatrick, Dennis	65 Fel	B L Tr	
May The Love Of Christ Dwell	Fitzpatrick, Dennis	65 Fel	B L Tr	
Message Of Love	Isele, Bill	71 Nal	B L Tr	
Mighty Fortress, A	Gilligan, Michael	67 Acp	B L L Tr	
Mighty Fortress, A	Luther, Martin	73 Acp	B L L Tr	
Mighty Fortress, A	Schneider, Kent E. (Arr)	69 Ccc	M B R L L Tr	
Mighty Fortress, A	Slater	75 Sac	M L Tr	Satb
Mini Motet From Micah	Beversdorf, Thomas	72 Smc	M L Tr	Satb
More Holiness Give Me	Wilson	Na Lor	M L Tr	Satb
More Like Jesus	London	Na Lor	M L Tr	Satb

More Like The Master	Hughes, Robert J.	Na Lor	M L Tr Satb
More Love To Thee	Thompson	Na Lor	M L Tr Satb
My Faith, It Is An Oaken Staff	Lynn, George	Na Abi	M L Tr Satb
My Father Is With Me	Hughes, Robert J.	Na Lor	M L Tr Satb
My God And I	Whitol/Peterson	Na Zon	L Tr Var
My Good Is To Be Near My God	Fitzpatrick, Dennis	65 Fel	B L Tr
My Heart Goes Out	Fitzpatrick, Dennis	65 Fel	B L Tr
My Heart Longs	Huijbers & Oosterhuis	74 Nal	M B L Tr
My Love For The Lord	Lohr, Al	54 Pic	M L Tr
My Peace, My Joy, My Love	Page, Paul F.	76 Rpb	M B R L L Tr
My Refuge, My Fortress	Fitzpatrick, Dennis	65 Fel	B L Tr
My Shepherd	Hamill, Paul	Na Abi	M L Tr Satb
My Shepherd I	Huijbers & Oosterhuis	74 Nal	M B L Tr
My Shepherd Ii	Huijbers & Oosterhuis	74 Nal	M B L Tr
My Shepherd Is The Lord (Psalm 23)	Hillebrand, Frank	75 Ahc	B R L L Tr
My Shepherd Will Supply My Need	Goemanne, Noel	72 Gia	M L Tr Satb+
My Son Has Gone Away	Dufford, Bob, S. J.	75 Nal	B R L Tr
My Soul Is Longing For Your Peace	Deiss, Lucien	65 Wlp	B R L Tr
My Soul Longs For You	Fitzpatrick, Dennis	65 Fel	B L Tr
My Soul Thirsts For You, O Lord	Fitzpatrick, Dennis	65 Fel	B L Tr
My Soul Wait Thou Only Upon God	Roff, Joseph	Na Abi	M L Tr Satb
My Trust Is In You, O Lord	Fitzpatrick, Dennis	65 Fel	B L Tr
Nearer To Thee	Eldridge, R.	75 Sil	R L L Tr
New Commandment, A	Burroughs	75 Maf	M L Tr Satb
No Greater Love	Smith, Lani	76 Lor	L Tr Satb+
No One Lives For Himself	Huijbers & Oosterhuis	74 Nal	M B R L Tr
None Shall Separate Us	Morgan	Na Lor	M L Tr Satb
Now Hear What God Will Give	Silvia, Helen	73 Acp	B L L Tr
O Be Joyful	Ellsworth, Eugene	Na Abi	M L Tr Satb
O Brother Man	Kirk, Theron	71 Smc	M L Tr Satb
O Fear The Lord, Ye His Saints	Wood	67 Aug	M L Tr Satb
O For A Closer Walk With God	Titcomb, Everett	Na Abi	M L Tr Sa
O For A Faith That Will Not Shrink	Lanier, Gary	Na Abi	M L Tr Satb
O God My God From The Dawn	Deiss, Lucien	65 Wlp	B L Tr
O God Of All Beauty	Roff, Joseph	Na Abi	M L Tr Satb
O God Of Love	Lovelace, Austin C.	72 Aug	M L Tr Solo
O God Of Love	Trued, S. Clarence	Na Abi	M L Tr Satb
O God Of The Quiet Spirit	Hughes, Robert J.	Na Lor	M L Tr Satb
O God Our Help	Silvia, Helen	73 Acp	B L L Tr
O God, You Are My God	Fitzpatrick, Dennis	65 Fel	B L Tr
O Holy Father	Lapo, Cecil E.	Na Abi	M L Tr Satb
O How Beautiful The Sky	Christiansen, P.	51 Aug	M L Tr Var
O Lord Give Us Your Love	Deiss, Lucien	70 Wlp	B L Tr
O Lord Hear Us Pray	Deiss, Lucien	70 Wlp	B L Tr
O Lord Of Hosts, Restore Us	Fitzpatrick, Dennis	65 Fel	B L Tr
O Lord Of Life	Burroughs	75 Sac	M L Tr Satb
O Lord Of Life (M)	Cabena, Barrie	Na Oxf	M L Tr Unis
O Lord Support Us All The Day Long	Young, Gordon	Na Abi	M L Tr Satb
O Lord, Be Kind To Me	Fitzpatrick, Dennis	65 Fel	B L Tr
O Lord, Hear My Prayer	Fitzpatrick, Dennis	65 Fel	B L Tr
O Lord, Look On The Face	Fitzpatrick, Dennis	65 Fel	B L Tr
O Lord, My Heart Is Not Proud	Fitzpatrick, Dennis	65 Fel	B L Tr
O Lord, Shield Of Our Help	Martin	Na Lor	M L Tr Satb
O Lord, Support Us	Martin	75 Sac	M L Tr Satb
O Lord, The Hope Of Israel	Lewis, John Leo	Na Gsc	B L Tr Satb+
O Love Of God	Thompson	Na Lor	M L Tr Satb
O Love, How Deep	Rogers	75 Sac	M L Tr Satb
O Love, How Deep	Smith	Na Lor	M L Tr Satb
O Love, How Deep	Young, Gordon	Na Lor	M L Tr Satb
O Men Of God, Be Strong!	Butler	75 Sac	M L Tr Satb
O Most Loving Father (Unacc)	Walter, Samuel	Na Abi	M L Tr Satb
O My God It Is You I Seek	Deiss, Lucien	65 Wlp	B R L Tr
O Perfect Love	Nystedt, Knut	72 Aug	M L Tr Solo
O Satisfy Us Early With Thy Mercy	Norden, Hugo	Na Abi	M L Tr Ttbb
O Take My Hand, Lord	Koller	Na Lor	M L Tr Satb
O Thou In Whose Presence	Ehret, Walter	75 Wrd	M L Tr Satb+
O Thou, From Whom All Goodness Flows	Lewis, John Leo	Na Gsc	B L Tr Satb+
O Trinity Of Blessed Light	Powell, Robert J.	Na Abi	M L Tr Satb
O Ye Little Flock (Md)	Amner, John	Na Oxf	M L Tr Full
Of Man's Mortalitie	Avshalomov, Jacob	52 Pic	M L Tr
Of The Kindness Of The Lord	Proulx, Richard	68 Aug	M L Tr Var
Oh Jerusalem	Tiffault	75 Pro	M L Tr Satb+
Oh, It's Good	Nix, Donna	74 Nal	B L Tr
Omnipresence	James, Allen	Na Abi	M L Tr Satb
Once Blind	Lewis, E.	75 Sil	L L Tr
One Faith	Landry, Carey (Rev.)	68 Nal	B L Tr
Only In God Is My Soul At Rest	Fitzpatrick, Dennis	65 Fel	B L Tr
Open Up Your Door	Lewis, E.	74 Sil	L L Tr
Open Your Heart	Gough, Nancy	73 Nal	B L Tr
Our Day Of Praise Is Done (E)	Harris, William H.	Na Oxf	M L Tr Satb
Our God Provides	Huijbers & Oosterhuis	74 Nal	M B R L Tr
Our Help	Huijbers & Oosterhuis	74 Nal	M B R L Tr
Pardon Me	Garza, Juliana, S. P.	73 Nal	B R L Tr
Pardon Your People	Landry, Carey (Rev.)	68 Nal	B R L Tr
Peace	Denton	Na Lor	M L Tr Satb
Peace	Kerner, Debby Melle	72 Mar	B L L Tr
Peace	Orland, Henry	Na See	M L Tr
Peace	Page, Paul F.	74 Rpb	M B R L L Tr
Peace Be To You	Garza, Juliana, S. P.	73 Nal	B R L Tr
Peace Be Unto You	Nystedt, Knut	65 Aug	M L Tr Satb
Peace Be Unto You	Walter, Samuel	Na Abi	M L Tr Satb
Peace Be Unto You	Wise, Judah L.	43 Pic	M L Tr
Peace I Give To Thee	Houser, Vic	72 Mar	R L L Tr
Peace I Give To You	Tracy, Shawn (Rev.)	72 Nal	B R L Tr
Peace I Give You	Cirou, Joseph	73 Acp	B L L Tr
Peace I Give You	Gilligan, Michael	67 Acp	B L L Tr
Peace I Leave With You	Nystedt, Knut	58 Aug	M L Tr Satb
Peace I Leave With You	Pelz, W.	63 Aug	M L Tr Satb
Peace I Leave With You	Wilhelm, Patricia	73 Pro	M L Tr Satb
Peace I Leave You	Fitzpatrick, Dennis	65 Fel	B L Tr
Peace Is Flowing Like A River	Landry, Carey (Rev.)	74 Nal	B R L Tr
Peace Like A River	Unknown	73 Mar	R L L Tr
Peace Within Thy Walls	Young, Gordon	75 Sac	M L Tr Satb
Peace (A Capella) Jn 14:27	Jergenson, Dale	76 Gia	M L L Tr Sab
Peace, Be Still	Palmer	Na Lor	M L Tr Satb
Peace, Love And Hope	Lewis, E.	74 Sil	R L L Tr
Peaceful Mind Tears Of Love	Lafferty, Karen Louise	75 Mar	R L L Tr
Peaceful Pastures	Sylvester, Erich	74 Nal	B R L Tr
Penitential Response	Smith, Roger	75 Nal	B R L Tr
People Of God	Huijbers & Oosterhuis	74 Nal	M B L Tr
People Of God	Schoenbachler, Tim	75 Nal	B R L Tr
People Of Zion	Blunt, Neil	69 Wlp	B L Tr
Peter (1-1:8)	Unknown	73 Mar	B L L Tr
Plan Of Love	Lafferty, Karen Louise	73 Mar	R L L Tr
Plowshares	Beebe	Na Wbp	L Tr
Prayer	Krider, Dale	Na Abi	M L Tr Satb
Prayer For Courage	Moody	69 Aug	M L Tr
Prayer For Peace	Dailey, Joe	75 Ahc	B R L L Tr
Prayer For Peace	Diamond, David	61 Som	M L Tr
Prayer For Peace	Fetler, Paul	69 Aug	M L Tr Satb
Prayer For Peace	Goemanne, Noel	72 Gia	M L Tr Sa(T)B+
Prayer For Peace	Lojewski/Lojeski	76 Hal	L Tr Satb
Prayer For Peace	Page, Paul F.	76 Rpb	M B R L L Tr
Prayer Of Humble Access, A	Wetherill	75 Sac	M L Tr Satb
Prayer Of St Augustine	Rickard, Jeffrey H.	76 Sac	L Tr Satb
Prayer Of St Francis	Peloquin, C Alexander	73 Gia	M L Tr Satb
Prayer Of St. Francis	Brown, Shirley L.	Na Fis	M L Tr
Prayer Of The Norwegian Child	Kountz, Richard	Na Gsc	B L Tr Var
Prayers I Make, The	Marshall	75 Sac	M L Tr Var
Promise Me Life	Patenaude, Andre, M. S	71 Nal	B R L Tr
Prosper The Work Of Our Hands	Fitzpatrick, Dennis	65 Fel	B L Tr
Protect Us, Lord, While We Are Awake	Fitzpatrick, Dennis	65 Fel	B L Tr
Psalm 119 (Happy Are They)	Anders	70 Aug	M L Tr U+Con
Psalm 128 (127)	Westendorf, Omer	65 Wlp	B L Tr
Psalm 131 (130) My Soul Longing	Deiss, Lucien	65 Wlp	B L Tr
Psalm 140 (Mixed Chor & Strgs)	Berger, Jean	63 Aug	M L Tr
Psalm 22	Theophane, Sr. M	71 Gia	M L Tr Var+
Psalm 23	Carter	75 Her	M L Tr Ssa
Psalm 23	Garlick, Antony	Na See	M L Tr
Psalm 23	Mason, Thom D	69 Gia	M L Tr 8pt+
Psalm 23	Peeters, Flor	74 Cfc	M L L Tr
Psalm 23	Toolan, Sr Suzanne	75 Rpb	M B R L L Tr
Psalm 23 (W/Org & Str. Bass)	Zimmerman	70 Aug	M L Tr Satb
Psalm 23 (22)	Westendorf, Omer	62 Wlp	B L Tr
Psalm 37	Leichtling, Alan	Na See	M L Tr
Psalm 42: Prayer For Strength And Light	Bohlen, D	Na Gia	M L Tr
Psalm 46 (God Is For Us A Refuge)	Anders	69 Aug	M L Tr Unis
Psalm 63 (62)	Westendorf/Trikass	64 Wlp	B L Tr
Psalm 83 (84)	Garza, Juliana, S. P.	73 Nal	B R L Tr
Psalm 83: How Lovely Is Your Dwelling	Peloquin, C Alexander	Na Gia	L Tr
Psalm 84 (How Lovely)	Proulx, Richard	72 Gia	M L Tr Satb
Psalm 84 (83)	Westendorf/Vermulst	64 Wlp	B L Tr
Psalm 90	Garlick, Antony	Na See	M L Tr
Psalm 91	Mcafee, Don	75 Sac	M L Tr Satb
Psalm 96 (95)	Westendorf/Parker	64 Wlp	B L Tr
Put On The Whole Armour Of God	Curry, R D	Na Gia	L Tr
Reach Out	Shelley, Tom	75 Ahc	B R L L Tr
Reconciliation	Pfautsch, Lloyd	Na Abi	M L Tr Satb
Rejoice In The Lord	Unknown	73 Mar	B L L Tr
Rejoice In The Lord Always	Moe, Daniel	Na Abi	M L Tr Satb
Rejoice, My Son	Fitzpatrick, Dennis	65 Fel	B L Tr
Remember Your Words, O Lord	Fitzpatrick, Dennis	65 Fel	B L Tr
Remembrance	Bassett, Leslie	Na Abi	M L Tr Satb
Rescue Me, My God, And Defend Me	Fitzpatrick, Dennis	65 Fel	B L Tr
Rest	Link, Wade Hampton	73 Mar	R L L Tr
Return To Joy	Hubert, Yvon	72 Fcc	R L L Tr
Rise Up, Jerusalem	Foley, John B., S. J.	70 Nal	B R L Tr
Rise Up, Jerusalem	Schoenbachler, Tim	75 Nal	B R L Tr
Rise Up, O Men Of God	Nelson, Ronald A.	Na Abi	M L Tr Satb
Rite Of Peace	Creed, Dan	73 Nal	B R L Tr
Rock Of Ages	Lynn, George	Na Abi	M L Tr Sab
Rock Of Ages	Nelson, Erick Martin	75 Mar	R L L Tr
Romans 8:38,39	Unknown	73 Mar	B L L Tr
Safe Under His Wing	St. Benedict's Farm	75 Sbf	B R L L Tr
Salem City	Gilligan, Michael	70 Acp	B L L Tr
Salem City	Silvia, Helen	73 Acp	B L L Tr
Save Me, O God	Strickler, David	46 Tcp	M L Tr
Savior, Like A Shepherd Lead Us	Rogers	75 Sac	M L Tr Satb
Searching For The Lord	Zsigray, Joe	74 Nal	B R L Tr
Secret Place Of God, The	Danielson, David G.	Na Zon	L Tr Satb
Seek And Ye Shall Find	Rettino, Ernest W.	73 Mar	B L L Tr
Seek The Lord	O'connor, Robert F.	75 Nal	B R L Tr
Set My Spirit Free	Unknown	73 Mar	R L L Tr
Shalom	Landry, Carey (Rev.)	68 Nal	B L Tr
Sheaves Of Peace (Psalm 23)	Hillebrand, Frank	75 Ahc	B R L L Tr
Shepherd Of Israel	Huijbers & Oosterhuis	74 Nal	M B L Tr
Shepherd Of Love	Peterson, John W.	76 Lor	L Tr Satb+
Shepherd Of Souls	Wilson, Roger C	Na Lor	M L Tr Sab
Show Me Thy Ways (W/Oboe, Guit)	Pelz, W.	70 Aug	M L Tr Satb
Silent Night	Schneider, Kent E.	75 Ccc	M B L L Tr
Simeon's Canticle	Schoenbachler, Tim	75 Nal	B R L Tr
Sing A Song Of Love	Zsigray, Joe	74 Nal	B R L Tr
Sing Out Hosannah	Shelley, Tom	75 Ahc	B R L L Tr
So Close To You And Me	Shaw, Jim	75 Fel	B R L L Tr
So Much	Bradford, W	74 Mar	R L L Tr
Soft Light Of Morning (Me)	Leaf, Robert	76 Gia	M L L Tr Satb+
Song For The Church	Butler, Charles F.	75 Mar	R L L Tr
Song Of Joy	Arthur, G & Angle, D	73 Mar	R L L Tr
Song Of Joy	Deiss, Lucien	65 Wlp	B R L Tr
Song Of Peace, A	Wood	75 Sac	M L Tr Satb

CATEGORIZED INDEX

Song Of The Shepherd	Orland, Henry	Na See	M L Tr	
Sons Of God, The	Bitgood, Roberta	75 Sac	M L Tr	Ttbb
Sparrow Finds A Home, The	Foley, John, S. J.	70 Nal	B R L Tr	
Sparrows	St. Benedict's Farm	75 Sbf	B R L L Tr	
Speak To One Another Of Psalms	Berger, Jean	62 Aug	M L Tr	Satb
Spread Your Love	Page, Paul F.	76 Rpb	M B R L L Tr	
Stand With Me	Isele, Bill	71 Nal	B L Tr	
Stay With Me	Sylvester, Erich	71 Nal	B R L Tr	
Stay With Your People, Lord	Zsigray, Joe	72 Nal	B R L Tr	
Stir Up Your Power	Fitzpatrick, Dennis	65 Fel	B L Tr	
Stranger, Share Our Fire	Moe, Daniel	69 Aug	M L Tr	Satb
Surely Goodness (Psalm 23:6)	Unknown	73 Mar	B L L Tr	
Sweet, Sweet Song	Butler, Charles F.	75 Mar	R L L Tr	
Swords Into Plowshares	Vernon, Knight	Na Gsc	B L Tr	Satb
Take Heart	Gilsdorf, Sr. Helen	73 Rpb	M B R L L Tr	
Talk With Us Lord	Ford, Virgil	Na Gsc	B L Tr	Satb
Teach Me To Love	Peterson, John W.	Na Zon	L Tr	Satb
Teach Me Your Law, O Lord	Fitzpatrick, Dennis	65 Fel	B L Tr	
Teach Me, Lord, To Do Your Will	Fitzpatrick, Dennis	65 Fel	B L Tr	
Temples Eternal	Christiansen, F. M.	34 Aug	M L Tr	Satb
Temples Of God	Nelson, Ronald A.	74 Aug	M L Tr	2pt+
The Angel Of The Lord Delivers	Fitzpatrick, Dennis	65 Fel	B L Tr	
The Body Of Christ	Cutrona, H	73 Mar	B L L Tr	
The Earth Is Full Of The Kindness	Fitzpatrick, Dennis	65 Fel	B L Tr	
The Eyes Of The Lord	Rettino, Ernest W.	73 Mar	B L L Tr	
The Gift Of Love	Hughes, Robert J.	Na Lor	M L Tr	Sab
The Glory Of The Lord Is Upon You	Fitzpatrick, Dennis	65 Fel	B L Tr	
The Good Man Speaks Wisdom	Fitzpatrick, Dennis	65 Fel	B L Tr	
The Greatest Of These Is Love	Moe, Daniel	58 Aug	M L Tr	Solo
The Hand Of The Lord Sustains	Fitzpatrick, Dennis	65 Fel	B L Tr	
The Joy Of The Lord	Deiss, Lucien	65 Wlp	B R L Tr	
The Joy Of The Lord	Fitzpatrick, Dennis	65 Fel	B L Tr	
The Just Man Shall Flourish	Fitzpatrick, Dennis	65 Fel	B L Tr	
The Just Man Shall Flourish (W/Inst)	Proulx, Richard	70 Aug	M L Tr	Unis
The Just Shall Grow	Fitzpatrick, Dennis	65 Fel	B L Tr	
The Lord Has Done Great Things	Fitzpatrick, Dennis	65 Fel	B L Tr	
The Lord Has Heard	Fitzpatrick, Dennis	65 Fel	B L Tr	
The Lord Is Just	Fitzpatrick, Dennis	65 Fel	B L Tr	
The Lord Is Loving And Merciful	Fitzpatrick, Dennis	65 Fel	B L Tr	
The Lord Is My Guardian	Fitzpatrick, Dennis	65 Fel	B R L Tr	
The Lord Is My Light	Fitzpatrick, Dennis	65 Fel	B L Tr	
The Lord Is My Light	St. Benedict's Farm	75 Sbf	B R L L Tr	
The Lord Is My Shepherd	Fitzpatrick, Dennis	65 Fel	B L Tr	
The Lord Is My Shepherd	Unknown	73 Mar	B L L Tr	
The Lord Is My Shepherd	Wilson, Roger C.	76 Lor	L Tr	Sab+
The Lord Is My True Shepherd	Lindusky, Eugene	65 Lit	B L Tr	
The Lord Led Forth His People	Fitzpatrick, Dennis	65 Fel	B L Tr	
The Lord My Faithful Shepherd Is	Jennings, K.	68 Aug	M L Tr	Satb
The Lord My Shepherd Is	Lovelace, Austin C.	61 Aug	M L Tr	Unis
The Lord Thy God In The Midst Of Thee	Rettino, Ernest W.	73 Mar	R L L Tr	
The Lord Will Give His Blessing	Fitzpatrick, Dennis	65 Fel	B L Tr	
The Love Of God Flows	Fitzpatrick, Dennis	65 Fel	B L Tr	
The Lovin' Man	Jory, B.	76 Sil	R L Tr	
The Mountain Of The Lord	Griffin, Jack	Na Gsc	B L Tr	Satb+
The Only Concern You Need To Have	Fitzpatrick, Dennis	65 Fel	B L Tr	
The Path Of The Just	Nystedt, Knut	69 Aug	M L Tr	Acap
The Peace That Passes Understanding	Kerner, Debby Melle	72 Mar	R L L Tr	
The People Of God	Butler, Eugene	74 Hal	L Tr	Satb
The Plan Of The Lords Stands	Fitzpatrick, Dennis	65 Fel	B L Tr	
The Prayer Of Manasseh	Berger Jean	Na Gsc	B L Tr	Satb
The Shepherd	Cutrona, H	73 Mar	R L L Tr	
The Truth Of The Lord Endureth Forever	Lekberg, Sven	Na Gsc	B L Tr	Satb
The Truth Will Make You Free	Gilsdorf, Sr. Helen	75 Rpb	M B R L L Tr	
The Wonder Of It All	Unknown	73 Mar	B L L Tr	
The Year Of Jubilee	Goemanne, Noel	75 Gia	L Tr	Sa(T)B
The Year Of Jubilee Has Come	Goemanne, Noel	74 Gia	M L L Tr	Sab
Thee Will I Love	Holz, WW	75 Sac	M L Tr	Satb
There Is No Greater Love	Peterson/Mickelson	Na Zon	L Tr	Satb
There Will Be Joy Over One Sinner	Fitzpatrick, Dennis	65 Fel	B L Tr	
There's A Love	Angle, D P	73 Mar	R L L Tr	
Therefore They Shall Come	Unknown	73 Mar	B R L L Tr	
They That Wait Upon The Lord	Berger, Jean	66 Aug	M L Tr	Satb
They That Wait Upon The Lord	Nelson, Ronald A.	Na Abi	M L Tr	Satb
This Is My Commandment	Trued	75 Sac	M L Tr	Satb
This Is My Commandment	Unknown	73 Mar	B R L L Tr	
Thou Dost Keep Him In Perfect Peace	Young, Robert H.	62 Gam	M L Tr	Satb
Thou Hidden Love Of God	Walter	76 Abi	M L Tr	Satb+
Though I Speak With The Tongues Of Men	Read, Gardner	Na Abi	M L Tr	Full
Though The Mountains May Fall	Schutte, Dan, S. J.	75 Nal	B R L Tr	
Thy Loving Kindness	Unknown	Mar	B R L L Tr	
To Bless The Earth	Lovelace, Austin C.	75 Sac	M L Tr	
To His Angels	Foley, John, S. J.	70 Nal	B R L Tr	
To Know Thou Art	Soteren, Leland B.	73 Aug	M L Tr	Solo
To The Hills I Lift Mine Eyes	Fryxell, Regina	Na Abi	M L Tr	Satb
To You Do I Raise My Eyes	Deiss, Lucien	65 Wlp	B R L Tr	
To You I Lift Up My Soul	Fitzpatrick, Dennis	65 Fel	B L Tr	
To You I Lift Up My Soul	Kavanaugh, John, S. J.	73 Nal	B R L Tr	
To You I Pray, O Lord	Fitzpatrick, Dennis	65 Fel	B L Tr	
Treasures In Heaven	Burroughs	75 Sac	M L Tr	Full
Tree Of Life	Toolan, Sr Suzanne	75 Rpb	M B R L L Tr	
Truly There Is A God	Fitzpatrick, Dennis	65 Fel	B L Tr	
Trust In God	Mark Riese	76 Lor	L Tr	Unis+
Trust In The Lord	Berger, Jean	61 Aug	M L Tr	Satb
Trust In The Lord	Brandon, George	73 Gia	M L Tr	Satb+
Trust In The Lord (Mixed Chor Acap)	Nystedt, Knut	69 Aug	M L Tr	
Turn Back, O Man	Copes, V. Earle	Na Abi	M L Tr	Sa(T)B
Turn To Me, O Man	Foley, John, S. J.	75 Nal	B R L Tr	
Twenty-Third Psalm	Acheson, Mark	47 Tcp	M L Tr	
Twenty-Third Psalm	Steinke, Greg	Na See	M L Tr	
Twenty-Third Psalm (W/Narrator)	Christiansen, P.	71 Aug	M L Tr	Satb
Under His Wings	Hughes, Robert J.	76 Lor	L Tr	Satb+
Unseen Presence, The	Fryxell, Regina	Na Abi	M L Tr	Satb
Unto Thee O Lord	Ford, Virgil	Na Gsc	B L Tr	Var
Unto Thee, O Lord	Willis	75 Sac	M L Tr	
Uphold Me In Life	Huijbers & Oosterhuis	74 Nal	B R L Tr	
Valleys Of Green	Schutte, Dan, S. J.	71 Nal	B R L Tr	
Walk In Love	Collard, Terry	71 Nal	B R L Tr	
Walk In Love	Fitzpatrick, Dennis	65 Fel	B L Tr	
Walk In Peace United	Purzycki, Krzysztof Z.	74 Mem	M L Tr	
Walkin' In The Light Of His Love	Purifoy, John	76 Wrd	B R L Tr	2pt+
Watch With Me	Wise, Joe	72 Nal	B R L Tr	
We Are His People (Icet)	Picca, Angelo Della	69 Wlp	B L Tr	
We Are The Body Of Christ	Fitzpatrick, Dennis	65 Fel	B L Tr	
We Are The People Of The Lord	Tracy, Shawn (Rev.)	72 Nal	B R L Tr	
We Find Thee, Lord In Others Need	Ambrose/Kraehenbuehl	76 Jsp	B L Tr	Satb
We Look For Light	Gilligan, Michael	67 Acp	B L L Tr	
We Look For Light	O'connell, T & Silvia	73 Acp	B L L Tr	
We Pray To You, O Lord 1	Deiss, Lucien	70 Wlp	B R L Tr	
We Would Be Building	Ayers, Jacob S.	Na Zon	L Tr	Satb
What Greater Love	Jones, S./Barosse, R.	75 Sil	R L L Tr	
Whatever You Ask For	Fitzpatrick, Dennis	65 Fel	B L Tr	
When The Terms Of Peace Are Made	Boyd, Jack	Na Gsc	B L Tr	Satb+
Whenever You Do This	O'sheil, Judy	66 Fel	B L Tr	
Where Charity And Love Abide	Deiss, Lucien	70 Wlp	B R L Tr	
Where Charity And Love Are Found	Maria Of The Cross, Sr.	73 Cfc	M L L Tr	
Where Charity And Love Prevail	Westendorf, Omer	61 Wlp	B L Tr	
Where I Am	Fitzpatrick, Dennis	65 Fel	B L Tr	
Where Love Is Living	Benoit, Paul	70 Acp	B L L Tr	
Where Love Is Living	Silvia, Helen	73 Acp	B L L Tr	
Where Two Or Three Are Gathered	Shelley, Tom	72 Ahc	B R L L Tr	
Who Shall Abide (W/Flute/Guit)	Pelz, W.	65 Aug	M L Tr	Sab+
Who Shall Separate Us From	Lynn, George	56 Smc	M L Tr	Satb
Why Art Thou Cast Down, O My Soul?	Berger, Jean	64 Aug	M L Tr	Satb
Why Art Thou Disquieted?	Mccusker, M	73 Mar	R L L Tr	
Wings Of Prayer	Smith, Lani	76 Lor	L Tr	Satb+
Wisdom Opened The Mouth Of The Dumb	Fitzpatrick, Dennis	65 Fel	B L Tr	
Wisdom Restored To Men	Fitzpatrick, Dennis	65 Fel	B L Tr	
With Song And Dance	Fritschel, J.	72 Aug	M L Tr	Satb
Woman, Has No One Condemned You	Fitzpatrick, Dennis	65 Fel	B L Tr	
Won't You Come And Stay, Lord?	Landry, Carey (Rev.)	68 Nal	B L Tr	
Wondrous Love	Christiansen, P.	58 Aug	M L Tr	Var
Wondrous Love	Pooler, Marie	62 Aug	M L Tr	Var
Yahweh Rejoices	Shelley, Tom	71 Ahc	B R L L Tr	
Yahweh, The Faithful One	Schutte, Dan, S. J.	70 Nal	B R L Tr	
You Are A Chosen Race	Fitzpatrick, Dennis	65 Fel	B L Tr	
You Are A Light For All The World	Fitzpatrick, Dennis	65 Fel	B L Tr	
You Are My Shield	Cull, Robert	73 Mar	R L L Tr	
You Are My Sons	Schutte, Dan, S. J.	70 Nal	B R L Tr	
You Are The Hope Of All	Mudd, C. P.	72 Nal	B R L Tr	
You Are The Light Of The World (4-Pt)	Silvia, Helen	73 Acp	B L L Tr	
You Have Put On Christ	Gilsdorf, Sr. Helen	75 Rpb	M B R L L Tr	
You Put Gladness Into My Heart	Fitzpatrick, Dennis	65 Fel	B L Tr	
You Save The Humble, O Lord	Fitzpatrick, Dennis	65 Fel	B L Tr	
You Will Be My People	Herbener, Marilyn	74 Rpb	M B R L L Tr	
You, O Lord, Will Keep Us	Fitzpatrick, Dennis	65 Fel	B L Tr	
You're A Friend To Me	Cull, Robert	74 Man	M L Tr	Choral
Your People Of Faith	Gutfreund, Ed (Rev.)	74 Nal	B R L Tr	

A Choral Prayer (A Cap)	Glarum, L Stanley	Na Gsc	B T Tr	Var
A Joyful Song	Leaf, Robert	69 Aug	M T Tr	Sa
A Mighty Fortress Is Our God	Bach, J. S.	Na Gsc	B T Tr	Satb+
A Mighty Fortress Is Our God	Luther, Martin	Na Gsc	B T Tr	Var
A Mighty Fortress Is Our God	Mueller, Carl F	Na Gsc	B T Tr	8mix
A Mighty Fortress Is Our God (Vv)	Luther/Westendorf, Omer	64 Wlp	B T Tr	
A Mighty Fortress Is Our God (W/Band)	Zimmermann	70 Aug	M T Tr	
A Prayer For Peace (Md)	Lord, David	Na Oxf	M T Tr	Satb
A Prayer For Today	Rosenmuller, Johann	Na Gsc	B T Tr	Ssatb+
A Prayer Of King Henry Vi (E)	Ley, Henry G.	Na Oxf	M T Tr	Satb
Abide With Me	Bish, D (Arr)	76 Bec	M T Tr	
Abide, O Dearest Jesus (Me)	Ehret, Walter	75 Gia	M L T Tr	Sab+
Abiding Joy	Byles, B D	Na Gsc	B T Tr	3mix
Aeterni Munera	Palestrina, Giovanni P	Na Kal	B T Tr	Satb
Ainsi Quon Oit Le Cerf Bruire	Goudimel, Claude	Na Gsc	B T Tr	Satb
All I Want	Work (Arr)	Na Lor	M T Tr	Satb
All Is Well	Wilson (Arr)	Na Lor	M T Tr	Satb
All My Heart	Jennings, K.	70 Aug	M T Tr	Satb
All Poor Men And Humble	Wetzler, Robert	67 Aug	M T Tr	Satb
All Shall Be Well	Wilson	Na Lor	M T Tr	Satb
All That's Good And Great And True	Thiman, Eric H.	Na Gsc	B T Tr	Satb+
Alma Dei Creatoria K 277	Mozart, Wolfgang A	Na Kal	B T Tr	Satb
Amazing Grace	Beck, John N	74 Bec	M T Tr	
Amazing Grace	Goemanne, Noel	73 Gia	M T Tr	Satbu
Amazing Grace	Smith	Na Lor	M T Tr	Satb
Amazing Grace (In 19 Rounds)	Trad/Tortolano	75 Gia	B L T Tr	2pt
Amazing Grace (New Britain Me)	Dean, T. W.	61 Gam	M T Tr	Satb
Amazing Grace Traditional	Decou, Harold	Na Zon	T Tr	Satb
An Anthem Of Faith	Mueller, Carl F	Na Gsc	B T Tr	Satb+
Ancient Prayer	Lipscomb, Helen	Na Gsc	B T Tr	Sab+
And Have Not Charity	Malotte, A H	Na Gsc	B T Tr	Ssa+
And His Mercy (Md)	Bach, J. S. (Arr)	Na Oxf	M T Tr	Ss
And The Best Is Love	Proulx, Richard	69 Aug	M T Tr	Unis
As The Bridegroom To His Chosen	Bevan/Cutts	37 Oxf	M B L T Tr	
As The Heart Panteth (From Ps 42)	Hawkins, Gordon	Na Oxf	M T Tr	Satb
Balm In Gilead	Rogers	Na Lor	M T Tr	
Be Not Afraid	Mendelssohn, F.	Na Gsc	B T Tr	Satb+
Be Not Afraid (Motet 4)	Bach, J. S.	Na Kal	B T Tr	Satb
Be Still, My Soul	Bish, D.	76 Bec	M T Tr	
Be Still, My Soul	Sibelius/Decou	Na Zon	T Tr	Satb
Be Still, My Soul, And Listen	Welch, Ray	Na Zon	T Tr	Full
Be Thou My Vision	Pooler, Marie	56 Aug	M T Tr	Var

CATEGORIZED INDEX

Beatitudes, The	Evans	Na Wbp		T Tr	
Behold, God Is My Salvation	Berger, L.	66 Aug	M	T Tr	Satb
Benediction (From Deuteronomy)	Hughes, Frank	58 Smc	M	T Tr	Satb
Benediction Avant La Repas. Bon Dieu	Le Jeune, C	Na Gsc	B	T Tr	Satb
Blessed Are The Merciful	Hiles, H	Na Gsc	B	T Tr	Satb
Blessed Are They	Conaway, G Wilkes	Na Gsc	B	T Tr	Satb+
Blessed Are They	Wetherill	75 Sac	M	T Tr	Satb
Blessed Are Those Who Believe	Newbury, Kent A.	Na Gsc	B	T Tr	Satb+
• Blessed He (From The Beatitudes)	Franck, Cesar	Na Gsc	B	T Tr	Satb+
Blessed Is Everyone That Feareth	Berger, Jean	65 Bbl	M	T Tr	Satb+
Blessed Is The Man (A Cap)	Glarum, L Stanley	Na Gsc	B	T Tr	Var
Blest Are The Pure In Heart	Huerter, C.	Na Gsc	B	T Tr	Satb+
Blest Is The Man Who Finds Wisdom	Lasso, Orlando Di	67 Fel	B	T Tr	
Bow Down Thine Ear	Frank, J L	Na Gsc	B	T Tr	Satb+
Bow Down Thine Ear	Parker, Horatio W	Na Gsc	B	T Tr	Satb+
Breathe On Me, Breath Of God	Price	Na Lor	M	T Tr	Satb
Build A Little Fence Of Trust	Berger, L.	73 Aug	M	T Tr	Satb
Build Thee More Stately Mansions	Andrews, Mark	Na Gsc	B	T Tr	Var
Built On A Rock	Christiansen, F. M.	53 Aug	M	T Tr	Satb
Built On A Rock	Johnston	Na Lor	M	T Tr	Satb
Built On A Rock	Lindeman-Brandon	65 Aug	M	T Tr	Sab
Built On A Rock	Lindeman/Rasley	Na Zon		T Tr	Satb
Built On A Rock The Church Doth Stand	Kuntz, Jeff	73 Pro	M	T Tr	Satb+
Built On A Rock The Church Doth Stand	Nystedt, Knut	62 Aug	M	T Tr	Satb
But I Have Trusted In Thy Mercy	Liszt, Franz	Na Gsc	B	T Tr	3mix
But The Lord Is Mindful Of His Own	Mendelssohn, F.	Na Gsc	B	T Tr	Var+
Cantata #104 Thou Guide (E & Germ)	Bach, J. S.	Na Kal	B	T Tr	Satb
Cantata #80 A Stronghold Sure (E&Germ)	Bach, J. S.	Na Kal	B	T Tr	Satb
Canticle Of Love, A	Thompson	Na Lor	M	T Tr	Satb
Cantiones Sacrea: In Te Domine	Schutz, Heinrich	Na Kal	B	T Tr	Satb
Cast Thy Burden Upon The Lord	Mendelssohn, F.	74 Gra	B R L	T Tr	Satb
Cast Thy Burden Upon The Lord	Mendelssohn, F.	Na Gsc	B	T Tr	Satb+
Celebration	Beck, John Ness	Na Gsc	B	T Tr	Full+
Chandos Anthem 2 (In The Lord I Put)	Handel, G. F.	Na Kal	B	T Tr	Satb
Channels Only	Gibbs/Peterson	Na Zon		T Tr	Satb
Children Of The Heavenly Father	Myrvik	46 Aug	M	T Tr	Satb
Children Of The Heavenly Father	Pooler, Marie	59 Aug	M	T Tr	U+Ds
Children Of The Heavenly Father	Traditional/Johnson	Na Zon		T Tr	Full
Church's One Foundation, The	Wesley/Rasley	Na Zon		T Tr	Satb
Close To Thee	Wilson, Roger C	Na Lor	M	T Tr	Satb
Come And Abide	Bach, J. S.	Na Lor	M	T Tr	
Come Holy Light (From J. Maccabeus)	Handel, G./Wiley (Arr)	75 Pro	M R	T Tr	Var+
Come To Me	Beethoven, L	Na Gsc	B	T Tr	Satb+
Come To The Savior, Make No Delay	Lynn, George (Arr)	56 Smc	M	T Tr	Satb
Come Unto Me	Coenen, W	Na Gsc	B	T Tr	Satb+
Come Unto Me	Liszt, Franz	Na Lor	M	T Tr	Satb
Come Unto Me	Schubert, Franz J.	Na Lor	M	T Tr	Satb
Come, Holy Light, Guide Divine	Handel, G. F. (Wiley)	73 Pro	M	T Tr	Ssa
Comfort Sweet (Cantata)	Bach, J. S.	75 Lps	B R	T Tr	Satb
Custodi Me, Domine	Lasso, Orlando Di	Na Gsc	B	T Tr	Satb
Depth Of Mercy	Johnson, Gary L.	74 Bfi	B L	T Tr	
Der Herr Ist Mein Hirte (Psalm 23)	Homilius, Gottfried	75 Bbl	M	T Tr	Satb
Do Justice (Cantata)	Bach, J. S.	75 Lps	B R	T Tr	Satb
Domine, Non Est Exaltum Cor Meum	Schutz, Heinrich	Na Kal	B	T Tr	Satb
Dona Nobis Pacem	Haydn, Joseph	Na Gsc	B	T Tr	Satb+
Dona Nobis Pacem	Haydn, Joseph	73 Pro	M	T Tr	Satb
Dona Nobis Pacem	Williams, Vaughan R.	Na Oxf	B	T Tr	Satb
Earth Abideth, The	Krenek, Ernst	61 Ron	M	T Tr	Ssa
Ease My Mind, Lord	Beck, J.	76 Bec	M	T Tr	
Eili, Eili	Na	Na Gsc	B	T Tr	Full
Elect Of God	Lorenz, E J	Na Gsc	B	T Tr	Satb+
En Priere	Faure, Gabriel	75 Bbl	M	T Tr	Satb+
Evening Hymn	Purcell, Henry (Arr)	Na Oxf	M	T Tr	Var
Evening Hymn (E)	Handel, G. F.	Na Oxf	M	T Tr	Satb
Ever-Loving Father	Brahms, Johannes	Na Gsc	B	T Tr	Satb+
Every Perfect Gift	Beck, J.	76 Bec	M	T Tr	
Exaudi Deus (Hear Me O Lord)	Grandi, Alessandro	Na Gsc	B	T Tr	Sattb+
Exsurge, Domine (Ps 44)	Byrd, William	Na Oxf	M	T Tr	Sattb
Faith	Malotte, A H	Na Gsc	B	T Tr	Var+
Faith Of Our Fathers	Hemy/Decou	Na Zon		T Tr	Ssatb
Faithful Shepherd, Guide Me	Stickles, William	Na Gsc	B	T Tr	Satb+
Fare Ye Well	Moore, Undine Smith	Na Wbp		T Tr	
Father Almighty	Franck, Cesar	Na Lor	M	T Tr	
Father, O Hear Me	Handel, G. F.	63 Aug	M	T Tr	Satb
Fear Not I Am With Thee	Foster, Will	Na Gsc	B	T Tr	Satb+
Fear Not, O Israel	Spicker, M	Na Gsc	B	T Tr	Full+
Fight The Good Fight	Martin	Na Lor	M	T Tr	
Flocks In Pastures Green Abiding (M)	Bach, J. S.	Na Oxf	M	T Tr	Satb
For All These Mercies We Will Sing	Handel, G. F.	Na Gsc	B	T Tr	Satb+
Fragrant The Prayer	Lekberg, Sven	73 Bbl	M	T Tr	Satb
From Heaven The Lord Looks Down	Nestor, Leo	70 Wlp	M	T Tr	
From Out Their Temples (Cantata)	Bach, J. S.	75 Lps	B R	T Tr	Satb
Garden Hymn (A Cap)	Van Iderstine, A. P.	Na Abi	M	T Tr	Satb
Gentle Hands	Wagner, Lavern J.	72 Sms	M R L	T Tr	
Give Ear O Lord, Unto My Pray'r	Handel, G. F.	Na Gsc	B	T Tr	Sab+
Give Ear To My Words	Newbury, Kent A.	Na Gsc	B	T Tr	Satb
Give Us Faith For Today	Wills, Arthur	Na Gsc	B	T Tr	Ssaa+
Give Us The Wings Of Faith (M)	Bullock, Ernest	Na Oxf	M	T Tr	Satb
Glorious Things Of Thee Are Spoken	Haydn/Decou	Na Zon		T Tr	Satb
Glroious Things Of Thee Are Spoken	Ayers, Jacob S.	75 Zon		T Tr	Satb
Go Thy Way (From Three Sacred Pieces)	Krenek, Ernst	73 Ron	M	T Tr	Satb
Go, Prayer Of Mine	Dexter	Na Lor	M	T Tr	Satb
God Be In My Head (E)	Rutter, John	Na Oxf	M	T Tr	Satb
God Be In Ny Head	Chapman, E T	Na Gsc	B	T Tr	Satb
God Bless The Little Things W/Organ Pi	Byles, B D	Na Gsc	B	T Tr	Var+
God Eternal Is My Refuge	Peninger, David	Na Gsc	B	T Tr	Satb+
God Has A Reason	Bell	Na Lor	M	T Tr	Satb
God Is Living, God Is Here! (Me)	Bach, J.S. (Arr Davies)	Na Oxf	M	T Tr	Satb
God Is Love	George	66 Aug	M	T Tr	Sa
God Is Love	Shelley, H R	Na Gsc	B	T Tr	Satb+

God Is My Guide	Schubert, Franz J.	Na Gsc	B	T Tr	Satb+
God Is My Strong Salvation (M)	Pfautsch, Lloyd	75 Abi	M	T Tr	Satb
God Is Our Eternal Refuge	Parks, Joe E.	Na Zon		T Tr	Satb
God Is Our Refuge	Macfarlane, W C	Na Gsc	B	T Tr	Satb+
God Is Our Strength And Song	Peninger, David	Na Gsc	B	T Tr	Satb+
God Is Wisdom God Is Love (From Ruth)	Gaul, A R	Na Gsc	B	T Tr	Satb+
God Of Love (Choral)	Fitzpatrick, Dennis	65 Fel	B	T Tr	
God Of Love My Shepherd Is, The	Thompson	Na Lor	M	T Tr	Satb
God Of Mercy	Bach, J.S. Arr Ehret	74 Aug	M	T Tr	Sab
God Of Our Life	Purday/Johnson	Na Zon		T Tr	Full
God Of The Pastures, Hear (Hymn)	Clare, T/Kraehenbuehl, D	76 Jsp	B	T Tr	Satb
God Which Has Prepared (Me)	Mudd	Na Oxf	M	T Tr	Satb
God, Give Me Understanding	Bell	Na Lor	M	T Tr	Satb
God, Give Us Christian Homes	Mckinney	Na Lor	M	T Tr	Satb
God, In Thee I Seek My Salvation	Haydn, Michael	Na Gsc	B	T Tr	Satb+
God's Blessing Sends Us Forth	Westendorf, Omer	64 Wlp	B	T Tr	
God's People (Collection/Church)	Kaiser/Brown	74 Wrd	B R	T Tr	Var+
Gracious God, Reveal Thy Will Unto Me	Lully-Ehret (Arr.)	Na Her	M	T Tr	Satb+
Grant Unto Me	Saint-Saens, Camille	Na Gsc	B	T Tr	Satb
Grant Unto Me (3rd Mov't)	Brahms, Johannes	Na Gsc	B	T Tr	Saatbb
Grant Us Thy Peace	Young, Gordon	75 Sac	M	T Tr	Satb
Grant, We Beseech Thee	Harker, F F	Na Gsc	B	T Tr	Satb+
Great Peace Have They	Macroberts	Na Lor	M	T Tr	Satb
Greatest Of These Is Love, The	Lorenz	Na Lor	M	T Tr	Satb
Guide Me, O Thou Great Jehovah	Hughes, Robert J.	Na Lor	M	T Tr	Satb
Guide Me, O Thou Great Jehovah	Smith	Na Lor	M	T Tr	Satb
Hand In Hand With God	Moore	Na Lor	M	T Tr	Satb
Hand In Hand With God	Rasley	Na Lor	M	T Tr	Satb
Hark, Hark, My Soul!	Shelley, H R	Na Gsc	B	T Tr	2chor
Haven Of Rest, The	Landon	Na Lor	M	T Tr	Satb
He Hideth My Soul	Landon	Na Lor	M	T Tr	Satb
He Leadeth Me	Lynn, George	56 Smc	M	T Tr	Satb
He Pled My Case	Daniels, T.	70 Sil	M	L T Tr	
He Shall Feed His Flock	Wilson	Na Lor	M	T Tr	Satb
He That Is Down Need Fear No Fall (Me)	Williams, Vaughan R.	Na Oxf	M	T Tr	Unis
He Walks With God	Hughes, Robert J.	Na Lor	M	T Tr	Satb
He Who Will Trust In God	Fitzpatrick, Dennis	65 Fel	B	T Tr	
He Will Surely Give Thee Peace (Md)	Pergolesi-Ehret	Na Gia	M	L T Tr	Satb+
He, Watching Over Israel	Mendelssohn, F.	Na Gsc	B	T Tr	Var+
Hear Me When I Call	Hall, King	Na Gsc	B	T Tr	Satb+
Hear Me, O Lord, The Great Support	Purcell, Henry	Na Gsc	B	T Tr	Satb+
Hear My Cry	Milligan, H	Na Gsc	B	T Tr	Satb+
Hear My Prayer	Greene, Maurice	74 Bbl	M	T Tr	Satb+
Hear My Prayer	James, Will	Na Gsc	B	T Tr	Var
Hear My Prayer	Mendelssohn, F.	Na Kal	B	T Tr	Satb
Hear My Prayer, O Lord	Newbury, Kent A.	Na Gsc	B	T Tr	Satb
Hear My Prayer, O My God	Jeppesen, Knud	75 Bbl	M	T Tr	Satb
Hear The Lambs	Sanford	Na Lor	M	T Tr	Satb
Hear Us, O Saviour	Hamblen, B.	Na Gsc	B	T Tr	Satb+
Heart Of God, The	Mcafee, Don	Na Lor	M	T Tr	Satb
Help Us, Jesus Christ, God's Son	Schutz/Heinrich	75 Sac	M	T Tr	Satb
Help Us, O God	Hayes-Douglas (Arr)	76 Pro	M	T Tr	Var+
Hence All Fears And Sadness	Bach, J. S.	Na Gsc	B	T Tr	Satb
Here Is Heavenly Joy (E)	Handel, G. F.	Na Oxf	M	T Tr	Sabu
His Eye Is On The Sparrow	Gabriel/Wilson	Na Lor	M	T Tr	Satb
Hold Thou My Hand	Briggs/Wilson	Na Lor	M	T Tr	Satb
Holy City, The	Adams/Decou	Na Zon		T Tr	Satb
Holy Father Hear My Cry	Chaffin, L G	Na Gsc	B	T Tr	Sab+
Holy Radiant Light	Gretchaninoff, A	Na Gsc	B	T Tr	Full
How Firm A Foundation	Na	Na Gsc	B	T Tr	Var+
How Firm A Foundation	Smith, Lani	Na Lor	M	T Tr	Satb
How Firm A Foundation	Thompson	Na Lor	M	T Tr	Var
How Firm A Foundation	Traditional/Decou	Na Zon		T Tr	Satb
How Firm A Foundation	Traditional/Peterson	75 Zon		T Tr	Ssatb
How Goodly Are Thy Tents	Pasquet, Jean	Na Gsc	B	T Tr	Satb+
How Lovely Is Thy Dwelling Place	Brahms/Tillinghast	Na Wbp		T Tr	
How Precious Is Thy Loving Kindness	Adler, Samuel	Na Oxf	M	T Tr	S-Satb
Hymn Of Peace, A	Jones	75 Her	M	T Tr	Ssa
Hymn To The Soul	Jenkins, Cyril	Na Gsc	B	T Tr	6mix
I Am Blessed By God's Love	Freeman	Na Lor	M	T Tr	Satb
I Am Content (Cantata)	Bach, J. S.	75 Lps	B R	T Tr	Satb
I Am Not Alone Today	Shea	Na Lor	M	T Tr	Sb
I Am The Good Shepherd	Wood	69 Aug	M	T Tr	Unis
I Am Trusting Thee, Lord Jesus	Smith, Lani	Na Lor	M	T Tr	Satb
I Ask For No More (Cantata)	Bach, J. S.	75 Lps	B R	T Tr	Satb
I Call With My Own Heart	Powell	Na Wbp		T Tr	
I Called Upon The Lord	Avery, S R	Na Gsc	B	T Tr	Satb
I Charge You, O Ye Daughters	Billings, William	74 Bbl	M	T Tr	Satb
I Found Him In My Heart	Adams	Na Lor	M	T Tr	Satb
I Have Been To The Mountaintop	Southbridge	Na Lor	M	T Tr	Satb
I Have Quieted My Soul	Thompson	Na Lor	M	T Tr	Satb
I Look To Thee In Every Need	Hughes, Robert J.	Na Lor	M	T Tr	Satb
I Love Thee	Traditional/Wyrtzen	Na Zon		T Tr	Satb
I Need Thee Every Hour	Heyward	Na Lor	M	T Tr	Satb
I Sat Down Under His Shadow (M)	Bairstow, E. C.	Na Oxf	M	T Tr	Satb
I Talked To God Last Night	Guion, David W.	Na Gsc	B	T Tr	Satb+
I Waited For The Lord (Ps 40)	Schutz, Heinrich	61 Smc	M	T Tr	Satb
I Will Bow And Be Simple	Na	Na Gsc	B	T Tr	Ssa+
I Will Give Peace	Ford	75 Pro	M	T Tr	Var+
I Will Lift Up Mine Eyes	Mueller, Carl F	Na Gsc	B	T Tr	Satb+
I Will Lift Up Mine Eyes	Pool, Kenneth	Na Zon		T Tr	Satb
I Will Lift Up Mine Eyes	Rogers, J H	Na Gsc	B	T Tr	Satb+
I Will Lift Up Mine Eyes	Wetherill	Na Lor	M	T Tr	Satb
I Will Love Thee O Lord	Glarum, L Stanley	Na Gsc	B	T Tr	Satb
I Would Seek God	Ford	Na Lor	M	T Tr	Satb
I've Discovered The Way Of Gladness	Hawkins	Na Lor	M	T Tr	Satb
If Ever The Sun Stops Shining	Hughes, Robert J.	Na Lor	M	T Tr	Satb
If I Have Wounded Any Soul	Gabriel	Na Lor	M	T Tr	Satb
If My Faith Is Strong And Sure	Carman, Albert	72 Sms	M R L	T Tr	
If Thou But Suffer God To Guide Thee	Bach, J. S.	Na Gsc	B	T Tr	Satb+

CATEGORIZED INDEX

If Thou Wilt Take My Hand (Alt Solo)	Elliott	Hof	M T Tr	Ssa
If Ye Love Me, Keep My Commandments	Fischer, Irwin	76 Cob	M T Tr	
If Ye Love Me, Keep My Commandments	Tallis, Thomas	Na Gsc	B T Tr	Satb
Ihr Kinderlein Kommet	Na	Na Gsc	B T Tr	Sab+
Immortal Love, For Ever Full	Matthews, H A	Na Gsc	B T Tr	Satb+
In A World That Needs Thy Love	Wallace, George	49 Smc	M T Tr	Satb
In Ecclesiis	Gabrieli, G	55 Bbl	B T Tr	Satb+
In God The Lord (Cantata)	Bach, J. S.	75 Lps	B R T Tr	Satb
In Heavenly Love	Boozer	75 Maf	M T Tr	Satb
In Heavenly Love	Mendelssohn, F.	35 Aug	M T Tr	Satb
In Heavenly Love Abiding	Douglas/Finnish Tune	76 Pro	M T Tr	Satb+
In Prayer	Faure, Gabriel	75 Bbl	M T Tr	Satb+
In Te Domine Speravi	Schutz, Heinrich	Na Gia	T Tr	
In Te, Domine, Speravi	Schutz, Heinrich	Na Gsc	B T Tr	Satb
In The Garden	Miles/Wilson	Na Lor	M T Tr	Var
In The Hollow Of Your Hand	Schmidt	Na Lor	M T Tr	Satb
In Thee, O Lord, Have I Put My Trust	Tours, B.	Na Gsc	B T Tr	Satb+
In Thine Arm I Rest Me	Bach, J. S.	Na Gsc	B T Tr	Ssatb
Incline Thine Ear To Me (S/Solo)	Himmel F.H.	Na Gsc	M T Tr	Satb+
Incline Your Ear	Wilkes, R. W.	Na Gsc	B T Tr	Ssa+
Interpreted By Love	Beck, John N	75 Bec	M T Tr	
Ist Nicht Ephraim Mein Teurer Sohn?	Schutz, Heinrich	Na Oxf	B T Tr	Satb
It Is Well With My Soul	London	Na Lor	M T Tr	Satb
It's A Gift To Be Simple	Wells, Tony	75 Maf	M T Tr	Satb
Iudica Me Deus (E & L) (Md)	Gorczycki, G.G.	76 Gia	M L T Tr	Satb+
Jesus Our Strength, Our Hope	Peninger, David	Na Gsc	B T Tr	Satb+
Joy	Christiansen, F. M.	33 Aug	M T Tr	Satb
Judge Me, O God	Mendelssohn, F.	Na Gsc	B T Tr	Var+
Just As I Am	Nolte	Na Lor	M T Tr	Satb
Just As I Am	Smith	Na Lor	M T Tr	Var
King Of Love My Shepherd Is, The	Follett, (Arr)	75 Pro	M T Tr	2pt+
King Of Love My Shepherd Is, The	Shelley	Na Lor	M T Tr	Var
King Of Love My Shepherd, The	Martin, Gilbert M.	76 Lor	T Tr	Satb+
Lass Dich Nur Nichts Nicht Dauren	Brahms, Johannes	Na Gsc	B T Tr	Satb+
Leaning On The Everlasting Arm	Bennett (Arr)	Hof	M T Tr	Satb
Let God Arise	Wills, Arthur	Na Gsc	B T Tr	Var
Let My Cry Come Before Thee	Newbury, Kent A.	Na Gsc	B T Tr	Ssa
Let Not Your Heart Be Troubled	Speaks, Oley	Na Gsc	B T Tr	Satb+
Let Nothing Disturb Thee	Lockwood, Normand	55 Smc	M T Tr	Satb
Let Nothing Ever Grieve Thee	Brahms, Johannes	Cfp	R T Tr	Satb+
Let The Word Of Christ	Newbury, Kent A.	Na Gsc	B T Tr	Satb
Let There Be Peace On Earth	Lojeski, Ed	74 Hal	T Tr	Var
Let Thy Hand Be Strengthened	Handel, G. F.	Na Gsc	B T Tr	Var+
Levavi Oculos Meos	Lasso, Orlando Di	Na Gsc	B T Tr	8mix
Lift Thine Eyes	Mendelssohn, F.	Na Gsc	B T Tr	Var+
Lift Thine Eyes (A Cap)	Mendelssohn, F.	Hof	M T Tr	Ssa
Lift Thine Eyes (Me)	Mendelssohn, F.	Na Oxf	M T Tr	2pt
Lift Up Your Heads	Andersen	53 Aug	M T Tr	Satb
Light Divine	Mascagni, Pietro	Na Gsc	B T Tr	8mix+
Like As The Heart Desireth The Water	Howells, Herbert I	Na Oxf	M T Tr	Satb
Lo, My Shepherd Is Divine	Haydn, Joseph	Na Gsc	B T Tr	Ssa+
Look Softly, Lord	Eliot	Na Lor	M T Tr	Satb
Look! See My God!	Wyrtzen, Don	Na Zon	T Tr	Satb
Lord Bless You And Keep You, The	Lutkin	Na Lor	M T Tr	Satb
Lord Hear My Voice	Wilson, James R.	Na Gsc	B T Tr	Satb
Lord Is In His Holy Temple, The	Bell	Na Lor	M T Tr	Satb
Lord Is My Shepherd, The	Erhardt	Na Lor	M T Tr	Var
Lord Is My Shepherd, The	Wilson	Na Lor	M T Tr	Satb
Lord Is Near To All, The	Haydn, Michael	75 Bbl	M T Tr	Satb
Lord Make Me An Instrument	Mallette	75 Pro	M T Tr	Satb+
Lord Of Life	Mitchell	74 Aug	M T Tr	Satb
Lord Of Nations Bless In Kindness	Farrell, Melvin	63 Wlp	B T Tr	
Lord We Implore Thee	Franck, Cesar	Na Gsc	B T Tr	Satb+
Lord, Be With Us Now	Lawrence, Anthony W.	76 Rpb	M B R L T Tr	
Lord, Hear Our Prayer To Thee	Avalos	76 Pro	M T Tr	3pt
Lord, Keep Us Steadfast	Luther–Johns	64 Aug	M T Tr	Sab
Lord, Keep Us Steadfast	Luther, M.–Distler	Na Aug	M T Tr	Sab
Lord, Let Me Know Mine End (Ps 39)	Greene, Maurice	Na Oxf	M T Tr	Ssatb
Lord, My Hope Is In Thee	Schutz, Heinrich	75 Maf	M T Tr	2pt
Lord, Thou Hast Been Our Dwelling	Mueller, Carl F	Na Gsc	B T Tr	Satb+
Lord, Walk With Me	Artman, Ruth	Na Wbp	T Tr	
Lord's My Shepherd, The	Irvine/Carmichael	Na Zon	T Tr	Satb
Love Divine	Beethoven, L	Na Gsc	B T Tr	Satb+
Love Divine	Prichard, R H	Na Gsc	B T Tr	Full
Love Thou Thy God (Cantata)	Bach, J. S.	75 Lps	B R T Tr	Satb
Ma Tovu (In 19 Lit Rounds)	Hebrew/Tortolano Ed	75 Gia	B L T Tr	4pt
Master Of Peace And Love	Bach, J. S.	Na Lor	M T Tr	Satb
Mercy And Truth	Thompson, V. D.	Na Gsc	B T Tr	Full
Mercy Lord, Upon Us	Mozart, Wolfgang A	Na Wbp	T Tr	
Mercy's Free (2 Voices)	Unknown/Tortolano	70 Gia	B L T Tr	Round
Mighty Fortress If Our God, A	Luther/Carmichael	Na Zon	T Tr	Satb
Mighty Fortress Is Our God, A	Hughes, Robert J.	Na Lor	M T Tr	Satb
Mighty Fortress, A	Luther/Rasley	Na Lor	M T Tr	Satb
Mighty Fortress, A	Wilson	Na Lor	M T Tr	Satb
More Love To Thee (P.D.)	Elrich, Dwight (Arr.)	74 Man	M T Tr	Choral
More Love To Thee, O Christ	Speaks, Oley	Na Gsc	B T Tr	Satb+
My Church Is A Holy Place	Dunlap, Fern Glasgow	Na Gsc	B T Tr	Satb+
My Eyes For Beauty Pine (Me)	Howells, Herbert	Na Oxf	M T Tr	Satb
My Father Walks Beside Me	Emig	Na Lor	M T Tr	Satb
My Father's Care (Norwegian)	Na	Na Lor	M T Tr	Unis
My God And I	Martin (Arr)	75 Sac	M T Tr	Satb
My God, My God, Look Upon Me	Blow, John	54 Bbl	M T Tr	Satb
My Heart Is Prepared	Harrer, Johann G	75 Bbl	M T Tr	Satb
My Jesus, I Love Thee	Rasley, John M.	Na Zon	T Tr	Satb
My Joy, My Life, My Crown (Md)	Montgomery, Bruce	Na Oxf	M T Tr	Satb
My Lord Is Like A Shepherd	Smith	Na Lor	M T Tr	Sab
My Master Hath A Garden	Thomson, Virgil	Na Gsc	B T Tr	Var+
My Shepherd Will Supply My Need	Pooler, Marie	63 Aug	M T Tr	Var
My Shepherd Will Supply My Need	Tortolano/Folk Tune	70 Gia	B L T Tr	Round
My Shepherd Will Supply My Need	Traditional/Rasley	Na Zon	T Tr	Satb
My Shepherd Will Supply My Need	Wilson	Na Lor	M T Tr	Satb
My Soul Longeth For Thee	Mendelssohn, F.	Na Gsc	B T Tr	Satb+
Nearer, Any God, To Thee	Street, Tilson	Na Gsc	B T Tr	Full
Non Vos Relinquos Orphanos (M)	Donati, Ignazio	Na Oxf	M T Tr	Ssa
Now Abideth Faith, Hope And Love	Shelley, H R	Na Gsc	B T Tr	Ssa+
O Blessed Lord	Schein, Johann H	75 Bbl	M T Tr	Full
O Brother Man (E)	Russell, Leslie	Na Oxf	M T Tr	Ss
O Dove Of Peace (Not H.Sp.)	Pickell, Ed	73 Pro	M T Tr	Satb+
O Father Blest	Nachtwey, Roger	65 Fel	B T Tr	
O For Closer Walk With God	Foster, M B	Na Gsc	B T Tr	Satb+
O God All Knowing & All Just	Westendorf, Omer	63 Wlp	B T Tr	
O God Be Merciful	Tye, Christopher	Na Oxf	M T Tr	Satb
O God Enfold Me In The Sun (Md)	Leighton, Kenneth	Na Oxf	M T Tr	Satb
O God Of Consolation (Choral)	Fitzpatrick, Dennis	65 Fel	B T Tr	
O God Of Love, O King Of Peace	Infante, Guy	74 Sms	M R L T Tr	
O God Of Peace	James	Na Lor	M T Tr	Satb
O God Our Help In Ages Past	Shipp, Clifford M.	62 Gam	M T Tr	Satb
O God Our Refuge & Our Strength	Gannon, Michael	63 Wlp	B T Tr	
O God, Beneath Thy Guiding Hand	Hatton, John	Na Gsc	B T Tr	Full+
O God, Our Help In Ages Past	Croft/Bolks	Na Zon	T Tr	Satb
O God, Our Help In Ages Past	Pice	Na Lor	M T Tr	Satb
O God, Our Help In Ages Past	Thompson	Na Lor	M T Tr	Satb
O God, Our Help In Ages Past	Young, Gordon	75 Her	M T Tr	Satb
O Hear We Lord God	Croce, Giovanni	Na Gsc	B T Tr	Satb+
O How Amiable (Ps 84) (Md)	Tompkins, Thomas	Na Oxf	M T Tr	Attb
O How Amiable Are Thy Dwellings	Barnby, Jos	Na Gsc	B T Tr	Var+
O How Lovely Are Your Dwellings	Andrews, Carroll T.	70 Gia	B L T Tr	Var
O Lord God Of My Salvation	Croft, William	75 Bbl	M T Tr	Ssaatb
O Love Of God, Most Full	Smith, Lani	76 Lor	T Tr	Satb+
O Love That Wilt Not Let Me Go	Grieb, Herbert	Na Gsc	B T Tr	Sab+
O Love That Wilt Not Let Me Go	Peace/Rasley	Na Zon	T Tr	Satb
O Love, How Deep (Opt Tpt)	Johnson (Arr), D.	72 Aug	M T Tr	Unis
O My Saints	Welch, James	67 Fel	B T Tr	
O One With God, The Father	Na	Na Gsc	B T Tr	Sa+
O Pray For The Peace Of Jerusalem	Howells, Herbert	Na Oxf	M T Tr	Satb
O Pray For The Peace Of Jerusalem	Tompkins, Thomas	54 Bbl	M T Tr	Satb
O Pray For The Peace Of Jerusalem (M)	Tompkins, Thomas	Na Oxf	M T Tr	Sstb
O Shepherd Of Israel	Morrison, C P	Na Gsc	B T Tr	Satb+
O Turn Away Mine Eyes (Md)	Bowie, William	Na Oxf	M T Tr	Unis
Oh, Lord, Make Me An Instrument	Sedores, Sil	61 Mca	M T Tr	
One Thing Have I Desired Of The Lord	Jeppesen, Knud	75 Bbl	M T Tr	Satb
One Thing I Ask Of The Lord	Schutz, Heinrich	75 Maf	M T Tr	2pt
Onward Ye Saints	Wetzler, Robert	60 Aug	M T Tr	Satb
Open My Heart (Me)	Bach, J.S. (Arr)	Na Oxf	M T Tr	Satb
Open Our Eyes	Macfarlane, W C	Na Gsc	B T Tr	Var+
Peace Be Multiplied	Hovhaness, Alan S.	74 Ron	M T Tr	Satb
Peace Be On Earth	Billings, William	Cfp	R T Tr	Satb
Peace I Leave With You	Roberts, J V	Na Gsc	B T Tr	Var+
Pleasure It Is	Thackray, Roy	Na Oxf	M T Tr	Unis
Plorans Ploravit (M)	Correa, Carlos	Na Oxf	M T Tr	Satb
Prayer	Mercer, M	Na Gsc	B T Tr	2eq+
Prayer Canon From Aroldo	Verdi, Giuseppe	67 Bbl	M T Tr	Full
Prayer For God's Blessing	Van Dyke, Paul C.	Na Gsc	B T Tr	Satb+
Prayer For Serenity	Bowles	75 Pro	M T Tr	Satb+
Prayer Of Penitence, A	Martin	Na Lor	M T Tr	
Prayer Of St. Francis	Wagner, Lavern J.	74 Sms	M R L T Tr	
Prepare My Mind And Heart For Prayer	Morgan	Na Lor	M T Tr	
Presence, The	Schoenfeld, William C.	Na Abi	M T Tr	Satb
Psalm 121	Schutz, Heinrich	Na Gsc	B T Tr	Satb+
Psalm 121 (I Will Lift Up Mine Eyes)	Rutter, John	Na Oxf	M T Tr	
Psalm 23	Berger, Jean	65 Bbl	M T Tr	Satb
Psalm 23	Creston, Paul	Na Gsc	B T Tr	Satb+
Psalm 23	Homilius, Gottfried A	75 Bbl	M T Tr	Satb
Psalm 23 From The Bay Psalm Book	Beeson, Jack	Na Oxf	M T Tr	Satb
Psalm 25	Zaumeyer, John	73 Hal	T Tr	Full
Psalm 31 From The Bay Psalm Book	Beeson, Jack	Na Oxf	M T Tr	Satb
Purer In Heart, O God	London	Na Lor	M T Tr	
Rejoice In The Lord	Glarum, L Stanley	Na Gsc	B T Tr	Satb+
Rejoice In The Lord Alway (M)	Anonymous	Na Oxf	M T Tr	Satb
Rejoice, Ye Pure In Heart	Messiter/Johnson	Na Zon	T Tr	Satb
Rise, God! Judge Thou The Earth	Tallis, Thomas	Na Gsc	B T Tr	Satb+
Rock Of Ages	Hastings/Rasley	Na Lor	M T Tr	
Rock Of Ages	Humperdinck	Na Lor	M T Tr	
Rock Of Ages (Arrangement)	Lewis, E.	75 Sil	R L T Tr	
Round Me Falls The Night	Thiman, Eric H.	Na Gsc	B T Tr	Var
Sabbath Bells	Stainer, Sir John	Na Lor	M T Tr	Var
Safe In The Arms Of Jesus	Burroughs	Na Lor	M T Tr	Satb
Savior, Again To Your Dear Name	Ellerton, J./Lee, John	70 Gia	B L T Tr	Satb
Saviour, Hear Us When We Pray	Strickland, Lily	Na Gsc	B T Tr	Satb
See Dearest God (Cantata)	Bach, J. S.	75 Lps	B R T Tr	Satb
Seek And Ye Shall Find	Tarner	Na Lor	M T Tr	Satb
Seek The Lord (E)	Tomblings, Philip	Na Oxf	M T Tr	U/2pt
Seek Ye The Lord	Burroughs	75 Sac	M T Tr	Satb
Seek Ye The Lord	Wyrtzen, Don	75 Sac	M T Tr	Satb
Seek Ye The Lord (Ten Solo)	Roberts	Na Gsc	M T Tr	Satb+
Seeking To Become	Spiritual/Artman	76 Hal	T Tr	Var
Selections From Canciones Sacrae (4vol)	Schutz, Heinrich	Na Kal	B T Tr	Satb
Send Out Thy Light	Gounod, Charles	Na Gsc	B T Tr	Satb+
Sheep And Lambs	Homer, Sidney	Na Gsc	B T Tr	Satb+
Sheep And Lambs May Safely Graze	Bach, J.S.	Na Gsc	B T Tr	Var+
Sheep May Safely Graze	Bach, J. S.	Na Lor	M T Tr	Satb
Siehe, Das Ist Gottes Lamm	Homilius, Gottfried	76 Bbl	M T Tr	Full
Solid Rock, The	Mccluskey	Na Lor	M T Tr	
Somebody's Knocking At Your Door	Wilson	Na Lor	M T Tr	Var
Song Of Peace, A	Sibelius, J	Na Lor	M T Tr	Var
Song Of Repentance	Bach, J. S.	52 Bbl	M T Tr	Satb
Spes Mea, Christe, Deus	Schutz, Heinrich	Na Kal	B T Tr	Satb
Stand In Awe	Lorenz	Na Lor	M T Tr	Satb
Steadfast And Good Is Jehovah	Goudimel, Claude	Na Gsc	B T Tr	Satb
Steal Away To Jesus	Na	Na Gsc	B T Tr	Satb

CATEGORIZED INDEX

Still, Still With Thee	Madsen, F J	Na Gsc	B	T Tr	3eq+
Still, Still With Thee	Shelley	Na Lor	M	T Tr	Satb
Supplication	Lokey	Na Lor	M	T Tr	Satb
Supplications	Na	Na Gsc	B	T Tr	Saatb
Sweet Hour Of Prayer	London	Na Lor	M	T Tr	Satb
Take Time To Be Holy	Smith	Na Lor	M	T Tr	Satb
Teach Me, O Lord (Ps 119 Md)	Hilton, John	Na Oxf	M	T Tr	Ssatb
The Beatitudes	Christiansen, P.	71 Aug	M	T Tr	Satb
The Beatitudes	Malotte, A H	Na Gsc	B	T Tr	Satb+
The Brotherhood Of Man	Handel, G. F.	75 Pro	M	T Tr	2pt+
The Church's One Foundation	Duro, John	Na Gsc	B	T Tr	Satb+
The Earth Is Full Of Goodness	Gannon, Michael	61 Wlp	B	T Tr	
The Expectation Of The Just	Lasso, Orlando Di	67 Fel	B	T Tr	
The Eyes Of All Wait Upon Thee	Berger, Jean	59 Aug	M	T Tr	Satb
The Faithful Shepherd (Cantata)	Bach, J. S.	75 Lps	B R	T Tr	Satb
The Good Shepherd	Barri, O	Na Gsc	B	T Tr	Var+
The Great Peace (E)	Bain, J.L.M. (Arr)	Na Oxf	M	T Tr	2pt
The Just Man Will Give His Heart	Lasso, Orlando Di	67 Fel	B	T Tr	
The King Of Love (In 19 Rounds)	Baker/Trad/Tortolano	75 Gia	B L	T Tr	2pt
The King Of Love My Shepherd Is	Shelley, H R	Na Gsc	B	T Tr	Satb+
The Lord Bless You	Bach, J. S.	70 Gia	M	T Tr	Satb
The Lord Is My Light	Allitsen, Frances	Na Gsc	B	T Tr	Var
The Lord Is My Light	Parker, Horatio W	Na Gsc	B	T Tr	Satb+
The Lord Is My Light	Speaks, Oley	Na Gsc	B	T Tr	Satb+
The Lord Is My Rock	Woodman, R. H.	Na Gsc	B	T Tr	Satb+
The Lord Is My Shepherd	Schubert, Franz J.	Na Gsc	B	T Tr	Var+
The Lord Is My Shepherd (Ps 23)	Schubert, Franz J.	Na Oxf	M	T Tr	Ssaa
The Lord Is My Shepherd 2 Voices	Trad/Tortolano Ed	75 Gia	B L	T Tr	Round
The Lord My Shepherd E'er Shall Be	Bach, J. S.	Na Gsc	B	T Tr	Ttbb
The Lord My Shepherd Is	Handel, G. F.	Na Gsc	B	T Tr	2chor
The Love Of God	Whikehart, Lewis E.	70 Gsc	B	T Tr	Satb
The Love Of God	Woodman, R. H.	Na Gsc	B	T Tr	Satb+
The Love Of My Lord To Me	Hughes, Robert J.	Na Lor	M	T Tr	Satb
The Mariner's Anthem (Moore)	Billings, William	Na Gsc	B	T Tr	Satb
The Prayer Perfect	Speaks, Oley	Na Gsc	B	T Tr	Var+
The Rightious (Der Gerechte)	Bach, J.C.(Gieringer)	41 Gsc	M	T Tr	Satb
The Twenty-Seventh Psalm(The Lord Is)	Edwards, Clara	Na Gsc	B	T Tr	Satb+
The Twenty-Third Psalm	Malotte, A H	Na Gsc	B	T Tr	Var+
The Twenty-Third Psalm	Williams, Vaughan R.	Na Oxf	M	T Tr	Satb
Thee Will I Love, O Lord	Little, Leonard	Na Gsc	B	T Tr	Ttbb
There Is A Love	Lang	Na Lor	M	T Tr	Satb
There's A Wideness In God's Mercy	Goemanne, Noel	72 Gia	M	T Tr	Var+
There's A Wideness In God's Mercy	Staton	73 Aug	M	T Tr	2pt
They That Put Their Trust In The Lord	Orr, Robin	Na Oxf	M	T Tr	Satb
They That Trust In The Lord	Adams	Na Lor	M	T Tr	Satb
They Who Considereth The Poor Shall Be	Morgan	Na Wbp		T Tr	
Thine, O Lord	Macfarlane, W C	Na Gsc	B	T Tr	Satb+
This Is My Father's World	Hughes, Robert J.	Na Lor	M	T Tr	Satb
This Is My Father's World	Johnson	Na Lor	M	T Tr	Satb
This Is My Father's World	Price, Benton	Na Lor	M	T Tr	Satb
This Is My Father's World	Sheppard/Hess	Na Zon		T Tr	Full
This Is My Father's World	Speehard/Johnson	Na Zon		T Tr	Satb
This Is My Song	Sibelius, Jean	76 Lor		T Tr	Satb+
Thou Alone Art Israel's Shield	Berger, Jean	75 Aug	M	T Tr	Satb
Thou Heart Of Compassion (Cantata)	Bach, J. S.	75 Lps	B R	T Tr	Satb
Thou Hope Of Every Contrite Heart	Thompson	Na Lor	M	T Tr	
Thou Refuge Of The Destitute	Des Pres, Josquin	Na Gsc	B	T Tr	Satb
Thou Visitest The Earth (Ps 65)	Greene, Maurice	Na Oxf	M	T Tr	Ss
Thou Wilt Keep Him	Peery	Na Lor	M	T Tr	
Thou Wilt Keep Him (A Cap) 1	Wyatt (Arr)	76 Pro	M	T Tr	Satb
Thou Wilt Keep Him In Perfect Peace	Hughes, Robert J.	Na Lor	M	T Tr	
Thou Wilt Keep Him In Perfect Peace	Speaks, Oley	Na Gsc	B	T Tr	Satb+
Thou Wilt Keep Him In Perfect Peace	Williams, C. L.	Na Gsc	B	T Tr	Satb
Though I Speak With The Tongues Of Men	Bairstow, E. C.	Na Oxf	M	T Tr	Satb
Though Your Sins Be As Scarlet	Mccluskey	Na Lor	M	T Tr	
Though Your Sins Be As Scarlet	Wilson	Na Lor	M	T Tr	
Through All The Changing Scenes	Hughes, Robert J.	Na Lor	M	T Tr	
Thus Saith The Lord Of Hosts	Rogers, J H	Na Gsc	B	T Tr	Satb+
Thy Love Brings Joy	Schutz, Heinrich	74 Aug	M	T Tr	Satb
Thy Love Shall Fail Me Never	Kilpatrick	Hof	M	T Tr	Satb
Thy Word Is A Lamp	Glarum, L Stanley	Na Gsc	B	T Tr	Satb
Tis Indeed The Gospel Truth	Bach, J. S.	75 Lps	B R	T Tr	Satb
Tis So Sweet To Trust In Jesus	Price	Na Lor	M	T Tr	
Tis So Sweet To Trust In Jesus (P. D.)	Elrich, Dwight (Arr.)	74 Man	M	T Tr	Choral
To Do God's Will	Berger, Jean	62 Aug	M	T Tr	Satb
To Mercy, Pity, Peace And Love	Fast, Willard S	Na Gsc	B	T Tr	Satb
To See The Lord	Martin	Na Lor	M	T Tr	
To You I Lift My Soul	Track, Gerhard	74 Hal		T Tr	Satb
To You I Lift Up My Soul & Ps 43	Lee, John	70 Gia	B L	T Tr	Satb
Tomorrow Shall Be My Dancing Day	Fissinger, Edwin (Arr)	75 Wlp	M	T Tr	Satb+
Troset Troset Mein Volk	Schutz, Heinrich	Na Gsc	B	T Tr	6mix
Trust	Sibelius, J	Na Gsc	B	T Tr	Var+
Trust In Him	Hamblen, B.	Na Gsc	B	T Tr	Var+
Trust In The Lord	Handel, G. F.	Na Gsc	B	T Tr	Ssa+
Trust Thou In God	Mendelssohn, F.	Na Gsc	B	T Tr	Satb+
Turn Not Thy Face	Sateren, Leland B.	56 Aug	M	T Tr	Satb
Twenty Third Psalm	Davis, K.K.	Na Wbp		T Tr	
Twenty-Third Psalm, The	Rozsa, Miklos	74 Bbl	M	T Tr	Satb
Two Dwellings	Martin	Na Lor	M	T Tr	Satb
Under His Wings	Smith	Na Lor	M	T Tr	Satb
Verleih Uns Frieden Genadiglich	Schutz, Heinrich	Na Gsc	B	T Tr	Satb
Vision Of Peace	Berger, Jean	49 Bbl	B	T Tr	Satb
We All Need God	Mccoy	Na Lor	M	T Tr	Sa
We Come To You With Longing	Vermulst, Jan	61 Wlp	B	T Tr	
We Lift Our Hearts To Thee	Kempinski, I	Na Gsc	B	T Tr	Var
We Love The Place Where Thine Honor	Brahms, Johannes	Na Oxf	M	T Tr	Ssa
We Need Thy Love	Darst	Na Lor	M	T Tr	Satb
We Wait For Thy Loving Kindness (Me)	Elvey, Stephen	Na Oxf	M	T Tr	Ss
What'e'er My God Ordains Is Right	Pachelbel, J	75 Sac	M	T Tr	
When Love Shines In	Hughes, Robert J.	Na Lor	M	T Tr	
When One Knows Thee	Glarum, L Stanley	Na Gsc	B	T Tr	Satb
Where Cross The Crowded Ways	Lynn-Zeuner	57 Smc	M	T Tr	Satb
Whispering Hope	Hawthorne	Na Lor	M	T Tr	
Who So Dwelleth	Goodenough, Forrest	51 Smc	M	T Tr	Satb
Why Art Thou So Heavy, O My Soul	Gibbons, Orlando	54 Bbl	M	T Tr	Satb
With A Holy Hush	Peterson, John W.	Na Zon		T Tr	Satb
With All Who Love Thy Name, O Lord	Smith	Na Lor	M	T Tr	
With My Hand In Thine	Wells	Na Lor	M	T Tr	
Within The Silence	Wilson	Na Lor	M	T Tr	
Without Love, No Feeling	Martin	Na Lor	M	T Tr	
Wonderful Peace	Hughes, Robert J.	Na Lor	M	T Tr	
Wonderful Words Of Life	London	Na Lor	M	T Tr	
Wondrous Love	Niles, John Jacob	Na Gsc	B	T Tr	Var+
Wondrous Love	Traditional/Decou	Na Zon	M	T Tr	Satb
Wondrous Love (Spiritual)	Lynn, George	56 Smc	M	T Tr	2pt
Ye Servants Of God (E)	Coleman, Henry	Na Oxf	M	T Tr	Satb
Ye Who Profess (Cantata)	Bach, J. S.	75 Lps	B R	T Tr	Satb
Yea, Though I Wander	Schumann-Christiansen	48 Aug	M	T Tr	Satb

Hymns and Psalms of Praise and Thanksgiving

A Child's Thanksgiving (E)	Baynon, Arthur	Na Oxf	M	C Tt	Unis
A Song Of Praise	Ford, Virgil	76 Abi	M	C Tt	2pt+
Children Of The Heavenly Father	Pooler, Marie	Na Abi	M	C Tt	Sa
Children's Voices Joyfully Sing	Leaf, Robert	67 Aug	M	C Tt	Unis
Clap Your Hands, All Ye Children	Hunnicutt, J.	71 Aug	M	C Tt	Unis
Come, Ye Children, Sweetly Singing	Rasley	Na Lor	M	C Tt	Unis
Does God Ever Laugh?	Curzio, Elaine	70 Van	B R	C Tt	
Everybody Sing Alleluia	Mcgrath, Roberta	75 Rpb	M B R L	C Tt	
God Who Made The Earth	Lewis, John Leo	Na Gsc	B	C Tt	Unis+
Hail To Thee	Comeau, Bill	67 Van	B R	C Tt	
Let The Children Sing	Bristol, Lee H.	Na Abi	M	C Tt	
Lord Thou Art Holy	Franck, Cesar	63 Gam	M	C Tt	Unis
Raise Your Hands	Miffleton, Jack	71 Wlp	B R	C Tt	
Song Of Blessing	Dreves, Veronica&Ellis	75 Rav	M B R L	C Tt	
Thank You Hymn	Blue, Robert	66 Fel	B R	C Tt	
The Big "G" Stands For	Comeau, Bill	67 Van	B R	C Tt	
A Little Less Of Me	Campbell, Glen	65 Bch		F Tt	
A New Song	Johnson, Gary L.	74 Bfi	B L	F Tt	
A Song Of Joy	Dunkin, Timothy L.	73 Fel	B	F Tt	
All Good Gifts	Schwartz, Stephen	71 Val	B R	F Tt	
All Of My Life	Germaine	66 Fel	B R	F Tt	
All Of Your People	Berlucchi, James	75 Wgm	B L	F Tt	
All The Days Of Our Lives	Hurd, Bob	73 Fel	B	F Tt	
All The World Acclaims Your Name	Shaltz, Gregory	74 Sms	M R L	F Tt	
All You Nations	Parker, Tom	68 Wlp	B R	F Tt	
Alle, Alle	Miffleton, Jack	67 Wlp	B R	F Tt	
Allelu	Farra, Mimi A.	71 Fis	M	F Tt	
Alleluia God Is Love	Russo, Robert	71 Jsp	B	F Tt	2pt
Alleluia!	Traditional/Mickelson	Na Zon		F Tt	Satb
Alleluia!	Traditional/Wyrtzen	Na Zon	M	F Tt	Satb
Alleluia, Sons Of God Arise	Farra, Mimi A.	71 Fis	M L	F Tt	
Allelujah Today	Pulkingham, Wes&Betty	74 Fis	M L	F Tt	
As A Child Before The Lord	Ste. Marie, Patricia	74 Sha	B R L	F Tt	
As Tears Go By	Jagger/Richard/Oldham	Na Esx		F Tt	
As The Sun	Miffleton, Jack	68 Acp	B L	F Tt	
As The Sun (4-Part Arr.)	Cirou, Joseph	70 Acp	B L	F Tt	
Awake, My Glory	Diemer Emma Lou	76 Abi	M	F Tt	Satb+
Bless The Lord	Blue, Robert	66 Fel	B	F Tt	
Bless The Lord, O My Soul	O'sheil, Judy	66 Fel	B	F Tt	
Bless Thou The Lord (Ps 103)	Pulkingham, Betty C.	72 Gia	M B R L	F Tt	Var+
Blowin' In The Wind	Dylan, Bob	62 Wbp		F Tt	
Brother John	Sparks	66 Mil		F Tt	
By My Side	Hamburger/Gordon	71 Val		F Tt	
Canticle Of Judith	Quinlan, Paul	66 Fel	B	F Tt	
Canticle Of The Sun	Temple, Sebastian	67 Fcc	B R L	F Tt	
Canticle Of The Three Young Men (Ver 1)	Uhl, Pat&Gilligan, M.	67 Acp	B L	F Tt	
Canticle Of The Three Young Men (Ver 2)	Uhl, Pat&Gilligan, M.	70 Acp	B R L	F Tt	
Catch A Little Sunshine	Edwards, Deanna	74 Fcc	R L	F Tt	
Celebrate	Wyrtzen, Don	Na Zon	M	F Tt	Satb
Celebrate Life	Tucciarone, Angel	73 Wlp	B R	F Tt	
Children Of The Day	Jacobs, Peter	71 Chd	B R L	F Tt	
Clap Your Hands	Johnson, Gary L.	75 Bfi	B R	F Tt	
Clap Your Hands	Repp, Ray	66 Fel	B R	F Tt	
Come All Ye Nations	Christmas, Charles	74 Wgm	B R L	F Tt	
Come Praise, Alleluia	Miller	67 Wlp	B	F Tt	
Come See The Joy We Have	Barbeau, Dennis	71 Jsp	B	F Tt	Guit
Day Is Done	Yarrow	Na Pep		F Tt	
Early In The Morning	Yarrow	62 Pep		F Tt	
Everything Is Beautiful	Stevens	70 Aha		F Tt	
Everywhere And Always	Holiday/Johnson	Na Zon	M	F Tt	Sab-Sc
Father, We Thank You	Reilly, Cyril A.	66 Fel	B	F Tt	
Follow Me	Denver, John	69 Clm		F Tt	
For Baby (For Bobbie)	Denver, John	65 Clm		F Tt	
For His Loving Kindness	Yantis, David	76 Yan	B	F Tt	
Forevermore	Repp, Ray	66 Fel	B R	F Tt	
Glorious God	Temple, Sebastian	67 Fcc	B R L	F Tt	Gia
Glory	Davis, Bob	73 Fcc	B R L	F Tt	
Glory	Wise, Joe	67 Wlp	B R	F Tt	
Glory (Sing To The Lord)	Farra, Mimi A.	73 Gia	M B R L	F Tt	Var+
Glory Hallelujah	Quinlan, Paul	65 Wlp	B R	F Tt	
Glory Hosanna	Silvia, Helen	73 Acp	B L	F Tt	
Glory To God	Christman, Charles	75 Wgm	B L	F Tt	
Glory To God	Quinlan, Paul	67 Fel	B R	F Tt	
Glory To God On High	Miffleton, Jack	71 Wlp	B	F Tt	
Glory To Jesus	Wagner, Lavern J.	72 Sms	M R L	F Tt	
Good-Bye	Jacobs, Peter	75 Chd	R L	F Tt	
Got To Shout About It	Fischer, John	69 Fel	B R	F Tt	

CATEGORIZED INDEX

Gotta' Give A Little	Lewis, E.	74 Sil	L F Tt	
Hallelujah, Yes, Praise The Lord	Wyrtzen, Don	75 Zon	M F Tt	Satb
Halleujah	Quinlan, Paul	65 Wlp	B R F Tt	
He Is Lord Of All	Aridas, Chris	73 Fel	B F Tt	
His Praise Is Higher Than The Highest	Vissing, Sr. Rosalie	74 Sha	B R L F Tt	
How Good It Is	Temple, Sebastian	67 Fcc	B R L F Tt	Gia
How Great Is Your Name	Temple, Sebastian	67 Fcc	B R L F Tt	Gia
How Wonderful And Great	Winberry, Mary & Malate	73 Fel	B F Tt	
Hurry Sundown	Harburg/Robinson	66 Nor	F Tt	
Hymn	Gold/Mason/Stookey	68 Pep	F Tt	
Hymn For A Prayer Meeting	Fitzgerald, Michael	74 Wgm	B R L F Tt	
Hymn Of Glory	Christmas, Charles	74 Wgm	B R L F Tt	
I Don't Know How To Love Him	Webber/Rice	70 Lds	F Tt	
I Praised The Earth	Mitchell, Ian	66 Fel	B R F Tt	
I Sing A Song To You, Lord	Beaumont, Fr. Richard	74 Sha	B R L F Tt	
I Sing Your Song	Silvia, Ray	73 Fel	B F Tt	
I Will Give Thanks	Tucciarone, Angel	76 Rpb	M B R L F Tt	
I Will Live To Sing Your Praise	Whitemore, Joan M.	74 Sms	M R L F Tt	
I Will Sing And Make Music	Ste. Marie, Patricia	74 Sha	B R L F Tt	
I Will Sing, I Will Sing	Dyer, Max	74 Fis	M L F Tt	
I Wish I Knew How It Would Feel	Taylor/Dallas	64 Dua	F Tt	
I'll Sing Praise To The Lord	Cunningham, Patrick	71 Gra	B R L F Tt	
I'm Being Guided	Hires, B.	74 Sil	R L F Tt	
I'm Gonna Sing	Coppock, Doug	Na Gia	B R L F Tt	
If I Had Wings	Yarrow/Yardley	67 Pep	F Tt	
In His Love	Ducote, Darryl	71 Fel	B R F Tt	
In Praise Of God	Meltz, Ken	72 Wlp	B F Tt	
It's A Great Day	Blue, Robert	66 Fel	B R F Tt	
Jacob's Song	Krieger, Jacob	73 Wgm	B R L F Tt	
Joy In Christ, Alleluia	Yantis, David	Na Yan	B F Tt	
Jubilee	Thiem, James	66 Fel	B F Tt	
Just Pretending	Jacobs, Peter	73 Chd	B R L F Tt	
King Of Kings (Glory Glory)	Russo, Robert	71 Jsp	B F Tt	+Guit
Late Winter, Early Spring	Denver/Taylor/Kniss	72 Clm	F Tt	
Let All The Earth	Ault, Gary	69 Fel	B R F Tt	
Let All The Earth Sing His Praise	Parker, Tom	68 Wlp	B R F Tt	
Let Everyone Praise (Ps 150)	Gerrish, James	71 Jsp	B F Tt	+Guit
Let It Be	Lennon/Mccartney	70 Nor	F Tt	
Let The Heavens Be Glad & Earth...	Parker, Tom	68 Wlp	B R F Tt	
Let The Hills Now Sing For Joy	Johnson, Gary L.	75 Bfi	B R F Tt	
Let Us Give Thanks	Howard, Brian	74 Fis	M L F Tt	
Let Your Song Ring Out	Miller, Dan	72 Fel	B R F Tt	
Lift Your Voice	Wise, Joe	68 Wlp	B F Tt	
Living God, The	Temple, Sebastian	67 Fcc	M B R L F Tt	Gia
Magnificat	Mitchell, Ian	66 Fel	B R F Tt	
My Simple Song	Montague, George T.	76 Gra	B R L F Tt	U/Guit
My Soul Doth Magnify	Pulkingham, B.C.(Arr)	72 Gia	M B R L F Tt	Var+
Now Sing With Joy	Gilligan, Michael	70 Acp	B R L F Tt	
Now Sing With Joy (4-Part Arr)	Burleigh, Harry T.	73 Acp	B L F Tt	
O Bless The Lord, My Soul	Schwartz, Stephen	71 Val	B R F Tt	
O Give Thanks	Johnson, Gary L.	74 Bfi	B L F Tt	
O Give Thanks Unto The Lord	Smith, Lani	Na Lor	M F Tt	Sab
O Lord How Great Is Your Name	Quinlan, Paul	65 Wlp	M B R F Tt	
O Lord, You Know Who I Am	Hurd, Bob	73 Fel	B R F Tt	
O, Praise The Lord	Quinlan, Paul	67 Fel	B R F Tt	
Pave The Way	Rowe, D.	76 Sil	R F Tt	
Pickin' The Sun Down	Weisberg/Sommers	74 Clm	F Tt	
Praise God	Wagner, Lavern J.	73 Sms	M R L F Tt	
Praise God	Winter, Miriam T.	71 Van	B R F Tt	
Praise God	Yantis, David	Na Yan	B F Tt	
Praise God From Whom All	Yantis, David	Na Yan	B F Tt	
Praise God, Praise Him Here Below	Quinlan, Paul	66 Fel	B L F Tt	
Praise God, Ps. 145	Ault, Gary	73 Fcc	B R L F Tt	
Praise Him	Wyrtzen, Don	Na Zon	M F Tt	Satb
Praise Him In The Morning	Traditional/Wyrtzen	75 Zon	M F Tt	Satb
Praise My God With The Tamborine	Davis, Diane	73 Gia	M B R L F Tt	Var+
Praise The Lord	Quinlan, Paul	65 Wlp	B R F Tt	
Praise The Lord	Winter, Miriam T.	67 Van	B R F Tt	
Praise The Lord In Many Voices	Quinlan, Paul	67 Van	B R F Tt	
Praise The Lord Who Lives Among Us	Wagner, Lavern J.	73 Sms	M R L F Tt	
Praise The Lord, My Brothers	Hanson, Mike	70 Fel	B R F Tt	
Praise Ye, The Lord	Quinlan, Paul	67 Van	B R F Tt	
Praise, The Holy Of Holies	Quinlan, Paul	65 Wlp	B R F Tt	
Presentation (Offertory)	Mitchell, Ian	68 Fel	B R F Tt	
Psalm 103 All Of My Life	Grace, Sister Mary	66 Fel	B F Tt	
Psalm 108	Hess, John H.	Na Zon	M F Tt	Unis
Psalm 113 Blest Be The Name	Quinlan, Paul	66 Fel	B F Tt	
Psalm 136 (O Give Thanks)	Thomerson, Kathleen	73 Gia	M B R L F Tt	Var+
Psalm 136 Praise God, Praise Him Here	Quinlan, Paul	66 Fel	B F Tt	
Psalm 145	Christmas, Charles	74 Wgm	B L F Tt	
Psalm 148	Aridas, Chris	73 Fel	B F Tt	
Psalm 47 Clap Your Hands	Quinlan, Paul	66 Fel	B R F Tt	
Psalm 47 Sing Halleluia, Praise	Quinlan, Paul	66 Fel	B F Tt	
Psalm 66 Shout Joyfully To God	Grace, Sister Mary	66 Fel	B F Tt	
Psalm 89 (I Will Celebrate)	Barrie, Karen M.	73 Kbr	M B R L F Tt	
Psalm 92 Glory To The Father	Quinlan, Paul	66 Fel	B R F Tt	
Psalm 96	Kohl, Jon	73 Fel	B F Tt	
Psalm 96 Sing To God A Joyous Song	Quinlan, Paul	66 Fel	B F Tt	
Psalm 98	Aridas, Chris	73 Fel	B F Tt	
Psalm 99 Holy, Holy Is The Lord	Quinlan, Paul	66 Fel	B F Tt	
Put My Memory In Your Pocket	Edwards, Deanna	74 Fcc	R L F Tt	
Reach For The Light	Lewis, E.	74 Sil	R L F Tt	
Rejoice With Me	Miller, Dan	72 Fel	B R F Tt	
Rejoice, Be Glad In The Lord	Fitzpatrick, Dennis	65 Fel	B R F Tt	
Rejoice, The Lord Is King	Mitchell, Ian	66 Fel	B R F Tt	
Rhymes And Reasons	Denver, John	69 Clm	F Tt	
Russ's Song	Stevens, Marsha J.	73 Chd	B R L F Tt	
Sabbath Prayer	Bock/Harnick	64 Nyt	F Tt	
Shout	Thiem, James	66 Fel	B F Tt	
Shout And Clap Your Hands	Scholtes, Peter	68 Fel	B R F Tt	
Shout From The Highest Mountain	Repp, Ray	66 Fel	B R F Tt	
Shout Joyfully To God	Whitemore, Joan M.	71 Sms	M R L F Tt	
Shout Out Your Joy	Ducote, Darryl	69 Fel	B R F Tt	
Shout Out, Sing Of His Glory	Meyer, Ron	70 Fel	B R F Tt	
Shout Praises To The Lord	Risewick, Jack M.	73 Fel	B F Tt	
Silver Packages	Jacobs, Hanneke	75 Chd	R L F Tt	
Sing Alleluia	Winberry, Mary	73 Fel	B F Tt	
Sing Alleluia To The King	Yantis, David	Na Yan	B F Tt	
Sing Alleluia! (Be Glad Within)	Gerrish, James	71 Jsp	B F Tt	+Guit
Sing Alleluia, Sing	Ault, Gary	73 Fcc	B R L F Tt	
Sing Hosanna, Halleluia	Repp, Ray	67 Fel	B R F Tt	
Sing Of Our God (Trinity)	Meyer, Ronald	68 Jsp	B F Tt	+Guit
Sing Out His Goodness	Ducote, Darryl	69 Fel	B R F Tt	
Sing Out The Glory Of The Lord	Kohl, Jon	73 Fel	B F Tt	
Sing Out, My Soul	Winberry, Mary	73 Fel	B F Tt	
Sing Out, My Soul, To The Lord	Repp, Ray	67 Fel	B R F Tt	
Sing Out, O Zion	Collins, J.T. & Peters	66 Fel	B F Tt	
Sing Out, Sing Out	Germaine	66 Fel	B R F Tt	
Sing Praise To The Lord	Wise, Joe	67 Wlp	B R F Tt	
Sing Praises To God	Kinley, Ken	73 Fel	B F Tt	
Sing To God	Quinlan, Paul	67 Van	B R F Tt	
Sing To God A Brand New Canticle	Quinlan, Paul	68 Nal	B R F Tt	
Sing To God A Joyous Song	Quinlan, Paul	66 Fel	B L F Tt	
Sing To The Lord	Fishel, Donald	74 Wgm	B R L F Tt	
Sing Unto The Lamb	Ste. Marie, Patricia	74 Sha	B R L F Tt	
Sing, Sing Alleluia	Newman, Nancy Carr	73 Gia	B R L F Tt	
Sing, Sing, Sing (Opt Brass)	Montague, George T.	72 Mcc	B R L F Tt	Unis+
Song For The Sun	Winter, Miriam T.	68 Van	B R F Tt	
Song Of Daniel	Uhl, Pat	67 Acp	B R L F Tt	
Song Of Praise	Berlucchi, James	75 Wgm	B R L F Tt	
Song Of Thanks	Quinlan, Paul	67 Fel	B R F Tt	
Song Of Thanksgiving	Ducote, Daryll	73 Fcc	B R L F Tt	
Squattin' Little Squillit	Wortley, Howard S.	Mem	F Tt	
Strongest Dream	Mccurdy, E.	50 Alm	F Tt	
Sunrise, Sunset	Bock/Harnick	64 Nyt	F Tt	
Sweet Surrender	Denver, John	74 Clm	F Tt	
Te Deum	Mitchell, Ian	66 Fel	B R F Tt	
Teach Your Children	Nash	70 Grm	F Tt	
Thank The Lord With Songs Of Praise	Hurd, Bob	73 Fel	B R F Tt	
Thank You	Kohl, Jon	73 Fel	B F Tt	
Thank You For Today	Winter, Miriam T.	71 Van	B R F Tt	
Thank You Lord	Davis, Diane	71 Fis	M L F Tt	
Thank You, Jesus	Winter, Miriam T.	67 Van	B R F Tt	
Thanks Be To God	Schaffer, Joe	67 Wlp	B F Tt	
Thanks To Thee	Corda, Mike (Lyrics)	72 Cor	M R F Tt	
Thanksgiving Song	Vissing, Sr. Rosalie	74 Sha	B R L F Tt	
The Circle Game	Mitchell	66 Siq	F Tt	
The First Time Ever	Mccoll	62 Stk	F Tt	
The Flesh Failures	Rado/Ragni/Macdermot	66 Uam	F Tt	
The Lord Be With You	Quinlan, Paul	67 Fel	B L F Tt	
The Morning After	Kasha/Hirshorn	72 Twe	F Tt	
The Search	Stevens, Marsha J.	71 Chd	B R L F Tt	
The Song Is Love	Stooky/Yarrow Et Al	67 Pep	F Tt	
The Song Of Moses (Ex 15)	Pulkingham, Betty C.	72 Gia	B R L F Tt	Var+
The Sound Of Jubilee	Blue, Robert	66 Fel	B F Tt	
The Universe Is Singing	Temple, Sebastian	69 Gia	B R L F Tt	Uguit
The Very Last Day	Yarrow/Stookey	63 Pep	F Tt	
Thou Art Holy	Johnson, Gary L.	74 Bfi	B L F Tt	
To God Be The Glory	Crosby, Doane	Fis	M L F Tt	
Tremble, Tremble Little Earth (Ps 114)	Quinlan, Paul	65 Wlp	B R F Tt	
Try A Little Kindness	Sapaugh, C/Austin, B	69 Bch	F Tt	
We Praise You Every Day	Caesar, Paul (Buddy)	70 Fel	B R F Tt	
We Say Thank You, Lord	Wagner, Lavern J.	74 Sms	M R L F Tt	
We Thank You (In Sunshine & Rain)	Temple, Sebastian	71 Gia	B R L F Tt	Var+
We'll Sing A New Song	Hershberg, Sarah	68 Fel	B R F Tt	
When I Sing	Miffleton, Jack	70 Wlp	B R F Tt	
Where Have All The Flowers Gone?	Seeger, Pete	61 Frm	F Tt	
Where Went The Days	Carter, W./Stevens, M.	73 Chd	B R L F Tt	
Wind Blowing Softly	Jacobs, Hanneke	75 Chd	R L F Tt	
Wonderful	Winter, Miriam T.	72 Van	B R F Tt	
Worthy Is The Lamb	Wyrtzen, Don	Na Zon	M F Tt	Satb
You Have Made Us	Shaltz, Gregory	74 Sms	M R L F Tt	
You've Got A Friend	King	71 Col	F Tt	
Your Love Reaches To The Heavens	Leyko, Patricia J.	76 Chh	B R L F Tt	
A Parade Of Miracles	Gaither/Gaither B/G	72 Gmc	M G Tt	
A Prayer For A Stranger	Oakes, Henry	75 Hhh	M B R G Tt	
Above All Else	Peterson/Carmichael	Na Zon	M G Tt	Satb
Above All Else	Peterson/Johnson	Na Zon	M G Tt	Sab
Adoration	Farrer, Carl	53 Man	B G Tt	Choral
Afterwhile	Mieir, Audrey	68 Man	B G Tt	
All Day Long My Heart Keeps Singing	Dunlop/Decou	Na Zon	M G Tt	Satb
All God's Children	Gaither-Milhuff/Gaithe	72 Gmc	M B R G Tt	Satb
Amen Hallelujah	Dunlop/Decou	Na Zon	M G Tt	Satb
Are You Ready?	Oakes, Henry	75 Hhh	M G Tt	
Blessed Father Great And Good	Fout, R.	74 Csm	M B L G Tt	
Clap Your Hand Children	Kerrick, Mary	75 Wrd	M G Tt	Var+
Come Dance And Sing	Na	Na Gsc	B G Tt	Satb+
Deep Down In My Heart	Clatterbuck/Johnson	Na Zon	M G Tt	Satb
Don't Let The Song Go Out Of Your Hear	Peterson, John W.	Na Zon	M G Tt	Satb
Get All Excited	Gaither/Gaither	72 Gmc	M B R G Tt	Var
Give Him The Glory	Hoffman/Johnson	Na Zon	M G Tt	Satb
Gloria	Atkinson, Condit	74 Gal	M G Tt	Satb
Glory, Hallelujah To The Lamb	Jones/Johnson	Na Zon	M G Tt	Satb
God Is So Good	Akers, Doris	56 Man	M B R G Tt	
God Is So Wonderful	Smith, I/Caldwell, W	75 Sem	R G Tt	
God's For Real Man	Schneider, Kent E.	69 Ccc	M B R L G Tt	
Great Is The Mystery	Williams	Na Zon	M G Tt	
Hallelujah	Amason, B.	74 Sil	R L G Tt	
Hallelujah, I Am Free	Crouch, Andrae	67 Man	R G Tt	

CATEGORIZED INDEX

Hallelujah, Praise The Lord	Spencer, Hal	73 Man	B G Tt	
His Name Is Wonderful	Mieir, Audrey	59 Man	M B R G Tt	
Holy, Holy (American Spiritual)	Follett (Arr)	76 Pro	M G Tt	Satb+
Holy, Holy, Holy	Owens, Jimmy	72 Lex	M R G Tt	
How Big Is God	Akers, Doris	60 Man	M B R G Tt	
How Great Thou Art	Hine, Stuart K.	53 Man	M B R G Tt	Var+
I Came To Praise The Lord	Gaither/Gaither	73 Gmc	M B R G Tt	Var
I Cannot Tell It All	Crouch, Andrae	67 Man	R G Tt	
I Hear Music	Stromberg, V.	Na Zon	M G Tt	Satb
I Just Feel Like Something Good Is	Gaither/Gaither	74 Gmc	M B R G Tt	
I Thank God For Amazing Grace	Smith, John Z.	65 Sto	G Tt	
I Thank My God	Lee, Johnnie	73 Mmc	M G Tt	
I Will Sing	Mieir, Audrey	68 Man	B G Tt	
I'll Sing	Smith/Childs	Na Zon	M G Tt	
I'm Singing For My Lord	Smith/Harper	Na Zon	M G Tt	
I'm So Happy	Mieir, Audrey	65 Man	B G Tt	
I've A Song	Gaither/Gaither B/G	62 Gmc	B G Tt	Satb
In His Name	Howe/Gould	Na Zon	M G Tt	
In My Heart	Peterson, John W.	Na Zon	M G Tt	Satb
In Your Reach	Hale, S.	76 Sil	R G Tt	
It's A Miracle	Gaither/Gaither B/G	75 Gmc	M B R G Tt	Var
It's No Secret	Cockerham, James	75 Sem	R G Tt	
Jesus Gives Me A Song	Grimes/Decou	Na Zon	M G Tt	Satb
Jesus, We Just Want To Thank You	Gaither/Gaither B/G	74 Gmc	M B R G Tt	Var
Joy	Elrich, Dwight (Arr.)	73 Man	M B R G Tt	Choral
Let All The Little Children Praise	Gaither/Gaither B/G	75 Gmc	M B R G Tt	Satb
Let Everything Within Me Cry Holy	Harrel, Melvin (Tr)	63 Gph	M R G Tt	
Let The People Praise	Red, Buryl	73 Wrd	M G Tt	Satb+
Let's Just Praise The Lord	Gaither/Gaither B/G	72 Gmc	M B R G Tt	Var
Melody Divine	Kerr/Boersma	Na Zon	M G Tt	Satb
Mother Take Your Rest	Ramey, Troy	75 Sem	R G Tt	
O For A Thousand Tongues To Sing	Glaser/Wesley/Carmicha	67 Wrd	B R G Tt	Full
Of God I Sing	Hamblen Stuart	Na Ham	M G Tt	
One Big Happy Family	Oakes, Henry	75 Hhh	M G Tt	
Our Thanks To Thee	Chiodo	Na Zon	M G Tt	
Power Medley	Herring, J.	76 Sil	R G Tt	
Praisallujah	Harper, Redd	Na Zon	M G Tt	
Praise Be To Jesus	Gaither/Gaither, G.	75 Gmc	M R G Tt	
Praise For The Lord	Gaither/Gaither	62 Gmc	M B R G Tt	Satb
Praise Him	Cockerham, J Robinson, S	75 Sem	R G Tt	
Praise The Lord	Oakes, Henry	75 Hhh	M G Tt	
Pray! Pray! Pray!	Johnson/Furman	Na Zon	M G Tt	
Reason For Singing, A	Ayers, David	Na Zon	M G Tt	Satb
Rejoice And Sing	Gonzalo, Carrie	69 Man	B G Tt	
Rise-Shine	Spiritual/Lundberg, J.	Na Zon	M G Tt	Satb
Run On	Cockerham, James	75 Sem	R G Tt	
Run On	Ramey, Troy	75 Sem	R G Tt	
Sing Gods Praise	Angell, Warren	75 Wrd	M G Tt	Satb+
Sometimes Alleluia	Girard, Chuck	74 Wrd	B R G Tt	Unis+
St. Matt. 5:16	Myring Charles	72 Jhm	M L G Tt	
Thank The Lord	Mcgill/Gilpin	Na Zon	M G Tt	
Thank The Lord	Oakes, Henry	75 Hhh	M G Tt	
Thank You, Lord	Sykes/Decou	Na Zon	M G Tt	Satb
Thanks For Sunshine	Gaither/Gaither B/G	74 Gmc	M B R G Tt	Var
The Lord Has Satisfied The Longing	Murphy, Charles	69 Gia	B R L G Tt	
The Train Is Gone	Ramey, Troy	75 Sem	R G Tt	
There's A New Song In My Heart	Peterson, John W.	Na Zon	M G Tt	Satb
This Is The Time I Must Sing	Gaither/Gaither B/G	75 Gmc	M R G Tt	
To God Let Praise Be Song	Handel/Lovecace	76 Wrd	M G Tt	Unis+
Trust In Him	Oakes, Henry	75 Hhh	M G Tt	
We'll All Praise God Together	Brandon, George	70 Gia	M G Tt	Udesc
We're Going To Sing	Mayfield, L.	Na Zon	M G Tt	Satb
We've Got A Great Big Wonderful God	Specner, Tim	63 Man	M B R G Tt	
When The Lord Laid His Hand On Me	Smith, I Mccarter, W	75 Sem	R G Tt	
Why Should I Sing Any Other Song?	Martin, Bruce	Na Zon	M G Tt	Satb
Worthy The Lamb	Gaither/Gaither B/G	74 Gmc	M B R G Tt	Satb
You Can Have A Song In Your Heart	Stanphill/Johnson	Na Zon	M G Tt	Satb
You're Gonna Need Somebody	Ramey, Troy	75 Sem	R G Tt	
A Blessing Song	Hurd, Bob	75 Fel	B R L L Tt	
A Canticle Of Thanksgiving (Opt Brs)	Pfautsch, Lloyd	Na Abi	M L Tt	Satb+
A Choral Ascription Of Praise	Marshall, Jane	Na Abi	M L Tt	Satb
A Hymn Of Praise	Pasquet, Jean	72 Hwg	M L Tt	Satb
A Hymn Of Thanks (High Voice)	Baumgartner, H. Leroy	Na Abi	M L Tt	Solo
A Joyful Sound	Misetich, Sr Marianne	76 Rpb	M B R L L Tt	
A Litany Of Thanksgiving	Schroth, G	70 Gia	M L Tt	Litany
A New Song	Copes, V. Earle	Na Abi	M L Tt	Satb
A Song Of Exaltation	Adler, Samuel	Na Abi	M L Tt	Satb
A Song Of Rejoicing	Candlyn, T. Frederick	Na Abi	M L Tt	Satb
A Thanksgiving Service (No 4540)	Fleming, Launa B.	75 Zon	B L Tt	
Adonai, Elohim	Bloch, Ernest	Na Gsc	B L Tt	5mix+
All Blessed Are You, O Lord	Deiss, Lucien	70 Wlp	B R L Tt	
All Creatures Of Our God And King	Bampton, Ruth	Na Abi	M L Tt	Satb
All Creatures Of Our God And King	Lorenz	Na Lor	M L Tt	2mel
All Glory, Laud, And Honor	Wilson	Na Lor	M L Tt	Satb
All Glory, Praise, And Honor	Fitzpatrick, Dennis	65 Fel	B L Tt	
All Honor To You, O Lord	Deiss, Lucien	70 Wlp	B R L Tt	
All Honor, Power To You, O Lord	Deiss, Lucien	70 Wlp	B R L Tt	
All Join Together	Fitzpatrick, Dennis	65 Fel	B L Tt	
All Men On Earth	Westendorf, Omer	70 Wlp	B L Tt	
All My Days	Schutte, Dan & Murray	71 Nal	B R L Tt	
All Of Creation	Shelley, Tom	75 Ahc	B R L L Tt	
All Of My Life	Grace, Sister Mary	67 Fel	B L L Tt	
All Praise To God	Caldwell, M	75 Sac	M L Tt	Satb
All Praise To Our Redeeming Lord	Ford, Virgil	Na Gsc	B L Tt	Satb
All Praise To The Lord Our God	Fitzpatrick, Dennis	65 Fel	B L Tt	
All Praise To You, Lord	Fitzpatrick, Dennis	65 Fel	B L Tt	
All Praise, Glory And Wisdom	Deiss, Lucien	70 Wlp	B R L Tt	
All That Has Life Praise God!	Schneider, Kent E.	69 Ccc	M B R L Tt	
All The Earth	Deiss, Lucien	65 Wlp	B R L Tt	
All The Nations	Mayhew, Kevin & Singers	75 Ahc	M B R L Tt	
All You Angels, Bless The Lord	Fitzpatrick, Dennis	65 Fel	B L Tt	
All You Nations	Deiss, Lucien	65 Wlp	B R L Tt	
Alleluia	Franck, Cesar	Na Lor	M L Tt	Satb
Alleluia	Garlick, Antony	Na See	M L Tt	
Alleluia	Hughes, Robert J.	Na Lor	M L Tt	Satb
Alleluia	Marshall	75 Sac	M L Tt	Sab
Alleluia	Ultan, Lloyd	Na See	M L Tt	
Alleluia	Williams	75 Her	M L Tt	Satb
Alleluia!	Hayes	75 Her	M L Tt	Satb
Alleluia!	Price	Na Lor	M L Tt	Satb
Alleluia! (E)	Hughes, Robert J.	Na Lor	M L Tt	Satb
Alleluia! Alleluia!	Eliot	Na Lor	M L Tt	Satb
Alleluia! In All Things	Peloquin, C Alexander	73 Gia	B L Tt	Var+
Alleluia-Psalm 57	Hurd, Bob	75 Fel	B R L L Tt	
Alleluia, Alleluia	Boyce	75 Her	M L Tt	Satb
Alleluia, Alleluia Blessed Be Our Lord	Deiss, Lucien	70 Wlp	B R L Tt	
Alleluia, Alleluia!	Larowe, Jane	Na Zon	L Tt	Satb
Alleluia, Praise To The Lord	Gutfreund, Ed (Rev.)	74 Nal	B R L Tt	
Almighty God, Which Has Me Brought (Me)	Ford, Thomas	Na Oxf	M L Tt	Satb
Amen, Praise The Lord	Kerner, Debby Melle	72 Mar	R L L Tt	
Arise My Soul, Arise!	Wood, Dale	Na Abi	M L Tt	Satb
Arise, Oh Ye Servants Of God (Me)	Floreen, John	Na Oxf	M L Tt	Satb
As Gentle As Silence	Mayhew, Kevin & Singers	75 Ahc	M B R L Tt	
Ask And You Will Receive	Mayhew, Kevin & Singers	75 Ahc	M B R L Tt	
At The Name Of Jesus	Fitzpatrick, Dennis	65 Fel	B L Tt	
Autumn Song	Mayhew, Kevin & Singers	75 Ahc	M B R L Tt	
Awake, O My Soul	Fitzpatrick, Dennis	65 Fel	B L Tt	
Be Glad And Rejoice	Fitzpatrick, Dennis	65 Fel	B L Tt	
Believing Souls, Rejoice And Sing	Landon	Na Lor	M L Tt	
Benediction	Beck, J N	75 Sac	M L Tt	Satb
Bless The Lord	Hurd, Bob	75 Fel	B R L L Tt	
Bless The Lord (4-Part Arrangement)	Silvia, Helen Trad Rus	67 Acp	B L L Tt	
Bless The Lord, Bless The Lord	Fitzpatrick, Dennis	65 Fel	B R L Tt	
Bless The Lord, O My Soul	Fitzpatrick, Dennis	65 Fel	B L Tt	
Bless The Lord, O My Soul	Young, Gordon	75 Sac	M L Tt	Satb
Bless The Lord, O My Soul (Med Voice)	Jordan, Alice	Na Abi	M L Tt	Solo
Bless Thou The Lord	Pasquet, Jean	62 Aug	M L Tt	Sab
Bless Ye The Lord (D)	Gore, Richard T	75 Abi	M L Tt	Satb
Blessed Are You	Schutte, Dan, S. J.	71 Nal	B R L Tt	
Blessed Are You	Tracy, Shawn (Rev.)	72 Nal	B R L Tt	
Blessed Art Thou	Mead, Edward G.	63 Som	M L Tt	
Blessed Be God	Deiss, Lucien	65 Wlp	B L Tt	
Blessed Be God	Page, Paul F.	75 Rpb	M B R L L Tt	
Blessed Be God	Zsigray, Joe	74 Nal	B R L Tt	
Blessed Be God Forever	Sylvester, Erich	71 Nal	B R L Tt	
Blessed Be God; He Gives Power	Fitzpatrick, Dennis	65 Fel	B L Tt	
Blessed Be Our Lord The God Of Israel	Deiss, Lucien	70 Wlp	B L Tt	
Blessed Be The Holy Trinity	Fitzpatrick, Dennis	65 Fel	B L Tt	
Blessed Be The Lord	Foley, John, S. J.	70 Nal	B R L Tt	
Blessed Be The Lord	Gilligan, M. (Text)	70 Acp	B L L Tt	
Blessed Be The Lord Forever	Newbury, Kent A.	76 Wlp	M L Tt	Satb
Blessed Be The Lord, The God Of Israel	Fitzpatrick, Dennis	65 Fel	B L Tt	
Blessed Be The Name Of The Lord	Anthony, Gregory	75 Rpb	M B R L L Tt	
Blessed Be The Name Of The Lord	Fitzpatrick, Dennis	65 Fel	B L Tt	
Blessed Be The Name Of The Lord	Ford, Virgil	Na Gsc	B L Tt	Satb
Blessed Be You Lord God	Collard, Terry	71 Nal	B R L Tt	
Blessing	Dailey, Joe	75 Ahc	B R L L Tt	
Blessing Over Water	Schoen, Frank (Rev.)	72 Cfc	M L L Tt	
Blest Be The Name Of The Lord	Quinlan, Paul	66 Fel	B L L Tt	
Blow Ye The Trumpet	Gore Richard	76 Abi	M L Tt	Satb+
Cantate Domino (L & E) A Cap	Kreutz, Robert	75 Wlp	M L Tt	Satb
Canticle Of Mary, Magnificat	St. Benedict's Farm	75 Sbf	B R L L Tt	
Canticle Of Praise	Anthony, Dick	Na Zon	L Tt	Satb
Canticle Of The Three Children	Deiss, Lucien	65 Wlp	B L Tt	
Chichester Psalms (First Movement)	Bernstein, Leonard	Na Gsc	B L Tt	Satb+
Children's Hymn Of Praise, The	Rasley	Na Lor	M L Tt	Sa
Choral Service For Thanksgiving, A	Wilson	Na Lor	M L Tt	
Christ Is The Spring	Winberry, Mary	73 Fel	B L Tt	
Christians, Sing Out With Exultation	Wolff, S. Drummond	66 Pic	M L Tt	
Clap Your Hands	Diercks, John	Na Abi	M L Tt	Satb
Clap Your Hands	Moore	75 Her	M L Tt	2mel
Clap Your Hands	Owens, Jimmy	72 Lex	M L Tt	
Come Let Us Tune Our Loftiest Song	Ford, Virgil	Na Gsc	B L Tt	Satb
Come Let's Rejoice (Md)	Amner, John	Na Oxf	M L Tt	Satb
Come Sing, Ye Choirs Exultant	Lewis, John Leo	Na Abi	M L Tt	Satb
Come, Let Us Sing To The Lord	Fitzpatrick, Dennis	65 Fel	B L Tt	
Come, My Soul	Nelson, Ronald A.	76 Aug	L Tt	2-Pt.+
Come, Sing, Praise The Lord	Shelley, Tom	75 Ahc	B R L L Tt	
Come, Sound His Praise Abroad	Burroughs, Bob	Na Zon	L Tt	Satb
Come, Ye That Love The Lord	Smith, Lani	76 Lor	L Tt	Satb+
Come, Your Hearts & Voices Raising	Krapf, Gerhard	68 Aug	M L Tt	Satb+
Creator God, We Give You Thanks	Burroughs	75 Maf	M L Tt	2pt
Cycle Of Holy Songs	Rorem, Ned	55 Som	M L Tt	
Day By Day I Will Sing Your Praise	Fitzpatrick, Dennis	65 Fel	B L Tt	
Declare His Glory	Peterson, John W.	Na Zon	L Tt	Satb
Do You Know?	Mayhew, Kevin & Singers	75 Ahc	M B R L Tt	
Earth With Joy Confesses	Lovelace, Austin C.	75 Sac	M L Tt	Sab
Eternal Father	Gilligan, Michael	73 Acp	B L L Tt	
Eternal Father (4-Part Arr.)	Dykes, John B.	73 Acp	B L L Tt	
Everlasting God	Fabing, Bob	74 Ahc	B R L L Tt	
Exaltation (S A Opt B)	Hadler	Na Lor	M L Tt	Sab
Exult, You Just, In The Lord	Fitzpatrick, Dennis	65 Fel	B L Tt	
Fanfare For A Holy Day	Young, Gordon	75 Sac	M L Tt	Satb
Fanfare For Thanksgiving	Glarum, L Stanley	Na Gsc	B L Tt	Var
Fanfare For The Seasons	Moore	75 Sac	M L Tt	Satb
Father Almighty	Schmal, Desmond	70 Acp	B L L Tt	
Father Almighty (4-Part Arr.)	Wojcik, Richard J.	73 Acp	B L L Tt	
Father, I Adore You	Coelho, Terrye	73 Mar	M R L L Tt	Round
Father, We Adore You	Landry, Carey (Rev.)	75 Nal	B R L Tt	

CATEGORIZED INDEX

Father, We Praise Thee	Pyle, Francis	55 Tcp	M L Tt	
Father, We Thank Thee	Goemanne, Noel	72 Gia	M L Tt	2eq+
For All That Has Been	Landry, Carey (Rev.)	68 Nal	B R L Tt	
For Ever, O Lord	Lewis, John Leo	Na Gsc	B L Tt	Satb+
For Health & Strength	Unknown	73 Mar	B L L Tt	
For The Beauty Of The Earth	Goemanne, Noel	74 Gia	M L Tt	Sab+
Forever His People Adore Him.	Greif, Jean A	65 Vrn	M L L Tt	
Forever I Will Sing	Zsigray, Joe	75 Nal	B R L Tt	
From All Who Dwell Beneath The Skies	Bourgeois, Louis	73 Acp	B L L Tt	
From All Who Dwell Beneath The Skies	Ken, Thomas	67 Acp	B L L Tt	
From The Rising Of The Sun	Herring, Bruce	75 Mar	R L L Tt	
From The Voices Of Children	Blunt, Neil	70 Wlp	B R L Tt	
From Whom All Blessings Flow	Wortley, Howard S.	75 Mem	M L Tt	
Give Praise To The Lord	Deiss, Lucien	65 Wlp	B R L Tt	
Give Praise To The Lord	Peloquin, C Alexander	Na Gia	L Tt	
Give Thanks	Gilsdorf, Sr. Helen	74 Rpb	M B R L L Tt	
Give Thanks To God The Father	Gilligan, Michael	67 Acp	B L L Tt	
Give Thanks To God The Father	Silvia, Helen	73 Acp	B L L Tt	
Give Thanks To The Lord	Gilligan, Michael	70 Acp	B L L Tt	
Give Thanks To The Lord	Roff, Joseph	67 Gia	M L Tt	Var+
Give Thanks To The Lord (4-Part Arr.)	Wurttemberg	73 Acp	B L Tt	
Give Thanks Unto The Lord (Ps. 136)	Starer, Robert	64 Som	M L Tt	
Giver Of All, We Thank Thee	Lovelace, Austin C.	75 Sac	M L Tt	Unis
Glorify The Lord With Me	Deiss, Lucien	65 Wlp	B R L Tt	
Glorious Is Thy Holy Name	Young, Gordon	75 Sac	M L Tt	Satb
Glory	Wood, Mike	76 Rpb	M B R L L Tt	
Glory Above The Heavens	Davis	75 Sac	M L Tt	Satb
Glory And Praise Forever	Zsigray, Joe	74 Nal	B R L Tt	
Glory And Praise To You Eternity	Deiss, Lucien	70 Wlp	B R L Tt	
Glory Be To God On High	Lovelace, Austin C.	Na Abi	M L Tt	Satb
Glory Be To God The Father (Me)	Leaf, Robert	76 Gia	M L L Tt	Satb+
Glory Be To The Father	Lekberg, Sven	Na Gsc	B L Tt	Satb
Glory To God	Powell, Robert J.	Na Abi	M L Tt	Satb
Glory To God In Highest	Deiss, Lucien	70 Wlp	B L Tt	Var
Glory To God In The Highest	Copely, R. Evan	Na Abi	M L Tt	Satb
Glory To God In The Highest (Opt Perc)	Ehret, Walter	76 Pro	M L Tt	Satb+
Glory To God In The Highest, Alleluia	Fitzpatrick, Dennis	65 Fel	B L Tt	
Glory To God On High	Repp, Ray	66 Fel	B R L Tt	
Glory To The Father	Quinlan, Paul	67 Fel	B R L L Tt	
God Be Magnified	Eckler, Greg	74 Man	R L Tt	
God Father, Be Thou Praised	Mytych, J F	Na Gia	L Tt	
God Lives!	Hughes, Robert J.	Na Lor	M L Tt	Satb
God Made Me!	Jothen, M.	75 Bec	M L Tt	
God Of Abraham Praise, The	Gore, Richard T.	Na Abi	M L Tt	Satb
God Of Might, We Praise Thy Name	Pfautsch, Lloyd	Na Abi	M L Tt	Satb
God, Hurrah (Mezzo Sop/Eng Horn/Cello)	Wetzler, Robert	Na Aug	M L Tt	Solo
God, Who Made The Earth	Cram	75 Sac	M L Tt	Sa
Gold For The Sun	Mayhew, Kevin & Singers	75 Ahc	M B R L Tt	
Great And Wonderful Are Thy Deeds	Newbury, Kent A.	75 Sac	M L Tt	Satb
Great Art Thou, O God (M)	Hoddinott, Alun	Na Oxf	M L Tt	Stab
Great Day	Patenaude, Andre, M. S	71 Nal	B R L Tt	
Great God Of Wonders	Peterson, John W.	Na Zon	L Tt	Satb
Great Is The Glory Of The Lord	Peterson, John W.	Na Zon	L Tt	Satb
Great Is The Lord	Unknown	73 Mar	B L L Tt	
Great Is The Lord	Young, Gordon	Na Lor	M L Tt	Satb
Great Jehovah Hear Thy Children's Pray	Slauson, Loyal	Na Zon	L Tt	Satb
Hail To The Lord's Anointed	Lovelace, Austin C.	75 Sac	M L Tt	Satb
Halalujah, Halalu El B'kod'sho	Lewandowski, L	Na Gsc	B L Tt	Satb+
Hallelujah (Psalm 150)	Wise, Judah L.	59 Pic	M L Tt	
Hallelujah! Praise! Selah! (Long)	Gossman/Mozart/Floria	75 Wrd	B R L Tt	Satb+
Hallelujah, Glory Hallelujah	Natalie Sleeth	76 Sac	L Tt	2pt+
Hallelujah, Praise The Lord	Thygerson	75 Her	M L Tt	Satb
Haul Away	Mayhew, Kevin & Singers	75 Ahc	M B R L Tt	-
He Comes Forth	Fitzpatrick, Dennis	65 Fel	B L Tt	
Hear Heaven Thunder	Gilligan, Michael (Tex	70 Acp	B R L L Tt	
Hear Heaven Thunder (4-Part Arr)	Billings, William	73 Acp	B L L Tt	
Hearts And Voices Raise (W/Percussion)	Young, C.	72 Aug	M L Tt	Satb
Heaven And Earth And Sea And Air	Meloy, Elizabeth	Na Abi	M L Tt	Satb
Heavenly Father	Unknown	Mar	B R L L Tt	
His Exaltation	Ives, Charles E.	56 Pic	M L Tt	
His Love Is Lasting (Psalm 136)	Hillebrand, Frank	75 Ahc	B R L L Tt	
His Mercy Endures Forever	Fitzpatrick, Dennis	65 Fel	B L Tt	
Holy God	Silvia, Helen	73 Acp	B L L Tt	
Holy Is The Lord	Baber, John O.	75 Hal	L Tt	Satb
Holy, Holy (Angelic Song)	Smith, Roger	75 Nal	B R L Tt	
Holy, Holy Is The Lord	Quinlan, Paul	67 Fel	B L L Tt	
Holy, Holy, Holy Lord (Hymn)	Temple, Sebastian	71 Gia	B R L L Tt	Satb+
Holy, Thou Art Holy	Kingery, Larry Delray	73 Mar	R L L Tt	
Honor Praise And Glory	Deiss, Lucien	65 Wlp	B R L Tt	
Honor The Lord With What You Have	Fitzpatrick, Dennis	65 Fel	B L Tt	
How Can I Keep From Singing	Gutfreund, Ed (Rev.)	74 Nal	B R L Tt	
How Excellent Is Thy Name	Donato, Anthony	66 Som	M L Tt	
How Good Is God	Blachura, James	75 Rpb	M B R L L Tt	
How Good It Is To Give Thanks To God	Foley, John, S. J.	70 Nal	B R L Tt	
How Great And Good Is He	Gilligan, Michael (Tex	70 Acp	B L L Tt	
How Great And Good Is He (4-Part Arr)	Bach, J. S.	73 Acp	B L L Tt	
How Great Is The Goodness	Fitzpatrick, Dennis	65 Fel	B L Tt	
How Great The Glory	Montague-Cunningham	72 Gra	B R L L Tt	Satb
How Great The Glory (Trinity)	Montague, George T.	72 Mcc	B R L L Tt	Satb
How Lovely Are Your Works	Winberry, M/Roff, J	74 Gia	B L L Tt	
Hymn Of Praise	Landry, Carey (Rev.)	74 Nal	B R L Tt	
Hymn Of Praise	Vernon, Sr. M	Na Gia	L Tt	
Hymn Of Praise: Psalm 135	Catalanello, Michael	76 Str	M L Tt	
Hymn Of Worship	Peterson, John W.	Na Zon	L Tt	Satb
Hymn To The Father	Ellis, Ron	76 Rav	B R L L Tt	
I Am Glad	Zimmermann	69 Aug	M L Tt	
I Bless You, Lord	Fitzpatrick, Dennis	65 Fel	B L Tt	
I Give You Thanks, O Lord	Fitzpatrick, Dennis	65 Fel	B L Tt	
I Praise You, Lord	Fitzpatrick, Dennis	65 Fel	B L Tt	
I Shout With Joy To You	Fitzpatrick, Dennis	65 Fel	B L Tt	
I Sing The Mighty Power Of God	Lipscomb, Helen	Na Gsc	B L Tt	Sab+
I Sing The Mighty Power Of God	Peininer	75 Sac	M L Tt	Satb
I Sing With All My Being	Patterson, Keith	76 Rpb	M B R L L Tt	
I Thank My God	Fabing, Bob	74 Ahc	B R L L Tt	
I Thank Thee, Lord	Copes, V. Earle	Na Abi	M L Tt	Satb
I Thank You, For You Deliver	Fitzpatrick, Dennis	65 Fel	B L Tt	
I Thank You, Lord	Wilkey, Terrence	73 Fel	B L Tt	
I Thank You, O Lord	Fitzpatrick, Dennis	65 Fel	B L Tt	
I Thank You, O Lord My God	Fitzpatrick, Dennis	65 Fel	B L Tt	
I Want To Sing	Deiss, Lucien	65 Wlp	B R L Tt	
I Will Extol Thee	Mead, Edward G.	63 Som	M L Tt	
I Will Give Glory To You	Fitzpatrick, Dennis	65 Fel	B L Tt	
I Will Give Glory To Your Name	Fitzpatrick, Dennis	65 Fel	B L Tt	
I Will Give Thanks	Blachura, James	75 Rpb	M B R L L Tt	
I Will Give Thanks	Diemer	75 Sac	M L Tt	Satb
I Will Magnify Thee (Md)	Gore, Richard T	75 Abi	M L Tt	Satb
I Will Rejoice In The Lord	Fitzpatrick, Dennis	65 Fel	B L Tt	
I Will Sing In The Morning	Lisicky, Paul	76 Rpb	M B R L L Tt	
I Will Sing Of The Lord	Foley, John, S. J.	72 Nal	B R L Tt	
I Will Sing Praise	Patenaude, Andre, M. S	71 Nal	B R L Tt	
I Will Sing Praise To My God	Fitzpatrick, Dennis	65 Fel	B L Tt	
I Will Sing Praise To You	Fitzpatrick, Dennis	65 Fel	B L Tt	
I Will Sing To The Lord	Fitzpatrick, Dennis	65 Fel	B L Tt	
I Will Sing Unto The Lord (Ps 104)	Amner, John	Na Oxf	M L Tt	Satb
I'll Praise My Maker (Opt Brs)	Pfautsch, Lloyd	Na Abi	M L Tt	Satb
I'm Gonna Praise His Name	Unknown	73 Mar	B L L Tt	
I'm Gonna Sing	Unknown	73 Mar	B L L Tt	
Immortal, Invisible	Lorenz, Ellen Jane	Na Abi	M L Tt	Satb
In Heaven Give Glory	Gilligan, Michael	70 Acp	B L L Tt	
In Heaven Give Glory	Wojcik, Richard J.	73 Acp	B L L Tt	
In Him Everything Was Created	Zsigray, Joe	73 Nal	B R L Tt	
In His Shelter	Huijbers & Oosterhuis	73 Nal	B R L Tt	
In Praise To God	Hunnicutt, J.	73 Aug	M L Tt	Satb+
In Thanksgiving I Go Around	Fitzpatrick, Dennis	65 Fel	B L Tt	
In The Mornin'	Shelley, Tom	72 Ahc	B R L L Tt	
In This Quiet Hour	Clark, Lynn	74 Wrd	B R L Tt	Unis+
It Is A Good Thing To Give Thanks	Lekberg, Sven	Na Gsc	B L Tt	Satb
It Is Good To Give Thanks	Berger, Jean	71 Aug	M L Tt	Satb+
It Is Good To Give Thanks	Cunningham, Patrick	76 Gra	B R L L Tt	
It Is Good To Give Thanks	Fitzpatrick, Dennis	65 Fel	B R L Tt	
It Is Good To Give Thanks	Twynham, R. F.	65 Lit	B L Tt	
Joy To Heaven	Deiss, Lucien	65 Wlp	B R L Tt	
Joy, Joy, Joy	Wojtowicz, Elaine	74 Rpb	M B R L L Tt	
Joyful Melody, A	Kirby	Na Lor	M L Tt	2mel
Joyful Psalmody	Mueller	75 Sac	M L Tt	Var
Jubilate	Hovland	66 Aug	M L Tt	Satb
Jubilate Deo	White, Louie	Na Abi	M L Tt	Satb
Jubilate Deo (Ps 100 W/Instruments)	Wood	70 Aug	M L Tt	Satb
Keep Not Thy Silence	Schwadron	75 Sac	M L Tt	Satb
Lauda Anima (Praise, My Soul)	Andrews, Mark	Na Gsc	B L Tt	Var+
Let All On Earth Their Voices Raise	Ford, Virgil	Na Gsc	B L Tt	Satb
Let All On Earth Their Voices Raise	Nachtwey, Roger	65 Fel	B L Tt	
Let All That Is Within Me	Mayhew, Kevin & Singers	75 Ahc	M B R L Tt	
Let All The Earth Rejoice (A Cap)	Harris, Kent	73 Pro	M L Tt	Satb
Let All The World In Every Corner Sing	Lekberg, Sven	Na Gsc	B L Tt	Satb
Let All Who Fear The Lord	Foley, John, S. J.	70 Nal	B R L Tt	
Let All With Sweet Accord	Rogers/White	76 Aug	L Tt	2pt+
Let Earth Rejoice	Ford, Virgil	70 Gsc	B L Tt	Satb
Let Earth Rejoice	Hughes, Howard	72 Gia	M L Tt	Usatb+
Let Every Heart Rejoice	Peterson, John W.	Na Zon	L Tt	Satb
Let God Arise	Gore, Richard	45 Tcp	M L Tt	
Let Heaven Rejoice	Dufford, Bob, S. J.	72 Nal	B R L Tt	
Let Me Sing Of Your Law, O My God	Deiss, Lucien	70 Wlp	B R L Tt	
Let The People Praise Thee	Mcafee, Don	75 Sac	M L Tt	Satb
Let The People Praise Thee	Wright, Bob	62 Gam	M L Tt	Satb
Let The Whole Creation Cry	Leaf, Robert	71 Aug	M L Tt	Sa
Let The Whole Creation Cry Glory (Md)	Boyajian, Gloria	75 Wlp	M L Tt	Satb+
Let Us Acclaim The Rock	Fitzpatrick, Dennis	65 Fel	B L Tt	
Let Us All Rejoice	Toolan, Sr Suzanne	75 Rpb	M B R L L Tt	
Let Us Bless The Lord	Deiss, Lucien	65 Wlp	B R L Tt	
Let Us Exalt Him (W/Opt Tpt, Perc)	Sisler, Hampson	75 Wlp	M L Tt	Satb+
Let Us Sing A New Song Unto The Lord	Arwood/Track	75 Hal	L Tt	Satb
Let Us Sing To The Lord	Emig	Na Lor	M L Tt	Sab
Let Us With A Gladsome Mind	Butler, Eugene	Na Abi	M L Tt	Satb
Let Us With Joy Our Voices Raise	Nachtwey, Roger	65 Fel	B L Tt	
Let Your Faithful Ones Bless You	Fitzpatrick, Dennis	65 Fel	B L Tt	
Lift Up Your Hearts, Ye People	Darst, S. Glen	68 Som	M L Tt	
Litany And Prayer	Kubik, Gail	56 Som	M L Tt	Litany
Litany Of Thanksgiving (W/Brs Etal)	Beck, John	Na Abi	M L Tt	Litany
Lord Dismiss Us With Thy Blessing	Ford, Virgil	Na Gsc	B L Tt	Satb
Lord Gave Me A Song To Sing, The	Vickers, Wendy	75 Nal	B R L Tt	
Lord It Is Good To Give Thanks To You	Zsigray, Joe	72 Nal	B R L Tt	
Lord Of The Worlds Above	Young, Gordon	75 Sac	M L Tt	Satb
Lord Our Lord	Ford, Virgil	Na Gsc	B L Tt	Satb
Lord, Give Them This Day	Billman, Mark	74 Wrd	B R L Tt	Solo+
Lord, We Praise Thee	Medley, Ann	75 Ast	M L Tt	
Lord, We Praise You For The Rhythm	Wetzler, Robert	71 Aug	M L Tt	2pt
Lost In Wonder, Love And Praise	Ford, Virgil	Na Gsc	B L Tt	Satb
Love Is Everlasting	Peloquin, C Alexander	67 Gia	B L Tt	Var+
Magnificat (W/Cont, Viols)	Leo/Bloesch	76 Aug	L Tt	Satb+
Make A Joyful Noise	Fetler, Paul	66 Aug	M L Tt	Satb
Make A Joyful Noise	Hopson	75 Sac	M L Tt	Satb
Make A Joyful Noise	Thygerson	75 Sac	M L Tt	Satb
Matthew 19:17	Rettino, Ernest W.	73 Mar	B L L Tt	
May The God Of Israel	Deiss, Lucien	65 Wlp	B L Tt	
May We Shout For Joy	Fitzpatrick, Dennis	65 Fel	B L Tt	
Miriam's Song	Herbener, Marilyn	74 Rpb	M B R L L Tt	
Monsoon Rain (Psalm 103)	Hillebrand, Frank	75 Ahc	B R L L Tt	
More Than Words	Strange, Joy Deanne	75 Mar	R L L Tt	
Most Glorious Lord Of Life (Me)	Harris, William H.	Na Oxf	M L Tt	Stb

CATEGORIZED INDEX

Title	Composer	Yr Pub	Codes	Voicing
Mountains And Hills	Schutte, Dan, S. J.	71 Nal	B R L Tt	
Mountains Will Sing, The	Gilligan, Michael	70 Acp	B L L Tt	
My Constant Joy	Caldwell, M	75 Sac	M L Tt	Unis
My God	Moultry, Prince Joseph	74 Nal	B R L Tt	
My God, How Wonderful Thou Art	Traditional/Rasley	Na Zon	L Tt	Satb
My God, I Thank Thee	Kirk, Theron	76 Pro	M L Tt	Satb+
My Heart Is Full Today	Proulx, Richard	71 Aug	M L Tt	
My Heart Is Longing To Praise	Sateren, Leland B.	57 Aug	M L Tt	Satb
My Love Song	Cull, Robert	74 Man	M L Tt	Choral
My Soul Doth Magnify	Blumenschein, W L	Na Gsc	B L Tt	Satb+
My Soul Give Thanks	Proulx, Richard	75 Gia	M L Tt	Var+
My Soul Gives Glory To The Lord	Harmonization Fel	67 Fel	B L L Tt	
My Soul Magnifies The Lord	Landry, Carey (Rev.)	75 Nal	B R L Tt	
Nature's Anthem Of Praise	Sullivan	Na Lor	M L Tt	Satb
New Song	Herring, Bruce	73 Mar	R L L Tt	
Not Alone For Mighty Empire	Hoffelt, Robert O.	Na Abi	M L Tt	Ttbb
Not To Us	Huijbers & Oosterhuis	74 Nal	M B R L Tt	
Now Jesus Said	Mayhew, Kevin & Singers	75 Ahc	M B R L Tt	
Now Thank We All Our God	Silvia, Helen	73 Acp	B L L Tt	
Now Thank We All Our God	Winkworth, Catherine	70 Acp	B L L Tt	
Now Will I Praise The Lord	Dietterich, Philip	Na Abi	M L Tt	Solo
O All Ye Works Of The Lord	Fetler, Paul	64 Aug	M L Tt	Satb
O Be Joyful	Hoag, Charles K	Na Gsc	B L Tt	6mix
O Be Joyful In The Lord	Lee	75 Sac	M L Tt	Satb
O Be Joyful In The Lord	Martin, Gilbert M.	76 Her	M L Tt	Satb+
O Bless The Lord	Cram	74 Aug	M L Tt	Satb
O Bless The Lord My Soul	Zsigray, Joe	75 Nal	B R L Tt	
O Blessed Lord (Md)	Crosse, Gordon	Na Oxf	M L Tt	Satb
O Christians Let Us Join In Song	Farrell, Melvin	55 Wlp	B L Tt	
O Clap For Joy!	Burroughs	75 Maf	M L Tt	Satb+
O Clap Your Hands	Mcafee, Don	75 Sac	M L Tt	Satb
O Clap Your Hands	Rohlig	63 Aug	M L Tt	Satb
O Come, Let Us Sing	Traditional/Engel	Na Zon	L Tt	Satb
O For A Thousand Tongues To Sing	Williams, David	66 Som	M L Tt	
O Give Thanks To The Lord	Track, Gerhard	73 Aug	M L Tt	
O Glorify The Lord	Mayhew, Kevin & Singers	75 Ahc	M B R L Tt	
O God O Lord	Lindh	76 Aug	L Tt	Satb+
O God Of All Above, Below	Butler, Eugene	Na Abi	M L Tt	Satb
O God Of All, We Thank You	Johnson, David N	76 Sac	L Tt	Satb+
O God Our Help	Watts, Isaac	70 Acp	B L L Tt	
O God, From Everlasting You Are	Fitzpatrick, Dennis	65 Fel	B L Tt	
O God, O Lord Of Heaven And Earth	Bender, Jan	69 Aug	M L Tt	Satb+
O God, Whose Presence Glows In All	Vick, Beryl Jr	Na Abi	M L Tt	Satb
O Gracious Lord	Huijbers & Oosterhuis	74 Nal	M B L Tt	
O Holy God, O Holy Might God	Fitzpatrick, Dennis	65 Fel	B L Tt	
O Lord Of Hosts	Quinlan, Paul	67 Fel	B L L Tt	
O Lord, From Everlasting	Fitzpatrick, Dennis	65 Fel	B L Tt	
O Lord, I Am In Awe Of Your Power	Fitzpatrick, Dennis	65 Fel	B L Tt	
O Lord, Our God	Schmutz, Albert	Na Abi	M L Tt	Satb
O Lord, Our Lord, How Wonderful	Fitzpatrick, Dennis	65 Fel	B R L Tt	
O Most Holy One And Only	Goemanne, Noel	72 Gia	M L Tt	Var+
O Praise God (Ps 150)	Gilbert, Norman	Na Oxf	M L Tt	Satb
O Praise The Lord	Corbitt	75 Sac	M L Tt	Satb
O Praise The Lord	Gelineau, Joseph	56 Gia	M L Tt	
O Praise The Lord	Mueller, Luise	Na Abi	M L Tt	Satb
O Praise The Lord (W/Brass, Org)	Slater, Richard W.	76 Wlp	M L Tt	Satb
O Sing A New Song	Black	75 Sac	M L Tt	Satb
O Sing All Ye Lands	Berger, Jean	62 Aug	M L Tt	Satb
O Sing The Glories Of Our Lord (Me)	Andrews, H. K.	Na Oxf	M L Tt	Satb
O Sing Unto The Lord	Alexander, Joseph	Na Abi	M L Tt	Satb
O Thank The Lord	Blachura, James	76 Rpb	M B R L L Tt	
O Thou In All Thy Might So Far	Walter	75 Sac	M L Tt	Satb
Oh, Bless The Lord, My Soul	Fitzpatrick, Dennis	67 Fel	B L Tt	
Omnes Gentes, Plaudite	White	75 Sac	M L Tt	2ch
On His Might	Goode, Jack C.	Na Abi	M L Tt	Satb
Open The Door	Peloquin, C Alexander	70 Gia	M L Tt	Satb
Our Father, By Whose Name	Hunnicutt, J.	74 Aug	M L Tt	Sa
Our God Is King (Notre Diev Fst Roi)	Wise, Judah L.	59 Pic	M L Tt	
Paean Of Praise (Church Anniversary)	Rasley, John M.	Na Zon	L Tt	Satb
Picture The Dawning	Page, Paul F.	76 Rpb	M B R L L Tt	
Pleasure It Is (E)	Cope, Cecil	Na Oxf	M L Tt	
Praise	Amann, M. Angelita	74 Rpb	M B R L L Tt	
Praise And Glory Alleluia	Fabing, Bob	70 Ahc	B R L L Tt	
Praise And Supplication	Couper, Alinda B.	Na Abi	M L Tt	Satb
Praise Be To You, O Lord	Fitzpatrick, Dennis	65 Fel	B L Tt	
Praise Book, A	Hazzard, Peter	Na See	M L Tt	
Praise God	Lynch, Michael & Martell	75 Rav	B R L L Tt	
Praise God With Loud Songs	Snell	73 Aug	M L Tt	Satb+
Praise God!	Bock	75 Sac	M L Tt	Satb
Praise Him	Jabusch, Willard F.	75 Rpb	M B R L L Tt	
Praise Him (Psalm 150)	Mckay	72 Aug	M L Tt	Full
Praise Him Now	Peterson, John W.	Na Zon	L Tt	Satb
Praise Our God	Gilligan, Michael	67 Acp	B L L Tt	
Praise Our God	Peterson/Colber-Johnsn	Na Zon	L Tt	Satb
Praise Our God Above (Pentatonic)	Hilty, Everett J	75 Wlp	M L Tt	Sa+
Praise The Father	Shelley, Tom	75 Ahc	B R L L Tt	
Praise The King Of Glory	Englert, Eugene	71 Aug	M L Tt	Satb
Praise The Lord	Amason, B.	74 Sil	R L L Tt	
Praise The Lord	Deiss, Lucien	65 Wlp	B R L Tt	
Praise The Lord	Kirk, Theron	73 Pro	M L Tt	Satb+
Praise The Lord (4-Part Arr)	Silvia, Helen	67 Acp	B L L Tt	
Praise The Lord All Nations	Neff	72 Aug	M L Tt	Satb
Praise The Lord For He Is Good	Manz, Paul	Na Con	B L Tt	Full
Praise The Lord My Soul	Foley, John, S. J.	75 Nal	B R L Tt	
Praise The Lord Of Heaven	Browne, Thomas	67 Acp	B L L Tt	
Praise The Lord Of Heaven	Darst, S. Glen	66 Som	M L Tt	
Praise The Lord Of Heaven (4-Part Arr)	Liturgical Press	73 Acp	B L L Tt	
Praise The Lord Through Every Nation	Slater, Richard	Na Abi	M L Tt	Satb
Praise The Lord Together	Unknown	73 Mar	R L L Tt	
Praise The Lord With Gladness (A Cap)	Unknown (#2815)	75 Pro	M L Tt	Satb
Praise The Lord With Gladness (A Cap)	Wiley	76 Pro	M L Tt	Satb+
Praise The Lord, His Glories Show	Burroughs, Bob	Na Abi	M L Tt	Satb
Praise The Lord, His Glories Show	Krogstad, Bob	75 Zon	L Tt	Satb
Praise The Lord, Now Come	Gilligan, Michael	70 Acp	B L L Tt	
Praise The Lord, Now Come (4-Part Arr)	Cirou, Joseph Et Al	73 Acp	B L L Tt	
Praise The Lord, O My Soul	Butler, Eugene	Na Abi	M L Tt	Satb
Praise The Lord, O My Soul	Ferris, W	Na Gia	L Tt	
Praise The Lord, Sing A Joyful Song	Hadley	76 Pro	M L Tt	Satb
Praise The Lord, Ye Congregation	Parks, Joe E.	Na Zon	L Tt	Satb
Praise The Savior	Darst, S. Glen	66 Som	M L Tt	
Praise To The Lord	Groom, Lester	Na Abi	M L Tt	Satb
Praise To The Lord (4-Part Arr)	Stralsund Gesangbuch	73 Acp	B L L Tt	
Praise To You Now And Evermore	Deiss, Lucien	65 Wlp	B L Tt	
Praise To You, Lord: You Have Given	Fitzpatrick, Dennis	65 Fel	B L Tt	
Praise Ye Jehovah	Agey, C. Buell	Na Abi	M L Tt	Sa-Tb
Praise Ye The Father	Darst, S. Glen	66 Som	M L Tt	
Praise Ye The Lord	Burroughs, Bob	Na Abi	M L Tt	U-Sa
Praise Ye The Lord	Butler, Eugene	Na Abi	M L Tt	Satb
Praise Ye The Lord	Henderson, K & Stovtam	73 Pro	M L Tt	Satb+
Praise Ye The Lord	Koch, Frederick	Na See	M L Tt	
Praise Ye The Lord!	Smith, Herb	Na Zon	L Tt	Satb
Praise Ye The Lord, Ye Children	Proulx, Richard	75 Aug	M L Tt	Unis+
Praise Ye, The Lord	Schneider, Kent E.	75 Ccc	M B R L L Tt	
Praise, Lord!	Landry, Carey (Rev.)	68 Nal	B R L Tt	
Praised Be The Father Of Our Lord	Hilf, Robert	74 Cfc	M L L Tt	
Praising God For Passing Sorrows	Amason, B.	75 Sil	R L L Tt	
Prayer And Praise	Amason, B.	75 Sil	R L L Tt	
Proclaim His Marvelous Deeds	Zsigray, Joe	72 Nal	B R L Tt	
Psalm Of Praise	Hedges, H	Na Gsc	B L Tt	Full+
Psalm Of Praise (Ps 150) W/Brs	Koch, Frederick	76 Wlp	M L Tt	Satb+
Psalm Of Praise, A	Davis, Allan	Na See	M L Tt	
Psalm One Hundred	Peloquin, C Alexander	74 Gia	B L Tt	Satb+
Psalm 100	Verdi, Ralph C. (Rev.)	72 Cfc	M R L L Tt	
Psalm 104 (103)	Tompkins, Thomas	64 Wlp	B L Tt	
Psalm 134, Behold Now, Bless The Lord	Proulx, Richard	73 Gia	M L Tt	Var+
Psalm 136 (135)	Westendorf/Takass	63 Wlp	B L Tt	
Psalm 149	Urquhart, Dan	Na See	M L Tt	
Psalm 150	Goode, Jack C.	Na Abi	M L Tt	Satb
Psalm 150	Jones, D H	Na Gsc	B L Tt	Full+
Psalm 150	Lohr, Al	66 Pic	M L Tt	
Psalm 150	Nabokov, Nicolas	Na See	M L Tt	
Psalm 150	Schutte, Dan, S. J.	69 Nal	B R L Tt	
Psalm 150 (M)	Cabena, Barrie	Na Oxf	M L Tt	Satb
Psalm 150 (Me)	Harper, John	Na Oxf	M L Tt	2pt
Psalm 150: Praise Ye The Lord	Track, Gerhard	Na Gia	L Tt	
Psalm 30	Pisk, Paul A.	54 Pic	M L Tt	
Psalm 34:1	Unknown	73 Mar	B L L Tt	
Psalm 45 (44)	Westendorf/Picca	64 Wlp	B L Tt	
Psalm 67	Pulsifer, Thomas	Na Abi	M L Tt	Satb
Psalm 8	Freed, Isadore	54 Som	M L Tt	
Psalm 97 (98)	Ripellino, D. & Schaef	75 Nal	B R L Tt	
Psalm 98	Warner	75 Sac	M L Tt	Satb
Psalm 98 (Joy To The World)	Nelson	71 Aug	M L Tt	Sa
Rejoice & Sing For Joy	Engler, Eugene	76 Aug	L Tt	Satb+
Rejoice Always In The Lord	Deiss, Lucien	65 Wlp	B R L Tt	
Rejoice And Be Merry (W/Oboe, Org)	Pelz, W.	71 Aug	M L Tt	Satb+
Rejoice Greatly	Petzold	69 Aug	M L Tt	Unis
Rejoice In The Lora	Rickard	Na Aug	M L Tt	Full
Rejoice In The Lord; Rejoice	Fitzpatrick, Dennis	65 Fel	B L Tt	
Rejoice, O Blessed Creation	Track, Gerhard	75 Hal	L Tt	Satb
Rejoice, O Jerusalem	Fitzpatrick, Dennis	65 Fel	B L Tt	
Rejoice, The Lord Is King	Wolff, S. Drummond	66 Pic	M L Tt	
Rejoice, Ye People (W/Insts)	Moe, Daniel	65 Aug	M L Tt	Satb
Rise Up And Sing Praise	Peterson, John W.	Na Zon	L Tt	Satb
Salvation, Glory & Power	Deiss, Lucien	70 Wlp	B R L Tt	
Shout Aloud To Heaven	Gilligan, Michael	70 Acp	B L L Tt	
Shout Aloud To Heaven (4-Part Arr)	Cirou, Joseph	73 Acp	B L L Tt	
Shout For Joy	Neighbor, Ardean	Na Gsc	B L Tt	Satb+
Shout For Joy	Peloquin, C Alexander	71 Gia	B L Tt	Satbu+
Shout For Joy Before The Lord	Neff	74 Aug	M L Tt	Satb
Shout Joyfully!	Landry, Carey (Rev.)	68 Nal	B R L Tt	
Show Forth The Glory	Carolan, Larry	74 Rpb	M B R L L Tt	
Sing A Brand New Song	Hurd, Bob	75 Fel	B R L L Tt	
Sing A New Song	Blachura, James	75 Rpb	M B R L L Tt	
Sing A New Song	Chapman, Keith	76 Her	M L Tt	Satb+
Sing A New Song	Schutte, Dan, S. J.	72 Nal	B R L Tt	
Sing A New Song Unto The Lord	Thygerson	75 Sac	M L Tt	Satb
Sing A Song Of Joy	Powell	64 Aug	M L Tt	2pt
Sing A Song Of Love	Krentel, Jerome	76 Str	M L Tt	
Sing Alleluia Forth	Dickey, Mark	Na Abi	M L Tt	Satb
Sing Brothers, Sing	Ferguson	75 Sac	M L Tt	Satb
Sing Gloria	Hunnicutt, J.	72 Aug	M L Tt	Sa
Sing Hallelujah	Stassen, Linda	74 Mar	R L L Tt	
Sing Joyfully To The Lord (Me)	Toolan, Sr Suzanne	75 Gia	M L L Tt	Satb+
Sing Of Him	Dufford, Bob, S. J.	73 Nal	B R L Tt	
Sing Praise	Page, Paul F.	76 Rpb	M B R L L Tt	
Sing Praise To God	Darst	75 Sac	M L Tt	Satb
Sing Praise To God Who Reigns Above	Mudde	58 Aug	M L Tt	Sab
Sing Praise!	Landry, Carey (Rev.)	71 Nal	M B R L Tt	
Sing To Him	Newbury, Kent A.	75 Her	M L Tt	Satb
Sing To Him Of Praise Eternal	Englert, Eugene	76 Gia	M L L Tt	Satb+
Sing To The Lord	Deiss, Lucien	70 Wlp	B R L Tt	
Sing To The Lord	Foley, John, S. J.	70 Nal	B R L Tt	
Sing To The Lord	Goode, Jack C.	Na Abi	M L Tt	Satb
Sing To The Lord (4-Part Arr)	Van Koert, Han	70 Acp	B L L Tt	
Sing To The Lord A New Song	Fitzpatrick, Dennis	65 Fel	B L Tt	
Sing To The Lord With Cheerful Voice	Young, Gordon	75 Sac	M L Tt	Satb
Sing Unto God	Fetler, Paul	59 Aug	M L Tt	Satb
Sing Unto The Lord A New Song	Mcafee, Don	75 Sac	M L Tt	Satb
Sing Unto The Lord A New Song	Stern	74 Aug	M L Tt	Satb

CATEGORIZED INDEX

Sing We Merrily (Ps 81)	Carpenter, Adrian	Na Oxf	M L Tt	Ssatb
Sing We Merrily (W/Brass, Org)	Proulx, Richard	71 Aug	M L Tt	Satb+
Sing We Merrily To God	Freestone	75 Sac	M L Tt	Satb
Sing We Merrily Unto God Our Strength	Hoag, Charles K	Na Gsc	B L Tt	Satb+
Sing With Joy To God	Fitzpatrick, Dennis	65 Fel	B L Tt	
Sing With Joy To God Our Strength	Fitzpatrick, Dennis	65 Fel	B L Tt	
Sing Ye Joyfully To The Lord	Young	66 Aug	M L Tt	Sa
Sing Ye Praises (W/Clavier/Rhythm)	Lovelace, Austin C.	74 Aug	M L Tt	Unis+
Sing, All Ye People	Miller, Thomas A.	Na Zon	L Tt	Satb
Sing, Men And Angels, Sing	Near, Gerald	69 Aug	M L Tt	Var
Sing, O Heavens (Md)	Amner, John	Na Oxf	M L Tt	Full
Singer Of The Universe	Butler, Eugene	Na Abi	M L Tt	Satb
Singers, Sing	Silvia, Helen	73 Acp	B L L Tt	
Singing Alleluia	Leaf, Robert	65 Aug	M L Tt	Unis
Solomon's Canticle	Iannaccone, Anthony	Na See	M L Tt	
Song Of Blessing	Wise, Joe	75 Nal	B R L Tt	
Song Of Daniel	Peloquin, C Alexander	Na Gia	L Tt	
Song Of Praise	Lipscomb, Helen	Na Gsc	B L Tt	2eq+
Song Of Praise (W/Perc)	Nystedt, Knut	75 Aug	M L Tt	Full
Song Of Thankfulness	Schneider, Kent E.	69 Ccc	M B R L L Tt	
Song Of Thanksgiving	Zsigray, Joe	73 Nal	B R L Tt	
Song Of Zachary	Nachtwey, Roger	65 Fel	B L Tt	
Song Of Zachary	Peloquin, C Alexander	Na Gia	L Tt	
Te Deum	Leonard, Clair	49 Tcp	M L Tt	
Te Deum	Polin, Claire	Na See	M L Tt	
Te Deum (Icet) W/ Organ (Me)	Peloquin, C Alexander	76 Gia	B L L Tt	2pt
Te Deum (You Are God: We Praise You)	Langlais, Jean	74 Cfc	M R L L Tt	
Te Deum Jubilar	Bernal Jimenez, Miguel	47 Som	M L Tt	Span
Te Deum Laudamus (Eng, Org, Guit)	Pulkingham, Betty C.	73 Gia	B R L L Tt	Satb+
Thank The Lord	Fabing, Bob	70 Ahc	B R L L Tt	
Thank You Jesus	Jones, Gary	75 Mar	R L L Tt	
Thanks Be To God.	Greif, Jean A	65 Vrn	M L L Tt	
Thanks Be To Thee, O God	Stuntz	75 Wlp	B L Tt	
Thanksgiving	Champagne, Claude	66 Pic	M L Tt	
Thanksgiving Hymn (Give Thanks To God)	Isele, David C.	74 Gia	B L L Tt	Satb+
Thanksgiving Litany	Murphy, Angela	76 Rpb	M B R L L Tt	Litany
Thanksgiving Song	Sydeman, William	Na See	M L Tt	
The Heavens Proclaim His Justice	Fitzpatrick, Dennis	65 Fel	B L Tt	
The Heavens Proclaim Your Wonders	Fitzpatrick, Dennis	65 Fel	B L Tt	
The Just Man Rejoices	Fitzpatrick, Dennis	65 Fel	B L Tt	
The Lord Bless Thee And Keep Thee	Smith, Gregg	Na Gsc	B L Tt	Sa+
The Lord Reigneth (Ps 99)	Mckinney, James C.	63 Gam	M L Tt	Satb
The Morning Sun	Williams, J.	76 Sil	L Tt	
The Praises Of A King	Lovelace, Austin C.	68 Aug	M L Tt	2pt
The Song Of David (1 Ck 29)	Guenther, Ralph R.	73 Pro	M L Tt	Satb+
There Is A World	Mayhew, Kevin & Singers	75 Ahc	M B R L Tt	
There Is None Like Him	Rivers, Clarence Jos.	Na Hol	M R L Tt	
They That Go Down To The Sea In Ships	Lawrence, Burton	Na Zon	L Tt	Satb
Thou Art My God (Ps 118-9) W/Tpts	Newbury, Kent A.	75 Wlp	M L Tt	Satb+
Thou O God Art Praised In Zion (Md)	Hare, Ian	Na Oxf	M L Tt	Satb
Time For Singing Has Come, The	Jordan, Alice	Na Abi	M L Tt	Unis
To Deum Laudamus	Proulx, Richard	75 Aug	M L Tt	Satb
To God Be The Glory (Opt Brass)	Brown, Leon F.	62 Smc	M L Tt	Satb
To God We Sing A New Song	Gilligan, Michael	70 Acp	B L L Tt	
To God We Sing A New Song (4-Part Arr)	Cirou, Joseph	73 Acp	B L L Tt	
To The Living God	Page, Paul F.	74 Rpb	M B R L L Tt	
To Thee Be Glory	Foley, John, S. J.	72 Nal	B R L Tt	
To You We Owe Our Hymn	Fitzpatrick, Dennis	65 Fel	B L Tt	
Trio Of Praise	Koch, Frederick	Na See	M L Tt	
Trumpeters And Singers Were As One	Powell, Robert J.	Na Abi	M L Tt	Satb
Two Holy Songs (Ps. 134, Ps. 150)	Rorem, Ned	55 Som	M L Tt	
Unto Thee Do We Cry	Graves, William	69 Smc	M L Tt	Ssa
Upon My Lips	Deiss, Lucien	65 Wlp	B R L Tt	
We Give You Thanks	Deiss, Lucien	70 Wlp	B L Tt	
We Give You Thanks, We Worship You	Deiss, Lucien	70 Wlp	B R L Tt	
We Magnify Our Father God	Peterson, John W.	Na Zon	L Tt	Satb
We Praise Thee, O God	Lipscomb, Helen	Na Gsc	B L Tt	2eq+
We Praise You Above All Forever	Fitzpatrick, Dennis	65 Fel	B L Tt	
We Praise You, O God	Fitzpatrick, Dennis	65 Fel	B L Tt	
We Praise You, O Lord	Fitzpatrick, Dennis	65 Fel	B L Tt	
We Rejoice And Adore You, O God	Fitzpatrick, Dennis	65 Fel	B L Tt	
We See The Lord	Byrne, James E	73 Jeb	M R L L Tt	
We Sing His Praise	Fitzpatrick, Dennis	65 Fel	B L Tt	
We Thank Thee	Peterson/Decou	Na Zon	L Tt	Satb
We Thank You	Wehr, David A.	Na Abi	M L Tt	Unis
We Thank You, O Lord	Fitzpatrick, Dennis	65 Fel	B L Tt	
We Will Celebrate	Zsigray, Joe	74 Nal	B R L Tt	
We Will Offer Praises To God	Fitzpatrick, Dennis	65 Fel	B L Tt	
What Great Marvels	Gilsdorf, Sr. Helen	75 Rpb	M B R L L Tt	
Where Has Your Lover Gone	Lynch, Michael B.	73 Rav	B L L Tt	
With A Joyful Heart	Deiss, Lucien	70 Wlp	B R L Tt	
With A Jubilant Song (Piano, Org, Tpt, Ti)	Leaf, Robert	71 Aug	M L Tt	Satb+
With A Voice Of Singing	Jennings, K.	64 Aug	M L Tt	Satb
With Cries Of Joy I Shout	Fitzpatrick, Dennis	65 Fel	B L Tt	
With Happy Voices Ringing	Staton, Kenneth	Na Abi	M L Tt	Unis
With Hearts Full Of Joy	Landry, Carey (Rev.)	68 Nal	B R L Tt	
With Joyful Lips, O Lord	Deiss, Lucien	65 Wlp	B R L Tt	
With Merry Dancing	Schutte, Dan, S. J.	71 Nal	B R L Tt	
With Words Of Praise	Deiss, Lucien	70 Wlp	B R L Tt	
Within Your Splendor	Deiss, Lucien	70 Wlp	B R L Tt	
Without Seeing You, We Love You	Deiss, Lucien	70 Wlp	B R L Tt	
Wonderful And Great	Deiss, Lucien	65 Wlp	B R L Tt	
Wonderful World	Eckler, Greg	74 Man	R L Tt	
Worship The Lord	Fitzpatrick, Dennis	65 Fel	B L Tt	
Worthy Is The Lamb	Dufford, Bob, S. J.	72 Nal	B R L Tt	
Yahweh Is A Saving Lord (Ps. 86)	Smith, Roger	75 Nal	B R L Tt	
Yahweh, Our God	Shelley, Tom	71 Ahc	B R L L Tt	
Ye Lands To The Lord	Pooler, Marie	56 Aug	M L Tt	Satb+
You Alone Are Holy	Deiss, Lucien	70 Wlp	B R L Tt	
You Are Blessed And Worthy	Fitzpatrick, Dennis	65 Fel	B L Tt	
You Are My God	Huijbers & Oosterhuis	74 Nal	M B L Tt	
You Are So Great, O God	Fitzpatrick, Dennis	65 Fel	B L Tt	
You Come As He	Fabing, Bob	74 Ahc	B R L L Tt	
You Have Favored Your Land	Fitzpatrick, Dennis	65 Fel	B L Tt	
You Have Made Children And Babes	Fitzpatrick, Dennis	65 Fel	B L Tt	
You're A Gift	Stevens, Russ	73 Chd	B R L L Tt	
You've Gotta Have What It Takes	Collard, Terry	71 Nal	B R L Tt	
Your Almighty Word, O Lord	Fitzpatrick, Dennis	65 Fel	B L Tt	
Your Name O Lord	Zsigray, Joe	74 Nal	B R L Tt	
Your Song That I Sing	Sylvester, Erich	74 Nal	B R L Tt	
Your Word, O Lord, Endures	Fitzpatrick, Dennis	65 Fel	B L Tt	
Zion Said	Ehret, Walter	Na Abi	M L Tt	Satb

A Choral Flourish (From Ps 33) (Md)	Williams, Vaughan R.	Na Oxf	M T Tt	Satb
A Hymn Of Praise (W/Org, Violins)	Couperin (Arr Jewell)	75 Wlp	M T Tt	Sab+
A Pages Road Song	Byles, B D	Na Gsc	B T Tt	Unis+
A Psalm Of Thanksgiving (Ps 145 & 104)	Darke, Harold	Na Oxf	M T Tt	Satb
A Seasonal Thanksgiving	Thiman, Eric H.	Na Gsc	B T Tt	Unis+
A Song Of Thanksgiving	Williams, Vaughan R.	Na Oxf	B T Tt	Satb
A Thanksgiving Day Ode	Woodman, R. H.	Na Gsc	B T Tt	Satb+
Above All Praise And Majesty (Me)	Mendelssohn, F.	Na Oxf	M T Tt	Full
Ad Cantus, Ad Choros	Biechteler, M S	Na Gsc	B T Tt	5mix+
Adoramus	Brahms, Johannes	54 Bbl	B T Tt	Ssaa
Adoramus Te (We Adore Thee)	Brahms, Johannes	Na Gsc	B T Tt	Ssaa
Adore And Be Still (C)	Gounod, Charles	Na Lor	M T Tt	Sa+
All Breathing Life	Bach, J. S.	Na Gsc	B T Tt	Satb
All Creatures Of Our God And King	Shaw	Na Gsc	B T Tt	Full
All From The Sun's Uprise	Tomblings, Philip	Na Oxf	M T Tt	Sab
All Glory Be To God On High	Praetorius, M.	Na Aug	M T Tt	Full
All Glory Laud & Honor (E)	Bach, J. S.	Na Oxf	M T Tt	S-Satb
All Glory Love And Power To Thee	Beethoven, L. (Douglas)	74 Pro	M L T Tt	3pt
All Glory To Jesus	Peterson/Mickelson	Na Zon	T Tt	Satb
All Glory, Laud, And Honor	Teschner/Decou	Na Zon	M T Tt	Satb
All Glory, Praise And Majesty	Bach, J. S.	Na Gsc	B T Tt	Ttbb+
All Hail The Power	Mueller, Carl F	Na Gsc	B T Tt	Satb+
All Hail The Power	Shrubsole (Arr Cartfor	53 Aug	M T Tt	Satb
All Lands And Peoples	Lovelace, Austin C.	64 Aug	M T Tt	2pt
All My Heart This Night Rejoices	Pooler, Marie	59 Aug	M T Tt	U+Ds
All Nature's Works His Praise Declare	Ehret, Walter	Na Lor	M T Tt	Satb
All People Clap Your Hands (Md)	Weelkes, Thomas	Na Oxf	M T Tt	Saatb
All People That On Earth Do Dwell	Bach, J. S.	Na Gsc	B T Tt	Satb+
All People That On Earth Do Dwell	Bourgeois/Johnson	Na Zon	T Tt	Full
All Praise And Thanks To God	Agey, C. Buell	Na Abi	M T Tt	Satb
All Praise To God, In Light Arrayed	Wagner, R.	Na Gsc	B T Tt	Satb+
All Praise To Our Redeeming Lord	Peninger, David	Na Gsc	B T Tt	Satb+
All Praise To Thee	Bach, J. S.	Na Aug	M T Tt	Satb
All Praise To Thee	Mueller, Carl F	Na Gsc	B T Tt	Satb+
All Praise To Thee	Tallis, Thomas	Na Gsc	B T Tt	Satb+
All Praise To Thee (Canon)	Tallis, Thomas	62 Aug	M T Tt	Var
All Things Are Thine	Darst	75 Sac	M T Tt	Satb
All Thy Works Shall Praise Thee (E & W)	Mathias, William	Na Oxf	M T Tt	Satb
Alla Trinite	Burney	Na Gsc	B T Tt	Satb
Alleluia	Christiansen, P.	70 Aug	M T Tt	Satb
Alleluia	Lekberg, Sven	75 Bbl	M T Tt	Satb
Alleluia	Obrecht, J	74 Gia	M T Tt	Fugue
Alleluia	Zaumeyer	Na Wbp	T Tt	
Alleluia Psallat	Hughes-Grainger	Na Gsc	B T Tt	Var
Alleluia Psallat (Alleluia Let Us Sing)	Grainger, P A	Na Gsc	B T Tt	Var+
Alleluia To The Lord Of Being	Fast, Willard S	Na Gsc	B T Tt	Satb
Alleluia!	Mozart, Wolfgang A	Na Lor	M T Tt	Sa
Alleluia! Hearts And Voices	Pasquet, Jean	Na Gsc	B T Tt	Satb+
Alleluia, Praise God	Scarlatti-Coggin	74 Aug	M T Tt	Satb
Alleluia, Rejoice & Sing (Piano + Perc)	Avalos (Arr)	75 Pro	M T Tt	3pt+
Alleluia, Sing A New Song	Gallus-Weldy	64 Aug	M T Tt	Full
Almighty And Everlasting God (Me)	Gibbons, Orlando	Na Oxf	M T Tt	Satb
Almighty God	Pedrette, Edward A	Na Gsc	B T Tt	Satb+
Almighty God, Who By Thy Son (Md)	Gibbons, Orlando	Na Oxf	M T Tt	Full
Amen, Amen My Lord (Opt Rhythm)	Ehret, Walter	76 Pro	M T Tt	Satb+
And Thou Shalt Love	Diercks, John	Na Abi	M T Tt	Satb
Angel's Chorus	Jenkins, Cyril	Na Gsc	B T Tt	Satb+
Angels Worship God In Heaven	Peterson, John W.	Na Zon	T Tt	Satb
Animation	Anonymous	75 Bbl	B T Tt	2pt
Anthem For A Harvest Festival (Me)	Ley, Henry G.	Na Oxf	M T Tt	Satb
Anthem For Thanksgiving, An	Billings, William	76 Bbl	M T Tt	Satb
Arise, My Soul, Arise!	Traditional/Decou	Na Zon	T Tt	Satb
Awake The Harp	Haydn, Joseph	Na Gsc	B T Tt	Satb+
Awake, Arise, Go Forth And Rejoice	Leaf, Robert	69 Aug	M T Tt	Unis
Balulalow	Cockshott, Gerald R.	57 Ron	M T Tt	
Be As A Lion	Hanson/Watson	Na Wbp	T Tt	
Be Glad	Fritschel	74 Aug	M T Tt	Full
Be Joyful!	Brandon, George	75 Sac	M T Tt	Unis
Be Thou Exalted	Handel, G.F./Douglas	75 Pro	M R T Tt	Satb+
Be Ye Glad And Rejoice O Ye Righteous	Coggin, Elwood	Na Gsc	B T Tt	Satb+
Be Ye Joyful, Earth And Sky	Bender, Jan	63 Aug	M T Tt	Satb
Before Jehovah's Awful Throne	Madan/Brandon	75 Pro	M T Tt	Satb+
Before The Lord Jehovah's Throne	Droste, Doreen	Na Abi	M T Tt	Satb
Begin, My Tongue, Some Heavenly Theme	Greatorex/Peterson	Na Zon	T Tt	Satb
Benedicite (Eng)	Williams, Vaughan R.	Na Oxf	B T Tt	Satb
Benedicite (Md)	Purcell, Henry	Na Oxf	M T Tt	Var
Benedicite In G (Md)	Jackson, Francis	Na Oxf	M T Tt	Satb
Benedicite, Omnia Opera	Sheppard, J Stanley	Na Gsc	B T Tt	Satb+
Benedicite, Omnia Opera Domini	Shephard	70 Gsc	M T Tt	Satb+
Benedictus Sit Deus K 117	Mozart, Wolfgang A	Na Kal	B T Tt	Satb
Benedixisti Domine	Gabrieli, G	Na Gsc	B T Tt	7mix+
Bless Now O Lord	Crotch, Dr William	Na Gsc	B T Tt	Sab+
Bless The Lord, O My Soul	Currie, Randolph	74 Bec	M T Tt	
Bless The Lord, O My Soul	Ippolitov-Ivanov, M	Na Gsc	B T Tt	Var
Bless The Lord, O My Soul	Ippolitov/Ivanov	70 Gia	M T Tt	Satb
Bless The Lord, O My Soul	Newbury, Kent A.	75 Wlp	M T Tt	Satb+
Bless The Lord, O My Soul (A Cap)	Ippolitoff-Ivanoff	Hof	M T Tt	Satb

Bless The Lord, O My Soul (Md)	Mathias, William	Na Oxf	M	T Tt	Satb
Bless The Lord, O My Soul (Me)	Gibbs, C. Armstrong	Na Oxf	M	T Tt	2pt
Blessed Art Thou, O Lord (Md)	Willan, Healey	Na Oxf	M	T Tt	Satb
Blessed Be The Lord	Gibbons, Orlando	Na Gsc	B	T Tt	Satb+
Blessing (Thanksgiving Or Gen)	Curran, P G	Na Gsc	B	T Tt	Var+
Blessing And Honor	Blake, George	Na Gsc	B	T Tt	Satb+
Blessing And Honor, Praise And Love	Brahms, Johannes	74 Gia	M	T Tt	Satb
Blessing Of The Trinity	Pasquet, Jean	Na Gsc	B	T Tt	Satb+
Blow Ye The Trumpet In Zion	Jackson, Francis	Na Oxf	M	T Tt	Satb
Bonum Est Confiteri	Palestrina, Giovanni P	Na Gsc	B	T Tt	5mix
Break Forth Into Joy	Hopson	75 Sac	M	T Tt	Satb
Break Forth Into Joy	Newbury, Kent A.	Na Gsc	B	T Tt	Satb+
Break Forth Into Joy	Simper, C	Na Gsc	B	T Tt	Satb+
Can't You Hear?	Price	Na Lor	M	T Tt	Satb
Canaan	Anonymous	75 Bbl	M	T Tt	Satb
Canon Alleluia (From Motet Exultate)	Mozart, Wolfgang A	76 Pro	M	T Tt	Ssa+
Cantabo Domino	Lewkovitch, Bernhard	Na Gsc	B	T Tt	Satb
Cantata #11 Lobet Gott (Eng/Germ)	Bach, J. S.	Na Kal	B	T Tt	Satb
Cantata #190 Sing To The Lord (E & Ger)	Bach, J. S.	Na Kal	B	T Tt	Satb
Cantata #28 Gottlob (Eng/Germ)	Bach, J. S.	Na Kal	B	T Tt	Satb
Cantata #79 The Lord Is A Sun (E & Ger)	Bach, J. S.	Na Kal	B	T Tt	Satb
Cantate Domini (Psalm 96)	Buxtehude, D.	Na Kal	B	T Tt	Satb
Cantate Domino	Conte, D. (Arr)	75 Bec	M	T Tt	
Cantate Domino	Hassler, H L	Na Gsc	B	T Tt	Ssaa
Cantate Domino	Pitoni, G/Ed Lee	75 Gia	M	T Tt	Satb
Cantate Domino	Pitoni, Giuseppe O	Na Gsc	B	T Tt	Satb
Cantate Domino	Schutz, Heinrich	Na Gsc	B	T Tt	Satb
Cantate Domino (O Sing Unto The Lord)	Anerio, Giovanni F	Na Gsc	B	T Tt	Satb
Cantate Domino (Ps 149)	Byrd, William	Na Oxf	M	T Tt	Full
Cantate, Domini Canticum Novum	Schutz, Heinrich	Na Kal	B	T Tt	Satb
Canticle Of Mary	Glarum, L Stanley	Na Gsc	B	T Tt	Var+
Canticle Of Praise, A	Rasley	Na Lor	M	T Tt	Satb
Cantique De Jean Racine	Faure, Gabriel	52 Bbl	M	T Tt	Satb
Carol Of Beauty (Md)	Sargent, Malcolm	Na Oxf	M	T Tt	Full
Chandos Anthem 1 (Be Joyful)	Handel, G. F.	Na Kal	B	T Tt	Satb
Chandos Te Deum (We Praise Thee)	Handel, G. F.	Na Kal	B	T Tt	Satb
Cherubim Song	Glinka, M	Na Gsc	B	T Tt	Full
Cherubim Song (A Cap)	Tschesnokoff-Cain	Hof	M	T Tt	Satb
Cherubim-Song	Bortniansky, D S	Na Gsc	B	T Tt	Var
Chorale Concertato On Praise The Lord	Manz, Paul	75 Con	B	T Tt	Ubr
Clap Your Hands	Christiansen, F. M.	32 Aug	M	T Tt	Satb
Clap Your Hands	Kerr, Phil	48 Gph	M	T Tt	
Clap Your Hands Ye People	Kiplinger	70 Gsc	M	T Tt	4pt+
Clap Your Hands, Stamp Your Feet	Nelson, Ronald A.	71 Aug	M	T Tt	Unis
Closing Doxology, The (Psalm 150)	Lockwood, Normand	52 Bbl	B	T Tt	Satb+
Come Let Us Sing	Mendelssohn, F.	Na Gsc	B	T Tt	Satb+
Come Let Us Worship	Proskinisomen, D	72 Gia	M	T Tt	Satb
Come Sound His Praise Abroad	Ford, Virgil	Na Gsc	B	T Tt	Satb
Come Ye Faithful, Raise The Strain	George	66 Aug	M	T Tt	Sa
Come Ye Faithful, Raise The Strain	Lindeman-Sateren	54 Aug	M	T Tt	Satb+
Come, Children, Praise Our Lord	Haydn, Michael	Na Gsc	B	T Tt	Ssa+
Come, Christians, Join To Sing	Traditional/Decou	Na Zon		T Tt	Satb
Come, Let Us Praise The Lord	Roff, Joseph	Na Gia		T Tt	
Come, My Spirit (Cantata)	Bach, J. S.	75 Lps	B R	T Tt	Satb
Come, Sing	Leaf, Robert	66 Aug	M	T Tt	Satb+
Come, Sing A Song Unto The Lord	Ayers, David	Na Zon		T Tt	Satb
Come, Sound His Praise Abroad	Harris, Kent	73 Pro	M	T Tt	Satb
Come, Thou Almighty King	De Giardin/Johnson	Na Zon		T Tt	Satb
Complainer	Ingalls, Jeremiah	75 Bbl	B	T Tt	Ttb
Concordi Laetitia (In 19 Rounds)	French/Tortolano Ed	75 Gia	B L	T Tt	2pt
Coronation Te Deum	Walton, William	Na Oxf	R	T Tt	Satb
Day Of Rejoicing (W/Trumpets)	Pelz, W.	69 Aug	M	T Tt	Satb
Deck, Thyself, My Soul, With Gladness	Handel, G. F.	Na Gsc	B	T Tt	Satb+
Dettingen Te Deum	Handel, G. F.	Na Kal	B	T Tt	Satb
Doxology (Hurrah To God)	Wetzler, Robert	70 Aug	M	T Tt	Unis
En Son Temple Sacre (Psalm 150)	Mauduit, Jacques	67 Bbl	M	T Tt	Ssatb
Eternal Trinity	Trued, Clarence	Na Gsc	B	T Tt	Satb
Exalt The Name Of The Lord	Butler	75 Her	M	T Tt	Sa
Exalt Ye	Glarum, L Stanley	Na Gsc	B	T Tt	Satb
Excelsus Super Omnes Gentes Dominus	Pergolesi, G B	Na Gsc	B	T Tt	Satb+
Exsultate Deo	Palestrina, Giovanni P	Na Gia		T Tt	
Exsultate Jubilate K 165	Mozart, Wolfgang A	Na Kal	B	T Tt	Satb
Exsultate Justi	Viadana, L	Na Gia		T Tt	
Exultate Deo	Najera, Edmund	Na Gsc	B	T Tt	Satb+
Exultate Deo	Palestrina, Giovanni P	Na Gsc	B	T Tt	Saatb
Exultate Deo	Scarlatti, Alessandro	Na Gsc	B	T Tt	Satb
Father, We Praise Thee	Jennings, C.	67 Aug	M	T Tt	Ssa
Father, We Praise Thee	Matthews, H A	Na Gsc	B	T Tt	Satb+
Father, We Praise Thee	Smith	Na Lor	M	T Tt	
Fear God & Give Glory To Him	Dieterich, Milton	58 Smc	M	T Tt	Satb
Fear Not, O Land	Rogers, J H	Na Gsc	B	T Tt	Satb+
Fecit Potentium	Senfl/Guettler	Wbp		T Tt	
Festival Anthem, Op. 109 No.3	Brahms, Johannes	Cfp	R	T Tt	Full
Festival Anthem, Op. 109 No. 1	Brahms, Johannes	Cfp	R	T Tt	Full
Festival Anthem, Op. 109 No.2	Brahms, Johannes	Cfp	R	T Tt	Full
Festival Hymn	Christiansen, P.	52 Aug	M	T Tt	Satb
Festival Hymn	Mendelssohn, F.	53 Bbl	M	T Tt	Satb
Festival Te Deum (Md)	Mathias, William	Na Oxf	M	T Tt	Satb
Festival Te Deum (On Trad. Themes)	Williams, Vaughan R.	Na Oxf	M	T Tt	Satb
Festival Te Deum No. 7	Buck, Dudley	Na Gsc	B	T Tt	Satb+
Fidelio	Lewer	75 Bbl	B	T Tt	Ttb
Fioucia From Three Folk Hymns	Robison	75 Bbl	B	T Tt	Sb+
Firmament Of Power	Davis, K.K.	Na Wbp		T Tt	
Follow Me	Infante, Guy	74 Sms	M R L	T Tt	
For The Beauty Of The Earth	Kocher/Davis, K.K.	Na Wbp		T Tt	
For The Beauty Of The Earth	Kocher/Decou	Na Zon		T Tt	Satb
For The Beauty Of The Earth	Kocher, C	Na Gsc	B	T Tt	Full+
Forever, O Lord (Ps 8)	Maunder, J. H.	73 Pro	M	T Tt	Satb
From All That Dwell Below The Skies	Grieb, Herbert	Na Gsc	B	T Tt	Satb+
From All That Dwell Below The Skies	Rasley, John M.	Na Zon		T Tt	Satb
From Glory To Glory Advancing	Humphries/Long	Na Gia		T Tt	
Fum, Fum, Fum	Nin-Culmell, Joaquin	59 Ron	M	T Tt	Satb
Gaudent In Coelis	Vittoria, T L	Na Gia		T Tt	
Give Laud Unto The Lord	Bullock, Ernest	Na Oxf	M	T Tt	Satb
Give Praise All Earthly Men	Saint-Saens, Camille	Na Gsc	B	T Tt	Var+
Glad Song	Mitchell	72 Aug	M	T Tt	Satb
Gloria Patri	Palestrina, Giovanni P	Na Gsc	B	T Tt	8mix
Gloria Sing All Our Voices	Bach, J. S.	Na Gsc	B	T Tt	Satb+
Glorious Things Of Thee Are Spoken	Coggin, Elwood	Na Gsc	B	T Tt	Satb+
Glory	Rimsky-Korsakoff/Amen	Na Wbp		T Tt	
Glory And Honor	Giorgi, Giovanni	Na Gsc	B	T Tt	Satb
Glory Be To God The Father	Bruckner, A./Ed Klein	67 Gia	B L	T Tt	Satb+
Glory To God	Handel, G. F.	Na Gsc	B	T Tt	Satb+
Glory To The Father	Saint-Saens, Camille	Na Gsc	B	T Tt	Var+
Glory To Thee My God This Night (Canon)	Tallis, Thomas	Na Oxf	M	T Tt	Satb
Glory To Thy Holy Name	Pasquet, Jean	Na Gsc	B	T Tt	Satb+
God Father, Praise And Glory	Goemanne, Noel	73 Gia	M	T Tt	Satb+
God Is A Spirit	Bennett, W S	Na Gsc	B	T Tt	Satb
God Is Great	Emig	Na Lor	M	T Tt	Unis
God Is Our Refuge, God Is Our Strength	Hopson	Na Wbp		T Tt	
God Of Abraham Praise, The	Beck, John N	75 Bec	M	T Tt	
God Of Everlasting Glory	Peterson/Wyrtzen	Na Zon		T Tt	Satb
God Of Grace And God Of Glory	Price	Na Lor	M	T Tt	Satb
God Of Light	Mueller, Carl F	Na Gsc	B	T Tt	2chor
God Of The Strong	Ford, Virgil	70 Gsc	M B	T Tt	Satb
God, Jehovah	Chadwick, George/Van C	75 Gal	M	T Tt	Satb
God, The Omnipotent	Lwoff/Lundberg	Na Zon		T Tt	Satb
God, Who Made Earth & Heaven	Bach, J.S./Ed Lee	73 Gia	B R L	T Tt	Satb+
Gods Glory And Honour	Frank, Marcel G	Na Gsc	B	T Tt	Full+
Good Christian Men, Rejoice & Sing	Johnson, D.	67 Aug	M	T Tt	Sab
Good Christians, Now Rejoice	Scheidt-Nelson	68 Aug	M	T Tt	Ss+
Great And Marvelous	Gaul, A R	Na Gsc	B	T Tt	Full+
Great Creator Of The World	Grieb, Herbert	Na Gsc	B	T Tt	Var+
Great God What Do I See And Hear	Na	Na Gsc	B	T Tt	Satb+
Great God, We Praise Your Holy Name	Bach, J. S.	63 Wlp	B	T Tt	
Great Is Jehovah	Schubert, Franz J.	Na Gsc	B	T Tt	Full+
Great Is The Father	Handel, G. F.	Na Lor	M	T Tt	Satb
Great Is The Lord	Matthews, H A	Na Gsc	B	T Tt	Satb+
Great Is The Lord	Mozart, Wolfgang A	76 Pro	M	T Tt	Satb
Great Is The Lord	Newbury, Kent A.	Na Gsc	B	T Tt	Satb+
Great Is The Lord	Schutz, Heinrich	75 Maf	M	T Tt	Satb
Great Is The Lord (Md)	Willan, Healey	Na Oxf	M	T Tt	Satb
Great Is The Lord Our Maker	Haydn, Michael	Na Gsc	B	T Tt	Satb+
Great Is Thy Faithfulness	Runyan/Landon	Na Lor	M	T Tt	Satb
Hail To The Brightness!	Mason/Mayfield	Na Zon		T Tt	Satb
Hallelujah	Beethoven, L	Na Lor	M	T Tt	Satb
Hallelujah Chorus	Handel/Johnson	Na Zon		T Tt	Satb
Hallelujah Chorus	Handel, G. F.	Na Gsc	B	T Tt	Var+
Hallelujah Chorus, The	Handel, G. F.	Na Lor	M	T Tt	Var
Hallelujah! Great And Marvelous	Brandon, George	75 Gia		T Tt	Sa(T)B+
Hallelujah, Amen	Handel, G. F.	Na Gsc	B	T Tt	Satb+
Halleujah (From Mount Of Olives)	Beethoven, L	Na Gsc	B	T Tt	Var+
Hark! Ten Thousand Harps And Voices	Mason/Decou	Na Zon		T Tt	Satb
Hark, Ten Thousand Harps And Voices	Cain	Na Lor	M	T Tt	Satb
Harvest Carol	Copes, V Earle	Na Gsc	B	T Tt	Satb
Have Ye Not Known?	Beck, John N	75 Bec	M	T Tt	
Heart And Lips (Cantata)	Bach, J. S.	75 Lps	B R	T Tt	Satb
Heavens Are Telling, The	Haydn, Joseph	Na Lor	M	T Tt	Satb
Hebrew Children	Na	Na Gsc	B	T Tt	Ssa
Helas Mamour (Old French)	Clement, Jacques	Na Gsc	B	T Tt	Ssaa
His Matchless Worth	Mozart, Wolfgang A	Na Zon		T Tt	Satb
Holy Art Thou	Handel, G. F.	Na Lor	M	T Tt	Satb
Holy Art Thou, O God!	Traditional/Rasley	Na Zon		T Tt	Satb
Holy God	Walworth, Clarence	67 Acp	B L	T Tt	
Holy God Of Sabboth (A Cap)	Dietterich, Philip	Na Abi	M	T Tt	S(Ora)
Holy God We Praise Thy Name	Pelz, W.	65 Aug	M	T Tt	Satb+
Holy God, We Praise Thy Name	Goemanne, Noel	74 Gia	M	T Tt	Sa(T)B+
Holy God, We Praise Thy Name	Mytych, J F	Na Gia		T Tt	
Holy God, We Praise Thy Name	Traditional/Johnson	Na Zon		T Tt	Satb
Holy Is The Lord	Schubert	Na Lor	M	T Tt	Var
Holy Is The Lord!	Bradbury/Peterson	Na Zon		T Tt	Satb
Holy Is Thy Name	Handel, G. F. (Duroche	Hof	M	T Tt	Ssa
Honor Him, Alleluia	Lehmeier, John	73 Hal		T Tt	Sab
How Can We Show Our Love To Thee	Ford, Virgil	Na Gsc	B	T Tt	Satb
How Excellent Is Thy Name	Mcafee, Don	75 Sac	M	T Tt	Satb
How Excellent Is Thy Name	Wilson, James R.	Na Gsc	B	T Tt	Satb
How Excellent Thy Name	Burroughs	75 Maf	M	T Tt	Satb
How Excellent Thy Name	Handel/Davis	Na Wbp		T Tt	
How Excellent Thy Name	Handel, G. F.	Na Gsc	B	T Tt	Var+
How Excellent Thy Name	Handel, G. F.	75 Maf	M R	T Tt	Satb
How Great Are Thy Wonders	Schumann-Christiansen	60 Aug	M	T Tt	Satb
How Lovely Is Thy Dwelling Place	Newbury, Kent A.	Na Gsc	B	T Tt	Satb
How Shall I Sing That Majesty	Lovelace, Austin C.	75 Sac	M	T Tt	Sab
Hymn Of Praise	Mendelssohn, F.	Na Kal	B	T Tt	Satb
Hymn Of Praise	Mytych, J F	67 Gia	M	T Tt	Sa+
Hymn Of Praise	Smith	Na Lor	M	T Tt	Satb
Hymn Of Praise	Tchaikovsky, P. I.	Na Gsc	B	T Tt	8mix+
Hymn Of Thanksgiving	Denton	Na Lor	M	T Tt	Satb
Hymn To The Godhead	Thompson	Na Lor	M	T Tt	Satb
Hymn To The Trinity	Thompson	Na Lor	M	T Tt	Satb
I Have The Joy (Arrangement)	Jansen, Geneva	74 Tal	R L	T Tt	
I Heard A Great Voice	Billings, William	Cfp	R	T Tt	Full
I Sing Of God	Price	Na Lor	M	T Tt	2mel
I Sing Of The Glory Of The Lord	Smith	Na Lor	M	T Tt	Sab
I Sing The Mighty Power Of God	Price	Na Lor	M	T Tt	Sab
I Sing The Mighty Power Of God	Traditional/Lundberg	Na Zon		T Tt	Satb
I Was Glad	Jothen, M.	75 Bec	M	T Tt	
I Will Arise	Lovelace, Austin C	75 Sac	M	T Tt	Sab
I Will Exalt Him	Handel, G. F.	Na Gsc	B	T Tt	Satb+
I Will Exalt Thee & Sing Unto The Lord	Tye, Christopher	Na Oxf	M	T Tt	Satb

CATEGORIZED INDEX

I Will Extol Thee	Costa, M	Na Gsc	B	T Tt	Satb+
I Will Extol Thee	Moe, Daniel	66 Aug	M	T Tt	Ttbb
I Will Extol Thee	Price	Na Lor	M	T Tt	Satb
I Will Give Thanks Unto The Lord	Campbell–Tipton	Na Gsc	B	T Tt	Satb+
I Will Magnify Thee	Vail	Na Lor	M	T Tt	Satb
I Will Praise The Lord	Schutz, Heinrich	Na Gsc	B	T Tt	Satb
I Will Praise The Lord	Telemann, Georg P	Na Gsc	B	T Tt	Sab
I Will Praise Thee	Hughes, Robert J.	Na Lor	M	T Tt	Unis
I Will Praise Thee, O Lord	Bowen	75 Her	M	T Tt	Satb
I Will Praise Thee, O Lord	Nystedt, Knut	58 Aug	M	T Tt	Satb
I Will Sing	Wilson	Na Lor	M	T Tt	Satb
I Will Sing Of Thee Thy Great Mercies	Mendelssohn, F.	Na Gsc	B	T Tt	Sab+
I Will Sing Praises	Telemann	75 Her	M	T Tt	Satb
I Will Sing Thee Songs Of Gladness	Dvorak, A	Na Gsc	B	T Tt	2pt+
I Will Sing To The Lord 1	Neff	73 Aug	M	T Tt	2pt
I Will Thank Thee, O Lord	Mendelssohn, F.	Na Gsc	B	T Tt	Var+
I Will Thank Thee, O Lord	Moir, F L	39 Gsc	B	T Tt	Satb+
I Will Wake Up The Sun	Hunnicutt, J.	72 Aug	M	T Tt	Unis
If Ye Be Merry	Liljestrand, Paul	Na Gsc	B	T Tt	Satb
Immortal, Invisible	Traditional/Decou	75 Zon		T Tt	Satb
In Dulci Jubilo	Buxtehude, D.	Na Kal	B	T Tt	Satb
In Mirth And In Gladness	Niedt, F E	Na Gsc	B	T Tt	Satb
In The Name Of The Lord	Nelson, Ronald A.	62 Aug	M	T Tt	Ss
In Thee Is Gladness	Gastoldi–Nelson	58 Aug	M	T Tt	Sab
In Thee Is Gladness (Gastoldi 1591)	Ley, Henry G.	Na Oxf	M	T Tt	Satb
Is There Anybody Here?	Smith	Na Lor	M	T Tt	Satb
It Is A Good Thing To Give Thanks	Schwartz, Paul	59 Ron	M	T Tt	Ttbb
Jesus, In Thy Dwelling Place Above	Infante, Guy	74 Sms	M R L	T Tt	
Join All The Glorious Names	Darwall/Wyrtzen	Na Zon		T Tt	Satb
Joy, Joy, Joy	Lorenz	Na Lor	M	T Tt	Satb
Joyful! Joyful!	Hampton, Calvin	75 Maf	M	T Tt	Satb
Joyful, Joyful, We Adore Thee	Beethoven/Johnson	Na Zon		T Tt	Satb
Joyfully Sing We His Praise!	Harris	75 Pro	M	T Tt	2pt+
Joyous Alleluia	Rocherolle, Eugenie	Na Wbp		T Tt	
Jubilate	Schilling, F	Na Gsc	B	T Tt	Satb+
Jubilate	Stanford, C V	Na Gsc	B	T Tt	Satb+
Jubilate (Russian)	Na	Na Lor	M	T Tt	Satb
Jubilate Deo	Gambino, James	55 Smc	M	T Tt	Satb
Jubilate Deo	Lasso, Orlando Di	Na Gia		T Tt	
Jubilate Deo (A Cap)	Gabrieli, G	Na Gsc	B	T Tt	8mix
Jubilate Deo (D)	Gardner, John	Na Oxf	M	T Tt	Satb
Jubilate Deo (D)	Preston, Simon	Na Oxf	M	T Tt	Satb
Jubilate Deo (Lat–Ger)	Lasso, Orlando Di	Cfp	R	T Tt	Satb
Jubilate Deo (M)	Cabena, Barrie	Na Oxf	M	T Tt	Unis
Jubilate Deo (Md)	Brown, Christopher	Na Oxf	M	T Tt	Satb
Jubilate Deo (Md)	Walton, William	Na Oxf	M	T Tt	Full
Jubilate Deo (Md)	Wickens, Dennis	Na Oxf	M	T Tt	Satb
Jubilate Deo (W/Brass)	Fetler, Paul	64 Aug	M	T Tt	Satb+
Jubilate Deo In C (M)	Britten, Benjamin	Na Oxf	M	T Tt	Satb
Jubilate Deo, Omnis Terra	Lasso, Orlando Di	Na Gsc	B	T Tt	Satb
Jubilemus Singuli	Gabrieli, G	Na Gsc	B	T Tt	8mix
Killingly	Jenks, Stephen	76 Bbl	M	T Tt	Satb
Kings Of The Earth And All People	Frank, Marcel G	Na Gsc	B	T Tt	Full+
Kittery (Lowens)	Billings, William	Na Gsc	B	T Tt	Satb
Lauda Anima Mea Dominum	Lasso, Orlando Di	Na Gsc	B	T Tt	Satb
Lauda Sion	Lasso, Orlando Di	Na Kal	B	T Tt	Satb
Lauda Sion (Cantata)	Mendelssohn, F.	Na Kal	B	T Tt	Satb
Laudamus	Mueller, Carl F	Na Gsc	B	T Tt	Var
Laudamus Te	Mueller	Na Gsc	M	T Tt	8pt
Laudate Alla Virgine (Female)	Verdi, Giuseppe	Na Kal	B	T Tt	
Laudate Dominum	Lasso, Orlando Di	Na Kal	B	T Tt	Satb
Laudate Dominum (M)	Mozart, Wolfgang A	Na Oxf	M	T Tt	Ssa
Laudate Dominum (Ps 150)	Brown, Christopher	Na Oxf	M	T Tt	Satb
Laudate Dominum (Ps 150) A Cap	Pitoni/Wiley (Arr)	76 Pro	M	T Tt	Satb
Laudate Pueri, Laudate Nomen Domini	Pergolesi, G B	Na Gsc	B	T Tt	Satb+
Laus Creatorum (Md)	Brown, Christopher	Na Oxf	M	T Tt	Satb
Legende	Tschaikowsky, P.	Hof	M	T Tt	Satb
Let All Men Rejoice	Brandon, George	Na Wbp		T Tt	
Let All On Earth Their Voices Raise	Robinson, C C	Na Gsc	B	T Tt	Satb+
Let All The Earth	Farrell, Melvin	55 Wlp	B	T Tt	
Let All The World In Every Corner Sing	Long, C. S.	Na Oxf	M	T Tt	2pt
Let All The World In Every Corner Sing	Roberton, Hugh S	Na Gsc	B	T Tt	Var
Let All The World In Every Corner Sing	Young, Carlton R.	Na Abi	M	T Tt	Satb
Let Christians All With Joyful Mirth	Held, Wilbur C	76 Bec	M	T Tt	
Let Man Exult With Heart And Voice	Beethoven, L	75 Her	M	T Tt	Satb
Let The Bright Seraphim	Deodatus Dutton, Jr.	76 Her	M	T Tt	Satb+
Let The People Praise Thee	Monhardt	63 Aug	M	T Tt	Satb
Let The Whole Creation Cry	Young	66 Aug	M	T Tt	Unis
Let Them Ever Sing For Joy	Newbury, Kent A.	Na Gsc	B	T Tt	Satb
Let Thy Merciful Ears (Me)	Mudd	Na Oxf	M	T Tt	Satb
Let Us All With Gladsome Voice	Track, Gerhard	70 Gia	M	T Tt	Sab+
Let Us Celebrate God's Name	Bruckner, Anton	68 Aug	M	T Tt	Satb
Let Us Now Our Voices Raise	Wennerberg/Douglas	76 Pro	M	T Tt	Satb
Let Us Praise Our Noble God	Farrell, Melvin/Burns	63 Wlp	B	T Tt	
Let Us Sing The New Song	Wyatt	75 Pro	M	T Tt	Var+
Lift The Cherubic Host	Gaul, A R	Na Gsc	B	T Tt	Var+
Lift Up Your Songs Of Praise	Saint–Saens, Camille	Na Lor	M	T Tt	Satb
Lift Your Glad Voices In Triumph	Jackson–Riedel	59 Aug	M	T Tt	Sab
Litany Glory Praise & Power K 125	Mozart, Wolfgang A	Na Kal	B	T Tt	Satb
Lobt Gott Mit Schall	Schutz, Heinrich	67 Bbl	M	T Tt	Satb
Lonsadle From Three Fuging–Tunes	Anonymous	75 Bbl	B	T Tt	Ttb
Lord Fill My Mouth With Words	Deiss, Lucien	70 Wlp	B R	T Tt	
Lord God We Praise Thy Goodness	Franck, Melchior	Na Gsc	B	T Tt	Satb
Lord God, Our Thanks To Thee We Raise	Johnson, Norman	Na Zon		T Tt	Satb
Lord God, We Worship Thee	Pooler, Marie	62 Aug	M	T Tt	Var
Lord Of All Power And Might	Talmadge, C. L.	Na Gsc	B	T Tt	Satb+
Lord We Give Thanks To Thee	Moore, Undine	Na Wbp		T Tt	
Lord, How Excellent Thy Name	Medler, Malcolm	Na Gsc	B	T Tt	Satb+
Love And Blessed Be Thou, King	Pasquet, Jean	Na Gsc	B	T Tt	Satb+
Magnificat	Bach, J. S.	Na Kal	B	T Tt	Satb

Magnificat	Durante, F. (D1755)	Na Kal	B	T Tt	Satb
Magnificat	Haydn, Michael	Na Gsc	B	T Tt	Ssa+
Magnificat	Pergolesi, G. B.	Na Kal	B	T Tt	Satb
Magnificat	Purcell, –Kleinsasser	74 Aug	M	T Tt	Full
Magnificat	Russel, Carlton	Na Gsc	B	T Tt	Satb
Magnificat	Vivaldi, A.	Na Kal	B	T Tt	Satb
Magnificat	White, Robert (1574)	Na Kal	B	T Tt	Satb
Magnificat (From Cantiones Sacrae)	Gardner, John	Na Oxf	M	T Tt	Satb
Magnificat And Nunc Dimittis (Eng)	Purcell, Henry	Cfp	R	T Tt	Satb+
Magnificat Anima Mea	Buxtehude, D.	Na Kal	B	T Tt	Satb
Magnificat Anima Mea Dominum	Pergolesi, G B	Na Gsc	B	T Tt	Satb+
Magnificat For 6 Voices (Organ Score)	Monteverdi, Claudio	Na Kal	B	T Tt	
Magnificat (C) (Lat)	Pachelbel, C. T.	Cfp	R	T Tt	Full+
Magnificat (Eng–Lat)	Buxtehude, D.	Cfp	R	T Tt	Solo+
Magnificat (Latin)	Bach, J. S.	Cfp	R	T Tt	Satb+
Make A Joyful Noise	Smith	Na Lor	M	T Tt	Satb
Make A Joyful Noise Unto The Lord (M)	Mathias, William	Na Oxf	M	T Tt	Satb
Make A Joyful Noise Unto The Lord (Me)	Orr, Robin	Na Oxf	M	T Tt	Ss
Make A Joyful Sound (5 Voices)	Praetorius/Tortolano	70 Gia	B L	T Tt	Round
May God Be Gracious (4 Voices)	Billings, W./Tortolano	70 Gia	B L	T Tt	Round
May Jesus Christ Be Praised	Barnby/Johnson	Na Zon		T Tt	Satb
May Jesus Christ Be Praised!	Barnby/Decou	75 Zon		T Tt	Satb
May The Words Of My Mouth	Rogers, J H	Na Gsc	B	T Tt	Satb+
Mihi Autem Nimis (Blessed Be Thy Name)	Tallis, Thomas	Na Oxf	M	T Tt	Sattb
Miriam's Song Of Triumph	Schubert, Franz J.	Na Kal	B	T Tt	
More Than Raiment	Petzold	73 Aug	M	T Tt	Satb
Morning Star	Boyer, D./Herring, J.	76 Sil	R	T Tt	
Morning Trumpet, The	White/Watkins	Na Zon		T Tt	Ssatb
Most High Omnipotent God	Robbins/Hampton	39 Gia	B L	T Tt	
My God, How Wonderful	Overby (Arr)	52 Aug	M	T Tt	Satb
My God, How Wonderful Thou Art	Christiansen, F. M.	68 Aug	M	T Tt	Satb
My Heart Sings With Joy (E & Ger)	Harrer/Harris (Arr)	75 Pro	M	T Tt	Var+
My Joy Is All In Thee (Cantata)	Bach, J. S.	75 Lps	B R	T Tt	Satb
My Lips Shall Speak Of Thy Praise (M)	Greene, Maurice	Na Oxf	M	T Tt	2pt
My Lord	Eilers, Joyce	75 Hal		T Tt	Sab
My Soul Doth Magnify The Lord	Saint–Saens, Camille	Na Gsc	B	T Tt	Stb+
My Soul, Praise The Lord (Me)	Williams, Vaughan R.	Na Oxf	M	T Tt	Satb
Natures Praise Of God	Beethoven, L	Na Gsc	B	T Tt	Ttbb
Non Nobis, Domine (Canon)	Byrd, William	Na Oxf	M	T Tt	3pts
Non Nobis, Domine (3 Voices)	Byrd, Wm/Tortolano	70 Gia	B L	T Tt	Round
Northfield	Ingalls, Jeremiah	75 Bbl	B	T Tt	Satb
Now Glad Of Heart	Powell, Robert J.	Na Gsc	B	T Tt	Satb+
Now In Joy We Sing Thy Praises	Farrell, Melvin	55 Wlp	B	T Tt	
Now Let Every Tongue Adore Thee	Bick	Hof	M	T Tt	Satb
Now Let The Vault Of Heaven Resound	Cassler, G. W.	59 Aug	M	T Tt	Satb
Now Sing We, Now Rejoice	Praetorius–Bliss	63 Aug	M	T Tt	Ss
Now Thank We All Our God	Burroughs, Bob	Na Abi	M	T Tt	Satb
Now Thank We All Our God	Cassler, G. W.	70 Aug	M	T Tt	Satb+
Now Thank We All Our God	Cruger (Arr Goodell)	Hof	M	T Tt	Var
Now Thank We All Our God	Cruger/Decou	Na Zon		T Tt	Satb
Now Thank We All Our God	Cruger, J	Na Gia		T Tt	
Now Thank We All Our God	Hughes, Robert J.	76 Lor		T Tt	Satb+
Now Thank We All Our God	Mendelssohn, F.	Na Wbp		T Tt	
Now Thank We All Our God	Mueller, Carl F	Na Gsc	B	T Tt	Var+
Now Thank We All Our God	Scheidt–Ehret	76 Abi	M	T Tt	Full+
Now Thank We All Our God (W/Tpts)	Goemanne, Noel (Arr)	75 Wlp	M	T Tt	Satb+
O Admirabile Commercium	Palestrina, Giovanni P	Na Kal	B	T Tt	
O Be Joyful In The Lord	Tours, B.	Na Gsc	B	T Tt	Sab
O Be Joyful In The Lord (M)	Nourse, John	Na Oxf	M	T Tt	Satb
O Be Joyful In The Lord (Md)	Leighton, Kenneth	Na Oxf	M	T Tt	Satb
O Be Joyful In The Lord (Ps 100 Me) 1	Willan, Healey	Na Oxf	M	T Tt	Satb
O Be Joyful In The Lord (Ps 100)	Longthorne, Brian	Na Oxf	M	T Tt	Satb
O Be Joyful In The Lord (Jubilate)	Boyce, William	Na Gsc	B	T Tt	Satb+
O Come Let Us Sing	Beck, J.	75 Bec	M	T Tt	
O Come Let Us Sing Unto The Lord	Berger, Jean	57 Bbl	M	T Tt	Satb
O Come, Let Us Sing	Root–Harris (Arr)	75 Pro	M	T Tt	Satb+
O Come, Loud Anthems Let Us Sing	Blake	Na Lor	M	T Tt	Satb
O Domine	Schein, Johann H	75 Bbl	M	T Tt	Full
O Father Thou Whose Hand	Gannon, Michael	63 Wlp	B	T Tt	
O For A Thousand Tongues	Glaser/Johnson	Na Zon		T Tt	Full
O For A Thousand Tongues	Thompson	Na Lor	M	T Tt	Satb
O For A Thousand Tongues	Ward	75 Sac	M	T Tt	Satb
O For A Thousand Tongues To Sing	Denton	Na Lor	M	T Tt	Satb
O For A Thousand Tongues To Sing	Hughes, Robert J.	Na Lor	M	T Tt	Satb
O For A Thousand Tongues To Sing	Wright, Bob	61 Smc	M	[Tt	Satb
O Give Thanks	Ford	Na Lor	M	T Tt	Satb
O Give Thanks	Powell	75 Sac	M	T Tt	Satb
O Give Thanks	Purcell, Henry	Na Lor	M	T Tt	Sabb
O Give Thanks Unto The Lord (Ps 105)	Tompkins, Thomas	Na Oxf	M	T Tt	Attb
O God Of Truth	Held, Wilbur C	75 Bec	M	T Tt	
O God The Father, Eternal One	Praetorius	69 Aug	M	T Tt	Full
O God, How Wonderful Thou Art	Brown, Leon, F.	62 Smc	M	T Tt	Satb
O God, The King Of Glory	Purcell, Henry	Na Gsc	B	T Tt	Satb+
O God, Thy Hands The Heavens Made	Wilson	Na Lor	M	T Tt	Satb
O God, Who Live Forever	Fitzpatrick, Dennis	65 Fel	B	T Tt	
O God, Wonderful Art Thou	Tompkins, Thomas	Na Oxf	M	T Tt	Saatb
O Holy Lord	Dett, R N	Na Gsc	B	T Tt	Full
O How Great Is The Lord Of All	Weldon, J (Coggin)	73 Pro	M	T Tt	Satb
O Light From Age To Age The Same	Shaw, Martin	Na Oxf	M	T Tt	Satb
O Lord And Master Of Us All	Southbridge	Na Lor	M	T Tt	Satb
O Lord From Whom All Good Things Come	Bales, Gerald	Na Oxf	M	T Tt	Satb
O Lord How Manifold	Barnby, Jos	Na Gsc	B	T Tt	Satb+
O Lord Most High, With All My Heart	Track, Gerhard	73 Gia	M	T Tt	Satb+
O Lord My God	Rush, John	Na Gsc	B	T Tt	Satb+
O Lord Of Hosts	Aichinger, Gregor	66 Som	M	T Tt	
O Lord, I Bow The Knee Of My Heart	Mundy, William	76 Bbl	M	T Tt	Saatb
O Lord, I Will Praise Thee (E)	Jacob, Gordon	Na Oxf	M	T Tt	Satb
O Lord, Open Thou Our Lips (M)	Ford, Virgil	75 Abi	M	T Tt	Satb
O Lord, Our Lord	Thompson	Na Lor	M	T Tt	Satb
O Lord, The Maker Of All Things (Me)	Mundy, William	Na Oxf	M	T Tt	Satb

O Lord, You Made The Rainbow	Pallock	Na Lor	M		T Tt	Var
O Mighty God, When I Behold The Wonder	Wedish/Decou	Na Zon			T Tt	Satb
O Nata Lux De Lumine (Me)	Tallis, Thomas	Na Oxf	M		T Tt	Sattb
O Not To Us, Good Lord (Opt Flute)	Telemann–Nelson	69 Aug	M		T Tt	Unis
O Praise God In His Holiness (M)	Paul, Leslie	Na Oxf	M		T Tt	Satb
O Praise God In His Holiness (Md)	White, Matthew	Na Oxf	M		T Tt	Full
O Praise God In His Holiness (Md)	White, Robert	Na Oxf	M		T Tt	Satb
O Praise God In His Holiness (Ps 150)	Gibbs, C. Armstrong	Na Oxf	M		T Tt	Var
O Praise God In His Holiness (Ps 150)	Lovelock, William	Na Oxf	M		T Tt	Satb
O Praise The Lord (Me)	Batten, Adrian	Na Oxf	M		T Tt	Satb
O Praise The Lord All Ye Heathen (Md)	Tompkins, Thomas	Na Oxf	M		T Tt	12pt
O Praise The Lord All Ye Nations	Johns	66 Aug	M		T Tt	Ssaa
O Praise The Lord All Ye Nations	Krapf, Gerhard	75 Abi	M		T Tt	Sab
O Praise The Lord Of Harvest	Johnson, D.	67 Aug	M		T Tt	Sab
O Praise The Lord Of Heaven	Billings, William	76 Bbi	M		T Tt	Satb
O Praise The Name Of The Lord	Lovelace, Austin C.	75 Sac	M		T Tt	Satb
O Rejoice In The Lord	King, R. (Coggin)	73 Pro	M		T Tt	Satb+
O Sapientia!	Noble, Harold	Na Gsc	B		T Tt	Full
O Sing Joyfully	Batten, Adrian	Na Oxf	M		T Tt	Satb
O Sing To God With Joy	Mischke/Vermulst, J.	61 Wlp	B		T Tt	
O Sing Unto The Lord	Hassler, H L	Na Gsc	B		T Tt	Satb
O Sing Unto The Lord	Hassler, H L	66 Som	M		T Tt	
O Sing Unto The Lord (M)	Mathias, William	Na Oxf	M		T Tt	Satb
O Sing Unto The Lord A New Song	Duke, John	Na Gsc	B		T Tt	Ssa+
O Sing Unto The Lord A New Song	Smith	Na Lor	M		T Tt	Satb
O Sing Unto The Lord A New Song	Willan	75 Cfp	M		T Tt	Satb+
O Sing Ye To The Lord	Croce, Giovanni	Na Gsc	B		T Tt	Satb
O That I Had A Thousand Voices	Konig–Nelson	56 Aug	M		T Tt	Sab
O Thou Most High	Christiansen, P.	Na Gsc	B		T Tt	Full
O Thou, In Whose Presence	Lewis, Freeman	Na Gsc	B		T Tt	8mix
O Thou, In Whose Presence	Traditional/Rasley	Na Zon			T Tt	Satb
O Thou, The True And Only Light	Mendelssohn, F.	Na Gsc	B		T Tt	Satb+
O Thou, To Whom In Ancient Time	Thiman, Eric H.	Na Gsc	B		T Tt	Satb+
O Wondrous Type	Petrich, Roger T.	Na Oxf	M		T Tt	Satb
O Worship The King	Barnes, E S	Na Gsc	B		T Tt	Satb+
O Worship The King	Haydn/Mayfield	Na Zon			T Tt	Satb
O Worship The King	Haydn, Michael	Na Gsc	B		T Tt	Full+
Of One That Is So Fair And Bright	Naylor, Bernard	Na Gsc	B		T Tt	Ssa
Oh For A Shout Of Joy	Mohr, J./Andrews	70 Gia	B	L	T Tt	Var
Omnes Gentes	Lully, J B	Na Gia			T Tt	
Once I Sang	Sateren, Leland B.	Na Gsc	B		T Tt	Satb
One Above All Others	Na	Na Gsc	B		T Tt	Sab+
One In Joyful Songs Of Praise	Koninkxop	61 Wlp	B		T Tt	
Our God Is Great (Swedish)	Na	Na Lor	M		T Tt	Var
Our Hymn Of Praise	Bergh	Hof	M		T Tt	Ssa
Our Lady's Song Of Praise	Arnandez/Chant	76 Jsp	B		T Tt	
Plaudite	Gabrieli, G	Na Gsc	B		T Tt	12mix
Power	White	75 Bbl	B		T Tt	Tb
Praise (Me)	Rowley, Alec	Na Oxf	M		T Tt	Satb
Praise God In Highest Heaven	Butler	75 Maf	M		T Tt	Satb
Praise God In His Holiness	Thompson	Na Lor	M		T Tt	Satb
Praise God In His Sanctuary	Thygerson	75 Sac	M		T Tt	Satb
Praise God With Sound (Psalm 117)	Schutz, Heinrich	67 Bbl	M		T Tt	Satb
Praise God, My Soul	Jeppesen, Knud	75 Bbl	M		T Tt	Satb
Praise God, Ye Christians	Praetorius, M	Na Gsc	B		T Tt	Satb
Praise Him Evermore	Brandon, George	70 Gia	M		T Tt	Stb+
Praise Him, Ye Nations	Mozart, Wolfgang A	Na Zon			T Tt	Satb
Praise My Soul The King Of Heaven	Goss, John	Na Gsc	B		T Tt	Sab+
Praise Shall Be Thine	Na	Na Lor	M		T Tt	2mel
Praise The Almighty (Cantata)	Bach, J. S.	75 Lps	B	R	T Tt	Satb
Praise The Grandeur Of Our God	Farrell, Melvin/Burns	61 Wlp	B	R	T Tt	
Praise The Lord	Hadler	Na Lor	M		T Tt	2mel
Praise The Lord	Praetorius, M	Na Gsc	B		T Tt	Satb
Praise The Lord	Randegger, A	Na Gsc	B		T Tt	Satb+
Praise The Lord (E)	Adler, Samuel	Na Oxf	M		T Tt	Sa
Praise The Lord (Judas Maccabeus)	Handel, G. F.	76 Pro	M		T Tt	Satb+
Praise The Lord (Motet 6)	Bach, J. S.	Na Kal	B		T Tt	Satb
Praise The Lord (Ps 117) 4 Voices	Caldara, A./Tortolano E	70 Gia	B	L	T Tt	Round
Praise The Lord For He Is Gracious	Mozart, Wolfgang A	Na Lor	M		T Tt	Sab
Praise The Lord My Soul (Cantata)	Bach, J. S.	75 Lps	B	R	T Tt	Satb
Praise The Lord Of Heaven	Thompson	Na Lor	M		T Tt	
Praise The Lord Who Is Present	Dullea, Dennis C., Jr.	72 Sms	M	R L	T Tt	
Praise The Lord! Ye Heavens	Haydn, Joseph	Na Oxf	M		T Tt	2pt
Praise The Lord, His Glories Show	Thiman, Eric H.	Na Gsc	B		T Tt	Satb+
Praise The Lord, O Jerusalem	Maunder	Na Lor	M		T Tt	
Praise The Lord, O My Soul	Child, W.(Arr Wienandt	63 Gam	M		T Tt	Satb
Praise The Lord, O My Soul	Watson, M.	Na Gsc	B		T Tt	Sab
Praise The Lord, O My Soul	Yeaman, W. Holladay	Na Gsc	B		T Tt	Satb+
Praise The Lord, O My Soul (Ps 103)	Tompkins, Thomas	Na Oxf	M		T Tt	Sstb
Praise The Lord, Ye Servants	Blow, John	Na Oxf	M		T Tt	Satb
Praise The Savior (P.D.)	Elrich, Dwight (Arr.)	74 Man	M		T Tt	Choral
Praise To God In The Highest (Me)	Campbell, S. S.	Na Oxf	M		T Tt	Satb
Praise To The Living God	Mueller, Carl F	Na Gsc	B		T Tt	Satb+
Praise To The Lord	Cassler, G. W.	70 Aug	M		T Tt	
Praise To The Lord	Christiansen, F. M.	57 Aug	M		T Tt	Satb
Praise To The Lord	Goemanne, Noel	74 Gia	M		T Tt	Satb+
Praise To The Lord	Na	Na Gsc	B		T Tt	Satb+
Praise To The Lord	Newbury, Kent A.	Na Gsc	B		T Tt	Satb+
Praise To The Lord	Toolan, Sr Suzanne	72 Gia	M		T Tt	Satbu+
Praise To The Lord (E)	Gilbert, Norman	Na Oxf	M		T Tt	Sab
Praise To The Lord God	Schutz, Heinrich	75 Maf	M		T Tt	2pt
Praise To The Lord, The Almighty	Gilbert, Norman	Na Oxf	M		T Tt	Satb
Praise To The Lord, The Almighty	Hebble	75 Sac	M		T Tt	Satb
Praise To The Lord, The Almighty	Hughes, Robert J.	Na Lor	M		T Tt	
Praise To The Lord, The Almighty	Thompson	Na Lor	M		T Tt	
Praise To The Lord, The Almighty	Wilson	Na Lor	M		T Tt	
Praise We The Name Of God	Bach, J.S./Coggin(Arr)	75 Pro	M		T Tt	Var+
Praise Ye	Christiansen, P.	60 Aug	M		T Tt	Satb
Praise Ye The Father	Gounod, Charles	Na Lor	M		T Tt	
Praise Ye The Father (Marche Romaine)	Gounod, Charles	Na Gsc	B		T Tt	Var
Praise Ye The Lord	Bernardi, Steffano	Na Gsc	B		T Tt	Ssatb
Praise Ye The Lord	Cherubini, L	Na Gsc	B		T Tt	Satb+
Praise Ye The Lord	Guenther, Ralph R.	73 Pro	M		T Tt	Satb+
Praise Ye The Lord	Karg/Elert	Na Lor	M		T Tt	
Praise Ye The Lord	Randegger, A	Na Gsc	B		T Tt	Satb+
Praise Ye The Lord	Saint–Saens, Camille	Na Gsc	B		T Tt	Satb+
Praise Ye The Lord	Schutz, Heinrich	75 Maf	M		T Tt	2pt
Praise Ye The Lord	Vulpius, Melchior	Na Gsc	B		T Tt	Satb
Praise Ye The Lord (E & Ger)	Gumpelzhaimer, A/Klein	67 Gia	B	L	T Tt	Satb+
Praise Ye The Lord (Ps 113)	Young, Gordon	Na Oxf	M		T Tt	Satb
Praise Ye The Lord (Ps 150)	Rutter, John	Na Oxf	M		T Tt	Satb
Praise Ye The Lord With Singing	Gumpelzhaimer, A	67 Gia	M		T Tt	Satb+
Praise Ye The Lord, Alleluia	Stroh, Virginia	65 Bbl	M		T Tt	Satb
Praise Ye The Lord, The Almighty	Traditional/Nichols	Na Zon			T Tt	Satb
Praise Ye The Lord, Ye Children (Me)	Tye, Christopher	Na Oxf	M		T Tt	Satb
Praise Ye The Triune God!	Fleming/Decou	Na Zon			T Tt	Satb
Praise Ye, Jehovah	Lyon	Na Lor	M		T Tt	
Praise!	Goss/Johnson	75 Zon			T Tt	Satb
Praise, My Soul, The King Of Heaven	Brandon, George	74 Gia	M		T Tt	Satb+
Praise, My Soul, The King Of Heaven	Gilbert, Norman	Na Oxf	M		T Tt	U+Sa
Praise, My Soul, The King Of Heaven	Goss/Mickelson	Na Zon			T Tt	Satb
Praise, Thou Zion (Cantata)	Bach, J. S.	75 Lps	B	R	T Tt	Satb
Praised Be My Lord	Thompson	Na Lor	M		T Tt	
Praised Be The Lord (Me)	Greene, Maurice	Na Oxf	M		T Tt	Unis
Prayer	Guion	46 Gsc	M		T Tt	Satb+
Prayer Of Thanksgiving	Na	Na Gsc	B		T Tt	Var+
Psalm Of Gratitude, A	Martin	Na Lor	M		T Tt	
Psalm Of Thanksgiving, A	Thompson	Na Lor	M		T Tt	
Psalm Praises	Martin	Na Lor	M		T Tt	
Psalm 100 (M)	Vaughan, Rodger	Na Oxf	M		T Tt	Satb
Psalm 103	Herrer, Johann G	75 Bbl	M		T Tt	Satb
Psalm 112 (Latin)	Handel, G. F.	Cfp		R	T Tt	Satb+
Psalm 117	Telemann, G.P.(D1767)	Na Kal	B		T Tt	Satb
Psalm 117 (Opt Brass Quartet)	Von Kreisler, Alex	69 Smc	M		T Tt	Satb
Psalm 117 O Praise The Lord	Mason, L	73 Gia	M		T Tt	Satb+
Psalm 135 O Praise The Lord	Handel, G. F.	Na Kal	B		T Tt	Satb
Psalm 148 (Praise Ye The Lord)	Glarum, L Stanley	Na Gsc	B		T Tt	Satb
Psalm 150	Franck, Cesar	Na Gsc	B		T Tt	Satb+
Psalm 150	Lockwood, Normand	52 Bbl	B		T Tt	Satb
Psalm 150	Mauduit, Jacques	67 Bbl	M		T Tt	Ssatb
Psalm 150	Purcell, Henry	Na Lor	M		T Tt	
Psalm 150 (French, German)	Franck, Cesar	Na Kal	B		T Tt	Satb
Psalm 150 (Md)	Mathias, William	Na Oxf	M		T Tt	Satb
Psalm 150 Based On A French Melody	Kodaly, Zoltan	Na Oxf	M		T Tt	Ssa
Psalm 31	Waters, James	Na Gsc	B		T Tt	Satb
Psalm 47 From The Bay Psalm Book	Beeson, Jack	Na Oxf	M		T Tt	Satb
Psalm 65 (Ainsworth Psalter)(Eng)	Goudimel Claude G.	Cfp		R	T Tt	Satb
Psalm 67 (Organ Or Piano Acc)	Beck, John Ness	Na Gsc	B		T Tt	Full+
Psalm 8	Frackenpohl, Arthur	55 Bbl	M		T Tt	Satb+
Psalm 85 (Md)	Smith, William	Na Oxf	M		T Tt	Saatb
Psalm 95	Mendelssohn, F.	Na Kal	B		T Tt	Satb
Psalm 96	Adler, Samuel	Na Gsc	B		T Tt	Satb+
Rejoice	Kirk, Theron	75 Pro	M		T Tt	2–Pt+
Rejoice Greatly	Woodward, H. H.	Na Gsc	B		T Tt	Sab+
Rejoice In His Word	Coggin, Elwood (Arr)	73 Pro	M		T Tt	Sab+
Rejoice In The Lord (Md)	Humfrey, Pelham	Na Oxf	M		T Tt	Satb
Rejoice In The Lord Always (M)	Purcell, Henry	Na Oxf	M		T Tt	Satb
Rejoice Now	Kirkston	66 Wlp	B		T Tt	
Rejoice, Earth And Heaven (Eng)	Buxtehude, D.	Cfp		R	T Tt	Solo+
Rejoice, O Church, Exalt In Glory	Wagner, Lavern J.	74 Sms	M	R L	T Tt	+Tpt
Rejoice, Rejoice, Believers	Martin	Na Lor	M		T Tt	
Rejoice, Ye Christian Brethren	Praetorius, M	Na Gsc	B		T Tt	Satb
Ring Out, Wild Bells	Newbury, Kent A.	Na Gsc	B		T Tt	Satb
Rockbridge	Chapin, Lucius	75 Bbl	M		T Tt	Ssb
Sanctum Et Terribile Nomen Ejus	Pergolesi, G B	Na Gsc	B		T Tt	5mix+
Scandalize My Name	Na	Na Gsc	B		T Tt	Full
Scarce Had The Daystar Risen	Gabrieli, Andrea	74 Bbl	M		T Tt	Satb
Short Service: Te Deum / Benedictus	Byrd, William	Na Oxf	M		T Tt	Full
Shout Praise And Glory	Andrews, Carroll T.	70 Gia	B	L	T Tt	Var
Shout The Glad Tidings	Williams	59 Aug	M		T Tt	Ss
Sing Alleluia For Your Soul	Friend	Na Wbp			T Tt	
Sing Alleluia Forth	Buck, Dudley	Na Gsc	B		T Tt	Stb+
Sing Alleluia!	Hughes, Robert J.	Na Lor	M		T Tt	
Sing Aloud To God	Erbach–Haldeman	69 Aug	M		T Tt	Satb
Sing Aloud To God	Haydn, Michael	Na Gsc	B		T Tt	Ssa+
Sing Aloud Unto God	Glarum, L Stanley	Na Gsc	B		T Tt	Var
Sing Aloud Unto God (Md)	Orr, Robin	Na Oxf	M		T Tt	Satb
Sing And Give Praise	Thompson	Na Lor	M		T Tt	
Sing And Rejoice (Md)	Silk, R. J.	Na Oxf	M		T Tt	Satb
Sing Gloria	Davis, K.K.	Na Wbp			T Tt	
Sing Glory To Our God	Husted, Richard S.	76 Chh	B	L	T Tt	
Sing Joyfully (Md)	Mundy, John	Na Oxf	M		T Tt	Saatb
Sing My Tongue The Ageless Story	Quinn, M.	61 Wlp	B		T Tt	
Sing Praise To God	Goemanne, Noel	73 Gia	M		T Tt	Satb+
Sing Praise To God	Martin	Na Lor	M		T Tt	
Sing Praise To God	Mcafee, Don	75 Maf	M		T Tt	Unis+
Sing Praise To God Who Reigns Above	Brahms, J.–Sateren	60 Aug	M		T Tt	Satb
Sing Praise To God Who Reigns Above	Whitlock, Percy	Na Oxf	M		T Tt	Satb
Sing Praise To God!	Traditional/Johnson	Na Zon			T Tt	Satb
Sing Praise To Our Creator	Francis	61 Wlp	B		T Tt	
Sing Praises	Billings, Wm/Van Camp	75 Aug	M		T Tt	Satb
Sing Praises To God A Cap	Tschaikowsky/Douglas	76 Pro	M	R	T Tt	Satb
Sing To The Lord	Haydn, Joseph	Na Gsc	B		T Tt	Satb+
Sing To The Lord	Schutz, Heinrich	Na Gsc	B		T Tt	8mix
Sing To The Lord (A Cap)	Wiley (Arr)	76 Pro	M		T Tt	Satb
Sing To The Lord A Joyful Song	Koert	61 Wlp	B		T Tt	
Sing To The Lord A Joyful Song (Md)	Rose, Michael	Na Oxf	M		T Tt	Eatb
Sing To The Lord A New Song	Hughes, Robert J.	Na Lor	M		T Tt	
Sing We	Powell	Na Wbp			T Tt	
Sing We All Now With One Accord	Praetorius, M	Na Gsc	B		T Tt	Satb

CATEGORIZED INDEX

Sing We Merrily (Ps 81)	Symons, Christopher	Na Oxf	M T Tt	Ss
Sing We The Praise Of God	Bach, J. S.	Na Gsc	B T Tt	Ttbb+
Sing With Fullness To God (5voices)	Dilasso, O./Tortolano	70 Gia	B L T Tt	Round
Sing Ye Merrily	Mendelssohn, F.	58 Aug	M T Tt	Full
Sing, O Sing To The Lord	Purcell, Henry	Na Kal	B T Tt	Satb
Singers Sing	Gannon, Michael	55 Wlp	B T Tt	
Singet Dem Herrn (Motet #1)	Bach, J. S.	Na Kal	B T Tt	Satb
Someone	Hughes, Robert J.	Na Lor	M T Tt	
Someone, Somewhere	Pollock	Na Lor	M T Tt	
Song Of Exhaltation	Beck, John Ness	Na Gsc	B T Tt	Satb+
Song Of Praise	Rasley, John M.	Na Zon	T Tt	Satb
Song Of Praise	Schutz, Heinrich	Na Gsc	B T Tt	8mix
Song Of Thanksgiving	Maunder	Na Kal	B T Tt	Satb
Song Of Thanksgiving, A	Richolson	Na Lor	M T Tt	
Sound Forth The Trumpet In Zion	Morley, T	74 Gia	M T Tt	Sab
Sound Over All Waters	Butler	Na Wbp	T Tt	
Sound The Trumpet, Strike The Cymbal	Schubert, Franz J.	Na Gsc	B T Tt	Satb+
Spem In Alium Nunquam Habui	Tallis, Thomas	Na Oxf	M T Tt	40pt
Spring Hill	Anonymous	75 Bbl	B T Tt	Sb
Stand Up And Bless The Lord (Me)	Turner C. Kenneth	Na Oxf	M T Tt	U/Sa
Sublime Alleluia, A	Young, Gordon	75 Sac	M T Tt	Satb
Such A Gay & Happy Tune	Follett (Arr)	76 Pro	M T Tt	Satb
Take It On Over	Martin	Na Lor	M T Tt	Unis
Tallis Canon (4 Voices)	Tallis, T./Tortolano	75 Gia	B L T Tt	Round
Te Deum	Berlioz, Hector	Na Kal	B R T Tt	Full
Te Deum	Bruckner, Anton (1896)	Na Kal	B R T Tt	Full
Te Deum	Dvorak, A.	Na Kal	B R T Tt	Satb
Te Deum	Harker, Clifford	Na Gsc	B T Tt	Satb+
Te Deum	Schuman, William	Na Gsc	B T Tt	Satb
Te Deum	Verdi, Giuseppe	Na Kal	B T Tt	Satb
Te Deum (Eng, Lat)	Haydn, J. (Ed Atkins)	Na Oxf	B T Tt	Satb
Te Deum (Md)	Nourse, John	Na Oxf	M T Tt	Satb
Te Deum (Md)	Tallis, Thomas	Na Oxf	M T Tt	Saatb
Te Deum And Benedictus	Williams, Vaughan R.	Na Oxf	M T Tt	Satbu
Te Deum And Jubilate (Md)	Farrant, John	Na Oxf	M T Tt	Satb
Te Deum In C Maj (D)	Britten, Benjamin	Na Oxf	M T Tt	Satb
Te Deum In D	Purcell, Henry	Na Kal	B T Tt	Satb
Te Deum In G (Md)	Williams, Vaughan R.	Na Oxf	M T Tt	Full
Te Deum Laudamus	Haydn, Joseph	Na Kal	B T Tt	Satb
Te Deum With Congregation (E)	Cabena, Barrie	Na Oxf	M T Tt	Unis
Te Deum (C) (Latin)	Bruckner, Anton	Cfp	R T Tt	Satb+
Te Deum, K 141	Mozart, Wolfgang A	54 Bbl	M T Tt	Satb+
Thanks Be To God	Mendelssohn, F.	Na Gsc	B T Tt	Satb+
Thanks Be To God (From Elijah)	Mendelssohn, F.	Na Gsc	M T Tt	Satb+
Thanks Be To Thee	Handel, G. F.	Na Gsc	B T Tt	Satb+
Thanks Be To Thee	Handel, G./Wiley (Arr)	75 Pro	M T Tt	Satb+
Thanks To God!	Hultman/Johnson	Na Zon	T Tt	Satb
Thanksgiving (From Holiday Motets)	Krenke, Ernst	67 Ron	B T Tt	Ssa
The Glory Of God In Nature	Beethoven, L	Na Gcr	B T Tt	Satb+
The God Of Abraham Praise	Goemanne, Noel	73 Gia	M T Tt	Sa(T)B+
The Greatness Of The Lord	Charles, Earnest	Na Gsc	B T Tt	Satb+
The Heavens Are Declaring	Beethoven, L	Na Gsc	B T Tt	Var+
The Heavens Are Telling	Haydn, Joseph	Na Gsc	B T Tt	Var+
The Heavens Are Telling (Creation)	Haydn, Joseph	Na Oxf	M T Tt	Sa
The Heavens Are Telling (3 Voices)	Telemann, G./Tortolano	70 Gia	B L T Tt	Round
The Heavens Declare (Cantata	Bach, J. S.	75 Lps	B R T Tt	Satb
The Heavens Declare The Glory	Schutz, Heinrich	Na Gsc	B T Tt	6mix
The Heavens Resounding	Beethoven/Christiansen	35 Aug	M T Tt	Satb
The Lord Is Exalted	West, J. E.	Na Gsc	B T Tt	Sab+
The Old Hundredth Psalm Tune (E)	Williams, Vaughan R.	Na Oxf	M T Tt	Var
The Omnipotence	Schubert, Franz J.	Na Gsc	B T Tt	Full+
The Only Lord	Daniels	74 Aug	M T Tt	Unis
The Psalms	Faure, J B	Na Gsc	B T Tt	Var+
The Righteous	Bach, J. C.	Na Gsc	B T Tt	Mix5
The Triumph Song (Anthem Of Praise)	Mueller	39 Gsc	M T Tt	Satb+
The Woods And Every Sweet-Smelling	West, J. E.	Na Gsc	B T Tt	Satb
Thee We Adore	James	Na Lor	M T Tt	Satb
There's A Song In The Air	Speaks, Oley	Na Gsc	B T Tt	Satb+
Thine Is The Glory	Elgar, E	Na Lor	M T Tt	Satb
Thine Is The Kingdom	Gaul, A.R.	Na Gsc	M T Tt	Satb+
This Be My Song	Peery	Na Lor	M T Tt	Satb
Thou Art God	Beck, John N	74 Bec	M T Tt	
Thou Art Mighty	Haydn, Michael	Na Gsc	B T Tt	Satb+
Thou Art Worthy	Mills, Pauline M.	66 Aso	M T Tt	
Thou God Of Wisdom (M)	Gibbons, Orlando	Na Oxf	M T Tt	Full
Thou Whose Redeeming Sacrifice	Rossini, Gioacchino	54 Bbl	M T Tt	Satb
Thou, O God, Art Praised In Sion (Ps65)	Corfe, Joseph (Arr)	Na Oxf	M T Tt	2pt
Thou, O God, Art Praised In Zion	Steel, Christopher	Na Gsc	B T Tt	Satb+
Thrice Holy Lord	Schutz/Hardwicke	75 Sac	M T Tt	Satb
Through North & South (4 Voices)	Billings, W./Tortolano	70 Gia	B L T Tt	Round
To God All Praise And Glory	Wilson	Na Lor	M T Tt	
To God Be The Glory	Brahms, Johannes	Na Lor	M T Tt	
To God Be The Glory	Hughes, Robert J.	Na Lor	M T Tt	
To God On High	Mendelssohn, F.	Na Gsc	B T Tt	Satb+
To Him Give Praise (Suite)	Fraser, Shena	Na Oxf	B T Tt	Ssa
To Raise A Grateful Song	Brandon, George	75 Pro	M T Tt	Sab+
To Thee O Lord, Our Hearts We Raise	Coleman, Henry	Na Oxf	M T Tt	Satb
To Thee, O Lord	Mendelssohn, F.	Na Gsc	B T Tt	Satb+
Traveler, The	Wood	Na Wbp	T Tt	
Trilogy Of Praise	Wetzler, Robert	Na Gsc	B T Tt	Full
Triumphal Hymn, Opus 55 (Eng/Germ)	Brahms, Johannes	Na Kal	B T Tt	Satb
Two Choral Songs	Bach, J. S.	52 Bbl	M T Tt	Satb
Two Hymns Of Praise	Rutter, John	Na Oxf	M T Tt	
Two Motets (Adoramus Te, Cantate)	Monteverdi, Claudio	Na Oxf	M T Tt	Satb
Two Te Deum And Magnificat	Parsley, Osbert (D1585)	Na Kal	B T Tt	Satb
Unto Thee Will I Sing	Glarum, L Stanley	Na Gsc	B T Tt	Var
Variants On An Irish Hymn	Beck, John N	73 Bec	M T Tt	
Vobis Datum Est	Porta, Costanzo	75 Bbl	M T Tt	Satb
We Adore Thee	Brahms, Johannes	64 Bbl	B T Tt	Ssaa
We Adore You No. 1	Lotti, Antonio	74 Bbl	M T Tt	Satb
We Adore You No. 2	Lotti, Antonio	74 Bbl	M T Tt	Satb
We Come To Praise His Name	Smith, G Riley, R	76 Tal	R L T Tt	
We Do Adore Thee	Lasso, Orlando Di	66 Som	M T Tt	
We Give Thanks To Thee	Glarum, L Stanley	Na Gsc	B T Tt	Var
We Plow The Fields	Lockwood, Normand	56 Smc	M T Tt	Satb
We Praise Thee, O God	Bach, J.S.-Jennings	67 Aug	M T Tt	Satb
We Praise Thee, O God	Johnson, D.	67 Aug	M T Tt	Sab
We Praise Thee, O God, Our Redeemer	Traditional/Shepard	Na Zon	T Tt	Satb
We Thank Thee	Byles, B D	Na Lor	M T Tt	Unis
We Thank Thee, Lord	Burroughs	Na Lor	M T Tt	Satb
We Thank Thee, O Lord	Price	Na Lor	M T Tt	Satb
We Walk Through The Meadow	Follett (Arr)	76 Pro	M T Tt	Sab
We Will Rejoice	Croft, William	75 Bbl	M T Tt	Satb
Whether Young Or Old	Moe, Daniel	73 Aug	M T Tt	Satb
Who Is Like Unto Thee (W/Keyboard)	Pergolesi-Ehret	Na Gia	M L T Tt	Satb+
Who Is Like Unto Thee, O Lord	Berger, Jean	66 Aug	M T Tt	Full
Why?	Moore/Anthony	Na Zon	T Tt	Satb
With Harp And Voice Of Psalms	Brandon, George	70 Gia	M T Tt	Sa(B)+
Worship The Lord In The Beauty	Smith	Na Lor	M T Tt	
Worthy Art Thou	Johnson, Gary L.	75 Bfi	B R T Tt	
Worthy Art Thou, O Lord God (W/Tmb)	Bruckner, Anton	Na Aug	M T Tt	Satb
Ye Servants Of God	Avalos (Arr)	76 Pro	M T Tt	Satb+
Ye Servants Of God	Haydn/Decou	Na Zon	M T Tt	Satb
Ye Tuneful Muses	Purcell, Henry	Na Kal	B T Tt	Satb
You Are Given To Know	Porta, Costanzo	75 Bbl	M T Tt	Satb
Young Lions, The	Beck, John N	72 Bec	M T Tt	

Hymns of Unity and Ecumenism

Hymn Of Unity (The Glory You Have)	Toolan, Sr Suzanne	71 Gia	B R L F Tu	Ar+
May All Your People Be One	Hurd, Bob	73 Fel	B R F Tu	
That We May Be One	Johnson, Gary L.	75 Bfi	B R F Tu	
Till All My People Are One	Repp, Ray	67 Fel	B R F Tu	
Where The Children Run Free	Summers, George	70 Gia	B R L F Tu	Var+
Love Will Bring Us Back	Sherberg, Jon	75 Wrd	B R G Tu	Satb+
Make Us One Father (W/Piano)	Johnson, Paul	73 Wrd	M G Tu	Satb+
Ecumenical Hymn To God Our Father	Dykes, John B.	73 Acp	B L L Tu	
Ecumenical Hymn To God Our Father	Wojcik, Richard J.	70 Acp	B L L Tu	
Ecumenical Hymn To God Our Father (4pt)	Bach, J. S.	73 Acp	B L L Tu	
From Sion Perfect In Beauty (M)	Kreutz, Robert	76 Gia	M L L Tu	Satb+
In Christ The Lord	Peloquin, C Alexander	65 Gia	M L Tu	Satbu+
Make Us One	Christiansen, P.	69 Aug	M L Tu	Satb
Prayer For Peace	Peloquin, C Alexander	65 Gia	M L Tu	Satbu+
Psalm For Unity	Peloquin, C Alexander	65 Gia	M L Tu	Satbu+
Psalm 132: Behold How Good It Is	Peloquin, C Alexander	Na Gia	L Tu	
Time For Building Bridges, A	Landry, Carey (Rev.)	74 Nal	B R L Tu	
Una Sancta (W/Keyboard Or Band)	Christiansen, P.	60 Aug	M L Tu	
Walls (You Have Made A Field)	Temple, Sebastian	71 Gia	B R L L Tu	Satb+
Anthem Of Unity	Beck, John Ness	Na Gsc	B T Tu	Satb+
Behold How Good And Joyful (Ps 133)	Vann, Stanley	Na Oxf	M T Tu	Satb
Let Us All Be One	Brandon, George	74 Gia	M T Tu	Satb+
Now Is The Time Approaching	Borthwick/Webb	76 Jsp	B T Tu	Satb
O God Of Every Race And Creed	Grieb, Herbert	Na Gsc	B T Tu	Satb+
Song Of Loyal Brotherhood	Mendelssohn, F.	Na Gsc	B T Tu	Satb
That They All May Be One	Mueller, Carl F	Na Gsc	B T Tu	Var+

Wedding Music

This section lists songs specifically oriented to weddings. See also category ZA and ZB for collections, and instrumental music.

Because We Are One	Wood, Mike	76 Rpb	M B R L F Tw	
Beginning Today	Ducote, Daryll-Balhoff	73 Fcc	B R L F Tw	
Behold, Thou Art Fair	Hershberg, Sarah	68 Fel	B F Tw	
Love One Another	Germaine	66 Fel	B R F Tw	
Psalm 128 Your Wife Shall Be	O'sheil, Judy	66 Fel	B F Tw	
Song Of Ruth	Ellis, Ron	73 Rav	B R L F Tw	
The Face Of God (Wedding Song)	Cunningham, Patrick	68 Gra	B R L F Tw	Solo
Treasures	Honeytree	73 Wrd	B R F Tw	Solo+
We Have Love (W/Piano)	Kershaw, Christopher	73 Wrd	B R F Tw	Solo+
Wedding Song	Ault, Gary	73 Fcc	B R L F Tw	
Whither Thou Goest	Hershberg, Sarah	68 Fel	B F Tw	
Hymn Of Love	Greif, Jean A	76 Vrn	M L G Tw	
Wedding Prayer, A	Smith/Ackley	Na Zon	M G Tw	
A Wedding Blessing	Pelz, W.	73 Aug	M L Tw	Solo
A Wedding Song	Carroll, J. R.	75 Gia	M L Tw	
Behold, Thus Is The Man Blessed	Ferris, W	Na Gia	L Tw	
Bless, O Lord, These Rings	Roff, Joseph	Na Gia	L Tw	
Blessing	Davis, Paulette	75 Rpb	M B R L L Tw	
Communion In A Minor, Ps 128	Cunningham, Patrick	69 Gra	B R L L Tw	Satb
Father Eternal, We Pray (A Cap)	Hunnicutt, J.	75 Gia	M L L Tw	Satb
Father, We Gather Here To Praise	Roff, Joseph	65 Lit	B L Tw	
Greet The Dawn	Schneider, Kent E.	75 Ccc	B L Tw	
Intrada In A Minor (Blessing)	Cunningham, Patrick	69 Gra	B R L L Tw	Satb
Jesus, Stand Beside Them	Lovelace, Austin C.	Na Abi	M L Tw	Solo
Life Is You	Ellis, Ron	76 Rav	B R L L Tw	
Lord, May Their Lives	Carroll, J. R.	Na Gia	L Tw	
Marriage (Response)	Picca, Angelo Della	68 Wlp	B L Tw	
May You See Your Children's Children	Fitzpatrick, Dennis	65 Fel	B L Tw	
Nuptial Blessing	Proulx, Richard	68 Aug	M L Tw	Solo
O God From Whom Mankind Derives	Kaan/Kraehenbuehl	76 Jsp	B L Tw	Satb
O God Of Love To Thee We Bow Low	Lovelace, Austin C.	Na Abi	M L Tw	Solo
O Ye Who Taste That Love Is Sweet	Lovelace, Austin C.	Na Abi	M L Tw	Solo
Our Father, By Whose Name	Lovelace, Austin C.	Na Abi	M L Tw	Solo

CATEGORIZED INDEX

Title	Composer	Pub	Codes
Psalm 128	Peeters, Flor	72 Cfc	M R L L Tw
Psalm 128	Wetzler, Robert	64 Aug	M L Tw Solo
Psalm 128 (127)	Deiss, Lucien	65 Wlp	B L Tw
Sacred Trust (A Wedding Song)	Kreutz, Robert	74 Gia	M L Tw Solo+
Set Me As A Seal	Smith, Gregg	Na Gsc	B L Tw Satb
Song Of Love	Schneider, Kent E.	75 Ccc	B L Tw
The Wedding Feast	Shelley, Tom	72 Ahc	B R L L Tw
There's A Time, There's A Moment	Lynch, Michael B.	69 Rav	B R L L Tw
To Share Their Joy (Wedding Song)	Landry, Carey (Rev.)	71 Nal	B R L Tw
Two Lives, One Moment	Jacobs, Peter	73 Chd	B R L L Tw
Wedded Souls	Saxe, Serge	52 Pic	M L Tw
Wedding Music For The Church Organist	Lovelace, Austin C.	Na Abi	M L Tw Solo+
Wedding Song	Verdi, Ralph C.	Na Gia	L Tw
Whither Thou Goest	Cassler, G. W.	55 Aug	M L Tw Solo
With These Rings	Shelley, Tom	71 Ahc	B R L L Tw
Behold You Are Charming	Des Pres, Josquin	Na Gsc	B T Tw Satb+
Cantata #195 Wedding Cantata (E & Ger)	Bach, J. S.	Na Kal	B T Tw
How Blest Are They (M)	Purcell, Henry	Na Oxf	M T Tw Satb
I Will Not Let Thee Go	Bach, J. C.	Na Gsc	B T Tw Full+
Love Divine (Me)	Vanderhoek, Bert	Na Oxf	M T Tw Unis
Music For Weddings	Dooner, A	Na Gia	T Tw
Now Joined By God	Westendorf, Omer	62 Wlp	B T Tw
Now You Will Feel No Rain (Wedding)	Wagner, Lavern J.	74 Sms	M R L T Tw
O Perfect Love	Barnby, Jos	Na Gsc	B T Tw Satb+
Psalm 121 And Wedding Responses	Mckie, William	Na Oxf	M T Tw Satb
Psalm 128	Berger, Jean	65 Bbl	M T Tw Satb
Set Me As A Seal	Grieb, Herbert	Na Gsc	B T Tw Satb+
Set Me As A Seal (4 Voices)	Billings, W./Tortolano	70 Gia	B L T Tw Round
Set Me As A Seal Upon Thine Heart	Walton, William	Na Oxf	M T Tw Satb
Sing Unto God (18 Minutes)	Handel, G.F. (Ed Stein)	Na Oxf	B T Tw Satb
Veniat Dilectus Meus (Come O Come)	Grandi, Alessandro	Na Gsc	B T Tw Sttb+
Wedding Chorus From Alceste	Handel, G. F.	73 Bbl	M T Tw Satb+
Wedding Motet	Fitzpatrick, Dennis	63 Fel	B T Tw
Wedding Prayer	Dunlap, Fern Glasgow	Na Gsc	B T Tw Satb+
Wedding Processional & Air (Org)	Bach, J.S.–Leupold	69 Aug	M T Tw Org
Wedding Responses	Guest, Douglas	Na Oxf	M T Tw Satb

General Topical Hymns

Here are hymns which do not fit into one of the other categories. They include morning songs, hymns about saints, catechetical songs and bible stories, as well as humorous songs.

Title	Composer	Pub	Codes
A Touch Of Lemon	Comeau, Bill	67 Van	B R C Tx
If God Could Be A Color	Haas, James E.	73 Mob	B C Tx
Spirit Of God	Haas, James E.	73 Mob	B C Tx
Sing For Joy	Haas, James E.	73 Mob	B C Tx
Come, Lord Jesus	Haas, James E.	73 Mob	B C Tx
God Has Visited His People	Haas, James E.	73 Mob	B C Tx
Go Forth	Haas, James E.	73 Mob	B C Tx
Abraham Sent Them Away	Temple, Sebastian	69 Fcc	R L C Tx
All Join Hands	Lewis, E.	75 Sil	S C Tx
Ana Abraham Cried	Temple, Sebastian	69 Fcc	R L C Tx
And Rachel Loved Him	Temple, Sebastian	69 Fcc	R L C Tx
Babble Babel	Temple, Sebastian	69 Fcc	R L C Tx
Birthday Song	Blunt, Neil	71 Wlp	B C Tx
Bringing Freedom	Comeau, Bill	67 Van	B R C Tx
Children's Prayer	Egoroff, A.	63 Som	M C Tx
Coat Of Many Colors	Hershberg, Sarah	69 Fcc	R L C Tx
Danny's Dance	Comeau, Bill	67 Van	B R C Tx
David, Swing Your Sling	North, Jack	75 Hal	C Tx 2-Pt.
Don't Send Those Kids To Sunday School	Hamblen Stuart	Na Ham	M C Tx
Dream, Pharoah, Dream	Temple, Sebastian	69 Fcc	R L C Tx
Dreamer	Comeau, Bill	67 Van	B R C Tx
Eastward In Eden	Temple, Sebastian	69 Fcc	R L C Tx
Famine Came Upon The Land	Temple, Sebastian	69 Fcc	R L C Tx
Fish Wish	Comeau, Bill	67 Van	B R C Tx
For Tommy: Thanks For The Chance!	Wise, Joe	72 Nal	B R C Tx
Gentle Guide (Mother's Day)	Hunt, Thomas	61 Gam	M C Tx Unis
Go On By	Hamblen Stuart	Na Ham	M C Tx
God Did!	Viger, Cathy	75 Rpb	M B R L C Tx
Great Person, A	Landry, Carey (Rev.)	75 Nal	B R C Tx
Halloween Song	Blunt, Neil	71 Wlp	B R C Tx
Hello Song	Blunt, Neil	71 Wlp	B R C Tx
I Went To Cincinnati	Wise, Joe	74 Nal	B R C Tx
In Sodom Town	Temple, Sebastian	69 Fcc	R L C Tx
It Is They	Temple, Sebastian	69 Fcc	R L C Tx
It's Cool In The Furnance (Musical)	Hawthorne/Red, Buryl	73 Wrd	B R C Tx Unis+
Jacob's Lament	Temple, Sebastian	69 Fcc	R L C Tx
Jacob's Ladder	Temple, Sebastian	69 Fcc	R L C Tx
Jello Man	Comeau, Bill	67 Van	B R C Tx
La La Life	Miffleton, Jack	71 Wlp	B R C Tx
Lion Hunt	Comeau, Bill	67 Van	B R C Tx
Listen, Listen	Landry, Carey (Rev.)	73 Nal	B R C Tx
Men In History (So The Bible Tells)	Lindsay Lisa	Na Ham	M C Tx
My Sons Abel And Cain	Temple, Sebastian	69 Fcc	R L C Tx
Noise Song, The	Wise, Joe	74 Nal	B R C Tx
Nursery Rhyme	Butler, Charles F.	73 Mar	R L C Tx
One Gentle, One Wild	Temple, Sebastian	69 Fcc	R L C Tx
Open Up Your Heart	Hamblen Stuart	Na Ham	M C Tx
Potter, Potter	Temple, Sebastian	69 Fcc	R L C Tx
Put On Love	Walker, Mary Lou	73 Pnp	C Tx
Quick, Quick	Temple, Sebastian	69 Fcc	R L C Tx
Ray The Rangy Rhino	Blunt, Neil	71 Wlp	B R C Tx
Red Balloon	Davis, Paulette	74 Rpb	M B R L C Tx
Red, Yellow, Purple And Green	Temple, Sebastian	69 Fcc	R L C Tx
Seed, The	Wise, Joe	74 Nal	B R C Tx
She's Just An Old Stump	Miffleton, Jack	71 Wlp	B R C Tx
Sidney The Silly Centipede	Miffleton, Jack	73 Wlp	B R C Tx
Sometimes I'd Like To Be A Clown	Miffleton, Jack	73 Wlp	B R C Tx
Song Of Sarah	Temple, Sebastian	69 Fcc	R L C Tx
Sons Of Jacob	Temple, Sebastian	69 Fcc	R L C Tx
Strangest Dream, The	Blunt, Neil	71 Wlp	B R C Tx
Take Time Out	Comeau, Bill	67 Van	B R C Tx
Talking Pets	Miffleton, Jack	71 Wlp	B R C Tx
The Alphabet Tree	Thiman, Eric H.	Na Gsc	B C Tx 2pt+
The Book Of Stories	Blue, Robert	66 Fel	B R C Tx
The Tree Song	Blue, Robert	66 Fel	B R C Tx
There Once Was A Man	Temple, Sebastian	69 Fcc	R L C Tx
Tomorrow And Tomorrow	Miffleton, Jack	71 Wlp	B R C Tx
What Can Make A Hippopotamus Smile	Wilkes, T. & Stevenson	73 Nal	B R C Tx
What Color Is God's Skin?	Landry, Carey (Rev.)	75 Nal	B R C Tx
What God Is Like	Walker, Mary Lou	73 Pnp	C Tx
Wind Song	Temple, Sebastian	69 Fcc	R L C Tx
Wrestlers, The	Landry, Carey (Rev.)	75 Nal	B R C Tx
You Are My Brother (Part 1)	Landry, Carey (Rev.)	75 Nal	B R C Tx
You Are My Brother (Part 3)	Landry, Carey (Rev.)	75 Nal	B R C Tx
You Are My Brother (Part 2)	Landry, Carey (Rev.)	75 Nal	B R C Tx
You've Got To Look Hard	Comeau, Bill	67 Van	B R C Tx
A Little Each Day	Yantis, David	Na Yan	B F Tx
A Soldier's Prayer	Redd, Gene C.	Na Sav	F Tx
A Special Kind Of Beautiful	Lewis, E.	74 Sil	L F Tx
Ain't Never Seen So Much Rain Before	Redd, Gc/Bid Causey	Na Sav	F Tx
All	Yantis, David	Na Yan	B F Tx
All The Roads Lead Home	Yantis, David	76 Yan	B F Tx
Along The Way	Hunkele	68 Wlp	B R F Tx
Amy's Song	Wood, Mike	76 Rpb	M B R L F Tx
An Appointed Time	Thiem, James	66 Fel	B F Tx
Away	Leyko, Patricia J.	76 Chh	B R L F Tx
Back To The Prairies	Smith–Harper	Na Zon	M F Tx
Balaam	Cunningham, Patrick	71 Gra	B R L F Tx
Ballad Of The Seasons	Winter, Miriam T.	71 Van	B R F Tx
Beyond A Dream	Yantis, David	Na Yan	B F Tx
Blue Town	Hershberg, Sarah	71 Fcc	R L F Tx
Bushel–Round	Miffleton, Jack	73 Wlp	B F Tx
Can I Show You	Stevens, Marsha J.	73 Chd	B R L F Tx
Carolina, Coming Home	Lewis, E.	74 Sil	L F Tx
Charlotte's Song	Parker, Tom	68 Wlp	B F Tx
Children Of The Lord	Winter, Miriam T.	71 Van	B R F Tx
Choices	Ellis, Ron	76 Rav	B R L F Tx
Come On Down	Davis, Bob	73 Fcc	B R L F Tx
Come Out Of Egypt	Jabusch, Willard F.	75 Rpb	M B R L F Tx
Come With Me	Meyer, Ron	76 Fel	B R F Tx
Come, Children, Hear Me	Repp, Ray	67 Fel	B R F Tx
Come, Then, My Son	Aridas, Chris	73 Fel	B F Tx
Country Blessing	Davis, Bob	73 Fcc	B R L F Tx
Creation	Bisignano/Furman	71 Wlp	B F Tx
Creed (1964 Text)	Winter, Miriam T.	66 Van	B R F Tx
Creed (64 Text)	Markaitis, Bruno	67 Van	B R F Tx
Cry Alice	Miffleton, Jack	69 Wlp	B F Tx
David's Song	Meltz, Ken	72 Wlp	B F Tx
Dayenu	Price, William	70 Acp	B L F Tx
Dayenu	Silvia, Helen	73 Acp	B L F Tx
Deborah	Hershberg, Sarah & Tem	68 Fel	B R F Tx
Dives And Lazarus (Folk Ballad)	Byrt, John	Na Oxf	B F Tx Equal
Do You Know?	Temple, Sebastian	63 Fcc	B R L F Tx Gia
Don't Be Afraid	Winter, Miriam T.	71 Van	B R F Tx
Don't Talk The Talk	Amason, B.	74 Sil	R L F Tx
Don't You Care	Hatfield, S & Mcnees, L	74 Man	R F Tx
Don't You Look All Around	Dunkin, Timothy L.	73 Fel	B F Tx
Doubting Thomas	Mccarthy, John	70 Van	B R F Tx
Down With Niniveh	Montague, George T.	68 Fel	B R F Tx
Ebb And Flow	Yantis, David	76 Yan	B F Tx
Esther	Hershberg, Sarah	68 Fel	B R F Tx
Eve's Lament	Hershberg, Sarah	68 Fel	B R F Tx
Even A Worm	Miffleton, Jack	73 Wlp	B F Tx
Every Day	Miller, Dan	73 Fel	B F Tx
Everything Is Beautiful	Lojeski, Ed	74 Hal	F Tx Satb
Face In The Crowd	Stevens, Marsha J.	75 Chd	R L F Tx
Fly (From Even A Worm)	Miffleton, Jack	73 Wlp	B F Tx
Folks Don't Kiss Old People Any More	Edwards, Deanna	74 Fcc	R L F Tx
Forevermore	Enlow, H./Hires, B.	74 Sil	R L F Tx
Freedom Song	Thiem, James	66 Fel	B R F Tx
Go Down Moses (Pd)	Kennedy–Cadwallader	72 Gia	B R L F Tx Var+
Go Tell Your People	Miffleton, Jack	68 Acp	B L F Tx
God Is A Fire Of Love	Temple, Sebastian	71 Gia	B R L F Tx Var+
God Is Moving On	Turner, Roy	67 Cam	M L F Tx
God Is Much Fairer	Finley, Ken	73 Fel	B F Tx
God Made The World	Miffleton, Jack	68 Wlp	B F Tx
God Made Us All	Miffleton, Jack	71 Wlp	B R F Tx
God Speaks	Winter, Miriam T.	71 Van	B R F Tx
God That Was Real	Wyrtzen, Don	Na Zon	M F Tx Satb
God Will Answer Prayer	Stewart, C H And H G	Na Lor	M F Tx Satb
Goin' Easy	Yantis, David	Na Yan	B F Tx
Gonna Sing My Lord	Wise, Joe	67 Wlp	B R F Tx
Grab Your Soap (From Even A Worm)	Miffleton, Jack	73 Wlp	B F Tx
Guide Me, O Thou Great Jehovah	Johnson, Gary L.	75 Bfi	B R F Tx
Happiness Song	Miller, Dan	73 Fel	B F Tx
Hard Feeling To Explain	Fischer, John	69 Fel	B R F Tx
Hell	Williams, J.	76 Sil	F Tx
Her Troubled Course	Ketchum, Teri	73 Msm	M R L F Tx
Hey Day	Miffleton, Jack	73 Wlp	B R F Tx
Hey Soul	Howard, Brian	74 Fis	M L F Tx
Holy Spirit Of The Living God	Temple, Sebastian	71 Gia	B R L F Tx Var+
Hosea	Norbet, Gregory	72 Wes	M B R L F Tx
I Know The Secret	Winter, Miriam T.	71 Van	B R F Tx
I Sing A Song Of Teilhard	Temple, Sebastian	69 Gia	B R L F Tx Uguit
I Wonder Why	Savals/Mattei/Blunt	68 Wlp	B R F Tx

Title	Author	Ref	Codes
I'll Hold You In My Arms	Edwards, Deanna	74 Fcc	R L F Tx
If We Saw Him	Tucciarone, Angel	73 Wlp	B F Tx
In Your Holy Place	Miffleton, Jack	69 Acp	B L F Tx
Irish Blessing	Dumin, Frank	70 Van	B F Tx
Is There Any Word	Ducote, Darryl	71 Fel	B R F Tx
Is There?	Hershberg, Sarah	71 Fcc	R L F Tx
It Must Be The Season Of The Lord	Phillips, David	73 Fel	B F Tx
It Only Takes A Hug	Miffleton, Jack	73 Wlp	B R F Tx
It's Mine, It's Mine	Sweeney	71 Wlp	B R F Tx
Jeremiah	Davis, Diane	72 Fis	M L F Tx
John Is My Name	Miffleton, Jack	73 Wlp	B R F Tx
Jonah	Montague, George T.	68 Fel	B R F Tx
Joy Of Heaven, The	Peterson, John W.	Na Zon	M F Ix Satb
Judith	Hershberg, Sarah	69 Fel	B R F Tx
Keep The Rumor Going (God Is Alive)	Edwin, Robert	67 Van	B R F Tx
Kum Ba Ya	Lojeski, Ed	74 Hal	F Tx Var
Laban's Lament	Hershberg, Sarah	68 Fel	B R F Tx
Let The Words Of My Mouth	Johnson, Gary L.	74 Bfi	B L F Tx
Let There Be Light	Gallegos, Jesse	73 Fel	B F Tx
Life	Hershberg, Sarah	71 Fcc	R L F Tx
Life Can Be Fun	Amason, B.	75 Sil	R L F Tx
Life Is A Makin' Do	Hershberg, Sarah	71 Fcc	R L F Tx
Like A Deer	Hanson, Mike	73 Fel	B F Tx
Listen To The Voices, That Want To Be	Welz, Joey—Wray, Link	71 Urs	M B R F Tx
Little Child	Ault, Gary	70 Fel	B R F Tx
Look All Around	Fischer, John	69 Fel	B R F Tx
Look Out Your Window	Repp, Ray	68 Fel	B R F Tx
Look To The Rainbow	Hunkele	67 Wlp	B R F Tx
Look To Your Soul (From Thoughts...)	Furman	71 Wlp	B R F Tx
Lookin' Back	Brigman, R.	74 Sil	R L F Tx
Lord Give Me Wings	Young, R. Otha	75 Ste	M R L F Tx
Lord Teach Us To Pray	Wise, Joe	71 Wlp	B R F Tx
Maleita's Song	Wise, Joe	67 Wlp	B R F Tx
May The Roads Rise Up (Irish Blessing)	Lynch, Michael B.	76 Rav	B R L F Tx
Mountain Country	Amason, B.	74 Sil	L F Tx
My Beloved Is Mine	O'sheil, Judy	66 Fel	B F Tx
My People	Wise, Joe	68 Wlp	B R F Tx
Nicodemus	Ylvisaker, J & A.	69 Van	B R F Tx
Nicodemus (P.D.)	Elrich, Dwight (Arr.)	73 Man	B F Tx Choral
Night	Winter, Miriam T.	68 Van	B R F Tx
No More Pain	Bowers, Julia	72 Sem	B F Tx
No Time Like The Present	Blunt, Neil	70 Wlp	B R F Tx
Now And Forever	Yantis, David	Na Yan	B F Tx
O My Achin Rib (Adams Complaint)	St. Benedict's Farm	75 Sbf	B R L F Tx
On The Road	Wood, Mike	76 Rpb	M B R L F Tx
One Day Soon	Lewis, E.	74 Sil	L F Tx
One From Among Us	Kleinpeter, Karen	73 Fel	B F Tx
Only These Two	Miffleton, Jack	71 Wlp	M B R F Tx
Open Up	Fischer, John	69 Fel	B R F Tx
Osee (Hosea)	Germaine	66 Fel	B R F Tx
Our Time Is Now	Winberry, Mary & Malat	73 Fel	B F Tx
Pasadena Kid	Hatfield, Steve	74 Man	R F Tx
Pause A While	Ault, Gary	69 Fel	B R F Tx
Peace Won't Come	Lewis, E./ Malool, G.	74 Sil	R L F Tx
People, Ask Me	Bisignano/Furman	71 Wlp	B R F Tx
Peter	Winter, Miriam T.	67 Van	B R F Tx
Peter And John	Stewart, Malcolm	69 Van	B R F Tx
Peter, Peter Hear Me	Mccarthy, John	70 Van	B R F Tx
Playground For People	Bisignano/Furman	71 Wlp	B F Tx
Preface (Jazz—Rock Mass)	Mitchell, Ian	68 Fel	B R F Tx
Pretend We're Young Again	Hershberg, Sarah	68 Fel	B R F Tx
Psalm 114 Israel Went Out	Quinlan, Paul	66 Fel	B F Tx
Psalm 126 These Are They	Grace, Sister Mary	66 Fel	B F Tx
Put On Your Boots	Barker, Sherrell	71 Fis	M L F Tx
Rain Song	Pulkingham, Betty C.	72 Fis	M L F Tx
Rainbow	Ducote, Daryll, Balhof	73 Fcc	B R L F Tx
Reap, Reap	Hershberg, Sarah	71 Fcc	R L F Tx
Rebuild The Temple	Cunningham, Patrick	68 Fel	B R F Tx
Reginas Song	Wise, Joe	67 Wlp	B R F Tx
Right To Live	Edwards, Deanna	74 Fcc	R L F Tx
Run, Christian, Run (4—Part Arr)	Silvia, Helen	73 Acp	B L F Tx
Sam Vel	Pulkingham, Betty C.	72 Fis	M L F Tx
Samson (Novelty Song)	St. Benedict's Farm	75 Sbf	B R L F Tx
Sarah	Hershberg, Sarah	68 Fel	B R F Tx
Sea Of Madness	Ketchum, Teri	74 Msm	M R L F Tx
Show Yourself To Me, Lord	Cockett, M/Mayhew, K.	69 Van	B R F Tx
So Said Amos The Prophet	Casey, F.J.	66 Fel	B F Tx
Song Of Daniel	Silvia, Helen	73 Acp	B L F Tx
Song Of Good News, The	Jabusch, Willard F.	67 Acf	M R F Tx
Song Of Hannah	Hershberg, Sarah	68 Fel	B R F Tx
Song Of Life	Enlow, H.	74 Sil	R L F Tx
Song Of My People	Pressel, Juliet	74 Wgm	B L F Tx
Song Of The City	Gilligan, Michael	70 Acp	B L F Tx
Song Of The City	Silvia, Helen	73 Acp	B L F Tx
Speak To Me, Wind	Winter, Miriam T.	66 Van	B R F Tx
Spirits Of The Night	Ketchum, Teri	74 Msm	M R L F Tx
Spread Your Wings	Lewis, E./ Malool, G.	74 Sil	L F Tx
St. John The Evangelist	Mccarthy, John	70 Van	B R F Tx
Stilled & Quiet Is My Soul Ps 139	Toolan, Sr Suzanne	71 Gia	B R L F Tx Ar+
Sunshine	Miffleton, Jack	73 Wlp	B R F Tx
T'was On A Cold And Wintry Night	Hershberg, Sarah	70 Fcc	R L F Tx
Tell Me Now	Kleinpeter, Karen	73 Fel	B F Tx
Ten Lepers	Winter, Miriam T.	66 Van	B R F Tx
The Apostle's Creed	Yantis, David	Na Yan	B F Tx
The Cold Cathedral	Fischer, John	69 Fel	B R F Tx
The Creed (Credo) (Jazz—Rock Mass)	Mitchell, Ian	68 Fel	B R F Tx
The Flowers Appear	Blue, Robert	66 Fel	B F Tx
The Four Seasons	Thiem, James	66 Fel	B F Tx
The Great Lights	Miffleton, Jack	73 Wlp	B R F Tx
The Hammer Song	Seeger, P/Hays, L.	58 Lud	F Tx
The Lord Bless You	Johnson, Gary L.	75 Bfi	B R F Tx
The Nicene Creed	Yantis, David	Na Yan	B F Tx
The Nicene Creed (Credo)	Blue, Robert	66 Fel	B F Tx
The Rich Young Ruler	Ylvisaker, J. & A.	69 Van	B R F Tx
The Road Of Life	Fischer, John	69 Fel	B R F Tx
The Silent Night	Belt, Thomas/Batastini	72 Gio	B R L F Tx Var+
The Times Are Always Changing	King, Charleen	72 Fel	B R F Tx
The Visit	Winter, Miriam T.	68 Van	B R F Tx
The Water Is Wide	Martin, Gilbert M	Na Lor	M F Tx Satb
The Wind Is Blowin'	Germaine	66 Fel	B R F Tx
These Two	Schaffer, Robert J.	69 Wlp	B R F Tx
Think Of It, Lord!	Ortlund, A.	Na Zon	M F Tx Satb
This World Outside	Wyrtzen, Don	Na Zon	M F Tx Satb
Thomas	Ylvisaker, J. & A.	69 Van	B R F Tx
Three Tents "One For Moses"	Winter, Miriam T.	68 Van	B R F Tx
Through All The World	Furman	71 Wlp	B F Tx
To Be Alive	Leyko, Patricia J.	76 Chh	B R L F Tx
To Be Alive	Repp, Ray	67 Fel	B R F Tx
To Cry Is To Die	Repp, Ray	66 Fel	B R F Tx
To Damascus	Casey, F. J.	66 Fel	B F Tx
To The Mountain	Jabusch, Willard F.	67 Acf	F Tx
To Whom Shall We Go	Jabusch, Willard F.	67 Acf	F Tx
Touch A Hand, Make A Friend	Lojeski, Ed	75 Hal	F Tx Var
Turn Your Eyes	Ducote, Darryl	69 Fel	B R F Tx
Turn, Turn, Turn	Seeger, Pete	62 Mel	F Tx
Wake Up	Miller, Don	72 Fel	B R F Tx
Wake Up, My People	Repp, Ray	67 Fel	B R F Tx
We Need Time	Repp, Ray	67 Fel	B R F Tx
What Can We Offer	Jabusch, Willard F.	67 Acf	F Tx
What Miracles Of Beauty	Mccarthy, John	70 Van	B R F Tx
What Would You Do	Lewis, E.	74 Sil	L F Tx
What You Gonna Do	Montague, George T.	68 Fel	B R F Tx
When I Witness	Yantis, David	Na Yan	B F Tx
Where Do I See God?	Yantis, David	Na Yan	B F Tx
Where In The World	Meilstrup/Marsh	Na Zon	M F Tx Satb
Where Is This Old World A—Goin?	Peterson/Peterson Sist	Na Zon	M F Tx Sab-Sa
Whither Bound St. James?	Mccarthy, John	70 Van	B R F Tx
Who Am I	Lewis, E.	74 Sil	L F Tx
Who Am I?	Hershberg, Sarah	71 Fcc	R L F Tx
Why, Oh Why	Repp, Ray	66 Fel	B R F Tx
Windows Of The Mind	Wyrtzen, Don	Na Zon	M F Tx Unis
Without Love	Wagner, Lavern J.	73 Sms	M R L F Tx
Woman Of Samaria	Casey, F. J.	66 Fel	B F Tx
Woman Of Stone	Hershberg, Sarah	71 Fcc	R L F Tx
Woman Of Valor	Hershberg, Sarah	68 Fel	B R F Tx
Wonderful World	Thiem, James	65 Fel	B F Tx
Your Word	Miffleton, Jack	75 Wlp	B R F Tx
Zaccheus (There Was A Man)	Winter, Miriam T.	66 Van	B R F Tx
A Few Things To Remember	Hamblen Stuart	Na Ham	M G Tx
A Little Thought Away	Benedetti, Quint	70 Abm	M R G Tx
Across The Shadows	Childs	Na Zon	M G Tx
Ain't Dat Good News	Traditional/Johnson	Na Zon	M G Tx Satb
Altar Of Faith	Casteel, K./Roth, P.	73 Csm	M B R L G Tx
Always Remembered	Smith/Harper	Na Zon	M G Tx
Answer Man, The	Harper, Redd	Na Zon	M G Tx
Answer, The	Peterson, John W.	Na Zon	M G Tx Satb
Believe Ye	Comer, John	74 Mam	R L G Tx
Better Start Believin'	Brock, Linda	74 Mam	R L G Tx
Black But Proud	Overstreet, Rev. L.	69 Sto	M G Tx
Bless You	Benedetti, Quint & Dic	68 Abm	M G Tx
But I Do Know	Calkin, Ruth	52 Man	M G Tx Choral
Calling (With Brass Acc)	Peterson/Decou	Na Zon	M G Tx Satb
Can I Have This Happiness	Akers, Doris	73 Man	B R G Tx
Can I Say	Cross, Danny	74 Mam	R L G Tx
Can It Be	Butler, Dorothy	68 Pmp	M B R L G Tx
Can We Be Identified	Butler, Dorothy	74 Pmp	M B L G Tx
Can You Believe?	Hendrix, James	70 Jhe	M R L G Tx
Carried Away	Mieir, Audrey	64 Man	M B G Tx
Carry On	Hendrix, James	70 Jhe	M R L G Tx
Chapel In The Hollow	Wrightman, N.	68 Csm	M B R L G Tx
Choose Life	Scholtes, Peter	68 Fel	B R G Tx
Choosing Rather	Mieir, Audrey	65 Man	B G Tx
Come Away, My Love	Gaither/Gaither B/G	70 Gmc	M B R G Tx Satb
Come On Over Yonder	Hendrix, James	74 Jhe	M R L G Tx
Daddy Sang Bass	Perkins, Carl	68 Ced	M R G Tx
De Animals A—Comin'	Bartholomew	Na Gsc	B G Tx Var
De Promis' Lan'	Na	Na Gsc	B G Tx Satb+
Dear God In Heaven	Tyacke Louis	71 Jhm	R L G Tx
Dedicated But Doomed	Peck, Barry	74 Mam	R L G Tx
Dig My Grave	Na	Na Gsc	B G Tx Var
Do—Don't Touch—A My Garment	Na	Na Gsc	B G Tx Ttbb
Don't Cry	Williams, Willie Jr.	69 Oak	B G Tx
Don't Disgrace My Mother's Name	Baskette Arvil	72 Jhm	R L G Tx
Don't Let Them Have Their Way	Wilt, Roberta	74 Pmp	M B R L G Tx
Don't Wait	Wilt, Roberta	74 Pmp	M B R L G Tx
Don't You Weep No More, Mary	Dett, R N	Na Gsc	B G Tx Satb
Elijah Rock	Na	Na Gsc	B G Tx Full
Evening Star	Atkinson, Condit	74 Gal	M G Tx Satb
Every Time I Feel De Spirit	Na	Na Gsc	B G Tx Full
Everybody Knows For Sure	Girard, Chuck	74 Wrd	B R G Tx Unis+
Everywhere	Crouch, Andrae	68 Man	B R G Tx
Fathers Table Grace	Sewell Homer/Jones O.	61 Oak	G Tx
Four Things	Atkinson, Condit	75 Gal	M G Tx Satb
Give Up	Goodman, Howard	57 Ced	M R G Tx
Go Down Moses	Na	Na Gsc	B G Tx Var
Go Down, Moses! (Negro Spiritual)	Na	Na Lor	M G Tx Sab
Go On My Child	Spratlen, Abbye	67 Jhe	M R L G Tx
God Is Alive	Mccarthy, J & Cavalier	67 Stm	M B R L G Tx
God Maketh No Mistake	Hendrix, James	71 Jhe	M R L G Tx

CATEGORIZED INDEX

God Spoke To Me One Day	Akers, Doris	54 Man	B G Tx	
God Will If You Will	Akers, Doris	58 Man	M B G Tx	
God's Little White Church	Knepp, David Lee	74 Pmp	M B R L G Tx	
God's Wonderful Plan	Ohler, Susan	74 Pmp	M B R L G Tx	
God's World Today	Ohler, Susan	74 Pmp	M B R L G Tx	
Gone Are The Days	Gonzalo, Carrie	69 Man	B G Tx	
Good News In The Kingdom	Sanford	Na Lor	M G Tx	Satb
Gospel Choir Favorites (No 5660)	Decou, Harold	Na Zon	B G Tx	
Grandma Stout	Lafferty, Karen Louise	75 Mar	R L G Tx	
Grasshopper Macclain	Hamblen Stuart	Na Ham	M G Tx	
Great Change	Ramey, Troy	72 Sem	R G Tx	
Great Day	Na	Na Gsc	B G Tx	Full
Have I Done My Best	Mieir, Audrey	58 Man	M B G Tx	
He Lived The Good Life (Jesus Musical)	Na	Na Zon	G Tx	
He That Hath Ears	Gaither/Gaither	64 Gmc	B G Tx	Satb
He's Got The Whole World In His Hands	Na	Na Gsc	B G Tx	Ttbb+
Higher Hands	Peterson, John W.	Na Zon	M G Tx	Var
I Believe	Hamblen Stuart	Na Ham	M G Tx	
I Believe In God	Laney E. C. Baxter Lil	74 Jhm	R L G Tx	
I Believe In Heaven	Floria, Cam	74 Wrd	B R G Tx	Satb+
I Believe In The Father	Lee, Danny	72 Man	M R G Tx	
I Cannot Tell	Gaither/Gaither, G.	63 Gmc	B G Tx	Satb
I Couldn't Hear Nobody Pray	Na	Na Gsc	B G Tx	Full
I Didn't Think It Could Be	Crouch, Andrae	71 Man	B R G Tx	
I Don't Know Why	Hamblen Stuart	Na Ham	M G Tx	
I Dreamed I Went To Heaven	Hubbard, H./S. Stevens	Na Sav	M G Tx	
I Love To Tell The Story	Fischer/Johnson	Na Zon	M G Tx	Ssatb
I Should Have Been Crucified	Jensen, Gordon	72 Jtb	M B R L G Tx	
I Talked To The Saviour	Butler, Dorothy	68 Pmp	M B R L G Tx	
I Won't Go Where They Are	Mieir, Audrey	72 Man	B R G Tx	
I'd Rather Fight Than Switch	Overstreet, Rev. L.	69 Sto	G Tx	
I'll Be Fightin' Old Satan 'til I Die	Sizemore, G/Sizemore,	47 Kmp	M B L G Tx	
I'll Tell It	Butler, Dorothy	74 Pmp	M B L G Tx	
I'm Gonna Put My Shoes On	Wortley, Howard S.	74 Mem	M G Tx	
If I Didn't Know	Akers, Doris	73 Man	B R G Tx	
If I Got My Ticket, Can I Ride?	Na	Na Gsc	B G Tx	Var+
If The Good Lord's Willing	Sewell Homer	65 Oak	G Tx	
Impatient Heart	Huntley/Campbell	Na Zon	M G Tx	
Imps Of Satan	Myring Charles	72 Jhm	M L G Tx	
In Rememberance	Mieir, Audrey	58 Man	M B G Tx	
In That Great Gettin' Up Mornin'	Na	Na Gsc	B G Tx	Ttbb
In The Autograph Of God	Stacey, Helen; Kent, R	68 Pmp	M B L G Tx	
In The Chapel Of The Dawn	Lee, Johnnie	74 Mmc	M G Tx	
It Rained	Akers, Doris	64 Man	B G Tx	
Joshua Fit De Battle Of Jericho	Kennedy-Cadwallader	72 Gia	B R L G Tx	Var+
Joshua Fit The Battle Of Jericho	Ferguson	75 Her	M G Tx	Satb
Joshua Fit The Battle Of Jericho	Spiritual/Drevits	Na Zon	M G Tx	Satb
Joy Comes In The Morning	Gaither/Gaither B/G	74 Gmc	M B R G Tx	Satb
Just A Dreamer	Mieir, Audrey	59 Man	M B G Tx	
Just One Look	Lee, Danny	72 Man	M G Tx	Choral
Keep In The Middle Of The Road	Na	Na Gsc	B G Tx	Ttbb
Let The Whole World Know	Peterson, John W.	Na Zon	M G Tx	Satb
Let's Go To Church On Sunday	Moye, Claud	67 Pmp	M B R L G Tx	
Little David (Spiritual)	Davenport, David N.	58 Smc	M G Tx	Ttbb
Look Up	Butler, Dorothy	67 Pmp	M B R L G Tx	
Lord Keep Your Hand On Me	Harper, Redd	Na Zon	M G Tx	
Lord Watch Over Mother	Rose Lon	74 Jhm	R L G Tx	
Lord, I Want To Be A Christian	Na	Na Gsc	B G Tx	7mix
Lord, Stay Close To Me	Brock, Linda	74 Mam	R L G Tx	
Love Like The Springtime	Taylor, R.	75 Sil	R L G Tx	
Mamma And Daddy Taught Me How To See	Barry, Jody	74 Man	R G Tx	
Mansion Over The Hilltop	Stanphill/Johnson	Na Zon	M G Tx	Satb
Master Of All Miracles	Butler, Dorothy	74 Pmp	M B L G Tx	
Me And Jesus	Hall, Tom T.	71 Chp	M B R L G Tx	
Merrill Dunlop Favorites (No 5252)	Dunlop, M.	Na Zon	G Tx	
Merrill Dunlop Favorites No 2 (No 5253)	Dunlop, M.	Na Zon	G Tx	
Merrill Dunlop's New Gospel Songs No 1	Dunlop, M.	Na Zon	G Tx	
Mine Just For The Asking	Akers, Doris	58 Man	M B R G Tx	
Mommy Why Doesn't Daddy Love Me	King Marian	70 Jhm	L G Tx	
Moses (Long)	Medema, Ken	73 Wrd	M G Tx	Satb+
Mother, You're God's Gift To Me	Borchers	Na Zon	M G Tx	
My Glory	Myring Charles	72 Jhm	M L G Tx	
My Guiding Star	Wayne, Millie	73 Pmp	M B R L G Tx	
My Lord, What A Morning	Na	Na Gsc	B G Tx	Ttbb
My Name Is John	Culverwell, Andrew	74 Man	B R G Tx	
My Need	Lovelace, Linda	74 Mam	R L G Tx	
No More	Mieir, Audrey	58 Man	M B G Tx	
No Time	Wyrtzen, Don	Na Zon	M G Tx	Satb
O Happy Day	Hawkins, Edwin R.	69 Uam	M B R L G Tx	
O Lord, Have Mercy On Me	Na	Na Gsc	B G Tx	9mix
Oh John	Na	Na Gsc	B G Tx	Full
Oh, Freedom!	Na	Na Gsc	B G Tx	5mix
Ol' Brother Jonah	Gaither/Gaither	68 Gmc	B R G Tx	Satb
Old Ark's A-Moverin'	Na	Na Gsc	B G Tx	Ttbb
Old Fashioned Sermons	Dyer	Na Zon	M G Tx	
Old Jordan	Smith	Na Lor	M G Tx	Sab
Old-Fashioned Meeting, The	Buffum/Carmichael	Na Zon	M G Tx	Satb
Only	Hubbard, H/S. Stevens	Na Sav	M G Tx	
Prayer Is The Answer	Akers, Doris	64 Man	B G Tx	
Reaching	Gaither/Gaither B/G	76 Gmc	M B R G Tx	
Roses While I'm Living	Jones, Casey	67 Pmp	M B R L G Tx	
Shadrack (A Cap)	Mcgimsey, R.	75 Wrd	M G Tx	Full
Show Me	Mieir, Audrey	72 Man	B G Tx	
Sing Little Children	Helser, K.	74 Sil	R L G Tx	
Smile Because God Loves You	Cram, W. Francis	74 Mam	M L G Tx	
Someone	Hamblen Stuart	Na Ham	M G Tx	
Someone	Peterson/Decou	Na Zon	M G Tx	Satb
Something Worth Living For	Gaither, William J	Na Lor	M G Tx	Satb
Something's Happened To Daddy	Gaither/Gaither B/G	71 Gmc	M B R G Tx	Satb
Soon One Mornin' Death Comes Creepin'	Kubik, Gail	Na Gsc	B G Tx	Full

Standing Far Off	Myring Charles	72 Jhm	M L G Tx	
Suppertime	Orr Vern	72 Jhm	L G Tx	
Swing Low, Sweet Chariot	Huntley	Na Gsc	B G Tx	Ttbb
Tell Me Why	St. Clair, Wendell	59 Man	M B G Tx	
That's Worth Everything	Gaither/Gaither B/G	74 Gmc	M B R G Tx	Satb
The Addict's Plea	Crouch, Andrae	67 Man	R G Tx	
The Battle Of Jericho (Traditional)	Bartholomew	Na Gsc	B G Tx	Var+
The Church In The Wildwood	Pitts, W./Carmichael	67 Wrd	B R G Tx	Full
The Face Of God	Benedetti, Quint	73 Abm	M G Tx	
The Great Someone	Butler, Dorothy	74 Pmp	M B L G Tx	
The Inner Place	Mieir, Audrey	75 Man	B G Tx	
The Mystery Of It All	Haag, Preston	55 Man	M G Tx	
The Old Ark	Marsters, Nancy (Arr)	76 Rpb	M B R L G Tx	
The Sabbath Of God	Shimmons, C	74 Csm	M B L G Tx	
The Voice Of God	Hendrix, James	71 Jhe	M R L G Tx	
The Warning Of Old	Ohler, Susan	74 Pmp	M B R L G Tx	
The Watch Bird	Llord, J./Dejesus, G	67 Csm	M B R L G Tx	
Then It Must Be So	Mieir, Audrey	64 Man	B G Tx	
There's Something About A Mountain	Gaither/Gaither B/G	72 Gmc	M B R G Tx	Satb
These Things Shall Pass	Hamblen Stuart	Na Ham	M G Tx	
This Book	Hamblen Stuart	Na Ham	M G Tx	
This I Believe	Johnson, Norman	Na Zon	M G Tx	Satb
Thomas	Culverwell, Andrew	73 Man	B R G Tx	
Through Some Other Eyes	Culverwell, Andrew	74 Man	B R G Tx	
Tinagera (She Is Young)	Girard, Chuck	74 Wrd	B R G Tx	Unis+
Tommy's Farewell	Butler, Dorothy	68 Pmp	M B R L G Tx	
Tomorrow Is In His Hands	Gaither/Gaither	63 Gmc	B G Tx	Satb
Too Late To Pray	Hall J., Coakley J.	74 Jhm	R L G Tx	
Tramping (Spiritual)	Na	Na Lor	M G Tx	2mel
Tried In The Fire	Stevens, Marsha J.	75 Chd	R L G Tx	
Two Spirituals	Kennedy, Matthew	Na Abi	M G Tx	Satb
Unless You Help Me Lord	Mieir, Audrey	68 Man	B G Tx	
Until Then	Hamblen Stuart	Na Ham	M G Tx	
Verily, Verily	Mcgranahan/Johnson	Na Zon	M G Tx	Satb
Voices	Amason, B.	75 Sil	R L G Tx	
Wade In The Water	Na	Na Gsc	B G Tx	Full
Wasn't That A Mighty Day	Dett, R N	Na Gsc	B G Tx	Satbb
Water Of Time	Rovison/Turner	74 Bri	M R G Tx	
We Have This Moment, Today	Gaither/Gaither, G.	75 Gmc	M R G Tx	
We're Goin' On A Picnic	White, Jack Noble	76 Rpb	M B R L G Tx	
What A Wonderful Feeling	Butler, Dorothy	68 Pmp	M B R L G Tx	
What Would I Do	Tricamo/Pallardy	75 Bri	M R G Tx	
Whatever It Takes	Chitwood, Joe	70 Man	M G Tx	
When God Makes The Morning	Evangeline/Sadler	Na Zon	M G Tx	
When I Looked Up	Butler, Dorothy	68 Pmp	M B R L G Tx	
When I See A Mountain	Hendrix, James	Na Gmp	M R L G Tx	Satb
Where They Love To Pray	Benedetti, Quint	72 Abm	M R G Tx	
Wicked Old Pharoah	Culverwell, Andrew	73 Man	B R G Tx	
Work For The Night	Mieir, Audrey	62 Man	M G Tx	
Workshop Of The Lord	Hamblen Stuart	Na Ham	M G Tx	
Would You Go	Mieir, Audrey	72 Man	B R G Tx	
Wrinkled And Old	Sizemore, G./Hall, T	44 Kmp	M B L G Tx	
Ye Shall Know The Truth	Dunlop, Merrill	Na Zon	M G Tx	Satb
Yesterday	Elrich, Dwight	72 Man	B R G Tx	
You Can See About Me	Lee, Danny	71 Man	B G Tx	
A Canticle Of Commemoration (A Cap)	Pfautsch, Lloyd	Na Abi	M L Tx	Var
A Cowboy's Dream	Herring, Bruce	75 Mar	R L L Tx	
A Hymn Of Youth	Wood	67 Aug	M L Tx	2pt
A Man Of Integrity	Moe, Daniel	73 Aug	M L Tx	Satb
A Rose Touched By The Sun's Warm Rays	Berger, Jean	62 Aug	M L Tx	Satb
A Treasure In A Field	Fabing, Bob	70 Ahc	B R L L Tx	
Above Him Stood The Seraphim (Me)	Dering, Richard	Na Oxf	M L Tx	2pt
Above The Hills Of Time (E)	Hughes, Robert J.	Na Lor	M L Tx	Satb
Abraham And Isaac	Pfautsch, Lloyd	Na Abi	M L Tx	Satb
According To Matthew	Ellis, Ron	72 Rav	B R L L Tx	
Aleatory Psalm (Chance Music)	Lamb, Gordon	75 Wlp	M L Tx	Satb
All Beautiful The March Of Days	Lapo, Cecil	Na Abi	M L Tx	Satb
All By Ourselves	Martin	Na Lor	M L Tx	Satb
All Poor Men & Humble	Christiansen, P.	76 Aug	L Tx	Satb
All The Ends Of The Earth	Peloquin, C Alexander	71 Gia	B L Tx	Satb+
All Things Have Their Time	Kavanaugh, John, S. J.	73 Nal	B R L Tx	
All Ye Servants Of The Lord	Young, Gordon	75 Sac	M L Tx	Satb
Almighty And Everlasting God	Roff, Joseph	69 Gia	M L Tx	Var+
Alone In The Still	Lohr, Al	55 Pic	M L Tx	
An Age Had Passed	Silvia, Helen	73 Acp	B L L Tx	
An Angel Offered Incense	Fitzpatrick, Dennis	65 Fel	B L Tx	
Anamnesis	Zsigray, Joe	75 Nal	B R L Tx	
Anamnesis	Mudd, C. P.	72 Nal	B R L Tx	
And Nobody Knows	Graham	Na Lor	M L Tx	Satb
And The King Was Moved	Dering, Richard	Na Oxf	M L Tx	Ssatb
And Then It Dawns On Me	Wise, Joe	72 Nal	B R L Tx	
Are Ye Able-Said The Master	Wilson	Na Lor	M L Tx	Satb
Are You Listening?	Angle, Dana P	73 Mar	R L L Tx	
As Candles Glow	Bender, Jan	63 Aug	M L Tx	Unis
As I Was A-Walking	Healey, D.	76 Aug	L Tx	Satb
Author Of Light (Md)	Cook, John	Na Oxf	M L Tx	Satb
Avak, The Healer	Hovhaness, Alan	45 Pic	M L Tx	
Babel	Smith, Gregg	Na Gsc	B L Tx	Satb+
Back And Forward	Gutfreund, Ed (Rev.)	74 Nal	B R L Tx	
Back Home	Fong, Preston Bing	75 Mar	R L L Tx	
Be Like The Sun	Fabing, Bob	74 Ahc	B R L L Tx	
Beyond The Wheeling Worlds Of Light	Buettell,	Na Lor	M L Tx	Satb
Bird In A Golden Sky	Lafferty, Karen Louise	74 Mar	R L L Tx	
Bless This House, O Lord	Fitzpatrick, Dennis	65 Fel	B L Tx	
Blessed Are Those Servants	Fitzpatrick, Dennis	65 Fel	B L Tx	
Bobbi's Song	Lafferty, Karen Louise	75 Mar	R L L Tx	
Brighten My Soul With Sunshine	Eilers, Joyce	75 Hal	L Tx	Sab
Bring A Little Sunshine	Shaw, Jim	75 Fel	B R L L Tx	
Bring Forth Abundant Fruit	Fitzpatrick, Dennis	65 Fel	B L Tx	

CATEGORIZED INDEX

Build Thee More Stately Mansions	Holmes	74 Hal	L Tx	Satb
Can It Be?	Diederich, Kelly W	75 Mar	R L L Tx	
Canaan's Land	Unknown	Pd Mar	B R L L Tx	
Canticle	Gulliksen, Kenn	75 Mar	R L L Tx	
Canticle 1	Leichtling, Alan	Na See	M L Tx	
Celebration	Krane, David	71 Som	M L Tx	
Choral Benedictions	Bitgood, Roberta	Na Abi	M L Tx	Satb
Choral Diptych (A Cap)	Harris	75 Pro	M L Tx	Satb
Chorale	Diamond, David	51 Som	M L Tx	
Christian Dost Thou See Them	Pfautsch, Lloyd	Na Abi	M L Tx	Satb
Come And Take	Patenaude, Andre, M.S.	71 Nal	B R L Tx	
Come Let Us Go	Landry, Carey (Rev.)	68 Nal	B R L Tx	
Come Life, Shaker Life	Sylvester, Erich	74 Nal	B R L Tx	
Come Where The Wind Is Free	Gilligan, M. (Text)	70 Acp	B L L Tx	
Come Where The Wind Is Free	Liturgical Press	73 Acp	B L L Tx	Satb
Come, Comes	Landry, Carey (Rev.)	68 Nal	B R L Tx	
Come, Rich And Poor	Silvia, Helen	73 Acp	B L L Tx	
Concluding Rite	Zsigray, Joe	73 Nal	B R L Tx	
Contemporary Prayer	Lewis, E.	74 Sil	L L Tx	
Creation, The	Waterman	Na Lor	M L Tx	Sa
Creed (Icet Text) Cong, Org	Hampton, Calvin	75 Gia	B L L Tx	Satb+
Creed (Icet) U Or Satb W/Org(Chant)	Lee, John	71 Gia	B L L Tx	Var
Crusade	Wilson	Na Lor	M L Tx	Satb
Daniel Prayed To God	Fitzpatrick, Dennis	65 Fel	B L Tx	
Day For Goodbye	Mudd, C. P. & Schleich	72 Nal	B R L Tx	
Days Of Man W/Solo	Healey, D.	76 Aug	L Tx	Satb
Dimensions In Music (No 5672)	Wyrtzen, Don	75 Zon	B L Tx	
Dirge In Woods	Heussenstamm, George	Na See	M L Tx	
Disclosure	Ives, Charles E.	54 Pic	M L Tx	
Do You Know?	Hughes, Robert J.	Na Lor	M L Tx	Satb
Down East	Ives, Charles E.	58 Pic	M L Tx	
Enormous Dreams (Psalm 131)	Hillebrand, Frank	75 Ahc	B R L L Tx	
Eternity To Live Or Die	Eldridge, R.	75 Sil	R L L Tx	
Eucharistic Prayer (Preface)	Isele, David C.	74 Gia	B L L Tx	Satb+
Eucharistic Prayer Ii	Blanchard, R. I.	73 Cfc	M L L Tx	
Eucharistic Prayer Iii	Blanchard, R. I.	71 Cfc	M R L L Tx	
Every Day	Page, Paul F.	74 Rpb	M B R L L Tx	
Everybody's Home	Unknown	73 Mar	B L L Tx	
Exhortation	Page, Paul F.	76 Rpb	M B R L L Tx	
Faith (Hb 11-12) (Md)	Bowie, William	Na Oxf	M L Tx	Satb
For A Reward	Fitzpatrick, Dennis	65 Fel	B L Tx	
For All The Saints	Williams, Vaughan	Na Lor	M L Tx	
For All The Saints	How, William H.	70 Acp	B L L Tx	
From Among The Branches	Germaine	66 Fel	B R L Tx	
From The Beginning	Ramseth, B.	76 Aug	L Tx	Unis+
From The Depths	Jabusch, Willard F.	67 Acf	L Tx	
Get On The Good Foot	Moultry, Prince Jos.	74 Nal	B R L Tx	
Get Out Of Yesterday	Lewis, E.	74 Sil	L L Tx	
Give Them, O Lord	Fitzpatrick, Dennis	65 Fel	B L Tx	
Glory Of Joy	Zunic, Sr. Mary Grace	74 Rpb	M B R L L Tx	
Glory To God	Rivers, Clarence Jos.	Na Wlp	L Tx	
God	Hutcheson, Jere	Na See	M L Tx	
God Deigning Men To Be (Apostles)	Damrosch, F.	76 Jsp	B L Tx	
God Is Everywhere	Gretchaninoff, A.	62 Som	M L Tx	
God Of Concrete	Lovelace, Austin C.	66 Aug	M L Tx	Unis
God Of Earth And Planets (Opt Flute)	Leaf, Robert	72 Aug	M L Tx	Sa
God Of The World	Wise, Judah L.	43 Pic	M L Tx	
God Spoke To Me Today	Hughes, Robert J.	Na Lor	M L Tx	Satb
God, Did You Hear	Hubert, Yvon	72 Fcc	R L L Tx	
God's Plan	Roff, Joseph	75 Sac	M L Tx	2mel
God's Word (4-Part Arr)	Luther, Martin	73 Acp	B L L Tx	
Golden Rules	Bacon, Ernst	56 Pic	M L Tx	
Good Morning, Zachary	Gutfreund, Ed (Rev.)	74 Nal	B R L Tx	
Good News	Nelson, Erick Martin	75 Mar	R L L Tx	
Good News	Sylvester, Erich	74 Nal	B R L Tx	
Goodbye	Cull, Robert	74 Mar	R L L Tx	
Goodbye	Butler, Charles F.	75 Mar	R L L Tx	
Guess What's Behind You	Hopkins, Edith	75 Mem	L Tx	
Hallowed And Gracious Is The Time	Williams, David	66 Som	M L Tx	
Harken Unto Me	Owen, Blythe	59 Tcp	M L Tx	
Have You Ever Heard	Arthur, Gary & Angle	73 Mar	R L L Tx	
He Cried	St. Benedict's Farm	75 Sbf	B R L L Tx	
He Gives Us The Water Of Learning	Fitzpatrick, Dennis	65 Fel	B L Tx	
He Is The Lord Of Life And Death	Fitzpatrick, Dennis	65 Fel	B L Tx	
He Lived To See The Christ	Fitzpatrick, Dennis	65 Fel	B L Tx	
He Who Is Of God	Fitzpatrick, Dennis	65 Fel	B L Tx	
He Who Sees Me	Fitzpatrick, Dennis	65 Fel	B L Tx	
He Who Would Valiant Be	Burroughs	75 Maf	M L Tx	Satb
Hear Mr. Lord, I'm Callin'	Shelley, Tom	71 Ahc	B R L L Tx	
Hear Us, O Lord, For You Are So Kind	Fitzpatrick, Dennis	65 Fel	B L Tx	
Hear Us, Oh Lord	Shelley, Tom	72 Ahc	B R L L Tx	
Hey Brothers!	Tlucek, Tim	75 Nal	B R L Tx	
High Time	Vickers, Wendy	75 Nal	B R L Tx	
Hinay Yom Hadin(Behold The Day Of Judg	Adler, Samuel	Na Gsc	B L Tx	
His Throne Shall Be	Fitzpatrick, Dennis	65 Fel	B L Tx	
Holy Way, The	O'connell, Timothy	67 Acp	B L L Tx	
How Blessed Are They Who Hear Gods Wd	Silvia, Helen	73 Acp	B L L Tx	
How Can This Be	Shelley, Tom	75 Ahc	B R L L Tx	
How Lovely Shines (W/Tpt, Org, Cong)	Bender, Jan	75 Con	B L Tx	Satb
Hymn For The Sick (4-Part Arr)	Dykes, John B.	73 Acp	B L L Tx	
Hymn For The Sick	Gilligan, Michael	70 Acp	B L L Tx	
Hymn For Winter	Clothier, Louita	Na Abi	M L Tx	Satb
Hymn To The Earth	Sibelius, Jean	45 Som	M L Tx	
I Believe	Young, Gordon	75 Sac	M L Tx	Satb
I Believe In One God (Creed)	Schneider, Kent E.	75 Ccc	B L Tx	
I Can't Spin A Web	Lewis	75 Sac	M L Tx	Sa
I Do Believe	St. Benedict's Farm	75 Sbf	B R L L Tx	
I Do Not Ask, O Lord	Verrees, Leon	47 Tcp	M L Tx	
I Have Plans, Says The Lord	Fitzpatrick, Dennis	65 Fel	B L Tx	
I Have Put My Words	Fitzpatrick, Dennis	65 Fel	B L Tx	
I Heard A Great Voice	Christiansen, P.	57 Aug	M L Tx	Satb
I Know What It's Like	Butler, Charles F.	75 Mar	R L L Tx	
I Know, O Lord	Fitzpatrick, Dennis	65 Fel	B L Tx	
I May Be Young	Moultry, Prince Joseph	74 Nal	B R L Tx	
I Said To The Man (E) 1	Harris, William H.	Na Oxf	M L Tx	Ttbb
I See That All Things Have Their End	Fitzpatrick, Dennis	65 Fel	B L Tx	
I Want To Call You	Huijbers & Oosterhuis	74 Nal	M B R L Tx	
I Will Meditate On Your Law	Fitzpatrick, Dennis	65 Fel	B L Tx	
I Will Not Forget You	Landry, Carey (Rev.)	74 Nal	B R L Tx	
I, The Lord, Am Your God	Fitzpatrick, Dennis	65 Fel	B L Tx	
If I Forget To Pray	Norman, Pierre	49 Som	M L Tx	
If You Continue In My Word	Busarow	68 Aug	M L Tx	Satb
If You Have Kept My Words	Fitzpatrick, Dennis	65 Fel	B L Tx	
If You Love Me, Simon Peter	Fitzpatrick, Dennis	65 Fel	B L Tx	
If You Want Life	Fitzpatrick, Dennis	65 Fel	B L Tx	
In All The World	Powell	74 Aug	M L Tx	Sa+
In Nature's Ebb And Flow	Alder, Samuel	68 Som	M L Tx	
In Thankful Remembrance (W/Brs Etal)	Lak	Na Abi	M L Tx	
In The Beginning	Graham, Robert	Na Abi	M L Tx	
In The Morning	Schutte, Dan, S.J.	70 Nal	B R L Tx	
In The Year That King Uzziah Died	Young, Gordon	Na Abi	M L Tx	Unis
Infinito	Polin, Claire	Na See	M L Tx	
It Was So Quiet	Harvey, Richard W.	Na Abi	M L Tx	Solo
It's A Long Road To Freedom	Winter, Miriam T.	66 Van	L Tx	
It's All About Love.	Smith, Lani	Na Lor	M B L Tx	Youth
It's Tough To Be A Friend Of The Proph	Blunt, Neil	72 Nal	B R L Tx	
Jacob's Ladder	Black	75 Sac	M L Tx	Satb
Jacob's Ladder	Wilson	Na Lor	M L Tx	Var
Jimmy	Nelson, Erick Martin	75 Mar	R L L Tx	
Joanie's Song	Gulliksen, Kenn	75 Mar	R L L Tx	
Job Was A True And Honest Man	Fitzpatrick, Dennis	65 Fel	B L Tx	
Jonah	Bacon, Ernst	56 Pic	M L Tx	
Joseph Dearest, Joseph Mine	Pfautsch, Lloyd	75 Sac	M L Tx	Satb
Joyful Dawning	Davis, Paulette	75 Rpb	M B R L L Tx	
Judah's Land	Johnson, D.	68 Aug	M L Tx	Satb
Keep Us Joyful	Hubert, Yvon	72 Fcc	R L L Tx	
Laborers Of Love	Lewis, E./Allen, T.	74 Sil	L L Tx	
Lamp Unto My Feet (W/Guitar)	Temple, Sebastian	71 Gia	B R L L Tx	Satb+
Lamparita Votiva (Lamp Of Prayer)	Heitmann, D. Roman	51 Pic	M L Tx	
Let It Shine	Chapman, Betsy	Na Bch	L Tx	
Let Me See	Rettino, Ernest W.	74 Mar	R L L Tx	
Let Me Tell Y'all	Moultry, Prince Joseph	74 Nal	B R L Tx	
Let Saints On Earth	Powell, Robert J.	Na Abi	M L Tx	Satb
Let There Be Light	Ives, Charles E.	55 Pic	M L Tx	
Let Your Father And Mother	Fitzpatrick, Dennis	65 Fel	B L Tx	
Lights Of Hanukkah	Wortley, Howard S.	74 Mem	M L Tx	
Lights Of The City, The	Gutfreund, Ed (Rev.)	74 Nal	B R L Tx	
Like Bells At Evening	Leaf, Robert	74 Aug	M L Tx	Satb
Listen Christian (Soc. Gospel)	Roff, Joseph	75 Gia	M L L Tx	Satb+
Listen With An Open Mind	Hughes, Robert J.	Na Lor	M L Tx	Sb
Listen You Nations	Fitzpatrick, Dennis	65 Fel	B L Tx	
Litany Of The Saints	Fitzpatrick, Dennis	63 Fel	B L Tx	
Living On The Bottle	Angle, Dana P	75 Mar	R L L Tx	
Long Ago A Prophet Sang	Grieb, Herbert	Na Abi	M L Tx	Satb
Long Song, The	Tracy, Shawn (Rev.)	72 Nal	B R L Tx	
Look All Around You	Shelley, Tom	72 Ahc	B R L L Tx	
Look Beyond	Ducote, Darryl	69 Fel	B R L Tx	
Look Down That Road	Blunt, Neil	72 Nal	B R L Tx	
Look Up, You Nations	Conley, Thomas P.	65 Fel	B L Tx	
Lord Is A Mighty God, The	Hastings	75 Sac	M L Tx	Satb
Lord Of No Beginning	Landry, Carey (Rev.)	71 Nal	B R L Tx	
Lord, Keep Us Steadfast In Thy Word	Near, Gerald	69 Aug	M L Tx	Sab
Lord, Lord, Lord	Nix, Donna	74 Nal	B L Tx	
Lord, My Lord	Landry, Carey (Rev.)	71 Nal	B R L Tx	
Love That Is Kept Inside	Landry, Carey (Rev.)	73 Nal	B R L Tx	
Lullaby	Gulliksen, Kenn	75 Mar	R L L Tx	
Man In The Dark (Musical)	Newman/Warne	Na Zon	B R L Tx	
May You Walk Worthily Of God	Fitzpatrick, Dennis	65 Fel	B L Tx	
Maybe	Butler, Charles F.	75 Mar	R L L Tx	
Meditation	Landry, Carey (Rev.)	69 Nal	B L Tx	
Meditation On Woodworth	Wetzler, Robert	Na Abi	M L Tx	Satb
Middle Of The Day	Cutrona, Henry	75 Mar	R L L Tx	
Migrant	Garza, Juliana, S. P.	73 Nal	B R L Tx	
Miracle	Isele, Bill	71 Nal	B L Tx	
Moment Of Time	Gulliksen, Kenn	75 Mar	R L L Tx	
More Than The Sunlight	Fong, Preston Bing	75 Mar	R L L Tx	
Morning Prayer	Ream, Albert W.	Na Abi	M L Tx	Satb
Morning Prayer	Caldwell, M	75 Sac	M L Tx	Satb
Motet	Chance, Nancy	Na See	M L Tx	
Mother's Day Carol	Ferguson	75 Sac	M L Tx	Satb
My Light	Hubert, Yvon	72 Fcc	R L L Tx	
My Will	Kerner, Debby Melle	72 Mar	R L L Tx	
Nameless Island	Hubert, Yvon	72 Fcc	R L L Tx	
Never Knew	Nelson, Erick Martin	75 Mar	R L L Tx	
New Is Old, The	Pfautsch, Lloyd	Na Abi	M L Tx	Satb
Nicene Creed (Sung Mass No. 2)	Fitzpatrick, Dennis	63 Fel	B L Tx	
No Time For Jesus	Lafferty, Karen Louise	73 Mar	R L L Tx	
Not To Us Lord	Quinlan, Paul	68 Fel	L Tx	
Nothing But Miracles	Hughes, Robert J.	Na Lor	M L Tx	Satb
Now Come To Me	O'connell, Timothy	70 Acp	B L L Tx	
Now Come To Me (4-Part Arr)	Cirou, Joseph/Silvia, H	73 Acp	B L L Tx	
Now Is The Time	Isele, Bill	71 Nal	B L Tx	
O Day Full Of Grace	Christiansen, F. M.	43 Aug	M L Tx	Satb
O Day Full Of Grace (W/String Bass)	Carlson, G.	72 Aug	M L Tx	Satb
O Day Full Of Grace	Johnson, D.	67 Aug	M L Tx	Sab
O Day Full Of Grace	Christiansen, P.	56 Aug	M L Tx	Satb
O Great Doctor, Blessed	Fitzpatrick, Dennis	65 Fel	B L Tx	
O Let Me Fly	Eliot	Na Lor	M L Tx	Sab
O Lord, Show Mercy To The Sick	Fitzpatrick, Dennis	65 Fel	B L Tx	
O Lord, Who Shall Dwell	Fitzpatrick, Dennis	65 Fel	B L Tx	

Old Gray Ford	Stipe, Thomas	74 Mar	R L L Tx	
On The Mountainside	Christiansen, P.	66 Aug	M L Tx	Satb
On Your Own	Strange, Joy Deanne	75 Mar	R L L Tx	
Once I Had A Dream	Fong, Preston Bing	75 Mar	R L L Tx	
One More Day	Mudd, C. P.	72 Nal	B R L Tx	
One Who Seeks, The	Hubert, Yvon	72 Fcc	R L L Tx	
Only A Shadow	Landry, Carey (Rev.)	71 Nal	M B R L Tx	
Open Like The Sky	Fabing, Bob	70 Ahc	B R L L Tx	
Open Up	Creed, Dan	73 Nal	B R L Tx	
Open Your Eyes	Shaw, Jim	73 Fel	B R L L Tx	
Our Star Of Faith (The Prayer Of Love)	Lohr, Al	55 Pic	M L Tx	
Patapan	Christiansen, P.	55 Aug	M L Tx	Satb
People Of Zion, Behold	Fitzpatrick, Dennis	65 Fel	B L Tx	
Peter, James And John	Butler, Charles F.	75 Mar	R L L Tx	
Petersham Place, (16)	Butler, Charles F.	75 Mar	R L L Tx	
Play Before The Lord	Dufford, Bob, S. J.	72 Nal	B R L Tx	
Poem Of Circumstance	Heussenstamm, George	Na See	M L Tx	
Poor Builder (Psalm 127)	Hillebrand, Frank	75 Ahc	B R L L Tx	
Possible Gospel, The	Blunt, Neil	72 Nal	B R L Tx	
Prayer	Diamond, David	68 Som	M L Tx	
Prayer	Lewis, E.	75 Sil	L L Tx	
Prayer (Prayer Of The Heart And Lips)	Andrews, Carroll T.	70 Gia	M L Tx	2pt
Prayers Of Steel	Christiansen, P.	50 Aug	M L Tx	Satb
Precious In The Sight Of The Lord	Fitzpatrick, Dennis	65 Fel	B L Tx	
Preface Dialogue	Hampton, Calvin	76 Gia	B L L Tx	Satb+
Promises	Kerner, Debby Melle	74 Mar	R L L Tx	
Prophetic Song	Turner, Robert	71 Pic	M L Tx	
Proverb 31	Gulliksen, Kenn	75 Mar	R L L Tx	
Psalm	Smit, Leo	51 Pic	M L Tx	
Psalm Concertato (In 3 Parts)	Moe, Daniel	70 Aug	M L Tx	Satb+
Psalm 107	Unknown	73 Mar	B L L Tx	
Psalm 19	Salisbury	68 Wrd	L Tx	
Psalm 4	Westendorf, Omer	63 Wlp	B L Tx	
Psalm 50	Christiansen, F. M.	Na Aug	M L Tx	Satb
Psalm 68	Rogers, Bernard	55 Som	M L Tx	
Re-Member Me	Wise, Joe	72 Nal	B R L Tx	
Reach Out	Lewis, E.	74 Sil	L L Tx	
Receive With Joy The Glory	Fitzpatrick, Dennis	65 Fel	B L Tx	
Rejoice In The Lord On The Feast	Fitzpatrick, Dennis	65 Fel	B L Tx	
Religion	Ives, Charles E.	54 Pic	M L Tx	
Remember All The People	Baumgartner, H. Leroy	Na Abi	M L Tx	Var
Remember Now Thy Creator	Adams	Na Lor	M L Tx	
Revelation (I Want You Should Know)	Tracy, Shawn (Rev.)	72 Nal	B R L Tx	
Rise Up	Silvia, Helen	73 Acp	B L L Tx	
Road To Freedom	Hubert, Yvon	72 Fcc	R L L Tx	
Root-Toot-To	Rettino, Ernest W.	73 Mar	B L L Tx	
Rosa Mundi	Polin, Claire	Na See	M L Tx	
Runnin'	Winter, Miriam T.	68 Van	L Tx	
Sail On Sailor	Mcvay, Lewis E	75 Mar	R L L Tx	
Save My People	Jaworski, Jack	71 Nal	B L Tx	
Saw You Never In The Twilight	Held, Wilbur C	68 Aug	M L Tx	Unis
Secret, The	Schoenfeld, William	Na Abi	M L Tx	Satb
Seven Verses	Krapf, Gerhard	76 Aug	L Tx	2pt
Signposts	Hemberg-Eskit	Na Gsc	B L Tx	Satb
Silver & Gold	Unknown	73 Mar	B L L Tx	
Sing Hosanna, Sing (Ps. 92)	Quinlan, Paul	68 Nal	B R L Tx	
Sing To The Mountains	Zsigray, Joe	75 Nal	B R L Tx	
Sittin' In The Pew	Angle, D & Herring, B	75 Mar	R L L Tx	
Six Sixty Six	Eldridge, R.	75 Sil	R L L Tx	
Smile	Stiltz, E.	74 Sil	R L L Tx	
So Dost Thou Give	Sateren, Leland B.	61 Aug	M L Tx	Satb
Some Other Man	Shelley, Tom	75 Ahc	B R L L Tx	
Some Seed Fell On Good Ground	Fitzpatrick, Dennis	65 Fel	B L Tx	
Somethin' Happened Today	Tucciarone, Angel	73 Wlp	B R L Tx	
Song At The Foot Of The Mountain	Huijbers & Oosterhuis	74 Nal	M B L Tx	
Song For Daniel, A	Davis, Allan	Na See	M L Tx	
Song For Martin (Moses)	Wise, Joe	73 Nal	B R L Tx	
Song For Pauline	Zsigray, Joe	75 Nal	B R L Tx	
Song For The Masses, A	Schoenbachler, Tim	75 Nal	B R L Tx	
Song For The New Year, A	Martin	75 Sac	M L Tx	Satb
Song Of All Seed	Huijbers & Oosterhuis	74 Nal	M B R L Tx	
Song Of The City	Huijbers & Oosterhuis	74 Nal	M B R L Tx	
Song Of The Journey	Huijbers & Oosterhuis	75 Nal	M B L Tx	
Sow A Seed	Vickers, Wendy	75 Nal	B R L Tx	
St. Joseph Was A Just Man	Westendorf, Omer	70 Wlp	B L Tx	
Sun Has Risen, The (4-Part Arr)	Cirou, Joseph Et Al	73 Acp	B L L Tx	
Sun Has Risen, The	Gilligan, Michael	67 Acp	B L L Tx	
Susan's Song (Based On Kahil Gibran)	Persinger, Susan	73 Nal	B R L Tx	
Testimony	Lafferty, Karen Louise	75 Mar	R L L Tx	
Testimony	Eldridge, R.	75 Sil	R L L Tx	
That's My God	Collard, Terry	71 Nal	B R L Tx	
The Ballad Of Luke Warm	Butler, Charles F.	71 Mar	R L L Tx	
The Ballad Of Paul	Gilsdorf, Sr. Helen	75 Rpb	M B R L L Tx	
The Business Of A Friend	Fabing, Bob	70 Ahc	B R L L Tx	
The Camp Meeting	Ives, Charles E.	58 Pic	M L Tx	
The Collection	Ives, Charles E.	58 Pic	M L Tx	
The Contemplation Song	Fabing, Bob	74 Ahc	B R L L Tx	
The Days Of Noah	Wickham, J M	75 Mar	R L L Tx	
The Drums Beat On	Shelley, Tom	72 Ahc	B R L L Tx	
The End Is The Beginning (Md)	Gardner, John	Na Oxf	M L Tx	Satb
The Fragile Joys	Dargomysky, A.	63 Som	M L Tx	
The Girl	Lafferty, Karen Louise	75 Mar	R L L Tx	
The History Of The Flood (W/Narration)	Lord, David	Na Oxf	B L Tx	Satb
The House Of Stars	Lohr, Al	59 Pic	M L Tx	
The King Desires Your Beauty	Fitzpatrick, Dennis	65 Fel	B L Tx	
The Lighted Hour	Lohr, Al	57 Pic	M L Tx	
The Lone, Wild Bird	Johnson (Arr)	66 Aug	M L Tx	Var
The Lord Anointed My Eyes	Fitzpatrick, Dennis	65 Fel	B L Tx	
The Lord Cried Out	Fitzpatrick, Dennis	65 Fel	B L Tx	
The Lord Loved Him And Clothed Him	Fitzpatrick, Dennis	65 Fel	B L Tx	
The Mark Of Time	Williams, J.	76 Sil	L Tx	
The Nicene Creed (Credo) (Sung Mass No 1)	Fitzpatrick, Dennis	63 Fel	B L Tx	
The Nicene Creed (Credo) (Chardin Mass)	Rudcki, Stanley	66 Fel	B L Tx	
The Present Hour	Sateren, Leland B.	76 Aug	L Tx	Ssatb+
The Present Tense (2 Pt Canon)	Nelson, Ronald A.	68 Aug	M L Tx	
The Prophet Isaiah	Rogers, Bernard	62 Som	M L Tx	
The Question	Fong, P B	75 Mar	R L L Tx	
The Runner	Lewis, E.	74 Sil	L L Tx	
The Season Of Tomorrow (W/Flute/Org)	Nelson, Ronald A.	74 Aug	M L Tx	Satb+
The Spacious Firmament (Md)	Drayton, Paul	Na Oxf	M L Tx	Full
The Stone Which The Builders Rejected	Fitzpatrick, Dennis	65 Fel	B L Tx	
The Vision Of Isaiah (Cantata)	Adler, Samuel	65 Smc	M L Tx	Satb
The Woman	Herring, J.	76 Sil	R L Tx	
The Word Of The Lord Is Pure	Fitzpatrick, Dennis	65 Fel	B L Tx	
The Work He Has Committed To Me	Fitzpatrick, Dennis	65 Fel	B L Tx	
The World Around Us	Shelley, Tom	72 Ahc	B R L L Tx	
The World Sees Nothing	Fitzpatrick, Dennis	65 Fel	B L Tx	
There Is A God	Track, Gerhard	68 Gia	M L Tx	Var+
There's A Light Upon The Mountains	Walter, Samuel	Na Abi	M L Tx	Unis
Think On These Things	Peterson, John W.	Na Zon	L Tx	Satb
This Day You Shall Know	Fitzpatrick, Dennis	65 Fel	B L Tx	
This Is A Holy Day	Sylvester, Erich	74 Nal	B R L Tx	
This Is My Gift	Wise, Joe	73 Nal	B R L Tx	
This Is The Faithful And Prudent	Fitzpatrick, Dennis	65 Fel	B L Tx	
This Is The God Who Gives A Home	Fitzpatrick, Dennis	65 Fel	B L Tx	
This Is The House Of God	Fitzpatrick, Dennis	65 Fel	B L Tx	
This Is The Wise Virgin	Fitzpatrick, Dennis	65 Fel	B L Tx	
This World My God (Evening)	Proulx, Richard	74 Gia	M L Tx	Var+
Thus Saith The Lord	Nystedt, Knut	58 Aug	M L Tx	Satb
Thy Word With Me Shall Always Stay	Berger	76 Aug	L Tx	Satb
To Speak His Word	Fabing, Bob	70 Ahc	B R L L Tx	
To The Work	Blakley	75 Sac	M L Tx	
Today The World Is Filled	Silvia, Helen	73 Acp	B L L Tx	
Trisagion	Traditional Byzantine	67 Acp	B L L Tx	
Trisagion (4-Part Arr)	Cirou, Joseph Et Al	73 Acp	B L L Tx	
Uncertain Tide	Garza, Juliana, S. P.	73 Nal	B R L Tx	
Under The Eastern Sky (Org & Opt Clar)	Nelson, Ronald A.	69 Aug	M L Tx	Unis
Until	Wise, Joe	73 Nal	B R L Tx	
Upon My Lap My Sovereign Sits	Peerson, Martin	66 Som	M L Tx	
Vision Of Saint Joan	Jaubiel, Charles	41 Tcp	M L Tx	
Voice Of The Lord	Hubert, Yvon	72 Fcc	R L L Tx	
Voice, The	Herforth	Na Lor	M L Tx	Satb
Voices	Landry, Carey (Rev.)	68 Nal	B R L Tx	
Watchman!	Ives, Charles E.	55 Pic	M L Tx	
We Three Are One	Sateren, Leland B.	55 Aug	M L Tx	Solo
We'll See The Light	Dailey, Joe	75 Ahc	B R L L Tx	
We're Goin' Home	Fabing, Bob	70 Ahc	B R L L Tx	
We've Been To The Mountain	Mcalister	69 Wlp	B R L Tx	
What I See	Chapman, Betsy	Na Bch	L Tx	
What I Tell You In Darkness	Fitzpatrick, Dennis	65 Fel	B L Tx	
What Is Your Name?	Huijbers & Oosterhuis	74 Nal	M B L Tx	
What Wondrous Sacrifice	Haubiel, Charles	45 Tcp	M L Tx	
Whatever You Do	Fitzpatrick, Dennis	65 Fel	B L Tx	
When God Is The Honored Guest (Mothers)	Denton, James	Na Lor	M L Tx	Satb
When It's Time	Garza, Juliana, S. P.	73 Nal	B R L Tx	
When We See	Gutfreund, Ed (Rev.)	74 Nal	B R L Tx	
Who Can Know Your Ways	Fitzpatrick, Dennis	65 Fel	B L Tx	
Who Is This That Cometh (Is 63)	Sisler, Hampson	75 Wlp	M L Tx	Satb+
Why Must You Go?	Nelson, E M	75 Mar	R L L Tx	
Why, O Lord, Do You Stand Aloof?	Peloquin, C Alexander	Na Gia	L Tx	
Why, O Lord?	Foley, John, S. J.	70 Nal	B R L Tx	
Will You Believe Me, Thomas?	Fabing, Bob	74 Ahc	B R L L Tx	
Winds Thru The Olive Trees	Wetzler, Robert	69 Aug	M L Tx	Unis
Wings Of Wood	Hurd, Bob	75 Fel	B R L L Tx	
Winter Meditation	Isele, Bill	71 Nal	B L Tx	
Wisdom Has Built Herself A House	Deiss, Lucien	70 Wlp	B R L Tx	
Wisdom Of God	Hubert, Yvon	72 Fcc	R L L Tx	
Woman, Woman	Landry, Carey (Rev.)	68 Nal	B L Tx	
Word Of The Lord, The	Huijbers & Oosterhuis	74 Nal	M B L Tx	
World In The Making	Hubert, Yvon	72 Fcc	R L L Tx	
World Within, A	Smith, Roger	75 Nal	B R L Tx	
Written In The Word	Rettino, Ernest W.	74 Mar	R L L Tx	
You Are A Child Of The Universe	Mudd, C. P.	72 Nal	B R L Tx	
You Are Fair In Every Way	Fitzpatrick, Dennis	65 Fel	B L Tx	
You Are Peter, The Rock	Fitzpatrick, Dennis	65 Fel	B L Tx	
You Are Righteous, O Lord	Lewis	75 Sac	M L Tx	
You Are The Temple	Hilty, Everett J.	Na Oxf	M L Tx	Sa
You Christians All	Gilligan, Michael	70 Acp	B L L Tx	
You Christians All	Silvia, Helen	73 Acp	B L L Tx	
You Gave Him His Heart's Desire	Fitzpatrick, Dennis	65 Fel	B L Tx	
You Love Right And Hate Wrong	Fitzpatrick, Dennis	65 Fel	B L Tx	
You Shall Go Before The Lord	Fitzpatrick, Dennis	65 Fel	B L Tx	
You Shall Say To The Sons Of Israel	Fitzpatrick, Dennis	65 Fel	B L Tx	
You're Caught In A World	Wickham, J & Angle, D	73 Mar	R L L Tx	
Your Wife Shall Bear A Son	Fitzpatrick, Dennis	65 Fel	B L Tx	
Your Word Is A Lamp To My Feet	Zsigray, Joe	72 Nal	B R L Tx	
Different Is Beautiful	Avery, R/Marsh, D	74 Prc	M L Tx	
Mrs. Jones	Avery, R/Marsh, D	71 Prc	M L Tx	
I Come Tired	Avery, R/Marsh, D	71 Prc	M L Tx	
Love Them Now	Avery, R/Marsh, D	70 Prc	M L Tx	
Love, O Love	Avery, R.Marsh, D	71 Prc	B L Tx	
Cries For Help	Avery, R/Marsh, D	70 Prc	M L Tx	
It Was Me	Avery, R/Marsh, D	70 Prc	M L Tx	
Be Still	Avery, R/Marsh, D	70 Prc	M L Tx	
The Great Parade	Avery, R/Marsh, D	71 Prc	M L Tx	
Psalm 23	Avery, R/Marsh, D	74 Prc	M L Tx	
This Is The Day	Avery, R/Marsh, D	72 Prc	B L Tx	
We're Here To Be Happy	Avery, R/Marsh, D	72 Prc	B L Tx	
Go And Be Happy	Avery, R/Marsh, D	72 Prc	B L Tx	
Lord Is It I	Avery, R/Marsh, D	72 Prc	B L Tx	

CATEGORIZED INDEX

Send Me	Avery, R/Marsh, D	72 Prc	B	L Tx	
John's Words Of Praise	Avery, R/Marsh, D	72 Prc	B	L Tx	
Paul's Prayer	Avery, R/Marsh, D	72 Prc	B	L Tx	
Separate And United	Avery, R/Marsh, D	72 Prc	B	L Tx	
Go Ye Therefore	Avery, R/Marsh, D	72 Prc	B	L Tx	
Join Hands	Avery, R/Marsh, D	72 Prc	B	L Tx	
As We Leave	Avery, R/Marsh, D	72 Prc	B	L Tx	
Glorious Amen	Avery, R/Marsh, D	72 Prc	B	L Tx	
Flexible Amen	Avery, R/Marsh, D	72 Prc	B	L Tx	
Solemn Amen	Avery, R/Marsh, D	72 Prc	B	L Tx	
Bell Amen	Avery, R/Marsh, D	72 Prc	B	L Tx	
Outcry Amen	Avery, R/Marsh, D	72 Prc	B	L Tx	
Simple Amen	Avery, R/Marsh, D	72 Prc	B	L Tx	
Welcome	Avery, R/Marsh, D	70 Prc	B	L Tx	
Doxology	Avery, R/Marsh, D	67 Prc	B	L Tx	
Gloria Patri	Avery, R/Marsh, D	67 Prc	B	L Tx	
Gentle Doxology	Avery, R/Marsh, D	72 Prc	B	L Tx	
Gentle Gloria Patri	Avery, R/Marsh, D	72 Prc	B	L Tx	
When You Least Expect Him	Avery, R/Marsh, D	72 Prc	B	L Tx	
Time To March Again	Avery, R/Marsh, D	71 Prc	B	L Tx	
Give A Little Something Special	Avery, R/Marsh, D	72 Prc	B	L Tx	
Jesus, White Boy	Avery, R/Marsh, D	67 Prc	B	L Tx	
When I'm Feeling Lonely	Avery, R/Marsh, D	67 Prc	B	L Tx	
Happy Birthday	Avery, R/Marsh, D	70 Prc	B	L Tx	
Sometimes	Avery, R/Marsh, D	70 Prc	B	L Tx	
Shines There Such A Light	Avery, R/Marsh, D	70 Prc	B	L Tx	
Mary, Too	Avery, R/Marsh, D	72 Prc	B	L Tx	
Advent Carol	Avery, R/Marsh, D	70 Prc	B	L Tx	
Born Again	Avery, R/Marsh, D	70 Prc	B	L Tx	
Come As A Child	Avery, R/Marsh, D	71 Prc	B	L Tx	
Thank You Lord	Avery, R/Marsh, D	70 Prc	B	L Tx	
I Was Glad	Avery, R/Marsh, D	70 Prc	B	L Tx	
I Can Be A Christian By Myself	Avery, R/Marsh, D	72 Prc	B	L Tx	
Passed Thru The Waters	Avery, R/Marsh, D	71 Prc	B	L Tx	
Join The Revolution	Avery, R/Marsh, D	70 Prc	B	L Tx	
Take Time	Avery, R/Marsh, D	67 Prc	B	L Tx	
My Kind Of Music	Avery, R/Marsh, D	71 Prc	B	L Tx	
If There Is A Holy Spirit	Avery, R/Marsh, D	67 Prc	B	L Tx	
And The Cock Begins To Crow	Avery, R/Marsh, D	70 Prc	B	L Tx	
O Let's Get On	Avery, R/Marsh, D	70 Prc	B	L Tx	
Who's That Guy	Avery, R/Marsh, D	70 Prc	B	L Tx	
The Other Side	Avery, R/Marsh, D	71 Prc	B	L Tx	
What Makes The Wind Blow	Avery, R/Marsh, D	70 Prc	B	L Tx	
Little Baby Boy	Avery, R/Marsh, D	67 Prc	B	L Tx	
We Are The Church	Avery, R/Marsh, D	72 Prc	B	L Tx	
Put Down Your Guns	Avery, R/Marsh, D	70 Prc	B	L Tx	
O God, O Son Of God	Avery, R/Marsh, D	71 Prc	B	L Tx	
Hosanna, Hallelujah!	Avery, R/Marsh, D	67 Prc	B	L Tx	
This Little Babe	Avery, R/Marsh, D	71 Prc	B	L Tx	
Hey! Hey! Anybody Listening?	Avery, R/Marsh, D	67 Prc	B	L Tx	
Every Morning Is Easter Morning	Avery, R/Marsh, D	72 Prc	B	L Tx	
Baby Sitter	Avery, R/Marsh, D	72 Prc	B	L Tx	
He's Alive	Avery, R/Marsh, D	70 Prc	B	L Tx	
Advent Proclamation	Avery, R/Marsh, D	69 Prc	B	L Tx	
Here He Comes	Avery, R/Marsh, D	70 Prc	B	L Tx	
Blood	Avery, R/Marsh, D	70 Prc	B	L Tx	
Taste The New Wine	Avery, R/Marsh, D	71 Prc	B	L Tx	
Love Them Now	Avery, R/Marsh, D	70 Prc	B	L Tx	
I Wonder Why	Avery, R/Marsh, D	70 Prc	B	L Tx	
Christ The Lord Is Risen	Avery, R/Marsh, D	67 Prc	B	L Tx	
Possibly, Probably	Avery, R/Marsh, D	70 Prc	B	L Tx	
Will Any Three Leaders	Avery, R/Marsh, D	72 Prc	B	L Tx	
Here We Go A-Caroling	Avery, R/Marsh, D	67 Prc	B	L Tx	
Let's Go!	Avery, R/Marsh, D	71 Prc	B	L Tx	
Shine, Star	Avery, R/Marsh, D	71 Prc	B	L Tx	
Walking Alone	Avery, R/Marsh, D	71 Prc	B	L Tx	
Explorer	Avery, R/Marsh, D	71 Prc	B	L Tx	
Sing Love Songs	Avery, R/Marsh, D	71 Prc	B	L Tx	
Thank You, Thank You	Avery, P/Marsh, D	67 Prc	B	L Tx	
The Rebel	Avery, R/Marsh, D	67 Prc	B	L Tx	
Mary, Mary	Avery, R/Marsh, D	67 Prc	B	L Tx	
Starlight	Avery, R/Marsh, D	70 Prc	B	L Tx	
Mission Possible	Avery, R/Marsh, D	71 Prc	B	L Tx	
Goodbye	Avery, R/Marsh, D	70 Prc	B	L Tx	
A Choral Hymn For Advent & Ascension	Ley, Henry G.	Na Oxf	M	T Tx	Satb
A Legend	Tchaikovsky, P. I.	Na Gsc	B	T Tx	Var
A Morning Prayer	Sibelius, J	Na Gsc	B	T Tx	8mix
A Mother's Song	Obenshain, Kathryn G	Na Lor	M	T Tx	Sa
A Prayer Of St. Richard Of Chichester	White, L. J.	Na Oxf	M	T Tx	Sa
A Song Of Hanukkah	Adler, Samuel	Na Gsc	B	T Tx	Satb
Absalom	Tompkins, Thomas	56 Bbl	M	T Tx	Ssatb
Achieved Is The Glorious Work	Haydn, Joseph	Na Gsc	B	T Tx	Satb+
Achieved Is The Glorious Work (Me)	Haydn, Joseph	Na Oxf	M	T Tx	2pt
Ah, Thou Poor World (Me)	Brahms, J. (Arr Russell)	Na Oxf	M	T Tx	Ssaa
Alleluia! Morn Of Beauty	Mueller, Carl F	Na Gsc	B	T Tx	Satb
Alleluia, I Heard A Voice (Md)	Weelkes, Thomas	Na Oxf	M	T Tx	Sstbb
Ancient Days	Jeffery/Pool	Na Zon		T Tx	Satb
Ancient Of Days	Weinandt	73 Aug	M	T Tx	Satb
And Did Those Feet In Ancient Time	Chorbajian, John	Na Gsc	B	T Tx	Full
And It Shall Come To Pass	Berger, L.	68 Aug	M	T Tx	Satb
Angelus Autem Domini Descendit	Anerio, Felice	75 Bbl	M	T Tx	Satb
Anthem For Springtime	Wells, Dana F.	Na Abi	M	T Tx	Satb
Arise, My Love, My Fair One	Near, Gerald	66 Aug	M	T Tx	Satb
Arise, Shine	Berger, L.	65 Aug	M	T Tx	Satb
As Joseph Was A-Walking (A Cap)	Grieb, Herbert	Na Gsc	B	T Tx	Sab
At Montserrat	Nicolau, A	Na Gsc	B	T Tx	6mix+
Athalia (Oratorio)	Handel, G. F.	Na Oxf	B	T Tx	Satb
Avina Malkaynu Chanayno	Adler, Samuel	Na Gsc	B	T Tx	Satb
Ayl Melech Yoshayv	Adler, Samuel	Na Gsc	B	T Tx	Satb
Band Of Angels	Hairston, Jester	Na Wbp		T Tx	
Be Joyful, O Earth	Warland	63 Aug	M	T Tx	Satb
Beautiful Valley, The	Sanders, Robert	67 Bbl	M	T Tx	Satb
Behold A Host	Grieg-Christiansen	Na Aug	M	T Tx	Satb
Belshazzar's Feast (Oratorio)	Walton, William	Na Oxf	B	T Tx	Satb
Benediction From Sacred Service	Bloch, Ernest	34 Bbl	M	T Tx	Satb+
Berlin (Moore) (Acap)	Billings, William	Na Gsc	B	T Tx	Satb
Blessed The Faithful	Schutz, Heinrich	Na Gsc	B	T Tx	6mix
Bound For Canaan's Land	Moore, Undine Smith	Na Wbp		T Tx	
Brother James's Air (Me)	Bain, J.L.M. (Arr)	Na Oxf	M	T Tx	
Bunker Hill	Law, Andrew	76 Bbl	M	T Tx	Satb
Caecilliam Cantata	Marenzio	Na Kal	R	T Tx	Satb
Choral Benedictions	Parthun And Owens	73 Aug	M	T Tx	Satb
City Of High Renown	Parker, Horatio/Van Cam	75 Gal	M	T Tx	Satb
Come And Behold	Christiansen, P.	74 Aug	M	T Tx	Satb
Come Now Let Us Reason Together (W/Org	Grieb, Herbert	Na Gsc	B	T Tx	Satb+
Come On Down, Zacchaeus	Leaf, Robert	72 Aug	M	T Tx	Unis
Come To Me	Vdorak/Hughes	Na Lor	M	T Tx	Satb
Come Unto Him (Messiah)	Handel, G. F. (Bick)	Hof	M	T Tx	Ssa
Consider The Lilies	Scott, J P	Na Gsc	B	T Tx	Satb+
Creation	Haydn, Joseph	Na Kal	B	T Tx	Satb
Credidi Propter	Stadler, Maximilian	Na Gsc	B	T Tx	Satb+
Credo	Scarlatti, D.	Na Kal	B	T Tx	Satb
Credo	Vivaldi, A.	Na Kal	B	T Tx	Satb
Crusader's Hymn	Wilson	Na Lor	M	T Tx	Satb
Daniel, Daniel, Servant Of The Lord	Moore, Undine Smith	Na Wbp		T Tx	
David (Unison)	Waterman	Na Lor	M	T Tx	Unis
Dear Lord, Who Once Upon The Lake	Thompson, V. D.	Na Gsc	B	T Tx	Satb+
Death Of Absalom, The	Sanders, Robert L	60 Bbl	M	T Tx	Satb
Dies Sanctificatus	Palestrina, Giovanni P	Na Gsc	B	T Tx	Satb
Dies Sanctificatus	Palestrina, Giovanni P	Na Gia		T Tx	
Diffusa Est Gratia	Nanini, G M	Na Gia		T Tx	
Dives And Lazarus (Cantata)	Hoddinott, A. & James	Na Oxf	B	T Tx	Satb
Dominica In Ramis	Padilla, Juan G.	68 Pic	M	T Tx	
Draw Nigh To Thy Jerusalem	Johnson, D	67 Aug	M	T Tx	Satb
Dum Transisset Sabatum	Taverner, John	Na Oxf	M	T Tx	Satbb
Earth And All Stars	Johnson, D.	70 Aug	M	T Tx	Unis
Earth Is The Lord's	Lovelace, Austin C.	74 Aug	M	T Tx	2pt
Elegerunt	Fitzpatrick, Dennis	63 Fel	B	T Tx	
Elijah (Oratorio)	Mendelssohn, F.	Na Kal	B	T Tx	Satb
Elijah (Ger)	Mendelssohn, F.	Cfp	R	T Tx	Satb+
Evening Shadows Gently Falling	Track, Gerhard	75 Hal		T Tx	Ssaa
Exaltation	Christiansen, F. M.	60 Aug	M	T Tx	Satb
Fall Softly, Snow	Moe, Daniel	63 Aug	M	T Tx	Satb
Fantasia On The Old 104th Psalm Tune	Williams, Vaughan R.	Na Oxf	B	T Tx	Satb
Festival Piece On "St. Ann"	Butler, Eugene	76 Her	M	T Tx	Satb+
Fight The Good Fight (E)	Rhodes, Harold	Na Oxf	M	T Tx	Satb
First And Second Preces And Psalms	Byrd, William	Na Kal	B	T Tx	Satb
First And Second Preces And Psalms	Gibbons, Orlando	Na Kal	B	T Tx	Satb
First Psalm	La Forge, F	Na Gsc	B	T Tx	Ttbb
For All The Saints	Williams, Vaughan R. N	Ag Sc	M	T Tx	Var
For All The Saints (M)	Williams, Vaughan R.	Na Oxf	M	T Tx	Var
Francis, Friend Of All Things	Westendorf, Omer	63 Wlp	B	T Tx	
Garden Hymn, The	Price	Na Lor	M	T Tx	Satb
Give Alms Of Thy Goods (Me)	Tye, Christopher	Na Oxf	M	T Tx	Satb
Go Forth With God! (Me)	Shaw, Martin	Na Oxf	M	T Tx	U+Des
God Bless You, Mother Dear	Landon	Na Lor	M	T Tx	Satb
God Grant You Many Years	Carroll, J. R.	72 Gia	M	T Tx	Satb
God Is God	Sateren, Leland B.	63 Aug	M	T Tx	Satb
God, Creator	Hunnicutt, J.	74 Aug	M	T Tx	Satb+
God, The Lord, Sent A Messenger	Anerio, Felix	75 Bbl	M	T Tx	Satb
God's Promise (E)	Adler, Samuel	Na Oxf	M	T Tx	
God's Word Shall Stand	Van Horn/Decou	Na Zon		T Tx	Satb
Great Service (Venite, Etc)	Byrd, William	Na Kal	B	T Tx	Satb
Happy And Blest Are They	Mendelssohn, F.	Na Gsc	B	T Tx	Satb+
Hark A Thrilling Voice Is Sounding	Wetzler, Robert	61 Aug	M	T Tx	Satb
Hark, The Vesper Hymn Is Stealing	Na	Na Gsc	B	T Tx	Satb+
Hashkivenu	Bernstein, Leonard	Na Wbp		T Tx	
Hast Thou Not Known?	Mueller, Carl F	Na Gsc	B	T Tx	Satb
Hayom Harat Olam	Adler, Samuel	Na Gsc	B	T Tx	Satb
He Is There	Burnham	75 Sac	M	T Tx	Var
He Who Would Valiant Be	Douglas-Near	66 Aug	M	T Tx	Satb
Heilig Ist Gott (Eng & Germ)	Bach, C.P.E. Ed. Stein	Na Oxf	B	T Tx	Full
Home And Mother	Dvorak	Na Lor	M	T Tx	Satb
Honor To The Hills	Ingalls, Jeremiah	75 Bbl	B	T Tx	Ttb
How Beautiful Upon The Mountains	Harker, F F	Na Gsc	B	T Tx	Var+
How Fair The Church	Schumann-Christiansen	68 Aug	M	T Tx	Full
How Gentle God's Commands	Ford, Virgil	Na Gsc	B	T Tx	Satb
How Lovely Are The Messengers	Mendelssohn, F.	Na Lor	M	T Tx	Satb
Hymn For Our Time	Beck, John Ness	Na Gsc	B	T Tx	Var+
Hymn Of Saint Teresa	Martin	75 Maf	M	T Tx	Satb
Hymn To David	Beck, John Ness	Na Gsc	B	T Tx	Full
Hymn To The Holy Innocents	Brown, Christopher	Na Oxf	B	T Tx	Satb
I Am	Williams, J.	76 Sil	R	T Tx	
I Am Come Into My Garden	Billings, William	74 Bbl	M	T Tx	Satb
I Believe In God	Denton	Na Lor	M	T Tx	Satb
I Believe In Miracles	Peterson, John W.	Na Lor	M	T Tx	Satb
I Can Believe	Nyboer	Na Lor	M	T Tx	2mel
I Just Come From The Fountain	Moore, Undine Smith	Na Wbp		T Tx	
I Love The Church	Sateren, Leland B.	52 Aug	M	T Tx	Satb
I Saw A Stranger Yester'en (A Cap)	Glarum, L Stanley	Na Gsc	B	T Tx	2pt
I Shall Not Care (Arr. Only)	Bergerson, Charles	75 Mam		R L T Tx	
I Think I Heard Him Say	Martin	Na Lor	M	T Tx	Satb
I Will Sing The Wondrous Story	Prichard/Johnson	75 Zon		T Tx	Satb
I'll Walk With God	Brodzsky	Na Wbp		T Tx	
I'm Standing In The Sun	Myers, Carmel	Na Gsc	B	T Tx	Ttbb
I've Been 'buked	Na	Na Gsc	B	T Tx	Satb
Immortal, Invisible	Wilson	Na Lor	M	T Tx	Satb
In Heaven Above	Christiansen, F. M.	25 Aug	M	T Tx	Satb
In Heaven Above	Norwegian	Na Lor	M	T Tx	Satb

In My Orchard, Pearl'd With Dew	Meyerowitz, Jan	53 Bbl	B	T Tx	Satb
In Times Like These	Jones	Na Lor	M	T Tx	Satb
Increase	Fischer, Irwin	76 Cob	M	T Tx	
Inveni David(Lat)	Bruckner, Anton	Cfp	R	T Tx	Ttbb+
Jacob's Vision	English	Na Lor	M	T Tx	Var
Jerusalem Morning	Na	Na Gsc	B	T Tx	Ttbb
Jesus Walked This Lonesome Valley	Dawson, William	Na Wbp		T Tx	
Jonah (Oratorio)	Carrissimi, Giacomo	Na Oxf	B	T Tx	Full
Joseph Dearest, Joseph Mine	Martin	Na Lor	M	T Tx	Sab
Joseph, Joseph, Dearest One	Calvisius, Seth	75 Bbl	M	T Tx	Full
Joseph, Lieber Joseph Mein	Calvisius, Seth	75 Bbl	M	T Tx	Full
Joseph, Patron Saint Of Workers	Mischke/Vermulst	63 Wlp	B	T Tx	
Keep His Commandments	Newbury, Kent A.	Na Gsc	B	T Tx	Satb
Kingsfold I Feel The Winds Of God	Beck, John N	75 Bec	M	T Tx	
Letter To Mother (Mother's Day)	Lockwood, Normand	56 Smc	M	T Tx	Satb
Leviathan (From Three Motets)	Krenek, Ernst	61 Ron	M	T Tx	Ssa
Listen To The Lambs	Dett, R N	Na Gsc	B	T Tx	Var
Little David, Play On Your Harp	Hughes, Robert J.	Na Lor	M	T Tx	Satb
Little Innocent Lamb	Na	Na Gsc	B	T Tx	Ttbb
Little Lamb	Artman, Ruth	Na Wbp		T Tx	
Look Down To Us St. Joseph	Gannon, Michael	63 Wlp	B	T Tx	
Lord Of Spirits	Reissiger-Christiansen	31 Aug	M	T Tx	Satb
Lost Child, The	Nin-Culmell, Joaquin	55 Ron	M	T Tx	Satb
Magnificat And Nunc Dimittis	Winter, John	Na Gsc	B	T Tx	Satb
May No Rash Intruder ("Solomon")	Handel, G. F.	Cfs	M	T Tx	Satb
Merciful Savior Hear Our Humble Prayer	Farrell, Melvin	55 Wlp	B	T Tx	
Messiah From Three Folk-Hymns	Anonymous	75 Bbl	B	T Tx	Sb
Mexican Psalm, A	Butler, Eugene	73 Hal		T Tx	Satb
Moment By Moment	Smith	Na Lor	M	T Tx	Satb
More Things Are Wrought By Prayer	Martin	Na Lor	M	T Tx	Satb
Morning Grace	Grieb, Herbert	Na Gsc	B	T Tx	2pt+
Morning Invocation	Buck, Dudley	Na Gsc	B	T Tx	3pt+
Morning Trumpet	White/Wood	Na Wbp		T Tx	
Motet No.1(Eng-Ger)	Bach, J. S.	Cfp	R	T Tx	Full+
Motet No.2(Eng-Ger)	Bach, J. S.	Cfp	R	T Tx	Full+
Motet No.3(Eng-Ger)	Bach, J. S.	Cfp	R	T Tx	Ssatb+
Motet No.4(Eng-Ger)	Bach, J. S.	Cfp	R	T Tx	Full+
Motet No.5(Eng-Ger)	Bach, J. S.	Cfp	R	T Tx	Full+
Motet No.6(Eng-Ger)	Bach, J. S.	Cfp	R	T Tx	Satb+
Motet O Beata	Palestrina, Giovanni P	Na Kal	B	T Tx	
Mother's Prayer, A	Wilson, I	Na Lor	M	T Tx	Satb
Mother's Song, A	Obenshain	Na Lor	M	T Tx	Sa
Mother's Task	Ashford	Na Lor	M	T Tx	Satb
Mothers Everywhere	Maker	Na Lor	M	T Tx	Sab
My Faith	Leaf, Robert	72 Aug	M	T Tx	Unis
Near To The Heart Of God	Mcafee/Mayfield	Na Zon		T Tx	Satb
Near To Thy Heart	Peterson/Decou	Na Zon		T Tx	Satb
Newport (From Four Plain-Tunes)	Read, Daniel	76 Bbl	M	T Tx	Satb
Now Praise We Great And Famous Men	Grieg-Bempton	Hof	M	T Tx	Sab
Now With The New Year Starting	Lynn, George	56 Smc	M	T Tx	Satb
Nunc Dimittis And Gloria (A Cap)	Tschesnokoff-Cain	Hof	M	T Tx	Satb
O Blessed Day Of Motherhood	Vick	Na Lor	M	T Tx	Satb
O God The King Of Glory (Md)	Gibbons, Orlando	Na Oxf	M	T Tx	Full
O God, The Rock Of Ages	Sateren, Leland B.	Na Aug	M	T Tx	Satb
O Happy Home	Rasley	Na Lor	M	T Tx	Satb
O Happy Man	Purcell, Henry	Na Gsc	B	T Tx	Satb+
O Joseph, Mighty Patron	Sr M. M. Keane/Wesley	70 Jsp	B	T Tx	
O Lord Of Light	Farrell, Melvin	61 Wlp	M B	T Tx	
O Son Of Man	Schaffer, Robert J.	69 Wlp	B R	T Tx	
O Ye People	Haydn, Michael	Na Gsc	B	T Tx	Satb
Old Irish Blessing	Agay	Na Wbp		T Tx	
On The Land And On The Sea	Meyerowitz, Jan	54 Bbl	M	T Tx	Satb
On Wings Of Living Light (W/Tpt)	Mitchell	74 Aug	M	T Tx	2pt
One God	Johnston	Na Lor	M	T Tx	Satb
One Sweetly Solemn Thought	Ambrise, R S	Na Gsc	B	T Tx	Var+
Oppression Shall Not Always Reign	Brandon, George	76 Abi	M	T Tx	Satb+
People Of God, The	Butler, Eugene	73 Hal		T Tx	Satb
Pilgrim Hymn	Bacon, Ernst	Na Gsc	B	T Tx	Unis+
Prayer For Mothers, A	Martens	Na Lor	M	T Tx	
Prayer, A	Reske	Na Lor	M	T Tx	
Primrose	Niles, John Jacob	Na Gsc	B	T Tx	Ssa+
Ride On, Jesus!	Na	Na Gsc	B	T Tx	6mix
Rise Up, O Men Of God	Jennings, K.	68 Aug	M	T Tx	Ttbb
Sacred Service Avodath Hakodesh	Bloch, Ernest	34 Bbl	B	T Tx	Var
Salve (Salutation)	Franco, Fernando	68 Pic	M	T Tx	
Samson (Eng/Germ) (Oratorio)	Handel, G. F.	Na Kal	B R	T Tx	Satb
Sanctification	Bloch, Ernest	62 Bbl	M	T Tx	Satb
Sanctorum Meritis	Palestrina, Giovanni P	Na Kal	B	T Tx	
Sandusky	Holyoke, Samuel	76 Bbl	M	T Tx	Atb
Saul. Sacred Concerto(Ger)	Schutz, Heinrich	Cfp	R	T Tx	Full+
Saviour, When Night Involves The Skies	Shelley, H R	Na Gsc	B	T Tx	Satb+
Seasons	Haydn, Joseph	Na Kal	B	T Tx	Satb
Second Service (Magnificat, Nunc)	Byrd, William	Na Kal	B	T Tx	Satb
Serve Bone	Lasso, Orlando Di	Na Gia		T Tx	
Sh'ma Yisroeyl	Schwadron, AA	Na Gsc	B	T Tx	Satb
Shadows Of Evening	Gannon, Michael	61 Wlp	B	T Tx	
Sherburne	Read, D	Na Gsc	B	T Tx	Satb
Sherburne	Read, Daniel	76 Bbl	M	T Tx	Satb
Short Service (Venite, Te Deum Etc)	Byrd, William	Na Kal	B	T Tx	Satb
Show Me A Window	Tarner	Na Lor	M	T Tx	
Sicut Rose & Ipsa Te Cogat Pietas	Lasso, Orlando Di	Na Gia		T Tx	
Silence Of God, The	Porter	Na Lor	M	T Tx	
Silent Devotion And Response	Bloch, Ernest	34 Bbl	M	T Tx	Satb+
Sinner You Can't Walk My Path	Moore, Undine Smith	Na Wbp		T Tx	
So Quietly He Came	Dexter	Na Lor	M	T Tx	
Song Of God, The	Rasley	Na Lor	M	T Tx	
Song Of Moses	Beck, John Ness	Na Gsc	B	T Tx	Full+
Song Of The Garo Christians	Cain, Noble	Na Gsc	B	T Tx	Satb
St. Paul (Oratorio, Germ/Eng)	Mendelssohn, F.	Na Kal	B	T Tx	Satb
Stay With Us	Bixel, James W.	74 Flp	M	T Tx	
Still, Still, Still	Wetzler, Robert	64 Aug	M	T Tx	Var
Striving After God	Moore, Undine Smith	Na Wbp		T Tx	
Summer Ended	Wood, Charles	Na Gsc	B	T Tx	Satb+
Sun Shines In Splendor, The	Elliot	Na Lor	M	T Tx	2mel
Tambourines To Glory	Moore, Undine Smith	Na Wbp		T Tx	
Thanks To God For My Mother	Loucks	Na Lor	M	T Tx	Satb
The Ballad Of Lazarus And The Rich Man	Mondoy, Robert	76 Rpb	M B R L	T Tx	
The Bells At Speyer	Senfl, Ludwig	Na Gsc	B	T Tx	6mix
The Binding (Oratorio)	Adler, Samuel	Na Oxf	B	T Tx	Ssatb
The Covenant Of The Rainbow (Cantata)	Crosse, Gordon	Na Oxf	B	T Tx	Satb
The Day Draws On With Golden Light (E)	Bairstow, E. C.	Na Oxf	M	T Tx	Satb
The Earth Is The Lord's	Couperin, F.(Nelson)	68 Aug	M	T Tx	Unis
The Earth Is The Lord's	Mitcheltree	71 Aug	M	T Tx	Ussa
The Feast Of Light	Adler, Samuel	Na Gsc	B	T Tx	Satb
The Godly Stranger	Cassler, G. W.	56 Aug	M	T Tx	Satb
The Great White Host	Grieg, E.	Na Gsc	B	T Tx	Satb+
The Just Men Have Taken Away	Lasso, Orlando Di	67 Fel	B	T Tx	
The Lamb	Schwadron, AA	Na Gsc	B	T Tx	Satb
The Miraculous Harvest	Niles, John Jacob	Na Gsc	B	T Tx	Satb
The Morning Trumpet	Na	Na Gsc	B	T Tx	Satb
The Pharisee And The Publican	Schutz, Heinrich	Na Gsc	B	T Tx	Satb+
The Play Of Daniel	Greenberg, Noah (Ed)	Na Oxf	B	T Tx	Satb
The Play Of Herod	Greenberg, N. & Smoldo	Na Oxf	B	T Tx	Satb
The Radiant Morn Hath Passed	Woodward, H. H.	Na Gsc	B	T Tx	Satb+
The Second Service (Te Deum, Jubilate)	Gibbons, Orlando	Na Kal	B	T Tx	Satb
The Short Service (Venite, Te Deum)	Gibbons, Orlando	Na Kal	B	T Tx	Satb
The Silent Sea	Neidlinger, W H	Na Gsc	B	T Tx	Var+
The Souls Of The Righteous (Me)	Williams, Vaughan R.	Na Oxf	M	T Tx	Var
The Sower (Cantata)	Darke-Aveling	Na Oxf	B	T Tx	Satb
The Tree Of Life (Cantata)	Merchant, W. M.	Na Oxf	B	T Tx	Satb
The Twelve (For Apostles)	Walton, William	Na Oxf	M	T Tx	Full
Then I Know	Martin	Na Lor	M	T Tx	Satb
Then Spake Solomon	Whettam, Graham	Na Gsc	B	T Tx	Satb+
There Be Four Things	Krenek, Ernst	73 Ron	M	T Tx	Satb
There Be Three Things	Krenek, Ernst	73 Ron	M	T Tx	Satb
There Is A Green Hill Far Away	Gounod, Charles	Na Gsc	B	T Tx	Satb+
There's A Wideness In God's Mercy	Tourjee/Johnson	Na Zon		T Tx	Satb
These Are Thy Glorious Works	Thompson	Na Lor	M	T Tx	Satb
They Gathered At The River	Wrynn, Paul	76 Rpb	M B R L	T Tx	
They Shall See The Glory Of The Lord	Rhodes	Na Wbp		T Tx	
Think On Me	Smith Charles N.	76 Abi	M	T Tx	Satb+
Third Service (Magnificat, Nunc Dim)	Byrd, William	Na Kal	B	T Tx	Satb
This Book Of The Law	Grieb, Herbert	Na Gsc	B	T Tx	Satb+
This Is My Commandment	Tallis, Thomas	Na Oxf	M	T Tx	Ssatb
This Train	Na	Na Gsc	B	T Tx	Ttbb
Thus Then The Law	Bach, J. S.	Na Gsc	B	T Tx	Ssa
To Our Fathers--And Thee	Lynn, George	56 Smc	M	T Tx	Satb
To The Sea In Ships	Krenek, Ernst	61 Ron	M	T Tx	Ssa
Tribute To Mother, A	Na	Na Lor	M	T Tx	Satb
Tu Es Petrus	Palestrina, Giovanni P	Na Gsc	B	T Tx	6mix
Tu Es Petrus	Palestrina, Giovanni P	Na Kal	B	T Tx	
Twilight And Dawn	Speaks, Oley	Na Gsc	B	T Tx	Satb+
Unsers Herzens Freude (Eng & Germ)	Bach, J. C.	Na Oxf	B	T Tx	Full
Upon This Rock	Beck, John Ness	Na Gsc	B	T Tx	Satb+
Ut Flos, Ut Rosa (Me) (Saints)	Crivelli, Giovanni B.	Na Oxf	M	T Tx	2pts
Uv' Shofar Gadol	Adler, Samuel	Na Gsc	B	T Tx	Satb
V'shom'ru	Ancis, S	Na Gsc	B	T Tx	Satb
Valiant-For-Truth (Md)	Williams, Vaughan R.	Na Oxf	M	T Tx	Satb
Veni Sanctus K 47	Mozart, Wolfgang A	Na Kal	B	T Tx	Satb
Vision Of Aeroplanes (Ezek 1)	Williams, Vaughan R.	Na Oxf	M	T Tx	Satb
Wade In De Water	Hairston, Jester	Na Wbp		T Tx	
Warrenton	Niles, John Jacob	Na Gsc	B	T Tx	Var+
We Come Unto Our Fathers' God	Rohlig, Harald	Na Abi	M	T Tx	
We've Got A Lot To Live For	Roesch	Na Lor	M	T Tx	
Were You There?	Na	Na Gsc	B	T Tx	Ttbb+
What Are These That Are Arrayed	Stainer, Sir John	Na Gsc	B	T Tx	Satb+
What Is A Man?	Jeppesen, Knud	75 Bbl	M	T Tx	Satb
What Is This Lovely Fragrance? (Me)	Willan, Healey	Na Oxf	M	T Tx	Satb
When David Heard That Absalom Was	Tompkins, Thomas	Na Gsc	B	T Tx	5mix
When From The Lips Of Truth	Fischer, Irwin	76 Cob	M	T Tx	
When Jesus Sat At Meat (Md) (Stmmag)	Nicholson, Richard	Na Oxf	M	T Tx	Ssatb
When Morning Gilds The Sky	Whitehead, Alfred	Na Gsc	B	T Tx	Satb+
When There's Love At Home	Denton	Na Lor	M	T Tx	
Where Cross The Crowded Ways	Johnson, D.	67 Aug	M	T Tx	Sab
Where Is Now Abel?	Alchinger, G/Ed	74 Gia	M	T Tx	Sab
Who Can Tell The Glory (Md)	Byrd, William	Na Oxf	M	T Tx	Ssatb
Who Knows The Answer?	Shea	Na Lor	M	T Tx	
Wisdom (From Three Motets)	Hovhaness, Alan S.	74 Ron	M	T Tx	Satb
Yes I'll Sing The Wondrous Story	Traditional/Mickelson	Na Zon	M	T Tx	Satb
You Got To Reap Just What You Sow	Dawson, William	Na Wbp		T Tx	

COLLECTIONS OF SACRED MUSIC

This section lists hymnals and other collections of sacred music, and also a small amount of instrumental music (collected and otherwise). Many of the collections listed here have been listed title by title in other parts of this book. In the listings below, ZA refers to the collections of music, and ZB refers to the instrumental material.

Collections of Hymns

Action No 1 (No 5121)	Na	Na Zon	C Za
Action No 2 (No 5122)	Na	Na Zon	C Za
Action No 3 (No 5123)	Na	Na Zon	C Za
Action No 4 (No 5124)	Na	Na Zon	C Za
Action No 5 (No 5125)	Na	Na Zon	C Za
Action No 6 (No 5126)	Na	Na Zon	C Za
Action No 7 (No 5127)	Na	Na Zon	C Za

CATEGORIZED INDEX

Adelante Juventud	Collected	Na Zon		C Za Span
Cherub Choir No 1 (No 5030)	Collected	Na Zon		C Za
Cherub Choir No 2 (No 5031)	Collected	Na Zon		C Za
Cherub Choir No 3 (No 5032)	Collected	Na Zon		C Za
Favoritos Juveniles (No 5372)	Collected	Na Zon		C Za Span
Happy Time Songs No 1 (No 5500)	Na	Na Zon		C Za
Happy Time Songs No 2 (No 5501)	Na	Na Zon		C Za
Hymn-Time For Tiny Tots (No 5521)	Collected	Na Zon		C Za
Hymnal For Boys And Girls No 1 5518	Collected	Na Zon		C Za
Hymnal For Boys And Girls No 2 (5525)	Peterson, John W.	Na Zon		C Za
Hymns For Youth	Hammersma, John	Na Erd	B	C Za 5-12
Junior Choir No 1 (No 5445)	Collected	Na Zon		C Za
Junior Choir No 2 (No 5446)	Collected	Na Zon		C Za
Junior Choir No 3 (No 5447)	Collected	Na Zon		C Za
Junior Choir No 4 (No 5448)	Collected	Na Zon		C Za
Junior Choir No 5 (No 5444)	Collected	Na Zon		C Za
Junior Choir No 6 (No 5451)	Collected	Na Zon		C Za
Junior Choir No 7 (No 5502)	Collected	Na Zon		C Za
Lively Choruses No 1 (No 5300)	Collected	Na Zon	B	C Za
Lively Choruses No 2 (No 5301)	Collected	Na Zon	B	C Za
Lively Choruses No 3 (No 5302)	Collected	Na Zon	B	C Za
Mass For Children (Icet)	Kreutz, Robert	69 Wlp	B	C Za
More Hymns And Anthems For Children's	Grime, William	Na Abi	M	C Za U-Sa
Rock On The Head	Wyrtzen, Don	Na Zon		C Za
Simple Songs For Toddlers No 1 (5572)	Collected	Na Zon	B	C Za
Simple Songs For Toddlers No 2 (5573)	Collected	Na Zon	B	C Za
Simple Songs For Toddlers No 3 (5574)	Collected	Na Zon	B	C Za
Simple Songs For Toddlers No 4 (5630)	Collected	Na Zon	B	C Za
Sing Time For Children (No 5014)	Na	Na Zon	R	C Za
Sing With Marcy (No 5455)	Tigner, Marcy	Na Zon	B	C Za
Sing-A-Long Songs As Used On The Child	Collected	Na Zon		C Za
Six Anthems For Junior Choir	Pfautsch, Lloyd	Na Abi	M	C Za U-Sa
Six Anthems For Junior Voices	Butler, Eugene	Na Abi	M	C Za Unis
Sunshine Choir No 1 (No 5520)	Na	Na Zon		C Za
Sunshine Choir No 2 (No 5523)	Na	Na Zon		C Za
The Children's Hymnbook	Hammersma, John	Na Erd	B	C Za Kt04
Three Anthems For Junior Choir	Gillette, James R.	Na Abi	M	C Za Sa
Three Junior Choir Anthems	Dressler, John	Na Abi	M	C Za
Top Songs For Children (No 5849)	Collected	Na Zon		C Za
Youth In Unison (No 5033)	Na	Na Zon		C Za
A Mass For All Occasions	Wagner, Lavern J.	71 Sms	M R L	F Za
Back To The Prairies And Other Country	Harper, Redd	Na Zon		F Za Span
Country And Western Hymnal	Bock, Fred	Na Zon		F Za
Country-Western Gospel Favorites (100)	Collected	75 Zon		F Za
Dias Especiales (No 5374)	Savage, Robert (Ed)	75 Zon		F Za Span
Eight Folksongs & Spirituals	Johnson (Arr), D.	75 Aug	M	F Za Tbb
Fifty Folk Favorites (No 5074)	Wyrtzen/Krogstad	Na Zon	B	F Za Youth
Folk Celebration (No 4355)	Bock, Fred	Na Zon	B	F Za Youth
Folk Songs Of Mike Mcgervey (4287)	Mcgervey	Na Zon	B	F Za
Four Folksongs And Spirituals	Johnson (Arr), D.	71 Aug	M	F Za Tbb
Hear Them Cryin'	Repp, Ray	72 Wrd	B R	F Za Unis+
Hip Pocket Hymnal (No 5313)	Na	Na Zon	B	F Za
Hymnal For Contemporary Christians	Wyrtzen-Johnson	Na Zon	B	F Za
It Wouldn't Be Enough (Collection)	Hiner, Robbie	76 Wrd	B R	F Za Satb+
Light Of The World (Musical)	Parks, Joe	Na Zon	B	F Za
Listen He's Here (No 4721)	Wyrtzen/Krogstad	Na Zon	B	F Za
Liturgy Of The Holy Spirit	Summerlin, E., Miller, W.	69 Van	B R	F Za
Living Waters (Scriptural Collec)	Toolan, Sr Suzanne	71 Gia	B R L	F Za Ar+
Love Was When/Love Is Now (No 4380)	Collected	Na Zon	B	F Za
Mass For Joy (W/Org, Guit)	Peloquin, C Alexander	68 Gia	B L	F Za Var+
Melchizedek Mass For The King	Pulkingham, Betty C.	73 Gia	B L	F Za Satb+
Missa A La Samba (W/Org, Bongos)	Peloquin, C Alexander	70 Gia	B L	F Za Var+
My Soapbox (No 5617)	Wyrtzen, Don	Na Zon	B	F Za
Now Sounds (No 4500)	Wsyrtzen/Walvoord	Na Zon	B	F Za
Pilgrim's Road	Wood, Mike	76 Rpb	M B R L	F Za
Revive Us Again	Christiansen, Ansgar	Na Zon		F Za
Sing Folk! No 1 (No 5075)	Collected	Na Zon	B	F Za
Sing Folk! No 2 (No 5076)	Collected	Na Zon	B	F Za
Sing Folk! No 3 (No 5077)	Collected	Na Zon	B	F Za
Smilin' More Everyday (No 5013)	Krogtlad, Bob	75 Zon	B	F Za
Songs From My Heart (W/Guitar)	Belt, Thomas	70 Gia	B R L	F Za Var+
Songs Of Erv Lewis (No 5139)	Lewis, Erv	Na Zon	B	F Za
Sounds Of Celebration No 1	Wyrtzen, Don	Na Zon	B	F Za
Teen Choir (No 5260)	Krogstad, Bob (Ed)	Na Zon	B	F Za Sab
Teen Favorites (No 5662)	Krogstad, Bob	Na Zon	B	F Za Sab
Teen Time Tunes (No 5733)	Na	Na Zon	B	F Za
Teenage Choir No 1 (No 5588)	Collected	Na Zon	B	F Za Sab
Teenage Choir No 2 (No 5583)	Collected	Na Zon	B	F Za Sab
Teenage Choir No 3 (No 5579)	Collected	Na Zon	B	F Za Sab
Teenage Choir No 4 (No 5578)	Collected	Na Zon	B	F Za Sab
Teenage Favorites No 1 (No 5586)	Na	Na Zon	B	F Za
Teenage Favorites No 2 (No 5587)	Na	Na Zon	B	F Za
Teenage Favorites No 3 (No 5607)	Na	Na Zon	B	F Za
Teenage Favorites No 4 (No 5610)	Na	Na Zon	B	F Za
The Country-Western Choir No 1 (5865)	Peterson, John W.	Na Zon	B	F Za
The Country-Western Choir No 2 (5872)	Collected	Na Zon	B	F Za
The Folk Hymnal (No 5767)	Johnson/Peterson	Na Zon	B	F Za Youth
The Gamble Folk Song Book (No 4515)	Collected	Na Zon	B	F Za
The Late Great Planet Earth Songbook	Bock, Fred (Ed)	Na Zon		F Za Unis
The Way I Feel (Collection)	Honeytree	74 Wrd	B R	F Za Unis+
Western Style Songs No 1 (No 5580)	Collected	Na Zon		F Za
Western Style Songs No 2 (No 5581)	Collected	Na Zon		F Za
Western Style Songs No 3 (No 5582)	Collected	Na Zon		F Za
Western Style Songs No 4 (No 5560)	Collected	Na Zon		F Za
What's It All About, Anyhow?	Na	Na Zon	B R	F Za
Who Wants To Be Free? (Musical)	Innes/Fasig	Na Zon	B R	F Za
Yesterday, Today And Tomorrow (No 5923)	Wyrtzen, Don	Na Zon	B	F Za
A Festival Of Carols For The Year	Caldwell, Mary E.	67 Wrd	B R	G Za Var+
Backpacker's Suite (Youth Musical)	Salsbury, Sonny	75 Wrd	B R	G Za Satb+
Burdens Are Lifted At Calvary	Moore, John	Na Zon		G Za Unis
Bus Sing (No 5135)	Decou, Harold	Na Zon	B	G Za
Canticos De Gozo E Inspiracion	Collected	Na Zon		G Za Span
Cantos De Evangelismo	Savage, Bob (Ed)	Na Zon		G Za Span
Celebration Songs (No 4360)	Wyrtzen, Don	Na Zon		G Za Unis
Children's Unison Choir No 1 (No 5793)	Collected	Na Zon		G Za
Children's Unison Choir No 2 (No 5798)	Collected	Na Zon		G Za
Children's Unison Choir No 3 (No 5800)	Collected	Na Zon		G Za
Children's Unison Choir No 4 (No 5893)	Collected	75 Zon		G Za
Choir Specials (No 5592)	Berntsen, W. R.	Na Zon	B	G Za
Christmas Organist (No 5950)	Decou/Johnson	Na Zon	B	G Za Organ
Cofre De Canticos	Savage, Bob (Ed)	Na Zon		G Za Span
Crowning Glory Hymnal	Na	Na Zon		G Za Unis+
Dallas Holm Songs	Holm, Dallas	Na Zon	B	G Za Youth
Doug Oldham Songbook (No 4336)	Peterson, John W.	75 Zon		G Za Solo
Duos Trios Y Cuartetos (No 5368)	Collected	Na Zon		G Za Span
Ecos De Victoria (No 5366)	Collected	Na Zon		G Za Span
Evangelism Arrangements No 1 (4000)	Souther, Billy	Na Zon	B	G Za
Evangelism Arrangements No 2 (4191)	Souther, Billy	Na Zon	B	G Za
Favorite Choir Arrangements No 1 (5427	Collected	Na Zon	B	G Za
Favorite Choir Arrangements No 2 (5465	Collected	Na Zon	B	G Za
Favorite Hymns For Crusades And Conf.	Decou, Harold (Col.)	Na Zon		G Za
Favorite Hymns Of Faith And Hope	Na Collected	Na Zon		G Za
Favorite Prophetic Songs For The Choir	Wyrtzen, Don	Na Zon	B	G Za
Favorite Spirituals No 1 (No 5593)	Johnson, Norman	Na Zon	B	G Za
Favorite Spirituals No 2 (No 5792)	Decou/Johnson	Na Zon	B	G Za
Favorites For Youth	Krogstad, Bob	75 Zon	B	G Za
Fifty Gospel Quartet Favorites	Na	Na Zon	B	G Za
Fifty Latin American Favorites (#5276)	Savage, Bob (Ed)	Na Zon		G Za Span
Fifty Men's Favorites No 4311	Na	Na Zon	B	G Za
Folio Of Gospel Choir Favorites	Peterson, John W.	Na Zon	B	G Za
Four Gospel Hymn Anthems	Lynn, George	Na Abi	M	G Za Satb
Gentle As Morning (Collection)	Kerr, Anita (Arr)	75 Wrd	B R	G Za Satb+
George Beverly Shea Gospel Solos (5433)	Shea, George Beverly	Na Zon		G Za Solo
George Beverly Shea Solos (No 5432)	Shea, George Beverly	Na Zon		G Za Solo
Gospel Choir Classics No 1 (No 5195)	Collected	Na Zon	B	G Za
Gospel Choir Classics No 2 (No 5196)	Collected	Na Zon	B	G Za
Gospel Choir Classics No 3 (No 5197)	Collected	Na Zon	B	G Za
Gospel Favorites For The Small Church	Rasley, John M.	Na Zon	B	G Za
Growing Pains (Youth Collection)	Owens, Jamie	76 Wrd	B R	G Za Satb+
Harold Decou Presents Choral Praises	Decou, Harold	Na Zon	B	G Za
He Touched Me And Other Songs (No 5416)	Gaither, William J	Na Zon		G Za Solo
He's Everything To Me (Coll)	Carmichael, Ralph (Ed)	74 Wrd	B	G Za Unis+
High Voice No 1 (No 5021)	Collected	Na Zon		G Za Solo
High Voice No 2 (No 5022)	Collected	Na Zon		G Za Solo
High Voice No 3 (No 5023)	Collected	Na Zon		G Za Solo
High Voice No 4 (No 5024)	Collected	Na Zon		G Za Solo
High Voice No 5 (No 5025)	Collected	Na Zon		G Za Solo
High Voice No 6 (No 5170)	Collected	Na Zon		G Za Solo
Himnos De Fe Y Alabanza	Collected	Na Zon		G Za Span
Hymns We Love To Sing (No 4400)	Collected	Na Zon		G Za
Inspiring Hymns	Na	Na Zon		G Za
Ira Stanphill Favorites No 1 (No 5495)	Stanphill, Ira	Na Zon		G Za Unis
Ira Stanphill Favorites No 2 (No 5496)	Stanphill, Ira	Na Zon		G Za Unis
Ira Stanphill Favorites No 3 (No 5497)	Stanphill, Ira	Na Zon		G Za Unis
Jesus Style Songs, Vol. 1	Accompaniment Ed.	76 Aug		G Za
Jesus Style Songs, Vol. 2	Accompaniment Ed.	76 Aug		G Za
John Mckay Choir Book (No 5034)	Na	Na Zon	B	G Za
John Mckay Sings Al Wilson (No 5016)	Wilson, Al	Na Zon		G Za Solo
John Mckay Sings Dorothy Harrison	Harrison, Dorothy	Na Zon		G Za Solo
John Mckay Sings Joyce Mott (No 5018)	Mott, Joyce	Na Zon		G Za Solo
John Mckay Solos (No 5020)	Na	Na Zon		G Za Solo
John Peterson's Folio Of Favorites	Collected	Na Zon		G Za Solo
John W Peterson's Song Favorites (5866)	Collected	Na Zon		G Za Solo
Let's Sing Duets No 1 (No 5080)	Na	Na Zon		G Za
Let's Sing Duets No 2 (No 5081)	Na	Na Zon		G Za
Let's Sing Duets No 3 (No 5082)	Na	Na Zon		G Za
Let's Sing Duets No 4 (No 5083)	Na	Na Zon		G Za
Let's Sing Duets No 5 (No 5084)	Na	Na Zon		G Za
Life Is A Symphony And Other Songs	Bisler, Beatrice Bush	Na Zon		G Za
Lift Your Voices (Men) (No 5470)	Na	Na Zon		G Za
Living Hymns For Crusades And Conf.	Na	Na Zon		G Za
Living Praise	Peterson, John W.	Na Zon		G Za
Love Song (Dunamis Music)	Girard/Johnston Et Al	72 Wrd	B R	G Za Var+
Low Voice No 1 (No 5221)	Collected	Na Zon		G Za Solo
Low Voice No 10 (No 5231)	Collected	Na Zon		G Za Solo
Low Voice No 11 (No 5232)	Collected	Na Zon		G Za Solo
Low Voice No 12 (No 5233)	Collected	Na Zon		G Za Solo
Low Voice No 13 (No 5234)	Collected	Na Zon		G Za Solo
Low Voice No 14 (No 5235)	Collected	Na Zon		G Za Solo
Low Voice No 15 (No 5236)	Collected	Na Zon		G Za Solo
Low Voice No 2 (No 5222)	Collected	Na Zon		G Za Solo
Low Voice No 3 (No 5223)	Collected	Na Zon		G Za Solo
Low Voice No 4 (No 5224)	Collected	Na Zon		G Za Solo
Low Voice No 5 (No 5225)	Collected	Na Zon		G Za Solo
Low Voice No 6 (No 5226)	Collected	Na Zon		G Za Solo
Low Voice No 7 (No 5227)	Collected	Na Zon		G Za Solo
Low Voice No 8 (No 5228)	Collected	Na Zon		G Za Solo
Low Voice No 9 (No 5229)	Collected	Na Zon		G Za Solo
Melodias De Bendicion (No 5369)	Collected	Na Zon		G Za Span
Miracle Melodies No 1	Peterson, John W.	Na Zon		G Za
Miracle Melodies No 2 (No 5191)	Peterson, John W.	Na Zon		G Za
Miracle Melodies No 3 (No 5192)	Peterson, John W.	Na Zon		G Za
Miracle Melodies No 4 (No 5193)	Peterson, John W.	Na Zon		G Za
Miracle Melodies No 5 (No 5194)	Peterson, John W.	Na Zon		G Za
Miracle Melodies No 6 (No 5198)	Peterson, John W.	Na Zon		G Za
Miracle Melodies No 7 (No 5199)	Peterson, John W.	Na Zon		G Za
Miracle Melodies No 8 (No 5201)	Peterson, John W.	Na Zon		G Za
Miracle Melodies No 9 (No 5203)	Peterson, John W.	75 Zon		G Za

CATEGORIZED INDEX

New Singspiration Sing-A-Long	Collected	Na Zon	G Za
New Sounds In Song (No 5665)	Boalt, Steve	Na Zon	B G Za
No Lonely Day (No 4504)	Wyrtzen, Don	Na Zon	B G Za
Now Sounds (Youth)	Collected	Na Zon	G Za
One Hundred Favorite Songs	Collected	76 Wrd	B R G Za Satb+
One Hundred Songs You Love	Carmichael, Ralph (Ed)	75 Wrd	B R G Za Unis+
Paul Mickelson's Arrangements For Men	Mickelson, Paul	Na Zon	B G Za
Praise And Celebration (No 4061)	Na	Na Zon	G Za
Praise Song (Collection)	Powell, Rick (Arr)	76 Wrd	B R G Za Satb+
Preludios Celestiales (No 5365)	Collected	Na Zon	G Za Span
Quartet Favorites No 1 (No 5430)	Peterson, John W.	Na Zon	B G Za
Quartet Favorites No 2 (No 5431)	Peterson, John W.	Na Zon	B G Za
Rapture (No 4700)	Collected	72 Zon	G Za Solo
Really Live (No 4351)	Wyrtzen, Don	Na Zon	B G Za
Sing 'n Celebrate! (Collection)	Brown Et Al.	71 Wrd	B R G Za Var+
Sing A New Song (No 5012)	Collected	Na Zon	G Za Solo
Sing Men! No 1 (No 5061)	Collected	Na Zon	B G Za
Sing Men! No 2 (No 5062)	Collected	Na Zon	B G Za
Sing Men! No 3 (No 5063)	Collected	Na Zon	B G Za
Sing Men! No 4 (No 5064)	Collected	Na Zon	B G Za
Sing Men! No 5 (No 5065)	Collected	Na Zon	B G Za
Sing Men! No 6 (No 5066)	Collected	Na Zon	B G Za
Sing! Make A Joyful Sound No 1 (5491)	Souther, Billy	Na Zon	B G Za
Sing! Make A Joyful Sound No 2 (5490)	Souther, Billy	Na Zon	B G Za
Sing! Make A Joyful Sound No 3 (5492)	Souther, Billy	Na Zon	B G Za
Sing! Make A Joyful Sound No 4 (5510)	Souther, Billy	Na Zon	B G Za
Singing Men (Male Quartets And Choirs)	Peterson, John W.	Na Zon	B G Za
Singing Youth	Peterson, John W.	Na Zon	G Za Youth
Singspiration Annual No 1 (No 5840)	Collected	Na Zon	G Za
Singspiration Annual No 2 (No 5841)	Collected	Na Zon	G Za
Singspiration Annual No 3 (No 5842)	Collected	Na Zon	G Za
Singspiration Annual No 4 (No 5848)	Collected	Na Zon	G Za
Singspiration Annual No 5 (No 5845)	Collected	Na Zon	G Za
Singspiration Annual No 6 (No 5839)	Collected	Na Zon	G Za
Singspiration Annual No 7 (No 5902)	Collected	Na Zon	G Za
Singspiration Annual No 8 (No 5914)	Collected	75 Zon	G Za
Singspiration No 1 (No 5001)	Collected	Na Zon	G Za
Singspiration No 10 (No 5010)	Collected	Na Zon	G Za
Singspiration No 11 (No 5011)	Collected	Na Zon	G Za
Singspiration No 12 (No 5012)	Collected	Na Zon	G Za
Singspiration No 2 (No 5002)	Collected	Na Zon	G Za
Singspiration No 3 (No 5003)	Collected	Na Zon	G Za
Singspiration No 4 (No 5004)	Collected	Na Zon	G Za
Singspiration No 5 (No 5005)	Collected	Na Zon	G Za
Singspiration No 6 (No 5006)	Collected	Na Zon	G Za
Singspiration No 7 (No 5007)	Collected	Na Zon	G Za
Singspiration No 8 (No 5008)	Collected	Na Zon	G Za
Singspiration No 9 (No 5009)	Collected	Na Zon	G Za
Sixteen Singing Men (No 5458)	Na	Na Zon	B G Za
Song Favorites For Low Voices	Peterson, John W.	Na Zon	G Za Solo
Songs And Hymns Of Praise And Worship	Na	Na Zon	G Za
Songs Everybody Loves No 1 (No 5418)	Collected	Na Zon	G Za
Songs Everybody Loves No 2 (No 5419)	Collected	Na Zon	G Za
Songs Everybody Loves No 3 (No 5420)	Collected	Na Zon	G Za
Songs Everybody Loves No 4 (No 5421)	Collected	Na Zon	G Za
Songs Everybody Loves No 5 (No 5426)	Collected	Na Zon	G Za
Songs Everybody Loves No 6 (No 5471)	Collected	Na Zon	G Za
Songs Everybody Loves No 7 (No 5474)	Collected	Na Zon	G Za
Songs For Men No 1 (No 5436)	Anthony, Dick	Na Zon	B G Za
Songs For Men No 2 (No 5437)	Anthony, Dick	Na Zon	B G Za
Songs For Men No 3 (No 5438)	Anthony, Dick	Na Zon	B G Za
Songs For Mixed Quartets No 2 (No 5749)	Collected	Na Zon	B G Za Satb
Songs For Our Revival And Evangelist.	Decou, Harold	Na Zon	G Za
Songs That Touch The Heart No 1	Collected	Na Zon	G Za
Songs That Touch The Heart No 2	Collected	Na Zon	G Za
Songs That Touch The Heart No 3	Collected	Na Zon	G Za
Songs That Touch The Heart No 4	Collected	Na Zon	G Za
Songs That Touch The Heart No 5	Collected	Na Zon	G Za
Songster Favorites (No 5439)	Johnson, Norman	Na Zon	B G Za
Stand Up And Sing (No 4062)	Musto, Steve	Na Zon	B G Za
Sunday Choir (No Zd-5472)	Huff, Ronn	Na Zon	B G Za
Take Me Back (Collection Youth)	Crouch, Andre	75 Wrd	B R G Za Var+
The American Country Hymn Book	Brown, A. (Ed)	75 Wrd	B R G Za Satb+
The Male Four (No Zd-5475)	Hughes, Robert J.	Na Zon	B G Za
The Melody Four Quartets For Men No 1	Na	Na Zon	B G Za
The Melody Four Quartets For Men No 2	Na	Na Zon	B G Za
The Melody Four Quartets For Men No 3	Na	Na Zon	B G Za
The Old Fashioned Revival Hour Quartet	Collected	Na Zon	B G Za
The Old Ralph Carmichael Quartet	Carmichael, Ralph	76 Wrd	B R G Za Ttbb+
The Sinner And The Song (Musical)	Stanphill, Ira	Na Zon	B R G Za
The Songs Of Mickey Holiday (No 4340)	Na	Na Zon	G Za Solo
Things We Deeply Feel (Youth Coll)	Archers	75 Wrd	B R G Za Var+
This Moment (Youth Collection)	Danniebelle	76 Wrd	B R G Za Var+
Top Songs For Duets 5774	Na	Na Zon	G Za
Top Songs For High Voice (No 5026)	Peterson, John W.	Na Zon	G Za Solo
Top Songs For Low Voice No 1 (No 5936)	Collected	Na Zon	G Za Solo
Top Songs For Low Voice No 2 (No 5941)	Collected	Na Zon	G Za Solo
Top Songs For Men (No 5831)	Peterson, John W.	Na Zon	B G Za
Top Songs For Soloists No 1 (No 5847)	Peterson, John W.	Na Zon	G Za Solo
Top Songs For Soloists No 2 (No 5832)	Peterson, John W.	Na Zon	G Za Solo
Top Songs For Trios (No 5777)	Peterson, John W.	Na Zon	G Za
Treble Trios No 1 (No 5041)	Na	Na Zon	G Za
Treble Trios No 2 (No 5042)	Na	Na Zon	G Za
Treble Trios No 3 (No 5043)	Na	Na Zon	G Za
Treble Trios No 4 (No 5044)	Na	Na Zon	G Za
Treble Trios No 5 (No 5045)	Na	Na Zon	G Za
Treble Trios No 6 (No 5046)	Na	Na Zon	G Za
Treble Trios No 7 (No 5091)	Na	Na Zon	G Za
Trios (No 5828)	Collected	Na Zon	G Za
Voces De Jubilo (No 5362)	Collected	Na Zon	G Za Span

Youth Favorites	Peterson, John W.	Na Zon	B G Za
A Collection Of Funeral Music	Lovelace, Austin C.	Na Abi	M L Za Organ
A Contemporary Psalm	Fetler, Paul	69 Aug	M L Za Satb+
A Festival Eucharist (Icet)(M)	Proulx, Richard	75 Gia	B L L Za Satb+
A Service Of Nine Lessons & Carols	Johnson, D.	69 Aug	M L Za Satb+
Alternate Responses And Te Deum	Sateren, Leland B.	72 Aug	B L Za
Anthems For Sab (5867)	Peterson, John W.	Na Zon	B L Za
Breakthrough (Musical) (No 4510)	Wyrtzen, Don	Na Zon	B R L Za
Cantata	Carter, John	64 Som	M L Za
Cathedral Chorus Marching Guitar Choir	Gutfreund, Ed (Rev.)	75 Nal	B R L L Za Humrs
Celebration Songs For Choir (No 5858)	Wyrtzen, Don	Na Zon	B L Za
Choral Mass (1970) Cong Ad Lib	Lee, John	70 Gia	B L L Za Satb+
Choral Prayers And Responses	Na	Na Lor	M L Za
Choral Responses For Christmas	Na	Na Lor	M L Za
Choral Responses For Easter	Na	Na Lor	M L Za
Choral Service For Watch Night, A	Wilson	Na Lor	M L Za
Choreographic Cantata (W/Perc,Org)	Lockwood, Normand	70 Aug	M L Za Satb
Congregation Mass (1970)	Lee, John	70 Gia	B L L Za U+Org
Contemporary Worship I-Hymns	Collected	Na Aug	M B L Za Joint
Contemporary Worship Ii-Holy Communi	Collected	Na Aug	B L Za Joint
Contemporary Worship Iii-Marriage	Collected	Na Aug	B L Za Joint
Contemporary Worship 4-Baptism,	Collected	Na Aug	B L Za Joint
Contemporary Worship 5: The Word	Collected	Na Aug	B L Za Joint
Easter Carol Mass (1964 Text)	Andrews, Carroll T.	66 Gia	B L L Za Var+
Eighteen Responses	Na	Na Lor	M L Za
Eleven Canzonets	Garlick, Antony	Na See	M L Za
Eleven Scriptural Songs	Collected	Na Cob	B L Za Solo
English High Mass.	Laverdiere, Armand	66 Vrn	B L L Za
Festival Anthems For Sab	Powell, Robert J.	Na Abi	M L Za Sab
Festival Mass (1965) W/Cantor	Peloquin, C Alexander	66 Gia	B L L Za U2pt+
Festival Mass (1972) W/Org	Lee, John	72 Gia	B L L Za Satb+
Five Hymns In Popular Style (Me)	Gardner, John	Na Oxf	M L Za Satb
Five Songs	Beeson, Jack	54 Pic	M L Za
Folio Of Choir Favorites	Peterson, John W.	Na Zon	B L Za
Folk Mass (Icet)	Kraehenbuehl, David	68 Jsp	B L Za +Guit
Four American Folk Hymns	Wade, Walter	Na Abi	M L Za U-Sa
Four Modern Anthems	Wells, Dana	Na Abi	M L Za Satb
Four Psalm Settings	Mawby, C	Na Gia	L Za
Fourteen Choral Responses	Mcafee, Don	75 Sac	M L Za Satb
Fresh Sounds	Harper, Jeanne&Pulkingh	Na Erd	B L Za More Of
God's Quiet Love (Collection)	Mann, Lynn/Mann, J.	76 Wrd	B R L Za Satb+
Gather 'round (88 Songs)	Page, Paul F. (Ed.)	76 Rpb	M B R L L Za
Great Hymns Of The Faith	Peterson, John W.	Na Zon	L Za
Good News (Original Anthems)	Leaf, Robert	74 Aug	M L Za
Hebrew Cantata	Shapero, Harold	66 Som	M L Za
Hebrew Melodies	Diamond, David	69 Som	M L Za
Hymn Anthems	Strickler, David	Na Abi	M L Za Satb
Hymn Descants Vol I	Bonham, Eugene	Na Abi	M L Za
Hymn Descants Vol Ii	Bonham, Eugene	Na Abi	M L Za
Hymns Of Thanks	Goemanne, Noel	70 Gia	M L Za Satb+
I Know That My Redeemer Lives	Collected	71 Gia	B L L Za U+Org
Introits (For Various Seasons)	Wetzler, Robert	65 Aug	B L Za
Introits And Graduals (Var Seasons)	Ensrud	60 Aug	B L Za
Jubilee Mass	Lee, John	74 Gia	B L L Za Sa+
Liturgical Mass	Goemanne, Noel	70 Wlp	B L Za
Love Alive (Collection)	Hawkins, Walter	76 Wrd	B R L Za Var+
Lyric Liturgy	Peloquin, C Alexander	Na Gia	L Za
Mass (To St. Anthony)	Harrison, Lou	74 Pic	M L Za
Mass For A Feast Day (Icet) Cong Opt	Kern, Jan	74 Gia	B L L Za Mixed
Mass For All Seasons	Lynch, Michael B.	75 Rav	M R L L Za
Mass For American Saint	Kreutz, Robert	69 Wlp	B L Za
Mass For Congregations (Icet)	Roff, Joseph	70 Gia	B L L Za
Mass For Parishes	Simutis, Leonard	70 Acp	B L L Za
Mass For Peace (E)	Maria Of The Cross	Na Oxf	M L Za 2pt
Mass For Two Voices (Icet)	Roff, Joseph	70 Gia	B L L Za 2pt
Mass In C Minor	Track, Gerhard	70 Gia	B L L Za Satb+
Mass In D (Easy)	Gentemann, Sr. Elaine	74 Gia	M L L Za Ssa
Mass In Honor Of All Saints	Schiavone, John	75 Gia	B L L Za Sab+
Mass In Honor Of Chicago	Rudski, Stanley	70 Acp	B L L Za
Mass In Honor Of Pope Paul Vi	Connor, Edward	70 Jsp	B L Za +Org
Mass In Honor Of St Joseph	Roff, Joseph	70 Gia	B L L Za Satbu+
Mass In Praise Of Holy Spirit	Schiavone, John	72 Gia	B L L Za Satb+
Mass In Praise Of Jesus Christ	Schiavone, John	74 Gia	B L L Za Sab+
Mass Of Celebration	Gelineau, Joseph	70 Acp	B L L Za
Mass Of Celebration (4-Part Arr)	Cirou, Joseph/Deeter T	73 Acp	B L L Za
Mass Of Freedom (Icet)	Jergenson, Dale	74 Gia	B L L Za Satb+
Mass Of Praise (Icet)	Pross, Daniel J.	71 Gia	B L L Za Var+
Mass Of Thanksgiving (Icet) Org, Cong	Kreutz, Robert	73 Gia	B L L Za Satb+
Mass Of The Bells Icet (W/Cantor/Cong)	Peloquin, C Alexander	72 Gia	B L L Za Satb+
Mass Volume Ii	Picca, Angelo Della	Na Wlp	B L Za
Mass, Roman Catholic English Text (E)	Merbecke, John	Na Oxf	M L Za Unis
Meditative Songs (Med Voice)	Burns, William K.	Na Abi	M L Za Solo
Messa A 4 Voci (A Cappella 1651)	Monteverdi, Claudio	74 Gia	B L L Za Satb
Missa Brevis	Palester, Roman	66 Som	M L Za
Missa Brevis	Track, Gerhard	Na Gia	L Za
Missa Brevis (Salzburg Mass) Lat & Icet	Track, Gerhard	73 Gia	B L L Za Full
Nine Easy Canons	Riedel	62 Aug	M L Za
Nineteen Choral Responses	Na	Na Lor	M L Za Satb
Nineteen Liturgical Rounds (2 Vols)	Tortolano, W	Na Gia	L Za
Norman Johnson Presents Choral Concep	Johnson, Norman	Na Zon	B L Za Satb
People's Mass (Icet)	Roff, Joseph	70 Gia	B L L Za U+Org
Peoples Mass (Icet)	Vermulst, Jan	61 Wlp	B L Za
Picture The Dawning	Page, Paul F.	76 Rpb	M B R L L Za
Psalm Praise (Var Settings)	Collected	73 Gia	M B L L Za Var
Psalms	Moore, Patrick	73 Nal	B R L Za
Psalms For The Church Year 1	Schalk, Carl (Ed)	75 Aug	B L Za Var+
Psalms For Today (Org, Guit Adlib)	Mantonti, C./Roff, J.	67 Gia	B L L Za Unis+
Responses 75-86 Psalms (Icet)	Picca, Angelo Della	70 Wlp	B L Za
Seasonal Responsorial Psalms (Chant)	Roff, Joseph	72 Gia	B L L Za Satb+

CATEGORIZED INDEX

Select Vocal Solos For The Church	Kugel, William F.	Na Abi	M L Za Solo
Selected Hymns In Large Type	Collected	64 Aug	M L Za
Seven Anthems For Treble Choirs	Beck, Theodore	75 Con	B L Za Var
Seven Choral Service Settings	Fryxell, Regina	Na Abi	M L Za Satb
Seven General Anthems For Unison–Trebl	Copley, R. Evan	Na Abi	M L Za Unis
Seven Psalms	Childs, David	Na Abi	M L Za Solo
Seven Sacred Solos	Goode, Jack C.	Na Abi	M L Za Solo
Seven Songs From Ancient Liturgies	Hytrek, S. Theophane	71 Cfc	M R L L Za
Sing And Praise Along The Way	Collected	63 Aug	M L Za
Singing Catechism	Collected	71 Aug	B L Za
Six Sacred Anthems For Male Voices	Cassler, G. W.	Na Abi	M L Za Ttbb
Six Songs	Bissell, Keith W.	60 Pic	M L Za
Solos For Christmas No 1	Peterson, John W.	Na Zon	L Za Solo
Solos For Christmas No 2	Peterson, John W.	Na Zon	L Za Solo
Solos For Easter	Peterson, John W.	Na Zon	L Za Solo
Song Favorites For Trios	Peterson, John W.	Na Zon	L Za Ssa
Songs For Special Days	Collected	Na Zon	L Za
Sounds For Now	Ford, Virgil	Na Abi	M L Za Unis
Sounds Of Living Waters	Harper, Jeanne&Pulkingh	Na Erd	B L Za Contemp
Special Trio Arrangements No 1 5422	Decou, Harold	Na Zon	L Za
Special Trio Arrangements No 2 5423	Decou, Harold	Na Zon	L Za
Special Trio Arrangements No 3 5424	Decou, Harold	Na Zon	L Za
The Contemporary Hymn Book	Yantis, David (Ed)	71 Wrd	B R L Za Unis+
The Gelineau Psalms	Gelineau, Joseph	56 Gia	M B R L L Za Var+
The Good Life (Musical)	Peterson, John W.	Na Zon	B R L Za
The Songs Of Mickey Holiday (4340)	Holiday, Mickey	Na Zon	B L Za
The Sound Of Singing (No 5965)	Peterson, John W.	Na Zon	B L Za Var
The Sound Of Singing (No 5994) Cantata	Peterson, John W.	Na Zon	B L Za Var
The Sunday Antiphonary (Icet)	Collected	75 Gia	B L L Za
Three Anthems Based On Canons	Copley, R. Evan	Na Abi	M L Za
Three Anthems Of Commitment	Young, Gordon	75 Sac	M L Za Satb
Three Anthems Of Praise	Copley, R. Evan	Na Abi	M L Za Satb
Three Anthems Of Praise	Wade, Walter	Na Abi	M L Za Sab
Three Introits For Festival Worship	Scott, Sarah	Na Abi	M L Za Satb
Three Motets	Diemente, Edward	Na See	M L Za
Three Psalms	White, Richard	75 Sac	M L Za Satb
Three Sacred Anthems (Ps 8, 19, 92)	Fissinger, Edwin	75 Wlp	M L Za Satb+
Three Sacred Solos For Medium Voice	Wells, Dana F.	Na Abi	M L Za Solo
Three Seasonal Songs	Hunnicutt	76 Aug	L Za Uorgfl
Three Songs For Sacred Occasions	Lorenz, Ellen Jane	Na Abi	M L Za Solo
Three Treble Choir Anthems	Powell, Robert J.	Na Abi	M L Za Sa
Three Wedding Motets	Dooner, A	Na Gia	L Za
Twelve Madrigals	Garlick, Antony	Na See	M L Za
Two Anthems	Diamond, David	69 Som	M L Za
Two Anthems From The Moravians	Nolte, Ewald V.	Na Abi	M L Za Satb
Two Easter Carols	Brown, Allanson G. Y.	Na Abi	M L Za Ssa
Two Hymns I/H St	Andrews, Carroll T.	73 Gia	M L Za Satb+
Two Introits	Atkinson, Gordon	Na Oxf	M L Za Un
Two Introits	Smith, Harold	69 Smc	M L Za Satb
Two Lenten Meditations	Wetzler, Robert	Na Abi	M L Za Satb
Two Proverbs	Leichtling, Alan	Na See	M L Za
Two Psalms (Ps. 146, Ps. 117)	Shapero, Harold	53 Som	M L Za
Two Psalms For High Voice	Triplett, Robert F.	Na Abi	M L Za Solo
Two Sacred Solos	Burns, William K.	Na Abi	M L Za Solo
Two Shabbat Songs	Zur, Menachem	Na See	M L Za
Two Songs (From Saint Paul)	Soler, Joseph	72 Som	M L Za
Two Songs For Medium Voice	Mcafee, Don	Na Abi	M L Za Solo
Worship Responses	Collected	54 Aug	M L Za Satb

A Heritage Of Folk Anthems (No 5833)	Rasley, John M.	Na Zon	B T Za
A Mass For Lent	Wagner, Lavern J.	71 Sms	M R L T Za
A Mighty Fortress (10 Chorales)	Bach, J. S./Ed. Lee	73 Gia	B R L T Za Satb+
All-Time Favorites For The Choir No 1	Vanhorn, Charles	Na Zon	B T Za
All-Time Favorites For The Choir No 2	Vanhorn, Charles	Na Zon	B T Za
All-Time Favorites For The Choir No 3	Vanhorn, Charles	Na Zon	B T Za
Anthems (Ave Maria, O Baptista)	Aston, Hugh	Na Kal	B T Za Satb
Anthems (Gaude Virgo, Te Deum, Ave)	Aston, Hugh	Na Kal	B T Za Satb
Anthems For Men's Voices Book Ii	Collected	Na Oxf	B T Za Ttbb
Anthems For Men's Voices Book 1	Collected	Na Oxf	B T Za Atb
Anthems For Special Occasions	Wehr, David A.	Na Abi	M T Za Satb
Anthems For Treble Voices (14)	Collected	Na Oxf	B T Za Sa
Anthems Of Faith (Collection, Md)	Lynn, George	75 Abi	M T Za Satb
Anthology Of Offertories And Motets	Meyer, V/Selner, J	Na Gia	T Za
Anthology Of Polyphonic Masters Book 1	Na	Na Gia	T Za 2,3pt
Arias From Church Cantatas (Sop W/Inst)	Bach, J. S.	Na Kal	B T Za
Beautiful Savior (Jr Choir W/Opt Rec)	Vick, Beryl Jr. (Arr)	73 Pro	M T Za 2pt+
Bread Of The World (10 Chorales)	Bach, J. S./Ed Lee	73 Gia	B R L T Za Satb+
Cantata #1 Wie Schoen (Eng/Germ)	Bach, J. S.	Na Kal	B T Za Satb
Cantata #115 Mache Dich (E & Germ)	Bach, J. S.	Na Kal	B T Za Satb
Cantata #150 Nach Dir (Eng & Germ)	Bach, J. S.	Na Kal	B T Za Satb
Cantata #169 Gott Soll (Eng & Germ)	Bach, J. S.	Na Kal	B T Za Satb
Cantata #198 Trauermusik (Eng & Germ)	Bach, J. S.	Na Kal	B T Za Satb
Cantata #21 My Spirit (Eng/Germ)	Bach, J. S.	Na Kal	B T Za Satb
Cantata #25 Es Ist Nichts (Eng/Germ)	Bach, J. S.	Na Kal	B T Za Satb
Cantata #27 Wer Weiss (Eng/Germ)	Bach, J. S.	Na Kal	B T Za Satb
Cantata #31 The Heaven's Laugh (E&Germ	Bach, J. S.	Na Kal	B T Za Satb
Cantata #33 Allein Zu Dir (Eng/Germ)	Bach, J. S.	Na Kal	B T Za Satb
Cantata #34 O Ewiges Feuer (Eng/Germ)	Bach, J. S.	Na Kal	B T Za Satb
Cantata #38 Aus Tiefer Not (Eng/Germ)	Bach, J. S.	Na Kal	B T Za Satb
Cantata #43 Gott Faehret (Eng/Germ)	Bach, J. S.	Na Kal	B T Za Satb
Cantata #45 Es Ist Gesagt (Eng/Germ)	Bach, J. S.	Na Kal	B T Za Satb
Cantata #50 Nun Ist (Eng/Germ)	Bach, J. S.	Na Kal	B T Za Satb
Cantata #54 Widerstehe (Eng/Germ)	Bach, J. S.	Na Kal	B T Za Satb
Cantata #55 Ich Armer Mensch (E & Ger)	Bach, J. S.	Na Kal	B T Za Satb
Cantata #56 (E & Germ)	Bach, J. S.	Na Kal	B T Za Satb
Cantata #6 Bide With Us (Eng/Germ)	Bach, J. S.	Na Kal	B T Za Satb
Cantata #64 Sehet (E & Germ)	Bach, J. S.	Na Kal	B T Za Satb
Cantata #65 Sie Merden (E & Germ)	Bach, J. S.	Na Kal	B T Za Satb
Cantata #68 Also Hat (E & Germ)	Bach, J. S.	Na Kal	B T Za Satb
Cantata #70 Wachet, Betet (E & Germ)	Bach, J. S.	Na Kal	B T Za Satb
Cantata #71 Gott Ist (E & Germ)	Bach, J. S.	Na Kal	B T Za Satb
Cantata #8 Liebster Gott (Eng/Germ)	Bach, J. S.	Na Kal	B T Za Satb
Cantata #82 Ich Hab Genug (Germ)	Bach, J. S.	Na Kal	B T Za Satb
Cantiones Quatuor Vocum (2 Volumes)	Byrd, William	Na Kal	B T Za Satb
Cantiones Quinque Vocum	Byrd, William	Na Kal	B T Za 5pts
Cantiones Sex Vocum (Peter & Paul)	Byrd, William	Na Kal	B T Za 6pts
Cantiones Trium Vocum	Byrd, William	Na Kal	B T Za 3pts
Children's Hymnary, The	Hartzler & Gaeddert	68 Flp	B T Za
Choir Favorites No 1 (No 5101)	Na	Na Zon	B T Za
Choir Favorites No 2 (No 5102)	Na	Na Zon	B T Za
Choir Favorites No 3 (No 5103)	Na	Na Zon	B T Za
Choir Favorites No 4 (No 5104)	Na	Na Zon	B T Za
Choir Favorites No 5 (No 5105)	Na	Na Zon	B T Za
Choir Favorites No 6 (No 5106)	Na	Na Zon	B T Za
Chorales	Bach, J. S.	Na Lps	M B T Za
Chorales	Bach, J. S.	Na Gsc	B T Za 2vol
Choruses From The Messiah (No 5955)	Johnson, Norman	Na Zon	B T Za Satb
Church Cantatas & Oratorios	Bach, J. S.	Na Lps	M B T Za
Complete Works Of Palestrina (74 Vol)	Palestrina, Giovanni P	Na Kal	B T Za
Concert From Four Folk-Hymns	Anonymous	75 Bbl	B T Za 2 Pt
Concordia Hymnal (34 Hymns)	Collected	32 Aug	B T Za
Congregational Mass In Dorian Mode	Cabena, Barrie	Na Oxf	M T Za Usatb
Coronation Mass K 317	Mozart, Wolfgang A	Na Kal	B T Za Satb
Coronation Mass (C) (Latin)	Mozart, Wolfgang A	Cfp	R T Za Satb+
Deck Thyself, My Soul (10 Chorales)	Bach, J.S./Ed Lee	73 Gia	B R L T Za Satb+
Deep North Spirituals (9)	Belcher	Cfp	R T Za Satb+
Descants For Choirs (No 5544)	Johnson, Norman	Na Zon	B T Za
Descants On Six Hymn Tunes	Cartford	69 Aug	M T Za
Eight Anthems	Gibbons, Orlando	Na Kal	B T Za Satb
Eight Hymns	Finck, Heinrich (D1527)	Na Kal	B T Za Satb
Eight Responses	Dressler, L R	Na Gsc	B T Za Satb
Eighty Six Prefaces From Missal	Kern, Jan (Music)	74 Gia	B L T Za Unis
Evening Service	Wills, Arthur	Na Oxf	M T Za
Evening Service For Verses	Heath, John	Na Oxf	M T Za
Evening Service In 'a Re' Magnificat	Rogers, Benjamin	Na Oxf	M T Za Satb
Evening Service In C: Magnificat Etc.	Stewart, C. Hylton	Na Oxf	M T Za Unis
Evening Service In E Flat	Bairstow, Edward C.	Na Oxf	M T Za Unis
Evening Service In Eb: Magnificat Etc.	Hunt, Thomas	Na Oxf	M T Za Satb
Evening Service; Magnificat Etc	Tye, Christopher	Na Oxf	M T Za Satb
Extended Bach Chorales (Eng, Welsh)	Bach, J.S. (Ed)	Na Oxf	M T Za Satb
Festal Responses (E)	Tallis, Thomas	Na Oxf	M T Za Satbb
Fifty Anthems For Mixed Voices	Jackson, Francis (Ed)	Na Oxf	B T Za Satb
Fifty Two Sacred Motets (Latin)	Collected Masters	Na Kal	B T Za Satb
Five Anthems	Taverner, John	Na Kal	B T Za Satb
Five Church Cantatas	Bach, J. S.	75 Lps	B R T Za Satb
Five Early American Hymn Tunes (E)	Lindsley, Charles E.	Na Oxf	M T Za Ttbb
Five Motets	Dressler, Gallus	Na Kal	B T Za Satb
Five Motets	Franck, Melchior	Na Kal	B T Za Satb
Five Sacred Choruses	Purcell, Henry	Na Kal	B T Za Satb
Five Sequences For The Virgin Mary	Anonymous	Na Oxf	M T Za Satb
Four Advent Chorales	Bach, J. S.	74 Gia	M T Za Sat
Four Anthems	Gibbons, Orlando	Na Kal	B T Za Satb
Four Canons	Riedel	62 Aug	M T Za Var
Four Choral Meditations–Lent	Andrews, Carroll T.	73 Gia	B T Za 2pt
Four Christmas Chorales	Bach, J. S.	70 Gia	M T Za Satb
Four Easter Chorales	Bach, J. S.	Na Gia	T Za
Four Folk-Hymns	Anon Robison	75 Bbl	B T Za 2 Pt
Four Motets	Des Pres, Josquin	Na Kal	B T Za Satb
Four Part Chorales (Germ Text)	Bach, J. S.	Na Kal	B T Za Satb
Four Psalms, Op. 74 (Eng)	Grieg, E.	Na Cfp	R T Za Satb
Four Settings Of Preces & Responses	Shaw, Watkins (Ed)	Na Oxf	M T Za Saatb
Four-Part Chorales (185)	Bach, J. S.	75 Lps	B T Za Satb
Fourteen Plainsong Hymns (E & L)	Lee, John (Ed)	75 Gia	B L T Za Unis+
Fourth Evening Service: Magnificat Etc	Batten, Adrian	Na Oxf	M T Za Satb
Fourth Mass, C Major (Latin)	Cherubini, M. L.	Na Kal	B T Za Satb
Gesangbuch Der Mennoniten	Epp, Henry H.	65 Flp	B T Za
Grand Mass K 427	Mozart, Wolfgang A	Na Kal	B T Za Satb
Great God Of Nations (10 Chorales)	Bach, J.S./Ed Lee	73 Gia	B R L T Za Satb+
Great Service (Complete D)	Byrd, William	Na Oxf	M T Za Full
Himnos De Fe Y Alabanza (No 5358)	Na	Na Zon	T Za
Hymn Descants Vol. Iii	Bonham, Eugene	Na Abi	M T Za U
Hymns And Songs For Church Schools	Collected	62 Aug	B T Za
Hymns For Grace And Glory	Collected	76 Abi	B T Za
Hymns For The Amusement Of Children	Oldham, Arthur & Smart	Na Oxf	B T Za Satb
Israel In Egypt (Oratorio)	Handel, G. F.	Na Kal	B R T Za Satb
It's Wedding Time No 1 (No 5493)	Collected	Na Zon	T Za Solo
It's Wedding Time No 2 (No 5494)	Collected	Na Zon	T Za Solo
Jesus Style Songs, Vol. 1	Collected	72 Aug	M T Za
John Rasley Presents A Choral Sampler	Na	Na Zon	B T Za
Jubilate Deo (Gregorian Rep)	Collected	74 Gia	B L T Za Unis
Judas Maccabaeus (Oratorio, Eng)	Handel, G. F.	Na Kal	B R T Za Satb
La Messe De Nostre Dame	De Machaut, Guillame	Na Oxf	B T Za Satb
Legendary Christmas Carols	Na	Na Lor	M T Za Satb
Lift Up Your Voice (32 Songs)	Collected	Na Cob	B T Za Solo
Liturgical Motets	Willan, Healey	Na Oxf	M T Za Satb
Magnificat And Nunc Dimittis	Gibbons, Orlando	Na Oxf	M T Za Satb
Magnificat And Nunc Dimittis (M)	Amner, John	Na Oxf	M T Za Ssatb
Magnificat And Nunc Dimittis (M)	Aston, Peter	Na Oxf	M T Za Satb
Magnificat And Nunc Dimittis (M)	Murrill, Herbert	Na Oxf	M T Za Satb
Magnificat And Nunc Dimittis (Md)	Byrd, William	Na Oxf	M T Za Full
Magnificat And Nunc Dimittis (Md)	Farrant, Richard	Na Oxf	M T Za Satb
Magnificat And Nunc Dimittis (Md)	Gardner, John	Na Oxf	M T Za Satb
Magnificat And Nunc Dimittis (Md)	Mathias, William	Na Oxf	M T Za Satb
Magnificat And Nunc Dimittis (Md)	Morley, Thomas	Na Oxf	M T Za Saatb
Magnificat And Nunc Dimittis (Md)	Tompkins, Thomas	Na Oxf	M T Za Satb
Magnificat And Nunc Dimittis (Md)	Weelkes, Thomas	Na Oxf	M T Za Saatb
Magnificat And Nunc Dimittis (Me)	Cook, E. T.	Na Oxf	M T Za Satb
Magnificat And Nunc Dimittis (Me)	Orr, Robin	Na Oxf	M T Za Satb
Magnificat And Nunc Dimittis (Me)	Wise, Michael	Na Oxf	M T Za Satbj
Magnificat And Nunc Dimittis Iii (Md)	Byrd, William	Na Oxf	M T Za Saatb

Magnificat And Nunc Dimittis In C	Greene, Maurice	Na Oxf	M		T Za	Full
Magnificat And Nunc Dimittis In Eb	Willan, Healey	Na Oxf	M		T Za	Satb
Mass	Charpentier, Marc-Anto	Na Oxf	B		T Za	Full
Mass (Guitar Or Clavier)	Burrell, Howard	Na Oxf	B		T Za	Sa
Mass #1 In F	Schubert, Franz J.	Na Kal	B		T Za	Satb
Mass And Te Deum	Aston, Hugh	Na Kal	B		T Za	Satb
Mass Corona Spinea	Taverner, John	Na Kal	B		T Za	Satb
Mass For Four Mixed Voices	Monteverdi, Claudio	Na Gia			T Za	
Mass For Four Voices	Tallis, Thomas	Na Kal	B		T Za	Satb
Mass For Peace	Miller	Na Kal	B		T Za	Satb
Mass For 4 Voices, Solo & Chorus	Saint-Saens, Camille	Na Kal	B		T Za	Satb
Mass Gloria Tibi Trinitas	Taverner, John	Na Kal	B		T Za	Satb
Mass Hymn Suites	Collected	68 Gia	B	L	T Za	U+Org
Mass In Ab And Eb	Schubert, Franz J.	Na Kal	B		T Za	Satb
Mass In B Minor	Bach, J. S.	Na Kal	B		T Za	Satb
Mass In B Minor (Latin)	Bach, J. S.	Cfp	R		T Za	Satb+
Mass In B-Flat	Haydn, Franz J	52 Bbl	B		T Za	Satb+
Mass In C (D)	Boatwright, Howard	Na Oxf	M		T Za	Full
Mass In C (Opus 86)	Beethoven, L	Na Kal	B R		T Za	Satb
Mass In C (Student's Mass)	Lotti, A. (D1740)	Na Kal	B		T Za	Satb
Mass In C K 258	Mozart, Wolfgang A	Na Kal	B		T Za	Satb
Mass In C Major	Beethoven, L	52 Bbl	B		T Za	
Mass In C Major	Schubert, Franz J.	Na Kal	B		T Za	Satb
Mass In C, Op 169	Rheinberger, J. G.	Na Kal	B		T Za	Satb
Mass In D	Bruckner, Anton	Na Kal	B		T Za	Full
Mass In D, Opus 86	Dvorak, A.	Na Kal	B		T Za	Satb
Mass In E Minor	Bruckner, Anton	Na Kal	B		T Za	Full
Mass In E Minor	Bruckner, Anton	52 Bbl	B		T Za	Full+
Mass In English (A Cap)	Tcherepnin, A.	75 Cfp	M		T Za	3pt
Mass In F	Bruckner, Anton	Na Kal	B		T Za	Full
Mass In G (In Bb)	Schubert, Franz J.	Na Kal	B		T Za	Satb
Mass In G Major No. 2	Schubert, Franz J.	52 Bbl	B		T Za	Satb+
Mass In Honor Of O.L. Visitation	Margaret, Sr. Mary	Na Wlp	B		T Za	
Mass Mater Christi	Taverner, John	Na Kal	B		T Za	Satb
Mass No. 10 In B-Flat Theresa Mass	Haydn, Franz J	52 Bbl	B		T Za	
Mass No. 2 In G Major	Schubert, Franz J.	52 Bbl	B		T Za	
Mass No. 1 (Bwv 233) (Latin)	Bach, J. S.	Cfp	R		T Za	Satb+
Mass No. 2 (Bwv 234) (Latin)	Bach, J. S.	Cfp	R		T Za	Satb+
Mass No. 2 (E) (Latin)	Bruckner, Anton	Cfp	R		T Za	Satb+
Mass No. 3 (Bwv 235) (Latin)	Bach, J. S.	Cfp	R		T Za	Satb+
Mass No. 3 (F) (Latin)	Bruckner, Anton	Cfp	R		T Za	Satb+
Mass No. 4 (Bwv 236) (Latin)	Bach, J. S.	Cfp	R		T Za	Satb+
Mass O Michaeli	Taverner, John	Na Kal	B		T Za	Satb
Mass Of Saint Andrew	Williamson, Malcolm	Na Gsc	B		T Za	Satb+
Mass Of The Redeemer (Cath, Ang)	Proulx, Richard	73 Gia	B	L	T Za	Sab+
Mass Of The Sacred Heart	Gounod, Charles	Na Kal	B		T Za	Satb
Mass Opus 147	Schumann, Robert	Na Kal	B		T Za	Satb
Mass Per Arma Justitiae	Marbeck, John	Na Kal	B		T Za	Satb
Mass Plain Song	Taverner, John	Na Kal	B		T Za	Satb
Mass Salve Intemerata	Tallis, Thomas (D1585)	Na Kal	B		T Za	Satb
Mass Sine Nomine	Taverner, John	Na Kal	B		T Za	Satb
Mass Small Devotion	Taverner, John	Na Kal	B		T Za	Satb
Mass St. Joanni De Deo	Haydn, Joseph	Na Kal	B		T Za	Satb
Mass The Western Wynde	Taverner, John (D1545)	Na Kal	B		T Za	Satb
Mass 12 (Eng)	Mozart, Wolfgang A	Na Kal	B		T Za	Satb
Mass 2 In G Major For Men's Voices	Gounod, Charles	Na Kal	B		T Za	Satb
Mass 6 In G Maj (4 Voices, Solo, Chor)	Gounod, Charles	Na Kal	B		T Za	Satb
Mass (C) (Latin)	Mozart, Wolfgang A	Cfp	R		T Za	Satb+
Mass, Op. 86 (C) (Latin)	Beethoven, L	Cfp	R		T Za	Satb+
Mass, Opus 44	Leighton, Kenneth	Na Oxf	B		T Za	Satb
Mass, Vesperae Sollenes K 339	Mozart, Wolfgang A	Na Kal	B		T Za	Satb
Mass, Videte Manus Meas	Aston, Hugh	Na Kal	B		T Za	Satb
Mennonite Hymnal, The	Collected	69 Flp	B		T Za	
Messe Breve In C Major 7	Gounod, Charles	Na Kal	B		T Za	Satb
Messe Solenelle	Gounod, Charles	Na Kal	B		T Za	Satb
Messiah (Eng-Ger)	Handel, G. F.	Cfp	R		T Za	Satb+
Messiah, The (Oratorio)	Handel, G. F.	Na Kal	B R		T Za	Satb
Missa "Aeterna Christi Munera" (Md)	Palestrina, Giovanni P	Na Oxf	M		T Za	Satb
Missa Brevis	Buxtehude, D.	Na Kal	B		T Za	Satb
Missa Brevis	Gabrieli, Andrea	Na Kal	B	L	T Za	Satb
Missa Brevis	Palestrina, Giovanni P	Na Kal	B		T Za	Satb
Missa Brevis	Pellegrini, P.	Na Kal	B		T Za	Satb
Missa Brevis (D)	Kelly, Bryan	Na Oxf	M		T Za	Satb
Missa Brevis (K192, 194, 220, 259, 275)	Mozart, Wolfgang A	Na Kal	B		T Za	Satb
Missa Brevis (Latin)	Brown, Christopher	Na Oxf	B		T Za	Satb
Missa Brevis (Md)	Preston, Simon	Na Oxf	M		T Za	Satb
Missa Brevis (Md)	Walton, William	Na Oxf	M		T Za	Full
Missa Brevis In A Major	Bach, J. S.	Na Kal	B		T Za	Satb
Missa Brevis In F Maj	Bach, J. S.	Na Kal	B		T Za	Satb
Missa Brevis In G M	Bach, J. S.	Na Kal	B		T Za	Satb
Missa Brevis In G Major	Bach, J. S.	Na Kal	B		T Za	Satb
Missa Carminum	Isaac, H. (D1517)	Na Kal	B		T Za	Satb
Missa Choralis	Liszt, Franz	Na Kal	B		T Za	Satb
Missa Da Pacem	Des Pres, Josquin	Na Kal	B		T Za	Satb
Missa De Beata Virgine	Des Pres, Josquin	Na Kal	B		T Za	Satb
Missa De Dominica K 321	Mozart, Wolfgang A	Na Kal	B		T Za	Satb
Missa Ecce Nunc Benedicite	Lasso, Orlando Di	Na Kal	B		T Za	Satb
Missa Festiva	Pert, Morris	Na Oxf	B		T Za	Ssaa
Missa Festivo	Gretchaninoff, A.	Na Kal	B		T Za	Satb
Missa Ich Stund	Handl, Jacob	Na Kal	B		T Za	Satb
Missa In F	Carpani, G. (D1825)	Na Kal	B		T Za	
Missa In G	Bernabei, G.E. (D1687)	Na Kal	B		T Za	Satb
Missa In G	Casciolini	Na Kal	B		T Za	Ssa
Missa In Hon. St. Josephi Op 21	Peeters, Flor	Na Kal	B		T Za	Satb
Missa In Summis	Finck, Heinrich	Na Kal	B		T Za	Satb
Missa Mi-Mi	Ockeghem	Na Kal	B		T Za	
Missa Pange Lingua	Des Pres, J. (D1521)	Na Kal	B		T Za	Satb
Missa Papae Marcelli	Palestrina, Giovanni P	Na Kal	B		T Za	Full
Missa Pro Defunctis	Casciolini	Na Kal	B		T Za	
Missa Pro Defunctis	Vittoria, Ludovica De	Na Kal	B		T Za	Satb

Missa Quinti Toni (5th Tone)	Lasso, Orlando Di	Na Kal	B		T Za	Satb
Missa Simile Est Regnum	Vittoria, Ludovica De	Na Kal	B		T Za	Satb
Missa Sine Nomine	Viadana, L. (D1627)	Na Kal	B		T Za	Satb
Missa Solemnis	Beethoven, L	Na Kal	B R		T Za	Satb
Missa Solemnis (Graner Mass)	Liszt, Franz	Na Kal	B		T Za	Satb
Missa Solemnis K 337	Mozart, Wolfgang A	Na Kal	B		T Za	Satb
Missa Solemnis (Latin)	Beethoven, L	Cfp	R		T Za	Satb+
Missa, La Bien Que J'ay	Goudimel, Claude	Na Kal	B		T Za	Satb
Missa, Quand Io Pens	Lasso, Orlando Di	Na Kal	B		T Za	Satb
Morning Service In D Minor	Williams, Vaughan R.	Na Oxf	M		T Za	Satb
Morning Service In Eb (Md)	Hunt, Thomas	Na Oxf	M		T Za	Satb
Motets	Bach, J. S.	Na Lps	M B		T Za	
Motets By Palestrina, Ten 4-Part	Palestrina, Harman (Ed)	Na Oxf	B		T Za	Satb
Mother's Hymns	Jacobus	Na Lor	M		T Za	Satb
New Plymouth Cantata	Meyerowitz, Jan	53 Bbl	B		T Za	Var
Nineteen Anthems In Four Vols	Tallis, Thomas	Na Kal	B		T Za	Satb
Nun Preiset Alle	Collected	68 Flp	M	L	T Za	
Old Netherlands Motets	Collected Masters	Na Kal	B		T Za	Satb
One Hundred Sacred Favorites (No 5661)	Johnson, Norman	Na Zon			T Za	
Paul Mickelson's Choral Arrangements	Na	Na Zon	B		T Za	
Popular Psalm Settings	Wills, Arthur	Na Gsc	B		T Za	Unis+
Praise For Today (Words, Music)	Collected	64 Aug	M		T Za	
Praise To The Lord (10 Chorales)	Bach, J.S./Ed Lee	73 Gia	B R	L	T Za	Satb+
Preces And Responses (M)	Naylor, Bernard	Na Oxf	M		T Za	Ssatb
Preces And Responses (M)	Reading, John	Na Oxf	M		T Za	Satb
Preces And Responses (Me)	Marlow, Richard	Na Oxf	M		T Za	Ttbb
Psalm 150	Bruckner, Anton	Na Kal	B		T Za	Full
Requiem Mass In C Minor	Cherubini, M. L.	Na Kal	B		T Za	Satb
Responses	Rhodes	Na Wbp			T Za	
Responses For The Church Service	Newbury, Kent A.	Na Gsc	B		T Za	Satb
Responses, With Preces By Gibbons	Barnard, John	Na Oxf	M		T Za	Saatb
Rounds For Church And Sunday School	Van Camp, L.	76 Bec	M		T Za	Round
Sacred A Capella Choruses (Germ/Eng)	Mendelssohn, F.	Na Kal	B		T Za	Satb
Sacred Choruses	Bruckner, Anton	Na Kal	B		T Za	Satb
Sacred Hymns	Dufay, Guilloume	Na Kal	B		T Za	Satb
Sacred Hymns (Seven)	Bruckner, Anton	Na Kal	B		T Za	Satb
Sacred Songs	Bach, J. S.	Na Lps	M B		T Za	
Sacred Songs (Geistliche Lieder)	Bach, J. S.	75 Lps	B		T Za	
Second Service: Magnificat & Nunc Dim.	Leighton, Kenneth	Na Oxf	M		T Za	Satb
Service Music For Sab Choir	Kirby (Ed)	70 Pro	B	L	T Za	Sab
Seven Hymn Tunes (In 2 Vols)	Dowland, John	Na Oxf	B		T Za	Satb
Seven Lenten Chorales	Bach, J. S.	70 Gia	M		T Za	Satb
Seven Sacred Motets	Lasso, Orlando Di	Na Kal	B		T Za	Satb
Seventeen Responses And Sentences	Na	Na Lor	M		T Za	Satb
Short Evening Service (Dorian Mode)	Tallis, Thomas	Na Oxf	M		T Za	Satb
Short Service (Md)	Gibbons, Orlando	Na Oxf	M		T Za	Satb
Short Service: Magnificat & Nunc	Amner, John	Na Oxf	M		T Za	Satb
Sing For Joy	Collected	74 Aug	M		T Za	
Sing His Praises No 1 (No 5060)	Till, Lee Roy	Na Zon	B		T Za	Satb
Sing His Praises No 2 (No 5768)	Till, Lee Roy	Na Zon	B		T Za	Satb
Singing In Seven Parts (No 5038)	Decou, Harold	Na Zon	B		T Za	
Six Christmas Songs	Williamson, Malcolm	Na Gsc	B		T Za	Unis+
Six Evening Hymns	Williamson, Malcolm	Na Gsc	B		T Za	Unis+
Six Motets	Bach, J. S.	75 Lps	B		T Za	Satb
Six Motets	Vaet, Jacobus	Na Kal	B		T Za	Satb
Six Motets In Polish And English	Chojnacki, J	Na Gia			T Za	
Six Polyphonic Motets	Na	Na Gia			T Za	
Six Short Anthems For The Seasons	Ley, Henry G.	Na Oxf	M		T Za	Var
Sixteen Choral Responses	Dethier	Na Lor	M		T Za	
Sixteenth-Century Anthem Book, A	Collected	Na Oxf	B		T Za	
Solemn Mass For Voices (Latin)	Franck, C.	Na Kal	B R		T Za	Satb
Songs For Kindergarten Children	Collected	Na Flp	R		T Za	
Songs Of Praises	Jones, Gj	Na Gsc	B		T Za	Satb
Standard Christmas Carols	Na	Na Lor	M		T Za	Var
Symphony Of Psalms	Stravinsky, Igor	Na Kal	B		T Za	
Tantum Ergo, 6 Settings (Eng-Lat)	Bruckner, Anton	Cfp	R		T Za	Satb+
Tantum Ergos (Six)	Bruckner, Anton	Na Kal	B		T Za	Satb
Ten Faux Bourdons On Well-Known Hymns	Willan, Healey	Na Oxf	M		T Za	Satb
Ten Four-Part Motets For The Year	Palestrina, Giovanni P	Na Oxf	M		T Za	Satb
The Baroque Song Book	Murphy, Ernest (Arr)	75 Maf	M		T Za	2pt
The Church Anthem Book (Boards)	Davies, W. & Ley, H.G.	Na Oxf	B		T Za	
The Cliff Barrows Choir No 2	Barrows, Cliff	Na Zon	B		T Za	
The Cliff Barrows Choir No 3 (No 5856)	Barrows, Cliff	75 Zon	B		T Za	
The Divine Liturgy	Roff, Joseph (Ed)	67 Gia	B	L	T Za	Satb+
The Falcon	Rutter, John	Na Oxf	B		T Za	Full
The New Christian Hymnal	Kuiper, H.J.	Na Erd	B		T Za	Prot.H
The Oxford Easy Anthem Book	Collected	Na Oxf	B		T Za	
Theresa Mass In B-Flat	Haydn, Franz J	52 Bbl	B		T Za	Satb+
Third Verse Service: Magnificat Etc	Batten, Adrian	Na Oxf	M		T Za	Saatb
Thirteen Amens & Alleluias	Praetorius, M./Ruening	74 Gia	B	L	T Za	Var+
Three Anthems	Marbeck, John	Na Kal	B		T Za	Satb
Three Folk-Hymns	Chapin, Robison	75 Bbl	B		T Za	Ssb
Three Fuging-Tunes	Ingalls, Anonymous	75 Bbl	B		T Za	Var
Three Introits	Whitlock, Percy	Na Oxf	M		T Za	Satb
Three Latin Renaissance Motets	Collected Harris Arr	76 Wlp	M		T Za	Ssaa
Three Magnificats	Taverner, John	Na Kal	B		T Za	Satb
Three Medieval Lyrics	Mathias, William (Tr W)	Na Oxf	B		T Za	Satb
Three Motets	Des Pres, Josquin	Na Kal	B		T Za	Satb
Three Motets	Gabrieli, G	Na Kal	B		T Za	Satb
Three Motets For Chorus & Solo	Mendelssohn, F.	Na Kal	B		T Za	Satb
Three Motets In Honor Of The Blessed	Lee, John	70 Gia	M		T Za	Satb
Three Part Choir No 1 (No 5813)	Peterson, John W.	Na Zon	B		T Za	Sab
Three Part Choir No 2 (No 5830)	Peterson, John W.	Na Zon	B		T Za	Sab
Three Part Choir No 3 (No 5829)	Peterson, John W.	Na Zon	B		T Za	Sab
Three Part Choir No 4 (No 4286)	Peterson, John W.	Na Zon	B		T Za	Sab
Three Passion Motets	Lasso, Orlando Di	Na Kal	B		T Za	Satb
Three Psalms	Des Pres, Josquin	Na Kal	B		T Za	Satb
Three Responses	Palestrina, Giovanni P	Na Gsc	B		T Za	Satb
Three Sacred Choruses	Martini, J.	Na Kal	B		T Za	Satb
Three Sacred Choruses, Op. 37 (Eng-Lat)	Brahms, Johannes	Na Cfp	R		T Za	Ssaa+

CATEGORIZED INDEX

Three Sacred Motets	Charpentier, Marc A.	Na Kal	B	T Za	
Three Short Holy Week Anthems	Newbury, Kent A.	Na Gsc	B	T Za	Satb
Three Songs Of Tribulation	Lewer, Dare	75 Bbl	B	T Za	Var
Twelve Canciones For Two Voices	Lasso, Orlando Di	Na Kal	B	T Za	2pt
Twelve Responses And Sentences	Whitney	Na Wbp		T Za	
Twenty Four Anthems For Sa Voices	Leger, Philip	Na Oxf	B	T Za	Sa
Twenty Responses (Elizabethan)	Ferguson	75 Sac	M	T Za	
Twenty Responses For General Worship	Na	Na Lor	M	T Za	Satb
Twenty-Five Anthems (In 4 Vols)	Gibbons, Orlando	Na Kal	B	T Za	Satb
Twenty-Five Anthems For Mixed Voices	Collected	Na Oxf	B	T Za	Satb
Twenty-One Service Responses	Evans	Na Wbp		T Za	
Two Anthems: (Me)	Barcrofte, George	Na Oxf	M	T Za	Satb
Two Carols	Copley, R. Evan	76 Abi	M	T Za	Satb+
Two Evening Hymns	Bourgeois, Louis (Arr)	Na Oxf	M	T Za	Ttbb
Two Marian Compositions (Lat)	Bruckner, Anton	Na Cfp	R	T Za	Satb+
Two Motets (Latin)	Bruckner, Anton	Na Cfp	R	T Za	Satb+
Two Motets 'in Diem Pacis' (D)	Mellers, Wilfred	Na Oxf	M	T Za	Satb
Two Motets In Honor Of Blessed Virgin	Lotti, A/Soriano, F	74 Gia	M	T Za	Satb
Two Sacred Pieces (Md)	Ravenscroft, Thomas	Na Oxf	M	T Za	Ssatb
Two Short Anthems (Me)	Bevan, Temple	Na Oxf	M	T Za	Satb
Two Songs For Mens Voices	Ingalls, Jeremiah	75 Bbl	B	T Za	Ttb
Two Songs Of Mourning From The	Ingalls, Jeremiah	75 Bbl	B	T Za	Ttb
Voices In Praise	Kirby (Ed)	69 Pro	M B	L T Za	Sab
We Sing To God (In 3 Volumes)	Weller (Ed)	66 Aug	B	T Za	Var
William Penn's Reflections (4 Pts)	Moe, Daniel	73 Aug	M	T Za	Satb

Instrumental Music

This section contains only a small amount of the available instrumental music. We include it as a small bonus, since the purpose of the book is to list primarily hymns and PARTICIPATIONAL music.

The Guitar Hymnal (No 5309)	Bay, Mel	Na Zon	B	F Zb	Guitar
Alleluia (No 5759)	Mickelson, Paul	Na Zon	B	G Zb	Organ
Brass Ensemble Packet No 1 (No 5441)	Decou, Harold	Na Zon	B	G Zb	Brass
Brass Ensemble Packet No 2 (No 5442)	Decou, Harold	Na Zon	B	G Zb	Brass
Brass Ensemble Packet No 3 (No 5443)	Decou, Harold	Na Zon	B	G Zb	Brass
Chapel Organist No 1 (No 5820)	Na	Na Zon	B	G Zb	Organ
Chapel Organist No 2 (No 5823)	Na	Na Zon	B	G Zb	Organ
Chapel Organist No 3 (No 5825)	Na	Na Zon	B	G Zb	Organ
Crusade Organist (No 5761)	Innes, John	Na Zon	B	G Zb	Organ
Deluxe Guitar Praise Book (No 5310)	Bay, Bill	Na Zon	B	G Zb	Guitar
Duets For Piano And Organ No 1 (5934)	Decou, Harold	Na Zon	B	G Zb	Orgpia
Duets For Piano And Organ No 2 (5931)	Decou, Harold	Na Zon	B	G Zb	Orgpia
Easy Organ Favorites (No 5412)	Decou, Harold	Na Zon	B	G Zb	Organ
Gospel Organist No 1 (No 5791)	Decou, Harold	Na Zon	B	G Zb	Organ
Gospel Organist No 2 (No 5796)	Decou, Harold	Na Zon	B	G Zb	Organ
Gospel Organist No 3 (No 5797)	Decou, Harold	Na Zon	B	G Zb	Organ
Gospel Organist No 4 (No 5799)	Decou, Harold	Na Zon	B	G Zb	Organ
Gospel Organist No 5 (No 5620)	Decou, Harold	Na Zon	B	G Zb	Organ
Guitar Christmas Carols (Nfo 4346)	Bay, Mel	Na Zon	B	G Zb	Uitar
Guitar Sing-A-Long (No 5540)	Peterson, John W.	Na Zon	B	G Zb	Guitar
Hymns For Brass Quartet (No 5760)	Schoen, Douglas E.	Na Zon	B	G Zb	Brass
Hymntime Piano No 1 (No 5745)	Bock, Fred	Na Zon	B	G Zb	Piano
Hymntime Piano No 2 (No 5746)	Bock, Fred	Na Zon	B	G Zb	Piano
Hymntime Piano No 3 (No 5747)	Bock, Fred	Na Zon	B	G Zb	Piano
Hymntime Piano No 4 (No 5748)	Bock, Fred	Na Zon	B	G Zb	Piano
Keyboard Rhapsodies (No 4701)	Atwood/Mickelson	Na Zon	B	G Zb	Orgpia
Keyboard Stylings For The Piano	Huff, Ronn And Donna	Na Zon	B	G Zb	Piano
My First Piano Hymnbook No 1 (No 5734)	Decou, Harold	Na Zon	B	G Zb	Piano
My Piano Hymnbook No 2 (No 5735)	Decou, Harold	Na Zon	B	G Zb	Piano
My Piano Hymnbook No 3 (No 5736)	Decou, Harold	Na Zon	B	G Zb	Piano
Organ Specials By Merrill Dunlop (5257)	Na	Na Zon	B	G Zb	Organ
Piano Duets At One Keyboard (No 5289)	Smith, Tedd	75 Zon	B	G Zb	Piano
Piano Solo Favorites No 1 (No 5814)	Na	Na Zon	B	G Zb	Piano
Piano Solo Favorites No 2 (No 5802)	Na	Na Zon	B	G Zb	Piano
Ring The Bells (No 5040)	Rasley, John M.	Na Zon	B	G Zb	Bell
Singspiration Guitar Hymnal (No 5785)	Collected	Na Zon	B	G Zb	Guit
Spirituals For Instrument	Braun, Richard	Na Yba	B	G Zb	

A Christmas Prelude (Easy)	Na	Na Abi	M	L Zb	Organ
A Festival Flourish	Ferris, W	Na Gia		L Zb	
A Meditation Upon The Passion	Powell	Na Abi	M	L Zb	Organ
Aria Da Chiesa	Hamill	Na Abi	M	L Zb	Organ
Aria For Organ	Malloch	Na Abi	M	L Zb	Organ
Ascensions	Mckay	Na Abi	M	L Zb	Organ
Can't Take It With You	Schneider, Kent E.	75 Ccc	M B	L Zb	
Chorale And Fugue On Lasst Uns	Bielawa	Na Abi	M	L Zb	Organ
Chorale Prelude On Angelus (Mod)	Powell	Na Abi	M	L Zb	Organ
Chorale Prelude On Bremen (Mod Diff)	Curry	Na Abi	M	L Zb	Organ
Chorale Prelude On Ein Feste Burg	Copley	Na Abi	M	L Zb	Organ
Chorale Prelude On O Trinity	Plettner	Na Abi	M	L Zb	Organ
Contemplations	Mckay	Na Abi	M	L Zb	Organ
Designs For Organ	Mcafee, Don	Na Abi	M	L Zb	Organ
Early American Compositions For Organ	Spong	Na Abi	M	L Zb	Organ
Eight Compositions For Organ	Young	Na Abi	M	L Zb	Organ
Ein Gebet	Schmutz	Na Abi	M	L Zb	Organ
Elegy For Organ	Powell	Na Abi	M	L Zb	Organ
Eleven Chorale Preludes	Copley	Na Abi	M	L Zb	Organ
Faithful Gather, The	Schneider, Kent E.	75 Ccc	M B	L Zb	
Fanfare-Improvisation On Azmon	Wyton	Na Abi	M	L Zb	Organ
Fantasia On Nun Danket	Grieb	Na Abi	M	L Zb	Organ
Fantasienne And Fughetta	Schmidt	Na Abi	M	L Zb	Organ
Fantasy On O Come All Ye Faithful	Rohlig	Na Abi	M	L Zb	Organ
Fantasy On Victimae Paschali (Diff)	Powell	Na Abi	M	L Zb	Organ
Festal Rhapsody	Candlyn	Na Abi	M	L Zb	Organ
Festival Prelude	Pfautsch, Lloyd	Na Abi	M	L Zb	Organ
Festival Prelude On I'll Praise	Pfautsch, Lloyd	Na Abi	M	L Zb	Organ
Fifteen Harmonizations On Hymns	Marshall	Na Abi	M	L Zb	Organ
Fifteen Preludes	Rohlig	Na Abi	M	L Zb	Organ
Fifty-Five Hymn Intonations	Rohlig	Na Abi	M	L Zb	Organ
Five Biblical Contemplations For Organ	Krapf, Gerhard	76 Sac	B	L Zb	Org
Four Chorale Preludes	Cummins	Na Abi	M	L Zb	Organ
Four Organ Preludes On Chorale Tunes	Lapo	Na Abi	M	L Zb	Organ
Four Preludes On Early American Tunes	Powell	Na Abi	M	L Zb	Organ
Four Preludes On Hymns Of The Church	Bielawa	Na Abi	M	L Zb	Organ
Four Psalm Preludes	Powell	Na Abi	M	L Zb	Organ
Four Psalm Preludes Set Ii	Powell	Na Abi	M	L Zb	Organ
Fugue In G	Bach, J. S.	75 Ccc	M B	L Zb	
Gaudeamus	Proulx, Richard	Na Gia		L Zb	
Good Christian Men Rejoice (Diff)	Rohlig	Na Abi	M	L Zb	Org+
Good Christian Men, Rejoice	Rohlig, Harald	Na Abi	M	L Zb	Organ
Gospel Rappings	Schneider, Kent E.	76 Ccc	M B	L Zb	
Gothic Fanfare	Groom, Lester	Na Abi	M	L Zb	Organ
Gothic Fanfare	Groom, Lester	Na Abi	M	L Zb	Organ
Grand Processional For Organ	Martin Shaw/Dale Wood	76 Sac	B	L Zb	Orgbrs
Greet A New Day	Schneider, Kent E.	75 Ccc	M B	L Zb	
Harmonizations On Hymn Tunes (15)	Marshall	Na Abi	M	L Zb	Organ
His Mercy Endureth Forever	Schmutz	Na Abi	M	L Zb	Organ
How Lovely Shines The Star (W/Ob)	Manz, Paul	Na Con	B	L Zb	Org
Hymn Intonations (55)	Rohlig	Na Abi	M	L Zb	Organ
Hymn-Tune Preludes (15)	Curry	Na Abi	M	L Zb	Organ
Improvisation On Father	Plettner	Na Abi	M	L Zb	Organ
Improvisation On Schonster Herr Jesu	Curry	Na Abi	M	L Zb	Organ
Improvisation On Unser Herrscher	Mckay	Na Abi	M	L Zb	Organ
Introduction And Passacaglia	Powell	Na Abi	M	L Zb	Organ
Introduction, Fugue And Variations	Bender, Jan	Na Abi	M	L Zb	Organ
Just As I Am (Woodworth) (Easy)	Johnson	Na Abi	M	L Zb	Organ
Lo, How A Rose E'er Blooming (Easy)	Davidson	Na Abi	M	L Zb	Organ
Lovers Are Special People	Schneider, Kent E.	75 Ccc	M B	L Zb	
Magnificat	Goode	Na Abi	M	L Zb	Organ
Meditation	Mccoy, Floyd	74 Smc	B	L Zb	Inst
Meditations On Psalm 37	Karhu	Na Abi	M	L Zb	Organ
Meditations On Sweet Rivers	Groom, Lester	Na Abi	M	L Zb	Organ
Mourning's Glory	Schneider, Kent E.	75 Ccc	M B	L Zb	
Nine Compositions For Organ	Walter	Na Abi	M	L Zb	Organ
Now Thank We All Our God	Rohlig, Harald	Na Abi	M	L Zb	Organ
Now Thank We All Our God (Mod Diff)	Rohlig	Na Abi	M	L Zb	Organ
O God, Thou Faithful God	Triplett	Na Abi	M	L Zb	Organ
Organ Offertories From The Baroque Era	Corina	Na Abi	M	L Zb	Organ
Organ Rarities, Volume I	Spong	Na Abi	M	L Zb	Organ
Partita On "St. Anne"	Manz, Paul	Na Con	B	L Zb	Org
Partita On St Paul	Peek	Na Abi	M	L Zb	Organ
Pastoral Preludes For Organ	Owens	Na Abi	M	L Zb	Organ
Pheres	Mcbride, James	75 Ccc	M B	L Zb	
Picardy Suite	Burns	Na Abi	M	L Zb	Organ
Prelude And Variations	Hampton, Calvin	75 Maf	M B	L Zb	Org
Prelude On A Southern Folk Hymn	Young	Na Abi	M	L Zb	Organ
Prelude On Amazing Grace	Lorenz	Na Abi	M	L Zb	Organ
Prelude On Christ Is Arisen (Diff)	Rohlig	Na Abi	M	L Zb	Organ
Prelude On Darwall	Candlyn	Na Abi	M	L Zb	Organ
Prelude On Hyfrydol	Candlyn	Na Abi	M	L Zb	Organ
Prelude On Mit Freuden Zart (Mod Easy)	Candlyn	Na Abi	M	L Zb	Organ
Prelude On O Store Gud	Lorenz	Na Abi	M	L Zb	Organ
Prelude On Rockingham	Candlyn	Na Abi	M	L Zb	Organ
Prelude On St Bernard	Candlyn	Na Abi	M	L Zb	Organ
Prelude On St Flavian	Candlyn	Na Abi	M	L Zb	Organ
Processional	Goode	Na Abi	M	L Zb	Organ
Processional March On St Dunstan's	Groom, Lester	Na Abi	M	L Zb	Organ
Projection 29	Schneider, Kent E.	69 Ccc	M B R L	L Zb	
Quiet Music For Organ	Read	Na Abi	M	L Zb	Organ
Sacred Dance (Lyric Liturgy)	Peloquin, C Alexander	74 Gia	B L	L Zb	Orgbrs
Sacred Harp Suite	Powell	Na Abi	M	L Zb	Organ
Six Easter Preludes	Powell	Na Abi	M	L Zb	Organ
Six Easter Preludes (Hymn-Tune Prelude	Powell	Na Abi	M	L Zb	Organ
Six Hymn-Tune Preludes	Walter	Na Abi	M	L Zb	Organ
Six Sacred Compositions For Organ,	Diercks	Na Abi	M	L Zb	Organ
Six Service Pieces For Organ	Roff, Joseph	Na Abi	M	L Zb	Organ
Sonata	Koloss	Na Abi	M	L Zb	Organ
Sonata I For Organ	Rohlig	Na Abi	M	L Zb	Organ
Soon A New Dawn	Schneider, Kent E.	76 Ccc	M B	L Zb	
Suite For Christmas (Mod)	Corina	Na Abi	M	L Zb	Organ
Suite For Organ	George	Na Abi	M	L Zb	Organ
Ten Chorale Improvisations (7 Sets)	Manz, Paul	Na Con	B	L Zb	Org
Ten Pieces For Organ	Rohlig	Na Abi	M	L Zb	Organ
The Seventh Seal	Mcbeth, W. Francis	72 Smc	M	L Zb	Band
The Spirit Of Christmas	Cailliet, Lucien	70 Smc	M	L Zb	Band
Thirty New Settings Of Familiar Hymns	Rohlig	Na Abi	M	L Zb	Organ
Three Chorale Preludes (Mod Diff)	Copley	Na Abi	M	L Zb	Organ
Three Christmas Preludes (Mod Easy)	Candlyn	Na Abi	M	L Zb	Organ
Three Duets For Organ And Harp	Bach C.P.E./Ludwig Alt	76 Sac	B	L Zb	
Three Festival Preludes	Groom, Lester	Na Abi	M	L Zb	Organ
Three Miniatures For Organ	Powell	Na Abi	M	L Zb	Organ
Three Organ Preludes On Hymn Tunes	Pfautsch, Lloyd	Na Abi	M	L Zb	Organ
Three Preludes And Fugues For Organ	Copley	Na Abi	M	L Zb	Organ
Three Unfamiliar Organ Compositions By	Mendelssohn, F.	Na Abi	M	L Zb	Organ
To Be Fed By Ravens	Mcbeth, W. Francis	75 Smc	M	L Zb	Band
Toccata For Nun Danket Alle Got	Cunningham, Patrick	76 Gra	B	L Zb	Organ
Toccata For Organ	Conley, James	Na Abi	M	L Zb	Organ
Totentanz	Krapf, Gerhard	Na Abi	M	L Zb	Organ
Transcriptions For Organ	Walter	Na Abi	M	L Zb	Organ
Triptych	Roff, Joseph	Na Abi	M	L Zb	Organ
Twelve Hymn Accompaniments	Withrow	Na Abi	M	L Zb	Organ
Twenty Hymn Preludes For Organ	Stearns, Peter Pindar	Na Cob	B	L Zb	Org
Two Christmas Preludes (Mod Easy)	Powell	Na Abi	M	L Zb	Organ
Two Compositions For Organ	Groom, Lester	Na Abi	M	L Zb	Organ
Two Preludes For Holy Week (Mod Diff)	Copes	Na Abi	M	L Zb	Organ
Variations On Gott Des Himmels	Merritt	Na Abi	M	L Zb	Organ

Title	Author			
Variations On Hymn Tunes By William	Baumgartner	Na Abi	M	L Zb Organ
Variations On Mit Freuden Zart	Withrow	Na Abi	M	L Zb Organ
Variations On Wer Nur Den Lieben Gott	Mcafee, Don	Na Abi	M	L Zb Organ
Variations To Adeste Fideles	Mcclenny/Hinson	Na Abi	M	L Zb Organ
Voluntaries For The Christian Year	Na	Na Abi	M	L Zb Organ
Voluntaries On Early American Hymns	Best	Na Abi	M	L Zb Organ
Wedding Music (In Two Volumes)	Johnson, D.	70 Aug	M	L Zb Org
Wedding Processional (Mod Easy)	Titcomb, Everett	Na Abi	M	L Zb Organ
Woodlawn Walk	Schneider, Kent E.	73 Ccc	M B R L	L Zb
You're In The Right Place	Schneider, Kent E.	75 Ccc	M B	L Zb
A Paraphrase Of "St. Elizabeth"	Hancock Gerre	76 Abi	B	T Zb Org
Adagio Religioso	Mozart, Wolfgang A	39 Smc	M	T Zb P+Ob
Adoration	Stainer, Sir John	74 Smc	B	T Zb Inst
American Hymns And Carols Of The 19th	Spong	76 Abi	B	T Zb Org
And In That Still Small Voice	Mendelssohn, F.	74 Smc	B	T Zb Inst
And Now Revived He Springs	Haydn, Joseph	61 Smc	M	T Zb P+Tm
Andante (From Sonata In A Minor)	Bach, J. S. (Arr Zvero	73 Smc	M	T Zb P+Fl
Brass Sounds Of Christmas	Tolosko/Wiskirchen	Na Gia		T Zb
Cantate Domino	Pitoni, Giuseppe	67 Smc	M	T Zb Bqrt
Chorale & Var. On Now Thank We	Cailliet, Lucien	74 Smc	M	T Zb Band
Chorale Prelude Arr For Brass	Brahms, Johannes	74 Smc	M	T Zb Band
Chorale Prelude In E Minor	Reed, Alfred	53 Smc	M	T Zb Band
Chorale Prelude On Bedford	Powell, Robert J.	75 Abi	M	T Zb Org
Chorale Prelude On Jesu Du, Du Bist	Roff, Joseph	76 Abi	B	T Zb Org
Chorale Prelude, "Wachet Auf"	Bach, J. S.	75 Maf	M	T Zb Band
Chorale—Prelude On "Bedford"	Powell	76 Abi	B	T Zb Org
Christmas Cameos Suite	Rhoads, William	71 Smc	M	T Zb Bqrt
Christmas Organist (No 5950)	Decou/Johnson	Na Zon		T Zb Org
Christmas Suite For Handbells	Brown, Charles	76 Abi		T Zb Bells
Complete Organ Works In 9 Vols.	Bach, J. S.	Na Kal	B	T Zb Org
Early American Hymn Tune	Mccoy, F. (Arr)	74 Smc		T Zb Inst
Easter Organist (No 5290)	Decou/Johnson	Na Zon	B	T Zb Organ
Elegy And Le Motif	Laxton	75 Nov	M	T Zb Org
Endure! Endure! (St Matt Passion)	Bach, J. S.	61 Smc	M	T Zb P+Tm
Ev'ry Valley (From Messiah)	Handel, G. F.	61 Smc	M	T Zb P+Tm
Festival Overture (Organ Solo)	Chapman	75 Cfp	M	T Zb
From Celestial Seats Descending	Handel, G. F.	61 Smc	M	T Zb P+Tm
Fugue In E Major	Handel, G. F.	75 Nov	M	T Zb Org
Glory To God	Bach, J. C. (Arr Mccoy)	74 Smc	B	T Zb Inst
God Is Watching Over Us	Mccoy, F. (Arr)	74 Smc	B	T Zb Inst
Haste Ye Shepherds	Bach, J. S. Arr Bevers	Smc	M	T Zb P+Tm
Herman Voss Presents Organ Favorites 1	Voss, Herman	Na Zon	B	T Zb Organ
Herman Voss Presents Organ Favorites 2	Voss, Herman	Na Zon	B	T Zb Organ
Hide Not Thy Face	Farrant, Richard	74 Smc	B	T Zb Inst
How Firm A Foundation	Steel, A. (Arr.)	59 Smc	M	T Zb Band
Hymn Preludes From Op 100	Peeters, Flor	75 Cfp	M	T Zb Org
Hymns For Brass Quartet	Vandre	76 Abi	B	T Zb Brass
Hymns Of Praise And Glory	Tolosko/Wiskirchen	Na Gia		T Zb
If With All Your Hearts	Mendelssohn, F.	73 Smc	M	T Zb P+Tm
In Faith I Steadfast Stand	Bach, J. S. (Arr Mccoy	74 Smc	B	T Zb Inst
It' Wedding Time No 1 (No 5493)	Na	Na Zon	B	T Zb Organ
It's Wedding Time No 2 (No 5494)	Na	Na Zon	B	T Zb Organ
Largo From "Xerxes"	Handel, G. F.	65 Smc	M	T Zb Tmqt
Lord, Grant Thy Blessing	Mason (Arr Mccoy)	74 Smc	M	T Zb Inst
Magnificat Du 3eme Et 4eme Ton	Corrette	75 Nov	M	T Zb Org
Music From "King Arthur"	Purcell, H. (Ratcliffe	75 Nov	M	T Zb Org
My Faith Looks Up To Thee	Mason, L. Arr Griffith	59 Smc	M	T Zb Band
Organ Solos (No 5801)	Bock, Fred	Na Zon	B	T Zb Organ
Organbook (Orgalbuchlein)	Bach, J. S.	Na Kal	M	T Zb Org
Piano Melodies (No 5788)	Johnson, Norman	Na Zon	B	T Zb Piano
Processional And Recessional	Tcherepnin, A.	75 Cfp	M	T Zb Org
Sabbath Music (Christian)	Karg—Elert (Adapted)	71 Smc	M	T Zb Band
Sacred Selections For Inst. Choir	Mccoy, Floyd (Arr)	65 Smc	B	T Zb Inst
Service Suite For Organ	Roff, Joseph	75 Abi	M	T Zb Org
Sixty Pieces For The Manuals	Stearns, P.	76 Cob		T Zb Coll.
Special Day Organist (No 5942)	Decou, Harold	Na Zon	B	T Zb Organis
Spirits & Places	Collected (Arr Bacon)	76 Wlp	M	T Zb Org
St. Anne's Fugue	Bach, J. S.	65 Smc	M	T Zb Band
Sunday Morning Organist No 2 (No 5817)	Decou, Harry	Na Zon	B	T Zb Organ
Sunday Morning Organist No 1 (No 5807)	Decou, Harry	Na Zon	B	T Zb Organ
Sunday Morning Organist No 3 (No 5286)	Decou, Harry	Na Zon	B	T Zb Organ
Sunday Morning Organist No 4 (No 5287)	Decou, Harry	Na Zon	B	T Zb Organ
Sunday Morning Organist No 5 (No 5288)	Decou, Harry	Na Zon	B	T Zb Organ
Tedd Smith's Hymn Transcriptions	Smith, T.	Na Zon	B	T Zb Piano
Tedd Smith's Piano Solo Arrangements	Smith, T.	Na Zon	B	T Zb Piano
Thanks Be To God	Mendelssohn, F.	74 Smc	B	T Zb Inst
The Enemy Said (Israel In Egypt)	Handel, G. F.	61 Smc L U R		T Zb P+Tm
Thine All The Glory	Billings, W. (Arr Mcco	74 Smc	B	T Zb Inst
Thine Own Way	Maunder, J. (Arr Mccoy)	74 Smc	B	T Zb Inst
Tis Thee I Would Be Praising	Bach, J. S. (Adapted)	61 Smc	M	T Zb P+Tm
Two Chorales For Concert Band	Butts, Carrol	72 Smc	M	T Zb Band
Violin Solo Favorites (No 5028)	Decou, Harold	Na Zon	B	T Zb Violin
Voluntaries Based On Hymn Tunes	Appleby—Hunt—Shipp	63 Gam	B	T Zb P+Or
When Jesus Wept (Round)	Billings, W. (Arr Mcco	74 Smc	B	T Zb Inst
With Songs And Honors	Haydn, J. (Arr Mccoy)	74 Smc	B	T Zb Inst

Title			Title			Title		
A Banquet Is Prepared	Nal	L Lo	A New Song	Abi	L Tt	Acclamation (A)	Rav	L Lj
A Blessing From Aaron	Wlp	F Tr	A New Song	Bfi	F Tt	Acclamation (C)	Rpb	L Li
A Blessing Song	Fel	L Tt	A New Song(Joy, Joy, Joy Is)	Gia	F Ss	Acclamation (D)	Rpb	L Li
A Brand New Promised Land	Ahc	L Sr	A Nun Takes The Veil	Gsc	T Tc	Acclamation(B)	Rav	L Lj
A Canticle Of Care	Ahc	L Tr	A Pages Road Song	Gsc	T Tt	Acclamation(C)	Rav	L Lj
A Canticle Of Commemoration (A Cap)	Abi	L Tx	A Parade Of Miracles	Gmc	G Tt	Acclamation(D)	Rav	L Lj
A Canticle Of Thanksgiving (Opt Brs)	Abi	L Tt	A Paraphrase Of "St. Elizabeth"	Abi	T Zb	Acclamations	Wlp	L Li
A Carol For Christmas Morn (5 Carols)	Gia	L Sc	A Pastoral Prayer	Gsc	L Tr	Acclamations	Acp	L Li
A Carol(Mary, The Mother, Sang To Her)	Gsc	T Sc	A Peace For All Mankind	Fel	F Tr	Acclamations (Icet)	Wlp	L Li
A Child Is Born	Wlp	L Sc	A People Marching To Freedom (Opt Brs)	Mcc	F La	Acclamations (Icet)	Wlp	L Li
A Child Is Born In Bethlehem	Aug	T Sc	A Prayer For A Stranger	Hhh	G Tt	Acclamations From Sacred Scripture	Cfc	L Le
A Child Is Born In Bethlehem	Aug	T Sc	A Prayer For Eastertide	Rpb	L Sr	According To Matthew	Rav	L Tx
A Child Is Born To Us	Fel	L Sc	A Prayer For Families	Abi	L Tr	Ach, Arme Welt(Alas, Poor World)	Gsc	T Sl
A Child This Day Is Born	Gsc	T Sc	A Prayer For Peace (Md)	Oxf	T Tr	Achieved Is The Glorious Work	Gsc	T Tx
A Child To Us Is Born	Gsc	T Sc	A Prayer For Today	Gsc	T Tr	Achieved Is The Glorious Work (Me)	Oxf	T Tx
A Child Was Born	Gsc	T Tj	A Prayer For Us (W/Bell,Timp,Brs)	Gia	L Tp	Across The Shadows	Zon	G Tx
A Child, O Virgin, You Bore	Fel	L Tm	A Prayer Of Dedication	Som	L Tc	Action No 1 (No 5121)	Zon	C Za
A Child's Message Of Easter (Cantata)	Zon	C Sr	A Prayer Of King Henry Vi (E)	Oxf	T Tr	Action No 2 (No 5122)	Zon	C Za
A Child's Noel	Gsc	T Sc	A Prayer Of St. Richard Of Chichester	Oxf	T Tx	Action No 3 (No 5123)	Zon	C Za
A Child's Prayer	Gsc	C Tr	A Prayer Of Supplication (Me)	Gia	L Sl	Action No 4 (No 5124)	Zon	C Za
A Child's Present To His Savior	Gsc	T Sc	A Prayer Song	Yan	T Tr	Action No 5 (No 5125)	Zon	C Za
A Child's Thanksgiving (E)	Oxf	C Tt	A Prayer To Jesus	Jhm	G Tj	Action No 6 (No 5126)	Zon	C Za
A Choral Ascription Of Praise	Abi	L Tt	A Promise Has Been Made	Fel	F Sa	Action No 7 (No 5127)	Zon	C Za
A Choral Flourish (From Ps 33) (Md)	Oxf	T Tt	A Psalm Of Thanksgiving (Ps 145 & 104)	Oxf	T Tt	Ad Cantus, Ad Choros	Gsc	T Tt
A Choral Hymn For Advent & Ascension	Oxf	T Tx	A Rose Touched By The Sun's Warm Rays	Aug	L Tx	Ad Flumina Babylonis	Gsc	T Sl
A Choral Prayer(A Cap)	Gsc	T Tr	A Seasonal Thanksgiving	Gsc	T Tt	Adagio Religioso	Smc	T Zb
A Christ Centered Life	Man	G Tc	A Service Of Nine Lessons & Carols	Aug	L Za	Adelante Juventud	Zon	C Za
A Christmas Cantata	Gam	L Sc	A Service Of Shadows	Sac	L Sl	Adeste Fideles	Gsc	T Sc
A Christmas Carol	Pic	L Sc	A Shelter For Me	Bfi	F Le	Adeste Fideles (W/Tpts,Org,Cong)	Con	T Sc
A Christmas Carol (In 5 Carols) E	Gia	L Sc	A Sky Without Sunlight	Fel	F Sl	Adeste Fideles (With Brass)	Aug	T Sc
A Christmas Concert	Lor	T Sc	A Soldier's Prayer	Sav	F Tx	Adonai, Elohim	Gsc	L Tt
A Christmas Fantasy	Abi	L Sc	A Son Is Born Of Mary	Aug	T Sc	Adoramus	Bbl	T Tt
A Christmas Folk Song	Gsc	G Sc	A Song For The Sabbath	Abi	L La	Adoramus	Gsc	T Sl
A Christmas Folk Song	Gsc	T Sc	A Song In Your Heart	Man	G Tr	Adoramus Te	Pro	T Sl
A Christmas Lullaby	Gsc	T Sc	A Song Of Exaltation	Abi	L Tt	Adoramus Te	Gsc	T Sl
A Christmas Mosaic	Her	T Sc	A Song Of Freedom	Wlp	F Tr	Adoramus Te	Gsc	T Sl
A Christmas Prelude (Easy)	Abi	L Zb	A Song Of Hanukkah	Gsc	T Tx	Adoramus Te (Lat & Eng)	Hof	T Sl
A Collection Of Funeral Music	Abi	L Za	A Song Of Joy	Fel	F Tt	Adoramus Te (We Adore Thee)	Gsc	T Tt
A Contemporary Psalm	Aug	L Za	A Song Of Mary & Jesus (W/Fl)	Wlp	T Sc	Adoramus Te (We Adore Thee)	Gsc	T Sl
A Cowboy's Dream	Mar	L Tx	A Song Of Praise	Abi	C Tl	Adoramus Te (We Adore Thee)	.Gsc	T Sl
A Cradle Hymn	Aug	T Sc	A Song Of Rejoicing	Abi	L Tt	Adoramus Te Christe	Gsc	T Sl
A Dedicatory Anthem	Sac	T Tc	A Song Of Thanksgiving	Oxf	T Tt	Adoramus Te Christe	Aug	T Sl
A Family Benediction	Abi	L Tr	A Song To The Lamb (W/Brass, Tim)	Hwg	L Sr	Adoramus Te Christe (Md)	Oxf	T Sl
A Family That Prays Together	Ivm	G Tr	A Song Unending (No 5953)	Zon	L Sc	Adoramus Te, Christe	Gia	T Tj
A Festival Eucharist (Icet)(M)	Gia	L Za	A Song Unending (No 5961)	Zon	L Sc	Adoramus Te, Christe	Gsc	T Sl
A Festival Flourish	Gia	L Zb	A Song Unending (No 5979)	Zon	L Sc	Adoramus Te, Christe (A Cap)	Abi	L Sl
A Festival Of Carols For The Year	Wrd	G Za	A Song Was Born Cantata (No 4455)	Zon	G Sc	Adoramus Te, No. 1	Bbl	T Tj
A Few Things To Remember	Ham	G Tx	A Special Kind Of Beautiful	Sil	F Tx	Adoramus Te, No. 2	Bbl	T Tj
A Few Words About Jesus	Sav	G Tj	A Star	Gia	T Sc	Adoration	Man	G Tt
A Flemish Carol	Aug	T Sc	A Star In The Sky	Aug	L Sc	Adoration	Smc	T Zb
A Friend Of Mine	Sem	G Tr	A Symbol Is This Child (Cantata)	Lps	T Sc	Adoration, The	Pro	T Sc
A Gift	Ahc	L To	A Thanksgiving Day Ode	Gsc	T Tt	Adore And Be Still (C)	Lor	T Tt
A Glimpse Of The Master	Gmc	G Tj	A Thanksgiving Service (No 4540)	Zon	L Tt	Advent Anthem	Aug	T Sa
A Great And Mighty Wonder	Aug	T Sc	A Thousand Stars (Opt Perc)	Pro	L Sc	Advent Carol	Prc	L Tx
A Great And Mighty Wonder	Gsc	T Sc	A Time For Joy! (W/Piano)	Pro	L Sc	Advent Carol	Gia	T Sa
A Great Sign Appeared In Heaven	Fel	L Lg	A Time Of Joy	Yan	F Tr	Advent Chorale, The (C)	Lor	T Sa
A Heritage Of Folk Anthems (No 5833)	Zon	L Za	A Tool In The Hands Of God	Yan	F Tc	Advent Glad Song (Heartily Rejoice)	Gia	F Sa
A Holy Stillness	Abi	L Tr	A Touch Of Lemon	Van	C Tx	Advent Proclamation	Prc	L Tx
A Hymn Of Praise	Hwg	L Tt	A Treasure In A Field	Ahc	L Tx	Advent Service	Aug	L Sa
A Hymn Of Praise (W/Org,Violins)	Wlp	T Tt	A Very Merry Christmas	Gsc	T Sc	Advent Song Op 84	Kal	T Sa
A Hymn Of Thanks (High Voice)	Abi	L Tt	A Virgin	Yan	F Tm	Aeterni Munera	Aug	T Tr
A Hymn Of Youth	Aug	L Tx	A Virgin Most Pure	Gsc	T Sc	After The Storm	Gmp	G Sl
A Hymn To The Risen Christ	Gsc	T Sr	A Virgin Pure And Fair (W/Flute)(E)	Gia	T Sc	Afterwhile	Man	G Tx
A Joyful Song	Aug	T Tr	A Voice Cries Out In The Wilderness	Wgm	F La	Against The Morn Is Come A King	Gsc	T Sc
A Joyful Sound	Rpb	L Tt	A Wealden Trio. Song Of The Women	Gsc	T Sc	Agnus Dei	Gsc	T Lm
A La Venue De Noel	Gsc	T Sc	A Wedding Blessing	Aug	L Tw	Agnus Dei	Gia	L Lm
A Legend	Gsc	T Tx	A Wedding Song	Gia	L Tw	Agnus Dei	Aug	T Lm
A Lenten Folk Song	Yan	F Sl	A Winter Carol	Pic	L Sc	Agnus Dei	Gsc	T Lm
A Light Shall Shine Upon Us	Fel	L Sa	A World Of Love	Hhh	G Tr	Agnus Dei	Gsc	T Lm
A Light Will Shine	Ahc	L Tj	Abba, Father	Acp	L Tr	Agnus Dei (Eng Mass)	Gia	L Lm
A Litany (M)	Oxf	T Sl	Abba, Father	Rpb	L Tr	Agnus Dei (Eng, Icet)	Gra	L Lm
A Litany Of Thanksgiving	Gia	L Tt	Abba, Father	Sha	F Lo	Agnus Dei (Mariachi Mass)	Fel	F Lm
A Little Bit Of Sunshine	Gmc	G Tr	Abba, Father (Rom 8:15-16)	Mel	F Tr	Agnus Dei (Mass For New Rite)	Gia	L Lm
A Little Christmas Cantata	Gsc	T Sc	Abba, Father(4-Part Arrangement)	Acp	L Tr	Agnus Dei (Mass For Schools)	Fel	C Lm
A Little Each Day	Yan	F Tx	Abide With Me	Bec	L Tr	Agnus Dei (Mass Of The Western Tribes)	Fel	F Lm
A Little Further On The Way	Wlp	F Tc	Abide With Me	Pic	L Tr	Agnus Dei (Missa Brevis)	Fel	T Lm
A Little Hymn To Mary	Aug	T Sc	Abide, O Dearest Jesus (Me)	Gia	T Tr	Agnus Dei (Sung Mass No. 2)	Fel	L Lm
A Little Less Of Me	Bch	F Tt	Abiding Joy	Gsc	T Tr	Agnus Dei (Thomas More Mass)	Fel	L Lm
A Little Thought Away	Abm	G Tx	Above All Else	Zon	G Tt	Agree With God And Be At Peace	Gsc	L Tr
A Long, Long Time Ago	Gsc	T Sc	Above All Else	Zon	G Tt	Ah Dearest Jesus	Gsc	T Sc
A Man Called Jesus	Gmc	G Tj	Above All Praise And Majesty (Me)	Oxf	T Tt	Ah Lord Thy Dear Sweet Angels Send	Gsc	T Sl
A Man Of Integrity	Aug	L Tx	Above Him Stood The Seraphim (Me)	Oxf	T Tx	Ah, Dearest Jesu, Holy Child	Aug	T Sc
A Mass For All Occasions	Sms	F Za	Above My Adversaries	Fel	L Sl	Ah, Dearest Jesus(A Cap)	Pro	L Sc
A Mass For Lent	Sms	T Za	Above The Hills Of Time (E)	Lor	L Tx	Ah, Holy Jesus	Aug	T Tj
A Meditation Upon The Passion	Abi	L Zb	Abraham And Isaac	Abi	L Tx	Ah, Jesus Lord, Thy Love To Me	Aug	T Tj
A Message Came To A Maiden Young	Aug	L Sa	Abraham Sent Them Away	Fcc	C Tx	Ah, Thou Poor World (Me)	Oxf	T Tx
A Mighty Fortress (Inst. Optional)	Aug	T La	Abroad The Regal Banners Fly	Abi	T Sr	Ain't Dat Good News	Zon	L Sr
A Mighty Fortress (10 Chorales)	Gia	T Za	Absalom	Bbl	T Tx	Ain't Gonna Lay My Armor Down	Mar	L Tc
A Mighty Fortress Is Our God	Gsc	T Tr	Accept O Lord	Wlp	F To	Ain't Got Time To Die	Gsc	G Tf
A Mighty Fortress Is Our God	Gsc	T Tr	Accept These Gifts, O Lord	Fel	L To	Ain't Never Seen So Much Rain Before	Sav	F Tx
A Mighty Fortress Is Our God	Gsc	T Tr	Accept, O Father In Thy Love	Wlp	T To	Ainsi Quon Oit Le Cerf Bruire	Gsc	T Tr
A Mighty Fortress Is Our God (Vv)	Wlp	T Tr	Acclamaciones (Memorial)	Gia	L Lj	Air	Bbl	T Sl
A Mighty Fortress Is Our God (W/Band)	Aug	T Tr	Acclamation	Rpb	L Li	Air Of Death	Bbl	T Tf
A Minuet Fut Fait Un Reveil	Gsc	T Sc	Acclamation	Rpb	L Li	Alabanzas Del Adviento	Pic	C Sa
A Morning Prayer	Gsc	T Tx	Acclamation	Rpb	L Lj	Alas! And Did My Savior Bleed(Me)	Gia	L Sl
A Mother's Song	Lor	T Tx	Acclamation	Rpb	L Li	Alas, And Did My Savior Bleed	Lor	L Sl
A National Hymn Of Victory	Gsc	T Tp	Acclamation	Rpb	L Li	Aleatory Psalm (Chance Music)	Wlp	L Tx
A New Commandment	Wlp	F Tr	Acclamation	Rpb	L Li	All	Yan	F Tx
A New Commandment I Give You	Fel	L Tr	Acclamation	Rpb	L Li	All Alone	Mar	L Sl
A New Heart Will I Give You	Gsc	T Sl	Acclamation	Rpb	L Li	All As God Wills (A Cap)	Gsc	L Tr

ALPHABETICAL INDEX OF TITLES

All Beautiful The March Of Days	Abi	L	Tx
All Blessed Are You, O Lord	Wlp	L	Tt
All Breathing Life	Gsc	T	Tt
All By Ourselves	Lor	L	Tx
All Creatures Of Our God And King	Abi	L	Tt
All Creatures Of Our God And King	Lor	L	Tt
All Creatures Of Our God And King	Gsc	T	Tt
All Day Long My Heart Keeps Singing	Zon	G	Tt
All Flesh Is Grass	Gsc	T	Sl
All For Jesus	Lor	L	Tj
All From Saba Shall Come	Gia	L	Sc
All From The Sun's Uprise	Oxf	T	Tt
All Glorious Is The King's Daughter	Fel	L	Tm
All Glory Be To God On High	Aug	T	Tt
All Glory Laud & Honor (E)	Oxf	T	Tt
All Glory Love And Power To Thee	Pro	T	Tt
All Glory To Jesus	Zon	T	Tt
All Glory, Laud, And Honor	Zon	T	Tt
All Glory, Laud, And Honor	Lor	L	Tt
All Glory, Praise And Majesty	Gsc	T	Tt
All Glory, Praise, And Honor	Fel	L	Tt
All Glory, Praise, And Honor	Acp	L	Tk
All Glory, Praise, And Honor	Acp	L	Tk
All God's Children	Gmc	G	Tt
All God's People (Me) (Evangelical)	Lor	L	Tc
All Good Gifts	Val	F	Tt
All Good Gifts Around Us	Lor	L	To
All Hail The Power	Gsc	T	Tt
All Hail The Power	Aug	T	Tt
All Hail The Power (Tune "Miles Lane")	Oxf	T	Tj
All Hail The Power Of Jesus' Name	Sac	T	Tj
All Hail The Power Of Jesus' Name	Zon	T	Tj
All Hail The Power Of Jesus' Name	Zon	T	Tj
All Hail The Power Of Jesus' Name	Lor	T	Tj
All Hail The Power Of Jesus' Name	Lor	T	Tj
All Hail The Power Of Jesus' Name	Lor	T	Tj
All Hail The Power Of Jesus' Name	Lor	T	Tj
All He Wants Is You	Man	T	Tc
All Honor To You, O Lord	Wlp	L	Tt
All Honor, Power To You, O Lord	Wlp	L	Tt
All I Am, I Give To You	Wlp	F	To
All I Know	Mar	L	Tr
All I Need Is You	Man	G	Tr
All I Want	Lor	T	Tr
All Is Well	Lor	T	Tr
All Join Hands	Sil	C	Tx
All Join Together	Fel	L	Tt
All Kings Shall Pay Him Homage	Fel	L	Sc
All Lands And Peoples	Aug	T	Tt
All Marveled At The Words	Fel	L	Tj
All Men On Earth	Wlp	L	Tt
All Men Seek God	Gia	L	Sc
All Men Shal. See The Salvation	Fel	L	Sa
All My Days	Nal	L	Tt
All My Enemies Shall Fall Back	Fel	L	Sl
All My Friends Have Forsaken Me	Elv	T	Sl
All My Heart	Aug	T	Tr
All My Heart Inflamed And Burning	Gsc	T	Ss
All My Heart This Night	Pro	T	Sc
All My Heart This Night Rejoices	Gsc	T	Sc
All My Heart This Night Rejoices	Aug	T	Tt
All My Heart This Night Rejoices	Gia	T	Sc
All My Hopes	Gmc	G	Tr
All My Trials	Hal	F	Sl
All Nature's Works His Praise Declare	Lor	T	Tt
All Of Creation	Ahc	L	Tt
All Of My Life	Fel	F	Tt
All Of My Life	Fel	L	Tt
All Of Seeing	Acp	L	Tr
All Of Seeing (4-Part Arr.)	Acp	L	Tr
All Of Your People	Wgm	F	Tt
All Our Hope Of Salvation	Acp	F	Tj
All Our Hope Of Salvation (4-Part Arr)	Acp	F	Tj
All Our Joy	Fel	F	To
All People Clap Your Hands (Md)	Oxf	T	Tt
All People That On Earth Do Dwell	Gsc	T	Tt
All People That On Earth Do Dwell	Zon	T	Tt
All Poor Men & Humble	Aug	L	Tx
All Poor Men And Humble	Aug	T	Tr
All Praise And Thanks To God	Abi	T	Tt
All Praise To God	Sac	L	Tt
All Praise To God, In Light Arrayed	Gsc	T	Tt
All Praise To Our Redeeming Lord	Gsc	L	Tt
All Praise To Our Redeeming Lord	Gsc	T	Tt
All Praise To Our Redeeming Lord	Pro	L	Tr
All Praise To The Lord Our God	Fel	L	Tt
All Praise To Thee	Aug	T	Tt
All Praise To Thee	Gsc	T	Tt
All Praise To Thee	Gsc	T	Tt
All Praise To Thee (Canon)	Aug	T	Tt
All Praise To You, Lord	Fel	L	Tt
All Praise, Glory And Wisdom	Wlp	L	Tt
All Shall Be Well	Lor	T	Tr
All That Has Life Praise God!	Ccc	L	Tt
All That I Am	Sil	G	To
All That I Am	Fcc	F	To
All That We Have	Fel	F	To
All That's Good And Great And True	Gsc	T	Tr
All That's Good And Great And True	Sac	L	Tr
All The Bright Morning Stars	Wlp	L	Tm
All The Days Of Our Lives	Fel	F	Tt
All The Earth	Wlp	L	Tt
All The Ends Of The Earth	Fel	L	Sc
All The Ends Of The Earth	Gia	L	Tx
All The Ends Of The Earth (Icet)	Wlp	L	Ld
All The Nations	Ahc	L	Tt
All The Nations Shall Come	Fel	L	Sc
All The Roads Lead Home	Yan	F	Tx
All The Way	Man	G	Tc
All The Way Down (Jonah 2)	Gia	L	Sl
All The Ways Of A Man(Long)	Aug	L	Tr
All The World Acclaims Your Name	Sms	F	Tt
All These Things	Wlp	F	To
All They From Saba Shall Come	Gsc	T	Sc
All Things Are Thine	Sac	T	Tt
All Things Are Thine	Tcp	L	To
All Things Bright And Beautiful	Gsc	C	Tr
All Things Bright And Beautiful	Sac	L	Tr
All Things Depend On You, O Lord	Fel	L	Tr
All Things Have Their Time	Nal	L	Tx
All Things New	Fel	F	Sc
All Things Work Together For Good	Gmc	G	Sl
All Thy Works Shall Praise Thee(E & W)	Oxf	T	Tt
All We Like Sheep Have Gone	Cfs	T	Sl
All Were Saved By This Water	Fel	L	Tb
All Ye Servants Of The Lord	Sac	L	Tx
All Ye That Pass By	Abi	T	Sl
All You Angels, Bless The Lord	Fel	L	Tt
All You Nations	Wlp	L	Tt
All You Nations	Wlp	F	Tt
All You Need	Man	G	Tc
All You Peoples, Clap Your Hands	Gia	L	Ld
All You Who Thirst	Fel	L	Tb
All Your Gifts Of Life	Nal	C	Tr
All-Time Favorites For The Choir No 1	Zon	T	Za
All-Time Favorites For The Choir No 2	Zon	T	Za
All-Time Favorites For The Choir No 3	Zon	T	Za
Alla Trinite	Gsc	T	Tt
Alle, Alle	Wlp	F	Tt
Alle, Alle, Alleluia (Gospel Accl.)	Nal	L	Lf
Allelu	Fis	F	Tt
Allelu	Fel	F	Sr
Allelu! Rejoice And Sing!	Her	T	Sc
Alleluia	Aug	T	Tt
Alleluia	Nal	L	Lf
Alleluia	Hal	L	Sc
Alleluia	Lor	L	Tt
Alleluia	See	L	Tt
Alleluia	Rpb	L	Lf
Alleluia	Lor	L	Tt
Alleluia	Gia	L	Lf
Alleluia	Bbl	T	Tt
Alleluia	Rpb	L	Lf
Alleluia	Rav	L	Lf
Alleluia	Sac	L	Tt
Alleluia	Gsc	T	Lf
Alleluia	Gia	T	Tt
Alleluia	Rpb	L	Lf
Alleluia	Rpb	L	Lf
Alleluia	Rpb	L	Lf
Alleluia	Nal	L	Lf
Alleluia	See	L	Tt
Alleluia	Her	L	Tt
Alleluia	Nal	L	Lf
Alleluia	Rpb	L	Lf
Alleluia	Sac	L	Sr
Alleluia	Wbp	T	Tt
Alleluia	Nal	L	Lf
Alleluia (A Cap)	Abi	T	Lf
Alleluia (Easter Day)	Fel	F	Sr
Alleluia (From "For Us A Child")	Pro	T	Sc
Alleluia (From Coronation Anthem No.2)	Gsc	T	Lf
Alleluia (Hearts And Voices)	Smc	T	Sr
Alleluia (Human Hands Cannot)	Gia	F	Tr
Alleluia (Icet)	Wlp	L	Lf
Alleluia (Icet)	Wlp	L	Lf
Alleluia (No 5759)	Zon	G	Zb
Alleluia (Notre Dame Mass)	Gia	L	Lf
Alleluia (3 Voices)	Gia	T	Lf
Alleluia (3 Voices)	Gia	T	Lf
Alleluia (8x)	Din	L	Lf
Alleluia Alleluia	Zon	G	Li
Alleluia And Psalm For Easter(E)	Gia	T	Lf
Alleluia From Brazilian Psalm	Gsc	L	Lf
Alleluia God Is Love	Jsp	F	Tt
Alleluia Haec Dies	Gsc	T	Sr
Alleluia No. 1	Wgm	L	Lf
Alleluia Noel	Gsc	T	Sc
Alleluia Psallat	Gsc	T	Tt
Alleluia Psallat(Alleluia Let Us Sing)	Gsc	T	Tt
Alleluia To Our King	Lor	L	Tk
Alleluia To The Lord Of Being	Gsc	T	Tt
Alleluia Verse (Christmas Vigil)(Icet)	Wlp	L	Lf
Alleluia(A Maj)	Rav	L	Lf
Alleluia(F Maj)	Rav	L	Lf
Alleluia!	Her	L	Tt
Alleluia!	Lor	T	Tt
Alleluia!	Lor	L	Tt
Alleluia!	Zon	F	Tt
Alleluia!	Zon	F	Tt
Alleluia! (E)	Lor	L	Tt
Alleluia! Alleluia!	Gia	L	Sr
Alleluia! Alleluia!	Lor	L	Tt
Alleluia! Alleluia! Alleluia!	Nal	L	Lf
Alleluia! Christ Has Risen	Acp	L	Sr
Alleluia! Christ Has Risen(4-Part Arr)	Acp	L	Sr
Alleluia! Christ Is Born	Sac	T	Sc
Alleluia! He Has Risen	Lor	L	Sr
Alleluia! Hearts And Voices	Gsc	T	Tt
Alleluia! Hearts To Heaven (E)	Oxf	T	Sr
Alleluia! In All Things	Gia	L	Tt
Alleluia! Jesus Is Lord	Acp	L	Tk
Alleluia! Jesus Is Lord (4-Part Arr.)	Acp	L	Tk
Alleluia! Let The Holy Anthem Rise!	Aug	T	Sr
Alleluia! Let The Song Of Glory Rise	Acp	L	Sr
Alleluia! Let The Song Of Glory Rise	Acp	L	Sr
Alleluia! Morn Of Beauty	Gsc	T	Tx
Alleluia! O Praise Ye The Lord	Sac	T	Sc
Alleluia! Sing To Jesus	Lor	L	Tj
Alleluia! Sing To Jesus	Fel	F	Tj
Alleluia! Sing To Jesus	Lor	T	Tj
Alleluia! Tulerunt Dominum	Gsc	T	Sr
Alleluia-Amen	See	L	Lf
Alleluia-Psalm 57	Fel	L	Tt
Alleluia/Amen	Rpb	L	Lf
Alleluia, Alleluia	Her	L	Tt
Alleluia, Alleluia	Gsc	T	Lf
Alleluia, Alleluia (Tone Special 148)	Fel	L	Lf
Alleluia, Alleluia Blessed Be Our Lord	Wlp	L	Tt
Alleluia, Alleluia Your Words O Lord	Wlp	L	Lf
Alleluia, Alleluia!	Zon	L	Tt
Alleluia, Alleluia, Alleluia	Wlp	L	Lf
Alleluia, Alleluia, Alleluia	Fel	L	Lf
Alleluia, Christ Is Risen	Bbl	T	Sr
Alleluia, For Christmas From Cantata	Gsc	T	Sc
Alleluia, I Heard A Voice (Md)	Oxf	T	Tx
Alleluia, Jesus Is King	Rpb	F	Tk
Alleluia, Jesus Lives	Aug	T	Sr
Alleluia, Praise God	Aug	T	Tt
Alleluia, Praise His Name	Vrn	F	Sr
Alleluia, Praise To The Lord	Nal	L	Tt
Alleluia, Rejoice & Sing (Piano +Perc)	Pro	T	Tt
Alleluia, Sing A New Song	Aug	T	Tt
Alleluia, Sing To Jesus	Gia	L	Tj
Alleluia, Sons Of God Arise	Fis	F	Tt
Alleluias (Accompaniment)	Gia	L	Lf
Alleluias (Sixteen)	Nal	L	Lf
Alleluja From Motet Exultate	Gsc	T	Lf
Allelujah Today	Fis	F	Tt
Allons, Gay Bergeres	Gsc	T	Sc
Alma Dei Creatoria K 277	Kal	T	Tr
Alma Redemptoris Mater	Pic	L	Tm
Alma Redemptoris Mater	Gsc	T	Tm
Almighty And Everlasting God	Gsc	L	Tr
Almighty And Everlasting God	Gia	L	Tx
Almighty And Everlasting God	Sac	L	Tr
Almighty And Everlasting God (Me)	Oxf	T	Tt
Almighty Father (From "Mass") (A Cap)	Gsc	L	Tr
Almighty God	Gsc	T	Tt
Almighty God, Unto Whom All Hearts	Abi	L	Lo
Almighty God, Which Has Me Brought(Me)	Oxf	L	Tt
Almighty God, Who By Thy Son (Md)	Oxf	T	Tt
Almighty God, Why By The Leading	Oxf	T	Sc
Almighty Lord And God Of Love (Me)	Oxf	T	Sl
Almighty Word (As By R.V. Williams)	Oxf	T	Sa
Alone (E)	Lor	L	Sr
Alone In The Garden	Lor	L	Sl
Alone In The Still	Pic	L	Tx
Along The Way	Wlp	F	Tx
Altar Of Faith	Csm	G	Tx
Alternate Responses And Te Deum	Aug	L	Za
Always Remembered	Zon	G	Tx
Am I A Soldier Of The Cross?	Zon	T	Tc
Am I A Soldier Of The Cross?	Zon	T	Tc
Am I A Soldier Of The Cross?	Lor	T	Sl
Amanda	Bbl	T	Tf
Amazing Day	Nal	L	Tc
Amazing Grace	Bec	T	Tr
Amazing Grace	Gia	T	Tr
Amazing Grace	Maf	T	Sl
Amazing Grace	Abi	T	Sl
Amazing Grace	Ccc	L	Lo
Amazing Grace	Lor	T	Tr
Amazing Grace	Nal	L	Tr
Amazing Grace	Zon	G	Tr
Amazing Grace	Zon	G	Tr
Amazing Grace (In 19 Rounds)	Gia	T	Tr
Amazing Grace (New Britain Me)	Gam	T	Tr
Amazing Grace Traditional	Zon	T	Tr
Amazing Grace!	Sac	T	Sl
Amen	Wlp	L	Lk
Amen	Snm	L	Lk
Amen	Rpb	L	Lk
Amen	Nal	L	Lk
Amen	Nal	L	Lk
Amen	Lor	G	Lf
Amen	Nal	L	Lk
Amen	Yan	F	Lk
Amen Hallelujah	Zon	G	Tt
Amen! (4-Part Arrangement)	Acp	L	Lk

ALPHABETICAL INDEX OF TITLES

Amen, Alleluia! Nal L Lk
Amen, Amen My Lord (Opt Rhythm) Pro T Tt
Amen, I Say To You Fel L Tr
Amen, Lord Nal L Lk
Amen, Praise The Lord Mar L Tt
America The Beautiful Gra T Tp
America The Beautiful Her T Tp
America The Beautiful Zon T Tp
America The Beautiful Zon G Tp
America, Your Torch Burns Yet Smc T Tp
American Genesis (Reconciliation) Mcc F Sl
American Hymns And Carols Of The 19th Abi T Zb
American Meditations Pic L Tp
American's Creed, The Her T Tp
Amy's Song Rpb F Tx
An Age Had Passed Acp L Sa
An Age Had Passed Acp L Tx
An Angel Came In Unto Mary (Me) Oxf T Tm
An Angel Came To Nazareth Acp L Tm
An Angel Came To Nazareth Acp L Tm
An Angel Offered Incense Fel L Tx
An Angel Speaks To The Shepherds Som L Sc
An Anthem For Communion Lor L Lo
An Anthem Of Faith Gsc T Tr
An Appointed Time Fel F Tx
An Early American Christmas Triptych Aug T Sc
An Easter Carillon (E) Oxf T Sr
An Easter Dialogue (W/Brass, Org) Cfp T Sr
An Easter Processional Hwg L Sr
An Easter Sequence (Eng, Lat) Oxf T Sr
Anamnesis Nal L Tx
Anamnesis Nal L Tx
Ancient Days Zon T Tx
Ancient Of Days Aug T Tx
Ancient Prayer Gsc T Tr
And Abraham Cried Fcc C Tx
And Can It Be? Zon G Sl
And Can It Be? Zon T Sl
And Can It Be? Abi T Sl
And Did Those Feet In Ancient Time Gsc T Tx
And Did'st Thou Love The Race (Me) Oxf L Sl
And God Shall Wipe Away All Tears Gsc T Sr
And Have Not Charity Gsc T Tr
And He Is Mine Man F Tr
And He Showed Me A Pure River Gsc T Sr
And His Mercy (Md) Oxf T Tr
And Holy Is His Name Sil G Sc
And I Will Follow (Psalm 23) Fel F La
And In That Still Small Voice Smc T Zb
And It Shall Come To Pass Aug T Tx
And Lo, The Star Aug T Sc
And Nobody Knows Lor L Tx
And Now Revived He Springs Smc T Zb
And One Bright Star Her L Sc
And Peace Shall Reign Again Lor L Sr
And Rachel Loved Him Fcc C Tx
And Rejoice! Her T Sc
And The Best Is Love Aug T Tr
And The Cock Begins To Crow Prc L Tx
And The Glory Of The Lord Pro T Sc
And The Glory Of The Lord Lor T Sc
And The Glory Of The Lord Cfs T Sc
And The Glory Of The Lord Gsc T Sc
And The Glory Of The Lord Aug T Sa
And The King Was Moved Oxf L Tx
And The Waters Keep On Running Gia L Tm
And The Word Was Made Flesh Van C Sc
And Then It Dawns On Me Nal L Tx
And Then Shall Your Light Gsc T Sr
And There Were Shepherds Lor L Sc
And This Shall Be A Sign Man C Sc
And Thou Shalt Love Abi T Tt
And With His Stripes Cfs T Sl
Andante (From Sonata In A Minor) Smc T Zb
Angel And The Shepherds, The Abi T Sc
Angel's Chorus Gsc T Tt
Angelic Bread Of Heaven Gia T Lo
Angelic Song (First Mass) Fel F Li
Angelic Song (Second Mass) Fel F Li
Angels And Shepherds Zon T Sc
Angels Are Singing Pro T Sc
Angels From The Realms Of Glory Gia T Sc
Angels From The Realms Of Glory Aug T Sc
Angels From The Realms Of Glory- Cfs T Sc
Angels Sang That Christmas Morn Ron T Sc
Angels Shall Keep Thee Wrd G Tr
Angels We Have Heard On High Aug T Sc
Angels We Have Heard On High Acp L Sc
Angels We Have Heard On High Lor T Sc
Angels We Have Heard On High Gsc T Sc
Angels We Have Heard On High Acp L Sc
Angels We Have Heard On High Pro T Sc
Angels We Have Heard On High Zon T Sc
Angels Worship God In Heaven Zon T Tt
Angels, From The Realms Of Glory Zon T Sc
Angelus Ad Pastores Ait Gsc T Sc
Angelus Ad Pastores Ait Gsc T Sc
Angelus Autem Domini Descendit Bbl T Tx
Angus Dei(Lamb Of God) (Deis) Gsc T Lm
Animation Bbl T Tt
Announce His Salvation Day After Day Fel L Tr
Anointed Of God Abi L Sc
Another Love Song Mar L Tr
Answer Man, The Zon G Tx
Answer, The Zon G Tx
Anthem For A Harvest Festival (Me) Oxf T Tt
Anthem For Communion, An Lor T Lo
Anthem For Springtime Abi T Tx
Anthem For Thanksgiving, An Bbl T Tt
Anthem Of Unity Gsc T Tu
Anthems (Ave Maria, O Baptista) Kal T Za
Anthems (Gaude Virgo, Te Deum, Ave) Kal T Za
Anthems For Men's Voices Book Ii Oxf T Za
Anthems For Men's Voices Book 1 Oxf T Za
Anthems For Sab (5867) Zon L Za
Anthems For Special Occasions Abi T Za
Anthems For Treble Voices (14) Oxf T Za
Anthems Of Faith (Collection,Md) Abi T Za
Anthology Of Offertories And Motets Gia T Za
Anthology Of Polyphonic Masters Book 1 Gia T Za
Antiphonal Carol Aug T Sc
Antiphons Rpb L Ld
Antiphons For Holy Week Lit L Sl
Are Not Our Hearts? Nal L Lo
Are Ye Able-Said The Master Lor L Tx
Are You Listening? Mar L Tx
Are You Ready? Mar L Sa
Are You Ready? Hhh G Tt
Are You Willing? Zon G Tc
Aria Da Chiesa Abi L Zb
Aria For Organ Abi L Zb
Arias From Church Cantatas(Sop W/Inst) Kal T Za
Arise And Follow Me Jhe G Tc
Arise My Soul, Arise! Abi L Tt
Arise, Come Sing In The Morning Nal L La
Arise, My Love, My Fair One Aug T Tx
Arise, My Soul, Arise! Zon T Tt
Arise, O Lord Gsc T Sl
Arise, O Lord, And Defend Me Fel L Sl
Arise, O Ye Servants Gsc T Sc
Arise, Oh Ye Servants Of God (Me) Oxf L Tt
Arise, Shine Aug T Tx
Arise, Shine Gsc T Sc
Arise, Shine, For Thy Light Pro T Sc
Arise, Shine, For Thy Light Has Come Aug T Sc
Arise,O Lord, And Help Us Fel L Sl
Arise,Shine! Lor L Sc
Army Of The Lord, The Ham G Tc
Art Thou The Christ Gsc T Tj
As A Child Chd L Tr
As A Child Before The Lord Sha F Tt
As A Doe (Ps 42) Gia F Tb
As A Family Rpb L Tr
As A Heart (Ps 42) (Sic) Smc T Tb
As A Heart Longs (3 Voices) (Sic) Gia T Tb
As A Husband Mar L Tr
As A Rose Among Thorns Fel T Sl
As By The Streams Of Babylon Gsc T Sl
As By The Streams Of Babylon (Acap) Gsc T Sl
As Candles Glow Aug L Tx
As Children Walk Ye In God's Love Gsc T Tc
As Flows The River Gmc G Tb
As For Me And My House Zon T Tc
As Gentle As Silence Ahc L Tt
As I Sat Under A Holly Tree Gsc L Sc
As I Was A-Walking Aug L Tx
As I Watched Beside My Sheep Pro T Sc
As It Began To Dawn Gsc T Sr
As It Began To Dawn Gsc T Sr
As It Began To Dawn (W/Bar Solo) Gsc T Sr
As Joseph Was A-Walking (A Cap) Gsc T Tx
As Lately We Watched Aug T Sc
As Men Of Old Their First Fruits Aug T To
As Only God Above Can Do Man G Tk
As Pants The Hart Gsc T Tb
As Tears Go By Esx F Tt
As The Bridegroom To His Chosen Oxf T Tr
As The Deer Nal L Tr
As The Heart Panteth Sac L Tb
As The Heart Panteth (From Ps 42) Oxf T Tr
As The Hills Are Round About Jerusalem Rpb L Ld
As The Lily Shines Fel T Tm
As The Rain Bec T Tb
As The Sun Acp F Tt
As The Sun (4-Part Arr.) Acp F Tt
As We Gather Nal L La
As We Grow Sil F Lo
As We Leave Prc L Tx
As We Pray Rav L Tr
As We Wait The Lord (Antiphon) Wlp L Tr
As With Gladness Men Of Old Abi T Sc
As With Gladness Men Of Old Zon T Sc
As Ye Sow Sil F Tr
Ascendit, Deus (Md) Oxf T Sr
Ascension Song Fel F Sr
Ascensions Abi L Zb
Ask And It Shall Be Given You Fel L Tr
Ask And It Shall Be Given You Gsc T To
Ask And You Will Receive Ahc L Tt
Ask Not What I Can Do Fel F Tj
Ask What You Will Man G Tr
Ask, And It Shall Be Given You Fis F Tr
Assumpta Est Maria Gsc T Tm
Assumpta Est Maria Kal T Tm
At All Times I Will Bless (Ps 34) Gra L Ld
At Calvary Zon G Sl
At Calvery Lor T Sr
At Jesus' Name Bfi T Tj
At Last We're In The Town Gsc T Sc
At Length There Dawns The Glorious Smc T Tp
At Montserrat Gsc T Tx
At Pentecost Gsc T Ss
At That First Eucharist Acp L Lo
At That First Eucharist (4part Arr.) Acp L Lo
At The Cradle Lor T Sc
At The Feet Of Jesus Her T Tj
At The Foot Of The Cross Gmc G Sl
At The Gospel Gia L Lf
At The Lamb's High Feast (Long)(Brass) Aug L Tk
At The Lamb's High Feast We Sing Acp L Sr
At The Lamb's High Feast We Sing Acp L Sr
At The Name Of Jesus Fel L Tt
At The Name Of Jesus Lor L Tj
At The Name Of Jesus Zon T Tj
At The Name Of Jesus Oxf T Tj
At Thy Feet Our God And Father Gsc L Tr
Athalia (Oratorio) Oxf T Tx
Audivi, Media Nocte (Md) Oxf T Sa
Aus Meiner Suden Tiefe Gsc T Sl
Austrian Shepherd's Carol Aug T Sc
Author Of Light (Md) Oxf L Tx
Autumn Song Ahc L Tt
Avak, The Healer Pic L Tx
Ave Maria Gsc T Tm
Ave Maria Gsc T Tm
Ave Maria Tcp L Tm
Ave Maria Acp L Tm
Ave Maria Rav L Tm
Ave Maria Gsc T Tm
Ave Maria Gia T Tm
Ave Maria Gsc T Tm
Ave Maria Gsc L Tm
Ave Maria Gsc T Tm
Ave Maria Gsc T Tm
Ave Maria Wbp T Tm
Ave Maria Gia T Tm
Ave Maria Nal L Tm
Ave Maria (In 19 Rounds) Gia T Tm
Ave Maria (Lat & Eng) Hof T Tm
Ave Maria (Lat Only)(M) Gia T Tm
Ave Maria (Lat) A Cap Gia T Tm
Ave Maria (Md) Oxf T Tm
Ave Maria (4-Part Arr.) Acp L Tm
Ave Maria, Father To Thee We Pray Gsc T Tm
Ave Maria, Full Of Grace Bbl T Tm
Ave Maria, Gratia Plena Bbl T Tm
Ave Maria, Op.12(Eng-Lat) Cfp T Tm
Ave Maria, Opus 12 (Female) Kal T Tm
Ave Maris Stella Gia T Tm
Ave Maris Stella Ron T Tm
Ave Maris Stella Gia T Tm
Ave Maris Stella Oxf T Tm
Ave Regina Coelorum (E & L) (Me) Gia T Tm
Ave Vera Virginitas Gia T Tc
Ave Verum Gia T Lo
Ave Verum Gia T Lo
Ave Verum Gsc T Lo
Ave Verum (Hail, True Body) Gia T Lo
Ave Verum (Me) Oxf T Lo
Ave Verum Corpus Gsc T Lo
Ave Verum Corpus Bbl T Lo
Ave Verum Corpus K 618 Kal T Lo
Ave Verum(Jesu Word Of God Incarnate) Gsc T Lo
Avina Malkaynu Chanayno Gsc T Tx
Awake And Live, O You Who Sleep Wlp L Tf
Awake Arise Gsc T Sr
Awake My Heart With Gladness (E) Oxf T Sr
Awake Sleeper Gra L Tb
Awake The Harp Gsc T Tt
Awake The Trumpet's Lofty Sound Gsc T Sc
Awake Up My Glory Gsc T Sr
Awake!Do Not Cast Us Off (Ps 44) Oxf T Sl
Awake, Arise, Go Forth And Rejoice Aug T Tt
Awake, Awake, Good People (Solo) Aug L La
Awake, My Glory Abi F Tt
Awake, My Soul Aug T La
Awake, My Soul! Lor L La
Awake, O My Soul Fel L Tt
Awake, Psaltry And Harp Aug T La
Awake, Thou That Sleepest Sac T Tb
Away Chh F Tx
Away In A Manger Zon T Sc
Away In A Manger Pro T Sc
Away In A Manger Aug T Sc
Away In A Manger Lor T Sc
Away In A Manger Gsc T Sc
Away Over In The Gloryland Zon G Sr
Away The Gloom Gsc T Sr
Away They Went With Weeping Wgm L Sl
Ayl Melech Yoshayv Gsc T Tx

Title	Code
Babble Babel	Fcc C Tx
Babe In A Manger	Abi L Sc
Babe In Bethlehem's Manger Laid	Pro T Sc
Babe Is Born, A	Sac T Sc
Babe Is Born, A	Pro T Sc
Babel	Gsc L Tx
Baby In The Cradle Lies (Opt A Cap)	Pro T Sc
Baby Jesu	Pro T Sc
Baby Sitter	Prc L Tx
Babylonian Captivity	Bbl T Sl
Back And Forward	Nal L Tx
Back Home	Mar L Tr
Back To The Prairies	Zon F Tx
Back To The Prairies And Other Country	Zon F Za
Backpacker's Suite(Youth Musical)	Wrd G Za
Balaam	Gra F Tx
Ballad Of The Prodigal Son	Van F Sl
Ballad Of The Seasons	Van F Sl
Ballad Of The Women	Van F Sl
Balm In Gilead	Lor T Tr
Balulalow	Gsc L Sc
Balulalow	Ron T Tt
Band Of Angels	Wbp T Tx
Banner Of The Lord	Mar L Tr
Baptism Prayer	Nal L Tb
Baptismal Acclamation	Chh C Tb
Baptized Into Union With Him	Fel L Tb
Battle Hymn Of The Republic	Wrd G Tp
Battle Hymn Of The Republic	Acp L Tp
Battle Hymn Of The Republic	Lor T Tp
Battle Hymn Of The Republic	Lor T Tp
Be A New Man	Wlp F Tr
Be Anxious Over Nothing	Man G Tr
Be As A Lion	Wbp T Tt
Be Aware	Wlp F Tc
Be Consoled My People	Wlp F Sl
Be Consoled, I Am Near	Nal L Tr
Be Filled With The Spirit	Gph T Ss
Be Filled With The Spirit	Aug T Ss
Be Filled With The Spirit	Nal L Ss
Be Glad	Aug T Tt
Be Glad And Rejoice	Fel L Tt
Be Glad Ye Heavens (Md)	Oxf T Sa
Be Glad, Be Happy	Rpb L Ld
Be Happy Today	Ham C Tr
Be Joyful!	Sac T Tt
Be Joyful, O Earth	Aug T Tx
Be Like The Sun	Ahc L Tx
Be Merciful O Lord (Icet)	Wlp L Ld
Be Merciful Unto Me (Md)	Oxf T Sl
Be Merciful Unto Me, O God	Aug T Sl
Be Not Afraid	Nal L Tr
Be Not Afraid	Gsc T Tr
Be Not Afraid (Motet 4)	Kal T Tr
Be Not Far From Me	Lor L Sl
Be Not Wise In Your Own Eyes	Abi L Tc
Be Of One Mind	Fel L Tr
Be Still	Prc L Tx
Be Still	Chh F Lo
Be Still And Know	Lor L Tr
Be Still My Heart	Zon G Tr
Be Still, My Soul	Bec T Tr
Be Still, My Soul	Zon T Tr
Be Still, My Soul, And Listen	Zon T Tr
Be Strong And Do Not Fear	Fel L Tr
Be Strong For Me	Rpb L Tj
Be Thou Exalted	Pro T Tt
Be Thou Faithful Unto Death	Gsc T Tc
Be Thou My Vision	Abi L Tc
Be Thou My Vision	Aug T Tr
Be Thou My Vision	Zon T Tc
Be With Me Lord (Icet)	Wlp L Ld
Be Ye Glad And Rejoice O Ye Righteous	Gsc T Tt
Be Ye Joyful	Aug T Tr
Be Ye Joyful, Earth And Sky	Aug T Tr
Be Ye Still	Chd F Tr
Be Ye Therefore Followers Of God	Gsc T Tc
Bearded Young Man	Mar L Tj
Beat The Drum	Gia T Sc
Beata Es Virgo	Gsc T Tm
Beatitudes	Fcc F Tr
Beatitudes	Wlp F Tr
Beatitudes	Rpb L Tr
Beatitudes	Van F Tr
Beatitudes, The	Lor L Tr
Beatitudes, The	Wbp L Tr
Beatitudes, The	Abi L Tr
Beatitudes, The	Lor L Tr
Beatitudes, The	Zon L Tr
Beatus Vir	Oxf T Tc
Beautiful City	Hal F Sr
Beautiful Garden Of Prayer, The	Lor L Tr
Beautiful Savior	Aug T Tj
Beautiful Savior	Lor T Tj
Beautiful Savior	Fel T Tj
Beautiful Savior	Lor T Tj
Beautiful Savior (Jr Choir W/Opt Rec)	Pro T Za
Beautiful Valley, The	Bbl T Tx
Beauty Is	Wlp F Tr
Because He Lives	Gmc G Sr
Because He Touched Me	Man T Tj
Because Of Love (W/Piano)	Wrd G Tr
Because Of Your Kindness	Fel L Tr
Because We Are One	Rpb F Tw
Because You Were Good	Fel L Sa
Become To Us The Living Bread	Jsp L Lo
Before Jehovah's Awful Throne	Pro T Tt
Before The Crucifix	Gsc T Sl
Before The Dawn	Lor L Sr
Before The Lord Jehovah's Throne	Abi T Tt
Before The Paling Of The Stars	Gsc T Sc
Before Us, Lord, The Sacrament	Lor L Lo
Begin, My Tongue, Some Heavenly Theme	Zon T Tt
Beginning Today	Fcc F Tw
Behind The Shadows	Man G Sl
Behold A Great Priest	Gra L La
Behold A Great Priest	Gia L La
Behold A Host	Aug T Tx
Behold A Mystical Rose	Wlp T Sc
Behold A Virgin Bearing Him	Wlp T Sa
Behold Among Men	Wlp L Tj
Behold He Bore Our Infirmities	Kal T Sl
Behold Him, The Name Of Whose	Fel L Tj
Behold How Good And How Pleasant	Fel L Tr
Behold How Good And Joyful (Ps 133)	Oxf T Tu
Behold I Stand At The Door	Gia F Ln
Behold Now, The House Of God	Aug L Tk
Behold O God This Lowly Bread	Wlp T To
Behold The Crucified!	Lor L Sl
Behold The Great Priest	Gia L La
Behold The Handmaid Of The Lord	Fel L Tm
Behold The High Priest	Fel L La
Behold The Lamb Of God	Zon T Tj
Behold The Lamb Of God	Gsc T Sl
Behold The Lord (From Come Follow)	Gia F Sc
Behold The Priest Of The Lord	Fel L La
Behold The Royal Cross On High	Wlp T Sl
Behold The Savior Of Mankind	Abi L Sl
Behold The Sorrow Of The Lord	Abi L Sl
Behold The Star!	Lor L Sc
Behold This Child Is Set For The Fall	Cfp T Sl
Behold You Are Charming	Gsc T Tw
Behold Your King Cantata	Zon L Sr
Behold! I Stand At The Door And Knock	Abi L Tj
Behold, A Simple Tender Babe	Gia L Sc
Behold, God Is My Salvation	Aug T Tr
Behold, God Is My Salvation	Hal L Tr
Behold, I Stand At The Door	Gsc T Sa
Behold, I Stand At The Door	Lor L Tj
Behold, I Stand At The Door And Knock	Mar L Tc
Behold, The Bridegroom Comes	Fel L Sj
Behold, The Grace Appears	Bbl T Tj
Behold, The Lord Shall Come	Fel L Sa
Behold, The Lord, The Ruler	Fel L Sc
Behold, The Star!	Fel F Tw
Behold, Thou Art Fair	Gia T Tw
Behold, Thus Art The Man Blessed	Gsc T Sa
Behold, Your God Will Come	Zon G Tj
Beholding Thee, Lord Jesus	Rpb C Ld
Believe	Wlp F Sl
Believe And Repent	Wrd G Tc
Believe In Your Heart	Mam G Tx
Believe Ye	Yan F Tr
Believing	Lor L Tt
Believing Souls, Rejoice And Sing	Prc L Tx
Bell Amen	Oxf T Sr
Bell Carol (Jr + Sr Choirs)	Pro T Sc
Bells Are Ringing (Perc)	Hof T Sc
Bells At Christmas (A Cap)	Maf L Sr
Bells Of Easter, The	Pro T Sc
Bells Of Paradise	Lor L Sr
Bells On Christmas Day, The	Her L Sc
Bells Ring Out Joyfully	Sil F Tr
Beloved	Aug L Tr
Beloved, Let Us Love (Solo)	Zon L Tr
Beloved, Let Us Love One Another	Oxf T Tx
Belshazzar's Feast (Oratorio)	Lor L Sl
Beneath The Cross Of Jesus	Lor L Sl
Beneath The Cross Of Jesus	Abi L Lo
Beneath The Forms Of Outward Rite	Oxf T Tt
Benedicite (Eng)	Oxf T Tt
Benedicite (Md)	Oxf T Tt
Benedicite In G (Md)	Gsc T Tt
Benedicite, Omnia Opera	Gsc T Tt
Benedicite, Omnia Opera Domini	Sac L Tt
Benediction	Smc T Tr
Benediction (From Deuteronomy)	Gsc T Tr
Benediction Avant La Repas. Bon Dieu	Bbl T Tx
Benediction From Sacred Service	Gsc T Li
Benedictus	Gsc T Li
Benedictus	Gsc T Li
Benedictus And Sanctus	Kal T Tt
Benedictus Sit Deus K 117	Gsc T Tt
Benedixisti Domine	Gsc T Tx
Berlin (Moore) (Acap)	Lor L Tr
Beside The Still Waters	Zon G Tr
Beside The Still Waters	Nal L Sr
Best Is Yet To Come, The	Cfp T Sr
Bethlehem	Lcr T Sc
Bethlehem Carol	Pro T Sc
Bethlehem Isn't Very Far	Mmc G Tx
Bethlehem Road	Gsc T Sc
Bethlehem Star, The	Lor L Sc
Bethlehem Star, The	Pro T Sc
Bethlehem Town	Gsc L Sc
Bethlehem,Galilee,Gethsemane	Gmc G Tj
Better Start Believin'	Mam G Tx
Between The Cross And Heaven	Gmc G Sl
Beulah Land	Zon G Sr
Beyond A Dream	Yan F Tx
Beyond The Cross	Man G Sl
Beyond The Wheeling Worlds Of Light	Lor L Tx
Beyond This Place	Man G Lo
Beyond Tomorrow	Zon G Sr
Biblical Litany To Our Lady	Wlp L Tm
Bid Me Come	Sbf L Tc
Big City Blues	Mar L Sl
Bird In A Golden Sky	Mar L Tx
Birth (From 'he Lived The Good Life')	Aug T Tb
Birth Of The King	Sav G Sc
Birthday Of A King, The	Lor T Sc
Birthday Of The King, The	Zon T Sc
Birthday Song	Wlp C Tx
Black But Proud	Sto G Tx
Bless Now O Lord	Gsc T Tt
Bless The Lord	Fel F Tt
Bless The Lord	Fel L Tt
Bless The Lord	Wlp G Le
Bless The Lord (4-Part Arrangement)	Acp L Tt
Bless The Lord, Bless The Lord	Fel L Tt
Bless The Lord, O My Soul	Bec T Tt
Bless The Lord, O My Soul	Fel L Tt
Bless The Lord, O My Soul	Gsc L Tt
Bless The Lord, O My Soul	Gia T Tt
Bless The Lord, O My Soul	Wlp T Tt
Bless The Lord, O My Soul	Fel F Tt
Bless The Lord, O My Soul	Zon L Tt
Bless The Lord, O My Soul	Sac L Tt
Bless The Lord, O My Soul (A Cap)	Hof T Tt
Bless The Lord, O My Soul (Md)	Oxf T Tt
Bless The Lord, O My Soul (Me)	Oxf T Tt
Bless The Lord, O My Soul (Med Voice)	Abi L Tt
Bless This House, O Lord	Fel L Tx
Bless Thou The Lord	Aug L Tt
Bless Thou The Lord (Ps 103)	Gia T Tt
Bless Us Mighty Father	Vrn L To
Bless Us, God Of Loving (Solo)	Aug L Tr
Bless Ye The Lord (D)	Abi L Tt
Bless You	Abm G Tx
Bless, O Lord, These Rings	Gia L Tw
Blessed Are The Faithful	Smc T Lo
Blessed Are The Merciful	Gsc T Tr
Blessed Are The Pure In Heart (Unacc)	Abi L Tr
Blessed Are They	Gsc T Tr
Blessed Are They	Sac T Tr
Blessed Are They Who Hear	Fel L Tr
Blessed Are Those	Wlp F Tr
Blessed Are Those Servants	Fel L Tx
Blessed Are Those Who Believe	Gsc T Tr
Blessed Are You	Nal L Tt
Blessed Are You	Nal L Tt
Blessed Are You Among Women	Fel L Tm
Blessed Art Thou	Som L Tt
Blessed Art Thou, O Lord (Md)	Oxf T Tt
Blessed Assurance	Lor T Tj
Blessed Assurance	Zon G Tj
Blessed Assurance	Lor T Tj
Blessed Assurance (Arrangement O.)	Mam T Tj
Blessed Assurance, Jesus Is Mine	Lor T Tj
Blessed Be God	Wlp L Tt
Blessed Be God	Rpb L Tt
Blessed Be God	Nal L Tt
Blessed Be God Forever	Nal L Tt
Blessed Be God; He Gives Power	Fel L Tt
Blessed Be Our Lord The God Of Israel	Wlp L Tt
Blessed Be The Day	Mar L Sr
Blessed Be The Holy Trinity	Fel L Tt
Blessed Be The Lord	Nal L Tt
Blessed Be The Lord	Gsc T Tt
Blessed Be The Lord	Acp L Tt
Blessed Be The Lord Forever	Wlp L Tt
Blessed Be The Lord, The God Of Israel	Fel L Tt
Blessed Be The Name Of The Lord	Rpb L Tt
Blessed Be The Name Of The Lord	Fel L Tt
Blessed Be The Name Of The Lord	Gsc L Tt
Blessed Be These Moments	Yan F Tr
Blessed Be You Lord God	Nal L Tt
Blessed Calvary	Zon G Sl
Blessed Father Great And Good	Csm G Tt
Blessed He(From The Beatitudes)	Gsc T Tr
Blessed Hope, The	Zon L Tr
Blessed Is Everyone That Feareth	Bbl T Tr
Blessed Is He That Comes	Sac L Sl
Blessed Is He That Cometh	Smc T Sl
Blessed Is He Who Cometh	Gsc T Lt
Blessed Is She Who Has Believed	Fel L Tm
Blessed Is The Man	Abi L Tr
Blessed Is The Man	Wgm L Lp
Blessed Is The Man (A Cap)	Gsc T Tr

ALPHABETICAL INDEX OF TITLES

Blessed Is The Man Who Has Endured	Fel	L Sl
Blessed Is The Nation	Fel	L Tp
Blessed Is The Woman Who Fears	Fel	L Tr
Blessed Jesu	Gsc	T Tj
Blessed Jesus	Gmc	G Tj
Blessed Jesus, At Thy Word	Gia	T Tj
Blessed Quietness	Zon	F Tr
Blessed Redeemer	Zon	G Tj
Blessed Redeemer	Lor	T Tj
Blessed Rest (Cantata)	Lps	T Tf
Blessed Sacrament, The	Fcc	F Lo
Blessed Saviour, Our Lord Jesus	Gsc	T Tj
Blessed The Faithful	Gsc	T Tx
Blessing	Ahc	L Tt
Blessing	Rpb	L Tw
Blessing (Thanksgiving Or Gen)	Gsc	T Tt
Blessing And Honor	Gsc	T Tt
Blessing And Honor, Praise And Love	Gia	T Tt
Blessing For Easter Morning, A	Sac	T Sr
Blessing Of St. Francis	Fcc	F Tr
Blessing Of The Trinity	Gsc	T Tt
Blessing Over Water	Cfc	L Tt
Blessings On The King	Rav	L Tk
Blessings On The King	Nal	L Tk
Blest Are The Pure In Heart	Gsc	T Tr
Blest Are The Pure In Heart	Lor	L Tc
Blest Be The Name Of The Lord	Fel	L Tt
Blest By The Hand Of The Lord	Rpb	L Tr
Blest Is The Man Who Finds Wisdom	Fel	T Tr
Blest Is The Man Who In Wisdom Shall	Fel	T Tc
Blood	Prc	L Tx
Blood Upon Your Hands	Ham	G Sl
Blow Ye The Trumpet	Abi	L Tt
Blow Ye The Trumpet Blow	Abi	L Tr
Blow Ye The Trumpet In Zion	Oxf	T Tt
Blow, Wind (W/Guitar)	Gia	F Ss
Blow, Winds, O Softly Blow (Trad)	Gsc	T Sc
Blow, Ye Winds, Softly	Lor	T Sc
Blowin' In The Wind	Wbp	F Tt
Blue Town	Fcc	F Tx
Bobbi's Song	Mar	L Tx
Boldly Let Us Come With Confidence	Fel	L La
Bonum Est Confiteri	Gsc	T Tt
Born A King	Abi	L Sc
Born A King	Zon	T Sc
Born A King (Cantata)	Zon	L Sc
Born Again	Prc	L Tx
Born Again	Wbp	T Tb
Born Again	Man	F Tb
Born Again	Jsp	F Tb
Born Again	Wlp	F Tb
Born In A Manger	Lor	L Sc
Born In A Manger (Gaelic Melody)	Lor	T Sc
Born In A Stable	Sac	L Sc
Born King Of Kings (E & Lat) (A Cap)	Pro	T Sc
Born To Be Crucified	Gmc	G Tj
Born To Die	Fel	F Sl
Born To Live And Die	Nal	L Tc
Born Today	Som	T Sc
Born Today	Lor	T Sc
Both Sides Now	Siq	F Tf
Bound For Canaan	Zon	G Sr
Bound For Canaan's Land	Wbp	T Tx
Boundless Mercy Traditional (Acap)	Gsc	T Sl
Bow Down Thine Ear	Gsc	T Tr
Bow Down Thine Ear	Gsc	T Tr
Bow Down Thine Ear, O Lord (Md)	Oxf	T Sl
Bow My Head, O Lord	Gsc	L Sl
Bow Thine Ear, O Lord (Md)	Oxf	T Sl
Branch Of Promise, The	Pro	T Sc
Branded By Jesus	Gmp	G Tc
Brass Ensemble Packet No 1 (No 5441)	Zon	G Zb
Brass Ensemble Packet No 2 (No 5442)	Zon	G Zb
Brass Ensemble Packet No 3 (No 5443)	Zon	G Zb
Brass Sounds Of Christmas	Gia	T Zb
Bread Of Heaven	Lor	L Lo
Bread Of Life	Lor	L Lo
Bread Of Life, The	Abi	L Lo
Bread Of Presence	Ccc	L Lo
Bread Of Tears	Aug	T Sl
Bread Of The World	Abi	L Lo
Bread Of The World	Abi	L Lo
Bread Of The World (10 Chorales)	Gia	T Za
Bread That's Cast Upon The Water	Man	G To
Bread To The Hungry	Rpb	L Lo
Bread You Have Given Us	Wlp	F Lo
Break Forth Into Joy	Sac	T Tt
Break Forth Into Joy	Gsc	T Tt
Break Forth Into Joy	Lor	L Sc
Break Forth Into Joy	Gsc	T Sc
Break Forth Into Joy	Gsc	T Tt
Break Forth O Beauteous Heavenly Light	Aug	T Sc
Break Forth O Beauteous Heavenly Light	Gsc	T Sc
Break Loose (W/Guitar)	Gia	F Tr
Break On Through	Wlp	F Tc
Break Open (A Choir In The Dawn)	Gia	F Sc
Break Thou The Bread Of Life	Smc	T Lo
Breakthrough (Musical) (No 4510)	Zon	L Za
Breast The Wave, Christian	Gsc	T Tc
Breath Of God	Aug	T Ss

Breathe On Me Breath Of God	Lor	T Ss
Breathe On Me, Breath Of God	Lor	T Tr
Breathe On Me, Breath Of God	Wbp	T Ss
Brethren, We Have Met To Worship	Zon	T La
Brevity	Bbl	T Tf
Bright & Glorious Is The Sky	Aug	L Sr
Bright & Joyful Is The Morn (Opt 2 Tpt	Pro	T Sc
Bright 'n' Shiny	Ham	C Tr
Brighten My Soul With Sunshine	Hal	L Tx
Brightest And Best	Gsc	T Sc
Brightest And Best	Pro	T Sc
Bring A Little Sunshine	Fel	L Tx
Bring A Torch, Jeannette	Pro	T Sc
Bring A Torch, Jeannette Isabella	Sac	T Sc
Bring A Torch, Jeannette...Acap	Wlp	T Sc
Bring Back The King	Man	G Tk
Bring Costly Offerings	Gsc	T To
Bring Forth Abundant Fruit	Fel	L Tx
Bring On	Wlp	F Sl
Bring To The Lord	Acp	F To
Bring To The Lord (4-Part Arr.)	Acp	F To
Bring Your Torches	Gsc	T Sc
Bringing Back The King	Zon	G Tk
Bringing Freedom	Van	C Tx
Bringing In The Sheaves	Zon	G Tc
British Children's Prayer	Gsc	C Tr
Brother James's Air (Me)	Oxf	T Tx
Brother Jesus	Nal	L Tj
Brother Jesus, I Am Small	Fel	C Tj
Brother John	Mil	F Tt
Brother, Brother	Nal	L Tr
Brother, Brother Mine	Fcc	F Tr
Brother, Watch The Light	Sil	L Tr
Brotherhood	Rpb	C Tr
Brothers All	Fcc	C Tr
Build A Little Fence Of Trust	Aug	T Tr
Build Thee More Stately Mansions	Gsc	T Tr
Build Thee More Stately Mansions	Hal	L Tx
Build Up The City Of Man	Nal	L Tr
Built On A Rock	Aug	T Tr
Built On A Rock	Lor	T Tr
Built On A Rock	Aug	T Tr
Built On A Rock	Zon	T Tr
Built On A Rock (W/Brass,Org)	Aug	L Tr
Built On A Rock The Church Doth Stand	Aug	L Tr
Built On A Rock The Church Doth Stand	Pro	T Tr
Built On A Rock The Church Doth Stand	Aug	T Tr
Built On The Rock	Abi	L Tr
Built On The Rock (E)	Oxf	T Tc
Bunker Hill	Bbl	T Tx
Burdens Are Lifted At Calvary	Zon	G Sl
Burdens Are Lifted At Calvary	Zon	G Za
Burst My Dreams	Ahc	L Tc
Burst Of Christ	Ccc	L Sc
Bus Sing (No 5135)	Zon	G Za
Bushel-Round	Wlp	F Tx
Busy Day	Van	C To
But As For Me, God Forbid(Gal 6:14)	Gia	F Sl
But For The Grace Of God	Ham	G Sl
But I Do Know	Man	G Tx
But I Have Trusted In Thy Mercy	Coo	T Tr
But I,When They Were Ill	Fel	L Tr
But Now Is Christ Risen	Zon	L Sr
But Our God Abideth In Heaven	Gsc	T Tk
But The Lord Is Mindful Of His Own	Gsc	T Tr
But Then Comes The Morning	Wlp	F Sr
Butterfly Song	Pnp	C Sr
By Babylon's Wave	Gsc	T Sl
By Faith We Can Know	Man	G Tr
By Grace	Man	G Sl
By My Side	Val	F Tt
By Springs Of Water	Aug	L Tb
By The Babylonian Rivers	Gsc	L Sl
By The Grace Of God	Urs	F Tr
By The Manger	Tcp	L Sc
By The River Of Babylon (E & L)	Gia	T Sl
By The Rivers Of Babylon	Fel	L Sl
By The Shores Of The Jordan	Som	L Sa
By The Streams Of Babylon	Gia	F Sl
By The Streams Of Babylon	Wlp	L Sl
By The Streams Of Babylon	Fel	F Sl
By The Waters Of Babylon	Bbl	T Sl
By The Waters Of Babylon	Bbl	T Sl
By The Waters Of Babylon (Piano)	Wlp	L Sl
By The Waters Of Babylon (3voices)	Gia	T Sl
By The Witness Of The Spirit	Gmc	G Ss
By The Wood Of The Cross	Fel	L Sl
By Their Fruit Shall Ye Know	Gia	F Tc
By Their Fruits Ye Shall Know Them	Gia	T Tc
By This Shall All Men Know	Fel	L Tr
By This We Died With Christ	Fel	L Tb
By Your Blood You Redeemed Us	Fel	L Tj
Caecilliam Cantata	Kal	T Tx
Caligarerunt Oculi Mei	Gsc	T Sl
Call His Name	Sav	F Tj
Call His Name Jesus	Lor	L Sc
Call On Jesus	Sem	G Tj
Call To Remembrance (Md)	Oxf	T Sl
Call To Worship (No 5027)	Zon	L Lp
Call Upon The Name	Mar	L Tr

Call, The	Sac	L Tc
Called	Nal	L Tc
Calling (With Brass Acc)	Zon	G Tx
Calm Assurance	Gmc	G Tr
Calm On The List'ning Ear Of Night	Gsc	T Sc
Calm On The Listening Ear	Pro	T Sc
Calvary	Zon	G Sl
Calvary	Gmc	G Sl
Calvary	Lor	T Sl
Calvary	Gsc	T Sl
Calvary	Gsc	G Sl
Calvary Love	Zon	G Sl
Calvary's Mountain	Aug	T Sl
Can I Have This Happiness	Man	G Tx
Can I Say	Mam	G Tx
Can I Show You	Chd	F Tx
Can It Be	Pmp	G Tx
Can It Be?	Mar	L Tx
Can We Be Identified	Pmp	G Tx
Can You Believe?	Jhe	G Tx
Can You Feel Him	Chd	F Tj
Can't Find The Time	Wrd	G Tc
Can't Take It With You	Ccc	L Zb
Can't Work Your Way To Heaven	Mar	L Sl
Can't You Hear?	Lor	T Tt
Canaan	Bbl	T Tt
Canaan's Land	Mar	L Tx
Canon Alleluia (From Motet Exultate)	Pro	T Tt
Cantabo Domino	Gsc	T Tt
Cantares De Pascua	Pic	L Sr
Cantata	Som	L Za
Cantata #1 Wie Schoen (Eng/Germ)	Kal	T Za
Cantata #104 Thou Guide (E & Germ)	Kal	T Tr
Cantata #106 God's Time Is Best (E&G)	Kal	T Sc
Cantata #11 Lobet Gott (Eng/Germ)	Kal	T Tt
Cantata #112 Der Herr (E & Germ)	Kal	T Tk
Cantata #115 Mache Dich (E & Germ)	Kal	T Za
Cantata #118 O Jesus Christ (E & Germ)	Kal	T Tj
Cantata #12 Weping (Eng/Germ)	Kal	T Sl
Cantata #140 Sleepers Awake (E & Ger)	Kal	T Sa
Cantata #142 To Us A Child Is Born	Kal	T Sc
Cantata #150 Nach Dir (Eng & Germ)	Kal	T Za
Cantata #151 Suesser Tod (Eng & Germ)	Kal	T Tf
Cantata #169 Gott Soll (Eng & Germ)	Kal	T Za
Cantata #180 Schmuecke Dich(Eng & Ger)	Kal	T Tk
Cantata #190 Sing To The Lord(E & Ger)	Kal	T Tt
Cantata #195 Wedding Cantata (E & Ger)	Kal	T Tw
Cantata #198 Trauermusik (Eng & Germ)	Kal	T Za
Cantata #21 My Spirit (Eng/Germ)	Kal	T Za
Cantata #25 Es Ist Nichts (Eng/Germ)	Kal	T Za
Cantata #26 Ach Wie Flueschtig	Kal	T Sl
Cantata #27 Wer Weiss (Eng/Germ)	Kal	T Za
Cantata #28 Gottlob (Eng/Germ)	Kal	T Tt
Cantata #31 The Heaven's Laugh (E&Germ	Kal	T Za
Cantata #33 Allein Zu Dir (Eng/Germ)	Kal	T Za
Cantata #34 O Ewiges Feuer (Eng/Germ)	Kal	T Za
Cantata #38 Aus Tiefer Not (Eng/Germ)	Kal	T Za
Cantata #4 Christ Lag (Eng/Germ)	Kal	T Sl
Cantata #41 Jesu Nun (Eng/Germ)	Kal	T Tj
Cantata #43 Gott Faehret (Eng/Germ)	Kal	T Za
Cantata #45 Es Ist Gesagt (Eng/Germ)	Kal	T Za
Cantata #50 Nun Ist (Eng/Germ)	Kal	T Za
Cantata #54 Widerstehe (Eng/Germ)	Kal	T Za
Cantata #55 Ich Armer Mensch (E & Ger)	Kal	T Za
Cantata #56 (E & Germ)	Kal	T Za
Cantata #6 Bide With Us (Eng/Germ)	Kal	T Za
Cantata #61 Nun Komm (E & Germ)	Kal	T Sa
Cantata #64 Sehet (E & Germ)	Kal	T Za
Cantata #65 Sie Merden (E & Germ)	Kal	T Za
Cantata #68 Also Hat (E & Germ)	Kal	T Za
Cantata #70 Wachet, Betet (E & Germ)	Kal	T Za
Cantata #71 Gott Ist (E & Germ)	Kal	T Za
Cantata #79 The Lord Is A Sun(E & Ger)	Kal	T Tt
Cantata #8 Liebster Gott (Eng/Germ)	Kal	T Za
Cantata #80 A Stronghold Sure (E&Germ)	Kal	T Tr
Cantata #81 Jesus Schlaeft (E & Ger)	Kal	T Tj
Cantata #82 Ich Hab Genug (Germ)	Kal	T Za
Cantata De Semana Santa	Pic	L Sl
Cantata For Easter	Oxf	T Sr
Cantata Of Peace W/Tpt	Abi	L Tr
Cantate Domini (Psalm 96)	Kal	T Tt
Cantate Domino	Bec	T Tt
Cantate Domino	Gsc	T Tt
Cantate Domino	Gia	T Tt
Cantate Domino	Smc	T Zb
Cantate Domino	Gsc	T Tt
Cantate Domino	Gsc	T Tt
Cantate Domino (L & E) A Cap	Wlp	L Tt
Cantate Domino (O Sing Unto The Lord)	Gsc	T Tt
Cantate Domino (Ps 149)	Oxf	T Tt
Cantate, Domini Canticum Novum	Kal	T Tt
Canticle	Mar	L Tx
Canticle For Easter, A	Sac	L Sr
Canticle Of Christmas	Her	T Sc
Canticle Of Judith	Fel	F Tt
Canticle Of Love, A	Lor	T Tr
Canticle Of Mary	Gsc	T Tt
Canticle Of Mary, Magnificat	Sbf	L Tt
Canticle Of Praise	Zon	L Tt
Canticle Of Praise, A	Lor	T Tt

ALPHABETICAL INDEX OF TITLES

Canticle Of The Gift (4-Part Arr.)	Acp	F	Sr
Canticle Of The Gift(Version 1)	Acp	F	Tj
Canticle Of The Gift(Version 2)	Acp	F	Tj
Canticle Of The Sun	Fcc	F	Tt
Canticle Of The Three Children	Wlp	L	Tt
Canticle Of The Three Young Men(Ver 1)	Acp	F	Tt
Canticle Of The Three Young Men(Ver 2)	Acp	F	Tt
Canticle 1	See	L	Tx
Canticles Of Christmas (Cantata)	Gam	L	Sc
Canticos De Gozo E Inspiracion	Zon	G	Za
Canticum Gaudii (W/Brass, Org)	Cfp	T	Sr
Cantiones Quatuor Vocum (2 Volumes)	Kal	T	Za
Cantiones Quinque Vocum	Kal	T	Za
Cantiones Sacrea: Heu Mihi Domine	Kal	T	Sl
Cantiones Sacrea: In Te Domine	Kal	T	Tr
Cantiones Sex Vocum (Peter & Paul)	Kal	T	Za
Cantiones Trium Vocum	Kal	T	Za
Cantique De Jean Racine	Bbl	T	Tt
Cantique De Noel	Lor	T	Sc
Cantique De Noel	Gsc	T	Sc
Cantique De Noel(O Holy Night)	Gsc	T	Sc
Cantos De Evangelismo	Zon	G	Za
Capernaum Comes Alive	Fis	F	Tj
Care Is All It Takes	Wlp	F	Tr
Careworn Mother Stood Attending	Gia	T	Sl
Carol Fantasy	Bec	T	Sc
Carol For Children, A	Her	L	Sc
Carol For Eastertide, A	Lor	T	Sr
Carol For Epiphany	Aug	T	Sc
Carol For Pentecost	Aug	T	Ss
Carol For The Christ-Child, A	Lor	L	Sc
Carol Of A Rose	Gsc	T	Sc
Carol Of Beauty (Md)	Oxf	T	Tt
Carol Of Christmas (No 5969)	Zon	L	Sc
Carol Of Christmas (No 5999)	Zon	L	Sc
Carol Of Christmas (No 6011)	Zon	L	Sc
Carol Of Joy (Aleria)	Aug	T	Sc
Carol Of Polish Grenadiers	Cfs	T	Sc
Carol Of Praise, A	Zon	T	Sc
Carol Of The Advent	Abi	T	Sc
Carol Of The Angels (Sop Soli)	Pro	T	Sc
Carol Of The Bagpipers	Zon	T	Sc
Carol Of The Bells	Lor	T	Sc
Carol Of The Bells	Lor	L	Sc
Carol Of The Bells (A Capella)	Cfs	T	Sc
Carol Of The Birds	Gsc	T	Sc
Carol Of The Gifts (In 5 Carols) E	Gia	L	Sc
Carol Of The Questioning Child	Gsc	L	Sc
Carol Of The Roses	Gsc	L	Sc
Carol Of The Russian Children	Gsc	T	Sc
Carol Of The Three Kings	Pro	T	Sc
Carol Of The Tree	Lor	L	Sc
Carol Of The Trees	Sac	L	Sc
Carol Of The Visitation	Gia	T	Sc
Carol Ye	Lor	L	Sc
Carol-Noel (A Capella)	Cfs	T	Sc
Carolina, Coming Home	Sil	F	Tx
Carols And Songs For Christmas	Bos	T	Sc
Carols For Christmas (Ssa)	Abi	T	Sc
Carols For Christmastide	Gia	L	Sc
Carols From Many Lands	Lor	T	Sc
Carols Of Christmas	Lor	L	Sc
Carried Away	Man	G	Tx
Carry Me Along	Mar	L	Tr
Carry On	Jhe	G	Tx
Cast Into The Deep	Gra	F	Tc
Cast Thy Burden Upon The Lord	Gsc	T	Tr
Cast Thy Burden Upon The Lord	Gra	T	Tr
Cast Your Care Upon The Lord	Fel	L	Tr
Catch A Little Sunshine	Fcc	F	Tt
Cathedral Chorus Marching Guitar Choir	Nal	L	Za
Cause Me To Come	Mar	L	Tc
Celebrate	Nal	L	Tr
Celebrate	Zon	F	Tt
Celebrate God	Nal	C	Tr
Celebrate Life	Van	C	Tr
Celebrate Life	Wlp	F	Tt
Celebration	Gsc	T	Tr
Celebration	Som	L	Tx
Celebration (Timmy's Song)	Rpb	F	Tr
Celebration Songs (No 4360)	Zon	G	Za
Celebration Songs For Choir (No 5858)	Zon	L	Za
Celestial Country	Pic	L	Sr
Celestial Visitor The	Lor	L	Sc
Centurion's Song	Sil	F	Le
Certainly	Man	G	Tc
Chandos Anthem 1 (Be Joyful)	Kal	T	Tt
Chandos Anthem 2 (In The Lord I Put)	Kal	T	Tr
Chandos Anthem 3 (Have Mercy On Me)	Kal	T	Sl
Chandos Te Deum (We Praise Thee)	Kal	T	Tt
Change It	Man	L	Tr
Channels Only	Zon	T	Tr
Chanson Des Anges	Gsc	T	Sc
Chanson Joyeuse Do Noel	Gsc	T	Sc
Chapel In The Hollow	Csm	G	Tx
Chapel Organist No 1 (No 5820)	Zon	G	Zb
Chapel Organist No 2 (No 5823)	Zon	G	Zb
Chapel Organist No 3 (No 5825)	Zon	G	Zb
Chariot Of Clouds	Zon	G	Sr
Chariots Of Clouds	Ahc	C	Sa

Charity	Mar	L	Tr
Charlotte's Song	Wlp	F	Tx
Cherry Tree Carol (Drama)	Aug	L	Sc
Cherub Choir No 1 (No 5030)	Zon	C	Za
Cherub Choir No 2 (No 5031)	Zon	C	Za
Cherub Choir No 3 (No 5032)	Zon	C	Za
Cherubim Song	Gsc	T	Tt
Cherubim Song (A Cap)	Hof	T	Tt
Cherubim-Song	Gsc	T	Tt
Chichester Psalms(First Movement)	Gsc	L	Tt
Child Of Bethlehem, The	Abi	L	Sc
Child Of Bethlehem, The	Maf	T	Sc
Child Of Bethlehem, The	Lor	L	Sc
Child Of God	Lor	L	Tb
Child Of Heaven	Lor	L	Sc
Child Of Hope, A	Lor	L	Sc
Child Of Morning	Van	F	Sc
Child Of The King, A	Zon	G	Tc
Child This Day Is Born, A	Lor	L	Sc
Child Was Born, A	Acp	L	Sc
Child Was Born, A	Acp	L	Sc
Child, The	Ccc	L	Tb
Child's Evening Prayer (M)	Oxf	C	Tr
Childhood Of Christ (Germ,Eng,Fr)	Kal	T	Tj
Children Gather Round	Sil	F	La
Children Of Light	Wlp	F	Tr
Children Of Sunlight	Nal	L	Tr
Children Of The Day	Chd	F	Tt
Children Of The Eighth Day	Nal	L	Sr
Children Of The Heavenly Father	Aug	T	Tr
Children Of The Heavenly Father	Aug	T	Tr
Children Of The Heavenly Father	Abi	C	Tt
Children Of The Heavenly Father	Zon	T	Tr
Children Of The King	Gam	C	Tk
Children Of The Lord	Nal	C	Tr
Children Of The Lord	Van	F	Tx
Children's Blessing	Gsc	C	Tr
Children's Hosanna, The	Lor	L	Sr
Children's Hymn Of Praise, The	Lor	L	Tt
Children's Hymnary, The	Flp	T	Za
Children's Prayer	Pro	C	Tr
Children's Prayer	Som	C	Tx
Children's Prayer	Aug	C	Tr
Children's Unison Choir No 1 (No 5793)	Zon	G	Za
Children's Unison Choir No 2 (No 5798)	Zon	G	Za
Children's Unison Choir No 3 (No 5800)	Zon	G	Za
Children's Unison Choir No 4 (No 5893)	Zon	G	Za
Children's Voices Joyfully Sing	Aug	C	Tt
Chimes Of The Holy Night	Lor	L	Sc
Choices	Rav	F	Tx
Choir Favorites No 1 (No 5101)	Zon	T	Za
Choir Favorites No 2 (No 5102)	Zon	T	Za
Choir Favorites No 3 (No 5103)	Zon	T	Za
Choir Favorites No 4 (No 5104)	Zon	T	Za
Choir Favorites No 5 (No 5105)	Zon	T	Za
Choir Favorites No 6 (No 5106)	Zon	T	Za
Choir Of Bethlehem, The	Lor	L	Sc
Choir Specials (No 5592)	Zon	G	Za
Choose Life	Nal	L	Tr
Choose Life	Fel	G	Tx
Choosing Rather	Man	G	Tx
Choral Benedictions	Abi	L	Tx
Choral Benedictions	Aug	T	Tx
Choral Diptych (A Cap)	Pro	L	Tx
Choral Fanfare On "Holy, Holy, Holy"	Lor	L	Li
Choral Mass (1970) Cong Ad Lib	Gia	L	Za
Choral Prayers And Responses	Lor	L	Za
Choral Responses For Christmas	Lor	L	Za
Choral Responses For Easter	Lor	L	Za
Choral Service For Thanksgiving, A	Lor	L	Tt
Choral Service For Watch Night, A	Lor	L	Za
Choral Stylings (No Zd-5473)	Zon	G	Tj
Choral Var On "Ah Holy Jesus" (Cruger)	Oxf	T	Sl
Chorale	Som	L	Tx
Chorale & Var. On Now Thank We	Smc	T	Zb
Chorale And Fugue On Lasst Uns	Abi	L	Zb
Chorale Concertato On Praise The Lord	Con	T	Tt
Chorale Prelude Arr For Brass	Smc	T	Zb
Chorale Prelude In E Minor	Smc	T	Zb
Chorale Prelude On Angelus (Mod)	Abi	L	Zb
Chorale Prelude On Bedford	Abi	T	Zb
Chorale Prelude On Bremen (Mod Diff)	Abi	L	Zb
Chorale Prelude On Ein Feste Burg	Abi	L	Zb
Chorale Prelude On Jesu Du, Du Bist	Abi	T	Zb
Chorale Prelude On O Trinity	Abi	L	Zb
Chorale Prelude, "Wachet Auf"	Maf	T	Zb
Chorale-Prelude On "Bedford"	Abi	T	Zb
Chorales	Lps	T	Za
Chorales	Gsc	T	Za
Chorales From The Christmas Oratorio	Gsc	T	Sc
Choreographic Cantata (W/Perc,Org)	Aug	L	Za
Chorus In The Skies, The	Lor	L	Sc
Chorus Of Angels	Gsc	T	Sr
Chorus Of The Angels	Gsc	T	Sc
Choruses From The Messiah (No 5955)	Zon	T	Za
Christ Arose (Easy)	Zon	L	Sr
Christ Arose (W/Piano)	Wrd	G	Sr
Christ Arose!	Lor	L	Sr
Christ Became Obedient (E) (Holy Wk)	Gra	L	Lg
Christ Became Obedient (Me)	Gia	T	Sl

Christ Became Obedient For Us	Gia	T	Sl
Christ Being Raised From The Dead	Oxf	L	Sr
Christ Child Is Born (Opt Orch Bells)	Pro	L	Sc
Christ Died For Our Sins	Nal	L	Sl
Christ Has Died	Gra	L	Lj
Christ Has Died	Acp	L	Lj
Christ Has Died (Acclamation)	Nal	L	Lj
Christ Has Died (Acclamation)	Nal	L	Lj
Christ Has Died (Icet)	Wlp	L	Lj
Christ Has Died (Icet)	Wlp	L	Lj
Christ Has Died (Icet)	Wlp	L	Lj
Christ Has Died (Icet) Ascap	Wlp	L	Lj
Christ Has Died (1 & 2)	Wlp	F	Lj
Christ Has Died #1	Chh	F	Lj
Christ Has Died #2	Chh	F	Lj
Christ Has Risen	Acp	L	Sr
Christ Has Risen (Choral)	Fel	T	Sr
Christ Has Risen From The Dead	Acp	L	Sr
Christ Has Risen From The Dead	Acp	L	Sr
Christ Hath A Garden	Gsc	T	Tj
Christ Hath Arisen	Gsc	T	Sr
Christ Hath Triumphed, Alleluia!	Lor	L	Sr
Christ In Me	Mar	L	Tj
Christ Is Arisen	Gsc	T	Sr
Christ Is Arisen (E & Ger)	Gia	T	Sr
Christ Is Arisen!	Abi	T	Sr
Christ Is Born	Lor	C	Sc
Christ Is Born	Pro	T	Sc
Christ Is Born	Her	L	Sc
Christ Is Born	Lor	L	Sc
Christ Is Born (No 4451)	Zon	L	Sc
Christ Is Born Of Maiden Fair	Gsc	T	Sc
Christ Is Born!	Lor	L	Sc
Christ Is King	Van	F	Tk
Christ Is Lord	Acp	F	Tk
Christ Is Made The Sure Foundation	Aug	T	Tj
Christ Is Made The Sure Foundation	Abi	T	Tj
Christ Is Made The Sure Foundation	Gsc	T	Tj
Christ Is My Rock	Van	F	Tj
Christ Is Near	Fel	F	Tr
Christ Is Our Leader	Acp	L	Tk
Christ Is Our Leader (4-Part Arr.)	Acp	L	Tj
Christ Is Our Peace (Hymn)	Jsp	L	Tr
Christ Is Risen	Lor	L	Sr
Christ Is Risen	Gia	L	Sr
Christ Is Risen	Zon	T	Sr
Christ Is Risen	Zon	T	Sr
Christ Is Risen (Bohemian Melody)	Gsc	T	Sr
Christ Is Risen From The Dead	Zon	T	Sr
Christ Is Risen Indeed	Maf	T	Sr
Christ Is Risen 1	Fis	F	Sr
Christ Is Risen!	Sac	L	Sr
Christ Is Risen!	Gsc	T	Sr
Christ Is Risen!	Lor	L	Sr
Christ Is Risen, Alleluia	Aug	T	Sr
Christ Is Risen, Alleluia!	Lor	L	Sr
Christ Is The Rock	Zon	G	Tj
Christ Is The Spring	Fel	L	Tt
Christ Is The World's Redeemer	Sac	L	Tj
Christ Is The World's True Light	Abi	L	Tj
Christ Is The World's True Light 1	Oxf	T	Tj
Christ Lives Through Me	Zon	G	Tr
Christ Liveth In Me	Zon	G	Tr
Christ Loves Us	Ahc	L	Tr
Christ On The Mount Of Olives (Germ)	Kal	T	Sl
Christ Our Leader (4-Part Arr.)	Acp	L	Tk
Christ Our Leader (4-Part Arr.)	Acp	L	Tk
Christ Our Light	Nal	L	Tj
Christ Our Lord And Brother	Acp	L	Tj
Christ Our Lord And Brother(4-Part Ar)	Acp	L	Tj
Christ Our Lord Has Died (Acclamation)	Nal	L	Lj
Christ Our Lord, Who Died To Save Us	Aug	T	Sl
Christ Our Passover (M)	Oxf	L	Sr
Christ Our Passover (Mass For N.Rite)	Gia	L	Le
Christ Our Passover (Md)	Abi	L	Sr
Christ Our Passover (Notre Dame Mass)	Gia	L	Le
Christ Our Passover (Org,Guit)	Gia	L	Le
Christ Our Prophet	Acp	L	Sa
Christ Our Prophet (4-Part Arr.)	Acp	L	Sa
Christ Returneth	Zon	G	Sa
Christ Rising Again (M)	Oxf	T	Sr
Christ Rising Again (Md)	Oxf	T	Sr
Christ Rose From Death	Fel	L	Sr
Christ The King	Yan	F	Tk
Christ The King Now Is Born	Pro	T	Sc
Christ The Light	Gia	L	Tj
Christ The Lord Hath Risen	Gsc	T	Sr
Christ The Lord In Silence Coming	Gia	T	Sc
Christ The Lord Is Born	Lor	L	Sc
Christ The Lord Is Born	Lor	L	Sc
Christ The Lord Is Ris'n (A Cap)	Cfp	T	Sr
Christ The Lord Is Risen	Prc	L	Tx
Christ The Lord Is Risen	Aug	T	Sr
Christ The Lord Is Risen	Aug	T	Sr
Christ The Lord Is Risen (W/Brs)	Cfp	T	Sr
Christ The Lord Is Risen Again	Bec	T	Sr
Christ The Lord Is Risen Again	Gia	T	Sr
Christ The Lord Is Risen Again	Oxf	T	Sr
Christ The Lord Is Risen Again	Aug	T	Sr
Christ The Lord Is Risen Again(Org,Br)	Aug	L	Sr

ALPHABETICAL INDEX OF TITLES

Christ The Lord Is Risen Today	Lor	L	Sr
Christ The Lord Is Risen Today	Lor	L	Sr
Christ The Lord Is Risen Today	Som	L	Sr
Christ The Lord Is Risen Today	Abi	T	Sr
Christ The Lord Is Risen Today	Lor	T	Sr
Christ The Lord Is Risen Today	Gsc	T	Sr
Christ The Lord Is Risen Today	Lor	T	Sr
Christ The Lord Is Risen Today	Zon	T	Sr
Christ The Lord Is Risen Today	Lor	L	Sr
Christ The Lord Is Risen Today (Easy)	Zon	T	Sr
Christ The Lord Is Risen Today (W/Opt	Zon	T	Sr
Christ The Lord Is Risen! (E)	Oxf	L	Sr
Christ The Lord Today Has Risen	Acp	L	Sr
Christ The Lord Today Has Risen	Acp	L	Sr
Christ The Lord, Is Risen Again	Gsc	T	Sr
Christ The Lord, Our Risen King	Fel	L	Sr
Christ The Sure Foundation	Aug	T	Tj
Christ Walked This Way Before	Lor	L	Sr
Christ Was Born On Christmas Day	Pro	T	Sc
Christ Was Born On Christmas Day	Gsc	T	Sc
Christ Was Born On Christmas Day	Gia	T	Sc
Christ Who Has Risen From The Dead	Wlp	L	Sr
Christ Who Knows All His Sheep	Gsc	T	Tj
Christ Whose Glory Fills The Skies	Abi	T	Sr
Christ Will Appear Again	Fel	L	Tk
Christ Will Come Again	Nal	L	Tj
Christ–Light	Fel	L	Tj
Christ, Be Thine The Glory	Gsc	T	Sr
Christ, For Our Sake	Fel	L	Sl
Christ, My Beloved	Gsc	T	Tj
Christ, Our Blessed Savior	Gsc	T	Sl
Christ, Our Lamb	Fel	L	Sr
Christ, Our Paschal Lamb	Gia	L	Sr
Christ, Our Passover	Fel	F	Sr
Christ, The Light Of The Nations	Gia	L	Tj
Christ, We Adore Thee	Lor	L	Tj
Christ, Whose Glory Fills The Skies	Oxf	T	Tk
Christ, Whose Glory Fills The Skies	Gsc	T	Tj
Christ's Body, Given Up For Us	Sms	T	Lo
Christe Jesu, Gaude Plurimum, Mater	Kal	T	Tj
Christe Jesu, Pastor Bone	Oxf	T	Tj
Christe, Adoramus Te	Abi	T	Sl
Christe, Qui Lux Es Et Dies (Md)	Oxf	T	Tj
Christian Dost Thou See Them	Abi	L	Tx
Christian Fellowship	Lor	L	Tr
Christian, The Morn Breaks Sweetly	Gsc	T	Tb
Christians Sound The Name That Saved	Wlp	T	Tj
Christians Tribulation	Sav	G	Sl
Christians, Sing Joyfully	Lor	L	Sr
Christians, Sing Out With Exultation	Pic	L	Tt
Christmas	Man	C	Sc
Christmas	Bbl	T	Sc
Christmas (From Holiday Motets)	Ron	T	Sc
Christmas Acclamation	Rpb	L	Sc
Christmas Alleluia	Hof	T	Sc
Christmas At The Cloisters	Gsc	L	Sc
Christmas Ballad	Nal	L	Sc
Christmas Ballad	Van	F	Sc
Christmas Bells	Man	C	Sc
Christmas Bells	Hof	T	Sc
Christmas Bells	Tcp	L	Sc
Christmas Bells With Joy Are Ringing	Sac	T	Sc
Christmas Bells, The	Sac	T	Sc
Christmas Cameos Suite	Smc	T	Zb
Christmas Candlelight Procession	See	L	Sc
Christmas Cantata In Spanish	Zon	G	Sc
Christmas Carol	Pic	L	Sc
Christmas Carol	Pic	L	Sc
Christmas Carols For Children (No 5805	Zon	C	Sc
Christmas Carols From The Masters	Lor	T	Sc
Christmas Chimes	Abi	L	Sc
Christmas Comes Anew	Gia	T	Sc
Christmas Concertato	Aug	L	Sc
Christmas Dawn	Sac	T	Sc
Christmas Day In The Morning	Lor	L	Sc
Christmas Ensemble S.S.A. & T.T.B.B.	Zon	T	Sc
Christmas Ensemble Ssa And Ttbb 5764	Zon	L	Sc
Christmas Eve Is Here	Gsc	T	Sc
Christmas Exultation, A	Sac	L	Sc
Christmas Fanfare	Her	L	Sc
Christmas Gloria, A	Lor	L	Sc
Christmas Hymn(While By My Sheep)	Gsc	T	Sc
Christmas In Bethlehem	Pro	T	Sc
Christmas In The Western World	Som	L	Sc
Christmas Introit	Lor	L	La
Christmas Invitation, The	Lor	L	Sc
Christmas Is A Beautiful Word	Abi	L	Sc
Christmas Is Coming	Gsc	T	Sc
Christmas Joy	Abi	L	Sc
Christmas Jubilate (Russian Melody)	Lor	T	Sc
Christmas Legend, A	See	L	Sc
Christmas Long Ago	Zon	T	Sc
Christmas Lullabies	Smc	T	Sc
Christmas Lullaby	Abi	L	Sc
Christmas Lullaby From China, A	Sac	L	Sc
Christmas Meditation	Lor	L	Sc
Christmas Morn (Spiritual)	Pro	G	Sc
Christmas Mosaic, A	Maf	T	Sc
Christmas Motet	Gsc	T	Sc
Christmas Night	Gsc	T	Sc
Christmas Night	Bbl	T	Sc
Christmas Night (Stille Nacht)	Gsc	T	Sc
Christmas Oratorio	Gsc	T	Sc
Christmas Oratorio	Kal	T	Sc
Christmas Oratorio	Kal	T	Sc
Christmas Oratorio	Kal	T	Sc
Christmas Oratorio(Ger)	Cfp	T	Sc
Christmas Organist (No 5950)	Zon	T	Zb
Christmas Organist (No 5950)	Zon	G	Za
Christmas Prayer	Som	L	Sc
Christmas Processional	Gia	L	Sc
Christmas Psalm (Today Is Born)	Gra	L	Ld
Christmas Rose, A	Maf	L	Sc
Christmas Season	Pic	L	Sc
Christmas So Wonderful Fair	Gsc	T	Sc
Christmas Song	Gsc	T	Sc
Christmas Song	Gsc	T	Sc
Christmas Song Of Songs The	Lor	L	Sc
Christmas Song, The	Lor	T	Sc
Christmas Story	Zon	L	Sc
Christmas Story, The	Abi	C	Sc
Christmas Suite For Handbells	Abi	T	Zb
Christmas Vigil Psalm (Icet)	Wlp	L	Ld
Christmas/Folk Style	Lor	C	Sc
Christus	Kal	T	Tj
Christus Factus Est	Gsc	T	Sl
Christus Factus Est	Gsc	T	Sl
Christus Factus Est	Gsc	T	Sl
Christus Factus Est (E & L) (Me)	Gia	T	Sl
Christus Factus Est Pro Nobis Obediens	Cfp	T	Sl
Christus Factus Est(Lat,Eng)	Gsc	T	Sl
Christus Resurgens (D)	Oxf	T	Sr
Church Cantatas & Oratorios	Lps	T	Za
Church In The Home	Zon	G	Tr
Church Is Where Men Are, The	Fcc	F	Tr
Church Of The Living God	Lor	L	Tc
Church Within Us	Ccc	L	Tr
Church, O Lord, Is Thine, The	Zon	L	Tr
Church's One Foundation, The	Acp	L	Tr
Church's One Foundation, The	Acp	L	Tr
Church's One Foundation, The	Lor	L	Tr
Church's One Foundation, The	Zon	T	Tr
Cinco Invocaciones Al Crucificado	Som	L	Sl
Citizens Of Heaven	Wlp	L	Tr
City Of High Renown	Gal	T	Tx
Clap Your Hand Children	Wrd	G	Tt
Clap Your Hands	Aug	T	Tt
Clap Your Hands	Abi	L	Tt
Clap Your Hands	Bfi	F	Tt
Clap Your Hands	Gph	T	Tt
Clap Your Hands	Her	L	Tt
Clap Your Hands	Lex	L	Tt
Clap Your Hands	Fel	F	Tk
Clap Your Hands	Fel	F	Tt
Clap Your Hands (Ascension)	Car	F	Sr
Clap Your Hands Ye People	Gsc	T	Tt
Clap Your Hands, All Ye Children	Aug	C	Tt
Clap Your Hands, Stamp Your Feet	Aug	T	Tt
Clean Heart(Ps 51)	Rav	L	Ld
Cleansing Wave, The	Zon	G	Tb
Climbin' Jacob's Ladder (P.D.)	Man	G	Lp
Close To Thee	Gmc	G	Tj
Close To Thee	Zon	G	Tr
Close To Thee	Lor	T	Tr
Close Your Eyes	Nal	C	Tr
Closer To God	Mar	L	Tr
Closing Doxology, The (Psalm 150)	Bbl	T	Tt
Coat Of Many Colors	Fcc	C	Tx
Coenam Cum Discipulis	Gsc	T	Lo
Cofre De Canticos	Zon	G	Za
Color Him Love (No 5019)	Zon	G	Tj
Colored Christmas Lights	Man	C	Sc
Columbia From Two Songs Of Mourning	Bbl	T	Sl
Come Alive	Sbf	L	Sr
Come All Ye Nations	Wgm	F	Tt
Come All You People	Rav	L	La
Come Along With Me To Jesus	Nal	C	Ln
Come And Abide	Lor	T	Tr
Come And Adore Him	Lor	T	Sc
Come And Behold	Aug	T	Tx
Come And Bless Us	Fel	F	Tj
Come And Gather, Little Children	Zon	L	Sc
Come And Go With Me	Nal	C	La
Come And Let Us Drink Of That New Rivr	Gsc	L	Tf
Come And Pray In Us,Spirit Of The Lord	Wlp	L	Ss
Come And Rescue Me	Fel	F	Sl
Come And Sing	Ahc	L	La
Come And Take	Nal	L	Tx
Come And Thank Him (Me)	Oxf	T	Sc
Come As A Child	Prc	L	Tx
Come As A Child	Yan	F	Tr
Come Away	Fel	F	Sr
Come Away, My Love	Gmc	G	Tx
Come Before The Table Of The Lord	Wlp	F	Lo
Come Beloved Monarch	Gsc	T	Sa
Come By Here	Acp	L	Lp
Come By Here	Acp	L	Tr
Come Closer Lord	Jhm	G	Tr
Come Creator Spirit	Jsp	L	Ss
Come Dance And Sing	Gsc	G	Tt
Come Down O Love (W/Piano)	Wrd	G	Ss
Come Down, Lord	Van	F	Sa
Come Down, O Love Divine	Her	T	Ss
Come Down, O Love Divine	Abi	T	Sa
Come Down, O Love Divine	Gia	L	Ss
Come Follow	Gia	F	Tc
Come Follow Me	Gia	F	Tc
Come Follow Me	Nal	L	Tc
Come Gracious Spirit	Aug	T	Ss
Come Hasten Ye Shepherds (Traditional)	Gsc	T	Sc
Come Heavenly Child	Abi	L	Sa
Come Holy Ghost	Gia	T	Ss
Come Holy Ghost	Gia	T	Ss
Come Holy Light (From J. Maccabeus)	Pro	T	Tr
Come Holy Spirit	Gia	F	Ss
Come Holy Spirit	Gia	T	Ss
Come Holy Spirit Come (Fire Of Love)	Gia	F	Ss
Come Holy Spirit, God And Lord	Aug	T	Ss
Come Home To God	Lor	L	Tr
Come In, Pilgrim	Fel	F	Sr
Come Jesus Christ	Wlp	L	Sa
Come Let Us Go	Nal	L	Tx
Come Let Us Join In Prayer Today	Wlp	L	La
Come Let Us Sing	Gsc	T	Tt
Come Let Us Tune Our Loftiest Song	Gsc	L	Tt
Come Let Us Tune Our Loftiest Song	Pro	T	Tk
Come Let Us Worship	Gia	T	Tt
Come Let's Rejoice (Md)	Oxf	L	Tt
Come Life, Shaker Life	Nal	L	Tx
Come Lord	Chh	F	Tr
Come Lord Jesus	Sha	F	Sa
Come My Friend	Rpb	L	La
Come Nearer	Gia	L	Tm
Come Now Let Us Reason Together(W/Org	Gsc	T	Tx
Come O Lord, O Come For Our Saving	Wlp	L	Sa
Come O Thou God Of Grace	Gsc	L	Tr
Come On Down	Mar	L	Tc
Come On Down	Fcc	F	Tx
Come On Down, Zacchaeus	Aug	T	Tx
Come On Home	Gmc	G	Tf
Come On In	Sil	F	La
Come On Over Yonder	Jhe	G	Tx
Come Out	Wlp	C	La
Come Out Of Egypt	Rpb	F	Tx
Come Praise, Alleluia	Wlp	F	Tt
Come Quickly Jesus	Mar	L	Tk
Come Rest A Little While	Sto	G	Tr
Come Save Me, Lord	Acp	L	Tr
Come Save Me, Lord	Acp	L	Sl
Come See Me	Gmc	G	Tr
Come See The Joy We Have	Jsp	F	Tt
Come Sing, Ye Choirs Exultant	Abi	L	Tt
Come Soothing Death	Gsc	T	Tf
Come Sound His Praise Abroad	Gsc	T	Tt
Come Sweet Death (Cantata)	Lps	T	Tf
Come Take My Yoke	Aug	T	Tc
Come Thou Almighty	Wrd	G	La
Come Thou Holy Spirit Come	Gia	T	Ss
Come Thou Holy Spirit Come	Nal	L	Ss
Come Thou Long–Expected Jesus	Som	L	Sa
Come To Bethlehem	Lor	L	Sc
Come To Jerusalem	Sha	F	La
Come To Me	Gsc	T	Tr
Come To Me	Lor	T	Ln
Come To Me	Bfi	F	Tr
Come To Me	Wes	F	Tj
Come To Me	Lor	T	Tx
Come To Me	Wlp	F	Tr
Come To Me All Who Are Weary	Nal	L	Tr
Come To Me All Who Labor	Wrd	G	Tr
Come To Me, All You Who Labor	Fel	L	Tr
Come To Me, I've Come To You	Nal	L	Tj
Come To Me, Jesus	Nal	L	Tj
Come To My House	Man	G	Lp
Come To My Table	Nal	L	Ln
Come To The Banquet (Chant)	Lit	T	Ln
Come To The Lord	Wlp	F	La
Come To The Lord	Acp	F	Lp
Come To The Lord (4–Part Arr.)	Acp	F	La
Come To The Manger	Aug	T	Sc
Come To The Mountain	Wlp	F	Tr
Come To The Running River	Acp	F	Tb
Come To The Running River	Acp	F	Ss
Come To The Savior, Make No Delay	Smc	T	Tr
Come To The Spirit (W/Piano)	Wrd	G	Ss
Come To The Springs Of Living Water	Van	F	Tb
Come To The Stable With Jesus	Gsc	T	Sc
Come To The Table Of The Lord	Nal	L	Ln
Come To The Tomb	Abi	L	Sr
Come To The Water	Rpb	L	Tb
Come Together	Lex	T	Lo
Come Together	Yan	F	Lo
Come Unto Him (Messiah)	Hof	T	Tx
Come Unto Me	Zon	T	Tc
Come Unto Me	Gsc	T	Tr
Come Unto Me	Cob	T	Lp
Come Unto Me	Gmc	G	La
Come Unto Me	Ham	G	Lp
Come Unto Me	Lor	T	Tr
Come Unto Me	Fis	T	La

Title	Code
Come Unto Me	Lor T Tr
Come Unto Me And Rest	Gph T Lp
Come Walk With Me In The Spirit	Mar L Ss
Come Where The Wind Is Free	Acp L Tx
Come Where The Wind Is Free	Acp L Tx
Come With Me	Fel F Tx
Come With Me	Man G Lp
Come With Me Into The Fields	Nal L Tc
Come With Rejoicing	Aug T La
Come With Your Heartache	Zon G Tr
Come Ye Faithful, Raise The Strain	Zon L Sr
Come Ye Faithful, Raise The Strain	Hwg L Sr
Come Ye Faithful, Raise The Strain	Aug T Tt
Come Ye Faithful, Raise The Strain	Aug T Tt
Come Ye Faithful, Raise The Strain	Zon T Sr
Come Ye Lofty, Come Ye Lowly	Pro T Sc
Come Ye Unto Me	Lor L Tr
Come You Faithful	Acp L La
Come You Faithful (4-Part Arr)	Acp L La
Come, All Ye Faithful	Lor T Sc
Come, All Ye Saints	Her L La
Come, Children, Hear Me	Fel F Tx
Come, Children, Praise Our Lord	Gsc T Tt
Come, Christians, Join To Sing	Gia L Lp
Come, Christians, Join To Sing	Zon T Tt
Come, Comes	Nal L Tx
Come, Enter My Father's House	Fel L Tf
Come, Faithful People, Come Away	Abi L Lp
Come, Follow Me	Fel L Tc
Come, Follow Me	Fel F Tc
Come, Holy Ghost	Gsc T Ss
Come, Holy Ghost, Creator Blest	Abi L Ss
Come, Holy Ghost, Draw Near Us	Sac L Ss
Come, Holy Ghost, In Love	Aug T Ss
Come, Holy Light, Guide Divine	Pro T Tr
Come, Holy Spirit	Gia T Ss
Come, Holy Spirit	Gra F Ss
Come, Holy Spirit	Gmc G Ss
Come, Holy Spirit	Lor G Ss
Come, Holy Spirit	Gia T Ss
Come, Holy Spirit	Acp L Ss
Come, Holy Spirit	Abi L Ss
Come, Holy Spirit	Zon G Ss
Come, Holy Spirit	Acp L Ss
Come, Holy Spirit	Gsc T Ss
Come, Jesu, Come (Motet 5)	Kal T Sa
Come, Let Us Bow Down	Gia L La
Come, Let Us Join	Som L Lp
Come, Let Us Praise The Lord	Gia T Tt
Come, Let Us Sing To The Lord	Fel L La
Come, Let Us Sing To The Lord	Zon F La
Come, Let Us Use The Grace Divine	Abi L Tr
Come, Let Us Worship	Gia T La
Come, Live In Us	Acp L Lo
Come, Live In Us (4-Part Arr.)	Acp L Lo
Come, Lord	Rpb L Tr
Come, Lord Jesus	Arc T Sa
Come, Lord Jesus	Mob C Tx
Come, Lord Jesus	Fel F Tk
Come, Lord Jesus	Nal F Sa
Come, Lord Jesus (The Night)	Van F Sa
Come, My Brothers	Fel F Tj
Come, My Soul	Aug T La
Come, My Spirit (Cantata)	Lps T Tt
Come, My Way, My Truth, My Life (Me)	Oxf T Tj
Come, O Blessed	Flp T Sr
Come, O Bride Of Christ	Fel L Tc
Come, O Come	Lor L Sa
Come, O Come, Lord Jesus, Come	Fel L Sa
Come, O Holy Spirit	Nal L Ss
Come, O Long Awaited Savior	Gia L Sa
Come, Peace Of God	Sac L Tr
Come, Redeemer Of Mankind	Fel L Sa
Come, Rich And Poor	Acp L Ln
Come, Rich And Poor	Acp L Tx
Come, Risen Lord	Aug T Sr
Come, Shake The Mountains	Acp L Sa
Come, Shake The Mountains	Acp L Tk
Come, Sing	Aug T Tt
Come, Sing A Song Unto The Lord	Zon T Tt
Come, Sing, Praise The Lord	Ahc L Tt
Come, Soothing Death	Aug T Tf
Come, Sound His Praise Abroad	Zon L Tt
Come, Sound His Praise Abroad	Pro T Tt
Come, Spirit Of The Living God	Gsc T Ss
Come, Spirit, Come	Ahc L Ss
Come, Then, My Son	Fel F Tx
Come, Thou Almighty King	Maf T Sa
Come, Thou Almighty King	Zon T Tt
Come, Thou Fount	Zon T Ss
Come, Thou Fount Of Every Blessing	Abi T Sa
Come, Thou Holy Spirit, Come	Lit T Ss
Come, Thou Holy Spirit, Come (Md)	Oxf T Ss
Come, Thou Long Expected Jesus	Abi T Sa
Come, Thou Long Expected Jesus	Abi L Sa
Come, Thou Long Expected Jesus (Me)	Oxf T Sa
Come, Thou Long-Expected Jesus	Gsc L Sa
Come, Thou Long-Expected Jesus	Aug T Sa
Come, Thou Long-Expected Jesus	Aug T Sa
Come, Thou Long-Expected Jesus	Aug T Sa
Come, Thou Spirit Everlasting	Sac T Ss
Come, Ye Blessed	Gsc T Sr
Come, Ye Children, Sweetly Singing	Lor C Tt
Come, Ye Disconsolate	Zon T Sl
Come, Ye Faithful	Lor L La
Come, Ye Faithful	Lor L La
Come, Ye Sinners, Poor And Needy	Lor L Tr
Come, Ye Sinners, Poor And Needy	Sac L Tr
Come, Ye Thankful People	Lor L La
Come, Ye Thankful People, Come	Aug T La
Come, Ye Thankful People, Come	Gsc T Lp
Come, Ye That Love The Lord	Lor L Tt
Come, Ye That Love The Lord	Zon T La
Come, Ye That Love The Lord	Sac L La
Come, Ye That Serve (Me) W/2 Tpts	Gia L La
Come, You Have My Father's Blessing	Aug L Tr
Come, Your Hearts & Voices Raising	Aug L Tt
Come,The Lord Is Waiting For Us	Vrn L Lo
Comfort Sweet (Cantata)	Lps T Tr
Comfort, O Lord (E)	Oxf T Sl
Coming Of Our Lord, The	Nal L Sa
Coming Together	Fel F La
Command Thine Angel That He Come	Bbl T Sc
Commitment (Flute Optional)	Aug T Tc
Committment Song	Ahc L Tc
Common Blessed Virgin Alleluia (Icet)	Wlp L Lf
Common Of Doctors (Icet) Psalm	Wlp L Ld
Common Of Doctors Alleluia (Icet)	Wlp L Lf
Common Of Martyrs Psalm (Icet)	Wlp L Ld
Common Of Pastors (Icet) Psalm	Wlp L Ld
Common Of Saints (Icet)	Wlp L Ld
Common Of Saints Psalm (2cet)	Wlp L Ld
Common Of Virgins (Icet) Psalm	Wlp L Ld
Common Of Virgins Alleluia Verse(Icet)	Wlp L Lf
Common Responses (Icet)	Wlp L Ld
Communion Anthem	Maf L Lo
Communion From Four Folk-Hymns	Bbl T Lo
Communion Hymn	Abi L Lo
Communion Hymn	Gsc T Lo
Communion Hymn Sequence For Choir	Lor L Lo
Communion Hymn(Bread Of The World)	Gsc L Lo
Communion In A Minor, Ps 128	Gra L Tw
Communion Meditations	Aug T Lo
Communion Muse	Nal L Lo
Communion Rite (Lyric Liturgy)	Gia L Lo
Communion Service	Oxf T Lo
Communion Service	Oxf T Lo
Communion Service (Alt Series 2)	Oxf T Lo
Communion Service (Mass Of Quiet Hour)	Oxf T Lo
Communion Service E E. Series 3 (Md)	Oxf T Lo
Communion Service In A Minor (M)	Oxf T Lo
Communion Service In C (Me)	Oxf T Lo
Communion Service In D (E)	Oxf T Lo
Communion Service In D (Me)	Oxf T Lo
Communion Service In D Minor	Oxf T Lo
Communion Service In E (Md)	Oxf T Lo
Communion Service In E Flat	Oxf T Lo
Communion Service In F With Kyrie	Oxf T Lo
Communion Service In G (Md)	Oxf T Lo
Communion Service, Series 3 (E)	Oxf T Lo
Communion Service, Series 3 (M)	Oxf T Lo
Communion Service, Series 3 (M)	Oxf T Ln
Communion Song (O Taste And See)	Gia L Lr
Communion With God	Lor L Tr
Community Song	Fel C Tr
Complainer	Bbl T Tt
Complete Holy Week Services (Chant)	Gia L Sl
Complete Love	Yan F Sl
Complete Organ Works In 9 Vols.	Kal T Zb
Complete Works Of Palestrina (74 Vol)	Kal T Za
Concert From Four Folk-Hymns	Bbl T Za
Concertato On "Adeste Fideles"	Aug L Sc
Concierto De Navidad	Pic L Sc
Concluding Rite	Nal L Tx
Concordi Laetitia (In 19 Rounds)	Gia T Tt
Concordia Hymnal (34 Hymns)	Aug T Za
Condemned	Man G Sl
Confitemini (From Holiday Motets)	Ron T Sl
Congregation Mass (1970)	Gia L Za
Congregational Mass In Dorian Mode	Oxf T Za
Conserva Me And Lamentationes	Kal T Sl
Consider The Lilies	Wgm L Tr
Consider The Lilies	Gsc T Tx
Consider The Lilies	Her L Tr
Consider, Lord	Som L Sl
Consume Me	Man G Tc
Contemplations	Abi L Zb
Contemporary Prayer	Sil L Tx
Contemporary Worship I-Hymns	Aug L Za
Contemporary Worship Ii-Holy Communion	Aug L Za
Contemporary Worship Iii-Marriage	Aug L Za
Contemporary Worship 4-Baptism,	Aug L Za
Contemporary Worship 5: The Word	Aug L Za
Contented	Gmc G Tr
Contentment In His Love	Zon G Tr
Cor Jesu	Gsc T Tj
Cordero De Dios	Gia L Lm
Corinthians On Love	Maf L Tr
Coronation Mass K 317	Kal T Za
Coronation Mass(C)(Latin)	Cfp T Za
Coronation Te Deum	Oxf T Tt
Corpus Christi Carol (Me)	Oxf L Lo
Cosmic Christ (You Are The Staff)	Gia F Tj
Could This Be A Special Night?	Her L Sc
Count Your Blessings	Man G Tr
Country And Western Hymnal	Zon F Za
Country Blessing	Fcc F Tx
Country-Western Gospel Favorites (100)	Zon F Za
Covenant Prayer	Rav L Tr
Coventry Carol	Bec T Sc
Coventry Carol	Gsc T Sc
Coventry Carol	Pro T Sc
Coverdale's Carol	Abi L Sc
Cradle Song Of The Virgin	Gsc T Sc
Cradle Song Of The Virgin (E&Ger)	Gsc T Sc
Cradled All Lowly	Abi L Sc
Crave, As Newborn Babes	Fel L Tb
Create In Me	Bfi L Ld
Create In Me	Abi L Ss
Create In Me	Ccc L To
Create In Me A Clean Heart	Aug T Sl
Create In Me A Clean Heart Willing	Yan F Sl
Create In Me A Clean Heart, O God	Gsc T Sl
Create In Me O God	Gsc T Sl
Created In His Image	Gmc G Tr
Creation	Wlp F Tx
Creation	Kal T Tx
Creation, The	Lor L Tx
Creator God, We Give You Thanks	Maf L Tt
Creator Of The Earth And Skies	Gia T Sl
Credidi Propter	Gsc T Tx
Credo	Kal T Tx
Credo	Kal T Tx
Creed (Icet Text) Cong, Org	Gia L Tx
Creed (Icet) U Or Satb W/Org(Chant)	Gia L Tx
Creed (1964 Text)	Van F Tx
Creed (64 Text)	Van F Tx
Cries For Help	Prc L Tx
Cross Was His Own, The	Lor L Sl
Cross Was Not The End, The	Lor L Sr
Cross, The	Lor L Sr
Crown Him Lord Of All	Lor L Tk
Crown Him Lord Of All	Aug T Tk
Crown Him Lord Of All!	Lor L Tk
Crown Him The King Of Kings	Acp L-Tk
Crown Him The King Of Kings	Acp L Tk
Crown Him With Many Crowns	Zon T Tk
Crown Him With Many Crowns	Wlp T Tk
Crown Him With Many Crowns	Gia T Tj
Crown Him With Many Crowns	Aug T Tk
Crown Him With Many Crowns	Sac T Tk
Crown Him With Many Crowns (Tpts,Org)	Aug L Tk
Crown With Thy Benediction	Aug L Tr
Crowning Glory Hymnal	Zon G Za
Crucifixion (Long)	Aug L Sl
Crucifixus	Gsc T Sl
Crucifixus	Gsc T Sl
Crucifixus	Aug T Sl
Crucifixus(From The Mass In B Minor)	Gsc T Sl
Crusade	Lor L Tx
Crusade Choir (No Zd-5474)	Zon T Tj
Crusade Organist (No 5761)	Zon G Zb
Crusader's Hymn	Lor T Tx
Crux Fidelis (E & L) (Me)	Gia T Sl
Cry Alice	Wlp L Tx
Cry Out To God(Ps 66)	Rav L Ld
Cry Out With Joy! (1s 12:1-6)	Gra L Ld
Cup Of Blessing That We Share	Wlp L Lo
Custodi Me, Domine	Gsc T Tx
Cycle Of Holy Songs	Som L Tt
Daddy Sang Bass	Ced G Tx
Daddy, Sing For Jesus	Sil G Tj
Daily Bread	Rpb F Lo
Dallas Holm Songs	Zon G Za
Daniel Prayed To God	Fel L Tx
Daniel, Daniel, Servant Of The Lord	Wbp T Tx
Danny's Dance	Van C Tx
Dare To Believe	Man G Tc
Dark/Light	Zon F Sl
Darkly Rose The Guilty Morning S	Gsc T Sl
Darkness Concealed The Earth	Lor T Sa
Darkness Now Has Taken Flight, The	Abi L Sr
Darkness Was Over All	Gsc T Sl
Darkness Was Over All	Som L Sl
Daughter Of Zion	Lor L Sa
David (Unison)	Lor T Tx
David, Swing Your Sling	Hal C Tx
David's Lamentation	Gsc T Sl
David's Lamentation	Cfp T Sl
David's Song	Fis F Le
David's Song	Wlp F Tx
Davide Penitente	Bbl T Sl
Davide Penitente K 469 (Eng/It/Germ)	Kal T Sl
Dawn Of Christmas, The	Lor L Sc
Day By Day	Zon L Tr
Day By Day	Val F Tr
Day By Day	Lor L Tr
Day By Day I Will Sing Your Praise	Fel L Tt
Day For Goodbye	Nal L Tx
Day Is Done	Pep F Tt

Title			
Day Of Brotherhood, The	Lor	L	Tr
Day Of Celebration, The	Fcc	L	Sr
Day Of Dawning Brotherhood	Sac	L	Tr
Day Of Pentecost	Aug	L	Ss
Day Of Rejoicing (W/Trumpets)	Aug	T	Tt
Day Of Resurrection, The	Zon	T	Sr
Day Of Sorrow	Elv	T	Sl
Dayenu	Acp	F	Tx
Dayenu	Acp	F	Tx
Days Of Man W/Solo	Aug	L	Tx
Daystar	Abi	L	Sa
De Animals A—Comin'	Gsc	G	Tx
De Profundis	Gsc	T	Sl
De Profundis (Out Of The Depths)	Gsc	T	Sl
De Profundis K 93	Kal	T	Sl
De Promis' Lan'	Gsc	G	Tx
De Propundis (From Holiday Motets)	Ron	T	Sl
De Spei	See	L	Tr
Dead, Mass Of, (Icet) Response	Wlp	L	Tf
Dear God In Heaven	Jhm	G	Tx
Dear Jesus Boy	Abi	L	Sc
Dear Little Jesus (Unison) (C)	Lor	L	Sc
Dear Lord	Mmc	G	Tr
Dear Lord And Father Of Mankind	Abi	L	Tr
Dear Lord, Be My Shepherd	Ham	G	Tr
Dear Lord, Who Once Upon The Lake	Gsc	T	Tx
Dearest Father, You Are Good	Fel	L	Tr
Dearest Jesu, Holy Child	Pro	T	Sc
Death I Do Not Fear Thee	Gsc	T	Tf
Death In The City	Fel	F	Sl
Death Is Swallowed Up	Fel	F	Tj
Death Of Absalom, The	Bbl	T	Tx
Death Shall No Longer Have	Fel	L	Sr
Death, Be Not Proud	Pic	L	Tf
Deborah	Fel	F	Tx
Decision	Man	L	Tc
Deck The Halls	Gsc	T	Sc
Deck Thyself, My Soul (10 Chorales)	Gia	T	Za
Deck, Thyself, My Soul, With Gladness	Gsc	T	Tt
Declare His Glory	Zon	L	Sr
Dedicated But Doomed	Mam	G	Tx
Dedication	Gsc	T	Tc
Dedication	Lor	L	Tc
Deep Down In My Heart	Zon	C	Tt
Deep In The Boding Night	Sac	L	Sl
Deep North Spirituals(9)	Cfp	T	Za
Deep River	Gsc	G	Sr
Deep Was The Silence	Zon	L	Sc
Deep Were His Wounds	Aug	T	Sl
Deeper And Deeper	Zon	T	Tc
Deeper In The Lord	Man	G	Tc
Deer Is Panting For The Stream, The	Sac	L	Tb
Defend My Cause, My God	Fel	L	Sl
Deliver Me, Lord, From Evil Men	Fel	L	Sl
Deliver Us, Good Lord (Me)	Oxf	T	Sl
Deliver Us, O God Of Israel	Nal	L	Sr
Deliver Us, O Lord (Me)	Oxf	T	Sl
Deluxe Guitar Praise Book (No 5310)	Zon	G	Zb
Depth Of Mercy	Bfi	T	Tr
Depth Of Mercy	Abi	L	Lo
Der Herr Ist Mein Hirte (Psalm 23)	Bbl	T	Tr
Descants For Choirs (No 5544)	Zon	T	Za
Descants On Six Hymn Tunes	Aug	T	Za
Descend O Spirit, Purging Flame	Jsp	L	Ss
Desert Highways Of The Night, The	Nal	L	Tr
Desert Shall Rejoice, The	Lor	L	Sa
Designs For Organ	Abi	L	Zb
Destiny	Zon	F	Tc
Dettingen Te Deum	Kal	T	Tt
Deus, Misereatur Nostri	Gsc	T	Sl
Devil, Devil Go Away	Man	C	Sl
Devoutly I Adore Thee	Gsc	T	Lo
Dias Especiales (No 5374)	Zon	F	Za
Did Jesus Weep For Me?	Lor	L	Sl
Did Not Our Heart Burn Within Us	Gsc	L	Sr
Did They Crucify My Lord?	Lor	T	Sl
Didn't My Lord Deliver Daniel	Gsc	G	Tx
Didst Thou Suffer Shame?	Her	T	Sl
Die With Us	Nal	L	Tc
Dies Irae, Dies Illa	Fel	L	Tk
Dies Sanctificatus	Pro	T	Sc
Dies Sanctificatus	Gsc	T	Sc
Dies Sanctificatus	Gia	T	Tx
Different Is Beautiful	Prc	L	Tx
Diffusa Est Gratia	Gsc	T	Ss
Diffusa Est Gratia	Gia	T	Tx
Dig My Grave	Gsc	G	Sr
Dimensions In Music (No 5672)	Zon	L	Tx
Ding Dong Merrily On High	Gsc	T	Sc
Dirge In Woods	See	L	Tx
Disclosure	Pic	L	Tx
Discovery	Zon	G	Tr
Dives And Lazarus (Cantata)	Oxf	T	Tx
Dives And Lazarus (Folk Ballad)	Oxf	F	Tx
Divine Priority, The	Zon	G	Tc
Do It With Your Love	Yan	F	Tr
Do Justice (Cantata)	Lps	L	Tr
Do Not Be Afraid Of Those	Fel	L	Tr
Do Not Be Anxious	Fel	L	Tr
Do Not Forsake Me, O Lord	Fel	L	Sl
Do Not Give Me Up, O Lord	Fel	L	Sl
Do This In Remembrance Of Me	Fel	L	Lo
Do This In Remembrance Of Me	Jsp	L	Ln
Do What He Wants You To Do	Lor	L	Tc
Do You Care?	Zon	G	Sl
Do You Feel The Change	Mar	L	Sl
Do You Have An Empty Heart?	Lor	L	Tr
Do You Know Jesus?	Ham	G	Tj
Do You Know?	Lor	L	Tx
Do You Know?	Ahc	L	Tt
Do You Know?	Gsc	T	Sr
Do You Know?	Fcc	F	Tx
Do You Really Love Me?	Nal	C	Tr
Do You Want Peace?	Zon	G	Tr
Do You Want To Be Free	Gia	F	Tr
Do—Don't Touch—A My Garment	Gsc	G	Tx
Doer Of The Lord	Mar	L	Tc
Does God Ever Laugh?	Van	C	Tt
Does Jesus Care	Lor	G	Tj
Does Jesus Care?	Lor	L	Tr
Dogwood Cross, The	Lor	L	Sl
Domine Memento Mei Jesu Think Of Me	Gsc	T	Sl
Domine Non Sum Dignus (E & L)(Md)	Gia	T	Lo
Domine, Non Est Exaltum Cor Meum	Kal	T	Tx
Dominica In Ramis	Pic	T	Tx
Don't Be Afraid	Van	F	Tx
Don't Cry	Oak	G	Tx
Don't Disgrace My Mother's Name	Jhm	G	Tx
Don't Forget To Pray	Pmp	G	To
Don't Let The Song Go Out Of Your Hear	Zon	G	Tt
Don't Let Them Have Their Way	Pmp	G	Tx
Don't Send Those Kids To Sunday School	Ham	C	Tx
Don't Spare Me	Man	G	Tc
Don't Stop Using Me	Man	G	Tc
Don't Talk The Talk	Sil	F	Tx
Don't Wait	Pmp	G	Tx
Don't Waste Your Precious Years	Man	G	Tc
Don't Worry (About Food)	Van	F	Tr
Don't You Care	Man	F	Tx
Don't You Look All Around	Fel	F	Tx
Don't You Weep No More, Mary	Gsc	G	Tx
Dona Nobis Pacem	Gsc	T	Tr
Dona Nobis Pacem	Pro	T	Tr
Dona Nobis Pacem	Oxf	T	Tr
Dona Nobis Pacem (In 19 Rounds)	Gia	T	Lm
Dona Nobis Pacem (Round)	Oxf	L	Lm
Dost Thou In A Manger Lie	Aug	T	Sc
Dost Thou In A Manger Lie?	Gsc	T	Sc
Doth Not Wisdom Cry	Gsc	T	Sl
Doubting Thomas	Van	F	Tx
Doug Oldham Songbook (No 4336)	Zon	G	Za
Down Deep In My Heart	Man	G	Tr
Down East	Pic	L	Tx
Down From His Glory	Zon	G	Sc
Down In Yon Forest	Gsc	F	Sc
Down With Nineveh	Fel	F	Tx
Doxology	Prc	L	Tx
Doxology	Nal	L	Le
Doxology	Nal	L	Le
Doxology	Chh	L	Lk
Doxology (Hurrah To God)	Aug	T	Tt
Doxology And "Amen"	Nal	L	Lk
Doxology And Amen (I)	Nal	L	Lk
Doxology And Amen (Ii)	Nal	L	Lk
Doxology And Great Amen	Nal	L	Lk
Doxology To The Lord's Prayer	Fel	L	Le
Doxology——Amen	Nal	L	Lk
Draw Near O Lord	Wlp	T	Sl
Draw Nigh To Thy Jerusalem	Aug	T	Sl
Dream Of Shalom	Aug	L	Tr
Dream, Pharoah, Dream	Fcc	C	Tx
Dreamer	Van	C	Tx
Dried Up Well	Mar	L	Sl
Drifting	Zon	G	Tc
Drink Deep Of The Fountain	Gra	F	Ss
Drop Down Ye Heavens	Gia	L	Sa
Drop Down, Ye Heaven (Is 45)	Oxf	T	Tm
Drop Down, Ye Heavens From Above	Aug	T	Sa
Drop, Drop Slow Tears	Oxf	T	Sl
Drop, Drop Slow Tears (A Cap)	Hwg	L	Sl
Drop, Drop, Slow Tears	Sac	T	Sl
Drop, Drop, Slow Tears	Abi	L	Sl
Drop, Drop, Slow Tears	Sac	L	Sl
Drop, Slow Tears	Gal	T	Sl
Duets For Piano And Organ No 1 (5934)	Zon	G	Zb
Duets For Piano And Organ No 2 (5931)	Zon	G	Zb
Dulcissime Et Benignissime Christe	Kal	T	Tj
Dum Transisset Sabatum	Oxf	T	Tx
Duos Trios Y Cuartetos (No 5368)	Zon	G	Za
Dusty Road, The	Zon	F	Tc
Dying You Destroyed Our Death	Gra	L	Lj
Dying You Destroyed Our Death	Wlp	L	Lj
Dying You Destroyed Our Death	Nal	L	Lj
Dying You Destroyed Our Death	Nal	L	Lj
E'en So, Lord Jesus, Quickly Come	Con	T	Tk
Each Man's Joy	Rpb	L	Tx
Each Step Of The Way	Zon	G	Tc
Each Winter As The Year Grows Older	Ucp	L	Sc
Early American Compositions For Organ	Abi	L	Zb
Early American Hymn Tune	Smc	T	Zb
Early American Hymnal	Gia	T	Tp
Early American Tune	Gsc	F	Sr
Early Easter Morning	Gsc	T	Sr
Early In The Morning	Sac	L	Sr
Early In The Morning	Pep	F	Tt
Early Spring, The	Lor	L	Sr
Early, O Lord, My Fainting Soul	Gsc	T	Sl
Earth Abideth, The	Ron	T	Tr
Earth And All Stars	Aug	T	Tx
Earth Is Full Of The Goodness, The	Nal	L	Ss
Earth Is The Lord's	Aug	L	Tx
Earth Is The Lord's	Sac	L	Tr
Earth Is The Lord's The	Flp	T	To
Earth Is The Lord's, The	Lor	L	Tk
Earth To Ashes	Aug	T	Sk
Earth With Joy Confesses	Sac	L	Tt
Earthen Vessels	Nal	L	Sl
Earthquake (Isaiah 52)	Gia	L	Ss
Ease My Mind, Lord	Bec	T	Tr
Easter	Pic	L	Sr
Easter (From Holiday Motets)	Ron	L	Sr
Easter (Most Glorious Lord)	Oxf	T	Sr
Easter Alleluia, An	Zon	T	Sr
Easter Anthem (Shaw)	Gsc	T	Sr
Easter Bell Carol	Abi	L	Sr
Easter Bells (Opt Group Lection)	Hof	L	Sr
Easter Cantata (W/Brass, Perc)	Cfp	T	Sr
Easter Cantata In Spanish	Zon	G	Sr
Easter Carol	Gsc	T	Sr
Easter Carol	Lor	L	Sr
Easter Carol	Sac	L	Sr
Easter Carol Mass (1964 Text)	Gia	L	Za
Easter Celebration Cantata	Zon	L	Sr
Easter Chorale	Gsc	T	Sr
Easter Dawn	Lor	L	Sr
Easter Dawning	Aug	T	Sr
Easter Day (A Cap)	Hwg	L	Sr
Easter Fanfare	Sac	L	Sr
Easter Fanfare: Christ The Lord	Aug	T	Sr
Easter Glory	Aug	T	Sr
Easter Hallelujah, The	Lor	L	Sr
Easter Hymn	Zon	T	Sr
Easter Hymn Of Praise (Opt Acc)	Abi	L	Sr
Easter Introit, An	Sac	L	La
Easter Morning	Aug	T	Sr
Easter Oratorio	Lps	T	Sr
Easter Oratorio (Eng)	Kal	T	Sr
Easter Organist (No 5290)	Zon	T	Zb
Easter Praise (E)	Lor	L	Sr
Easter Song	Sac	L	Sr
Easter Song	Rav	L	Sr
Easter Song	Van	F	Sr
Easter Song! (Cantata)	Zon	L	Sr
Eastward In Eden	Fcc	C	Tx
Easy Organ Favorites (No 5412)	Zon	G	Zb
Ebb And Flow	Yan	F	Tx
Ecce Ascendimus Jerusalem	Gsc	T	Sl
Ecce Dominus Veniet (E,L)(Md)	Gia	L	Sa
Ecce Nunc Tempus	Caa	T	Sl
Ecce Quomodo Moritur	Gsc	T	Tf
Ecce Quomodo Moritur Justus (Me)	Oxf	T	Sl
Ecce Sacerdos Magnus	Gia	T	Tc
Ecce Virgo Concipiet	Gsc	T	Tm
Ecce! Quomodo Moritur Justus	Gsc	T	Tf
Ecce, Quomodo (Lo Now, So Is)	Gsc	T	Tf
Echo Alleluia	Sac	L	Lf
Echo Carol, The	Lor	T	Sc
Echo Holy Holy	Nal	L	Li
Echo Of Christmas The	Lor	L	Sc
Echoing Alleluia	Abi	L	Lf
Ecos De Victoria (No 5366)	Zon	G	Za
Ecumenical Hymn To God Our Father	Acp	L	Tu
Ecumenical Hymn To God Our Father	Acp	L	Tu
Ecumenical Hymn To God Our Father(4pt)	Acp	L	Tu
Ego Sum Panis Vitae	Gsc	T	Lo
Ego Sum Panis Vivus	Gia	T	Lo
Eight Alleluias, Gospel Acclamations	Cfc	L	Lf
Eight Anthems	Kal	T	Za
Eight Compositions For Organ	Abi	L	Zb
Eight Folksongs & Spirituals	Aug	F	Za
Eight Hymns	Kal	T	Za
Eight Responses	Gsc	T	Za
Eighteen Responses	Lor	L	Za
Eighty Six Prefaces From Missal	Gia	T	Za
Eili, Eili	Gsc	T	Tr
Ein Gebet	Abi	L	Zb
El Nino Perdido	Ron	T	Sc
Elect Of God	Gsc	T	Tr
Elegerunt	Fel	T	Tx
Elegy	Gsc	T	Tf
Elegy And Le Motif	Nov	T	Zb
Elegy For Organ	Abi	L	Zb
Eleven Canzonets	See	L	Za
Eleven Chorale Preludes	Abi	L	Zb
Eleven Scriptural Songs	Cob	L	Za
Elijah (Oratorio)	Kal	T	Tx
Elijah Rock	Gsc	G	Tx
Elijah(Ger)	Cfp	T	Tx
Emitte Spiritum Tuum (Lat, Eng)	Hof	T	Ss

ALPHABETICAL INDEX OF TITLES

Title	Code
Emmanuel	Aug T Sa
Emmanuel	Wlp F Le
Emmanuel Come Save Your People	Wlp L Le
Emmaus Road	Lor L Sr
En Priere	Bbl T Tr
En Son Temple Sacre (Psalm 150)	Bbl T Tt
Endure! Endure! (St Matt Passion)	Smc T Zb
Enduring Faith	Abi L Tr
English High Mass.	Vrn L Za
Enlighten Mine Eyes	Gia L Tf
Enormous Dreams (Psalm 131)	Ahc L Tx
Enter And Sing To The Lord	Rpb F La
Enter O People Of God	Wlp L La
Enter With The Blest (Tannhouser)	Smc T Tf
Entrance Song For Christmas	Gra L La
Entrata Festiva	Cfp L La
Ephesions Hymn (Blessed Be)	Gia F Tj
Ephesions Hymn Ii (May Christ)	Gia F Tj
Epiphany (From Holiday Motets)	Ron T Sc
Epiphany Adoration (Solo)	Aug L Sc
Epiphany Carol (E)	Oxf T Sc
Epiphany Prayer, An	Sac L Sc
Epistle (Response)	Wlp F Ld
Es Ist Nun Aus	Bbl L Sl
Esther	Fel F Tx
Estote Fortes In Bello	Gsc T Tc
Et Verbum Caro Factum Est	Gsc L Sc
Eternal Father	Acp L Tt
Eternal Father (4-Part Arr.)	Acp L Tt
Eternal God	Abi L Tr
Eternal God (W/Choral Spking)	Abi L Tr
Eternal God, Whose Power Upholds	Abi L Tr
Eternal God, Whose Power Upholds	Gia L Tk
Eternal Hope	Sac L Tr
Eternal Rest (Introit)(Funeral-Folk)	Fel F Tf
Eternal Trinity	Gsc T Tt
Eternity To Live Or Die	Sil L Tx
Eucharist, Most Holy.	Vrn L Lo
Eucharistic Acclamation (Simple)	Wlp L Lj
Eucharistic Acclamation (Solemn)	Wlp L Lj
Eucharistic Prayer (Preface)	Gia L Tx
Eucharistic Prayer Ii	Cfc L Tx
Eucharistic Prayer Iii	Cfc L Tx
Ev'ry Valley (From Messiah)	Smc T Zb
Evangelism Arrangements No 1 (4000)	Zon G Za
Evangelism Arrangements No 2 (4191)	Zon G Za
Eve's Lament	Fel F Tx
Even A Worm	Wlp F Tx
Even For One	Lor L Sr
Even So Lord Jesus Quickly Come	Gra L Sa
Even So, Lord Jesus	Aug L Sa
Even So, Lord Jesus, Come	Gmc G Sa
Even So, Lord Jesus, Come	Lor G Sa
Even Then	Nal L Tr
Even Though I Am Tormented	Fel L Sl
Evening Hymn	Oxf T Tr
Evening Hymn (E)	Oxf T Tr
Evening Prayer	Nal C Tr
Evening Service	Oxf T Za
Evening Service For Verses	Oxf T Za
Evening Service In 'a Re' Magnificat	Oxf T Za
Evening Service In C: Magnificat Etc.	Oxf T Za
Evening Service In E Flat	Oxf T Za
Evening Service In Eb: Magnificat Etc.	Oxf T Za
Evening Service; Magnificat Etc	Oxf T Za
Evening Shadows Gently Falling	Hal T Tx
Evening Song	Rpb F Tr
Evening Star	Gal G Tx
Ever-Loving Father	Gsc T Tr
Everlasting God	Ahc L Tt
Everlasting Joy	Lor L Sc
Everlasting Mercy	Mam G Tr
Evermore (I Love The Feelin')	Wrd G Tr
Every Day	Fel F Tx
Every Day	Rpb L Tx
Every Day I Will Praise You (Ps 145)	Rpb L Ld
Every Good & Perfect Gift (M)	Wlp L To
Every Knee Shall Bow	Wrd G Tj
Every Man's Work Shall Be Made	Oxf L Tc
Every Morning Is Easter Morning	Prc L Tx
Every Perfect Gift	Bec T Tr
Every Person Is Gift	Nal L Tr
Every Time I Feel De Spirit	Gsc G Tx
Every Time I Feel The Spirit	Zon G Ss
Every Time I Think About Jesus	Aug G Tj
Every Valley	Nal L Sa
Everybody Knows For Sure	Wrd G Tx
Everybody Sing Alleluia	Rpb C Tt
Everybody's Got To Grow	Wlp F Tx
Everybody's Home	Mar L Tx
Everything Is Beautiful	Hal F Tx
Everything Is Beautiful	Aha F Tx
Everything Will Be All Right	Sav G Tr
Everywhere	Man G Tx
Everywhere And Always	Zon F Tt
Exalt The Name Of The Lord	Her L Tt
Exalt Ye	Gsc T Tt
Exaltation	Aug T Tx
Exaltation	Lor L Tt
Exaltation (S A Opt B)	Lor L Tt
Exaudi Deus (Hear Me O Lord)	Gsc T Tr
Excelsus Super Omnes Gentes Dominus	Gsc T Tt
Except The Lord Build The House	Gsc L Tt
Exciting Savior	Lor F Tj
Exhortation	Rpb L Tx
Exit	Bbl T Tf
Explorer	Prc L Tx
Exsultate Deo	Gia T Tt
Exsultate Jubilate K 165	Kal T Tt
Exsultate Justi	Gia T Tt
Exsurge, Domine (Ps 44)	Oxf T Tr
Exult, You Just, In The Lord	Fel L Tt
Exultate Deo	Gsc T Tt
Exultate Deo	Gsc T Tt
Exultate Deo	Gsc T Tt
Exultet(Easter Proclamation)	Rav L Sr
Eye Has Not Seen	Fel T Sr
Eye Hasn't Seen	Nal L Sr
Eye Hath Not Seen	Gsc T Sr
Eye Hath Not Seen (A Cap)	Abi L Tt
Eyes Have Not Seen	Vrn G Tf
Ezekiel	Fel F Sl
Face In The Crowd	Chd T Tr
Face To Face	Ham G Sr
Face To Face (Psalm 42-43)	Ahc L Lo
Fair Easter	Gsc T Sr
Fairest Lord Jesus	Lor T Tj
Fairest Lord Jesus	Zon T Tj
Faith	Gsc T Tr
Faith (Hb 11-12) (Md)	Oxf L Tx
Faith (Hb 11:1-3,6)	Wlp L Tx
Faith Of Our Fathers	Acp L Tr
Faith Of Our Fathers	Zon T Tr
Faith Of Our Fathers (4-Part Arr.)	Acp L Tr
Faith, Hope And Charity	Fcc F Tr
Faith, Hope And Love (Lyric Liturgy)	Gia L Tr
Faith, Tears And Resurrection Cantata	Zon G Sr
Faithful Cross	Fel T Sl
Faithful Cross	Fel F Sl
Faithful Gather, The	Ccc L Zb
Faithful Shepherd, Guide Me	Gsc T Tr
Fall Softly, Snow	Aug T Tx
Famine Came Upon The Land	Fcc C Tx
Fanfare & Choral Procession (W/Brass)	Aug L La
Fanfare For A Holy Day	Sac L Tt
Fanfare For Thanksgiving	Gsc L Tt
Fanfare For The Seasons	Sac L Tt
Fanfare-Improvisation On Azmon	Abi L Zb
Fantasia On Nun Danket	Abi L Zb
Fantasia On The Old 104th Psalm Tune	Oxf T Tx
Fontasienne And Fughetta	Abi L Zb
Fantasy On O Come All Ye Faithful	Abi L Zb
Fantasy On Victimae Paschali (Diff)	Abi L Zb
Fare Ye Well	Wbp T Tr
Father	Wgm F Tr
Father Almighty	Lor T Tr
Father Almighty	Acp L Tt
Father Almighty (4-Part Arr.)	Acp L Tt
Father Eternal, We Pray (A Cap)	Gia L Tw
Father In Heaven	Wlp L Tr
Father Lead Me Day By Day	Abi L Tr
Father Most Merciful	Gsc T Lo
Father Of Peace	Rav L Tr
Father Of The Human Family	Jsp L Tb
Father While This Bread Is Readied	Wlp L Lo
Father, Bless Our Homes (Hymn)	Jsp L Tr
Father, Bless This Work	Fel F Tj
Father, Eternal, Ruler Of Creation	Aug L La
Father, Forgive Them	Smc T Sl
Father, God Of All Things Living	Wlp T Lo
Father, Hear Us Pray	Som L To
Father, I Adore You	Mar L Tt
Father, I Put My Life In Your Hands	Cfc L Ld
Father, I Will Obey	Gia T Sl
Father, If This Cup	Fel L Sl
Father, If This Cup (Choral)	Fel T Sl
Father, Keep Them Holy	Fel L Tr
Father, May They Be One	Fel L Tr
Father, May We Be One In Christ	Fel L Tr
Father, Mercy	Nal L Tr
Father, O Hear Me	Aug T Tr
Father, O Hear Me	Abi L Sl
Father, Once More Within	Gsc T La
Father, Thy Will Be Done	Van F Sl
Father, We Adore You	Nal L Tt
Father, We Gather Here To Praise	Lit L Tw
Father, We Praise Thee	Aug T Tt
Father, We Praise Thee	Gsc T Tt
Father, We Praise Thee	Tcp L Tt
Father, We Praise Thee	Lor T Tt
Father, We Thank Thee	Gia L Tt
Father, We Thank You	Fel F Tt
Fathers Table Grace	Oak G Tx
Favorite Choir Arrangements No 1 (5427)	Zon G Za
Favorite Choir Arrangements No 2 (5465)	Zon G Za
Favorite Christmas Carols	Gia T Sc
Favorite Hymns For Crusades And Conf.	Zon G Za
Favorite Hymns Of Faith And Hope	Zon G Za
Favorite Prophetic Songs For The Choir	Zon G Za
Favorite Spirituals No 1 (No 5593)	Zon G Za
Favorite Spirituals No 2 (No 5792)	Zon G Za
Favorites For Youth	Zon G Za
Favoritos Juveniles (No 5372)	Zon C Za
Fear God & Give Glory To Him	Smc T Tt
Fear Not	Fel F Tr
Fear Not I Am With Thee	Gsc T Tr
Fear Not; The Lord Will Protect	Fel L Tr
Fear Not, Little Flock	Fel F Tr
Fear Not, O Israel	Gsc T Tt
Fear Not, O Land	Gsc T Tt
Fear Thou Not	Man G Tr
Feast Of Joy	Aug L Tr
Fecit Potentium	Wbp T Tt
Feed My Lambs	Nal L Tc
Feed Us Now, O Son Of God	Gal T Lo
Feel The Place Of The Nails	Fel L Sr
Feeling At Home In The Presence	Gmc G Tj
Fellowship Divine	Zon G Lo
Festal Alleluia, A	Lor L Sr
Festal Responses (E)	Oxf T Za
Festal Rhapsody	Abi L Zb
Festival Anthem On Crown Him	Aug T La
Festival Anthem, Op. 109 No.3	Cfp T Tt
Festival Anthem, Op.109 No.1	Cfp T Tt
Festival Anthem, Op.109 No.2	Cfp T Tt
Festival Anthems For Sab	Abi L Za
Festival Hymn	Aug T Tt
Festival Hymn	Bbl T Tt
Festival Introits	Abi L La
Festival Mass (1965) W/Cantor	Gia L Za
Festival Mass (1972) W/Org	Gia L Za
Festival Of Christmas	Lor L Sc
Festival Of Lessons And Carols	Lor L Sc
Festival Overture (Organ Solo)	Cfp T Zb
Festival Piece On "St. Ann"	Her T Tx
Festival Prelude	Abi L Zb
Festival Prelude On I'll Praise	Abi L Zb
Festival Te Deum (Md)	Oxf T Tt
Festival Te Deum (On Trad. Themes)	Oxf T Tt
Festival Te Deum No. 7	Gsc T Tt
Fidelia	Bbl T Tt
Fierce Was The Wild Billow	Gsc T Sl
Fifteen Harmonizations On Hymns	Abi L Zb
Fifteen Preludes	Abi L Zb
Fifty Anthems For Mixed Voices	Oxf T Za
Fifty Folk Favorites (No 5074)	Zon F Za
Fifty Gospel Quartet Favorites	Zon G Za
Fifty Just Men	Fcc C Sl
Fifty Latin American Favorites (#5276)	Zon G Za
Fifty Men's Favorites No 4311	Zon G Za
Fifty Two Sacred Motets (Latin)	Kal T Za
Fifty-Five Hymn Intonations	Abi L Zb
Fight Is On, The (W/Opt Trumpet Trio)	Zon G Tc
Fight The Good Fight	Abi L Tc
Fight The Good Fight	Zon T Tc
Fight The Good Fight	Lor T Tr
Fight The Good Fight (E)	Oxf T Tx
Filhas De Maria	Som L Tm
Fill It With Sunshine	Nal C Tr
Fill Me, Holy Spirit	Yan F Ss
Fill My Cup, Lord	Wrd G Ln
Fill My House	Jas T Lo
Fill The Pots With Water	Van F Tb
Fill The World With Light (Epiphany)	Pro L Sc
Fill Us With Your Love (Ps 90)	Gra L Ld
Final Doxology	Gia L Lk
Fioucia From Three Folk Hymns	Bbl T Tt
Fire Of Love	Nal L Ss
Firmament Of Power	Wbp T Tt
First And Second Preces And Psalms	Kal T Tx
First And Second Preces And Psalms	Kal T Tx
First Noel, The	Acp L Sc
First Noel, The	Acp L Sc
First Noel, The (C)	Lor T Sc
First Psalm	Gsc T Tx
First, The Last, The	Abi L Tj
Fish Wish	Van C Tx
Fisherman	Gia F Tc
Fishers Of Men	Sac L Tc
Five Anthems	Kal T Za
Five Biblical Contemplations For Organ	Sac L Zb
Five Church Cantatas	Lps T Za
Five Early American Hymn Tunes (E)	Oxf T Za
Five Hymns In Popular Style (Me)	Oxf L Za
Five Minutes More	Zon G Sr
Five Motets	Kal T Za
Five Motets	Kal T Za
Five Sacred Choruses	Kal T Za
Five Sequences For The Virgin Mary	Oxf T Za
Five Songs	Pic L Za
Fix Me, Jesus	Gsc G Ts
Flag To Follow, A (W/Opt Brs & Percuss	Zon G Tp
Flee Into Egypt Land (Christmas)	Jhe T Sc
Flexible Amen	Prc L Tx
Flies The Dove (From Young Carpenter)	Wlp F Ss
Fling Wide The Gates	Cfs T Sl
Fling Wide The Gates	Gsc T Sl
Flocks In Pastures Green Abiding (M)	Oxf T Sc
Flower Of Jesse	Gsc T Sc
Flowing Free (Love Is Flowing)	Gia F Ss

ALPHABETICAL INDEX OF TITLES

Fly (From Even A Worm)	Wlp	F	Tx
Fold To Thy Heart Thy Brother	Gsc	L	Lo
Folio Of Choir Favorites	Zon	L	Za
Folio Of Gospel Choir Favorites	Zon	G	Za
Folk Celebration (No 4355)	Zon	F	Za
Folk Mass (Icet)	Jsp	L	Za
Folk Songs Of Mike Mcgervey (4287)	Zon	F	Za
Folks Don't Kiss Old People Any More	Fcc	F	Tx
Follow All The Way	Man	G	Tc
Follow Christ	Fcc	F	Tc
Follow Me	Clm	F	Tt
Follow Me	Sms	T	Tt
Follow Me	Lor	L	Tc
Follow Me	Van	F	Tc
Follow Me (Cantata) (No 4275)	Zon	L	Tc
Follow On	Lor	G	Tc
Follow On	Zon	G	Tc
Follow The Road	Lor	L	Tc
Follow You	Mar	L	Tc
Follow, I Will Follow Thee	Zon	G	Tc
Footsteps Of Jesus	Lor	L	Tc
For A Pearl Of Great Price	Fel	L	Tc
For A Reward	Fel	L	Tx
For All That Has Been	Nal	L	Tt
For All The Saints	Acp	L	Tx
For All The Saints	Lor	L	Tx
For All The Saints	Sc	T	Tx
For All The Saints (M)	Oxf	T	Tx
For All These Mercies We Will Sing	Gsc	T	Tr
For As The Rain Cometh Down	Gsc	L	Sa
For Baby (For Bobbie)	Clm	F	Tt
For By Grace	Zon	L	Tr
For Ever, O Lord	Gsc	L	Tt
For God So Loved The World	Lym	T	Sc
For He Shall Give His Angels Charge	Aug	T	Sl
For Health & Strength	Mar	L	Tt
For His Loving Kindness	Yan	F	Tt
For His Mercy Will Never End	Fel	L	Tr
For Spacious Skies	Lor	L	Tp
For The Beauty Of The Earth	Gia	L	Tt
For The Beauty Of The Earth	Wbp	T	Tt
For The Beauty Of The Earth	Zon	T	Tt
For The Beauty Of The Earth	Gsc	T	Tt
For The Bread	Abi	L	Lo
For The Christ Child	Pio	L	Sc
For The Healing Of The Nations	Jsp	L	Tr
For The Healing Of The Nations	Gal	L	Tr
For The People Of God	Gia	L	Tr
For Theirs Is The Kingdom Of Heaven	Gsc	L	Ll
For Those Tears I Died	Chd	G	Tj
For Thy Great Mercy(Double Chorus)	Gsc	T	Sl
For Tommy: Thanks For The Chance!	Nal	C	Tx
For Unto Us A Child Is Born	Lor	T	Sc
For Unto Us A Child Is Born	Gsc	T	Sc
For Unto Us A Child Is Born	Pro	T	Sc
For We Are One	Fel	F	Tr
For We Have Seen His Star	Gsc	T	Sc
For With Time Our Father Has Brought	Mar	L	Tr
For You Are My God	Nal	L	Tr
For You Shall Go Out In Joy	Gsc	T	Sc
For Your Light Has Come	Aug	T	Sc
Forbidden Fruit	Fcc	C	Sl
Forever	Wlp	F	Tr
Forever Gone	Man	G	Sl
Forever His People Adore Him.	Vrn	L	Tt
Forever I Will Sing	Nal	L	Tt
Forever I Will Sing(Ps 89)	Rav	L	Ld
Forever I Will Sing(Ps 89)	Rav	L	Ld
Forever Together With Him	Zon	F	Sr
Forever With Jesus	Gmc	G	Tf
Forever, O Lord (Ps 8)	Pro	T	Tt
Forevermore	Sil	F	Tx
Forevermore	Fel	F	Tt
Forget The Sins Of Our Past	Fel	L	Sl
Forgive Me (E)	Lor	L	Sr
Forgive My Lord	Wrd	G	Sl
Forgive Our Sins As We Forgive	Gia	L	Sl
Forming God's People	Fel	L	Tr
Forth In Thy Name	Lor	T	Tc
Forth In Thy Name, O Lord	Abi	L	Tc
Forth In Thy Name, O Lord	Lor	L	Tc
Forty Days To Easter	Lor	T	Sl
Forward Into Light	Pic	L	Tc
Foundation	Abi	T	Tp
Four Advent Chorales	Gia	T	Za
Four American Folk Hymns	Abi	L	Za
Four Anthems	Kal	T	Za
Four Canons	Aug	T	Za
Four Canticles For Christmas	Sac	L	Sc
Four Carols	Pic	L	Sc
Four Carols For A Holy Night	Gsc	T	Sc
Four Choral Meditations—Lent	Gia	T	Za
Four Chorale Preludes	Abi	L	Zb
Four Christmas Chorales	Gia	T	Za
Four Easter Chorales	Gia	T	Za
Four Folk—Hymns	Bbl	T	Za
Four Folksongs And Spirituals	Aug	F	Za
Four Gospel Hymn Anthems	Abi	G	Za
Four Modern Anthems	Abi	L	Za
Four Motets	Kal	T	Za
Four Organ Preludes On Chorale Tunes	Abi	L	Zb
Four Part Chorales (Germ Text)	Kal	T	Za
Four Preludes On Early American Tunes	Abi	L	Zb
Four Preludes On Hymns Of The Church	Abi	L	Zb
Four Psalm Preludes	Abi	L	Zb
Four Psalm Preludes Set Ii	Abi	L	Zb
Four Psalm Settings	Gia	L	Za
Four Psalms, Op. 74 (Eng)	Cfp	T	Za
Four Settings Of Preces & Responses	Oxf	T	Za
Four Things	Gal	G	Tx
Four—Part Chorales (185)	Lps	T	Za
Fourteen Choral Responses	Sac	L	Za
Fourteen Plainsong Hymns (E & L)	Gia	T	Za
Fourth Evening Service: Magnificat Etc	Oxf	T	Za
Fourth Mass, C Major (Latin)	Kal	T	Za
Fragrant The Prayer	Bbl	T	Tr
Francis, Friend Of All Things	Wlp	T	Tx
Free Child	Wlp	F	Tr
Free From Fear	Fel	L	Tr
Free Me	Yan	F	Tr
Free To Go Home	Gmc	G	Tf
Freedom Song	Fel	F	Tx
Freely Will I Offer	Fel	L	To
Fresh Sounds	Erd	L	Za
Friend Song	Fel	C	Tr
Friendly Beasts, The (C)	Lor	T	Sc
Friends	Mar	L	Tr
Friends	Mar	L	Tr
Friends Are Like Flowers	Nal	C	Tr
Friends I Know	Ham	G	Tr
Friends, Friends	Nal	C	Tr
Friendship Hymn (I Shall Not Call)	Gia	F	Tr
From All That Dwell Below The Skies	Gsc	T	Tt
From All That Dwell Below The Skies	Zon	T	Tt
From All Who Dwell Beneath The Skies	Acp	L	Tt
From All Who Dwell Beneath The Skies	Acp	L	Tt
From Among The Branches	Fel	L	Tx
From An Indirect Love	Nal	L	Tr
From Celestial Seats Descending	Smc	T	Zb
From Despair To Hope	Rpb	L	Sl
From East To West	Sac	L	Sc
From Egypt's Bondage Come	Gsc	T	Tb
From Glory To Glory Advancing	Gia	T	Tt
From Heaven Above	Abi	L	Sc
From Heaven An Angel (Hungarian Carol)	Gsc	T	Sc
From Heaven On High	Gsc	T	Sc
From Heaven The Lord Looks Down	Wlp	T	Tr
From Isaiah (In Three Parts)	Aug	T	Sa
From My Distress	Fel	L	Sl
From My Heart	Zon	G	Tr
From Out Their Temples (Cantata)	Lps	T	Tr
From Sion Perfect In Beauty (M)	Gia	L	Tu
From The Beginning	Aug	L	Tx
From The Deep, Lord (Cantata)	Lps	T	Sl
From The Depths	Acp	L	Sl
From The Depths	Acf	L	Tx
From The Depths	Fel	L	Sl
From The Depths (4—Part Arr.)	Acp	L	Sl
From The Depths Do I Cry	Wlp	L	Sl
From The Rising Of The Sun	Mar	L	Tt
From The Rising Of The Sun	Abi	L	Sc
From The Voices Of Children	Wlp	L	Tt
From Wanton Sin	Fel	L	Sl
From Where Is His Wisdom	Fel	L	Tj
From Whom All Blessings Flow	Mem	L	Tt
Fugue In E Major	Nov	T	Zb
Fugue In G	Ccc	L	Zb
Full Stature	Abi	L	Tr
Fum, Fum, Fum	Gsc	T	Sc
Fum, Fum, Fum	Ron	T	Tt
Funeral Anthem For Queen Caroline	Kal	T	Tf
Funeral Anthem On The Death	Bbl	T	Tf
Funeral Hymn	Bbl	T	Tf
Gabriel Angelus	Gia	T	Tm
Gabriel's Message	Gsc	T	Sc
Galatians 2:20	Mar	L	Tj
Galilee (Jesus Took A Walk)	Wrd	G	Tc
Garden	Mar	L	Tr
Garden Hymn	Gsc	T	Tj
Garden Hymn (A Cap)	Abi	T	Tr
Garden Hymn, The	Lor	T	Tx
Garden Hymn, The	Sac	L	Tr
Gatatumba (Andalusian Carol)	Gsc	F	Sc
Gates Of Heaven Are Open	Hof	L	Sr
Gates Of Jerusalem, The	Maf	T	Sr
Gates Of Jerusalem, The	Lor	T	Sr
Gather 'round	Rpb	L	La
Gather 'round (88 Songs)	Rpb	L	Za
Gather Us From Among The Nations	Fel	L	Sl
Gathering Home	Ham	G	Tf
Gathering Song	Fcc	F	La
Gathering Song (W/ Org, Perc)	Gia	L	La
Gaude Maria	Gia	T	Tm
Gaudeamus	Gia	L	Zb
Gaudent In Coelis	Gia	T	Tt
General Intercessions	Wlp	L	Lh
General Intercessions	Wlp	L	Lh
General Intercessions(Notre Dame Mass)	Gia	L	Lh
Gentle As Morning (Collection)	Wrd	G	Za
Gentle Doxology	Prc	L	Tx
Gentle Gloria Patri	Prc	L	Tx
Gentle Guide (Mother's Day)	Gam	C	Tx
Gentle Hands	Sms	T	Tr
Gentle Holy Spirit	Bfi	T	Ss
Gentle Jesus	Lor	T	Sc
Gentle Jesus, Meek And Mild	Abi	T	Tj
Gentle Love Song, A	Nal	L	Tr
Gentle Mary	Pro	F	Sc
Gentle Mary Catalan Folk—Song	Gsc	T	Sc
Gentle Rains	Rav	L	Lo
Gentle Savior, Hold My Hand	Smc	T	Tj
Gentle Shepherd	Gmc	G	Tr
Gentle Shepherd (Narration)	Lor	G	Tr
George Beverly Shea Gospel Solos(5433)	Zon	G	Za
George Beverly Shea Solos (No 5432)	Zon	G	Za
German Magnificat	Oxf	T	Tm
German Requiem (Eng & Ger)	Cfp	T	Tf
Gesangbuch Der Mennoniten	Flp	T	Za
Get All Excited	Gmc	G	Tt
Get On Board	Nal	L	Tc
Get On The Good Foot	Nal	L	Tx
Get On The Right Road	Pmp	G	Sl
Get Out Of Yesterday	Sil	L	Tx
Get Up And Live	Fel	L	Tr
Get Up, Jerusalem	Wlp	F	Sa
Get Yourself Together	Man	L	Tr
Gettin' It Together In Jesus	Sil	L	Tj
Getting High On Love	Gia	F	Tr
Getting Used To The Family Of God	Gmc	G	Tr
Giant Love Ball Song	Nal	C	Tr
Gift Of Joy	Van	F	To
Gift Of Light	Aug	T	Sc
Gift Of Love	Lor	T	Sc
Gift Of Love, The	Lor	L	Tr
Gift Of Peace	Fel	F	Tr
Gift Of Wheat From Thy Teeming Fields	Wlp	T	To
Gifts	Nal	L	To
Gifts Of Bread And Wine	Fel	F	To
Gifts We Shall Bring	Gia	T	Sc
Give A Little Something Special	Prc	L	Tx
Give Alms Of Thy Goods (Me)	Oxf	T	Tx
Give Ear O Lord, Unto My Pray'r	Gsc	T	Tr
Give Ear To My Words	Gsc	T	Tr
Give Ear, O Lord	Som	L	Tr
Give God A Chance And Be Made Glad	Sto	G	Tr
Give Him The Glory	Zon	G	Tt
Give It Life	Rpb	L	Tr
Give Laud Unto The Lord	Oxf	T	Tt
Give Light To My Eyes	Fel	L	Sl
Give Me An Answer (Psalm4)	Ahc	L	Tr
Give Me Jesus	Lor	T	Tj
Give Me Jesus (Spiritual)	Aug	G	Tj
Give Me Justice, O God	Fel	L	Sl
Give Me More Of Thee	Mar	L	Ss
Give Me Your Hand	Fel	C	Lo
Give Peace, O Lord	Fel	L	Tr
Give Peace, O Lord (Ps 122)	Gra	F	Tr
Give Praise All Earthly Men	Gsc	T	Tt
Give Praise To The Lord	Wlp	L	Tt
Give Praise To The Lord	Gia	L	Tt
Give Praise Unto The Lord (A Cap)	Pro	T	Sc
Give Thanks	Rpb	L	Tt
Give Thanks To God The Father	Acp	L	Tt
Give Thanks To God The Father	Acp	L	Tt
Give Thanks To The Lord	Acp	L	Tt
Give Thanks To The Lord	Gia	L	Tt
Give Thanks To The Lord (Ps107)	Gra	L	Ld
Give Thanks To The Lord (4—Part Arr.)	Acp	L	Tt
Give Thanks Unto The Lord (Ps. 136)	Som	L	Tt
Give The Bread Of Life	Wlp	L	Ln
Give The King Your Final Judgment	Acp	L	Tk
Give The King Your Final Judgment	Acp	L	Tk
Give The King Your Final Judgment(4pt)	Acp	L	Tk
Give The King Your Final Judgment(4pt)	Acp	L	Tk
Give The Lord Glory(Ps 96)	Rav	L	Ld
Give Them Rest	Fel	L	Tf
Give Them Rest (Choral)	Fel	T	Tf
Give Them, O Lord	Fel	L	Tx
Give To The Winds Thy Fears (Opt Acc)	Abi	L	Sl
Give Unto The Humble	Gsc	T	Sl
Give Unto The Lord	Gsc	T	To
Give Up	Ced	G	Tx
Give Us Faith For Today	Gsc	T	Tr
Give Us The Wings Of Faith (M)	Oxf	T	Tr
Give Your Heart To Jesus (Rock)	Wrd	F	Tc
Giver Of All, We Thank Thee	Sac	L	Tt
Glad Song	Aug	T	Tt
Glad Tidings Of Great Joy	Pro	T	Sc
Glimpse Of Jesus	Man	G	Tj
Gloria	Gal	G	Tt
Gloria	Aug	T	Lc
Gloria	Gia	L	Lc
Gloria	Aug	T	Lc
Gloria	Gia	L	Lc
Gloria	Gsc	T	Lc
Gloria	Gsc	T	Lc
Gloria	Gsc	T	Sc
Gloria	Gsc	T	Lc
Gloria	Oxf	T	Lc
Gloria	Kal	T	Lc

ALPHABETICAL INDEX OF TITLES

Title	Code		Title	Code
Gloria	Oxf T Lc		Glory To God	Cfc L Lc
Gloria	Nal L Lc		Glory To God	Abi L Tt
Gloria	Nal L Lc		Glory To God	Fel F Tt
Gloria (A Cappella, Long)	Aug L Lc		Glory To God	Wlp L Tx
Gloria (D)	Oxf T Lc		Glory To God	Lor L Sc
Gloria (Eng Mass)	Gia L Lc		Glory To God	Ccc L Lc
Gloria (Eng, Icet) Opt Brass	Gra L Lc		Glory To God	Nal L Lc
Gloria (From Celebration)	Gia L Lc		Glory To God	Abi L Lc
Gloria (From The Twelfth Mass)	Lor T Lc		Glory To God	Ahc L Lc
Gloria (Icet) From Community Mass	Gia L Lc		Glory To God	Sbf L Lc
Gloria (Latin)	Oxf L Lc		Glory To God	Nal L Lc
Gloria (Liturgy Of Joy)	Fel L Lc		Glory To God	Nal L Lc
Gloria (Lyric Liturgy)	Gia L Lc		Glory To God	Yan F Lc
Gloria (Mariachi Mass)	Fel F Lc		Glory To God ("Messiah")	Pro T Sc
Gloria (Mass For King Of Glory)Org/Gui	Gia F Lc		Glory To God (American Saint)(Icet)	Wlp L Lc
Gloria (Mass For New Rite)	Fel C Lc		Glory To God (Angelic Hymn)	Gia L Lc
Gloria (Mass For Schools)	Oxf T Lc		Glory To God (Bcl)	Wlp L Lc
Gloria (Md)	Oxf T Lc		Glory To God (Cel Of Unity)	Gia L Lc
Gloria (Missa Brevis)	Fel T Lc		Glory To God (Chardin Mass)	Fel L Lc
Gloria (Notre Dame Mass)	Gia L Lc		Glory To God (Child Mass)	Gia L Lc
Gloria (Sung Mass No.2)	Fel L Lc		Glory To God (Choir Alone) (M)	Wlp L Lc
Gloria (Thomas More Mass)	Fel L Lc		Glory To God (Community Mass)	Gia L Lc
Gloria (W/Fl,Cello)	Gia L Lc		Glory To God (Danish Amen Mass)	Jsp L Lc
Gloria A Dios (Chant)	Gia L Lc		Glory To God (Folk Mass No.4)	Fel F Lc
Gloria A La Samba (W/Org, Bongos)	Gia F Lc		Glory To God (Icet)	Wlp L Lc
Gloria And Alleluia	Gsc L Lc		Glory To God (Icet)	Jsp L Lc
Gloria And Sanctus/Benedictus	Gia T Lc		Glory To God (Icet)(Mass Of Hope) M	Wlp L Lc
Gloria From Messa A 4 Voci Da Cappella	Gia T Lc		Glory To God (Lyric Mass)	Gia L Lc
Gloria In Excelsis	Ron T Lc		Glory To God (Mass Assembly)(Icet)	Wlp L Lc
Gloria In Excelsis	Lor L Sc		Glory To God (Missa Bossa Nova)	Fel F Lc
Gloria In Excelsis	Gsc T Lc		Glory To God (Opt Brs/Timp)	Gia L Lc
Gloria In Excelsis	Gsc T Lc		Glory To God (People's Mass)(Icet)	Wlp L Lc
Gloria In Excelsis	Maf T Lc		Glory To God (Sung Mass No.1)	Fel L Lc
Gloria In Excelsis ("12th Mass")	Cfs T Lc		Glory To God (W/Cantor) Dominic Mass	Gia L Lc
Gloria In Excelsis (Md)	Oxf T Lc		Glory To God (1964 Text)	Van F Lc
Gloria In Excelsis Deo	Sac L Sc		Glory To God (64 Text)	Van F Lc
Gloria In Excelsis Deo	Gsc T Lc		Glory To God In Highest	Wlp L Tt
Gloria In Excelsis Deo	Ron T Sc		Glory To God In The Highest	Abi L Tt
Gloria In Excelsis Deo	Lor T Lc		Glory To God In The Highest	Wlp T Lc
Gloria Of The Bells Icet	Gia L Lc		Glory To God In The Highest	Maf T Lc
Gloria Patri	Prc L Tx		Glory To God In The Highest	Lor T Lc
Gloria Patri	Gsc T Tt		Glory To God In The Highest	Gsc T Lc
Gloria Patri	Gsc T Lc		Glory To God In The Highest	Pro T Lc
Gloria Patri	Gsc T Tt		Glory To God In The Highest	Gsc T Lc
Gloria Sing All Our Voices	Gsc L Lc		Glory To God In The Highest (Opt Perc)	Pro T Lc
Gloria Tibi(From Mass)	Her T Sc		Glory To God In The Highest, Alleluia	Fel L Tt
Gloria To God On High	Gsc T Lc		Glory To God In The Highest, Glory	Maf T Lc
Gloria(Mass In B Flat)	Aug T Sr		Glory To God On High	Wlp F Tt
Glorification	Wlp L Tt		Glory To God On High	Aug T Lc
Glorify The Lord With Me	Prc L Tx		Glory To God On High	Fel L Tt
Glorious Amen	Zon G Tr		Glory To God We Sing	Zon T Sc
Glorious Church, A	Fcc F Tt		Glory To God(Icet)(Holy Spirit Mass)	Wlp L Lc
Glorious God	Gia F Tj		Glory To God(Mass For All Seasons)	Gia L Lc
Glorious In Majesty (Trad Jewish)	Sac L Tt		Glory To God(New Mass)	Gia L Lc
Glorious Is Thy Holy Name	Lor L Sc		Glory To God(Vianney Mass)	Gia L Lc
Glorious Message, The	Wlp L Tm		Glory To Jesus	Sms F Tt
Glorious Mysteries	Pro T Sc		Glory To Our Risen King	Sac L Sr
Glorious Song, The	Pro T Sc		Glory To The Father	Fel L Tt
Glorious Star Is Beaming	Oxf T Sc		Glory To The Father	Gsc T Tt
Glorious The Day When Christ Was Born	Gsc T Tt		Glory To The King Of Kings	Lor L Tk
Glorious Things Of Thee Are Spoken	Zon T Tt		Glory To The Lamb (Cantata) (No 4269)	Zon L Sr
Glorious Things Of Thee Are Spoken	Fcc F Tt		Glory To The Risen Lord	Van F Sr
Glory	Wbp T Tt		Glory To Thee (Me) 1	Oxf L Sc
Glory	Wlp F Tt		Glory To Thee My God This Night(Canon)	Oxf T Tt
Glory	Rpb L Tt		Glory To Thy Holy Name	Gsc T Tt
Glory	Yan F Lc		Glory To You	Rpb L Lg
Glory (Sing To The Lord)	Gia F Tt		Glory To You, Word Of God(Icet)	Wlp L Lg
Glory Above The Heavens	Sac L Tt		Glory, Glory (A Capella)	Mcc G Le
Glory And Honor	Gsc T Tt		Glory,Hallelujah To The Lamb	Zon G Sr
Glory And Praise Forever	Nal L Tt		Glroious Things Of Thee Are Spoken	Zon T Tr
Glory And Praise To You	Wlp L Lg		Go And Be Happy	Prc L Tx
Glory And Praise To You	Nal L Lg		Go Down Moses	Gsc G Sc
Glory And Praise To You (Icet)	Wlp L Lg		Go Down Moses (Pd)	Gia F Tx
Glory And Praise To You Eternity	Wlp L Tt		Go Down, Moses! (Negro Spiritual)	Lor G Tx
Glory And Triumph	Sac T Sr		Go Forth	Mob C Tx
Glory Around His Head, The	Bbl T Sr		Go Forth	Yan F Tc
Glory Be To God	Gia T Lc		Go Forth (Mission Song)	Jsp L Tx
Glory Be To God On High	Abi L Tt		Go Forth With God! (Me)	Oxf T Tx
Glory Be To God On High (Jazz-Rock)	Fel F Lc		Go Forth, People Of God	Rpb T Tc
Glory Be To God The Father	Gia T Tt		Go In Joy	Bfi F Tr
Glory Be To God The Father (Me)	Gia L Tt		Go In Peace	Nal L Tr
Glory Be To Israel	Fel F Sc		Go In Peace	Yan F Tr
Glory Be To The Father	Gsc L Tt		Go In Peace And Love (W/Guitar)	Gia L Tr
Glory Be To The Father.	Vrn L Lp		Go Little Prayer, Go	Csm G To
Glory Bound (From Psalm 29)	Wlp F Sr		Go Make Of All Disciples	Abi L Tr
Glory Hallelujah	Wlp F Tt		Go Now In Peace	Nal L Tr
Glory Hallelujah To The Lamb	Zon T Sr		Go On By	Ham C Tx
Glory Hosanna	Acp F Tt		Go On My Child	Jhe G Tx
Glory Hosanna	Acp F Tt		Go Out To The Whole World	Rpb L Tc
Glory Land	Fel F Sr		Go Tell Everyone	Van F Tc
Glory Of Joy	Rpb L Tx		Go Tell It In The City	Abi L Tr
Glory Of The Star The	Lor L Sc		Go Tell It On The Mountain	Pro G Sc
Glory To God	Smc T Zb		Go Tell It On The Mountain	Zon G Tc
Glory To God	Cfc L Lc		Go Tell It On The Mountain	Zon G Tc
Glory To God	Wgm F Tt		Go Tell The Untold Millions	Acp F Tx
Glory To God	Gia L Lc		Go Tell Your People	Acp F Tt
Glory To God	Lor L Sc		Go Tell Your People (4-Part Arr)	Acp F Tj
Glory To God	Lor T Sc		Go Thy Way (From Three Sacred Pieces)	Ron T Tr
Glory To God	Gsc T Tt		Go To Dark Gethsemane	Bfi T Sl
Glory To God	Cfc L Lc		Go To Dark Gethsemane	Lor T Sl
			Go To Dark Gethsemane	Lor T Sl

Title	Code
Go Ye And Teach All Nations	Lor T Tc
Go Ye Into All The World	Aug T Tc
Go Ye Therefore	Prc L Tc
Go Ye Therefore	Sac L Tc
Go You Also Into My Vineyard	Fel L Tc
Go, Make All Nations	Fel L Tc
Go, Prayer Of Mine	Lor T Tr
Go, Tell It On The Mountain	Lor G Sc
God	See L Tx
God And Man At Table	Sta F Tk
God Arises	Fel F Tk
God Ascends Amid Shouts Of Joy	Fel L Sr
God Be In My Head	Abi L Tr
God Be In My Head (A Cap)	Abi L Tr
God Be In My Head (E)	Oxf L Tr
God Be In Ny Head	Gsc T Tr
God Be Magnified	Man L Tt
God Be Merciful	Aug T Sl
God Be Merciful Unto Us	Ron T Sl
God Be Merciful Unto Us	Abi L Tr
God Bless Our Land	Gsc L Tp
God Bless Our Native Land	Gsc L Tp
God Bless The Little Things W/Organ Pi	Gsc T Tp
God Bless You, Mother Dear	Lor T Tx
God Deigning Men To Be (Apostles)	Jsp L Tx
God Did!	Rpb C Tx
God Don't Care Who You Are	Mar G Tr
God Doth Not Slumber Nor Sleep	Zon G Tr
God Dwells In The Hearts	Rpb F Tr
God Eternal Is My Refuge	Gsc T Tr
God Father, Be Thou Praised	Gia L Tt
God Father, Praise And Glory	Gia T Tt
God Forbid That I Should Boast	Acp L Sl
God Forbid That I Should Boast (4pt)	Acp L Sl
God Gave (Me) The Song	Gmc G Ss
God Gave Him Life Again!	Sac L Sr
God Give Ye Merry Christmastide	Pro T Sc
God Gives Freely	Rpb F To
God Gives His People Strength	Van F Lp
God Grant You Many Years	Gia T Tx
God Has A Reason	Lor T Tr
God Has Been Good To Me	Bul G Tr
God Has Blessed You Forever	Fel L Tr
God Has Blessings Of All Kind	Sto G Tr
God Has Called You	Fis F Tc
God Has Ears To Listen	Sac L Tr
God Has Made Us One In His Love	Sha F Tr
God Has My Heart (Cantata)	Lps T Tc
God Has Visited His People	Mob C Tx
God Himself Is With Us	Lor L Tr
God In A Star	Lor L Sc
God Is A Fire Of Love	Gia F Tx
God Is A Spirit	Gsc T Tr
God Is Alive	Van C Tr
God Is Alive	Stm G Tx
God Is Alive	Wlp F Tr
God Is Before Me	Lor L Tr
God Is Building A House	Nal C Tr
God Is Everywhere	Zon G Tr
God Is Everywhere	Som L Tx
God Is Everywhere	Lor L Tr
God Is God	Aug T Tx
God Is Great	Lor T Tt
God Is Here—Let's Celebrate	Aug T La
God Is In His Holy Temple	Sac L Tc
God Is In His Holy Temple	Gsc T Ss
God Is In This Holy Place	Gia L La
God Is In This Place	Sac L Tc
God Is Living, God Is Here! (Me)	Oxf T Tr
God Is Love	Ahc L Tr
God Is Love	Wlp L Tr
God Is Love	Aug T Tr
God Is Love	Rpb L Tr
God Is Love	Nal L Tr
God Is Love	Aug L Tr
God Is Love	Sti G Ln
God Is Love	Gsc T Tr
God Is Love	Lor L Tr
God Is Love	Mar L Tr
God Is Merciful	Gsc T Sl
God Is Moving On	Cam F Tx
God Is Much Fairer	Fel F Tx
God Is My Guide	Gsc T Tr
God Is My Life	Wlp F Tr
God Is My Strong Salvation	Wbp T La
God Is My Strong Salvation (A Cap)	Abi L Tr
God Is My Strong Salvation (M)	Abi L Tr
God Is Not Dead	Sac L Tk
God Is Our Eternal Refuge	Zon L Tr
God Is Our Father	Nal C Tr
God Is Our Refuge	Nal L Tr
God Is Our Refuge	Gsc T Tr
God Is Our Refuge And Strength	Sac L Tr
God Is Our Refuge, God Is Our Strength	Wbp T Tt
God Is Our Saviour	Jhm G Tr
God Is Our Strength And Song	Gsc T Tr
God Is So Good	Man G Tr
God Is So Good	Mar G Tr
God Is So Wonderful	Sem G Tt
God Is Unique And One	Gal L Tr

ALPHABETICAL INDEX OF TITLES

Title	Code		
God Is Watching Over Us	Smc	T	Zb
God Is Wisdom God Is Love(From Ruth)	Gsc	T	Tr
God Is Working His Purpose Out	Abi	L	Tr
God Knows All About Tomorrow	Zon	G	Tr
God Lives!	Lor	L	Tt
God Loves A Cheerful Giver	Van	F	Tc
God Loves To Talk To Boys While	Gmc	G	Tr
God Loves You	Hhh	G	Tr
God Made Me!	Bec	L	Tt
God Made The World	Wlp	F	Tx
God Made Us All	Wlp	F	Tx
God Maketh No Mistake	Jhe	G	Tx
God Mounts His Throne	Gia	L	Sr
God Mounts His Throne (Icet)	Wlp	L	Ld
God Mounts His Throne (Ps47)	Gra	L	Ld
God Of Abraham Praise, The	Bec	T	Tt
God Of Abraham Praise, The	Abi	L	Tt
God Of All Grace	Gsc	T	Sl
God Of Concrete	Aug	L	Tx
God Of Earth And Planets (Opt Flute)	Aug	L	Tx
God Of Everlasting Glory	Zon	T	Tt
God Of Grace And God Of Glory	Lor	T	Tt
God Of Light	Gsc	T	Tt
God Of Love (Choral)	Fel	T	Tr
God Of Love My Shepherd Is, The	Lor	T	Tr
God Of Love, King Of Peace	Sac	L	Tr
God Of Mercy	Aug	T	Tr
God Of Might, We Praise Thy Name	Abi	L	Tt
God Of Our Fathers	Bec	T	Tp
God Of Our Fathers	Acp	L	Tp
God Of Our Fathers	Zon	T	Tp
God Of Our Fathers	Lor	T	Tp
God Of Our Fathers	Acp	L	Tp
God Of Our Fathers (4-Part Arr)	Acp	T	Tp
God Of Our Fathers (4-Part Arr)	Acp	L	Tp
God Of Our Life	Zon	T	Tr
God Of The Earth	Abi	L	Tr
God Of The Earth	Sac	L	To
God Of The Pastures, Hear (Hymn)	Jsp	T	Tr
God Of The Strong	Gsc	T	Tt
God Of The World	Pic	L	Tx
God Our Father	Gsc	T	Sl
God Put His Hand On My Shoulder	Zon	G	Tr
God Reigns	Wlp	L	Sr
God Rest Ye Merry, Gentlemen	Lor	T	Sc
God Rest You Merrie Gentlemen	Gsc	T	Sc
God Rest You Merry Gentlemen	Pro	T	Sc
God Rest You Merry Gentlemen	Zon	T	Sc
God Reveals Himself To Me	Man	G	Tr
God Shall Wipe Away All Tears	Gsc	T	Sr
God So Loved (No 4278) (Musical)	Zon	L	Tj
God So Loved The World	Gia	T	Sl
God So Loved The World	Fel	L	Sl
God So Loved The World	Gsc	T	Sa
God So Loved The World	Lor	T	Sl
God So Loved The World	Cfs	T	Sl
God So Loved The World	Aug	T	Sl
God So Loved The World	Gsc	T	Sl
God Speaks	Van	F	Tx
God Spoke To Me One Day	Man	G	Tx
God Spoke To Me Today	Lor	L	Tx
God Supplies What I Need	Gmp	G	Tr
God That Was Real	Zon	F	Tx
God The Father	Fel	F	Lh
God Unlimited (Smile On Me)	Gia	F	Tr
God Which Has Prepared (Me)	Oxf	T	Tr
God Who By Your Holy Spirit	Jsp	F	Tc
God Who Made Earth (W/Piano)	Wrd	G	Tr
God Who Made The Earth	Gsc	C	Tt
God Will Answer Prayer	Lor	F	Tx
God Will Come Into Your Heart	Man	L	Tb
God Will If You Will	Man	G	Tx
God Will Take Care Of You	Lor	L	Tr
God With Us (Opt Brs)	Abi	L	Sc
God/Man (Satb) (No 4520) Cantata	Zon	L	Sc
God, Creator	Aug	T	Tx
God, Did You Hear	Fcc	L	Tx
God, Give Me Understanding	Lor	T	Tr
God, Give Us Christian Homes	Lor	T	Tr
God, Hear Me Calling (Psalm 55)	Rpb	L	Sl
God, Hurrah (Mezzo Sop/Eng Horn/Cello)	Aug	L	Tt
God, In Thee I Seek My Salvation	Gsc	T	Tr
God, Jehovah	Gal	T	Tt
God, The Lord, Sent A Messenger	Bbl	T	Tx
God, The Omnipotent	Zon	T	Tt
God, Who Made Earth & Heaven	Gia	T	Tt
God, Who Made The Earth	Sac	L	Tt
God's Afterglow	Man	G	Tr
God's Been Good To Me	Tal	G	Tr
God's Blessing Sends Us Forth	Wlp	T	Tr
God's Final Call	Zon	G	Tf
God's For Real Man	Ccc	G	Tt
God's Gift Of Love	Lor	T	Sc
God's Great Love	Man	G	Tr
God's Great Love Came Down At Xmas	Mmc	G	Sc
God's Holy Mountain We Ascend	Wlp	T	La
God's House	Lor	L	Tr
God's Infant Son	Gsc	T	Sc
God's Little White Church	Pmp	G	Tx
God's Love For Me	Man	G	Tr
God's Love Gift (No 4369) Cantata	Zon	L	Sc
God's Love Is Such A Beautiful Thing	Man	G	Tr
God's Love Is The Love For Me	Sto	G	Tr
God's People(Collection/Church)	Wrd	T	Tr
God's Place	Rpb	L	Tc
God's Plan	Sac	L	Tx
God's Promise (E)	Oxf	T	Tx
God's Quiet Love (Collection)	Wrd	L	Za
God's Son Has Made Me Free	Aug	T	Tb
God's Wonderful Plan	Pmp	G	Tx
God's Word (4-Part Arr)	Acp	L	Tx
God's Word Shall Stand	Zon	T	Tx
God's World Today	Pmp	G	Tx
Gods Glory And Honour	Gsc	T	Tt
Goin' Easy	Yan	F	Tx
Goin' Home	Urs	F	Sr
Goin' Home On A Cloud	Gsc	T	Sr
Goin' Home To The Master	Mar	L	Tf
Going His Way	Man	G	Tc
Going Home	Gmc	G	Tf
Going Home	Mar	L	Tf
Going To That Holy Land	Sil	G	Sr
Gold For The Sun	Ahc	L	Tt
Golden Harps Are Sounding	Pro	T	Sc
Golden Morning	Fel	F	Sr
Golden Rules	Pic	L	Tx
Golden Slumbers Carol	Som	L	Sc
Gone Are The Days	Man	G	Tx
Gone, Buried, Lost	Man	G	Tf
Gonna Ride That Heavenly Train	Her	G	Sr
Gonna Sing My Lord	Wlp	F	Tx
Good Christian Men Rejoice	Gsc	T	Sc
Good Christian Men Rejoice (Diff)	Abi	L	Zb
Good Christian Men Rejoice & Sing (E)	Oxf	T	Sr
Good Christian Men, Rejoice	Zon	T	Sc
Good Christian Men, Rejoice	Lor	T	Sc
Good Christian Men, Rejoice	Pro	T	Sc
Good Christian Men, Rejoice	Aug	T	Sc
Good Christian Men, Rejoice	Abi	L	Zb
Good Christian Men, Rejoice & Sing	Aug	T	Tt
Good Christians, Now Rejoice	Aug	T	Tt
Good Folk On Earth Below	Hof	L	Sc
Good Friday Meditation	Lor	T	Sl
Good King Wenceslas	Gsc	T	Sc
Good Lady Poverty	Fcc	F	Tc
Good Life, The	Zon	G	Tb
Good Lord, Shall I Ever Be The One	Abi	L	Tt
Good Morning, Zachary	Nal	L	Tx
Good News	Mar	L	Tx
Good News	Nal	L	Tx
Good News (Original Anthems)	Aug	L	Za
Good News In The Kingdom	Lor	G	Tx
Good Shepherd, The	Abi	L	Tj
Good Shepherd, We Love You (Org,Flute)	Gra	L	Lp
Good Tidings	Aug	L	Sc
Good Tidings Of Joy	Lor	L	Sc
Good To Me	Lor	L	Tr
Good-Bye	Chd	F	Tt
Goodbye	Prc	L	Tx
Goodbye	Mar	L	Tx
Goodbye	Mar	L	Tx
Gospel Acclamation (Notre Dame Mass)	Gia	L	Lg
Gospel Acclamation In A Maj	Rav	L	Lf
Gospel Acclamation Verses A,B,C	Gia	L	Lf
Gospel Acclamations	Cfc	L	Lf
Gospel Acclamations, Bvm	Cfc	L	Lf
Gospel Acclamations, Confirmation, Etc	Cfc	L	Lf
Gospel Acclamations, Good Friday, Etc.	Cfc	L	Lg
Gospel Acclamations, Holy Orders	Cfc	L	Lf
Gospel Choir Classics No 1 (No 5195)	Zon	G	Za
Gospel Choir Classics No 2 (No 5196)	Zon	G	Za
Gospel Choir Classics No 3 (No 5197)	Zon	G	Za
Gospel Choir Favorites (No 5660)	Zon	G	Tx
Gospel Favorites For The Small Church	Zon	G	Za
Gospel Halleluia	Fel	C	Lf
Gospel Organist No 1 (No 5791)	Zon	G	Zb
Gospel Organist No 2 (No 5796)	Zon	G	Zb
Gospel Organist No 3 (No 5797)	Zon	G	Zb
Gospel Organist No 4 (No 5799)	Zon	G	Zb
Gospel Organist No 5 (No 5620)	Zon	G	Zb
Gospel Rappings	Ccc	L	Zb
Gospel Song Of Christmas, The	Lor	G	Sc
Gospel Trumpet, The	Abi	L	Tr
Got To Get In Touch	Nal	C	Tr
Got To Shout About It	Fel	F	Tt
Gothic Fanfare	Abi	L	Zb
Gothic Fanfare	Abi	L	Zb
Gotta' Give A Little	Sil	F	Tt
Grab Your Soap (From Even A Worm)	Wlp	F	Tx
Grace And Peace	Rpb	L	Tr
Gracious God, Reveal Thy Will Unto Me	Her	T	Tr
Gracious Love	Med	L	Tr
Gracious Spirit, Holy Ghost	Sac	T	Ss
Gracious Spirit, Love Divine	Lor	L	Ss
Gradual And Alleluia	Rpb	L	Lf
Graduale: Sancta Maria, K. 273	Bbl	T	Tm
Grand Mass K 427	Kal	T	Za
Grand Processional For Organ	Sac	L	Zb
Grandma Stout	Mar	G	Tx
Grant To Us (A Heart Renewed)	Wlp	L	Sl
Grant Unto Me	Gsc	T	Tr
Grant Unto Me (3rd Mov't)	Gsc	T	Tr
Grant Us Peace	Her	L	Tr
Grant Us Peace	Acp	L	Tr
Grant Us Peace (4-Part Arr)	Acp	L	Tr
Grant Us Thy Peace	Sac	T	Tr
Grant Us Thy Spirit	Smc	T	Ss
Grant We Beseech Thee Merciful Lord	Abi	L	Tr
Grant, We Beseech Thee	Gsc	T	Tr
Grasshopper Macclain	Ham	G	Tx
Great Amen	Wlp	L	Lk
Great Amen	Fel	L	Lk
Great Amen	Wlp	L	Lk
Great Amen	Wlp	L	Lk
Great Amen	Chh	F	Lk
Great Amen	Acp	F	Lk
Great Amen	Rpb	L	Lk
Great Amen (Icet)	Wlp	L	Lk
Great Amen (Mus For Euch Prayer Acc)	Gia	L	Lk
Great Amen (4-Part Arr)	Acp	L	Lk
Great Amen For Advent	Acp	L	Lk
Great Amen For Advent (4-Part Arr)	Acp	L	Lk
Great Amen For Christmas And Epiphany	Acp	L	Lk
Great Amen For Christmas And Epiphany	Acp	L	Lk
Great Amen For Easter	Acp	L	Lk
Great Amen For Easter (4-Part Arr)	Acp	L	Lk
Great Amen For Pentecost	Acp	L	Lk
Great Amen For Pentecost (4-Part Arr)	Acp	L	Lk
Great Amen's Through The Year	Acp	L	Lk
Great Amens Through The Year (4-Part)	Acp	L	Lk
Great And Marvelous	Gsc	T	Tt
Great And Wonderful Are Thy Deeds	Sac	L	Tt
Great Art Thou, O God (M)	Oxf	L	Tt
Great Change	Sem	G	Tx
Great Commission, The	Abi	L	Tc
Great Creator Of The World	Gsc	T	Tt
Great Day	Gsc	G	Tx
Great Day	Nal	L	Tt
Great Day (A Cap)	Pro	T	Sc
Great Day In Bethlehem	Fcc	F	Sc
Great Day In Bethlehem (Cantata)	Gia	F	Sc
Great God Of Nations	Gsc	T	Tp
Great God Of Nations(10 Chorales)	Gia	T	Za
Great God Of Wonders	Zon	L	Tt
Great God What Do I See And Hear	Gsc	T	Tt
Great God, We Praise Your Holy Name	Wlp	T	Tt
Great Hymns Of The Faith	Zon	L	Za
Great Is Jehovah	Gsc	T	Tt
Great Is The Father	Lor	T	Tt
Great Is The Glory Of The Lord	Zon	L	Tt
Great Is The Lord	Gsc	T	Tt
Great Is The Lord	Pro	T	Tt
Great Is The Lord	Gsc	T	Tt
Great Is The Lord	Maf	T	Tt
Great Is The Lord	Mar	L	Tt
Great Is The Lord	Lor	L	Tt
Great Is The Lord (Md)	Oxf	T	Tt
Great Is The Lord Our Maker	Gsc	T	Tt
Great Is The Mystery	Zon	G	Tt
Great Is Thy Faithfulness	Lor	T	Tt
Great Is Thy Reward	Gsc	T	Sr
Great Jehovah Hear Thy Children's Pray	Zon	L	Tt
Great Joy	Sav	G	Tr
Great King Of Peace	Lit	L	Tr
Great Peace Have They	Lor	T	Tr
Great Peace Have They	Gsc	T	Tf
Great Person, A	Nal	C	Tx
Great Service (Complete D)	Oxf	T	Za
Great Service (Venite, Etc)	Kal	T	Tx
Great Shepherd Of A Loyal Flock	Wlp	T	La
Great Things Happen!	Nal	L	Tc
Greater Love Than This	Fel	L	Sl
Greatest Of These Is Love, The	Lor	T	Tr
Green Growing Plants	Rpb	C	Tr
Greet A New Day	Ccc	L	Zb
Greet The Dawn	Ccc	L	Tw
Greet The Risen Lord With Joy	Acp	F	Sr
Greet The Risen Lord With Joy 4-Part	Acp	F	Sr
Grief Is In My Heart	Gsc	T	Sl
Grieve Not The Holy Spirit	Gsc	T	Ss
Grow Closer	Man	G	Tc
Grow In Love	Hal	L	Tr
Growing For Jesus	Pmp	G	Tc
Growing Pains (Youth Collection)	Wrd	G	Za
Guess What's Behind You	Mem	L	Tx
Guide Me	Nal	L	Tr
Guide Me Jesus	Sil	T	Tj
Guide Me, O Thou Great Jehovah	Lor	T	Tr
Guide Me, O Thou Great Jehovah	Bfi	F	Tx
Guide Me, O Thou Great Jehovah	Lor	T	Tr
Guide My Head	Gsc	G	Tc
Guide Us	Fel	F	Tr
Guiding Christ Our Shepherd, The	Abi	L	Tj
Guiding Light	Mar	L	Tr
Guitar Christmas Carols (Nfo 4346)	Zon	G	Zb
Guitar Sing-A-Long (No 5540)	Zon	G	Zb
Hacia Belen Va Un Borrico	Gsc	T	Sc
Haec Dies (From Holiday Motets)	Ron	T	Sc
Haec Dies (Md)	Oxf	T	Sr
Hail Blessed Lady	Wlp	T	Tm

Title	Code
Hail Christ, Our Royal Priest & King	Wlp T Tk
Hail Festal Day	Gsc T Le
Hail His Coming, King Of Glory	Wbp T Tk
Hail Holy Queen	Wlp L Tm
Hail Holy Queen Enthroned (Vv)	Wlp L Tm
Hail Maiden Mary	Gia L Tm
Hail Mary	Gia T Tm
Hail Mary	Fel L Tm
Hail Mary	Nal C Tm
Hail Mary	Gia L Tm
Hail Mary	Eph L Tm
Hail Mary (E & Lat)	Gia T Tm
Hail Mary Full Of Grace	Wlp T Tm
Hail Mary.	Vrn T Tm
Hail Mary, Gentle Woman	Nal L Tm
Hail The Day	Gsc T Sr
Hail The Long Expected Star (Me)	Gia T Sc
Hail Thee Festival Day (W/Org,Perc)	Gia L Lp
Hail Thee, Spirit, Lord Eternal	Aug L Ss
Hail To The Brightness!	Zon T Tt
Hail To The King	Zon T Sr
Hail To The Lord's Anointed	Sac L Tt
Hail To The Lord's Anointed	Zon T La
Hail To Thee	Van C Tt
Hail To Thee, Glad Day	Smc T Sr
Hail, All Hail The Glorious Morn	Gsc T Sc
Hail, Alpha And Omega	Sac L Tj
Hail, Dear Virgin (W/Organ)	Bbl T Tm
Hail, Glorious King (No 5964)	Zon L Tm
Hail, Holy Mother	Fel L Tm
Hail, Holy Queen	Gsc T Tm
Hail, Mary (Unison Or Choral)	Fel T Tm
Hail, Noble Flesh	Gia T Lo
Hail, O Hail True Body	Som T Lo
Hail, O Hail True Body (Md)	Oxf T Lo
Hail, Queen Of Heaven, Be Joyful	Som T Tm
Hail, Queen Of Heaven, Rejoice	Gia T Tm
Hail, Thou Once—Despised Jesus	Zon L Sr
Hail, True Body Born Of Mary	Gsc T Lo
Hail, True Virginity	Gia L Tm
Hail, Virgin Mary	Bbl T Tm
Halalujoh, Halalu El B'kod'sho	Gsc L Tt
Halay, When To God I Send A Plea	Fel L Ld
Hallelujah	Sil G Tt
Hallelujah	Lor T Tt
Hallelujah (Psalm 150)	Pic L Tt
Hallelujah Chorus	Zon T Tt
Hallelujah Chorus	Gsc T Tt
Hallelujah Chorus ("Messiah")	Cfs T Lf
Hallelujah Chorus, The	Lor T Tt
Hallelujah For The Cross	Zon G Sl
Hallelujah For The Cross (No 5959)	Zon L Sr
Hallelujah I Love Him (W/Piano)	Wrd G Sl
Hallelujah To The King	Man G Tk
Hallelujah! Christ Is Risen (Brs)	Elv T Sr
Hallelujah! Great And Marvelous	Gia T Tt
Hallelujah! We Shall Rise	Zon G Sr
Hallelujah! What A Savior!	Lor T Tj
Hallelujah! What A Savior! (No 5978)	Zon L Sr
Hallelujah!Praise!Selah!(Long)	Wrd L Tt
Hallelujah, Amen	Gsc T Tt
Hallelujah, Glory Hallelujah	Sac L Tt
Hallelujah, Hallelujah, Jesus Christ	Mar L Sr
Hallelujah, I Am Free	Man G Tt
Hallelujah, I Want To Sing	Cam G Le
Hallelujah, Jesus Is King!	Gia F Tk
Hallelujah, Praise The Lord	Man G Tt
Hallelujah, Praise The Lord	Her L Tt
Hallelujah, What A Savior	Zon T Sr
Hallelujah, Yes, Praise The Lord	Zon F Tt
Halleluyah, Christ Is Risen	Zon T Sr
Halleujah	Wlp F Tt
Halleujah (From Mount Of Olives)	Gsc T Tt
Hallowed And Gracious Is The Time	Som L Tx
Halloween Song	Wlp C Tx
Hammering	Sac T Sl
Hammering (Spiritual)	Lor G Sr
Hamshire, (Good Friday) W/Viol,Cello	Bbl T Sl
Hand In Hand With God	Lor T Tr
Hand In Hand With God	Lor T Tr
Handful Of Clay	Fel F Sl
Handful Of Sunshine, A.	Ham C Tr
Happiness	Gmc G Tr
Happiness (Musical)	Zon L Tc
Happiness Is The Lord	Zon G Tr
Happiness Song	Fel F Tx
Happy Am I	Zon F Tr
Happy And Blest Are They	Gsc T Tx
Happy Are The Children Of The Lord	Ahc L Tr
Happy Are They	Fel L Tr
Happy Are They Who Hope In The Lord	Nal L Tr
Happy Birthday	Prc L Tr
Happy Birthday, Gentle Saviour	Zon G Sc
Happy Birthday, Merry Christmas	Man C Sc
Happy In Jesus	Mar L Tr
Happy In The Lord	Mar L Tr
Happy Is He Who Regards (Ps 41)	Gra L Ld
Happy Is He Whose Fault Is Taken	Gra L Ld
Happy Is The Man	Nal L Tr
Happy Is The Man	Nal L Tr
Happy Lord	Wlp F Tr
Happy The Heart	Nal C Tr
Happy The Man	Aug L Tr
Happy The Man (Ps 1) W/Guitar	Gra F Tc
Happy The Man Who Delights	Fel L Tr
Happy The Man Who Fears	Fel L Tr
Happy Time Songs No 1 (No 5500)	Zon C Za
Happy Time Songs No 2 (No 5501)	Zon C Za
Happy Xmas	Mcl F Sc
Happy, Happy	Mar L Tr
Hard Feeling To Explain	Fel F Tx
Hard Time Smiling	Wlp F Sl
Harden Not Your Hearts(Ps 95)	Rav L Ld
Hark A Thrilling Voice Is Sounding	Aug T Tx
Hark The Glad Sound	Gsc T Sc
Hark The Herald Angels Sing	Bbl T Sc
Hark The Herald Angels Sing	Pro T Sc
Hark Ye! What News The Angels Bring	Pro T Sc
Hark! A Thrilling Voice	Abi T Sc
Hark! Ten Thousand Harps And Voices	Zon T Tt
Hark! The Glad Sound	Zon L Sc
Hark! The Herald Angels Sing	Lor T Sc
Hark, Angel Carols	Aug T Sc
Hark, Hark, My Soul!	Gsc T Tr
Hark, Ten Thousand Harps And Voices	Lor T Tt
Hark, The Glad Sound	Lor T Sa
Hark, The Herald Angels Sing	Zon T Sc
Hark, The Vesper Hymn Is Stealing	Gsc T Tx
Harken Unto Me	Tcp L Tx
Harmonizations On Hymn Tunes (15)	Abi L Zb
Harold Decou Presents Choral Praises	Zon G Za
Harvest Carol	Gsc T Tt
Harvest Time	Mar L Tc
Hashkivenu	Wbp T Tx
Hast Thou Not Known?	Gsc T Tx
Haste Thee O Lord (In 19 Rounds)	Gia T Sa
Haste Thee, O God (Me)	Oxf T Sl
Haste Thee, O God (Me)	Oxf T Sl
Haste Ye Shepherds	Smc T Zb
Haul Away	Ahc L Tt
Have A Little Talk With The Lord	Zon G Tr
Have A Nice Day	Man F Tr
Have Faith	Hhh G Tr
Have Faith In God	Man G Tr
Have Faith In God	Zon G Tr
Have Faith In God	Abi L Tr
Have Faith, Don't Cry	Ham G Tr
Have I Done My Best	Man G Tx
Have I Done My Best For Jesus	Zon G Tc
Have Mercy O Lord, Have Mercy	Wlp L Sl
Have Mercy On Me	Gia L Ld
Have Mercy On Me	Gia T Sl
Have Mercy On Us, O Lord	Wlp L Sl
Have Mercy Upon Me, O God (M)	Oxf T Sl
Have Mercy Upon Me, O Lord (Ps. 31)	Som L Tr
Have Mercy Upon Us	Gsc L Sl
Have Mercy, Lord, On Me	Fel L Sl
Have Pity On Me, O Lord	Fel L Sl
Have Thine Own Way, Lord	Lor T Sl
Have Thine Own Way, Lord	Lor T Sl
Have Ye Not Known?	Bec T Tt
Have You Any Room For Jesus?	Lor T Tj
Have You Ever Been	Fel F Sr
Have You Ever Heard	Mar L Tx
Have You Ever Thought (About Jesus)	Gia F Tj
Have You Had A Gethsemane?	Gmc G Sl
Have You Seen Him	Msm F Tj
Haven Of Rest, The	Lor T Tr
Hayom Harat Olam	Gsc T Tx
He Asked Life Of You	Fel L Tf
He Belongs To Me	Man G Tr
He Bought My Soul At Calvary	Ham G Sl
He Bought The Whole Field	Van F Tc
He Brought Me Out	Zon G Sl
He Called Me From Birth	Fel L Tc
He Came	Nal L Tj
He Came	Nal L Tj
He Came Among Us W/Solo	Aug L Sa
He Cared For Me	Zon G Tr
He Changed My Life	Zon G Tc
He Comes	Var F Sa
He Comes Forth	Fel L Tr
He Comes To Me	Mon G Lo
He Cried	Sbf L Tr
He Didn't Have To Do It	Gmc G Sl
He Endured The Cross	Aug T Sl
He Fed Them With Most Precious Wheat	Gia L Lo
He Feeds Us With The Finest Of Wheat	Fel L Ln
He Filled My Life With Ecstasy	Gmc G Tr
He Gives Us Bread Which Comes	Fel L Ln
He Gives Us The Water Of Learning	Fel L Tx
He Had It Planned Long Ago	Man G Sa
He Has Borne Our Woes	Gia L Sl
He Has Life Restored	Wlp F Sr
He Has Made A Special Place For Me	Lor T Sr
He Has Risen As He Said	Fel L Sr
He Heals The Broken Hearted (Ps147)	Gra L Ld
He Heard My Voice	Fel L Sl
He Hideth My Soul	Lor T Tr
He Is Able	Zon T Tk
He Is All I Need	Lor T Tj
He Is Born	Aug T Sc
He Is Born (W/ Finger Cymbals)	Pro T Sc
He Is Born, Christ Is Born Today	Sac T Sc
He Is Coming Again	Man G Sa
He Is Everywhere (God Is Love)	Pic L Tr
He Is Here	Lex T La
He Is Here Among Us	Wlp F La
He Is Lord	Mar L Sr
He Is Lord (Verses)	Gra T Ln
He Is Lord Of All	Fel F Tt
He Is Risen	Aug L Sr
He Is Risen	Nal L Sr
He Is Risen	Gsc T Sr
He Is Risen	Nal L Sr
He Is Risen	Aug T Sr
He Is Risen	Zon T Sr
He Is Risen (E)	Oxf L Sr
He Is Risen, Alleluia (Opt Brass)	Abi L Sr
He Is Risen, Alleluia (W/Org)	Gia L Sr
He Is The Lord Of Life And Death	Fel L Tx
He Is There	Sac T Tx
He Is Your Brother	Fcc F Tr
He Knoweth	Man G Tr
He Knows And He Cares	Man G Tr
He Knows What He's Doin All The Time	Zon G Tr
He Laid His Hand On Me	Lor L Tr
He Leadeth Me	Smc T Tr
He Leadeth Me	Lor L Tc
He Lifted Me	Lor L Tr
He Lifted Me (P.D.)	Man G Tr
He Lived The Good Life (Jesus Musical)	Zon G Tx
He Lived To See The Christ	Fel L Tx
He Lives	Lor T Sr
He Lives	Mar L Sr
He Loves Me	Man G Tr
He Loves You, My Friend	Zon F Tr
He Lovingly Guards Every Footstep	Zon G Tr
He Never Said A Mumblin' Word	Lor G Sl
He Pled My Case	Sil T Tr
He Really Has Set Me Free	Man G Sr
He Said (God Is My Father)	Jsp F Tj
He Said He Would Deliver Me	Sav G Sl
He Satisfied That Longing In My Soul	Man G Sr
He Saved Me Because He Loves Me	Fel L Sr
He Says He Is God	Nal L Tj
He Shall Call On Me	Fel L Tr
He Shall Come Down	Zon L Sa
He Shall Come Down Like Rain	Gsc T Sa
He Shall Feed His Flock	Pro T Sc
He Shall Feed His Flock	Lor T Tr
He Shall Reign Forever	Lor T Tk
He Shall Return As He Has Left	Fel L Sr
He Shall Rule From Sea To Sea	Gia L Sr
He Smiled On Me	Gsc T Tj
He That Descended (Md)	Oxf L Tk
He That Endureth	Man G Tr
He That Hath Ears	Gmc G Tx
He That Is Down Need Fear No Fall (Me)	Oxf T Tr
He That Is Down Needs Fear No Fall (E)	Oxf L Tr
He That Overcomes	Wrd G Tf
He That Shall Endure	Gsc T Tc
He That Would Love Life	Abi L Tr
He The Pearly Gates Will Open	Zon G Tf
He Touched Me	Gmc G Tr
He Touched Me And Other Songs(No 5416)	Zon G Za
He Walks With God	Lor T Tr
He Was Alone	Gsc T Tj
He Was Despised	Gsc T Sl
He Was Despised	Lor T Sl
He Was More Then Just A Man	Man G Tj
He Was Silent (Choral)	Fel T Sl
He Was There	Ham G Tj
He Was Wounded For Our Transgressions	Zon T Sl
He Was Wounded For Our Transgressions	Zon T Sr
He Who Abides In Me	Fel L Tr
He Who Abides In Me	Fel F Tr
He Who Believes In Me.	Fel L Tr
He Who Believes In Me.	Vrn G Lp
He Who Believes In Me, From Within	Fel L Ld
He Who Does Justice (Ps 15)	Gra L Ld
He Who Drinks Of The Water	Fel L Ss
He Who Eats My Flesh	Fel L Lo
He Who Follows Me	Fel L Tc
He Who Follows Me	Gia L Tc
He Who Is Of God	Fel L Tx
He Who Sees Me	Fel T Tr
He Who Will Trust In God	Fel L Tr
He Who With Weeping Soweth	Gsc T Sl
He Who Would Valiant Be	Maf L Tx
He Who Would Valiant Be	Aug T Tx
He Who Would Valiant Be	Abi L Tx
He Whom Joyous Shepherds Praised	Aug T Sc
He Will Heal	Zon G Tr
He Will Receive The Blessing	Gia L Tc
He Will Surely Give Thee Peace (Md)	Gia T Tr
He, Watching Over Israel	Gsc T Tr
He'll Break Through The Blue	Zon G Sa
He'll Help You Out (If You Just Don't)	Sil F Tj

ALPHABETICAL INDEX OF TITLES

He'll Make A Way	Zon	G Tr
He'll Make My Dream Come True	Man	G Sr
He'll Never Fail	Man	G Tr
He'll Never Leave Me	Man	G Tr
He'll Understand, And Say, "Well Done"	Lor	T Sr
He's A Light Unto My Pathway	Man	G Tr
He's Alive	Prc	L Tx
He's Alive	Mar	L Sr
He's All I Need	Mam	G Tj
He's Back In The Land Of The Living	Gal	L Sr
He's Everything To Me (Coll)	Wrd	G Za
He's Everywhere	Man	G Tr
He's Filling Up Heaven With Sinners	Zon	G Tc
He's For Real	Pro	L Sc
He's Got The Whole World In His Hands	Lor	F Tr
He's Got The Whole World In His Hands	Gsc	G Tx
He's Got The Whole World In His Hands	Acp	F Tr
He's Got The Whole World In His Hands	Zon	F Tr
He's My Friend	Lor	G Tr
He's Risen	Nal	L Sr
He's Risen, Christ Jesus The Lord	Aug	L Sr
He's Standing At The Door	Wgm	F Tj
He's Still The King Of Kings	Gmc	G Tk
He's The Reason To Go On	Mar	L Tc
He's Willing	Man	G Tr
Head That Once Was Crowned With Thorns	Abi	T Sr
Headin Down The Trail	Zon	F Tc
Heal Your People	Nal	L Tr
Healer, The	Zon	G Tr
Healing Love Of Jesus, The	Zon	G Tr
Healing Of The Nations	Ams	T Sl
Hear Heaven Thunder	Acp	L Tt
Hear Heaven Thunder (4-Part Arr)	Acp	L Tt
Hear Me	Fel	L Tr
Hear Me When I Call	Gsc	T Tr
Hear Me, O Lord	Maf	T Sl
Hear Me, O Lord, The Great Support	Gsc	T Tr
Hear Mr. Lord, I'm Callin'	Ahc	L Tx
Hear My Call	Van	F Sl
Hear My Cry	Gsc	T Tr
Hear My Cry	Her	L Sl
Hear My Prayer	Smc	T Sl
Hear My Prayer	Bbl	T Tr
Hear My Prayer	Gsc	T Tr
Hear My Prayer	Kal	T Tr
Hear My Prayer, O Lord	Gsc	T Tr
Hear My Prayer, O My God	Bbl	T Tr
Hear Now Our Cry	Gsc	T Sl
Hear O Israel	Chh	L Ld
Hear Oh Hear	Gsc	T Sc
Hear Our Prayer	Lor	T To
Hear The Bells! See The Star!	Maf	L Sc
Hear The Glad Tidings	Her	L Sc
Hear The Lambs	Lor	T Tr
Hear Them Cryin'	Wrd	F Za
Hear Us As We Pray	Gsc	L Tr
Hear Us, O Father	Aug	T Sl
Hear Us, O Lord	Gia	T Sl
Hear Us, O Lord, For You Are So Kind	Fel	L Tx
Hear Us, O Saviour	Gsc	T Tr
Hear Us, Oh Lord	Ahc	L Tx
Hear Us, Our Father	Sac	L Tr
Hear Ye Him	Lor	L Tc
Hear Ye Jesus Is The Lamb Of God	Bbl	T Tj
Hear, O Heavens (Is 1, M)	Oxf	T Sl
Hear, O Lord	Fel	F Sl
Hear, O Lord (Ps 30) (Md)	Oxf	T Sl
Heart And Lips (Cantata)	Lps	T Tt
Heart Divine	Lor	T Tj
Heart Of Christ	Jsp	L Tj
Heart Of Christ	Wlp	T Tj
Heart Of God, The	Lor	T Tr
Heart Of Love, A	Zon	F Tr
Heart's Adoration	Oxf	T Sc
Hearts And Voices Raise (W/Percussion)	Aug	L Tt
Hearts To Heaven And Voices Raise	Abi	T Sr
Heaven	Man	G Sr
Heaven And Earth And Sea And Air	Abi	L Tt
Heaven Came Down	Zon	G Tr
Heaven Haven	Pic	L Sr
Heaven In My Heart	Zon	G Ss
Heaven Is Way Out There	Sem	G Tr
Heaven My Home	Abi	L Sr
Heaven Will Be My Home	Sav	G Tf
Heaven's Lights Ahead	Jhm	G Sr
Heavenly Father	Mar	L Tt
Heavenly Father Hear Us	Nal	L Tr
Heavens Are Telling, The	Lor	T Tt
Heavens Drop Dew From Above	Wlp	L Sa
Hebrew Cantata	Som	L Za
Hebrew Children	Gsc	T Tt
Hebrew Melodies	Som	L Za
Heed My Call For Help	Nal	L Tr
Heilig	Gsc	T Li
Heilig Ist Gott (Eng & Germ)	Oxf	T Tx
Helas Mamour (Old French)	Gsc	T Tt
Helas! Mon Dieu.	Oxf	T Sl
Hell	Sil	F Tx
Hello Song	Wlp	C Tx
Help Me Know The Way	Wlp	F Sl
Help Me Speedily	Man	G Sl
Help Me To Light A Candle	Mmc	G Tr
Help My Unbelief	Van	F Tr
Help Thou My Unbelief	Ham	G Tr
Help Us, Jesus Christ, God's Son	Sac	T Tr
Help Us, O God	Pro	T Tr
Help Us, O God, Our Savior	Fel	L Sl
Help Us, O Lord, Deliver Us	Gsc	T Sl
Help Us, O Lord, To See	Fcc	L Tr
Hence All Fears And Sadness	Gsc	T Tr
Hence With Earthly Treasure	Gsc	T To
Her Troubled Course	Msm	F Tx
Herald Of Good Tiding (W/Tpts)	Cfp	L Sa
Heralds Of Christ	Zon	L Tc
Here Am I Oh Lord(Ps 40)	Rav	L Ld
Here At The Table Of The Lord	Gia	L Lo
Here Comes Jesus	Wrd	G Sl
Here Comes Jesus	Zon	F Tj
Here He Comes	Prc	L Tx
Here Is A Great Priest	Gia	L La
Here Is All Of Me	Man	G Tc
Here Is Heavenly Joy (E)	Oxf	T Tr
Here Is My Life	Nal	L Tc
Here We Are	Fel	F La
Here We Go A-Caroling	Prc	L Tx
Here Yet Awhile	Gsc	T Sl
Here Yet Awhile (St Mt Passion)	Cfs	T Sl
Here, Mid The Ass And Oxen Mild	Gsc	T Sc
Herman Voss Presents Organ Favorites 1	Zon	T Zb
Herman Voss Presents Organ Favorites 2	Zon	T Zb
Heute Ist Christus Der Herr Geboren	Gsc	T Sc
Hey Brothers!	Nal	L Tx
Hey Day	Wlp	F Tx
Hey God!	Van	C Tr
Hey Joy	Wlp	F Tr
Hey Soul	Fis	F Tx
Hey! Hey! Anybody Listening?	Prc	L Tx
Hey, Manger Child	Lor	G Sc
Hi God!	Nal	C La
Hide Not Thou Thy Face	Oxf	L Sl
Hide Not Thy Face	Smc	T Zb
Hide Not Your Face From Me	Fel	L Sl
Hiding In The Arms Of Jesus	Csm	G Tj
High Time	Nal	L Tx
High Voice No 1 (No 5021)	Zon	G Za
High Voice No 2 (No 5022)	Zon	G Za
High Voice No 3 (No 5023)	Zon	G Za
High Voice No 4 (No 5024)	Zon	G Za
High Voice No 5 (No 5025)	Zon	G Za
High Voice No 6 (No 5170)	Zon	G Za
Higher Hands	Zon	G Tx
Higher Road, The	Zon	G Tc
Hilariter	Gsc	T Sr
Himnos De Fe Y Alabanza	Zon	G Za
Himnos De Fe Y Alabanza (No 5358)	Zon	T Za
Hinay Yom Hadin(Behold The Day Of Judg	Gsc	L Tx
Hip Pocket Hymnal (No 5313)	Zon	F Za
His Angels Will Protect You	Fel	L Tr
His Are The Thousand Sparkling Rills	Aug	L Tp
His Banner Over Me Is Love	Nal	C Tr
His Delight Is In The Law Of The Lord	Abi	L Tr
His Exaltation	Pic	L Tt
His Eye Is On The Sparrow	Lor	T Tr
His Hands	Ham	G Sl
His Light Still Shines	Sil	F Tj
His Love Is All Around	Lor	L Tr
His Love Is Endless	Zon	F Tr
His Love Is Everlasting (Icet)	Wlp	L Ld
His Love Is Lasting (Psalm 136)	Ahc	L Tt
His Love Is Wonderful To Me	Zon	G Tr
His Matchless Worth	Zon	T Tt
His Mercy Endures Forever	Fel	L Tt
His Mercy Endureth Forever	Abi	L Zb
His Nail-Pierced Hands	Man	G Sl
His Name Is Love	Zon	F Tr
His Name Is The Sweetest I Know	Gmp	G Tj
His Name Is Wonderful	Man	G Tt
His Peace We Share	Rav	L Tr
His Praise Is Higher Than The Highest	Sha	F Tt
His Saving Power Revealed (Ps98)	Gra	L Ld
His Sovereign Love	Zon	G Tr
His Throne Shall Be	Fel	L Tx
His Will	Gmc	G Tr
His Yoke Is Easy	Zon	L Sl
Ho! Everyone That Is Thirsty	Zon	G Ss
Ho! Everyone That Thirsteth	Gia	F Ss
Ho, Every One That Thirsteth	Gsc	T Tb
Hodie	Pic	L Sc
Hodie Apparuit	Gsc	T Sc
Hodie Christus	Gsc	T Sc
Hodie Christus Natus Est	Gsc	T Sc
Hodie Christus Natus Est	Gsc	T Sc
Hodie Christus Natus Est	Bbl	T Sc
Hold My Hand, Dear Lord	Zon	G Tr
Hold Out Your Light	Zon	G Tc
Hold Thou My Hand	Lor	T Tr
Holiday And Holy Day	Her	L Sc
Holy	Nal	L Li
Holy	Nal	L Li
Holy	Nal	L Li
Holy	Nal	L Li
Holy Art Thou	Lor	T Tt
Holy Art Thou, O God!	Zon	T Tt
Holy Child, The (W/ Opt Flute)	Pro	T Sc
Holy City, The	Zon	T Tr
Holy City, The	Lor	T Tk
Holy City, The	Kal	T Sr
Holy Easter Morning	Lor	T Sr
Holy Father Hear My Cry	Gsc	T Tr
Holy God	Acp	L Tt
Holy God	Acp	T Tt
Holy God Of Sabbath (A Cap)	Abi	T Tt
Holy God We Praise Thy Name	Aug	T Tt
Holy God, We Praise Thy Name	Gia	T Tt
Holy God, We Praise Thy Name	Gia	T Tt
Holy God, We Praise Thy Name	Zon	T Tt
Holy Hands	Man	G Sl
Holy Holy (Icet)	Jsp	L Li
Holy Holy Lord	Chh	F Li
Holy Infant Of Bethlehem	Sac	L Sc
Holy Is The Lord	Hal	L Tt
Holy Is The Lord	Lor	T Tt
Holy Is The Lord!	Zon	T Tt
Holy Is Thy Name	Hof	T Tt
Holy Manna	Lor	T Lo
Holy Mary, Now We Crown You	Wlp	L Tm
Holy Mother Of God, Intercede	Fel	L Tm
Holy Mother Of Our Redeemer	Wlp	L Tm
Holy Night!	Sac	L Sc
Holy Radiant Light	Gsc	T Tr
Holy Redeemer! Be Thy Rest	Abi	T Sl
Holy Spirit	Sil	G Ss
Holy Spirit	Man	G Ss
Holy Spirit	Sil	F Ss
Holy Spirit Of The Living God	Gia	F Tx
Holy Spirit Song	Chd	F Ss
Holy Spirit, Hear Us	Lor	L Ss
Holy Spirit, Now Outpoured	Zon	L Ss
Holy Spirit, Truth Divine	Fel	L Ss
Holy Way, The	Acp	L Tx
Holy, Holy	Nal	L Li
Holy, Holy	Nal	L Li
Holy, Holy	Nal	L Li
Holy, Holy	Nal	L Li
Holy, Holy (American Spiritual)	Pro	G Tt
Holy, Holy (Angelic Song)	Nal	L Tt
Holy, Holy (Icet)	Jsp	L Li
Holy, Holy (Opt Brs/Timp)	Gia	L Li
Holy, Holy I	Nal	L Li
Holy, Holy Is The Lord	Fel	L Tt
Holy, Holy, God Of Hosts	Vrn	L Li
Holy, Holy, Holy	Gam	L La
Holy, Holy, Holy	Fcc	F Li
Holy, Holy, Holy	Rpb	L Li
Holy, Holy, Holy	Wlp	L Tr
Holy, Holy, Holy	Gia	L Li
Holy, Holy, Holy	Rpb	L Li
Holy, Holy, Holy	Nal	L Li
Holy, Holy, Holy	Nal	L Li
Holy, Holy, Holy	Rpb	L Li
Holy, Holy, Holy	Rav	L Li
Holy, Holy, Holy	Rav	L Li
Holy, Holy, Holy	Rpb	L Li
Holy, Holy, Holy	Acp	F Li
Holy, Holy, Holy	Gsc	T Li
Holy, Holy, Holy	Nal	L Li
Holy, Holy, Holy	Lex	G Tt
Holy, Holy, Holy	Rpb	L Li
Holy, Holy, Holy	Rpb	L Li
Holy, Holy, Holy	Gia	L Li
Holy, Holy, Holy	Lor	T Li
Holy, Holy, Holy	Ccc	L Li
Holy, Holy, Holy	Gsc	T Li
Holy, Holy, Holy	Sbf	L Li
Holy, Holy, Holy	Abi	L Lo
Holy, Holy, Holy	Wlp	F Li
Holy, Holy, Holy	Yan	F Li
Holy, Holy, Holy (Cel Of Unity)	Gia	L Li
Holy, Holy, Holy (Celebration Lit)	Yan	F Li
Holy, Holy, Holy (Chardin Mass)	Fel	L Li
Holy, Holy, Holy (Child Mass)	Gia	L Li
Holy, Holy, Holy (Community Mass)	Gia	L Li
Holy, Holy, Holy (Cong+Choir)	Abi	T Li
Holy, Holy, Holy (Folk Mass No. 4)	Fel	F Li
Holy, Holy, Holy (Funeral Folk Mass)	Fel	F Li
Holy, Holy, Holy (Hymn Tune Mass)	Fel	L Li
Holy, Holy, Holy (Icet)	Wlp	L Li
Holy, Holy, Holy (Icet)	Wlp	L Li
Holy, Holy, Holy (Icet)	Wlp	L Li
Holy, Holy, Holy (Icet)	Wlp	L Li
Holy, Holy, Holy (Icet)	Wlp	L Li
Holy, Holy, Holy (Icet)	Wlp	L Li
Holy, Holy, Holy (Jazz-Rock Mass)	Fel	F Li
Holy, Holy, Holy (Lord God Sabaoth)	Gia	F Li
Holy, Holy, Holy (Lyric Mass)	Gia	L Li
Holy, Holy, Holy (Me)	Oxf	T Li
Holy, Holy, Holy (Missa Bossa Nova)	Fel	F Li
Holy, Holy, Holy (Short Mass)	Gia	L Li
Holy, Holy, Holy (Sung Mass No.1)	Fel	L Li
Holy, Holy, Holy (W/Cantor)(Dominic)	Gia	L Li

Title	Code	Title	Code	Title	Code
Holy, Holy, Holy (W/Rhythm)	Aug C Li	How Far Is It To Bethlehem?	Gsc T Sc	Hymn Of Praise (Second Mass)	Fel F Lc
Holy, Holy, Holy (1964 Text)	Van F Li	How Far Is It To Bethlehem?	Aug L Sc	Hymn Of Praise: Psalm 135	Str L Tt
Holy, Holy, Holy (3pt Rhythm)	Pro L Li	How Far Is It To Bethlehem?	Aug T Sc	Hymn Of Saint Teresa	Maf T Tx
Holy, Holy, Holy (4-Part Arr)	Acp L Li	How Firm A Foundation	Gsc T Tr	Hymn Of Thanksgiving	Lor T Tt
Holy, Holy, Holy (4-Part Arr)	Acp L Li	How Firm A Foundation	Lor T Tr	Hymn Of The Initiants	Gsc T Tb
Holy, Holy, Holy (64 Text)	Van F Li	How Firm A Foundation	Smc T Zb	Hymn Of The Universe	Wgm F Tk
Holy, Holy, Holy (67th Street Mass)	Fel F Li	How Firm A Foundation	Lor T Tr	Hymn Of Unity (The Glory You Have)	Gia F Tu
Holy, Holy, Holy Lord	Gia L Li	How Firm A Foundation	Zon T Tr	Hymn Of Worship	Zon L Tt
Holy, Holy, Holy Lord (Hymn)	Gia L Li	How Firm A Foundation	Zon T Tr	Hymn Preludes From Op 100	Cfp T Zb
Holy, Holy, Holy Lord God Almighty	Gsc T Li	How Firm A Foundation	Abi L Tr	Hymn To David	Gsc T Tx
Holy, Holy, Holy Lord(Vianney Mass)	Gia L Li	How Gentle God's Commands	Gsc T Tx	Hymn To Mary	Rav L Im
Holy, Holy, Holy(Mass For All S.)	Gia L Li	How Godly Is The House Of God	Ron T Lp	Hymn To The Earth	Som L Tx
Holy, Holy, Holy(New Mass)	Gia L Li	How Good Is God	Rpb L Tt	Hymn To The Father	Rav L Tt
Holy, Holy, Holy!	Zon T Li	How Good Is The Lord	Nal L Tr	Hymn To The Godhead	Lor T Tt
Holy, Holy, Holy, Lord God	Acp L Li	How Good It Is	Fcc F Tt	Hymn To The Holy Innocents	Oxf T Tx
Holy, Thou Art Holy	Mar L Tt	How Good It Is To Give Thanks To God	Nal L Tt	Hymn To The Saviour	Gsc L Tj
Home And Mother	Lor T Tx	How Good, How Delightful It Is	Wgm F Tr	Hymn To The Soul	Gsc T Tr
Homecoming In Glory	Pmp G Sr	How Goodly Are Thy Tents	Gsc T Tr	Hymn To The Trinity	Lor T Tt
Homo Natus De Muliere	Oxf T Tj	How Great And Good Is He	Acp L Tt	Hymn-Time For Tiny Tots (No 5521)	Zon C Za
Honey In That Rock	Man F Tr	How Great And Good Is He (4-Part Arr)	Acp L Tt	Hymn-Tune Preludes (15)	Abi L Zb
Honey In The Rock	Mar G Tr	How Great Are Thy Wonders	Aug T Tt	Hymnal For Boys And Girls No 1 5518	Zon C Za
Honor And Praise (From Come Follow)	Gia F Tk	How Great Is The Goodness	Fel L Tt	Hymnal For Boys And Girls No 2 (5525)	Zon C Za
Honor Him, Alleluia	Hal T Tt	How Great Is Your Name	Fcc F Tt	Hymnal For Contemporary Christians	Zon F Za
Honor Praise And Glory	Wlp L Tt	How Great The Glory	Gra L Tt	Hymns And Songs For Church Schools	Aug T Za
Honor The Lord With What You Have	Fel L Tt	How Great The Glory (Trinity)	Mcc L Tt	Hymns For Brass Quartet	Abi T Zb
Honor To The Hills	Bbl T Tx	How Great The Name Of Christ Our Lord	Gia T Sc	Hymns For Brass Quartet (No 5760)	Zon G Zb
Hope Is Finding Him	Wlp F Tj	How Great The Sign Of God's Love	Cfc L Tr	Hymns For Grace And Glory	Abi T Za
Hope Of Our Days	Rpb L Tr	How Great Thou Art	Man G Tt	Hymns For The Amusement Of Children	Oxf T Za
Hope Of The World	Abi T Tj	How I Have Longed	Van F Sl	Hymns For Youth	Erd C Za
Hope Of The World	Abi L Tr	How I Rejoiced	Nal L La	Hymns Of Praise And Glory	Gia T Zb
Hope Of.Life	Rpb L Tr	How I Rejoiced When I Heard Them Say	Fel L La	Hymns Of Thanks	Gia L Za
Hope Thou In God	Lor L Tr	How Long O Lord	Wlp T Sl	Hymns We Love To Sing (No 4400)	Zon G Za
Hosanna	Gsc T Le	How Long Will It Be?	Zon G Sa	Hymntime Piano No 1 (No 5745)	Zon G Zb
Hosanna	Aug L Le	How Long Wilt Thou Forget Me	Gsc T Sl	Hymntime Piano No 2 (No 5746)	Zon G Zb
Hosanna	Aug L Le	How Long Wilt Thou Forget Me	Gsc T Sl	Hymntime Piano No 3 (No 5747)	Zon G Zb
Hosanna	Gsc T Sr	How Long Wilt Thou Forget Me?	Lor T Sl	Hymntime Piano No 4 (No 5748)	Zon G Zb
Hosanna	Lor T Sl	How Long, O Lord	Fel L Sl	I Am	Sms T Tj
Hosanna	Gsc T Sr	How Long, O Lord	Fel F Sa	I Am	Sil T Tx
Hosanna	Rpb L Le	How Lovely Are The Messengers	Gsc T Sa	I Am Alpha And Omega	Gsc T Sa
Hosanna	Aug L Le	How Lovely Are The Messengers	Gsc T Tc	I Am At Peace With My Neighbor	Fel L Tr
Hosanna	Gsc T Li	How Lovely Are The Messengers	Lor T Tx	I Am Blessed By God's Love	Lor T Tr
Hosanna	Zon T Sl	How Lovely Are Those Dwellings	Zon T Sr	I Am Come Into My Garden	Bbl T Tx
Hosanna	Aug L Le	How Lovely Are Your Works	Gia L Tt	I Am Content (Cantata)	Lps T Tr
Hosanna	Mar L Le	How Lovely Is Thy Dwelling Place	Wbp T Tr	I Am Determined	Man G Tc
Hosanna	Lds F Li	How Lovely Is Thy Dwelling Place	Gsc T Tt	I Am Glad	Aug L Tt
Hosanna (Folk Communion Service)	Aug F Lo	How Lovely Is Thy Dwelling Place	Gsc T Tt	I Am In His Hands	Man G Tr
Hosanna (Lat)	Gsc T Sr	How Lovely Is Thy Dwelling Place	Gia L Tr	I Am My Brother's Brother	Fel L Tr
Hosanna Be The Children's Song	Sac L Sl	How Lovely Is Your Dwelling Place	Fel L Tr	I Am Not Alone Today	Lor T Tr
Hosanna Filio David (Choral)	Fel T Sl	How Lovely Is Your Dwelling Place	Sha F Tr	I Am One For Whom You Died	Mam G Tj
Hosanna For Joy	Nal L Le	How Lovely Shines (W/Tpt,Org,Cong)	Con L Tx	I Am Persuaded	Ham G Tc
Hosanna In The Highest	Chh T Li	How Lovely Shines The Star (W/Ob)	Con L Zb	I Am Persuaded	Man G Tr
Hosanna In The Highest	Wlp F Le	How Many Miles Must We Go?	Her L Sc	I Am Resolved	Zon G Tc
Hosanna In The Highest!	Lor T Sl	How Much He Cared	Man G Sl	I Am So Glad	Bec T Sc
Hosanna To The King	Lor T Sl	How Much He Cares	Man G Sl	I Am So Glad Each Christmas Eve	Aug L Sc
Hosanna To The Son Of David	Fel L Sl	How Precious Is Thy Loving Kindness	Oxf T Tr	I Am The Alpha And The Omega	Aug T Tj
Hosanna To The Son Of David	Aug L Sl	How Sacred A Feast	Gia T Ln	I Am The Bread Of Life	Sac L Lo
Hosanna To The Son Of David	Oxf T Sl	How Shall I Fitly Meet Thee	Gsc T Sc	I Am The Bread Of Life	Gia T Lo
Hosanna We Sing	Lor T Sl	How Shall I Sing That Majesty	Sac T Tt	I Am The Bread Of Life	Gia F Ln
Hosanna!	Nal L Le	How Still And Tiny	Gia T Sc	I Am The Door	Sac L Tj
Hosanna! Blessed Is He!	Lor T Sl	How Still The Garden Of Gethsemane	Abi T Sl	I Am The Good Shepherd	Sac L Tr
Hosanna! Hosanna!	Lor T Sl	How Sweet Is The Voice Of My Lord	Pro L Tr	I Am The Good Shepherd	Fel L Tj
Hosanna! O Blessed Is He	Aug L Le	How Sweet It Is	Man G Tr	I Am The Good Shepherd	Wlp F Tj
Hosanna, Blessed Is He	Aug L Le	How Sweet The Name	Bfi T Tj	I Am The Good Shepherd	Aug T Tr
Hosanna, Hallelujah!	Prc L Tx	How Sweet The Name Of Jesus Sounds(P.D	Man T Tj	I Am The Handmaid Of The Lord	Sha F Tr
Hosanna, Hosanna, Hosanna	Wlp L Le	How Unto Bethlehem	Gsc T Sc	I Am The Light	Aug T Tj
Hosanna, Loud Hosanna	Sac L Sl	How Wonderful And Great	Fel F Tt	I Am The Light Of The World	Sac L Tj
Hosanna, Loud Hosanna	Lor T Sl	Howl My Soul	Van F Sl	I Am The Living Bread	Fel L Ln
Hosanna, Loud Hosanna!	Lor T Sl	Humbly Let Us Voice Our Homage	Wlp T Lo	I Am The Living Bread	Wlp F Lo
Hosanna, Son Of David	Aug L Le	Humbly We Adore Thee	Wlp T Lo	I Am The Resurrection	Fel L Sr
Hosannah To The Son Of David (Md)	Oxf T Sl	Humbly We Adore You	Fel T Lo	I Am The Resurrection	Fel F Ln
Hosea	Wes F Tx	Huron Indian Carol	Sac T Sc	I Am The Resurrection And The Life	Oxf T Sr
How Amiable Are Thy Tabernacles	Abi L Tc	Hurry Sundown	Nor F Tr	I Am The Resurrection And The Life	Zon T Sr
How Beauteous Are Their Feet	Gsc T Sa	Hush My Dear	Abi T Sc	I Am The Resurrection And The Life	Cfp T Sr
How Beautiful Upon The Mountains	Gsc T Tx	Hush, My Babe	Sac L Sc	I Am The Resurrection And The Life	Sac L Sr
How Big Is God	Man G Tt	Hushing Carol	Gsc T Sc	I Am The Rose Of Sharon	Gsc T Tj
How Big Is God	Ham G Tr	Hymn	Pep F Tt	I Am The Rose Of Sharon	Bbl T Tj
How Blessed Are They Who Hear God's Wd	Acp L Tx	Hymn Anthems	Abi L Za	I Am The Salvation Of My People	Fel L Tt
How Blessed Are They Who Hear Gods Wd	Acp L Tx	Hymn Descants Vol i	Abi L Za	I Am The True Vine	Fel L Ln
How Blest Are They	Aug L Tr	Hymn Descants Vol ii	Abi L Za	I Am The Vine	Wlp F Tr
How Blest Are They (M)	Oxf T Tw	Hymn Descants Vol. iii	Abi T Za	I Am The Vine	Sac L Lo
How Brightly Shines The Morning Star	Acp L Lr	Hymn For A Prayer Meeting	Wgm F Tt	I Am The Way	Acp F Tj
How Brightly Shines The Morning Star	Acp L Lr	Hymn For Ascensiontide (E)	Oxf T Sr	I Am The Way (From No Time Like...)	Wlp F Tj
How Calm And Beautiful The Morn	Gsc T Sr	Hymn For Our Time	Gsc T Tx	I Am The Way (4-Part Arr)	Acp F Sl
How Can I Be A Friend?	Jsp F Tr	Hymn For The Sick	Acp L Tx	I Am The Way, The Truth, And The Life	Sac L Tj
How Can I Keep From Singing	Nal L Tt	Hymn For The Sick (4-Part Arr)	Acp L Tx	I Am Thine	Sav G Tc
How Can Sinner Know	Gsc T Sl	Hymn For Winter	Abi L Tx	I Am Trusting Thee, Lord Jesus	Lor T Tr
How Can This Be	Ahc L Tx	Hymn Intonations (55)	Abi L Zb	I Am Willing, Lord (W/Piano)	Wrd G Tc
How Can We Show Our Love To Thee	Gsc T Tt	Hymn Of Consecration	Maf T Tc	I Am With You	Zon L Lo
How Can You Really Care? (Ps. 6)	Nal L Sl	Hymn Of Glory	Wgm F Tt	I Am Your Light (Opt Brass)	Gra F Tc
How Dark Was The Stable?	Ahc L Sc	Hymn Of Joy (Let Us Live In Christ)	Gia F Tr	I Am...Because	Gmc G Tc
How Excellent Is Thy Name	Som L Tt	Hymn Of Love.	Vrn G Tw	I Ask For No More (Cantata)	Lps T Tr
How Excellent Is Thy Name	Sac L Tt	Hymn Of Nativity	Som L Sc	I Ask God	Gmp G Tr
How Excellent Is Thy Name	Gsc T Tt	Hymn Of Peace, A	Her T Tr	I Believe	Ham G Tx
How Excellent Thy Name	Maf T Tt	Hymn Of Praise	Nal L Tt	I Believe	Bfi F Tc
How Excellent Thy Name	Wbp T Tt	Hymn Of Praise	Kal L Tt	I Believe	Sac L Tt
How Excellent Thy Name	Maf T Tt	Hymn Of Praise	Gia T Tt	I Believe Heaven's God's Will	Jhm G Sr
How Excellent Thy Name	Gsc T Tt	Hymn Of Praise	Lor T Tt	I Believe In A Hill Called Mt. Calvary	Gmc G Sl
How Fair The Church	Aug T Tx	Hymn Of Praise	Gsc T Tt	I Believe In God	Lor T Tr
How Faithful God	Nal L Tr	Hymn Of Praise	Gia L Tt	I Believe In God	Jhm G Tx
How Far Is It To Bethlehem?	Sac T Sc	Hymn Of Praise (First Mass)	Fel F Lc	I Believe In Heaven	Wrd G Tx

ALPHABETICAL INDEX OF TITLES

Title	Code
I Believe In Miracles	Zon G Tr
I Believe In Miracles	Lor T Tx
I Believe In One God (Creed)	Ccc L Tx
I Believe In The Father	Man G Tx
I Believe In The Sun	Nal C Tr
I Believe In You	Nal C Tc
I Believe It	Gmc G Tr
I Believe That I Shall See(Ps 27)	Rav L Ld
I Believe That Jesus Died For Me	Zon G Sl
I Believe That My Redeemer Lives	Fel L Sr
I Believe That My Redeemer Lives	Rpb L Tf
I Believe That My Redeemer Lives	Gia L Sr
I Believe What The Bible Says	Gmc G Tr
I Believe, Help Thou My Belief	Gmc G Tr
I Belong To Jesus	Man G Tc
I Belong To Jesus	Jhm G Tj
I Bind My Heart	Gia T Tc
I Bind Unto Myself Today	Abi L Tc
I Bless You, Lord	Fel L Tt
I Bring Gifts To You, Lord	Fel L To
I Built A Garden	Van F Sl
I Call On You, O God	Fel L Sl
I Call With My Own Heart	Wbp T Tr
I Call You Friends	Sms F Tr
I Called Upon The Lord	Gsc T Tr
I Came To Praise The Lord	Gmc G Tt
I Can Be A Christian By Myself	Prc L Tx
I Can Believe	Lor T Tx
I Can Know	Zon L Tr
I Can't Spin A Web	Sac L Tx
I Cannot Fail The Lord	Man G Tr
I Cannot Tell	Gmc G Tx
I Cannot Tell It All	Man G Tt
I Caused Thy Grief	Aug L Sl
I Charge You, O Ye Daughters	Bbl T Tr
I Come Tired	Prc L Tx
I Come To Thee Jesus (Opt Bel,Ob,Perc)	Pro T Sc
I Come With Joy	Aug L La
I Come, O Lord, Unto Thee	Sac L Lp
I Could Hardly See The Road	Gmc G Tc
I Could Never Outlove The Lord	Gmc G Tr
I Couldn't Hear Nobody Pray	Gsc G Tx
I Cried To God In Tribulation	Gsc T Sl
I Depend Upon My God	Zon G Tr
I Didn't Think It Could Be	Man G Tx
I Do Believe	Sbf L Tx
I Do Not Ask, O Lord	Tcp L Tx
I Don't Deserve His Love	Sil T Tj
I Don't Know How To Love Him	Lds F Tt
I Don't Know Why	Ham G Tx
I Don't Know Why Jesus Loved Me	Lex T Tj
I Done Got Over	Sav G Tf
I Dreamed I Went To Heaven	Sav G Tx
I Find No Fault In Him	Man G Sl
I Found Him In My Heart	Lor T Tr
I Found Joy (W/Piano)	Wrd G Sr
I Found Life In Christ	Man G Tb
I Found My Life In Jesus	Rav G Tj
I Found The Lord	Sil F Tj
I Found The Truth	Man G Tr
I Gave My Life To Jesus	Zon G Tc
I Give My All To Thee (W/Piano)	Wrd G Tc
I Give Myself Unto Prayer	Sac L Tr
I Give You Thanks, O Lord	Fel L Tt
I Go To The Father	Fel L Sl
I Got My Religion In Time	Her T Tc
I Got Shoes	Gsc G Tk
I Guess God Thought Of Everything	Gmc G Tr
I Have A Dream	Abi L Tr
I Have A Father Who Can	Gmp G Tr
I Have A Friend	Sto G Tr
I Have Arisen And Am With You	Fel L Sr
I Have Been To The Mountaintop	Lor T Tr
I Have Come To Set Fire	Fel L Ss
I Have Decided To Follow Jesus	Zon G Tc
I Have Faith	Nal L Tc
I Have Given You An Example	Fel L Sl
I Have Plans, Says The Lord	Fel L Tx
I Have Put My Words	Fel L Tx
I Have Quieted My Soul	Lor T Tr
I Have The Joy (Arrangement)	Tal T Tt
I Have Waited For The Lord (Ps 40)	Gra L Ld
I Hear Jesus Calling My Name	Jhm G Tj
I Hear Music	Zon G Tt
I Heard A Great Voice	Cfp T Tt
I Heard A Great Voice	Aug L Tx
I Heard God Today	Man G Tr
I Heard The Lord	Wgm F Tj
I Heard The Voice	Abi L Tc
I Heard The Voice Of Jesus Say	Lor T Tj
I Hide Me Jesus In Thy Name	Gsc T Tj
I Hold The Kingdom	Gia L Tc
I Ieiunio Et Fletu (M)	Oxf T Sl
I In Them	Rpb L Tr
I Just Come From The Fountain	Wbp T Tx
I Just Feel Like Something Good Is	Gmc G Tt
I Just Got Religion	Man G Tb
I Just Love My Jesus	Man G Tc
I Know A Fount' So Wondrous Blest	Man G Ss
I Know He Cares	Man G Tr
I Know He Holdeth Me	Zon G Tr
I Know He's Mine	Man G Tj
I Know Jesus	Sil F Tj
I Know My Friend Jesus Is Piloting Me	Mam G Tj
I Know Not Where The Road May Lead	Abi L Tc
I Know That My Redeemer (W/Org)	Cfp T Sr
I Know That My Redeemer Lives	Gia L Za
I Know That My Redeemer Lives	Gsc T Sr
I Know That My Redeemer Lives	Zon T Sr
I Know That My Redeemer Lives (M)	Oxf T Sr
I Know That My Redeemer Liveth	Lor T Sr
I Know That My Redeemer Liveth	Aug T Sr
I Know The Father Loves Me	Fcc F Tr
I Know The Lord's Laid His Hand On Me	Lor G Tc
I Know The Secret	Van F Tx
I Know The Story	Man G Sr
I Know What It's Like	Mar L Tx
I Know Where I'm Goin	Zon F Tc
I Know Where I'm Going	Lor F Tc
I Know Where I'm Going	Zon F Tc
I Know, O Lord	Fel L Tx
I Know, They're Gone	Zon G Sl
I Lift My Eyes To The Mt (Psalm 121)	Ahc L Tr
I Lift My Soul	Acp F To
I Lift My Soul (4-Part Arr)	Acp F To
I Lift Up My Eyes	Fel F Tr
I Lift Up My Eyes To The Hills	Aug L Tr
I Like God's Love	Nal C Tr
I Like The Sound Of America	Wrd C Tp
I Long For Thy Salvation	Gsc T Sa
I Long To Find Perfect Peace	Man G Tr
I Longed To Find The Risen Lord	Smc T Sr
I Look To God	Van F Tr
I Look To Thee In Every Need	Lor T Tr
I Look Up To Thee	Hof L Tr
I Looked For Someone	Fel L Sl
I Lost It All To Find Everthing	Gmc G Tc
I Love America (Musical)	Zon L Tp
I Love Him	Mam G Tj
I Love Him (With All My Heart)	Sil L Tj
I Love Him Because He First Loved Me	Man C Tr
I Love The Church	Aug T Tx
I Love Thee	Zon T Tr
I Love Thy Kingdom, Lord	Gsc T Tk
I Love Thy Kingdom, Lord	Zon T Tk
I Love Thy Kingdom, Lord	Sac L Tk
I Love To Take A Walk	Mar G Tj
I Love To Tell The Story	Zon G Tx
I Love You Lord My Strength (Ps 18)	Gra L Ld
I Love You, O Lord, My Strength	Fel L Tr
I Make My Vows To The Lord	Fel L Tc
I May Be Young	Nal L Tx
I Met My Master	Lor L Tc
I Mingle My Drink With Tears	Fel L Sl
I Must Go On	Gmp G Tc
I Must Tell Jesus	Lor T Tj
I Need Thee Every Hour	Lor T Tr
I Place All My Trust	Nal L Tr
I Praise You, Lord	Fel L Tt
I Praised The Earth	Fel F Tt
I Pray To You, O Lord	Fel L Tr
I Rejoiced (Psalms 121 & 122)	Rpb L Ld
I Remember The Time	Man G Sr
I Renew My Vows To You, Lord	Fel L Tc
I Said To The Man (E) 1	Oxf L Tx
I Sat Down Under His Shadow (M)	Oxf T Tr
I Saw A Stranger Yester'en	Gal T Sc
I Saw A Stranger Yester'en(A Cap)	Gsc T Tx
I Saw The Cross Of Jesus	Lor T Sl
I Saw The Holy City	Fel F Sr
I Saw The New Jerusalem	Wlp L Tm
I Saw Three Ships	Gsc T Sc
I See That All Things Have Their End	Fel L Tx
I See Your Face	Man L Tr
I Shall Be Content	Fel L Tr
I Shall Never Let Go His Hand	Man G Tc
I Shall Not Care(Arr.Only)	Mam T Tx
I Shall Not Die, But Live	Fel L Tf
I Should Have Been Crucified	Jtb G Tx
I Shout With Joy To You	Fel L Tt
I Sing A Song Of Teilhard	Gia F Tx
I Sing A Song To You, Lord	Sha F Tt
I Sing Of A Maiden	Gsc T Sc
I Sing Of God	Lor T Tt
I Sing Of The Glory Of The Lord	Lor T Tt
I Sing The Mighty Power Of God	Gsc L Tt
I Sing The Mighty Power Of God	Sac L Tt
I Sing The Mighty Power Of God	Lor T Tt
I Sing The Mighty Power Of God	Zon T Tt
I Sing With All My Being	Rpb L Tt
I Sing Your Song	Fel F Tt
I Sought My God	Nal L Tr
I Sought The Lord	Abi L Tr
I Sought The Lord	Gmc G Tr
I Stopped Dying And Started Living	Man G Tb
I Sure Do Love The Lord	Man G Tr
I Talked To God Last Night	Gsc T Tr
I Talked To The Saviour	Pmp G Tx
I Thank God For Amazing Grace	Sto G Tt
I Thank My God	Ahc L Tt
I Thank My God	Mmc G Tt
I Thank Thee, Lord	Abi L Tt
I Thank You, For You Deliver	Fel L Tt
I Thank You, Lord	Fel L Tt
I Thank You, O Lord	Fel L Tt
I Thank You, O Lord My God	Fel L Tt
I Think I Heard Him Say	Lor T Tx
I Trust In You	Wlp F Tr
I Trust In You, O God	Fel L Tr
I Wait For The Lord	Abi L Sa
I Waited And Waited For The Lord	Fel L Tr
I Waited For The Lord	Gsc T Sa
I Waited For The Lord (Ps 40)	Smc T Tr
I Walk Along With Jesus	Zon G Tc
I Walk The Glory Road	Zon G Tc
I Walked Today Where Jesus Walked	Gsc T Tj
I Want Jesus To Walk With Me	Lor G Tj
I Want Jesus To Walk With Me	Abi L Tc
I Want More Of Jesus	Mar L Tj
I Want To Be Ready	Lor T Sr
I Want To Be There	Ham G Sr
I Want To Be There	Zon G Sr
I Want To Be Your Friend	Nal L Tr
I Want To Call You	Nal L Tx
I Want To Do What He Commands	Pmp G To
I Want To Go To Heaven	Jhm G Sr
I Want To Serve The Lord	Lor L Tc
I Want To Sing	Wlp L Tt
I Want To Walk	Nal C Tc
I Want To Walk As A Child	Fis F Tc
I Was Glad	Prc L Tx
I Was Glad	Bec T Tt
I Was Glad (Ps 122)	Oxf T La
I Was Hungry,And You Fed Me.	Vrn G Tr
I Was There When The Spirit Came	Man G Ss
I Went To Cincinnati	Nal C Tx
I Will Arise	Sac T Tt
I Will Arise (So Early)	Gia F La
I Will Arise And Go To Jesus	Zon G Lp
I Will Be As The Dew	Aug T Sa
I Will Be Like A Father & Mother	Gra F Tb
I Will Bear Witness, O Lord	Fel L Tc
I Will Bow And Be Simple	Gsc T Tr
I Will Breathe Into You	Fel L Ss
I Will Call Upon The Lord	Fel L Tr
I Will Come Again	Bfi F Tk
I Will Come Again (Cantata)	Zon G Sa
I Will Exalt Him	Gsc T Tt
I Will Exalt Thee & Sing Unto The Lord	Oxf T Tt
I Will Extol Thee	Gsc T Tt
I Will Extol Thee	Som L Tt
I Will Extol Thee	Aug T Tt
I Will Extol Thee	Lor T Tt
I Will Give Glory To You	Fel L Tt
I Will Give Glory To Your Name	Fel L Tt
I Will Give My Baby	Ahc L Sc
I Will Give Peace	Pro T Tr
I Will Give Thanks	Rpb L Tt
I Will Give Thanks	Sac L Tt
I Will Give Thanks	Rpb F Tt
I Will Give Thanks Unto The Lord	Gsc T Tt
I Will Give You A New Commandment (Me)	Oxf T Ss
I Will Go Forward And Walk	Gra F Tc
I Will Go To The Altar Of God	Gra L La
I Will Go To The Altar Of God	Fel L La
I Will Go To The Mountain	Mem L Lp
I Will Hope In God	Fel L Tr
I Will Lift Mine Eyes	Gsc T Sr
I Will Lift Up Mine Eyes	Sac L Tr
I Will Lift Up Mine Eyes	Maf L Tr
I Will Lift Up Mine Eyes	Gsc T Tr
I Will Lift Up Mine Eyes	Abi L Tr
I Will Lift Up Mine Eyes	Zon T Tr
I Will Lift Up Mine Eyes	Gsc T Tr
I Will Lift Up Mine Eyes	Lor T Tr
I Will Lift Up Mine Eyes (Ps 121)	Pro L Tr
I Will Lift Up Mine Eyes Unto The Hill	Oxf L Tr
I Will Lift Up My Eyes	Bos L Sl
I Will Live To Sing Your Praise	Sms F Tt
I Will Love Thee O Lord	Gsc T Tr
I Will Magnify Thee	Lor T Tt
I Will Magnify Thee (Md)	Abi L Tt
I Will Meditate On Your Law	Fel L Tx
I Will Not Forget You	Nal L Tx
I Will Not Leave You Friendless	Fel L Ss
I Will Not Let Thee Go	Gsc T Tw
I Will Not Question	Man G Tr
I Will Offer A Heart	Fel L To
I Will Offer In His House	Fel L To
I Will Offer Joyful Sacrifice	Fel L To
I Will Offer Sacrifice	Fel L To
I Will Offer Sacrifice (Ps 27)	Gra F To
I Will Pour Clean Water On You	Fel L Tb
I Will Pour Out My Spirit	Aug T Ss
I Will Praise The Lord	Gsc T Tt
I Will Praise The Lord	Gsc T Tt
I Will Praise Thee	Lor T Tt
I Will Praise Thee, O Lord	Her T Tt
I Will Praise Thee, O Lord	Aug T Tt
I Will Praise You Lord (Ps 22 End)	Gra L Ld

Title	Code
I Will Put Enmity	Fel L Tm
I Will Rejoice In The Lord	Fel L Tt
I Will Serve Thee	Gmc G Tc
I Will Serve Thee	Lor G Tc
I Will Sing	Man G Tt
I Will Sing	Lor T Tt
I Will Sing And Make Music	Sha F Tt
I Will Sing In The Morning	Rpb L Tt
I Will Sing Of My Redeemer	Lor T Tj
I Will Sing Of The Lord	Nal G Tt
I Will Sing Of The Mercies Of The Lord	Sac L Tr
I Will Sing Of Thee Thy Great Mercies	Gsc T Tt
I Will Sing Praise	Nal L Tt
I Will Sing Praise To My God	Fel L Tt
I Will Sing Praise To You	Fel L Tt
I Will Sing Praises	Her T Tt
I Will Sing The Wondrous Story	Zon T Tx
I Will Sing Thee Songs Of Gladness	Gsc T Tt
I Will Sing To The Lord	Fel L Tt
I Will Sing To The Lord 1	Aug T Tt
I Will Sing Unto The Lord (Ps 104)	Oxf L Tt
I Will Sing, I Will Sing	Fis F Tt
I Will Thank Thee, O Lord	Gsc T Tt
I Will Thank Thee, O Lord	Gsc T Tt
I Will Wake Up The Sun	Aug T Tt
I Will Walk In God's Presence	Gra L Ld
I Wish I Knew How It Would Feel	Dua F Tt
I Wish That I Had Been There	Sav G Sl
I Wish You Jesus	Ham G Tj
I Won't Go Where They Are	Man G Tx
I Won't Move Unless He Tells Me	Man G Tc
I Wonder As I Wander	Gsc T Sc
I Wonder As I Wander	Aug L Sc
I Wonder How It Felt	Gmc G Sl
I Wonder If It's Happened Yet To You	Zon G Ss
I Wonder Why	Prc L Tx
I Wonder Why	Wlp F Tx
I Would Be True	Zon L Tx
I Would Renew The Whole World	Gra F Ss
I Would Seek God	Lor T Tr
I, The Lord, Am Your God	Fel L Tr
I'd Do It All Over Again	Gmc G Tc
I'd Like To Teach The World To Sing	Cke F Tr
I'd Like To Walk Around	Sem G Tc
I'd Rather Fight Than Switch	Sto G Tx
I'll Be Fightin' Old Satan 'til I Die	Kmp G Tx
I'll Be There	Nal L Tr
I'll Fashion Me A People	Fcc C Lo
I'll Go	Sem G Tc
I'll Go Now	Zon G Lp
I'll Hold You In My Arms	Fcc F Tx
I'll Keep Christmas In My Heart Always	Zon G Sc
I'll Keep On Serving	Sem G Tc
I'll Live For Him	Sac L Tc
I'll Live For Jesus	Zon L Tc
I'll Never Be Lonely	Mar L Tr
I'll Never Be Lonely	Man G Sl
I'll Never Be The Same Again	Zon F Tb
I'll Never Contented Be	Fel F Tr
I'll Never Forget	Man G Tr
I'll Never Leave You	Mar L Tc
I'll Praise My Maker (Opt Brs)	Abi L Tt
I'll Raise You Up (Calypso)	Gia F Sr
I'll Sing	Zon G Tt
I'll Sing Praise To The Lord	Gra F Tt
I'll Tell It	Pmp G Tx
I'll Trust And Never Be Afraid	Zon F Tc
I'll Trust And Never Be Afraid	Zon G Tr
I'll Understand	Man G Tr
I'll Walk Into That Sunset	Gmc G Tc
I'll Walk With God	Wbp T Tx
I'll Wear A New White Robe	Jhm G Sr
I'm A Happy, Happy Christian	Zon G Tr
I'm A Promise	Gmc G Ss
I'm A Soldier	Zon G Tc
I'm A–Goin To Glory	Zon G Sr
I'm Almost Home	Gmc G Sr
I'm Being Guided	Sil F Tt
I'm But A Stranger Here	Lor L Tf
I'm Coming	Gmc G Sa
I'm Feasting On The Living Bread	Mar L Lo
I'm Following The Son	Sil F Tc
I'm Free	Gmc G Ss
I'm Glad To Know There's A Heaven	Man G Sr
I'm Going About My Father's Business	Man G Tr
I'm Going To Fly Away To Heaven	Jhm G Sr
I'm Going To Make It Through	Jhm G Sr
I'm Gonna Keep On	Gmc G Tc
I'm Gonna Let My Love Shine	Lor T Tc
I'm Gonna Praise His Name	Mar L Tt
I'm Gonna Put My Shoes On	Mem G Tr
I'm Gonna Ride That Train To Heaven	Kmp G Sr
I'm Gonna Sing	Gia F Tt
I'm Gonna Sing	Mar L Tt
I'm Gonna' Take A Trip	Man G Sr
I'm Here To Stay	Man G Tc
I'm His To Command	Zon G Tc
I'm Living, I'm Living	Wlp F Sr
I'm Not Afraid	Fel L Tr
I'm Not Afraid Anymore	Zon G Tr
I'm Not Afraid Of The Dark Any More	Ham C Tf
I'm Not Alone	Fis F Tr
I'm Not Alone	Zon G Tr
I'm Not Satisfied Yet	Man G Tc
I'm On My Way To Heaven Anyhow	Sem G Tr
I'm Ready To Follow	Wlp F Tc
I'm Sheltered In His Arms	Sav G Tr
I'm Singing For My Lord	Zon G Tt
I'm So Glad I Found An Altar Of Prayer	Gmc G Tr
I'm So Happy	Zon G Tr
I'm So Happy	Man G It
I'm Standing In The Sun	Gsc T Tx
I'm Still Growing	Gmp G To
I'm Thankful	Hhh G To
I'm Watching For His Coming	Jhm G Sr
I've A Song	Gmc G Tt
I've Been 'buked	Gsc T Tx
I've Been Born Again	Mam G Tb
I've Been On The Mountain	Gmc G Tr
I've Been Sealed	Mar L Sr
I've Been To Calvary	Gmc G Sl
I've Been Touched By His Hand	Yan F Tj
I've Discovered The Way Of Gladness	Lor T Tr
I've Found Something	Man G Tb
I've Got A Light	Rpb C La
I've Got It	Man G Ss
I've Got Jesus	Man G Tj
I've Got Jesus	Lor L Tc
I've Got So Many Million Years	Ham G Sr
I've Got The Liberty	Mar L Tr
I've Just Come From The Place	Gmc G Tr
I've Just Seen Jesus	Gmc G Tj
Ich Aber Bin Eland(Lord, God I Am Wear	Gsc T Sl
If Any Man Come After Me	Mar L Tc
If Anyone Serves Me	Fel L Tc
If Anyone Thirst	Fel L Lo
If Anyone Wishes To Come After Me	Gia L Tc
If Ever The Sun Stops Shining	Lor T Tr
If God Be For Us, Who Shall Be Against	Gsc T Tc
If God Could Be A Color	Mob C Tx
If God Is For Us	Nal L Tr
If I Created You	Man L Tr
If I Didn't Know	Man G Tx
If I Forget To Pray	Som L Tx
If I Got My Ticket, Can I Ride?	Gsc G Tx
If I Had All The World's Money	Gia F Ss
If I Had Not Jesus	Man G Tj
If I Had Wings	Pep F Tt
If I Have My Jesus(From Two Litanies)	Bbl T Tj
If I Have Wounded Any Soul	Lor T Tr
If I Should Go To Heaven	Kmp G Sr
If I Speak With The Tongues Of Men	Tcp L Tr
If I Wanted To Hide	Sbf L Ss
If I, The Lord And Master	Fel L Sl
If It Keeps Gettin' Better	Gmc G Tc
If My Faith Is Strong And Sure	Sms T Tr
If My People	Man G Tr
If My People	Zon L Tp
If My People (Musical)	Wrd G Tp
If One Member Suffers	Fel L Tr
If Only You'll Answer Me	Fel F Sl
If The Christ Should Come To Me	Lor T Sa
If The Good Lord's Willing	Oak G Tx
If The Lord Does Not Build	Nal L Tc
If The Lord Wills	Gsc L Tr
If The World Could Only Be Happy	Pro L Tr
If There Is A Holy Spirit	Prc L Tx
If Thou Be Jesus	Pmp G Tj
If Thou But Suffer God To Guide Thee	Gsc T Tr
If Today You Hear His Voice (Alt Solo)	Hof T Tr
If Today You Hear His Voice (Icet)	Wlp L Ld
If We Are Humble	Fel L Tr
If We Have One Another	Nal L Tr
If We Saw Him	Wlp F Tx
If With All Your Hearts	Smc T Zb
If With All Your Hearts	Gsc T Sl
If With All Your Hearts	Aug T Sl
If With All Your Hearts	Lor T Sl
If Ye Be Merry	Gsc T Tt
If Ye Love Me (Me)	Oxf T Ss
If Ye Love Me, Keep My Commandments	Cob T Tr
If Ye Love Me, Keep My Commandments	Gsc T Tr
If Ye Then Be Risen (Opt Acc)	Abi T Sr
If You Abide (W/Piano)	Wrd G Tr
If You Bring Your Gift To The Altar	Wlp L To
If You Continue In My Word	Aug L Tx
If You Give Of Your Bread	Fcc L To
If You Have Kept My Words	Fel L Tx
If You Have Risen With Christ	Fel L Tb
If You Keep Our Transgressions	Wlp L Sl
If You Know Christ	Man G Tj
If You Love Me, Keep My Word	Jsp F Tr
If You Love Me, Simon Peter	Fel L Tx
If You Really Love Him	Man G Tr
If You Receive My Words	Aug L Tr
If You Want Life	Fel L Tx
If You Will Believe	Mar L Tr
If You Would Come After Me	Fel L Tc
If You Would Serve God	Fel L Tc
If You'll Take My Hand	Chd F Tj
Ihr Kinderlein Kommet	Gsc T Tr
Immaculate Mary (Modern Text)	Gsc T Tm
Immanuel	Bfi T Lp
Immortal Love	Aug L Tr
Immortal Love	Sac L Sl
Immortal Love	Abi L Tt
Immortal Love, For Ever Full	Gsc T Tr
Immortal, Invisible	Abi L Tt
Immortal, Invisible	Zon T Tt
Immortal, Invisible	Lor T Tx
Impatient Heart	Zon G Tx
Improperium	Maf T Sl
Improvisation On Father	Abi L Zb
Improvisation On Schonster Herr Jesu	Abi L Zb
Improvisation On Unser Herrscher	Abi L Zb
Imps Of Satan	Jhm G Tx
In A Cave (W/Opt Flute)	Zon T Sc
In A Manger He Is Sleeping	Lor T Sc
In A World That Needs Thy Love	Smc T Tr
In Adam We Have All Been One	Jsp L Tr
In Ages Now Long Past	Acp L Sa
In All The World	Aug L Tx
In Assumptione B. Mariae& In Festo	Kal T Tm
In Bethlehem	Lor T Sc
In Bethlehem Is Born A King 1	Aug T Sc
In Bethlehem That Fair City	Gsc T Sc
In Christ The Lord	Gia L Tu
In Christ The Prince Of Peace	Acp L Tj
In Christ The Prince Of Peace (4–Part	Acp L Tj
In Christ There Is No East Or West	Sac L Lo
In Christ There Is No East Or West	Abi L Tr
In Christ There Is No East Or West	Zon G Lo
In Dulci Jubilo	Kal T Tr
In Dulci Jubilo	Gsc T Sc
In Ecclesiis	Gsc T La
In Ecclesiis	Bbl T Tr
In Excelsis Gloria	Aug T Sc
In Faith I Steadfast Stand	Smc T Zb
In Festo Purificationis	Kal T Sc
In God The Lord (Cantata)	Lps T Tr
In God's Tomorrow	Gmc G Sr
In Heaven Above	Aug T Tx
In Heaven Above	Lor T Tx
In Heaven Give Glory	Acp L Tt
In Heaven Give Glory	Acp L Tt
In Heavenly Love	Maf T Tr
In Heavenly Love	Aug T Tr
In Heavenly Love Abiding	Pro T Tr
In Him Everything Was Created	Nal L Tt
In Him Who Strengthens Me	Ahc L Tr
In His Care	Aug L Tr
In His Love	Fel F Tt
In His Name	Zon G Tt
In His Presence	Zon G Tr
In His Shelter	Nal L Tt
In Holy Splendor (Ccd)	Wlp F Sc
In Honour Of A King	Gsc L Sr
In Jesus	Lor T Tj
In Jesus Name	Mar L Tj
In Jesus' Name	Man G Tj
In Love We Gather	Wlp L La
In Love With The Lover Of My Soul	Zon G Tr
In Manibus Tuis (Eng) Ps 31	Gra L Ld
In Memoriam	Tcp L Tf
In Memory Of The Savior's Love	Abi L Lo
In Memory Of The Savior's Love	Sac L Sl
In Mirth And In Gladness	Gsc T Tt
In My Father's House	Gsc T Sr
In My Garden	Sac L Tr
In My Heart	Zon G Tt
In My Heart There Rings A Melody	Lor T Tj
In My Name	Fel F Tc
In My Old Age, O God	Fel L Tf
In My Orchard, Pearl'd With Dew	Bbl T Tx
In Nativitate Mariae Virginis	Kal T Tm
In Nature's Ebb And Flow	Som L Tx
In Night's Deep Silence	Gia T Sc
In Nomine Jesu	Gia T Tj
In Nomine Jesu(At Jesus' Holy Name)	Gia T Tj
In Paradisum	Fel T Tf
In Paradisum	Ron T Tf
In Peace & Joy	Aug L Tr
In Pleasant Places	Zon G Tx
In Praise Of Easter (5 Movements)	Jfs L Sr
In Praise Of God	Wlp F Tt
In Praise To God	Aug L Tt
In Prayer	Bbl T Tr
In Remembrance	Man G Tx
In Remembrance Of Me	Bfi F Lo
In Remembrance Of Me	Zon L Lo
In Resurrectione Domini	Bbl T Sr
In Sodom Town	Fcc C Tx
In Te Domine Speravi	Gia T Tr
In Te, Domine, Speravi	Gsc T Tr
In Tears Of Grief (St.Matt Pass) (Md)	Oxf T Sl
In Thankful Remembrance (W/Brs Etal)	Abi L Tx
In Thanksgiving I Go Around	Fel L Tt
In That Great Gettin' Up Mornin'	Gsc G Sk
In That Great Gettin' Up Mornin'	Aug G Tk
In That Lovely Far–Off City	Gsc T Sc

ALPHABETICAL INDEX OF TITLES

In The Arms Of My Brothers Fel F Tr
In The Autograph Of God Pmp G Tx
In The Beginning Abi L Tx
In The Beginning Van F Sc
In The Bleak Mid-Winter Gsc T Sc
In The Chapel Of The Dawn Mmc G Tx
In The Cross Of Christ I Glory Zon T Sl
In The Day Of The Lord Nal L Tk
In The End Of The Sabbath Gsc T Sr
In The End You Will Receive Me Fel L Tf
In The Garden Lor T Tr
In The Glow Of His Love Cor F Tr
In The Hollow Of Your Hand Lor T Tr
In The Home Where They Love To Pray Mdm G Tp
In The Image Of God Zon G Tr
In The Lord We Will Live Acp F Lo
In The Lord We Will Live (4-Part Arr) Acp L Tr
In The Midst Of The Assembly Fel L Tr
In The Month Of December Fel F Sc
In The Mornin' Ahc L Tt
In The Morning Nal L Tx
In The Name Of The Lord Aug T Tt
In The Night Christ Came Walking(Acap) Gsc T Tj
In The Peace Of Christ Wlp L Tr
In The Presence (Ps 116) Rav L Ld
In The Presence Of God Nal L La
In The Presence Of The Master Gmc G Tr
In The Stillness Gsc T Sc
In The Stillness Of The Night Man G Sc
In The Stillness Of The Night Lor T Sc
In The Upper Room Gmc G Tr
In The Upper Room Lor G Tr
In The Year That King Uzziah Died Abi L Tx
In Thee Is Gladness Aug T Tt
In Thee Is Gladness (Gastoldi 1591) Oxf T Tt
In Thee O Lord Have I Put My Trust Gia L Tr
In Thee, O Lord, Do I Put My Trust Aug L Tr
In Thee, O Lord, Have I Put My Trust Gsc T Tr
In These Times Sem G Tc
In Thine Arm I Rest Me Gsc T Tr
In This Bread (We Share The Cross) Gia L Lo
In This Old Troubled World Zon G Tj
In This Quiet Hour Wrd L Tt
In This Season Of Lent. Vrn L Sl
In Times Like These Lor T Tx
In Times Like These Zon G Tc
In Venisti Enim Gratiam Gsc T Tm
In You Do I Find My Reward Wlp F Tr
In Your Great Mercy Fel L Tr
In Your Holy Place Acp F Tx
In Your Holy Place (4-Part Arr) Acp F La
In Your Kindness Save Me, Lord Fel L Sl
In Your Reach Sil G Tt
Incarnatio (Dum Medium Silentium) Oxf T Sc
Incline Thine Ear To Me (S/Solo) Gsc T Tr
Incline Your Ear Gsc T Tr
Increase Cob T Tx
Infant Christus W/Solo Aug L Sc
Infant Holy Gsc T Sc
Infant Jesus Abi L Sc
Infinito See L Tx
Ingrediente (Choral) Fel T Sl
Initiation Prayer Rpb L Tb
Innkeeper, The Sac L Sc
Innocentes Pro Christo Gsc T Sc
Inspiring Hymns Zon G Za
Instrument Of Thy Peace, An Sac L Tr
Insult Has Broken My Heart Fel L Sl
Intercession Prayer For Cath. Church Wlp L Lh
Interpreted By Love Bec T Tr
Into Our Hearts, O Spirit Come Wlp L Ss
Into The Woods My Master Went Lor T Tj
Into Your Hands Wlp L Sl
Into Your Hands Fel F Sl
Into Your Hands, O Lord Fel L Sl
Intrada In A Minor (Blessing) Gra L Tw
Introduction And Passacaglia Abi L Zb
Introduction To Canon Acclamation Rpb L Le
Introduction, Fugue And Variations Abi L Zb
Introductory Rite Nal L La
Introit For Easter Abi T Sr
Introit For The New Year (M) Oxf T La
Introits (For Various Seasons) Aug L Za
Introits And Graduals (Var Seasons) Aug L Za
Introits For Lent And Easter Abi L La
Inveni David(Lat) Cfp T Tx
Ira Stanphill Favorites No 1 (No 5495) Zon G Za
Ira Stanphill Favorites No 2 (No 5496) Zon G Za
Ira Stanphill Favorites No 3 (No 5497) Zon G Za
Irish Blessing Van F Tx
Is He Satisfied With Me Ham G Tc
Is It Nothing (O Vos Omnes) Gia T Sl
Is It Nothing All Of You Who Pass By Gsc T Sl
Is It Nothing To You Gsc T Sl
Is Not The Cup That We Bless Fel L Lo
Is There Any Peace Anywhere Man G Tr
Is There Any Word Fel F Tx
Is There Anybody Here? Lor T Tt
Is There Room In Your Heart? Gmc G Tr
Is There? Fcc F Tx
Is This America Oak G Tp
Isaiah 40:31 Mar L Tr
Isaiah 43 Wgm L Lp
Isn't The Love Of Jesus Something Zon G Tj
Israel In Egypt (Oratorio) Kal T Za
Israel, Rely On Yahweh Wgm L Ld
Ist Nicht Ephraim Mein Teurer Sohn? Oxf T Tr
It Came Upon The Midnight Clear Gsc T Sc
It Fell Upon A Winter's Day Pro T Sc
It Happened Gmc G Tb
It Is A Good Thing To Give Thanks Gsc L Tt
It Is A Good Thing To Give Thanks Ron T Tt
It Is A Great Day Of Joy Van F Sr
It Is A Thing Most Wonderful Sac L Tr
It Is Finished Gmc G Sl
It Is Glory Just To Walk With Him Zon G Tr
It Is Good To Give Thanks Aug L Tt
It Is Good To Give Thanks Gra L Tt
It Is Good To Give Thanks Fel L Tt
It Is Good To Give Thanks Lit L Tt
It Is Good To Give Thanks To You Gra L Ld
It Is Jesus Man G Tj
It Is My Faith Wlp F Tr
It Is Not Too Late Van F Sl
It Is The Joyful Eastertime Aug L Sr
It Is They Fcc C Tx
It Is Well With My Soul Zon G Tr
It Is Well With My Soul Lor T Tr
It Is You, O Lord Gia L Tc
It Matters To Him Man G Tr
It May Be Today Zon G Sa
It Must Be The Season Of The Lord Fel F Tx
It Only Takes A Hug Wlp F Tx
It Rained Man G Tx
It Was For You Sil T Sl
It Was Jesus Zon G Tj
It Was Me Prc L Tx
It Was So Quiet Abi L Tx
It Will Be Worth It All Gmc G Sr
It Won't Be Long(We'll Be Goin') Wrd G Sa
It Wouldn't Be Enough (Collection) Wrd F Za
It' Wedding Time No 1 (No 5493) Zon T Zb
It's A Brand New Day Ham G Tc
It's A Brand New Day Nal L Tk
It's A Brand New Day Van F Sr
It's A Brand-New World Fcc F Tk
It's A Gift To Be Simple Maf T Tr
It's A Glorious Alleluia! Lor L Sc
It's A Great Day Fel F Tt
It's A Long Road To Freedom Van L Tx
It's A Miracle Gmc G Tt
It's A Sign Of Love Fel F La
It's A Wonderful, Wonderful Life Zon G Tr
It's A Young World Zon F Tr
It's All About Love. Lor L Tx
It's All Right Nal L Tr
It's But A Road Yan F Tc
It's Christmas Csm G Sc
It's Cool In The Furnance(Musical) Wrd C Tx
It's Easy When You Rhyme With Dove Wlp C Tr
It's Gonna' Be A Morning To Remember Man G Sr
It's Gotta Happen Within Zon F Tb
It's Just Like Moses On The Mountain Gra G Sr
It's Just Like My Lord Gmc G Tj
It's Mine, It's Mine Wlp F Tx
It's No Secret Sem G Tt
It's No Wonder Gmc G Tj
It's Not An Easy Road Zon G Tc
It's So Nice To Have Jesus Wrd G Sa
It's The Lord's Thing. Lor F Sc
It's Tough To Be A Friend Of The Proph Nal L Tx
It's Up To Us Wlp C Tc
It's Wedding Time No 1 (No 5493) Zon T Za
It's Wedding Time No 2 (No 5494) Zon T Za
It's Wedding Time No 2 (No 5494) Zon T Zb
It's Yours For The Asking Zon F Ss
Iudica Me Deus (E & L) (Md) Gia T Tr
Ivory Palaces Lor T Sr
Ivory Places Lor T Sr
Jacob's Ladder Sac L Tx
Jacob's Ladder Fcc C Tx
Jacob's Ladder Lor L Tx
Jacob's Lament Fcc C Tx
Jacob's Song Wgm F Tt
Jacob's Vision Lor T Tx
Jello Man Van C Tx
Jeremiah Fis F Tx
Jeremiah Sings The Blues Fel L Sl
Jeremiah 31:12 Mar L Tr
Jerusalem Fel F Sl
Jerusalem Rpb L Sl
Jerusalem Lor T Sl
Jerusalem Gsc L Sl
Jerusalem Van F Sl
Jerusalem Morning Gsc T Tx
Jerusalem O Turn Thee To The Lord Gsc T Sl
Jerusalem The Golden Gsc T Sr
Jerusalem, Jerusalem (+Ps 130) Gia T Sl
Jerusalem, My Happy Home Acp F Tf
Jerusalem, My Happy Home Aug T Tk
Jerusalem, My Happy Home Sac L Sr
Jesse Tree Song Wlp C Sc
Jesu By Thee I Would Be Blessed Gsc T Tj
Jesu Dulcis Memoria Gsc T Tj
Jesu Dulcis Memoria Bbl T Tj
Jesu Dulcis Memoria (E & Lat) Oxf L Lo
Jesu Joy Of Man's Desiring Gsc T Tj
Jesu Priceless Treasure Gsc T Tj
Jesu Word Of God Incarnate(Ave Verum) Gsc T Tj
Jesu, Creator Of The World Gia L Tj
Jesu, Friend Of My Delight Sac L Tj
Jesu, Gentlest Saviour Gsc T Tj
Jesu, Grant Me This I Pray Oxf T Sl
Jesu, Grant Me This I Pray (Md) Oxf T Sl
Jesu, Jesu, Dulcissime Bbl T Tj
Jesu, Jesu, Why Did You Die? Gsc L Sr
Jesu, Joy And Treasure(Eng) Cfp T Tj
Jesu, Joy Of Man's Desiring Lor T Tj
Jesu, Joy Of Man's Desiring Gsc T Tj
Jesu, Joy Of Man's Desiring (E) Gia T Tj
Jesu, Joy Of Man's Desiring (E) Oxf T Tj
Jesu, Lover Of My Soul (E) Oxf T Tj
Jesu, My Heart's Treasure Kal T Tj
Jesu, My Little One(In 5 Carols) E Gia L Sc
Jesu, Our Blessed Hope Of Heaven Aug L Tj
Jesu, Priceless Treasure Aug T Tj
Jesu, Priceless Treasure (Motet 3) Kal T Tj
Jesu, The Very Thought Is Sweet Sac L Tj
Jesu, The Very Thought Of Thee (M) Oxf T Lo
Jesu, The Very Thought Of Thee (Me) Oxf T Ln
Jesu, The Very Thought Of Thee (Me) Oxf T Tj
Jesu, Thou My Heart's Delight Aug T Tj
Jesu, Word Of God Incarnate Gsc T Lo
Jesus Str L Lo
Jesus Gmc G Tj
Jesus Mar L Tj
Jesus Chd L Tj
Jesus And Me Zon G Tj
Jesus Calls Us Gsc T Tc
Jesus Calls Us Bbl T Tc
Jesus Calls Us Lor T Tc
Jesus Calls Us (W/Bass Solo) Gsc T Tc
Jesus Can Sil L Tj
Jesus Cares Zon G Tj
Jesus Christ Mar L Tj
Jesus Christ Is Born Gsc T Sc
Jesus Christ Is Lord Gia F Tk
Jesus Christ Is Risen Today (+ Tpts) Aug T Sr
Jesus Christ Is Risen Today (W/Inst) Abi T Sr
Jesus Christ Is The Same Today Sil F Tj
Jesus Christ Our Lord & God (Hymn) Jsp L Tj
Jesus Christ The Faithful Witness Wlp L Tj
Jesus Christ, King Of Kings Sha F Tk
Jesus Christ, Our King Gia F Tk
Jesus Descended From Majesty Glorious Mam G Tj
Jesus Died Sav G Sl
Jesus Died On Calvary's Mountain Lor T Sl
Jesus Gave His Life Away Fel L Sl
Jesus Gives Me A Song Zon G Tt
Jesus Has Come Fel F Sr
Jesus Has Something For You Yan F Tj
Jesus Heal Us Rav L Tr
Jesus I Am Yours Chh F Tc
Jesus In Me Fel F Tr
Jesus In The Mornin' Ahc L Tj
Jesus Is A Friend Of Mine Cpc G Tj
Jesus Is A Loving Lord Wgm F Tj
Jesus Is A Precious Name Zon G Tj
Jesus Is A Wonderful Landlord Pdm G Tj
Jesus Is A-Drivin' Out Satan Fis F Tk
Jesus Is All That We Need Mar L Tj
Jesus Is All The World To Me Lor L Tj
Jesus Is Born Man C Sc
Jesus Is Born Gsc T Sc
Jesus Is Born The King! Lor L Sc
Jesus Is Born Today Man G Sc
Jesus Is Coming (Musical) Zon G Sa
Jesus Is Coming (Theme Ii) Zon G Sa
Jesus Is Coming Again Zon G Sa
Jesus Is Coming Again Zon G Sa
Jesus Is Everything Sem G Tj
Jesus Is Knocking Jhm G Tj
Jesus Is Lord Sha F Tk
Jesus Is Lord Of All Gmc G Tk
Jesus Is Lord Of All Lor G Tk
Jesus Is Mine Nal L Tj
Jesus Is My Song Fel F Tj
Jesus Is Our Prayer Rav L Tj
Jesus Is Soon Coming Fis F Tk
Jesus Is Standing Here Mar L Tj
Jesus Is The Answer Wrd G Tj
Jesus Is The Friend Of Sinners Zon G Tj
Jesus Is The Morning Mar L Tj
Jesus Is The Name Man G Tj
Jesus Is The One Mar L Tj
Jesus Is The One Who Saves Wgm F Tj
Jesus Is Waiting Zon G Tj
Jesus Joy Mar L Tj
Jesus Joy Of Loving Hearts Gsc T Tj
Jesus Knows Zon G Tj

ALPHABETICAL INDEX OF TITLES

Title	Code
Jesus Led Me All The Way	Zon G Tc
Jesus Loves Me	Zon G Tr
Jesus Loves Me (Arrangement)	Sil L Tj
Jesus Loves Me As I Am	Rpb C Tj
Jesus My Lord	Fel F Sr
Jesus My Lord	Mam G Tj
Jesus Our Strength, Our Hope	Gsc T Tr
Jesus Paid It All	Zon L Sl
Jesus Paid It All	Sil G Tj
Jesus Pleases	Csm G Tj
Jesus Prayed	Pmp G Tj
Jesus Prayed As They Slept	Gmp G Sl
Jesus Precious Savior	Wrd G Tj
Jesus Remember Me	Rav L Sl
Jesus Said To His Mother	Fel L Sl
Jesus Said Unto The People	Gsc T Tj
Jesus Saves	Lor T Tj
Jesus Saves	Lor G Tj
Jesus Sends His Sunlight	Jhm G Tj
Jesus Shall Reign	Zon T Tk
Jesus Shall Reign	Lor T Tk
Jesus Shall Reign	Sac T Tk
Jesus Song	Fel F Le
Jesus Speaks From The Cross	Lor T Sl
Jesus Style Songs, Vol. 1	Aug G Za
Jesus Style Songs, Vol. 1	Aug T Za
Jesus Style Songs, Vol. 2	Aug G Za
Jesus The Christ Is Born	Gsc F Sc
Jesus The Christ Is Born	Gsc T Sc
Jesus The King Passes By	Zon L Tk
Jesus The Very Thought Of Thee	Wrd G Tj
Jesus Told Me So	Zon G Tj
Jesus Took My Sins Away	Zon F Sl
Jesus Walked	Lor T Tj
Jesus Walked This Lonesome Valley	Wbp T Tx
Jesus We're Waiting For You	Gia F Sa
Jesus Went With Them	Fel L Lp
Jesus Wher'e'er Thy People Meet	Gsc L La
Jesus Will Come	Zon G Tj
Jesus Will Come Thru	Fel F Tj
Jesus Will Fix It After Awhile	Sto G Tj
Jesus Will Move Every	Sav G Ss
Jesus You Are Here	Wlp F Tj
Jesus! Name Of Wondrous Love	Abi L Tj
Jesus—My Joy	Zon T Tj
Jesus, Admired And Noble King	Gia T Tk
Jesus, Be My Friend	Urs L Tj
Jesus, Bright And Morning Star	Sac T Sc
Jesus, By Thy Cross (Cantata)	Lps T Sl
Jesus, Come Abide With Me	Lor T Sr
Jesus, Come Our Way	Fcc L Tj
Jesus, Come To Us.	Vrn L Lo
Jesus, How Dear You Are	Zon G Tj
Jesus, I Believe What You Said	Gmc G Tj
Jesus, I Come	Lor T Tc
Jesus, I Heard You Had A Big House	Gmc G Sr
Jesus, I Love Thee	Zon T Tj
Jesus, I Love You	Fis F Tj
Jesus, I Need You	Nal L Tj
Jesus, In Our Hands	Nal L Tj
Jesus, In Thy Dwelling Place Above	Sms T Tt
Jesus, In Thy Dying Woes	Aug T Sl
Jesus, Jesus	Nal C Tj
Jesus, Jesus	Man G Tj
Jesus, Jesus My Lord	Krg T Tj
Jesus, Jesus Rest Your Head	Gsc F Sc
Jesus, Jesus, Rest Your Head	Lor T Sc
Jesus, Jesus, Rock Of Ages	Man L Tj
Jesus, Lead The Way	Gia L Tj
Jesus, Lead Us	Sac T Tc
Jesus, Let Our Souls Be Fed	Aug T Lo
Jesus, Let Your Light Shine	Sil G Tj
Jesus, Lover Of My Soul	Lor T Tj
Jesus, Lover Of My Soul	Lor T Tj
Jesus, My Comforter	Man G Tr
Jesus, My Lord, My God, My All	Sac T Tj
Jesus, My Saviour, Look On Me	Gsc T Tj
Jesus, My Wonderful Lord	Man G Tk
Jesus, Name All Names Above	Aug T Tj
Jesus, Name Of Wondrous Love	Sac T Tj
Jesus, O Precious Name (New Year)	Smc T Tj
Jesus, Of A Maid Thou Wouldst Be Born	Abi L Sc
Jesus, Our Lord, Is Risen Today!	Sac L Sr
Jesus, Our Lord, We Adore Thee	Gsc T Sc
Jesus, Our Savior	Cfp T Sl
Jesus, Priceless Treasure	Gia T Tj
Jesus, Priceless Treasure	Fel T Tj
Jesus, Refuge Of The Weary	Aug T Tj
Jesus, Son Of God	Lor T Tj
Jesus, Stand Beside Them	Abi L Tw
Jesus, Still Lead On	Zon T Tc
Jesus, The Very Thought Of Thee	Zon T Tj
Jesus, Thou Blessed Name Of Mercy	Sac L Tj
Jesus, Thou Joy Of Loving Hearts	Zon T Tj
Jesus, Thou Joy Of Loving Hearts	Lor T Tj
Jesus, Thou Joy Of Loving Hearts	Aug T Tj
Jesus, Thy Blood And Righteousness	Zon T Sl
Jesus, Thy Boundless Love To Me	Sac T Tj
Jesus, We Just Want To Thank You	Gmc G Tt
Jesus, We Look To Thee	Lor T Tj
Jesus, White Boy	Prc L Tx
Jesus, Wonderful Lord	Zon G Tj
Jesus, You Have The Power To Heal	Nal C Tj
Jimmy	Mar L Tx
Joanie's Song	Mar L Tx
Job Was A True And Honest Man	Fel L Tx
Job's Story	Bfi F Sl
John	Van F Sa
John Is My Name	Wlp F Tx
John Mckay Choir Book (No 5034)	Zon G Za
John Mckay Sings Al Wilson (No 5016)	Zon G Za
John Mckay Sings Dorothy Harrison	Zon G Za
John Mckay Sings Joyce Mott (No 5018)	Zon G Za
John Mckay Solos (No 5020)	Zon G Za
John Peterson's Folio Of Favorites	Zon G Za
John Rasley Presents A Choral Sampler	Zon T Za
John The Baptist	Rpb L Sa
John The Baptist	Fel F Sa
John The Baptizer	Van F Sa
John W Peterson's Song Favorites(5866)	Zon G Za
John Wesley Covenant Service, The	Abi T Tc
John's Words Of Praise	Prc L Tx
Join All The Glorious Names	Zon T Tt
Join Hands	Prc L Tx
Join The Revolution	Prc L Tx
Jonah	Pic L Tx
Jonah	Fel F Tx
Jonah (Oratorio)	Oxf T Tx
Joseph Dearest, Joseph Mine	Abi L Sc
Joseph Dearest, Joseph Mine	Lor T Tx
Joseph Dearest, Joseph Mine	Sac L Tx
Joseph Est Bien Marie	Gsc T Sc
Joseph, Joseph, Dearest One	Bbl T Tx
Joseph, Lieber Joseph Mein	Bbl T Tx
Joseph, Patron Saint Of Workers	Wlp T Tx
Joseph, Take Mary As Your Wife	Fel L Sa
Joshua Fit De Battle Of Jericho	Gia G Tx
Joshua Fit The Battle Of Jericho	Her G Tx
Joshua Fit The Battle Of Jericho	Zon G Tx
Joy	Aug T Tr
Joy	Man G Tt
Joy (Love Is All Around)	Gia F To
Joy Comes In The Morning	Gmc G Tx
Joy Dawned Again On Easter Day	Sac L Sr
Joy Giving Light	Wlp L Tj
Joy In Christ, Alleluia	Yan F Tt
Joy In The Camp	Gmc G Tr
Joy In The Morning	Msm F Tr
Joy Is Like The Rain	Van F Sa
Joy Is The Spirit Of Love	Lor L Tr
Joy Joy Joy	Mar F Tr
Joy Of A Sinner Set Free, The	Zon G Sl
Joy Of Heaven, The	Zon F Tx
Joy Of The Lord, The	Nal C Tr
Joy To All People!	Lor L Sc
Joy To Heaven	Wlp L Tt
Joy To The World	Lor T Sc
Joy To The World	Her T Sc
Joy To The World	Lor T Sc
Joy To The World	Zon T Sc
Joy To The World	Acp F Sc
Joy To The World	Acp F Sc
Joy To The World (No 5944)	Zon L Sc
Joy To The World (No 5945)	Zon L Sc
Joy To The World (No 6012)	Zon L Sc
Joy To You O Virgin Mary	Wlp L Tm
Joy, Joy, Joy	Nal L Tr
Joy, Joy, Joy	Lor T Tt
Joy, Joy, Joy	Rpb L Tt
Joy, Real Joy	Gmc G Tr
Joyful Dawning	Rpb L Tx
Joyful Melody, A	Lor L Tt
Joyful Mysteries	Wlp T Tm
Joyful Psalmody	Sac L Tt
Joyful! Joyful!	Maf T Tt
Joyful, Joyful, We Adore Thee	Zon T Tt
Joyfully Sing We His Praise!	Pro T Tt
Joyous Alleluia	Wbp T Tt
Joyous Carol (Divided Parts)	Cfs T Sc
Joyous Celebration	Mem L Tr
Joyous Christmas Carol	Pro L Sc
Joyous Christmas Song	Aug L Sc
Joyous Coming Of Our Lord	Wlp F Sa
Jubilate	Aug L Tt
Jubilate	Gsc T Tt
Jubilate	Gsc T Tt
Jubilate (Russian)	Lor T Tt
Jubilate Deo	Smc T Tt
Jubilate Deo	Gia T Tt
Jubilate Deo	Abi L Tt
Jubilate Deo (A Cap)	Gsc T Tt
Jubilate Deo (D)	Oxf T Tt
Jubilate Deo (D)	Oxf T Tt
Jubilate Deo (Gregorian Rep)	Gia T Za
Jubilate Deo (Lat-Ger)	Cfp T Tt
Jubilate Deo (M)	Oxf T Tt
Jubilate Deo (Md)	Oxf T Tt
Jubilate Deo (Md)	Oxf T Tt
Jubilate Deo (Md)	Oxf T Tt
Jubilate Deo (Ps 100 W/Instruments)	Aug L Tt
Jubilate Deo (W/Brass)	Aug T Tt
Jubilate Deo (W/Brs)	Abi L Sr
Jubilate Deo In C (M)	Oxf T Tt
Jubilate Deo, Omnis Terra	Gsc T Tt
Jubilation!	Lor F Sr
Jubilee	Fel F Tt
Jubilee Mass	Gia L Za
Jubilemus Singuli	Gsc T Tt
Judah's Land	Aug L Tx
Judas Iscariot	Van F Sl
Judas Maccabaeus (Oratorio,Eng)	Kal T Za
Judas, Mercator Pessimus	Gsc T Sl
Judas, Why?	Van F Sl
Judge Eternal, Throned	Jsp L Tr
Judge Me O God	Gsc T Sl
Judge Me, O God	Gsc T Tr
Judge Me, O God (W/Sop Solo)	Gsc T Sl
Judge Us With Mercy, Lord	Fel L Sl
Judgment Anthem	Bbl T Tk
Judith	Fel F Tx
Junior Choir No 1 (No 5445)	Zon C Za
Junior Choir No 2 (No 5446)	Zon C Za
Junior Choir No 3 (No 5447)	Zon C Za
Junior Choir No 4 (No 5448)	Zon C Za
Junior Choir No 5 (No 5444)	Zon C Za
Junior Choir No 6 (No 5451)	Zon C Za
Junior Choir No 7 (No 5502)	Zon C Za
Just A Closer Walk	Man G Tr
Just A Closer Walk With Thee	Hal G Tc
Just A Closer Walk With Thee	Lor F Tj
Just A Closer Walk With Thee	Zon G Tj
Just A Dreamer	Man G Tx
Just A Wayward Lamb	Zon G Sl
Just As A Heart	Bbl T Lo
Just As I Am	Lor T Tr
Just As I Am	Lor T Tr
Just As I Am (Woodworth) (Easy)	Abi L Zb
Just For You	Lor T Tc
Just One Day At A Time	Gsc T Tc
Just One Look	Man G Tx
Just Pretending	Chd F Tt
Just Take His Hand Again	Man G Tr
Just Trust And Obey	Man G Tr
Justum Deduxit Dominus	Gsc T Tc
Kedron	Gsc T Sc
Keep Alive (Psalm 128)	Ahc L Tr
Keep Christ In Christmas	Lor L Sa
Keep Christ In Christmas	Zon L Sc
Keep His Commandments	Gsc T Tx
Keep In Mind	Wlp L Sr
Keep In Mind	Ccc L Lj
Keep In The Middle Of The Road	Gsc G Tx
Keep Me At The Foot Of The Cross	Man G Sl
Keep Me Safe (Psalm 16)	Rpb L Ld
Keep Me Safe O God (Ps 16)	Gra L Ld
Keep Not Thy Silence	Sac L Tt
Keep On Holding On	Man G Tc
Keep On Holding On	Sil G Tc
Keep The Faith On Movin'	Nal L Tc
Keep The Rumor Going (God Is Alive)	Van F Tx
Keep This In Mind	Ham G Sr
Keep Us Joyful	Fcc L Tx
Keyboard Rhapsodies (No 4701)	Zon G Zb
Keyboard Stylings For The Piano	Zon G Zb
Killingly	Bbl T Tt
King All Glorious	Gsc T Tk
King All-Glorious	Lor L Sc
King All-Glorious	Lor T Sr
King Forever	Lor L Sc
King In The Stable, The	Lor L Sc
King Indeed, A (Easy)	Zon L Sc
King Is Riding By, The	Lor T Sr
King Of All Kings	Ham G Tk
King Of Creation	Wgm F Tk
King Of Glory Cantata (No 5990)	Zon L Sr
King Of Glory, King Of Peace (Me)	Oxf T Tk
King Of Glory, The	Lor T Tk
King Of Glory, The	Abi L Sc
King Of Glory, The	Acf F Tk
King Of Kings	Wgm F Tk
King Of Kings	Lor T Tk
King Of Kings	Gsc T Tk
King Of Kings (Glory Glory)	Jsp F Tt
King Of Kings (No 4294)	Zon L Sc
King Of Kings, Lord Of Lords	Str L Tk
King Of Love My Shepherd Is, The	Pro T Tr
King Of Love My Shepherd Is, The	Lor T Tr
King Of Love My Shepherd, The	Lor T Tr
King Of Love, The	Lor T Tk
King Shall Come When Morning Dawns,The	Sac L Tk
King, All Glorious (W/Solos)	Gsc T Tk
King's Highway	Wgm F Tk
Kingdom Of Children	Mar L Tk
Kingdom Song	Fel F Sr
Kings Of The Earth And All People	Gsc T Tt
Kings Of The Orient Three	Gsc T Sc
Kingsfold I Feel The Winds Of God	Bec T Tx
Kittery (Lowens)	Gsc T Tt
Kneel At The Manger	Lor T Sc
Knight Of Bethlehem, The	Maf L Sc

Title	Code
Knight Without A Sword	Abi L Tc
Knock, Knock	Fis F Tr
Knock, Knock	Van F Ss
Know That I Am God	Fel L Tr
Known Only To Him	Ham G Sl
Komm Susser Tod!	Aug T Tf
Komm, Heiliger Geist, Herre Gott	Gsc T Ss
Kum Ba Ya	Hal F Tx
Kum Ba Yah	Zon F Lo
Kum—Bah—Yah	Lor F Tr
Kyrie	Gsc T Lb
Kyrie	Gsc T Lb
Kyrie	Oxf T Lb
Kyrie	Her T Lb
Kyrie	Gsc T Lb
Kyrie	Gsc T Lb
Kyrie	Nal L Lb
Kyrie (Eng Mass)	Gia L Lb
Kyrie (Eng, Icet Pen Rite C)	Gra L Lb
Kyrie (Lord, Have Mercy)	Nal L Lb
Kyrie (Mariachi Mass)	Fel F Lb
Kyrie (Mass For New Rite)	Gia L Lb
Kyrie (Mass For Schools)	Fel C Lb
Kyrie (Mass Of The Western Tribes)	Fel F Lb
Kyrie (Missa Brevis)	Fel L Lb
Kyrie (Sung Mass No.2)	Fel L Lb
Kyrie (Thomas More Mass)	Fel L Lb
Kyrie (With Narrator)	Aug L Lb
Kyrie (3fold) Mass For King	Gia L Lb
Kyrie (6fold) Mass For King	Gia L Lb
Kyrie (9fold) Mass For King	Gia L Lb
Kyrie Eleison	Her T Lb
Kyrie Eleison	Sac T Lb
Kyrie Eleison	Wlp L Lb
Kyrie Eleison	Wbp T Lb
Kyrie Eleison	Her L Lb
Kyrie From "Missa Secunda"	Her T Lb
Kyrie From Missa Super L'homme Arme	Bbl T Lb
Kyrie I (Notre Dame Mass)	Gia L Lb
Kyrie I (Rite A)	Gia L Lb
Kyrie Ii (Notre Dame Mass)	Gia L Lb
Kyrie Ii (Rite C)	Gia L Lb
Kyrie In D Minor	Gsc T Lb
La La Life	Wlp C Tx
La Messe De Nostre Dame	Oxf T Za
La Nana	Gsc T Sc
La Virgin Lava Panales	Gsc T Sc
Laban's Lament	Fel F Tx
Laborers Of Love	Sil L Tx
Lacrymosa	Gsc T Sl
Lamb Of Calvary	Sac T Lm
Lamb Of God	Gsc T Lm
Lamb Of God	Aug L Lm
Lamb Of God	Nal L Lm
Lamb Of God	Fcc F Lm
Lamb Of God	Rpb L Lm
Lamb Of God	Aug L Lm
Lamb Of God	Nal L Lm
Lamb Of God	Gia L Lm
Lamb Of God	Gia L Lm
Lamb Of God	Rpb L Lm
Lamb Of God	Fel F Lm
Lamb Of God	Som T Lm
Lamb Of God	Gsc T Lm
Lamb Of God	Nal L Lm
Lamb Of God	Rpb L Lm
Lamb Of God	Rpb L Lm
Lamb Of God	Gia L Lm
Lamb Of God	Ccc L Lm
Lamb Of God	Sbf L Lm
Lamb Of God	Nal L Lm
Lamb Of God	Wlp F Lm
Lamb Of God	Rpb L Lm
Lamb Of God	Nal L Lm
Lamb Of God	Nal L Lm
Lamb Of God (Agnus Dei) (Sung Mass No1	Fel L Lm
Lamb Of God (Cel Of Unity)	Gia L Lm
Lamb Of God (Chardin Mass)	Fel L Lm
Lamb Of God (Child Mass)	Gia L Lm
Lamb Of God (Community Mass)	Gia L Lm
Lamb Of God (Folk Mass No.4)	Fel F Lm
Lamb Of God (Icet)	Wlp L Lm
Lamb Of God (Icet)	Jsp L Lm
Lamb Of God (Icet)	Wlp L Lm
Lamb Of God (Icet)	Wlp F Lm
Lamb Of God (Icet)	Wlp L Lm
Lamb Of God (Icet) (Me)	Wlp L Lm
Lamb Of God (Liturgy Of Joy)	Fel L Lm
Lamb Of God (Lyric Mass)	Gia L Lm
Lamb Of God (Mass For All Seasons)	Gia L Lm
Lamb Of God (Missa Bossa Nova)	Fel F Lm
Lamb Of God (New Mass)	Gia L Lm
Lamb Of God (Notre Dame Mass)	Gia L Lm
Lamb Of God (Opt Brs/Timp)	Gia L Lm
Lamb Of God (Short Mass)	Gia L Lm
Lamb Of God (Vianney Mass)	Gia L Lm
Lamb Of God (W/Cantor)Dominic Mass	Gia L Lm
Lamb Of God (With Rhythm Inst)	Aug L Lm
Lamb Of God (1964 Text)	Van F Lm
Lamb Of God (64 Text)	Van F Lm
Lamb Of God (67th Street Mass)	Fel F Lm
Lamb Of God! Thou Shalt Remain Forever	Abi L Tj
Lamb Of God, For Sinners Slain	Gia T Sl
Lamb Of God, I Took To Thee	Gsc L Tj
Lamb, The	Abi L Sl
Lambs Also Love Thee, The	Her T Sc
Lament	Wlp T Sl
Lamentation	Bbl T Sl
Lamentation	Bbl T Sl
Lamentation Over Boston	Cfp T Sl
Lamentations	Fel F Sl
Lamentations	See L Sl
Lamentations	Nal L Sl
Lamentations	Fel T Sl
Lamentations For 5 & 6 Voices	Kal T Sl
Lamp Unto My Feet (W/Guitar)	Gia L Tx
Lamparita Votiva (Lamp Of Prayer)	Pic L Tx
Land Of Our Loyalty	Lor T Tp
Land Without Water (Psalm 63)	Ahc L Sl
Largo From "Xerxes"	Smc T Zb
Lass Dich Nur Nichts Nicht Dauren	Gsc T Tr
Last Supper	Bec T Lo
Last Trip To Jerusalem	Aug L Sl
Last Words Of Christ	Kal T Sl
Late Winter, Early Spring	Clm F Tt
Lauda Anima (Praise, My Soul)	Gsc T Tt
Lauda Anima Mea Dominum	Gsc T Tt
Lauda Sion	Kal T Tt
Lauda Sion (Cantata)	Kal T Tt
Lauda, Sion, Salvatorem	Fel T Lo
Laudamus	Gsc T Tt
Laudamus Te	Gsc T Tt
Laudate Alla Virgine (Female)	Kal T Tt
Laudate Dominum	Kal T Tt
Laudate Dominum (M)	Oxf T Tt
Laudate Dominum (Ps 150)	Oxf T Tt
Laudate Dominum (Ps 150) A Cap	Pro T Tt
Laudate Pueri, Laudate Nomen Domini	Gsc T Tt
Laus Creatorum (Md)	Oxf T Tt
Lay Down Your Staffs, O Shepherds	Gsc T Sc
Lay Your Burden Down	Wrd G Sl
Le Message Des Anges	Gsc T Sc
Lead By The Master's Hand	Jhm G Tr
Lead Me To Calvary	Lor T Sl
Lead Me, Lord	Gsc T Tc
Lead Me, O Lead Me	Zon G Tc
Lead Me, Savior	Lor T Tj
Lead On, Lord Jesus	Man G Tc
Lead On, O King Eternal	Lor T Tc
Lead On, O King Eternal	Aug L Tk
Lead On, O King Eternal	Lor T Tc
Lead On, O King Eternal	Zon T Tk
Lead On, O King Eternal	Gsc T Tk
Lead On, O King Eternal	Lor T Tc
Lead The Way (W/Piano)	Wrd G Tc
Lead Us On, O Lord	Nal L Tc
Leaning On The Everlasting Arm	Hof T Tr
Leaning On The Everlasting Arms	Zon G Tr
Leaning On The Everlasting Arms	Zon F Tr
Leave It In The Hands Of The Lord	Fcc F Tr
Leave, Then, Thy Foolish Ranges	Gsc T Sl
Leaves A-Fallin' (Good Friday)	Gia F Sl
Legendary Christmas Carols	Lor T Za
Legende	Hof T Za
Lengthen The Cords And Strengthen The	Zon G Tc
Lent (From Holiday Motets)	Ron T Sl
Lenten Holy	Nal L Sl
Lenten Invocation	Rav L Sl
Lenten Invocation	Rav L Sl
Lenten Invocation	Rav L Sl
Leoni	Gia T Sr
Let All Men Rejoice	Wbp T Tt
Let All Men Sing God's Praises	Gsc T Sc
Let All Mortal Flesh Keep Silence	Sac T Lo
Let All Mortal Flesh Keep Silence	Aug L Lo
Let All Mortal Flesh Keep Silence	Lor T Lo
Let All Mortal Flesh Keep Silence	Gsc T Lo
Let All Mortal Flesh Keep Silence	Acp L Lo
Let All Mortal Flesh Keep Silence	Gia L Ln
Let All Mortal Flesh Keep Silence	Acp L Lo
Let All Mortal Flesh Keep Silence	Gia L Lo
Let All Mortal Flesh Keep Silence	Zon T Sc
Let All On Earth	Gia L Sc
Let All On Earth Their Voices Raise	Gsc L Tt
Let All On Earth Their Voices Raise	Fel L Tt
Let All On Earth Their Voices Raise	Gsc T Tt
Let All That Is Within Me	Ahc L Tt
Let All The Earth	Fel F Tt
Let All The Earth	Wlp T Tt
Let All The Earth Rejoice (A Cap)	Pro L Tt
Let All The Earth Rejoice & Sing	Wlp L Sr
Let All The Earth Sing His Praise	Wlp F Tt
Let All The Little Children Praise	Gmc G Tt
Let All The World In Every Corner Sing	Oxf T Tt
Let All The World In Every Corner Sing	Gsc L Tt
Let All The World In Every Corner Sing	Gsc T Tt
Let All The World In Every Corner Sing	Abi T Tt
Let All Together Praise Our God	Lor T Sc
Let All Who Fear The Lord	Nal L Tt
Let All With Sweet Accord	Aug L Tt
Let Christians All With Joyful Mirth	Bec T Tt
Let Earth Receive Her King	Lor T Sc
Let Earth Rejoice	Gsc L Tt
Let Earth Rejoice	Gia L Tt
Let Every Heart Rejoice	Zon L Tt
Let Everyone Praise (Ps 150)	Jsp F Tt
Let Everything Within Me Cry Holy	Gph G Tt
Let Go	Mar L Tc
Let God Arise	Tcp L Tt
Let God Arise	Gsc T Tr
Let God Take Over	Gmp G Tc
Let God Tune Your Heartstrings	Zon G Tr
Let Heaven Rejoice	Nal L Tt
Let Him Who Would Come After Me	Fel L Tc
Let Hymns Of Joy	Fel T Sr
Let Hymns Of Joy Of Grief Succeed	Gia T Sr
Let It Be	Nor F Tt
Let It Shine	Bch L Tx
Let Man Exult With Heart And Voice	Her T Tt
Let Me Bathe In The Water	Bri G Tb
Let Me Do It With Love	Nal L Tr
Let Me Introduce You	Zon F Tr
Let Me Lord	Rpb L Tr
Let Me See	Mar L Tx
Let Me Sing Of Your Law, O My God	Wlp L Tt
Let Me Sow Love	Yan F Tr
Let Me Tell Y'all	Nal L Tx
Let Me Walk	Mar L Tc
Let Mount Zion Rejoice	Lor T Sa
Let My Complaint Come Before Thee	Oxf T Sl
Let My Cry Come Before Thee	Gsc T Sl
Let My Heart Be Broken	Man G Sl
Let My Prayer Come Before You	Fel L Sl
Let My Prayer Come Like Incense	Wlp L Tr
Let My Tongue Be Silenced (Ps137)	Gra L Ld
Let My Tongue Be Silenced(Ps 137)	Rav L Ld
Let Not Your Heart Be Troubled	Gsc T Tr
Let Nothing Disturb Thee	Sac L Tr
Let Nothing Disturb Thee	Smc T Tr
Let Nothing Ever Grieve Thee	Cfp T Tr
Let Our Gladness Know No End	Aug T Sc
Let Saints On Earth	Abi L Tx
Let The Bright Seraphim	Her T Tt
Let The Children Sing	Abi C Tt
Let The Earth Hear His Voice Cantata	Zon L Tc
Let The Earth Resound	Gia T Sc
Let The Heavens Be Glad	Gia L Sc
Let The Heavens Be Glad (Ccd)	Wlp F Ld
Let The Heavens Be Glad & Earth...	Wlp F Tt
Let The Hills Now Sing For Joy	Bfi F Tt
Let The Light Of Thy Countenance	Gia L Tr
Let The Little Children Come	Gra F Tb
Let The Old Man Die	Mar L Sl
Let The Peace Of God	Wlp L Tr
Let The People Praise	Wrd G Tt
Let The People Praise Thee	Sac L Tt
Let The People Praise Thee	Aug T Tt
Let The People Praise Thee	Gam L Tt
Let The Savior In (Old Dutch Melody)	Lor T Tj
Let The Thought Of My Heart	Fel L To
Let The Whole Creation Cry	Aug L Tt
Let The Whole Creation Cry	Aug T Tt
Let The Whole Creation Cry Glory (Md)	Wlp L Tt
Let The Whole World Know	Zon G Tx
Let The Word Of Christ	Gsc T Tr
Let The Words Of My Mouth	Bfi F Tx
Let Them Ever Sing For Joy	Gsc T Tt
Let There Be Light	Fel L Tx
Let There Be Light	Pic L Tx
Let There Be Peace	Van F Tr
Let There Be Peace On Earth	Hal T Tr
Let There Be Peace On Earth	Jan F Tr
Let This Mind Be In You (Me)	Oxf L Tr
Let Thy Hand Be Strengthened	Gsc T Tr
Let Thy Love Flow Down	Sac L Tr
Let Thy Merciful Ears (Me)	Oxf T Tt
Let Thy Merciful Ears, O Lord, Be Open	Abi L Tr
Let Thy Mercy, O Lord, Be Upon Us	Gia T Sl
Let Trumpets Sound	Van F Sr
Let Us Acclaim The Rock	Fel L Tt
Let Us All Be One	Gia L Tu
Let Us All Rejoice	Rpb L Tt
Let Us All With Gladsome Voice	Gia T Tt
Let Us Be Happy (Opttri)Org	Aug L Tr
Let Us Bless The Lord	Wlp L Tt
Let Us Break Bread	Ccc L Lo
Let Us Break Bread Together	Gia F Lo
Let Us Break Bread Together	Fel C Lo
Let Us Break Bread Together	Gia L Lo
Let Us Break Bread Together	Hal T Lo
Let Us Break Bread Together	Van F Lo
Let Us Break Bread Together	Fel F Lo
Let Us Break Bread Together	Abi L Lo
Let Us Break Bread Together	Gsc G Lo
Let Us Break Bread Together	Lor G Lo
Let Us Break Bread Together	Maf L Ln
Let Us Break Bread Together	Aug T Ln
Let Us Break Bread Together	Acp F Lo

Title	Code
Let Us Break Bread Together (Arr)	Gia F Lo
Let Us Celebrate God's Name	Aug T Tt
Let Us Enter The House Of The Lord	Gia L La
Let Us Exalt Him (W/Opt Tpt,Perc)	Wlp L Tt
Let Us Give Thanks	Fis F Tt
Let Us Go Rejoicing (Icet)	Wlp L Ld
Let Us Keep Silence	Sac L Tr
Let Us Look Up And Live (Opt Tpts)	Aug L Tr
Let Us Make Music For God	Sms F La
Let Us Now Our Voices Raise	Pro T Tt
Let Us Now Praise Famous Men	Gam L Tf
Let Us Now Praise Famous Men (A Cap)	Abi T Tp
Let Us Only Glory	Fel L Sl
Let Us Praise Our Noble God	Wlp T Tt
Let Us Pray	Zon F Tr
Let Us Pray For The Usa	Pmp G Tp
Let Us Serve The Lord	Fel L Tc
Let Us Sing A New Song Unto The Lord	Hal L Tt
Let Us Sing The New Song	Pro T Tt
Let Us Sing To The Lord	Lor L Tt
Let Us Stand In Prayer	Gia L La
Let Us With A Gladsome Mind	Abi L Tt
Let Us With Joy Our Voices Raise	Fel L Tt
Let Your Eye Be To The Lord	Aug L Sl
Let Your Faithful Ones Bless You	Fel L Th
Let Your Father And Mother	Fel L Tx
Let Your Song Ring Out	Fel F Sc
Let's Celebrate Easter	Zon T Sr
Let's Get Together	Irv F Tr
Let's Go To Church On Sunday	Pmp G Tx
Let's Go!	Prc L Tx
Let's Join In Songs Of Love	Gmp G Lp
Let's Just Praise The Lord	Gmc G Tr
Let's Keep Growing	Man L Tc
Let's Make Peace	Fcc F Tr
Let's Sing Duets No 1 (No 5080)	Zon G Za
Let's Sing Duets No 2 (No 5081)	Zon G Za
Let's Sing Duets No 3 (No 5082)	Zon G Za
Let's Sing Duets No 4 (No 5083)	Zon G Za
Let's Sing Duets No 5 (No 5084)	Zon G Za
Letter To Mother (Mother's Day)	Smc T Tx
Levavi Oculos Meos	Gsc T Tr
Leviathan (From Three Motets)	Ron T Tx
Libera Me (Choral)	Fel T Sl
Libera Me (Unison)	Fel T Sl
Life	Fcc F Tx
Life Can Be Fun	Sil F Tx
Life Eternal	Man G Sr
Life In Jesus	Mar L Tj
Life Is A Circle	Ccc L Tf
Life Is A Makin' Do	Fcc F Tx
Life Is A Symphony And Other Songs	Zon G Za
Life Is You	Rav L Tw
Life Without You	Fcc L Sl
Lift The Cherubic Host	Gsc T Tt
Lift Thine Eyes	Gsc T Tr
Lift Thine Eyes (A Cap)	Hof T Tr
Lift Thine Eyes (Me)	Oxf T Tr
Lift Up Jesus	Gmc G Sl
Lift Up Your Eyes	Smc T Tk
Lift Up Your Hands, O Ye Gates	Gsc T La
Lift Up Your Heads	Aug T Tr
Lift Up Your Heads	Lor T Sa
Lift Up Your Heads	Lor T Sa
Lift Up Your Heads	Gsc T Sa
Lift Up Your Heads (Ps 24)	Oxf T Sr
Lift Up Your Heads (Ps 24) (Md)	Oxf L Tr
Lift Up Your Heads, O Ye Gates	Gsc T La
Lift Up Your Heads, O Ye Gates	Zon L La
Lift Up Your Heads, O Ye Gates	Cfp T Sl
Lift Up Your Heads, O Ye Gates	Zon L La
Lift Up Your Heads, Ye Gates Of Brass	Aug L La
Lift Up Your Hearts	Van F Tr
Lift Up Your Hearts, Ye People	Som L Tt
Lift Up Your Songs Of Praise	Lor T Tt
Lift Up Your Voice (32 Songs)	Cob T Za
Lift Up, O Gates	Fel L La
Lift Your Glad Voices In Triumph	Aug T Tt
Lift Your Voice	Wlp F Tt
Lift Your Voices (Men) (No 5470)	Zon G Za
Light	Fel F Sc
Light	Gsc L Tr
Light Divine	Gsc T Tr
Light Has Come	Rav L Lp
Light Of Christ	Fel L La
Light Of The World	Val F Tc
Light Of The World (Musical)	Zon F Za
Light Of The World (No 4292)	Zon F Tc
Lighten Mine Eyes	Abi L Tf
Lighter Side Of Darkness	Mar L Sl
Lights Of Hanukkah	Mem L Tx
Lights Of The City, The	Nal L Tx
Lightshine (Musical)	Wrd G Tj
Like A Deer	Fel F Tx
Like A Deer In Winter (Ps. 41)	Nal L Tr
Like A Father	Wlp F Tr
Like A River Glorious	Zon T Ss
Like As The Heart Desireth The Water	Oxf T Tr
Like Bells At Evening	Aug L Tx
Like Cedars They Shall Stand	Nal L Sc
Like Dew Before The Daystar	Fel L Sc
Like In Noah's Days	Wlp L Tr
Like Olive Branches	Lor T Sr
Lilies (Mumma)	Zon G Tj
Lily Of The Valley, The	Lor T Tj
Lily Of The Valley, The	Man G Sl
Linger A Little Longer	Van C Tx
Lion Hunt	Gsc F Sc
Lippai, Wake Up!	Chh F Tr
Listen And Hear	Gia L Tx
Listen Christian (Soc. Gospel)	Zon F Za
Listen He's Here (No 4721)	Wlp F Tr
Listen Lord	Fel L Tj
Listen To Him	Sms F To
Listen To My Words	Aug L Sl
Listen To My Words, Lord	Gsc T Tx
Listen To The Lambs	Fel F Tr
Listen To The Silence	Urs F Tx
Listen To The Voices, That Want To Be	Rav L La
Listen To The Word	Fel L Sl
Listen To Their Sighs	Lor L Tx
Listen With An Open Mind	Fel L Tx
Listen You Nations	Nal C Tx
Listen, Listen	Kal L Lh
Litania K 243	Kal T Lh
Litaniae Laurentanae K 195	Nal L Lh
Litany	Gia L Lh
Litany	Som L Tt
Litany And Prayer	Rpb L Lo
Litany For Breaking Bread	Abi L Sr
Litany For Easter (A Cap)	Sta F Tk
Litany For The Lord's Coming	Kal T Tt
Litany Glory Praise & Power K 125	Jsp L Tr
Litany Of Comfort	Abi L Tt
Litany Of Thanksgiving (W/Brs Etal)	Fel L Tm
Litany Of The Blessed Virgin	Vrn G Lo
Litany Of The Eucharist	Vrn L Ss
Litany Of The Holy Spirit.	Fel L Tx
Litany Of The Saints	Fel F Ss
Litany Of The Spirit	Oxf T Ss
Litany To The Holy Spirit (E)	Prc L Tx
Little Baby Boy	Ham C Sl
Little Black Sheep	Gsc T Sc
Little Brother Jesus	Fel F Sc
Little Child	Gia L Sc
Little Child Sleeping Boy(E)	Smc G Tx
Little David (Spiritual)	Lor T Tx
Little David, Play On Your Harp	Hhh G Tr
Little Hands	Gsc T Tx
Little Innocent Lamb	Wbp T Tx
Little Lamb	Lor T Sc
Little Lord Jesus	Ham C Tj
Little Lost Sheep	Gsc T Sc
Little White Dove	Pro C Sc
Littlest Christmas Tree	Wlp L Za
Liturgical Mass	Oxf T Za
Liturgical Motets	Gia L Lo
Liturgy Of Eucharist (Lyric Liturgy)	Van F Za
Liturgy Of The Holy Spirit	Wlp L Le
Liturgy Of The Word (Icet)	Man G Tc
Live In Me	Acp F Tr
Live In The Light	Acp F Tr
Live In The Light (4-Part Arr)	Fel F Tr
Live With The Lord	Nal L Tr
Live With Us	Oxf T Tc
Live Your Life For Him Always (E)	Zon C Za
Lively Choruses No 1 (No 5300)	Zon C Za
Lively Choruses No 2 (No 5301)	Zon C Za
Lively Choruses No 3 (No 5302)	Sac L Tj
Living Christ, The	Lor T Tc
Living For Jesus	Fcc F Tt
Living God, The	Zon G Za
Living Hymns For Crusades And Conf.	Mar L Tx
Living On The Bottle	Zon G Za
Living Praise	Gia L Ss
Living Spirit	Gia F Ss
Living Spirit (Blessed Be The God)	Gia F Ss
Living Spirit, The	Nal L Ss
Living Water	Zon F Ss
Living Water(Lenten Invocation)	Rav L Sl
Living Waters (Scriptural Collec)	Gia F Za
Living Words (Mary,Simon,Etc)	Gia F Tr
Llanfair	Gia T Sr
Lo The Angel Said To The Shepherds	Gsc T Sc
Lo The Tomb Is Empty	Gsc T Sr
Lo! God Is Here	Lor L La
Lo! God Is Here!	Maf G La
Lo! He Comes In Clouds Descending	Bbl T Sa
Lo! Star-Led Chiefs (Me)	Oxf T Sc
Lo, A Child Is Born	Bbl T Sc
Lo, Angels Bread (Eng Only)	Gia T Lo
Lo, Angels' Bread	Gia T Lo
Lo, God Is Here	Zon T La
Lo, God Is Here!	Gsc T La
Lo, How A Rose	Bec T Sc
Lo, How A Rose	Aug T Sc
Lo, How A Rose (4 Voices)	Gia T Sc
Lo, How A Rose E'er Blooming	Sac T Sc
Lo, How A Rose E'er Blooming	Hof T Sc
Lo, How A Rose E'er Blooming	Gia T Sc
Lo, How A Rose E'er Blooming (E)	Gia T Sc
Lo, How A Rose E'er Blooming (Easy)	Abi L Zb
Lo, How A Rose Ere Blooming	Aug T Sc
Lo, I Am The Voice Of One Crying	Gsc T Sa
Lo, I Am With You Always	Abi L Tr
Lo, My Shepherd Is Divine	Gsc T Tr
Lo, Our Savior King Is Here	Wlp T Tj
Lo, Round The Throne A Glorious Band	Gsc T Sr
Lo, The Angel Said To The Shepherds	Gsc T Sc
Lobt Gott Mit Schall	Bbl T Tt
Locus Este A Deo Factus Est(Lat)	Cfp T Tc
Lone Calvary	Jhm G Sl
Lonely	Man G Sl
Lonely Days	Rpb F Sl
Lonesome Valley	Lor T Sl
Long Ago A Prophet Sang	Abi L Tx
Long Ago In Bethlehem	Sac T Sc
Long Ago In Bethlehem	Her L Sc
Long Black Train A-Comin'	Pmp G Tf
Long Live The Lord	Wlp L Sr
Long Song, The	Nal L Tx
Long Time Ago	Lor T Sc
Long Time Ago	Sac L Sc
Long Way Home (Psalm 126)	Ahc L Tx
Long Years Ago	Gsc L Sc
Longing For God	Wlp L Tr
Lonsdale From Three Fuging-Tunes	Bbl T Tt
Look All Around	Fel L Tt
Look All Around You	Ahc L Tx
Look And Live	Zon G Tb
Look Around	Fel F Sr
Look At Jesus	Gia F Sl
Look At My Gifts	Rav L To
Look Behind You	Sil F Tr
Look Beyond	Fel L Tx
Look Down That Road	Nal L Tx
Look Down To Us St. Joseph	Wlp T Tx
Look For Him	Zon F Tr
Look For Me	Zon G Tr
Look For Me In Lowly Men	Cfc L Tr
Look On Me, O Lord	Fel L Sl
Look Out Your Window	Fel F Tx
Look Softly, Lord	Lor T Tr
Look To The Lamb Of God	Zon G Sl
Look To The Lord	Fel L Tr
Look To The Lord And Be Strengthened	Fel L Tr
Look To The Mountains	Van F Tr
Look To The Rainbow	Wlp F Tx
Look To The Rock (From Isaiah)	Mcc F Tc
Look To The Skies Above	Lor L To
Look To Your Soul (From Thoughts...)	Wlp F Tx
Look Toward Me	Nal L Tr
Look Toward Me (Psalm 25)	Rpb L Ld
Look Up	Pmp G Tx
Look Up	Cor F Sa
Look Up	Zon F Tj
Look Up And See Jesus	Fel F Tr
Look Up To The Lord	Fel L Tx
Look Up, You Nations	Yan F Tr
Look Within	Aug T Sr
Look Ye Saints, The Sight Is Glorious	Zon T Tr
Look! See My God!	Sil F Tx
Lookin' Back	Oak G Tj
Looking Reaching For My Lord	Wrd G Tp
Lord Achieve Your Purpose(Org)	Sms F Ld
Lord Be Not Far From Me	Nal L Tr
Lord Be With Us	Lor T Tr
Lord Bless You And Keep You, The	Wlp F Lj
Lord By Your Cross	Nal L Lj
Lord By Your Cross	Nal L Lj
Lord By Your Cross	Nal L Lj
Lord By Your Cross	Wlp L Lj
Lord By Your Cross And Resurrection	Gra L Lj
Lord Christ, When First Thou Cam'st	Aug T Sc
Lord Christ, When First Thou Cam'st	Gsc T Sc
Lord Dismiss Us With Thy Blessing	Gsc L Tt
Lord Don't Lift Your Spirit From Me	Man G Ss
Lord Doth Reign, The (Opt Acc)	Abi L Tr
Lord Every Nation (Icet)	Wlp L Ld
Lord Every Nation(Ps 72)	Rav L Ld
Lord Fill My Mouth With Words	Wlp T Tt
Lord For Thy Tender Mercies Sake	Gsc T Sl
Lord Gave Me A Song To Sing, The	Nal L Tx
Lord Give Me A Heart Of Flesh	Wlp F Sl
Lord Give Me Wings	Ste F Tx
Lord God We Praise Thy Goodness	Gsc T Tt
Lord God We Worship Thee	Gia T La
Lord God, Our Thanks To Thee We Raise	Zon T Tt
Lord God, We Worship Thee	Aug T Tt
Lord Has Done Great Things(Ps 126)	Rav L Ld
Lord Has Risen In Glory, The	Acp F Sr
Lord Have Mercy	Flp T Lb
Lord Have Mercy	Fcc L Lb
Lord Have Mercy	Rpb L Lb
Lord Have Mercy	Gia L Lb
Lord Have Mercy	Aug T Lb
Lord Have Mercy	Rpb L Lb
Lord Have Mercy	Nal L Lb
Lord Have Mercy	Rpb L Lb

ALPHABETICAL INDEX OF TITLES

Lord Have Mercy	Rpb	L	Lb
Lord Have Mercy	Gia	L	Lb
Lord Have Mercy	Ccc	L	Lb
Lord Have Mercy	Nal	L	Lb
Lord Have Mercy	Nal	L	Lb
Lord Have Mercy	Sbf	L	Lb
Lord Have Mercy	Nal	L	Lb
Lord Have Mercy	Yan	F	Lb
Lord Have Mercy (Kyrie)	Fel	L	Lb
Lord Have Mercy (Kyrie)	Fel	F	Lb
Lord Have Mercy (Kyrie)	Fel	F	Lb
Lord Have Mercy (Kyrie)(Chardin Mass)	Fel	L	Lb
Lord Have Mercy (Kyrie)(Folk Mass #4)	Fel	L	Lb
Lord Have Mercy (Kyrie)(Funeral Folk)	Fel	F	Lb
Lord Have Mercy (Kyrie)(Hymn Tune)	Fel	T	Lb
Lord Have Mercy (Kyrie)(Jazz-Rock)	Fel	F	Lb
Lord Have Mercy On Us	Acp	L	Lb
Lord Have Mercy Upon Us	Gsc	T	Sa
Lord Have Mercy (Cel Of Unity)	Gia	L	Lb
Lord Have Mercy (Child Mass)	Gia	L	Lb
Lord Have Mercy (Community Mass)	Gia	L	Lb
Lord Have Mercy (Danish Amen)	Jsp	L	Lb
Lord Have Mercy (Icet)	Jsp	L	Lb
Lord Have Mercy (Icet)	Wlp	L	Lb
Lord Have Mercy (Icet)	Wlp	L	Lb
Lord Have Mercy (Icet)	Wlp	L	Lb
Lord Have Mercy (Icet)	Wlp	F	Lb
Lord Have Mercy (Icet)	Wlp	L	Lb
Lord Have Mercy (Icet)	Wlp	F	Lb
Lord Have Mercy (Lyric Mass)	Gia	L	Lb
Lord Have Mercy (Mass For All Seasons)	Gia	L	Lb
Lord Have Mercy (New Mass)	Gia	L	Lb
Lord Have Mercy (Short Mass)	Gia	L	Lb
Lord Have Mercy (Threefold)	Wlp	L	Lb
Lord Have Mercy (Twofold)	Wlp	L	Lb
Lord Have Mercy (Upon Me)	Gia	F	Lb
Lord Have Mercy (W/Cantor)(Dominic)	Gia	L	Lb
Lord Have Mercy (1964 Text)	Van	F	Lb
Lord Have Mercy (3 Fold)	Van	F	Lb
Lord Have Mercy (4 Voices)	Gia	T	Lb
Lord Have Mercy – 2nd Version	Rpb	L	Lb
Lord Have Mercy On Us (2-Part Arr)	Acp	L	Lb
Lord Have Mercy On Us All	Nal	L	Lb
Lord Have Mercy 2	Nal	L	Lb
Lord Have Mercy(Opt Brs/Timp)	Gia	L	Lb
Lord Have Mercy(Vianney Mass)	Gia	L	Lb
Lord Have Your Way With Me	Man	F	Tk
Lord Hear My Voice	Gsc	T	Tr
Lord Hosanna In The Highest	Gsc	T	Li
Lord I Love The Habitation	Gam	T	Tc
Lord I've Come To Your Garden	Wlp	F	Tr
Lord In Thy Presence Lead Us	Gsc	T	Lo
Lord In Thy Resurrection	Gsc	T	Sr
Lord In Your Tenderness	Wlp	L	Tr
Lord Is A Mighty God, The	Sac	L	Tx
Lord Is Compassionate, The	Nal	L	Tr
Lord Is Counting On You, The	Ham	C	Tc
Lord Is Drawing Near, The	Acp	L	Sa
Lord Is Drawing Near, The (4-Part Arr)	Acp	L	Sa
Lord Is Good, The	Sac	L	Tr
Lord Is In His Holy Temple, The	Lor	T	Tr
Lord Is It I	Prc	L	Tx
Lord Is King, The	Abi	L	Tk
Lord Is King, The	Abi	T	Tk
Lord Is King, The	Zon	T	Tk
Lord Is Merciful, The	Lor	T	Sr
Lord Is My Hope, The	Nal	L	Tr
Lord Is My Light And My Salvation, The	Nal	L	Tr
Lord Is My Light, The	Lor	L	Tr
Lord Is My Light, The	Lor	L	Tr
Lord Is My Light, The	Sac	L	Tr
Lord Is My Shepherd (Ps 23)	Rav	L	Ld
Lord Is My Shepherd, The	Lor	T	Tr
Lord Is My Shepherd, The	Nal	L	Tr
Lord Is My Shepherd, The	Lor	L	Tr
Lord Is My Shepherd, The	Sac	L	Tr
Lord Is My Shepherd, The	Lor	T	Tr
Lord Is My Shepherd, The	Zon	F	Tr
Lord Is My Shepherd, The	Nal	L	Tr
Lord Is My Strength, The	Sac	L	Tr
Lord Is Near To All, The	Bbl	T	Tr
Lord Is Nigh, The	Sac	L	Sa
Lord Is Risen Today, The	Lor	T	Sr
Lord Is Thy Keeper, The	Sac	L	Tr
Lord Is With Us, The	Sac	L	Tr
Lord It Is Good To Give Thanks To You	Nal	L	Tt
Lord Jesus By Thy Passion	Aug	T	Sl
Lord Jesus Christ In Thee Alone	Gsc	T	Tj
Lord Jesus Come From "Lyric Liturgy"	Gia	L	Tj
Lord Jesus On The Cross Was Hung	Gsc	T	Sl
Lord Jesus Think On Me	Gal	T	Tj
Lord Jesus, Receive My Spirit	Fel	L	Tf
Lord Jesus, Think On Me	Abi	T	Sl
Lord Jesus, Think On Me	Lor	T	Tj
Lord Jesus, Think On Me	Gsc	L	Tj
Lord Jesus, Think On Me	Gsc	T	Tj
Lord Jesus, Think On Me	Lor	T	Tj
Lord Jesus, Think On Me (High Voice)	Abi	L	Tj
Lord Keep Me In The Holy Band	Sto	G	Tr
Lord Keep Your Hand On Me	Zon	G	Tx
Lord Let Me Walk	Wlp	F	Tc
Lord Let Us See Your Kindness (Icet)	Wlp	L	Ld
Lord Make Me An Instrument	Pro	T	Tr
Lord Make Me Know Your Ways	Sha	F	Ld
Lord Make Us Ready	Wlp	F	Sa
Lord Makes Me Happy! The	Zon	F	Tr
Lord Most High (Opt Brs)	Abi	L	Tc
Lord Of All	Gsc	L	Tk
Lord Of All Being	Abi	L	Tr
Lord Of All Nations	Jsp	L	Tr
Lord Of All Power And Might	Gsc	T	Tt
Lord Of All, You Gave Us This	Her	T	Tp
Lord Of Glory Is My Light, The	Abi	L	Tr
Lord Of Life	Aug	T	Tr
Lord Of Nations Bless In Kindness	Wlp	T	Tr
Lord Of No Beginning	Nal	L	Tx
Lord Of Our Life	Gsc	L	Tr
Lord Of Spirits	Aug	T	Tx
Lord Of The Dance	Van	F	Tj
Lord Of The Worlds Above	Sac	L	Tt
Lord Of The Years	Gsc	T	Tk
Lord Our Lord	Gsc	L	Tt
Lord Rabboni	Wlp	F	Tj
Lord Reigneth, The	Abi	L	Tk
Lord Reigns, The	Sac	L	Tk
Lord Send Me	Zon	G	Tc
Lord Send Out Your Spirit (Icet)	Wlp	L	Ld
Lord Send Out Your Spirit(Ps 104)	Rav	L	Ld
Lord Speak To Me	Wrd	G	Tc
Lord Take Our Lives	Sil	T	Tc
Lord Teach Us To Pray	Wlp	F	Tx
Lord Thou Art Holy	Gam	C	Tt
Lord To Thee I Make My Moan (M)	Oxf	T	Sl
Lord Watch Over Mother	Jhm	G	Tx
Lord We Gather At Your Altar	Wlp	T	La
Lord We Give Thanks To Thee	Wbp	T	Tt
Lord We Implore Thee	Gsc	T	Tr
Lord Will Give Us Peace, The	Fcc	L	Tr
Lord You Are Good And Forgiving	Gra	L	Ld
Lord You Are My Refuge	Nal	L	Tr
Lord You Have Blessed Us	Gia	F	Tr
Lord You Have The Word (Icet)	Wlp	L	Ld
Lord, Be With Us Now	Rpb	T	Tr
Lord, Behold Us (E)	Oxf	L	Tr
Lord, Bless This Little Child	Bfi	F	Tb
Lord, Build Me A Cabin In Glory	Ivm	T	Sr
Lord, By Whose Breath	Aug	L	Ss
Lord, By Your Cross And Resurrection	Nal	L	Lj
Lord, Create In Me A Clean Heart	Maf	T	Sl
Lord, Do Not Forget Forever	Fel	L	Sl
Lord, Don't Move That Mountain	Man	G	Tr
Lord, For Thy Tender Mercies	Gsc	T	Sl
Lord, For Thy Tender Mercy's Sake (E)	Oxf	T	Sl
Lord, From Your Cross, Look Upon Us	Gia	L	Sl
Lord, Give Them This Day	Wrd	L	Tt
Lord, Give Us Strength	Nal	L	Tr
Lord, Grant Thy Blessing	Smc	T	Zb
Lord, Have Mercy Upon Us	Abi	L	Lo
Lord, Have Mercy; Save My Soul	Fel	F	Tr
Lord, Hear Our Prayer To Thee	Pro	T	Tr
Lord, How Excellent Thy Name	Gsc	T	Tt
Lord, I Am Not Worthy	Ahc	L	Sl
Lord, I Can Suffer	Gsc	T	Sl
Lord, I Cry Unto Thee	Abi	L	Sl
Lord, I Love Your Law	Fel	L	Tr
Lord, I Pray	Ham	G	Tr
Lord, I Trust Thee (From Passion)	Oxf	T	Sl
Lord, I Want A Diadem	Zon	G	Sr
Lord, I Want To Be A Christian	Gsc	G	Tx
Lord, If I But Thee May Have	Gsc	T	Sl
Lord, If You Remember Sins	Fel	L	Sl
Lord, Inspire Our Worship	Ccc	L	Lp
Lord, Jesus Christ(Offertory)(Funeral)	Fel	F	To
Lord, Keep Me Thine Own	Man	G	Tc
Lord, Keep My Mind On Thee	Man	G	Tc
Lord, Keep Us Steadfast	Aug	T	Tr
Lord, Keep Us Steadfast	Aug	T	Tr
Lord, Keep Us Steadfast In Thy Word	Aug	L	Tx
Lord, Let Me Know Mine End (Ps 39)	Oxf	T	Tr
Lord, Let Your Face Shine (Ps 4)	Gra	L	Ld
Lord, Lord, Lord	Nal	L	Tx
Lord, Make Be A Better Man Today	Bri	G	To
Lord, Make Me An Instrument	Som	L	Tr
Lord, Make Me An Instrument	Aug	L	Tr
Lord, Make Me Your Vessel	Man	G	To
Lord, May Their Lives	Gia	L	Tw
Lord, May We Follow	Maf	L	Tc
Lord, My Hope Is In Thee	Maf	T	Tr
Lord, My Lord	Nal	L	Tx
Lord, Open Thou Our Eyes	Lor	L	Tc
Lord, Redeemer Of All Who Know Thee	Gsc	T	Sl
Lord, Remember Us	Aug	T	Sl
Lord, Send Out Your Spirit	Gra	F	Ld
Lord, Send Out Your Spirit	Gia	L	Ld
Lord, Speak To Me	Maf	L	Tr
Lord, Speak To Me	Sac	L	Tr
Lord, Speak To Me That I May Speak	Abi	L	Tr
Lord, Stay Close To Me	Mam	G	Tx
Lord, Surround Us With Holy Symbols	Aug	L	Lo
Lord, Take My Heart	Aug	T	Tc
Lord, Thou Hast Been Our Dwelling	Gsc	T	Sl
Lord, Thou Hast Been Our Dwelling	Gsc	T	Tr
Lord, Walk With Me	Wbp	T	Tr
Lord, We Are Glad For Those Who Laugh	Aug	L	Tr
Lord, We Are Not The Same	Bfi	T	Tc
Lord, We Beseech Thee (Me)	Oxf	T	Sl
Lord, We Praise Thee	Ast	L	Tt
Lord, We Praise You For The Rhythm	Aug	L	Tt
Lord, When The Wise Men Came	Oxf	T	Sc
Lord, Whom Need I Fear	Fel	F	Ld
Lord, Will You Come To Us	Fel	L	Tr
Lord, You Have The Words	Gia	L	Ld
Lord, You Have The Words	Gia	L	Ld
Lord, You Have The Words (Ps 19)	Gra	L	Ld
Lord, You Live	Nal	L	Sr
Lord, You See Me	Fel	F	Tr
Lord, Your Love Is Eternal	Gra	L	Ld
Lord's My Shepherd (Ps 23)Opt Guit	Pro	F	Ld
Lord's My Shepherd, The	Zon	T	Tr
Lord's My Shepherd, The	Sac	L	Tr
Lord's Prayer	Fcc	F	Ll
Lord's Prayer	Ccc	L	Ll
Lord's Prayer	Hal	T	Ll
Lord's Prayer (Mass For New Rite)	Gia	L	Ll
Lord's Prayer (Notre Dame Mass)	Gia	L	Ll
Lord's Prayer (Org Or Guitar)	Aug	L	Ll
Lord's Prayer For Hours	Cfc	L	Ll
Lord's Prayer For Mass (Icet)	Cfc	L	Ll
Lord's Prayer Icet	Gia	L	Ll
Lord's Prayer 1	Wlp	T	Ll
Lord's Prayer 2	Wlp	T	Ll
Lord's Prayer, The	Aug	L	Ll
Lord's Prayer, The	Gra	F	Ll
Lord's Prayer, The	Lor	T	Ll
Lord's Prayer, The	Nal	L	Ll
Lord's Supper, The	Maf	L	Lo
Lose Youself In Me	Nal	L	Tc
Lost Child, The	Ron	T	Tx
Lost In The Night	Aug	L	Sl
Lost In The Night	Zon	G	Sl
Lost In Wonder, Love And Praise	Gsc	L	Tt
Lost Millions Still Untold	Zon	G	Tc
Lost-But Still He Loves You	Zon	F	Sl
Love	Wgm	L	Lo
Love	Bfi	F	Tr
Love	Fel	F	Tj
Love Alive (Collection)	Wrd	L	Za
Love All The Brethren	Gmc	G	Lo
Love And Blessed Be Thou, King	Gsc	T	Tt
Love Came Down At Christmas	Sac	T	Sc
Love Came Down At Christmas	Aug	L	Sc
Love Came Down At Christmas	Sac	T	Sc
Love Came Down At Christmas	Sac	T	Sc
Love Came Down At Christmas	Aug	T	Sc
Love Came Down At Christmas	Wrd	G	Sc
Love Came Down At Christmas	Gsc	T	Sc
Love Came Down At Christmas	Aug	L	Sc
Love Came Down At Chris..mas (W/Inst)	Aug	L	Sc
Love Came Down(Musical)	Wrd	G	Sc
Love Divine	Gsc	T	Tr
Love Divine	Gsc	T	Tr
Love Divine (God Incarnate)	Gia	F	Sc
Love Divine (Me)	Oxf	T	Tw
Love Divine, All Loves Excelling	Aug	L	Tr
Love For Life	Zon	F	Tr
Love Found A Way	Zon	G	Tj
Love Gift, The	Lor	L	Sc
Love In Grief	Aug	L	Sl
Love Is A Gift	Fcc	L	To
Love Is Almost Worth The Dying	Fel	F	Sl
Love Is Come Again	Gsc	T	Sr
Love Is Everlasting	Gia	L	Tt
Love Is God's Answer	Sil	G	Tr
Love Is Like A Circle	Rpb	F	Tr
Love Is Patient	Fel	F	Tr
Love Is The Way	Acp	F	Tr
Love Is The Way (4-Part Arr)	Acp	F	Tr
Love Knows No Season	Gia	F	Tr
Love Like The Springtime	Sil	G	Tx
Love Must Rule In Man's Heart	Lor	L	Tr
Love Not The World	Gsc	T	Sr
Love Of Jesus, All Divine	Gsc	T	Tj
Love Of My Lord To Me, The	Lor	L	Tr
Love Of The Lord	Fcc	L	Tr
Love One Another	Str	L	Tr
Love One Another	Mar	L	Tr
Love One Another	Fel	F	Tw
Love Song (Dunamis Music)	Wrd	G	Za
Love That Is Kept Inside	Nal	L	Tx
Love That Never Fades Away	Sil	F	Tr
Love That Wilt Not Let Me Go	Lor	L	Tr
Love The Lord With All Your Heart	Fel	L	Tr
Love Them Now	Prc	L	Tx
Love Them Now	Prc	L	Tx
Love Thou Thy God (Cantata)	Lps	T	Tr
Love Transcending (No 5954)	Zon	L	Sc
Love Transcending (No 5974)	Zon	L	Sc
Love Transcending (No 5975)	Zon	L	Sc
Love Walks The World In Flesh	Aug	L	Tj
Love Was When	Zon	F	Tr

ALPHABETICAL INDEX OF TITLES

Love Was When/Love Is Now (No 4380)	Zon	F	Za
Love Will Bring Us Back	Wrd	G	Tu
Love Your Brother	Lor	L	Sr
Love Your Brother	Van	F	Tr
Love, Love	Mar	L	Tr
Love, Love, Love	Aug	L	Tr
Love, O Love	Prc	L	Tx
Loved By The Lord	Van	F	Tr
Loved Ones Are Waiting	Sav	G	Tf
Lovely Appear(The Redemption)	Gsc	T	Sa
Lovely Child, Holy Child	Aug	L	Sc
Lovers Are Special People	Ccc	L	Zb
Lovest Thou Me?	Gmc	G	Tc
Lovest Thou Me?	Lor	G	Tc
Loving Shepherd Of Thy Sheep	Oxf	L	Tr
Loving Shepherd Of Thy Sheep (E)	Oxf	L	Sr
Low Voice No 1 (No 5221)	Zon	G	Za
Low Voice No 10 (No 5231)	Zon	G	Za
Low Voice No 11 (No 5232)	Zon	G	Za
Low Voice No 12 (No 5233)	Zon	G	Za
Low Voice No 13 (No 5234)	Zon	G	Za
Low Voice No 14 (No 5235)	Zon	G	Za
Low Voice No 15 (No 5236)	Zon	G	Za
Low Voice No 2 (No 5222)	Zon	G	Za
Low Voice No 3 (No 5223)	Zon	G	Za
Low Voice No 4 (No 5224)	Zon	G	Za
Low Voice No 5 (No 5225)	Zon	G	Za
Low Voice No 6 (No 5226)	Zon	G	Za
Low Voice No 7 (No 5227)	Zon	G	Za
Low Voice No 8 (No 5228)	Zon	G	Za
Low Voice No 9 (No 5229)	Zon	G	Za
Lower Your Eyes	Van	F	Sl
Lowly People You Save (Ps 18)	Gra	F	Ld
Lullaby	Mar	L	Tx
Lullaby At Christmas	Abi	L	Sc
Lullaby For Jesus	Gia	T	Sc
Lullaby Of The Spirit	Fel	F	Ss
Lullaby On Christmas Eve	Aug	L	Sc
Lullaby, Jesus Dear	Gsc	T	Sc
Lyric Liturgy	Gia	L	Za
Ma Tovu (In 19 Lit Rounds)	Gia	T	Tr
Madonna	Tcp	L	Tm
Magdalen, Cease From Sobs And Sighs	Oxf	T	Sr
Magdalena Op 22 No 6	Gsc	T	Sr
Magnificat	Kal	T	Tt
Magnificat	Fel	L	Tm
Magnificat	Kal	T	Tt
Magnificat	Nal	L	Tm
Magnificat	Abi	L	Zb
Magnificat	Gsc	T	Tt
Magnificat	Fel	F	Tt
Magnificat	Kal	T	Tt
Magnificat	Aug	T	Tt
Magnificat	Gsc	T	Tt
Magnificat	Kal	T	Tt
Magnificat	Kal	T	Tt
Magnificat	Oxf	T	Tm
Magnificat (From Cantiones Sacrae)	Oxf	T	Tt
Magnificat (Long)	Gia	T	Tm
Magnificat (Luke), The	Nal	L	Tm
Magnificat (W/Cont,Viols)	Aug	L	Tt
Magnificat And Nunc Dimittis	Oxf	T	Za
Magnificat And Nunc Dimittis	Gsc	T	Tx
Magnificat And Nunc Dimittis (M)	Oxf	T	Za
Magnificat And Nunc Dimittis (M)	Oxf	T	Za
Magnificat And Nunc Dimittis (M)	Oxf	T	Za
Magnificat And Nunc Dimittis (Md)	Oxf	T	Za
Magnificat And Nunc Dimittis (Md)	Oxf	T	Za
Magnificat And Nunc Dimittis (Md)	Oxf	T	Za
Magnificat And Nunc Dimittis (Md)	Oxf	T	Za
Magnificat And Nunc Dimittis (Md)	Oxf	T	Za
Magnificat And Nunc Dimittis (Md)	Oxf	T	Za
Magnificat And Nunc Dimittis (Md)	Oxf	T	Za
Magnificat And Nunc Dimittis (Me)	Oxf	T	Za
Magnificat And Nunc Dimittis (Me)	Oxf	T	Za
Magnificat And Nunc Dimittis (Me)	Oxf	T	Za
Magnificat And Nunc Dimittis Iii (Md)	Oxf	T	Za
Magnificat And Nunc Dimittis In C	Oxf	T	Za
Magnificat And Nunc Dimittis In Eb	Oxf	T	Za
Magnificat And Nunc Dimittis(Eng)	Cfp	T	Tt
Magnificat Anima Mea	Kal	T	Tt
Magnificat Anima Mea Dominum	Gsc	T	Tt
Magnificat Du 3eme Et 4eme Ton	Nov	T	Zb
Magnificat For 6 Voices (Organ Score)	Kal	T	Tt
Magnificat In D	Lps	T	Tm
Magnificat No. 1	Pic	T	Tm
Magnificat(C)(Lat)	Cfp	T	Tt
Magnificat(Eng-Lat)	Cfp	T	Tt
Magnificat(Latin)	Cfp	T	Tt
Make A Joyful Noise	Aug	L	Tt
Make A Joyful Noise	Sac	L	Tt
Make A Joyful Noise	Lor	T	Tt
Make A Joyful Noise	Sac	L	Tt
Make A Joyful Noise Unto The Lord (M)	Oxf	T	Tt
Make A Joyful Noise Unto The Lord (Me)	Oxf	T	Tt
Make A Joyful Sound (5 Voices)	Gia	T	Tt
Make Known Your Way	Nal	L	Tr
Make Me A Channel Of Your Peace	Fcc	F	Tr
Make Me Your Own (I Give You)	Gia	L	To
Make Of Us O Lord A New People	Nal	L	To
Make Up Your Mind	Man	L	Tc
Make Us One	Aug	L	Tu
Make Us One Father (W/Piano)	Wrd	G	Tu
Make We Joy Now In This Feast	Gsc	T	Sc
Maleita's Song	Wlp	F	Tx
Mamma And Daddy Taught Me How To See	Man	G	Tx
Man Born Of A Woman, A	Bbl	T	Tj
Man In The Dark (Musical)	Zon	L	Tx
Man Of Sorrows	Aug	L	Sl
Man Of The Lord	Mar	L	Tc
Man On The Cross, The	Sac	L	Sl
Man's Redemption	Gsc	T	Sc
Manger And Star	Abi	L	Sc
Manger Carol, A	Lor	T	Sc
Manger King, The	Lor	L	Sc
Mansion Over The Hilltop	Zon	G	Tx
Many Are We Yet One We Are	Nal	L	Lo
Many Shall Come From The East And West	Gsc	T	Sc
Many Signs Jesus Worked	Fel	L	Tj
Many Times I Have Turned	Rpb	F	Sl
Marana-Tha	Acp	F	Sa
Marana-Tha	Acp	F	Tk
Maranatha	Wlp	L	Sa
Maranatha	Wlp	F	Sa
March Of Freedom	Smc	T	Tp
March Of The Kings	Gsc	T	Sc
March Of The Kings	Gsc	T	Sc
March Of The Three Kings	Pro	L	Sc
March On With Christ	Lor	T	Tc
Marching To Zion	Zon	G	Lp
Maria Magdalene Et Altera Maria	Bbl	T	Sr
Maria Magdalene Et Altera Maria	Bbl	T	Sr
Marriage (Response)	Wlp	L	Tw
Mary	Nal	L	Tm
Mary	Wlp	F	Tm
Mary (Optional Instruments)	Aug	L	Tm
Mary Had A Baby	Lor	G	Tj
Mary Had A Baby	Gsc	G	Sc
Mary Had A Baby Boy (E)	Pro	F	Sc
Mary Laid Her Child	Gsc	T	Sc
Mary The Dawn	Acp	L	Tm
Mary The Dawn (4-Part Arr)	Acp	L	Tm
Mary, Filled With Grace	Acp	L	Tm
Mary, Filled With Grace	Acp	L	Tm
Mary, Mary	Prc	L	Tx
Mary, Mary	Abi	L	Sc
Mary, Mother Of The Word	Gra	F	Tm
Mary, Too	Prc	L	Tx
Mary, We Must Go	Gsc	T	Tm
Mary, Your Child Is God	Ahc	L	Tm
Mary's Boy Child	Hal	F	Sc
Mary's Gift (A Christmas Carol)	Pic	L	Sc
Mary's Lament	Aug	L	Tm
Mary's Little Boy Child	Sch	F	Sc
Mary's Lullaby	Maf	T	Sc
Mary's Lullaby	Gia	L	Sc
Mary's Lullaby	Man	L	Sc
Mary's Manger Song	Gsc	T	Sc
Mary's Nowell	Gsc	T	Sc
Mary's Salutation (E & Germ)	Oxf	T	Tm
Mary's Soliloquy (From The Cantata)	Gsc	T	Sc
Mary's Song	Ahc	L	Tm
Mary's Song	Ccc	L	Sl
Marys Little Baby	Gsc	T	Sc
Mass	Oxf	T	Za
Mass (Guitar Or Clavier)	Oxf	T	Za
Mass (To St. Anthony)	Pic	L	Za
Mass #1 In F	Kal	T	Za
Mass And Te Deum	Kal	T	Za
Mass Corona Spinea	Kal	T	Za
Mass For A Feast Day (Icet) Cong Opt	Gia	L	Za
Mass For All Seasons	Rav	L	Za
Mass For American Saint	Wlp	L	Za
Mass For Children (Icet)	Wlp	C	Za
Mass For Congregations (Icet)	Gia	L	Za
Mass For Four Mixed Voices	Gia	T	Za
Mass For Four Voices	Kal	T	Za
Mass For Joy (W/Org,Guit)	Gia	F	Za
Mass For Parishes	Acp	L	Za
Mass For Peace	Kal	T	Za
Mass For Peace (E)	Oxf	L	Za
Mass For Two Voices (Icet)	Gia	L	Za
Mass For 4 Voices, Solo & Chorus	Kal	T	Za
Mass Gloria Tibi Trinitas	Kal	T	Za
Mass Hymn Suites	Gia	T	Za
Mass In Ab And Eb	Kal	T	Za
Mass In B Minor	Kal	T	Za
Mass In B Minor(Latin)	Cfp	T	Za
Mass In B-Flat	Bbl	T	Za
Mass In C (D)	Oxf	T	Za
Mass In C (Opus 86)	Kal	T	Za
Mass In C (Student's Mass)	Kal	T	Za
Mass In C K 258	Kal	T	Za
Mass In C Major	Bbl	T	Za
Mass In C Major	Kal	T	Za
Mass In C Minor	Gia	L	Za
Mass In C, Op 169	Kal	T	Za
Mass In D	Kal	T	Za
Mass In D (Easy)	Gia	L	Za
Mass In D, Opus 86	Kal	T	Za
Mass In E Minor	Kal	T	Za
Mass In E Minor	Bbl	T	Za
Mass In English (A Cap)	Cfp	T	Za
Mass In F	Kal	T	Za
Mass In G (In Bb)	Kal	T	Za
Mass In G Major No. 2	Bbl	T	Za
Mass In Honor Of All Saints	Gia	L	Za
Mass In Honor Of Chicago	Acp	L	Za
Mass In Honor Of O.L. Visitation	Wlp	T	Za
Mass In Honor Of Pope Paul Vi	Jsp	L	Za
Mass In Honor Of St Joseph	Gia	L	Za
Mass In Praise Of Holy Spirit	Gia	L	Za
Mass In Praise Of Jesus Christ	Gia	L	Za
Mass Is Ended, The	Fcc	F	Lp
Mass Mater Christi	Kal	T	Za
Mass No. 10 In B-Flat Theresa Mass	Bbl	T	Za
Mass No. 2 In G Major	Bbl	T	Za
Mass No.1(Bwv 233)(Latin)	Cfp	T	Za
Mass No.2(Bwv 234)(Latin)	Cfp	T	Za
Mass No.2(E)(Latin)	Cfp	T	Za
Mass No.3(Bwv 235)(Latin)	Cfp	T	Za
Mass No.3(F)(Latin)	Cfp	T	Za
Mass No.4(Bwv 236)(Latin)	Cfp	T	Za
Mass O Michaeli	Kal	T	Za
Mass Of Celebration	Acp	L	Za
Mass Of Celebration (4-Part Arr)	Acp	L	Za
Mass Of Freedom (Icet)	Gia	L	Za
Mass Of Praise (Icet)	Gia	L	Za
Mass Of Resurrection	Gia	L	Tf
Mass Of Saint Andrew	Gsc	T	Za
Mass Of Thanksgiving (Icet)Org,Cong	Gia	L	Za
Mass Of The Bells Icet (W/Cantor/Cong)	Gia	L	Za
Mass Of The Redeemer (Cath,Ang)	Gia	T	Za
Mass Of The Sacred Heart	Kal	T	Za
Mass Opus 147	Kal	T	Za
Mass Per Arma Justitiae	Kal	T	Za
Mass Plain Song	Kal	T	Za
Mass Salve Intemerata	Kal	T	Za
Mass Sine Nomine	Kal	T	Za
Mass Small Devotion	Kal	T	Za
Mass St. Joanni De Deo	Kal	T	Za
Mass The Western Wynde	Kal	T	Za
Mass Volume Ii	Wlp	L	Za
Mass 12 (Eng)	Kal	T	Za
Mass 2 In G Major For Men's Voices	Kal	T	Za
Mass 6 In G Maj (4 Voices,Solo,Chor)	Kal	T	Za
Mass(C)(Latin)	Cfp	T	Za
Mass, Op. 86(C)(Latin)	Cfp	T	Za
Mass, Opus 44	Oxf	T	Za
Mass, Roman Catholic English Text (E)	Oxf	L	Za
Mass, Vesperae Sollenes K 339	Kal	T	Za
Mass, Videte Manus Meas	Kal	T	Za
Master Hath Called Us, The	Lor	T	Tc
Master Of All Miracles	Pmp	G	Tx
Master Of Eager Youth	Maf	T	Tc
Master Of Peace And Love	Lor	T	Tr
Master, Speak! Thy Servant Heareth	Abi	L	Tr
Master, What Shall I Do?	Lor	T	Tc
Master's Pace, The (Opt Guitar)	Pro	F	Tc
Master's Touch, The	Zon	F	Tj
Masters In This Hall (In 19 Rounds)	Gia	T	Sc
Mater Patris Et Filia	Gsc	T	Tm
Matthew 19:17	Mar	L	Tt
May All Your People Be One	Fel	F	Tu
May Choirs Of Angels Bring You	Fel	L	Tf
May Eternal Light Shine	Fel	L	Tf
May God Be Gracious (4 Voices)	Gia	T	Tt
May God Bless You And Keep You	Zon	G	Tr
May God Grant Us Peace	Pmp	G	Tr
May God Have Mercy Upon Us	Gsc	L	Tr
May God Have Pity On Us	Gia	L	Ld
May I Be Firm In Keeping Your Law	Fel	L	Tr
May Jesus Christ Be Praised	Zon	T	Tt
May Jesus Christ Be Praised!	Zon	T	Tt
May Light Eternal (Funeral Folk Mass)	Fel	F	Tf
May Magnificat	Oxf	T	Tm
May No Rash Intruder ("Solomon")	Cfs	T	Tx
May The Angels	Nal	L	Tf
May The Angels	Nal	L	Tf
May The God Of Israel	Wlp	L	Tt
May The God Of Israel Join You	Fel	L	Tm
May The Lord Bless & Keep You	Wlp	F	Tr
May The Lord Bless Us (Ps 126)	Gra	L	Ld
May The Lord Bless Us With Peace	Fel	L	Tr
May The Love Of Christ Dwell	Fel	L	Tr
May The Roads Rise Up	Rpb	F	Tr
May The Roads Rise Up(Irish Blessing)	Rav	F	Tx
May The Words Of My Mouth	Gsc	T	Tt
May This Sacrifice Of Ours	Fel	L	To
May We All One Bread, One Body Be	Fel	L	Ln
May We Shout For Joy	Fel	L	Tt
May You See Your Children's Children	Fel	L	Tw
May You Walk Worthily Of God	Fel	L	Tx
May Your Priests Be Clothed	Fel	L	Tc
Maybe	Mar	L	Tx
Me And Jesus	Chp	G	Tx
Meditabor	Gsc	T	Sl
Meditation	Abi	L	Sr
Meditation	Nal	L	Tx
Meditation	Smc	L	Zb

ALPHABETICAL INDEX OF TITLES

Meditation On "Passion Chorale"	Sac	L Sl
Meditation On Woodworth	Abi	L Tx
Meditations On Psalm 37	Abi	L Zb
Meditations On Sweet Rivers	Abi	L Zb
Meditative Songs (Med Voice)	Abi	L Za
Meet Me In Heaven	Man	G Sr
Mein Herz Ist Bereit	Bbl	T Tc
Melchizedek Mass For The King	Gia	F Za
Melodias De Bendicion (No 5369)	Zon	G Za
Melody Divine	Zon	G Tt
Members Of One Mystic Body	Wlp	L Lo
Memorial Acclamation	Rpb	L Lj
Memorial Acclamation	Rpb	L Lj
Memorial Acclamation	Rpb	L Lj
Memorial Acclamation (Christ Has Died)	Gia	L Lj
Memorial Acclamation (Christ Has Died)	Gia	L Lj
Memorial Acclamation 1	Fel	L Lj
Memorial Acclamation 1	Fel	L Lj
Memorial Acclamation 2	Fel	L Lj
Memorial Acclamation 2	Fel	L Lj
Memorial Acclamation 3	Fel	L Lj
Memorial Acclamation 3	Fel	L Lj
Memorial Acclamation 4	Fel	L Lj
Memorial Acclamation 4	Fel	L Lj
Memorial Acclamation(Christ Has Died)	Gia	L Lj
Memorial Acclamations	Acp	L Lj
Memorial Acclamations (Icet)	Wlp	L Lj
Memorial Acclamations I-Iv	Gia	L Lj
Memories Of Christmas	Lor	T Sc
Memories Of The Manger	Lor	L Sc
Men For The Crisis Hour	Lor	T Tc
Men In History (So The Bible Tells)	Ham	C Tx
Men Of Faith	Nal	L Tc
Men Of Old	Gsc	L Sc
Mennonite Hymnal, The	Flp	T Za
Mensch, Vom Weibe Geboren, Der	Bbl	T Sl
Merciful Savior Hear Our Humble Prayer	Wlp	T Tx
Mercy And Truth	Gsc	T Tr
Mercy Lord, Upon Us	Wbp	T Tr
Mercy's Free (2 Voices)	Gia	T Tr
Merrill Dunlop Favorites (No 5252)	Zon	G Tx
Merrill Dunlop Favorites No 2(No 5253)	Zon	G Tx
Merrill Dunlop's New Gospel Songs No 1	Zon	G Tx
Merrily On High	Lor	T Sc
Merrily On High	Zon	T Sc
Merry Christmas	Zon	T Sc
Merry Merry Christmas	Man	C Sc
Messa A 4 Voci (A Cappella 1651)	Gia	L Za
Message Of Love	Nal	L Tr
Message Of The Bells	Hof	T Sr
Messe Breve In C Major 7	Kal	T Za
Messe Solenelle	Kal	T Za
Messiah From Three Folk-Hymns	Bbl	T Tx
Messiah(Eng-Ger)	Cfp	T Za
Messiah-Singspiration's Abridged Ed.	Zon	T Tj
Messiah, The (Oratorio)	Kal	T Za
Mexican Christmas Procession	Aug	L Sc
Mexican Psalm, A	Hal	T Tx
Middle Of The Day	Mar	L Tx
Midnight, Sleeping Bethlehem	Aug	L Sc
Midst The Deep Silence (Handbells)	Aug	L Sc
Mighty Fortress If Our God, A	Zon	T Tr
Mighty Fortress Is Our God, A	Lor	T Tr
Mighty Fortress, A	Acp	L Tr
Mighty Fortress, A	Lor	T Tr
Mighty Fortress, A	Acp	L Tr
Mighty Fortress, A	Ccc	L Tr
Mighty Fortress, A	Sac	L Tr
Mighty Fortress, A	Lor	T Tr
Migrant	Nal	L Tx
Mihi Autem Nimis (Blessed Be Thy Name)	Oxf	T Tt
Miles Coverdale's Carol	Gsc	T Sc
Mine Just For The Asking	Man	G Tx
Mini Motet From Micah	Smc	L Tr
Minor Carol, The	Zon	T Sc
Miracle	Nal	L Tx
Miracle Melodies No 1	Zon	G Za
Miracle Melodies No 2 (No 5191)	Zon	G Za
Miracle Melodies No 3 (No 5192)	Zon	G Za
Miracle Melodies No 4 (No 5193)	Zon	G Za
Miracle Melodies No 5 (No 5194)	Zon	G Za
Miracle Melodies No 6 (No 5198)	Zon	G Za
Miracle Melodies No 7 (No 5199)	Zon	G Za
Miracle Melodies No 8 (No 5201)	Zon	G Za
Miracle Melodies No 9 (No 5203)	Zon	G Za
Miracle Of Bethlehem, The	Lor	L Sc
Miracle Of Love, The	Lor	L Sc
Miriam's Song	Rpb	L Tt
Miriam's Song Of Triumph	Kal	T Tt
Miserere Mei (Ps 51)	Oxf	T Sl
Miserere Mei Deus	Gsc	T Sl
Miserere: Psalm 51 (Eng)	Str	L Sl
Misericordia Dominis K 222	Kal	T Sl
Missa "Aeterna Christi Munera" (Md)	Oxf	T Za
Missa A La Samba (W/Org,Bongos)	Gia	F Za
Missa Brevis	Kal	T Za
Missa Brevis	Kal	T Za
Missa Brevis	Som	L Za
Missa Brevis	Kal	T Za
Missa Brevis	Kal	T Za
Missa Brevis	Gia	L Za
Missa Brevis (D)	Oxf	T Za
Missa Brevis (K192,194,220,259,275)	Kal	T Za
Missa Brevis (Latin)	Oxf	T Za
Missa Brevis (Md)	Oxf	T Za
Missa Brevis (Md)	Oxf	T Za
Missa Brevis (Salzburg Mass)Lat & Icet	Gia	L Za
Missa Brevis In A Major	Kal	T Za
Missa Brevis In F Maj	Kal	T Za
Missa Brevis In G M	Kal	T Za
Missa Brevis In G Major	Kal	T Za
Missa Carminum	Kal	T Za
Missa Choralis	Kal	T Za
Missa Da Pacem	Kal	T Za
Missa De Beata Virgine	Kal	T Za
Missa De Dominica K 321	Kal	T Za
Missa Ecce Nunc Benedicite	Kal	T Za
Missa Festiva	Oxf	T Za
Missa Festivo	Kal	T Za
Missa Ich Stund	Kal	T Za
Missa In F	Kal	T Za
Missa In G	Kal	T Za
Missa In G	Kal	T Za
Missa In Hon. St. Josephi Op 21	Kal	T Za
Missa In Summis	Kal	T Za
Missa Mi-Mi	Kal	T Za
Missa Pange Lingua	Kal	T Za
Missa Papae Marcelli	Kal	T Za
Missa Pro Defunctis	Kal	T Za
Missa Pro Defunctis	Kal	T Za
Missa Puer Qui Natus Est Nobis	Kal	T Sc
Missa Quinti Toni (5th Tone)	Kal	T Za
Missa Simile Est Regnum	Kal	T Za
Missa Sine Nomine	Kal	T Za
Missa Solemnis	Kal	T Za
Missa Solemnis (Graner Mass)	Kal	T Za
Missa Solemnis K 337	Kal	T Za
Missa Solemnis(Latin)	Cfp	T Za
Missa Super L'homme Arme Kyrie	Bbl	T Le
Missa Super L'homme Arme Kyrie Ii	Bbl	T Lb
Missa, La Bien Que J'ay	Kal	T Za
Missa, Quand Io Pens	Kal	T Za
Missas Est Gabriel	Gsc	T Sc
Mission Possible	Prc	L Tx
Mistletoe And Holly Bright	Gsc	T Sc
Mit Weinen Hebt Sichs An	Bbl	T Sl
Moist With One Drop Of Thy Blood	Abi	L Lo
Moment By Moment	Lor	T Tx
Moment Of Birth	Nal	L Tb
Moment Of Time	Mar	L Tx
Mommy Why Doesn't Daddy Love Me	Jhm	G Tx
Monsoon Rain(Psalm 103)	Ahc	L Tt
Monstra Te Esse Matrem	Pic	T Tm
More Holiness Give Me	Lor	L Tr
More Hymns And Anthems For Children's	Abi	C Za
More Like Jesus	Lor	L Tr
More Like The Master	Lor	L Tr
More Love To Thee	Zon	G Tr
More Love To Thee	Lor	L Tr
More Love To Thee (P.D.)	Man	T Tr
More Love To Thee, O Christ	Gsc	T Tr
More Than Raiment	Aug	T Tt
More Than The Sunlight	Mar	L Tx
More Than Words	Mar	L Tt
More Things Are Wrought By Prayer	Lor	T Tx
Morning Grace	Gsc	T Tx
Morning Has Broken	Hal	F Lp
Morning Has Broken	Lor	T Lo
Morning Invocation	Gsc	T Tx
Morning Prayer	Sac	L Tx
Morning Prayer	Abi	L Tx
Morning Service In D Minor	Oxf	T Za
Morning Service In Eb (Md)	Oxf	T Za
Morning Star	Sil	T Tt
Morning Trumpet	Wbp	T Tx
Morning Trumpet, The	Zon	T Tt
Morning-Song For The Christ Child	Gsc	T Sc
Morning, Mourning	Fel	F Sl
Mortality	Bbl	T Tf
Moses (Long)	Wrd	G Tx
Moses Offered Sacrifice	Fel	L To
Moses Pleaded With God	Fel	L Sl
Most Glorious Lord Of Life (Md)	Oxf	T Sr
Most Glorious Lord Of Life (Me)	Oxf	L Tt
Most Glorious Lord Of Life!	Oxf	T Sr
Most High Omnipotent God	Gia	T Tt
Motet	See	L Tx
Motet No.1(Eng-Ger)	Cfp	T Tx
Motet No.2(Eng-Ger)	Cfp	T Tx
Motet No.3(Eng-Ger)	Cfp	T Tx
Motet No.4(Eng-Ger)	Cfp	T Tx
Motet No.5(Eng-Ger)	Cfp	T Tx
Motet No.6(Eng-Ger)	Cfp	T Tx
Motet O Beata	Kal	T Tx
Motet Super Dixit Maria	Kal	T Tm
Motets	Lps	T Za
Motets By Palestrina, Ten 4-Part	Oxf	T Za
Mother Of God (W/Org)	Mcc	T Tm
Mother Of Holy Hope	Wlp	L Tm
Mother Take Your Rest	Sem	G Tt
Mother, You're God's Gift To Me	Zon	G Tx
Mother's Day Carol	Sac	L Tx
Mother's Hymns	Lor	T Za
Mother's Prayer, A	Lor	T Tx
Mother's Song, A	Lor	T Tx
Mother's Task	Lor	T Tx
Mothers Everywhere	Lor	T Tx
Mount Calvery	Lor	T Sl
Mountain Country	Sil	F Tx
Mountains And Hills	Nal	L Tt
Mountains Will Sing, The	Acp	L Tt
Mourning's Glory	Ccc	L Zb
Move To A Better Home	Sem	G Tf
Mrs. Jones	Prc	L Tx
Music Filled The Sky (E)	Gia	L Sc
Music For Christmas	Bbl	T Sc
Music For Eucharistic Prayer	Gia	L Le
Music For Palm Sunday	Gia	T Sl
Music For Reception Ceremonies	Gia	L Tc
Music For The Lord's Supper	Gam	L Lo
Music For Weddings	Gia	T Tw
Music From "King Arthur"	Nov	T Zb
Music Of Bethlehem, The	Lor	L Sc
Music Of Christmas, The	Lor	L Sc
Must Jesus Bear Another Cross?	Gsc	T Sl
Must Jesus Bear The Cross Alone?	Abi	L Sl
Mustard Seed Faith	Zon	G Tr
My Beloved Is Mine	Fel	F Tx
My Beloved Spoke (Sg 2:10-14)	Gia	F Tr
My Blessed Savior (Cantata)	Lps	T Tj
My Cactus Christmas Tree	Zon	F Sc
My Christmas Prayer	Lor	L Sc
My Church Is A Holy Place	Gsc	T Tr
My Constant Joy	Sac	L Tt
My Country, Tis Of Thee	Zon	T Tp
My Days Are Gone Like A Shadow (Md)	Oxf	T Sl
My Eyes For Beauty Pine (Me)	Oxf	T Tr
My Faith	Aug	T Tx
My Faith Looks Up To Thee	Gam	T Tj
My Faith Looks Up To Thee	Smc	T Zb
My Faith Still Holds	Gmc	G Tr
My Faith, It Is An Oaken Staff	Abi	L Tr
My Father	Ham	G Tr
My Father Is With Me	Lor	L Tr
My Father Walks Beside Me	Lor	T Tr
My Father's Care (Norwegian)	Lor	T Tr
My First Piano Hymnbook No 1 (No 5734)	Zon	G Zb
My Flesh Is Food	Fel	L Lo
My Friend And I	Wrd	G Tr
My Friend Of Calvary	Lor	T Sl
My Gift For You	Sms	F To
My Glory	Jhm	G Tx
My God	Nal	L Tt
My God And I	Sac	T Tr
My God And I	Zon	L Tr
My God Is A Rock	Acp	F Tr
My God Is A Rock	Acp	F Tr
My God Is Standing Over Me	Bri	G Tr
My God Is There	Mmc	G Tr
My God Shall Raise Me Up	Gsc	T Sl
My God Shall Supply	Man	G Tr
My God, Accept My Heart	Abi	L Tc
My God, And Is Thy Table Spread (Me)	Oxf	T Ln
My God, How Wonderful	Aug	T Tt
My God, How Wonderful Thou Art	Aug	T Tt
My God, How Wonderful Thou Art	Zon	L Tt
My God, I Thank Thee	Pro	L Tt
My God, My God	Fel	C Ld
My God, My God	Gia	L Ld
My God, My God (Icet)	Wlp	L Ld
My God, My God (Ps 22)	Gra	L Ld
My God, My God, Look Upon Me	Bbl	T Tr
My God, My God, Why Have You	Fel	L Sl
My God, My God, Why Have You Abandoned	Cfc	L Sl
My Good Is To Be Near My God	Fel	L Tr
My Guiding Star	Pmp	G Tx
My Heart Ever Faithful	Lor	T Tc
My Heart Ever Faithful(From Cantata 6)	Oxf	T Tc
My Heart Goes Out	Fel	L Tr
My Heart Is A Manger	Gsc	L Sc
My Heart Is Filled With Jesus' Love	Man	G Tr
My Heart Is Fixed	Gmc	G Tc
My Heart Is Full Today	Aug	L Tt
My Heart Is Longing To Praise	Aug	L Tt
My Heart Is Prepared	Bbl	T Tr
My Heart Longs	Nal	L Tr
My Heart Sings Hosanna	Zon	T Sl
My Heart Sings With Joy (E & Ger)	Pro	T Tt
My Heart Stands Ready	Sha	F Tc
My Heart Would Sing Of Jesus	Zon	G Tj
My Hope And Trust	Acp	F Tr
My House Shall Be Called	Fel	L Sl
My Jesus	Aug	T Tj
My Jesus, I Love Thee	Zon	T Tr
My Jesus, I Love Thee	Lor	T Tj
My Joy Is All In Thee (Cantata)	Lps	T Tt
My Joy, My Life, My Crown (Md)	Oxf	T Tr
My Kind Of Music	Prc	L Tx
My Light	Fcc	L Tx
My Light And Salvation (Ps27)	Gra	L Ld

ALPHABETICAL INDEX OF TITLES

Title	Code
My Lips Shall Speak Of Thy Praise (M)	Oxf T Tt
My Little Lamb	Abi L Sc
My Lord	Hal T Tt
My Lord Has Set Me Free	Lor T Sr
My Lord Is Alive	Rpb L Tf
My Lord Is Like A Shepherd	Lor T Tr
My Lord Is Long A Comin'	Fel F Tk
My Lord Is Mighty	Ham G Tk
My Lord Jesus	Sil F Tj
My Lord Said (Come With Me)	Gia F Tc
My Lord Will Come Again	Wlp F Sa
My Lord, My God, My All	Zon L Tc
My Lord, My Love, Is Crucified!	Lor T Sl
My Lord, What A Morning	Gsc G Tx
My Lord, What A Morning	Lor T Sr
My Love For The Lord	Pic L Tr
My Love Song	Man L Tt
My Lover & My Master	Gia F Tj
My Master Hath A Garden	Gsc T Tr
My Master Was So Very Poor	Lor T Tj
My Melody Of Longing	Zon G Sr
My Name Is John	Man G Tx
My Need	Mam G Tx
My Own Way	Wrd G Tc
My Peace, My Joy, My Love	Rpb L Tr
My People	Nal L Sl
My People	Rpb L Sl
My People	Wlp F Tx
My Piano Hymnbook No 2 (No 5735)	Zon G Zb
My Piano Hymnbook No 3 (No 5736)	Zon G Zb
My Redeemer	Lor T Tj
My Redeemer Liveth	Lor T Sr
My Refuge, My Fortress	Fel L Tr
My Religion's Not Old–Fashioned	Ham G Tr
My Reward	Gmp G Tf
My Shepherd	Abi L Tr
My Shepherd	Zon F Tr
My Shepherd I	Nal L Tr
My Shepherd Ii	Nal L Tr
My Shepherd Is The Lord	Wlp L Tf
My Shepherd Is The Lord (Psalm 23)	Ahc L Tr
My Shepherd Will Supply My Need	Gia L Tr
My Shepherd Will Supply My Need	Aug T Tr
My Shepherd Will Supply My Need	Gia T Tr
My Shepherd Will Supply My Need	Zon T Tr
My Shepherd Will Supply My Need	Lor T Tr
My Simple Song	Gra F Tt
My Sins Are Blotted Out, I Know	Zon G Sl
My Sins Are Blotted Out, I Know	Zon G Sl
My Sins Are Gone	Zon G Sl
My Soapbox (No 5617)	Zon F Za
My Son Has Gone Away	Nal L Tr
My Song Is Love Unknown	Sac L Sr
My Song Of Assurance	Man G Tr
My Sons Abel And Cain	Fcc C Tx
My Soul Doth Magnify	Gsc L Tt
My Soul Doth Magnify	Abi L Sa
My Soul Doth Magnify	Gia F Tt
My Soul Doth Magnify The Lord	Gsc T Tt
My Soul Give Thanks	Gia L Tt
My Soul Gives Glory To The Lord	Fel L Tt
My Soul Is Athirst	Fel L Tb
My Soul Is Exceeding Sorrowful	Aug T Sl
My Soul Is Longing For Your Peace	Wlp L Tr
My Soul Is Thirsting (Ps 63)	Rav L Ld
My Soul Is Thirsting For You (Icet)	Wlp L Ld
My Soul Is Waiting For The Lord	Wlp L Sa
My Soul Longeth For Thee	Gsc T Tr
My Soul Longs For You	Fel L Tr
My Soul Longs For Your Salvation	Fel L Sl
My Soul Magnifies The Lord	Nal L Tt
My Soul Thirsteth For God	Lor T Tb
My Soul Thirsts For God (Ps 42)	Gam L Tb
My Soul Thirsts For The Lord	Wlp F Ld
My Soul Thirsts For You, O Lord	Fel L Tr
My Soul Wait Thou Only Upon God	Abi L Tr
My Soul, Praise The Lord (Me)	Oxf T Tt
My Soul, There Is A Country	Oxf L Sr
My Spirit Thirsts	Bbl T Tb
My Spirit Will Not Haunt The Mound	Som L Tf
My Sweet Lord	Mcl F Tj
My Task	Lor L Tc
My Testimony Song	Zon G Tc
My Time Is Come	Bbl T Tf
My Total Life	Ham G Tc
My Trust Is In You, O Lord	Fel L Tr
My Truth And My Mercy Go With Him	Fel L Tc
My Will	Mar L Tx
My Wonderful Jesus	Man G Tj
Mysteries Of The Rosary	Wlp T Tm
Name Of Jesus, The	Bec T Tj
Name Of Jesus, The	Zon G Tj
Nameless Island	Fcc L Tx
Narrow Road	Lor L Tc
Narrow Way, The	Zon G Tc
Nativity, The	Lor L Sc
Nature's Anthem Of Praise	Lor L Tt
Natures Praise Of God	Gsc T Tt
Naught That Country Needeth	Pic L Tp
Nazareth	Gsc T Sc
Near To The Heart Of God	Zon T Tx
Near To The Heart Of God (A Cap)	Wrd G Tr
Near To Thy Heart	Zon T Tx
Nearer To Thee	Sil L Tr
Nearer, Any God, To Thee	Gsc T Tr
Nearer, My God, To Thee	Sac T Tf
Never In A Million Years	Zon G Sl
Never Knew	Mar L Tx
Never Knew The Day	Mar L Sl
Never Shall A Man	Nal L Sl
Never Was A Child So Lovely	Gsc T Sc
New	Zon F Tr
New Commandment, A	Maf L Tr
New Coventry	Gsc T Sc
New Creation, A	Lor T Tb
New Day	Zon G Sr
New Day Dawning	Wlp F Sr
New Hope	Nal C Tr
New Is Old, The	Abi L Tx
New Life	Ahc L Tb
New Life	Chd F Sr
New Life	Nal L Tb
New Life	Rpb L Tb
New Life, The	Lor L Tb
New Plymouth Cantata	Bbl T Za
New Singspiration Sing–A–Long	Zon G Za
New Song	Mar L Tt
New Sounds In Song (No 5665)	Zon G Za
New Tomorrow, A	Zon F Sr
New Way Of Life, A	Sav G Tc
Newborn Baby	Lor L Sc
Newborn, The	Sac T Sc
Newport (From Four Plain–Tunes)	Bbl T Tx
Nicene Creed (Sung Mass No.2)	Fel L Tx
Nicodemus	Van F Tx
Nicodemus (P.D.)	Man F Tx
Night	Van F Tx
Night In The Desert	Gsc T Sl
Night Of Holy Memories	Lor L Sc
Night Of Miracles (No 5976)	Zon L Sc
Night Of Miracles Spanish Edition	Zon L Sc
Night Of Miracles–Dramatization (5921)	Zon L Sc
Night Of The Star	Lor L Sc
Night So Dark And Hour So Late	Zon L Sc
Nightingale Carol	Gsc L Sc
Nine Compositions For Organ	Abi L Zb
Nine Easy Canons	Aug L Za
Nineteen Anthems In Four Vols	Kal T Za
Nineteen Choral Responses	Lor L Za
Nineteen Liturgical Rounds (2 Vols)	Gia L Za
No Cradle Song	Lor L Sc
No Dark Valleys	Man G Sl
No End To God's Love	Gmc G Tr
No Greater Love	Lor L Sr
No Greater Love	Gmc G Tr
No Greater Love	Lor L Tr
No Greater Love (No 5977)	Zon L Sr
No Greater Love (No 5984)	Zon L Sr
No Greater Love (No 5992)	Zon L Sr
No Help	Abi L Sl
No Lonely Day (No 4504)	Zon G Za
No Longer Alone	Van F Sc
No Longer Will I Call You Servants	Gia L Tc
No Man Is An Island	Som L Lo
No More	Man G Tx
No More Death	Zon G Sr
No More Pain	Sem F Tx
No More Sorrow Over There	Mam G Sr
No One But The Lord	Man G Tr
No One But You	Man G Tc
No One Can Ever Be Equal To Jesus	Sto G Tj
No One Lives For Himself	Nal L Tr
No One Understands Like Jesus	Lor L Tj
No Room In The Inn	Gsc T Sc
No Room In The Inn	Lor L Sc
No Room In The Inn	Zon T Sc
No Shadows Yonder	Gsc T Tf
No Shadows Yonder (From Holy City)	Cfs T Sr
No Tears Tomorrow	Zon G Sr
No Time	Zon G Tx
No Time For Jesus	Mar L Tx
No Time Like The Present	Wlp F Tx
No Turning Back	Lor L Tc
No Vacancy	Fel F Sc
Noel	Acp L Sc
Noel	Lor L Sc
Noel	Acp L Sc
Noel (Ox And Donkey's Carol) W/Inst	Aug T Sc
Noel Noel	Gsc T Sc
Noel Noel A Saviour Is Born	Gsc T Sc
Noel Noel Bells Are Ringing	Gsc T Sc
Noel Nouvelet	Aug T Sc
Noel!	Lor T Sc
Noel, A	Her L Sc
Noise Song, The	Nal C Tx
Nolo Mortem Peccatoris (M)	Oxf T Sl
Non Nobis, Domine (Canon)	Oxf T Tt
Non Nobis, Domine (3 Voices)	Gia T Tt
Non Vos Relinquos Orphanos (M)	Oxf T Tr
None Other Lamb	Aug L Sl
None Other Lamb	Sac L Sl
None Other Lamb (No 4271)	Zon T Sr
None Shall Separate Us	Lor L Tr
Norman Johnson Presents Choral Concept	Zon L Za
Northfield	Bbl T Tt
Norwegian Christmas Carol, A	Lor T Sc
Nos Qui Sumus In Hoc Mundo	Gsc T Sl
Not A Sparrow Falleth (Mat 10)	Gia F Tr
Not All Of Those Who Say Lord, Lord	Vrn G Sl
Not Alone For Mighty Empire	Abi L Tt
Not Here For Long	Man G Tf
Not On Bread Alone	Fel L Sl
Not To The Hills	Zon L Tc
Not To Us	Nal L Tt
Not To Us Lord	Fel L Tx
Nothin' Left To Fear	Ccc L Sr
Nothing Between	Zon G Tr
Nothing But Miracles	Lor L Tx
Now Abideth Faith, Hope And Love	Gsc T Tr
Now And Forever	Yan F Tx
Now April Has Come	Gsc T Sr
Now Come To Me	Acp L Tx
Now Come To Me (4–Part Arr)	Acp L Tx
Now Every Child That Dwells	Gia T Sc
Now Glad Of Heart	Gsc T Tt
Now He Is Born	Van F Sc
Now Hear What God Will Give	Acp L Tr
Now I Belong To Jesus	Lor L Tc
Now If Christ Be Preached	Gsc T Sr
Now In Joy We Sing Thy Praises	Wlp T Tt
Now In The Name Of Him	Jsp L Tb
Now Is Christ Risen	Zon T Sr
Now Is Christ Risen (W/Instruments)	Aug L Sr
Now Is Christ Risen Cantata	Zon L Sr
Now Is The Time	Nal L Tx
Now Is The Time Approaching	Jsp T Tu
Now It Is Christmas Time	Aug L Sc
Now Jesus Said	Ahc L Tt
Now Joined By God	Wlp T Tw
Now Let Every Tongue Adore Thee	Hof T Tt
Now Let The Vault Of Heaven Resound	Aug T Tt
Now Praise We Christ, The Holy One	Aug T Tj
Now Praise We Great And Famous Men	Hof T Tx
Now Praise We Great And Famous Men	Sac T Tp
Now Proclaim His Birth In Song	Sac L Sc
Now Quit Your Care	Abi T Sl
Now Sing We All Noel	Sac L Sc
Now Sing We, Now Rejoice	Aug T Tt
Now Sing With Joy	Acp F Tt
Now Sing With Joy (4–Part Arr)	Acp F Tt
Now Sing, All Saints	Zon T Sr
Now Sounds (No 4500)	Zon F Za
Now Sounds (Youth)	Zon G Za
Now Tell Us, Gentle Mary (Instruments)	Aug L Sr
Now Thank We All Our God	Abi T Tt
Now Thank We All Our God	Aug T Tt
Now Thank We All Our God	Hof T Tt
Now Thank We All Our God	Zon T Tt
Now Thank We All Our God	Gia T Tt
Now Thank We All Our God	Lor T Tt
Now Thank We All Our God	Wbp T Tt
Now Thank We All Our God	Gsc T Tt
Now Thank We All Our God	Abi L Zb
Now Thank We All Our God	Abi T Tt
Now Thank We All Our God	Acp L Tt
Now Thank We All Our God	Acp L Tt
Now Thank We All Our God (Mod Diff)	Abi L Zb
Now Thank We All Our God (W/Tpts)	Wlp T Tt
Now The Green Blade Riseth (Arr)	Oxf T Sr
Now The Morning Son Is Here	Acp L Tj
Now We Are Met	Pro L La
Now Will I Praise The Lord	Abi L Tt
Now With The New Year Starting	Smc T Tx
Now You Will Feel No Rain (Wedding)	Sms T Tw
Now, Arise Ye Shepherds Mild	Gsc T Sc
Nox Praecessit	Gsc T Sa
Number One (Prophecy)	Mcc F Tr
Nun Preiset Alle	Flp T Za
Nunc Dimittis	Tcp L Tf
Nunc Dimittis	Hal T Tf
Nunc Dimittis And Gloria (A Cap)	Hof T Tx
Nuptial Blessing	Aug L Tw
Nursery Rhyme	Mar C Tx
O Admirabile Commercium	Kal T Tt
O All Ye Works Of The Lord	Aug L Tt
O Antiphons	Wlp L Sa
O Antiphons	Rpb L Sa
O Be Joyful	Abi L Tr
O Be Joyful	Gsc L Tt
O Be Joyful In The Lord	Sac L Tt
O Be Joyful In The Lord	Her L Tt
O Be Joyful In The Lord	Gsc T Tt
O Be Joyful In The Lord (M)	Oxf T Tt
O Be Joyful In The Lord (Md)	Oxf T Tt
O Be Joyful In The Lord (Ps 100 Me) 1	Oxf T Tt
O Be Joyful In The Lord (Ps 100)	Oxf T Tt
O Be Joyful In The Lord(Jubilate)	Gsc T Tt
O Bless The Lord	Aug L Tt
O Bless The Lord (Ps 103)	Gra L Ld
O Bless The Lord My Soul	Nal L Tt

ALPHABETICAL INDEX OF TITLES

Title	Code
O Bless The Lord, My Soul	Val F Tt
O Blessed Day Of Motherhood	Lor T Tx
O Blessed Jesus	Bbl T Tt
O Blessed Jesus	Som T Tj
O Blessed Lord	Bbl T Tt
O Blessed Lord (Md)	Oxf L Tt
O Bone Jesu	Bbl T Tj
O Bone Jesu	Gsc T Tj
O Bone Jesu (Oh Loving Jesus)	Gsc T Tj
O Bread Of Angels	Wlp T Lo
O Bread Of Angels	Gia T Lo
O Bread Of Life	Aug L Ln
O Bread Of Life	Wlp L Lo
O Breath Of Life	Zon T Ss
O Brother Man	Smc L Tr
O Brother Man	Wlp T Tp
O Brother Man	Lor G Tr
O Brother Man (E)	Oxf T Tr
O Brother Man!	Lor G Tr
O Cast Me Not Away(2nd Mov't)	Gsc T Sl
O Christ Our King	Acp L Tk
O Christ Our King (4-Part Arr)	Acp L Tk
O Christ Who Holds The Open Gate	Gsc T Tj
O Christ Your Church Is Waiting Still	Acp L Sa
O Christ Your Church Is Waiting Still	Acp L Sa
O Christ, Eternal King	Gia L Tj
O Christ, I Look To Thee	Sac L Tj
O Christ, Our Hope	Aug L Tj
O Christ, Who Art The Light & Day (M)	Oxf T Sl
O Christ, Why Should A Manger Be?	Lor L Sc
O Christians Let Us Join In Song	Wlp L Tt
O Clap For Joy!	Maf L Tt
O Clap Your Hands	Sac L Tt
O Clap Your Hands	Aug L Tt
O Clap Your Hands (Ps 47)	Oxf T Sr
O Clap Your Hands (Ps 47)	Oxf T Sr
O Clap Your Hands (With Doxology) (Md)	Oxf T Sr
O Come All Ye Faithful (W/Org, Tpt)	Aug T Sc
O Come And Dwell In Me	Gsc L Lo
O Come And Mourn	Gsc L Sl
O Come And Mourn	Smc T Sl
O Come And Mourn With Me	Lor T Sl
O Come And Mourn With Me Awhile	Aug T Sl
O Come Emmanuel	Gsc T Sa
O Come Let Us Sing	Bec T Tt
O Come Let Us Sing	Sac L La
O Come Let Us Sing Unto The Lord	Bbl T Tt
O Come To My Heart (No 6010) Cantata	Zon T Sc
O Come Ye To The Cross	Abi T Sl
O Come, All Ye Children	Aug L La
O Come, All Ye Faithful	Bec T Sc
O Come, All Ye Faithful	Lor T Sc
O Come, All Ye Faithful	Gsc T Sc
O Come, All Ye Faithful	Acp F Sc
O Come, All Ye Faithful	Lor T Sc
O Come, All Ye Faithful	Zon T Sc
O Come, All Ye Faithful (4 Part Arr)	Acp F Sc
O Come, Emmanuel (Ancient Hymn)	Lor T Sa
O Come, Emmanuel (E)	Oxf L Sa
O Come, Good Spirit	Lit L Tb
O Come, Holy Spirit(W/Contin & Violin)	Aug L Ss
O Come, Let Us Sing	Sac L La
O Come, Let Us Sing	Pro T Tt
O Come, Let Us Sing	Zon L Tt
O Come, Let Us Sing To The Lord	Gia L La
O Come, Let Us Sing Unto The Lord	Oxf L La
O Come, Let Us Worship	Gsc T La
O Come, Loud Anthems Let Us Sing	Lor T Tt
O Come, O Come Emmanuel	Aug T Sa
O Come, O Come Emmanuel	Maf L Sa
O Come, O Come Emmanuel	Acp L Sa
O Come, O Come Emmanuel	Acp L Sa
O Come, O Come Immanuel	Zon T Sa
O Cross Thou Only Hope	Bbl T Sl
O Crux Ave	Bbl T Sl
O Crux Ave, Spes Unica	Bbl T Sl
O Day Full Of Grace	Aug L Tx
O Day Full Of Grace	Aug L Tx
O Day Full Of Grace	Aug L Tx
O Day Full Of Grace (W/String Bass)	Aug L Tx
O Day Of God, Draw Nigh	Sac T Tk
O Day Of Rest And Gladness	Zon T Lp
O Dearest Lord	Abi L Sl
O Dearest Lord, Thy Sacred Head	Aug T Sl
O Death, Rock Me Asleep	Som L Tf
O Deepest Woe	Sac T Sl
O Divine Redeemer	Lor T Tj
O Divine Redeemer	Gsc T Tj
O Domine	Bbl T Tt
O Domine Jesu Christe	Gsc T Tj
O Dove Of Peace (Not H.Sp.)	Pro T Tr
O Ever Radiant Virgin	Wlp L Tm
O Faithful Cross	Gia L Sl
O Faithful Cross (A Cap) (E)	Gia L Sl
O Father Blest	Fel T Tr
O Father Thou Whose Hand	Wlp T Tt
O Fear The Lord, Ye His Saints	Aug L Tr
O Food Of Men Wayfaring	Pro L Lo
O Food We Pilgrims Pray For	Gia T Ln
O For A Closer Walk With God	Abi L Tr
O For A Faith That Will Not Shrink	Abi L Tr
O For A Thousand Tongues	Zon T Tt
O For A Thousand Tongues	Lor T Tt
O For A Thousand Tongues	Sac T Tt
O For A Thousand Tongues To Sing	Lor T Tt
O For A Thousand Tongues To Sing	Wrd G Tt
O For A Thousand Tongues To Sing	Lor T Tt
O For A Thousand Tongues To Sing	Som L Tt
O For Closer Walk With God	Smc T Tr
O For The Wings Of A Dove	Gsc T Sl
O Give Me A Soapbox	Zon F Tc
O Give Thanks	Lor T Tt
O Give Thanks	Bfi F Tt
O Give Thanks	Sac T Tt
O Give Thanks	Lor T Tt
O Give Thanks To The Lord	Aug L Tt
O Give Thanks Unto The Lord	Lor F Tt
O Give Thanks Unto The Lord (Ps 105)	Oxf T Tt
O Glorify The Lord	Ahc L Tt
O Glorious Love	Zon G Tr
O Glorious Night	Gia L Sc
O Glorious Resurrection Day	Zon L Sr
O God All Knowing & All Just	Wlp T Tr
O God Be Merciful	Oxf T Tr
O God Enfold Me In The Sun (Md)	Oxf T Tr
O God From Whom Mankind Derives	Jsp L Tw
O God My God From The Dawn	Wlp T Tr
O God O Lord	Aug L Tt
O God Of All Above, Below	Abi L Tr
O God Of All Beauty	Abi L Tr
O God Of All, We Thank You	Sac L Tt
O God Of Consolation (Choral)	Fel T Tr
O God Of Earth And Altar	Acp L To
O God Of Earth And Altar (4 Part Arr)	Acp L To
O God Of Every Race And Creed	Gsc T Tu
O God Of Love	Aug L Tr
O God Of Love	Abi L Tr
O God Of Love To Thee We Bow Low	Abi L Tw
O God Of Love, O King Of Peace	Sms T Tr
O God Of Peace	Lor T Tr
O God Of The Quiet Spirit	Lor L Tr
O God Of Truth	Bec T Tt
O God Our Help	Acp L Tt
O God Our Help	Acp L Tt
O God Our Help In Ages Past	Aug T La
O God Our Help In Ages Past	Gam T La
O God Our Refuge & Our Strength	Wlp T Tr
O God The Father, Eternal One	Aug T Tt
O God The King Of Glory (Md)	Oxf T Tx
O God Upholding These U.S.	Wlp T Tp
O God Who Called The Hebrews	Wlp T Sl
O God, Beneath Thy Guiding Hand	Gsc T Tr
O God, From Everlasting You Are	Fel L Tt
O God, Have Mercy And Bless Us	Fel L Sl
O God, Hear My Prayer, Deliver Me	Fel L Sl
O God, How Wonderful Thou Art	Smc T Tt
O God, O Lord Of Heaven And Earth	Aug L Tt
O God, O Son Of God	Prc L Tx
O God, Our Help In Ages Past	Aug T La
O God, Our Help In Ages Past	Zon T Tr
O God, Our Help In Ages Past	Lor T Tr
O God, Our Help In Ages Past	Lor T Tr
O God, Our Help In Ages Past	Her T Tr
O God, Our Help In Ages Past (Brass)	Elv T La
O God, Pity Us (Ps67)	Gra L Ld
O God, Please Rescue Me	Fel L Sl
O God, Save Me With Your Name	Gra L Ld
O God, The King Of Glory	Gsc T Tt
O God, The Rock Of Ages	Aug T Tx
O God, Thou Art My God	Smc T Tb
O God, Thou Faithful God	Abi L Zb
O God, Thou Hast The Dawn Of Life	Lor L Sr
O God, Thy Hands The Heavens Made	Lor T Tt
O God, Who By The Leading Of A Star	Oxf L Sc
O God, Who Live Forever	Fel T Tt
O God, Whose Presence Glows In All	Abi L Tt
O God, Wonderful Art Thou	Oxf L Tt
O God, You Are My God	Fel L Tr
O God, You Have Rejected Us	Fel L Sl
O Gracious King	Lor T Tk
O Gracious Lord	Nal L Tt
O Great Doctor, Blessed	Fel L Tx
O Hail Sacred Cross	Bbl T Sl
O Hail, Mary	Bbl T Tm
O Happy Day	Uam G Tx
O Happy Day	Zon G Tb
O Happy Home	Lor T Tx
O Happy Man	Gsc T Tx
O Hear We Lord God	Gsc T Tr
O Heart Of Christ	Wlp T Tj
O Holy Banquet	Gia L Lo
O Holy Child	Aug L Sc
O Holy Father	Abi L Tr
O Holy God, O Holy Might God	Fel L Tr
O Holy Jesu	Gsc T Tj
O Holy Lord	Gsc T Tt
O Holy Savior	Zon T Tj
O Holy Spirit Come To Us	Wlp T Ss
O Holy Spirit Of God	Abi L Ss
O Holy Spirit Sent From Heaven	Gsc L Ss
O Holy Spirit, Come To Us	Fel L Ss
O How Amiable (Me)	Oxf T Tc
O How Amiable (Ps 84)	Oxf T Tc
O How Amiable (Ps 84) (Md)	Oxf T Tr
O How Amiable Are Thy Dwellings	Gsc T Tr
O How Beautiful The Sky	Aug L Tr
O How Blessed Is This Place	Aug L Tc
O How Great Is The Lord Of All	Pro T Tt
O How Happy Are They Who The Savior	Lor T Tc
O How I Love Jesus	Zon G Tj
O How Lovely Are Your Dwellings	Gia T Tr
O How Shall I Receive Thee	Gia L Sa
O I Would Sing Of Mary's Child	Aug L Sc
O Jesu Mi Dulcissime	Gsc T Tj
O Jesu, Look	Oxf T Sl
O Jesus Christ, To Thee May Hymns	Aug T Tj
O Jesus King Of Gentleness	Gsc L Tk
O Jesus, King Most Wonderful	Aug T Tk
O Jesus, King Of Gentleness	Gsc T Tj
O Jesus, Thou Are Standing	Gsc T Tj
O Jesus, Thou Art Standing	Lor L Tj
O Jesus, Thou Son Of God	Maf T Tj
O Joseph, Mighty Patron	Jsp T Tx
O Joyful Day Of Our Salvation (Cant)	Lps T Sr
O Joyful Day! (Christmas Motet)	Gsc T Sc
O King Of Might & Splendor	Wlp T To
O King Of Might & Splendor	Gia T To
O King Of Might And Splendor	Gia T To
O Lamb Of God	Abi T Lo
O Lamb Of God	Gia F Lm
O Lamb Of God	Gsc T Lm
O Lamb Of God	Gsc T Lm
O Lamb Of God	Abi L Lo
O Lamb Of God	Yan F Lm
O Lamb Of God (Agnus Dei)	Fel L Lm
O Lamb Of God Most Holy	Gsc T Tj
O Let Me Fly	Lor L Tr
O Let Me Tread In The Right Path (Me)	Oxf T Sl
O Let's Get On	Prc L Tx
O Light From Age To Age The Same	Oxf T Tt
O Listen, Brother	Abi F Sc
O Little One Sweet	Gsc T Sc
O Little Town Of Bethlehem	Gsc T Sc
O Little Town Of Bethlehem	Zon T Sc
O Little Town Of Bethlehem	Lor T Sc
O Little Town Of Bethlehem (Easy)	Zon T Sc
O Living Water	Sha F Ss
O Look To Golgotha	Aug T Sl
O Lord	Wlp F Tr
O Lord Amen	Mar L Tc
O Lord And Master Of Us All	Lor T Tt
O Lord Be Not Mindful	Wlp L Sl
O Lord From Whom All Good Things Come	Oxf T Tt
O Lord Give Us Light	Wlp F Tr
O Lord Give Us Your Love	Wlp L Tr
O Lord God Of My Salvation	Bbl T Tr
O Lord God Of My Salvation	Gsc T Sl
O Lord Have Mercy	Wlp L Sl
O Lord Hear Us Pray	Wlp L Tr
O Lord How Great Is Your Name	Wlp F Tt
O Lord How Manifold	Gsc T Tt
O Lord In Thy Wrath (Md)	Oxf T Sl
O Lord Most High, With All My Heart	Gia T To
O Lord Most High, With All My Heart	Gia T Tt
O Lord My God	Gsc T Tt
O Lord Of Hosts	Som T Tt
O Lord Of Hosts	Fel L Tt
O Lord Of Hosts, Restore Us	Fel L Tr
O Lord Of Life	Sac L Tr
O Lord Of Life (M)	Oxf L Tr
O Lord Of Life (Who Wills New Life)	Jsp L Tb
O Lord Of Light	Wlp T Tx
O Lord Our Governor	Gsc T Tk
O Lord Support Us All The Day Long	Abi L Tt
O Lord Who Drew From Jesus' Side	Wlp T Tj
O Lord With Wondrous Mystery	Wlp T Lo
O Lord You Know Our Weakness	Wlp T Sl
O Lord, Be Kind To Me	Fel L Tr
O Lord, Do Not Be Far From Me	Fel L Sl
O Lord, Do Not Deal With Us	Fel L Sl
O Lord, From Everlasting	Fel L Tt
O Lord, Give Him Eternal Life	Fel L Tf
O Lord, Give Thy Holy Spirit (Me)	Oxf T Ss
O Lord, Have Mercy On Me	Gsc G Tx
O Lord, Hear My Prayer	Fel L Tr
O Lord, How Good It Is To Be Here	Fel L La
O Lord, How Numerous Are My Foes	Bbl T Sl
O Lord, I Am In Awe Of Your Power	Fel L Tt
O Lord, I Am Unworthy	Fel L Lo
O Lord, I Bow The Knee Of My Heart	Bbl T Tt
O Lord, I Will Praise Thee (E)	Oxf T Tt
O Lord, Jesus Christ	Som T Tj
O Lord, Let My Enemies See	Fel L Sl
O Lord, Look On The Face	Fel L Tr
O Lord, My Heart Is Not Proud	Fel L Tr
O Lord, My Trust Is In Thy Mercy	Gsc T Sl
O Lord, Open Thou Our Lips (M)	Abi T Tt
O Lord, Our God	Abi L Tt

Title			
O Lord, Our Lord	Lor	T	Tt
O Lord, Our Lord, How Wonderful	Fel	L	Tt
O Lord, Shield Of Our Help	Lor	L	Tr
O Lord, Show Mercy To The Sick	Fel	L	Tx
O Lord, Support Us	Sac	L	Tt
O Lord, The Hope Of Israel	Gsc	L	Tr
O Lord, The Maker Of All Things (Me)	Oxf	T	Tt
O Lord, Thou Art My God And King	Aug	T	Tk
O Lord, Thou Hast Searched Me	Abi	L	Tc
O Lord, Who Shall Dwell	Fel	L	Tx
O Lord, You Know Who I Am	Fel	F	Tt
O Lord, You Made The Rainbow	Lor	T	Tt
O Love Of God	Lor	L	Tr
O Love Of God, Most Full	Lor	T	Tr
O Love That Triumphs Over Loss (A Cap)	Abi	L	Sl
O Love That Wilt Not Let Me Go	Gsc	T	Tr
O Love That Wilt Not Let Me Go	Zon	T	Tr
O Love, How Deep	Sac	L	Tr
O Love, How Deep	Lor	L	Tr
O Love, How Deep	Lor	L	Tr
O Love, How Deep (Opt Tpt)	Aug	T	Tr
O Lovely Son Of God	Gsc	T	Sc
O Loving Jesus	Gia	T	Sl
O Magnum Mysterium	Gsc	T	Sc
O Magnum Mysterium	Gsc	T	Sc
O Man, Rejoice	Abi	L	Sc
O Man, You Have Been Told	Fel	F	Tr
O Maria Mater Gratiae	Gsc	T	Tm
O Mary Don't You Weep	Gia	G	Tm
O Mary Of All Women	Wlp	T	Tm
O Master Let Me Walk With Thee	Gsc	T	Tj
O Master, Let Me Walk With Thee	Lor	T	Tc
O Master, Let Me Walk With Thee	Gsc	T	Tc
O Men Of God, Be Strong!	Sac	L	Tr
O Mighty God, When I Behold The Wonder	Zon	T	Tt
O Most Holy One And Only	Gia	L	Tt
O Most Loving Father (Unacc)	Abi	L	Tr
O My Achin Rib(Adams Complaint)	Sbf	F	Tx
O My God It Is You I Seek	Wlp	L	Tr
O My Lord	Fel	F	Tr
O My Lord	Wlp	F	Tr
O My Saints	Fel	T	Tr
O Nata Lux De Lumine	Gsc	T	Sc
O Nata Lux De Lumine (Lat & Eng)	Gsc	T	Sc
O Nata Lux De Lumine (Me)	Oxf	T	Tt
O Newborn Child	Abi	L	Sc
O Night Of Holy Memory	Lor	T	Sc
O Not To Us, Good Lord (Opt Flute)	Aug	T	Tt
O One With God, The Father	Gsc	T	Tr
O Perfect Love	Gsc	T	Tw
O Perfect Love	Aug	L	Tr
O Praise God (Ps 150)	Oxf	L	Tt
O Praise God In His Holiness (M)	Oxf	T	Tt
O Praise God In His Holiness (Md)	Oxf	T	Tt
O Praise God In His Holiness (Md)	Oxf	T	Tt
O Praise God In His Holiness (Ps 150)	Oxf	T	Tt
O Praise The Lord	Sac	L	Tt
O Praise The Lord	Gia	L	Tt
O Praise The Lord	Abi	L	Tt
O Praise The Lord (Me)	Oxf	T	Tt
O Praise The Lord (W/Brass,Org)	Wlp	L	Tt
O Praise The Lord All Ye Heathen (Md)	Oxf	T	Tt
O Praise The Lord All Ye Nations	Aug	T	Tt
O Praise The Lord All Ye Nations	Abi	T	Tt
O Praise The Lord Of Harvest	Aug	T	Tt
O Praise The Lord Of Heaven	Bbl	T	Tt
O Praise The Name Of The Lord	Sac	T	Tt
O Pray For The Peace Of Jerusalem	Oxf	T	Tr
O Pray For The Peace Of Jerusalem	Bbl	T	Tr
O Pray For The Peace Of Jerusalem (M)	Oxf	T	Tr
O Quam Gloriosum	Gsc	T	Tm
O Quam Gloriosum Est Regnum	Kal	T	Tk
O Queen Of Heaven	Bbl	T	Tm
O Queen Of Heaven	Wlp	T	Tm
O Redeemer Divine	Bbl	T	Tj
O Rejoice In The Lord	Pro	T	Tr
O Rejoice Ye Christians Loudly	Gsc	T	Sc
O Rest In The Lord	Gsc	T	Tt
O Rex Gloriae	Oxf	T	Tk
O Sacrament Most Holy (Music)	Wlp	T	Lo
O Sacred Feast (Eng Only)	Gia	T	Lo
O Sacred Head	Aug	T	Sl
O Sacred Head	Lor	T	Sl
O Sacred Head Now Wounded	Gsc	T	Sl
O Sacred Head Surrounded	Wlp	T	Sl
O Sacred Head, Now Wounded	Zon	T	Sl
O Sacrum Convivium	Maf	T	Lo
O Sacrum Convivium (Md)	Oxf	T	Lo
O Sacrum Convivium (Me)	Oxf	T	Lo
O Salutaris Hostia	Bbl	T	Lo
O Salutaris Hostia (Md)	Oxf	T	Lo
O Sanctissima	Gsc	T	Tm
O Sapientia!	Gsc	T	Tt
O Satisfy Us Early With Thy Mercy	Abi	L	Tr
O Savior Our Refuge	Gsc	T	Sl
O Savior, Precious Savior	Smc	T	Tj
O Savior, Throw The Heavens Wide	Gsc	T	Tj
O Saviour Of The World(A Cap)	Gsc	T	Tj
O Shepherd Of Israel	Gsc	T	Tr
O Shepherds	Aug	L	Sc
O Sing A New Song	Sac	L	Tt
O Sing All Ye Lands	Aug	L	Tt
O Sing Joyfully	Oxf	T	Tt
O Sing The Glories Of Our Lord (Me)	Oxf	L	Tt
O Sing To God With Joy	Wlp	T	Tt
O Sing Unto The Lord	Abi	L	Tt
O Sing Unto The Lord	Gsc	T	Tt
O Sing Unto The Lord	Som	T	Tt
O Sing Unto The Lord (M)	Oxf	T	Tt
O Sing Unto The Lord A New Song	Gsc	T	Tt
O Sing Unto The Lord A New Song	Lor	T	Tt
O Sing Unto The Lord A New Song	Cfp	T	Tt
O Sing Ye To The Lord	Gsc	T	Tt
O Sleep, My Fairest One	Lor	L	Sc
O Son Of Man	Wlp	T	Tx
O Sons And Daughters	Gsc	L	Ss
O Spirit, Who From Jesus Came	Gsc	L	Ss
O Spotless Lamb	Aug	T	Sl
O Star Of Bethlehem	Hal	L	Sc
O Sweet Jesus	Wgm	F	Sl
O Take My Hand, Lord	Lor	L	Tr
O Tannenbaum	Gsc	T	Sc
O Taste And See	Gsc	T	Lo
O Taste And See	Lor	L	Lo
O Taste And See (From 5 Anthems)	Gia	L	Lo
O Taste And See (Ps 34)	Oxf	T	Ln
O Thank The Lord	Rpb	L	Tt
O That I Had A Thousand Voices	Aug	T	Tt
O The Deep, Deep Love Of Jesus	Lor	L	Tj
O Thou Eternal Christ, Ride On!	Abi	L	Tk
O Thou In All Thy Might So Far	Sac	L	Tt
O Thou In Whose Presence	Wrd	L	Tr
O Thou Most High	Gsc	T	Tt
O Thou That Art The Light Eternal	Gsc	T	Tj
O Thou That Tellest	Gsc	T	Sa
O Thou That Tellest Good Tidings	Lor	T	Sc
O Thou To Whose All-Searching Sight	Abi	L	Sl
O Thou, From Whom All Goodness Flows	Gsc	L	Tr
O Thou, In Whose Presence	Gsc	T	Tt
O Thou, In Whose Presence	Zon	T	Tt
O Thou, The True And Only Light	Gsc	T	Tt
O Thou, To Whom In Ancient Time	Gsc	T	Tt
O To Be Like Thee	Lor	T	Sl
O Trinity Of Blessed Light	Abi	L	Tr
O Turn Away Mine Eyes (Md)	Oxf	T	Tr
O Virgin Mother, He Whom The World	Fel	L	Tm
O Virgin's Son	Fel	L	Tj
O Vos Omnes	Gsc	T	Sl
O Vos Omnes	Gsc	T	Sl
O Vos Omnes	Gsc	T	Sl
O Vos Omnes (Accompanied)	Elv	T	Sl
O Vos Omnes (Come Ye People)	Gsc	T	Sl
O Vos Omnes (Lam 1, V. 12) (Md)	Oxf	T	Sl
O Vos Omnes (M)	Oxf	T	Sl
O Welcome Light (Cantata)	Lps	T	Sa
O Welt, Ich Muss Dich Lassen	Gsc	T	Tf
O What A Happening	Van	F	Sc
O Where Are Kings And Empires Now	Abi	L	Sr
O Wonder Of This Christman Night	Gsc	L	Sc
O Wondrous Life	Zon	G	Tj
O Wondrous Type	Oxf	T	Tt
O World I Must Be Parting (E&Ger)	Gsc	T	Tf
O Worship The King	Gsc	T	Tt
O Worship The King	Zon	T	Tt
O Worship The King	Gsc	T	Tt
O Worship The King (Me)	Abi	T	Tk
O Ye Little Flock (Md)	Oxf	L	Tt
O Ye People	Gsc	T	Tx
O Ye Who Taste That Love Is Sweet	Abi	L	Tw
O, How Amiable	Gsc	T	Tc
O, Let Him In	Fel	F	Tj
O, Praise The Lord	Fel	F	Tt
O, To Be Like Thee	Gmc	G	Tc
O'er Bethlehem A Star (Polish Carol)	Pro	T	Sc
Obituary Of Mrs. Prayer Meeting	Pmp	G	Tf
Of God I Sing	Ham	G	Tt
Of Man's Mortalitie	Pic	L	Tr
Of My Hands	Fel	F	To
Of One That Is So Fair And Bright	Gsc	T	Sc
Of The Father's Love Begotten	Gsc	T	Sc
Of The Father's Love Begotten	Bec	T	Sc
Of The Glorious Body Telling	Oxf	T	Lo
Of The Glorious Body Telling	Aug	T	Lo
Of The Kindness Of The Lord	Aug	L	Tr
Of Your Love	Yan	F	Tr
Offer To God Praise As Your Sacrifice	Fel	F	To
Offer Unto God	Aug	L	To
Offering	Rpb	L	To
Offertorium, Salve Regina	Kal	T	Tm
Often They Fought Me	Fel	L	Sl
Oh Come And Mourn With Us	Wbp	T	Sl
Oh For A Shout Of Joy	Gia	T	Tt
Oh How He Loves You And Me	Wrd	G	Tr
Oh Jerusalem	Pro	L	Tr
Oh John	Gsc	G	Tx
Oh Lord, I Long To See Your Face	Sms	F	Tr
Oh That I Knew	Man	L	Tr
Oh, Bless The Lord, My Soul	Fel	L	Tt
Oh, Freedom!	Gsc	G	Tx
Oh, He's A Wonderful Savior	Zon	G	Sl
Oh, How I Love Jesus	Nal	C	Tj
Oh, It's Good	Nal	L	Tr
Oh, Let Me Walk With Thee	Man	G	Lp
Oh, Little Child Of Bethlehem	Gsc	T	Sc
Oh, Lord, Make Me An Instrument	Mca	T	Tr
Oh, Senora (Blessed Lady)	Pic	T	Tm
Oh, That Out Of Zion	Fel	L	Sl
Oh, Yes, Lord Jesus Lives	Nal	C	Sr
Ol' Brother Jonah	Gmc	G	Tx
Old Ark's A-Moverin'	Gsc	G	Tx
Old Book And The Old Faith, The	Zon	G	Sl
Old Fashioned Sermons	Zon	G	Tx
Old Gray Ford	Mar	L	Tx
Old Irish Blessing	Wbp	T	Tx
Old Jordan	Lor	G	Tx
Old Netherlands Motets	Kal	T	Za
Old Rugged Cross, The	Lor	T	Sl
Old-Fashioned Meeting, The	Zon	G	Tx
Old-Time Religion, The	Zon	G	Tr
Olive Tree Lullaby	Gsc	L	Sc
Omnes Amici Mei Dereliquerunt Me	Gsc	T	Sl
Omnes De Saba Venient	Oxf	T	Sc
Omnes Gentes	Gia	T	Tt
Omnes Gentes, Plaudite	Sac	L	Tt
Omnipresence	Abi	L	Tr
On A Day When Men Were Counted	Sac	L	Sc
On A Morning Long Ago	Gsc	T	Sc
On A Pallet Of Straw	Ron	T	Sc
On A Rugged Hill	Zon	T	Sl
On All The Earth Thy Spirit Pour	Gia	T	Ss
On And On	Man	G	Tc
On Belief	Zon	F	Tr
On Calvary's Hill	Aug	T	Sl
On Christmas Night	Abi	L	Sc
On Christmas Night, We Laud & Sing	Pro	T	Sc
On Easter Morn	Gsc	T	Sr
On His Might	Abi	L	Tt
On Jordan's Stormy Banks	Lor	L	Sa
On That First Bright Easter Day	Gsc	C	Sr
On The Cross	Zon	G	Sl
On The Day When The Radiant Star	Wlp	T	Tf
On The Land And On The Sea	Bbl	T	Tx
On The Mount Of Olive Groves	Van	F	Sl
On The Mount Of Olives (E & Lat)	Gia	T	Sl
On The Mountainside	Aug	L	Tx
On The Other Side Of Time	Lor	T	Tf
On The Road	Rpb	F	Tx
On The Way To Bethlehem	Sac	T	Sc
On The Way To Jerusalem	Lor	T	Sl
On The Way To Jerusalem	Gsc	T	Sl
On The Way To The Mountain	Fcc	L	Lp
On The Willows	Val	F	Sl
On The Wood His Arms Are Stretched	Aug	T	Sl
On This Blessed Easter Day	Lor	L	Sr
On This Day Of Glory (W/3 Tpts)	Aug	T	Sr
On This Fair Night The Angels Sing(Me)	Gia	T	Sc
On Wings Of Living Light (W/Tpt)	Aug	T	Tx
On Your Own	Mar	L	Tx
Once A Fair Maiden	Gsc	T	Sc
Once Blind	Sil	L	Tr
Once I Had A Dream	Mar	L	Tx
Once I Sang	Gsc	T	Tt
Once In Royal David's City	Sac	T	Sc
Once In Royal David's City	Lor	T	Sc
Once In Royal David's City	Gsc	T	Sc
Once In Royal David's City	Aug	L	Sc
Once To Every Man And Nation	Gsc	T	Tp
One Above All Others	Gsc	T	Sc
One Big Happy Family	Hhh	G	Tt
One Bread, One Body Are We.	Vrn	G	Lo
One Day Nearer Home	Ham	G	Sr
One Day Soon	Sil	F	Tr
One Faith	Nal	L	Tr
One From Among Us	Fel	F	Tx
One Gentle, One Wild	Fcc	C	Tx
One God	Lor	T	Tx
One Hundred Favorite Songs	Wrd	G	Za
One Hundred Sacred Favorites (No 5661)	Zon	T	Za
One Hundred Songs You Love	Wrd	G	Za
One Hundredth Psalm, The	Sac	T	La
One In Joyful Songs Of Praise	Wlp	T	Tt
One More Day	Nal	L	Tx
One Night So Long Ago	Maf	T	Sc
One O'er All The Earth	Abi	L	Lo
One Of The Soldiers	Fel	L	Sl
One Small Child	Lor	F	Sc
One Star	Lor	T	Sc
One Step Beyond	Pmp	G	Sr
One Sweetly Solemn Thought	Gsc	T	Tx
One Tender Moment	Man	G	Tr
One There Is Above All Others	Smc	T	Sl
One Thing Have I Desired Of The Lord	Bbl	T	Tr
One Thing I Ask Of The Lord	Fel	L	Tc
One Thing I Ask Of The Lord	Maf	T	Tr
One Way	Man	G	Tj
One Way	Lor	T	Tj
One Way	Man	G	Tj
One Who Seeks, The	Fcc	L	Tx
One, Two, Three, Jesus Loves Me	Mar	L	Tj

Title			
Only	Sav	G	Tx
Only A Shadow	Nal	L	Tx
Only Begotten, Word Of God Eternal	Aug	L	Tj
Only God	Man	G	Tr
Only In God Is My Soul At Rest	Fel	L	Tx
Only In The Midst Of The World	Ccc	L	La
Only One Life	Zon	G	Tc
Only These Two	Wlp	F	Tx
Only Trust Him	Zon	G	Tr
Onward Ye Saints	Aug	T	Tr
Onward, Christian Soldiers	Lor	T	Tc
Onward, Christian Soldiers	Lor	T	Tc
Onward, Christian Soldiers	Lor	T	Tc
Onward, Christian Soldiers	Lor	T	Tc
Onward,Christian Soldiers	Zon	T	Tc
Open Like The Sky	Ahc	L	Tx
Open My Eyes	Lor	T	Tb
Open My Eyes	Lor	T	Tb
Open My Eyes, That I May See	Lor	T	Tb
Open My Heart (Me)	Oxf	T	Tr
Open Now Thy Gates Of Beauty	Sac	T	La
Open Our Eyes	Gsc	T	Tr
Open The Door	Gia	L	Tt
Open The Gates Of Justice	Fel	L	La
Open The Gates Of The Temple	Lor	T	Sr
Open The Gates Of The Temple	Zon	T	La
Open Up	Nal	L	Tx
Open Up	Fel	F	Tx
Open Up Your Door	Sil	L	Tr
Open Up Your Heart	Ham	C	Tx
Open Up Your Heart(W/Guitar)	Gia	F	Sc
Open Your Eyes	Fel	L	Tx
Open Your Heart	Nal	L	Tr
Oppression Shall Not Always Reign	Abi	T	Tx
Ora Pro Nobis	Bbl	T	Tm
Organ Offertories From The Baroque Era	Abi	L	Zb
Organ Rarities, Volume I	Abi	L	Zb
Organ Solos (No 5801)	Zon	T	Zb
Organ Specials By Merrill Dunlop(5257)	Zon	G	Zb
Organbook (Orgelbuchlein)	Kal	T	Zb
Os Justi (The Just Mouth)	Gsc	T	Sl
Osee (Hosea)	Fel	F	Tx
Ou Sen Vont Ces Gais Bergers	Gsc	T	Sc
Our Blest Redeemer (Trad Irish Tune)	Oxf	T	Tj
Our Church Proclaims God's Love And	Abi	T	Tx
Our Day Of Praise Is Done (E)	Oxf	L	Tr
Our Days Are As A Shadow	Kal	T	Sl
Our Eyes Are On You, O Lord	Fel	L	Sl
Our Father	Ahc	L	Ll
Our Father	Wlp	L	Ll
Our Father	Rpb	L	Ll
Our Father	Fel	L	Ll
Our Father	Nal	L	Ll
Our Father	Nal	L	Ll
Our Father	Acp	L	Ll
Our Father	Acp	L	Ll
Our Father	Rpb	L	Ll
Our Father	Wlp	F	Ll
Our Father	Rpb	L	Ll
Our Father	Wlp	F	Ll
Our Father	Nal	L	Ll
Our Father	Bbl	T	Ll
Our Father	Fel	L	Ll
Our Father	Ahc	L	Ll
Our Father	Sbf	L	Ll
Our Father	Gsc	T	Ll
Our Father	Van	F	Ll
Our Father	Van	F	Ll
Our Father	Wlp	L	Ll
Our Father	Yan	F	Ll
Our Father	Nal	L	Ll
Our Father (Icet)	Wlp	L	Ll
Our Father (Organ + Guitar)	Gia	L	Ll
Our Father (Unison Or Choral)	Fel	L	Ll
Our Father In Heaven	Rpb	L	Ll
Our Father Thou In Heaven Above	Gsc	T	Ll
Our Father(D Maj)	Rav	L	Ll
Our Father(E Maj)	Rav	L	Ll
Our Father, By Whose Name	Aug	T	Tt
Our Father, By Whose Name	Abi	L	Tw
Our Father, The Lords Prayer	Ahc	L	Ll
Our Father's Care	Lor	T	Ll
Our God Is A God Of Love	Nal	C	Tr
Our God Is Great (Swedish)	Lor	T	Tt
Our God Is King (Notre Diev Est Roi)	Pic	L	Tt
Our God Provides	Nal	L	Tr
Our Help	Nal	L	Tr
Our Hymn Of Praise	Hof	T	Tt
Our Lady's Song Of Praise	Jsp	T	Tt
Our Lord Did Suffer Death	Sac	T	Sl
Our Lord Is Risen	Sac	L	Sr
Our Sacrifice Of Praise	Zon	G	To
Our Soul Has Been Resuced	Fel	L	Sl
Our Star Of Faith (The Prayer Of Love)	Pic	L	Tx
Our Thanks To Thee	Zon	G	Tt
Our Time Is Now	Fel	F	Tx
Out Of Darkness (Cantata On Ps 130)	Kal	T	Sl
Out Of The Deep (D)	Oxf	L	Sl
Out Of The Deep (M)	Oxf	T	Sl
Out Of The Depths	Sac	L	Sl
Out Of The Depths	Acp	L	Sl
Out Of The Depths	Acp	L	Sl
Out Of The Depths	Maf	T	Sl
Out Of The Depths (A Cap)	Hal	T	Sl
Out Of The Depths (From Come Follow)	Gia	F	Sl
Out Of The Depths (2 Voices)	Gia	T	Sl
Out Of The Depths I Cry (Ps 129)	Wlp	T	Sl
Out Of The Depths I Cry To Thee	Gsc	T	Sl
Out Of The Depths I Cry To Thee	Gsc	T	Sl
Out Of The Depths I Cry To You	Fel	L	Sl
Out Of The Depths We Cry, Lord	Aug	T	Sl
Out Of Your Sleep Arise And Wake	Gsc	L	Sc
Outcry Amen	Prc	L	Tx
Over The Hills (Uber's Gebirg)	Gsc	T	Tm
Over The Hills Maria Went	Gsc	T	Tm
Over The Sunset Mountains	Zon	G	Tf
Overshadowed (A Cap)	Wrd	G	Sl
Padre Nuestro	Gia	L	Ll
Paean Of Praise (Church Anniversary)	Zon	L	Tt
Palm Sunday	Van	F	Sl
Palm Sunday Procession	Gsc	T	Sl
Palm Sunday Processional	Nal	L	Sl
Palms, The	Lor	T	Sl
Pange Lingua,Eucharistic Hymn(Lat)	Cfp	T	Lo
Panis Angelicus	Gia	L	Lo
Panis Angelicus (E&L) (Md)	Gia	T	Lo
Panis Angelicus (Prayer For Peace)	Hof	T	Lo
Paradise	Zon	G	Sr
Paradise	Gsc	T	Sr
Parce Mihi Domini (Job's Complaint)	Pic	T	Sl
Pardon Me	Nal	L	Tr
Pardon Peace	Wlp	F	Sl
Pardon Your People	Nal	L	Tr
Parousia Song	Fel	F	Tk
Part The Waters (W/Piano)	Wrd	G	Sl
Partita On "St. Anne"	Con	L	Zb
Partita On St Paul	Abi	L	Zb
Partners With The Lord	Ham	G	Tc
Pasadena Kid	Man	F	Tx
Pasch Of The New Law	Wlp	L	Sr
Pass It On	Lex	L	Tc
Pass My Love Around	Yan	F	Lo
Passed Thru The Waters	Prc	L	Tx
Passion Chorale	Gsc	T	Sl
Passion Chorale, The	Lor	T	Sl
Passiontide Carol	Gsc	T	Sr
Pastoral Preludes For Organ	Abi	L	Zb
Pastores A Belen	Gsc	T	Sc
Pastores, Dicite, Quidnam Vidistis?	Gsc	T	Sc
Patapan	Aug	L	Tx
Pater Noster	Gsc	T	Ll
Patter, Patter	Fcc	C	Tx
Paul Mickelson's Arrangements For Men	Zon	G	Za
Paul Mickelson's Choral Arrangements	Zon	T	Za
Paul's Prayer	Prc	L	Tx
Pause A While	Fel	F	Tx
Pave The Way	Sil	F	Tt
Peace	Wlp	C	Tr
Peace	Lor	L	Tr
Peace	Gia	F	Tr
Peace	Mar	L	Tr
Peace	See	L	Tr
Peace	Rpb	L	Tr
Peace Be Multiplied	Ron	T	Tr
Peace Be On Earth	Cfp	T	Tr
Peace Be To You	Nal	L	Tr
Peace Be Unto You	Aug	L	Tr
Peace Be Unto You	Abi	L	Tr
Peace Be Unto You	Pic	L	Tr
Peace Give I To Thee	Mar	F	Tr
Peace Hymn (Truly I Assure You)	Gia	F	Tr
Peace I Give To Thee	Mar	L	Tr
Peace I Give To You	Nal	L	Tr
Peace I Give You	Acp	L	Tr
Peace I Give You	Acp	L	Tr
Peace I Leave With You	Aug	L	Tr
Peace I Leave With You	Aug	L	Tr
Peace I Leave With You	Gsc	T	Tr
Peace I Leave With You	Prc	L	Tr
Peace I Leave With You (Ps 23)	Gra	F	Ld
Peace I Leave You	Fel	L	Tr
Peace In Your World	Zon	F	Tr
Peace Is Flowing Like A River	Nal	L	Tr
Peace Like A River	Lor	G	Tr
Peace Like A River	Mar	L	Tr
Peace Of Lord	Abi	L	Sc
Peace Of The Lord (Reigns On High)	Jsp	F	Tr
Peace Song	Fel	C	Tr
Peace Time	Nal	C	Tr
Peace To All	Wlp	T	Tr
Peace To His People (Ps85)	Gra	L	Ld
Peace To You	Fel	F	Tr
Peace Upon Earth	Van	F	Sc
Peace We Share	Fel	F	Tr
Peace Within	Mam	G	Tr
Peace Within Thy Walls	Sac	L	Tr
Peace Won't Come	Sil	F	Tx
Peace(A Capella) Jn 14: 27	Gia	L	Tr
Peace, Be Still	Lor	L	Tr
Peace, Joy, Happiness	Wlp	F	Tr
Peace, Love And Hope	Sil	L	Tr
Peace, My Friends	Fel	F	Tr
Peacebird	Fcc	C	Ss
Peaceful Eve So Still & Holy (E)	Gia	T	Sc
Peaceful Mind Tears Of Love	Mar	L	Tr
Peaceful Postures	Nal	L	Tr
Pearly Mansions	Mar	L	Sr
Pen. Rite And Lit. Of Word	Gia	L	Le
Penitential Psalms (3)	Kal	T	Sl
Penitential Response	Nal	L	Tr
Penitential Song	Fel	L	Sl
Penitential Tears Of St. Peter (3 Vol)	Kal	T	Sl
Pentecost	Nal	L	Ss
Pentecost Day	Fel	F	Ss
People Everywhere Are Gathered	Sil	F	La
People Of God	Nal	L	Tr
People Of God	Nal	L	Tr
People Of God, The	Hal	T	Tr
People Of Praise (New Year)	Gra	F	Tc
People Of Zion	Wlp	L	Tr
People Of Zion, Behold	Fel	L	Tx
People, Ask Me	Wlp	F	Tx
People's Mass (Icet)	Gia	L	Za
Peoples Mass (Icet)	Wlp	L	Za
Peregrinus (Acting Version)	Oxf	T	Sr
Perfect Through Suffering	Cfp	T	Sl
Peter	Van	F	Tx
Peter (1 – 1:8)	Mar	L	Tr
Peter & The Angel	Van	F	Sr
Peter And John	Van	F	Tx
Peter, James And John	Mar	L	Tx
Peter, Peter Hear Me	Van	F	Tx
Petersham Place, (16)	Mar	L	Tx
Petitions For Help	Aug	L	Lh
Pheres	Ccc	L	Zb
Piano Duets At One Keyboard (No 5289)	Zon	G	Zb
Piano Melodies (No 5788)	Zon	T	Zb
Piano Solo Favorites No 1 (No 5814)	Zon	G	Zb
Piano Solo Favorites No 2 (No 5802)	Zon	G	Zb
Picardy Suite	Abi	L	Zb
Pickin' The Sun Down	Clm	F	Tt
Pickin' Up The Pieces	Mar	L	Sl
Picture The Dawning	Rpb	L	Za
Picture The Dawning	Rpb	L	Tt
Pie Jesu(God Of Mercy)	Gsc	T	Tx
Pilgrim Hymn	Gsc	T	Tx
Pilgrim Song	Van	F	Tr
Pilgrim's Farewell	Bbl	T	Tf
Pilgrim's Journey (Cantata)	Oxf	T	Tc
Pilgrim's Road	Rpb	F	Za
Pilgrim's Song	Rpb	F	Tc
Pilgrimage	Fel	F	Tb
Place Your Hope In Me	Sha	F	Tr
Plan Of Love	Mar	L	Tr
Planctus Mariae (Latin & English)	Oxf	T	Sl
Planets, Stars And Airs Of Space	Gsc	T	Sc
Planted Wheat (Trad Hb Mel)	Gia	F	Sr
Plaudite	Gsc	T	Tt
Play Before The Lord	Nal	L	Tx
Playground For People	Wlp	F	Tx
Please Accept Our Gifts	Fel	F	To
Pleasure It Is	Oxf	T	Tr
Pleasure It Is (E)	Oxf	L	Tt
Plegaria A La Virgen	Pic	T	Tm
Plenty Of Room In The Family	Gmc	G	Lo
Plorans Ploravit (M)	Oxf	T	Tr
Plowshares	Wbp	L	Tr
Po' Mo'ner Got A Home At Las'	Gsc	G	Tf
Poem Of Circumstance	See	L	Tx
Poor Builder (Psalm 127)	Ahc	L	Tx
Popular Psalm Settings	Gsc	T	Za
Popule Meus	Gsc	T	Sl
Possible Gospel, The	Nal	L	Tx
Possibly, Probably	Prc	L	Tx
Post Septuagesima & In Annuntiatione	Kal	T	Tm
Power	Bbl	T	Tt
Power Medley	Sil	G	Tt
Praisallujah	Zon	G	Tt
Praise	Rpb	L	Tt
Praise (Me)	Oxf	T	Tt
Praise And Celebration (No 4061)	Zon	G	Za
Praise And Elation	Bec	T	Sc
Praise And Glory Alleluia	Ahc	L	Tt
Praise And Honor	Rpb	L	Lg
Praise And Honor To You (Icet)	Wlp	L	Lg
Praise And Supplication	Abi	L	Tt
Praise Be To Jesus	Gmc	G	Tt
Praise Be To You, O Lord	Fel	L	Tt
Praise Book, A	See	L	Tt
Praise For The Lord	Gmc	G	Tt
Praise For Today (Words, Music)	Aug	T	Za
Praise God	Rav	L	Tt
Praise God	Sms	F	Tt
Praise God	Van	F	Tt
Praise God	Yan	F	Tt
Praise God From Whom All	Yan	F	Tt
Praise God In Highest Heaven	Maf	T	Tt
Praise God In His Holiness	Lor	T	Tt
Praise God In His Sanctuary	Sac	T	Tt
Praise God With Loud Songs	Aug	L	Tt

ALPHABETICAL INDEX OF TITLES

Praise God With Sound (Psalm 117) Bbl T Tt
Praise God! Sac L Tt
Praise God, My Soul Bbl T Tt
Praise God, Praise Him Here Below Fel F Tt
Praise God, Ps. 145 Fcc F Tt
Praise God, Ye Christians Gsc T Tt
Praise Him Sem G Tt
Praise Him Rpb L Tt
Praise Him Zon F Tt
Praise Him (From Come Follow) Gia G Lg
Praise Him (Psalm 150) Aug L Tt
Praise Him Evermore Gia T Tt
Praise Him In The Morning Zon F Tt
Praise Him Now Zon L Tt
Praise Him, Ye Nations Zon T Tt
Praise My God With The Tamborine Gia F Tt
Praise My Soul The King Of Heaven Gsc T Tt
Praise Our God Lor T Sr
Praise Our God Acp L Tt
Praise Our God Zon L Tt
Praise Our God Above (Pentatonic) Wlp L Tt
Praise Shall Be Thine Lor T Tt
Praise Song Rav L La
Praise Song (Collection) Wrd G Za
Praise The Almighty (Cantata) Lps T Tt
Praise The Father Ahc L Tt
Praise The Grandeur Of Our God Wlp T Tt
Praise The King Of Glory Aug L Tt
Praise The Lord Sil L Tt
Praise The Lord Wlp L Tt
Praise The Lord Lor T Tt
Praise The Lord Pro L Tt
Praise The Lord Hhh G Tt
Praise The Lord Gsc T Tt
Praise The Lord Wlp F Tt
Praise The Lord Gsc T Tt
Praise The Lord Van F Tt
Praise The Lord (E) Oxf T Tt
Praise The Lord (Judas Maccabeus) Pro T Tt
Praise The Lord (Motet 6) Kal T Tt
Praise The Lord (Ps 117) 4 Voices Gia T Tt
Praise The Lord (4-Part Arr) Acp L Tt
Praise The Lord All Nations Aug L Tt
Praise The Lord For He Is Good Gra L Ld
Praise The Lord For He Is Good Con L Tt
Praise The Lord For He Is Gracious Lor T Tt
Praise The Lord In Many Voices Van F Tt
Praise The Lord My Soul Nal L Tt
Praise The Lord My Soul (Cantata) Lps T Tt
Praise The Lord My Soul (Ps146) Gra L Ld
Praise The Lord Of Heaven Acp L Tt
Praise The Lord Of Heaven Som L Tt
Praise The Lord Of Heaven Lor T Tt
Praise The Lord Of Heaven (4-Part Arr) Acp L Tt
Praise The Lord Through Every Nation Abi L Tt
Praise The Lord Together Mar L Tt
Praise The Lord Who Heals(Ps 147) Rav L Ld
Praise The Lord Who Is Present Sms T Tt
Praise The Lord Who Lives Among Us Sms F Tt
Praise The Lord Who Reigns Above(Acap) Abi L Tk
Praise The Lord With Gladness (A Cap) Pro L Tt
Praise The Lord With Gladness (A Cap) Pro L Tt
Praise The Lord! Ye Heavens Oxf T Tt
Praise The Lord, His Glories Show Abi L Tt
Praise The Lord, His Glories Show Zon L Tt
Praise The Lord, His Glories Show Gsc T Tt
Praise The Lord, My Brothers Fel F Tt
Praise The Lord, Now Come Acp L Tt
Praise The Lord, Now Come (4-Part Arr) Acp L Tt
Praise The Lord, O Jerusalem Lor T Tt
Praise The Lord, O My Soul Abi L Tt
Praise The Lord, O My Soul Gam T Tt
Praise The Lord, O My Soul Gia L Tt
Praise The Lord, O My Soul Gsc T Tt
Praise The Lord, O My Soul Gsc T Tt
Praise The Lord, O My Soul (Ps 103) Oxf T Tt
Praise The Lord, Sing A Joyful Song Pro L Tt
Praise The Lord, Ye Congregation Zon L Tt
Praise The Lord, Ye Servants Oxf T Tt
Praise The Savior Abi L Sr
Praise The Savior Som L Tt
Praise The Savior (P.D.) Man T Tt
Praise To God In The Highest (Me) Oxf T Tt
Praise To The Living God Gsc T Tt
Praise To The Lord Aug T Tt
Praise To The Lord Aug T Tt
Praise To The Lord Gia T Tt
Praise To The Lord Abi L Tt
Praise To The Lord Gsc T Tt
Praise To The Lord Gsc T Tt
Praise To The Lord Gia T Tt
Praise To The Lord (E) Oxf T Tt
Praise To The Lord (10 Chorales) Gia T Za
Praise To The Lord (4-Part Arr) Acp L Tt
Praise To The Lord God Maf T Tt
Praise To The Lord, The Almighty Oxf T Tt
Praise To The Lord, The Almighty Sac T Tt
Praise To The Lord, The Almighty Lor T Tt
Praise To The Lord, The Almighty Lor T Tt
Praise To The Lord, The Almighty Lor T Tt

Praise To You Lord Jesus Christ Icet Wlp L Lg
Praise To You Now And Evermore Wlp L Tt
Praise To You, Lord;You Have Given Fel L Tt
Praise We Christ's Immortal Body Wlp T Lo
Praise We The Name Of God Pro T Tt
Praise Ye Aug T Tt
Praise Ye Jehovah Abi L Tt
Praise Ye The Father Som L Tt
Praise Ye The Father Lor T Tt
Praise Ye The Father(Marche Romaine) Gsc T Tt
Praise Ye The Lord Gsc T Tt
Praise Ye The Lord Abi L Tt
Praise Ye The Lord Abi L Tt
Praise Ye The Lord Gsc T Tt
Praise Ye The Lord Pro T Tt
Praise Ye The Lord Pro L Tt
Praise Ye The Lord Lor T Tt
Praise Ye The Lord See L Tt
Praise Ye The Lord Gsc T Tt
Praise Ye The Lord Gsc T Tt
Praise Ye The Lord Maf T Tt
Praise Ye The Lord Gsc T Tt
Praise Ye The Lord (E & Ger) Gia T Tt
Praise Ye The Lord (Ps 113) Oxf T Tt
Praise Ye The Lord (Ps 150) Oxf T Tt
Praise Ye The Lord With Singing Gia T Tt
Praise Ye The Lord! Zon L Tt
Praise Ye The Lord, Alleluia Bbl T Tt
Praise Ye The Lord, The Almighty Zon T Tt
Praise Ye The Lord, Ye Children Aug L Tt
Praise Ye The Lord, Ye Children (Me) Oxf T Tt
Praise Ye The Triune God! Zon T Tt
Praise Ye, Jehovah Lor T Tt
Praise Ye, The Lord Van F Tt
Praise Ye, The Lord Ccc L Tt
Praise! Zon T Tt
Praise, Lord! Nal L Tt
Praise, My Soul, The King Of Heaven Gia T Tt
Praise, My Soul, The King Of Heaven. Oxf T Tt
Praise, My Soul, The King Of Heaven Zon T Tt
Praise, The Holy Of Holies Wlp F Tt
Praise, Thou Zion (Cantata) Lps T Tt
Praised Be My Lord Lor T Tt
Praised Be The Father Of Our Lord Cfc L Tt
Praised Be The Lord (Me) Oxf T Tt
Praises For The Risen Christ Sac L Sr
Praises To The Giver Lor T To
Praising God For Passing Sorrows Sil L Tt
Pray For The Peace Of Jerusalem Gra F Ld
Pray For The Peace Of Jerusalem Bfi F Ld
Pray! Pray! Pray! Zon G Tt
Prayer Som L Tx
Prayer Gsc T Tt
Prayer Abi L Tr
Prayer Sil L Tx
Prayer Gsc T Tr
Prayer (From Celebration) Gia L Tc
Prayer (Prayer Of The Heart And Lips) Gia L Tx
Prayer And Praise Sil L Tt
Prayer Canon From Aroldo Bbl T Tr
Prayer For Courage Aug L Tr
Prayer For God's Blessing Gsc T Tr
Prayer For Mercy (First Mass) Fel F Lb
Prayer For Mercy (Second Mass) Fel F Lb
Prayer For Mothers, A Lor T Tx
Prayer For Our Country, A Lor T Tp
Prayer For Peace Ahc L Tr
Prayer For Peace Som L Tr
Prayer For Peace Aug L Tr
Prayer For Peace Gia L Tr
Prayer For Peace Hal L Tr
Prayer For Peace Rpb L Tr
Prayer For Peace Gia L Tu
Prayer For Peace Fcc F Tr
Prayer For Serenity Pro T Tr
Prayer Intonations Abi L Le
Prayer Is A Part Of Man Sem G Tr
Prayer Is The Answer Man G Tx
Prayer Of Humble Access, A Sac L Tr
Prayer Of Penitence, A Lor T Tr
Prayer Of Petition (Kyrie) Fel F Lb
Prayer Of St Augustine Sac L Tr
Prayer Of St Francis Gia L Tr
Prayer Of St. Francis Fis L Tr
Prayer Of St. Francis Van F Tr
Prayer Of St. Francis Fcc F Tr
Prayer Of St. Francis Sms T Tr
Prayer Of Thanksgiving Gsc T Tt
Prayer Of The Faithful Fel L Lh
Prayer Of The Faithful (Response) Wlp L Lh
Prayer Of The Faithful For Advent Acp L Lh
Prayer Of The Faithful For Advent Acp L Lh
Prayer Of The Faithful For Christmas Acp L Lh
Prayer Of The Faithful For Christmas Acp L Lh
Prayer Of The Faithful For Easter Acp L Lh
Prayer Of The Faithful For Easter Acp L Lh
Prayer Of The Faithful For Lent Acp L Lh
Prayer Of The Faithful For Lent (4pt) Acp L Lh
Prayer Of The Faithful For Ordinary Acp L Lh
Prayer Of The Faithful For Ordinary Tm Acp L Lh

Prayer Of The Faithful For Pentecost Acp L Lh
Prayer Of The Faithful For Pentecost Acp L Lh
Prayer Of The Norwegian Child Gsc L Tr
Prayer On Christmas Eve Aug L Sc
Prayer To Jesus (Me) Oxf T Sl
Prayer To Our Father Wlp F Tr
Prayer, A Lor T Tx
Prayers I Make, The Sac L Tr
Prayers Of Steel Aug L Tx
Preces And Responses (M) Oxf T Za
Preces And Responses (M) Oxf T Za
Preces And Responses (Me) Oxf T Za
Precious Crimson Fountain Mam G Sl
Precious In The Sight Of The Lord Fel L Tx
Preface (Jazz-Rock Mass) Fel F Tx
Preface & Eucharistic Acclamations Acp L Le
Preface Dialogue Gia L Tx
Preface, Sanctus, Benedictus Gia L Le
Prelude And Variations Maf L Zb
Prelude On A Southern Folk Hymn Abi L Zb
Prelude On Amazing Grace Abi L Zb
Prelude On Christ Is Arisen (Diff) Abi L Zb
Prelude On Darwall Abi L Zb
Prelude On Hyfrydol Abi L Zb
Prelude On Mit Freuden Zart (Mod Easy) Abi L Zb
Prelude On O Store Gud Abi L Zb
Prelude On Psalms Gsc T Sc
Prelude On Rockingham Abi L Zb
Prelude On St Bernard Abi L Zb
Prelude On St Flavian Abi L Zb
Preludios Celestiales (No 5365) Zon G Za
Prepare For The Coming Fel F Sa
Prepare Him Room Lor L Sc
Prepare My Mind And Heart For Prayer Lor T Tr
Prepare Now Your Finest Chamber Bbl T Lo
Prepare The Way O Zion Zon T Sl
Prepare The Way Of The Lord Gsc T Sa
Prepare Ye (Cantata) Lps T Sa
Prepare Ye The Way Rpb L Sa
Prepare Ye The Way Gia L Sa
Prepare Ye The Way Of The Lord Gsc T Sa
Prepare Ye The Way Of The Lord Val F Sa
Prepare You For The Day Fel F Sa
Prepare! The Lord Is Near Rpb L Sa
Preparing Now Wlp F Sa
Presence, The Abi T Tr
Presentation (Offertory) Fel F Tt
Pretend We're Young Again Fel F Tx
Pretty Me Up On The Inside Lord Ham G Sl
Prevent Us, O Lord, In All Our Doings Oxf T Sl
Priest And Bishop Gia L La
Priestly People Wlp L Tc
Primrose Gsc T Tx
Prince Of Peace (Born In Bethlehem) Gia F Sc
Prince Of Peace (Cantata) Zon L Sc
Prince Of Peace Is Born Today Her T Sc
Prince Of Peace, The Lor L Sc
Prince Of Peace, The Lor L Sc
Pro Adventus & Post Nativitatem Dom Kal T Sc
Pro Nobis Puer Natus Est Sac T Sc
Proba Me Deus Gsc T Sl
Procession Of Palms Gsc T Sr
Processional Abi L Zb
Processional & Alleluia(Xmas & Easter) Oxf T Lp
Processional "Let There Be Light" Pic L La
Processional And Recessional Cfp T Zb
Processional March On St Dunstan's Abi L Zb
Processional Psalm Gia L La
Processional Psalm For Lent (E) Gia T Sl
Proclaim His Great Love Wrd G Sr
Proclaim His Marvelous Deeds Nal L Tt
Proclaim To The World Acp L Tc
Proclaim To The World (4-Part Arr) Acp L Tc
Projection 29 Ccc L Zb
Promise Fulfilled, The Bec T Sc
Promise Me Life Nal L Tr
Promise Of Salvation Wlp F Sa
Promised Land Bec T Sr
Promised One, The Lor L Sc
Promised One, The Lor L Sc
Promises Mar L Tx
Promises Of God (W/Piano) Wrd G Sr
Promises Of Love Man G Tr
Promises To Keep Ham G Tc
Prope Est Dominus Bbl T Sa
Proper Offertories Of The Sundays Gia L Sa
Prophetic Song Pic L Tx
Prosper The Work Of Our Hands Fel L Tr
Protect Me From Those Who Do Evil Fel L Sl
Protect Our Country, O Lord Fel L Tp
Protect Us, Lord, While We Are Awake Fel L Tr
Proverb 31 Mar L Tx
Psalm Pic L Tx
Psalm Concertato (In 3 Parts) Aug L Tx
Psalm For Advent, To You, O Lord Gia L Sa
Psalm For Epiphany Gia L Ld
Psalm For Unity Gia L Tu
Psalm Of Gratitude, A Lor T Tt
Psalm Of Praise Gsc L Tt
Psalm Of Praise (Ps 150)W/Brs Wlp L Tt

Psalm Of Praise, A	See L Tt	Psalm 23	Bbl T Tr
Psalm Of Thanksgiving, A	Lor L Tt	Psalm 23	Gia L Tr
Psalm One Hundred	Gia L Tt	Psalm 23	Cfc L Tr
Psalm Praise (Var Settings)	Gia L Za	Psalm 23	Rpb L Tr
Psalm Praises	Lor T Tt	Psalm 23 (W/Org & Str. Bass)	Aug L Tr
Psalm 1 He Is Like A Tree	Fel F Tr	Psalm 23 (22)	Wlp L Tr
Psalm 100	Zon F La	Psalm 23 From The Bay Psalm Book	Oxf T Tr
Psalm 100	See L La	Psalm 23 The Lord Is My Shepherd	Fel F Tr
Psalm 100	Cfc L La	Psalm 23 The Lord Is My Shepherd (2)	Fel F Tr
Psalm 100	Aug L La	Psalm 24	Abi L Tk
Psalm 100 (M)	Oxf T Tt	Psalm 24 (Lift Up Your Heads)	Aug L La
Psalm 100 (Spoken/Song)	Wrd G Lp	Psalm 25	Hal T Tr
Psalm 100 (99)	Wlp L La	Psalm 27 Christ—Light	Fel C Tj
Psalm 100 The Lord Be With You	Fel F La	Psalm 30	Pic L Tt
Psalm 102 (Becker Psalter) Eng	Gia T Sl	Psalm 30 I Praise You, O Lord	Fel F Ld
Psalm 103	Bbl T Tt	Psalm 31	Gsc T Tt
Psalm 103	Rav L Ld	Psalm 31 From The Bay Psalm Book	Oxf T Tr
Psalm 103	Rpb C Ld	Psalm 32 (Becker Psalter)Eng	Gia T Sl
Psalm 103 All Of My Life	Fel F Tt	Psalm 33	Rpb C Ld
Psalm 104	Rpb L Ld	Psalm 33	Gia L Ld
Psalm 104 (103)	Wlp L Tt	Psalm 34	Cfc L Ln
Psalm 107	Mar L Tx	Psalm 34	Gsc T Sl
Psalm 108	Zon F Tt	Psalm 34	Sil L Lo
Psalm 109 O Lord God	Fel F To	Psalm 34 I Looked To God	Fel F Tr
Psalm 11 Run Like A Deer	Fel F La	Psalm 34:1	Mar L Tr
Psalm 112(Latin)	Cfp L Tt	Psalm 37	See L Tr
Psalm 113 Blest Be The Name	Fel F Tt	Psalm 38 (Becker Psalter)Eng	Gia T Sl
Psalm 114 Israel Went Out	Fel L Tx	Psalm 39 When My Heart Was Burning	Fel F Sl
Psalm 117	Kal T Tt	Psalm 4	Wlp L Tx
Psalm 117 (Opt Brass Quartet)	Smc T Tt	Psalm 40	Man G Ld
Psalm 117 O Praise The Lord	Gia T Tt	Psalm 40 (M)	Oxf T Sl
Psalm 118 (W/Brs)	Abi L Sr	Psalm 41	Rpb L Ld
Psalm 119 (Happy Are They)	Aug L Tr	Psalm 42	Mar L Tb
Psalm 121	Zon L Lp	Psalm 42 (41)	Wlp L Tb
Psalm 121	Gsc T Tr	Psalm 42 As A Heart	Kal T Tb
Psalm 121 (I Will Lift Up Mine Eyes)	Oxf T Tr	Psalm 42:Prayer For Strength And Light	Gia L Tr
Psalm 121 (Unacc)	Abi L La	Psalm 45(44)	Wlp L Tt
Psalm 121 And Wedding Responses	Oxf T Tw	Psalm 46 (God Is For Us A Refuge)	Aug L Tr
Psalm 121: Let Us Go To God's House	Gia L Ld	Psalm 47 (O Clap Your Hands) W/Brass	Aug T Sr
Psalm 122: Hail Jerusalem!	Str L La	Psalm 47 Clap Your Hands	Fel F Tt
Psalm 126 These Are They	Fel F Ix	Psalm 47 From The Bay Psalm Book	Oxf T Tt
Psalm 126 (126)	Wlp L La	Psalm 47 Sing Halleluia, Praise	Fel F Tt
Psalm 128	Bbl T Tw	Psalm 50	Aug L Tx
Psalm 128	Cfc L Tw	Psalm 51	Rav L Ld
Psalm 128	Aug L Tw	Psalm 51	Maf T Sl
Psalm 128 (127)	Wlp L Tw	Psalm 51 (Becker Psalter)Eng	Gia T Sl
Psalm 128 (127)	Wlp L Tr	Psalm 51 (50)	Wlp L Sl
Psalm 128 Your Wife Shall Be	Fel L Tw	Psalm 51 Have Mercy, Lord	Fel F Sl
Psalm 13	Som L Sl	Psalm 6 (Becker Psalter) Eng	Gia T Sl
Psalm 13	Ron T Sl	Psalm 63 (62)	Wlp L Tr
Psalm 13	Sac L Sl	Psalm 63 You Are The God	Fel F Tr
Psalm 13 Lord How Long	Kal T Sl	Psalm 65 (From Come Follow)	Gia F Ld
Psalm 13 Lord, How Long Wilt Thou	Gsc T Sl	Psalm 65(Ainsworth Psalter)(Eng)	Cfp T Tt
Psalm 130	Abi L Sl	Psalm 66 Shout Joyfully To God	Fel F Tt
Psalm 130	Aug L Sl	Psalm 67	Abi L Tt
Psalm 130 (Becker Psalter) Eng	Gia T Sl	Psalm 67 (Organ Or Piano Acc)	Gsc T Tt
Psalm 130 From The Depths	Fel F Sl	Psalm 68	Som L Tx
Psalm 131 (130) My Soul Longing	Wlp L Tr	Psalm 8	Bbl T Tt
Psalm 131 Like A Child	Fel F Tr	Psalm 8	Som L Tt
Psalm 132: Behold How Good It Is	Gia L Tu	Psalm 80 Maranatha	Fel F Tk
Psalm 134, Behold Now, Bless The Lord	Gia L Tt	Psalm 83 (84)	Nal L Tr
Psalm 135 O Praise The Lord	Kal T Tt	Psalm 83: How Lovely Is Your Dwelling	Gia L Tr
Psalm 136 (O Give Thanks)	Gia T Tt	Psalm 84 (How Lovely)	Gia L Tr
Psalm 136 (135)	Wlp L Tt	Psalm 84 (How Lovely)	Gia F Ld
Psalm 136 Praise God, Praise Him Here	Fel F Tt	Psalm 84 (O How Amiable)	Fis F Tr
Psalm 139	Abi L Tc	Psalm 84 (83)	Wlp L Tr
Psalm 140 (Mixed Chor & Strgs)	Aug L Tx	Psalm 84 O Lord Of Hosts	Fel F Tr
Psalm 143 (Becker Psalter) Eng	Gia T Sl	Psalm 85 (Md)	Oxf T Tt
Psalm 145	Wgm F Tt	Psalm 89 (I Will Celebrate)	Kbr F Tt
Psalm 148	Fel L Tt	Psalm 90	See L Tr
Psalm 148 (From Come Follow)	Gia F Ld	Psalm 91	Sac L Tr
Psalm 148 (Praise Ye The Lord)	Gsc T Tt	Psalm 92 Glory To The Father	Fel F Tr
Psalm 149	See L Tt	Psalm 95	Bbl T La
Psalm 150	Kal T Za	Psalm 95	Kal T Tt
Psalm 150	Gsc T Tt	Psalm 96	Gsc T Tt
Psalm 150	Rpb L Ld	Psalm 96	Fel F Tt
Psalm 150	Abi L Tt	Psalm 96 (95)	Wlp L Tr
Psalm 150	Gsc L Tt	Psalm 96 Sing To God A Joyous Song	Fel F Tt
Psalm 150	Bbl T Tt	Psalm 96 This Is The Day	Fel F Sr
Psalm 150	Pic L Tt	Psalm 97 (98)	Nal L Tr
Psalm 150	Bbl T Tt	Psalm 98	Fel F Tt
Psalm 150	See L Tt	Psalm 98	Cfc L La
Psalm 150	Lor L Tt	Psalm 98	Ccc L Ld
Psalm 150	Nal L Tt	Psalm 98	Pic L Sc
Psalm 150 (Alleluia)	Wlp L Lf	Psalm 98	Sac L Tt
Psalm 150 (French, German)	Kal L Tt	Psalm 98 (D)	Oxf L Sa
Psalm 150 (M)	Oxf L Tt	Psalm 98 (Joy To The World)	Aug L Tt
Psalm 150 (Md)	Oxf T Tt	Psalm 99 Holy, Holy Is The Lord	Fel F Tt
Psalm 150 (Me)	Oxf L Tt	Psalms	Nal L Za
Psalm 150 (W/Triple Alleluia)	Wlp L Lf	Psalms For Advent	Gia L Ld
Psalm 150 Based On A French Melody	Oxf T Tt	Psalms For The Church Year 1	Aug L Za
Psalm 150: Praise Ye The Lord	Gia L Tt	Psalms For Today (Org,Guit Adlib)	Gia L Za
Psalm 19	Wrd L Tx	Puer Natus Est Nobis	Bbl T Sc
Psalm 19 Drop Down Dew	Fel F Sa	Puer Nobis	Abi L Sc
Psalm 22	Gia L Tr	Puer Nobis Nascitur (In 19 Rounds)	Gia T Sc
Psalm 23	Prc L Tx	Pueri Concinite	Gsc T Sc
Psalm 23	Bbl T Tr	Pure As Crystal Water	Sil T Tb
Psalm 23	Her L Tr	Pure Light (Of The Son Of God)	Gia F Tc
Psalm 23	Gsc L Tr	Purer In Heart, O God	Lor L Tt
Psalm 23	See L Tr	Purge Me, O Lord (Me)	Oxf T Sl

Purge Ut Therefore The Old Leaven	Cfp T Sr
Put Down Your Guns	Prc L Tx
Put Forth, O God, Thy Spirit's Might	Lor T Ss
Put Forth, O God, Thy Spirit's Might	Abi L Ss
Put My Memory In Your Pocket	Fcc F Tt
Put On Love	Pnp C Tx
Put On The Whole Armour Of God	Gia L Tr
Put On Your Boots	Fis F Tx
Put To Shame And Confusion	Fel L Sl
Put Your Hand In The Hand	Her G Tj
Qonswe Od Qonswea	Zon T Sc
Quartet Favorites No 1 (No 5430)	Zon G Za
Quartet Favorites No 2 (No 5431)	Zon G Za
Queen Of Heaven	Gia T Tm
Queen Of Heaven (E & Lat)	Gia T Tm
Queen Of Heaven (Regina Coeli) Eng	Wlp L Tm
Quem Vidistis, Pastores?	Gsc T Sc
Quick, Quick	Fcc C Tx
Quiet Carol, The (German)	Lor T Sc
Quiet Hour (When The Day Is Done)	Wrd G Tr
Quiet Music For Organ	Abi L Zb
Quiet Time (W/Piano)	Wrd G Tr
Quiet Time, A	Zon G Tr
Quietly He Came	Rpb L Sc
Quoniam Ad Te Clamabo, Domine	Gsc T Sl
Quotiescumque	Fel T Lo
Rain Song	Fis F Tx
Rainbow	Fcc F Tx
Rainy Day Song	Van C Sl
Raise Your Hands	Wlp C Tt
Rally Round The Cross	Zon G Sl
Rapture (No 4700)	Zon G Za
Ray The Rangy Rhino	Wlp C Tx
Re—Member Me	Nal L Tx
Reach For The Light	Sil F Tt
Reach Out	Sil L Tx
Reach Out	Ahc L Tr
Reach Out!	Nal C Tr
Reaching	Gmc G Tx
Reaching For My Crown	Sto G Sr
Reaching Out	Yan F Tr
Ready	Man G Tc
Real Peace	Man G Tr
Really Live	Zon F Tr
Really Live (No 4351)	Zon G Za
Reap, Reap	Fcc F Tx
Reason For Singing, A	Zon G Tt
Reborn	Mam G Tb
Rebuild The Temple	Fel F Tx
Receive In Your Heart	Jsp F Tr
Receive Now The Body Of Christ	Gia T Lo
Receive The Holy Spirit	Gia L Ss
Receive With Joy The Glory	Fel L Tx
Receive Ye The Body Of Christ	Gia L Lo
Recessional	Sac L Tc
Reconciliation	Abi L Tr
Recreation (Sin & Penance)	Mcc F Sl
Red Balloon	Rpb C Tx
Red, Yellow, Purple And Green	Fcc C Tx
Redeem Me, O Lord;Give Me Life	Fel L Sl
Redeem Me, O Lord, And Have Pity	Fel L Sl
Redeemed	Sil L Sl
Redeemed	Zon G Sl
Redeemer King	Acp L Tk
Redeemer King	Acp L Tk
Redeemer Of The Nations	Wlp T Sa
Redeemer Shall Come, The	Lor T Sc
Redeeming Love	Gmc G Sl
Redeeming Love	Lor G Sl
Redemption Anthem	Bbl T Sr
Redemption Song (Exodus)	Gra F Sr
Regeneration	Aug L Tb
Regina Coeli	Bbl T Tm
Regina Coeli	Gsc T Tm
Regina Coeli K 276	Kal T Tm
Regina, Coeli	Gia T Tm
Reginas Song	Wlp F Tx
Reign, Master Jesus	Fel L Tk
Rejoice	Pro T Tt
Rejoice	Yan F Tr
Rejoice & Sing For Joy	Aug L Tt
Rejoice Always	Wgm F La
Rejoice Always In The Lord	Wlp L Tt
Rejoice And Be Merry (W/Oboe,Org)	Aug L Tt
Rejoice And Sing	Gsc T Sc
Rejoice And Sing	Man G Tt
Rejoice Believers (M)	Gia L Sa
Rejoice Greatly	Aug L Tt
Rejoice Greatly	Gsc T Tt
Rejoice In His Word	Pro T Tt
Rejoice In Hope	Gia L La
Rejoice In The Lord	Gsc L Tr
Rejoice In The Lord	Aug L Tt
Rejoice In The Lord	Mar L Tr
Rejoice In The Lord (Md)	Oxf T Tt
Rejoice In The Lord Alway (M)	Oxf T Tt
Rejoice In The Lord Always	Abi L Tr
Rejoice In The Lord Always	Nal C Tt
Rejoice In The Lord Always (M)	Oxf T Tt
Rejoice In The Lord On The Feast	Fel L Tx

ALPHABETICAL INDEX OF TITLES

Rejoice In The Lord; Rejoice Fel L Tt
Rejoice Now Wlp T Tt
Rejoice O Virgin Mary Wlp L Tm
Rejoice Today With One Accord Aug L Sc
Rejoice With Me Fel F Tt
Rejoice You're Free Zon G Tr
Rejoice! Rejoice! Maf L Sc
Rejoice! The Lord Is King! Zon T Tk
Rejoice!For We Are Saved Pro L Sr
Rejoice, Be Glad In The Lord Fel F Tt
Rejoice, Earth And Heaven(Eng) Cfp T Tt
Rejoice, For Christ Is Born! Lor T Sc
Rejoice, Give Thanks And Sing Bec T Sc
Rejoice, My Friends Fcc F La
Rejoice, My Son Fel L Tr
Rejoice, O Blessed Creation Hal L Tt
Rejoice, O Church, Exalt In Glory Sms T Tt
Rejoice, O Jerusalem Fel L Tt
Rejoice, O Queen Of Heaven Gia T Tm
Rejoice, Our Lord Is Born Lor T Sc
Rejoice, Queen Of Heaven Gia T Tm
Rejoice, Rejoice This Glad Easter Day Aug L Sr
Rejoice, Rejoice. Vrn L Sr
Rejoice, Rejoice, Believers Lor T Tt
Rejoice, The Lord Is King Gia T Tk
Rejoice, The Lord Is King Sac T Tk
Rejoice, The Lord Is King Fel F Tt
Rejoice, The Lord Is King Lor T Sc
Rejoice, The Lord Is King Pic L Tt
Rejoice, The Messiah Is Coming Fel F Sa
Rejoice, Ye Christian Brethren Gsc T Tt
Rejoice, Ye People (W/Insts) Aug L Tt
Rejoice, Ye Pure In Heart Zon T Tr
Rejoice, You Pure In Heart Gia L Sr
Rejoice, You're A Child Of The King Gmc G Tb
Religion Pic L Tx
Remain In Me Sha F Lo
Remember All The People Abi L Tx
Remember Me Sbf L Sl
Remember Me, Lord, When You Come Fel L Sl
Remember Now Thy Creator Lor L Tx
Remember Us Rpb L Tk
Remember Us O Lord Wlp L Sl
Remember Your Mercies O Lord (Ps 25) Gra L Ld
Remember Your Words, O Lord Fel L Tr
Remember, Man, That You Are Dust Fel L Sl
Remember, O Thou Man Gsc T Sl
Remembrance Abi L Tr
Renew A Right Spirit Within Me Gsc T Sl
Reproaches, The Acp L Sl
Reproaches, The Acp L Sl
Requiem Kal T Tf
Requiem Kal T Tf
Requiem Kal T Tf
Requiem Som L Tf
Requiem Kal T Tf
Requiem (Eng Or Germ) Kal T Tf
Requiem Aeternam–Christe Eleison Cfs T Tf
Requiem In D Minor Kal T Tf
Requiem In D Minor (Male) Kal T Tf
Requiem Mass (Latin) Kal T Tf
Requiem Mass In C Minor Kal T Za
Requiem(Latin) Cfp T Tf
Rescue Me From My Enemies Nal L Sl
Rescue Me, My God, And Defend Me Fel L Tr
Rescue The Perishing Zon G Tc
Response To The First Reading Rpb L Ld
Response: Stations Of The Cross Rpb L Sl
Responses Wbp T Za
Responses For The Church Service Gsc T Za
Responses 75–86 Psalms (Icet) Wlp L Za
Responses 87–88 Gospel Acclamation Wlp L Lf
Responses, With Preces By Gibbons Oxf T Za
Responsorial Psalm For Christmas Gra L Ld
Responsorial Psalms Ritual Masses Wlp L Ld
Responsorium Gsc T Lf
Rest Mar L Tr
Restore My Church Fcc F Tr
Restore Us Rpb L Sl
Resurrection Van C Sr
Resurrection Fel F Sr
Resurrection (Life W/New Direction) Gia F Sr
Resurrection Alleluia Zon T Sr
Resurrection Morn Lor T Sr
Resurrection Psalm Gia L Ld
Return Again Man G Sl
Return To Joy Fcc L Tr
Return To Your People, O Lord Nal L Sl
Return, O Lord, And Save My Life Fel L Sl
Revelation (I Want You Should Know) Nal L Tx
Revelation Motet Bbl T Sr
Revelation Six Six Six Jhm G Tk
Revive Us Again Zon F Za
Rhymes And Reasons Clm F Tt
Ride On (He Came Riding) Gia F Tj
Ride On In Majesty Aug L Tk
Ride On King Jesus! Lor T Sr
Ride On! Lor T Sr
Ride On, Eternal King Aug L Tk
Ride On, Jesus! Gsc T Tx
Ride On, King Jesus Zon T Sr
Ride On, King Jesus (Spiritual) Aug G Tk
Ride On, Ride On In Majesty Lor T Sr
Ride On, Ride On In Majesty Sac T Sr
Ride On, Ride On In Majesty Gsc T Tk
Ride On, Ride On In Majesty(Opt Tpt) Aug T Tj
Right Hand Of The Lord, The Acp F Sr
Right Hand Of The Lord,The(4–Part Arr) Acp F Sr
Right On With Number One! Lor L Tc
Right To Live Fcc F Tx
Ring Out Wild Bells Gsc T Sc
Ring Out, Wild Bells Gsc T Tt
Ring The Bells Zon T Sc
Ring The Bells (East) Zon T Sc
Ring The Bells (No 5040) Zon G Zb
Ring Ye Joy Bells Hof L Sr
Ring, Bells, O Ring Zon T Sc
Ring, Christmas Bells Sac L Sc
Ring, Ye Bells Sac L Sc
Rise Up Acp L Sa
Rise Up Acp L Tx
Rise Up And Sing Praise Zon L Tt
Rise Up My Love (From Sg) Gia T Sr
Rise Up, Jerusalem Nal L Tr
Rise Up, Jerusalem Nal L Tr
Rise Up, My Love Gia T Sr
Rise Up, O Men Of God Aug T Tx
Rise Up, O Men Of God Abi L Tr
Rise Up, O Men Of God! Lor L Tc
Rise Up, Shepherd Maf T Sc
Rise Up, Shepherd, And Follow Lor T Sc
Rise–Shine Zon G Tt
Rise, God! Judge Thou The Earth Gsc T Tr
Rise, O Lord! (From Come Follow) Gia F Sl
Risen Christ! Sac L Sr
Risen Christ, The Lor T Sr
Risen Today Lor T Sr
Rite Of Peace Nal L Tr
Road To Freedom Fcc L Tx
Rock & Roll Preacher Wrd G Tc
Rock Of Ages Lor T Tr
Rock Of Ages Lor T Tr
Rock Of Ages Abi L Tr
Rock Of Ages Mar L Tr
Rock Of Ages (Arrangement) Sil T Tr
Rock On The Head Zon C Za
Rockbridge Bbl T Tt
Roger's Alleluia (Gospel Acclamation) Nal L Lf
Roll That Stone Away Van F Sr
Rolled Away (Revisited) Zon F Sr
Romans 8:14,15 Mar L Ss
Romans 8:38,39 Mar L Tr
Room At The Cross For You Zon G Tb
Root–Toot–To Mar L Tx
Rosa Mundi See L Tx
Rose Of Christmas, The Lor L Sc
Roses While I'm Living Pmp G Tx
Roun' De Glory Manger Gsc G Sc
Round Me Falls The Night Gsc T Tr
Rounds For Church And Sunday School Bec T Za
Royal Banners Forward Go, The Abi L Tk
Rule Over My Soul Mar L Tk
Run Deep On Well Of Mercy Wrd G Tb
Run On Sem G Tt
Run On Sem G Tt
Run, Christian, Run Acp F Tc
Run, Christian, Run (4–Part Arr) Acp F Tx
Run, Come, See(1) Fel C La
Run, Come, See(2) Fel C La
Runnin' Van L Tx
Russ's Song Chd F Tt
Russian Alleluia (Victimae) Car F Sr
Russian Christmas Hymn Gsc T Sc
Sabbath Bells Lor T Tr
Sabbath Music (Christian) Smc T Zb
Sabbath Prayer Nyt F Tt
Sacred A Capella Choruses (Germ/Eng) Kal T Za
Sacred Choruses Kal T Za
Sacred Dance (Lyric Liturgy) Gia L Zb
Sacred Harp Suite Abi L Zb
Sacred Hymns Kal T Za
Sacred Hymns (Seven) Kal T Za
Sacred Selections For Inst. Choir Smc T Zb
Sacred Service Avodath Hakodesh Bbl T Tx
Sacred Songs Lps T Za
Sacred Songs (Geistliche Lieder) Lps T Za
Sacred Trust(A Wedding Song) Gia L Tw
Sadness Song Fel F Sl
Safe In His Precious Arms Man G Tr
Safe In The Arms Of Jesus Lor T Tr
Safe Under His Wing Sbf L Tr
Said The Lord Fcc F Lo
Sail On Sailor Mar L Tx
Saint Matthew Passion Bbl T Sl
Saints & Sinners (Cantata) Lps T Sl
Salem City Acp L Tr
Salem City Acp L Tr
Salvation Belongeth Unto The Lord Abi L Sl
Salvation Is Created Gsc T Sl
Salvation Is For All Lor T Sl
Salvation Song Fel F Sr
Salvation, Glory & Power Wlp L Tt
Salvator Mundi (Md) Oxf T Sl
Salve (Salutation) Pic T Tx
Salve Regina Gsc T Tm
Sam Vel Fis F Tx
Samson (Novelty Song) Sbf F Tx
Samson (Eng/Germ) (Oratorio) Kal T Tx
Sancta Maria Pic L Tm
Sancta Maria Graduale Bbl T Tm
Sancta Maria Mater Dei K 273 Kal T Tm
Sancta Maria, Mater Dei Gsc T Tm
Sanctification Bbl T Tx
Sanctorum Meritis Kal T Tx
Sanctum Et Terrible Nomen Ejus Gsc T Tt
Sanctus Gia L Li
Sanctus Lor T Li
Sanctus Aug T Li
Sanctus Gsc T Li
Sanctus Gsc T Li
Sanctus Gsc T Li
Sanctus Gsc T Li
Sanctus Gsc T Li
Sanctus Nal L Li
Sanctus (B Minor Mass) Gsc T Li
Sanctus (Eng Mass) Gia L Li
Sanctus (Eng, Icet) Gra L Li
Sanctus (From Missa Brevis In G Maj) Pro T Li
Sanctus (Holy, Holy, Holy) Gsc T Li
Sanctus (Mariachi Mass) Fel F Li
Sanctus (Mass For New Rite) Gia L Li
Sanctus (Mass In Bm) Cfs T Li
Sanctus (Mass Of Schools) Fel C Li
Sanctus (Mass Of The Western Tribes) Fel F Li
Sanctus (Missa Brevis) Fel T Li
Sanctus (Mus For Euch Prayer Acc) Gia L Li
Sanctus (Notre Dame Mass) Gia L Li
Sanctus (Sung Mass No.2) Fel L Li
Sanctus (Thomas More Mass) Fel L Li
Sanctus (W/Fl,Cello) Gia L Li
Sanctus & Benedictus (St Cec Mass) Cfs T Li
Sanctus And Benedictus (St.Cec) Gsc T Li
Sanctus And Osanna Gsc T Li
Sanctus In D Oxf T Li
Sanctus(From Mass) Gsc L Li
Sanctus, The Abi L Li
Sandals Zon F Tj
Sandusky Bbl T Tx
Santo, Santo, Santo Gia L Li
Sarah Fel F Tx
Saul. Sacred Concerto(Ger) Cfp T Tx
Save Me Wlp F Sl
Save Me My God Wlp F Sl
Save Me, O God Tcp L Tr
Save Me, O God, By Thy Name Gsc L Sl
Save Me, O Lord! Som L Sl
Save Me, O Lord, And Rescue Me Fel L Sl
Save Me, O Lord, From The Hands Fel L Sl
Save My People Nal L Tx
Save The Mission Fel L Tc
Save The People Val F Tp
Save Us, O Lord Gsc T Sl
Save Us, O Lord, Our God Fel L Sl
Saved, Saved Zon G Sl
Savior Of My Soul Mar L Tj
Savior Of The Nations, Come Aug L Sa
Savior Of The Nations, Come Aug T Sa
Savior Of The World Sav G Tj
Savior, Again To Your Dear Name Gia T Tr
Savior, I Long To Be Lor T Tj
Savior, Lead Me Lor T Tc
Savior, Like A Shepherd Lead Us Sac L Tr
Savior, Teach Me Day By Day (M) Abi T Tj
Saviour, Hear Us When We Pray Gsc T Tr
Saviour, Like A Shepherd Lead Us Gsc T Tc
Saviour, When Night Involves The Skies Gsc T Tx
Saw Ye My Savior Aug L Sr
Saw Ye My Savior? (W/Flute) Aug T Sl
Saw You Never In The Twilight Aug L Tx
Scandalize My Name Gsc T Tt
Scarce Had The Daystar Risen Bbl T Tt
Scripture Response, Alleluia Wlp F Lf
Sea Of Madness Msm F Tx
Search Le, O Lord Lor T Sl
Search Me, O God Gsc T Sl
Search Me, O God Lor T Sl
Searching For The Lord Nal L Tr
Seasonal Responsorial Psalms (Chant) Gia L Za
Seasons Kal T Tx
Seasons Of Rapture Zon F Sa
Second Service (Magnificat, Nunc) Kal T Tx
Second Service: Magnificat & Nunc Dim. Oxf T Za
Secret Place Of God, The Zon L Tr
Secret, The Abi L Tx
See Dearest God (Cantata) Lps T Tr
See How The Virgin Waits Rpb F Sa
See Jesus The Savior Gsc F Sc
See Me Through Man G Tc
See That Babe In The Lowly Manger Gsc T Sc
See The Land Abi L Sl

ALPHABETICAL INDEX OF TITLES

See What God Can Do	Zon	G	Tr
See What Love	Aug	T	Sl
See What Love Hath The Father	Gsc	T	Sa
See Your People (Ministry)	Lit	L	Tc
See, The Fields Are White	Gra	F	Tc
See, Your King Shall Come	Fel	L	Sa
Seed, The	Nal	C	Tx
Seek And Ye Shall Find	Mar	L	Tr
Seek And Ye Shall Find	Lor	T	Tr
Seek First His Kingdom	Bfi	F	Tr
Seek First The Kingdom	Van	F	Tc
Seek The Lord	Nal	L	Tr
Seek The Lord (E)	Oxf	T	Tr
Seek Ye First	Zon	G	Tk
Seek Ye First	Mar	L	Tk
Seek Ye First The Kingdom Of God	Gia	T	Tk
Seek Ye The Lord	Sac	T	Tr
Seek Ye The Lord	Lor	T	Sl
Seek Ye The Lord	Aug	T	Sl
Seek Ye The Lord	Gsc	T	Sl
Seek Ye The Lord	Lor	T	Sl
Seek Ye The Lord	Sac	T	Tr
Seek Ye The Lord (Ten Solo)	Gsc	T	Tr
Seeking To Become	Hal	T	Tr
Select Vocal Solos For The Church	Abi	L	Za
Selected Hymns In Large Type	Aug	L	Za
Selected Music For Funerals	Gia	L	Tf
Selections From Canciones Sacrae(4vol)	Kal	T	Tr
Send Forth Thy Spirit	Gsc	T	Ss
Send Forth Thy Spirit, O Lord	Gsc	T	Ss
Send Forth Your Life-Giving Spirit	Fel	L	Ss
Send Forth Your Light And Your Truth	Fel	L	La
Send Forth Your Spirit, O Lord	Wlp	L	Ss
Send Me	Prc	L	Tx
Send Out Thy Light	Gsc	T	Tr
Send Out Thy Light	Lor	T	Tb
Send Out Thy Light (Short Anthem)	Smc	L	Sa
Send The Light Gabriel	Zon	G	Tc
Send Thy Holy Breath	Zon	L	Ss
Senor, Ten Piedad	Gia	L	Lm
Sent Forth By God's Blessing	Wlp	T	Tc
Separate And United	Prc	L	Tx
Serene Alleluias	Gia	L	Lf
Sermon On The Mount	Fel	F	Tr
Servant Of All	Mar	L	Tc
Servant Song	Nal	L	Tj
Servant-King, The	Acp	L	Tj
Servant-King, The	Acp	L	Tj
Serve Bone	Gia	T	Tx
Serve Each Other In Loving Kindness	Fel	F	Tr
Serve The Lord With Fear	Fel	F	Tr
Service And Strength	Gsc	T	Ss
Service Music For Sab Choir	Pro	T	Za
Service Suite For Organ	Abi	T	Zb
Set Me As A Seal	Gsc	T	Tw
Set Me As A Seal	Gsc	L	Tw
Set Me As A Seal (4 Voices)	Gia	T	Tw
Set Me As A Seal Upon Thine Heart	Oxf	T	Tw
Set My Spirit Free	Mar	L	Tr
Seven Anthems For Treble Choirs	Con	L	Za
Seven Choral Service Settings	Abi	L	Za
Seven French Noels	Gia	T	Sc
Seven General Anthems For Unison-Trebl	Abi	L	Za
Seven Hymn Tunes (In 2 Vols)	Oxf	T	Za
Seven Last Words	Kal	T	Sl
Seven Last Words	Kal	T	Sl
Seven Last Words, The	Lor	T	Sl
Seven Lenten Chorales	Gia	T	Za
Seven Psalms	Abi	L	Za
Seven Sacred Motets	Kal	T	Za
Seven Sacred Solos	Abi	L	Za
Seven Sayings From The Cross	Lor	T	Sl
Seven Songs From Ancient Liturgies	Cfc	L	Za
Seven Times	Van	F	Tr
Seven Verses	Aug	L	Tx
Seven Words From The Cross	Aug	L	Sl
Seven Words From The Cross	Abi	T	Sl
Seven Words Of Love	Abi	T	Sl
Seventeen Responses And Sentences	Lor	T	Za
Sh'ma Yisroeyl	Gsc	T	Tx
Shadow Scenes Of The Saviour's Birth	Zon	T	Sc
Shadows Of Evening	Wlp	T	Tx
Shadrack (A Cap)	Wrd	G	Tx
Shall I Crucify Him?	Lor	T	Sl
Shall I Crucify My Savior?	Lor	T	Sl
Shall We Gather At The River	Zon	G	La
Shall We Gather At The River	Smc	T	Sr
Shall We Gather At The River?	Lor	G	Sr
Shalom	Wlp	F	Tr
Shalom	Nal	L	Tr
Shalom	Acp	F	Tr
Shalom	Acp	F	Tr
She Was America	Sil	L	Tp
She's Just An Old Stump	Wlp	C	Tx
Sheaves Of Peace (Psalm 23)	Ahc	L	Tr
Sheep And Lambs	Gsc	T	Tr
Sheep And Lambs May Safely Graze	Gsc	T	Tr
Sheep May Safely Graze	Lor	T	Tr
Shelter Of Your Arms	Mam	G	Tr
Shepherd Boy	Man	C	Sc

Shepherd Of Israel	Nal	L	Tr
Shepherd Of Love	Lor	L	Tr
Shepherd Of Love	Zon	G	Tr
Shepherd Of Souls	Lor	L	Tr
Shepherd Of Souls In Love Come Feed	Wlp	T	Lo
Shepherd, Hark	Gsc	T	Sc
Shepherd's Alleluia	Nal	L	Sc
Shepherd's Nativity Song, The	Maf	T	Sc
Shepherds Come A-Running	Aug	L	Sc
Shepherds In The Field	Lor	T	Sc
Shepherds Tell Your Wondrous Story	Abi	T	Sc
Shepherds Went Their Hasty Way, The	Abi	L	Sc
Shepherds' Carol, The	Lor	C	Sc
Shepherds' Carol, The	Lor	T	Sc
Sherburne	Gsc	T	Tx
Sherburne	Bbl	T	Tx
Shine Shine Shine	Zon	G	Tc
Shine, Star	Prc	L	Tx
Shines There Such A Light	Prc	L	Tx
Short Communion Service W/Congregation	Oxf	T	Lo
Short Communion Service: Kyrie Etc	Oxf	T	Lo
Short Evening Service (Dorian Mode)	Oxf	T	Za
Short Service (Md)	Oxf	T	Za
Short Service (Venite, Te Deum Etc)	Kal	T	Tx
Short Service: Magnificat & Nunc	Oxf	T	Za
Short Service: Te Deum/ Benedictus	Oxf	T	Tt
Shout	Fel	F	Tt
Shout Aloud To Heaven	Acp	L	Tt
Shout Aloud To Heaven (4-Part Arr)	Acp	L	Tt
Shout And Clap Your Hands	Fel	F	Tt
Shout For Joy	Gsc	L	Tt
Shout For Joy	Gia	L	Tt
Shout For Joy Before The Lord	Aug	L	Tt
Shout For Joy, For He Comes	Fel	L	Sa
Shout From The Highest Mountain	Fel	F	Tt
Shout Joyfully To God	Sms	F	Tt
Shout Joyfully!	Nal	L	Tt
Shout Out Your Joy	Fel	F	Tt
Shout Out, Sing Of His Glory	Fel	F	Tt
Shout Praise And Glory	Gia	T	Tt
Shout Praises To The Lord	Fel	F	Tt
Shout The Glad Tidings	Aug	T	Tt
Shout The Good News	Van	F	Tc
Show A Little Bit Of Love And Kindness	Zon	G	Tr
Show A Little Love	Zon	G	Tc
Show Forth The Glory	Rpb	L	Tt
Show Forth, O God, Your Power	Fel	L	Tk
Show Me	Man	G	Tx
Show Me A Window	Lor	T	Tx
Show Me The Way	Zon	G	Tc
Show Me The Way	Lor	T	Sl
Show Me The Way To Thee	Abi	L	Tc
Show Me Thy Ways (W/Oboe,Guit)	Aug	L	Tr
Show Us Your Mercy, Lord	Fel	L	Sl
Show Yourself In Me	Sil	L	Tj
Show Yourself To Me, Lord	Van	F	Tx
Sic Deus Dilexit Mundum	Gia	T	Sl
Sicut Cervus	Gsc	T	Tb
Sicut Cervus	Bbl	T	Lo
Sicut Rose & Ipsa Te Cogat Pietas	Gia	T	Tx
Sidney The Silly Centipede	Wlp	C	Tx
Siehe, Das Ist Gottes Lamm	Bbl	T	Tr
Sign Of His Life In The World, The	Fcc	L	Lo
Sign Of Total Giving	Fel	F	Lo
Signposts	Gsc	L	Tx
Silence Of God, The	Lor	T	Tx
Silent Devotion And Response	Bbl	T	Tx
Silent Night	Sac	T	Sc
Silent Night	Maf	T	Sc
Silent Night	Lor	T	Sc
Silent Night	Ccc	L	Tr
Silent Night (Full, Original Arr)	Aug	T	Sc
Silent Night (4-Part Arr)	Acp	T	Sc
Silent Night Holy Night	Zon	T	Sc
Silent The Night	Van	F	Sc
Silesian Lullaby	Ron	T	Sc
Silver & Gold	Mar	L	Tt
Silver And Gold Have I None	Nal	C	To
Silver Packages	Chd	F	Tt
Simeon's Canticle	Nal	L	Tr
Simon The Cyrenean Speaks	Sac	L	Sl
Simple Amen	Prc	L	Tx
Simple Christmas Song	Rav	F	Sc
Simple Gifts	Lor	T	To
Simple Gifts	Abi	L	To
Simple Gifts	Rpb	C	To
Simple Gifts	Nal	L	To
Simple Joys	Chh	F	To
Simple Songs For Toddlers No 1 (5572)	Zon	C	Za
Simple Songs For Toddlers No 2 (5573)	Zon	C	Za
Simple Songs For Toddlers No 3 (5574)	Zon	C	Za
Simple Songs For Toddlers No 4 (5630)	Zon	C	Za
Sin's Darkest Valley	Pmp	G	Sl
Since By Man Came Death	Gsc	T	Sr
Since God Came Into My Heart	Sem	G	Tc
Since I Found My Life In Him	Man	G	Tc
Since I Met Jesus	Mar	L	Tj
Since Jesus Passed By	Gmc	G	Tj
Since The Savior Found Me	Zon	G	Tr
Since We All Believe In Jesus	Zon	G	Tr

Sing 'n Celebrate! (Collection)	Wrd	G	Za
Sing A Brand New Song	Fel	L	Tt
Sing A New Song	Rpb	L	Tt
Sing A New Song	Her	L	Tt
Sing A New Song	Nal	L	Tt
Sing A New Song (Gonna Love)	Gia	F	Tr
Sing A New Song (No 5012)	Zon	G	Za
Sing A New Song Unto The Lord	Sac	L	Tt
Sing A Simple Song	Nal	C	Tr
Sing A Song Of Christmas	Dis	T	Sc
Sing A Song Of Joy	Aug	L	Tt
Sing A Song Of Love	Str	L	Tt
Sing A Song Of Love	Nal	L	Tr
Sing Alleluia	Fel	F	Tt
Sing Alleluia For Your Soul	Wbp	F	Tt
Sing Alleluia Forth	Gsc	T	Tt
Sing Alleluia Forth	Abi	L	Tt
Sing Alleluia To The King	Yan	F	Tt
Sing Alleluia!	Lor	T	Tt
Sing Alleluia! (Be Glad Within)	Jsp	F	Tt
Sing Alleluia, Jesus Lives	Sac	L	Sr
Sing Alleluia, Sing	Fcc	F	Tt
Sing Allelujah Christ Is Born	Gsc	T	Sc
Sing Aloud To God	Aug	T	Tt
Sing Aloud To God	Gsc	T	Tt
Sing Aloud Unto God	Gsc	T	Tt
Sing Aloud Unto God (Md)	Oxf	T	Tt
Sing And Give Praise	Lor	T	Tt
Sing And Praise Along The Way	Aug	L	Za
Sing And Rejoice	Sac	L	Sc
Sing And Rejoice (Md)	Oxf	T	Tt
Sing Brothers, Sing	Sac	L	Tt
Sing Folk! No 1 (No 5075)	Zon	F	Za
Sing Folk! No 2 (No 5076)	Zon	F	Za
Sing Folk! No 3 (No 5077)	Zon	F	Za
Sing For Joy	Aug	T	Za
Sing For Joy	Mob	C	Tx
Sing Freedom (Christ Calls)	Gia	F	Tc
Sing Gloria	Wbp	T	Tt
Sing Gloria	Aug	L	Tt
Sing Glory Hallelujah	Lor	T	Sc
Sing Glory To Our God	Chh	T	Tt
Sing Gods Praise	Wrd	G	Tt
Sing Hallelujah	Mar	L	Tt
Sing Hallelujah, Praise The Lord	Gsc	T	Sr
Sing His Praises No 1 (No 5060)	Zon	T	Za
Sing His Praises No 2 (No 5768)	Zon	T	Za
Sing Hosanna	Mam	G	Tr
Sing Hosanna (W/Org, Opt 3 Tpts)	Aug	L	Le
Sing Hosanna, Halleluia	Fel	F	Tt
Sing Hosanna, Sing (Ps. 92)	Nal	L	Tx
Sing Joy!	Sac	T	Sc
Sing Joy, Sing Love	Gia	L	Sc
Sing Joyfully (Md)	Oxf	T	Tt
Sing Joyfully To The Lord	Gia	L	Ld
Sing Joyfully To The Lord (Me)	Gia	L	Tt
Sing Little Children	Sil	G	Tx
Sing Love Songs	Prc	L	Tx
Sing Men! No 1 (No 5061)	Zon	G	Za
Sing Men! No 2 (No 5062)	Zon	G	Za
Sing Men! No 3 (No 5063)	Zon	C	Za
Sing Men! No 4 (No 5064)	Zon	G	Za
Sing Men! No 5 (No 5065)	Zon	G	Za
Sing Men! No 6 (No 5066)	Zon	G	Za
Sing My Song To Jesus	Mam	G	Tj
Sing My Tongue The Ageless Story	Wlp	T	Tt
Sing Noel, Merry Noel	Gsc	T	Sc
Sing Of Birth	Van	F	Sc
Sing Of Him	Nal	L	Tt
Sing Of Mary	Acp	L	Tm
Sing Of Mary	Acp	L	Tm
Sing Of Our God (Trinity)	Jsp	F	Tt
Sing Out His Goodness	Fel	F	Tt
Sing Out Hosannah	Ahc	L	Tr
Sing Out The Glory Of The Lord	Fel	F	Tt
Sing Out Use Your Voice Now	Gia	L	La
Sing Out, My Soul	Fel	F	Tt
Sing Out, My Soul, To The Lord	Fel	F	Tt
Sing Out, O Zion	Fel	F	Tt
Sing Out, Sing Out	Fel	F	Tt
Sing Praise	Rpb	L	Tt
Sing Praise To God	Sac	L	Tt
Sing Praise To God	Gia	T	Tt
Sing Praise To God	Lor	T	Tt
Sing Praise To God	Maf	T	Tt
Sing Praise To God Who Reigns Above	Aug	T	Tt
Sing Praise To God Who Reigns Above	Aug	L	Tt
Sing Praise To God Who Reigns Above	Oxf	T	Tt
Sing Praise To God!	Zon	T	Tt
Sing Praise To Our Creator	Wlp	T	Tt
Sing Praise To The Lord	Wlp	F	Tt
Sing Praise!	Nal	L	Tt
Sing Praises	Aug	T	Tt
Sing Praises To God	Fel	F	Tt
Sing Praises To God A Cap	Pro	T	Tt
Sing Praises To Our King	Lor	T	Sc
Sing Softly	Gsc	L	Sc
Sing The Praise Of Jesus	Gia	F	Tj
Sing Time For Children (No 5014)	Zon	C	Za
Sing To God	Van	F	Tt

ALPHABETICAL INDEX OF TITLES

Sing To God A Brand New Canticle	Nal	F	Tt
Sing To God A Joyous Song	Fel	F	Tt
Sing To Him	Her	L	Tt
Sing To Him Of Praise Eternal	Gia	L	Tt
Sing To Mary, Mother Most Merciful	Wlp	T	Tm
Sing To The Lord	Wlp	L	Tt
Sing To The Lord	Wgm	F	Tt
Sing To The Lord	Nal	L	Tt
Sing To The Lord	Sms	T	La
Sing To The Lord	Abi	L	Tt
Sing To The Lord	Gsc	T	Tt
Sing To The Lord	Gsc	T	Tt
Sing To The Lord (A Cap)	Pro	T	Tt
Sing To The Lord (Ascension)	Fel	L	Sr
Sing To The Lord (3 Voices)	Gia	T	Sr
Sing To The Lord (4-Part Arr)	Acp	L	Tt
Sing To The Lord A Joyful Song	Wlp	T	Tt
Sing To The Lord A Joyful Song (Md)	Oxf	T	Tt
Sing To The Lord A New Song	Gra	L	Ld
Sing To The Lord A New Song	Fel	L	Tt
Sing To The Lord A New Song	Lor	T	Tt
Sing To The Lord With Cheerful Voice	Sac	L	Tt
Sing To The Mountains	Nal	L	Tx
Sing Unto God	Aug	L	Tt
Sing Unto God (18 Minutes)	Oxf	T	Tw
Sing Unto The Lamb	Sha	F	Tt
Sing Unto The Lord A New Song	Sac	L	Tt
Sing Unto The Lord A New Song	Aug	L	Tt
Sing Up All Now Alleluia	Gia	T	Sr
Sing We	Wbp	T	Tt
Sing We A Song Of High Revolt	Jsp	L	Sl
Sing We All Noel	Abi	T	Sc
Sing We All Now With One Accord	Gsc	T	Tt
Sing We Merrily (Ps 81)	Oxf	L	Tt
Sing We Merrily (Ps 81)	Oxf	T	Tt
Sing We Merrily (W/Brass, Org)	Aug	L	Tt
Sing We Merrily To God	Sac	L	Tt
Sing We Merrily Unto God Our Strength	Gsc	L	Tt
Sing We Noel	Her	L	Sc
Sing We Now Hosanna	Sac	L	Sl
Sing We Now Of Christmas	Lor	T	Sc
Sing We The Praise Of God	Gsc	T	Tt
Sing We The Virgin Mary	Gsc	T	Sc
Sing We To Christ The King	Gsc	T	Sc
Sing With Fullness To God (5voices)	Gia	T	Tt
Sing With Joy To God	Fel	L	Tt
Sing With Joy To God (Ps81)	Gra	L	Ld
Sing With Joy To God Our Strength	Fel	L	Tt
Sing With Marcy (No 5455)	Zon	C	Za
Sing With The Spirit	Abi	L	Ss
Sing With Wonder And Delight	Lor	T	Sc
Sing Ye Joyfully To The Lord	Aug	L	Tt
Sing Ye Merrily	Aug	T	Tt
Sing Ye Nowell!	Bec	T	Sc
Sing Ye Praises (W/Clavier/Rhythm)	Aug	L	Tt
Sing! Make A Joyful Sound No 1 (5491)	Zon	G	Za
Sing! Make A Joyful Sound No 2 (5490)	Zon	G	Za
Sing! Make A Joyful Sound No 3 (5492)	Zon	G	Za
Sing! Make A Joyful Sound No 4 (5510)	Zon	G	Za
Sing-A-Long Songs As Used On The Child	Zon	C	Za
Sing, All Ye People	Zon	L	Tt
Sing, Christians, Sing	Sbf	F	Sr
Sing, Heaven Imperial (Md)	Oxf	T	Sa
Sing, Men And Angels, Sing	Aug	L	Tt
Sing, My Tongue (Choral)	Fel	T	Sl
Sing, O Heavens	Gsc	T	Sc
Sing, O Heavens (Md)	Oxf	L	Tt
Sing, O Sing	Gsc	L	Sc
Sing, O Sing To The Lord	Kal	T	Tt
Sing, Sing Alleluia	Gia	F	Tk
Sing, Sing Alleluia	Gia	F	Tt
Sing, Sing For Christmas	Lor	T	Sc
Sing, Sing, Sing (Opt Brass)	Mcc	F	Tt
Sing, Soul Of Mine! The Lord Is Risen	Aug	L	Sr
Sing, This Blessed Morn.	Gsc	T	Sc
Singer Of The Universe	Abi	L	Tt
Singers Sing	Wlp	T	Tt
Singers, Sing	Acp	L	Sc
Singers, Sing	Acp	L	Tt
Singet Dem Herrn (Motet #1)	Kal	T	Tt
Singing Alleluia	Aug	L	Tt
Singing Catechism	Aug	L	Za
Singing In Seven Parts (No 5038)	Zon	T	Za
Singing Men (Male Quartets And Choirs)	Zon	G	Za
Singing Youth	Zon	G	Za
Singspiration Annual No 1 (No 5840)	Zon	G	Za
Singspiration Annual No 2 (No 5841)	Zon	G	Za
Singspiration Annual No 3 (No 5842)	Zon	G	Za
Singspiration Annual No 4 (No 5848)	Zon	G	Za
Singspiration Annual No 5 (No 5845)	Zon	G	Za
Singspiration Annual No 6 (No 5839)	Zon	G	Za
Singspiration Annual No 7 (No 5902)	Zon	G	Za
Singspiration Annual No 8 (No 5914)	Zon	G	Za
Singspiration Guitar Hymnal (No 5785)	Zon	G	Zb
Singspiration No 1 (No 5001)	Zon	G	Za
Singspiration No 10 (No 5010)	Zon	G	Za
Singspiration No 11 (No 5011)	Zon	G	Za
Singspiration No 12 (No 5012)	Zon	G	Za
Singspiration No 2 (No 5002)	Zon	G	Za
Singspiration No 3 (No 5003)	Zon	G	Za
Singspiration No 4 (No 5004)	Zon	G	Za
Singspiration No 5 (No 5005)	Zon	G	Za
Singspiration No 6 (No 5006)	Zon	G	Za
Singspiration No 7 (No 5007)	Zon	G	Za
Singspiration No 8 (No 5008)	Zon	G	Za
Singspiration No 9 (No 5009)	Zon	G	Za
Sinner You Can't Walk My Path	Wbp	T	Tx
Sir Christmas	Gsc	T	Sc
Sitivit Anima Mea	Bbl	T	Tb
Sittin' In The Pew	Mar	L	Tx
Six Anthems For Junior Choir	Abi	C	Za
Six Anthems For Junior Voices	Abi	C	Za
Six Christmas Songs	Gsc	T	Za
Six Early American Anthems	Wlp	T	Tp
Six Easter Preludes	Abi	L	Zb
Six Easter Preludes (Hymn-Tune Prelude	Abi	L	Zb
Six Evening Hymns	Gsc	T	Za
Six Hymn-Tune Preludes	Abi	L	Zb
Six Motets	Lps	T	Za
Six Motets	Kal	T	Za
Six Motets In Polish And English	Gia	T	Za
Six Polyphonic Motets	Gia	T	Za
Six Sacred Anthems For Male Voices	Abi	L	Za
Six Sacred Compositions For Organ	Abi	L	Zb
Six Service Pieces For Organ	Abi	L	Zb
Six Short Anthems For The Seasons	Oxf	T	Za
Six Sixty Six	Sil	L	Tx
Six Songs	Pic	L	Za
Sixteen Choral Responses	Lor	T	Za
Sixteen Singing Men (No 5458)	Zon	G	Za
Sixteenth-Century Anthem Book, A	Oxf	T	Za
Sixty Pieces For The Manuals	Cob	T	Zb
Sleep Celestial Infant (Mex-Am Carol)	Pro	F	Sc
Sleep In Peace, O Heavenly Child	Gsc	T	Sc
Sleep My Little One	Smc	T	Sc
Sleep Of The Child Jesus	Lor	T	Sc
Sleep Of The Child Jesus	Abi	L	Sc
Sleep Well, Thou Lovely Heavenly Babe	Gia	T	Sc
Sleep, Holy Babe	Gsc	T	Sc
Sleep, Little Jesus	Sac	T	Sc
Sleep, Little Lord	Gsc	T	Sc
Sleep, My Jesus, Sleep	Pro	T	Sc
Sleep, My Savior, Sleep	Zon	T	Sc
Sleepers Awake (Cantata)	Lps	T	Sr
Sleepers Wake (From Cantata 140)	Gsc	T	Sa
Sleepers, Wake, A Voice Is Calling	Gsc	T	Sa
Slow Down (In The Midst...)	Wrd	G	Tr
Slumber, O Holy Jesu	Sac	T	Sc
Slumber, O Holy Jesu (Christmas)	Abi	L	Sc
Smile	Sil	L	Tx
Smile Because God Loves You	Mam	G	Tx
Smile Song	Yan	F	Tr
Smile, Jesus Loves You	Man	G	Tr
Smilin' More Everyday (No 5013)	Zon	F	Za
Snow Lay On The Ground, The	Lor	T	Sc
So Close To You And Me	Fel	L	Tr
So Dark The Night	Abi	L	Sc
So Dost Thou Give	Aug	L	Tx
So Full Of Song	Van	F	Tr
So Great A Gift (No 5985) Cantata	Zon	L	Sc
So Let Me Live	Lor	T	Sr
So Lonely	Fel	L	Sl
So Lowly Doth The Savior Ride	Sac	L	Sl
So Much	Mar	L	Tr
So Quietly He Came	Lor	T	Tx
So Said Amos The Prophet	Fel	F	Tx
So Send I You (No 6002)	Zon	G	Tc
So Send I You (With Brass)	Zon	G	Tc
So Soon It Is Over	Man	G	Tf
Soft Light Of Morning (Me)	Gia	L	Tr
Softly The Winds Blew (Polish Carol)	Pro	T	Sc
Sold Out To Jesus	Pmp	G	Tc
Soldiers Of Christ, Arise	Gsc	L	Tc
Soldiers Of Christ, Arise	Lor	T	Tc
Soldiers Of Christ, Arise!	Abi	L	Tc
Solemn Amen	Prc	L	Tx
Solemn Mass For Voices (Latin)	Kal	T	Za
Solid Rock, The	Lor	T	Tr
Solid Rock, The	Zon	F	Tr
Solomon's Canticle	See	L	Tt
Solos For Christmas No 1	Zon	L	Za
Solos For Christmas No 2	Zon	L	Za
Solos For Easter	Zon	L	Za
Solus Ad Victimam (Me)	Oxf	T	Sl
Some Beautiful Morning	Mmc	G	Sr
Some Day	Jhm	G	Tk
Some Other Man	Ahc	L	Tx
Some Seed Fell On Good Ground	Fel	L	Tx
Some Young Carpenter	Wlp	F	Tj
Somebody Heard My Prayer	Zon	G	Tr
Somebody Loves You	Man	G	Tr
Somebody's Knocking At Your Door	Lor	T	Tr
Someday	Fel	L	Sa
Someday I'll See His Face	Man	G	Sr
Someday My Lord Will Come	Wrd	G	Sa
Someone	Ham	G	Tx
Someone	Lor	T	Tr
Someone	Zon	G	Tx
Someone Watches Over Me	Sem	G	Tr
Someone, Somewhere	Lor	T	Tt
Someone's Callin'	Mar	L	Tc
Somethin' Happened Today	Wlp	L	Tx
Something Beautiful	Gmc	G	Tj
Something For Jesus	Lor	T	Tc
Something More	Mar	L	Tc
Something New For Christmas (No 5594)	Zon	L	Sc
Something To Be Thankful For	Man	G	To
Something To Remember At Xmas	Pmp	G	Sc
Something Worth Living For	Lor	G	Tx
Something Worth Living For	Gmc	G	Tc
Something's Happened To Daddy	Gmc	G	Tx
Sometimes	Prc	L	Tx
Sometimes	Fel	F	Sl
Sometimes	Zon	G	Sl
Sometimes Alleluia	Wrd	G	Tt
Sometimes I Feel Like A Motherless Ch.	Gsc	T	Sl
Sometimes I'd Like To Be A Clown	Wlp	C	Tx
Sometimes, O Lord	Rpb	L	Sl
Somewhere Beyond The Sun	Ham	G	Sr
Somewhere In Heaven	Zon	G	Sa
Son Come Down (Guitar Or Piano)	Gia	F	Tj
Son Come Out	Mar	L	Sl
Son Of God	Acp	L	Tj
Son Of God	Gsc	T	Tj
Son Of God	Acp	L	Tj
Son Of God!	Nal	L	Tj
Son Of God, Eternal Savior	Lor	T	Tj
Son, Why Have You Treated Us So	Fel	L	Sc
Sonata	Abi	L	Zb
Sonata I For Organ	Abi	L	Zb
Song At The Foot Of The Mountain	Nal	L	Tx
Song Favorites For Low Voices	Zon	G	Za
Song Favorites For Trios	Zon	L	Za
Song For Daniel, A	See	L	Tx
Song For Martin (Moses)	Nal	L	Tx
Song For Pauline	Nal	L	Tx
Song For The Church	Mar	L	Tr
Song For The Masses, A	Nal	L	Tx
Song For The New Year, A	Sac	L	Tx
Song For The Sun	Van	F	Tt
Song From St. Matthew	Gsc	T	Sc
Song Of All Seed	Nal	L	Tx
Song Of Baptism	Nal	L	Tb
Song Of Bethlehem, A	Lor	C	Sc
Song Of Blessing	Rav	C	Tt
Song Of Blessing	Nal	L	Tt
Song Of Christian Men	Nal	L	Tc
Song Of Commitment	Wlp	L	Tc
Song Of Covenant	Rpb	L	Tc
Song Of Daniel	Gia	L	Tt
Song Of Daniel	Acp	F	Tx
Song Of Daniel	Acp	F	Tt
Song Of Deliverance	Lor	T	Sr
Song Of Deliverance, A	Sac	L	Sr
Song Of Exhaltation ,	Gsc	T	Tt
Song Of Glory	Van	F	Sc
Song Of God, The	Lor	T	Tx
Song Of God's Kingdom (From St. Paul)	Gia	F	Tr
Song Of Good News, The	Acf	F	Tx
Song Of Hannah	Fel	F	Tx
Song Of Hope	Gia	L	Sr
Song Of Jesus Christ	Nal	L	Tj
Song Of Job (From Come Follow)	Gia	G	Sl
Song Of Joy	Mar	L	Tr
Song Of Joy	Wlp	L	Tr
Song Of Life	Sil	F	Tx
Song Of Love	Ccc	L	Tw
Song Of Love, Hope & Good Cheer	Yan	F	Tr
Song Of Loveliness	Van	F	Tr
Song Of Loyal Brotherhood	Gsc	T	Tu
Song Of Mary	Fel	L	Tm
Song Of Mary	Van	F	Tm
Song Of Mary (W/Insts)	Aug	L	Tm
Song Of Moses	Gsc	T	Tx
Song Of My People	Wgm	F	Tx
Song Of New Life	Nal	L	Tb
Song Of Peace, A	Lor	T	Tr
Song Of Peace, A	Sac	L	Tr
Song Of Praise	Wgm	F	Tt
Song Of Praise	Gsc	L	Tt
Song Of Praise	Zon	T	Tt
Song Of Praise	Gsc	T	Tt
Song Of Praise (W/Perc)	Aug	L	Tt
Song Of Repentance	Bbl	T	Tr
Song Of Repentance	Fis	F	Tr
Song Of Ruth	Rav	F	Tw
Song Of Sarah	Fcc	C	Tx
Song Of Tears And Triumph	Nal	L	Sr
Song Of Thankfulness	Ccc	L	Tt
Song Of Thanks	Fel	F	Tt
Song Of Thanksgiving	Fcc	F	Tt
Song Of Thanksgiving	Kal	T	Tt
Song Of Thanksgiving	Nal	L	Tt
Song Of Thanksgiving, A	Lor	T	Tt
Song Of The Angels	Lor	T	Sc
Song Of The Angels, The	Lor	T	Sc
Song Of The Angels, The	Lor	L	Sc
Song Of The City	Acp	F	Tx
Song Of The City	Nal	L	Tx
Song Of The City	Acp	F	Tx

ALPHABETICAL INDEX OF TITLES

Song Of The Crib	Aug L Sc
Song Of The Garo Christians	Gsc T Tx
Song Of The Holy Night	Lor L Sc
Song Of The Holy Spirit	Nal L Ss
Song Of The Journey	Nal L Tx
Song Of The Loving Father	Nal C Tr
Song Of The Passion (M)	Oxf T Tj
Song Of The Prodigal	Man G Sl
Song Of The Shepherd	See L Tr
Song Of The Shepherd Boy	Sac L Sc
Song Of The Shepherds, The	Zon L Sc
Song Of The Stable Boy	Van F Sc
Song Of The Thankful(Come Follow)	Gia F Sl
Song Of The Three Young Men	Gia L Ld
Song Of The Wounded	Nal L Sl
Song Of Trust	Fel F Tr
Song Of Watchfulness	Rav L Sa
Song Of Zachary	Fel L Tt
Song Of Zachary	Gia L Tt
Song That The Angels Sang, The	Lor T Sc
Song To The Lamb Of God (First Mass)	Fel F Lm
Song To The Lamb Of God (Second Mass)	Fel F Lm
Songs And Hymns Of Praise And Worship	Zon G Za
Songs Everybody Loves No 1 (No 5418)	Zon G Za
Songs Everybody Loves No 2 (No 5419)	Zon G Za
Songs Everybody Loves No 3 (No 5420)	Zon G Za
Songs Everybody Loves No 4 (No 5421)	Zon G Za
Songs Everybody Loves No 5 (No 5426)	Zon G Za
Songs Everybody Loves No 6 (No 5471)	Zon G Za
Songs Everybody Loves No 7 (No 5474)	Zon G Za
Songs For Kindergarten Children	Flp T Za
Songs For Men No 1 (No 5436)	Zon G Za
Songs For Men No 2 (No 5437)	Zon G Za
Songs For Men No 3 (No 5438)	Zon G Za
Songs For Mixed Quartets No 2(No 5749)	Zon G Za
Songs For Our Revival And Evangelist.	Zon G Za
Songs For Special Days	Zon L Za
Songs From My Heart (W/Guitar)	Gia F Za
Songs Of Erv Lewis (No 5139)	Zon F Za
Songs Of Praise The Angels Sang	Som L Sc
Songs Of Praises	Gsc T Za
Songs That Touch The Heart No 1	Zon G Za
Songs That Touch The Heart No 2	Zon G Za
Songs That Touch The Heart No 3	Zon G Za
Songs That Touch The Heart No 4	Zon G Za
Songs That Touch The Heart No 5	Zon G Za
Songster Favorites (No 5439)	Zon G Za
Sonnet (On Hearing The Dies Irae Sung)	Gsc T Tf
Sons Of Cain	Fel F Sl
Sons Of God	Fel F Ln
Sons Of God, The	Sac L Tr
Sons Of Jacob	Fcc C Tx
Sonshine	Mar L Tj
Soon A New Dawn	Ccc L Zb
Soon I'll See His Face	Man G Sr
Soon One Mornin' Death Comes Creepin'	Gsc G Tx
Sorrow And Grief	Bbl T Sl
Sorrow's Tear (From Three Songs)	Bbl T Sl
Sorrowful Mysteries	Wlp T Tm
Sorrowful Now Is My Soul	Som T Sl
Sorrowful Road, The	Abi L Sl
Sorsum Corda (English)	Gia F Le
Soul Of My Savior	Gia T Tj
Soul, Array Thyself	Gsc T Tf
Souls Of The Righteous	Aug T Sr
Sound Forth The Trumpet In Zion	Gia T Tt
Sound Over All Waters	Wbp T Tt
Sound The Trumpet (2 Pt Acc)	Elv T Sr
Sound The Trumpet, Strike The Cymbal	Gsc T Tt
Soundings For New Beginnings	Ccc L Ld
Sounds For Now	Abi L Za
Sounds Of Celebration No 1	Zon F Za
Sounds Of Living Waters	Erd L Za
Sow A Seed	Nal L Tx
Sparrow Finds A Home, The	Nal L Tr
Sparrows	Sbf L Tr
Speak To Me, Wind	Van F Tx
Speak To One Another Of Psalms	Aug L Tr
Speak, Lord	Gmc G Tr
Special Day Organist (No 5942)	Zon T Zb
Special Trio Arrangements No 1 5422	Zon L Za
Special Trio Arrangements No 2 5423	Zon L Za
Special Trio Arrangements No 3 5424	Zon L Za
Spem In Alium Nunquam Habui	Oxf T Tt
Spes Mea, Christe, Deus	Kal T Tr
Spirit Boundless	Aug L Ss
Spirit Comes, The	Nal L Ss
Spirit Divine	Sac T Ss
Spirit Is A-Movin', The	Nal L Ss
Spirit Move	Fcc F Ss
Spirit Of Action	Acp F Ss
Spirit Of Action 4-Part Arr	Acp L Ss
Spirit Of God	Mob C Tx
Spirit Of God	Gsc T Ss
Spirit Of God	Lor T Ss
Spirit Of God	Van F Ss
Spirit Of God, This Very Hour	Lor T Ss
Spirit Of Life	Nal L Ss
Spirit Of Life (Violin)	Abi L Ss
Spirit Of Light And Life	Rpb L Ss

Spirit Of Strength	Acp L Ss
Spirit Of Strength	Acp L Ss
Spirit Of The Lord	Van F Ss
Spirit Of The Lord, The	Lor T Ss
Spirit Of The Lord, The (Unacc)	Abi L Ss
Spirits & Places	Wlp T Zb
Spirits Of The Night	Msm F Tx
Spirituals For Instrument	Yba G Zb
Splendor Of Creation	Wlp L Tm
Sponsus (The Bridegroom)Acting Version	Oxf T Tk
Spread A Little Love Around	Man G Tr
Spread The Word	Zon G Tc
Spread Thou Mighty Word (Hymn)	Jsp T Tc
Spread Your Love	Rpb L Tr
Spread Your Wings	Sil F Tx
Spring Hill	Bbl T Tt
Springs Of Living Water	Zon G Ss
Springs Of Water (Icet)	Wlp L Ld
Sprinkle, Me, Lord	Fel L Tb
Squattin' Little Squillit	Mem F Tt
St John Passion, The	Abi T Sl
St. Anne's Fugue	Smc T Zb
St. Francis Prayer	Wlp F Tr
St. John Passion (Germ/Eng)	Kal T Sl
St. John Passion(Ger)	Cfp T Sl
St. John The Evangelist	Van F Tx
St. John's Passion	Kal T Sl
St. Joseph Was A Just Man	Wlp L Tx
St. Mark Passion (W/Soli)	Cfp T Sl
St. Matt. 5:16	Jhm G Tt
St. Matthew Passion (Eng)	Kal T Sl
St. Matthew Passion(Ger)	Cfp T Sl
St. Paul (Oratorio, Germ/Eng)	Kal T Tx
Stabat Mater	Bbl T Tm
Stabat Mater	Kal T Sl
Stabat Mater	Kal T Sl
Stabat Mater	Gsc T Tm
Stabat Mater	Oxf T Sl
Stabat Mater	Som L Tm
Stabat Mater	Kal T Sl
Stabat Mater	Kal T Sl
Stabat Mater (Unfinished)	Kal T Sl
Stabat Mater (W/Sop Solo)	Cfp T Sl
Stabat Mater Dolorosa	Fel T Tm
Stabat Mater 1	Kal T Sl
Stand By Me, Jesus	Ste F Tj
Stand In Awe	Lor T Tr
Stand On His Promise	Wlp L Ss
Stand Up	Wlp C Le
Stand Up And Bless The Lord	Aug L La
Stand Up And Bless The Lord	Zon L La
Stand Up And Bless The Lord (Me)	Oxf T Tt
Stand Up And Sing (No 4062)	Zon G Za
Stand Up For Jesus	Lor T Tc
Stand Up For Jesus	Lor T Tc
Stand Up For Jesus(W/Opt Trumpet Trio)	Zon G Tc
Stand Up, Stand Up For Jesus	Sac T Tc
Stand With Me	Nal L Tr
Standard Christmas Carols	Lor T Za
Standin' In The Need O' Prayer	Gsc T Sl
Standing Far Off	Jhm G Tx
Star In The East	Gsc T Sc
Star In The Night, A	Lor T Sc
Star In The Sky, A	Lor L Sc
Star Of Bethlehem, Op 164 Eng	Kal T Sc
Star Of The East	Lor T Sc
Star Of The Orient	Gsc T Sc
Star Of The Silent Night	Lor L Sc
Star Upon The Ocean	Wlp T Tm
Star, A Shepherd, A Lamb, A	Lor T Sc
Starlight	Prc L Tx
Stars Shone Bright, The (Norwegian)	Lor T Sc
Stay With Me	Nal L Tr
Stay With Me Jesus	Sem G Tj
Stay With Us	Flp T Tx
Stay With Your People, Lord	Nal L Tr
Steadfast And Good Is Jehovah	Gsc T Tr
Steadfast In Your Paths (Ps 17)	Gra F Ld
Steal Away	Zon G Tr
Steal Away To Jesus	Gsc T Tr
Stephen Was A Stable-Boy	Gsc T Sc
Steward's Prayer, The	Abi L To
Still, Still (Arr)	Gia T Sc
Still, Still With Thee	Gsc T Tr
Still, Still With Thee	Lor T Tr
Still, Still, Still	Aug T Tx
Still,Still,Still	Hal L Sc
Stilled & Quiet Is My Soul Ps 139	Gia F Tx
Stir Up Your Power	Fel L Tr
Story Of Love, The	Lor L Sc
Stranger, Share Our Fire	Aug L Tr
Strangest Dream	Alm F Tt
Strangest Dream, The	Fcc C Tx
Streams In The Desert	Gia F Sc
Streams Of Babylon (Psalm 137)	Ahc L Sl
Streams Of Life	Mar L Ss
Strengthen, O God	Gia L Ss
Strengthen, O God, What You	Fel L Ss
Strife Is O'er, The	Zon T Sr
Striving After God	Wbp T Tx

Strong Son Of God, Immortal Love	Som L Tj
Sublime Alleluia, A	Sac T Tt
Subvenite (Choral)	Fel T Tf
Such A Gay & Happy Tune	Pro T Tt
Suffer The Children	Wrd G Tj
Suffering Servant Song, The	Nal L Tj
Suite For Christmas (Mod)	Abi L Zb
Suite For Organ	Abi L Zb
Summer Ended	Gsc T Tx
Sun Has Risen, The	Acp L Tx
Sun Has Risen, The (4-Part Arr)	Acp L Tx
Sun Of My Soul (A Cap)	Wrd G Tr
Sun Shines In Splendor, The	Lor T Tx
Sunday Carol (A Cap)	Pro L Lp
Sunday Choir (No Zd-5472)	Zon G Za
Sunday Morning Orangist No 2 (No 5817)	Zon T Zb
Sunday Morning Organist No 1 (No 5807)	Zon T Zb
Sunday Morning Organist No 3 (No 5286)	Zon T Zb
Sunday Morning Organist No 4 (No 5287)	Zon T Zb
Sunday Morning Organist No 5 (No 5288)	Zon T Zb
Sunday School Sinner	Jhm G Sl
Sundown (Bar Solo,Orch Or Piano)	Gia L Sl
Sunlight	Zon G Tr
Sunrise On A Hill	Lor T Sr
Sunrise, Sunset	Nyt F Tt
Sunshine	Wlp F Tx
Sunshine Choir No 1 (No 5520)	Zon C Za
Sunshine Choir No 2 (No 5523)	Zon C Za
Sunshine In My Soul	Zon G Tr
Super Flumina Babylonis	Maf T Sl
Suppertime	Jhm G Tx
Supplication	Lor T Tr
Supplications	Gsc T Tr
Surely God Is In This Place	Lor T La
Surely God Is In This Place	Lor T La
Surely Goodness (Psalm 23:6)	Mar L Tr
Surely Goodness And Mercy	Zon G Tr
Surely Goodness And Mercy (Crusade Ed)	Zon G Tr
Surely He Has Borne Our Griefs	Aug L Sl
Surely He Hath Borne Our Griefs	Gsc T Sl
Surely He Hath Borne Our Griefs	Cfs T Sl
Surely He Hath Borne Our Griefs	Sac T Sl
Surely He Hath Borne Our Griefs	Gsc T Sl
Surely I Can Believe	Man G Tr
Surely The Lord Is In This Place	Abi L Tc
Surely The Lord Is In This Place	Sac L Tc
Surely, God Is In This Holy Place	Gam L Tc
Surrender	Man G Tc
Surrexit Dominus	Gia T Sr
Surrexit Pastor Bonus	Gsc T Sr
Susan's Song (Based On Kahil Gibran)	Nal L Tx
Sweet Hour Of Prayer	Lor T Tr
Sweet Is Thy Mercy	Gsc T Sl
Sweet Jesu, King Of Bliss (E)	Oxf T Tj
Sweet Jesus	Man G Tj
Sweet Jesus	Bec T Tj
Sweet Jesus (Your Spirit)	Fis F Ss
Sweet Jesus Morning	Mar L Tj
Sweet Little Boy Jesus	Gsc T Sc
Sweet Little Jesus Baby	Maf G Sc
Sweet Marie And Her Baby	Gsc T Sc
Sweet Music	Lor T Sr
Sweet Peace	Man G Tr
Sweet Rivers	Gsc T Ss
Sweet Spirit, Comfort Me	Gsc T Ss
Sweet Summer Rain	Mar L Ss
Sweet Surrender	Clm F Tt
Sweet Sweet Sound	Rav L Lo
Sweet Was The Song	Gsc T Sc
Sweet Was The Song (W/Solo)	Cfs T Sc
Sweet Was The Song The Virgin Sang	Aug L Sc
Sweet Wine	Sbf L Lo
Sweet, Sweet Song	Mar L Tr
Sweet, Sweet Spirit	Man G Ss
Sweeter Than The Day Before	Gmc G Tj
Sweetest Name I Know	Mar L Tj
Swing Down Sweet Chariot	Mar L Tf
Swing Low Sweet Chariot	Pmp G Sr
Swing Low, Sweet Chariot	Gsc G Tx
Swing Low, Sweet Chariot	Abi L Sr
Swords Into Plowshares	Gsc L Tr
Symphonia Sacra: Mein Sohn, Warum	Oxf T Sc
Symphony Of Psalms	Kal T Za
Syriac Acclamation	Gra L Lj
T'was On A Cold And Wintry Night	Fcc F Tx
Take Courage	Van F Sc
Take From Us, Lord	Bbl T Tc
Take Heart	Rpb L Tr
Take It On Over	Lor T Tt
Take It To Jesus	Lor T Tj
Take Me Back (Collection Youth)	Wrd G Za
Take My Hand	Fcc F Tr
Take My Hand	Fel F Tr
Take My Hands	Fcc F To
Take My Life	Bfi F To
Take My Life And Let It Be	Lor T Tc
Take My Life And Let It Be	Zon T Tc
Take My Life And Let It Be	Zon F Tc
Take My Life Precious Jesus	Wrd G Tc
Take Our Bread	Wlp F To

ALPHABETICAL INDEX OF TITLES

Take Our Gifts	Wlp	F	To
Take Our Hands	Wgm	L	To
Take The Child And His Mother	Fel	L	Sc
Take Thou Our Minds, Dear Lord	Sac	L	Tc
Take Time	Prc	L	Tx
Take Time Out	Wlp	C	Tx
Take Time To Be Holy	Lor	T	Tr
Take Time To Pray	Zon	G	Tr
Take Up Thy Cross	Lor	T	Tc
Take Up Thy Cross	Lor	T	Sl
Take Up Thy Cross	Lor	T	Tc
Take Up Your Cross And Follow Me	Zon	G	Tc
Take Us, O Lord	Gia	T	Sl
Take, Lord, Receive	Nal	L	To
Taken Up In Glory	Gia	L	Sr
Talk With Us Lord	Gsc	L	Tr
Talking Pets	Van	C	Tx
Tallis Canon (4 Voices)	Gia	T	Tt
Tambourines To Glory	Wbp	T	Tx
Tantum Ergo	Kal	T	Lo
Tantum Ergo	Gsc	T	Lo
Tantum Ergo	Gia	T	Lo
Tantum Ergo, Opus 65, No. 2	Bbl	T	Lo
Tantum Ergo, 6 Settings(Eng-Lat)	Cfp	T	Za
Tantum Ergos (Six)	Kal	T	Za
Taste And See	Rpb	L	Lo
Taste And See	Gia	L	Ld
Taste And See (Icet)	Wlp	L	Ld
Taste And See (Ps 34)	Gra	F	Ln
Taste And See (Ps 34)	Rav	L	Ld
Taste And See How Good The Lord Is	Fel	L	Ln
Taste The New Wine	Prc	L	Tx
Te Deum	Kal	T	Tt
Te Deum	Kal	T	Tt
Te Deum	Kal	T	Tt
Te Deum	Gsc	T	Tt
Te Deum	Tcp	L	Tt
Te Deum	Fel	F	Tt
Te Deum	See	L	Tt
Te Deum	Gsc	T	Tt
Te Deum	Kal	T	Tt
Te Deum (Eng, Lat)	Oxf	T	Tt
Te Deum (Icet) W/ Organ (Me)	Gia	L	Tt
Te Deum (Md)	Oxf	T	Tt
Te Deum (Md)	Oxf	T	Tt
Te Deum (You Are God: We Praise You)	Cfc	L	Tt
Te Deum And Benedictus	Oxf	T	Tt
Te Deum And Jubilate (Md)	Oxf	T	Tt
Te Deum In C Maj (D)	Oxf	T	Tt
Te Deum In D	Kal	T	Tt
Te Deum In G (Md)	Oxf	T	Tt
Te Deum Jubilar	Som	L	Tt
Te Deum Laudamus	Kal	T	Tt
Te Deum Laudamus (Eng,Org,Guit)	Gia	L	Tt
Te Deum With Congregation (E)	Oxf	T	Tt
Te Deum(C)(Latin)	Cfp	T	Tt
Te Deum, K 141	Bbl	T	Tt
Teach All Nations	Sac	L	Tc
Teach Me O Lord	Gsc	T	Sl
Teach Me Thy Way	Lor	T	Sl
Teach Me To Die	Fcc	F	Sl
Teach Me To Love	Zon	L	Tr
Teach Me To Love Thee More	Lor	T	Sl
Teach Me To Pray	Lor	T	Sl
Teach Me Your Law, O Lord	Fel	L	Tr
Teach Me Your Ways (Ps 25)	Rav	L	Ld
Teach Me, Fill Me, Use Me, Lord	Lor	L	Tc
Teach Me, Lord, To Do Your Will	Fel	L	Tr
Teach Me, Lord, To Wait	Ham	G	Sl
Teach Me, O Lord (Ps 119 Md)	Oxf	T	Tr
Teach Me, O Lord (Ps 119 Me)	Oxf	T	Sa
Teach Your Children	Grm	F	Tt
Tear Down The Walls	Mar	L	Sl
Tedd Smith's Hymn Transcriptions	Zon	T	Zb
Tedd Smith's Piano Solo Arrangements	Zon	T	Zb
Teen Choir (No 5260)	Zon	F	Za
Teen Favorites (No 5662)	Zon	F	Za
Teen Time Tunes (No 5733)	Zon	F	Za
Teenage Choir No 1 (No 5588)	Zon	F	Za
Teenage Choir No 2 (No 5583)	Zon	F	Za
Teenage Choir No 3 (No 5579)	Zon	F	Za
Teenage Choir No 4 (No 5578)	Zon	F	Za
Teenage Favorites No 1 (No 5586)	Zon	F	Za
Teenage Favorites No 2 (No 5587)	Zon	F	Za
Teenage Favorites No 3 (No 5607)	Zon	F	Za
Teenage Favorites No 4 (No 5610)	Zon	F	Za
Teilhard's Offering	Gia	F	To
Teilhard's Vision	Gia	F	Tj
Tell It Out (All Creation Has Ears)	Gia	F	Tc
Tell Me Now	Fel	F	Tx
Tell Me That Name Again	Gmc	G	Tj
Tell Me Why	Man	G	Tx
Tell The Blessed Tidings	Aug	L	Sc
Tell The Good News	Zon	G	Tc
Tell The World	Fel	F	Ss
Temples Eternal	Aug	L	Tr
Temples Of God	Aug	L	Tr
Temptation	Man	G	Sl
Temptation Of Christ, The	Abi	L	Sl
Ten Chorale Improvisations (7 Sets)	Con	L	Zb

Ten Faux Bourdons On Well-Known Hymns	Oxf	T	Za
Ten Four-Part Motets For The Year	Oxf	T	Za
Ten Lepers	Van	F	Tx
Ten Pieces For Organ	Abi	L	Zb
Ten Thousand Angels	Lor	T	Sr
Tenderly	Zon	G	Tr
Tenebrae Factae Sunt	Gsc	T	Sl
Tenebrae Factae Sunt	Gsc	T	Sa
Testimony	Sil	L	Tx
Testimony	Mar	L	Tx
Thank God For The Promise Of Spring	Gmc	G	Sr
Thank The Lord	Ahc	L	Tt
Thank The Lord	Zon	G	Tt
Thank The Lord	Hhh	G	Tt
Thank The Lord With Songs Of Praise	Fel	F	Tt
Thank You	Fel	F	Tt
Thank You For Today	Van	F	Tt
Thank You Hymn	Fel	C	Tt
Thank You Jesus	Mar	L	Tt
Thank You Lord	Prc	L	Tx
Thank You Lord	Fis	F	Tt
Thank You, Jesus	Fcc	L	Tj
Thank You, Jesus	Van	F	Tt
Thank You, Jesus, You're My Friend	Sil	L	Tj
Thank You, Lord	Zon	G	Tt
Thank You, Thank You	Prc	L	Tx
Thanks Be To Christ (Your Body)	Jsp	L	Ln
Thanks Be To God	Smc	T	Zb
Thanks Be To God	Gsc	T	Tt
Thanks Be To God	Wlp	F	Tt
Thanks Be To God (From Elijah)	Gsc	T	Tt
Thanks Be To God.	Vrn	L	Tt
Thanks Be To Thee	Gsc	T	Tt
Thanks Be To Thee	Pro	T	Tt
Thanks Be To Thee, O God	Wlp	L	Tt
Thanks For Sunshine	Gmc	G	Tt
Thanks To Calvary	Gmc	G	Sl
Thanks To God For My Mother	Lor	T	Tx
Thanks To God!	Zon	T	Tt
Thanks To Thee	Cor	F	Tt
Thanksgiving	Pic	L	Tt
Thanksgiving (From Holiday Motets)	Ron	T	Tt
Thanksgiving Hymn (Give Thanks To God)	Gia	L	Tt
Thanksgiving Litany	Rpb	L	Tt
Thanksgiving Song	See	L	Tt
Thanksgiving Song	Sha	F	Tt
Thanksgiving To God For His House, A	Her	L	Tc
That Beautiful Name	Zon	T	Sc
That Easter Day	Acp	L	Sr
That Easter Day	Acp	L	Sr
That Easter Day With Joy Was Bright	Aug	T	Sr
That Easter Day With Joy Was Bright	Aug	T	Sr
That Easter Morn At Break Of Day(Tpt)	Aug	T	Sr
That Glorious Day	Pdm	L	Sr
That God Doth Love The World We Know	Oxf	T	Sr
That Holy Night	Lor	T	Sc
That I May Too Arise	Lor	L	Sr
That Lonesome Valley	Ham	G	Sl
That One Bright Star	Lor	L	Sc
That The World Might Be Renewed	Nal	L	Sr
That They All May Be One	Gsc	T	Tu
That Virgin's Child	Gsc	T	Sr
That We May Be One	Bfi	F	Tu
That's How Real God Can Be	Sil	G	Tr
That's My God	Nal	L	Tx
That's What Jesus Means To Me	Gmc	G	Tj
That's Worth Everything	Gmc	G	Tx
The "Leroy" Kyrie	Oxf	T	Sl
The Acclamations (Christ Has Died)	Gia	L	Lj
The Addict's Plea	Man	G	Tx
The Alphabet Tree	Wlp	C	Tx
The American Country Hymn Book	Wrd	G	Za
The Angel Of The Lord Delivers	Fel	L	Tr
The Angel's Carol	Cfp	T	Sc
The Angel's Song	Aug	T	Sc
The Angels And The Shepherds	Her	T	Sc
The Angels And The Shepherds	Gsc	T	Sc
The Angels Song	Gsc	T	Sc
The Apostle's Creed	Yan	F	Tx
The Appeal Of The Crucified	Gsc	T	Sl
The Babe	Gsc	T	Sc
The Bagpiper's Carol (Arr)	Gia	L	Sc
The Baker Woman	Van	F	Tm
The Ballad Of Lazarus And The Rich Man	Rpb	T	Tx
The Ballad Of Luke Warm	Mar	L	Tx
The Ballad Of Paul	Rpb	L	Tx
The Banquet Of The Lord	Fel	F	Lo
The Baptism Song	Ahc	L	Tb
The Baroque Song Book	Maf	T	Za
The Battle Of Jericho (Traditional)	Gsc	G	Tx
The Beatitudes	Aug	T	Tr
The Beatitudes	Gsc	T	Tr
The Beatitudes	Sms	F	Tr
The Beatitudes (From Come Follow)	Gia	F	Tr
The Bell Doth Toll	Som	L	Sl
The Bells At Speyer	Gsc	T	Tx
The Bells Of Heaven	Gsc	T	Sc
The Bells Ring Out For Christmas	Gsc	T	Sc
The Big "G" Stands For	Van	C	Tt
The Binding (Oratorio)	Oxf	T	Tx

The Birth	Van	F	Sc
The Birth Of Our Lord And Saviour	Gsc	T	Sc
The Birthday Of A King	Gsc	T	Sc
The Birthday Of The King (No 5524)	Zon	C	Sc
The Blessed Bird	Gsc	T	Sc
The Blessed Christ Is Risen Today	Gia	T	Sr
The Blessing-Song Cycle	Som	L	Sc
The Blood Will Never Lose It's Power	Man	G	Sr
The Body Of Christ	Mar	L	Tr
The Body Of Christ	Yan	F	Lo
The Body Song	Fis	F	Tr
The Bones You Have Crushed	Fel	L	Sl
The Book Of Stories	Gsc	C	Tx
The Boys' Carol	Gsc	T	Sc
The Bread Is One	Gia	L	Lo
The Breath Of God	Wbc	G	Ss
The Broken Vessel	Man	G	Sl
The Brotherhood Of Man	Pro	T	Tr
The Business Of A Friend	Ahc	L	Tx
The Butterfly Song	Fis	F	Sr
The Call (How Brightly Deep)	Gia	F	Tc
The Camp Meeting	Pic	L	Tx
The Canticle Of Canticles	Fel	F	Tr
The Carol Of The Angels	Gsc	T	Sc
The Carol Of The Birds	Gsc	T	Sc
The Carpenter	Ahc	L	Tj
The Cherry-Tree Carol	Gsc	F	Sc
The Child Of Love	Aug	T	Sc
The Children Of The Hebrews	Fel	L	Sl
The Children's Hymnbook	Erd	C	Za
The Christ Hymn	Ahc	L	Tj
The Christ Of Every Crisis	Gmc	G	Sl
The Christ-Child Lay On May's Lap	Gia	L	Sc
The Christ-Childs Lullaby	Gsc	T	Sc
The Christmas Choir No 1 (No 5949)	Zon	L	Sc
The Christmas Choir No 2 (No 5890)	Zon	L	Sc
The Christmas Nightingale	Gsc	T	Sc
The Christmas Symbol	Aug	T	Sc
The Church Anthem Book (Boards)	Oxf	T	Za
The Church In The Wildwood	Wrd	G	Tx
The Church Triumphant	Gmc	G	Sr
The Church's One Foundation	Gsc	T	Tr
The Circle Game	Siq	F	Tt
The Cliff Barrows Choir (No 5843)	Zon	T	Sl
The Cliff Barrows Choir No 2	Zon	T	Za
The Cliff Barrows Choir No 3 (No 5856)	Zon	T	Za
The Cold Cathedral	Fel	F	Tx
The Collection	Pic	L	Tx
The Coming Of Christ (3 Pts)	Van	F	Sa
The Contemplation Song	Ahc	L	Tx
The Contemporary Hymn Book	Wrd	L	Za
The Country-Western Choir No 1 (5865)	Zon	F	Za
The Country-Western Choir No 2 (5872)	Zon	F	Za
The Covenant Of The Rainbow (Cantata)	Oxf	T	Tx
The Cradle	Aug	T	Sc
The Creed(Credo) (Jazz-Rock Mass)	Fel	F	Tx
The Crucifixion	Chd	L	Sl
The Crucifixion (No 5808)	Zon	T	Sl
The Cuckoo Carol	Gsc	T	Sc
The Dancing Heart	Cam	G	Ss
The Darkest Night (E) W/Keyboard	Gia	L	Sc
The Daughters Of Kings	Fel	L	Tm
The Day Draws On With Golden Light (E)	Oxf	T	Tx
The Day Of Resurrection	Gia	L	Sr
The Day Of The Lord	Fel	F	Sa
The Days Of Noah	Mar	L	Tx
The Death Of God (W/Narrator)	Oxf	L	Sl
The Desert Shall Blossom	Aug	T	Sr
The Dirge Of David	Fel	L	Sl
The Divine Liturgy	Gia	T	Za
The Donkey	Gsc	T	Sl
The Door You Try To Open	Yan	F	Tr
The Dove	Gsc	T	Sc
The Dream Of God	Fel	F	Sl
The Drums Beat On	Ahc	L	Tx
The Earth Feared	Gia	T	Sr
The Earth Feared	Gia	L	Sr
The Earth Feared And Was Silent	Gia	T	Sr
The Earth Feared And Was Silent	Gia	L	Sr
The Earth Is Filled	Rpb	F	Tr
The Earth Is Full Of Goodness	Wlp	T	Tr
The Earth Is Full Of The Kindness	Fel	L	Tr
The Earth Is The Lord's	Aug	T	Tx
The Earth Is The Lord's	Gsc	T	Tk
The Earth Is The Lord's	Aug	T	Tx
The Earth Shall Be Filled	Gia	L	Sa
The Earth Was Fearful And Silent	Fel	L	Sr
The Easter Anthems	Oxf	T	Sr
The Easter Choir (No 5330)	Zon	T	Sr
The Easter Song	Fel	L	Sr
The Eastern Heavens Are All Aglow	Gsc	T	Sc
The Embodied Word (Nar,Flute,Perc)	Aug	L	Sc
The Empty Cave	Aug	L	Sr
The End Is The Beginning (Md)	Oxf	L	Tx
The Enemy Said (Israel In Egypt)	Smc	T	Zb
The Everlasting Arms Of God	Man	G	Tr
The Expectation Of The Just	Fel	T	Tr
The Eyes Of All Wait Upon Thee	Aug	T	Tr
The Eyes Of The Lord	Mar	L	Tr
The Face Of God	Mdm	F	Tr

ALPHABETICAL INDEX OF TITLES

The Face Of God	Abm	G	Tx
The Face Of God (Wedding Song)	Gra	F	Tw
The Faithful Shall Rejoice In Glory	Fel	L	Tk
The Faithful Shepherd (Cantata)	Lps	T	Tr
The Falcon	Oxf	T	Za
The Family Of God	Gmc	G	Lo
The Father Had But One Son	Fel	F	Sl
The Feast Of Light	Gsc	T	Tx
The Fire Of Love	Gia	L	Ss
The Fire Of Love	Gia	F	Tr
The First And Great Commandment	Mmc	G	Tr
The First Christmas	Gsc	T	Sc
The First Christmas Morn	Gsc	T	Sc
The First Noel	Gsc	T	Sc
The First Of His Signs	Fel	L	Tj
The First Time Ever	Stk	F	Tt
The Flesh Failures	Uam	F	Tt
The Flowers Appear	Fel	F	Tx
The Folk Hymnal (No 5767)	Zon	F	Za
The Foot Washing Song (Chant)	Gia	F	Tr
The Four Freedoms(Musical)	Wrd	L	Tp
The Four Seasons	Fel	F	Tx
The Fragile Joys	Som	L	Tx
The Friendly Beasts (Arr)	Gia	T	Sc
The Friendly Beasts (Trad Old English)	Gsc	T	Sc
The Gamble Folk Song Book (No 4515)	Zon	F	Za
The Garden Of My Heart	Wrd	G	Tr
The Gelineau Psalms	Gia	L	Za
The Gift Of Christmas	Gsc	T	Sc
The Gift Of Christmas Morn	Gsc	T	Sc
The Gift Of Love	Lor	L	Tr
The Gifts Of God	Cor	F	Ss
The Girl	Mar	L	Tx
The Glorious Deeds Of The Lord (Ps78)	Gra	L	Ld
The Glory Of Easter (No 5983)	Zon	L	Sr
The Glory Of God In Nature	Gsc	T	Tt
The Glory Of Our King	Aug	T	Tk
The Glory Of The Lord (Md) W/Brs	Gia	L	Sc
The Glory Of The Lord Is Upon You	Fel	L	Tr
The Glory Of This Day	Aug	T	Sr
The God Of Abraham	Mcc	F	Tc
The God Of Abraham Praise	Gia	T	Tt
The God Whom Earth & Sea & Sky	Gia	T	Tm
The God Whom Earth & Sea & Sky	Wlp	T	Tm
The Godly Stranger	Aug	T	Tx
The Good Life (Musical)	Zon	L	Za
The Good Man Speaks Wisdom	Fel	L	Tr
The Good Shepherd	Gsc	T	Tr
The Good Shepherd (Me)	Gia	L	Tj
The Great Day Of The Lord Is Near	Gsc	T	Sa
The Great Judgment Day	Pmp	G	Tk
The Great Lights	Wlp	F	Tx
The Great Parade	Prc	L	Tx
The Great Peace (E)	Oxf	T	Tr
The Great Someone	Pmp	G	Tx
The Great White Host	Gsc	T	Tx
The Greatest Of These Is Love	Aug	L	Tr
The Greatest Story Yet Untold(Cantata)	Zon	L	Tc
The Greatest Wonder (W/Piano)	Wrd	G	Tj
The Greatness Of The Lord	Gsc	T	Tt
The Guitar Hymnal (No 5309)	Zon	F	Zb
The Halo	Gsc	T	Sc
The Hammer Song	Lud	F	Tx
The Hand Of The Lord Feeds Us	Gra	L	Ld
The Hand Of The Lord Sustains	Fel	L	Tr
The Head That Once Was Crowned	Gia	T	Sl
The Heavens Are Declaring	Gsc	T	Tt
The Heavens Are Telling	Gsc	T	Tt
The Heavens Are Telling (Creation)	Oxf	T	Tt
The Heavens Are Telling (3 Voices)	Gia	T	Tt
The Heavens Declare (Cantata	Lps	T	Tt
The Heavens Declare The Glory	Gsc	T	Tt
The Heavens Proclaim His Justice	Fel	L	Tt
The Heavens Proclaim Your Wonders	Fel	L	Tt
The Heavens Rejoiced	Gia	L	Sc
The Heavens Resounding	Aug	T	Tt
The Hebrew Children Spread	Fel	L	Sl
The History Of The Flood (W/Narration)	Oxf	L	Tx
The Holly And The Ivy	Gsc	T	Sc
The Holly Carol	Gsc	T	Sc
The Holy Child	Gsc	T	Sc
The Holy City (From Revelations)	Gra	L	Sa
The Horsemen	Mar	L	Sr
The House Of Our Lord	Sac	L	Tc
The House Of Stars	Pic	L	Tx
The Icy December (Arr)	Gia	T	Sc
The Incarnation (No 5952) Cantata	Zon	L	Sc
The Infant Christ	Gsc	T	Sc
The Inner Place	Man	G	Tx
The Innkeeper's Carol	Gsc	T	Sc
The Joy In Serving The Lord	Gmc	G	Tc
The Joy Of The Lord	Wlp	L	Tr
The Joy Of The Lord	Fel	L	Tr
The Joy Song	Yan	F	Tr
The Joyous News Of Christmas (No 5055)	Zon	L	Sc
The Judgement Day	Sil	F	Sa
The Just Man Rejoices	Fel	L	Tt
The Just Man Shall Flourish	Fel	L	Tr
The Just Man Shall Flourish (W/Inst)	Aug	L	Tr
The Just Man Will Give His Heart	Fel	T	Tr
The Just Men Have Taken Away	Fel	T	Tx
The Just Shall Always Be Remembered	Fel	L	Tf
The Just Shall Grow	Fel	L	Tr
The King Desires Your Beauty	Fel	L	Tx
The King Is Coming	Gmc	G	Sa
The King Of Love	Rpb	G	Tk
The King Of Love (In 19 Rounds)	Gia	T	Tr
The King Of Love My Shepherd Is	Gia	T	Tj
The King Of Love My Shepherd Is	Aug	L	Tk
The King Of Love My Shepherd Is	Gsc	T	Tr
The King Of Love My Shepherd Is (Me)	Oxf	T	Sr
The King Shall Rejoice	Kal	T	Tk
The Kingdom Of God	Sha	F	Tk
The Kingdom Of Jesus	Chh	F	Tk
The Lamb	Gsc	T	Sl
The Lamb	Gsc	T	Tj
The Lamb	Gsc	T	Tx
The Lament Of Job	Gsc	T	Sl
The Lamentations Of Jeremiah (Lat & E)	Oxf	T	Sl
The Last Commandment (Cantata)	Zon	L	Tc
The Last Day (We're A Pilgrim)	Gia	L	Sa
The Last Supper	Som	L	Sl
The Late Great Planet Earth Songbook	Zon	F	Za
The Law Of God Is Perfect	Gra	L	Ld
The Light Has Come (Service)	Aug	L	Sc
The Light Of Bethlehem	Gsc	T	Sc
The Light Of Christ	Wgm	L	Tj
The Lighted Hour	Pic	L	Tx
The Lily Of The Valley	Lor	G	Tj
The Lion And The Lamb	Fel	F	Tk
The Little Drummer Boy	Bel	F	Sc
The Little Family	Gsc	T	Sr
The Little King	Gsc	T	Sc
The Little King Of The World	Aug	C	Sc
The Little Saviour	Gsc	L	Sc
The Lone, Wild Bird	Aug	L	Tx
The Longer I Serve Him	Gmc	G	Tc
The Lord Anointed My Eyes	Fel	L	Tx
The Lord Ascendeth Up On High	Sac	L	Sr
The Lord Be With You	Fel	F	Tt
The Lord Bless Thee And Keep Thee	Gsc	L	Tt
The Lord Bless You	Gia	T	Tr
The Lord Bless You	Bfi	F	Tx
The Lord Bless You	Fel	F	Tr
The Lord Bless You And Keep You	Gsc	L	Le
The Lord Bless You And Keep You	Gsc	T	Le
The Lord Came Down	Mam	G	Tj
The Lord Cried Out	Fel	L	Tx
The Lord Has Brought Us	Fel	L	Tk
The Lord Has Chosen Him	Gia	L	Tc
The Lord Has Delivered	Fel	L	Tk
The Lord Has Done Great Things	Gra	L	Ld
The Lord Has Done Great Things	Fel	L	Tr
The Lord Has Heard	Fel	L	Tr
The Lord Has Made Known	Fel	L	Sc
The Lord Has Risen	Fel	L	Sr
The Lord Has Satisfied The Longing	Gia	G	Tt
The Lord Has Set His Throne	Gra	F	Ld
The Lord Has Sworn	Fel	L	Sc
The Lord Has Sworn	Gia	L	Tc
The Lord Into His Garden (Md)	Pro	T	Tj
The Lord Is A Great & Mighty King	Gia	F	Tk
The Lord Is Come (W/Guitar)	Gia	F	Sc
The Lord Is Exalted	Gsc	T	Tt
The Lord Is God	Fel	L	Tk
The Lord Is Good (Ps 71)	Gia	L	Sl
The Lord Is Here	Sbf	F	La
The Lord Is In This Place (W/Brs)	Abi	L	La
The Lord Is Just	Fel	L	Tr
The Lord Is King	Fel	L	Tk
The Lord Is King (Psalm 93) W/Brs	Gra	L	Ld
The Lord Is Loving And Merciful	Fel	L	Tr
The Lord Is My Guardian	Fel	L	Tr
The Lord Is My Light	Man	G	Tr
The Lord Is My Light	Gsc	T	Tr
The Lord Is My Light	Gam	L	Sl
The Lord Is My Light	Fel	L	Tr
The Lord Is My Light	Gsc	T	Tr
The Lord Is My Light	Gsc	T	Tr
The Lord Is My Light	Cof	L	Tr
The Lord Is My Portion	Gia	L	Tc
The Lord Is My Rock	Gsc	T	Tr
The Lord Is My Shepherd	Mam	G	Tr
The Lord Is My Shepherd	Fel	L	Tr
The Lord Is My Shepherd	Wlp	F	Tr
The Lord Is My Shepherd	Fel	F	Tr
The Lord Is My Shepherd	Gsc	T	Tr
The Lord Is My Shepherd	Mar	L	Tr
The Lord Is My Shepherd	Lor	L	Tr
The Lord Is My Shepherd (Ps 23)	Oxf	T	Tr
The Lord Is My Shepherd 2 Voices	Gia	T	Tr
The Lord Is My Shepherd(1)	Fel	C	Ld
The Lord Is My True Shepherd	Lit	L	Tr
The Lord Is Near To All	Fel	L	Sa
The Lord Is Present In His Sanctuary	Chm	F	La
The Lord Is Ris'n Indeed	Cfp	T	Sr
The Lord Is Ris'n Indeed (A Cap)	Cfp	T	Sr
The Lord Is Risen	Wlp	F	Sr
The Lord Is Still Around	Mam	G	Tj
The Lord Is Takin' Us Home	Fel	F	Sr
The Lord Led Forth His People	Fel	L	Tr
The Lord Led Forth His People In Joy	Fel	L	Tk
The Lord Loved Him And Clothed Him	Fel	L	Tx
The Lord My Faithful Shepherd Is	Aug	L	Tr
The Lord My Shepherd E'er Shall Be	Gsc	T	Tr
The Lord My Shepherd Is	Gsc	T	Tr
The Lord My Shepherd Is	Aug	L	Tr
The Lord Of Evolution	Gia	F	Tk
The Lord Of The Dance	Gal	F	Sl
The Lord Our God Is King Of Kings	Aug	L	Tk
The Lord Reigneth	Aug	L	Tk
The Lord Reigneth (Ps 99)	Gam	L	Tt
The Lord Said To Me (Ccd)	Wlp	F	Sc
The Lord Said To Me (Icet)	Gia	L	Sc
The Lord Said You Are My Son	Gia	T	Sc
The Lord Thundered	Fel	L	Tk
The Lord Thy God In The Midst Of Thee	Mar	L	Tr
The Lord Will Give His Blessing	Fel	L	Tr
The Lord's Prayer	Fel	F	Ll
The Lord's Prayer	Fel	L	Ll
The Lord's Prayer	Gsc	T	Ll
The Lord's Prayer	Ham	C	Ll
The Lord's Prayer	Gsc	T	Ll
The Lord's Prayer	Gsc	T	Ll
The Lord's Prayer	Gia	L	Ll
The Lord's Prayer	Cfc	L	Ll
The Lord's Prayer	Gia	T	Ll
The Lord's Prayer	Yan	F	Ll
The Lord's Prayer (Bcp) Adapted	Oxf	T	Ll
The Lord's Prayer (E)	Oxf	L	Ll
The Lord's Prayer (E)	Oxf	T	Ll
The Lord's Prayer (First Mass)	Fel	F	Ll
The Lord's Prayer (Jazz–Rock Mass)	Fel	F	Ll
The Lord's Prayer (Liturgy Of Joy)	Fel	C	Ll
The Lord's Prayer (Merbecke)	Oxf	L	Ll
The Lord's Prayer (Missa Bossa Nova)	Fel	F	Ll
The Lord's Prayer (Second Mass)	Fel	F	Ll
The Lords Prayer (Spiritual)	Oxf	G	Ll
The Love Of Christ	Fel	F	La
The Love Of Christ Has Joined	Fel	L	La
The Love Of God	Gsc	T	Tr
The Love Of God	Gsc	T	Tr
The Love Of God Flows	Fel	L	Tr
The Love Of God Will Rise	Fel	F	Tr
The Love Of My Lord To Me	Lor	T	Tr
The Lovin' Man	Sil	L	Tr
The Lute–Book Lullaby	Sac	T	Sc
The Magic Morning	Gsc	T	Sc
The Magic Touch	Man	G	Tb
The Male Four (No Zd-5475)	Zon	G	Za
The Man Next Door	Sbf	F	Tj
The Man Of Galilee	Man	G	Tj
The Mariner's Anthem (Moore)	Gsc	T	Tr
The Mark Of Time	Sil	L	Tx
The May Carol	Gsc	T	Sr
The Meek Shall Possess The Land	Fel	L	Tk
The Melody Four Quartets For Men No 1	Zon	G	Za
The Melody Four Quartets For Men No 2	Zon	G	Za
The Melody Four Quartets For Men No 3	Zon	G	Za
The Memorare	Gia	L	Tm
The Miracle	Man	C	Sc
The Miracle (No 4312)	Zon	L	Sr
The Miraculous Harvest	Gsc	T	Tx
The Morning After	Twe	F	Tt
The Morning Of The Day Of Days	Gsc	T	Sr
The Morning Son	Sil	L	Tj
The Morning Star	Gsc	T	Sc
The Morning Sun	Sil	L	Tt
The Morning Trumpet	Gsc	T	Tx
The Mother Of Jesus Was There	Gra	F	Tm
The Mountain Of The Lord	Gsc	L	Tr
The Moving Of The Breath Of God	Man	G	Ss
The Mystery Of It All	Man	G	Tx
The Name Of Jesus	Sbf	L	Tj
The Name Of Jesus (Arrangement)	Tal	T	Tj
The Nativity	Gsc	T	Sc
The New Amen Song	Yan	F	Lk
The New Christian Hymnal	Erd	T	Za
The New Creation	Fel	F	Sr
The New Morn (The Sun Came Over)	Gia	F	Sr
The Newborn Babe	Kal	T	Sc
The Nicene Creed	Yan	F	Tx
The Nicene Creed(Credo)	Fel	F	Tx
The Nicene Creed(Credo)(Chardin Mass)	Fel	L	Tx
The Nicene Creed(Credo)(Sung Mass No1)	Fel	L	Tx
The Night The Angels Sang (No 5986)	Zon	L	Sc
The Old Ark	Rpb	G	Tx
The Old Fashioned Revival Hour Quartet	Zon	G	Za
The Old Hundredth Psalm Tune (E)	Oxf	T	Tt
The Old Ralph Carmichael Quartet	Wrd	G	Za
The Old Rugged Cross Made	Gmc	G	Sl
The Omnipotence	Gsc	T	Tt
The One I Love	Man	G	Tr
The Only Concern You Need To Have	Fel	L	Tr
The Only Lord	Aug	T	Tt
The Other Side	Prc	L	Tx
The Oxen. A Carol	Gsc	T	Sc
The Oxford Easy Anthem Book	Oxf	T	Za
The Passion According To St John	Oxf	T	Sl
The Passion According To St Luke	Oxf	T	Sl

ALPHABETICAL INDEX OF TITLES

The Passion According To St Matthew	Oxf	T Sl
The Passion According To St. Mark	Aug	L Sl
The Passion Of Christ (1716)	Oxf	T Sl
The Past Is Dark	Gsc	T Sl
The Path Of The Just	Aug	L Tr
The Peace Of Christ Be With You	Yan	F Tr
The Peace That Jesus Gives (A Cap)	Wrd	G Tr
The Peace That Passes Understanding	Mar	L Tr
The People Of God	Hol	L Tr
The Perfect Will	Man	G Tr
The Pharisee And The Publican	Gsc	T Tx
The Pilgrim Way	Smc	T Tf
The Plan Of The Lords Stands	Fel	L Tr
The Play Of Daniel	Oxf	T Tx
The Play Of Herod	Oxf	T Tx
The Power Of Jesus	Man	G Tj
The Praises Of A King	Aug	L Tt
The Prayer Of Manasseh	Gsc	L Tr
The Prayer Perfect	Gsc	T Tr
The Prayer To St. Ignatius	Ahc	L Tc
The Present Hour	Aug	L Tx
The Present Tense (2 Pt Canon)	Aug	L Tx
The Prophet Isaiah	Som	L Tx
The Psalms	Gsc	T Tt
The Question	Mar	L Tx
The Race That Long In Darkness Pined	Abi	F Sa
The Radiant Morn Hath Passed	Gsc	T Tx
The Rebel	Prc	L Tx
The Redeemer Shall Come	Lor	L Sa
The Reproaches	Rpb	L Sl
The Reproaches (Prophecy)	Gra	F Sl
The Rest Of Our Lives	Wgm	F Tc
The Resurrection	Gsc	T Sr
The Resurrection	Som	L Sr
The Resurrection	Gsc	T Sr
The Resurrection (W/Insts)	Aug	L Sr
The Resurrection According To St Mat	Gsc	T Sr
The Resurrection Morn	Gmc	G Sr
The Rich Young Ruler	Van	F Tx
The Right Choice	Sto	G Tc
The Right Hand Of The Lord (Canon)	Gia	T Sr
The Righteous	Gsc	T Tt
The Rightious (Der Gerechte)	Gsc	T Tr
The Road I'm On	Fel	F Sl
The Road Of Christ	Ahc	L Tc
The Road Of Life	Fel	F Tx
The Robin And The Thorn	Gsc	T Sr
The Rock Holler	Fel	C Lp
The Rock Of My Salvation	Sil	G Tr
The Runner	Sil	L Tx
The Sabbath Of God	Csm	G Tx
The Saints You Gave	Fel	L Sr
The Salvation Of The Just	Fel	L Sr
The Savior Is Waiting (A Cap)	Wrd	G Tc
The Search	Chd	F Tt
The Season Of Tomorrow (W/Flute/Org)	Aug	L Tx
The Second Service (Te Deum, Jubilate)	Kal	T Tx
The Seed That Falls (Psalm 65)	Rpb	L Ld
The Seven Last Words From The Cross	Oxf	T Sl
The Seven Seals Revealed	Pmp	G Tk
The Sevenfold Amen	Gsc	T Lk
The Seventh Seal	Smc	L Zb
The Shadows Of The Cross (Tenebrae)	Abi	T Sl
The Shepherd	Mar	L Tr
The Shepherd Boy Sings In The Valley	Som	L Sl
The Shepherd On The Hill	Gsc	T Sc
The Shepherd's Vigil (W/C Inst)	Aug	L Sc
The Shepheras Saw A Star	Gsc	T Sc
The Shepherds' Adoration	Aug	L Sc
The Shepherds' Chorus	Gsc	T Sc
The Shepherds' Farewell	Gsc	T Sc
The Short Service (Venite, Te Deum)	Kal	T Tx
The Silent Night	Gia	F Tx
The Silent Sea	Gsc	T Tx
The Silver Bells	Gsc	T Sc
The Sinner And The Song (Musical)	Zon	G Za
The Smile On His Face	Man	G Tj
The Snow Lay On The Ground	Aug	T Sc
The Snow Lay On The Ground (Me)	Gia	T Sc
The Son In My Life	Mar	L Tj
The Song Is Love	Pep	F Tt
The Song Of David (1 Ck 29)	Pro	L Tt
The Song Of Joshua	Gra	F Tc
The Song Of Mary	Gsc	T Tm
The Song Of Mary	Aug	L Tm
The Song Of Moses (Ex 15)	Gia	F Tt
The Song Of The Birds	Gsc	T Sc
The Songs Of Mickey Holiday (No 4340)	Zon	G Za
The Songs Of Mickey Holiday (4340)	Zon	L Za
The Sorrows Of Mary (M)	Oxf	T Tm
The Sorrows Of My Heart (Ps 25) (E)	Oxf	T Sl
The Sorrows Of My Heart Are Enlarged	Gia	L Sl
The Souls Of The Just	Fel	L Tf
The Souls Of The Righteous (Me)	Oxf	T Tx
The Sound Of Jubilee	Fel	F Tt
The Sound Of Singing (No 5965)	Zon	L Za
The Sound Of Singing (No 5994) Cantata	Zon	L Za
The Sounding Skies W/Organ Or Piano	Gsc	L Sc
The Sower	Van	F Tc
The Sower (Cantata)	Oxf	T Tx
The Spacious Firmament (Md)	Oxf	L Tx
The Spelling Of Christmas	Gsc	T Sc
The Spirit Also Helpeth (Motet 2)	Kal	T Ss
The Spirit And The Bride	Wgm	F Ss
The Spirit And The Bride	Mcc	F Ss
The Spirit Breathes Where He Will	Fel	L Ss
The Spirit Came One Morn'	Ahc	L Ss
The Spirit Of Christmas	Smc	L Zb
The Spirit Of God Rests Upon Me	Wlp	L Ss
The Spirit Of Jesus Is In This Place	Gmc	G Ss
The Spirit Of The Lord	Fel	F Ss
The Spirit Of The Lord	Mcc	F Ss
The Spirit Of The Lord	Yan	F Ss
The Spirit Of The Lord (Hath Set Me)	Gia	F Ss
The Spirit Of The Lord (W/Guit,Fl)	Aug	F Ss
The Spirit Of The Lord Fills	Fel	L Ss
The Spirit Of The Lord Is Upon Me	Fel	L Ss
The Spirit Will Come To Guide You	Fel	L Ss
The Spirit Will Teach You All Things	Fel	L Ss
The Star	Sav	G Sc
The Star Road	Gsc	T Sc
The Stone Which The Builders Rejected	Fel	L Tx
The Stones Will Shout Out	Fel	F Sl
The Story Of Christmas (No 5882)	Zon	L Sc
The Story–Tellin' Man (Musical)	Wrd	C Tj
The Strife Is O'er	Gsc	T Sr
The Sufferings Of The Present	Abi	T Sl
The Sufferings Of The Present (Me)	Abi	T Sl
The Sun Shall Be No More Thy Light	Gsc	T Sr
The Sunday Antiphonary (Icet)	Gia	L Za
The Sussex Carol	Gsc	T Sc
The Sweetest Peace Of Mind	Mmc	G Tr
The Sycamore Tree	Gsc	T Sc
The Temple Of God (E)	Oxf	T Tc
The Three Gifts (W/Keyboard)	Gia	L Sc
The Three Kings	Oxf	T Sc
The Three Kings	Gsc	T Sc
The Three Kings	Oxf	T Sc
The Three Kings Of Orient (Opt Perc)	Pro	F Sc
The Three Lilies	Gsc	T Sr
The Three Part Christmas Choir (5932)	Zon	T Sc
The Time Has Come	Wlp	F Sa
The Times And The Seasons (No 5668)	Zon	G Sa
The Times Are Always Changing	Fel	F Tx
The Touch Of His Hand	Mam	G Tj
The Train Is Gone	Sem	G Tt
The Tree Of Life	Fel	F Sr
The Tree Of Life (Cantata)	Oxf	T Tx
The Tree Song	Fel	C Tx
The Triumph Song (Anthem Of Praise)	Gsc	T Tt
The Triumph–Song	Gsc	T Sr
The Truth Of The Lord Endureth Forever	Gsc	L Tr
The Truth Will Make You Free	Rpb	L Tr
The Twelve (For Apostles)	Oxf	T Tx
The Twenty–Seventh Psalm(The Lord Is)	Gsc	T Tr
The Twenty–Third Psalm	Gsc	T Tr
The Twenty–Third Psalm	Oxf	T Tr
The Universe Is Singing	Gia	F Tt
The Very Last Day	Pep	F Tt
The Via Dolorosa	Mmc	G Sl
The Victory Dance	Van	F Sr
The Vineyard Of The Lord (Ps 80)	Gra	L Ld
The Vision Of Isaiah (Cantata)	Smc	L Tx
The Visit	Van	F Tx
The Visitor.	Lor	F Sc
The Voice Of God	Jhe	G Tx
The Voices Of Christmas	Som	L Sc
The Waiting Soul	Pic	L To
The Warning Of Old	Pmp	G Tx
The Watch Bird	Csm	G Tx
The Water Is Wide	Lor	F Tx
The Water That I Shall Give You	Fel	L Tb
The Water That I Will Give You	Fel	L Tb
The Waters Are Troubled	Gmc	G Tb
The Way I Feel (Collection)	Wrd	F Za
The Wedding Banquet (I Cannot Come)	Van	F Tc
The Wedding Feast	Ahc	L Tw
The Wedding In The Sky	Pmp	G Tk
The Whole Armor (Spir, War)	Fis	F Tc
The Wind Blows	Wlp	F Ss
The Wind Is Blowin'	Fel	F Tx
The Woman	Sil	L Tx
The Wonder Of Christmas (No 5970)	Zon	L Sc
The Wonder Of It All	Mar	L Tr
The Woods And Every Sweet–Smelling	Gsc	T Tt
The Word	Fel	F Tr
The Word (In The Beginning)	Gia	F Tr
The Word (Though The Rivers)	Gia	L Sr
The Word Is The Life	Fel	F Tj
The Word Of God (Opt Insts)	Aug	L Sc
The Word Of God Endureth	Man	G Le
The Word Of The Lord Is Pure	Fel	L Tx
The Word Was Made Flesh	Fel	L Sc
The Words From The Cross	Aug	L Sl
The Work He Has Committed To Me	Fel	L Tx
The World Around Us	Ahc	L Tx
The World Sees Nothing	Fel	L Tx
The Year Of Jubilee	Gia	L Tr
The Year Of Jubilee Has Come	Gia	L Tr
Thee We Adore	Lor	T Tt
Thee We Adore (A Cap)	Abi	T Sl
Thee Will I Love	Sac	L Tr
Thee Will I Love, O Lord	Gsc	T Tr
Their Bodies Lie In Peace	Fel	L Tf
Their Message Goes Forth	Fel	L Tc
Their Sweetest Hour	Zon	G Tr
Then Did Priests Make Offering (M)	Oxf	T To
Then I Know	Lor	T Tx
Then It Must Be So	Man	G Tx
Then Round About The Starry Throne	Gsc	T Sr
Then Shall The King Say Unto Them	Gsc	T Sr
Then Spake Solomon	Gsc	T Tx
Then The Lord Stood By Me	Zon	G Tc
There Are But Three Things That Last	Wlp	F Tr
There Be Four Things	Ron	T Tx
There Be Three Things	Ron	T Tx
There Came A Star (W/Solos,Trios)	Lor	L Sc
There Is A Child	Gsc	T Sc
There Is A Fountain	Zon	G Ss
There Is A God	Gia	L Tx
There Is A Green Hill Far Away	Gsc	T Tx
There Is A Land	Gsc	L Sr
There Is A Love	Lor	T Tr
There Is A Name	Man	G Tj
There Is A New Wind Blowin'	Yan	F Ss
There Is A River	Sac	L Tc
There Is A World	Ahc	L Tt
There Is No Future In Gaining	Sto	G Sl
There Is No Greater Love	Zon	G Sl
There Is No Greater Love	Zon	L Tr
There Is No Need To Walk Alone	Sto	G Tr
There Is No One Like Jesus	Wrd	G Tj
There Is No Room	Zon	L Sl
There Is None Like Him	Hol	L Tt
There Is One Lord	Wlp	L Tb
There Is Rachel Weeping	Fel	L Sc
There Might Have Been A Stranger	Abi	L Sc
There Never Was A Christmas Day	Man	C Sc
There Once Was A Man	Fel	F Sl
There Once Was A Man	Fel	C Tx
There Shall Be Showers Of Blessing	Zon	G Tr
There Shall Be Star Come Out Of Jacob	Gsc	T Sa
There Was A Pig	Gsc	T Sc
There Were Ninety And Nine	Lor	G Tr
There Were Shepherds	Gsc	T Sc
There Were Three Lights	Lor	T Sc
There Will Be Joy Over One Sinner	Fel	L Tr
There'll Always Be A Christmas (4291)	Zon	L Sc
There'll Be Bread	Man	L Sr
There's A Light Upon The Mountains	Abi	L Tx
There's A Love	Mar	L Tr
There's A New Song In My Heart	Zon	G Tt
There's A Place In God's Heart	Ham	C Tr
There's A Power Working In My Life	Gmp	G Ss
There's A River Of Life (Vv)	Fis	G Ss
There's A Song In The Air	Zon	T Sc
There's A Song In The Air	Gsc	T Tt
There's A Time, There's A Moment	Rav	L Tw
There's A Voice In The Wilderness	Sac	L Sa
There's A Wideness	Fel	F Tr
There's A Wideness In God's Mercy	Gia	T Tr
There's A Wideness In God's Mercy	Aug	T Tr
There's A Wideness In God's Mercy	Zon	T Tx
There's Glory In My Soul	Mam	G Sr
There's No Sitting On The Fence	Man	L Tc
There's Nothing Like The Holy Ghost	Sav	G Ss
There's Room At The Cross For You	Lor	T Sl
There's Something About A Mountain	Gmc	G Tx
There's Something About God	Bul	G Tr
There's Something About That Name	Gmc	G Tj
Therefore They Shall Come	Mar	L Tr
Theresa Mass In B–Flat	Bbl	T Za
These Are Thy Glorious Works	Lor	T Tx
These Forty Days Of Lent	Wlp	T Sl
These Things I Have Spoken Unto You	Mar	L Ss
These Things Shall Pass	Ham	G Tx
These Times Must Come	Man	G Sa
These Two	Wlp	F Tx
They Ate And Were	Fel	L Lo
They Came From Sheba	Fel	L Sc
They Cast Their Nets	Van	F Tc
They Cried To The Lord	Fel	L Sl
They Divide My Garments	Fel	L Sl
They Follow Me	Aug	L Tc
They Gathered At The River	Rpb	T Tx
They Gossip About Me	Fel	L Sl
They Have Taken Away My Lord	Gsc	T Sr
They Kingdom Come	Gsc	L Ll
They Sang That Night In Bethlehem	Gsc	T Sc
They Shall Be Mine	Sav	G Tc
They Shall See The Glory Of The Lord	Wbp	T Tx
They Shall Walk	Sac	L Tc
They That Go Down To The Sea In Ships	Zon	L Tt
They That Put Their Trust In The Lord	Oxf	T Tr
They That Sow In Tears	Gmc	G Sl
They That Sow In Tears	Lor	G Sl
They That Sow In Tears	Gsc	T Tf
They That Trust In The Lord	Lor	T Tr
They That Wait Upon The Lord	Aug	L Tr
They That Wait Upon The Lord	Abi	L Tr

ALPHABETICAL INDEX OF TITLES

They Took Him Up To Jerusalem	Fel	L	Sc
They Were Filled With The Holy	Fel	L	Ss
They Who Considereth The Poor Shall Be	Wbp	T	Tr
They'll Know We Are Christians	Zon	F	Ss
They'll Know We Are Christians	Fel	F	Lo
Thine Accounting (Cantata)	Lps	T	Sr
Thine All The Glory	Smc	T	Zb
Thine Be The Glory (W/Piano)	Wrd	F	Tf
Thine Forever	Aug	L	Tc
Thine Is The Glory	Lor	T	Tt
Thine is The Glory (Easy)	Zon	T	Sr
Thine Is The Kingdom	Gsc	T	Tt
Thine Is The Kingdom (Holy City)	Cfs	T	Tk
Thine Own Way	Smc	T	Zb
Thine, O Lord	Gsc	T	Tr
Things I Have Left Undone, The	Zon	G	Tr
Things We Deeply Feel(Youth Coll)	Wrd	G	Za
Think Of God	Zon	G	Tr
Think Of It, Lord!	Zon	F	Tx
Think Of The Goodness Of God	Sav	G	Tr
Think On Me	Abi	T	Tx
Think On These Things	Zon	L	Tx
Third Service (Magnificat, Nunc Dim)	Kal	T	Tx
Third Verse Service: Magnificat Etc	Oxf	T	Za
Thirteen Amens & Alleluias	Gia	T	Za
Thirty New Settings Of Familiar Hymns	Abi	L	Zb
This Be My Song	Lor	T	Tt
This Book	Ham	G	Tx
This Book Of The Law	Gsc	T	Tx
This Bread Commits Us To Christ	Fel	L	Lo
This Christmastide	Lor	T	Sc
This Could Be The Dawning Of That Day	Gmc	G	Sa
This Day	Gsc	T	Sc
This Day A Rose Of Judah	Acp	L	Sc
This Day A Rose Of Judah	Acp	L	Sc
This Day God Made	Nal	L	Sr
This Day God Made	Wlp	L	Sr
This Day Our Lord Is Born(Piano/Cinst)	Aug	L	Sc
This Day We Welcome A Little Child	Gia	T	Sc
This Day You Shall Know	Fel	L	Tx
This Glad Day (Md)	Oxf	T	Sr
This Glorious Christmas Night	Gsc	T	Sc
This Holy Day	Gsc	T	Sc
This I Believe	Zon	G	Tx
This Is A Holy Day	Nal	L	Tx
This Is His Promise	Sil	T	Tj
This Is Jesus	Lor	T	Tj
This Is My Body	Jsp	L	Ln
This Is My Body	Nal	L	Lo
This Is My Commandment	Nal	C	Tr
This Is My Commandment	Oxf	T	Tx
This Is My Commandment	Sac	L	Tr
This Is My Commandment	Mar	L	Tr
This Is My Father's World	Lor	T	Tr
This Is My Father's World	Lor	T	Tr
This Is My Father's World	Lor	T	Tr
This Is My Father's World	Zon	T	Tr
This Is My Father's World	Zon	T	Tr
This Is My Gift	Nal	L	Tx
This Is My Song	Lor	T	Tr
This Is Our Accepted Time	Wlp	T	Sa
This Is Real	Yan	F	Tr
This Is The Birthday Of The Lord	Pro	T	Sc
This Is The Covenant	Aug	L	Lo
This Is The Day	Prc	L	Tx
This Is The Day	Maf	T	Sr
This Is The Day	Som	T	Sr
This Is The Day	Nal	C	Sr
This Is The Day	Ccc	L	Sr
This Is The Day	Wlp	F	Sr
This Is The Day	Nal	L	Sr
This Is The Day	Nal	L	Sr
This Is The Day	Gia	L	Ld
This Is The Day	Fel	F	Sr
This Is The Day	Fel	F	Sr
This Is The Day	Gia	L	Sr
This Is The Day	Rpb	L	Sr
This Is The Day	Mar	L	Sr
This Is The Day (M)	Abi	T	La
This Is The Day (Ps 118) (Me)	Oxf	T	Sr
This Is The Day (W/ Perc,Bells,Org)	Gia	L	Ld
This Is The Day (W/Flute)	Aug	T	Sr
This Is The Day That The Lord	Fel	F	Sr
This Is The Day The Lord Has Made	Wlp	L	Ld
This Is The Day The Lord Has Made	Gia	L	Sr
This Is The Day The Lord Has Made	Wlp	L	Ld
This Is The Day The Lord Has Made	Aug	T	Sr
This Is The Day The Lord Hath Made	Gmc	G	Sr
This Is The Day The Lord Hath Made	Aug	L	Sr
This Is The Day The Lord Hath Made	Zon	L	Sr
This Is The Day When Christ Was Born	Gia	T	Sc
This Is The Day Which The Lord	Fel	L	Sr
This Is The Day Which The Lord Hath	Gsc	L	Sr
This Is The Day Which The Lord Hath	Aug	L	Sr
This Is The Faithful And Prudent	Fel	L	Tx
This Is The Feast Of Victory(Opt Tpt)	Aug	L	Tk
This Is The God Who Gives A Home	Fel	L	Tx
This Is The House Of God	Fel	L	Tx
This Is The Land I Love	Lor	T	Tp
This Is The Lord	Sac	L	Sc
This Is The Lord's Own Day	Gsc	L	Lp
This Is The Record Of John (M)	Oxf	T	Sa
This Is The Time I Must Sing	Gmc	G	Tt
This Is The Wise Virgin	Fel	L	Tx
This Is What We Bring	Acp	L	To
This Is What We Bring (4-Part Arr)	Acp	L	To
This Is Why I Want To Go	Zon	G	Tc
This Joyful Eastertide	Gsc	T	Sr
This Little Babe	Prc	L	Tx
This Little Babe (W/Guitar)	Aug	F	Sc
This Moment (Youth Collection)	Wrd	G	Za
This Most Glorious Day	Hal	T	Sr
This Night	Aug	L	Sc
This Night Did God Become A Child	Aug	L	Sc
This Ole House	Ham	G	Sr
This Ship Of Mine	Ham	G	Tc
This Train	Gsc	T	Tx
This World My God (Evening)	Gia	L	Tx
This World Outside	Zon	F	Tx
This, The Bread I Give You	Fel	L	Lo
Tho' Autumn's Coming On	Ham	G	Sl
Thomas	Man	G	Tx
Thomas	Van	F	Tx
Those Who Sow In Tears	Fel	L	Sl
Thou Alone Art Israel's Shield	Aug	T	Tr
Thou Art God	Bec	T	Tt
Thou Art Holy	Bfi	F	Tt
Thou Art Jesus, Savior And Lord	Aug	T	Tj
Thou Art Mighty	Gsc	T	Tt
Thou Art My God (Ps 118-9)W/Tpts	Wlp	L	Tt
Thou Art The Kindler	Fcc	L	Tj
Thou Art The Living Christ	Lor	T	Sr
Thou Art The Way	Gsc	T	Tj
Thou Art There	Bfi	G	Le
Thou Art Worthy	Asa	T	Tt
Thou Art Worthy	Aug	L	Tk
Thou Dost Keep Him In Perfect Peace	Gam	L	Tr
Thou God Of Wisdom (M)	Oxf	T	Tt
Thou Heart Of Compassion (Cantata)	Lps	T	Tr
Thou Hidden Love Of God	Abi	L	Tr
Thou Hope Of Every Contrite Heart	Lor	T	Tr
Thou Knowest Lord, The Secrets	Gsc	T	Sl
Thou Knowest, Lord, The Secrets	Oxf	T	Tf
Thou O God Art Praised In Zion (Md)	Oxf	L	Tt
Thou Refuge Of The Destitute	Gsc	T	Tr
Thou Sanctified Fire	Gsc	T	Ss
Thou Visitest The Earth (Ps 65)	Oxf	T	Tr
Thou Whose Redeeming Sacrifice	Bbl	T	Tt
Thou Wilt Keep Him	Lor	T	Tr
Thou Wilt Keep Him (A Cap) 1	Pro	T	Tr
Thou Wilt Keep Him In Perfect Peace	Gsc	T	Tf
Thou Wilt Keep Him In Perfect Peace	Abi	T	Sl
Thou Wilt Keep Him In Perfect Peace	Lor	T	Tr
Thou Wilt Keep Him In Perfect Peace	Gsc	T	Tr
Thou Wilt Keep Him In Perfect Peace	Gsc	T	Tr
Thou, O God, Art Praised In Sion(Ps65)	Oxf	T	Tt
Thou, O God, Art Praised In Zion	Gsc	T	Tt
Thou, Who Hast Loved The Little Child	Abi	L	Tb
Though Deep Has Been My Falling	Gsc	T	Sl
Though I Speak With The Tongues Of Men	Oxf	T	Tr
Though I Speak With The Tongues Of Men	Abi	L	Tr
Though I Walk Amid Distress	Fel	L	Sl
Though The Mountains May Fall	Nal	L	Tr
Though Your Sins Be As Scarlet	Lor	T	Tr
Though Your Sins Be As Scarlet	Lor	T	Tr
Three Anthems	Kal	T	Za
Three Anthems Based On Canons	Abi	L	Za
Three Anthems For Junior Choir	Abi	C	Za
Three Anthems Of Commitment	Sac	L	Za
Three Anthems Of Praise	Abi	L	Za
Three Anthems Of Praise	Abi	L	Za
Three Bell Carols For Junior Choirs	Lor	T	Sc
Three Carols For Christmas Nad New Yr	Abi	L	Sc
Three Chorale Preludes (Mod Diff)	Abi	L	Zb
Three Christmas Anthems For Sa Voices	Abi	L	Sc
Three Christmas Carols	Gia	L	Sc
Three Christmas Preludes (Mod Easy)	Abi	L	Zb
Three Duets For Organ And Harp	Sac	L	Zb
Three Early American Christmas Carols	Abi	T	Sc
Three Festival Preludes	Abi	L	Zb
Three Folk-Hymns	Bbl	T	Za
Three Fuging-Tunes	Bbl	T	Za
Three Introits	Oxf	T	Za
Three Introits For Festival Worship	Abi	L	Za
Three Junior Choir Anthems	Abi	C	Za
Three Kings	Gsc	T	Sc
Three Latin Renaissance Motets	Wlp	T	Za
Three Magnificats	Kal	T	Za
Three Medieval Lyrics	Oxf	T	Za
Three Men Died On A Hillside	Fel	F	Sl
Three Miniatures For Organ	Abi	L	Zb
Three Motets	Kal	T	Za
Three Motets	See	L	Za
Three Motets	Kal	T	Za
Three Motets For Chorus & Solo	Kal	T	Za
Three Motets In Honor Of The Blessed	Gia	T	Za
Three Organ Preludes On Hymn Tunes	Abi	L	Zb
Three Original Carols For Junior Choir	Sac	L	Sc
Three Part Choir No 1 (No 5813)	Zon	T	Za
Three Part Choir No 2 (No 5830)	Zon	T	Za
Three Part Choir No 3 (No 5829)	Zon	T	Za
Three Part Choir No 4 (No 4286)	Zon	T	Za
Three Passion Motets	Kal	T	Za
Three Preludes And Fugues For Organ	Abi	L	Zb
Three Psalms	Kal	T	Za
Three Psalms	Sac	L	Za
Three Responses	Gsc	T	Za
Three Riders, The	Sac	L	Sc
Three Sacred Anthems (Ps 8,19,92)	Wlp	L	Za
Three Sacred Choruses	Kal	T	Za
Three Sacred Choruses, Op.37 (Eng-Lat)	Cfp	T	Za
Three Sacred Motets	Kal	T	Za
Three Sacred Solos For Medium Voice	Abi	L	Za
Three Seasonal Songs	Aug	L	Za
Three Short Holy Week Anthems	Gsc	T	Za
Three Songs For Sacred Occasions	Abi	L	Za
Three Songs Of Tribulation	Bbl	T	Za
Three Tents "One For Moses"	Van	F	Tx
Three Treble Choir Anthems	Abi	L	Za
Three Unfamiliar Organ Compositions By	Abi	L	Zb
Three Wedding Motets	Gia	L	Za
Three Wise Kings (E)	Oxf	L	Sc
Thrice Holy Lord	Sac	T	Tt
Throned Upon The Awful Tree	Sac	L	Sl
Through All The Changing Scenes	Lor	T	Tr
Through All The World	Wlp	F	Tx
Through Bitter Tribulation	Lps	T	Sl
Through It All	Man	G	Tr
Through Midnite Silence (Opt Oboe)	Pro	T	Sc
Through My Tears	Gmc	G	Sl
Through North & South (4 Voices)	Gia	T	Tt
Through Some Other Eyes	Man	G	Tx
Through The Eyes Of A Child	Pro	L	Sc
Throughout These Days	Acp	L	Sl
Throughout These Days	Acp	L	Sl
Throw Out The Lifeline	Zon	G	Tc
Thus Said The Lord	Gsc	T	Tj
Thus Saith The Lord	Aug	L	Tx
Thus Saith The Lord Of Hosts	Gsc	T	Tr
Thus Then The Law	Gsc	T	Tx
Thy Cross	Zon	G	Sl
Thy Giving Power	Smc	T	Ss
Thy Kingdom Come	Aug	T	Tk
Thy Kingdom Come (Opt Tpt)	Aug	L	Tk
Thy Kingdom Come On Earth	Aug	L	Tk
Thy Kingdom Come, O Lord	Aug	L	Tk
Thy Kingdom Come, O Lord	Abi	L	Tk
Thy Little Ones Dear Lord Are We	Gia	T	Sc
Thy Little Ones, Dear Lord, Are We	Aug	C	Tr
Thy Love Brings Joy	Aug	T	Tr
Thy Love Shall Fail Me Never	Hof	T	Tr
Thy Loving Kindness	Mar	L	Tr
Thy Way, Not Mine, O Lord	Gsc	T	Tc
Thy Will Be Done	Her	L	Sl
Thy Will Be Done	Gsc	L	Ll
Thy Will Be Done	Gsc	T	Ll
Thy Will Be Done	Sil	G	Tr
Thy Word Is A Lamp	Gsc	T	Tr
Thy Word With Me Shall Always Stay	Aug	L	Tx
Tidings Of Comfort And Joy	Lor	L	Sc
Till All My People Are One	Fel	F	Tu
Till He Comes	Zon	G	Tc
Time For Building Bridges, A	Nal	L	Tu
Time For Joy	Pro	L	Sc
Time For Singing Has Come, The	Abi	L	Tt
Time Is Short; Eternity's Long	Pmp	G	Sr
Time Stood Still On Calvary's Hill	Man	G	Sl
Time To Die	Wlp	F	Tf
Time To March Again	Prc	L	Tx
Tinagera (She Is Young)	Wrd	G	Tx
Tis A Gift To Be Simple (4-Part Arr)	Acp	F	Tr
Tis Christmas This Night	Van	F	Sc
Tis Finished	Gsc	T	Sl
Tis Finished! So The Savior Cried	Aug	T	Sl
Tis Indeed The Gospel Truth	Lps	T	Tr
Tis Midnight	Abi	L	Sl
Tis Noel Again!	Pro	T	Sc
Tis So Sweet To Trust In Jesus	Zon	G	Tr
Tis So Sweet To Trust In Jesus	Lor	T	Tr
Tis So Sweet To Trust In Jesus (P. D.)	Man	T	Tr
Tis Thee I Would Be Praising	Smc	T	Zb
Tis Well (Cantata)	Lps	T	Sr
Titus 3:5	Mar	L	Tb
To A Virgin, Meek And Mild	Aug	T	Tm
To Be A Friend	Wlp	C	Tr
To Be Alive	Chh	F	Tx
To Be Alive	Fel	F	Tx
To Be At Peace With God	Gmp	G	Tr
To Be Fed By Ravens	Smc	L	Zb
To Be Redeemed	Gia	F	Sr
To Be Used Of God	Man	G	Tc
To Be What You Want Me To Be	Zon	F	Tc
To Be Your Body	Wlp	F	Lo
To Bless The Earth	Sac	L	Tr
To Christ The King	Acp	L	Tk
To Christ The King (4-Part Arr)	Acp	L	Tk
To Christ, Glory & Power	Wlp	L	Tj
To Come, O Lord, To Thee	Gsc	T	La
To Cry Is To Die	Fel	F	Tx
To Damascus	Fel	F	Tx

Title	Code
To Deum Laudamus	Aug L Tt
To Do God's Will	Aug T Tr
To God All Praise And Glory	Lor T Tt
To God Almighty We Confess	Wlp T Tt
To God Be The Glory	Lor T Tt
To God Be The Glory	Fis F Tt
To God Be The Glory	Lor T Tt
To God Be The Glory (Opt Brass)	Smc L Tt
To God Let Praise Be Song	Wrd G Tt
To God On High	Gsc T Tt
To God We Sing A New Song	Acp L Tt
To God We Sing A New Song (4—Part Arr)	Acp L Tt
To Greet The Babe So Holy	Abi L Sc
To Him Give Praise (Suite)	Oxf T Tr
To His Angels	Nal L Tr
To Jesus Christ Our Sovereign King	Gia T Tk
To Jesus Christ Our Sovereign King	Acp L Tk
To Jesus Christ Our Sovereign King	Acp L Tk
To Jesus Holy	Wlp T Tj
To Know Thou Art	Aug L Tr
To Mercy, Pity, Peace And Love	Gsc T Tr
To Our Fathers—And Thee	Smc T Tx
To Our King Immortal	Aug L Tk
To Raise A Grateful Song	Pro T Tt
To Rise Again	Wlp F Sr
To See The Lord	Lor T Tr
To Share Their Joy (Wedding Song)	Nal L Tw
To Speak His Word	Ahc L Tx
To The Hills I Lift Mine Eyes	Abi L Tr
To The Lamb Who Was Slain	Fel L Tk
To The Living God	Rpb L Tt
To The Lord I Cry	Gia L To
To The Mountain	Acf F Tx
To The Mountain Lord!	Gra F Lp
To The Name That Guides Our Nation	Acp L Tp
To The Name That Guides Our Nation	Acp L Tp
To The Sea In Ships	Ron T Tx
To The Town Of Bethlehem	Gia T Sc
To The Work	Sac L Tx
To The Work	Zon G Tc
To Thee Be Glory	Nal L Tt
To Thee O Lord, Our Hearts We Raise	Oxf T Tt
To Thee The Holy Ghost, We Now Pray	Gsc T Ss
To Thee, O Lord	Gsc T Tt
To Thee, O Lord, Our Hearts We Raise	Lor T To
To Us A Child Is Given (Cantata)	Lps T Sc
To Us Is Born (W/Bells)	Abi T Sc
To Us Is Born Immanuel	Gsc T Sc
To Whom Shall We Go	Acf F Tx
To You Do I Raise My Eyes	Wlp L Tr
To You I Cry, O Lord	Fel L Sl
To You I Lift My Soul	Hal T Tr
To You I Lift Up My Soul	Fel L Tr
To You I Lift Up My Soul	Nal L Tr
To You I Lift Up My Soul & Ps 43	Gia T Tr
To You I Pray, O Lord	Fel L Tr
To You We Owe Our Hymn	Fel L Tt
To You Will I Offer	Fel L To
To You, O Lord (Icet)	Wlp L Ld
To You, O Lord, I Lift My Soul	Gia L To
To Your Table	Ahc L Ln
To Zion Jesus Came	Lor T Tr
Toccata For Nun Danket Alle Got	Gra L Zb
Toccata For Organ	Abi L Zb
Today I Followed Jesus	Sil G Tj
Today I Walked In His Footsteps	Sil G Tj
Today In Bethlehem	Abi L Sc
Today Is The Crown Of Creation	Nal L Sr
Today Is The First Day	Man G Tc
Today The World Is Filled	Acp L Sc
Today The World Is Filled	Acp L Tx
Today There Is Ringing	Aug T Sr
Together Again(Scotty's Song)	Rpb F Tr
Tommy's Farewell	Pmp G Tx
Tomorrow And Tomorrow	Fcc C Tx
Tomorrow Christ Is Coming	Aug L Tk
Tomorrow Is In His Hands	Gmc G Tx
Tomorrow Shall Be My Dancing Day	Wlp T Sc
Too Late To Pray	Jhm G Tx
Top Songs For Children (No 5849)	Zon C Za
Top Songs For Duets 5774	Zon G Za
Top Songs For High Voice (No 5026)	Zon G Za
Top Songs For Low Voice No 1 (No 5936)	Zon G Za
Top Songs For Low Voice No 2 (No 5941)	Zon G Za
Top Songs For Men (No 5831)	Zon G Za
Top Songs For Soloists No 1 (No 5847)	Zon G Za
Top Songs For Soloists No 2 (No 5832)	Zon G Za
Top Songs For Trios (No 5777)	Zon G Za
Totentanz	Abi L Zb
Touch A Hand, Make A Friend	Hal F Tx
Touch Me Just Now	Man G Tx
Touch Me Savior	Man G Tj
Touch Of His Hand, The	Zon G Tr
Touch Them With Love	Urs F Tr
Tous Les Bourgeois De Chastres	Gsc T Sc
Traditional German Carol	Gsc T Sc
Tramping (Spiritual)	Lor G Tx
Transcriptions For Organ	Abi L Zb
Traveler, The	Wbp T Tt
Travelin' Road (Cantata)	Zon L Tc
Travelin' 40 Days	Ccc L Sl
Traveling On	Man G Tc
Treasure Of Heaven, The	Zon G Sr
Treasures	Wrd F Tw
Treasures In Heaven	Sac L Tr
Treble Trios No 1 (No 5041)	Zon G Za
Treble Trios No 2 (No 5042)	Zon G Za
Treble Trios No 3 (No 5043)	Zon G Za
Treble Trios No 4 (No 5044)	Zon G Za
Treble Trios No 5 (No 5045)	Zon G Za
Treble Trios No 6 (No 5046)	Zon G Za
Treble Trios No 7 (No 5091)	Zon G Za
Tree Of Life	Rpb L Tr
Tremble, Tremble Little Earth (Ps 114)	Wlp F Tt
Tribute To Mother, A	Lor T Tx
Tried In The Fire	Chd G Tx
Trilogy Of Praise	Gsc T Tt
Trio Of Praise	See L Tt
Trios (No 5828)	Zon G Za
Triptych	Abi L Zb
Trisagion	Acp L Tx
Trisagion (Mass For New Rite)	Gia L Le
Trisagion (Notre Dame Mass)	Gia L Le
Trisagion (4—Part Arr)	Acp L Tx
Tristis Est Anima Mea	Gsc T Sl
Tristis Est Anima Mea	Bbl T Sl
Tristis Est Anima Mea	Kal T Sl
Triumph	Bbl T Sr
Triumph Of The Cross (Psalm) (Icet)	Wlp L Ld
Triumph Of The Cross Alleluia (Icet)	Wlp L Lf
Triumphal Hymn, Opus 55 (Eng/Germ)	Kal T Tt
Troset Troset Mein Volk	Gsc T Tr
Trouble	Man G Sl
Trouble, Lord	Gia F Sl
True Fasting	Abi L Sl
Truly There Is A God	Fel L Tr
Truly Trust	Man G Tr
Truly, We Shall Be In Paradise	Gsc L Sr
Trumpet Of God	Lor T Tk
Trumpeters And Singers Were As One	Abi L Tt
Trust	Gsc T Tr
Trust And Obey	Fel F Tr
Trust God And Come Before Him	Wlp T La
Trust In God	Lor L Tr
Trust In Him	Mam G Tr
Trust In Him	Gsc T Tr
Trust In Him	Hhh G Tr
Trust In Me	Man G Tr
Trust In The Lord	Aug L Tr
Trust In The Lord	Gia L Tr
Trust In The Lord	Gsc T Sl
Trust In The Lord	Fis F Tr
Trust In The Lord	Gsc T Tr
Trust In The Lord (Mixed Chor Acap)	Aug L Tr
Trust In The Lord (Prov 3)	Gia F Tr
Trust Thou In God	Gsc T Tr
Trusting Jesus	Lor T Tj
Trusting Jesus	Zon G Tj
Trusting Jesus A	Zon T Tj
Try A Little Kindness	Bch F Tt
Try Jesus	Man G Tj
Try Jesus	Zon G Tj
Trying To Make Heaven My Home	Her G Sr
Tu Es Petrus	Kal T Tx
Tu Es Petrus	Gsc T Tx
Turn Back To God, America	Zon G Tp
Turn Back, O Man	Abi L Tr
Turn Back, O Man	Val F Sl
Turn It Over To Jesus	Yan F Tj
Turn Not Thy Face	Aug T Tr
Turn Thy Face From My Sins (M)	Oxf T Sl
Turn To Me, O Man	Nal L Tr
Turn Ye Even To Me	Gsc T Sl
Turn Your Eyes	Fel F Tx
Turn Your Eyes Upon Jesus	Zon T Tj
Turn Your Thoughts To Those Who	Bbl T Tf
Turn, Turn, Turn	Mel F Tx
Twas In The Moon Of Wintertime	Gia T Sc
Twas On One Sunday Morning	Lor T Sr
Twelve Benediction Amens (E—Md)	Oxf T Lk
Twelve Canciones For Two Voices	Kal L Za
Twelve Days Of Christmas, The	Abi L Sc
Twelve Hymn Accompaniments	Abi L Zb
Twelve Madrigals	See L Za
Twelve Responses And Sentences	Wbp T Za
Twenty Four Anthems For Sa Voices	Oxf L Za
Twenty Hymn Preludes For Organ	Cob L Zb
Twenty Responses (Elizabethan)	Sac T Za
Twenty Responses For General Worship	Lor T Za
Twenty Third Psalm	Wbp T Tr
Twenty—Five Anthems (In 4 Vols)	Kal T Za
Twenty—Five Anthems For Mixed Voices	Oxf T Za
Twenty—One Service Responses	Wbp T Za
Twenty—Third Psalm	Tcp L Tr
Twenty—Third Psalm	Van F Ld
Twenty—Third Psalm	See L Tr
Twenty—Third Psalm (W/Narrator)	Aug L Tr
Twenty—Third Psalm, The	Bbl T Tr
Twilight And Dawn	Gsc T Tx
Two Anthems	Som L Za
Two Anthems For Children's Voices	Abi C Sc
Two Anthems From The Moravians	Abi L Za
Two Anthems: (Me)	Oxf T Za
Two Carols	Abi T Za
Two Carols	Gia T Sc
Two Choral Songs	Bbl L Za
Two Chorales For Concert Band	Smc T Zb
Two Christmas Carols	Abi L Sc
Two Christmas Preludes (Mod Easy)	Abi L Zb
Two Compositions For Organ	Abi L Zb
Two Dwellings	Lor I Ir
Two Easter Anthems	Cfp T Sr
Two Easter Anthems (A Cap)	Cfp T Sr
Two Easter Carols	Abi L Za
Two Evening Hymns	Oxf T Za
Two Holy Songs (Ps. 134, Ps. 150)	Som L Tt
Two Hymns For The Bicentennial	Wlp T Tp
Two Hymns I/H St	Gia L Za
Two Hymns Of Praise	Oxf T Tt
Two Introits	Oxf L Za
Two Introits	Smc L Za
Two Junior Choir Anthems	Sac L Za
Two Lenten Meditations	Abi L Za
Two Lives, One Moment	Chd L Tw
Two Marian Compositions (Lat)	Cfp T Za
Two Motets (Adoramus Te, Cantate)	Oxf T Tt
Two Motets (Latin)	Cfp T Za
Two Motets 'in Diem Pacis' (D)	Oxf T Za
Two Motets From Kancjonaxy	Gia T Sc
Two Motets In Honor Of Blessed Virgin	Gia T Sc
Two Preludes For Holy Week (Mod Diff)	Abi L Zb
Two Proverbs	See L Za
Two Psalms (Ps. 146, Ps. 117)	Som L Za
Two Psalms For High Voice	Abi L Za
Two Roads	Mar L Tc
Two Sacred Pieces (Md)	Oxf T Za
Two Sacred Solos	Abi L Za
Two Shabbat Songs	See L Za
Two Short Anthems (Me)	Oxf T Za
Two Songs (From Saint Paul)	Som L Za
Two Songs For Medium Voice	Abi L Za
Two Songs For Mens Voices	Bbl T Za
Two Songs Of Mourning From The	Bbl T Za
Two Spirituals	Abi G Tx
Two Te Deum And Magnificat	Kal T Tt
Two—Fold Kyrie	Gia L Lb
Ubi Caritas Et Amor (Eng & Lt)(M)	Gia T Sl
Ukrainian Bell Carol	Lor T Sc
Una Sancta (W/Keyboard Or Band)	Aug L Tu
Unbounded Grace	Zon F Tr
Uncertain Tide	Nal L Tx
Unconditional Love	Yan F Tr
Under His Wings	Lor L Tr
Under His Wings	Lor T Tr
Under The Eastern Sky (Org & Opt Clar)	Aug L Tx
Under The Shadow (Of My Wing)	Chd F Tr
Unfold Ye Portals ("Redemption")	Cfs T Tk
Unfold Ye Portals(The Redemption)	Gsc T La
Unfold, Unfold! Take In His Light	Gsc T Tc
Unfold, Ye Portals	Lor T La
Unites Us All Together As One	Wlp F Lo
Universal Lord, The	Sac L Tk
Unless A Man Be Born Again	Fel L Tb
Unless You Help Me Lord	Man G Tx
Unseen Presence, The	Abi L Tr
Unsers Herzens Freude (Eng & Germ)	Oxf T Tx
Until	Nal L Tx
Until Then	Gmc G Sa
Until Then	Ham G Tx
Until We Meet Again(I'll Pray For You)	Zon G Tr
Unto Christ The Victim (Victimae)	Oxf T Sr
Unto Thee Do We Cry	Smc L Tt
Unto Thee O Lord	Gsc L Tr
Unto Thee Will I Cry (Ps 28)	Oxf T Sl
Unto Thee Will I Sing	Gsc T Tr
Unto Thee, O Lord	Sac L Tr
Unto Us A Boy Is Born	Gia L Sc
Unto Us A Boy Is Born	Gsc L Sc
Unto Us A Child Is Born	Maf L Sc
Unto Us A Child Is Born	Wlp L Sc
Untold Millions, Still Untold	Man G Tc
Up The Hill Of Calvary With Love	Elv L Sl
Up To Jerusalem (Lk 18:3)	Wlp F Sl
Up, O Jerusalem	Fel L Sa
Up, Up And Away	Man G Tx
Uphold Me In Life	Nal L Tr
Upon Easter Day	Gia L Sr
Upon My Lap My Sovereign Sits	Som L Tx
Upon My Lips	Wlp L Tt
Upon This Rock	Gsc T Tx
Upper Room, The	Lor T Sr
Upright Is The Word	Gra L Ld
Ut Flos, Ut Rosa (Me) (Saints)	Oxf T Tx
Uv' Shofar Gadol	Gsc T Tx
V'shom'ru	Gsc T Tx
Valiant—For-Truth (Md)	Oxf T Tx
Valleys Of Green	Nal L Tr
Vamos Al Portal	Gsc T Sc
Variants On An Irish Hymn	Bec T Tt
Variations On Gott Des Himmels	Abi L Zb

ALPHABETICAL INDEX OF TITLES

Variations On Hymn Tunes By William Abi L Zb
Variations On Mit Freuden Zart Abi L Zb
Variations On Wer Nur Den Lieben Gott Abi L Zb
Variations To Adeste Fideles Abi L Zb
Vaterunser, Das Bbl T Ll
Veni Sanctus K 47 Kal T Tx
Veni, Sancte Spiritus Fel T Ss
Veni, Virgo Sacrata Bbl T Tm
Veniat Dilectus Meus(Come O Come) Gsc T Tw
Venite Ad Me Omnes Gsc T Sl
Venite Adoremus Sac T Sc
Verbum Caro Factum Est Gsc T Sc
Verbum Caro In A Minor Gia T Tj
Verbum Caro In G Gia T Tj
Verbum Patris Humanatur Gsc T Sc
Vere Languores Nostros Gsc T Sl
Verily, Verily Zon G Tx
Verily, Verily, I Say Unto You Oxf T Lo
Verleih Uns Frieden Genadiglich Gsc T Tr
Vexilla Regis Prodeunt(Lat) Cfp T Sr
Via Crucis Kal T Sl
Victimae Paschali Laudes Fel T Sr
Victimae Paschali Laudes Gia T Sr
Victory Ahead Zon G Sr
Videntes Stellam (Md) Oxf T Sc
Vidi Aquam Aug L Tb
Vidimus Stellam Ron T Sc
Vigil Assumption–Alleluia (Vv)(Icet) Wlp L Lf
Vigil Assumption–Psalm (Icet) Wlp L Ld
Vigil Pentecost Alleluia (Vv)(Icet) Wlp L Lf
Vigil Pentecost Psalm (Icet) Wlp L Ld
Vigil Peter & Paul Alleluia (Vv)(Icet) Wlp L Lf
Vigil Peter & Paul Psalm (Icet) Wlp L Ld
Vigilate Aug T Sl
Vineyard Of The Lord (Ps 80) Rav L Ld
Violet In The Snow Nal C Sc
Violin Solo Favorites (No 5028) Zon T Zb
Virga Jesse Floruit(Lat) Cfp T Sc
Virgen Lava Panales, La Ron T Tm
Virgin Full Of Grace Wlp T Tm
Virgin Mother Gia T Tm
Vision Of Aeroplanes (Ezek 1) Oxf T Tx
Vision Of Peace Bbl T Tr
Vision Of Saint Joan Tcp L Tx
Visions Of Eternity Pmp G Tk
Visit, The Nal C Sc
Visitatio Sepulchri (Acting Version) Oxf T Sr
Vital Spark Of Heav'nly Flame (A Cap) Abi L Ss
Vobis Datum Est Bbl T Tt
Voces De Jubilo (No 5362) Zon G Za
Voice Of The Lord Fcc L Tx
Voice, The Lor L Tx
Voices Sil G Tx
Voices Nal L Tx
Voices In Praise Pro T Za
Voices Of The Sky Gsc T Sc
Voluntaries Based On Hymn Tunes Gam T Zb
Voluntaries For The Christian Year Abi L Zb
Voluntaries On Early American Hymns Abi L Zb
Von Himmel Hoch (In 5 Carols) Me Gia T Sc
Vow Song Ahc L Tc
Vox In Rama (E & L) (M) Gia T Sc
Wade In De Water Wbp T Tx
Wade In The Water Gsc G Tx
Wade In The Water Van F Tb
Wait For The Lord With Courage Fel L Sa
Waiting Fel F Sa
Wake Awake Acp L Sa
Wake Awake For Night Is Flying Aug T Sc
Wake Awake The Night Is Dying Wlp T Sa
Wake Up Fel F Tx
Wake Up, My People Fel F Tx
Wake, Awake Aug T Sc
Wake, Awake (W/Str Bass) Aug T Sc
Wake, O Shepherds (W/Violin) Aug T Sc
Wake, O Wake (Wachet Auf) (Me) Oxf T Sc
Wake, Ye Shepherds Gsc T Sc
Waken, Little Shepherd Gsc T Sc
Walk In Light (God Is Light) Gia F Tr
Walk In Love Nal L Tr
Walk In Love Fel L Tr
Walk In Peace United Mem L Tr
Walk In Sunlight (Cantata) Wrd C Sc
Walk In The Light Gsc L Tc
Walk In The Sunshine Man G Tb
Walk On Sha F Lp
Walk On The Pathway Sav G Tc
Walk On The Water Gmc G Tr
Walk With Me Lor T Tj
Walk With The Years Lor L Tc
Walk With Us, Lord Lor T Tj
Walk With Your God Lor T Tc
Walk Worthy Gsc T Tc
Walkin' And Talkin' With Jesus Man G Tj
Walkin' Down The Line Man G Tc
Walkin' In The Light Of His Love Wrd L Tr
Walking Alone Prc L Tx
Walking On Higher Ground Sil G Tc
Walls (You Have Made A Field) Gia L Tu
Walpole (From Two Plain–Tunes) Bbl T Sl
Wanna Go To Heaven? Man G Sr
War Requiem (Russian–English) Kal T Tp
Warrenton Gsc T Tx
Washington Bbl T Tp
Wasn't That A Mighty Day Gsc G Tx
Wasn't That A Mighty Day! Her F Sc
Watch With Me Nal L Tr
Watch Ye, Pray Ye (Cantata) Lps T Sl
Watchman! Pic L Tx
Water Of Life Van F Tb
Water Of Time Bri G Tx
Water Pot (John 2) Mcc F Tj
Waters Of Love (God's Power) Jsp T Tb
Way Of All Flesh Fel F Sl
Way Of Christ, The Lor T Tc
Wayfaring Stranger Gsc T Sl
Wayfaring Stranger, The Zon G Sl
We Adore Thee Zon T Sl
We Adore Thee Bbl T Tt
We Adore You Gia T Tj
We Adore You Gia T Tj
We Adore You (E & Lat) Gia T Sl
We Adore You (E & Lat) Gia T Sl
We Adore You No. 1 Bbl T Tt
We Adore You No. 2 Bbl T Tt
We Adore You, Jesus Christ Gia T Sl
We Adore You, O Christ Fel L Sl
We Adore You, O Christ Gia T Tj
We Adore You, O Lord Jesus Christ Gia T Sl
We All Need God Lor T Tr
We All Stand At Your Table Wlp F Ln
We Are All Held In His Hand Wlp F Tr
We Are His People Gia L Ld
We Are His People (Icet) Wlp L Tr
We Are Hungry Fel L Lo
We Are One Fcc F Lo
We Are The Body Of Christ Fel L Tr
We Are The Body Of Christ Nal C Lo
We Are The Church Prc L Tx
We Are The Light Of The World. Vrn G Lp
We Are The People Of The Lord Nal L Tr
We Are Your Bread Wlp F To
We Believe That Thou Shalt Come Gsc T Sa
We Belong To You O Risen Lord Gra L Tc
We Beseech Thee Val F To
We Come And Go Sil F Tr
We Come Praising God Yan F La
We Come To Join In Your Banquet Wlp F Ln
We Come To Praise His Name Tal T Tt
We Come To Praise His Name (Jud Mac) Pro T La
We Come To You With Longing Wlp T Tr
We Come To Your Table Nal L Ln
We Come To Your Table Nal C Ln
We Come Unto Our Fathers' God Abi T Tx
We Do Adore Thee Som T Tt
We Don't Have Much Farther To Go Zon G Sr
We Find Thee, Lord In Others Need Jsp L Tr
We Gather At Your Table, Lord Sac L La
We Gather Together Rpb L La
We Gather Together Fel F Ln
We Gather Together Wlp T La
We Gather Together (4–Part Arr) Acp L La
We Give An Offering To Jesus Nal L To
We Give Thanks To Thee Gsc T Tt
We Give Thanks To Thee, O Lord Abi L Sl
We Give You Thanks Wlp L Tt
We Give You Thanks, We Worship You Wlp L Tt
We Go Into The House Of The Lord Wlp F La
We Greet You (Litany Of Bvm) Wlp L Tm
We Hasten, O Jesu (From Cantata 78) Oxf T Tj
We Have A King Rpb F Tk
We Have A Strong City (Is 26) Oxf L Tc
We Have All Been To The Water Rpb L Tb
We Have An Anchor Zon G Tr
We Have Been A–Rambling Gsc T Sc
We Have Come Mar L Tc
We Have Love (W/Piano) Wrd F Tw
We Have Seen His Star In The East Fel L Sc
We Have Seen His Star In The East Gsc L Sc
We Have This Moment, Today Gmc G Tx
We Know That Christ Is Raised (W/Perc) Aug T Sr
We Lift Our Hearts To Thee Gsc T Tr
We Long For You, O Lord Fel L Lo
We Look For Light Acp L Tr
We Look For Light Acp L Tr
We Love The Place Where Thine Honor Oxf T Tr
We Love The Place, O God Gsc T Tc
We Magnify Our Father God Zon L Tt
We Need Thy Love Lor T Tr
We Need Time Fel F Tx
We Offer Bread And Wine Ahc L To
We Offer You Our Gifts. Vrn L To
We Offer You The Prayer Fel L To
We Place Our Selves (Sub Tuum) Wlp L Tm
We Plow The Fields Smc T Tt
We Praise Thee, O God Aug T Tt
We Praise Thee, O God Aug T Tt
We Praise Thee, O God Gsc L Tt
We Praise Thee, O God, Our Redeemer Zon T Tt
We Praise You Above All Forever Fel L Tt
We Praise You Every Day Fel F Tt
We Praise You Lord For Jesus Jsp T Tb
We Praise You, O God Fel L Tt
We Praise You, O Lord Fel L Tt
We Pray To You, O Lord 1 Wlp L Tr
We Reach Out For Love Rpb F Tr
We Rejoice And Adore You, O God Fel L Tt
We Say Thank You, Lord Sms F Tt
We See The Lord Jeb L Tt
We See You O Lord Nal L Tj
We Shall Enter Your Courts Fel L La
We Shall Overcome Acp F Tr
We Sing His Praise Fel L Tt
We Sing In Celebration Bec T Sc
We Sing Now At Christmas Aug L Sc
We Sing To God (In 3 Volumes) Aug T Za
We Stand In Need Rav L Lo
We Thank Thee Lor T Tt
We Thank Thee Hof T Tp
We Thank Thee Zon L Tt
We Thank Thee, Lord Lor T Tt
We Thank Thee, O Lord Lor T Tt
We Thank You Abi L Tt
We Thank You (In Sunshine & Rain) Gia F Tt
We Thank You, O Lord Fel L Tt
We Three Are One Aug L Tx
We Three Kings Ccc L Sc
We Three Kings Abi T Sc
We Three Kings Of Orient Are Cfs T Sc
We Wait For The Coming Of Jesus Lor T Sa
We Wait For Thy Loving Kindness (M) Oxf T Tc
We Wait For Thy Loving Kindness (Me) Oxf T Tr
We Walk Through The Meadow Pro T Tt
We Welcome Glad Easter Lor T Sr
We Will Celebrate Nal L Tt
We Will Hear Your Word Wlp F Le
We Will Offer Praises To God Fel L Tt
We Will Rejoice Bbl T Tt
We Would Be Building Zon L Tr
We Would Offer Thee This Day Sac T To
We'll All Praise God Together Gia G Tt
We'll See The Light Ahc L Tx
We'll Sing A New Song Fel F Tt
We'll Talk It Over Zon G Tr
We're Called To Be That City Wlp L Tc
We're Gathered Together Rpb L La
We're Goin' Home Ahc L Tx
We're Goin' On A Picnic Rpb G Tx
We're Going To Sing Zon G Tt
We're Gonna March Down Fel F La
We're Here To Be Happy Prc L Tx
We're Marching To Zion Zon G Lp
We've A Story To Tell To The Nations Zon G Tc
We've Been To The Mountain Wlp L Tx
We've Got A Great Big Wonderful God Man G Tt
We've Got A Lot To Live For Lor T Tx
Weary Marching Up The Calvary Road Zon T Sl
Wedded Souls Pic L Tw
Wedding Chorus From Alceste Bbl T Tw
Wedding Motet Fel T Tw
Wedding Music (In Two Volumes) Aug L Zb
Wedding Music For The Church Organist Abi L Tw
Wedding Prayer Gsc T Tw
Wedding Prayer, A Zon G Tw
Wedding Processional (Mod Easy) Abi L Zb
Wedding Processional & Air (Org) Aug T Tw
Wedding Responses Oxf T Tw
Wedding Song Fcc F Tw
Wedding Song Gia L Tw
Weep, Little Children, Weep Fcc F Sl
Weeping Nature (From Three Songs) Bbl T Sl
Welcome Prc L Tx
Welcome Happy Morning Gsc T Sr
Welcome Happy Morning (Md) Oxf T Sr
Welcome In Nal L Lp
Welcome Son Of Mary Wlp T Sc
Welcome To The Family Man L Tb
Welcome Welcome Dear Redeemer Gsc T Sa
Welcome, Happy Morning Zon T Sr
Welcome, Lord (W/Guitar) Gia L La
Well Done, Come Home Ham G Tf
Well Done, Good And Faithful Fel L Tf
Well Done, Good And Faithful Fel T Tf
Well, It's A New Day Wlp L La
Were You There Smc G Sl
Were You There Hal T Sl
Were You There? Hof G Sl
Were You There? Abi L Sl
Were You There? Gsc T Tx
Were You There? Zon G Sl
Were You There? Nal L Sl
Were You There? (No 4014) Zon G Sl
Were You There? (Spiritual) Lor G Sl
Western Style Songs No 1 (No 5580) Zon F Za
Western Style Songs No 2 (No 5581) Zon F Za
Western Style Songs No 3 (No 5582) Zon F Za
Western Style Songs No 4 (No 5560) Zon F Za
Westminster Carol Lor T Sc
What A Friend Lor T Tj
What A Friend We Have In Jesus (Arr.) Sil G Tj

ALPHABETICAL INDEX OF TITLES

What A Great Thing It Is Fel F Tr
What A Wonderful Feeling Pmp G Tx
What A Wonderful Savior! Zon T Tj
What A Wonderful Way To Go Man G Tc
What Are These That Are Arrayed Gsc T Tx
What Can A Man Say? Fel F Sl
What Can I Do For My Country? Ham G Tp
What Can I Give Him? Lor T Sc
What Can I Give Him? Lor T Sc
What Can Keep Us? Nal L Tc
What Can Make A Hippopotamus Smile Wlp C Tx
What Can We Offer Acf F Tx
What Child Is This? Lor T Sc
What Child Is This? Maf T Sc
What Child Is This? Lor T Sc
What Child Is This? Gsc T Sc
What Child Is This? Aug T Sc
What Child Is This? Zon T Sc
What Child Is This? Lor T Sc
What Child Is This? (W/Perc) Aug T Sc
What Color Is God's Skin? Nal C Tx
What Could Be Better Fis F Tr
What Did You Say Was The Baby's Name? Gmc G Sc
What Do You Do Fel F Sl
What God Is Like Nal C Tx
What Grace Is This Zon G Tr
What Great Marvels Rpb L Tt
What Greater Love Sil L Tr
What Has God Given Me? Nal L To
What Have You Given Wlp F To
What I See Bch L Tx
What I Tell You In Darkness Fel L Tx
What If Christ Came Tonight Pmp G Tk
What Is A Man? Bbl T Tx
What Is It Troubles Thee (Cantata) Lps T Sl
What Is This Lovely Fragrance? (Me) Oxf T Tx
What Is This Pleasant Fragrance? Gsc T Sc
What Is Your Name? Nal L Tx
What Kind Of King? Abi L Sc
What Love Have We Denied To The Lord Acp F Sl
What Love Have We Denied To The Lord Acp F Sl
What Makes A Man Turn His Back On God Man G Sl
What Makes Love Grow? Nal C Lo
What Makes The Wind Blow Prc L Tx
What Miracles Of Beauty Van F Tx
What Pain Our Master Didst Endure Aug T Sl
What Return Shall I Make To The Lord? Gia L Tc
What Shall I Do? Nal C Tc
What Shall I Render Abi L To
What Shall We Give Fel F To
What Shall We Give Gsc T Sc
What Songs Were Sung Gsc T Sc
What Star Is This? Zon T Sc
What The Future Hath W/Organ Acc Gsc L Sr
What Then Of Your Soul? Yan F Sl
What Think Ye Of Christ? Lor T Sr
What Wondrous Love Gia T Tf
What Wondrous Love Abi L Sl
What Wondrous Love Is This Lor T Sl
What Wondrous Sacrifice Tcp L Tx
What Would I Do Bri G Tx
What Would I Do Without Jesus? Zon G Tj
What Would You Do Sil F Tx
What Would You Have Us Do? Nal L Tc
What You Gave Us Acp L To
What You Gonna Call Yo Pretty Little Gsc T Sc
What You Gonna Do Fel F Tx
What You Hear In The Dark Nal L Tc
What'e'er My God Ordains Is Right Sac T Tr
What's It All About, Anyhow? Zon F Za
Whatcha Gonna Do Man L Sl
Whatever It Takes Man G Tx
Whatever You Ask For Fel L Tr
Whatever You Do Fel L Tx
Whatsoever Things Gia L Lm
Whatsoever You Do Acf F Lo
When Christ Was Born Of Mary Free Gsc T Sc
When Christmas Morn Is Dawning Aug T Sc
When David Heard Gsc T Sl
When David Heard That Absalom Was Gsc T Tx
When Earth's Last Picture Is Painted Ham G Sa
When From Our Exile Nal L Sl
When From The Lips Of Truth Cob T Tx
When God Calls Us Home Pmp G Sr
When God Is The Honored Guest(Mothers) Lor L Tx
When God Makes The Morning Zon G Tx
When God Seems So Near Gmc G Tr
When He Shall Come Zon L Sa
When His Salvation Bringing Zon T Sl
When I Can Read My Title Clear Zon T Tf
When I Climb Them Golden Stairs Jhm G Sr
When I Get To Heaven Mar L Sr
When I Had Fallen Low Indeed Acp L Sl
When I Had Fallen Low Indeed Acp L Sl
When I Looked Up Pmp G Tx
When I Met My Savior Zon G Tj
When I Prayed Through Gmc G Tr
When I Remember Zon T Sl
When I See A Mountain Gmp G Tx
When I Sing Wlp F Tt
When I Stood At Calvary Lor T Sl
When I Survey The Wondrous Cross Gsc T Sl
When I Survey The Wondrous Cross Sac T Sl
When I Survey The Wondrous Cross Sac T Sl
When I Think Of Calvary Gmc G Sl
When I Walk Through The Valley Wlp F Sl
When I Was Sinkin' Down Gsc T Sl
When I Witness Yan F Tx
When I'm Feeling Lonely Prc L Tx
When I've Changed My Address To Heaven Zon G Tf
When Israel Nal L Sr
When It's Time Nal L Tx
When Jesus Breaks The Morning Gmc G Sa
When Jesus In The Garden Gsc T Sl
When Jesus Knelt Aug L Tj
When Jesus Left His Father's Throne Aug T Sc
When Jesus Left His Father's Throne 1 Aug L Sc
When Jesus Lived In Galilee Gsc T Sc
When Jesus Sat At Meat (Md) (Stmmag) Oxf T Tx
When Jesus Wept Gsc T Sl
When Jesus Wept (In 19 Rounds) Gia T Sl
When Jesus Wept (Med Voice) Abi L Sl
When Jesus Wept (Round) Smc T Zb
When Lights Are Lit On Christmas Eve Zon L Sc
When Love Came Down Lor L Sc
When Love Shines In Lor T Tr
When Love Shines In Zon G Tr
When Love Was Born Lor L Sc
When Love Was Born Zon T Sc
When Mary Magdalene Bbl T Sr
When Mary Through The Garden Went (Me) Oxf T Sr
When Morning Gilds The Skies Lor T La
When Morning Gilds The Skies Lor T La
When Morning Gilds The Sky Gsc T Tx
When My Lord Picks Up The Phone Ham G Tr
When My Weak Eyes Can See That Cross Acp L Sl
When My Weak Eyes Can See That Cross Acp L Sl
When One Knows Thee Gsc T Tr
When The Great Trumpet Sound Jhe G Tk
When The Lord Laid His Hand On Me Sem G Tt
When The Lord Of Love Was Here Lor L Tj
When The Lord Turned Again (Me) Oxf T Sr
When The Lord Was Born Gia T Sc
When The Morning Comes Fel F Sr
When The Roll Is Called Up Yonder Zon G Tf
When The Son Of Man Shall Come (D) Oxf T Sa
When The Spirit Moves You Wgm F Ss
When The Terms Of Peace Are Made Gsc L Tr
When There's Love At Home Lor T Tx
When This World Ends Oak G Tk
When We Eat This Bread Nal L Lj
When We Eat This Bread Wlp F Lj
When We Eat This Bread Nal L Lj
When We Eat This Bread Wlp F Lj
When We Eat This Bread Wlp F Lj
When We Eat This Bread Nal L Lj
When We Eat This Bread Nal L Lj
When We Eat This Bread (Icet) Wlp L Lj
When We In Spirit View Thy Passion Abi L Sl
When We See Nal L Tx
When We See Christ Zon G Sr
When Wilt Thou Save The People? Gsc T Sl
When Woe Assails Us Through And Throug Gsc T Sl
When You Least Expect Him Prc L Tx
When You Pray Man G Tr
When, His Salvation Bringing Abi L Sl
Whence Art Thou My Maiden? (Arr) Gia T Sc
Whenever You Do This Fel L Tr
Where Are You Going Man G Tc
Where Charity And Love Abide Wlp L Tr
Where Charity And Love Are Lit L La
Where Charity And Love Are Found Cfc L Tr
Where Charity And Love Prevail Wlp L Tr
Where Cross The Crowded Ways Aug T Tx
Where Cross The Crowded Ways Smc T Tr
Where Do I Go From Here Man G Tc
Where Do I See God? Yan F Tx
Where Do You Want Me Ahc L Tc
Where Does The Uttered Music Go? Oxf T Tc
Where Else Would I Go Chd F Tj
Where Has Your Lover Gone Rav L Tt
Where Have All The Flowers Gone? Frm F Tt
Where Have You Gone, My Lonely Lord? Lor T Sl
Where He Leads I'll Follow Zon G Tc
Where I Am Fel L Tr
Where In The World Zon F Tx
Where Is He? Zon L Sc
Where Is Love Today? Zon F Tr
Where Is Now Abel? Gia T Tx
Where Is This Old World A-Goin? Zon F Tx
Where Love Is Living Acp L Tr
Where Love Is Living Acp L Tr
Where Our Lord May Go Zon T Tc
Where Shall I Find The Christ Child? Abi L Sc
Where The Children Run Free Gia F Tu
Where The Seasons Never Change Hum G Sr
Where The Spirit Leads Van C Ss
Where There Is Charity And Love Fel T Sl
Where They Love To Pray Abm G Tx
Where Two Or Three Nal L Lo
Where Two Or Three Fel F La
Where Two Or Three Are Gathered Wlp L La
Where Two Or Three Are Gathered Ahc L Tr
Where Two Or Three Are Gathered Gia F La
Where Was Jesus Jhm G Tj
Where Went The Days Chd F Tt
Where Were You Going Sav G Sl
Where Were You, O Shepherd? Abi L Sc
Whereever Faithful Men Assemble Fel L La
Wherefore Hath The Light Been Granted Gsc T Tb
Wherever He Leads I'll Go Lor T Tc
Whether Young Or Old Aug T Tt
While Angels Sing Aug T Sc
While By My Sheep Aug T Sc
While By My Sheep Gsc T Sc
While By Our Sheep Zon T Sc
While I Did Watch My Sheep Gsc T Sc
While I Sup With Thee Lor L Lo
While Shepherds Watch'd Their Flocks Bbl T Sc
While Shepherds Watched Smc T Sc
While Shepherds Watched Their Flocks Abi L Sc
While Shepherds Watched Their Flocks Gsc T Sc
While Standing At The Cross Lor T Sl
Whisper One Name Man G Tj
Whispering Hope Lor T Tr
Whispering Hope (A Cap) Wrd G Sl
Whither Bound St. James? Van F Tx
Whither Shall I Go Smc L Ss
Whither Thou Goest Aug L Tw
Whither Thou Goest Fel F Tw
Who Am I Sil F Tx
Who Am I? Fcc F Tx
Who At My Door Is Standing? Lor T Tj
Who Can Behold Aug T Sl
Who Can Know Your Ways Fel L Tx
Who Can Tell The Glory (Md) Oxf T Tx
Who Do You Say That I Am Man G Tj
Who Follows Me Fel T Tc
Who Is He That Stands Triumphant Acp L Tk
Who Is He That Stands Triumphant? Acp L Sr
Who Is Like Unto Thee (W/Keyboard) Gia T Tt
Who Is Like Unto Thee, O Lord Aug T Tt
Who Is On The Lord's Side? Zon T Tc
Who Is On The Lord's Side? Zon T Tc
Who Is This Man Fel F Tj
Who Is This Man? Sac T Tj
Who Is This That Comes In Glory? Sac T Sr
Who Is This That Cometh (Is 63) Wlp L Tx
Who Knows The Answer? Lor T Tx
Who Passes Yonder Through The Throng? Hwg L Sl
Who Shall Abide (W/Flute/Guit) Aug L Tr
Who Shall Separate Us From Smc L Tr
Who So Dwelleth Smc T Tr
Who Wants To Be Free? (Musical) Zon F Za
Who Will Bow And Bend Gsc T Tc
Who Will Come To Bethlehem? Gsc T Sc
Who Will Deliver Me? Fcc L Sl
Who Will Dwell On God's Mountain? Wlp F Ld
Who's Goin To Walk That Road With Me? Zon G Tc
Who's That Guy Prc L Tx
Whoever Eats This Bread Fel L Lo
Whoever Would Be Great Among You(Guit) Aug F Tr
Whom Shall I Fear (Ps 27) Rav L Ld
Whom Shall I Send? Aug T Tc
Why Art Thou Cast Down, O My Soul? Aug L Tr
Why Art Thou Disquieted? Mar L Tr
Why Art Thou So Heavy, O My Soul Bbl T Tr
Why Art Thou So Heavy, O My Soul (M) Oxf T Sl
Why Did Jesus Come To Earth Fel F Sa
Why Do I Sing? Zon G Tc
Why Do The Nations Rage? Abi L Sc
Why Have You Forsaken Me Fel F Sl
Why I Love Jesus Pmp G Tj
Why Limit God? Yan F Tr
Why Must You Go? Mar L Tx
Why Not Now? Zon F Tc
Why Rage Fiercely The Heathen Aug T Sc
Why Should He Love Me So? Lor T Sl
Why Should I Sing Any Other Song? Zon G Tt
Why Should I Worry Or Fret? Gmc G Tr
Why Thus Cradled Here? Abi L Sc
Why, O Lord, Do You Stand Aloof? Gia L Tx
Why, O Lord? Nal L Tx
Why, Oh Why Fel F Tx
Why? Zon T Tt
Wicked Old Pharoah Man G Tx
Will Any Three Leaders Prc L Tx
Will He Know Me Man G Tj
Will I Have To Pay Jhm G Sl
Will It Be Soon? Zon G Sa
Will You Be Ready? Zon F Sa
Will You Be There Pmp G Sr
Will You Believe Me, Thomas? Ahc L Tx
William Penn's Reflections (4 Pts) Aug T Za
Willing To Go Man G Tc
Willow Tree Fcc F Sl
Wilt Not Thou Turn Again? Abi L Sl
Wind Blowing Softly Chd F Tt
Wind Song Pnp C Tx
Windows Of The Mind Zon F Tx

Title			
Winds Through The Olive Trees	Lor	T	Sc
Winds Thru The Olive Trees	Aug	L	Tx
Wings Of Prayer	Zon	G	Tr
Wings Of Prayer	Lor	L	Tr
Wings Of Wood	Fel	L	Tx
Wings Over America	Kmp	F	Tp
Winter Meditation	Nal	L	Tx
Winter Song	Nal	L	Sc
Wisdom (From Three Motets)	Ron	T	Tx
Wisdom Has Built Herself A House	Wlp	L	Tx
Wisdom Of God	Fcc	L	Tx
Wisdom Opened The Mouth Of The Dumb	Fel	L	Tr
Wisdom Restored To Men	Fel	L	Tr
Wise Men From The East (Guit,Trio)	Pro	L	Sc
Wise Men Still Seek Him	Zon	T	Sc
With A Holy Hush	Zon	T	Tr
With A Joyful Heart	Wlp	L	Tt
With A Jubilant Song(Piano,Org,Tpt,Ti)	Aug	L	Tt
With A Voice Of Singing	Aug	L	Tt
With All My Heart	Rav	L	Sc
With All Who Love Thy Name, O Lord	Lor	T	Tx
With An Everlasting Love	Gia	L	Tc
With Awe And Confidence	Gia	L	To
With Broken Heart And Contrite Sigh	Sac	T	Sl
With Cries Of Joy I Shout	Fel	L	Tt
With Gifts We Enter Your Courts	Fel	L	To
With Gladness And Rejoicing	Fel	L	Lo
With God On Our Side	Rav	L	Sc
With Happy Voices Ringing	Abi	L	Tt
With Harp And Voice Of Psalms	Gia	T	Tt
With Hearts Full Of Joy	Nal	L	Tt
With Honest Heart	Fel	L	To
With Jesus, Our Brother	Ahc	L	Tj
With Joyful Lips, O Lord	Wlp	L	Tt
With Joyful Voice (Opt Tpts)	Elv	T	Sr
With Merry Dancing	Nal	L	Tt
With My Hand In Thine	Lor	T	Tr
With My Holy Oil	Fel	L	Tc
With Song And Dance	Aug	L	Tr
With Songs And Honors	Smc	T	Zb
With The Blessing Of God	Chh	T	Lp
With The Lord There Is Mercy (Icet)	Wlp	L	Ld
With These Our Lenten Prayers	Wlp	L	Sl
With These Rings	Ahc	L	Tw
With Weeping Life Begins	Bbl	L	Sl
With Words Of Praise	Wlp	L	Tt
Within The Silence	Lor	T	Tr
Within Your Splendor	Wlp	L	Tt
Without Clouds	Fel	L	Sl
Without Love	Sms	F	Tx
Without Love, No Feeling	Lor	T	Tr
Without Seeing You, We Love You	Wlp	L	Tt
Witness (Md) Spiritual	Wlp	L	Tc
Witness Song	Fel	F	Tc
Woe Is Me (Me)	Oxf	L	Sl
Woman Of Samaria	Fel	F	Tx
Woman Of Stone	Fcc	F	Tx
Woman Of Valor	Fel	F	Tx
Woman, Has No One Condemned You	Fel	L	Tr
Woman, Woman	Nal	L	Tx
Won't You Come And Stay, Lord?	Nal	L	Tr
Wonder Of The Ages, The	Lor	T	Sc
Wonder Of The Star, The	Lor	L	Sc
Wonder When He's Coming	Lor	L	Sa
Wonderful	Van	F	Tt
Wonderful And Great	Wlp	L	Tt
Wonderful Blessing, A	Zon	G	Tr
Wonderful Guest	Man	G	Tj
Wonderful Is Jesus	Zon	L	Tj
Wonderful Peace	Lor	T	Tr
Wonderful Wonderful Jesus (A Cap)	Wrd	G	Tj
Wonderful Words Of Life	Lor	T	Tr
Wonderful World	Man	L	Tt
Wonderful World	Fel	F	Tx
Wondering Why	Wlp	F	Sl
Wondrous Cross, The	Lor	T	Sc
Wondrous Is The Life In Heaven	Gsc	T	Sr
Wondrous Is Your Presence	Gia	F	Tj
Wondrous Love	Aug	L	Tr
Wondrous Love	Maf	F	Tr
Wondrous Love	Lor	T	Sl
Wondrous Love	Gsc	T	Tr
Wondrous Love	Aug	L	Tr
Wondrous Love	Zon	T	Sl
Wondrous Love (A Cap)	Abi	L	Sl
Wondrous Love (Spiritual)	Smc	T	Tr
Wondrous Spirit	Nal	L	Ss
Woodlawn Walk	Ccc	L	Zb
Word Of Light	Fel	F	Tr
Word Of The Lord, The	Nal	L	Tx
Word Was God, The	Sac	L	Tj
Word Who Is Life, The	Nal	L	Tj
Words From The Cross, The	Abi	L	Sl
Words Of Institution	Nal	L	Lo
Words Of Jesus (Cantata)	Gam	L	Sl
Work For The Night	Man	G	Tx
Work Through Me	Man	G	Tc
Workshop Of The Lord	Ham	G	Tx
World In The Making	Fcc	L	Tx
World Is The Gift	Fcc	L	To
World Within, A	Nal	L	Tx
World's Redeemer, The	Lor	L	Sc
Worship Responses	Aug	L	Za
Worship The Christ—Child	Lor	T	Sc
Worship The Lord	Fel	L	Tt
Worship The Lord In The Beauty	Lor	T	Tt
Worthy Art Thou	Bfi	T	Tt
Worthy Art Thou, O Lord God (W/Tmb)	Aug	T	Tt
Worthy Is The Lamb	Nal	L	Tt
Worthy Is The Lamb	Zon	F	Tt
Worthy The Lamb	Gmc	G	Tt
Would You Go	Man	G	Tx
Wounded For Me	Zon	T	Sl
Wrestlers, The	Fcc	T	Tx
Wrinkled And Old	Kmp	G	Tx
Written In The Book Of Love	Zon	F	Tr
Written In The Word	Mar	L	Tx
Ya Viene La Vieja	Gsc	T	Sc
Yahweh Is A Saving Lord (Ps. 86)	Nal	L	Tt
Yahweh Rejoices	Ahc	L	Tr
Yahweh, Our God	Fel	F	To
Yahweh, Our God	Ahc	L	Tr
Yahweh, The Faithful One	Nal	L	Tr
Ye Folk Afar	Abi	L	Sc
Ye Lands To The Lord	Aug	L	Tt
Ye Servants Of God	Pro	T	Tt
Ye Servants Of God	Zon	T	Tt
Ye Servants Of God	Maf	T	Tc
Ye Servants Of God	Lor	T	Lp
Ye Servants Of God (E)	Oxf	T	Tt
Ye Shall Know The Truth	Zon	G	Tx
Ye Shepherds, Ye Wise Men!(Opt Flute)	Pro	T	Sc
Ye Sons And Daughters	Gia	L	Sr
Ye Sons And Daughters (Choral)	Fel	T	Sr
Ye Tuneful Muses	Kal	T	Tt
Ye Watchers And Ye Holy Ones (Me)	Oxf	T	Sr
Ye Were Sometimes Darkness (Eph4)	Gia	F	Tc
Ye Who Pass By	Som	T	Sl
Ye Who Profess (Cantata)	Lps	T	Tr
Yea, Though I Wander	Aug	T	Tr
Yes I Shall Arise	Wlp	L	Sl
Yes I Will Arise	Rpb	L	Tf
Yes I'll Know Him	Sav	G	Sa
Yes I'll Sing The Wondrous Story	Zon	T	Tx
Yes To You, My Lord	Nal	C	Tc
Yes To You, My Lord	Wlp	F	Tc
Yes, Amen	Fel	F	Lk
Yes, He Did	Zon	G	Sl
Yes, Lord	Fel	F	Tc
Yes, Lord (I Heard You Calling)	Gia	L	Sl
Yes, Lord, Alleluia	Rpb	L	Lf
Yes, Lord, Amen	Nal	L	Tc
Yes, Lord, Yes	Nal	C	Tc
Yesterday	Man	G	Tx
Yesterday	Sbf	L	Tc
Yesterday, Today & Tomorrow (Hb 13:8)	Wlp	F	Tj
Yesterday,Today And Tomorrow (No 5923)	Zon	F	Za
Yesterday's Gone	Zon	G	Tj
Yet I Believe	Van	F	Tr
You Alone Are Holy	Wlp	L	Tt
You Are A Child Of The Universe	Nal	L	Tx
You Are A Chosen Race	Fel	L	Tr
You Are A Light For All The World	Fel	L	Tr
You Are A Priest Forever	Nal	L	Sa
You Are All Beautiful	Wlp	L	Tm
You Are Blessed And Worthy	Fel	L	Tt
You Are Blessed, O Virgin Mary	Fel	L	Tm
You Are Fair In Every Way	Fel	L	Tx
You Are Given To Know	Bbl	T	Tr
You Are Loved	Fel	F	Tr
You Are My Brother (Part 1)	Nal	C	Tx
You Are My Brother (Part 2)	Nal	C	Tx
You Are My Brother (Part 3)	Nal	C	Tx
You Are My God	Nal	L	Tt
You Are My People	Fel	F	Tr
You Are My Shield	Mar	L	Tr
You Are My Son	Fel	L	Sc
You Are My Son	Wlp	L	Tj
You Are My Sons	Nal	L	Tr
You Are Near	Nal	L	Sa
You Are Peter, The Rock	Fel	L	Tx
You Are Righteous, O Lord	Sac	L	Tx
You Are Shepherd	Fel	F	Tr
You Are So Great, O God	Fel	L	Tt
You Are The Answer	Fcc	F	Tj
You Are The Honor	Wlp	L	Tm
You Are The Hope Of All	Nal	L	Tr
You Are The Joy Of Jesus	Chh	F	Tr
You Are The Light Of The World	Acp	F	Tj
You Are The Light Of The World	Gsc	T	Tc
You Are The Light Of The World (4–Pt)	Acp	L	Tr
You Are The Only Son	Acp	L	Tj
You Are The Only Son (4–Part Arr)	Acp	L	Tj
You Are The Temple	Oxf	L	Tx
You Are The Way	Nal	L	Tj
You Are With Me	Sms	F	Lo
You Ask Me Why	Man	C	Sc
You Ask My Why (I Keep Smilin')	Wrd	G	Tr
You Broke The Reign Of Death	Wlp	L	Sr
You Can Have A Song In Your Heart	Zon	G	Tt
You Can See About Me	Man	G	Tx
You Can't Beat God Giving	Man	G	To
You Can't Buy A Savior	Fel	F	Tj
You Can't Love Without Giving	Ham	C	To
You Christians All	Acp	L	Tx
You Christians All	Acp	L	Tx
You Come As He	Ahc	L	Tt
You Drew Me Clear (Ps30)	Gra	L	Ld
You Fill The Day	Wlp	F	Ss
You Gave Him His Heart's Desire	Fel	L	Tx
You Gave Us Lord Your Sacred Heart	Jsp	L	Tj
You Give Us Bread, O Lord	Gsc	T	Sl
You Got To Cross That Lonesome Valley	Gsc	T	Sl
You Got To Have Jesus In Your Heart	Csm	G	Tj
You Got To Reap Just What You Sow	Wbp	T	Tx
You Gotta Walk	Man	G	Tc
You Have Crowned Him With Glory	Fel	L	Sr
You Have Favored Your Land	Fel	L	Tt
You Have Made Children And Babes	Fel	L	Tt
You Have Made Us	Sms	F	Tt
You Have Mercy On All	Fel	L	Sl
You Have Put On Christ	Rpb	L	Tr
You Have Set On His Head	Fel	L	Sr
You Have To Rise And Go	Man	G	Tc
You Heavens Open From Above	Wlp	T	Sa
You I Carry, O Lord (Ancient Text)	Wlp	L	Ln
You Knew Me Before I Was Born(Ps 139)	Rav	L	Tx
You Love Right And Hate Wrong	Ham	G	Tb
You Must Be Born Again	Man	G	Sl
You Ought To Walk Right	Man	G	Sl
You Put Gladness Into My Heart	Fel	L	Tr
You Save The Humble, O Lord	Fel	L	Tr
You Shall Go Before The Lord	Fel	L	Tx
You Shall Make Them Princes	Fel	L	Sr
You Shall Say To The Sons Of Israel	Fel	L	Tx
You Were There	Mar	L	Sl
You Who Have Followed Me	Fel	L	Tc
You Will Be My People	Rpb	L	Tr
You Will Show Me The Path To Life	Nal	L	Sr
You, Lord Are The Way	Wlp	L	Tc
You, O Lord, Are Near	Fel	L	Sa
You, O Lord, Will Keep Us	Fel	L	Tr
You're A Friend To Me	Man	L	Tr
You're A Gift	Chd	L	Tt
You're Always At Home	Chh	F	Tr
You're Caught In A World	Mar	L	Tx
You're Enough	Mar	L	Tj
You're Gonna Need Somebody	Gam	G	Tt
You're In The Right Place	Ccc	L	Zb
You're Something Special	Gmc	G	Tr
You've Got A Friend	Col	F	Tt
You've Got To Look Hard	Van	C	Tt
You've Gotta Have What It Takes	Nal	L	Tt
Young Lions, The	Bec	T	Tt
Your Almighty Word, O Lord	Fel	L	Tt
Your Holy Cross	Gia	L	Sl
Your Holy Death	Wlp	L	Sl
Your Light Has Come, O Jerusalem	Fel	L	Sc
Your Love Reaches To The Heavens	Chh	F	Tt
Your Name O Lord	Nal	L	Tt
Your People Of Faith	Nal	L	Tr
Your Shining Hour	Man	G	Sr
Your Song That I Sing	Nal	L	It
Your Wife Shall Bear A Son	Fel	L	Tx
Your Will Be Done	Fel	F	Tx
Your Will Be Done	Fcc	F	Tr
Your Word	Wlp	F	Tx
Your Word Is A Lamp To My Feet	Nal	L	Tx
Your Word, O Lord, Endures	Fel	L	Tt
Your Words, O Lord	Wlp	L	Le
Yours Are The Heavens	Fel	L	Tk
Yours Are The Heavens	Gia	L	Sc
Yours Are The Heavens	Gia	L	Sc
Yours Is Princely Power	Gia	L	Sc
Yours Is Princely Power (Ccd)	Wlp	F	Sc
Yours Is The Kingdom	Wlp	F	Tk
Youth Favorites	Zon	G	Za
Youth In Unison (No 5033)	Zon	C	Za
Yuletide Memories	Lor	L	Sc
Zaccheus (There Was A Man)	Van	F	Tx
Zion Said	Abi	L	Tt
Zion Sing	Wlp	L	Sa

COMPOSER INDEX

Acheson, Mark	Twenty-Third Psalm
Ackroyd, Mary	Jesus Is A-Drivin' Out Sata
Adam, Ad	Cantique De Noel
Adam, Adolphe	Cantique De Noel
Adam, Adolphe	Christmas Song, The
Adams	I Found Him In My Heart
Adams	Remember Now Thy Creator
Adams	They That Trust In The Lord
Adams/Decou	Holy City, The
Adams/Krogstad	Jesus Took My Sins Away
Adams, Harvey	Holy City, The
Aderholt, Norman	He Was More Then Just A Man
Adkins/Opel	Go Make Of All Disciples
Adler	Listen To My Words, Lord
Adler, Samuel	A Song Of Exaltation
Adler, Samuel	A Song Of Hanukkah
Adler, Samuel	Avina Malkaynu Chanayno
Adler, Samuel	Awake!Do Not Cast Us Off
Adler, Samuel	Ayl Melech Yoshayv
Adler, Samuel	God's Promise (E)
Adler, Samuel	Hayom Harat Olam
Adler, Samuel	Hinay Yom Hadin
Adler, Samuel	How Precious Is Thy Loving
Adler, Samuel	Praise The Lord (E)
Adler, Samuel	Psalm 40 (M)
Adler, Samuel	Psalm 96
Adler, Samuel	The Binding (Oratorio)
Adler, Samuel	The Feast Of Light
Adler, Samuel	The Vision Of Isaiah (Canta
Adler, Samuel	Uv' Shofar Gadol
Agay	Old Irish Blessing
Ager, Laurence	In Honour Of A King
Ager, Laurence	The Little Saviour
Agey, C. Buell	All Praise And Thanks To Go
Agey, C. Buell	Eternal God, Whose Power Up
Agey, C. Buell	Praise Ye Jehovah
Aguilera, Irene	In The Arms Of My Brothers
Aguilera, Irene	Your Will Be Done
Ahearn, Dennis	A Promise Has Been Made
Ahlwen/Johnson	He The Pearly Gates Will Op
Ahnfelt/Johnson	Day By Day
Aichinger, G	Assumpta Est Maria
Aichinger, Gregor	O Lord Of Hosts
Akers, Doris	All You Need
Akers, Doris	Ask What You Will
Akers, Doris	Bread That's Cast Upon The
Akers, Doris	Can I Have This Happiness
Akers, Doris	Deeper In The Lord
Akers, Doris	Don't Stop Using Me
Akers, Doris	God Is So Good
Akers, Doris	God Spoke To Me One Day
Akers, Doris	God Will If You Will
Akers, Doris	Grow Closer
Akers, Doris	He Knows And He Cares
Akers, Doris	He's A Light Unto My Pathwa
Akers, Doris	He's Everywhere
Akers, Doris	Honey In That Rock
Akers, Doris	How Big Is God
Akers, Doris	I Cannot Fail The Lord
Akers, Doris	I Just Got Religion
Akers, Doris	I Know The Story
Akers, Doris	I Stopped Dying And Started
Akers, Doris	I Sure Do Love The Lord
Akers, Doris	I Was There When The Spirit
Akers, Doris	I Won't Move Unless He Tell
Akers, Doris	I'm Glad To Know There's A
Akers, Doris	I'm Not Satisfied Yet
Akers, Doris	I've Found Something
Akers, Doris	If I Didn't Know
Akers, Doris	Is There Any Peace Anywhere
Akers, Doris	It Is Jesus
Akers, Doris	It Rained
Akers, Doris	Jesus Is Born Today
Akers, Doris	Jesus Is The Name
Akers, Doris	Lead On, Lord Jesus
Akers, Doris	Life Eternal
Akers, Doris	Lord, Keep My Mind On Thee
Akers, Doris	Meet Me In Heaven
Akers, Doris	Mine Just For The Asking
Akers, Doris	My Heart Is Filled With Jes
Akers, Doris	My Song Of Assurance
Akers, Doris	No One But The Lord
Akers, Doris	Prayer Is The Answer
Akers, Doris	Sweet Jesus
Akers, Doris	Sweet Peace
Akers, Doris	Sweet, Sweet Spirit
Akers, Doris	The Lord Is My Light
Akers, Doris	The Smile On His Face
Akers, Doris	These Times Must Come
Akers, Doris	Trouble
Akers, Doris	Walk In The Sunshine
Akers, Doris	Wanna Go To Heaven?
Akers, Doris	You Can't Beat God Giving
Akers, Doris (Arr.)	Climbin' Jacob's Ladder
Akers,D And Jackson,M	Lord, Don't Move That Mount
Albrecht, K	The Earth Feared And Was
Alchinger, G/Ed	Where Is Now Abel?
Alder, Samuel	In Nature's Ebb And Flow
Alexander/Shaw	All Things Bright And Beaut
Alexander, Joseph	O Sing Unto The Lord
Allegri, G	Miserere Mei Deus
Allem/Carmichael	When I Met My Savior
Allen/Pallardy	Lord, Make Be A Better Man
Allen, Lanny	God Who Made Earth (W/Piano
Allen, Lanny	Psalm 100 (Spoken/Song)
Allen, Peter(Swenson)	Feed Us Now, O Son Of God
Allitsen	Lord Is My Light, The
Allitsen, Frances	The Lord Is My Light
Amann, M. Angelita	Go Forth, People Of God
Amann, M. Angelita	Praise
Amann, M. Angelita	Prepare! The Lord Is Near
Amason, B.	Don't Talk The Talk
Amason, B.	Going To That Holy Land
Amason, B.	Hallelujah
Amason, B.	He'll Help You Out
Amason, B.	I Found The Lord
Amason, B.	Jesus Christ Is The Same To
Amason, B.	Life Can Be Fun
Amason, B.	Mountain Country
Amason, B.	Praise The Lord
Amason, B.	Praising God For Passing So
Amason, B.	Prayer And Praise
Amason, B.	Voices
Ambrise, R S	One Sweetly Solemn Thought
Ambrose/Kraehenbuehl	We Find Thee, Lord In Other
Amner, John	Christ Rising Again (Md)
Amner, John	Come Let's Rejoice (Md)
Amner, John	He That Descended (Md)
Amner, John	Hear, O Lord (Ps 30) (Md)
Amner, John	I Will Sing Unto The Lord
Amner, John	Lift Up Your Heads (Ps 24)
Amner, John	Magnificat And Nunc Dimitti
Amner, John	O Ye Little Flock (Md)
Amner, John	Short Service: Magnificat &
Amner, John	Sing, O Heavens (Md)
Amner, John	Woe Is Me (Me)
Ancis, S	V'shom'ru
Anders	Psalm 119 (Happy Are They)
Anders	Psalm 46 (God Is For Us A R
Andersen	Lift Up Your Heads
Anderson	He Whom Joyous Shepherds Pr
Anderson, Clyde	There Once Was A Man
Anderson, Ruth	Passiontide Carol
Anderson, Ruth	The Holly Carol
Andreasen, Bodil	I Know A Fount' So Wondrous
Andrews, Carroll T.	Easter Carol Mass (1964 Tex
Andrews, Carroll T.	Father, I Will Obey
Andrews, Carroll T.	Four Choral Meditations-Len
Andrews, Carroll T.	Glory To God(Mass For All S
Andrews, Carroll T.	Glory To God (Lyric Mass)
Andrews, Carroll T.	Glory To God (Child Mass)
Andrews, Carroll T.	Glory To God(New Mass)
Andrews, Carroll T.	Glory To God(Vianney Mass)
Andrews, Carroll T.	Hail Mary
Andrews, Carroll T.	Holy, Holy, Holy(Mass For A
Andrews, Carroll T.	Holy, Holy, Holy (Child Mas
Andrews, Carroll T.	Holy, Holy, Holy Lord(Viann
Andrews, Carroll T.	Holy, Holy, Holy (Lyric Mas
Andrews, Carroll T.	Holy, Holy, Holy(New Mass)
Andrews, Carroll T.	Lamb Of God (Vianney Mass)
Andrews, Carroll T.	Lamb Of God (Mass For All S
Andrews, Carroll T.	Lamb Of God (New Mass)
Andrews, Carroll T.	Lamb Of God (Lyric Mass)
Andrews, Carroll T.	Lamb Of God (Child Mass)
Andrews, Carroll T.	Lord Have Mercy (New Mass)
Andrews, Carroll T.	Lord Have Mercy (Lyric Mass
Andrews, Carroll T.	Lord Have Mercy (Child Mass
Andrews, Carroll T.	Lord Have Mercy (Mass For A
Andrews, Carroll T.	Lord Have Mercy(Vianney
Andrews, Carroll T.	O Glorious Night
Andrews, Carroll T.	O How Lovely Are Your Dwell
Andrews, Carroll T.	O Loving Jesus
Andrews, Carroll T.	Peaceful Eve So Still & Hol
Andrews, Carroll T.	Prayer (Prayer Of The Heart
Andrews, Carroll T.	Rejoice, O Queen Of Heaven
Andrews, Carroll T.	Shout Praise And Glory
Andrews, Carroll T.	Take Us, O Lord
Andrews, Carroll T.	The Earth Feared
Andrews, Carroll T.	The Heavens Rejoiced
Andrews, Carroll T.	The Snow Lay On The Ground
Andrews, Carroll T.	This Is The Day When Christ
Andrews, Carroll T.	Two Hymns I/H St
Andrews, Carroll T.	We Adore You, Jesus Christ
Andrews, H. K.	O Sing The Glories Of Our
Andrews, Mark	Build Thee More Stately Man
Andrews, Mark	Lauda Anima (Praise, My Sou
Androzzo A Bazel	I Wish You Jesus
Androzzo A Bazel	My Total Life
Androzzo A Bazel	Pretty Me Up On The Inside
Anerio, F./Ehret(Ed)	Christ Became Obedient (Me)
Anerio, Felice	Angelus Autem Domini Descen
Anerio, Felice	Christus Factus Est
Anerio, Felix	God, The Lord, Sent A Messe
Anerio, G	Ave Maris Stella
Anerio, Giovanni F	Cantate Domino (O Sing Unto
Angell, W.M.	Hallelujah I Love Him (W/Pi
Angell, Warren	Sing Gods Praise
Angle, D & Herring, B	Sittin' In The Pew
Angle, D P	Son Come Out
Angle, D P	There's A Love
Angle, Dana P	Are You Listening?
Angle, Dana P	Bearded Young Man
Angle, Dana P	Do You Feel The Change
Angle, Dana P	I've Been Sealed
Angle, Dana P	Living On The Bottle
Anon Robison	Four Folk-Hymns
Anon/Kraehenbuehl	This Is My Body
Anthony, Dick	Canticle Of Praise
Anthony, Dick	Songs For Men No 1 (No 5436
Anthony, Dick	Songs For Men No 2 (No 5437
Anthony, Dick	Songs For Men No 3 (No 5438
Anthony, Gregory	Blessed Be The Name Of The
Appleby-Hunt-Shipp	Voluntaries Based On Hymn
Arcadelt, J	Ave Maria
Arcadelt, J	Hail Mary
Arcadelt,J./Ed Klein	Hail Mary (E & Lat)
Arceneaux, Tommy	Come, Lord Jesus
Archer, Violet	Sweet Jesu, King Of Bliss
Archers	Things We Deeply Feel
Aridas, Chris	Come And Bless Us
Aridas, Chris	Come, Then, My Son
Aridas, Chris	He Is Lord Of All
Aridas, Chris	Lord, Whom Need I Fear
Aridas, Chris	Peace We Share
Aridas, Chris	Psalm 148
Aridas, Chris	Psalm 98
Aridas, Chris	Yahweh, Our God
Armitage	Sing Hosanna (W/Org, Opt 3
Armstrong, M	Let Us Break Bread Together
Armstrong, Thomas	Christ, Whose Glory Fills
Arnandez/Chant	Our Lady's Song Of Praise
Arnatt, Ronald	Gloria And Sanctus/Benedict
Arnatt, Ronald	Gospel Acclamations
Arnel/Decou	Am I A Soldier Of The Cross
Arnel/Peterson	Am I A Soldier Of The Cross
Arthur, G & Angle, D	Song Of Joy
Arthur, Gary	Closer To God
Arthur, Gary	Jesus Is All That We Need
Arthur, Gary & Angle	Have You Ever Heard
Arthur, Gary & Angle	If You Will Believe
Arthur, Gary & Angle,	Come On Down
Artman (Arr)	Grow In Love
Artman, Ruth	Little Lamb
Artman, Ruth	Lord, Walk With Me
Arwood/Track	Let Us Sing A New Song Unto
Ashfield, Robert	Of The Father's Love Begott
Ashford	Lift Up Your Heads
Ashford	Mother's Task
Ashford	My Task
Aston, Hugh	Anthems (Ave Maria, O Bapti
Aston, Hugh	Anthems (Gaude Virgo, Te De
Aston, Hugh	Mass And Te Deum
Aston, Hugh	Mass, Videte Manus Meas
Aston, Peter	Balulalow
Aston, Peter	Magnificat And Nunc Dimitti
Atkinson, Condit	Evening Star
Atkinson, Condit	Four Things
Atkinson, Condit	Gloria
Atkinson, Gordon	Two Introits
Attwood, Thomas	O God, Who By The Leading
Attwood, Thos	Teach Me O Lord
Atwood/Mickelson	Keyboard Rhapsodies (No 470
Auerbach	Bells Ring Out Joyfully
Auerbach	Prince Of Peace Is Born Tod
Ault, Gary	All That We Have
Ault, Gary	Come In, Pilgrim
Ault, Gary	Glory Land
Ault, Gary	Golden Morning
Ault, Gary	Have You Ever Been
Ault, Gary	I Know The Father Loves Me
Ault, Gary	Jesus Has Come
Ault, Gary	Let All The Earth
Ault, Gary	Little Child
Ault, Gary	Pause A While
Ault, Gary	Praise God, Ps. 145
Ault, Gary	Sign Of Total Giving
Ault, Gary	Sing Alleluia, Sing
Ault, Gary	Spirit Move
Ault, Gary	Tell The World
Ault, Gary	The Love Of God Will Rise
Ault, Gary	The New Creation
Ault, Gary	The Spirit Of The Lord
Ault, Gary	Wedding Song
Ault, Gary	You Are Loved
Avalos	Lord, Hear Our Prayer To Th
Avalos (Arr)	Alleluia, Rejoice & Sing
Avalos (Arr)	Ye Servants Of God
Avery, S R	I Called Upon The Lord
Avshalomov Jacob	I Saw A Stranger Yester'en
Avshalomov, Jacob	Of Man's Mortalitie
Ayers, David	Come, Sing A Song Unto The
Ayers, David	Reason For Singing, A
Ayers, Jacob	None Other Lamb (No 4271)
Ayers, Jacob S.	Come Ye Faithful, Raise The
Ayers, Jacob S.	Glroious Things Of Thee Are
Ayers, Jacob S.	We Adore Thee
Ayers, Jacob S.	We Would Be Building
Baber, John O.	Holy Is The Lord
Bach C.P.E./Ludwig Alt	Three Duets For Organ
Bach-Lorenz	Everlasting Joy

COMPOSER INDEX

Composer	Title
Bach/Black	Alleluia! O Praise Ye The
Bach/Christiansen	My Jesus
Bach/Rasley	Come Unto Me
Bach, C.P.E. Ed. Stein	Heilig Ist Gott (Eng & Germ
Bach, J. C.	Air
Bach, J. C.	Air Of Death
Bach, J. C.	By The Waters Of Babylon
Bach, J. C.	Es Ist Nun Aus
Bach, J. C.	Man Born Of A Woman, A
Bach, J. C.	Mensch, Vom Weibe Geboren,
Bach, J. C.	Mit Weinen Hebt Sichs An
Bach, J. C.	My Time Is Come
Bach, J. C.	Unsers Herzens Freude (Eng
Bach, J. C.	With Weeping Life Begins
Bach, J. C.	I Will Not Let Thee Go
Bach, J. C.	The Righteous
Bach, J. C.(Arr Mccoy)	Glory To God
Bach, J. S.	A Mighty Fortress Is Our Go
Bach, J. S.	A Symbol Is This Child (Can
Bach, J. S.	Ah Dearest Jesus
Bach, J. S.	Ah Lord Thy Dear Sweet Ange
Bach, J. S.	All Breathing Life
Bach, J. S.	All Glory Laud & Honor (E)
Bach, J. S.	All Glory, Praise And Majes
Bach, J. S.	All People That On Earth Do
Bach, J. S.	All Praise To Thee
Bach, J. S.	All They From Saba Shall Co
Bach, J. S.	Alleluia, For Christmas Fro
Bach, J. S.	Arias From Church Cantatas
Bach, J. S.	Awake My Heart With Gladnes
Bach, J. S.	Be Not Afraid (Motet 4)
Bach, J. S.	Blessed Rest (Cantata)
Bach, J. S.	Break Forth O Beauteous Hea
Bach, J. S.	Break Forth O Beauteous Hea
Bach, J. S.	Cantata #1 Wie Schoen (Eng
Bach, J. S.	Cantata #104 Thou Guide (E
Bach, J. S.	Cantata #106 God's Time Is
Bach, J. S.	Cantata #11 Lobet Gott (Eng
Bach, J. S.	Cantata #112 Der Herr (E &
Bach, J. S.	Cantata #115 Mache Dich (E
Bach, J. S.	Cantata #118 O Jesus Christ
Bach, J. S.	Cantata #12 Weping (Eng/Ger
Bach, J. S.	Cantata #140 Sleepers Awake
Bach, J. S.	Cantata #142 To Us A Child
Bach, J. S.	Cantata #150 Nach Dir (Eng
Bach, J. S.	Cantata #151 Suesser Tod (E
Bach, J. S.	Cantata #169 Gott Soll (Eng
Bach, J. S.	Cantata #180 Schmuecke Dich
Bach, J. S.	Cantata #190 Sing To The Lo
Bach, J. S.	Cantata #195 Wedding Cantat
Bach, J. S.	Cantata #198 Trauermusik (E
Bach, J. S.	Cantata #21 My Spirit (Eng
Bach, J. S.	Cantata #25 Es Ist Nichts
Bach, J. S.	Cantata #26 Ach Wie Fluesch
Bach, J. S.	Cantata #27 Wer Weiss (Eng
Bach, J. S.	Cantata #28 Gottlob (Eng/Ge
Bach, J. S.	Cantata #31 The Heaven's La
Bach, J. S.	Cantata #33 Allein Zu Dir
Bach, J. S.	Cantata #34 O Ewiges Feuer
Bach, J. S.	Cantata #38 Aus Tiefer Not
Bach, J. S.	Cantata #4 Christ Lag (Eng
Bach, J. S.	Cantata #41 Jesu Nun (Eng/G
Bach, J. S.	Cantata #43 Gott Faehret (E
Bach, J. S.	Cantata #45 Es Ist Gesagt
Bach, J. S.	Cantata #50 Nun Ist (Eng/Ge
Bach, J. S.	Cantata #54 Widerstehe (Eng
Bach, J. S.	Cantata #55 Ich Armer Mensc
Bach, J. S.	Cantata #56 (E & Germ)
Bach, J. S.	Cantata #6 Bide With Us (En
Bach, J. S.	Cantata #61 Nun Komm (E & G
Bach, J. S.	Cantata #64 Sehet (E & Germ
Bach, J. S.	Cantata #65 Sie Merden (E &
Bach, J. S.	Cantata #68 Also Hat (E & G
Bach, J. S.	Cantata #70 Wachet, Betet
Bach, J. S.	Cantata #71 Gott Ist (E & G
Bach, J. S.	Cantata #79 The Lord Is A S
Bach, J. S.	Cantata #8 Liebster Gott (E
Bach, J. S.	Cantata #80 A Stronghold Su
Bach, J. S.	Cantata #81 Jesus Schlaeft
Bach, J. S.	Cantata #82 Ich Hab Genug
Bach, J. S.	Chorale Prelude, "Wachet Au
Bach, J. S.	Chorales
Bach, J. S.	Chorales
Bach, J. S.	Chorales From The Christmas
Bach, J. S.	Christmas Oratorio
Bach, J. S.	Christmas Oratorio
Bach, J. S.	Christmas Oratorio(Ger)
Bach, J. S.	Church Cantatas & Oratorios
Bach, J. S.	Come And Abide
Bach, J. S.	Come And Thank Him (Me)
Bach, J. S.	Come Soothing Death
Bach, J. S.	Come Sweet Death (Cantata)
Bach, J. S.	Come, Jesu, Come (Motet 5)
Bach, J. S.	Come, My Spirit (Cantata)
Bach, J. S.	Come, Soothing Death
Bach, J. S.	Comfort Sweet (Cantata)
Bach, J. S.	Complete Organ Works In 9 V
Bach, J. S.	Crucifixus(From The Mass In
Bach, J. S.	Death I Do Not Fear Thee
Bach, J. S.	Do Justice (Cantata)
Bach, J. S.	Easter Oratorio
Bach, J. S.	Easter Oratorio (Eng)
Bach, J. S.	Ecumenical Hymn To God Our
Bach, J. S.	Endure! Endure! (St Matt Pa
Bach, J. S.	Five Church Cantatas
Bach, J. S.	Flocks In Pastures Green Ab
Bach, J. S.	Four Advent Chorales
Bach, J. S.	Four Christmas Chorales
Bach, J. S.	Four Easter Chorales
Bach, J. S.	Four Part Chorales (Germ Te
Bach, J. S.	Four-Part Chorales (185)
Bach, J. S.	From Out Their Temples (Can
Bach, J. S.	From The Deep, Lord (Cantat
Bach, J. S.	Fugue In G
Bach, J. S.	Gloria Sing All Our Voices
Bach, J. S.	God Has My Heart (Cantata)
Bach, J. S.	Great God, We Praise Your H
Bach, J. S.	Heart And Lips (Cantata)
Bach, J. S.	Hence All Fears And Sadness
Bach, J. S.	Hence With Earthly Treasure
Bach, J. S.	Here Yet Awhile
Bach, J. S.	Here Yet Awhile (St Mt Pass
Bach, J. S.	How Great And Good Is He
Bach, J. S.	How Shall I Fitly Meet Thee
Bach, J. S.	I Am Content (Cantata)
Bach, J. S.	I Ask For No More (Cantata)
Bach, J. S.	I Know That My Redeemer Liv
Bach, J. S.	If Thou But Suffer God To G
Bach, J. S.	In God The Lord (Cantata)
Bach, J. S.	In Thine Arm I Rest Me
Bach, J. S.	Jesu Joy Of Man's Desiring
Bach, J. S.	Jesu Priceless Treasure
Bach, J. S.	Jesu, Joy Of Man's Desiring
Bach, J. S.	Jesu, Joy Of Man's Desiring
Bach, J. S.	Jesu, Joy Of Man's Desiring
Bach, J. S.	Jesu, Priceless Treasure
Bach, J. S.	Jesu, Priceless Treasure (M
Bach, J. S.	Jesus, By Thy Cross (Cantat
Bach, J. S.	Live Your Life For Him Alwa
Bach, J. S.	Love Thou Thy God (Cantata)
Bach, J. S.	Magnificat
Bach, J. S.	Magnificat In D
Bach, J. S.	Magnificat(Latin)
Bach, J. S.	Mass In B Minor
Bach, J. S.	Mass In B Minor(Latin)
Bach, J. S.	Mass No.1(Bwv 233)(Latin)
Bach, J. S.	Mass No.2(Bwv 234)(Latin)
Bach, J. S.	Mass No.3(Bwv 235)(Latin)
Bach, J. S.	Mass No.4(Bwv 236)(Latin)
Bach, J. S.	Master Of Peace And Love
Bach, J. S.	Missa Brevis In A Major
Bach, J. S.	Missa Brevis In F Maj
Bach, J. S.	Missa Brevis In G M
Bach, J. S.	Missa Brevis In G Major
Bach, J. S.	Mistletoe And Holly Bright
Bach, J. S.	Motet No.1(Eng-Ger)
Bach, J. S.	Motet No.2(Eng-Ger)
Bach, J. S.	Motet No.3(Eng-Ger)
Bach, J. S.	Motet No.4(Eng-Ger)
Bach, J. S.	Motet No.5(Eng-Ger)
Bach, J. S.	Motet No.6(Eng-Ger)
Bach, J. S.	Motets
Bach, J. S.	My Blessed Savior (Cantata)
Bach, J. S.	My Heart Ever Faithful
Bach, J. S.	My Joy Is All In Thee (Cant
Bach, J. S.	O Joyful Day Of Our Salvati
Bach, J. S.	O Rejoice Ye Christians Lou
Bach, J. S.	O Sacred Head Now Wounded
Bach, J. S.	O Welcome Light (Cantata)
Bach, J. S.	Organbook (Orgalbuchlein)
Bach, J. S.	Out Of The Depths I Cry To
Bach, J. S.	Passion Chorale
Bach, J. S.	Planets, Stars And Airs Of
Bach, J. S.	Praise The Almighty (Cantat
Bach, J. S.	Praise The Lord (Motet 6)
Bach, J. S.	Praise The Lord My Soul (Ca
Bach, J. S.	Praise, Thou Zion (Cantata)
Bach, J. S.	Prelude On Psalms
Bach, J. S.	Prepare Ye (Cantata)
Bach, J. S.	Rejoice And Sing
Bach, J. S.	Sacred Songs
Bach, J. S.	Sacred Songs (Geistliche Li
Bach, J. S.	Saint Matthew Passion
Bach, J. S.	Saints & Sinners (Cantata)
Bach, J. S.	Sanctus (B Minor Mass)
Bach, J. S.	Sanctus (Mass In Bm)
Bach, J. S.	Sanctus In D
Bach, J. S.	See Dearest God (Cantata)
Bach, J. S.	Seven Lenten Chorales
Bach, J. S.	Sheep And Lambs May Safely
Bach, J. S.	Sheep May Safely Graze
Bach, J. S.	Sing We The Praise Of God
Bach, J. S.	Singet Dem Herrn (Motet #1)
Bach, J. S.	Six Motets
Bach, J. S.	Sleepers Awake (Cantata)
Bach, J. S.	Sleepers Wake From Cantata
Bach, J. S.	Song Of Repentance
Bach, J. S.	St. Anne's Fugue
Bach, J. S.	St. John Passion (Germ/Eng)
Bach, J. S.	St. John Passion(Ger)
Bach, J. S.	St. Matthew Passion (Eng)
Bach, J. S.	St. Matthew Passion(Ger)
Bach, J. S.	The Faithful Shepherd (Cant
Bach, J. S.	The Heavens Declare (Cantat
Bach, J. S.	The Lord Bless You
Bach, J. S.	The Lord My Shepherd E'er
Bach, J. S.	The Spirit Also Helpeth (Mo
Bach, J. S.	Thine Accounting (Cantata)
Bach, J. S.	Thou Heart Of Compassion
Bach, J. S.	Thou Sanctified Fire
Bach, J. S.	Through Bitter Tribulation
Bach, J. S.	Thus Then The Law
Bach, J. S.	Tis Indeed The Gospel Truth
Bach, J. S.	Tis Well (Cantata)
Bach, J. S.	To Us A Child Is Given (Can
Bach, J. S.	Two Choral Songs
Bach, J. S.	Watch Ye, Pray Ye (Cantata)
Bach, J. S.	What Is It Troubles Thee
Bach, J. S.	Ye Who Profess (Cantata)
Bach, J. S. Alt.	At The Lamb's High Feast We
Bach, J. S. (Adapted)	Tis Thee I Would Be Praisin
Bach, J. S. (Arr Mccoy	In Faith I Steadfast Stand
Bach, J. S. (Arr Zvero	Andante (From Sonata In A M
Bach, J. S. (Kirk)	Alleluia (From "For Us A Ch
Bach, J. S. Arr Bevers	Haste Ye Shepherds
Bach, J. S./Ed Lee	Bread Of The World (10 Chor
Bach, J. S./Ed. Lee	A Mighty Fortress (10 Chora
Bach, J.C.(Gieringer)	The Rightious (Der Gerechte
Bach, J.S. (Arr Dawes)	In Tears Of Grief (St.Matt
Bach, J.S. (Arr)	And His Mercy (Md)
Bach, J.S. (Arr)	King Of Glory, King Of Peac
Bach, J.S. (Arr)	My Heart Ever Faithful(From
Bach, J.S. (Arr)	Open My Heart (Me)
Bach, J.S. (Arr)	Wake, O Wake (Wachet Auf)
Bach, J.S. (Ed)	Extended Bach Chorales (Eng
Bach, J.S. Arr Ehret	God Of Mercy
Bach, J.S.(Arr Davies)	God Is Living, God Is Here!
Bach, J.S.(Arr Davies)	We Hasten, O Jesu (From Can
Bach, J.S.(Treharne)	Jesu, Joy Of Man's Desiring
Bach, J.S.-Christensen	Komm Susser Tod!
Bach, J.S.-Jennings	We Praise Thee, O God
Bach, J.S.-Leupold	Wedding Processional & Air
Bach, J.S.-Sateren	Jesu, Thou My Heart's Delig
Bach, J.S.-Thoburn	O Spotless Lamb
Bach, J.S./Coggin(Arr)	Praise We The Name Of God
Bach, J.S./Ed Lee	Blessed Jesus, At Thy Word
Bach, J.S./Ed Lee	Deck Thyself, My Soul (10 C
Bach, J.S./Ed Lee	God, Who Made Earth & Heave
Bach, J.S./Ed Lee	Great God Of Nations(10 Cho
Bach, J.S./Ed Lee	Jesus, Priceless Treasure
Bach, J.S./Ed Lee	Lord God We Worship Thee
Bach, J.S./Ed Lee	Praise To The Lord (10 Chor
Bach, J.S./Ed Lee	The God Whom Earth & Sea &
Bach, Johann (1604)	Our Days Are As A Shadow
Back, Sven-Erik	Domine Memento Mei Jesu Thi
Back, Sven-Erik	Ecce Ascendimus Jerusolymam
Back, Sven-Erik	Ego Sum Panis Vitae
Back, Sven-Erik	Et Verbum Caro Factum Est
Back, Sven-Erik	Nox Praecessit
Bacon/Emerson/Williams	Two Hymns For The Bicentenn
Bacon, Ernst	A Christmas Carol
Bacon, Ernst	Golden Rules
Bacon, Ernst	Jonah
Bacon, Ernst	Pilgrim Hymn
Bain, J.L.M. (Arr)	Brother James's Air (Me)
Bain, J.L.M. (Arr)	The Great Peace (E)
Bainton-Luther-Laberge	Von Himmel Hoch (In 5 Carol
Bairstow, E. C.	I Sat Down Under His Shadow
Bairstow, E. C.	Jesu, The Very Thought Of T
Bairstow, E. C.	The Day Draws On With Golde
Bairstow, E. C.	The King Of Love My Shepher
Bairstow, E. C.	Though I Speak With The Ton
Bairstow, Edward C.	Communion Service In E Flat
Bairstow, Edward C.	Evening Service In E Flat
Baker	Silent Night
Baker	Three Original Carols For J
Baker/Decou	Jesus, Thou Joy Of Loving
Baker/Trad/Tortolano	The King Of Love (In 19 Rou
Baker, Dave	Love Is Patient
Baksa, Robert	Psalm 13
Baldwin, Bonnie	Long Black Train A-Comin'
Bales, Gerald	O Lord From Whom All Good
Bales, Richard	Mary's Gift (A Christmas Ca
Balhoff, Mike & Ducote	Love Is Almost Worth The Dy
Ball	New Creation, A
Ball	Our Father's Care
Ball	Worship The Christ-Child
Ball, Albert C	Alleluia Noel
Bampton, Ruth	All Creatures Of Our God An
Bancroft, H. Hugh	The Temple Of God (E)
Barbeau, Dennis	Come See The Joy We Have
Barbeau, Dennis	Peace Of The Lord (Reigns O
Barbee, N	Judge Me O God
Barber, Samuel	A Nun Takes The Veil
Barber, Samuel	Agnus Dei
Barber, Samuel	Easter Chorale
Barber, Samuel	Lamb Of God
Barcrofte, George	Two Anthems: (Me)
Barg Paula	Like In Noah's Days
Barker, Sherrell	David's Song

COMPOSER INDEX

Barker, Sherrell	Put On Your Boots
Barnard, John	Responses, With Preces By G
Barnby(Arr Squires)	King, All Glorious (W/Solos
Barnby/Decou	May Jesus Christ Be Praised
Barnby/Johnson	May Jesus Christ Be Praised
Barnby, Jos	Awake Up My Glory
Barnby, Jos	King All Glorious
Barnby, Jos	O How Amiable Are Thy Dwell
Barnby, Jos	O Lord How Manifold
Barnby, Jos	O Perfect Love
Barnby, Jos	Sweet Is Thy Mercy
Barnes, Charles	Unto Thee Will I Cry (Ps 28
Barnes, E S	O Worship The King
Barnes, E S	Three Kings
Barnett	And Can It Be?
Barraclough	Trumpet Of God
Barraclough/Mccluskey	Ivory Palaces
Barraclough/Wilson	Ivory Places
Barri, O	The Good Shepherd
Barrie, Karen M.	Psalm 89 (I Will Celebrate)
Barrows, Cliff	The Cliff Barrows Choir (No
Barrows, Cliff	The Cliff Barrows Choir No
Barrows, Cliff	The Cliff Barrows Choir No
Barry, Jody	I'm Gonna' Take A Trip
Barry, Jody	It's Gonna' Be A Morning To
Barry, John	Alleluia, Jesus Is King
Barry, Rev. John	A Prayer For Eastertide
Barry,Jody	Mamma And Daddy Taught Me
Bartholomew	De Animals A-Comin'
Bartholomew	The Battle Of Jericho (Trad
Bash/Laycock	By The Babylonian Rivers
Baskette Arvil	Don't Disgrace My Mother's
Bassett, Leslie	Remembrance
Batozynski	Emmanuel
Batozynski, Lawrence	Glory To God
Batten, Adrian	Deliver Us, O Lord (Me)
Batten, Adrian	Fourth Evening Service: Mag
Batten, Adrian	Haste Thee, O God (Me)
Batten, Adrian	Let My Complaint Come Befor
Batten, Adrian	Lord, We Beseech Thee (Me)
Batten, Adrian	O Praise The Lord (Me)
Batten, Adrian	O Sing Joyfully
Batten, Adrian	Short Communion Service: Ky
Batten, Adrian	Third Verse Service: Magnif
Batten, Adrian	When The Lord Turned Again
Battishill, Jonathan	How Long Wilt Thou Forget M
Bauman/Batastini	Complete Holy Week Services
Baumer/Blunt	Free Child
Baumgartner	Variations On Hymn Tunes By
Baumgartner, H. Leroy	A Hymn Of Thanks (High Voic
Baumgartner, H. Leroy	His Delight Is In The Law O
Baumgartner, H. Leroy	Remember All The People
Baumgartner, H. Leroy	When, His Salvation Bringin
Baumgartner, Leroy	Thou, Who Hast Loved The Li
Baxter, D./Hamblen, S	Promises To Keep
Bay, Bill	Deluxe Guitar Praise Book
Bay, Mel	Guitar Christmas Carols (Nf
Bay, Mel	The Guitar Hymnal (No 5309)
Baynon, Arthur	A Child's Thanksgiving (E)
Beaumont, Fr. Richard	I Sing A Song To You, Lord
Beck, J N	Benediction
Beck, J N	On The Way To Bethlehem
Beck, J.	As The Rain
Beck, J.	Ease My Mind, Lord
Beck, J.	Every Perfect Gift
Beck, J.	Name Of Jesus, The
Beck, J.	O Come Let Us Sing
Beck, J. (Arr)	Of The Father's Love Begott
Beck, John	Litany Of Thanksgiving (W/B
Beck, John N	Amazing Grace
Beck, John N	God Of Abraham Praise, The
Beck, John N	Have Ye Not Known?
Beck, John N	Interpreted By Love
Beck, John N	Kingsfold I Feel The Winds
Beck, John N	Thou Art God
Beck, John N	Variants On An Irish Hymn
Beck, John N	Young Lions, The
Beck, John Ness	A Child's Noel
Beck, John Ness	A New Heart Will I Give You
Beck, John Ness	Anthem Of Unity
Beck, John Ness	Celebration
Beck, John Ness	Hosanna
Beck, John Ness	Hymn For Our Time
Beck, John Ness	Hymn To David
Beck, John Ness	Once In Royal David's City
Beck, John Ness	Psalm 67 (Organ Or Piano Ac
Beck, John Ness	Song Of Exhaltation
Beck, John Ness	Song Of Moses
Beck, John Ness	Upon This Rock
Beck, Theodore	Seven Anthems For Treble Ch
Beck, W. Leonard	An Easter Carillon (E)
Beckhard	Christmas In Bethlehem
Beckhard (Arr)	God Give Ye Merry Christmas
Beebe	Plowshares
Beeson, Jack	Five Songs
Beeson, Jack	Psalm 23 From The Bay Psalm
Beeson, Jack	Psalm 31 From The Bay Psalm
Beeson, Jack	Psalm 47 From The Bay Psalm
Beethoven/Christiansen	The Heavens Resounding
Beethoven/Glazer	Born Again
Beethoven/Johnson	Joyful, Joyful, We Adore Th
Beethoven, L	Christ On The Mount Of Oliv
Beethoven, L	Come To Me
Beethoven, L	Elegy
Beethoven, L	Hallelujah
Beethoven, L	Halleujah (From Mount Of Ol
Beethoven, L	Let Man Exult With Heart An
Beethoven, L	Love Divine
Beethoven, L	Mass In C (Opus 86)
Beethoven, L	Mass In C Major
Beethoven, L	Mass, Op. 86(C)(Latin)
Beethoven, L	Missa Solemnis
Beethoven, L	Missa Solemnis(Latin)
Beethoven, L	Natures Praise Of God
Beethoven, L	The Glory Of God In Nature
Beethoven, L	The Heavens Are Declaring
Beethoven, L.(Douglas)	All Glory Love And Power To
Belcher	Deep North Spirituals(9)
Belcher, Supply	While Shepherds Watched The
Bell	God Has A Reason
Bell	God, Give Me Understanding
Bell	Lord Is In His Holy Temple,
Bell	Walk With Your God
Belt, Thomas	A New Song(Joy, Joy, Joy Is
Belt, Thomas	Alleluia (Human Hands Canno
Belt, Thomas	Blow, Wind (W/Guitar)
Belt, Thomas	Break Loose (W/Guitar)
Belt, Thomas	Do You Want To Be Free
Belt, Thomas	God Unlimited (Smile On Me)
Belt, Thomas	Joy (Love Is All Around)
Belt, Thomas	Love Divine (God Incarnate)
Belt, Thomas	Open Up Your Heart(W/Guitar
Belt, Thomas	Resurrection (Life W/New Di
Belt, Thomas	Sing Freedom (Christ Calls)
Belt, Thomas	Songs From My Heart (W/Guit
Belt, Thomas	Streams In The Desert
Belt, Thomas	The Lord Is Come (W/Guitar)
Belt, Thomas/Batastini	Break Open (A Choir In The
Belt, Thomas/Batastini	Come Holy Spirit
Belt, Thomas/Batastini	Fisherman
Belt, Thomas/Batastini	Getting High On Love
Belt, Thomas/Batastini	Leaves A-Fallin' (Good Frid
Belt, Thomas/Batastini	Love Knows No Season
Belt, Thomas/Batastini	Ride On (He Came Riding)
Belt, Thomas/Batastini	Sing A New Song (Gonna Love
Belt, Thomas/Batastini	Son Come Down (Guitar Or Pi
Belt, Thomas/Batastini	The New Morn (The Sun Came
Belt, Thomas/Batastini	The Silent Night
Belt, Thomas/Batastini	Trouble, Lord
Bender, Jan	As Candles Glow
Bender, Jan	Be Ye Joyful, Earth And Sky
Bender, Jan	Christmas Concertato
Bender, Jan	How Lovely Shines (W/Tpt,Or
Bender, Jan	In Thee, O Lord, Do I Put M
Bender, Jan	Introduction, Fugue And Var
Bender, Jan	O God, O Lord Of Heaven And
Benedetti/Devore	The Face Of God
Benedetti, Quint	A Little Thought Away
Benedetti, Quint	In The Home Where They Love
Benedetti, Quint	The Face Of God
Benedetti, Quint	Where They Love To Pray
Benedetti, Quint & Dic	Bless You
Benedict, Em	And This Shall Be A Sign
Benedict, Em	Christmas Bells
Benedict, Em	Happy Birthday, Merry Chris
Benedict, Em	Jesus Is Born
Benedict, Em	The Miracle
Benedict, Em	There Never Was A Christmas
Benedict, Em	You Ask Me Why
Benedict, Em & Ford,Ol	Christmas
Benedict, Em And Ford	Shepherd Boy
Benham, Asahel	Redemption Anthem
Bennard/Wilson	Old Rugged Cross, The
Bennard,Mrs.George	Lord, Keep Me Thine Own
Bennett (Arr)	Leaning On The Everlasting
Bennett, Richard R.	The Sorrows Of Mary (M)
Bennett, W S	God Is A Spirit
Benoit, Paul	Where Love Is Living
Benson	Choir Of Bethlehem, The
Bentel, Franklin	God Be In My Head
Benton Price	Hope Thou In God
Benton Price	Trusting Jesus
Berchem, Jachet	O Lord, Jesus Christ
Berger	Thy Word With Me Shall Alwa
Berger, Jean	A Rose Touched By The Sun's
Berger, Jean	Alleluia From Brazilian Psa
Berger, Jean	Blessed Is Everyone That Fe
Berger, Jean	Cherry Tree Carol (Drama)
Berger, Jean	From Isaiah (In Three Parts
Berger, Jean	How Amiable Are Thy Taberna
Berger, Jean	It Is Good To Give Thanks
Berger, Jean	O Come Let Us Sing Unto The
Berger, Jean	O Sing All Ye Lands
Berger, Jean	Psalm 128
Berger, Jean	Psalm 140 (Mixed Chor & Str
Berger, Jean	Psalm 23
Berger, Jean	Psalm 95
Berger, Jean	Speak To One Another Of Psa
Berger, Jean	Take From Us, Lord
Berger, Jean	The Eyes Of All Wait Upon T
Berger, Jean	The Prayer Of Manasseh
Berger, Jean	The Word Of God (Opt Insts)
Berger, Jean	They Kingdom Come
Berger, Jean	They That Wait Upon The Lor
Berger, Jean	This Is The Covenant
Berger, Jean	Thou Alone Art Israel's Shi
Berger, Jean	To Do God's Will
Berger, Jean	Trust In The Lord
Berger, Jean	Vision Of Peace
Berger, Jean	Who Is Like Unto Thee, O Lo
Berger, Jean	Whom Shall I Send?
Berger, Jean	Why Art Thou Cast Down, O M
Berger, L.	And It Shall Come To Pass
Berger, L.	Arise, Shine
Berger, L.	Behold, God Is My Salvation
Berger, L.	Build A Little Fence Of Tru
Bergerson, Charles	I Shall Not Care(Arr.Only)
Bergh	Our Hymn Of Praise
Berlioz, Hector	Childhood Of Christ (Germ,E
Berlioz, Hector	Requiem
Berlioz, Hector	Te Deum
Berlioz, Hector	The Shepherds' Farwell
Berlucchi, James	A Voice Cries Out In The Wi
Berlucchi, James	All Of Your People
Berlucchi, James	He's Standing At The Door
Berlucchi, James	Jesus Is The One Who Saves
Berlucchi, James	Song Of Praise
Bernabei, G.E.(D1687)	Missa In G
Bernal Jimenez, Miguel	Te Deum Jubilar
Bernard/Dykes/Carmicha	Jesus The Very Thought Of
Bernardi, Steffano	Praise Ye The Lord
Bernardi, Steffano	Thus Said The Lord
Bernstein, Leonard	Almighty Father (From "Mass
Bernstein, Leonard	Chichester Psalms(First Mov
Bernstein, Leonard	Gloria Tibi(From Mass)
Bernstein, Leonard	Hashkivenu
Bernstein, Leonard	Sanctus(From Mass)
Berntsen, W. R.	Choir Specials (No 5592)
Berry, Wallace	No Man Is An Island
Berti,G./Ed. Klein	We Adore You (E & Lat)
Besig	If The World Could Only Be
Besig	Time For Joy
Besig, Don	A Time For Joy! (W/Piano)
Besig, Don	Children's Prayer
Best	Voluntaries On Early Americ
Beuerle	O Shepherds
Beuerle	The Shepherd's Vigil (W/C I
Bevan/Cutts	As The Bridegroom To His Ch
Bevan, Temple	Two Short Anthems (Me)
Bevans, William	Psalm 24
Beversdorf, Thomas	Mini Motet From Micah
Beverst	Gloria In Excelsis Deo
Beverst	One Hundredth Psalm, The
Biber, C H	Tenebrae Factae Sunt
Bick	Now Let Every Tongue Adore
Biechteler, M S	Ad Cantus, Ad Choros
Bielawa	Chorale And Fugue On Lasst
Bielawa	Four Preludes On Hymns Of T
Biggs, John	Gospel Acclamations, Good F
Biggs, John	Meditabor
Billings (Ed. Daniel)	The Lord Is Ris'n Indeed (A
Billings (Ed. Daniel)	Two Easter Anthems (A Cap)
Billings, William	Anthem For Thanksgiving, An
Billings, William	Berlin (Moore) (Acap)
Billings, William	Bethlehem
Billings, William	David's Lamentation
Billings, William	David's Lamentation
Billings, William	Easter Anthem (Shaw)
Billings, William	Hear Heaven Thunder (4-Part
Billings, William	I Am Come Into My Garden
Billings, William	I Am The Rose Of Sharon
Billings, William	I Am The Rose Of Sharon
Billings, William	I Charge You, O Ye Daughter
Billings, William	I Heard A Great Voice
Billings, William	Kittery (Lowens)
Billings, William	Lamentation Over Boston
Billings-Wienandt	Lift Up Your Eyes
Billings,W./Tortolano	May God Be Gracious (4 Voic
Billings, William	O Praise The Lord Of Heaven
Billings, William	Peace Be On Earth
Billings,W./Tortolano	Set Me As A Seal (4 Voices)
Billings, Wm/Van Camp	Sing Praises
Billings, William	The Angel's Carol
Billings, William	The Lord Is Ris'n Indeed
Billings, William	The Mariner's Anthem (Moore
Billings, W. (Arr Mcco	Thine All The Glory
Billings,W./Tortolano	Through North & South (4 Vo
Billings, William	Two Easter Anthems
Billings, William	When Jesus Wept (Med Voice)
Billings, W. (Arr Mcco	When Jesus Wept (Round)
Billings,W./Tortolano	When Jesus Wept (In 19 Roun
Billings, William	When Jesus Wept
Billman, Mark	Lord, Give Them This Day
Billman,M./Brown,C.	It's So Nice To Have Jesus
Binckes	This Is The Lord
Bingham	Perfect Through Suffering
Bish, D (Arr)	Abide With Me
Bish, D.	Be Still, My Soul
Bish, D.	Carol Fantasy
Bish, D.	Lo, How A Rose

COMPOSER INDEX

Bishop, M. & Weatherly	Christmas Lullabies
Bisignano/Furman	Creation
Bisignano/Furman	Hard Time Smiling
Bisignano/Furman	People, Ask Me
Bisignano/Furman	Playground For People
Bisler, Beatrice Bush	Life Is A Symphony And Othe
Bissell, Keith W.	Six Songs
Bitgood, Roberta	Bring A Torch, Jeannette Is
Bitgood, Roberta	Choral Benedictions
Bitgood, Roberta	Lord, May We Follow
Bitgood, Roberta	Sons Of God, The
Bitgood, Roberta	They Shall Walk
Bixel, James W.	Come, O Blessed
Bixel, James W.	Earth Is The Lord's, The
Bixel, James W.	Lord Have Mercy
Bixel, James W.	Stay With Us
Bixler/Mickelson	It May Be Today
Bizet, G	Angus Dei(Lamb Of God) (Dei
Blachura, James	How Good Is God
Blachura, James	I Will Give Thanks
Blachura, James	O Thank The Lord
Blachura, James	Sing A New Song
Black	Jacob's Ladder
Black	O Come, Let Us Sing
Black	O Sing A New Song
Black/Decou	When The Roll Is Called Up
Black/Mercer	Look To The Lamb Of God
Blades, Jack	Live In Me
Blake	O Come, Loud Anthems Let Us
Blake	Son Of God, Eternal Savior
Blake	There Were Three Lights
Blake	Way Of Christ, The
Blake, George	Blessing And Honor
Blake, George	Love Of Jesus, All Divine
Blake, Kevin	Psalm 100
Blakley	God Is Before Me
Blakley	Spirit Of God, This Very Ho
Blakley	To The Work
Blanchard	Sleep, Little Jesus
Blanchard, R. I.	Eucharistic Prayer ii
Blanchard, R. I.	Eucharistic Prayer iii
Blanchard, R. I.	Gospel Acclamations, Bvm
Blanchard, R. I.	Psalm 34
Blanchard, Richard	Fill My Cup, Lord
Blattert, Cloutier	Acclamations From Sacred Sc
Blevins D. Coakley J.	A Prayer To Jesus
Bliss/Rasley	It Is Well With My Soul
Bliss/Wyrtzen	Hallelujah, What A Savior
Bloch, Ernest	Adonai, Elohim
Bloch, Ernest	Benediction From Sacred Ser
Bloch, Ernest	Sacred Service Avodath Hako
Bloch, Ernest	Sanctification
Bloch, Ernest	Silent Devotion And Respons
Bloom, C G L	Jesu, Creator Of The World
Blow, John	Be Merciful Unto Me (Md)
Blow, John	My Days Are Gone Like A Sha
Blow, John	My God, My God, Look Upon M
Blow, John	Praise The Lord, Ye Servant
Blue, Robert	Bless The Lord
Blue, Robert	Christ–Light
Blue, Robert	Community Song
Blue, Robert	Give Me Your Hand
Blue, Robert	Gloria (Liturgy Of Joy)
Blue, Robert	Gospel Halleluia
Blue, Robert	I Saw The Holy City
Blue, Robert	It's A Great Day
Blue, Robert	Lamb Of God (Liturgy Of Joy
Blue, Robert	Let Us Break Bread Together
Blue, Robert	Magnificat
Blue, Robert	Prayer Of Petition (Kyrie)
Blue, Robert	Psalm 23 The Lord Is My She
Blue, Robert	Psalm 27 Christ–Light
Blue, Robert	Psalm 96 This Is The Day
Blue, Robert	Run, Come, See(1)
Blue, Robert	Run, Come, See(2)
Blue, Robert	Thank You Hymn
Blue, Robert	The Canticle Of Canticles
Blue, Robert	The Flowers Appear
Blue, Robert	The Lord Is My Shepherd(1)
Blue, Robert	The Lord's Prayer (Liturgy
Blue, Robert	The Nicene Creed(Credo)
Blue, Robert	The Rock Holler
Blue, Robert	The Sound Of Jubilee
Blue, Robert	The Tree Song
Blue, Robert	There Once Was A Man
Blue, Robert	We're Gonna March Down
Blue, Robert	Witness Song
Blue, Robert	Yes, Amen
Blumenschein, W L	My Soul Doth Magnify
Blunt, Neil	Birthday Song
Blunt, Neil	Children Of Light
Blunt, Neil	From The Voices Of Children
Blunt, Neil	Halloween Song
Blunt, Neil	Hello Song
Blunt, Neil	I Want To Be Your Friend
Blunt, Neil	It's Tough To Be A Friend O
Blunt, Neil	It's Up To Us
Blunt, Neil	Look Down That Road
Blunt, Neil	No Time Like The Present
Blunt, Neil	Peace
Blunt, Neil	People Of Zion
Blunt, Neil	Possible Gospel, The
Blunt, Neil	Ray The Rang, Rhino
Blunt, Neil	Song Of Commitment
Blunt, Neil	St. Francis Prayer
Blunt, Neil	Take Time Out
Blunt, Neil	What Has God Given Me?
Boalt	Christ Is Born
Boalt/Wyrtzen	Blessed Quietness
Boalt, Steve	New Sounds In Song (No 5665
Boatwright, Howard	Mass In C (D)
Boccardi, Donald	Christ Is Our Peace (Hymn)
Bock	Meditation On "Passion Chor
Bock	Praise God!
Bock/Harnick	Sabbath Prayer
Bock/Harnick	Sunrise, Sunset
Bock, Fred	Country And Western Hymnal
Bock, Fred	Folk Celebration (No 4355)
Bock, Fred	Hymntime Piano No 1 (No 574
Bock, Fred	Hymntime Piano No 2 (No 574
Bock, Fred	Hymntime Piano No 3 (No 574
Bock, Fred	Hymntime Piano No 4 (No 574
Bock, Fred	Organ Solos (No 5801)
Bock, Fred (Ed)	The Late Great Planet Earth
Bodycombe, Aneurin	O Master Let Me Walk With
Boeringer	Jesu, The Very Thought Is
Boeringer, James	What Kind Of King?
Bohlen, D	Psalm 42:Prayer For Strengt
Bollbach/Decou	Ring The Bells
Bollbach/Rasley	Ring The Bells (East)
Bolz, Hariett	Sweet Jesus
Bonham, Eugene	Hymn Descants Vol I
Bonham, Eugene	Hymn Descants Vol Ii
Bonham, Eugene	Hymn Descants Vol. Iii
Bonta, Stephen	In The Bleak Mid–Winter
Bonta, Stephen	Sir Christmas
Booth–Clibborn, W.E.	The Breath Of God
Boozer	In Heavenly Love
Boozer	Mary's Lullaby
Borchers	Mother, You're God's Gift T
Borthwick/Webb	Now Is The Time Approaching
Bortniansky, D S	Cherubim–Song
Bottenberg	Acclamations (Icet)
Bottenberg	Christ Has Died (Icet)
Bottenberg	God Himself Is With Us
Boud, Ron	It's Gotta Happen Within
Bougher	Be Still My Heart
Bourgeois/Johnson	All People That On Earth Do
Bourgeois, Louis	From All Who Dwell Beneath
Bourgeois, Louis(Arr)	Two Evening Hymns
Bowen	I Will Praise Thee, O Lord
Bowers, Jane	To Be Redeemed
Bowers, Julia	I'd Like To Walk Around
Bowers, Julia	No More Pain
Bowie, William	Faith (Hb 11–12) (Md)
Bowie, William	O Turn Away Mine Eyes (Md)
Bowie, William	The Sorrows Of My Heart (Ps
Bowie, William	Welcome Happy Morning (Md)
Bowles	Prayer For Serenity
Boyajian, Gloria	Let The Whole Creation Cry
Boyce	Alleluia, Alleluia
Boyce, William	By The Waters Of Babylon
Boyce, William	O Be Joyful In The Lord(Jub
Boyce,W./Tortolano	As A Heart Longs (3 Voices)
Boyce,W./Tortolano Ed	Alleluia (3 Voices)
Boyd/Wall	Let Me Bathe In The Water
Boyd, Jack	When The Terms Of Peace Are
Boyd, Jack (Arr)	Bring A Torch, Jeannette...
Boyer,D./Herring,J.	Morning Star
Bradbury/Peterson	Holy Is The Lord!
Bradbury/Wyrtzen	Jesus Loves Me
Bradford, W	So Much
Brahms/Tillinghast	How Lovely Is Thy Dwelling
Brahms, J. & Klein, M.	Come Holy Spirit
Brahms, J.(Deis)	Cradle Song Of The Virgin
Brahms, J.–Sateren	Sing Praise To God Who Reig
Brahms, J./Goldman	Joyous Christmas Carol
Brahms, Johannes	Ach, Arme Welt(Alas, Poor W
Brahms, Johannes	Adoramus
Brahms, Johannes	Adoramus Te (We Adore Thee)
Brahms, Johannes	Ave Maria
Brahms, Johannes	Ave Maria, Op.12(Eng–Lat)
Brahms, Johannes	Ave Maria, Opus 12 (Female)
Brahms, Johannes	Blessing And Honor, Praise
Brahms, Johannes	Chorale Prelude Arr For Bra
Brahms, Johannes	Come, Holy Spirit
Brahms, Johannes	Cradle Song Of The Virgin
Brahms, Johannes	Create In Me O God
Brahms, Johannes	Ever–Loving Father
Brahms, Johannes	Festival Anthem, Op. 109 No
Brahms, Johannes	Festival Anthem, Op.109 No.
Brahms, Johannes	Festival Anthem, Op.109 No.
Brahms, Johannes	German Requiem (Eng & Ger)
Brahms, Johannes	Grant Unto Me (3rd Mov't)
Brahms, Johannes	How Long Wilt Thou Forget M
Brahms, Johannes	How Lovely Is Thy Dwelling
Brahms, Johannes	Ich Aber Bin Eland(Lord, Go
Brahms, Johannes	Lass Dich Nur Nichts Nicht
Brahms, Johannes	Let Nothing Ever Grieve The
Brahms, Johannes	Magdalena Op 22 No 6
Brahms, Johannes	O Blessed Jesus
Brahms, Johannes	O Bone Jesu
Brahms, Johannes	O Bone Jesu (Oh Loving Jesu
Brahms, Johannes	O Cast Me Not Away(2nd Mov'
Brahms, Johannes	O Queen Of Heaven
Brahms, Johannes	O Savior, Throw The Heavens
Brahms, Johannes	Psalm 13 Lord, How Long Wi
Brahms, Johannes	Regina Coeli
Brahms, Johannes	Requiem (Eng Or Germ)
Brahms, Johannes	Three Sacred Choruses, Op.3
Brahms, Johannes	To God Be The Glory
Brahms, Johannes	Triumphal Hymn, Opus 55 (En
Brahms, Johannes	We Adore Thee
Brahms, Johannes	We Love The Place Where Thi
Brahms, Johannes	When Woe Assails Us Through
Brahms, Johannes	Wherefore Hath The Light Be
Brahms,J.(Arr Russell)	Ah, Thou Poor World (Me)
Brahms,J./Goldman(Arr)	On Christmas Night, We Laud
Brandon, George	Advent Carol
Brandon, George	Be Joyful!
Brandon, George	Branch Of Promise, The
Brandon, George	Carol Of The Visitation
Brandon, George	Fill The World With Light
Brandon, George	Halle'ujah! Great And Marve
Brandon, George	Hope Of The World
Brandon, George	Let All Men Rejoice
Brandon, George	Let Us All Be One
Brandon, George	Lord Is King, The
Brandon, George	On All The Earth Thy Spirit
Brandon, George	Oppression Shall Not Always
Brandon, George	Praise Him Evermore
Brandon, George	Praise, My Soul, The King O
Brandon, George	Rejoice Today With One Acco
Brandon, George	The Day Of Resurrection
Brandon, George	The Head That Once Was Crow
Brandon, George	The Sounding Skies W/Organ
Brandon, George	To Raise A Grateful Song
Brandon, George	True Fasting
Brandon, George	Trust In The Lord
Brandon, George	We'll All Praise God Togeth
Brandon, George	What The Future Hath W/Orga
Brandon, George	With Awe And Confidence
Brandon, George	With Harp And Voice Of Psal
Brandon, George (Arr)	Hail The Long Expected Star
Brandt	Bethlehem Carol
Brandt Dorothea	Babe In A Manger
Brandt Dorothea	Manger And Star
Brandt, Dorothea	Enduring Faith
Braun, Richard	Spirituals For Instrument
Brebeuf, St Jean De	Jesus Is Born
Brenner/Kraehenbuehl	Descend O Spirit, Purging F
Briggs/Wilson	Hold Thou My Hand
Briggs, S.	I Know Jesus
Brigman, R.	Lookin' Back
Bristol, Lee	Lord, Speak To Me That I Ma
Bristol, Lee H.	Let The Children Sing
Britten, Benjamin	A Wealden Trio. Song Of The
Britten, Benjamin	Corpus Christi Carol (Me)
Britten, Benjamin	Jubilate Deo In C (M)
Britten, Benjamin	Sweet Was The Song
Britten, Benjamin	Te Deum In C Maj (D)
Britten, Benjamin	The Oxen. A Carol
Britten, Benjamin	The Sycamore Tree
Brock	I'll Keep Christmas In My H
Brock, E C	I Want To Do What He Comman
Brock, Linda	Better Start Believin'
Brock, Linda	He's All I Need
Brock, Linda	I Love Him
Brock, Linda	Lord, Stay Close To Me
Brock, Linda	No More Sorrow Over There
Brock, Linda	Peace Within
Brock, Linda	Shelter Of Your Arms
Brock, Linda	Sing Hosanna
Brock, Linda	The Lord Came Down
Brock, Linda	Trust In Him
Brodzsky	I'll Walk With God
Brokering	Love, Love, Love
Brooks/Dailey	Come To The Spirit (W/Piano
Broome, Ed	Lo The Tomb Is Empty
Brosseau, Jean	Rejoice Believers (M)
Broughton	Go, Tell It On The Mountain
Broughton	Ride On!
Broughton, Edward	Forth In Thy Name
Broughton, Edward	Joy To The World
Brown Et Al.	Sing 'n Celebrate! (Collect
Brown/Rasley	Follow, I Will Follow Thee
Brown, A. (Ed)	The American Country Hymn B
Brown, Allanson G. Y.	And Dids't Thou Love The Ra
Brown, Allanson G. Y.	Two Easter Carols
Brown, C.F.	Part The Waters (W/Piano)
Brown, Charles	Christmas Suite For Handbel
Brown, Charles	Gentle Jesus, Meek And Mild
Brown, Charles	Jesus, Of A Maid Thou Would
Brown, Charles	Take My Life Precious Jesus
Brown, Christopher	Gloria (Latin)
Brown, Christopher	Hymn To The Holy Innocents
Brown, Christopher	Jubilate Deo (Md)
Brown, Christopher	Laudate Dominum (Ps 150)
Brown, Christopher	Laus Creatorum (Md)
Brown, Christopher	Missa Brevis (Latin)

Brown, E Bouldin	The Holy Child
Brown, J/Descroquettes	Carols For Christmastide
Brown, J/Descroquettes	Three Christmas Carols
Brown, Leon F.	Blessed Is He That Cometh
Brown, Leon F.	To God Be The Glory (Opt Br
Brown, Leon, F.	O God, How Wonderful Thou A
Brown, Sally	Father
Brown, Shirley L.	Prayer Of St. Francis
Brown, Shirley L.	The Foot Washing Song (Chan
Brown, Shirley L.	The Whole Armor (Spir, War)
Browne, Thomas	Praise The Lord Of Heaven
Bruckner, A./Ed Klein	Glory Be To God The Father
Bruckner, A./Ed Klein	God So Loved The World
Bruckner, A./Ed Klein	On The Mount Of Olives (E &
Bruckner, A./Ed Klein	Rise Up My Love (From Sg)
Bruckner, Anton	Christus Factus Est
Bruckner, Anton	Christus Factus Est Pro Nob
Bruckner, Anton	Glory Be To God
Bruckner, Anton	Inveni David(Lat)
Bruckner, Anton	Jesus, Our Savior
Bruckner, Anton	Let Us Celebrate God's Name
Bruckner, Anton	Locus Este A Deo Factus Est
Bruckner, Anton	Mass In D
Bruckner, Anton	Mass In E Minor
Bruckner, Anton	Mass In E Minor
Bruckner, Anton	Mass In F
Bruckner, Anton	Mass No.2(E)(Latin)
Bruckner, Anton	Mass No.3(F)(Latin)
Bruckner, Anton	Os Justi (The Just Mouth)
Bruckner, Anton	Pange Lingua,Eucharistic Hy
Bruckner, Anton	Psalm 150
Bruckner, Anton	Requiem In D Minor
Bruckner, Anton	Rise Up, My Love
Bruckner, Anton	Sacred Choruses
Bruckner, Anton	Sacred Hymns (Seven)
Bruckner, Anton	Tantum Ergo, 6 Settings(Eng
Bruckner, Anton	Tantum Ergos (Six)
Bruckner, Anton	Te Deum(C)(Latin)
Bruckner, Anton	Two Marian Compositions (La
Bruckner, Anton	Two Motets (Latin)
Bruckner, Anton	Vexilla Regis Prodeunt(Lat)
Bruckner, Anton	Virga Jesse Floruit(Lat)
Bruckner, Anton	Worthy Art Thou, O Lord God
Bruckner, Anton (1896)	Te Deum
Bruckner,A./Ed Klein	Seek Ye First The Kingdom O
Brumbaugh, Harley	No Greater Love
Brumel, Antoine	Mater Patris Et Filia
Brun, Johann N.	How Blessed Are They Who He
Brusseau	His Sovereign Love
Buchanan, Annabel M.	Jerusalem, My Happy Home
Buck	Communion Hymn(Bread Of The
Buck, Daniel	I Lift My Soul
Buck, Dudley	Communion Hymn
Buck, Dudley	Darkly Rose The Guilty Morn
Buck, Dudley	Festival Te Deum No. 7
Buck, Dudley	He Shall Come Down Like Rai
Buck, Dudley	Morning Invocation
Buck, Dudley	Sing Alleluia Forth
Buckhaus	He Is All I Need
Bucky, Frida Sarsen	The Blessing-Song Cycle
Buettell	Beatitudes, The
Buettell	Beyond The Wheeling Worlds
Buettell	Cross, The
Buffum/Carmichael	Old-Fashioned Meeting, The
Bull, John	Almighty God, Why By The Le
Bullock, Ernest	Drop, Drop Slow Tears
Bullock, Ernest	Give Laud Unto The Lord
Bullock, Ernest	Give Us The Wings Of Faith
Bullock, Ernest	Good Christian Men Rejoice
Burgin, D	Streams Of Life
Burgin, D & Rios, D	Something More
Burke, John	Come Heavenly Child
Burke, John T.	Where Were You, O Shepherd?
Burleigh, Harry T.	Now Sing With Joy (4-Part A
Burney	Alla Trinite
Burnham	Christmas Fanfare
Burnham	He Is There
Burnham	Manger Carol, A
Burnham	Thanksgiving To God For His
Burnham	Who Is This Man?
Burns	Carol Of The Bells
Burns	Picardy Suite
Burns, James	Common Of Saints Psalm (2ce
Burns, James	Triumph Of The Cross (Psalm
Burns, James	Triumph Of The Cross Allelu
Burns, R. H.	Branded By Jesus
Burns, William K.	Behold! I Stand At The Door
Burns, William K.	Meditative Songs (Med Voice
Burns, William K.	O Man, Rejoice
Burns, William K.	Two Sacred Solos
Burrell, Howard	Mass (Guitar Or Clavier)
Burroughs	Christmas Rose, A
Burroughs	Come, Thou Almighty King
Burroughs	Creator God, We Give You Th
Burroughs	Drop, Drop, Slow Tears
Burroughs	Gloria
Burroughs	He Who Would Valiant Be
Burroughs	How Excellent Thy Name
Burroughs	How Far Is It To Bethlehem?
Burroughs	Knight Of Bethlehem, The
Burroughs	Lo! God Is Here!
Burroughs	Lord's Supper, The
Burroughs	My Lord, My Love, Is Crucif
Burroughs	New Commandment, A
Burroughs	None Other Lamb
Burroughs	O Christ, I Look To Thee
Burroughs	O Clap For Joy!
Burroughs	O Come And Mourn With Me
Burroughs	O Lord Of Life
Burroughs	Safe In The Arms Of Jesus
Burroughs	Seek Ye The Lord
Burroughs	Treasures In Heaven
Burroughs	We Thank Thee, Lord
Burroughs, Bob	Come, Sound His Praise Abro
Burroughs, Bob	God So Loved (No 4278) (Mus
Burroughs, Bob	Heaven My Home
Burroughs, Bob	In Memory Of The Savior's L
Burroughs, Bob	Now Thank We All Our God
Burroughs, Bob	Praise The Lord, His Glorie
Burroughs, Bob	Praise Ye The Lord
Busarow	If You Continue In My Word
Butler	Come, Peace Of God
Butler	Exalt The Name Of The Lord
Butler	Glory To Our Risen King
Butler	I Will Lift Up Mine Eyes
Butler	Let All Mortal Flesh Keep S
Butler	Lord Is Good, The
Butler	Lord Reigns, The
Butler	O Come Let Us Sing
Butler	O Day Of God, Draw Nigh
Butler	O Men Of God, Be Strong!
Butler	Out Of The Depths
Butler	Praise God In Highest Heave
Butler	Sound Over All Waters
Butler/Krogstad	Let Me Introduce You
Butler, Charles Franci	All Alone
Butler, Charles F.	Friends
Butler, Charles F.	Goodbye
Butler, Charles F.	I Know What It's Like
Butler, Charles F.	Jesus Christ
Butler, Charles F.	Let The Old Man Die
Butler, Charles F.	Maybe
Butler, Charles F.	Nursery Rhyme
Butler, Charles F.	Pearly Mansions
Butler, Charles F.	Peter, James And John
Butler, Charles F.	Petersham Place, (16)
Butler, Charles F.	Someone's Callin'
Butler, Charles F.	Song For The Church
Butler, Charles F.	Sweet, Sweet Song
Butler, Charles F.	The Ballad Of Luke Warm
Butler, Dorothy	Can It Be
Butler, Dorothy	Can We Be Identified
Butler, Dorothy	Homecoming In Glory
Butler, Dorothy	I Talked To The Saviour
Butler, Dorothy	I'll Tell It
Butler, Dorothy	If Thou Be Jesus
Butler, Dorothy	Jesus Prayed
Butler, Dorothy	Let Us Pray For The Usa
Butler, Dorothy	Look Up
Butler, Dorothy	Master Of All Miracles
Butler, Dorothy	One Step Beyond
Butler, Dorothy	Sin's Darkest Valley
Butler, Dorothy	Sold Out To Jesus
Butler, Dorothy	Something To Remember At Xm
Butler, Dorothy	The Great Someone
Butler, Dorothy	The Wedding In The Sky
Butler, Dorothy	Tommy's Farewell
Butler, Dorothy	Visions Of Eternity
Butler, Dorothy	What A Wonderful Feeling
Butler, Dorothy	What If Christ Came Tonight
Butler, Dorothy	When I Looked Up
Butler, Dorothy	Will You Be There
Butler, Eugene	Behold, God Is My Salvation
Butler, Eugene	Festival Piece On "St. Ann"
Butler, Eugene	Forth In Thy Name, O Lord
Butler, Eugene	Hark! A Thrilling Voice
Butler, Eugene	Jesus, Name Of Wondrous Lov
Butler, Eugene	Let Us With A Gladsome Mind
Butler, Eugene	Mexican Psalm, A
Butler, Eugene	O God Of All Above, Below
Butler, Eugene	People Of God, The
Butler, Eugene	Praise The Lord, O My Soul
Butler, Eugene	Praise Ye The Lord
Butler, Eugene	Singer Of The Universe
Butler, Eugene	Six Anthems For Junior Voic
Butler, Eugene	The People Of God
Butterworth/Krogstad	Lord Makes Me Happy! The
Butts, Carrol	Two Chorales For Concert Ba
Buxtehude, D.	Cantate Domini (Psalm 96)
Buxtehude, D.	Command Thine Angel That He
Buxtehude, D.	In Dulci Jubilo
Buxtehude, D.	Jesu, Joy And Treasure(Eng)
Buxtehude, D.	Jesu, My Heart's Treasure
Buxtehude, D.	Magnificat Anima Mea
Buxtehude, D.	Magnificat(Eng-Lat)
Buxtehude, D.	Missa Brevis
Buxtehude, D.	Rejoice, Earth And Heaven(E
Buxtehude, D.	The Newborn Babe
Buxtehude, D.	Wake Awake For Night Is Fly
Buxtehude, D.(D1707)	Behold He Bore Our Infirmit
Byles, B D	A Carol(Mary, The Mother, S
Byles, B D	A Child's Present To His So
Byles, B D	A Christmas Folk Song
Byles, B D	A Pages Road Song
Byles, B D	Abiding Joy
Byles, B D	Be Still And Know
Byles, B D	Before The Paling Of The St
Byles, B D	Bethlehem Road
Byles, B D	Easter Carol
Byles, B D	God Bless The Little Things
Byles, B D	We Thank Thee
Byrd, William	Be Glad Ye Heavens (Md)
Byrd, William	Bow Thine Ear, O Lord (Md)
Byrd, William	Cantate Domino (Ps 149)
Byrd, William	Cantiones Quatuor Vocum
Byrd, William	Cantiones Quinque Vocum
Byrd, William	Cantiones Sex Vocum (Peter
Byrd, William	Cantiones Trium Vocum
Byrd, William	Exsurge, Domine (Ps 44)
Byrd, William	First And Second Preces And
Byrd, William	Great Service (Complete D)
Byrd, William	Great Service (Venite, Etc)
Byrd, William	Hail, O Hail True Body (Md)
Byrd, William	In Assumptione B. Mariae& I
Byrd, William	In Festo Purificationis
Byrd, William	In Nativitate Mariae V Irgi
Byrd, William	Magnificat And Nunc Dimitti
Byrd, William	Magnificat And Nunc Dimitti
Byrd, William	Miserere Mei (Ps 51)
Byrd, William	Non Nobis, Domine (Canon)
Byrd, William	O Christ, Who Art The Light
Byrd, William	Post Septuagesima & In Annu
Byrd, William	Prevent Us, O Lord, In All
Byrd, William	Pro Adventus & Post Nativit
Byrd, William	Second Service (Magnificat,
Byrd, William	Short Service (Venite, Te D
Byrd, William	Short Service: Te Deum/ Ben
Byrd, William	Sing, Heaven Imperial (Md)
Byrd, William	Teach Me, O Lord (Ps 119 Me
Byrd, William	Then Did Priests Make Offer
Byrd, William	Third Service (Magnificat,
Byrd, William	This Glad Day (Md)
Byrd, William	Unto Christ The Victim (Vic
Byrd, William	Who Can Tell The Glory (Md)
Byrd, William (Ehret)	Dies Sanctificatus
Byrd, Wm/Kendall	Vigilate
Byrd, Wm/Tortolano	Non Nobis, Domine (3 Voices
Byrne, James E	We See The Lord
Byrt, John	Dives And Lazarus (Folk Bal
Bystrom	My Melody Of Longing
Cabena, Barrie	Congregational Mass In Dori
Cabena, Barrie	Introit For The New Year (M
Cabena, Barrie	Jubilate Deo (M)
Cabena, Barrie	Loving Shepherd Of Thy Shee
Cabena, Barrie	O Lord Of Life (M)
Cabena, Barrie	Psalm 150 (M)
Cabena, Barrie	Te Deum With Congregation
Cabena, Barrie	Twelve Benediction Amens
Cadwallader, Ann	Come Follow Me
Cadwallader, Ann	My Beloved Spoke (Sg 2:10-1
Cadwallader, Ann	My Lover & My Master
Caesar, Paul	Rejoice, My Friends
Caesar, Paul (Buddy)	Look Up To The Lord
Caesar, Paul (Buddy)	We Praise You Every Day
Cailliet, Lucien	Chorale & Var. On Now Thank
Cailliet, Lucien	The Spirit Of Christmas
Cain	Celestial Visitor The
Cain	Communion With God
Cain	Hark, Ten Thousand Harps An
Cain, Nobie	In The Night Christ Came Wa
Cain, Nobie	March Of The Kings
Cain, Nobie	Song Of The Garo Christians
Caldara, Antonio	Stabat Mater
Caldara,A./Tortolano E	Praise The Lord (Ps 117) 4
Caldwell, M	All Praise To God
Caldwell, M	Hear Us, Our Father
Caldwell, M	I Am The Good Shepherd
Caldwell, M	Jesu, Friend Of My Delight
Caldwell, M	Lo, How A Rose E'er Bloomin
Caldwell, M	Morning Prayer
Caldwell, M	My Constant Joy
Caldwell, M	Risen Christ!
Caldwell, Mary E.	A Festival Of Carols For Th
Calkin, Ruth	But I Do Know
Calkin, Ruth H.	How Much He Cares
Calvisius, Seth	Joseph, Joseph, Dearest One
Calvisius, Seth	Joseph, Lieber Joseph Mein
Camp/Decou	That Beautiful Name
Campbell	He'll Understand, And Say,
Campbell-Tipton	I Will Give Thanks Unto The
Campbell/Johnson	And Can It Be?
Campbell, Glen	A Little Less Of Me
Campbell, Helen; Goebo	Jesus Is A Loving Lord
Campbell, Robert, Alt.	At The Lamb's High Feast We
Campbell, S. S.	Praise To God In The Highes
Campian, T	As By The Streams Of Babylo
Candlyn	Festal Rhapsody
Candlyn	Prelude On Darwall
Candlyn	Prelude On Hyfrydol
Candlyn	Prelude On Mit Freuden Zart

COMPOSER INDEX

Candlyn	Prelude On Rockingham
Candlyn	Prelude On St Bernard
Candlyn	Prelude On St Flavian
Candlyn	Three Christmas Preludes (M
Candlyn, T. Fred	Child Of Bethlehem, The
Candlyn, T. Frederick	A Song Of Rejoicing
Canning, Thomas	John Wesley Covenant Servic
Cannon, Jack D.	Be Thou My Vision
Cantata	Unto Us A Child Is Born
Caperton, Florence	Two Anthems For Children's
Carey, T/Mel, L./Kelly	If I Should Go To Heaven
Carissimi, Giacomo	Beatus Vir
Carissimi, Giacomo	O Come Ye To The Cross
Carleton	Memories Of Christmas
Carleton	My Christmas Prayer
Carleton	Night Of The Star
Carleton	Star In The Sky, A
Carleton	Wonder Of The Star, The
Carlson	Communion Meditations
Carlson	Jesus, Refuge Of The Weary
Carlson	Mary's Lament
Carlson	On The Cross
Carlson	Wake, Awake (W/Str Bass)
Carlson, G.	He Came Among Us W/Solo
Carlson, G.	O Day Full Of Grace (W/Stri
Carman, Albert	If My Faith Is Strong And S
Carmichael, Ralph	The Old Ralph Carmichael Qu
Carmichael, Ralph	The Savior Is Waiting (A Ca
Carmichael, Ralph (Ed)	He's Everything To Me (Coll
Carmichael,R./Floria,C	My Friend And I
Carmichael,Ralph (Ed)	One Hundred Songs You Love
Carmony	Behold The Crucified!
Carmony	Jesus Speaks From The Cross
Carmony	Kneel At The Manger
Carolan, Larry	Show Forth The Glory
Carpani, G. (D1825)	Missa In F
Carpenter, Adrian	Sing We Merrily (Ps 81)
Carr/Decou	Old Book And The Old Faith,
Carr, Nancy	Sing, Sing Alleluia
Carrier	While Standing At The Cross
Carrissimi, Giacomo	Jonah (Oratorio)
Carroll, J. R.	A Wedding Song
Carroll, J. R.	Agnus Dei
Carroll, J. R.	Come, Let Us Worship
Carroll, J. R.	Gloria
Carroll, J. R.	God Grant You Many Years
Carroll, J. R.	Lord, May Their Lives
Carroll, J. R.	Receive Now The Body Of Chr
Carroll, J. R.	Sanctus
Carroll, J. R.	Seven French Noels
Carroll, J. R.	Two-Fold Kyrie
Carter	Gloria
Carter	Psalm 23
Carter	The Lord Of The Dance
Carter, J.	Last Supper
Carter, J.	Promised Land
Carter, J. (Arr)	Christ The Lord Is Risen Ag
Carter, J. (Arr)	Promise Fulfilled, The
Carter, John	Cantata
Carter, W./Stevens, M.	Where Went The Days
Cartford	Descants On Six Hymn Tunes
Casciolini	Missa In G
Casciolini	Missa Pro Defunctis
Casciolini, C	Lo, Angels' Bread
Casciolini,C./Ed Lee	Lo, Angels Bread (Eng Only)
Casey, F. J.	So Said Amos The Prophet
Casey, F. J.	To Damascus
Casey, F. J.	Woman Of Samaria
Cassler, G. W.	Adeste Fideles (With Brass)
Cassler, G. W.	Awake, Awake, Good People
Cassler, G. W.	Built On A Rock (W/Brass,Or
Cassler, G. W.	Built On A Rock The Church
Cassler, G. W.	Cradled All Lowly
Cassler, G. W.	Crown With Thy Benediction
Cassler, G. W.	Drop Down, Ye Heavens From
Cassler, G. W.	Earth To Ashes
Cassler, G. W.	Gospel Trumpet, The
Cassler, G. W.	Holy, Holy, Holy (Cong+Choi
Cassler, G. W.	Infant Christus W/Solo
Cassler, G. W.	Infant Jesus
Cassler, G. W.	Love Divine, All Loves Exce
Cassler, G. W.	Now Let The Vault Of Heaven
Cassler, G. W.	Now Thank We All Our God
Cassler, G. W.	O God, Our Help In Ages Pas
Cassler, G. W.	Praise The Savior
Cassler, G. W.	Praise To The Lord
Cassler, G. W.	Six Sacred Anthems For Male
Cassler, G. W.	The Godly Stranger
Cassler, G. W.	While By My Sheep
Cassler, G. W.	Whither Thou Goest
Casteel, K./Roth, P.	Altar Of Faith
Casteel, K./Roth, P.	Hiding In The Arms Of Jesus
Caswell/Hampton	Come Thou Holy Spirit Come
Catalanello, Michael	Hymn Of Praise: Psalm 135
Catalanello, Michael	Jesus
Catalanello, Michael	King Of Kings, Lord Of Lord
Catalanello, Michael	Love One Another
Catalanello, Michael	Miserere: Psalm 51 (Eng)
Catalanello, Michael	Psalm 122: Hail Jerusalem!
Cato, Jim & Esther	Blessed Assurance (Arrangem
Cavalieri, Angelo	A Thousand Stars (Opt Perc)
Cavalli, Francesco	Salve Regina
Cavnar, James	Away They Went With Weeping
Chadwick, George/Van C	God, Jehovah
Chaffin, L G	Holy Father Hear My Cry
Champagne, Claude	Easter
Champagne, Claude	For The Christ Child
Champagne, Claude	Thanksgiving
Chance, Nancy	Motet
Chapin, Lucius	Rockbridge
Chapin, Robison	Three Folk-Hymns
Chaplin, M W	Noel Noel A Saviour Is Born
Chaplin, M W	Sing We To Christ The King
Chapman	Festival Overture (Organ So
Chapman, Betsy	Let It Shine
Chapman, Betsy	What I See
Chapman, E T	God Be In Ny Head
Chapman, Keith	Sing A New Song
Chapman, Marie B.	The Pilgrim Way
Chardin	The Fire Of Love
Charles, Earnest	Lord Of The Years
Charles, Earnest	The Greatness Of The Lord
Charpentier, Marc A.	Three Sacred Motets
Charpentier, Marc-Anto	Mass
Chaumont, James	Suffering Servant Song, The
Chavira, Eli	Traveling On
Chenoweth, Wilbur	Noel Noel
Chenoweth, Wilbur	Noel Noel Bells Are Ringing
Cherubini, L	Give Unto The Humble
Cherubini, L	Lamb Of God, For Sinners Sl
Cherubini, L	Pie Jesu(God Of Mercy)
Cherubini, L	Praise Ye The Lord
Cherubini, M. L.	Fourth Mass, C Major (Latin
Cherubini, M. L.	Requiem Mass In C Minor
Cherubini, M.L.(D1842)	Requiem In D Minor (Male)
Chesterton, Gilbert K.	O God Of Earth And Altar
Chew, D	These Things I Have Spoken
Chihara	Kyrie Eleison
Child, W.(Arr Wienandt	Praise The Lord, O My Soul
Childs	Across The Shadows
Childs	Blessed Redeemer
Childs	From My Heart
Childs	Paradise
Childs	Seek Ye First
Childs	Thy Cross
Childs, David	Seven Psalms
Chiodo	Our Thanks To Thee
Chitwood, Joe	God's Love For Me
Chitwood, Joe	I Remember The Time
Chitwood, Joe	No Dark Valleys
Chitwood, Joe	Oh, Let Me Walk With Thee
Chitwood, Joe	The Everlasting Arms Of God
Chitwood, Joe	Whatever It Takes
Chojnacki, J	Six Motets In Polish And En
Chopin	God's Gift Of Love
Chorbajian, John	And Did Those Feet In Ancie
Chorbajian, John	De Profundis (Out Of The De
Chorbajian, John	The Lamb
Chorbajian, John	When David Heard
Christiansen, Ansgar	Revive Us Again
Christiansen, F. M.	A Cradle Hymn
Christiansen, F. M.	Beautiful Savior
Christiansen, F. M.	Built On A Rock
Christiansen, F. M.	Clap Your Hands
Christiansen, F. M.	Exaltation
Christiansen, F. M.	Glorification
Christiansen, F. M.	Hosanna
Christiansen, F. M.	Immortal Love
Christiansen, F. M.	In Heaven Above
Christiansen, F. M.	Joy
Christiansen, F. M.	Lamb Of God
Christiansen, F. M.	Lost In The Night
Christiansen, F. M.	Love In Grief
Christiansen, F. M.	My God, How Wonderful Thou
Christiansen, F. M.	O Bread Of Life
Christiansen, F. M.	O Day Full Of Grace
Christiansen, F. M.	Offer Unto God
Christiansen, F. M.	Praise To The Lord
Christiansen, F. M.	Psalm 50
Christiansen, F. M.	Regeneration
Christiansen, F. M.	Temples Eternal
Christiansen, F. M.	The Christmas Symbol
Christiansen, F. M.	This Night
Christiansen, F. M.	Thy Kingdom Come, O Lord
Christiansen, F. M.	Today There Is Ringing
Christiansen, F.M. & P	Let All Mortal Flesh Keep S
Christiansen, P.	A Flemish Carol
Christiansen, P.	Agnus Dei
Christiansen, P.	All Poor Men & Humble
Christiansen, P.	Alleluia
Christiansen, P.	Angels We Have Heard On Hig
Christiansen, P.	Bread Of Tears
Christiansen, P.	Come And Behold
Christiansen, P.	Easter Morning
Christiansen, P.	Festival Hymn
Christiansen, P.	I Heard A Great Voice
Christiansen, P.	Joyous Christmas Song
Christiansen, P.	Kyrie (With Narrator)
Christiansen, P.	Lord Jesus By Thy Passion
Christiansen, P.	Lord's Prayer, The
Christiansen, P.	Lullaby On Christmas Eve
Christiansen, P.	Make Us One
Christiansen, P.	Mexican Christmas Processio
Christiansen, P.	O Come, O Come Emmanuel
Christiansen, P.	O Day Full Of Grace
Christiansen, P.	O God Our Help In Ages Past
Christiansen, P.	O How Beautiful The Sky
Christiansen, P.	O Thou Most High
Christiansen, P.	On The Mountainside
Christiansen, P.	Patapan
Christiansen, P.	Praise Ye
Christiansen, P.	Prayers Of Steel
Christiansen, P.	Song Of The Crib
Christiansen, P.	The Beatitudes
Christiansen, P.	The Cradle
Christiansen, P.	The Desert Shall Blossom
Christiansen, P.	Thy Kingdom Come On Earth
Christiansen, P.	Twenty-Third Psalm (W/Narra
Christiansen, P.	Una Sancta (W/Keyboard Or B
Christiansen, P.	Vidi Aquam
Christiansen, P.	While Angels Sing
Christiansen, P.	Wondrous Love
Christie-Hoffman	We Thank Thee
Christman, Charles	Glory To God
Christmas, Charles	Come All Ye Nations
Christmas, Charles	Hymn Of Glory
Christmas, Charles	King Of Creation
Christmas, Charles	King Of Kings
Christmas, Charles	King's Highway
Christmas, Charles	O Sweet Jesus
Christmas, Charles	Psalm 145
Christmas, Charles	The Spirit And The Bride
Christy (Arr)	While I Did Watch My Sheep
Cirou, J & O'connell	You Are The Only Son
Cirou, J & Silvia, H	We Shall Overcome
Cirou, Joseph	As The Sun (4-Part Arr.)
Cirou, Joseph	Canticle Of The Gift (4-Par
Cirou, Joseph	Christ Has Risen From The D
Cirou, Joseph	Christ Is Our Leader (4-Par
Cirou, Joseph	Come Save Me, Lord
Cirou, Joseph	Come To The Lord (4-Part Ar
Cirou, Joseph	Come, Live In Us (4-Part Ar
Cirou, Joseph	God Forbid That I Should Bo
Cirou, Joseph	Great Amen For Advent (4-Pa
Cirou, Joseph	Great Amen For Christmas An
Cirou, Joseph	Great Amen For Pentecost (4
Cirou, Joseph	Love Is The Way (4-Part Arr
Cirou, Joseph	Memorial Acclamations
Cirou, Joseph	Out Of The Depths
Cirou, Joseph	Peace I Give You
Cirou, Joseph	Prayer Of The Faithful For
Cirou, Joseph	Preface & Eucharistic Accla
Cirou, Joseph	Reproaches, The
Cirou, Joseph	Shout Aloud To Heaven (4-Pa
Cirou, Joseph	Spirit Of Action 4-Part Arr
Cirou, Joseph	Throughout These Days
Cirou, Joseph	To God We Sing A New Song
Cirou, Joseph Et Al	Now The Morning Son Is Here
Cirou, Joseph Et Al	O God Of Earth And Altar (4
Cirou, Joseph Et Al	Praise The Lord, Now Come
Cirou, Joseph Et Al	Silent Night (4-Part Arr)
Cirou, Joseph Et Al	Sun Has Risen, The (4-Part
Cirou, Joseph Et Al	To Christ The King (4-Part
Cirou, Joseph Et Al	To The Name That Guides Our
Cirou, Joseph Et Al	Trisagion (4-Part Arr)
Cirou, Joseph Et Al	We Gather Together (4-Part
Cirou, Joseph Et Al	When My Weak Eyes Can See T
Cirou, Joseph Et Al	You Are The Only Son (4-Par
Cirou, Joseph Fr. M.J.	All Of Seeing (4-Part Arr.)
Cirou, Joseph/Deeter T	Mass Of Celebration (4-Part
Cirou, Joseph/Oconnell	Lord Have Mercy On Us (2-Pa
Cirou, Joseph/Silvia H	Mary The Dawn (4-Part Arr)
Cirou, Joseph/Silvia H	Right Hand Of The Lord,The
Cirou, Joseph/Silvia H	This Is What We Bring (4-Pa
Cirou, Joseph/Silvia,H	Great Amen For Easter (4-Pa
Cirou, Joseph/Silvia,H	Great Amens Through The Yea
Cirou, Joseph/Silvia,H	Now Come To Me (4-Part Arr)
Cirou, Joseph, Lyrica	Christ The Lord Today Has R
Cirou, Joseph,Wesley,	Church's One Foundation, Th
Clapp Donald C.	Foundation
Clare,T/Kraehenbuehl,D	God Of The Pastures, Hear
Clark, Eugene L.	Let The Earth Hear His Voic
Clark, Eugene L.	The Greatest Story Yet Unto
Clark, Eugene L.	The Last Commandment (Canta
Clark, Lynn	In This Quiet Hour
Clarkson/Fischer	Lord Send Me
Clatterback, R.	Pure As Crystal Water
Clatterbuck/Johnson	Deep Down In My Heart
Clayton	Now I Belong To Jesus
Clement, Jacques	Helas Mamour (Old French)
Clements, John	The Lord's Prayer (E)
Clibborn	Down From His Glory
Clothier	Sing, Soul Of Mine! The Lor
Clothier, Louita	Hymn For Winter
Coakley J. Blevins D.	God Is Our Saviour
Coakley J. Blevins D.	I Hear Jesus Calling My Nam
Coakley J. Blevins D.	I Want To Go To Heaven
Coakley J. Blevins D.	I'm Going To Fly Away To He
Coakley J. Blevins D.	I'm Going To Make It Throug
Coakley J. Blevins D.	I'm Watching For His Coming

COMPOSER INDEX

Coakley J. Blevins D.	Jesus Is Knocking
Coburn Bill	Bright 'n' Shiny
Cockerham/Barber/Robin	In These Times
Cockerham, J	Call On Jesus
Cockerham, J Barber, F	I'll Go
Cockerham, James	I'll Keep On Serving
Cockerham, James	It's No Secret
Cockerham, James	Run On
Cockerham, James	Since God Came Into My Hear
Cockerham,J Robinson,G	Jesus Is Everything
Cockerham,J Robinson,S	Praise Him
Cockerham,J/Robinson,G	A Friend Of Mine
Cockett,M./Pearson,J.	Glory To The Risen Lord
Cockett,M/Mayhew,K.	Let Trumpets Sound
Cockett,M/Mayhew,K.	Lower Your Eyes
Cockett,M/Mayhew,K.	Show Yourself To Me, Lord
Cockett,M/Pearson, J.	Fill The Pots With Water
Cockshott, Gerald R.	Angels Sang That Christmas
Cockshott, Gerald R.	Balulalow
Cockshott, Gerald R.	Gloria In Excelsis
Coelho, Terrye	Father, I Adore You
Coelho, Terrye	If Any Man Come After Me
Coenen, W	Come Unto Me
Coggin	It Is A Thing Most Wonderfu
Coggin (Arr)	Angels Are Singing
Coggin (Arr)	Baby In The Cradle Lies (Op
Coggin (Arr)	Sleep, My Jesus, Sleep
Coggin, Elwood	Be Ye Glad And Rejoice O Ye
Coggin, Elwood	Glorious Things Of Thee Are
Coggin, Elwood	Thou Wilt Keep Him In Perfe
Coggin, Elwood (Arr)	Rejoice In His Word
Coggin, Elwood (Arr)	Softly The Winds Blew (Poli
Cole Ann. Myring Charl	Jesus Sends His Sunlight
Cole, Gail	The Lord Is Present In His
Cole,Bill/Mann,Johnny	The Four Freedoms(Musical)
Coleman, Henry	Jesu, Lover Of My Soul (E)
Coleman, Henry	To Thee O Lord, Our Hearts
Coleman, Henry	Ye Servants Of God (E)
Collard, Terry	Blessed Be You Lord God
Collard, Terry	Come To Me, Jesus
Collard, Terry	Feed My Lambs
Collard, Terry	Fire Of Love
Collard, Terry	He's Risen
Collard, Terry	Holy, Holy
Collard, Terry	Lamb Of God
Collard, Terry	Mary
Collard, Terry	Spirit Comes, The
Collard, Terry	That's My God
Collard, Terry	Walk In Love
Collard, Terry	We Give An Offering To Jesu
Collard, Terry	You've Gotta Have What It T
Collins (Arr)	Babe In Bethlehem's Manger
Collins, David	Hallelujah To The King
Collins, J.T. & Peters	Sing Out, O Zion
Collins, Ray	Holy, Holy, Holy
Colom/Johnson	Weary Marching Up The Calva
Comeau, Bill	A Touch Of Lemon
Comeau, Bill	Bringing Freedom
Comeau, Bill	Busy Day
Comeau, Bill	Danny's Dance
Comeau, Bill	Dreamer
Comeau, Bill	Fish Wish
Comeau, Bill	Hail To Thee
Comeau, Bill	Jello Man
Comeau, Bill	Lion Hunt
Comeau, Bill	Rainy Day Song
Comeau, Bill	Talking Pets
Comeau, Bill	The Big "G" Stands For
Comeau, Bill	You've Got To Look Hard
Comeau, Josephine	He Said (God Is My Father)
Comer, John	Believe Ye
Conaway, G Wilkes	Blessed Are They
Conkey/Burkwall	In The Cross Of Christ I Gl
Conley, David	My Faith Looks Up To Thee
Conley, James	Toccata For Organ
Conley, Thomas P.	Look Up, You Nations
Connaughton/O'riordan	Roll That Stone Away
Connor, Edward	Mass In Honor Of Pope Paul
Conte, D. (Arr)	Cantate Domino
Cook, E. T.	Christ Being Raised From Th
Cook, E. T.	Magnificat And Nunc Dimitti
Cook, John	Author Of Light (Md)
Cooke, Arnold	Loving Shepherd Of Thy Shee
Cooke, Arnold	Three Wise Kings (E)
Coombe, C W	And God Shall Wipe Away All
Coombe, C W	Brightest And Best
Coombs, C W	As It Began To Dawn (W/Bar
Coomes, Thomas William	Jesus Is Standing Here
Cooney	I Am The Way (From No Time
Cooper, David S.	Sancta Maria
Cooper, Ken	He's For Real
Cope, Cecil	He Is Risen (E)
Cope, Cecil	Pleasure It Is (E)
Copeland	Their Sweetest Hour
Copely, R. Evan	Glory To God In The Highest
Copes	Two Preludes For Holy Week
Copes, C. Earle	Eternal God
Copes, V Earle	Harvest Carol
Copes, V Earle	When I Survey The Wondrous
Copes, V. Earle	A New Song
Copes, V. Earle	Eternal God (W/Choral Spkin
Copes, V. Earle	For The Bread
Copes, V. Earle	Go Tell It In The City
Copes, V. Earle	Hope Of The World
Copes, V. Earle	I Thank Thee, Lord
Copes, V. Earle	Psalm 121 (Unacc)
Copes, V. Earle	Turn Back, O Man
Copley	Chorale Prelude On Ein Fest
Copley	Eleven Chorale Preludes
Copley	Three Chorale Preludes (Mod
Copley	Three Preludes And Fugues F
Copley, R. Evan	Jesus Christ Is Risen Today
Copley, R. Evan	Salvation Belongeth Unto Th
Copley, R. Evan	Seven General Anthems For U
Copley, R. Evan	This Is The Day (M)
Copley, R. Evan	Three Anthems Based On Cano
Copley, R. Evan	Three Anthems Of Praise
Copley, R. Evan	Two Carols
Coppock, Doug	Christ Is Risen 1
Coppock, Doug	I'm Gonna Sing
Coppock, Doug	Jesus Is Soon Coming
Corbeil, Pierre De	The Little King
Corbitt	O Praise The Lord
Corda, M And Lenke, W	The Gifts Of God
Corda, Mike (Lyrics)	In The Glow Of His Love
Corda, Mike (Lyrics)	Thanks To Thee
Corda,M. And Flint,J.	Look Up
Corfe, Joseph (Arr)	Thou, O God, Art Praised In
Corigliano, John	Christmas At The Cloisters
Corina	Organ Offertories From The
Corina	Suite For Christmas (Mod)
Corina, John	He That Would Love Life
Corina, John	Psalm 118 (W/Brs)
Cornelius, Peter	Christmas Song
Cornelius, Peter	The Infant Christ
Cornelius, Peter (Arr)	The Three Kings
Cornell	The Angel's Song
Cornell, G.	We Sing In Celebration
Correa, Carlos	O Vos Omnes (M)
Correa, Carlos	Plorans Ploravit (M)
Corrette	Magnificat Du 3eme Et 4eme
Corsi, J	Adoramus Te, Christe
Corss/Rasley	I Will Come Again (Cantata)
Costa, M	I Will Extol Thee
Costeley, Guillaume	Allons, Gay Bergeres
Costeley, Guillaume	Now, Arise Ye Shepherds Mil
Cothran, Jeff (Arr)	Glorious In Majesty (Trad J
Cothran, Jeff(Wds,Arr)	Planted Wheat (Trad Hb Mel)
Coulthard, Jean	Child's Evening Prayer (M)
Couper	In Christ There Is No East
Couper, Alinda B.	Christmas Joy
Couper, Alinda B.	Festival Introits
Couper, Alinda B.	Praise And Supplication
Couperin (Arr Jewell)	A Hymn Of Praise (W/Org,Vio
Couperin, F. (Hines)	O Vos Omnes (Accompanied)
Couperin, F.(Nelson)	The Earth Is The Lord's
Cram	Blessed Is He That Comes
Cram	God, Who Made The Earth
Cram	Master Of Eager Youth
Cram	O Bless The Lord
Cram, Fisk	Precious Crimson Fountain
Cram, W. Francis	Smile Because God Loves You
Cram, W. Francis	There's Glory In My Soul
Cram, Wilbur	I Know My Friend Jesus Is P
Cram, Wilbur & Francis	I Am One For Whom You Died
Cram, Wilbur & Francis	Jesus Descended From Majest
Cram, Wilbur, Fisk	The Lord Is My Shepherd
Crawford, John	Psalm 98 (D)
Creed, Dan	Alleluia
Creed, Dan	Alleluias (Sixteen)
Creed, Dan	Doxology
Creed, Dan	Holy, Holy
Creed, Dan	Open Up
Creed, Dan	Rite Of Peace
Creed, Dan (Arr.)	This Day God Made
Creed, Dan & Fletcher,	Jesus, I Need You
Creston, Paul	Devoutly I Adore Thee
Creston, Paul	Hail, Holy Queen
Creston, Paul	Psalm 23
Crivelli, Giovanni	O Maria Mater Gratiae
Crivelli, Giovanni B.	Ut Flos, Ut Rosa (Me) (Sain
Croce, Giovanni	Is It Nothing All Of You Wh
Croce, Giovanni	O Hear We Lord God
Croce, Giovanni	O Sing Ye To The Lord
Croft/Bolks	O God, Our Help In Ages Pas
Croft, William	O Lord God Of My Salvation
Croft, William	We Will Rejoice
Cromie, Marguerite Big	How Great The Sign Of God's
Crosby, Doane	To God Be The Glory
Cross, Danny	Can I Say
Cross, Danny	The Lord Is Still Around
Cross, Richart (Alt)	Behold A Mystical Rose
Crosse, Gordon	O Blessed Lord (Md)
Crosse, Gordon	The Covenant Of The Rainbow
Crotch, Dr William	Bless Now O Lord
Crotch, William (Arr)	Comfort, O Lord (E)
Crotch, William (Arr)	Lo! Star-Led Chiefs (Me)
Crouch, Andrae	Everywhere
Crouch, Andrae	Hallelujah, I Am Free
Crouch, Andrae	He That Endureth
Crouch, Andrae	How Sweet It Is
Crouch, Andrae	I Cannot Tell It All
Crouch, Andrae	I Didn't Think It Could Be
Crouch, Andrae	I Don't Know Why Jesus Love
Crouch, Andrae	I Find No Fault In Him
Crouch, Andrae	I Just Love My Jesus
Crouch, Andrae	I Love Him Because He First
Crouch, Andrae	I Shall Never Let Go His Ha
Crouch, Andrae	I'll Never Forget
Crouch, Andrae	I've Got It
Crouch, Andrae	I've Got Jesus
Crouch, Andrae	Lord Don't Lift Your Spirit
Crouch, Andrae	One Way
Crouch, Andrae	Psalm 40
Crouch, Andrae	Someday I'll See His Face
Crouch, Andrae	The Addict's Plea
Crouch, Andrae	The Blood Will Never Loose
Crouch, Andrae	The Broken Vessel
Crouch, Andrae	The Power Of Jesus
Crouch, Andrae	There Is A Name
Crouch, Andrae	Through It All
Crouch, Andrae	What Makes A Man Turn His B
Crouch, Andre	Take Me Back (Collection Yo
Crouch,A./Floria,C.	It Won't Be Long(We'll Be G
Crouch,A&S/Floria,C.	Jesus Is The Answer
Crow	Baby Jesu
Cruger (Arr Goodell)	Now Thank We All Our God
Cruger/Decou	Now Thank We All Our God
Cruger, J	Now Thank We All Our God
Cruger, J.	Ah, Holy Jesus
Csonka, Paul	Cantata De Semana Santa
Csonka, Paul	Concierto De Navidad
Cui, C	Angelic Bread Of Heaven
Cull, Robert	All I Need Is You
Cull, Robert	Another Love Song
Cull, Robert	Goodbye
Cull, Robert	Here Is All Of Me
Cull, Robert	Let's Keep Growing
Cull, Robert	My Love Song
Cull, Robert	You Are My Shield
Cull, Robert	You're Enough
Cull, Robert	Welcome To The Family
Cull, Robert	You're A Friend To Me
Culross, David	Calvary
Culverwell, Andrew	All The Way
Culverwell, Andrew	Born Again
Culverwell, Andrew	Come To My House
Culverwell, Andrew	He Had It Planned Long Ago
Culverwell, Andrew	He Really Has Set Me Free
Culverwell, Andrew	I Found The Truth
Culverwell, Andrew	I Know He's Mine
Culverwell, Andrew	I See Your Face
Culverwell, Andrew	If I Created You
Culverwell, Andrew	My Name Is John
Culverwell, Andrew	The Man Of Galilee
Culverwell, Andrew	There'll Be Bread
Culverwell, Andrew	There's No Sitting On The F
Culverwell, Andrew	Thomas
Culverwell, Andrew	Through Some Other Eyes
Culverwell, Andrew	Trust In Me
Culverwell, Andrew	Whatcha Gonna Do
Culverwell, Andrew	Who Do You Say That I Am
Culverwell, Andrew	Wicked Old Pharoah
Culverwell, Andrew	You Gotta Walk
Cummins	Four Chorale Preludes
Cunningham/Quinn	Out Of The Depths I Cry (Ps
Cunningham, Pat, Carol	Cast Into The Deep
Cunningham, Patrick	Agnus Dei (Eng, Icet)
Cunningham, Patrick	America The Beautiful
Cunningham, Patrick	At All Times I Will Bless
Cunningham, Patrick	Awake Sleeper
Cunningham, Patrick	Balaam
Cunningham, Patrick	Behold A Great Priest
Cunningham, Patrick	By The Streams Of Babylon
Cunningham, Patrick	Christ Became Obedient (E)
Cunningham, Patrick	Christ Has Died
Cunningham, Patrick	Christmas Psalm (Today Is B
Cunningham, Patrick	Come And Rescue Me
Cunningham, Patrick	Come, Holy Spirit
Cunningham, Patrick	Communion In A Minor, Ps 12
Cunningham, Patrick	Cry Out With Joy! (Is 12:1-
Cunningham, Patrick	Drink Deep Of The Fountain
Cunningham, Patrick	Dying You Destroyed Our Dea
Cunningham, Patrick	Entrance Song For Christmas
Cunningham, Patrick	Even So Lord Jesus Quickly
Cunningham, Patrick	Fill Us With Your Love (Ps
Cunningham, Patrick	Give Peace, O Lord (Ps 122)
Cunningham, Patrick	Give Thanks To The Lord (Ps
Cunningham, Patrick	Gloria (Eng, Icet) Opt Bras
Cunningham, Patrick	God Mounts His Throne (Ps47
Cunningham, Patrick	Good Shepherd, We Love You
Cunningham, Patrick	Happy Is He Who Regards (Ps
Cunningham, Patrick	Happy Is He Whose Fault Is
Cunningham, Patrick	He Heals The Broken Hearted
Cunningham, Patrick	He Is Lord (Verses)
Cunningham, Patrick	He Who Does Justice (Ps 15)
Cunningham, Patrick	His Saving Power Revealed
Cunningham, Patrick	I Am Your Light (Opt Brass)
Cunningham, Patrick	I Have Waited For The Lord
Cunningham, Patrick	I Love You Lord My Strength

Cunningham, Patrick	I Will Be Like A Father & M
Cunningham, Patrick	I Will Go Forward And Walk
Cunningham, Patrick	I Will Go To The Altar Of G
Cunningham, Patrick	I Will Offer Sacrifice (Ps
Cunningham, Patrick	I Will Praise You Lord (Ps
Cunningham, Patrick	I Will Walk In God's Presen
Cunningham, Patrick	I Would Renew The Whole Wor
Cunningham, Patrick	I'll Sing Praise To The Lor
Cunningham, Patrick	Icet Responsorial Antiphons
Cunningham, Patrick	In Manibus Ivis (Eng) Ps 31
Cunningham, Patrick	Intrada In A Minor (Blessin
Cunningham, Patrick	It Is Good To Give Thanks
Cunningham, Patrick	It Is Good To Give Thanks T
Cunningham, Patrick	It's Just Like Moses On The
Cunningham, Patrick	Keep Me Safe O God (Ps 16)
Cunningham, Patrick	Kyrie (Eng, Icet Pen Rite C
Cunningham, Patrick	Let My Tongue Be Silenced
Cunningham, Patrick	Let The Little Children Com
Cunningham, Patrick	Lord By Your Cross And Resu
Cunningham, Patrick	Lord You Are Good And Forgi
Cunningham, Patrick	Lord, Let Your Face Shine
Cunningham, Patrick	Lord, Send Out Your Spirit
Cunningham, Patrick	Lord, You Have The Words (P
Cunningham, Patrick	Lord, Your Love Is Eternal
Cunningham, Patrick	Lord's Prayer, The
Cunningham, Patrick	Lowly People You Save (Ps 1
Cunningham, Patrick	Mary, Mother Of The Word
Cunningham, Patrick	May The Lord Bless Us (Ps 1
Cunningham, Patrick	My God, My God (Ps 22)
Cunningham, Patrick	My Light And Salvation (Ps2
Cunningham, Patrick	O Bless The Lord (Ps 103)
Cunningham, Patrick	O God, Pity Us (Ps67)
Cunningham, Patrick	O God, Save Me With Your Na
Cunningham, Patrick	Out Of The Depths (From Com
Cunningham, Patrick	Peace I Leave With You (Ps
Cunningham, Patrick	Peace To His People (Ps85)
Cunningham, Patrick	People Of Praise (New Year)
Cunningham, Patrick	Praise The Lord For He Is G
Cunningham, Patrick	Praise The Lord My Soul (Ps
Cunningham, Patrick	Pray For The Peace Of Jerus
Cunningham, Patrick	Rebuild The Temple
Cunningham, Patrick	Redemption Song (Exodus)
Cunningham, Patrick	Remember Your Mercies O Lor
Cunningham, Patrick	Responsorial Psalm For Chri
Cunningham, Patrick	Sanctus (Eng, Icet)
Cunningham, Patrick	See, The Fields Are White
Cunningham, Patrick	Sing To The Lord A New Song
Cunningham, Patrick	Sing With Joy To God (Ps81)
Cunningham, Patrick	Steadfast In Your Paths (Ps
Cunningham, Patrick	Syriac Acclamation
Cunningham, Patrick	Taste And See (Ps 34)
Cunningham, Patrick	The Day Of The Lord
Cunningham, Patrick	The Dream Of God
Cunningham, Patrick	The Face Of God (Wedding So
Cunningham, Patrick	The Glorious Deeds Of The L
Cunningham, Patrick	The Hand Of The Lord Feeds
Cunningham, Patrick	The Law Of God Is Perfect
Cunningham, Patrick	The Lord Has Done Great Thi
Cunningham, Patrick	The Lord Has Set His Throne
Cunningham, Patrick	The Lord Is King (Psalm 93)
Cunningham, Patrick	The Mother Of Jesus Was The
Cunningham, Patrick	The Reproaches (Prophecy)
Cunningham, Patrick	The Song Of Joshua
Cunningham, Patrick	The Vineyard Of The Lord (P
Cunningham, Patrick	To The Mountain Lord!
Cunningham, Patrick	Toccata For Nun Danket Alle
Cunningham, Patrick	Upright Is The Word
Cunningham, Patrick	We Belong To You O Risen Lo
Cunningham, Patrick	You Drew Me Clear (Ps30)
Curphey, Geraldine	Lord Of Glory Is My Light,
Curran, P G	Blessing (Thanksgiving Or G
Curran, P G	The Resurrection
Currie, R. (Arr)	God Of Our Fathers
Currie, Randolph	Bless The Lord, O My Soul
Currie, Randolph	Come Down, O Love Divine
Currie, Randolph	Coventry Carol
Currie, Randolph	Hymn Of Consecration
Curry	Chorale Prelude On Bremen
Curry	Hymn-Tune Preludes (15)
Curry	Improvisation On Schonster
Curry, Lawrence	In Christ There Is No East
Curry, R D	Put On The Whole Armour Of
Curry, R D	Whatsoever Things
Curry, Sheldon	Lord Speak To Me
Curry, W Lawrence	A Hymn To The Risen Christ
Curry, W Lawrence	Against The Morn Is Come A
Curry, W Lawrence	Great God Of Nations
Curry,S./Brown,C.	Give Your Heart To Jesus (R
Curzio, Elaine	And The Word Was Made Flesh
Curzio, Elaine	Celebrate Life
Curzio, Elaine	Does God Ever Laugh?
Curzio, Elaine	God Is Alive
Curzio, Elaine	Hey God!
Curzio, Elaine	Resurrection
Curzio, Elaine	Where The Spirit Leads
Cutler-Lynn	At Length There Dawns The G
Cutrona, H	The Body Of Christ
Cutrona, H	The Shepherd
Cutrona, Henry	Middle Of The Day
Czajanek, Victor	Christmas So Wonderful Fair
Dailey, Joe	A Light Will Shine
Dailey, Joe	Blessing
Dailey, Joe	Committment Song
Dailey, Joe	God Is Love
Dailey, Joe	Happy Are The Children Of T
Dailey, Joe	New Life
Dailey, Joe	Our Father
Dailey, Joe	Prayer For Peace
Dailey, Joe	The Christ Hymn
Dailey, Joe	We'll See The Light
Daingerfield Richard	The Kingdom Of Jesus
Dalby, Martin	And He Showed Me A Pure Riv
Dale,A./Richards,H.	Go Tell Everyone
Damrosch, F.	God Deigning Men To Be (Apo
Dan Reta. Laney E.C.	I Believe Heaven's God's Wi
Daniels	The Only Lord
Daniels, E.	It Was For You
Daniels, Mabel	Carol Of A Rose
Daniels, T.	He Pled My Case
Danielsen	Come Ye Unto Me
Danielson, David G.	Secret Place Of God, The
Danniebelle	This Moment (Youth Collecti
Dare, Elkanah K	Babylonian Captivity
Dare, Elkanah K	Hark The Herald Angels Sing
Dargomysky, A.	The Fragile Joys
Darke-Aveling	The Sower (Cantata)
Darke, Harold	A Psalm Of Thanksgiving (Ps
Darke, Harold	Communion Service In A Mino
Darke, Harold	Communion Service In E (Md)
Darke, Harold	Communion Service In F With
Darst	All Hail The Power Of Jesus
Darst	All Things Are Thine
Darst	Gracious Spirit, Holy Ghost
Darst	I Am The Light Of The World
Darst	Immortal Love
Darst	Jesus, Lead Us
Darst	Jesus, Thou Joy Of Loving H
Darst	Sing Praise To God
Darst	Take Thou Our Minds, Dear L
Darst	We Need Thy Love
Darst, S. Glen	Come Thou Long-Expected Jes
Darst, S. Glen	Come, Let Us Join
Darst, S. Glen	Lift Up Your Hearts, Ye Peo
Darst, S. Glen	Praise The Lord Of Heaven
Darst, S. Glen	Praise The Savior
Darst, S. Glen	Praise Ye The Father
Darst, S. Glen	Strong Son Of God, Immortal
Darst, W. Glen	Come Ye Faithful, Raise The
Darst, W. Glen	Father, Hear Us Pray
Darwall/Berntsen	Rejoice! The Lord Is King!
Darwall/Wyrtzen	Join All The Glorious Names
Davenport, David N.	Little David (Spiritual)
David N Johnson	O God Of All, We Thank You
David N. Johnson	Lord Of All, You Gave Us Th
David, Elmer L	Marys Little Baby
Davidson	Did They Crucify My Lord?
Davidson	Lo, How A Rose E'er Bloomin
Davidson, Ray	O Holy Spirit Of God
Davies, W. & Ley, H.G.	The Church Anthem Book (Boa
Davies,Westbrook,Frost	Three Carols For Christmas
Davis	Glory Above The Heavens
Davis	God Is In This Place
Davis	Hail His Coming, King Of Gl
Davis F. Clark	O Listen, Brother
Davis, Allan	Psalm Of Praise, A
Davis, Allan	Song For Daniel, A
Davis, Bob	Brother, Brother Mine
Davis, Bob	Come On Down
Davis, Bob	Country Blessing
Davis, Bob	Gathering Song
Davis, Bob	Glory
Davis, Bob	Holy, Holy, Holy
Davis, Bob	Lamb Of God
Davis, Bob	Lord Have Mercy
Davis, Bob	Lord's Prayer
Davis, Diane	God Has Called You
Davis, Diane	I'm Not Alone
Davis, Diane	Jeremiah
Davis, Diane	Praise My God With The Tamb
Davis, Diane	Thank You Lord
Davis, Diane	The Lord Is A Great & Might
Davis, K K	Renew A Right Spirit Within
Davis, K.K.	Firmament Of Power
Davis, K.K.	Sing Gloria
Davis, K.K.	Twenty Third Psalm
Davis, Katherine	Grant We Beseech Thee Merci
Davis, Katherine	I Sought The Lord
Davis, Katherine K.	Let Thy Merciful Ears, O Lo
Davis, M.J.	Because Of Love (W/Piano)
Davis, Paulette	Blessing
Davis, Paulette	Christmas Acclamation
Davis, Paulette	Holy, Holy, Holy
Davis, Paulette	Joyful Dawning
Davis, Paulette	Lamb Of God
Davis, Paulette	Lord Have Mercy
Davis, Paulette	Quietly He Came
Davis, Paulette	Red Balloon
Dawson, William	Jesus Walked This Lonesome
Dawson, William	You Got To Reap Just What Y
Day	God Is Everywhere
Day	Let God Tune Your Heartstri
Day	Things I Have Left Undone,
De Clerambault	He Is Born, Christ Is Born
De Giardin/Johnson	Come, Thou Almighty King
De Lassus, O	Improperium
De Lassus, O	Super Flumina Babylonis
De Machaut, Guillame	La Messe De Nostre Dame
De Vere, Aubrey	Who Is He That Stands Trium
De Victoria	Kyrie Eleison
Dean, T. W.	A Christmas Cantata
Dean, T. W.	Amazing Grace (New Britain
Dean, T. W.	Canticles Of Christmas (Can
Dean, T. W.	Let Us Now Praise Famous Me
Dean, T. W.	Music For The Lord's Supper
Dean, T. W.	The Lord Is My Light
Dean, T. W.	Words Of Jesus (Cantata)
Dearnley, C. & Wicks A	Communion Service, Series 3
Decius-Pooler	Lamb Of God
Decou/Johnson	Christmas Ensemble S.S.A. &
Decou/Johnson	Christmas Organist (No 5950
Decou/Johnson	Christmas Organist (No 5950
Decou/Johnson	Easter Organist (No 5290)
Decou/Johnson	Favorite Spirituals No 2 (N
Decou, Harold	Amazing Grace Traditional
Decou, Harold	Brass Ensemble Packet No 1
Decou, Harold	Brass Ensemble Packet No 2
Decou, Harold	Brass Ensemble Packet No 3
Decou, Harold	Bus Sing (No 5135)
Decou, Harold	Christmas Story
Decou, Harold	Duets For Piano And Organ N
Decou, Harold	Duets For Piano And Organ N
Decou, Harold	Easter Celebration Cantata
Decou, Harold	Easy Organ Favorites (No 54
Decou, Harold	God's Love Gift (No 4369) C
Decou, Harold	Gospel Choir Favorites (No
Decou, Harold	Gospel Organist No 1 (No 57
Decou, Harold	Gospel Organist No 2 (No 57
Decou, Harold	Gospel Organist No 3 (No 57
Decou, Harold	Gospel Organist No 4 (No 57
Decou, Harold	Gospel Organist No 5 (No 56
Decou, Harold	Hark, The Herald Angels Sin
Decou, Harold	Harold Decou Presents Chora
Decou, Harold	May God Bless You And Keep
Decou, Harold	My First Piano Hymnbook No
Decou, Harold	My Piano Hymnbook No 2 (No
Decou, Harold	My Piano Hymnbook No 3 (No
Decou, Harold	No Tears Tomorrow
Decou, Harold	Send The Light Gabriel
Decou, Harold	Singing In Seven Parts (No
Decou, Harold	Songs For Our Revival And E
Decou, Harold	Special Day Organist (No 59
Decou, Harold	Special Trio Arrangements N
Decou, Harold	Special Trio Arrangements N
Decou, Harold	Special Trio Arrangements N
Decou, Harold	Violin Solo Favorites (No 5
Decou, Harold (Col.)	Favorite Hymns For Crusades
Decou, Harry	Sunday Morning Orangist No
Decou, Harry	Sunday Morning Organist No
Decou, Harry	Sunday Morning Organist No
Decou, Harry	Sunday Morning Organist No
Decou, Harry	Sunday Morning Organist No
Defalco, Elinor	Receive In Your Heart
Dehan, Christopher	Place Your Hope In Me
Dehan, Sheila	I Am The Handmaid Of The Lo
Deiss, Lucien	A Child Is Born
Deiss, Lucien	Acclamations
Deiss, Lucien	All Blessed Are You, O Lord
Deiss, Lucien	All Honor To You, O Lord
Deiss, Lucien	All Honor, Power To You, O
Deiss, Lucien	All Praise, Glory And Wisdo
Deiss, Lucien	All The Bright Morning Star
Deiss, Lucien	All The Earth
Deiss, Lucien	All You Nations
Deiss, Lucien	Alleluia, Alleluia Blessed
Deiss, Lucien	Alleluia, Alleluia Your Wor
Deiss, Lucien	Alleluia, Alleluia, Allelui
Deiss, Lucien	Amen
Deiss, Lucien	As We Wait The Lord (Antiph
Deiss, Lucien	Awake And Live, O You Who S
Deiss, Lucien	Behold Among Men
Deiss, Lucien	Biblical Litany To Our Lady
Deiss, Lucien	Blessed Be God
Deiss, Lucien	Blessed Be Our Lord The God
Deiss, Lucien	Canticle Of The Three Child
Deiss, Lucien	Christ Has Died (Icet)
Deiss, Lucien	Christ Who Has Risen From T
Deiss, Lucien	Citizens Of Heaven
Deiss, Lucien	Come And Pray In Us,Spirit
Deiss, Lucien	Come Jesus Christ
Deiss, Lucien	Come O Lord, O Come For Our
Deiss, Lucien	Emmanuel Come Save Your Peo
Deiss, Lucien	Eucharistic Acclamation (Si
Deiss, Lucien	Eucharistic Acclamation (So
Deiss, Lucien	From The Depths Do I Cry
Deiss, Lucien	General Intercessions
Deiss, Lucien	Give Praise To The Lord
Deiss, Lucien	Give The Bread Of Life
Deiss, Lucien	Glorify The Lord With Me
Deiss, Lucien	Glory And Praise To You
Deiss, Lucien	Glory And Praise To You Ete

Deiss, Lucien	Glory To God (Icet)
Deiss, Lucien	Glory To God In Highest
Deiss, Lucien	Glory To God(Icet)(Holy Spi
Deiss, Lucien	God Is Love
Deiss, Lucien	God Reigns
Deiss, Lucien	Grant To Us (A Heart Renewe
Deiss, Lucien	Great Amen (Icet)
Deiss, Lucien	Hail Holy Queen
Deiss, Lucien	Have Mercy O Lord, Have Mer
Deiss, Lucien	Have Mercy On Us, O Lord
Deiss, Lucien	Heavens Drop Dew From Above
Deiss, Lucien	Holy Mother Of Our Redeemer
Deiss, Lucien	Holy, Holy, Holy
Deiss, Lucien	Honor Praise And Glory
Deiss, Lucien	Hosanna, Hosanna, Hosanna
Deiss, Lucien	I Saw The New Jerusalem
Deiss, Lucien	I Want To Sing
Deiss, Lucien	If You Bring Your Gift To T
Deiss, Lucien	If You Keep Our Transgressi
Deiss, Lucien	In The Peace Of Christ
Deiss, Lucien	Intercession Prayer For Cat
Deiss, Lucien	Into Your Hands
Deiss, Lucien	Jesus Christ The Faithful W
Deiss, Lucien	Joy Giving Light
Deiss, Lucien	Joy To Heaven
Deiss, Lucien	Joy To You O Virgin Mary
Deiss, Lucien	Keep In Mind
Deiss, Lucien	Kyrie Eleison
Deiss, Lucien	Lamb Of God (Icet)
Deiss, Lucien	Let Me Sing Of Your Law, O
Deiss, Lucien	Let Us Bless The Lord
Deiss, Lucien	Like Olive Branches
Deiss, Lucien	Liturgy Of The Word (Icet)
Deiss, Lucien	Long Live The Lord
Deiss, Lucien	Longing For God
Deiss, Lucien	Lord Fill My Mouth With Wor
Deiss, Lucien	Lord Have Mercy (Threefold)
Deiss, Lucien	Lord Have Mercy (Twofold)
Deiss, Lucien	Lord In Your Tenderness
Deiss, Lucien	Maranatha
Deiss, Lucien	May The God Of Israel
Deiss, Lucien	Mother Of Holy Hope
Deiss, Lucien	My Shepherd Is The Lord
Deiss, Lucien	My Soul Is Longing For Your
Deiss, Lucien	My Soul Is Waiting For The
Deiss, Lucien	O Antiphons
Deiss, Lucien	O Ever Radiant Virgin
Deiss, Lucien	O God My God From The Dawn
Deiss, Lucien	O Lord Be Not Mindful
Deiss, Lucien	O Lord Give Us Your Love
Deiss, Lucien	O Lord Have Mercy
Deiss, Lucien	O Lord Hear Us Pray
Deiss, Lucien	O My God It Is You I Seek
Deiss, Lucien	On The Day When The Radiant
Deiss, Lucien	Our Father
Deiss, Lucien	Our Father (Icet)
Deiss, Lucien	Pasch Of The New Law
Deiss, Lucien	Praise The Lord
Deiss, Lucien	Praise To You Now And Everm
Deiss, Lucien	Prayer Of The Faithful (Res
Deiss, Lucien	Priestly People
Deiss, Lucien	Psalm 128 (127)
Deiss, Lucien	Psalm 131 (130) My Soul Lon
Deiss, Lucien	Queen Of Heaven (Regina Cae
Deiss, Lucien	Rejoice Always In The Lord
Deiss, Lucien	Rejoice O Virgin Mary
Deiss, Lucien	Remember Us O Lord
Deiss, Lucien	Salvation, Glory & Power
Deiss, Lucien	Send Forth Your Spirit, O L
Deiss, Lucien	Sing To The Lord
Deiss, Lucien	Song Of Joy
Deiss, Lucien	Splendor Of Creation
Deiss, Lucien	The Joy Of The Lord
Deiss, Lucien	The Spirit Of God Rests Upo
Deiss, Lucien	There Is One Lord
Deiss, Lucien	This Is The Day The Lord Ha
Deiss, Lucien	To Christ, Glory & Power
Deiss, Lucien	To You Do I Raise My Eyes
Deiss, Lucien	Unto Us A Child Is Born
Deiss, Lucien	Upon My Lips
Deiss, Lucien	We Give You Thanks
Deiss, Lucien	We Give You Thanks, We Wors
Deiss, Lucien	We Greet You (Litany Of Bvm
Deiss, Lucien	We Place Our Selves (Sub Tu
Deiss, Lucien	We Pray To You, O Lord 1
Deiss, Lucien	Where Charity And Love Abid
Deiss, Lucien	Where Two Or Three Are Gath
Deiss, Lucien	Wisdom Has Built Herself A
Deiss, Lucien	With A Joyful Heart
Deiss, Lucien	With Joyful Lips, O Lord
Deiss, Lucien	With Words Of Praise
Deiss, Lucien	Within Your Splendor
Deiss, Lucien	Without Seeing You, We Love
Deiss, Lucien	Wonderful And Great
Deiss, Lucien	Yes I Shall Arise
Deiss, Lucien	You Alone Are Holy
Deiss, Lucien	You Are All Beautiful
Deiss, Lucien	You Are The Honor
Deiss, Lucien	You Broke The Reign Of Deat
Deiss, Lucien	You I Carry, O Lord (Ancien
Deiss, Lucien	You, Lord Are The Way
Deiss, Lucien	Your Holy Death
Deiss, Lucien	Your Words, O Lord
Deiss, Lucien	Zion Sing
Dejong	O Sacrament Most Holy (Musi
Dejong (Music)	Glorious Mysteries
Del Castillo, Fructos	Monstra Te Esse Matrem
Demone, Richard	O Come, O Come Emmanuel
Demone, Richard	Wondrous Love
Denton	Christ The Lord Is Risen To
Denton	Come, Ye Faithful
Denton	First Noel, The (C)
Denton	God In A Star
Denton	He Lifted Me
Denton	Hymn Of Thanksgiving
Denton	I Believe In God
Denton	I Saw The Cross Of Jesus
Denton	I Want To Be Ready
Denton	Jesus Is Born The King!
Denton	Jesus Saves
Denton	Joy To All People!
Denton	King Forever
Denton	Let All Mortal Flesh Keep S
Denton	Long Time Ago
Denton	O Brother Man!
Denton	O Christ, Why Should A Mang
Denton	O For A Thousand Tongues To
Denton	O God, Thou Hast The Dawn O
Denton	Peace
Denton	Praise Our God
Denton	Song Of The Angels
Denton	What Wondrous Love Is This
Denton	When Morning Gilds The Skie
Denton	When There's Love At Home
Denton, James	Daughter Of Zion
Denton, James	Jesus Saves
Denton, James	We Wait For The Coming Of J
Denton, James	When God Is The Honored Gue
Denver/Taylor/Kniss	Late Winter, Early Spring
Denver, John	Follow Me
Denver, John	For Baby (For Bobbie)
Denver, John	Rhymes And Reasons
Denver, John	Sweet Surrender
Deodatus Dutton, Jr.	Let The Bright Seraphim
Dering, Richard	Above Him Stood The Seraphi
Dering, Richard	And The King Was Moved
Derosa, Judy	Our Father
Des Pres, Josquin	Behold You Are Charming
Des Pres, Josquin	Hail, True Body Born Of Mar
Des Pres, Josquin	Kyrie From Missa Super L'ho
Des Pres, J.(D1521)	Missa Pange Lingua
Des Pres, Josquin	Missa Super L'homme Arme Ky
Des Pres, Josquin	O Domine Jesu Christe
Des Pres, Josquin	Ave Vera Virginitas
Des Pres, Josquin	Ave Verum (Hail, True Body)
Des Pres, Josquin	Four Motets
Des Pres, Josquin	Missa Da Pacem
Des Pres, Josquin	Missa De Beata Virgine
Des Pres, Josquin	Three Motets
Des Pres, Josquin	Three Psalms
Des Pres, Josquin	Thou Refuge Of The Destitut
Dethier	Sixteen Choral Responses
Dett, R N	As By The Streams Of Babylo
Dett, R N	As Children Walk Ye In God'
Dett, R N	Don't You Weep No More, Mar
Dett, R N	Listen To The Lambs
Dett, R N	O Holy Lord
Dett, R N	Wasn't That A Mighty Day
Detweiler, Janice	Love One Another
Devictoria, Tomas L.	Jesu, The Very Thought Of T
Devictoria, Tomas L.	O Sacrum Convivium (Me)
Devictoria, Tomas L.	Of The Glorious Body Tellin
Dexter	Go, Prayer Of Mine
Dexter	So Quietly He Came
Di Lasso, Orlano	Adoramus Te, Christe (A Cap
Diamond, David	Chorale
Diamond, David	Hebrew Melodies
Diamond, David	My Spirit Will Not Haunt Th
Diamond, David	Prayer
Diamond, David	Prayer For Peace
Diamond, David	The Shepherd Boy Sings In T
Diamond, David	Two Anthems
Dickey, Mark	Sing Alleluia Forth
Dickin,M/Kraehenbuehl	O Lord Of Life (Who Wills N
Diederich, Kelly W	Can It Be?
Diemente, E	Music For Palm Sunday
Diemente, Edward	Three Motets
Diemer	Babe Is Born, A
Diemer	I Will Give Thanks
Diemer Emma Lou	Awake, My Glory
Diercks	Six Sacred Compositions For
Diercks, John	And Thou Shalt Love
Diercks, John	Clap Your Hands
Diercks, John H.	He Is Risen, Alleluia (Opt
Diercks, John H.	Lord, I Cry Unto Thee
Diercks, John H.	Why Do The Nations Rage?
Dieterich, Milton	Fear God & Give Glory To Hi
Dietterich, Philip	Carol Of The Advent
Dietterich, Philip	Come Down, O Love Divine
Dietterich, Philip	Holy God Of Sabboth (A Cap)
Dietterich, Philip	Immortal Love
Dietterich, Philip	Now Will I Praise The Lord
Dietterich, Philip	O Love That Triumphs Over L
Dietterich, Philip	Sanctus, The
Dietterich, Philip	Wilt Not Thou Turn Again?
Diggle, R	Let All Mortal Flesh Keep S
Dilasso, O. Arr Avalos	Adoramus Te
Dilasso,O./Tortolano	Sing With Fullness To God
Distler	O Christ, Our Hope
Doane/Heacock	To The Work
Doane/Mayfield	Rescue The Perishing
Doane/Rasley	More Love To Thee
Dodd Jimmie	He Was There
Dodd/Johnson	New Day
Donati, Ignazio	Alleluia Haec Dies
Donati, Ignazio	Non Vos Relinquos Orphanos
Donato, Anthony	How Excellent Is Thy Name
Donato, Anthony	The Last Supper
Dooner, A	Music For Weddings
Dooner, A	Three Wedding Motets
Dosogne, R	Let All On Earth
Dougherty, Celius	The First Christmas
Dougherty, Mary/S/A	Hope Of Our Days
Douglas (Arr)	This Is The Birthday Of The
Douglas-Near	He Who Would Valiant Be
Douglas/Finnish Tune	In Heavenly Love Abiding
Dowdy	Easter Song
Dowland, John	Seven Hymn Tunes (In 2 Vols
Drayton, Paul	Easter Day (A Cap)
Drayton, Paul	Jesu Dulcis Memoria (E & La
Drayton, Paul	Lord, Behold Us (E)
Drayton, Paul	My Soul, There Is A Country
Drayton, Paul	The Spacious Firmament (Md)
Dreisoerner, Charles	Mother Of God (W/Org)
Dresden	Great Amen
Drese/Rasley	Jesus, Still Lead On
Dressler, Gallus	Five Motets
Dressler, John	First, The Last, The
Dressler, John	Spirit Of Life (Violin)
Dressler, John	Three Junior Choir Anthems
Dressler, L R	Eight Responses
Dretke, Leora	Sing Allelujah Christ Is Bo
Dreves,Veronica&Ellis	Song Of Blessing
Droste, Doreen	Before The Lord Jehovah's T
Droste, Doreen	Come, Holy Ghost, Creator B
Drury,M/Kraehenbuehl	Become To Us The Living Bre
Dubois	Christ, We Adore Thee
Dubois, T	Adoramus Te Christe
Dubois,Theodore(D1924)	Seven Last Words
Ducote, Darryl	All Our Joy
Ducote, Darryl	In His Love
Ducote, Darryl	In My Name
Ducote, Darryl	Is There Any Word
Ducote, Darryl	Look Beyond
Ducote, Darryl	Shout Out Your Joy
Ducote, Darryl	Sing Out His Goodness
Ducote, Darryl	Turn Your Eyes
Ducote, Darryl	When The Morning Comes
Ducote, Darryl	Without Clouds
Ducote, Darryl	Yes, Lord
Ducote, Daryll	Beatitudes
Ducote, Daryll	Song Of Thanksgiving
Ducote, Daryll-Balhoff	Beginning Today
Ducote, Daryll, Balhof	Rainbow
Dufay, Guillaume	Missa Super L'homme Arme Ky
Dufay, Guillaume	Sacred Hymns
Dufford, Bob, S. J.	Be Not Afraid
Dufford, Bob, S. J.	Doxology
Dufford, Bob, S. J.	Every Valley
Dufford, Bob, S. J.	Father, Mercy
Dufford, Bob, S. J.	Holy
Dufford, Bob, S. J.	Let Heaven Rejoice
Dufford, Bob, S. J.	My People
Dufford, Bob, S. J.	My Son Has Gone Away
Dufford, Bob, S. J.	Play Before The Lord
Dufford, Bob, S. J.	Return To Your People, O Lo
Dufford, Bob, S. J.	Sing Of Him
Dufford, Bob, S. J.	Worthy Is The Lamb
Duke, John	O Sing Unto The Lord A New
Dullea, Dennis C., Jr.	Praise The Lord Who Is Pres
Dumin, Frank	Irish Blessing
Dumin, Frank	Prayer Of St. Francis
Duncan, Leo	Safe In His Precious Arms
Duncan, Leo	You Ought To Walk Right
Duncan, Leo L.	By Faith We Can Know
Duncan, Leo L.	Count Your Blessings
Dunkin, Timothy L.	A Song Of Joy
Dunkin, Timothy L.	Don't You Look All Around
Dunlap, Fern Glasgow	My Church Is A Holy Place
Dunlap, Fern Glasgow	Wedding Prayer
Dunlop/Carmichael	My Sins Are Blotted Out, I
Dunlop/Decou	All Day Long My Heart Keeps
Dunlop/Decou	Amen Hallelujah
Dunlop/Decou	Christ Is Risen From The De
Dunlop/Decou	Contentment In His Love
Dunlop/Ferrin	My Sins Are Blotted Out, I
Dunlop/Johnson	Lord, I Want A Diadem
Dunlop/Meckelson	He Was Wounded For Our Tran
Dunlop, M.	Merrill Dunlop Favorites (N
Dunlop, M.	Merrill Dunlop Favorites No

COMPOSER INDEX

Dunlop, M.	Merrill Dunlop's New Gospel
Dunlop, Merrill	I Believe That Jesus Died F
Dunlop, Merrill	Ye Shall Know The Truth
Durante, F.(D1755)	Magnificat
Durante, Francesco	For Thy Great Mercy(Double
Durante, Francesco	Kyrie
Duro, John	The Church's One Foundation
Durocher	Easter Bells (Opt Group Lec
Durocher	I Look Up To Thee
Durocher	Ring Ye Joy Bells
Dvorak	Home And Mother
Dvorak, A	All My Heart Inflamed And B
Dvorak, A	Blessed Jesu
Dvorak, A	I Will Sing Thee Songs Of G
Dvorak, A.	Mass In D, Opus 86
Dvorak, A.	Requiem
Dvorak, A..	Te Deum
Dvorak, A. (D1904)	Stabat Mater
Dvorak, Anton	Heart Divine
Dyer	Old Fashioned Sermons
Dyer, Max	I Will Sing, I Will Sing
Dykes	Hosanna We Sing
Dykes, John B.	Ecumenical Hymn To God Our
Dykes, John B.	Eternal Father (4-Part Arr.
Dykes, John B.	Holy, Holy, Holy (4-Part Ar
Dykes, John B.	Hymn For The Sick (4-Part A
Dylan, Bob	Blowin' In The Wind
Ebeling (Kirk Arr)	Christ Is Born
Ebeling-Beckhard	All My Heart This Night
Eberlin, Ernst	God Our Father
Eberlin, Ernst	Grief Is In My Heart
Eberlin, Ernst	O Savior Our Refuge
Eberlin, Ernst	Trust In The Lord
Eccard, J	Christ Is Arisen
Eccard, J	O Lamb Of God Most Holy
Eccard, J	Over The Hills Maria Went
Eccard, J.	Over The Hills (Uber's Gebi
Eccard, Johann	Mary's Salutation (E & Germ
Eccard, Johannes	O Lamb Of God
Eckler, Greg	Decision
Eckler, Greg	Get Yourself Together
Eckler, Greg	God Be Magnified
Eckler, Greg	Make Up Your Mind
Eckler, Greg	Wonderful World
Eckler, Greg & Felex,J	I'm Going About My Father's
Eddins, Martha A.	Jesus Is A Wonderful Landlo
Eddins, Martha A.	That Glorious Day
Edmunds, John	O Death, Rock Me Asleep
Edwards	Christ Is The Rock
Edwards	Church In The Home
Edwards, Clara	Awake Arise
Edwards, Clara	Dedication
Edwards, Clara	I Will Lift Mine Eyes
Edwards, Clara	The Eastern Heavens Are All
Edwards, Clara	The Twenty-Seventh Psalm(Th
Edwards, Deanna	Catch A Little Sunshine
Edwards, Deanna	Folks Don't Kiss Old People
Edwards, Deanna	He Is Your Brother
Edwards, Deanna	I'll Hold You In My Arms
Edwards, Deanna	It's A Brand-New World
Edwards, Deanna	Peacebird
Edwards, Deanna	Put My Memory In Your Pocke
Edwards, Deanna	Right To Live
Edwards, Deanna	Take My Hand
Edwards, Deanna	Teach Me To Die
Edwin, Robert	Keep The Rumor Going (God I
Edwin, Robert	Twenty-Third Psalm
Effinger, C	By Springs Of Water
Effinger, C	Mary's Soliloquy (From The
Egoroff, A.	Children's Prayer
Ehret, Walter	Abide, O Dearest Jesus (Me)
Ehret, Walter	Alas! And Did My Savior Ble
Ehret, Walter	All Nature's Works His Prai
Ehret, Walter	Alleluia! Alleluia!
Ehret, Walter	Amen, Amen My Lord (Opt Rhy
Ehret, Walter	Angels From The Realms Of G
Ehret, Walter	Christ The Lord Is Risen To
Ehret, Walter	Christmas Comes Anew
Ehret, Walter	Gifts We Shall Bring
Ehret, Walter	Glory To God In The Highest
Ehret, Walter	Grant Us Peace
Ehret, Walter	Hear The Bells! See The Sta
Ehret, Walter	Holiday And Holy Day
Ehret, Walter	Holy, Holy, Holy (3pt Rhyth
Ehret, Walter	In Bethlehem Is Born A King
Ehret, Walter	O How Shall I Receive Thee
Ehret, Walter	O Thou In Whose Presence
Ehret, Walter	One Night So Long Ago
Ehret, Walter	Sing Up All Now Alleluia
Ehret, Walter	Sleep Well, Thou Lovely Hea
Ehret, Walter	Sweet Little Jesus Baby
Ehret, Walter	The Friendly Beasts (Arr)
Ehret, Walter	This Day Our Lord Is Born(P
Ehret, Walter	This Day We Welcome A Littl
Ehret, Walter	Twas In The Moon Of Wintert
Ehret, Walter	We Gather At Your Table, Lo
Ehret, Walter	Zion Said
Ehret, Walter (Arr)	A Virgin Pure And Fair (W/F
Ehret, Walter (Arr)	It Fell Upon A Winter's Day
Eilers (Adapted)	Still,Still,Still
Eilers, Joyce	Alleluia
Eilers, Joyce	Brighten My Soul With Sunsh
Eilers, Joyce	Joy To The World
Eilers, Joyce	My Lord
Eilers, Joyce	Silent Night
Eilers, Joyce E	Thy Will Be Done
Eimer	Emmanuel
Elbert, Edwin	Heart Of Christ
Eldridge, R.	As We Grow
Eldridge, R.	Brother, Watch The Light
Eldridge, R.	Eternity To Live Or Die
Eldridge, R.	Holy Spirit
Eldridge, R.	Nearer To Thee
Eldridge, R.	Six Sixty Six
Eldridge, R.	Testimony
Eldridge, R.	Thank You, Jesus, You're My
Elgar, E	Thine Is The Glory
Eliot	Alleluia! Alleluia!
Eliot	Early Spring, The
Eliot	Look Softly, Lord
Eliot	O Let Me Fly
Ellerton,J./Lee,John	Savior, Again To Your Dear
Elliot	God Rest Ye Merry, Gentleme
Elliot	Sun Shines In Splendor, The
Elliott	Christmas Alleluia
Elliott	Christmas Bells
Elliott	If Thou Wilt Take My Hand
Ellis	Shall I Crucify Him?
Ellis, Ron	According To Matthew
Ellis, Ron	Alleluia(A Maj)
Ellis, Ron	Alleluia(F Maj)
Ellis, Ron	Choices
Ellis, Ron	Clean Heart(Ps 51)
Ellis, Ron	Cry Out To God(Ps 66)
Ellis, Ron	Easter Song
Ellis, Ron	Exultet(Easter Proclamation
Ellis, Ron	Forever I Will Sing(Ps 89)
Ellis, Ron	Gentle Rains
Ellis, Ron	Harden Not Your Hearts(Ps 9
Ellis, Ron	His Peace We Share
Ellis, Ron	Hymn To Mary
Ellis, Ron	Hymn To The Father
Ellis, Ron	I Found My Life In Jesus
Ellis, Ron	Jesus Heal Us
Ellis, Ron	Jesus Is Our Prayer
Ellis, Ron	Jesus Remember Me
Ellis, Ron	Lenten Invocation
Ellis, Ron	Let My Tongue Be Silenced(P
Ellis, Ron	Life Is You
Ellis, Ron	Light Has Come
Ellis, Ron	Listen To The Word
Ellis, Ron	Lord Every Nation(Ps 72)
Ellis, Ron	My Soul Is Thirsting (Ps 63
Ellis, Ron	Our Father(E Maj)
Ellis, Ron	Simple Christmas Song
Ellis, Ron	Song Of Ruth
Ellis, Ron	Song Of Watchfulness
Ellis, Ron	Taste And See (Ps 34)
Ellis, Ron	With All My Heart
Ellis,Ron & Ellis,Rob	In The Presence (Ps 116)
Ellis,Ron&Ellis, Rob	Lenten Invocation
Ellis,Ron&Lynch,M.	Covenant Prayer
Ellis,Ron&Lynch,M.	Lord Send Out Your Spirit(P
Ellis,Ron&Lynch,M.	You Knew Me Before I Was Bo
Ellsworth Eugene	Our Church Proclaims God's
Ellsworth, A. Eugene	A Family Benediction
Ellsworth, A. Eugene	God Be In My Head (A Cap)
Ellsworth, Eugene	O Be Joyful
Ellsworth, Eugene	Show Me The Way To Thee
Elmore	Hail, Alpha And Omega
Elmore	Living Christ, The
Elrich, Dwight (Arr.)	How Sweet The Name Of Jesus
Elrich, Dwight (Arr.)	Joy
Elrich, Dwight (Arr.)	Nicodemus (P.D.)
Elrich, Dwight (Arr.)	Praise The Savior (P.D.)
Elrich, Dwight (Arr.)	Tis So Sweet To Trust In Je
Elrich, Dwight(Arr.)	He Lifted Me (P.D.)
Elrich, Dwight(Arr.)	More Love To Thee (P.D.)
Elrich,Dweight	Yesterday
Elvey	Arise, Shine, For Thy Light
Elvey/Wyrtzen	Crown Him With Many Crowns
Elvey, George J.	Crown Him The King Of Kings
Elvey, Stephen	We Wait For Thy Loving Kind
Emerson	Christ Is Risen
Emerson	Lift Up Your Heads
Emery	What Can I Give Him?
Emery, Dorothy R.	So Dark The Night
Emery, John	Make We Joy Now In This Fea
Emig	Child Of God
Emig	Children's Hosanna, The
Emig	Christians, Sing Joyfully
Emig	Come To Bethlehem
Emig	God Is Great
Emig	Hosanna To The King
Emig	King Of Glory, The
Emig	Let Us Sing To The Lord
Emig	My Father Walks Beside Me
Emig	Shepherds' Carol, The
Emig	Song Of Bethlehem, A
Emig	Walk With Me
Eneberg/Johnson	Love For Life
Eneberg, Gale	It's A Young World
Eneberg, Gale	Peace In Your World
Engel, J.	By The Shores Of The Jordan
Engler, Eugene	Alleluia! Let The Holy Anth
Engler, Eugene	Come, Christians, Join To S
Engler, Eugene	Rejoice & Sing For Joy
Engler, Eugene	Rejoice, You Pure In Heart
Engler, Eugene	The King Of Love My Shepher
Englert, Eugene	Acclamations (Icet)
Englert, Eugene	Christ Has Died (Icet)
Englert, Eugene	Christ Is Made The Sure Fou
Englert, Eugene	Come, Ye That Serve (Me)
Englert, Eugene	Dying You Destroyed Our Dea
Englert, Eugene	He Is Risen, Alleluia (W/Or
Englert, Eugene	Lord By Your Cross (Icet)
Englert, Eugene	Lord, From Your Cross, Look
Englert, Eugene	Lord's Prayer For Mass (Ice
Englert, Eugene	Music Filled The Sky (E)
Englert, Eugene	O Faithful Cross (A Cap) (E
Englert, Eugene	Praise The King Of Glory
Englert, Eugene	Sing To Him Of Praise Etern
Englert, Eugene	When We Eat This Bread (Ice
English	Jacob's Vision
English	What Child Is This?
English, Tina	Quiet Time (W/Piano)
Enlow, H.	Song Of Life
Enlow, H.	The Morning Son
Enlow, H./Hires, B.	Forevermore
Ensrud	Introits And Graduals (Var
Epp, Henry H.	Gesangbuch Der Mennoniten
Erbach-Holdeman	Sing Aloud To God
Erhardt	Lord Is My Shepherd, The
Erickson/Gotrich	Wonderful Blessing, A
Esquivel, Juan De	O Quam Gloriosum
Esquivel, Juan De	O Vos Omnes
Esserwein, Philip	Abba, Father
Eulalia, Sister	Ave Maria
Evangeline/Sadler	When God Makes The Morning
Evans	Beatitudes, The
Evans	Twenty-One Service Response
Evelyn F Tarner	Walk With The Years
Evenson	Thine Forever
Evers, J. Clifford	Accept, O Father In Thy Lov
Exner, Max	I Have A Dream
Exner, Max	Where Shall I Find The Chri
F.E.L.	Holy, Holy, Holy (Hymn Tune
Faber-Mathews	Oh Come And Mourn With Us
Faber, Frederick	Faith Of Our Fathers
Fabing, Bob	A Brand New Promised Land
Fabing, Bob	A Canticle Of Care
Fabing, Bob	A Gift
Fabing, Bob	A Treasure In A Field
Fabing, Bob	Be Like The Sun
Fabing, Bob	Burst My Dreams
Fabing, Bob	Chariots Of Clouds
Fabing, Bob	Come And Sing
Fabing, Bob	Everlasting God
Fabing, Bob	I Thank My God
Fabing, Bob	In Him Who Strengthens Me
Fabing, Bob	Mary's Song
Fabing, Bob	Open Like The Sky
Fabing, Bob	Praise And Glory Alleluia
Fabing, Bob	Thank The Lord
Fabing, Bob	The Business Of A Friend
Fabing, Bob	The Contemplation Song
Fabing, Bob	The Prayer To St. Ignatius
Fabing, Bob	To Speak His Word
Fabing, Bob	We're Goin' Home
Fabing, Bob	Where Do You Want Me
Fabing, Bob	Will You Believe Me, Thomas
Fabing, Bob	You Come As He
Farjeon, E/Sowerby	Now Every Child That Dwells
Farmer, Floyd	All Ye That Pass By
Farmer, H	Gloria(Mass In B Flat)
Farmer, H	Lord For Thy Tender Mercies
Farmer, John	The Lord's Prayer (Bcp) Ada
Farner	Dear Little Jesus (Unison)
Farquharson	Father Of The Human Family
Farquharson	Father, Bless Our Homes (Hy
Farra, Mimi A.	Allelu
Farra, Mimi A.	Alleluia, Sons Of God Arise
Farra, Mimi A.	Flowing Free (Love Is Flowi
Farra, Mimi A.	Glory (Sing To The Lord)
Farra, Mimi A.	Hallelujah, Jesus Is Lord!
Farra, Mimi A.	Have You Ever Thought (Abou
Farra, Mimi A.	Holy, Holy, Holy (Lord God
Farra, Mimi A.	I Will Arise (So Early)
Farra, Mimi A.	If I Had All The World's Mo
Farra, Mimi A.	Let Us Break Bread Together
Farra, Mimi A.	Lord Have Mercy (Upon Me)
Farra, Mimi A.	Lord You Have Blessed Us
Farra, Mimi A.	My Lord Said (Come With Me)
Farra, Mimi A.	Not A Sparrow Falleth (Mat
Farra, Mimi A.	O Lamb Of God
Farra, Mimi A.	O Mary Don't You Weep
Farra, Mimi A.	Peace
Farra, Mimi A.	Prince Of Peace (Born In Be
Farra, Mimi A.	Pure Light (Of The Son Of G
Farra, Mimi A.	The Spirit Of The Lord (Hat

Farra, Mimi A.	Trust In The Lord
Farra, Mimi A.	Trust In The Lord (Prov 3)
Farra, Mimi A.	Ye Were Sometimes Darkness
Farrant, John	Te Deum And Jubilate (Md)
Farrant, Richard	Hide Not Thou Thy Face
Farrant, Richard	Hide Not Thy Face
Farrant, Richard	Magnificat And Nunc Dimitti
Farrant,R./Ed Lee	O Sacred Feast (Eng Only)
Farrell, Melvin	Christians Sound The Name T
Farrell, Melvin	Crown Him With Many Crowns
Farrell, Melvin	Draw Near O Lord
Farrell, Melvin	Hail Holy Queen Enthroned
Farrell, Melvin	Heart Of Christ
Farrell, Melvin	Holy Mary, Now We Crown You
Farrell, Melvin	Humbly Let Us Voice Our Hom
Farrell, Melvin	Humbly We Adore Thee
Farrell, Melvin	Let All The Earth
Farrell, Melvin	Let All The Earth Rejoice &
Farrell, Melvin	Lo, Our Savior King Is Here
Farrell, Melvin	Lord Of Nations Bless In Ki
Farrell, Melvin	Merciful Savior Hear Our Hu
Farrell, Melvin	Now In Joy We Sing Thy Prai
Farrell, Melvin	O Christians Let Us Join In
Farrell, Melvin	O God Upholding These U.S.
Farrell, Melvin	O Heart Of Christ
Farrell, Melvin	O Holy Spirit Come To Us
Farrell, Melvin	O Lord Of Light
Farrell, Melvin	O Queen Of Heaven
Farrell, Melvin	O Sacred Head Surrounded
Farrell, Melvin	Praise We Christ's Immortal
Farrell, Melvin	To God Almighty We Confess
Farrell, Melvin	Virgin Full Of Grace
Farrell, Melvin	Wake Awake The Night Is Dyi
Farrell, Melvin	You Heavens Open From Above
Farrell, Melvin/Burns	Father, God Of All Things L
Farrell, Melvin/Burns	Let Us Praise Our Noble God
Farrell, Melvin/Burns	Praise The Grandeur Of Our
Farrell, Melvin/Goeman	Father While This Bread Is
Farrell, Melvin/Picca	O God Who Called The Hebrew
Farrell,M. &Van Hulse,	Behold O God This Lowly Bre
Farrer, Carl	Adoration
Farrer, Carl	Holy Hands
Farrer, Carl	Touch Me Savior
Farrer,C And Miller,C.	He'll Make My Dream Come Tr
Fasig, Bill	Faith, Tears And Resurrecti
Fast, Willard S	Alleluia To The Lord Of Bei
Fast, Willard S	To Mercy, Pity, Peace And L
Faure	Tantum Ergo
Faure, G	My Friend Of Calvary
Faure, Gabriel	Cantique De Jean Racine
Faure, Gabriel	En Priere
Faure, Gabriel	In Prayer
Faure, Gabriel	O Redeemer Divine
Faure, Gabriel	Tantum Ergo, Opus 65, No. 2
Faure, Gabriel(D1924)	Requiem
Faure, J B	The Psalms
Faure,G	Palms, The
Fenstermaker, John	What Child Is This?
Ferguson	All Things Bright And Beaut
Ferguson	At The Feet Of Jesus
Ferguson	Blessing For Easter Morning
Ferguson	Christmas Exultation, A
Ferguson	Deep In The Boding Night
Ferguson	Eternal Hope
Ferguson	Hammering
Ferguson	Hosanna, Loud Hosanna
Ferguson	Joshua Fit The Battle Of Je
Ferguson	Mother's Day Carol
Ferguson	Sing Brothers, Sing
Ferguson	Twenty Responses (Elizabeth
Ferris, W	A Festival Flourish
Ferris, W	Behold, Thus Is The Man Ble
Ferris, W	Hail, Noble Flesh
Ferris, W	Praise The Lord, O My Soul
Ferris, W	Serene Alleluias
Ferris, William	Drop Down Ye Heavens
Ferris, William	Enlighten Mine Eyes
Ferris, William	In Thee O Lord Have I Put M
Ferris, William	O Taste And See (From 5 Ant
Ferris, William	The Lord Said To Me (Icet)
Ferris, William	The Sorrows Of My Heart Are
Fetler, Paul	A Contemporary Psalm
Fetler, Paul	A Great And Mighty Wonder
Fetler, Paul	Dream Of Shalom
Fetler, Paul	Easter Fanfare: Christ The
Fetler, Paul	Hosanna
Fetler, Paul	Jubilate Deo (W/Brass)
Fetler, Paul	Make A Joyful Noise
Fetler, Paul	Noel (Ox And Donkey's Carol
Fetler, Paul	O All Ye Works Of The Lord
Fetler, Paul	Prayer For Peace
Fetler, Paul	Sing Unto God
Fetler, Paul	The Words From The Cross
Fillmore/Johnson	I Am Resolved
Fillmore/Wilson	Beautiful Garden Of Prayer,
Finch, John D.	If You Know Christ
Finck, Heinrich	Missa In Summis
Finck,Heinrich(D1527)	Eight Hymns
Finley, Ken	Ask Not What I Can Do
Finley, Ken	God Is Much Fairer
Finley, Ken	O My Lord
Finley, Ken	Why Did Jesus Come To Earth
Finley, Ken	Why Have You Forsaken Me
Fischer	Jesus Will Come
Fischer/Johnson	I Love To Tell The Story
Fischer, C A	The Song Of Mary
Fischer, Irwin	Come Unto Me
Fischer, Irwin	If Ye Love Me, Keep My Comm
Fischer, Irwin	Increase
Fischer, Irwin	When From The Lips Of Truth
Fischer, John	Alleluia (Easter Day)
Fischer, John	Born To Die
Fischer, John	Death In The City
Fischer, John	Death Is Swallowed Up
Fischer, John	Got To Shout About It
Fischer, John	Hard Feeling To Explain
Fischer, John	Jesus In Me
Fischer, John	Jesus Is My Song
Fischer, John	Jesus My Lord
Fischer, John	Light
Fischer, John	Look All Around
Fischer, John	No Vacancy
Fischer, John	Open Up
Fischer, John	Salvation Song
Fischer, John	Sons Of Cain
Fischer, John	The Cold Cathedral
Fischer, John	The Lord's Prayer
Fischer, John	The Road Of Life
Fischer, John	The Word
Fischer, John	Trust And Obey
Fischer, John	Way Of All Flesh
Fiscus	Do You Have An Empty Heart?
Fiscus, Donna	Exciting Savior
Fishel, Donald	Alleluia No. 1
Fishel, Donald	Sing To The Lord
Fishel, Donald	The Light Of Christ
Fiske, Milton	Christ The Lord Is Risen To
Fiske, Milton	Golden Slumbers Carol
Fiske, Milton	Songs Of Praise The Angels
Fissinger, Edwin	Three Sacred Anthems (Ps 8,
Fissinger, Edwin (Arr)	Tomorrow Shall Be My Dancin
Fissinger, Edwin (Arr)	Witness (Md) Spiritual
Fitch, Donald	Glory To God (Choir Alone)
Fitzgerald, Michael	How Good, How Delightful It
Fitzgerald, Michael	Israel, Rely On Yahweh
Fitzgerald, Michael	When The Spirit Moves You
Fitzgerald, Michael &	Hymn Of The Universe
Fitzgerald,M/Farra,M.	As A Doe (Ps 42)
Fitzgerald,Michael	Hymn For A Prayer Meeting
Fitzpatrick, Dennis	A Child Is Born To Us
Fitzpatrick, Dennis	A Child, O Virgin, You Bore
Fitzpatrick, Dennis	A Great Sign Appeared In He
Fitzpatrick, Dennis	A Light Shall Shine Upon Us
Fitzpatrick, Dennis	A New Commandment I Give Yo
Fitzpatrick, Dennis	Above My Adversaries
Fitzpatrick, Dennis	Accept These Gifts, O Lord
Fitzpatrick, Dennis	Agnus Dei (Sung Mass No. 2)
Fitzpatrick, Dennis	All Glorious Is The King's
Fitzpatrick, Dennis	All Glory, Praise, And Hono
Fitzpatrick, Dennis	All Join Together
Fitzpatrick, Dennis	All Kings Shall Pay Him Hom
Fitzpatrick, Dennis	All Marveled At The Words
Fitzpatrick, Dennis	All Men Shall See The Salva
Fitzpatrick, Dennis	All My Enemies Shall Fall B
Fitzpatrick, Dennis	All Praise To The Lord Our
Fitzpatrick, Dennis	All Praise To You, Lord
Fitzpatrick, Dennis	All The Ends Of The Earth
Fitzpatrick, Dennis	All The Nations Shall Come
Fitzpatrick, Dennis	All Things Depend On You, O
Fitzpatrick, Dennis	All Were Saved By This Wate
Fitzpatrick, Dennis	All You Angels, Bless The L
Fitzpatrick, Dennis	All You Who Thirst
Fitzpatrick, Dennis	Alleluia, Alleluia (Tone Sp
Fitzpatrick, Dennis	Alleluia, Alleluia, Allelui
Fitzpatrick, Dennis	Amen, I Say To You
Fitzpatrick, Dennis	An Angel Offered Incense
Fitzpatrick, Dennis	Announce His Salvation Day
Fitzpatrick, Dennis	Arise, O Lord, And Defend M
Fitzpatrick, Dennis	Arise,O Lord, And Help Us
Fitzpatrick, Dennis	Ask And It Shall Be Given Y
Fitzpatrick, Dennis	At The Name Of Jesus
Fitzpatrick, Dennis	Awake, O My Soul
Fitzpatrick, Dennis	Baptized Into Union With Hi
Fitzpatrick, Dennis	Be Glad And Rejoice
Fitzpatrick, Dennis	Be Of One Mind
Fitzpatrick, Dennis	Be Strong And Do Not Fear
Fitzpatrick, Dennis	Because Of Your Kindness
Fitzpatrick, Dennis	Because You Were Good
Fitzpatrick, Dennis	Behold Him, The Name Of Who
Fitzpatrick, Dennis	Behold How Good And How Ple
Fitzpatrick, Dennis	Behold The Handmaid Of The
Fitzpatrick, Dennis	Behold The High Priest
Fitzpatrick, Dennis	Behold The Priest Of The Lo
Fitzpatrick, Dennis	Behold, The Bridegroom Come
Fitzpatrick, Dennis	Behold, The Lord Shall Come
Fitzpatrick, Dennis	Behold, The Lord, The Ruler
Fitzpatrick, Dennis	Bless The Lord, Bless The L
Fitzpatrick, Dennis	Bless The Lord, O My Soul
Fitzpatrick, Dennis	Bless This House, O Lord
Fitzpatrick, Dennis	Blessed Are They Who Hear
Fitzpatrick, Dennis	Blessed Are Those Servants
Fitzpatrick, Dennis	Blessed Are You Among Women
Fitzpatrick, Dennis	Blessed Be God; He Gives Po
Fitzpatrick, Dennis	Blessed Be The Holy Trinity
Fitzpatrick, Dennis	Blessed Be The Lord, The Go
Fitzpatrick, Dennis	Blessed Be The Name Of The
Fitzpatrick, Dennis	Blessed Is She Who Has Beli
Fitzpatrick, Dennis	Blessed Is The Man Who Has
Fitzpatrick, Dennis	Blessed Is The Nation
Fitzpatrick, Dennis	Blessed Is The Woman Who Fe
Fitzpatrick, Dennis	Boldly Let Us Come With Con
Fitzpatrick, Dennis	Bring Forth Abundant Fruit
Fitzpatrick, Dennis	But I,When They Were Ill
Fitzpatrick, Dennis	By The Rivers Of Babylon
Fitzpatrick, Dennis	By The Wood Of The Cross
Fitzpatrick, Dennis	By This Shall All Men Know
Fitzpatrick, Dennis	By This We Died With Christ
Fitzpatrick, Dennis	By Your Blood You Redeemed
Fitzpatrick, Dennis	Cast Your Care Upon The Lor
Fitzpatrick, Dennis	Christ Has Risen (Choral)
Fitzpatrick, Dennis	Christ Rose From Death
Fitzpatrick, Dennis	Christ Will Appear Again
Fitzpatrick, Dennis	Christ, For Our Sake
Fitzpatrick, Dennis	Christ, Our Lamb
Fitzpatrick, Dennis	Come To Me, All You Who Lab
Fitzpatrick, Dennis	Come, Enter My Father's Hou
Fitzpatrick, Dennis	Come, Follow Me
Fitzpatrick, Dennis	Come, Let Us Sing To The Lo
Fitzpatrick, Dennis	Come, O Bride Of Christ
Fitzpatrick, Dennis	Come, O Come, Lord Jesus, C
Fitzpatrick, Dennis	Come, Redeemer Of Mankind
Fitzpatrick, Dennis	Crave, As Newborn Babes
Fitzpatrick, Dennis	Daniel Prayed To God
Fitzpatrick, Dennis	Day By Day I Will Sing Your
Fitzpatrick, Dennis	Death Shall No Longer Have
Fitzpatrick, Dennis	Defend My Cause, My God
Fitzpatrick, Dennis	Deliver Me, Lord, From Evil
Fitzpatrick, Dennis	Dies Irae, Dies Illa
Fitzpatrick, Dennis	Do Not Be Afraid Of Those
Fitzpatrick, Dennis	Do Not Be Anxious
Fitzpatrick, Dennis	Do Not Forsake Me, O Lord
Fitzpatrick, Dennis	Do Not Give Me Up, O Lord
Fitzpatrick, Dennis	Do This In Remembrance Of M
Fitzpatrick, Dennis	Doxology To The Lord's Pray
Fitzpatrick, Dennis	Elegerunt
Fitzpatrick, Dennis	Even Though I Am Tormented
Fitzpatrick, Dennis	Exult, You Just, In The Lor
Fitzpatrick, Dennis	Faithful Cross
Fitzpatrick, Dennis	Father, If This Cup
Fitzpatrick, Dennis	Father, If This Cup (Choral
Fitzpatrick, Dennis	Father, Keep Them Holy
Fitzpatrick, Dennis	Father, May They Be One
Fitzpatrick, Dennis	Father, May We Be One In Ch
Fitzpatrick, Dennis	Fear Not; The Lord Will Pro
Fitzpatrick, Dennis	Feel The Place Of The Nails
Fitzpatrick, Dennis	For A Pearl Of Great Price
Fitzpatrick, Dennis	For A Reward
Fitzpatrick, Dennis	For His Mercy Will Never En
Fitzpatrick, Dennis	Forget The Sins Of Our Past
Fitzpatrick, Dennis	Freely Will I Offer
Fitzpatrick, Dennis	From My Distress
Fitzpatrick, Dennis	From Wanton Sin
Fitzpatrick, Dennis	From Where Is His Wisdom
Fitzpatrick, Dennis	Gather Us From Among The Na
Fitzpatrick, Dennis	Give Light To My Eyes
Fitzpatrick, Dennis	Give Me Justice, O God
Fitzpatrick, Dennis	Give Peace, O Lord
Fitzpatrick, Dennis	Give Them Rest
Fitzpatrick, Dennis	Give Them Rest (Choral)
Fitzpatrick, Dennis	Give Them, O Lord
Fitzpatrick, Dennis	Gloria (Sung Mass No.2)
Fitzpatrick, Dennis	Glory To God (Sung Mass No.
Fitzpatrick, Dennis	Glory To God In The Highest
Fitzpatrick, Dennis	Go You Also Into My Vineyar
Fitzpatrick, Dennis	Go, Make All Nations
Fitzpatrick, Dennis	God Ascends Amid Shouts Of
Fitzpatrick, Dennis	God Has Blessed You Forever
Fitzpatrick, Dennis	God Of Love (Choral)
Fitzpatrick, Dennis	God So Loved The World
Fitzpatrick, Dennis	Great Amen
Fitzpatrick, Dennis	Greater Love Than This
Fitzpatrick, Dennis	Hail Mary
Fitzpatrick, Dennis	Hail, Holy Mother
Fitzpatrick, Dennis	Hail, Mary (Unison Or Chora
Fitzpatrick, Dennis	Happy The Man Who Delights
Fitzpatrick, Dennis	Happy The Man Who Fears
Fitzpatrick, Dennis	Have Mercy, Lord, On Me
Fitzpatrick, Dennis	Have Pity On Me, O Lord
Fitzpatrick, Dennis	He Asked Life Of You
Fitzpatrick, Dennis	He Called Me From Birth
Fitzpatrick, Dennis	He Comes Forth
Fitzpatrick, Dennis	He Feeds Us With The Finest
Fitzpatrick, Dennis	He Gives Us Bread Which Com
Fitzpatrick, Dennis	He Gives Us The Water Of Le
Fitzpatrick, Dennis	He Has Risen As He Said
Fitzpatrick, Dennis	He Heard My Voice
Fitzpatrick, Dennis	He Is The Lord Of Life And
Fitzpatrick, Dennis	He Lived To See The Christ
Fitzpatrick, Dennis	He Saved Me Because He Love
Fitzpatrick, Dennis	He Shall Call On Me

COMPOSER INDEX

Fitzpatrick, Dennis	He Shall Return As He Has L
Fitzpatrick, Dennis	He Was Silent (Choral)
Fitzpatrick, Dennis	He Who Abides In Me
Fitzpatrick, Dennis	He Who Believes In Me
Fitzpatrick, Dennis	He Who Believes In Me, From
Fitzpatrick, Dennis	He Who Drinks Of The Water
Fitzpatrick, Dennis	He Who Eats My Flesh
Fitzpatrick, Dennis	He Who Follows Me
Fitzpatrick, Dennis	He Who Is Of God
Fitzpatrick, Dennis	He Who Sees Me
Fitzpatrick, Dennis	He Who Will Trust In God
Fitzpatrick, Dennis	Hear Us, O Lord, For You Ar
Fitzpatrick, Dennis	Help Us, O God, Our Savior
Fitzpatrick, Dennis	Hide Not Your Face From Me
Fitzpatrick, Dennis	His Angels Will Protect You
Fitzpatrick, Dennis	His Mercy Endures Forever
Fitzpatrick, Dennis	His Throne Shall Be
Fitzpatrick, Dennis	Holy Mother Of God, Interce
Fitzpatrick, Dennis	Holy, Holy, Holy (Sung Mass
Fitzpatrick, Dennis	Honor The Lord With What Yo
Fitzpatrick, Dennis	Hosanna Filio David (Choral
Fitzpatrick, Dennis	Hosanna To The Son Of David
Fitzpatrick, Dennis	How Great Is The Goodness
Fitzpatrick, Dennis	How I Rejoiced When I Heard
Fitzpatrick, Dennis	How Long, O Lord
Fitzpatrick, Dennis	How Lovely Is Your Dwelling
Fitzpatrick, Dennis	I Am At Peace With My Neigh
Fitzpatrick, Dennis	I Am The Good Shepherd
Fitzpatrick, Dennis	I Am The Living Bread
Fitzpatrick, Dennis	I Am The Resurrection
Fitzpatrick, Dennis	I Am The Salvation Of My Pe
Fitzpatrick, Dennis	I Am The True Vine
Fitzpatrick, Dennis	I Believe That My Redeemer
Fitzpatrick, Dennis	I Bless You, Lord
Fitzpatrick, Dennis	I Bring Gifts To You, Lord
Fitzpatrick, Dennis	I Call On You, O God
Fitzpatrick, Dennis	I Give You Thanks, O Lord
Fitzpatrick, Dennis	I Go To The Father
Fitzpatrick, Dennis	I Have Arisen And Am With Y
Fitzpatrick, Dennis	I Have Come To Set Fire
Fitzpatrick, Dennis	I Have Given You An Example
Fitzpatrick, Dennis	I Have Plans, Says The Lord
Fitzpatrick, Dennis	I Have Put My Words
Fitzpatrick, Dennis	I Know, O Lord
Fitzpatrick, Dennis	I Looked For Someone
Fitzpatrick, Dennis	I Love You, O Lord, My Stre
Fitzpatrick, Dennis	I Make My Vows To The Lord
Fitzpatrick, Dennis	I Mingle My Drink With Tear
Fitzpatrick, Dennis	I Praise You, Lord
Fitzpatrick, Dennis	I Pray To You, O Lord
Fitzpatrick, Dennis	I Renew My Vows To You, Lor
Fitzpatrick, Dennis	I See That All Things Have
Fitzpatrick, Dennis	I Shall Be Content
Fitzpatrick, Dennis	I Shall Not Die, But Live
Fitzpatrick, Dennis	I Shout With Joy To You
Fitzpatrick, Dennis	I Thank You, For You Delive
Fitzpatrick, Dennis	I Thank You, O Lord
Fitzpatrick, Dennis	I Thank You, O Lord My God
Fitzpatrick, Dennis	I Trust In You, O God
Fitzpatrick, Dennis	I Waited And Waited For The
Fitzpatrick, Dennis	I Will Bear Witness, O Lord
Fitzpatrick, Dennis	I Will Breathe Into You
Fitzpatrick, Dennis	I Will Call Upon The Lord
Fitzpatrick, Dennis	I Will Give Glory To You
Fitzpatrick, Dennis	I Will Give Glory To Your N
Fitzpatrick, Dennis	I Will Go To The Alter Of G
Fitzpatrick, Dennis	I Will Hope In God
Fitzpatrick, Dennis	I Will Meditate On Your Law
Fitzpatrick, Dennis	I Will Not Leave You Friend
Fitzpatrick, Dennis	I Will Offer A Heart
Fitzpatrick, Dennis	I Will Offer In His House
Fitzpatrick, Dennis	I Will Offer Joyful Sacrifi
Fitzpatrick, Dennis	I Will Offer Sacrifice
Fitzpatrick, Dennis	I Will Pour Clean Water On
Fitzpatrick, Dennis	I Will Put Enmity
Fitzpatrick, Dennis	I Will Rejoice In The Lord
Fitzpatrick, Dennis	I Will Sing Praise To My Go
Fitzpatrick, Dennis	I Will Sing Praise To You
Fitzpatrick, Dennis	I Will Sing To The Lord
Fitzpatrick, Dennis	I, The Lord, Am Your God
Fitzpatrick, Dennis	If Anyone Serves Me
Fitzpatrick, Dennis	If Anyone Thirst
Fitzpatrick, Dennis	If I, The Lord And Master
Fitzpatrick, Dennis	If One Member Suffers
Fitzpatrick, Dennis	If We Are Humble
Fitzpatrick, Dennis	If You Have Kept My Words
Fitzpatrick, Dennis	If You Have Risen With Chri
Fitzpatrick, Dennis	If You Love Me, Simon Peter
Fitzpatrick, Dennis	If You Want Life
Fitzpatrick, Dennis	If You Would Come After Me
Fitzpatrick, Dennis	If You Would Serve God
Fitzpatrick, Dennis	In My Old Age, O God
Fitzpatrick, Dennis	In Paradisum
Fitzpatrick, Dennis	In Thanksgiving I Go Around
Fitzpatrick, Dennis	In The End You Will Receive
Fitzpatrick, Dennis	In The Midst Of The Assembl
Fitzpatrick, Dennis	In Your Great Mercy
Fitzpatrick, Dennis	In Your Kindness Save Me, L
Fitzpatrick, Dennis	Ingrediente (Choral)
Fitzpatrick, Dennis	Insult Has Broken My Heart
Fitzpatrick, Dennis	Into Your Hands, O Lord
Fitzpatrick, Dennis	Is Not The Cup That We Bles
Fitzpatrick, Dennis	It Is Good To Give Thanks
Fitzpatrick, Dennis	Jesus Said To His Mother
Fitzpatrick, Dennis	Jesus Went With Them
Fitzpatrick, Dennis	Jesus, Priceless Treasure
Fitzpatrick, Dennis	Job Was A True And Honest M
Fitzpatrick, Dennis	Joseph, Take Mary As Your W
Fitzpatrick, Dennis	Judge Us With Mercy, Lord
Fitzpatrick, Dennis	Kyrie (Sung Mass No.2)
Fitzpatrick, Dennis	Lamb Of God (Agnus Dei) (Su
Fitzpatrick, Dennis	Let Hymns Of Joy
Fitzpatrick, Dennis	Let My Prayer Come Before Y
Fitzpatrick, Dennis	Let The Thought Of My Heart
Fitzpatrick, Dennis	Let Us Acclaim The Rock
Fitzpatrick, Dennis	Let Us Only Glory
Fitzpatrick, Dennis	Let Us Serve The Lord
Fitzpatrick, Dennis	Let Your Faithful Ones Bles
Fitzpatrick, Dennis	Let Your Father And Mother
Fitzpatrick, Dennis	Libera Me (Choral)
Fitzpatrick, Dennis	Libera Me (Unison)
Fitzpatrick, Dennis	Lift Up, O Gates
Fitzpatrick, Dennis	Like Dew Before The Daystar
Fitzpatrick, Dennis	Listen To Him
Fitzpatrick, Dennis	Listen To Their Sighs
Fitzpatrick, Dennis	Listen You Nations
Fitzpatrick, Dennis	Litany Of The Blessed Virgi
Fitzpatrick, Dennis	Litany Of The Saints
Fitzpatrick, Dennis	Look On Me, O Lord
Fitzpatrick, Dennis	Look To The Lord
Fitzpatrick, Dennis	Look To The Lord And Be Str
Fitzpatrick, Dennis	Lord Have Mercy (Kyrie)
Fitzpatrick, Dennis	Lord Jesus, Receive My Spir
Fitzpatrick, Dennis	Lord, Do Not Forget Forever
Fitzpatrick, Dennis	Lord, I Love Your Law
Fitzpatrick, Dennis	Lord, If You Remember Sins
Fitzpatrick, Dennis	Lord, Will You Come To Us
Fitzpatrick, Dennis	Love The Lord With All Your
Fitzpatrick, Dennis	Many Signs Jesus Worked
Fitzpatrick, Dennis	May Choirs Of Angels Bring
Fitzpatrick, Dennis	May Eternal Light Shine
Fitzpatrick, Dennis	May I Be Firm In Keeping Yo
Fitzpatrick, Dennis	May The God Of Israel Join
Fitzpatrick, Dennis	May The Lord Bless Us With
Fitzpatrick, Dennis	May The Love Of Christ Dwel
Fitzpatrick, Dennis	May This Sacrifice Of Ours
Fitzpatrick, Dennis	May We All One Bread, One B
Fitzpatrick, Dennis	May We Shout For Joy
Fitzpatrick, Dennis	May You See Your Children's
Fitzpatrick, Dennis	May You Walk Worthily Of Go
Fitzpatrick, Dennis	May Your Priests Be Clothed
Fitzpatrick, Dennis	Memorial Acclamation 1
Fitzpatrick, Dennis	Memorial Acclamation 2
Fitzpatrick, Dennis	Memorial Acclamation 3
Fitzpatrick, Dennis	Memorial Acclamation 4
Fitzpatrick, Dennis	Moses Offered Sacrifice
Fitzpatrick, Dennis	Moses Pleaded With God
Fitzpatrick, Dennis	My Flesh Is Food
Fitzpatrick, Dennis	My God, My God, Why Have Yo
Fitzpatrick, Dennis	My God, My God, Why Have Yo
Fitzpatrick, Dennis	My Good Is To Be Near My Go
Fitzpatrick, Dennis	My Heart Goes Out
Fitzpatrick, Dennis	My House Shall Be Called
Fitzpatrick, Dennis	My Refuge, My Fortress
Fitzpatrick, Dennis	My Soul Is Athirst
Fitzpatrick, Dennis	My Soul Longs For You
Fitzpatrick, Dennis	My Soul Longs For Your Salv
Fitzpatrick, Dennis	My Soul Thirsts For You, O
Fitzpatrick, Dennis	My Trust Is In You, O Lord
Fitzpatrick, Dennis	My Truth And My Mercy Go Wi
Fitzpatrick, Dennis	Nicene Creed (Sung Mass No.
Fitzpatrick, Dennis	Not On Bread Alone
Fitzpatrick, Dennis	O God Of Consolation (Chora
Fitzpatrick, Dennis	O God, From Everlasting You
Fitzpatrick, Dennis	O God, Have Mercy And Bless
Fitzpatrick, Dennis	O God, Hear My Prayer, Deli
Fitzpatrick, Dennis	O God, Please Rescue Me
Fitzpatrick, Dennis	O God, Who Live Forever
Fitzpatrick, Dennis	O God, You Are My God
Fitzpatrick, Dennis	O God, You Have Rejected Us
Fitzpatrick, Dennis	O Great Doctor, Blessed
Fitzpatrick, Dennis	O Holy God, O Holy Might Go
Fitzpatrick, Dennis	O Holy Spirit, Come To Us
Fitzpatrick, Dennis	O Lord Of Hosts, Restore Us
Fitzpatrick, Dennis	O Lord, Be Kind To Me
Fitzpatrick, Dennis	O Lord, Do Not Be Far From
Fitzpatrick, Dennis	O Lord, Do Not Deal With Us
Fitzpatrick, Dennis	O Lord, From Everlasting
Fitzpatrick, Dennis	O Lord, Give Him Eternal Li
Fitzpatrick, Dennis	O Lord, Hear My Prayer
Fitzpatrick, Dennis	O Lord, How Good It Is To B
Fitzpatrick, Dennis	O Lord, I Am In Awe Of Your
Fitzpatrick, Dennis	O Lord, I Am Unworthy
Fitzpatrick, Dennis	O Lord, Let My Enemies See
Fitzpatrick, Dennis	O Lord, Look On The Face
Fitzpatrick, Dennis	O Lord, My Heart Is Not Pro
Fitzpatrick, Dennis	O Lord, Our Lord, How Wonde
Fitzpatrick, Dennis	O Lord, Show Mercy To The S
Fitzpatrick, Dennis	O Lord, Who Shall Dwell
Fitzpatrick, Dennis	O Virgin Mother, He Whom Th
Fitzpatrick, Dennis	Offer To God Praise As Your
Fitzpatrick, Dennis	Often They Fought Me
Fitzpatrick, Dennis	Oh, Bless The Lord, My Soul
Fitzpatrick, Dennis	Oh, That Out Of Zion
Fitzpatrick, Dennis	One Of The Soldiers
Fitzpatrick, Dennis	One Thing I Ask Of The Lord
Fitzpatrick, Dennis	Only In God Is My Soul At R
Fitzpatrick, Dennis	Open The Gates Of Justice
Fitzpatrick, Dennis	Our Eyes Are On You, O Lord
Fitzpatrick, Dennis	Our Father (Unison Or Chora
Fitzpatrick, Dennis	Our Soul Has Been Resuced
Fitzpatrick, Dennis	Out Of The Depths I Cry To
Fitzpatrick, Dennis	Peace I Leave You
Fitzpatrick, Dennis	People Of Zion, Behold
Fitzpatrick, Dennis	Praise Be To You, O Lord
Fitzpatrick, Dennis	Praise To You, Lord;You Hav
Fitzpatrick, Dennis	Prayer Of The Faithful
Fitzpatrick, Dennis	Precious In The Sight Of Th
Fitzpatrick, Dennis	Prosper The Work Of Our Han
Fitzpatrick, Dennis	Protect Me From Those Who D
Fitzpatrick, Dennis	Protect Our Country, O Lord
Fitzpatrick, Dennis	Protect Us, Lord, While We
Fitzpatrick, Dennis	Put To Shame And Confusion
Fitzpatrick, Dennis	Quotiescumque
Fitzpatrick, Dennis	Receive With Joy The Glory
Fitzpatrick, Dennis	Redeem Me, O Lord;Give Me L
Fitzpatrick, Dennis	Redeem Me, O Lord, And Have
Fitzpatrick, Dennis	Rejoice In The Lord On The
Fitzpatrick, Dennis	Rejoice In The Lord; Rejoic
Fitzpatrick, Dennis	Rejoice, Be Glad In The Lor
Fitzpatrick, Dennis	Rejoice, My Son
Fitzpatrick, Dennis	Rejoice, O Jerusalem
Fitzpatrick, Dennis	Remember Me, Lord, When You
Fitzpatrick, Dennis	Remember Your Words, O Lord
Fitzpatrick, Dennis	Remember, Man, That You Are
Fitzpatrick, Dennis	Rescue Me, My God, And Defe
Fitzpatrick, Dennis	Return, O Lord, And Save My
Fitzpatrick, Dennis	Sanctus (Sung Mass No.2)
Fitzpatrick, Dennis	Save Me, O Lord, And Rescue
Fitzpatrick, Dennis	Save Me, O Lord, From The H
Fitzpatrick, Dennis	Save Us, O Lord, Our God
Fitzpatrick, Dennis	See, Your King Shall Come
Fitzpatrick, Dennis	Send Forth Your Life-Giving
Fitzpatrick, Dennis	Send Forth Your Light And Y
Fitzpatrick, Dennis	Serve Each Other In Loving
Fitzpatrick, Dennis	Serve The Lord With Fear
Fitzpatrick, Dennis	Shout For Joy, For He Comes
Fitzpatrick, Dennis	Show Forth, O God, Your Pow
Fitzpatrick, Dennis	Show Us Your Mercy, Lord
Fitzpatrick, Dennis	Sing To The Lord (Ascension
Fitzpatrick, Dennis	Sing To The Lord A New Song
Fitzpatrick, Dennis	Sing With Joy To God
Fitzpatrick, Dennis	Sing With Joy To God Our St
Fitzpatrick, Dennis	Sing, My Tongue (Choral)
Fitzpatrick, Dennis	Some Seed Fell On Good Grou
Fitzpatrick, Dennis	Son, Why Have You Treated U
Fitzpatrick, Dennis	Sprinkle, Me, Lord
Fitzpatrick, Dennis	Stabat Mater Dolorosa
Fitzpatrick, Dennis	Stir Up Your Power
Fitzpatrick, Dennis	Strengthen, O God, What You
Fitzpatrick, Dennis	Subvenite (Choral)
Fitzpatrick, Dennis	Take The Child And His Moth
Fitzpatrick, Dennis	Taste And See How Good The
Fitzpatrick, Dennis	Teach Me Your Law, O Lord
Fitzpatrick, Dennis	Teach Me, Lord, To Do Your
Fitzpatrick, Dennis	The Angel Of The Lord Deliv
Fitzpatrick, Dennis	The Bones You Have Crushed
Fitzpatrick, Dennis	The Children Of The Hebrews
Fitzpatrick, Dennis	The Daughters Of Kings
Fitzpatrick, Dennis	The Earth Is Full Of The Ki
Fitzpatrick, Dennis	The Earth Was Fearful And S
Fitzpatrick, Dennis	The Faithful Shall Rejoice
Fitzpatrick, Dennis	The First Of His Signs
Fitzpatrick, Dennis	The Glory Of The Lord Is Up
Fitzpatrick, Dennis	The Good Man Speaks Wisdom
Fitzpatrick, Dennis	The Hand Of The Lord Sustai
Fitzpatrick, Dennis	The Heavens Proclaim His Ju
Fitzpatrick, Dennis	The Heavens Proclaim Your W
Fitzpatrick, Dennis	The Hebrew Children Spread
Fitzpatrick, Dennis	The Joy Of The Lord
Fitzpatrick, Dennis	The Just Man Rejoices
Fitzpatrick, Dennis	The Just Man Shall Flourish
Fitzpatrick, Dennis	The Just Shall Always Be Re
Fitzpatrick, Dennis	The Just Shall Grow
Fitzpatrick, Dennis	The King Desires Your Beaut
Fitzpatrick, Dennis	The Lord Anointed My Eyes
Fitzpatrick, Dennis	The Lord Cried Out
Fitzpatrick, Dennis	The Lord Has Brought Us
Fitzpatrick, Dennis	The Lord Has Delivered
Fitzpatrick, Dennis	The Lord Has Done Great Thi
Fitzpatrick, Dennis	The Lord Has Heard
Fitzpatrick, Dennis	The Lord Has Made Known
Fitzpatrick, Dennis	The Lord Has Risen
Fitzpatrick, Dennis	The Lord Has Sworn
Fitzpatrick, Dennis	The Lord Is God
Fitzpatrick, Dennis	The Lord Is Just
Fitzpatrick, Dennis	The Lord Is King
Fitzpatrick, Dennis	The Lord Is Loving And Merc
Fitzpatrick, Dennis	The Lord Is My Guardian
Fitzpatrick, Dennis	The Lord Is My Light

COMPOSER INDEX

Composer	Title
Fitzpatrick, Dennis	The Lord Is My Shepherd
Fitzpatrick, Dennis	The Lord Is Near To All
Fitzpatrick, Dennis	The Lord Led Forth His Peop
Fitzpatrick, Dennis	The Lord Led Forth His Peop
Fitzpatrick, Dennis	The Lord Loved Him And Clot
Fitzpatrick, Dennis	The Lord Thundered
Fitzpatrick, Dennis	The Lord Will Give His Bles
Fitzpatrick, Dennis	The Lord's Prayer
Fitzpatrick, Dennis	The Love Of God Flows
Fitzpatrick, Dennis	The Meek Shall Possess The
Fitzpatrick, Dennis	The Nicene Creed(Credo)(Sun
Fitzpatrick, Dennis	The Only Concern You Need T
Fitzpatrick, Dennis	The Plan Of The Lords Stand
Fitzpatrick, Dennis	The Saints You Gave
Fitzpatrick, Dennis	The Salvation Of The Just
Fitzpatrick, Dennis	The Souls Of The Just
Fitzpatrick, Dennis	The Spirit Breathes Where H
Fitzpatrick, Dennis	The Spirit Of The Lord Fill
Fitzpatrick, Dennis	The Spirit Of The Lord Is U
Fitzpatrick, Dennis	The Spirit Will Come To Gui
Fitzpatrick, Dennis	The Spirit Will Teach You A
Fitzpatrick, Dennis	The Stone Which The Builder
Fitzpatrick, Dennis	The Water That I Shall Give
Fitzpatrick, Dennis	The Water That I Will Give
Fitzpatrick, Dennis	The Word Of The Lord Is Pur
Fitzpatrick, Dennis	The Word Was Made Flesh
Fitzpatrick, Dennis	The Work He Has Committed T
Fitzpatrick, Dennis	The World Sees Nothing
Fitzpatrick, Dennis	Their Bodies Lie In Peace
Fitzpatrick, Dennis	Their Message Goes Forth
Fitzpatrick, Dennis	There Is Rachel Weeping
Fitzpatrick, Dennis	There Will Be Joy Over One
Fitzpatrick, Dennis	They Ate And Were
Fitzpatrick, Dennis	They Came From Sheba
Fitzpatrick, Dennis	They Cried To The Lord
Fitzpatrick, Dennis	They Divide My Garments
Fitzpatrick, Dennis	They Gossip About Me
Fitzpatrick, Dennis	They Took Him Up To Jerusal
Fitzpatrick, Dennis	They Were Filled With The H
Fitzpatrick, Dennis	This Bread Commits Us To Ch
Fitzpatrick, Dennis	This Day You Shall Know
Fitzpatrick, Dennis	This Is The Day Which The L
Fitzpatrick, Dennis	This Is The Faithful And Pr
Fitzpatrick, Dennis	This Is The God Who Gives A
Fitzpatrick, Dennis	This Is The House Of God
Fitzpatrick, Dennis	This Is The Wise Virgin
Fitzpatrick, Dennis	This, The Bread I Give You
Fitzpatrick, Dennis	Those Who Sow In Tears
Fitzpatrick, Dennis	Though I Walk Amid Distress
Fitzpatrick, Dennis	To The Lamb Who Was Slain
Fitzpatrick, Dennis	To You I Cry, O Lord
Fitzpatrick, Dennis	To You I Lift Up My Soul
Fitzpatrick, Dennis	To You I Pray, O Lord
Fitzpatrick, Dennis	To You We Owe Our Hymn
Fitzpatrick, Dennis	To You Will I Offer
Fitzpatrick, Dennis	Truly There Is A God
Fitzpatrick, Dennis	Unless A Man Be Born Again
Fitzpatrick, Dennis	Up, O Jerusalem
Fitzpatrick, Dennis	Veni, Sancte Spiritus
Fitzpatrick, Dennis	Victimae Paschali Laudes
Fitzpatrick, Dennis	Wait For The Lord With Cour
Fitzpatrick, Dennis	Walk In Love
Fitzpatrick, Dennis	We Adore You, O Christ
Fitzpatrick, Dennis	We Are The Body Of Christ
Fitzpatrick, Dennis	We Have Seen His Star In Th
Fitzpatrick, Dennis	We Offer You The Prayer
Fitzpatrick, Dennis	We Praise You Above All For
Fitzpatrick, Dennis	We Praise You, O God
Fitzpatrick, Dennis	We Praise You, O Lord
Fitzpatrick, Dennis	We Rejoice And Adore You, O
Fitzpatrick, Dennis	We Shall Enter Your Courts
Fitzpatrick, Dennis	We Sing His Praise
Fitzpatrick, Dennis	We Thank You, O Lord
Fitzpatrick, Dennis	We Will Offer Praises To Go
Fitzpatrick, Dennis	Wedding Motet
Fitzpatrick, Dennis	Well Done, Good And Faithfu
Fitzpatrick, Dennis	What I Tell You In Darkness
Fitzpatrick, Dennis	Whatever You Ask For
Fitzpatrick, Dennis	Whatever You Do
Fitzpatrick, Dennis	Where I Am
Fitzpatrick, Dennis	Whereever Faithful Men Asse
Fitzpatrick, Dennis	Who Can Know Your Ways
Fitzpatrick, Dennis	Whoever Eats This Bread
Fitzpatrick, Dennis	Wisdom Opened The Mouth Of
Fitzpatrick, Dennis	Wisdom Restored To Men
Fitzpatrick, Dennis	With Cries Of Joy I Shout
Fitzpatrick, Dennis	With Gifts We Enter Your Co
Fitzpatrick, Dennis	With Gladness And Rejoicing
Fitzpatrick, Dennis	With Honest Heart
Fitzpatrick, Dennis	With My Holy Oil
Fitzpatrick, Dennis	Woman, Has No One Condemned
Fitzpatrick, Dennis	Worship The Lord
Fitzpatrick, Dennis	Ye Sons And Daughters (Chor
Fitzpatrick, Dennis	You Are A Chosen Race
Fitzpatrick, Dennis	You Are A Light For All The
Fitzpatrick, Dennis	You Are Blessed And Worthy
Fitzpatrick, Dennis	You Are Blessed, O Virgin M
Fitzpatrick, Dennis	You Are Fair In Every Way
Fitzpatrick, Dennis	You Are My Son
Fitzpatrick, Dennis	You Are Peter, The Rock
Fitzpatrick, Dennis	You Are So Great, O God
Fitzpatrick, Dennis	You Gave Him His Heart's De
Fitzpatrick, Dennis	You Give Us Bread, O Lord
Fitzpatrick, Dennis	You Have Crowned Him With G
Fitzpatrick, Dennis	You Have Favored Your Land
Fitzpatrick, Dennis	You Have Made Children And
Fitzpatrick, Dennis	You Have Mercy On All
Fitzpatrick, Dennis	You Have Set On His Head
Fitzpatrick, Dennis	You Love Right And Hate Wro
Fitzpatrick, Dennis	You Put Gladness Into My He
Fitzpatrick, Dennis	You Save The Humble, O Lord
Fitzpatrick, Dennis	You Shall Go Before The Lor
Fitzpatrick, Dennis	You Shall Make Them Princes
Fitzpatrick, Dennis	You Shall Say To The Sons O
Fitzpatrick, Dennis	You Who Have Followed Me
Fitzpatrick, Dennis	You, O Lord, Are Near
Fitzpatrick, Dennis	You, O Lord, Will Keep Us
Fitzpatrick, Dennis	Your Almighty Word, O Lord
Fitzpatrick, Dennis	Your Light Has Come, O Jeru
Fitzpatrick, Dennis	Your Wife Shall Bear A Son
Fitzpatrick, Dennis	Your Word, O Lord, Endures
Fitzpatrick, Dennis	Yours Are The Heavens
Five French Noels	A La Venue De Noel
Five French Noels	A Minuet Fut Fait Un Reveil
Five French Noels	Joseph Est Bien Marie
Five French Noels	Ou Sen Vont Ces Gais Berger
Five French Noels	Tous Les Bourgeois De Chast
Flanagan, William	Heaven Haven
Fleming (Arr)	Every Time I Think About Je
Fleming (Arr)	Give Me Jesus (Spiritual)
Fleming (Arr)	Ride On, King Jesus (Spirit
Fleming/Decou	Praise Ye The Triune God!
Fleming, Launa B.	A Thanksgiving Service (No
Fletcher	Noel, A
Fletcher, Grant	By The Waters Of Babylon (P
Floreen, John	Arise, Oh Ye Servants Of Go
Floria, C.	Every Knee Shall Bow
Floria, C.	Forgive My Lord
Floria, Cam	Believe In Your Heart
Floria, Cam	I Believe In Heaven
Floria,C./Holben,L.	He That Overcomes
Floria,C./Sherberg,J.	My Own Way
Floyd, Phillip	Servant Of All
Foley Et Al (Arr)	Swing Low Sweet Chariot
Foley, Brian	Immaculate Mary (Modern Tex
Foley, John B., S. J.	Rise Up, Jerusalem
Foley, John, S. J.	Blessed Be The Lord
Foley, John, S. J.	Deliver Us, O God Of Israel
Foley, John, S. J.	Earthen Vessels
Foley, John, S. J.	For You Are My God
Foley, John, S. J.	Heed My Call For Help
Foley, John, S. J.	Holy
Foley, John, S. J.	How Good It Is To Give Than
Foley, John, S. J.	I Will Sing Of The Lord
Foley, John, S. J.	If God Is For Us
Foley, John, S. J.	Lamb Of God
Foley, John, S. J.	Let All Who Fear The Lord
Foley, John, S. J.	Look Toward Me
Foley, John, S. J.	Lord Is My Shepherd, The
Foley, John, S. J.	Magnificat
Foley, John, S. J.	Never Shall A Man
Foley, John, S. J.	Praise The Lord My Soul
Foley, John, S. J.	Rescue Me From My Enemies
Foley, John, S. J.	Sing To The Lord
Foley, John, S. J.	Sparrow Finds A Home, The
Foley, John, S. J.	Take, Lord, Receive
Foley, John, S. J.	This Is My Body
Foley, John, S. J.	To His Angels
Foley, John, S. J.	To Thee Be Glory
Foley, John, S. J.	Turn To Me, O Man
Foley, John, S. J.	Why, O Lord?
Follett (Arr)	Hark Ye! What News The Ange
Follett (Arr)	Holy, Holy (American Spirit
Follett (Arr)	How Sweet Is The Voice Of M
Follett (Arr)	I Come To Thee Jesus (Opt B
Follett (Arr)	Such A Gay & Happy Tune
Follett (Arr)	Tis Noel Again!
Follett (Arr)	We Walk Through The Meadow
Follett, Charles (Arr)	O'er Bethlehem A Star (Poli
Follett,(Arr)	King Of Love My Shepherd Is
Fong, P B	Sweet Jesus Morning
Fong, P B	The Question
Fong, Preston Bing	All I Know
Fong, Preston Bing	Back Home
Fong, Preston Bing	Can't Work Your Way To Heav
Fong, Preston Bing	Dried Up Well
Fong, Preston Bing	Happy In Jesus
Fong, Preston Bing	Let Go
Fong, Preston Bing	Lighter Side Of Darkness
Fong, Preston Bing	More Than The Sunlight
Fong, Preston Bing	Once I Had A Dream
Forcucci, Samuel (Arr)	The Three Kings Of Orient
Ford	Alleluia! He Has Risen
Ford	God Is My Strong Salvation
Ford	I Will Give Peace
Ford	I Would Seek God
Ford	Jesus, We Look To Thee
Ford	O Give Thanks
Ford	O Jesus, King Of Gentleness
Ford	Salvation Is For All
Ford	Teach Me, Fill Me, Use Me.
Ford, Paul	Our Father
Ford, Thomas	Almighty God, Which Has Me
Ford, Virgil	A Song Of Praise
Ford, Virgil	Agree With God And Be At Pe
Ford, Virgil	All As God Wills (A Cap)
Ford, Virgil	All Praise To Our Redeeming
Ford, Virgil	Almighty And Everlasting Go
Ford, Virgil	At Thy Feet Our God And Fat
Ford, Virgil	Be Not Wise In Your Own Eye
Ford, Virgil	Blessed Be The Name Of The
Ford, Virgil	Come Let Us Tune Our Loftie
Ford, Virgil	Come O Thou God Of Grace
Ford, Virgil	Come Sound His Praise Abroa
Ford, Virgil	God Of The Strong
Ford, Virgil	How Can Sinner Know
Ford, Virgil	How Can We Show Our Love To
Ford, Virgil	How Gentle God's Commands
Ford, Virgil	I Heard The Voice
Ford, Virgil	I Hide Me Jesus In Thy Name
Ford, Virgil	If The Lord Wills
Ford, Virgil	Jesus Wher'e'er Thy People
Ford, Virgil	Let All On Earth Their Voic
Ford, Virgil	Let Earth Rejoice
Ford, Virgil	Long Years Ago
Ford, Virgil	Lord Dismiss Us With Thy Bl
Ford, Virgil	Lord Of Our Life
Ford, Virgil	Lord Our Lord
Ford, Virgil	Lost In Wonder, Love And Pr
Ford, Virgil	Men Of Old
Ford, Virgil	O Come And Dwell In Me
Ford, Virgil	O Jesus King Of Gentleness
Ford, Virgil	O Lord, Open Thou Our Lips
Ford, Virgil	Sounds For Now
Ford, Virgil	Talk With Us Lord
Ford, Virgil	This Is The Day Which The L
Ford, Virgil	Thy Will Be Done
Ford, Virgil	Tis Midnight
Ford, Virgil	Unto Thee O Lord
Ford,T/Tortonalo	Haste Thee O Lord (In '19 Ro
Forsblad (Arr)	Babe Is Born, A
Forsyth, J	The Lord's Prayer
Forsythe, Kenneth	Jesus Is A Friend Of Mine
Fortunate, Lou	Born Again
Fortunate, Lou	Do This In Remembrance Of M
Fortunate, Lou	Go Forth (Mission Song)
Fortunate, Lou	How Can I Be A Friend?
Fortunate, Lou	If You Love Me, Keep My Wor
Foster	Christmas Day In The Mornin
Foster, Anthony	Dona Nobis Pacem (Round)
Foster, M B	As It Began To Dawn
Foster, M B	O For Closer Walk With God
Foster, Will	Fear Not I Am With Thee
Foster, Will	Hear My Prayer
Foster, Will	Thy Will Be Done
Fout, R.	Blessed Father Great And Go
Fox, Baynard (Keene)	Up The Hill Of Calvary With
Fox, Luacine Clark	There Came A Star (W/Solos,
Fr. M.J.,Alt-Gilligan	All Of Seeing
Frackenpohl, Arthur	Psalm 8
Francis	Sing Praise To Our Creator
Franck-Ehret	The Sufferings Of The Prese
Franck, C.	Solemn Mass For Voices (Lat
Franck, C. (Hoffman)	Panis Angelicus (Prayer For
Franck, Cesar	Alleluia
Franck, Cesar	At The Cradle
Franck, Cesar	Blessed He(From The Beatitu
Franck, Cesar	Father Almighty
Franck, Cesar	Father Most Merciful
Franck, Cesar	Lord Thou Art Holy
Franck, Cesar	Lord We Implore Thee
Franck, Cesar	Panis Angelicus
Franck, Cesar	Psalm 150
Franck, Cesar	Psalm 150 (French, German)
Franck, Cesar	Welcome Welcome Dear Redeem
Franck, Cesarll	O Breath Of Life
Franck, Melchior	Five Motets
Franck, Melchior	Jesu By Thee I Would Be Ble
Franck, Melchior	Lord God We Praise Thy Good
Franck, Melchior	Lord Jesus Christ In Thee A
Franck, Melchior	Our Father Thou In Heaven A
Franck, Melchior	Out Of The Depths I Cry To
Franck, Melchior	Revelation Motet
Franco, Fernando	Oh, Senora (Blessed Lady)
Franco, Fernando	Parce Mihi Domini (Job's Co
Franco, Fernando	Plegaria A La Virgen
Franco, Fernando	Salve (Salutation)
Frank, J L	Bow Down Thine Ear
Frank, Marcel	Lord, Make Me An Instrument
Frank, Marcel G	Gods Glory And Honour
Frank, Marcel G	Kings Of The Earth And All
Franklin/Decou	In A Cave (W/Opt Flute)
Franzmann/Kraehenbuehl	In Adam We Have All Been On
Fraser, Jeffrey D.	Our Blest Redeemer (Trad Ir
Fraser, Shena	To Him Give Praise (Suite)
Frazier, M. (Arr)	O Come, All Ye Faithful
Frederick, Donald	A Prayer Of Dedication
Freed, Isadore	Psalm 8
Freeman	I Am Blessed By God's Love
Freeman, Eileen	Litany For Breaking Bread

COMPOSER INDEX

Freestone	Let Nothing Disturb Thee
Freestone	Sing We Merrily To God
Freestone G. S.	Lord Jesus, Think On Me
French/Tortolano Ed	Concordi Laetitia (In 19 Ro
French/Tortolano Ed	Masters In This Hall (In 19
French, Carol	Friendly Beasts, The (C)
Freydt (Ed Nolte)	When We In Spirit View Thy
Friend	Sing Alleluia For Your Soul
Frischman/Deiss	General Intercessions
Frischmann, C. G.	Spread Thou Mighty Word (Hy
Fritschel	Be Glad
Fritschel	In Peace & Joy
Fritschel, J.	With Song And Dance
Frohbieter	Blow Ye The Trumpet Blow
Fryxell, Regina	Daystar
Fryxell, Regina	Seven Choral Service Settin
Fryxell, Regina	Thou Wilt Keep Him In Perfe
Fryxell, Regina	To The Hills I Lift Mine Ey
Fryxell, Regina	Unseen Presence, The
Fuller (Arr)	As I Watched Beside My Shee
Furman	Hope Is Finding Him
Furman	Look To Your Soul (From Tho
Furman	Through All The World
Furman	Wondering Why
Fux, Johann J	O Hail, Mary
Gabriel	If I Have Wounded Any Soul
Gabriel/Wilson	His Eye Is On The Sparrow
Gabrieli, Andrea	Lo The Angel Said To The Sh
Gabrieli, Andrea	Maria Magdalene Et Altera M
Gabrieli, Andrea	Missa Brevis
Gabrieli, Andrea	Scarce Had The Daystar Rise
Gabrieli, G	Beata Es Virgo
Gabrieli, G	Benedictus
Gabrieli, G	Benedixisti Domine
Gabrieli, G	Hodie Christus Natus Est
Gabrieli, G	In Ecclesiis
Gabrieli, G	In Ecclesiis
Gabrieli, G	Jubilate Deo (A Cap)
Gabrieli, G	Jubilemus Singuli
Gabrieli, G	O Jesu Mi Dulcissime
Gabrieli, G	Plaudite
Gabrieli, G	Three Motets
Gaddy, Carol	The Greatest Wonder (W/Pian
Gadsby, H	O Lord Our Governor
Gadwood, Gary	Hear Oh Hear
Gaither B/G,R. Powell	I Guess God Thought Of Ever
Gaither D,Sickal	Created In His Image
Gaither-Milhuff/Gaithe	All God's Children
Gaither-R.Allen	Have You Had A Gethsemane?
Gaither/Gaither	A Glimpse Of The Master
Gaither/Gaither	All My Hopes
Gaither/Gaither	As Flows The River
Gaither/Gaither	Born To Be Crucified
Gaither/Gaither	Calvary
Gaither/Gaither	Get All Excited
Gaither/Gaither	Happiness
Gaither/Gaither	He Filled My Life With Ecst
Gaither/Gaither	He That Hath Ears
Gaither/Gaither	He Touched Me
Gaither/Gaither	I Believe It
Gaither/Gaither	I Come To Praise The Lord
Gaither/Gaither	I Just Feel Like Something
Gaither/Gaither	I'd Do It All Over Again
Gaither/Gaither	I'll Walk Into That Sunset
Gaither/Gaither	I'm Gonna Keep On
Gaither/Gaither	I've Been To Calvary
Gaither/Gaither	I've Just Come From The Pla
Gaither/Gaither	I've Just Seen Jesus
Gaither/Gaither	If It Keeps Gettin' Better
Gaither/Gaither	In God's Tomorrow
Gaither/Gaither	In The Upper Room
Gaither/Gaither	Is There Room In Your Heart
Gaither/Gaither	It Will Be Worth It All
Gaither/Gaither	Jesus
Gaither/Gaither	Joy In The Camp
Gaither/Gaither	Lovest Thou Me?
Gaither/Gaither	No End To God's Love
Gaither/Gaither	No Greater Love
Gaither/Gaither	O, To Be Like Thee
Gaither/Gaither	Ol' Brother Jonah
Gaither/Gaither	Praise For The Lord
Gaither/Gaither	Since Jesus Passed By
Gaither/Gaither	Speak, Lord
Gaither/Gaither	Tell Me That Name Again
Gaither/Gaither	That's What Jesus Means To
Gaither/Gaither	The Joy In Serving The Lord
Gaither/Gaither	The Longer I Serve Him
Gaither/Gaither	Tomorrow Is In His Hands
Gaither/Gaither	What Did You Say Was The Ba
Gaither/Gaither	When I Prayed Through
Gaither/Gaither	When I Think Of Calvary
Gaither/Gaither	When Jesus Breaks The Morni
Gaither/Gaither	Why Should I Worry Or Fret?
Gaither/Gaither B/G	A Little Bit Of Sunshine
Gaither/Gaither B/G	A Parade Of Miracles
Gaither/Gaither B/G	Because He Lives
Gaither/Gaither B/G	Bethlehem,Galilee,Gethseman
Gaither/Gaither B/G	Between The Cross And Heave
Gaither/Gaither B/G	Blessed Jesus
Gaither/Gaither B/G	By The Witness Of The Spiri
Gaither/Gaither B/G	Calm Assurance
Gaither/Gaither B/G	Close To Thee
Gaither/Gaither B/G	Come Away, My Love
Gaither/Gaither B/G	Come On Home
Gaither/Gaither B/G	Come See Me
Gaither/Gaither B/G	Come, Holy Spirit
Gaither/Gaither B/G	Contented
Gaither/Gaither B/G	Even So, Lord Jesus, Come
Gaither/Gaither B/G	Feeling At Home In The Pres
Gaither/Gaither B/G	Forever With Jesus
Gaither/Gaither B/G	Free To Go Home
Gaither/Gaither B/G	Gentle Shepherd
Gaither/Gaither B/G	Getting Used To The Family
Gaither/Gaither B/G	God Gave (Me) The Song
Gaither/Gaither B/G	God Loves To Talk To Boys W
Gaither/Gaither B/G	Going Home
Gaither/Gaither B/G	He's Still The King Of King
Gaither/Gaither B/G	I Am...Because
Gaither/Gaither B/G	I Believe, Help Thou My Bel
Gaither/Gaither B/G	I Could Hardly See The Road
Gaither/Gaither B/G	I Could Never Outlove The L
Gaither/Gaither B/G	I Lost It All To Find Evert
Gaither/Gaither B/G	I Sought The Lord
Gaither/Gaither B/G	I Will Serve Thee
Gaither/Gaither B/G	I Wonder How It Felt
Gaither/Gaither B/G	I'm A Promise
Gaither/Gaither B/G	I'm Almost Home
Gaither/Gaither B/G	I'm Coming
Gaither/Gaither B/G	I'm Free
Gaither/Gaither B/G	I'm So Glad I Found An Alta
Gaither/Gaither B/G	I've A Song
Gaither/Gaither B/G	I've Been On The Mountain
Gaither/Gaither B/G	In The Presence Of The Most
Gaither/Gaither B/G	It Happened
Gaither/Gaither B/G	It Is Finished
Gaither/Gaither B/G	It's A Miracle
Gaither/Gaither B/G	It's Just Like My Lord
Gaither/Gaither B/G	Jesus Is Lord Of All
Gaither/Gaither B/G	Jesus, I Believe What You S
Gaither/Gaither B/G	Jesus, I Heard You Had A Bi
Gaither/Gaither B/G	Jesus, We Just Want To Than
Gaither/Gaither B/G	Joy Comes In The Morning
Gaither/Gaither B/G	Joy, Real Joy
Gaither/Gaither B/G	Let All The Little Children
Gaither/Gaither B/G	Let's Just Praise The Lord
Gaither/Gaither B/G	Lift Up Jesus
Gaither/Gaither B/G	Love All The Brethren
Gaither/Gaither B/G	My Faith Still Holds
Gaither/Gaither B/G	My Heart Is Fixed
Gaither/Gaither B/G	Plenty Of Room In The Famil
Gaither/Gaither B/G	Reaching
Gaither/Gaither B/G	Rejoice, You're A Child Of
Gaither/Gaither B/G	Something's Happened To Dad
Gaither/Gaither B/G	Thank God For The Promise O
Gaither/Gaither B/G	Thanks For Sunshine
Gaither/Gaither B/G	Thanks To Calvary
Gaither/Gaither B/G	That's Worth Everything
Gaither/Gaither B/G	The Christ Of Every Crisis
Gaither/Gaither B/G	The Church Triumphant
Gaither/Gaither B/G	The Family Of God
Gaither/Gaither B/G	The King Is Coming
Gaither/Gaither B/G	The Old Rugged Cross Made
Gaither/Gaither B/G	The Resurrection Morn
Gaither/Gaither B/G	The Spirit Of Jesus Is In T
Gaither/Gaither B/G	The Waters Are Troubled
Gaither/Gaither B/G	There's Something About A M
Gaither/Gaither B/G	There's Something About Tha
Gaither/Gaither B/G	They That Sow In Tears
Gaither/Gaither B/G	This Could Be The Dawning O
Gaither/Gaither B/G	This Is The Day The Lord Ha
Gaither/Gaither B/G	This Is The Time I Must Sin
Gaither/Gaither B/G	Through My Tears
Gaither/Gaither B/G	Until The Day Breaks
Gaither/Gaither B/G	Walk On The Water
Gaither/Gaither B/G	When God Seems So Near
Gaither/Gaither B/G	Worthy The Lamb
Gaither/Gaither B/G	You're Something Special
Gaither/Gaither, G.	A Man Called Jesus
Gaither/Gaither, G.	Come Unto Me
Gaither/Gaither, G.	I Cannot Tell
Gaither/Gaither, G.	Praise Be To Jesus
Gaither/Gaither, G.	Redeeming Love
Gaither/Gaither, G.	Something Beautiful
Gaither/Gaither, G.	We Have This Moment, Today
Gaither, D.Oldham	I Believe In A Hill Called
Gaither, William J	Come, Holy Spirit
Gaither, William J	Even So, Lord Jesus, Come
Gaither, William J	Gentle Shepherd (Narration)
Gaither, William J	He Touched Me And Other Son
Gaither, William J	I Will Serve Thee
Gaither, William J	In The Upper Room
Gaither, William J	Jesus Is Lord Of All
Gaither, William J	Lovest Thou Me?
Gaither, William J	Redeeming Love
Gaither, William J	Something Worth Living For
Gaither, William J	They That Sow In Tears
Gallegos, Jesse	Let There Be Light
Gallus-Weldy	Alleluia, Sing A New Song
Gallus,J/Jacob,H	Diffusa Est Gratia
Gallus,J/Jacob,H	Ecce Quomodo Moritur
Gallus,J/Jacob,H	Lord In Thy Resurrection
Gallus,J/Jacob,H	Pueri Concinite
Gambino, James	Jubilate Deo
Gannon, Michael	Behold A Virgin Bearing Him
Gannon, Michael	Into Our Hearts, O Spirit C
Gannon, Michael	Joyful Mysteries
Gannon, Michael	Look Down To Us St. Joseph
Gannon, Michael	Mysteries Of The Rosary
Gannon, Michael	O Bread Of Angels
Gannon, Michael	O Bread Of Life
Gannon, Michael	O Father Thou Whose Hand
Gannon, Michael	O God Our Refuge & Our Stre
Gannon, Michael	O Lord With Wondrous Myster
Gannon, Michael	O Mary Of All Women
Gannon, Michael	Shadows Of Evening
Gannon, Michael	Singers Sing
Gannon, Michael	Sorrowful Mysteries
Gannon, Michael	Star Upon The Ocean
Gannon, Michael	The Earth Is Full Of Goodne
Gannon, Michael	This Is Our Accepted Time
Gannon, Michael	To Jesus Holy
Gannon, Michael	Welcome Son Of Mary
Gardiner/Carmichael	Jesus, Thy Blood And Righte
Gardner, Don	A Christmas Folk Song
Gardner, John	Cantata For Easter
Gardner, John	Five Hymns In Popular Style
Gardner, John	I Will Lift Up Mine Eyes Un
Gardner, John	Jubilate Deo (D)
Gardner, John	Magnificat (From Cantiones
Gardner, John	Magnificat And Nunc Dimitti
Gardner, John	The End Is The Beginning (M
Gardner, John	We Have A Strong City (Is 2
Garlick, Antony	Alleluia
Garlick, Antony	Eleven Canzonets
Garlick, Antony	Psalm 100
Garlick, Antony	Psalm 23
Garlick, Antony	Psalm 90
Garlick, Antony	Twelve Madrigals
Garrett, G M	Prepare Ye The Way Of The L
Garza, Juliana, S. P.	Celebrate
Garza, Juliana, S. P.	Communion Muse
Garza, Juliana, S. P.	It's All Right
Garza, Juliana, S. P.	Migrant
Garza, Juliana, S. P.	Our Father
Garza, Juliana, S. P.	Pardon Me
Garza, Juliana, S. P.	Peace Be To You
Garza, Juliana, S. P.	Psalm 83 (84)
Garza, Juliana, S. P.	Uncertain Tide
Garza, Juliana, S. P.	We Come To Your Table
Garza, Juliana, S. P.	When It's Time
Gasparini, Q	We Adore You
Gasparini, Quirino	Adoramus Te (We Adore Thee)
Gasparini,Q./Ed Klein	We Adore You (E & Lat)
Gassman/Mozart/Floria	Hallelujah!Praise!Selah!(Lo
Gastoldi-Nelson	In Thee Is Gladness
Gaul, A R	God Is Wisdom God Is Love(F
Gaul, A R	Great And Marvelous
Gaul, A R	Lift The Cherubic Host
Gaul, A R	Love Not The World
Gaul, A R	No Shadows Yonder
Gaul, A R	They That Sow In Tears
Gaul, A.R.	Thine Is The Kingdom
Gaul, Harvey	No Shadows Yonder (From Hol
Gaul, Harvey	The Three Lilies
Gaul, Harvey	Thine Is The Kingdom (Holy
Gaul, Harvey(D1945)	Holy City, The
Gavitt/Johnson	I'm So Happy
Gay, Wm. & A.	Each Winter As The Year Gro
Gelineau, Joseph	Mass Of Celebration
Gelineau, Joseph	O Praise The Lord
Gelineau, Joseph	The Gelineau Psalms
Gemignani, Michael	God Who By Your Holy Spirit
Gentemann, Sr. Elaine	Gloria
Gentemann, Sr. Elaine	Glory To God
Gentemann, Sr. Elaine	Holy, Holy, Holy Lord
Gentemann, Sr. Elaine	Holy, Holy, Holy
Gentemann, Sr. Elaine	Lamb Of God
Gentemann, Sr. Elaine	Lamb Of God
Gentemann, Sr. Elaine	Lord Have Mercy
Gentemann, Sr. Elaine	Lord Have Mercy
Gentemann, Sr. Elaine	Mass In D (Easy)
Gentemann, Sr. Elaine	Music For Reception Ceremon
Gentemann, Sr. Elaine	Rejoice, Queen Of Heaven
Gentemann, Sr. Elaine	Were You There
Geoboro, Jean	Take Our Hands
George	Come Ye Faithful, Raise The
George	God Is Love
George	It Is The Joyful Eastertime
George	Stand Up And Bless The Lord
George	Suite For Organ
George, Graham	Fight The Good Fight
Germaine	All Of My Life
Germaine	Fear Not
Germaine	From Among The Branches
Germaine	Gift Of Peace
Germaine	I'll Never Contented Be
Germaine	Jerusalem
Germaine	Love One Another
Germaine	My Lord Is Long A Comin'
Germaine	Osee (Hosea)

COMPOSER INDEX

Germaine	Resurrection
Germaine	Sing Out, Sing Out
Germaine	Song Of Trust
Germaine	The Father Had But One Son
Germaine	The Wind Is Blowin'
Germaine	Who Is This Man
Germaine	You Are My People
Gerrish, James	Come Creator Spirit
Gerrish, James	Enter And Sing To The Lord
Gerrish, James	Let Everyone Praise (Ps 150
Gerrish, James	Sing Alleluia! (Be Glad Wit
Gesangbuch (Canavati)	Carol Of The Three Kings
Gevaert, F A	Cantique De Noel
Gevaert, F A	Chanson Joyeuse Do Noel
Gevaert, F A	Le Message Des Anges
Gevaert, F A	Sleep Of The Child Jesus
Gibbons, Orlando	Almighty And Everlasting Go
Gibbons, Orlando	Almighty God, Who By Thy So
Gibbons, Orlando	Blessed Be The Lord
Gibbons, Orlando	Come, Holy Spirit
Gibbons, Orlando	Eight Anthems
Gibbons, Orlando	First And Second Preces And
Gibbons, Orlando	Four Anthems
Gibbons, Orlando	Hosannah To The Son Of Davi
Gibbons, Orlando	I Am The Resurrection And T
Gibbons, Orlando	Lift Up Your Heads (Ps 24)
Gibbons, Orlando	Magnificat And Nunc Dimitti
Gibbons, Orlando	O Clap Your Hands (With Dox
Gibbons, Orlando	O God The King Of Glory (Md
Gibbons, Orlando	O Lord In Thy Wrath (Md)
Gibbons, Orlando	Short Service (Md)
Gibbons, Orlando	The Second Service (Te Deum
Gibbons, Orlando	The Short Service (Venite,
Gibbons, Orlando	This Is The Record Of John
Gibbons, Orlando	Thou God Of Wisdom (M)
Gibbons, Orlando	Twenty-Five Anthems (In 4 V
Gibbons, Orlando	Why Art Thou So Heavy, O My
Gibbs	Behold The Savior Of Mankin
Gibbs/Peterson	Channels Only
Gibbs, Alan	Christ Our Passover (M)
Gibbs, C. Armstrong	Bless The Lord, O My Soul
Gibbs, C. Armstrong	Easter (Most Glorious Lord)
Gibbs, C. Armstrong	O Praise God In His Holines
Gibson,S./Brown,C.	Jesus Precious Savior
Gilbert, Norman	Christ The Lord Is Risen!
Gilbert, Norman	Glory To Thee (Me) 1
Gilbert, Norman	O Praise God (Ps 150)
Gilbert, Norman	Praise To The Lord (E)
Gilbert, Norman	Praise To The Lord, The Alm
Gilbert, Norman	Praise, My Soul, The King O
Gilchrist, W W	Except The Lord Build The H
Giles, Nathaniel	Almighty Lord And God Of Lo
Gillette, James R.	Three Anthems For Junior Ch
Gilliam, R L	Lord Of All
Gilligan, M. (Text)	Alleluia! Christ Has Risen
Gilligan, M. (Text)	Alleluia! Jesus Is Lord
Gilligan, M. (Text)	Alleluia! Let The Song Of G
Gilligan, M. (Text)	An Age Had Passed
Gilligan, M. (Text)	An Angel Came To Nazareth
Gilligan, M. (Text)	Blessed Be The Lord
Gilligan, M. (Text)	Christ Has Risen
Gilligan, M. (Text)	Christ Has Risen From The D
Gilligan, M. (Text)	Christ Our Leader
Gilligan, M. (Text)	Christ Our Lord And Brother
Gilligan, M. (Text)	Christ The Lord Today Has R
Gilligan, M. (Text)	Church's One Foundation, Th
Gilligan, M. (Text)	Come To The Running River
Gilligan, M. (Text)	Come Where The Wind Is Free
Gilligan, M. (Text)	Come, Holy Spirit
Gilligan, M. (Text)	Come, Rich And Poor
Gilligan, M. (Text)	Come, Shake The Mountains
Gilligan, Michael	All Glory, Praise, And Hono
Gilligan, Michael	Angels We Have Heard On Hig
Gilligan, Michael	Ave Maria
Gilligan, Michael	Child Was Born, A
Gilligan, Michael	Christ Is Our Leader
Gilligan, Michael	Christ Our Prophet
Gilligan, Michael	Come By Here
Gilligan, Michael	Come Save Me, Lord
Gilligan, Michael	Eternal Father
Gilligan, Michael	From The Depths
Gilligan, Michael	Give Thanks To God The Fath
Gilligan, Michael	Give Thanks To The Lord
Gilligan, Michael	Give The King Your Final Ju
Gilligan, Michael	Grant Us Peace
Gilligan, Michael	Great Amen For Advent
Gilligan, Michael	Great Amen For Christmas An
Gilligan, Michael	Great Amen For Easter
Gilligan, Michael	Great Amen For Pentecost
Gilligan, Michael	Great Amen's Through The Ye
Gilligan, Michael	How Brightly Shines The Mor
Gilligan, Michael	Hymn For The Sick
Gilligan, Michael	In Ages Now Long Past
Gilligan, Michael	In Heaven Give Glory
Gilligan, Michael	Live In The Light
Gilligan, Michael	Lord Have Mercy On Us
Gilligan, Michael	Lord Is Drawing Near, The
Gilligan, Michael	Marana-Tha
Gilligan, Michael	Mary The Dawn
Gilligan, Michael	Mary, Filled With Grace
Gilligan, Michael	Mighty Fortress, A
Gilligan, Michael	Mountains Will Sing, The
Gilligan, Michael	Noel
Gilligan, Michael	Now Sing With Joy
Gilligan, Michael	O Christ Your Church Is Wai
Gilligan, Michael	Out Of The Depths
Gilligan, Michael	Peace I Give You
Gilligan, Michael	Praise Our God
Gilligan, Michael	Praise The Lord, Now Come
Gilligan, Michael	Prayer Of The Faithful For
Gilligan, Michael	Prayer Of The Faithful For
Gilligan, Michael	Prayer Of The Faithful For
Gilligan, Michael	Prayer Of The Faithful For
Gilligan, Michael	Prayer Of The Faithful For
Gilligan, Michael	Prayer Of The Faithful For
Gilligan, Michael	Proclaim To The World
Gilligan, Michael	Redeemer King
Gilligan, Michael	Rise Up
Gilligan, Michael	Salem City
Gilligan, Michael	Servant-King, The
Gilligan, Michael	Shout Aloud To Heaven
Gilligan, Michael	Sing Of Mary
Gilligan, Michael	Son Of God
Gilligan, Michael	Song Of The City
Gilligan, Michael	Spirit Of Strength
Gilligan, Michael	Sun Has Risen, The
Gilligan, Michael	This Day A Rose Of Judah
Gilligan, Michael	To God We Sing A New Song
Gilligan, Michael	To The Name That Guides Our
Gilligan, Michael	Today The World Is Filled
Gilligan, Michael	Wake Awake
Gilligan, Michael	We Look For Light
Gilligan, Michael	What Love Have We Denied To
Gilligan, Michael	When I Had Fallen Low Indee
Gilligan, Michael	You Christians All
Gilligan, Michael (Tex	Glory Hosanna
Gilligan, Michael (Tex	Hear Heaven Thunder
Gilligan, Michael (Tex	How Great And Good Is He
Gilmour/Kirk	He Brought Me Out
Gilsdorf, Sr. Helen	Abba, Father
Gilsdorf, Sr. Helen	As The Hills Are Round Abou
Gilsdorf, Sr. Helen	Be Glad, Be Happy
Gilsdorf, Sr. Helen	Come To The Water
Gilsdorf, Sr. Helen	Every Day I Will Praise You
Gilsdorf, Sr. Helen	Give Thanks
Gilsdorf, Sr. Helen	Go Out To The Whole World
Gilsdorf, Sr. Helen	God, Hear Me Calling (Psalm
Gilsdorf, Sr. Helen	Grace And Peace
Gilsdorf, Sr. Helen	I In Them
Gilsdorf, Sr. Helen	Jerusalem
Gilsdorf, Sr. Helen	John The Baptist
Gilsdorf, Sr. Helen	O Antiphons
Gilsdorf, Sr. Helen	Psalm 150
Gilsdorf, Sr. Helen	Restore Us
Gilsdorf, Sr. Helen	Spirit Of Light And Life
Gilsdorf, Sr. Helen	Take Heart
Gilsdorf, Sr. Helen	The Ballad Of Paul
Gilsdorf, Sr. Helen	The Truth Will Make You Fre
Gilsdorf, Sr. Helen	What Great Marvels
Gilsdorf, Sr. Helen	Yes, Lord, Alleluia
Gilsdorf, Sr. Helen	You Have Put On Christ
Giorgi, Giovanni	Glory And Honor
Girard/Johnston Et Al	Love Song (Dunamis Music)
Girard, Chuck	Evermore (I Love The Feelin
Girard, Chuck	Everybody Knows For Sure
Girard, Chuck	Galilee (Jesus Took A Walk)
Girard, Chuck	Lay Your Burden Down
Girard, Chuck	Quiet Hour (When The Day Is
Girard, Chuck	Rock & Roll Preacher
Girard, Chuck	Slow Down (In The Midst...)
Girard, Chuck	Sometimes Alleluia
Girard, Chuck	Tinagera (She Is Young)
Girard, Chuck	You Ask My Why (I Keep Smil
Glarum	Be Merciful Unto Me, O God
Glarum, L Stanley	A Choral Prayer(A Cap)
Glarum, L Stanley	Ask And It Shall Be Gi.en Y
Glarum, L Stanley	Blessed Is The Man (A Cap)
Glarum, L Stanley	Canticle Of Mary
Glarum, L Stanley	Exalt Ye
Glarum, L Stanley	Fanfare For Thanksgiving
Glarum, L Stanley	I Saw A Stranger Yester'en
Glarum, L Stanley	I Will Love Thee O Lord
Glarum, L Stanley	King Of Glory, The
Glarum, L Stanley	Lord Hosanna In The Highest
Glarum, L Stanley	Master, Speak! Thy Servant
Glarum, L Stanley	Psalm 148 (Praise Ye The Lo
Glarum, L Stanley	Rejoice In The Lord
Glarum, L Stanley	Sing Aloud Unto God
Glarum, L Stanley	Thy Word Is A Lamp
Glarum, L Stanley	Unto Thee Will I Sing
Glarum, L Stanley	We Give Thanks To Thee
Glarum, L Stanley	When One Knows Thee
Glaser/Johnson	O For A Thousand Tongues
Glaser/Wesley/Carmicha	O For A Thousand Tongues To
Glees, Robert	My Hope And Trust
Glinka, M	Cherubim Song
Goeboro, Jean	Consider The Lilies
Goeboro, Jean	Love
Goemanne, Noel	Agnus Dei (Eng Mass)
Goemanne, Noel	Alleluia, Sing To Jesus
Goemanne, Noel	Amazing Grace
Goemanne, Noel	Christ Is Risen
Goemanne, Noel	Come Holy Ghost
Goemanne, Noel	Crown Him With Many Crowns
Goemanne, Noel	Father, We Thank Thee
Goemanne, Noel	For The Beauty Of The Earth
Goemanne, Noel	Gloria (Eng Mass)
Goemanne, Noel	Gloria (W/Fl,Cello)
Goemanne, Noel	Glory To God (Opt Brs/Timp)
Goemanne, Noel	Glory To God (W/Cantor) Dom
Goemanne, Noel	God Father, Praise And Glor
Goemanne, Noel	Great Amen
Goemanne, Noel	Holy God, We Praise Thy Nam
Goemanne, Noel	Holy, Holy (Opt Brs/Timp)
Goemanne, Noel	Holy, Holy, Holy (Icet)
Goemanne, Noel	Holy, Holy, Holy (W/Cantor)
Goemanne, Noel	Hymns Of Thanks
Goemanne, Noel	Kyrie (Eng Mass)
Goemanne, Noel	Kyrie I (Rira)
Goemanne, Noel	Kyrie Ii (Rirc)
Goemanne, Noel	Lamb Of God
Goemanne, Noel	Lamb Of God (Opt Brs/Timp)
Goemanne, Noel	Lamb Of God (W/Cantor)Domin
Goemanne, Noel	Leoni
Goemanne, Noel	Let Us Break Bread Together
Goemanne, Noel	Liturgical Mass
Goemanne, Noel	Llanfair
Goemanne, Noel	Lord Have Mercy (W/Cantor)
Goemanne, Noel	Lord Have Mercy(Opt Brs/Tim
Goemanne, Noel	My Shepherd Will Supply My
Goemanne, Noel	O Lord Who Drew From Jesus'
Goemanne, Noel	O Most Holy One And Only
Goemanne, Noel	Praise To The Lord
Goemanne, Noel	Prayer For Peace
Goemanne, Noel	Rejoice, The Lord Is King
Goemanne, Noel	Sanctus (Eng Mass)
Goemanne, Noel	Sanctus (W/Fl,Cello)
Goemanne, Noel	Sing Praise To God
Goemanne, Noel	Sing To The Lord
Goemanne, Noel	Song Of Hope
Goemanne, Noel	The God Of Abraham Praise
Goemanne, Noel	The Year Of Jubilee
Goemanne, Noel	The Year Of Jubilee Has Com
Goemanne, Noel	There's A Wideness In God's
Goemanne, Noel	To Jesus Christ Our Soverei
Goemanne, Noel	Unto Us A Boy Is Born
Goemanne, Noel	What Wondrous Love
Goemanne, Noel (Arr)	Now Thank We All Our God (W
Gold/Mason/Stookey	Hymn
Golden, James Reed	I'll Never Be Lonely
Golden, James Reed	Never Knew The Day
Goldsmith, J.	Amen
Gonzalo, Carrie	A Christ Centered Life
Gonzalo, Carrie	Don't Waste Your Precious Y
Gonzalo, Carrie	Gone Are The Days
Gonzalo, Carrie	He'll Never Leave Me
Gonzalo, Carrie	I Belong To Jesus
Gonzalo, Carrie	I Found Life In Christ
Gonzalo, Carrie	Jesus, My Comforter
Gonzalo, Carrie	Jesus, My Wonderful Lord
Gonzalo, Carrie	Rejoice And Sing
Goodban-Hardwicke	Now We Are Met
Goode	Born A King
Goode	Magnificat
Goode	Processional
Goode, Jack	Prayer Intonations
Goode, Jack C.	On His Might
Goode, Jack C.	Psalm 150
Goode, Jack C.	Seven Sacred Solos
Goode, Jack C.	Sing To The Lord
Goodell (Arr)	Were You There?
Goodenough, Forrest	Thy Giving Power
Goodenough, Forrest	Who So Dwelleth
Goodhall, Clare	The Lamb
Goodman, Howard	Give Up
Goossen, Frederic	American Meditations
Goossen, Frederic	Death, Be Not Proud
Goossen, Frederic	Hodie
Gorczycki, G.G.	Ave Maria (Lat Only)(M)
Gorczycki, G.G.	Iudica Me Deus (E & L) (Md)
Gore Richard	Blow Ye The Trumpet
Gore Richard	My Soul Doth Magnify
Gore, Richard	Let God Arise
Gore, Richard T	Bless Ye The Lord (D)
Gore, Richard T	I Will Magnify Thee (Md)
Gore, Richard T.	God Of Abraham Praise, The
Goss/Johnson	Praise!
Goss/Mickelson	Praise, My Soul, The King O
Goss/Peterson	Who Is On The Lord's Side?
Goss, John	God So Loved The World
Goss, John	O Saviour Of The World(A Ca
Goss, John	Praise My Soul The King Of
Gottschalk	In His Presence
Goudimel Claude G.	Psalm 65(Ainsworth Psalter)
Goudimel, C W	Psalm 34
Goudimel, Claude	Ainsi Quon Oit Le Cerf Brui
Goudimel, Claude	Missa, La Bien Que J'ay
Goudimel, Claude	Steadfast And Good Is Jehov
Gough, Nancy	Open Your Heart
Gough, Nancy	Our Father

PAGE 157

COMPOSER INDEX

Composer	Title
Gounod, Charles	Adore And Be Still (C)
Gounod, Charles	Ave Maria. Father To Thee W
Gounod, Charles	Ave Verum(Jesu Word Of God
Gounod, Charles	Benedictus And Sanctus
Gounod, Charles	Bethlehem
Gounod, Charles	Blessed Is He Who Cometh
Gounod, Charles	By Babylon's Wave
Gounod, Charles	Cor Jesu
Gounod, Charles	Gloria In Excelsis Deo
Gounod, Charles	Glory To God
Gounod, Charles	Jerusalem O Turn Thee To Th
Gounod, Charles	Jesu Word Of God Incarnate
Gounod, Charles	Lovely Appear(The Redemptio
Gounod, Charles	Mass Of The Sacred Heart
Gounod, Charles	Mass 2 In G Major For Men's
Gounod, Charles	Mass 6 In G Maj (4 Voices,S
Gounod, Charles	Messe Breve In C Major 7
Gounod, Charles	Messe Solenelle
Gounod, Charles	Nazareth
Gounod, Charles	O Divine Redeemer
Gounod, Charles	O Divine Redeemer
Gounod, Charles	Out Of Darkness (Cantata On
Gounod, Charles	Praise Ye The Father
Gounod, Charles	Praise Ye The Father(Marche
Gounod, Charles	Ring Out Wild Bells
Gounod, Charles	Sanctus
Gounod, Charles	Sanctus
Gounod, Charles	Sanctus & Benedictus (St Ce
Gounod, Charles	Sanctus And Benedictus (St.
Gounod, Charles	Send Out Thy Light
Gounod, Charles	Send Out Thy Light
Gounod, Charles	There Is A Green Hill Far A
Gounod, Charles	Unfold Ye Portals ("Redempt
Gounod, Charles	Unfold Ye Portals(The Redem
Gounod, Charles	Unfold, Ye Portals
Graap, Augustine	Clap Your Hands (Ascension)
Graap, Augustine	Russian Alleluia (Victimae)
Grace, Sister Mary	All Of My Life
Grace, Sister Mary	Fear Not, Little Flock
Grace, Sister Mary	He Who Abides In Me
Grace, Sister Mary	Psalm 1 He Is Like A Tree
Grace, Sister Mary	Psalm 103 All Of My Life
Grace, Sister Mary	Psalm 109 O Lord God
Grace, Sister Mary	Psalm 126 These Are They
Grace, Sister Mary	Psalm 66 Shout Joyfully To
Graham	Alleluia To Our King
Graham	And Nobody Knows
Graham	Christmas Lullaby From Chin
Graham	Long Ago In Bethlehem
Graham	My Master Was So Very Poor
Graham	Shepherds Tell Your Wondrou
Graham	Sing We Now Hosanna
Graham	Sing With Wonder And Deligh
Graham, Robert	Behold The Sorrow Of The Lo
Graham, Robert	Christmas Story, The
Graham, Robert	How Still The Garden Of Get
Graham, Robert	Hush My Dear
Graham, Robert	In The Beginning
Graham, Robert	Sing Joy!
Graham, Robert	The Voices Of Christmas
Grainer, J	Hosanna
Grainger, P A	Alleluia Psallat(Alleluia L
Grandi, Alessandro	Exaudi Deus(Hear Me O Lord)
Grandi, Alessandro	Veniat Dilectus Meus(Come O
Grant, Don	Were You There? (No 4014)
Grape/Rasley	Jesus Paid It All
Grauert	O Holy Child
Graun-Wetzler	He Endured The Cross
Graun-Wienandt, Karl H	Lord I Love The Habitation
Graun, K. H.	Blessed Are The Faithful
Graun, Karl H	He Was Despised
Graves-Track, G.	We Sing Now At Christmas
Graves, William	Unto Thee Do We Cry
Greatorex/Peterson	Begin, My Tongue, Some Heav
Green, F.P.	Glorious The Day When Chris
Green, James R.	The Shadows Of The Cross (T
Green, Russell	Drop, Drop Slow Tears (A Ca
Greenberg, N. & Smoldo	The Play Of Herod
Greenberg, Noah (Ed)	The Play Of Daniel
Greene C & M Renfro	Come Closer Lord
Greene, Maurice	Hear My Prayer
Greene, Maurice	Lord, Let Me Know Mine End
Greene, Maurice	Magnificat And Nunc Dimitti
Greene, Maurice	My Lips Shall Speak Of Thy
Greene, Maurice	Praised Be The Lord (Me)
Greene, Maurice	Thou Visitest The Earth (Ps
Greestone	Love Came Down At Christmas
Gregor	Hosanna
Gregorian Mel/Lee(Arr)	Jerusalem, Jerusalem (+Ps 1
Gregory, D.	O King Of Might & Splendor
Greif,Jean A	Alleluia, Praise His Name
Greif,Jean A	Bless Us Mighty Father
Greif,Jean A	Come,The Lord Is Waiting Fo
Greif,Jean A	Eucharist, Most Holy.
Greif,Jean A	Eyes Have Not Seen
Greif,Jean A	Forever His People Adore Hi
Greif,Jean A	Glory Be To The Father.
Greif,Jean A	Hail Mary.
Greif,Jean A	He Who Believes In Me.
Greif,Jean A	Holy, Holy, God Of Hosts
Greif,Jean A	Hymn Of Love.
Greif,Jean A	I Was Hungry,And You Fed Me
Greif,Jean A	In This Season Of Lent.
Greif,Jean A	Jesus, Come To Us.
Greif,Jean A	Litany Of The Eucharist.
Greif,Jean A	Litany Of The Holy Spirit.
Greif,Jean A	Not All Of Those Who Say Lo
Greif,Jean A	One Bread, One Body Are We.
Greif,Jean A	Rejoice, Rejoice.
Greif,Jean A	Thanks Be To God.
Greif,Jean A	We Are The Light Of The Wor
Greif,Jean A	We Offer You Our Gifts.
Gresens	Come To The Manger
Gretchaninoff, A	Holy Radiant Light
Gretchaninoff, A.	God Is Everywhere
Gretchaninoff, A.	Missa Festivo
Grieb	Fantasia On Nun Danket
Grieb	The Angels Song
Grieb	Three Riders, The
Grieb, Herbert	A Christmas Lullaby
Grieb, Herbert	As Joseph Was A-Walking (A
Grieb, Herbert	Come Now Let Us Reason Toge
Grieb, Herbert	Early Easter Morning
Grieb, Herbert	From All That Dwell Below T
Grieb, Herbert	Great Creator Of The World
Grieb, Herbert	Hail Festal Day
Grieb, Herbert	How Calm And Beautiful The
Grieb, Herbert	Kings Of The Orient Three
Grieb, Herbert	Little White Dove
Grieb, Herbert	Long Ago A Prophet Sang
Grieb, Herbert	Morning Grace
Grieb, Herbert	No Room In The Inn
Grieb, Herbert	O God Of Every Race And Cre
Grieb, Herbert	O Love That Wilt Not Let Me
Grieb, Herbert	Set Me As A Seal
Grieb, Herbert	This Book Of The Law
Grieb, Herbert	This Holy Day
Grieb, Herbert	Walk Worthy
Grieg	My Lord Has Set Me Free
Grieg E.	Four Psalms, Op. 74 (Eng)
Grieg-Bempton	Now Praise We Great And Fam
Grieg-Christiansen	Behold A Host
Grieg-Overby	God's Son Has Made Me Free
Grieg, E.	The Great White Host
Griffin, Jack	The Mountain Of The Lord
Grime, William	More Hymns And Anthems For
Grimes/Decou	Jesus Gives Me A Song
Grimes, Travis	Early In The Morning
Grimm, Johann D.	Lamb Of God! Thou Shalt Rem
Grimm, Johann D.	The Child Of Love
Groom, Lester	Gothic Fanfare
Groom, Lester	Gothic Fanfare
Groom, Lester	Meditations On Sweet Rivers
Groom, Lester	Praise To The Lord
Groom, Lester	Processional March On St Du
Groom, Lester	Three Festival Preludes
Groom, Lester	Two Compositions For Organ
Gruber/Decou	Silent Night Holy Night
Gruber/Gruber	Silent Night
Gruber, F.-Track, G.	Silent Night (Full, Origina
Grum/Smith	Victory Ahead
Grundy, S.K.	I Found Joy (W/Piano)
Gryniewicz, Tom & Elle	Rejoice Always
Guenther, Ralph R.	Praise Ye The Lord
Guenther, Ralph R.	The Song Of David (1 Ck 29)
Guerrero, Francisco	Ecce Nunc Tempus
Guerrero, Francisco	Missa Puer Qui Natus Est No
Guerrero, Francisco	Vamos Al Portal
Guest, Douglas	Wedding Responses
Guion	Prayer
Guion, David W.	I Talked To God Last Night
Gulliksen, Kenn	As A Husband
Gulliksen, Kenn	Canticle
Gulliksen, Kenn	Charity
Gulliksen, Kenn	Joanie's Song
Gulliksen, Kenn	Lullaby
Gulliksen, Kenn	Man Of The Lord
Gulliksen, Kenn	Moment Of Time
Gulliksen, Kenn	O Lord Amen
Gulliksen, Kenn	Proverb 31
Gulliksen, Kenn	We Have Come
Gulliksen, Kenn	You Were There
Gumma	Rise Up, O Men Of God!
Gumpelzhaimer, A	Praise Ye The Lord With Sin
Gumpelzhaimer, Adam	Coenam Cum Discipulis
Gumpelzhaimer,A/Klein	Praise Ye The Lord (E & Ger
Gunter/Johnson	Minor Carol, The
Gurney-Douglas	Come Ye Lofty, Come Ye Lowl
Gustafson, Dwight	The House Of Our Lord
Gutfreund, Ed (Rev.)	Alleluia, Praise To The Lor
Gutfreund, Ed (Rev.)	Back And Forward
Gutfreund, Ed (Rev.)	Cathedral Chorus Marching G
Gutfreund, Ed (Rev.)	Children Of Sunlight
Gutfreund, Ed (Rev.)	From An Indirect Love
Gutfreund, Ed (Rev.)	Good Morning, Zachary
Gutfreund, Ed (Rev.)	How Can I Keep From Singing
Gutfreund, Ed (Rev.)	In The Day Of The Lord
Gutfreund, Ed (Rev.)	Lights Of The City, The
Gutfreund, Ed (Rev.)	Lord Have Mercy On Us All
Gutfreund, Ed (Rev.)	When We See
Gutfreund, Ed (Rev.)	Your People Of Faith
Haag	Mustard Seed Faith
Haag, Preston	Glimpse Of Jesus
Haag, Preston	Going His Way
Haag, Preston	The Mystery Of It All
Habecker, Marilyn P.	The Birthday Of The King (N
Habjan, Germaine	Come, Lord Jesus
Hadle	Hosanna, Loud Hosanna!
Hadler	Christmas/Folk Style
Hadler	Exaltation (S A Opt B)
Hadler	Good To Me
Hadler	Merrily On High
Hadler	Praise The Lord
Hadler	Prepare Him Room
Hadler	Three Bell Carols For Junio
Hadley	Praise The Lord, Sing A Joy
Hager	Holy, Holy, Holy (W/Rhythm)
Hager	Lamb Of God (With Rhythm In
Hairston/Lojeski(Arr)	Mary's Boy Child
Hairston, Jester	Band Of Angels
Hairston, Jester	Mary's Little Boy Child
Hairston, Jester	Wade In De Water
Hale, Leonard	Heaven Is Way Out There
Hale, S.	Beloved
Hale, S.	I Love Him (With All My Hea
Hale, S.	In Your Reach
Hale, S.	Jesus Loves Me (Arrangement
Hale, S.	Love Is God's Answer
Hale, S.	The Rock Of My Salvation
Hall J. Barnett	Heaven's Lights Ahead
Hall J., Coakley J.	Too Late To Pray
Hall, Alan	Short Communion Service W/C
Hall, Arthur	Sing With The Spirit
Hall, King	Hear Me When I Call
Hall, King	O Lord, My Trust Is In Thy
Hallstrom, Henry	Christ The Lord Is Risen To
Hamblen Stuart	A Few Things To Remember
Hamblen Stuart	Army Of The Lord, The
Hamblen Stuart	Blood Upon Your Hands
Hamblen Stuart	But For The Grace Of God
Hamblen Stuart	Dear Lord, Be My Shepherd
Hamblen Stuart	Do You Know Jesus?
Hamblen Stuart	Don't Send Those Kids To Su
Hamblen Stuart	Face To Face
Hamblen Stuart	Friends I Know
Hamblen Stuart	Gathering Home
Hamblen Stuart	Go On By
Hamblen Stuart	Grasshopper Macclain
Hamblen Stuart	Handful Of Sunshine, A.
Hamblen Stuart	Have Faith, Don't Cry
Hamblen Stuart	He Bought My Soul At Calvar
Hamblen Stuart	His Hands
Hamblen Stuart	How Big Is God
Hamblen Stuart	I Am Persuaded
Hamblen Stuart	I Believe
Hamblen Stuart	I Don't Know Why
Hamblen Stuart	I Want To Be There
Hamblen Stuart	I'm Not Afraid Of The Dark
Hamblen Stuart	I've Got So Many Million Ye
Hamblen Stuart	Is He Satisfied With Me
Hamblen Stuart	It's A Brand New Day
Hamblen Stuart	Keep This In Mind
Hamblen Stuart	King Of All Kings
Hamblen Stuart	Known Only To Him
Hamblen Stuart	Little Black Sheep
Hamblen Stuart	Little Lost Sheep
Hamblen Stuart	Lord Is Counting On You, Th
Hamblen Stuart	Lord, I Pray
Hamblen Stuart	My Father
Hamblen Stuart	My Lord Is Mighty
Hamblen Stuart	My Religion's Not Old-Fashi
Hamblen Stuart	Of God I Sing
Hamblen Stuart	One Day Nearer Home
Hamblen Stuart	Open Up Your Heart
Hamblen Stuart	Partners With The Lord
Hamblen Stuart	Someone
Hamblen Stuart	Somewhere Beyond The Sun
Hamblen Stuart	Teach Me, Lord, To Wait
Hamblen Stuart	That Lonesome Valley
Hamblen Stuart	These Things Shall Pass
Hamblen Stuart	This Book
Hamblen Stuart	This Ole House
Hamblen Stuart	This Ship Of Mine
Hamblen Stuart	Tho' Autumn's Coming On
Hamblen Stuart	Until Then
Hamblen Stuart	Well Done, Come Home
Hamblen Stuart	What Can I Do For My Countr
Hamblen Stuart	When Earth's Last Picture I
Hamblen Stuart	When My Lord Picks Up The P
Hamblen Stuart	Where The Seasons Never Cha
Hamblen Stuart	Workshop Of The Lord
Hamblen Stuart	You Can't Love Without Givi
Hamblen Stuart	You Must Be Born Again
Hamblen Suzy	Be Happy Today
Hamblen Suzy	Come Unto Me
Hamblen Suzy	Help Thou My Unbelief
Hamblen Suzy	The Lord's Prayer
Hamblen Suzy	There's A Place In God's He
Hamblen, B.	Hear Us, O Saviour
Hamblen, B.	Trust In Him

COMPOSER INDEX

Composer	Title
Hamburger/Gordon	By My Side
Hamill	Aria Da Chiesa
Hamill, Paul	My Shepherd
Hamill, Paul	Were You There?
Hammerschmidt	An Easter Dialogue (W/Brass
Hammerschmidt/Pooler	Glory And Triumph
Hammersma, John	Hymns For Youth
Hammersma, John	The Children's Hymnbook
Hampton, Calvin	Agnus Dei (Mass For New Rit
Hampton, Calvin	At The Gospel
Hampton, Calvin	Christ Is Risen Indeed
Hampton, Calvin	Christ Our Passover (Mass F
Hampton, Calvin	Creed (Icet Text) Cong, Org
Hampton, Calvin	Gloria (Mass For New Rite)
Hampton, Calvin	Hail Thee Festival Day (W/O
Hampton, Calvin	Joyful! Joyful!
Hampton, Calvin	Kyrie (Mass For New Rite)
Hampton, Calvin	Lord, Speak To Me
Hampton, Calvin	Lord's Prayer (Mass For New
Hampton, Calvin	Lord's Prayer Icet
Hampton, Calvin	Memorial Acclamation (Chris
Hampton, Calvin	Preface Dialogue
Hampton, Calvin	Prelude And Variations
Hampton, Calvin	Sanctus (Mass For New Rite)
Hampton, Calvin	This Is The Day
Hampton, Calvin	Trisagion (Mass For New Rit
Hanchett, Inez; Laney	Lead By The Master's Hand
Hancock Gerre	A Paraphrase Of "St. Elizab
Hancock, Gerre	A Song To The Lamb (W/Brass
Handel	Glory To God
Handel/Davis	How Excellent Thy Name
Handel/Ed Johnson	Behold The Lamb Of God
Handel/Johnson	Hallelujah Chorus
Handel/Johnson	Messiah-Singspiration's Abr
Handel/Lovecace	To God Let Praise Be Song
Handel/Montgomery	Thine Is The Glory (Easy)
Handel, G. F.	All We Like Sheep Have Gone
Handel, G. F.	Alleluia (From Coronation A
Handel, G. F.	And The Clory Of The Lord
Handel, G. F.	And The Glory Of The Lord
Handel, G. F.	And The Glory Of The Lord
Handel, G. F.	And The Glory Of The Lord
Handel, G. F.	And The Glory Of The Lord
Handel, G. F.	And With His Stripes
Handel, G. F.	Athalia (Oratorio)
Handel, G. F.	Awake The Trumpet's Lofty S
Handel, G. F.	Behold The Lamb Of God
Handel, G. F.	Chandos Anthem 1 (Be Joyful
Handel, G. F.	Chandos Anthem 2 (In The Lo
Handel, G. F.	Chandos Anthem 3 (Have Merc
Handel, G. F.	Chandos Te Deum (We Praise
Handel, G. F.	Deck, Thyself, My Soul, Wit
Handel, G. F.	Dettingen Te Deum
Handel, G. F.	Ev'ry Valley (From Messiah)
Handel, G. F.	Evening Hymn (E)
Handel, G. F.	Father, O Hear Me
Handel, G. F.	For All These Mercies We Wi
Handel, G. F.	For Unto Us A Child Is Born
Handel, G. F.	For Unto Us A Child Is Born
Handel, G. F.	For Unto Us A Child Is Born
Handel, G. F.	From Celestial Seats Descen
Handel, G. F.	Fugue In E Major
Handel, G. F.	Funeral Anthem For Queen Ca
Handel, G. F.	Funeral Anthem On The Death
Handel, G. F.	Give Ear O Lord, Unto My Pr
Handel, G. F.	Glory Around His Head, The
Handel, G. F.	Glory To Cod
Handel, G. F.	Glory To God ("Messiah")
Handel, G. F.	Great Is The Father
Handel, G. F.	Hallelujah Chorus
Handel, G. F.	Hallelujah Chorus ("Messiah
Handel, G. F.	Hallelujah Chorus, The
Handel, G. F.	Hallelujah, Amen
Handel, G. F.	He Shall Feed His Flock
Handel, G. F.	Here Is Heavenly Joy (E)
Handel, G. F.	Holy Art Thou
Handel, G. F.	Holy, Holy, Holy (Me)
Handel, G. F.	How Excellent Thy Name
Handel, G. F.	How Excellent Thy Name
Handel, G. F.	I Know That My Redeemer Liv
Handel, G. F.	I Know That My Redeemer Liv
Handel, G. F.	I Will Exalt Him
Handel, G. F.	Israel In Egypt (Oratorio)
Handel, G. F.	Judas Maccabaeus (Oratorio,
Handel, G. F.	Largo From "Xerxes"
Handel, G. F.	Let Thy Hand Be Strengthene
Handel, G. F.	Lift Up Your Hands, O Ye Ga
Handel, G. F.	Lift Up Your Heads, O Ye Ga
Handel, G. F.	Lord, I Trust Thee (From Pa
Handel, G. F.	May No Rash Intruder ("Solo
Handel, G. F.	Messiah(Eng-Ger)
Handel, G. F.	Messiah, The (Oratorio)
Handel, G. F.	O Thou That Tellest
Handel, G. F.	O Thou That Tellest Good Ti
Handel, G. F.	Praise The Lord (Judas Macc
Handel, G. F.	Psalm 112(Latin)
Handel, G. F.	Psalm 135 O Praise The Lord
Handel, G. F.	Samson (Eng/Germ) (Oratorio
Handel, G. F.	Since By Man Came Death
Handel, G. F.	Soul, Array Thyself
Handel, G. F.	Surely He Hath Borne Our Gr
Handel, G. F.	Surely He Hath Borne Our Gr
Handel, G. F.	Thanks Be To Thee
Handel, G. F.	The Brotherhood Of Man
Handel, G. F.	The Enemy Said (Israel In E
Handel, G. F.	The King Shall Rejoice
Handel, G. F.	The Lord My Shepherd Is
Handel, G. F.	The Passion Of Christ (1716
Handel, G. F.	Trust In The Lord
Handel, G. F.	We Believe That Thou Shalt
Handel, G. F.	Wedding Chorus From Alceste
Handel, G. F. (Bick)	Come Unto Him (Messiah)
Handel, G. F. (Duroche	Holy Is Thy Name
Handel, G. F. (Wiley)	Come, Holy Light, Guide Div
Handel, G. F. (Wiley)	We Come To Praise His Name
Handel, G. F./Hardwick	Born King Of Kings (E & Lat
Handel, G./Wiley (Arr)	Come Holy Light (From J. Ma
Handel, G./Wiley(Arr)	Thanks Be To Thee
Handel, G.F.(Christy)	Then Round About The Starry
Handel, G.F./Douglas	Be Thou Exalted
Handel, George F.	St John Passion, The
Handel,G.F.(Ed Stein)	Sing Unto God (18 Minutes)
Handl, J. (Gieringer)	Ecce, Quomodo (Lo Now, So I
Handl, Jacob	Ecce Quomodo Moritur Justus
Handl, Jacob	In Nomine Jesu
Handl, Jacob	In Nomine Jesu(At Jesus' Ho
Handl, Jacob	Missa Ich Stund
Handl, Jacob	Omnes De Saba Venient
Handl, Jacob	Surrexit Dominus
Handl, Jacob	This Is The Day
Haney, J/Thompson, S.	A Few Words About Jesus
Hankinson	Child Of Bethlehem, The
Hanson/Watson	Be As A Lion
Hanson, Mike	Gifts Of Bread And Wine
Hanson, Mike	Like A Deer
Hanson, Mike	Praise The Lord, My Brother
Hanson, Mike	What Shall We Give
Haper	Until We Meet Again(I'll Pr
Harburg/Robinson	Hurry Sundown
Hardwicke (Arr)	Glorious Star Is Beaming
Hardwicke (Arr)	Through Midnite Silence (Op
Hardwicke (Arr)	Ye Shepherds, Ye Wise Men!
Hare, Ian	Thou O God Art Praised In Z
Harker, Clifford	Te Deum
Harker, F F	As It Began To Dawn
Harker, F F	Calm On The List'ning Ear O
Harker, F F	Grant, We Beseech Thee
Harker, F F	How Beautiful Upon The Moun
Harker, F F	Turn Ye Even To Me
Harmon, P.	And Holy Is His Name
Harmon, P.	Look Behind You
Harmonization Fel	My Soul Gives Glory To The
Harper/Barnett	My Cactus Christmas Tree
Harper, John	Psalm 150 (Me)
Harper, Redd	Answer Man, The
Harper, Redd	Are You Willing?
Harper, Redd	Back To The Prairies And Ot
Harper, Redd	Each Step Of The Way
Harper, Redd	Five Minutes More
Harper, Redd	I Walk The Glory Road
Harper, Redd	I'm A Happy, Happy Christia
Harper, Redd	Jesus Told Me So
Harper, Redd	Lord Keep Your Hand On Me
Harper, Redd	My Testimony Song
Harper, Redd	Praisallujah
Harper, Redd	Quiet Time, A
Harper, Redd	Rally Round The Cross
Harper, Redd	See What God Can Do
Harper, Redd	Shine Shine Shine
Harper, Redd	Show Me The Way
Harper, Redd	Turn Back To God, America
Harper, Redd	Walkin' And Talkin' With Je
Harper, Redd	What Would I Do Without Jes
Harper,Jeanne&Pulkingh	Fresh Sounds
Harper,Jeanne&Pulkingh	Sounds Of Living Waters
Harrel, Melvin (Tr)	Let Everything Within Me Cr
Harrer/Harris (Arr)	My Heart Sings With Joy (E
Harrer, Johann G	Mein Herz Ist Bereit
Harrer, Johann G	My Heart Is Prepared
Harries, David	O Come, Let Us Sing Unto Th
Harrington/Johnson	There's A Song In The Air
Harris	Ah, Dearest Jesus(A Cap)
Harris	Choral Diptych (A Cap)
Harris	Joyfully Sing We His Praise
Harris	O Food Of Men Wayfaring
Harris (Arr)	Gentle Mary
Harris, Kent	Come, Sound His Praise Abro
Harris, Kent	Glorious Song, The
Harris, Kent	Let All The Earth Rejoice
Harris, William H.	He That Is Down Needs Fear
Harris, William H.	I Said To The Man (E) 1
Harris, William H.	Most Glorious Lord Of Life
Harris, William H.	Our Day Of Praise Is Done
Harrison	My Sweet Lord
Harrison, Dorothy	John Mckay Sings Dorothy Ha
Harrison, Lou	Alma Redemptoris Mater
Harrison, Lou	Mass (To St. Anthony)
Hartzler & Gaeddert	Children's Hymnary, The
Harvey, Richard W.	It Was So Quiet
Harzer, B. Resinerius	St. John's Passion
Haskins/Decou	Since The Savior Found Me
Hassler	Kyrie From "Missa Secunda"
Hassler-Christiansen	O Sacred Head
Hassler/Bach	O Sacred Head
Hassler/Peterson	O Sacred Head, Now Wounded
Hassler, H L	Angelus Ad Pastores Ait
Hassler, H L	Blessed Saviour, Our Lord J
Hassler, H L	Cantate Domino
Hassler, H L	Gloria
Hassler, H L	O Sing Unto The Lord
Hassler, H L	O Sing Unto The Lord
Hassler, H L	Verbum Caro Factum Est
Hassler, H.L.(D1612)	Motet Super Dixit Maria
Hassler,H.L./Ed Klein	Christ Is Arisen (E & Ger)
Hastings	Lord Is A Mighty God, The
Hastings/Rasley	Rock Of Ages
Hatfield, & Mcnees, L.	And He Is Mine
Hatfield, S & Mcnees,L	Don't You Care
Hatfield, Steve	Lord Have Your Way With Me
Hatfield, Steve	My Wonderful Jesus
Hatfield, Steve	Pasadena Kid
Hatfield, Steve	Smile, Jesus Loves You
Hatfield, Steve	Try Jesus
Hatfield, Steve	Walkin' Down The Line
Hatfield,S & Mcnees,L	Have A Nice Day
Hatfield,Steve & Mcnee	His Nail-Pierced Hands
Hatton/Williams	Jesus Shall Reign
Hatton, John	O God, Beneath Thy Guiding
Haubiel, Charles	Madonna
Haubiel, Charles	What Wondrous Sacrifice
Haubrick & Wagner	Listen To My Words
Havergal/Decou	Welcome, Happy Morning
Havey, Marguerite	O Spirit, Who From Jesus Ca
Hawkins	I've Discovered The Way Of
Hawkins, Gordon	As The Heart Panteth (From
Hawkins, Walter	Love Alive (Collection)
Hawthorne	Whispering Hope
Hawthorne/Red, Buryl	It's Cool In The Furnance(M
Hawthorne/Red, Buryl	Lightshine (Musical)
Hawthorne, Alice	Whispering Hope (A Cap)
Haxby, Wm. G.	While I Sup With Thee
Haydn-Coggin	Glory To God In The Highest
Haydn/Decou	Glorious Things Of Thee Are
Haydn/Decou	Ye Servants Of God
Haydn/Mayfield	O Worship The King
Haydn/Yungton	Day Of Resurrection, The
Haydn, Franz J	Mass In B-Flat
Haydn, Franz J	Mass No. 10 In B-Flat There
Haydn, Franz J	Theresa Mass In B-Flat
Haydn, J. (Arr Mccoy)	With Songs And Honors
Haydn, J. (Ed Atkins)	Te Deum (Eng, Lat)
Haydn, J.-Ehret	Lord Have Mercy
Haydn, Joseph	Achieved Is The Glorious Wo
Haydn, Joseph	Achieved Is The Glorious Wo
Haydn, Joseph	Agnus Dei
Haydn, Joseph	And Now Revived He Springs
Haydn, Joseph	Awake The Harp
Haydn, Joseph	Creation
Haydn, Joseph	Darkness Concealed The Eart
Haydn, Joseph	Dona Nobis Pacem
Haydn, Joseph	Dona Nobis Pacem
Haydn, Joseph	Heavens Are Telling, The
Haydn, Joseph	Kyrie
Haydn, Joseph	Kyrie
Haydn, Joseph	Kyrie Eleison
Haydn, Joseph	Last Words Of Christ
Haydn, Joseph	Lo, My Shepherd Is Divine
Haydn, Joseph	Mass St. Joanni De Deo
Haydn, Joseph	Praise The Lord! Ye Heavens
Haydn, Joseph	Sanctus
Haydn, Joseph	Seasons
Haydn, Joseph	Sing To The Lord
Haydn, Joseph	Stabat Mater
Haydn, Joseph	Te Deum Laudamus
Haydn, Joseph	The Heavens Are Telling
Haydn, Joseph	The Heavens Are Telling (Cr
Haydn, Michael	Come, Children, Praise Our
Haydn, Michael	Darkness Was Over All
Haydn, Michael	Ecce! Quomodo Moritur Justu
Haydn, Michael	God Is Merciful
Haydn, Michael	God, In Thee I Seek My Salv
Haydn, Michael	Great Is The Lord Our Maker
Haydn, Michael	Help Us, O Lord, Deliver Us
Haydn, Michael	I Cried To God In Tribulati
Haydn, Michael	Lord Is Near To All, The
Haydn, Michael	Magnificat
Haydn, Michael	O Joyful Day! (Christmas Mo
Haydn, Michael	O Worship The King
Haydn, Michael	O Ye People
Haydn, Michael	Omnes Amici Mei Dereliqueru
Haydn, Michael	Prope Est Dominus
Haydn, Michael	Sing Aloud To God
Haydn, Michael	Sleep In Peace, O Heavenly
Haydn, Michael	Son Of God
Haydn, Michael	Thou Art Mighty
Haydn, Michael	Tristis Est Anima Mea
Haydn, Michael(Ehret)	Day Of Sorrow
Hayes	Alleluia!
Hayes-Douglas (Arr)	Help Us, O God
Hayes, Twila	Take My Hand

COMPOSER INDEX

Hayes, William	Bow Down Thine Ear, O Lord
Hays/Mickelson	Lily Of The Valley, The
Hazzard, Peter	Praise Book, A
Headington, C.	Man's Redemption
Healey, D.	As I Was A-Walking
Healey, D.	Days Of Man W/Solo
Heath, John	Evening Service For Verses
Hebble	Praise To The Lord, The Alm
Hebble, Robert	Glory To God (Cel Of Unity)
Hebble, Robert	Holy, Holy, Holy (Cel Of Un
Hebble, Robert	Lamb Of God (Cel Of Unity)
Hebble, Robert	Lord Have Mercy (Cel Of Uni
Heber, Reginald	Holy, Holy, Holy, Lord God
Hebrew/Tortolano Ed	Ma Tovu (In 19 Lit Rounds)
Heckel, M.P.&Carroll,J	Little Child Sleeping Boy(E
Heckel, M.P.&Carroll,J	The Darkest Night (E) W/Key
Heckel, M.P.&Carroll,J	The Three Gifts (W/Keyboard
Hedges, H	Behold, The Star!
Hedges, H	Psalm Of Praise
Hegarty, David H	Jesus, Jesus, Rest Your Hea
Hegarty, David H	Redeemer Shall Come, The
Hegarty, David H	The Redeemer Shall Come
Hegedus, A	Proper Offertories Of The S
Hegenbart, Alex	Lord Of All Being
Hegenbart, Alex F	Sing, O Sing
Hegenbart, Alex F.	Meditation
Heins/Lorenz	Where Our Lord May Go
Heitmann, D. Roman	Lamparita Votiva (Lamp Of P
Held, Wilbur C	A Message Came To A Maiden
Held, Wilbur C	Advent Service
Held, Wilbur C	Dost Thou In A Manger Lie
Held, Wilbur C	His Are The Thousand Sparkl
Held, Wilbur C	Let Christians All With Joy
Held, Wilbur C	O God Of Truth
Held, Wilbur C	Saw You Never In The Twilig
Heller	Cross Was His Own, The
Hellreigel, Martin	To Jesus Christ Our Soverei
Helser, K.	Sing Little Children
Hemberg-Eskit	Signposts
Hemy/Decou	Faith Of Our Fathers
Hemy, Henri	Faith Of Our Fathers (4-Par
Henderson & Stoutamire	I Will Lift Up Mine Eyes (P
Henderson, K & Stovtam	Praise Ye The Lord
Hendrix, James	After The Storm
Hendrix, James	Arise And Follow Me
Hendrix, James	Can You Believe?
Hendrix, James	Carry On
Hendrix, James	Come On Over Yonder
Hendrix, James	Flee Into Egypt Land (Chris
Hendrix, James	God Maketh No Mistake
Hendrix, James	I Ask God
Hendrix, James	I Have A Father Who Can
Hendrix, James	I Must Go On
Hendrix, James	I'm Still Growing
Hendrix, James	Jesus Prayed As They Slept
Hendrix, James	Let God Take Over
Hendrix, James	Let's Join In Songs Of Love
Hendrix, James	My Reward
Hendrix, James	The Voice Of God
Hendrix, James	There's A Power Working In
Hendrix, James	To Be At Peace With God
Hendrix, James	When I See A Mountain
Hendrix, James	When The Great Trumpet Soun
Henson, Jack E.	Sing A Song Of Christmas
Herbener, Marilyn	Miriam's Song
Herbener, Marilyn	You Will Be My People
Herbert	Let Mount Zion Rejoice
Herbert, Oscar A.	Something To Be Thankful Fo
Herbst, Martin	From The Depths (4-Part Arr
Herforth	Voice, The
Herklots/Lowens	Forgive Our Sins As We Forg
Hernaman, Claudia F.	Throughout These Days
Herrer, Johann G	Psalm 103
Herring, Bruce	A Cowboy's Dream
Herring, Bruce	From The Rising Of The Sun
Herring, Bruce	He's The Reason To Go On
Herring, Bruce	Jesus Is The One
Herring, Bruce	New Song
Herring, Bruce & Angie	Harvest Time
Herring, J.	Power Medley
Herring, J.	Redeemed
Herring, J.	The Woman
Herrmann, William	A Child This Day Is Born
Hershberg, Sarah	Behold, Thou Art Fair
Hershberg, Sarah	Blue Town
Hershberg, Sarah	Coat Of Many Colors
Hershberg, Sarah	Esther
Hershberg, Sarah	Eve's Lament
Hershberg, Sarah	Great Day In Bethlehem
Hershberg, Sarah	Is There?
Hershberg, Sarah	Judith
Hershberg, Sarah	Laban's Lament
Hershberg, Sarah	Life
Hershberg, Sarah	Life Is A Makin' Do
Hershberg, Sarah	Pretend We're Young Again
Hershberg, Sarah	Reap, Reap
Hershberg, Sarah	Sarah
Hershberg, Sarah	Song Of Hannah
ershberg, Sarah	T'was On A Cold And Wintry
shberg, Sarah	The Lion And The Lamb
Hershberg, Sarah	We'll Sing A New Song
Hershberg, Sarah	Weep, Little Children, Weep
Hershberg, Sarah	Whither Thou Goest
Hershberg, Sarah	Who Am I?
Hershberg, Sarah	Willow Tree
Hershberg, Sarah	Woman Of Stone
Hershberg, Sarah	Woman Of Valor
Hershberg, Sarah & Tem	Deborah
Herter, J	In Night's Deep Silence
Herter, J	Two Motets From Kancjonaxy
Herter, J. (Ed)	Ecce Dominus Veniet (E,L)(M
Herzogenberg	Christmas Song
Hess, John H.	Psalm 108
Heussenstamm, George	Dirge In Woods
Heussenstamm, George	Poem Of Circumstance
Hewlett, W H	Fierce Was The Wild Billow
Heyward	I Need Thee Every Hour
Hiles, H	Blessed Are The Merciful
Hilf, Robert	Memorial Acclamation
Hilf, Robert	Praised Be The Father Of Ou
Hillebrand, Frank	Enormous Dreams (Psalm 131)
Hillebrand, Frank	Face To Face (Psalm 42-43)
Hillebrand, Frank	Give Me An Answer (Psalm4)
Hillebrand, Frank	His Love Is Lasting (Psalm
Hillebrand, Frank	I Lift My Eyes To The Mt (P
Hillebrand, Frank	Keep Alive (Psalm 128)
Hillebrand, Frank	Land Without Water (Psalm 6
Hillebrand, Frank	Long Way Home (Psalm 126)
Hillebrand, Frank	Monsoon Rain(Psalm 103)
Hillebrand, Frank	My Shepherd Is The Lord (Ps
Hillebrand, Frank	Poor Builder (Psalm 127)
Hillebrand, Frank	Sheaves Of Peace (Psalm 23)
Hillebrand, Frank	Streams Of Babylon (Psalm 1
Hillebrand, Frank	Vow Song
Hilton, John	Call To Remembrance (Md)
Hilton, John	Lord, For Thy Tender Mercy'
Hilton, John	Teach Me, O Lord (Ps 119 Md
Hilty, Everett J	Praise Our God Above (Penta
Hilty, Everett J.	Built On The Rock (E)
Hilty, Everett J.	O Come, Emmanuel (E)
Hilty, Everett J.	The Lord's Prayer (Merbecke
Hilty, Everett J.	You Are The Temple
Himmel F.H.	Incline Thine Ear To Me (S
Hine	Easter Dawn
Hine, Stuart K.	How Great Thou Art
Hiner,Robbie	It Wouldn't Be Enough (Coll
Hires, B.	I'm Being Guided
Hoag, Charles K	Gloria
Hoag, Charles K	May God Have Mercy Upon Us
Hoag, Charles K	O Be Joyful
Hoag, Charles K	Sing Softly
Hoag, Charles K	Sing We Merrily Unto God Ou
Hoddinott, A. & James	Dives And Lazarus (Cantata)
Hoddinott, Alun	Every Man's Work Shall Be M
Hoddinott, Alun	Great Art Thou, O God (M)
Hoddinott, Alun	Out Of The Deep (D)
Hoffelt, Robert O.	Not Alone For Mighty Empire
Hoffman	Petitions For Help
Hoffman/Decou	What A Wonderful Savior!
Hoffman/Johnson	Give Him The Glory
Hoffmeister, L A	Arise, O Lord
Hokanson, Margrethe	As With Gladness Men Of Old
Holben,Larry/Tewson,B.	Suffer The Children
Holden/Decou	All Hail The Power Of Jesus
Holden/Jess	All Hail The Power Of Jesus
Holden, Oliver	Behold, The Grace Appears
Holden, Oliver	Christmas
Holden, Oliver	Funeral Hymn
Holiday/Johnson	Everywhere And Always
Holiday/Johnson	I Know Where I'm Goin
Holiday/Johnson	It's Yours For The Asking
Holiday, Mickey	Happy Am I
Holiday, Mickey	The Songs Of Mickey Holiday
Holland/Kraehenbuehl	Judge Eternal, Throned
Holloway, Robin	The Death Of God (W/Narrato
Holm, Dallas	Dallas Holm Songs
Holman, Derek	Away The Gloom
Holman, Derek	Christ Hath A Garden
Holman, Derek	Christ, My Beloved
Holman, Derek	Let This Mind Be In You (Me
Holmes	Build Thee More Stately Man
Holst, Imogen	As I Sat Under A Holly Tree
Holst, Imogen	Out Of Your Sleep Arise And
Holt, Evelyn	Nunc Dimittis
Holton	Chimes Of The Holy Night
Holton	Chorus In The Skies, The
Holton	Music Of Bethlehem, The
Holton	Prince Of Peace, The
Holton	World's Redeemer, The
Holyoke, Samuel	Lo! He Comes In Clouds Desc
Holyoke, Samuel	Sandusky
Holz, W W	Thee Will I Love
Homer, Sidney	Sheep And Lambs
Homilius, Gottfried	Der Herr Ist Mein Hirte (Ps
Homilius, Gottfried	Hear Ye Jesus Is The Lamb O
Homilius, Gottfried	Siehe, Das Ist Gottes Lamm
Homilius, Gottfried A	Psalm 23
Honeytree	The Way I Feel (Collection)
Honeytree	Treasures
Hooper	Great Amen
Hooper	Memorial Acclamations (Icet
Hooper	Now Praise We Christ, The H
Hooper, W.L.	Come Down O Love (W/Piano)
Hope,Johnnie/Lambert,O	Down Deep In My Heart
Hopkins-Cassler	Thy Kingdom Come
Hopkins-Nightingale	We Three Kings Of Orient Ar
Hopkins, Edith	Guess What's Behind You
Hopkins, John L	Lift Up Your Heads
Hopper, E./Dell, V.	Go Little Prayer, Go
Hopson	Break Forth Into Joy
Hopson	God Is Our Refuge, God Is O
Hopson	Make A Joyful Noise
Hopson, Hal	Communion Hymn
Hopson, Hal H.	Christmas Bells With Joy Ar
Horder, Mervyn	Bread Of The World
Horn, Richard	Alleluia
Houser, Vic	Peace Give I To Thee
Houser, Vic	Peace I Give To Thee
Hovdesven	Carol Of The Tree
Hovdesven	Lord, Take My Heart
Hovdesven, E A	Fold To Thy Heart Thy Broth
Hovdesven, E A	My Heart Is A Manger
Hovdesven, E A	Nightingale Carol
Hovdesven, E A	Olive Tree Lullaby
Hovhaness, Alan	Avak, The Healer
Hovhaness, Alan S.	God Be Merciful Unto Us
Hovhaness, Alan S.	Peace Be Multiplied
Hovhaness, Alan S.	Wisdom (From Three Motets)
Hovland	Jubilate
How, William H.	For All The Saints
Howard, Brian	Hey Soul
Howard, Brian	Let Us Give Thanks
Howard, Brian	The Butterfly Song
Howard, Brian	What Could Be Better
Howe-Steefe	Battle Hymn Of The Republic
Howe/Gould	In His Name
Howell, Richard D.	Sleep Of The Child Jesus
Howells, Herbert	My Eyes For Beauty Pine (Me
Howells, Herbert	O Pray For The Peace Of Jer
Howells, Herbert I	Like As The Heart Desireth
Howorth, Wayne	The Angels And The Shepherd
Hruby (Arr)	Holy Child, The (W/ Opt Flu
Hruby, Dolores	Your Holy Cross
Hubbard/G.C.Redd/Merr.	I Am Thine
Hubbard/Redd/Merriw.	I'm Sheltered In His Arms
Hubbard,H.	Birth Of The King
Hubbard,H./G.C. Redd	Everything Will Be All Righ
Hubbard,H./G.C. Redd	Heaven Will Be My Home
Hubbard,H./G.C. Redd	Jesus Died
Hubbard,H./G.C. Redd	There's Nothing Like The Ho
Hubbard,H./S. Stevens	I Done Got Over
Hubbard,H./S. Stevens	I Dreamed I Went To Heaven
Hubbard,H/G.C.Redd	Loved Ones Are Waiting
Hubbard,H/G.C.Redd	Walk On The Pathway
Hubbard,H/R.Merriw.	They Shall Be Mine
Hubbard,H/S.Stevens	Only
Hubert, Yvon	Day Of Celebration, The
Hubert, Yvon	God, Did You Hear
Hubert, Yvon	Help Us, O Lord, To See
Hubert, Yvon	If You Give Of Your Bread
Hubert, Yvon	Jesus, Come Our Way
Hubert, Yvon	Keep Us Joyful
Hubert, Yvon	Life Without You
Hubert, Yvon	My Light
Hubert, Yvon	Nameless Island
Hubert, Yvon	On The Way To The Mountain
Hubert, Yvon	One Who Seeks, The
Hubert, Yvon	Return To Joy
Hubert, Yvon	Road To Freedom
Hubert, Yvon	Sign Of His Life In The Wor
Hubert, Yvon	Thank You, Jesus
Hubert, Yvon	Thou Art The Kindler
Hubert, Yvon	Voice Of The Lord
Hubert, Yvon	Who Will Deliver Me?
Hubert, Yvon	Wisdom Of God
Hubert, Yvon	World In The Making
Hubert, Yvon	World Is The Gift
Hudson/Decou	Glorious Church, A
Hudson/Decou	His Yoke Is Easy
Huerter, C.	Blest Are The Pure In Heart
Huerter, C.	Lord In Thy Presence Lead U
Huff, Ronn	Sunday Choir (No Zd-5472)
Huff, Ronn And Donna	Keyboard Stylings For The P
Hughes-Grainger	Alleluia Psallat
Hughes/Decou	Calvary Love
Hughes/Thygerson	Song Of The Shepherd Boy
Hughes, D/Trad	Creator Of The Earth And Sk
Hughes, Dvorak	Come To Me
Hughes, Frank	Benediction (From Deuterono
Hughes, H/Wilson, P	Christ The Lord In Silence
Hughes, Howard	By The Streams Of Babylon
Hughes, Howard	Great Amen (Mus For Euch Pr
Hughes, Howard	Let Earth Rejoice
Hughes, Howard	Let Us Enter The House Of T
Hughes, Howard	Memorial Acclamation(Christ
Hughes, Howard	Psalms For Advent
Hughes, Howard	Sanctus (Mus For Euch Praye
Hughes, Howard	Taste And See
Hughes, Howard (Bro.)	Gospel Acclamations, Confir
Hughes, Miki	Gift Of Love

COMPOSER INDEX

Hughes, Miki	Joy Is The Spirit Of Love
Hughes, Miki	Look To The Skies Above
Hughes, Miki	Wonder When He's Coming
Hughes, Robert J Et Al	All God's People (Me) (Evan
Hughes, Robert J.	Above The Hills Of Time (E)
Hughes, Robert J.	Alas, And Did My Savior Ble
Hughes, Robert J.	All Hail The Power Of Jesus
Hughes, Robert J.	Alleluia
Hughes, Robert J.	Alleluia! (E)
Hughes, Robert J.	Alleluia! Sing To Jesus
Hughes, Robert J.	Angels We Have Heard On Hig
Hughes, Robert J.	At The Name Of Jesus
Hughes, Robert J.	Beautiful Savior
Hughes, Robert J.	Blessed Assurance
Hughes, Robert J.	Born In A Manger
Hughes, Robert J.	Born In A Manger (Gaelic Me
Hughes, Robert J.	Child This Day Is Born, A
Hughes, Robert J.	Christ Arose!
Hughes, Robert J.	Christ Hath Triumphed, Alle
Hughes, Robert J.	Christ The Lord Is Risen To
Hughes, Robert J.	Church Of The Living God
Hughes, Robert J.	Come, O Come
Hughes, Robert J.	Do You Know?
Hughes, Robert J.	Does Jesus Care
Hughes, Robert J.	Forth In Thy Name, O Lord
Hughes, Robert J.	Gift Of Love, The
Hughes, Robert J.	God Is Everywhere
Hughes, Robert J.	God Lives!
Hughes, Robert J.	God Spoke To Me Today
Hughes, Robert J.	Guide Me, O Thou Great Jeho
Hughes, Robert J.	He Laid His Hand On Me
Hughes, Robert J.	He Lives
Hughes, Robert J.	He Walks With God
Hughes, Robert J.	Hear Ye Him
Hughes, Robert J.	I Look To Thee In Every Nee
Hughes, Robert J.	I Must Tell Jesus
Hughes, Robert J.	I Will Praise Thee
Hughes, Robert J.	If Ever The Sun Stops Shini
Hughes, Robert J.	In Jesus
Hughes, Robert J.	It's A Glorious Alleluia!
Hughes, Robert J.	Jesus Died On Calvary's Mou
Hughes, Robert J.	Jesus Shall Reign
Hughes, Robert J.	Keep Christ In Christmas
Hughes, Robert J.	Listen With An Open Mind
Hughes, Robert J.	Little David, Play On Your
Hughes, Robert J.	Lo! God Is Here
Hughes, Robert J.	Lord Is My Shepherd, The
Hughes, Robert J.	Lord Jesus, Think On Me
Hughes, Robert J.	Love Of My Lord To Me, The
Hughes, Robert J.	Love Your Brother
Hughes, Robert J.	March On With Christ
Hughes, Robert J.	Master Hath Called Us, The
Hughes, Robert J.	Mighty Fortress Is Our God,
Hughes, Robert J.	More Like The Master
Hughes, Robert J.	My Father Is With Me
Hughes, Robert J.	Narrow Road
Hughes, Robert J.	No Cradle Song
Hughes, Robert J.	No Turning Back
Hughes, Robert J.	Nothing But Miracles
Hughes, Robert J.	Now Thank We All Our God
Hughes, Robert J.	O For A Thousand Tongues To
Hughes, Robert J.	O God Of The Quiet Spirit
Hughes, Robert J.	O How Happy Are They Who Th
Hughes, Robert J.	O Jesus, Thou Art Standing
Hughes, Robert J.	O Master, Let Me Walk With
Hughes, Robert J.	O The Deep, Deep Love Of Je
Hughes, Robert J.	On This Blessed Easter Day
Hughes, Robert J.	Once In Royal David's City
Hughes, Robert J.	One Way
Hughes, Robert J.	Onward, Christian Soldiers
Hughes, Robert J.	Open My Eyes, That I May Se
Hughes, Robert J.	Praise To The Lord, The Alm
Hughes, Robert J.	Prince Of Peace, The
Hughes, Robert J.	Ride On, Ride On In Majesty
Hughes, Robert J.	Rise Up, Shepherd, And Foll
Hughes, Robert J.	Risen Today
Hughes, Robert J.	Savior, I Long To Be
Hughes, Robert J.	Savior, Lead Me
Hughes, Robert J.	Sing Alleluia!
Hughes, Robert J.	Sing To The Lord A New Song
Hughes, Robert J.	Someone
Hughes, Robert J.	Song Of The Angels, The
Hughes, Robert J.	Stand Up For Jesus
Hughes, Robert J.	Story Of Love, The
Hughes, Robert J.	Take My Life And Let It Be
Hughes, Robert J.	Take Up Thy Cross
Hughes, Robert J.	That Holy Night
Hughes, Robert J.	That One Bright Star
Hughes, Robert J.	The Gift Of Love
Hughes, Robert J.	The Love Of My Lord To Me
Hughes, Robert J.	The Male Four (No Zd-5475)
Hughes, Robert J.	This Is My Father's World
Hughes, Robert J.	This Is The Land I Love
Hughes, Robert J.	Thou Wilt Keep Him In Perfe
Hughes, Robert J.	Through All The Changing Sc
Hughes, Robert J.	To God Be The Glory
Hughes, Robert J.	To Thee, O Lord, Our Hearts
Hughes, Robert J.	Under His Wings
Hughes, Robert J.	What Child Is This?
Hughes, Robert J.	When Love Shines In
Hughes, Robert J.	When Morning Gilds The Skie
Hughes, Robert J.	Wonder Of The Ages, The
Hughes, Robert J.	Wonderful Peace
Huijbers & Oosterhuis	As The Deer
Huijbers & Oosterhuis	Even Then
Huijbers & Oosterhuis	God Is Our Refuge
Huijbers & Oosterhuis	Guide Me
Huijbers & Oosterhuis	Happy Is The Man
Huijbers & Oosterhuis	He Says He Is God
Huijbers & Oosterhuis	How Faithful God
Huijbers & Oosterhuis	I Want To Call You
Huijbers & Oosterhuis	In His Shelter
Huijbers & Oosterhuis	My Heart Longs
Huijbers & Oosterhuis	My Shepherd I
Huijbers & Oosterhuis	My Shepherd Ii
Huijbers & Oosterhuis	No One Lives For Himself
Huijbers & Oosterhuis	Not To Us
Huijbers & Oosterhuis	O Gracious Lord
Huijbers & Oosterhuis	Our God Provides
Huijbers & Oosterhuis	Our Help
Huijbers & Oosterhuis	People Of God
Huijbers & Oosterhuis	Shepherd Of Israel
Huijbers & Oosterhuis	Song At The Foot Of The Mou
Huijbers & Oosterhuis	Song Of All Seed
Huijbers & Oosterhuis	Song Of The City
Huijbers & Oosterhuis	Song Of The Holy Spirit
Huijbers & Oosterhuis	Song Of The Journey
Huijbers & Oosterhuis	Uphold Me In Life
Huijbers & Oosterhuis	What Is Your Name?
Huijbers & Oosterhuis	When From Our Exile
Huijbers & Oosterhuis	When Israel
Huijbers & Oosterhuis	Winter Song
Huijbers & Oosterhuis	Word Of The Lord, The
Huijbers & Oosterhuis	You Are My God
Hultman/Johnson	Thanks To God!
Humber, Yvon	Lord Will Give Us Peace, Th
Humber, Yvon	Love Is A Gift
Humber, Yvon	Love Of The Lord
Humfrey, Pelham	Hear, O Heavens (Is 1, M)
Humfrey, Pelham	Rejoice In The Lord (Md)
Humperdinck	Rock Of Ages
Humphries/Long	From Glory To Glory Advanci
Hunkele	Along The Way
Hunkele	Come To The Lord
Hunkele	Happy Lord
Hunkele	Listen Lord
Hunkele	Look To The Rainbow
Hunkele	Lord Rabboni
Hunkele	Mary
Hunkele	New Day Dawning
Hunkele	Pardon Peace
Hunkele	Shalom
Hunkele	Take Our Gifts
Hunnicutt	Three Seasonal Songs
Hunnicutt, J.	Carol For Epiphany
Hunnicutt, J.	Carol For Pentecost
Hunnicutt, J.	Clap Your Hands, All Ye Chi
Hunnicutt, J.	Father Eternal, We Pray (A
Hunnicutt, J.	God, Creator
Hunnicutt, J.	I Will Wake Up The Sun
Hunnicutt, J.	In Praise To God
Hunnicutt, J.	Midst The Deep Silence (Han
Hunnicutt, J.	Now Tell Us, Gentle Mary
Hunnicutt, J.	Our Father, By Whose Name
Hunnicutt, J.	Sing Gloria
Hunnicutt, J.	Sing Joy, Sing Love
Hunnicutt, J.	Surely He Has Borne Our Gri
Hunt, Thomas	Evening Service In Eb: Magn
Hunt, Thomas	Gentle Guide (Mother's Day)
Hunt, Thomas	Morning Service In Eb (Md)
Huntley	Swing Low, Sweet Chariot
Huntley/Campbell	Beyond Tomorrow
Huntley/Campbell	Impatient Heart
Huntley/Newman	Jesus Is Waiting
Huntley/Newman	Rejoice You're Free
Hurd, Bob	A Blessing Song
Hurd, Bob	All The Days Of Our Lives
Hurd, Bob	Alleluia—Psalm 57
Hurd, Bob	Bless The Lord
Hurd, Bob	By The Streams Of Babylon
Hurd, Bob	Jeremiah Sings The Blues
Hurd, Bob	Jesus Gave His Life Away
Hurd, Bob	John The Baptist
Hurd, Bob	Lamentations
Hurd, Bob	May All Your People Be One
Hurd, Bob	O Lord, You Know Who I Am
Hurd, Bob	O, Let Him In
Hurd, Bob	Penitential Song
Hurd, Bob	Sing A Brand New Song
Hurd, Bob	Someday
Hurd, Bob	Thank The Lord With Songs O
Hurd, Bob	The Banquet Of The Lord
Hurd, Bob	Wings Of Wood
Hurford, Peter	Litany To The Holy Spirit
Hurford, Peter	Magdalen, Cease From Sobs A
Husted, Richard S.	Baptismal Acclamation
Husted, Richard S.	Doxology
Husted, Richard S.	Hear O Israel
Husted, Richard S.	Sing Glory To Our God
Husted, Richard S.	With The Blessing Of God
Hutcheson, Jere	God
Hutson, Joan	God Is Love
Hydn/Hirt	Kyrie Eleison
Hytrek, S. Theophane	Glory To God
Hytrek, S. Theophane	Seven Songs From Ancient Li
Iannaccone, Anthony	Solomon's Canticle
Indian Melodies	Agnus Dei (Mass Of The West
Indian Melodies	Kyrie (Mass Of The Western
Indian Melodies	Sanctus (Mass Of The Wester
Infante, Guy	Follow Me
Infante, Guy	I Am
Infante, Guy	Jesus, In Thy Dwelling Plac
Infante, Guy	O God Of Love, O King Of Pe
Ingalls, Anonymous	Three Fuging—Tunes
Ingalls, Jeremiah	Columbia From Two Songs Of
Ingalls, Jeremiah	Complainer
Ingalls, Jeremiah	Honor To The Hills
Ingalls, Jeremiah	Lamentation
Ingalls, Jeremiah	Northfield
Ingalls, Jeremiah	Two Songs For Mens Voices
Ingalls, Jeremiah	Two Songs Of Mourning From
Ingegneri, Marc A	Caligarerunt Oculi Mei
Ingegneri, Marc A	Tenebrae Factae Sunt
Innes/Fasig	Who Wants To Be Free? (Musi
Innes, John	Crusade Organist (No 5761)
Innes, John	Prince Of Peace (Cantata)
Ippolitoff—Ivanoff	Bless The Lord, O My Soul
Ippolitov—Ivanov, M	Bless The Lord, O My Soul
Ippolitov—Ivanov, M	Russian Christmas Hymn
Ippolitov/Ivanov	Bless The Lord, O My Soul
Ironside/Schuler/Carmi	Overshadowed (A Cap)
Irvine/Carmichael	Lord's My Shepherd, The
Irwin	He'll Make A Way
Irwin	Healer, The
Irwin	I Gave My Life To Jesus
Irwin	It Was Jesus
Irwin	Narrow Way, The
Irwin	We Don't Have Much Farther
Isaac, H. (D1517)	Missa Carminum
Isaac, Heinrich	O Welt, Ich Muss Dich Lasse
Isaac, Heinrich	Ora Pro Nobis
Isaac, Henricus	O World I Must Be Parting
Isaak/Andrews	O Food We Pilgrims Pray For
Isele, Bill	Called
Isele, Bill	Gifts
Isele, Bill	Live With Us
Isele, Bill	Lord, Give Us Strength
Isele, Bill	Message Of Love
Isele, Bill	Miracle
Isele, Bill	Moment Of Birth
Isele, Bill	Now Is The Time
Isele, Bill	Pentecost
Isele, Bill	Son Of God!
Isele, Bill	Song Of New Life
Isele, Bill	Stand With Me
Isele, Bill	That The World Might Be Ren
Isele, Bill	Winter Meditation
Isele, David C.	Alleluia (Notre Dame Mass)
Isele, David C.	Christ Our Passover (Notre
Isele, David C.	Communion Song (O Taste And
Isele, David C.	Eucharistic Prayer (Preface
Isele, David C.	Final Doxology
Isele, David C.	General Intercessions(Notre
Isele, David C.	Gloria (Notre Dame Mass)
Isele, David C.	Gospel Acclamation (Notre D
Isele, David C.	Kyrie I (Notre Dame Mass)
Isele, David C.	Kyrie Ii (Notre Dame Mass)
Isele, David C.	Lamb Of God (Notre Dame Mas
Isele, David C.	Lord's Prayer (Notre Dame M
Isele, David C.	Memorial Acclamation (Chris
Isele, David C.	Sanctus (Notre Dame Mass)
Isele, David C.	Sing Out Use Your Voice Now
Isele, David C.	Thanksgiving Hymn (Give Tha
Isele, David C.	Trisagion (Notre Dame Mass)
Ives, Charles E.	Abide With Me
Ives, Charles E.	Celestial Country
Ives, Charles E.	Disclosure
Ives, Charles E.	Down East
Ives, Charles E.	Forward Into Light
Ives, Charles E.	His Exaltation
Ives, Charles E.	Let There Be Light
Ives, Charles E.	Naught That Country Needeth
Ives, Charles E.	Processional "Let There Be
Ives, Charles E.	Religion
Ives, Charles E.	The Camp Meeting
Ives, Charles E.	The Collection
Ives, Charles E.	The Waiting Soul
Ives, Charles E.	Watchman!
Iwin	Somebody Heard My Prayer
Jabusch, Willard F.	Come Out Of Egypt
Jabusch, Willard F.	From The Depths
Jabusch, Willard F.	God Dwells In The Hearts
Jabusch, Willard F.	King Of Glory, The
Jabusch, Willard F.	Many Times I Have Turned
Jabusch, Willard F.	Praise Him
Jabusch, Willard F.	See How The Virgin Waits
Jabusch, Willard F.	Song Of Good News, The
Jabusch, Willard F.	To The Mountain
Jabusch, Willard F.	To Whom Shall We Go
Jabusch, Willard F.	We Have A King

COMPOSER INDEX

Jabusch, Willard F.	What Can We Offer
Jabusch, Willard F.	Whatsoever You Do
Jackson–Riedel	Lift Your Glad Voices In Tr
Jackson, Francis	Benedicite In G (Md)
Jackson, Francis	Blow Ye The Trumpet In Zion
Jackson, Francis	Communion Service E E. Seri
Jackson, Francis	Communion Service In G (Md)
Jackson, Francis (Ed)	Fifty Anthems For Mixed Voi
Jacob, Gordon	O Lord, I Will Praise Thee
Jacobs, Hanneke	Can You Feel Him
Jacobs, Hanneke	Silver Packages
Jacobs, Hanneke	Wind Blowing Softly
Jacobs, Peter	As A Child
Jacobs, Peter	Children Of The Day
Jacobs, Peter	Good–Bye
Jacobs, Peter	Holy Spirit Song
Jacobs, Peter	If You'll Take My Hand
Jacobs, Peter	Just Pretending
Jacobs, Peter	New Life
Jacobs, Peter	The Crucifixion
Jacobs, Peter	Two Lives, One Moment
Jacobs, Peter	Under The Shadow (Of My Win
Jacobus	Mother's Hymns
Jagger/Richard/Oldham	As Tears Go By
James	Christian Fellowship
James	Communion Hymn Sequence For
James	Lord Is My Light, The
James	My Soul Thirsteth For God
James	O God Of Peace
James	Song Of Deliverance
James	Thee We Adore
James, Allen	Echoing Alleluia
James, Allen	Omnipresence
James, Allen	Twelve Days Of Christmas, T
James, W.	Jesus, Our Lord, We Adore T
James, Will	Hear My Prayer
Jankins	Sweet Was The Song (W/Solo)
Jansen, Geneva	I Have The Joy (Arrangement
Jansen, Geneva	The Name Of Jesus (Arrangem
Jaubiel, Charles	Vision Of Saint Joan
Jaworski, Jack	Save My People
Jeffery/Pool	Ancient Days
Jenkins, Cyril	Angel's Chorus
Jenkins, Cyril	Hymn To The Soul
Jenkins, Cyril	Night In The Desert
Jenks, Stephen	Killingly
Jenks, Stephen	Sorrow's Tear (From Three S
Jenks, Stephen	Weeping Nature (From Three
Jennings, C.	Father, We Praise Thee
Jennings, K	I Lift Up My Eyes To The Hi
Jennings, K.	All My Heart
Jennings, K.	Arise, Shine, For Thy Light
Jennings, K.	For He Shall Give His Angel
Jennings, K.	He Is Risen
Jennings, K.	Love Came Down At Christmas
Jennings, K.	Rise Up, O Men Of God
Jennings, K.	The Lord My Faithful Shephe
Jennings, K.	With A Voice Of Singing
Jeppesen, Knud	Hear My Prayer, O My God
Jeppesen, Knud	O Lord, How Numerous Are My
Jeppesen, Knud	One Thing Have I Desired Of
Jeppesen, Knud	Praise God, My Soul
Jeppesen, Knud	What Is A Man?
Jergenson, Dale	Mass Of Freedom (Icet)
Jergenson, Dale	Peace(A Capella) Jn 14: 27
Jergenson, Dale	The Lament Of Job
Jergenson, Dale (Arr)	Lo, How A Rose E'er Bloomin
John Iv (Ed Tortolano)	Crux Fidelis (E & L) (Me)
Johns	O Praise The Lord All Ye Na
Johnson	Ah, Jesus Lord, Thy Love To
Johnson	Cross Was Not The End, The
Johnson	Just As I Am (Woodworth)
Johnson	Lead On, O King Eternal
Johnson	This Is My Father's World
Johnson (Arr)	The Lone, Wild Bird
Johnson (Arr), D.	Eight Folksongs & Spiritual
Johnson (Arr), D.	Four Folksongs And Spiritua
Johnson (Arr), D.	O Love, How Deep (Opt Tpt)
Johnson (Traditional)	Good Christian Men, Rejoice
Johnson/Drevits	My Heart Sings Hosanna
Johnson/Furman	Pray! Pray! Pray!
Johnson/Peterson	The Folk Hymnal (No 5767)
Johnson, D	Draw Nigh To Thy Jerusalem
Johnson, D.	A Service Of Nine Lessons &
Johnson, D.	A Star In The Sky
Johnson, D.	Christ The Lord Is Risen
Johnson, D.	Crown Him With Many Crowns
Johnson, D.	Earth And All Stars
Johnson, D.	Good Christian Men, Rejoice
Johnson, D.	Hosanna (Folk Communion Ser
Johnson, D.	I Am The Light
Johnson, D.	Judah's Land
Johnson, D.	Lead On, O King Eternal
Johnson, D.	Lord Christ, When First Tho
Johnson, D.	Lord's Prayer (Org Or Guita
Johnson, D.	Lovely Child, Holy Child
Johnson, D.	O Day Full Of Grace
Johnson, D.	O Dearest Lord, Thy Sacred
Johnson, D.	O Praise The Lord Of Harves
Johnson, D.	Ride On, Ride On In Majesty
Johnson, D.	Saw Ye My Savior
Johnson, D.	Saw Ye My Savior? (W/Flute)
Johnson, D.	Souls Of The Righteous
Johnson, D.	Sweet Was The Song The Virg
Johnson, D.	The King Of Love My Shepher
Johnson, D.	This Is The Day (W/Flute)
Johnson, D.	Thy Kingdom Come (Opt Tpt)
Johnson, D.	To A Virgin, Meek And Mild
Johnson, D.	We Praise Thee, O God
Johnson, D.	Wedding Music (In Two Volum
Johnson, D.	When Jesus Left His Father'
Johnson, D.	When Jesus Left His Father'
Johnson, D.	Where Cross The Crowded Way
Johnson, Gary L.	A New Song
Johnson, Gary L.	A Shelter For Me
Johnson, Gary L.	At Jesus' Name
Johnson, Gary L.	Clap Your Hands
Johnson, Gary L.	Come To Me
Johnson, Gary L.	Create In Me
Johnson, Gary L.	Depth Of Mercy
Johnson, Gary L.	Gentle Holy Spirit
Johnson, Gary L.	Go In Joy
Johnson, Gary L.	Go To Dark Gethsemane
Johnson, Gary L.	Guide Me, O Thou Great Jeho
Johnson, Gary L.	How Sweet The Name
Johnson, Gary L.	I Believe
Johnson, Gary L.	I Will Come Again
Johnson, Gary L.	Immanuel
Johnson, Gary L.	In Remembrance Of Me
Johnson, Gary L.	Job's Story
Johnson, Gary L.	Let The Hills Now Sing For
Johnson, Gary L.	Let The Words Of My Mouth
Johnson, Gary L.	Lord, Bless This Little Chi
Johnson, Gary L.	Lord, We Are Not The Same
Johnson, Gary L.	Love
Johnson, Gary L.	O Give Thanks
Johnson, Gary L.	Pray For The Peace Of Jerus
Johnson, Gary L.	Seek First His Kingdom
Johnson, Gary L.	Take My Life
Johnson, Gary L.	That We May Be One
Johnson, Gary L.	The Lord Bless You
Johnson, Gary L.	Thou Art Holy
Johnson, Gary L.	Thou Art There
Johnson, Gary L.	Worthy Art Thou
Johnson, Hall	Ain't Got Time To Die
Johnson, Hall	Po' Mo'ner Got A Home At La
Johnson, Jeff	Holy, Holy, Holy
Johnson, Jeff	Prepare Ye The Way
Johnson, Jeff	We Have All Been To The Wat
Johnson, Norman	Call To Worship (No 5027)
Johnson, Norman	Choruses From The Messiah
Johnson, Norman	Church, O Lord, Is Thine, T
Johnson, Norman	Descants For Choirs (No 554
Johnson, Norman	Favorite Spirituals No 1 (N
Johnson, Norman	Fight The Good Fight
Johnson, Norman	Glory To The Lamb (Cantata)
Johnson, Norman	Heralds Of Christ
Johnson, Norman	Holy, Holy, Holy!
Johnson, Norman	Lord God, Our Thanks To The
Johnson, Norman	Norman Johnson Presents Cho
Johnson, Norman	Now Is Christ Risen
Johnson, Norman	One Hundred Sacred Favorite
Johnson, Norman	Piano Melodies (No 5788)
Johnson, Norman	Songster Favorites (No 5439
Johnson, Norman	This I Believe
Johnson, Norman	Will It Be Soon?
Johnson, P. (Arr)	Christ Arose (W/Piano)
Johnson, Paul	Acclamation (C)
Johnson, Paul	Make Us One Father (W/Piano
Johnson, Robert S.	Christus Resurgens (D)
Johnson, Robert S.	Incarnatio (Dum Medium Sile
Johnson,B/Johnson,M.	As Ye Sow
Johnston	All Hail The Power Of Jesus
Johnston	Built On A Rock
Johnston	Christmas Gloria, A
Johnston	He Was Despised
Johnston	In Bethlehem
Johnston	Jesus, Come Abide With Me
Johnston	King In The Stable, The
Johnston	Manger King, The
Johnston	On The Other Side Of Time
Johnston	One God
Johnston/Lebar	Merry Christmas
Joiner, W./ Clement, D	Love That Never Fades Away
Jones	Hymn Of Peace, A
Jones	In Times Like These
Jones	Pro Nobis Puer Natus Est
Jones R.	His Love Is Endless
Jones/Anthony	In Times Like These
Jones/Decou	Keep Christ In Christmas
Jones/Johnson	Glory Hallelujah To The Lam
Jones/Johnson	Glory,Hallelujah To The Lam
Jones, Barry	One, Two, Three, Jesus Love
Jones, Casey	Roses While I'm Living
Jones, D H	Psalm 150
Jones, G. Thaddeus	My God, My God, Why Have Yo
Jones, Gary	Thank You Jesus
Jones, Gj	Songs Of Praises
Jones, Richmond	Let Us Pray
Jones, S./ Barosse, R.	What Greater Love
Jordan	America The Beautiful
Jordan	Rejoice, The Lord Is King
Jordan	Ring, Christmas Bells
Jordan, Alice	All Things Are Thine
Jordan, Alice	Beatitudes, The
Jordan, Alice	Bless The Lord, O My Soul
Jordan, Alice	See The Land
Jordan, Alice	Time For Singing Has Come,
Jory, B.	The Lovin' Man
Jothen, M.	God Made Me!
Jothen, M.	I Am So Glad
Jothen, M.	I Was Glad
Jothen, M.	Rejoice, Give Thanks And Si
Jothen, M.	Sing Ye Nowell!
Judd, Percy	When Mary Through The Garde
Kaan/Kraehenbuehl	For The Healing Of The Nati
Kaan/Kraehenbuehl	Now In The Name Of Him
Kaan/Kraehenbuehl ,	O God From Whom Mankind Der
Kaan/Kraehenbuehl	Sing We A Song Of High Revo
Kaan, Fred	For The Healing Of The Nati
Kaan, Fred/Metcalf	He's Back In The Land Of Th
Kaan, Fred/Peloquin A.	The Good Shepherd (Me)
Kaan, Fred/Shaw	God Is Unique And One
Kabalewsky	War Requiem (Russian–Englis
Kaiser/Brown	God's People(Collection/Chu
Kaiser, Kurt	Angels Shall Keep Thee
Kaiser, Kurt	Oh How He Loves You And Me
Kaiser, Kurt	Pass It On
Kaiser,K./Brown,C.	I Am Willing, Lord (W/Piano
Karg–Elert (Adapted)	Sabbath Music (Christian)
Karg/Elert	Praise Ye The Lord
Karhu	Meditations On Psalm 37
Kasha/Hirshorn	The Morning After
Kathe Willis/Eielrs	O Star Of Bethlehem
Kavanaugh, John, S. J.	A Banquet Is Prepared
Kavanaugh, John, S. J.	All Things Have Their Time
Kavanaugh, John, S. J.	God Is Love
Kavanaugh, John, S. J.	To You I Lift Up My Soul
Kay, Ulysses	Christmas Carol
Kearney, Peter	Fill My House
Kechley, Gerald	Drop, Slow Tears
Keel, Richard	Hear Now Our Cry
Keel, Richard	The Resurrection According
Keene	Headin Down The Trail
Kellam ,Iam	An Angel Came In Unto Mary
Kellenbenz, Eugene(Ed)	Early American Hymnal
Kelly, Bryan	Communion Service, Series 3
Kelly, Bryan	Missa Brevis (D)
Kelly, Columba (Rev.)	Lord's Prayer For Hours
Kempinski, I	We Lift Our Hearts To Thee
Ken, Thomas	From All Who Dwell Beneath
Kenhow, Beulah	God Has Been Good To Me
Kenhow, Beulah	There's Something About God
Kennedy	Glory To God In The Highest
Kennedy	Rise Up, Shepherd
Kennedy	Star Of The East
Kennedy–Cadwallader	Go Down Moses (Pd)
Kennedy–Cadwallader	Joshua Fit De Battle Of Jer
Kennedy, Matthew	Two Spirituals
Kennerly	Blow, Ye Winds, Softly
Kennerly	Lord's Prayer, The
Kenney	Bethlehem Star, The
Kern, Jan	Mass For A Feast Day (Icet)
Kern, Jan (Music)	Eighty Six Prefaces From Mi
Kerner, Debby Melle	Amen, Praise The Lord
Kerner, Debby Melle	Are You Ready?
Kerner, Debby Melle	Behold, I Stand At The Door
Kerner, Debby Melle	Blessed Be The Day
Kerner, Debby Melle	Come Walk With Me In The Sp
Kerner, Debby Melle	For With Time Our Father Ha
Kerner, Debby Melle	Friends
Kerner, Debby Melle	Hallelujah, Hallelujah, Jes
Kerner, Debby Melle	Jesus
Kerner, Debby Melle	My Will
Kerner, Debby Melle	Peace
Kerner, Debby Melle	Promises
Kerner, Debby Melle	The Horsemen
Kerner, Debby Melle	The Peace That Passes Under
Kerr	I'm His To Command
Kerr	Touch Of His Hand, The
Kerr/Boersma	In Love With The Lover Of M
Kerr/Boersma	Melody Divine
Kerr, Phil	Clap Your Hands
Kerr,Anita (Arr)	Gentle As Morning (Collecti
Kerrick, Mary	Clap Your Hand Children
Kershaw, Christopher	We Have Love (W/Piano)
Ketchum, Teri	Have You Seen Him
Ketchum, Teri	Her Troubled Course
Ketchum, Teri	Joy In The Morning
Ketchum, Teri	Sea Of Madness
Ketchum, Teri	Spirits Of The Night
Kettering, E L	Song From St. Matthew
Kilpatrick	Thy Love Shall Fail Me Neve
King	Good Friday Meditation
King	Psalm 47 (O Clap Your Hands
King	You've Got A Friend
King (Arr)	Great Day (A Cap)
King Marian	Mommy Why Doesn't Daddy Lov
King, Charleen	The Times Are Always Changi
King, Charleen	The Word Is The Life

COMPOSER INDEX

King, Lew	Proclaim His Great Love
King, R. (Coggin)	O Rejoice In The Lord
Kingery, Larry Delray	Holy, Thou Art Holy
Kinley, Ken	Sing Praises To God
Kinsman (Arr)	Calm On The Listening Ear
Kinsman, Elmer F.	To Greet The Babe So Holy
Kinsman, Franklin	The Sufferings Of The Prese
Kiplinger	Clap Your Hands Ye People
Kirby	Joyful Melody, A
Kirby	Master's Pace, The (Opt Gui
Kirby (Ed)	Service Music For Sab Choir
Kirby (Ed)	Voices In Praise
Kirby, George	O Jesu, Look
Kirk, Theron (Arr)	Bells Are Ringing (Perc)
Kirk, Theron	Christ Was Born On Christma
Kirk, Theron	Dearest Jesu, Holy Child
Kirk, Theron (Arr)	He Is Born (W/ Finger Cymba
Kirk, Theron	Hear The Glad Tidings
Kirk, Theron	Lord Is With Us, The
Kirk, Theron	My God, I Thank Thee
Kirk, Theron	O Brother Man
Kirk, Theron	Praise The Lord
Kirk, Theron	Rejoice
Kirk, Theron	Sunday Carol (A Cap)
Kirkpatrick	Earth Is The Lord's, The
Kirkpatrick/Bolkds	Tis So Sweet To Trust In Je
Kirkpatrick/Decou	Away In A Manger
Kirkpatrick/Decou	When Love Shines In
Kirkpatrick/Mercer	Redeemed
Kirkpatrick/Wilson	Lead Me To Calvary
Kirkpatrick/Yungton	We Have An Anchor
Kirkston	Rejoice Now
Kirschke/Krogstad	Living Water
Kirschkel/Krogstad	Written In The Book Of Love
Kitson, C. H.	Jesu, Grant Me This I Pray
Kittrell, Christine	Call His Name
Kleinpeter, Karen	One From Among Us
Kleinpeter, Karen	Tell Me Now
Klemm, G	A Child's Prayer
Klevdal/Blake	Dusty Road, The
Knapp	Open The Gates Of The Templ
Knapp/Decou	Blessed Assurance
Knapp/Decou	Cleansing Wave, The
Knapp/Johnson	Open The Gates Of The Templ
Knepp, David Lee	God's Little White Church
Knepp, David Lee	Why I Love Jesus
Knudsen/Johnson	When Lights Are Lit On Chri
Koch, Frederick	Praise Ye The Lord
Koch, Frederick	Psalm Of Praise (Ps 150)W/B
Koch, Frederick	Trio Of Praise
Kocher/Davis, K.K.	For The Beauty Of The Earth
Kocher/Decou	For The Beauty Of The Earth
Kocher/Johnson	As With Gladness Men Of Old
Kocher, C	For The Beauty Of The Earth
Kocher, Conrad, Alt.	Christ Our Prophet (4-Part
Kodaly, Zoltan	Psalm 150 Based On A French
Koert	Sing To The Lord A Joyful S
Kohl, Jon	Jesus Song
Kohl, Jon	Light Of Christ
Kohl, Jon	Psalm 96
Kohl, Jon	Sing Out The Glory Of The L
Kohl, Jon	Thank You
Koller	O Take My Hand, Lord
Koloss	Sonata
Konig-Nelson	O That I Had A Thousand Voi
Koninkxop	One In Joyful Songs Of Prai
Korgstad/Kirschke	Happiness (Musical)
Korgstad, Bob	Hark! The Glad Sound
Korgstad, Bob	Psalm 121
Korhonen, J	Alleluia
Korhonen, J	Come, O Long Awaited Savior
Kortkamp	Lord Is Merciful, The
Kostos, Patti	Agnus Dei (Mass For Schools
Kostos, Patti	Gloria (Mass For Schools)
Kostos, Patti	Kyrie (Mass For Schools)
Kostos, Patti	My God, My God
Kostos, Patti	Sanctus (Mass Of Schools)
Kostos, Patti	The Road I'm On
Kountz, Richard	Carol Of The Questioning Ch
Kountz, Richard	Carol Of The Roses
Kountz, Richard	God Bless Our Land
Kountz, Richard	Hushing Carol
Kountz, Richard	Prayer Of The Norwegian Chi
Kraehenbuehl/Frischman	Glory To God (Danish Amen M
Kraehenbuehl/Frischman	Holy Holy (Icet)
Kraehenbuehl/Frischman	Lamb Of God (Icet)
Kraehenbuehl/Frischman	Lord Have Mercy (Danish Ame
Kraehenbuehl, David	Folk Mass (Icet)
Kraehenbuehl, David	Glory To God (Icet)
Kraehenbuehl, David	Holy, Holy (Icet)
Kraehenbuehl, David	Lord Have Mercy (Icet)
Krag, Lynch	Sweet Jesus (Your Spirit)
Kramper, Jerry	Come Follow
Kramper, Jerry	Honor And Praise (From Come
Kramper, Jerry	Psalm 148 (From Come Follow
Kramper, Jerry	Psalm 65 (From Come Follow)
Kramper, Jerry	Song Of God's Kingdom (From
Kramper, Jerry	Song Of The Thankful(Come F
Kramper, Jerry	The Beatitudes (From Come F
Krane, David	Celebration
Kranz, James R.	Our Father
Krapf, Gerhard	Come, Your Hearts & Voices
Krapf, Gerhard	Five Biblical Contemplation
Krapf, Gerhard	From Heaven Above
Krapf, Gerhard	O Praise The Lord All Ye Na
Krapf, Gerhard	Savior Of The Nations, Come
Krapf, Gerhard	Seven Verses
Krapf, Gerhard	Totentanz
Kremser, E	Hymn To The Saviour
Krenek, Ernst	Christmas (From Holiday Mot
Krenek, Ernst	Confitemini (From Holiday M
Krenek, Ernst	De Propundis (From Holiday
Krenek, Ernst	Earth Abideth, The
Krenek, Ernst	Easter (From Holiday Motets
Krenek, Ernst	Epiphany (From Holiday Mote
Krenek, Ernst	Gloria In Excelsis Deo
Krenek, Ernst	Go Thy Way (From Three Sacr
Krenek, Ernst	Haec Dies (From Holiday Mot
Krenek, Ernst	In Paradisum
Krenek, Ernst	Lent (From Holiday Motets)
Krenek, Ernst	Leviathan (From Three Motet
Krenek, Ernst	There Be Four Things
Krenek, Ernst	There Be Three Things
Krenek, Ernst	To The Sea In Ships
Krenek, Ernst	Vidimus Stellam
Krenke, Ernst	Thanksgiving (From Holiday
Krentel, Jerome	Sing A Song Of Love
Kreutz, Robert	Cantate Domino (L & E) A Ca
Kreutz, Robert	Common Blessed Virgin Allel
Kreutz, Robert	Common Of Virgins (Icet) Ps
Kreutz, Robert	Common Of Virgins Alleluia
Kreutz, Robert	From Sion Perfect In Beauty
Kreutz, Robert	Glory To God (American Sain
Kreutz, Robert	Holy, Holy, Holy (Icet)
Kreutz, Robert	Lamb Of God (Icet)
Kreutz, Robert	Let My Prayer Come Like Inc
Kreutz, Robert	Lord Have Mercy (Icet)
Kreutz, Robert	Mass For American Saint
Kreutz, Robert	Mass For Children (Icet)
Kreutz, Robert	Mass Of Thanksgiving (Icet)
Kreutz, Robert	Sacred Trust(A Wedding Song
Kreutz, Robert	The Memorare
Kreutz, Robert	To You, O Lord, I Lift My S
Kreutz, Robert	Vigil Peter & Paul Alleluia
Kreutzer, Conradin	This Is The Lord's Own Day
Krider, Dale	Prayer
Krieger, Jacob	Glorious Message, The
Krieger, Jacob	I Heard The Lord
Krieger, Jacob	Jacob's Song
Krieger, Jacob	Jesus, Jesus My Lord
Krogstad, Bob	Favorites For Youth
Krogstad, Bob	Praise The Lord, His Glorie
Krogstad, Bob	Teen Favorites (No 5662)
Krogstad, Bob (Ed)	Teen Choir (No 5260)
Krogtlad, Bob	Smilin' More Everyday (No 5
Kubik, Gail	Litany And Prayer
Kubik, Gail	Soon One Mornin' Death Come
Kugel, William F.	Select Vocal Solos For The
Kuhnau, Johann	Sorrow And Grief
Kuhnau, Johann	Tristis Est Anima Mea
Kuiper, H.J.	The New Christian Hymnal
Kuntz, Jeff	Built On A Rock The Church
Kush, Joseph	Our Father
La Berge, Nellie J.	A Carol For Christmas Morn
La Berge, Nellie J.	A Christmas Carol (In 5 Car
La Forge, F	Before The Crucifix
La Forge, F	First Psalm
La Rowe, Jane	King Of Glory Cantata (No 5
Laberge, Nellie J.	Carol Of The Gifts (In 5 Ca
Laberge, Nellie J.	Jesu, My Little One(In 5 Ca
Lafferty, Karen Louise	Bird In A Golden Sky
Lafferty, Karen Louise	Bobbi's Song
Lafferty, Karen Louise	Garden
Lafferty, Karen Louise	Grandma Stout
Lafferty, Karen Louise	Jesus Joy
Lafferty, Karen Louise	No Time For Jesus
Lafferty, Karen Louise	Peaceful Mind Tears Of Love
Lafferty, Karen Louise	Plan Of Love
Lafferty, Karen Louise	Seek Ye First
Lafferty, Karen Louise	Sweet Summer Rain
Lafferty, Karen Louise	Testimony
Lafferty, Karen Louise	The Girl
Lak	In Thankful Remembrance (W/
Lalande, Michael R.	Lord Have Mercy Upon Us
Lallouette, J F	O Sacrum Convivium
Lamb	Christmas Mosaic, A
Lamb, Gordon	Aleatory Psalm (Chance Musi
Lamb, Richard	A Christmas Mosaic
Lambillotte/Andrews	O Bread Of Angels
Landgrave,P.	There Is No One Like Jesus
Landon	Believing Souls, Rejoice An
Landon	Dogwood Cross, The
Landon	Fairest Lord Jesus
Landon	Footsteps Of Jesus
Landon	Glory Of The Star The
Landon	God Bless You, Mother Dear
Landon	God Will Take Care Of You
Landon	Haven Of Rest, The
Landon	He Hideth My Soul
Landon	In A Manger He Is Sleeping
Landon	It Is Well With My Soul
Landon	Mary Had A Baby
Landon	More Like Jesus
Landon	Noel!
Landon	Purer In Heart, O God
Landon	Shall I Crucify My Savior?
Landon	Sweet Hour Of Prayer
Landon	Wonderful Words Of Life
Landon	Wondrous Love
Landon (Arr)	Go To Dark Gethsemane
Landon, Stewart	Noel
Landon, Stewart	O To Be Like Thee
Landry, Carey (Rev.)	All Your Gifts Of Life
Landry, Carey (Rev.)	Alle, Alle, Alleluia (Gospe
Landry, Carey (Rev.)	Amen, Lord
Landry, Carey (Rev.)	Are Not Our Hearts?
Landry, Carey (Rev.)	Born To Live And Die
Landry, Carey (Rev.)	Brother Jesus
Landry, Carey (Rev.)	Brother, Brother
Landry, Carey (Rev.)	Build Up The City Of Man
Landry, Carey (Rev.)	Celebrate God
Landry, Carey (Rev.)	Children Of The Lord
Landry, Carey (Rev.)	Choose Life
Landry, Carey (Rev.)	Christ Has Died (Acclamatio
Landry, Carey (Rev.)	Come Along With Me To Jesus
Landry, Carey (Rev.)	Come And Go With Me
Landry, Carey (Rev.)	Come Follow Me
Landry, Carey (Rev.)	Come Let Us Go
Landry, Carey (Rev.)	Come, Comes
Landry, Carey (Rev.)	Come, Lord Jesus
Landry, Carey (Rev.)	Come, O Holy Spirit
Landry, Carey (Rev.)	Desert Highways Of The Nigh
Landry, Carey (Rev.)	Do You Really Love Me?
Landry, Carey (Rev.)	Doxology And Amen (I)
Landry, Carey (Rev.)	Doxology And Amen (Ii)
Landry, Carey (Rev.)	Echo Holy Holy
Landry, Carey (Rev.)	Every Person Is Gift
Landry, Carey (Rev.)	Father, We Adore You
Landry, Carey (Rev.)	For All That Has Been
Landry, Carey (Rev.)	Friends Are Like Flowers
Landry, Carey (Rev.)	Friends, Friends
Landry, Carey (Rev.)	Giant Love Ball Song
Landry, Carey (Rev.)	God Is Building A House
Landry, Carey (Rev.)	God Is Our Father
Landry, Carey (Rev.)	Got To Get In Touch
Landry, Carey (Rev.)	Great Person, A
Landry, Carey (Rev.)	Great Things Happen!
Landry, Carey (Rev.)	Hail Mary
Landry, Carey (Rev.)	Hail Mary, Gentle Woman
Landry, Carey (Rev.)	Heal Your People
Landry, Carey (Rev.)	Hi God!
Landry, Carey (Rev.)	His Banner Over Me Is Love
Landry, Carey (Rev.)	Holy, Holy, Holy
Landry, Carey (Rev.)	Holy, Holy, Holy
Landry, Carey (Rev.)	How Good Is The Lord
Landry, Carey (Rev.)	Hymn Of Praise
Landry, Carey (Rev.)	I Believe In The Sun
Landry, Carey (Rev.)	I Like God's Love
Landry, Carey (Rev.)	I Sought My God
Landry, Carey (Rev.)	I Want To Walk
Landry, Carey (Rev.)	I Will Not Forget You
Landry, Carey (Rev.)	Jesus, Jesus
Landry, Carey (Rev.)	Jesus, You Have The Power T
Landry, Carey (Rev.)	Joy Of The Lord, The
Landry, Carey (Rev.) V	Joy, Joy, Joy
Landry, Carey (Rev.)	Lead Us On, O Lord
Landry, Carey (Rev.)	Listen, Listen
Landry, Carey (Rev.)	Litany
Landry, Carey (Rev.)	Lord Of No Beginning
Landry, Carey (Rev.)	Lord, My Lord
Landry, Carey (Rev.)	Lord, You Live
Landry, Carey (Rev.)	Lose Youself In Me
Landry, Carey (Rev.)	Love That Is Kept Inside
Landry, Carey (Rev.)	Make Of Us O Lord A New Peo
Landry, Carey (Rev.)	Meditation
Landry, Carey (Rev.)	Men Of Faith
Landry, Carey (Rev.)	My Soul Magnifies The Lord
Landry, Carey (Rev.)	New Hope
Landry, Carey (Rev.)	New Life
Landry, Carey (Rev.)	Oh, How I Love Jesus
Landry, Carey (Rev.)	Oh, Yes, Lord Jesus Lives
Landry, Carey (Rev.)	One Faith
Landry, Carey (Rev.)	Only A Shadow
Landry, Carey (Rev.)	Our God Is A God Of Love
Landry, Carey (Rev.)	Pardon Your People
Landry, Carey (Rev.)	Peace Is Flowing Like A Riv
Landry, Carey (Rev.)	Peace Time
Landry, Carey (Rev.)	Praise, Lord!
Landry, Carey (Rev.)	Reach Out!
Landry, Carey (Rev.)	Shalom
Landry, Carey (Rev.)	Shepherd's Alleluia
Landry, Carey (Rev.)	Shout Joyfully!
Landry, Carey (Rev.)	Silver And Gold Have I None
Landry, Carey (Rev.)	Sing A Simple Song
Landry, Carey (Rev.)	Sing Praise!
Landry, Carey (Rev.)	Song Of Baptism
Landry, Carey (Rev.)	Song Of Christian Men
Landry, Carey (Rev.)	Song Of Jesus Christ
Landry, Carey (Rev.)	Song Of The Loving Father
Landry, Carey (Rev.)	Spirit Is A-Movin', The

COMPOSER INDEX

Composer	Title
Landry, Carey (Rev.)	Spirit Of Life
Landry, Carey (Rev.)	This Is My Commandment
Landry, Carey (Rev.)	This Is The Day
Landry, Carey (Rev.)	Time For Building Bridges,
Landry, Carey (Rev.)	To Share Their Joy (Wedding
Landry, Carey (Rev.)	Violet In The Snow
Landry, Carey (Rev.)	Voices
Landry, Carey (Rev.)	We Are The Body Of Christ
Landry, Carey (Rev.)	We Come To Your Table
Landry, Carey (Rev.)	We See You O Lord
Landry, Carey (Rev.)	What God Is Like
Landry, Carey (Rev.)	What Makes Love Grow?
Landry, Carey (Rev.)	What Shall I Do?
Landry, Carey (Rev.)	What Would You Have Us Do?
Landry, Carey (Rev.)	When We Eat This Bread
Landry, Carey (Rev.)	Where Two Or Three
Landry, Carey (Rev.)	With Hearts Full Of Joy
Landry, Carey (Rev.)	Woman, Woman
Landry, Carey (Rev.)	Won't You Come And Stay, Lo
Landry, Carey (Rev.)	Word Who Is Life, The
Landry, Carey (Rev.)	Yes, Lord, Yes
Landry, Carey (Rev.)	You Are My Brother (Part 1)
Landry, Carey (Rev.)	You Are My Brother (Part 2)
Landry, Carey (Rev.)	You Are My Brother (Part 3)
Landry, Carey (Rev)	In The Presence Of God
Lane	There Were Ninety And Nine
Laney E. C. Baxter Lil	I Believe In God
Laney E.C. Drake R.	Revelation Six Six Six
Laney E. C. Angus Beth	Sunday School Sinner
Lang	There Is A Love
Lang, C Tilghman	On That First Bright Easter
Lang, C Tilghman	The Earth Is The Lord's
Lang, C. S.	Jesu, The Very Thought Of T
Lang, C. S.	Let All The World In Every
Langlais, Jean	Te Deum (You Are God: We Pr
Lanier	I'll Live For Him
Lanier	Word Was God, The
Lanier, Gary	If You Abide (W/Piano)
Lanier, Gary	O For A Faith That Will Not
Lanier, Gary	Promises Of God (W/Piano)
Lant's Roll/Tortolano	Lord Have Mercy (4 Voices)
Lapo	Four Organ Preludes On Chor
Lapo, Cecil	All Beautiful The March Of
Lapo, Cecil E.	Christmas Lullaby
Lapo, Cecil E.	Drop, Drop, Slow Tears
Lapo, Cecil E.	Easter Hymn Of Praise (Opt
Lapo, Cecil E.	Joseph Dearest, Joseph Mine
Lapo, Cecil E.	Lullaby At Christmas
Lapo, Cecil E.	O Holy Father
Larowe, Jane	Alleluia, Alleluia!
Larowe, Jane	The Incarnation (No 5952) C
Lasso, Orlando Di	Adoramus Te Christe (Md)
Lasso, Orlando Di	Adoramus Te, Christe
Lasso, Orlando Di	As A Rose Among Thorns
Lasso, Orlando Di	As The Lily Shines
Lasso, Orlando Di	Aus Meiner Suden Tiefe
Lasso, Orlando Di	Blest Is The Man Who Finds
Lasso, Orlando Di	Blest Is The Man Who In Wis
Lasso, Orlando Di	By The River Of Babylon (E
Lasso, Orlando Di	Christ Hath Arisen
Lasso, Orlando Di	Custodi Me, Domine
Lasso, Orlando Di	Eye Has Not Seen
Lasso, Orlando Di	Hodie Apparuit
Lasso, Orlando Di	Jubilate Deo
Lasso, Orlando Di	Jubilate Deo (Lat-Ger)
Lasso, Orlando Di	Jubilate Deo, Omnis Terra
Lasso, Orlando Di	Lauda Anima Mea Dominum
Lasso, Orlando Di	Lauda Sion
Lasso, Orlando Di	Laudate Dominum
Lasso, Orlando Di	Let Him Who Would Come Afte
Lasso, Orlando Di	Levavi Oculos Meos
Lasso, Orlando Di	Missa Ecce Nunc Benedicite
Lasso, Orlando Di	Missa Quinti Toni (5th Tone
Lasso, Orlando Di	Missa, Quand Io Pens
Lasso, Orlando Di	Nos Qui Sumus In Hoc Mundo
Lasso, Orlando Di	Penitential Psalms (3)
Lasso, Orlando Di	Penitential Tears Of St. Pe
Lasso, Orlando Di	Proba Me Deus
Lasso, Orlando Di	Serve Bone
Lasso, Orlando Di	Seven Sacred Motets
Lasso, Orlando Di	Sicut Rose & Ipsa Te Cogat
Lasso, Orlando Di	Sorrowful Now Is My Soul
Lasso, Orlando Di	Surrexit Pastor Bonus
Lasso, Orlando Di	The Expectation Of The Just
Lasso, Orlando Di	The Just Man Will Give His
Lasso, Orlando Di	The Just Men Have Taken Awa
Lasso, Orlando Di	Though Deep Has Been My Fal
Lasso, Orlando Di	Three Passion Motets
Lasso, Orlando Di	Tristis Est Anima Mea
Lasso, Orlando Di	Twelve Canciones For Two Vo
Lasso, Orlando Di	Venite Ad Me Omnes
Lasso, Orlando Di	We Do Adore Thee
Lasso, Orlando Di	Who Follows Me
Lat, E	Christe, Adoramus Te
Latham/Decou	Blessed Calvary
Latin-Tortolano Ed	Dona Nobis Pacem (In 19 Rou
Latrobe	Holy Redeemer! Be Thy Rest
Laverdiere,Armand	English High Mass.
Law, Andrew	Bunker Hill
Lawrence, Anthony W.	Lord, Be With Us Now
Lawrence, Burton	They That Go Down To The Se
Laxton	Elegy And Le Motif
Le Jeune, C	Benediction Avant La Repas.
Leaf	God Of Love, King Of Peace
Leaf, Robert	A Joyful Song
Leaf, Robert	Awake, Arise, Go Forth And
Leaf, Robert	Children's Prayer
Leaf, Robert	Children's Voices Joyfully
Leaf, Robert	Come On Down, Zacchaeus
Leaf, Robert	Come With Rejoicing
Leaf, Robert	Come, Sing
Leaf, Robert	Glory Be To God The Father
Leaf, Robert	God Is Here-Let's Celebrate
Leaf, Robert	God Of Earth And Planets (O
Leaf, Robert	Good News (Original Anthems
Leaf, Robert	I Will Pour Out My Spirit
Leaf, Robert	Let The Whole Creation Cry
Leaf, Robert	Let Us Be Happy (Opttri)Org
Leaf, Robert	Let Us Look Up And Live (Op
Leaf, Robert	Like Bells At Evening
Leaf, Robert	My Faith
Leaf, Robert	O How Blessed Is This Place
Leaf, Robert	On This Day Of Glory (W/3 T
Leaf, Robert	Rejoice, Rejoice This Glad
Leaf, Robert	Ride On, Eternal King
Leaf, Robert	Singing Alleluia
Leaf, Robert	Soft Light Of Morning (Me)
Leaf, Robert	That Easter Morn At Break O
Leaf, Robert	The Lord Our God Is King Of
Leaf, Robert	This Night Did God Become A
Leaf, Robert	To Our King Immortal
Leaf, Robert	When Jesus Knelt
Leaf, Robert	With A Jubilant Song(Piano,
Lee	Huron Indian Carol
Lee	O Be Joyful In The Lord
Lee, Anthony	Amazing Grace
Lee, Danny	God Will Come Into Your Hea
Lee, Danny	Holy Spirit
Lee, Danny	I Believe In The Father
Lee, Danny	In The Stillness Of The Nig
Lee, Danny	Jesus, Jesus, Rock Of Ages
Lee, Danny	Just One Look
Lee, Danny	Keep On Holding On
Lee, Danny	Lord, Make Me Your Vessel
Lee, Danny	One Way
Lee, Danny	Somebody Loves You
Lee, Danny	Spread A Little Love Around
Lee, Danny	Where Are You Going
Lee, Danny	You Can See About Me
Lee, John	Acclamaciones (Memorial)
Lee, John	Behold, A Simple Tender Bab
Lee, John	Choral Mass (1970) Cong Ad
Lee, John	Christ Became Obedient For
Lee, John	Congregation Mass (1970)
Lee, John	Cordero De Dios
Lee, John	Creed (Icet) U Or Satb W/Or
Lee, John	Festival Mass (1972) W/Org
Lee, John	Gloria (Icet) From Communit
Lee, John	Gloria A Dios (Chant)
Lee, John	Glory To God (Community Mas
Lee, John	Holy, Holy, Holy (Community
Lee, John	Holy, Holy, Holy (Short Mas
Lee, John	Jubilee Mass
Lee, John	Lamb Of God (Community Mass
Lee, John	Lamb Of God (Short Mass)
Lee, John	Let Hymns Of Joy Of Grief S
Lee, John	Lord Have Mercy (Community
Lee, John	Lord Have Mercy (Short Mass
Lee, John	Mary's Lullaby
Lee, John	O King Of Might And Splendo
Lee, John	Padre Nuestro
Lee, John	Santo, Santo, Santo
Lee, John	Senor, Ten Piedad
Lee, John	The Blessed Christ Is Risen
Lee, John	The Christ-Child Lay On May
Lee, John	Thine Be The Glory (W/Piano
Lee, John	This Is The Day The Lord Ha
Lee, John	Three Motets In Honor Of Th
Lee, John	To You I Lift Up My Soul &
Lee, John	Yours Are The Heavens
Lee, John (Ed)	Fourteen Plainsong Hymns (E
Lee, Johnnie	Bethlehem Isn't Very Far
Lee, Johnnie	Dear Lord
Lee, Johnnie	God's Great Love Came Down
Lee, Johnnie	Help Me To Light A Candle
Lee, Johnnie	I Thank My God
Lee, Johnnie	In The Chapel Of The Dawn
Lee, Johnnie	My God Is There
Lee, Johnnie	Some Beautiful Morning
Lee, Johnnie	The First And Great Command
Lee, Johnnie	The Sweetest Peace Of Mind
Lee, Johnnie	The Via Dolorosa
Leger, Philip	Twenty Four Anthems For Sa
Lehman, Louis P.	Wonderful Guest
Lehmeier, John	Honor Him, Alleluia
Leichtling, Alan	Canticle 1
Leichtling, Alan	Psalm 37
Leichtling, Alan	Two Proverbs
Leighton, Kenneth	An Easter Sequence (Eng, La
Leighton, Kenneth	Communion Service In D (E)
Leighton, Kenneth	Mass, Opus 44
Leighton, Kenneth	O Be Joyful In The Lord (Md
Leighton, Kenneth	O God Enfold Me In The Sun
Leighton, Kenneth	Second Service: Magnificat
Leighton, Kenneth	Solus Ad Victimam (Me)
Leist, Warren C	O Little One Sweet
Lejeune, Claude	Helas! Mon Dieu.
Lekberg, Sven	Alleluia
Lekberg, Sven	Bow My Head, O Lord
Lekberg, Sven	For As The Rain Cometh Down
Lekberg, Sven	Four Carols For A Holy Nigh
Lekberg, Sven	Fragrant The Prayer
Lekberg, Sven	Gloria And Alleluia
Lekberg, Sven	Glory Be To The Father
Lekberg, Sven	Have Mercy Upon Us
Lekberg, Sven	It Is A Good Thing To Give
Lekberg, Sven	Let All The World In Every
Lekberg, Sven	O Wonder Of This Christman
Lekberg, Sven	The Truth Of The Lord Endur
Lekberg, Sven	Walk In The Light
Lemmel/Johnson	Turn Your Eyes Upon Jesus
Lennon/Mccartney	Let It Be
Lenzo, Joseph	Send Out Thy Light (Short A
Leo/Bloesch	Magnificat (W/Cont.Viols)
Leo, Leornardo	Christus Factus Est (E & L)
Leonard, Clair	If I Speak With The Tongues
Leonard, Clair	Te Deum
Leontovich-Wilhousky	Carol Of The Bells (A Capel
Leontovich, M	Ukrainian Bell Carol
Leupold	Lift Up Your Heads, Ye Gate
Lewandowski, L	Halalujoh, Halalu El B'kod'
Lewer	Fidelia
Lewer, Dare	Three Songs Of Tribulation
Lewis	God Has Ears To Listen
Lewis	I Am The Door
Lewis	I Can't Spin A Web
Lewis	Innkeeper, The
Lewis	There Is A River
Lewis	You Are Righteous, O Lord
Lewis, E.	A Special King Of Beautiful
Lewis, E.	All Join Hands
Lewis, E.	All That I Am
Lewis, E.	Carolina, Coming Home
Lewis, E.	Come On In
Lewis, E.	Contemporary Prayer
Lewis, E.	Get Out Of Yesterday
Lewis, E.	Gettin' It Together In Jesu
Lewis, E.	Gotta' Give A Little
Lewis, E.	Guide Me Jesus
Lewis, E.	His Light Still Shines
Lewis, E.	I'm Following The Son
Lewis, E.	Jesus Can
Lewis, E.	Jesus Paid It All
Lewis, E.	Jesus, Let Your Light Shine
Lewis, E.	Keep On Holding On
Lewis, E./ Allen, T.	Laborers Of Love
Lewis, E.	Lord Take Our Lives
Lewis, E.	Once Blind
Lewis, E.	One Day Soon
Lewis, E.	Open Up Your Door
Lewis, E./ Malool, G.	Peace Won't Come
Lewis, E.	Peace, Love And Hope
Lewis, E.	Prayer
Lewis, E.	Reach For The Light
Lewis, E.	Reach Out
Lewis, E.	Rock Of Ages (Arrangement)
Lewis, E./ Malool, G.	She Was America
Lewis, E.	Show Yourself In Me
Lewis, Erv	Songs Of Erv Lewis (No 5139
Lewis, E./ Malool, G.	Spread Your Wings
Lewis, E.	The Runner
Lewis, E.	This Is His Promise
Lewis, E.	Thy Will Be Done
Lewis, E.	Today I Followed Jesus
Lewis, E.	Today I Walked In His Foots
Lewis, E.	What Would You Do
Lewis, E.	Who Am I
Lewis, Freeman	O Thou, In Whose Presence
Lewis, Jesse D	Spirit Of God
Lewis, John Leo	Come Sing, Ye Choirs Exulta
Lewis, John Leo	Come, Thou Long-Expected Je
Lewis, John Leo	For Ever, O Lord
Lewis, John Leo	God Who Made The Earth
Lewis, John Leo	Lamb Of God, I Took To Thee
Lewis, John Leo	Lord Jesus, Think On Me
Lewis, John Leo	My Little Lamb
Lewis, John Leo	O Lord, The Hope Of Israel
Lewis, John Leo	O Thou, From Whom All Goodn
Lewis, John Leo	O Worship The King (Me)
Lewis, John Leo	Save Me, O God, By Thy Name
Lewis, John Leo	Savior, Teach Me Day By Day
Lewis, John Leo	Soldiers Of Christ, Arise
Lewis, John Leo	There Is A Land
Lewis, John Leo	There Might Have Been A Str
Lewis,E./Taylor,R.	Walking On Higher Ground
Lewkovitch, Bernhard	Cantabo Domino
Lewkovitch, Bernhard	Stabat Mater
Ley, Henry G.	A Choral Hymn For Advent &
Ley, Henry G.	A Prayer Of King Henry Vi (
Ley, Henry G.	Anthem For A Harvest Festiv

COMPOSER INDEX

Ley, Henry G.	Come, Thou Long Expected Je
Ley, Henry G.	In Thee Is Gladness (Gastol
Ley, Henry G.	Six Short Anthems For The S
Leyko, Patricia J.	Away
Leyko, Patricia J.	Be Still
Leyko, Patricia J.	Christ Has Died #1
Leyko, Patricia J.	Christ Has Died #2
Leyko, Patricia J.	Come Lord
Leyko, Patricia J.	Great Amen
Leyko, Patricia J.	Holy Holy Lord
Leyko, Patricia J.	Hosanna In The Highest
Leyko, Patricia J.	Jesus I Am Yours
Leyko, Patricia J.	Listen And Hear
Leyko, Patricia J.	Simple Joys
Leyko, Patricia J.	To Be Alive
Leyko, Patricia J.	You Are The Joy Of Jesus
Leyko, Patricia J.	You're Always At Home
Leyko, Patricia J.	Your Love Reaches To The He
Liberstein, Jerry	Psalm 131 Like A Child
Licht, Myrtha B	Fair Easter
Licht, Myrtha B	The Dove
Licht, Myrtha B	The Halo
Liddell	I Depend Upon My God
Lile, Bobby	As Only God Above Can Do
Liljestrand, Paul	Follow Me (Cantata) (No 427
Liljestrand, Paul	If Ye Be Merry
Liljestrand, Paul	O Come To My Heart (No 6010
Lillenas/Carmichael	The Peace That Jesus Gives
Lillenas/Carmichael(Ar	The Garden Of My Heart
Lillenas/Johnson	It Is Glory Just To Walk Wi
Lindeman-Brandon	Built On A Rock
Lindeman-Cassler	Easter Glory
Lindeman-Leupold	Alleluia, Jesus Lives
Lindeman-Sateren	Come Ye Faithful, Raise The
Lindeman/Rasley	Built On A Rock
Linder, Kristina & F.	Love
Lindh	O God O Lord
Lindsay Lisa	Men In History (So The Bibl
Lindsley, Charles E.	Five Early American Hymn Tu
Lindusky, Eugene	The Lord Is My True Shepher
Link, Wade Hampton	Rest
Lipscomb, Helen	A Pastoral Prayer
Lipscomb, Helen	Ancient Prayer
Lipscomb, Helen	Bethlehem Town
Lipscomb, Helen	I Sing The Mighty Power Of
Lipscomb, Helen	Jesu, Jesu, Why Did You Die
Lipscomb, Helen	O Come And Mourn
Lipscomb, Helen	O Holy Spirit Sent From Hea
Lipscomb, Helen	Song Of Praise
Lipscomb, Helen	We Have Seen His Star In Th
Lipscomb, Helen	We Praise Thee, O God
Lisicky, Paul	Alleluia
Lisicky, Paul	Glory To You
Lisicky, Paul	Holy, Holy, Holy
Lisicky, Paul	I Will Sing In The Morning
Lisicky, Paul	Look Toward Me (Psalm 25)
Lisicky, Paul	My People
Lisicky, Paul	The Seed That Falls (Psalm
Lisicky, Paul	We Gather Together
Lisicky, Paul	We're Gathered Together
Liszt, Franz	But I Have Trusted In Thy M
Liszt, Franz	Come Unto Me
Liszt, Franz	Missa Choralis
Liszt, Franz	Missa Solemnis (Graner Mass
Liszt, Franz	Psalm 13 Lord How Long
Liszt, Franz	Via Crucis
Litherland, Donna	Follow On
Little, Leonard	Thee Will I Love, O Lord
Liturgical Press	Come Where The Wind Is Free
Liturgical Press	O Christ Your Church Is Wai
Liturgical Press	Praise The Lord Of Heaven (
Liturgical Press	When I Had Fallen Low Indee
Liturgical Press, Alt.	All Glory, Praise, And Hono
Llord, J./Dejesus, G	The Watch Bird
Llord, J./Dejesus, G.	It's Christmas
Locke, Matthew	Turn Thy Face From My Sins
Locke, Matthew	When The Son Of Man Shall C
Locklair	In Praise Of Easter (5 Move
Lockwood, Normand	Alleluia (Hearts And Voices
Lockwood, Normand	Alleluia, Christ Is Risen
Lockwood, Normand	As A Heart (Ps 42)
Lockwood, Normand	Break Thou The Bread Of Lif
Lockwood, Normand	Choreographic Cantata (W/Pe
Lockwood, Normand	Closing Doxology, The (Psal
Lockwood, Normand	Hail To Thee, Glad Day
Lockwood, Normand	Hosanna
Lockwood, Normand	Hosanna (Lat)
Lockwood, Normand	Jesus, O Precious Name (New
Lockwood, Normand	Let Nothing Disturb Thee
Lockwood, Normand	Letter To Mother (Mother's
Lockwood, Normand	Psalm 150
Lockwood, Normand	We Plow The Fields
Lockwood, Normand(Arr)	While Shepherds Watched
Loes/Decou	Love Found A Way
Logan	He Cared For Me
Lohr, Al	Alone In The Still
Lohr, Al	Christmas Season
Lohr, Al	He Is Everywhere (God Is Lo
Lohr, Al	My Love For The Lord
Lohr, Al	Our Star Of Faith (The Pray
Lohr, Al	Psalm 150
Lohr, Al	The House Of Stars
Lohr, Al	The Lighted Hour
Lojeski/Ed(Arr)	Were You There
Lojeski, Ed	Beautiful City
Lojeski, Ed	Everything Is Beautiful
Lojeski, Ed	Just A Closer Walk With The
Lojeski, Ed	Kum Ba Ya
Lojeski, Ed	Let There Be Peace On Earth
Lojeski, Ed	Morning Has Broken
Lojeski, Ed	Touch A Hand, Make A Friend
Lojeski, Ed (Arr.)	All My Trials
Lojeski, Ed(Arr)	Let Us Break Bread Together
Lojewski	Glory To God (Mass Assembly
Lojewski	Holy, Holy, Holy (Icet)
Lojewski	Lamb Of God (Icet)
Lojewski	Lord Have Mercy (Icet)
Lojewski/Lojeski	Prayer For Peace
Lojewski, Harry V	Agnus Dei (Mariachi Mass)
Lojewski, Harry V	Gloria (Mariachi Mass)
Lojewski, Harry V	Sanctus (Mariachi Mass)
Lojewski, Harry V.	Kyrie (Mariachi Mass)
Lokey	Supplication
Lokey	Walk With Us, Lord
Lona	Sing Glory Hallelujah
Longthorne, Brian	O Be Joyful In The Lord (Ps
Loosemore, Henry	Why Art Thou So Heavy, O My
Lopez, Francisco	Magnificat No. 1
Lord, David	A Prayer For Peace (Md)
Lord, David	Most Glorious Lord Of Life!
Lord, David	The History Of The Flood (W
Lorenz	All Creatures Of Our God An
Lorenz	Carols Of Christmas
Lorenz	Christmas Invitation, The
Lorenz	Church's One Foundation, Th
Lorenz	Come, All Ye Faithful
Lorenz	Easter Hallelujah, The
Lorenz	Echo Of Christmas The
Lorenz	Festal Alleluia, A
Lorenz	Gloria In Excelsis Deo
Lorenz	Good Christian Men, Rejoice
Lorenz	Gospel Song Of Christmas, T
Lorenz	Greatest Of These Is Love,
Lorenz	Jesus Is All The World To M
Lorenz	Joy, Joy, Joy
Lorenz	Open My Eyes
Lorenz	Praises To The Giver
Lorenz	Prelude On Amazing Grace
Lorenz	Prelude On O Store Gud
Lorenz	Stand In Awe
Lorenz	Sunrise On A Hill
Lorenz	Wondrous Cross, The
Lorenz/Rasley	Name Of Jesus, The
Lorenz, E J	Elect Of God
Lorenz, E J	Seven Sayings From The Cros
Lorenz, Ellen Jane	Immortal, Invisible
Lorenz, Ellen Jane	One O'er All The Earth
Lorenz, Ellen Jane	Three Songs For Sacred Occa
Lorenz, Matthias	Give The King Your Final Ju
Lotti, A	Crucifixus
Lotti, A	Gaude Maria
Lotti, A	Hail, Queen Of Heaven, Rejo
Lotti, A	Queen Of Heaven
Lotti, A & Weber, R.	Kyrie (Missa Brevis)
Lotti, A & Weber, R.	Sanctus (Missa Brevis)
Lotti, A.	Gloria (Missa Brevis)
Lotti, A. (D1740)	Mass In C (Student's Mass)
Lotti, A./ Ed Klein	Queen Of Heaven (E & Lat)
Lotti, A/Soriano, F	Two Motets In Honor Of Bles
Lotti, Antonio	Adoramus Te, No. 1
Lotti, Antonio	Adoramus Te, No. 2
Lotti, Antonio	We Adore You No. 1
Lotti, Antonio	We Adore You No. 2
Lotti, Antonio	Ye Who Pass By
Loucks	God's House
Loucks	My Redeemer Liveth
Loucks	Thanks To God For My Mother
Lovelace, Austin C.	A Collection Of Funeral Mus
Lovelace, Austin C.	A Prayer For Families
Lovelace, Austin C.	All Lands And Peoples
Lovelace, Austin C.	Beneath The Forms Of Outwar
Lovelace, Austin C.	Christ Is Risen!
Lovelace, Austin C.	Christ Is The World's Redee
Lovelace, Austin C.	Christ Whose Glory Fills Th
Lovelace, Austin C.	Come To The Tomb
Lovelace, Austin C.	Come, Thou Long Expected Je
Lovelace, Austin C.	Concertato On "Adeste Fidel
Lovelace, Austin C.	Darkness Now Has Taken Flig
Lovelace, Austin C.	Dear Lord And Father Of Man
Lovelace, Austin C.	Earth Is The Lord's
Lovelace, Austin C.	Earth With Joy Confesses
Lovelace, Austin C.	From East To West
Lovelace, Austin C.	Giver Of All, We Thank Thee
Lovelace, Austin C.	Glory Be To God On High
Lovelace, Austin C.	God Is In His Holy Temple
Lovelace, Austin C.	God Is Working His Purpose
Lovelace, Austin C.	God Of Concrete
Lovelace, Austin C.	Hail To The Lord's Anointed
Lovelace, Austin C.	Hark, Angel Carols
Lovelace, Austin C.	How Shall I Sing That Majes
Lovelace, Austin C.	I Come With Joy
Lovelace, Austin C	I Will Arise
Lovelace, Austin C.	Jesus, Stand Beside Them
Lovelace, Austin C.	King Shall Come When Mornin
Lovelace, Austin C.	Lord Is My Shepherd, The
Lovelace, Austin C.	Love Came Down At Christmas
Lovelace, Austin C.	None Other Lamb
Lovelace, Austin C.	O Dearest Lord
Lovelace, Austin C.	O God Of Love To Thee We Bo
Lovelace, Austin C.	O God Of Love
Lovelace, Austin C.	O I Would Sing Of Mary's Ch
Lovelace, Austin C.	O Praise The Name Of The Lo
Lovelace, Austin C.	O Thou Eternal Christ, Ride
Lovelace, Austin C.	O Ye Who Taste That Love Is
Lovelace, Austin C.	On A Day When Men Were Coun
Lovelace, Austin C.	Only Begotten, Word Of God
Lovelace, Austin C.	Our Father, By Whose Name
Lovelace, Austin C.	Praise The Lord Who Reigns
Lovelace, Austin C.	Sing Ye Praises (W/Clavier/
Lovelace, Austin C	Spirit Divine
Lovelace, Austin C.	The Lord My Shepherd Is
Lovelace, Austin C.	The Praises Of A King
Lovelace, Austin C.	There's A Voice In The Wild
Lovelace, Austin C.	Throned Upon The Awful Tree
Lovelace, Austin C.	To Bless The Earth
Lovelace, Austin C.	Tomorrow Christ Is Coming
Lovelace, Austin C.	Universal Lord, The
Lovelace, Austin C.	Wedding Music For The Churc
Lovelace, Austin C.	When I Survey The Wondrous
Lovelace, Austin C.	Who Can Behold
Lovelace, Linda	Everlasting Mercy
Lovelace, Linda	My Need
Lovelock, William	O Praise God In His Holines
Low, James L	I Want To Serve The Lord
Lowden/Wilson	Living For Jesus
Lowry/Ayers	We're Marching To Zion
Lowry/Decou	Follow On
Lowry/Decou	Shall We Gather At The Rive
Lowry/Decou	When I Can Read My Title Cl
Lowry/Johnson	Christ Arose (Easy)
Lucht	Do You Care?
Lucht	Jesus, How Dear You Are
Lully-Ehret(Arr.)	Gracious God, Reveal Thy Wi
Lully, J B	Omnes Gentes
Luther-Johns	Lord, Keep Us Steadfast
Luther/Carmichael	Mighty Fortress If Our God,
Luther/Rasley	Mighty Fortress, A
Luther/Westendorf,Omer	A Mighty Fortress Is Our Go
Luther, M. (Swift)	Away In A Manger
Luther, M.-Distler	Lord, Keep Us Steadfast
Luther, M.-Johnson	A Mighty Fortress (Inst. Op
Luther, Martin	A Mighty Fortress Is Our Go
Luther, Martin	God's Word (4-Part Arr)
Luther, Martin	Mighty Fortress, A
Lutkin	Into The Woods My Master We
Lutkin	Lord Bless You And Keep You
Lutkin, Peter	The Lord Bless You And Keep
Luvas	When Christmas Morn Is Dawn
Lvoff, A Von	O Holy Jesu
Lwoff/Lundberg	God, The Omnipotent
Lynch, Michael B.	Acclamation (A)
Lynch, Michael B.	Acclamation(B)
Lynch, Michael B.	Acclamation(C)
Lynch, Michael B.	Acclamation(D)
Lynch, Michael B.	Alleluia
Lynch, Michael B.	As We Pray
Lynch, Michael B.	Ave Maria
Lynch, Michael B.	Blessings On The King
Lynch, Michael B.	Come All You People
Lynch, Michael B.	Father Of Peace
Lynch, Michael B.	Forever I Will Sing(Ps 89)
Lynch, Michael B.	Give The Lord Glory(Ps 96)
Lynch, Michael B.	Gospel Acclamation In A Maj
Lynch, Michael B.	Here Am I Oh Lord(Ps 40)
Lynch, Michael B.	Holy, Holy, Holy
Lynch, Michael B.	Holy, Holy, Holy
Lynch, Michael B.	I Believe That I Shall See(
Lynch, Michael B.	Lenten Invocation
Lynch, Michael B.	Living Water(Lenten Invocat
Lynch, Michael B.	Lord Has Done Great Things(
Lynch, Michael B.	Lord Is My Shepherd (Ps 23)
Lynch, Michael B.	Mass For All Seasons
Lynch, Michael B.	May The Roads Rise Up(Irish
Lynch, Michael B.	Our Father(D Maj)
Lynch, Michael B.	Praise Song
Lynch, Michael B.	Praise The Lord Who Heals(P
Lynch, Michael B.	Psalm 103
Lynch, Michael B.	Psalm 51
Lynch, Michael B.	Teach Me Your Ways (Ps 25)
Lynch, Michael B.	There's A Time, There's A M
Lynch, Michael B.	Vineyard Of The Lord (Ps 80
Lynch, Michael B.	We Stand In Need
Lynch, Michael B.	Where Has Your Lover Gone
Lynch, Michael B.	Whom Shall I Fear (Ps 27)
Lynch, Michael B.	With God On Our Side
Lynch,Michael&Blanc,M.	Look At My Gifts
Lynch,Michael&Martell	Praise God
Lynn-Zeuner	Where Cross The Crowded Way
Lynn, George	Amazing Grace
Lynn, George	And Can It Be?

COMPOSER INDEX

Lynn, George	Anthems Of Faith (Collectio
Lynn, George	Come, Let Us Use The Grace
Lynn, George	Father, Forgive Them
Lynn, George	Four Gospel Hymn Anthems
Lynn, George	Gentle Savior, Hold My Hand
Lynn, George	He Leadeth Me
Lynn, George	I Longed To Find The Risen
Lynn, George	Lord Doth Reign, The (Opt A
Lynn, George	Must Jesus Bear The Cross A
Lynn, George	My Faith, It Is An Oaken St
Lynn, George	Now With The New Year Start
Lynn, George	One There Is Above All Othe
Lynn, George	Rock Of Ages
Lynn, George	Sleep My Little One
Lynn, George	To Our Fathers--And Thee
Lynn, George	Who Shall Separate Us From
Lynn, George	Why Thus Cradled Here?
Lynn, George	Wondrous Love (Spiritual)
Lynn, George (Arr)	Come To The Savior, Make No
Lynn, George (Arr)	Shall We Gather At The Rive
Lyon	Praise Ye, Jehovah
Mabry	And Peace Shall Reign Again
Macfarlane	Jesus Calls Us (W/Bass Solo
Macfarlane, W C	God Is Our Refuge
Macfarlane, W C	Ho, Every One That Thirstet
Macfarlane, W C	Jesus Calls Us
Macfarlane, W C	O Rest In The Lord
Macfarlane, W C	Open Our Eyes
Macfarlane, W C	Saviour, Like A Shepherd Le
Macfarlane, W C	Thine, O Lord
Maclellan (Arr)	Put Your Hand In The Hand
Maconchy, Elizabeth	I Sing Of A Maiden
Maconchy, Elizabeth	This Day
Macroberts	Before Us, Lord, The Sacram
Macroberts	Great Peace Have They
Madan/Brandon	Before Jehovah's Awful Thro
Madsen, F J	Still, Still With Thee
Mahler, Gustov	Canticle Of Christmas
Mahoney, Patrick	Lord Have Mercy
Mahoney, Patrick	Our Father
Maker	Mothers Everywhere
Maker-Wetgzler	Christ Is Risen, Alleluia
Maker, F C	Arise, Shine
Malan/Johnson	Take My Life And Let It Be
Mallette	Lord Make Me An Instrument
Malloch	Aria For Organ
Malloch, David J.	Christmas Chimes
Malone, Miriam	I Rejoiced (Psalms 121 & 12
Malone, Miriam	New Life
Malotte, A H	And Have Not Charity
Malotte, A H	Faith
Malotte, A H	The Beatitudes
Malotte, A H	The Lord's Prayer
Malotte, A H	The Twenty-Third Psalm
Manion, Tim, S. J.	Blessings On The King
Mann, Lynn/Mann,J.	God's Quiet Love (Collectio
Manton, Robert	In Memoriam
Mantonti,C./Roff,J.	Psalms For Today (Org,Guit
Manz, Paul	Antiphonal Carol
Manz, Paul	Chorale Concertato On Prais
Manz, Paul	E'en So, Lord Jesus, Quickl
Manz, Paul	How Lovely Shines The Star
Manz, Paul	I Caused Thy Grief
Manz, Paul	Partita On "St. Anne"
Manz, Paul	Praise The Lord For He Is G
Manz, Paul	Ten Chorale Improvisations
Manz, Paul	The Lord Reigneth
Marbeck, John	Mass Per Arma Justitiae
Marbeck, John	Three Anthems
Marcello, Benedetto	Heart's Adoration
Marenzio	Caecilliam Cantata
Marenzio, Luca	Born Today
Marenzio, Luca	O Rex Gloriae
Margaret, Sr. Mary	Mass In Honor Of O.L. Visit
Maria Of The Cross	Mass For Peace (E)
Maria Of The Cross,Sr.	Where Charity And Love Are
Marian, Sister	Hear Me
Marier, Theodore	Eight Alleluias, Gospel Acc
Marier, Theodore	Glory To God
Mark Riese	Trust In God
Markaitis, Bruno	Creed (64 Text)
Markaitis, Bruno	Glory To God (64 Text)
Markaitis, Bruno	Holy, Holy, Holy (64 Text)
Markaitis, Bruno	Lamb Of God (64 Text)
Markaitis, Bruno	Lord Have Mercy (3 Fold)
Marlow, Richard	Preces And Responses (Me)
Marsh, Donald T.	Look For Him
Marsh, Donald T.	New Tomorrow, A
Marshall	Alleluia
Marshall	Fifteen Harmonizations On H
Marshall	Harmonizations On Hymn Tune
Marshall	Instrument Of Thy Peace, An
Marshall	Prayers I Make, The
Marshall	We Would Offer Thee This Da
Marshall, Jane	A Choral Ascription Of Prai
Marshall, Jane	Blessed Is The Man
Marshall, Jane	Give To The Winds Thy Fears
Marshall, Jane	He Who Would Valiant Be
Marshall, Jane	Lord Most High (Opt Brs)
Marshall, Paul A.	Song Of The Shepherds, The
Marsters, Nancy (Arr)	The Old Ark
Martens	Prayer For Mothers, A
Martens	Star In The Night, A
Marth, Helen J	In The Stillness
Martin	All By Ourselves
Martin	Amazing Grace!
Martin	And One Bright Star
Martin	Anthem For Communion, An
Martin	Arise,Shine!
Martin	Awake, My Soul!
Martin	Beatitudes, The
Martin	Could This Be A Special Nig
Martin	Do What He Wants You To Do
Martin	Easter Praise (E)
Martin	Epiphany Prayer, An
Martin	Fight The Good Fight
Martin	Hosanna In The Highest!
Martin	Hymn Of Saint Teresa
Martin	I Think I Heard Him Say
Martin	Joseph Dearest, Joseph Mine
Martin	Joy To The World
Martin	Kum-Bah-Yah
Martin	Let Us Keep Silence
Martin	Love Gift, The
Martin	Man On The Cross, The
Martin	More Things Are Wrought By
Martin	My Redeemer
Martin	Newborn, The
Martin	O Lord, Shield Of Our Help
Martin	O Lord, Support Us
Martin	Passion Chorale, The
Martin	Praises For The Risen Chris
Martin	Prayer Of Penitence, A
Martin	Psalm Of Gratitude, A
Martin	Psalm Praises
Martin	Rejoice, For Christ Is Born
Martin	Rejoice, Rejoice, Believers
Martin	Shall We Gather At The Rive
Martin	Simple Gifts
Martin	Sing Praise To God
Martin	Song For The New Year, A
Martin	Take It On Over
Martin	Then I Know
Martin	To See The Lord
Martin	Two Dwellings
Martin	Without Love, No Feeling
Martin (Arr)	My God And I
Martin Shaw/Dale Wood	Grand Processional For Orga
Martin/Blake	My Shepherd
Martin, Bruce	Lost Millions Still Untold
Martin, Bruce	New
Martin, Bruce	Why Should I Sing Any Other
Martin, G C	The Great Day Of The Lord I
Martin, G M	A Dedicatory Anthem
Martin, Gilbert M	An Anthem For Communion
Martin, Gilbert M	He's Got The Whole World In
Martin, Gilbert M	Love Came Down At Christmas
Martin, Gilbert M	Morning Has Broken
Martin, Gilbert M	The Water Is Wide
Martin, Gilbert M.	Blest Are The Pure In Heart
Martin, Gilbert M.	I'm But A Stranger Here
Martin, Gilbert M.	King Of Love My Shepherd, T
Martin, Gilbert M.	O Be Joyful In The Lord
Martin, Gilbert M.	Put Forth, O God, Thy Spiri
Martin, Gilbert M.	The Lute-Book Lullaby
Martin, Gilbert M.	When The Lord Of Love Was H
Martin, Warren	Psalm 13
Martini, J.	Three Sacred Choruses
Mascagni, Pietro	Light Divine
Mascagni, Pietro	Regina Coeli
Mason (Arr Mccoy)	Lord, Grant Thy Blessing
Mason-Riedel	O Look To Golgotha
Mason/Decou	Hark! Ten Thousand Harps An
Mason/Decou	There Is A Fountain
Mason/Johnson	Joy To The World
Mason/Mayfield	Hail To The Brightness!
Mason, L	Psalm 117 O Praise The Lord
Mason, L. Arr Griffith	My Faith Looks Up To Thee
Mason, Thom D	Psalm 23
Massie-Tortolano	Puer Nobis Nascitur (In 19
Mathias, William	All Thy Works Shall Praise
Mathias, William	Bless The Lord, O My Soul (
Mathias, William	Communion Service In C (Me)
Mathias, William	Festival Te Deum (Md)
Mathias, William	Gloria (Md)
Mathias, William	Magnificat And Nunc Dimitti
Mathias, William	Make A Joyful Noise Unto Th
Mathias, William	O Salutaris Hostia (Md)
Mathias, William	O Sing Unto The Lord (M)
Mathias, William	Psalm 150 (Md)
Mathias, William(Tr W)	Three Medieval Lyrics
Mathis, Ola	His Name Is The Sweetest I
Matthews/Decou	Do You Want Peace?
Matthews, David	Christ Is Born Of Maiden Fa
Matthews, H A	Eye Hath Not Seen
Matthews, H A	Father, Once More Within
Matthews, H A	Father, We Praise Thee
Matthews, H A	Great Is The Lord
Matthews, H A	Immortal Love, For Ever Ful
Matthews, H A	Sleep, Holy Babe
Matthews, H A	Voices Of The Sky
Matthews, H A	Welcome Happy Morning
Mauduit, Jacques	En Son Temple Sacre (Psalm
Mauduit, Jacques	Psalm 150
Maunder	On The Way To Jerusalem
Maunder	Praise The Lord, O Jerusale
Maunder	Song Of Thanksgiving
Maunder, J H	On The Way To Jerusalem
Maunder, J. (Arr Mccoy	Thine Own Way
Maunder, J. H.	Forever, O Lord (Ps 8)
Mawby, C	Four Psalm Settings
Mayfield, L.	We're Going To Sing
Mayhew, K. (Arr)	Let Us Break Bread Together
Mayhew,Kevin & Singers	All The Nations
Mayhew,Kevin & Singers	As Gentle As Silence
Mayhew,Kevin & Singers	Ask And You Will Receive
Mayhew,Kevin & Singers	Autumn Song
Mayhew,Kevin & Singers	Do You Know?
Mayhew,Kevin & Singers	Gold For The Sun
Mayhew,Kevin & Singers	Haul Away
Mayhew,Kevin & Singers	How Dark Was The Stable?
Mayhew,Kevin & Singers	I Will Give My Baby
Mayhew,Kevin & Singers	Let All That Is Within Me
Mayhew,Kevin & Singers	Now Jesus Said
Mayhew,Kevin & Singers	O Glorify The Lord
Mayhew,Kevin & Singers	The Carpenter
Mayhew,Kevin & Singers	There Is A World
Mcafee/Carmichael	Near To The Heart Of God (A
Mcafee/Mayfield	Near To The Heart Of God
Mcafee, D	Bells Of Easter, The
Mcafee, D	Corinthians On Love
Mcafee, D	I Will Lift Up Mine Eyes
Mcafee, Don	A Winter Carol
Mcafee, Don	Almighty God, Unto Whom All
Mcafee, Don	Built On The Rock
Mcafee, Don	Communion Anthem
Mcafee, Don	Designs For Organ
Mcafee, Don	Earth Is The Lord's The
Mcafee, Don	Fourteen Choral Responses
Mcafee, Don	Gates Of Jerusalem, The
Mcafee, Don	Go Ye Therefore
Mcafee, Don	Heart Of God, The
Mcafee, Don	Holy Infant Of Bethlehem
Mcafee, Don	How Excellent Is Thy Name
Mcafee, Don	Let The People Praise Thee
Mcafee, Don	Lord Is Nigh, The
Mcafee, Don	O Clap Your Hands
Mcafee, Don	Psalm 139
Mcafee, Don	Psalm 51
Mcafee, Don	Psalm 91
Mcafee, Don	Ride On, Ride On In Majesty
Mcafee, Don	Sing Praise To God
Mcafee, Don	Sing Unto The Lord A New So
Mcafee, Don	Two Christmas Carols
Mcafee, Don	Two Songs For Medium Voice
Mcafee, Don	Variations On Wer Nur Den L
Mcalister	O Lord Give Us Light
Mcalister	We've Been To The Mountain
Mcbeth, W. Francis	The Seventh Seal
Mcbeth, W. Francis	To Be Fed By Ravens
Mcbride, James	Amazing Grace
Mcbride, James	Pheres
Mcbride, James	This Is The Day
Mccabe, John	Mary Laid Her Child
Mccabe, Michael	Alleluia! Christ Is Born
Mccarthy, J & Cavalier	God Is Alive
Mccarthy, John	Doubting Thomas
Mccarthy, John	It Is A Great Day Of Joy
Mccarthy, John	It Is Not Too Late
Mccarthy, John	Judas, Why?
Mccarthy, John	Now He Is Born
Mccarthy, John	On The Mount Of Olive Grove
Mccarthy, John	Peter, Peter Hear Me
Mccarthy, John	St. John The Evangelist
Mccarthy, John	They Cast Their Nets
Mccarthy, John	Tis Christmas This Night
Mccarthy, John	What Miracles Of Beauty
Mccarthy, John	Whither Bound St. James?
Mcclenny/Hinson	Variations To Adeste Fidele
Mccluskey	Come, Ye Sinners, Poor And
Mccluskey	Solid Rock, The
Mccluskey	Though Your Sins Be As Scar
Mccluskey	When I Stood At Calvary
Mccoll	The First Time Ever
Mccormick	Song Of Deliverance, A
Mccoy	We All Need God
Mccoy, F. (Arr)	Early American Hymn Tune
Mccoy, F. (Arr)	God Is Watching Over Us
Mccoy, Floyd	Meditation
Mccoy, Floyd (Arr)	Sacred Selections For Inst.
Mccurdy, E.	Strangest Dream
Mccusker, M	Why Art Thou Disquieted?
Mccusker, M & Ugartech	Sonshine
Mcfarland	Holy Easter Morning
Mcfeeters Arr	Gentle Mary Catalan Folk-So
Mcgervey	Folk Songs Of Mike Mcgervey
Mcgill	Only One Life
Mcgill/Gilpin	Thank The Lord
Mcgimsey, R.	Shadrack (A Cap)
Mcgranahan/Decou	Bringing Back The King

Mcgranahan/Decou	There Shall Be Showers Of B	Mendelssohn, F.	In Heavenly Love	Mieir, Audrey	Gone, Buried, Lost
Mcgranahan/Johnson	Christ Liveth In Me	Mendelssohn, F.	Judge Me, O God	Mieir, Audrey	Have Faith In God
Mcgranahan/Johnson	Hallelujah For The Cross	Mendelssohn, F.	Kyrie	Mieir, Audrey	Have I Done My Best
Mcgranahan/Johnson	Verily, Verily	Mendelssohn, F.	Kyrie In D Minor	Mieir, Audrey	He Belongs To Me
Mcgranahan/Mickelson	Christ Returneth	Mendelssohn, F.	Lacrymosa	Mieir, Audrey	He Comes To Me
Mcgranahan, J. (Field)	Hallelujah! Christ Is Risen	Mendelssohn, F.	Lauda Sion (Cantata)	Mieir, Audrey	He Is Coming Again
Mcgrath, J J	The Earth Feared	Mendelssohn, F.	Lift Thine Eyes	Mieir, Audrey	He Knoweth
Mcgrath, Roberta	Believe	Mendelssohn, F.	Lift Thine Eyes (A Cap)	Mieir, Audrey	He Loves Me
Mcgrath, Roberta	Brotherhood	Mendelssohn, F.	Lift Thine Eyes (Me)	Mieir, Audrey	He'll Never Fail
Mcgrath, Roberta	Everybody Sing Alleluia	Mendelssohn, F.	My Soul Longeth For Thee	Mieir, Audrey	He's Willing
Mcgrath, Roberta	Holy, Holy, Holy	Mendelssohn, F.	Now Thank We All Our God	Mieir, Audrey	Help Me Speedily
Mcgrath, Roberta	I've Got A Light	Mendelssohn, F.	O Come, Let Us Worship	Mieir, Audrey	His Name Is Wonderful
Mcgrath, Roberta	Psalm 103	Mendelssohn, F.	O For The Wings Of A Dove	Mieir, Audrey	How Much He Cared
Mcguire, Margie, Ccw	Happy The Heart	Mendelssohn, F.	O Thou, The True And Only L	Mieir, Audrey	I Am Determined
Mcguire, Thomas	Holy Spirit, Truth Divine	Mendelssohn, F.	On This Fair Night The Ange	Mieir, Audrey	I Am In His Hands
Mcguire, Thomas	Memorial Acclamation 3	Mendelssohn, F.	Psalm 42 As A Heart	Mieir, Audrey	I Am Persuaded
Mcguire,D./Mcguire,W.	My Lord Jesus	Mendelssohn, F.	Psalm 95	Mieir, Audrey	I Heard God Today
Mckay,D./Mcguire,W.	Ascensions	Mendelssohn, F.	Sacred A Capella Choruses	Mieir, Audrey	I Know He Cares
Mckay	Contemplations	Mendelssohn, F.	Sancta Maria, Mater Dei	Mieir, Audrey	I Long To Find Perfect Peac
Mckay	Improvisation On Unser Herr	Mendelssohn, F.	Sanctus	Mieir, Audrey	I Will Not Question
Mckay	Praise Him (Psalm 150)	Mendelssohn, F.	Sanctus And Osanna	Mieir, Audrey	I Will Sing
Mckay, John (Ed)	Color Him Love (No 5019)	Mendelssohn, F.	See What Love	Mieir, Audrey	I Won't Go Where They Are
Mckenna/Traditional	Careworn Mother Stood Atten	Mendelssohn, F.	See What Love Hath The Fath	Mieir, Audrey	I'll Never Be Lonely
Mckenzie, Louis A	Love Is The Way	Mendelssohn, F.	Sing Ye Merrily	Mieir, Audrey	I'll Understand
Mckie, William	Psalm 121 And Wedding Respo	Mendelssohn, F.	Sleepers, Wake, A Voice Is	Mieir, Audrey	I'm Here To Stay
Mckie, William	We Wait For Thy Loving Kind	Mendelssohn, F.	Song Of Loyal Brotherhood	Mieir, Audrey	I'm So Happy
Mckinney	God, Give Us Christian Home	Mendelssohn, F.	St. Pual (Oratorio, Germ/En	Mieir, Audrey	If I Had Not Jesus
Mckinney/Wilson	Wherever He Leads I'll Go	Mendelssohn, F.	Thanks Be To God	Mieir, Audrey	If You Really Love Him
Mckinney, James C.	The Lord Reigneth (Ps 99)	Mendelssohn, F.	Thanks Be To God	Mieir, Audrey	In Jesus' Name
Mcphail	Teach Me To Pray	Mendelssohn, F.	Thanks Be To God (From Elij	Mieir, Audrey	In Rememberance
Mcspadden,Boyd & Helen	Heaven	Mendelssohn, F.	There Shall Be Star Come Ou	Mieir, Audrey	It Matters To Him
Mcvay, Lewis E	Sail On Sailor	Mendelssohn, F.	Three Motets For Chorus & S	Mieir, Audrey	Jesus, Jesus
Mead, Edward	God Of The Earth	Mendelssohn, F.	Three Unfamiliar Organ Comp	Mieir, Audrey	Just A Dreamer
Mead, Edward G.	Blessed Art Thou	Mendelssohn, F.	To God On High	Mieir, Audrey	Just Take His Hand Again
Mead, Edward G.	Christmas Prayer	Mendelssohn, F.	To Thee, O Lord	Mieir, Audrey	Just Trust And Obey
Mead, Edward G.	I Will Extol Thee	Mendelssohn, F.	Trust Thou In God	Mieir, Audrey	Keep Me At The Foot Of The
Meador, C.	I Don't Deserve His Love	Mendelssohn, F.	Why Rage Fiercely The Heath	Mieir, Audrey	Let My Heart Be Broken
Mede.na, Ken	Moses (Long)	Menotti, Gian Carlo	The Shepherds' Chorus	Mieir, Audrey	Linger A Little Longer
Medema, Ken	The Story—Tellin' Man (Musi	Merbecke, John	Mass, Roman Catholic Englis	Mieir, Audrey	My God Shall Supply
Medema,K./Brown,C.	Lead The Way (W/Piano)	Mercer, M	Prayer	Mieir, Audrey	No More
Medler, Malcolm	Lord, How Excellent Thy Nam	Merchant, W. M.	The Tree Of Life (Cantata)	Mieir, Audrey	No One But You
Medley, Ann	Lord, We Praise Thee	Merrick, Frank	Epiphany Carol (E)	Mieir, Audrey	Not Here For Long
Medling, Rebecca	Amen	Merritt	Variations On Gott Des Himm	Mieir, Audrey	Oh That I Knew
Medling, Rebecca	Amen	Merritt, Charles	On Christmas Night	Mieir, Audrey	On And On
Medling, Rebecca	Hosanna	Merritt, Charles	Simple Gifts	Mieir, Audrey	One Tender Moment
Medling, Rebecca	Lamb Of God	Merriweather, Roy	Great Joy	Mieir, Audrey	Promises Of Love
Meilstrup/Johnson	Where Is Love Today?	Merton,T./Peloquin C A	All The Way Down (Jonah 2)	Mieir, Audrey	Ready
Meilstrup/Marsh	Where In The World	Merton,T./Peloquin C A	Earthquake (Isaiah 52)	Mieir, Audrey	Real Peace
Meilstrup, David G.	I Can Know	Merton,T./Peloquin C A	Sundown (Bar Solo,Orch Or P	Mieir, Audrey	Return Again
Melby	Savior Of The Nations, Come	Merton,T./Peloquin C A	The Lord Is Good (Ps 71)	Mieir, Audrey	See Me Through
Melby, J.	Bright & Glorious Is The Sk	Messiter/Johnson	Rejoice, Ye Pure In Heart	Mieir, Audrey	Show Me
Mellers, Wilfred	Two Motets 'in Diem Pacis'	Meyer/Johnson	Ho! Everyone That Is Thirst	Mieir, Audrey	So Soon It Is Over
Meloy, Elizabeth	Heaven And Earth And Sea An	Meyer, Ron	All Things New	Mieir, Audrey	Surrender
Meltz, Ken	A Song Of Freedom	Meyer, Ron	Christ Is Near	Mieir, Audrey	Temptation
Meltz, Ken	Believe And Repent	Meyer, Ron	Come With Me	Mieir, Audrey	The Inner Place
Meltz, Ken	Come To The Mountain	Meyer, Ron	Forming God's People	Mieir, Audrey	The Moving Of The Breath Of
Meltz, Ken	David's Song	Meyer, Ron	Get Up And Live	Mieir, Audrey	The One I Love
Meltz, Ken	Epistle (Response)	Meyer, Ron	Listen To The Silence	Mieir, Audrey	The Perfect Will
Meltz, Ken	Father In Heaven	Meyer, Ron	Look Around	Mieir, Audrey	The Word Of God Endureth
Meltz, Ken	He Has Life Restored	Meyer, Ron	Shout Out, Sing Of His Glor	Mieir, Audrey	Then It Must Be So
Meltz, Ken	In Praise Of God	Meyer, Ron	The Stories Will Shout Out	Mieir, Audrey	Time Stood Still On Calvary
Meltz, Ken	In You Do I Find My Reward	Meyer, Ronald	Sing Of Our God (Trinity)	Mieir, Audrey	To Be Used Of God
Meltz, Ken	Maranatha	Meyer, V/Selner, J	Anthology Of Offertories An	Mieir, Audrey	Today Is The First Day
Meltz, Ken	May The Lord Bless & Keep Y	Meyerowitz, Jan	Ave Maria, Full Of Grace	Mieir, Audrey	Touch Me Just Now
Meltz, Ken	Our Father	Meyerowitz, Jan	Ave Maria, Gratia Plena	Mieir, Audrey	Truly Trust
Meltz, Ken	The Time Has Come	Meyerowitz, Jan	Ave Maris Stella	Mieir, Audrey	Unless You Help Me Lord
Meltz, Ken	This Is The Day	Meyerowitz, Jan	How Godly Is The House Of G	Mieir, Audrey	Untold Millions, Still Unto
Mendelssohn, F.	Above All Praise And Majest	Meyerowitz, Jan	If I Have My Jesus(From Two	Mieir, Audrey	When You Pray
Mendelssohn, F.	Advent Chorale, The (C)	Meyerowitz, Jan	In My Orchard, Pearl'd With	Mieir, Audrey	Where Do I Go From Here
Mendelssohn, F.	And In That Still Small Voi	Meyerowitz, Jan	Music For Christmas	Mieir, Audrey	Whisper One Name
Mendelssohn, F.	Be Not Afraid	Meyerowitz, Jan	New Plymouth Cantata	Mieir, Audrey	Will He Know Me
Mendelssohn, F.	But Our God Abideth In Heav	Meyerowitz, Jan	On A Pallet Of Straw	Mieir, Audrey	Willing To Go
Mendelssohn, F.	But The Lord Is Mindful Of	Meyerowitz, Jan	On The Land And On The Sea	Mieir, Audrey	Work For The Night
Mendelssohn, F.	Cast Thy Burden Upon The Lo	Meyerowitz, Jan (Ed)	Silesian Lullaby	Mieir, Audrey	Work Through Me
Mendelssohn, F.	Cast Thy Burden Upon The Lo	Michaelides, Peter	Lamentations	Mieir, Audrey	Would You Go
Mendelssohn, F.	Christus	Mickelson, Paul	Alleluia (No 5759)	Mieir, Audrey	You Have To Rise And Go
Mendelssohn, F.	Come Let Us Sing	Mickelson, Paul	Paul Mickelson's Arrangemen	Mieir, Audrey	Your Shining Hour
Mendelssohn, F.	Elijah (Oratorio)	Mickelson, Paul	The Miracle (No 4312)	Mieir, Audrey (Arr.)	Just A Closer Walk
Mendelssohn, F.	Elijah(Ger)	Mieir, Audrey	A Song In Your Heart	Mierzwa, Ronald	Jesus Loves Me As I Am
Mendelssohn, F.	Festival Hymn	Mieir, Audrey	Afterwhile	Miffleton, Jack	A Blessing From Aaron
Mendelssohn, F.	Gloria In Excelsis	Mieir, Audrey	All He Wants Is You	Miffleton, Jack	All These Things
Mendelssohn, F.	Happy And Blest Are They	Mieir, Audrey	Be Anxious Over Nothing	Miffleton, Jack	Alle, Alle
Mendelssohn, F.	Hark The Herald Angels Sing	Mieir, Audrey	Because He Touched Me	Miffleton, Jack	As The Sun
Mendelssohn, F.	He That Shall Endure	Mieir, Audrey	Beyond The Cross	Miffleton, Jack	Beatitudes
Mendelssohn, F.	He, Watching Over Israel	Mieir, Audrey	Beyond This Place	Miffleton, Jack	Break On Through
Mendelssohn, F.	Hear My Prayer	Mieir, Audrey	Bring Back The King	Miffleton, Jack	Bring On
Mendelssohn, F.	Heilig	Mieir, Audrey	By Grace	Miffleton, Jack	Bring To The Lord
Mendelssohn, F.	How Lovely Are The Messenge	Mieir, Audrey	Carried Away	Miffleton, Jack	Bushel—Round
Mendelssohn, F.	How Lovely Are The Messenge	Mieir, Audrey	Certainly	Miffleton, Jack	Care Is All It Takes
Mendelssohn, F.	How Lovely Are The Messenge	Mieir, Audrey	Choosing Rather	Miffleton, Jack	Christ Has Died (1 & 2)
Mendelssohn, F.	How Lovely Are Those Dwelli	Mieir, Audrey	Come With Me	Miffleton, Jack	Christ Is Lord
Mendelssohn, F.	Hymn Of Praise	Mieir, Audrey	Condemned	Miffleton, Jack	Come Out
Mendelssohn, F.	I Waited For The Lord	Mieir, Audrey	Consume Me	Miffleton, Jack	Cry Alice
Mendelssohn, F.	I Will Sing Of Thee Thy Gre	Mieir, Audrey	Dare To Believe	Miffleton, Jack	Even A Worm
Mendelssohn, F.	I Will Thank Thee, O Lord	Mieir, Audrey	Don't Save Me	Miffleton, Jack	Everybody's Got To Grow
Mendelssohn, F.	If With All Your Hearts	Mieir, Audrey	Fear Thou Not	Miffleton, Jack	Flies The Dove (From Young
Mendelssohn, F.	If With All Your Hearts	Mieir, Audrey	Follow All The Way	Miffleton, Jack	Fly (From Even A Worm)
Mendelssohn, F.	If With All Your Hearts	Mieir, Audrey	Forever Gone	Miffleton, Jack	Glory To God On High
Mendelssohn, F.	If With All Your Hearts	Mieir, Audrey	God's Afterglow	Miffleton, Jack	Go Tell Your People
Mendelssohn, F.	If With All Your Hearts	Mieir, Audrey	God's Great Love	Miffleton, Jack	God Made The World

COMPOSER INDEX

Miffleton, Jack	God Made Us All
Miffleton, Jack	Grab Your Soap (From Even A
Miffleton, Jack	Great Amen
Miffleton, Jack	Green Growing Plants
Miffleton, Jack	Greet The Risen Lord With J
Miffleton, Jack	Hey Day
Miffleton, Jack	Hey Joy
Miffleton, Jack	Holy, Holy, Holy
Miffleton, Jack	I Am The Good Shepherd
Miffleton, Jack	I Am The Living Bread
Miffleton, Jack	I Am The Vine
Miffleton, Jack	I Trust In You
Miffleton, Jack	I'm Ready To Follow
Miffleton, Jack	In Holy Splendor (Ccd)
Miffleton, Jack	In Your Holy Place
Miffleton, Jack	It Is My Faith
Miffleton, Jack	It Only Takes A Hug
Miffleton, Jack	It's Easy When You Rhyme Wi
Miffleton, Jack	Jesse Tree Song
Miffleton, Jack	John Is My Name
Miffleton, Jack	La La Life
Miffleton, Jack	Like A Father
Miffleton, Jack	Lord By Your Cross
Miffleton, Jack	Lord I've Come To Your Gard
Miffleton, Jack	Lord Let Me Walk
Miffleton, Jack	Only These Two
Miffleton, Jack	Raise Your Hands
Miffleton, Jack	Scripture Response, Allelui
Miffleton, Jack	She's Just An Old Stump
Miffleton, Jack	Sidney The Silly Centipede
Miffleton, Jack	Some Young Carpenter
Miffleton, Jack	Sometimes I'd Like To Be A
Miffleton, Jack	Spirit Of Action
Miffleton, Jack	Stand On His Promise
Miffleton, Jack	Stand Up
Miffleton, Jack	Sunshine
Miffleton, Jack	The Alphabet Tree
Miffleton, Jack	The Great Lights
Miffleton, Jack	The Wind Blows
Miffleton, Jack	There Are But Three Things
Miffleton, Jack	To Be A Friend
Miffleton, Jack	Up To Jerusalem (Lk 18:3)
Miffleton, Jack	We're Called To Be That Cit
Miffleton, Jack	Well, It's A New Day
Miffleton, Jack	What Can Make A Hippopotamu
Miffleton, Jack	When I Sing
Miffleton, Jack	When We Eat This Bread
Miffleton, Jack	Yesterday, Today & Tomorrow
Miffleton, Jack	You Are My Son
Miffleton, Jack	You Are The Light Of The Wo
Miffleton, Jack	Your Word
Miffleton, Jack	Yours Is The Kingdom
Miffleton, Jack Et Al	But Then Comes The Morning
Miles/Mclellan	Look For Me
Miles/Wilson	In The Garden
Miles, Gary	Song Of Repentance
Milgrove-Riedel	Glory To God On High
Milgrove/Douglas (Arr)	Bright & Joyful Is The Morn
Milhuff/Gaither	His Will
Milhuff/Gaither	It's No Wonder
Milkey, E T	Christmas Is Coming
Miller	Come Praise, Alleluia
Miller	Mass For Peace
Miller	Sing, Sing For Christmas
Miller/Jackson	Let There Be Peace On Earth
Miller, Dan	Come, Follow Me
Miller, Dan	Every Day
Miller, Dan	Happiness Song
Miller, Dan	Happy Are They
Miller, Dan	Jesus Will Come Thru
Miller, Dan	Let Your Song Ring Out
Miller, Dan	Morning, Mourning
Miller, Dan	Peace To You
Miller, Dan	Rejoice With Me
Miller, Dan	Rejoice, The Messiah Is Com
Miller, Dan	Sadness Song
Miller, Dan	Sometimes
Miller, Dan	Wake Up
Miller, John	The Gift Of Christmas Morn
Miller, M R	Two Carols
Miller, Thomas A.	Sing, All Ye People
Millet Arr	The Song Of The Birds
Milligan, H	Hear My Cry
Mills, Pauline M.	Thou Art Worthy
Milner, Anthony	Most Glorious Lord Of Life
Minor/Johnson	Bringing In The Sheaves
Mischke/Papale	Cup Of Blessing That We Sha
Mischke/Vermulst	Joseph, Patron Saint Of Wor
Mischke/Vermulst	Trust God And Come Before H
Mischke/Vermulst, J.	O Sing To God With Joy
Misetich,Sr Marianne	A Joyful Sound
Mitchell	Both Sides Now
Mitchell	Glad Song
Mitchell	Lord Of Life
Mitchell	Love Came Down At Christmas
Mitchell	On Wings Of Living Light (W
Mitchell	The Circle Game
Mitchell, Ian	Alleluia! Sing To Jesus
Mitchell, Ian	Christ, Our Passover
Mitchell, Ian	Eternal Rest (Introit)(Fune
Mitchell, Ian	Faithful Cross
Mitchell, Ian	Glory Be To God On High (Ja
Mitchell, Ian	Holy, Holy, Holy (Funeral F
Mitchell, Ian	Holy, Holy, Holy (Jazz-Rock
Mitchell, Ian	I Praised The Earth
Mitchell, Ian	Lamb Of God
Mitchell, Ian	Let Us Break Bread Together
Mitchell, Ian	Lord Have Mercy (Kyrie)(Fu
Mitchell, Ian	Lord Have Mercy (Kyrie)(Ja
Mitchell, Ian	Lord, Jesus Christ(Offertor
Mitchell, Ian	Magnificat
Mitchell, Ian	May Light Eternal (Funeral
Mitchell, Ian	Preface (Jazz-Rock Mass)
Mitchell, Ian	Presentation (Offertory)
Mitchell, Ian	Rejoice, The Lord Is King
Mitchell, Ian	Te Deum
Mitchell, Ian	The Creed(Credo) (Jazz-Rock
Mitchell, Ian	The Lord's Prayer (Jazz-Roc
Mitchell, Ian	There's A Wideness
Mitchell, Ian	Three Men Died On A Hillsid
Mitcheltree	The Earth Is The Lord's
Moats	Gentle Jesus
Moe, Daniel	A Man Of Integrity
Moe, Daniel	Cantata Of Peace W/Tpt
Moe, Daniel	Fall Softly, Snow
Moe, Daniel	Fanfare & Choral Procession
Moe, Daniel	God Be Merciful
Moe, Daniel	I Am The Alpha And The Omeg
Moe, Daniel	I Will Extol Thee
Moe, Daniel	Let Your Eye Be To The Lord
Moe, Daniel	Lord Is My Strength, The
Moe, Daniel	O Jesus Christ, To Thee May
Moe, Daniel	Psalm Concertato (In 3 Part
Moe, Daniel	Rejoice In The Lord Always
Moe, Daniel	Rejoice, Ye People (W/Insts
Moe, Daniel	Stranger, Share Our Fire
Moe, Daniel	The Glory Of This Day
Moe, Daniel	The Greatest Of These Is Lo
Moe, Daniel	Whether Young Or Old
Moe, Daniel	William Penn's Reflections
Moffatt	All For Jesus
Moffatt	Alone (E)
Moffatt	Call His Name Jesus
Moffatt	I Will Sing Of My Redeemer
Moffatt	Miracle Of Love, The
Moffatt	O Come, All Ye Faithful
Moffatt	Who At My Door Is Standing?
Moffatt, James	I Know Where I'm Going
Moffatt, James	Peace Like A River
Mohr, J./Andrews	Oh For A Shout Of Joy
Moir, F L	I Will Thank Thee, O Lord
Monaco, Richard	All Flesh Is Grass
Monaco, Richard	Lord, Thou Hast Been Our Dw
Monday, Robert	Acclamation
Monday, Robert	Keep Me Safe (Psalm 16)
Monday, Robert	Psalm 104
Monday, Robert	The Ballad Of Lazarus And T
Monhardt	Let The People Praise Thee
Monk, William H. Alt.	Alleluia! Jesus Is Lord (4-
Monk, William Henry	Hail The Day
Montague-Cunningham	How Great The Glory
Montague, George T.	A People Marching To Freedo
Montague, George T.	American Genesis (Reconcili
Montague, George T.	Down With Niniveh
Montague, George T.	Ezekiel
Montague, George T.	Glory, Glory (A Capella)
Montague, George T.	How Great The Glory (Trinit
Montague, George T.	If Only You'll Answer Me
Montague, George T.	Jonah
Montague, George T.	Look To The Rock (From Isai
Montague, George T.	My Simple Song
Montague, George T.	Number One (Prophecy)
Montague, George T.	O Man, You Have Been Told
Montague, George T.	Prepare You For The Day
Montague, George T.	Recreation (Sin & Penance)
Montague, George T.	Sing, Sing, Sing (Opt Brass
Montague, George T.	The God Of Abraham
Montague, George T.	The Holy City (From Revelat
Montague, George T.	The Lord Is Takin' Us Home
Montague, George T.	The Spirit And The Bride
Montague, George T.	The Spirit Of The Lord
Montague, George T.	Water Pot (John 2)
Montague, George T.	What Can A Man Say?
Montague, George T.	What Do You Do
Montague, George T.	What You Gonna Do
Monteverdi, Claudio	Angelus Ad Pastores Ait
Monteverdi, Claudio	Gloria From Messa A 4 Voci
Monteverdi, Claudio	Hodie Christus Natus Est
Monteverdi, Claudio	Holy, Holy, Holy
Monteverdi, Claudio	Lamb Of God
Monteverdi, Claudio	Lamb Of God
Monteverdi, Claudio	Magnificat For 6 Voices (Or
Monteverdi, Claudio	Mass For Four Mixed Voices
Monteverdi, Claudio	Messa A 4 Voci (A Cappella
Monteverdi, Claudio	Two Motets (Adoramus Te, Ca
Montgomery-Scott	Angels From The Realms Of G
Montgomery, Bruce	My Joy, My Life, My Crown (
Montsalvatge, Xavier	Cinco Invocaciones Al Cruci
Moody	Prayer For Courage
Moore	Clap Your Hands
Moore	Fanfare For The Seasons
Moore	Fishers Of Men
Moore	Four Canticles For Christma
Moore	Hand In Hand With God
Moore	Hear My Cry
Moore/Anthony	Why?
Moore/Decou	Burdens Are Lifted At Calva
Moore, D	O Lovely Son Of God
Moore, John	Burdens Are Lifted At Calva
Moore, Patrick	Psalms
Moore, Undine	Lord We Give Thanks To Thee
Moore, Undine Smith	Bound For Canaan's Land
Moore, Undine Smith	Daniel, Daniel, Servant Of
Moore, Undine Smith	Fare Ye Well
Moore, Undine Smith	I Just Come From The Founta
Moore, Undine Smith	Sinner You Can't Walk My Pa
Moore, Undine Smith	Striving After God
Moore, Undine Smith	Tambourines To Glory
Morales, Cristobal De	Ecce Virgo Concipiet
Morales, Cristobal De	Lo, A Child Is Born
Morales, Cristobal De	Missas Est Gabriel
Morales, Cristobal De	O Cross Thou Only Hope
Morales, Cristobal De	O Crux Ave, Spes Unica
Morales, Cristobal De	O Magnum Mysterium
Morales, Cristobal De	Pastores, Dicite, Quidnam V
Morales, Cristobal De	Puer Natus Est Nobis
Morgan	I Am The Vine
Morgan	None Shall Separate Us
Morgan	Prepare My Mind And Heart F
Morgan	Sing Praises To Our King
Morgan	They Who Considereth The Po
Morgan, Justin	Amanda
Morgan, Justin	Judgment Anthem
Morley, T	Sound Forth The Trumpet In
Morley, Thomas	Magnificat And Nunc Dimitti
Morley, Thomas	Nolo Mortem Peccatoris (M)
Morley, Thomas	Out Of The Deep (M)
Morley, Thomas	Thou Knowest Lord, The Secr
Morris/Mayfield	Fight Is On, The (W/Opt Tru
Morrison, C P	O Shepherd Of Israel
Mott, Joyce	John Mckay Sings Joyce Mott
Moultrie, Gerard	Let All Mortal Flesh Keep S
Moultry, Prince Jos.	Get On The Good Foot
Moultry, Prince Joseph	Amen
Moultry, Prince Joseph	He Is Risen
Moultry, Prince Joseph	Holy, Holy, Holy
Moultry, Prince Joseph	I May Be Young
Moultry, Prince Joseph	Jesus Is Mine
Moultry, Prince Joseph	Kyrie (Lord, Have Mercy)
Moultry, Prince Joseph	Lamb Of God
Moultry, Prince Joseph	Let Me Tell Y'all
Moultry, Prince Joseph	Lord By Your Cross
Moultry, Prince Joseph	Lord Have Mercy 2
Moultry, Prince Joseph	My God
Moultry, Prince Joseph	This Is The Day
Moultry, Prince Joseph	When We Eat This Bread
Mountain/Decou	Like A River Glorious
Moussorgsky, Modest	Gates Of Jerusalem, The
Mouton, Jean	Ave Maria
Moye, Claud	Let's Go To Church On Sunda
Moye, Claud	Obituary Of Mrs. Prayer Mee
Moyer, J. Edward	Surely The Lord Is In This
Mozart, Wolfgang A	Adagio Religioso
Mozart, Wolfgang A	Alleluia!
Mozart, Wolfgang A	Alleluja From Motet Exultat
Mozart, Wolfgang A	Alma Dei Creatoria K 277
Mozart, Wolfgang A	Ave Verum
Mozart, Wolfgang A	Ave Verum
Mozart, Wolfgang A	Ave Verum (Me)
Mozart, Wolfgang A	Ave Verum Corpus
Mozart, Wolfgang A	Ave Verum Corpus
Mozart, Wolfgang A	Ave Verum Corpus K 618
Mozart, Wolfgang A	Benedictus Sit Deus K 117
Mozart, Wolfgang A	Canon Alleluia (From Motet
Mozart, Wolfgang A	Coronation Mass K 317
Mozart, Wolfgang A	Coronation Mass(C)(Latin)
Mozart, Wolfgang A	Davide Penitente
Mozart, Wolfgang A	Davide Penitente K 469 (Eng
Mozart, Wolfgang A	De Profundis
Mozart, Wolfgang A	De Profundis K 93
Mozart, Wolfgang A	Exsultate Jubilate K 165
Mozart, Wolfgang A	Gloria (From The Twelfth Ma
Mozart, Wolfgang A	Gloria In Excelsis
Mozart, Wolfgang A	Gloria In Excelsis ("12th M
Mozart, Wolfgang A	Graduale: Sancta Maria, K.
Mozart, Wolfgang A	Grand Mass K 427
Mozart, Wolfgang A	Great Is The Lord
Mozart, Wolfgang A	His Matchless Worth
Mozart, Wolfgang A	Jesu, Word Of God Incarnate
Mozart, Wolfgang A	Justum Deduxit Dominus
Mozart, Wolfgang A	Kyrie
Mozart, Wolfgang A	Laudate Dominum (M)
Mozart, Wolfgang A	Litania K 243
Mozart, Wolfgang A	Litaniae Laureltanae K 195
Mozart, Wolfgang A	Litany Glory Praise & Power
Mozart, Wolfgang A	Mass In C K 258
Mozart, Wolfgang A	Mass 12 (Eng)
Mozart, Wolfgang A	Mass(C)(Latin)
Mozart, Wolfgang A	Mass, Vesperae Sollenes K 3
Mozart, Wolfgang A	Mercy Lord, Upon Us

COMPOSER INDEX

Mozart, Wolfgang A	Misericordia Dominis K 222
Mozart, Wolfgang A	Missa Brevis (K192,194,220,
Mozart, Wolfgang A	Missa De Dominica K 321
Mozart, Wolfgang A	Missa Solemnis K 337
Mozart, Wolfgang A	O Lord Most High, With All
Mozart, Wolfgang A	Praise Him, Ye Nations
Mozart, Wolfgang A	Praise The Lord For He Is G
Mozart, Wolfgang A	Regina Coeli K 276
Mozart, Wolfgang A	Requiem Aeternam-Christe El
Mozart, Wolfgang A	Requiem Mass (Latin)
Mozart, Wolfgang A	Requiem(Latin)
Mozart, Wolfgang A	Sancta Maria Graduale
Mozart, Wolfgang A	Sancta Maria Mater Dei K 27
Mozart, Wolfgang A	Sanctus (From Missa Brevis
Mozart, Wolfgang A	Te Deum, K 141
Mozart, Wolfgang A	The First Christmas Morn
Mozart, Wolfgang A	Veni Sanctus K 47
Mozart,W.A./Tortolano	Ave Maria (In 19 Rounds)
Muczynski, R	Alleluia
Mudd	God Which Has Prepared (Me)
Mudd	Let Thy Merciful Ears (Me)
Mudd, C. P.	Anamnesis
Mudd, C. P.	Children Of The Eighth Day
Mudd, C. P.	Get Up, Jerusalem
Mudd, C. P.	Lament
Mudd, C. P.	One More Day
Mudd, C. P.	The Lord Is Risen
Mudd, C. P.	What Can Keep Us?
Mudd, C. P.	You Are A Child Of The Univ
Mudd, C. P.	You Are The Hope Of All
Mudd, C. P. & Schleich	Day For Goodbye
Mudde	Sing Praise To God Who Reig
Mueller	Joyful Psalmody
Mueller	Laudamus Te
Mueller	The Triumph Song (Anthem Of
Mueller, Carl F	A Mighty Fortress Is Our Go
Mueller, Carl F	All Hail The Power
Mueller, Carl F	All My Heart This Night Rej
Mueller, Carl F	All Praise To Thee
Mueller, Carl F	Alleluia! Morn Of Beauty
Mueller, Carl F	An Anthem Of Faith
Mueller, Carl F	Christ Is Risen!
Mueller, Carl F	Create In Me A Clean Heart,
Mueller, Carl F	God Bless Our Native Land
Mueller, Carl F	God Is In His Holy Temple
Mueller, Carl F	God Of Light
Mueller, Carl F	Hast Thou Not Known?
Mueller, Carl F	He Is Risen
Mueller, Carl F	I Will Lift Up Mine Eyes
Mueller, Carl F	Judge Me, O God (W/Scp Solo
Mueller, Carl F	Laudamus
Mueller, Carl F	Lo, God Is Here!
Mueller, Carl F	Lord, Thou Hast Been Our Dw
Mueller, Carl F	Now Thank We All Our God
Mueller, Carl F	Once To Every Man And Natio
Mueller, Carl F	Praise To The Living God
Mueller, Carl F	Search Me, O God
Mueller, Carl F	Sing Hallelujah, Praise The
Mueller, Carl F	That They All May Be One
Mueller, Carl F	The Light Of Bethlehem
Mueller, Carl F	The Lord Bless You And Keep
Mueller, Carl F	The Lord's Prayer
Mueller, Carl F	The Triumph-Song
Mueller, Carl F	When Wilt Thou Save The Peo
Mueller, Luise	A Song For The Sabbath
Mueller, Luise	Come, Holy Spirit
Mueller, Luise	Depth Of Mercy
Mueller, Luise	O Praise The Lord
Mundy, John	Sing Joyfully (Md)
Mundy, William	O Lord, I Bow The Knee Of M
Mundy, William	O Lord, The Maker Of All Th
Murphy, Angela	Psalm 33
Murphy, Angela	Thanksgiving Litany
Murphy, Charles	Behold The Lord (From Come
Murphy, Charles	But As For Me, God Forbid(G
Murphy, Charles	Praise Him (From Come Follo
Murphy, Charles	Rise, O Lord! (From Come Fo
Murphy, Charles	Song Of Job (From Come Foll
Murphy, Charles	The Lord Has Satisfied The
Murphy, Ernest (Arr)	The Baroque Song Book
Murphy, J A	Behold A Great Priest
Murray/Lee,John	O King Of Might & Splendor
Murrill, Herbert	Magnificat And Nunc Dimitti
Musto, Steve	Stand Up And Sing (No 4062)
Myers, Carmel	I'm Standing In The Sun
Myers, Gordon	Let Us Break Bread Together
Myring Charles	Imps Of Satan
Myring Charles	My Glory
Myring Charles	Some Day
Myring Charles	St. Matt. 5:16
Myring Charles	Standing Far Off
Myring, Charles	Lone Calvary
Myrow, Gerald	March Of Freedom
Myrvik	Children Of The Heavenly Fa
Mytych, J F	God Father, Be Thou Praised
Mytych, J F	Holy God, We Praise Thy Nam
Mytych, J F	Hymn Of Praise
Mytych, J F	O Christ, Eternal King
Nabokov, Nicolas	Psalm 150
Nachtwey - Fitzpatrick	Lauda, Sion, Salvatorem
Nachtwey, Roger	Christ The Lord, Our Risen
Nachtwey, Roger	Let All On Earth Their Voic
Nachtwey, Roger	Let Us With Joy Our Voices
Nachtwey, Roger	Memorial Acclamation 2
Nachtwey, Roger	Memorial Acclamation 4
Nachtwey, Roger	O Father Blest
Nachtwey, Roger	O Virgin's Son
Nachtwey, Roger	Song Of Mary
Nachtwey, Roger	Song Of Zachary
Nachtwey, Roger	The Love Of Christ Has Join
Nachtwey, Roger	Where There Is Charity And
Nachtwey, Roger(Arr.)	Beautiful Savior
Nachtwey, Roger;Harm.,	Humbly We Adore You
Naggin, Elwood	Come Beloved Monarch
Najera, Edmund	Ad Flumina Babylonis
Najera, Edmund	Exultate Deo
Najera, Edmund	In Dulci Jubilo
Nanini, G M	Diffusa Est Gratia
Nankivell, Louise	Be Filled With The Spirit
Nardella, Faith	Alleluia! Christ Has Risen
Nardella, Faith	Christ Our Leader (4-Part A
Nardella, Faith	God Of Our Fathers
Nardella, Faith	Servant-King, The
Nares/Tortolano Ed	By The Waters Of Babylon (3
Narum & Jennings	The Light Has Come (Service
Narum And Preus	Even So, Lord Jesus
Nasanni	The Sussex Carol
Nash	Teach Your Children
Nasteley, Guillaume	Coventry Carol
Natalie Sleeth	Hallelujah, Glory Halleluja
Nathan/Mcgranahan	Come Unto Me And Rest
Naylor, Bernard	Of One That Is So Fair And
Naylor, Bernard	Preces And Responses (M)
Naylor, Bernard	Service And Strength
Neale	The God Whom Earth & Sea &
Neale/Smith, K.	Come And Let Us Drink Of Th
Neale/Wood, D.	Christ Is Made The Sure Fou
Neale, John M.	Come You Faithful
Neale, John M.	O Come, O Come Emmanuel
Neale, John N.	That Easter Day
Neander/Rasley	Christ Is Risen
Neander, J. (Carlton)	With Joyful Voice (Opt Tpts
Near, Gerald	An Easter Processional
Near, Gerald	Arise, My Love, My Fair One
Near, Gerald	Come, Risen Lord
Near, Gerald	Lord, Keep Us Steadfast In
Near, Gerald	Sing, Men And Angels, Sing
Near, Gerald	This Is The Day The Lord Ha
Neff	I Will Sing To The Lord 1
Neff	Jesus, Thou Joy Of Loving H
Neff	My Soul Is Exceeding Sorrow
Neff	Praise The Lord All Nations
Neff	Shout For Joy Before The Lo
Neff	The Empty Cave
Neidinger/Johnson	Birthday Of The King, The
Neidlinger	Birthday Of A King, The
Neidlinger	O Little Town Of Bethlehem
Neidlinger, W H	The Birthday Of A King
Neidlinger, W H	The Silent Sea
Neighbor, Ardean	Shout For Joy
Nelson	Psalm 98 (Joy To The World)
Nelson ,Ronald	The Passion According To St
Nelson/Ogilvy	Think Of God
Nelson, E M	Why Must You Go?
Nelson, Erick Martin	Carry Me Along
Nelson, Erick Martin	Follow You
Nelson, Erick Martin	Going Home
Nelson, Erick Martin	Good News
Nelson, Erick Martin	He Lives
Nelson, Erick Martin	Jimmy
Nelson, Erick Martin	Never Knew
Nelson, Erick Martin	Pickin' Up The Pieces
Nelson, Erick Martin	Rock Of Ages
Nelson, Paul	For Theirs Is The Kingdom O
Nelson, Ronald A.	Awake, My Soul
Nelson, Ronald A.	Be Filled With The Spirit
Nelson, Ronald A.	Clap Your Hands, Stamp Your
Nelson, Ronald A.	Come, My Soul
Nelson, Ronald A.	Come, Ye Thankful People, C
Nelson, Ronald A.	For Your Light Has Come
Nelson, Ronald A.	Hosanna
Nelson, Ronald A.	Hosanna To The Son Of David
Nelson, Ronald A.	Hosanna! O Blessed Is He
Nelson, Ronald A.	How Far Is It To Bethlehem?
Nelson, Ronald A.	In The Name Of The Lord
Nelson, Ronald A.	Introit For Easter
Nelson, Ronald A.	Introits For Lent And Easte
Nelson, Ronald A.	Psalm 24 (Lift Up Your Head
Nelson, Ronald A.	Rise Up, O Men Of God
Nelson, Ronald A.	Temples Of God
Nelson, Ronald A.	The Present Tense (2 Pt Can
Nelson, Ronald A.	The Season Of Tomorrow (W/F
Nelson, Ronald A.	They That Wait Upon The Lor
Nelson, Ronald A.	This Is The Feast Of Victor
Nelson, Ronald A.	Under The Eastern Sky (Org
Nelson, Ronald A.	We Know That Christ Is Rais
Nelson, Ronald A.	Whoever Would Be Great Amon
Nestor, Leo	From Heaven The Lord Looks
Neumann, Alfred	Truly, We Shall Be In Parad
Neumann, D. & Tlucek,	Living Spirit, The
Nevin, Geo B	Jesus, My Saviour, Look On
Newbury, Kent A.	Awake, Thou That Sleepest
Newbury, Kent A.	Behold, I Stand At The Door
Newbury, Kent A.	Behold, Your God Will Come
Newbury, Kent A.	Bless The Lord, O My Soul
Newbury, Kent A.	Blessed Are Those Who Belie
Newbury, Kent A.	Blessed Be The Lord Forever
Newbury, Kent A.	Break Forth Into Joy
Newbury, Kent A.	Christ Is Born
Newbury, Kent A.	Come Thou Almighty
Newbury, Kent A.	Faith (Hb 11:1-3,6)
Newbury, Kent A.	For We Have Seen His Star
Newbury, Kent A.	For You Shall Go Out In Joy
Newbury, Kent A.	Give Ear To My Words
Newbury, Kent A.	Gloria
Newbury, Kent A.	God Is Our Refuge And Stren
Newbury, Kent A.	Great And Wonderful Are Thy
Newbury, Kent A.	Great Is The Lord
Newbury, Kent A.	Hear My Prayer, O Lord
Newbury, Kent A.	Hosanna
Newbury, Kent A.	How Lovely Is Thy Dwelling
Newbury, Kent A.	I Long For Thy Salvation
Newbury, Kent A.	Keep His Commandments
Newbury, Kent A.	Let My Cry Come Before Thee
Newbury, Kent A.	Let The Word Of Christ
Newbury, Kent A.	Let Them Ever Sing For Joy
Newbury, Kent A.	O Lamb Of God
Newbury, Kent A.	Palm Sunday Procession
Newbury, Kent A.	Praise To The Lord
Newbury, Kent A.	Prepare The Way Of The Lord
Newbury, Kent A.	Responses For The Church Se
Newbury, Kent A.	Ring Out, Wild Bells
Newbury, Kent A.	Save Us, O Lord
Newbury, Kent A.	Send Forth Thy Spirit, O Lo
Newbury, Kent A.	Sing To Him
Newbury, Kent A.	Thou Art My God (Ps 118-9)W
Newbury, Kent A.	Three Short Holy Week Anthe
Newbury, Kent A.	Ye Servants Of God
Newbury, Kent A.	You Are The Light Of The Wo
Newman/Huntley	I Know, They're Gone
Newman/Warne	Man In The Dark (Musical)
Newman, Nancy Carr	Sing, Sing Alleluia
Nicholson	Try Jesus
Nicholson, Richard	When Jesus Sat At Meat (Md)
Nicolai-Christiansen	Wake, Awake
Nicolai, Philip	How Brightly Shines The Mor
Nicolau, A	At Montserrat
Niedt, F E	In Mirth And In Gladness
Niles	Little Brother Jesus
Niles	See Jesus The Savior
Niles (Warrell)	Jesus The Christ Is Born
Niles (Warrell)	Jesus, Jesus Rest Your Head
Niles-Horton	Carol Of Polish Grenadiers
Niles, John Jacob	A National Hymn Of Victory
Niles, John Jacob	Flower Of Jesse
Niles, John Jacob	Gabriel's Message
Niles, John Jacob	In Bethlehem That Fair City
Niles, John Jacob	In That Lovely Far-Off City
Niles, John Jacob	Jesus The Christ Is Born
Niles, John Jacob	Never Was A Child So Lovely
Niles, John Jacob	Once A Fair Maiden
Niles, John Jacob	Primrose
Niles, John Jacob	Sing We The Virgin Mary
Niles, John Jacob	Star In The East
Niles, John Jacob	Sweet Little Boy Jesus
Niles, John Jacob	Sweet Marie And Her Baby
Niles, John Jacob	The Bells Of Heaven
Niles, John Jacob	The Blessed Bird
Niles, John Jacob	The Carol Of The Angels
Niles, John Jacob	The Carol Of The Birds
Niles, John Jacob	The Little Family
Niles, John Jacob	The May Carol
Niles, John Jacob	The Miraculous Harvest
Niles, John Jacob	The Nativity
Niles, John Jacob	The Robin And The Thorn
Niles, John Jacob	The Shepherd On The Hill
Niles, John Jacob	Waken, Little Shepherd
Niles, John Jacob	Warrenton
Niles, John Jacob	Wayfaring Stranger
Niles, John Jacob	What Songs Were Sung
Niles, John Jacob	When Jesus Lived In Galilee
Niles, John Jacob	Wondrous Love
Niles, John Jacob	You Got To Cross That Lones
Nin-Culmell, Joaquin	El Nino Perdido
Nin-Culmell, Joaquin	Fum, Fum, Fum
Nin-Culmell, Joaquin	Lost Child, The
Nin-Culmell, Joaquin	Virgen Lava Panales, La
Nishol/Leader/Decou	We've A Story To Tell To Th
Nix, Donna	Lord Have Mercy
Nix, Donna	Lord, Lord, Lord
Nix, Donna	Oh, It's Good
Noble, Harold	My God Shall Raise Me Up
Noble, Harold	O Sapientia!
Noble, Harold	Sweet Spirit, Comfort Me
Noble, J. & Hopson, H.	A Prayer Of Supplication (M
Noel, M-C, Richards H.	The Baker Woman
Nolan, J. & Huck, G.	Come To The Banquet (Chant
Nolte	Dawn Of Christmas, The
Nolte	Just As I Am
Nolte	King All-Glorious

Nolte	Memories Of The Manger	Ono/Lennon	Happy Xmas	Palestrina, Giovanni P	Aeterni Munera
Nolte	Star Of The Silent Night	Opie, M P	Communion Hymn	Palestrina, Giovanni P	All My Friends Have Forsake
Nolte, Ewald V.	Two Anthems From The Moravi	Orland, Henry	Christmas Candlelight Proce	Palestrina, Giovanni P	Alleluia! Tulerunt Dominum
Norbet, Gregory	Come To Me	Orland, Henry	Christmas Legend, A	Palestrina, Giovanni P	Alma Redemptoris Mater
Norbet, Gregory	Hosea	Orland, Henry	Peace	Palestrina, Giovanni P	Assumpta Est Maria
Norden, Hugo	O Satisfy Us Early With Thy	Orland, Henry	Song Of The Shepherd	Palestrina, Giovanni P	Ave Maria
Nordman	Search Le, O Lord	Orr Vern	Suppertime	Palestrina, Giovanni P	Ave Maria
Norman	Christ Walked This Way Befo	Orr, Robin	Magnificat And Nunc Dimitti	Palestrina, Giovanni P	Ave Maris Stella
Norman, Pierre	If I Forget To Pray	Orr, Robin	Make A Joyful Noise Unto Th	Palestrina, Giovanni P	Benedictus
North, Jack	David, Swing Your Sling	Orr, Robin	Sing Aloud Unto God (Md)	Palestrina, Giovanni P	Bonum Est Confiteri
Norwegian	In Heaven Above	Orr, Robin	They That Put Their Trust I	Palestrina, Giovanni P	Come, Holy Ghost
Nourse, John	O Be Joyful In The Lord (M)	Ortlip, Stephen	At Pentecost	Palestrina, Giovanni P	Come, Thou Holy Spirit, Com
Nourse, John	Te Deum (Md)	Ortlund	Trusting Jesus A	Palestrina, Giovanni P	Complete Works Of Palestrin
Nyboer	I Can Believe	Ortlund, A.	He Shall Come Down	Palestrina, Giovanni P	Crucifixus
Nyquist, R.	Bells Of Paradise	Ortlund, A.	Think Of It, Lord!	Palestrina, Giovanni P	Dies Sanctificatus
Nyquist, R.	Good Christian Men, Rejoice	Orton, Irv	Just One Day At A Time	Palestrina, Giovanni P	Dies Sanctificatus
Nystedt, Knut	All The Ways Of A Man(Long)	Osborne/Dailey	Run Deep On Well Of Mercy	Palestrina, Giovanni P	Ego Sum Panis Vivus
Nystedt, Knut	Built On A Rock The Church	Osiander, Lucas	Komm, Heiliger Geist, Herre	Palestrina, Giovanni P	Exsultate Deo
Nystedt, Knut	Good Christian Men, Rejoice	Ovens/Decou	Wounded For Me	Palestrina, Giovanni P	Exultate Deo
Nystedt, Knut	Hear Us, O Father	Overby (Arr)	My God, How Wonderful	Palestrina, Giovanni P	Gloria Patri
Nystedt, Knut	Hosanna, Blessed Is He	Overholt	Ten Thousand Angels	Palestrina, Giovanni P	Haec Dies (Md)
Nystedt, Knut	I Will Be As The Dew	Overstreet, Rev. L.	Black But Proud	Palestrina, Giovanni P	Hodie Christus
Nystedt, Knut	I Will Praise Thee, O Lord	Overstreet, Rev. L.	God Has Blessings Of All Ki	Palestrina, Giovanni P	Hodie Christus Natus Est
Nystedt, Knut	If You Receive My Words	Overstreet, Rev. L.	I'd Rather Fight Than Switc	Palestrina, Giovanni P	Innocentes Pro Christo
Nystedt, Knut	O Come All Ye Faithful (W/O	Overstreet, Rev. L.	Reaching For My Crown	Palestrina, Giovanni P	Jesus, Admired And Noble Ki
Nystedt, Knut	O Perfect Love	Overstreet, Rev. L.	There Is No Future In Gaini	Palestrina, Giovanni P	Just As A Heart
Nystedt, Knut	Peace Be Unto You	Owen, Blythe	Harken Unto Me	Palestrina, Giovanni P	Missa "Aeterna Christi Mune
Nystedt, Knut	Peace I Leave With You	Owens	Pastoral Preludes For Organ	Palestrina, Giovanni P	Missa Brevis
Nystedt, Knut	Seven Words From The Cross	Owens, Barbara	Three Early American Christ	Palestrina, Giovanni P	Missa Papae Marcelli
Nystedt, Knut	Song Of Praise (W/Perc)	Owens, Dewey	Christ Is Made The Sure Fou	Palestrina, Giovanni P	Motet O Beata
Nystedt, Knut	The Path Of The Just	Owens, J&C	Lord Achieve Your Purpose(O	Palestrina, Giovanni P	My Spirit Thirsts
Nystedt, Knut	Thus Saith The Lord	Owens, Jamie	Growing Pains (Youth Collec	Palestrina, Giovanni P	O Admirabile Commercium
Nystedt, Knut	Trust In The Lord (Mixed Ch	Owens, Jimmie	He Satisfied That Longing I	Palestrina, Giovanni P	O Bone Jesu
Nystedt, Ronald	Lord, By Whose Breath	Owens, Jimmy	He Is Here	Palestrina, Giovanni P	O Vos Omnes
Nystedt, Ronald	Now Is Christ Risen (W/Inst	Owens, Jimmy	Holy, Holy, Holy	Palestrina, Giovanni P	Panis Angelicus (E&L) (Md)
O'connell, T & Silvia	We Look For Light	Owens, Jimmy	Come Together	Palestrina, Giovanni P	Popule Meus
O'connell, Timothy	Acclamations	Owens, Jimmy & Carol	If My People (Musical)	Palestrina, Giovanni P	Sanctorum Meritis
O'connell, Timothy	Holy Way, The	Owens, Jimmy & Carol	Lord Jesus, Think On Me (Hi	Palestrina, Giovanni P	Sanctus
O'connell, Timothy	Now Come To Me	Owens, Sam Batt	Behind The Shadows	Palestrina, Giovanni P	Sicut Cervus
O'connor, Robert F.	Seek The Lord	Owens,J & Hopkins,Mrs.	Jesus Knows	Palestrina, Giovanni P	Sicut Cervus
O'hara, Geoffrey	Art Thou The Christ	Pace	Jesus Knows	Palestrina, Giovanni P	Sitivit Anima Mea
O'hara, Geoffrey	Come To The Stable With Jes	Pachelbel, C. T.	Magnificat(C)(Lat)	Palestrina, Giovanni P	Strife Is O'er, The
O'hara, Geoffrey	He Smiled On Me	Pachelbel, J	What'e'er My God Ordains Is	Palestrina, Giovanni P	Ten Four-Part Motets For Th
O'hara, Geoffrey	I Walked Today Where Jesus	Padilla, Juan G.	Dominica In Ramis	Palestrina, Giovanni P	The Strife Is O'er
O'hara, Geoffrey	Must Jesus Bear Another Cro	Page, Arthur	From Egypt's Bondage Come	Palestrina, Giovanni P	Three Responses
O'hara, Geoffrey	The Star Road	Page, Jodi	Living Words (Mary,Simon,Et	Palestrina, Giovanni P	Tu Es Petrus
O'neill,J/Kraehenbuehl	We Praise You Lord For Jesu	Page, Paul F.	Acclamation	Palestrina, Giovanni P	Tu Es Petrus
O'sheil, Judy	Ascension Song	Page, Paul F.	Acclamation	Palestrina, Giovanni P	Videntes Stellam (Md)
O'sheil, Judy	Bless The Lord, O My Soul	Page, Paul F.	Acclamation (D)	Palestrina, Giovanni P	We Adore You, O Christ
O'sheil, Judy	For We Are One	Page, Paul F.	Alleluia	Palestrina, Giovanni P	We Give Thanks To Thee, O L
O'sheil, Judy	Friend Song	Page, Paul F.	Alleluia/Amen	Palestrina, Harman(Ed)	Motets By Palestrina, Ten 4
O'sheil, Judy	Kingdom Song	Page, Paul F.	Antiphons	Pollock	Come Home To God
O'sheil, Judy	My Beloved Is Mine	Page, Paul F.	As A Family	Pollock	O Lord, You Made The Rainbo
O'sheil, Judy	Peace Song	Page, Paul F.	Be Strong For Me	Pollock	Someone, Somewhere
O'sheil, Judy	Please Accept Our Gifts	Page, Paul F.	Beatitudes	Palmer	Peace, Be Still
O'sheil, Judy	Psalm 128 Your Wife Shall B	Page, Paul F.	Blessed Be God	Paminger, Leonhard	Christmas Motet
O'sheil, Judy	Psalm 19 Drop Down Dew	Page, Paul F.	Blest By The Hand Of The Lo	Papp, Akos G.	Good Lord, Shall I Ever Be
O'sheil, Judy	Psalm 63 You Are The God	Page, Paul F.	Bread To The Hungry	Parente, Sr. Elizabeth	Ave Maria
O'sheil, Judy	Psalm 80 Maranatha	Page, Paul F.	Come My Friend	Parker	Jerusalem
O'sheil, Judy	Whenever You Do This	Page, Paul F.	Come, Lord	Parker, Henry	Jerusalem
Oakeley, Frederick	O Come, All Ye Faithful	Page, Paul F.	Each Man's Joy	Parker, Horatio W	Bow Down Thine Ear
Oakes, Henry	A Prayer For A Stranger	Page, Paul F.	Every Day	Parker, Horatio W	The Lord Is My Light
Oakes, Henry	A World Of Love	Page, Paul F.	Exhortation	Parker, Jerry	Gracious Love
Oakes, Henry	Are You Ready?	Page, Paul F.	Gather 'round	Parker, Tom	All You Nations
Oakes, Henry	God Loves You	Page, Paul F.	Give It Life	Parker, Tom	Be Consoled My People
Oakes, Henry	Have Faith	Page, Paul F.	Great Amen	Parker, Tom	Charlotte's Song
Oakes, Henry	I'm Thankful	Page, Paul F.	Holy, Holy, Holy	Parker, Tom	Come Before The Table Of Th
Oakes, Henry	Little Hands	Page, Paul F.	Holy, Holy, Holy	Parker, Tom	Let All The Earth Sing His
Oakes, Henry	One Big Happy Family	Page, Paul F.	Hope Of.Life	Parker, Tom	Let The Heavens Be Glad & E
Oakes, Henry	Praise The Lord	Page, Paul F.	I Believe That My Redeemer	Parker, Tom	Lord Make Us Ready
Oakes, Henry	Thank The Lord	Page, Paul F.	Initiation Prayer	Parker, Tom	Our Father
Oakes, Henry	Trust In Him	Page, Paul F.	Introduction To Canon Accla	Parker, Tom	Save Me My God
Obenshain	Mother's Song, A	Page, Paul F.	Lamb Of God	Parker, Tom	We Come To Join In Your Ban
Obenshain	Shepherds In The Field	Page, Paul F.	Lamb Of God	Parker, Tom	When I Walk Through The Val
Obenshain, Kathryn G	A Mother's Song	Page, Paul F.	Let Me Lord	Parker,Horatio/Van Cam	City Of High Renown
Obrecht, J	Alleluia	Page, Paul F.	Lord Have Mercy	Parks/Johnson	Destiny
Obrecht, J	Hear Us, O Lord	Page, Paul F.	Lord Have Mercy	Parks, J.	In Remembrance Of Me
Ockeghem	Missa Mi-Mi	Page, Paul F.	My Peace, My Joy, My Love	Parks, Joe	A Song Was Born Cantata (No
Ogden/Decou	Where He Leads I'll Follow	Page, Paul F.	Offering	Parks, Joe	Light Of The World (Musical
Ogden/Peterson	Look And Live	Page, Paul F.	Our Father	Parks, Joe	Light Of The World (No 4292
Ohler, Susan	Don't Forget To Pray	Page, Paul F.	Peace	Parks, Joe	The Joyous News Of Christma
Ohler, Susan	Get On The Right Road	Page, Paul F.	Picture The Dawning	Parks, Joe E.	Away Over In The Gloryland
Ohler, Susan	God's Wonderful Plan	Page, Paul F.	Picture The Dawning	Parks, Joe E.	God Is Our Eternal Refuge
Ohler, Susan	God's World Today	Page, Paul F.	Prayer For Peace	Parks, Joe E.	I Know He Holdeth Me
Ohler, Susan	Growing For Jesus	Page, Paul F.	Remember Us	Parks, Joe E.	King Indeed, A (Easy)
Ohler, Susan	May God Grant Us Peace	Page, Paul F.	Response To The First Readi	Parks, Joe E.	Praise The Lord, Ye Congreg
Ohler, Susan	The Great Judgment Day	Page, Paul F.	Response: Stations Of The C	Parsley, Osbert(D1585)	Conserva Me A Clean Heart
Ohler, Susan	The Seven Seals Revealed	Page, Paul F.	Simple Gifts	Parsley, Osbert(D1585)	Two Te Deum And Magnificat
Ohler, Susan	The Warning Of Old	Page, Paul F.	Sing Praise	Parsons/Johnson	Heaven In My Heart
Ohler, Susan	Time Is Short; Eternity's L	Page, Paul F.	Sometimes, O Lord	Parsons, Robert	Ave Maria (Md)
Ohler, Susan	When God Calls Us Home	Page, Paul F.	Spread Your Love	Parthun	Adoramus Te Christe
Okolo/Kulaks, A	Rejoice, Our Lord Is Born	Page, Paul F.	The King Of Love	Parthun And Owens	Choral Benedictions
Oldham/Gaither	At The Foot Of The Cross	Page, Paul F.	The Reproaches	Pasquet, Jean	A Hymn Of Praise
Oldham, Arthur & Smart	Hymns For The Amusement Of	Page, Paul F.	To The Living God	Pasquet, Jean	Alleluia! Hearts And Voices
Oldham, D/Gaither	Something Worth Living For	Paget, Michael	Miles Coverdale's Carol	Pasquet, Jean	Bless Thou The Lord
Oldroyd, George	Communion Service (Mass Of	Paino, Paul	He Is Able	Pasquet, Jean	Blessing Of The Trinity
Oldroyd, George	Prayer To Jesus (Me)	Palester, Roman	Missa Brevis	Pasquet, Jean	Create In Me A Clean Heart
Oldroyd, George	Song Of The Passion (M)	Palestrina, Giovanni P	Adoramus	Pasquet, Jean	Glory To Thy Holy Name
Oldroyd, George	Ye Watchers And Ye Holy One	Palestrina, Giovanni P	Adoramus Te (Lat & Eng)	Pasquet, Jean	How Goodly Are Thy Tents
Olivier, John H.	Alleluia			Pasquet, Jean	Hymn Of The Initiants

COMPOSER INDEX

Pasquet, Jean	In My Father's House
Pasquet, Jean	Love And Blessed Be Thou, K
Pasquet, Jean	The Shepherds Saw A Star
Pasquet, Jean	Then Shall The King Say Unt
Pasquet, Jean (Arr)	O God, Our Help In Ages Pas
Patenaude, A. & Charbo	He Is Risen
Patenaude, Andre, M. S	Amazing Day
Patenaude, Andre, M.	As We Gather
Patenaude, Andre, M.	Christmas Ballad
Patenaude, Andre, M. S	Great Day
Patenaude, Andre, M. S	I Have Faith
Patenaude, Andre, M. S	I Place All My Trust
Patenaude, Andre, M. S	I Will Sing Praise
Patenaude, Andre, M. S	Promise Me Life
Patenaude, Andre, M. S	This Is The Day
Patenaude, Andre, M. S	Wondrous Spirit
Patenaude, Andre, M.S.	Come And Take
Patterson	Follow The Road
Patterson	That I May Too Arise
Patterson, Keith	Acclamation
Patterson, Keith	I Sing With All My Being
Patterson, Keith	Lord Have Mercy
Patterson, Keith	Lord Have Mercy - 2nd Versi
Patterson, Keith	Memorial Acclamation
Paul, Leslie	O Praise God In His Holines
Paxson, Theodore	He Was Alone
Paynter, J.(Text Hopk)	May Magnificat
Peace/Lorenz	Love That Wilt Not Let Me G
Peace/Rasley	O Love That Wilt Not Let Me
Pearce/Johnson	When He Shall Come
Peck, Barry	Dedicated But Doomed
Peck, Barry	I've Been Born Again
Peck, Barry	Jesus My Lord
Peck, Barry	Reborn
Peck, Barry	Sing My Song To Jesus
Peck, Barry	The Touch Of His Hand
Peck, Judy	Up, Up And Away
Pedrette, Edward A	Almighty God
Pedrette, Edward A	Is It Nothing To You
Peek	Partita On St Paul
Peek	The Race That Long In Darkn
Peek/Decou	I Would Be True
Peek, Richard	Come, Faithful People, Come
Peek, Richard	Come, Thou Fount Of Every B
Peek, Richard	Lo, I Am With You Always
Peek, Richard	Psalm 130
Peek, Richard	Royal Banners Forward Go, T
Peerson, Martin	Upon My Lap My Soveraigne S
Peery	Behold The Star!
Peery	For Spacious Skies
Peery	In The Stillness Of The Nig
Peery	This Be My Song
Peery	Thou Wilt Keep Him
Peeters, Flor	Canticum Gaudii (W/Brass, O
Peeters, Flor	Entrata Festiva
Peeters, Flor	Hymn Preludes From Op 100
Peeters, Flor	I Know That My Redeemer (W
Peeters, Flor	In Excelsis Gloria
Peeters, Flor	Missa In Hon. St. Josephi O
Peeters, Flor	Prayer On Christmas Eve
Peeters, Flor	Psalm 128
Peeters, Flor	Psalm 23
Peeters, Flor	This Is The Day Which The L
Peininer	I Sing The Mighty Power Of
Pekiel, B/Herter, J	How Great The Name Of Chris
Pekiel, B/Herter, J	Let The Earth Resound
Pellegrini, Francis	Litany Of Comfort
Pellegrini, P.	Missa Brevis
Peloquin, C Alexander	A Prayer For Us (W/Bell,Tim
Peloquin, C Alexander	All The Ends Of The Earth
Peloquin, C Alexander	Alleluia! In All Things
Peloquin, C Alexander	Beat The Drum
Peloquin, C Alexander	Christ The Light
Peloquin, C Alexander	Christ, The Light Of The Na
Peloquin, C Alexander	Come Nearer
Peloquin, C Alexander	Communion Rite (Lyric Litur
Peloquin, C Alexander	Faith, Hope And Love (Lyric
Peloquin, C Alexander	Festival Mass (1965) W/Cant
Peloquin, C Alexander	Gathering Song (W/ Org, Per
Peloquin, C Alexander	Give Praise To The Lord
Peloquin, C Alexander	Gloria (From Celebration)
Peloquin, C Alexander	Gloria (Lyric Liturgy)
Peloquin, C Alexander	Gloria A La Samba (W/Org, B
Peloquin, C Alexander	Gloria Of The Bells Icet
Peloquin, C Alexander	God Is In This Holy Place
Peloquin, C Alexander	God Mounts His Throne
Peloquin, C Alexander	Have Mercy On Me
Peloquin, C Alexander	How Still And Tiny
Peloquin, C Alexander	I Believe That My Redeemer
Peloquin, C Alexander	In Christ The Lord
Peloquin, C Alexander	Litany
Peloquin, C Alexander	Liturgy Of Eucharist (Lyric
Peloquin, C Alexander	Lord Jesus Come From "Lyric
Peloquin, C Alexander	Lord, Send Out Your Spirit
Peloquin, C Alexander	Lord, You Have The Words
Peloquin, C Alexander	Love Is Everlasting
Peloquin, C Alexander	Lullaby For Jesus
Peloquin, C Alexander	Lyric Liturgy
Peloquin, C Alexander	Mass For Joy (W/Org.Guit)
Peloquin, C Alexander	Mass Of Resurrection
Peloquin, C Alexander	Mass Of The Bells Icet (W/C
Peloquin, C Alexander	Missa A La Samba (W/Org,Bon
Peloquin, C Alexander	My God, My God
Peloquin, C Alexander	Open The Door
Peloquin, C Alexander	Pen. Rite And Lit. Of Word
Peloquin, C Alexander	Prayer (From Celebration)
Peloquin, C Alexander	Prayer For Peace
Peloquin, C Alexander	Prayer Of St Francis
Peloquin, C Alexander	Psalm For Advent, To You, O
Peloquin, C Alexander	Psalm For Epiphany
Peloquin, C Alexander	Psalm For Unity
Peloquin, C Alexander	Psalm One Hundred
Peloquin, C Alexander	Psalm 132: Behold How Good
Peloquin, C Alexander	Psalm 83: How Lovely Is You
Peloquin, C Alexander	Receive The Holy Spirit
Peloquin, C Alexander	Rejoice In Hope
Peloquin, C Alexander	Resurrection Psalm
Peloquin, C Alexander	Sacred Dance (Lyric Liturgy
Peloquin, C Alexander	Shout For Joy
Peloquin, C Alexander	Song Of Daniel
Peloquin, C Alexander	Song Of Zachary
Peloquin, C Alexander	Taste And See
Peloquin, C Alexander	Te Deum (Icet) W/ Organ (Me
Peloquin, C Alexander	The Bread Is One
Peloquin, C Alexander	The Lord's Prayer
Peloquin, C Alexander	This Is The Day
Peloquin, C Alexander	To The Town Of Bethlehem
Peloquin, C Alexander	We Are His People
Peloquin, C Alexander	When The Lord Was Born
Peloquin, C Alexander	Why, O Lord, Do You Stand A
Pelz, W.	A Wedding Blessing
Pelz, W.	At The Lamb's High Feast (L
Pelz, W.	Christ The Lord Is Risen
Pelz, W.	Christ The Lord Is Risen Ag
Pelz, W.	Come, You Have My Father's
Pelz, W.	Crown Him With Many Crowns
Pelz, W.	Day Of Rejoicing (W/Trumpet
Pelz, W.	Father, Eternal, Ruler Of C
Pelz, W.	Feast Of Joy
Pelz, W.	He Is Risen
Pelz, W.	He's Risen, Christ Jesus Th
Pelz, W.	Holy God We Praise Thy Name
Pelz, W.	Jesus Christ Is Risen Today
Pelz, W.	Peace I Leave With You
Pelz, W.	Rejoice And Be Merry (W/Obo
Pelz, W.	Show Me Thy Ways (W/Oboe,Gu
Pelz, W.	The Embodied Word (Nar,Flut
Pelz, W.	Who Shall Abide (W/Flute/Gu
Peninger	Easter Fanfare
Peninger	In Memory Of The Savior's L
Peninger	My Song Is Love Unknown
Peninger	O Deepest Woe
Peninger	Open Now Thy Gates Of Beaut
Peninger	When I Survey The Wondrous
Peninger, David	All Praise To Our Redeeming
Peninger, David	God Eternal Is My Refuge
Peninger, David	God Is Our Strength And Son
Peninger, David	Jesus Joy Of Loving Hearts
Peninger, David	Jesus Our Strength, Our Hop
Peninger, David	Trying To Make Heaven My Ho
Pergolesi	Glory To God In The Highest
Pergolesi (Ed Agey)	Abroad The Regal Banners Fl
Pergolesi-Ehret	He Will Surely Give Thee Pe
Pergolesi-Ehret	Who Is Like Unto Thee (W/Ke
Pergolesi, G B	Alleluia, Alleluia
Pergolesi, G B	Excelsus Super Omnes Gentes
Pergolesi, G B	Gloria
Pergolesi, G B	Gloria Patri
Pergolesi, G B	Glory To God In The Highest
Pergolesi, G B	Kyrie
Pergolesi, G B	Laudate Pueri, Laudate Nome
Pergolesi, G B	Magnificat Anima Mea Dominu
Pergolesi, G B	Sanctum Et Terrible Nomen E
Pergolesi, G. B.	Glory To God In The Highest
Pergolesi, G. B.	Magnificat
Pergolesi, G. B.	Stabat Mater
Pergolesi, G.B.(D1736)	Stabat Mater (Unfinished)
Pergolesi, G-Riedel	O Come And Mourn With Me Aw
Pergolesi, Giovanni B.	Alleluia (A Cap)
Perkins, Carl	Daddy Sang Bass
Perrin	Jesus Walked
Perry	Beautiful Savior
Perry	Christ Is Risen!
Perry, Julia	Stabat Mater
Persinger, Susan	Susan's Song (Based On Kahi
Pert, Morris	Missa Festiva
Perti (Arr Beveridge)	O Vos Omnes (Come Ye People
Perti, G A	Adoramus Te
Perti, G A	O Vos Omnes
Perti, G A	We Adore You
Peter Jacobs	Jesus
Peterson/Anthony	God's Final Call
Peterson/Anthony	I Believe In Miracles
Peterson/Carmichael	Above All Else
Peterson/Carmichael	Go Tell The Untold Millions
Peterson/Carmichael	Oh, He's A Wonderful Savior
Peterson/Colber-Johnsn	Praise Our God
Peterson/Decou	Calling (With Brass Acc)
Peterson/Decou	Heaven Came Down
Peterson/Decou	Holy Spirit, Now Outpoured
Peterson/Decou	I'm Not Alone
Peterson/Decou	It's Not An Easy Road
Peterson/Decou	Jesus Is Coming Again
Peterson/Decou	Near To Thy Heart
Peterson/Decou	Someone
Peterson/Decou	Springs Of Living Water
Peterson/Decou	We Thank Thee
Peterson/Decou	When I Remember
Peterson/Decou	Wings Of Prayer
Peterson/Draper	There Is No Greater Love
Peterson/Erb	Have A Little Talk With The
Peterson/Johnson	Above All Else
Peterson/Mayfield	I'm A Soldier
Peterson/Mickelson	All Glory To Jesus
Peterson/Mickelson	In The Image Of God
Peterson/Mickelson	Jesus Is Coming Again
Peterson/Mickelson	There Is No Greater Love
Peterson/Mickelson	What Grace Is This
Peterson/Parks	Isn't The Love Of Jesus Som
Peterson/Peterson Sist	Where Is This Old World A-G
Peterson/Smith	Surely Goodness And Mercy
Peterson/Smith/Carmich	Surely Goodness And Mercy
Peterson/Wyrtzen	Forever Together With Him
Peterson/Wyrtzen	God Of Everlasting Glory
Peterson/Wyrtzen	I Love America (Musical)
Peterson/Wyrtzen	Lost-But Still He Loves You
Peterson/Wyrtzen	Will You Be Ready?
Peterson/Yungton/Decou	Jesus Led Me All The Way
Peterson, John W.	A Song Unending (No 5953)
Peterson, John W.	A Song Unending (No 5961)
Peterson, John W.	A Song Unending (No 5979)
Peterson, John W.	Angels Worship God In Heave
Peterson, John W.	Answer, The
Peterson, John W.	Anthems For Sab (5867)
Peterson, John W.	As For Me And My House
Peterson, John W.	Beatitudes, The
Peterson, John W.	Behold Your King Cantata
Peterson, John W.	Beloved, Let Us Love One An
Peterson, John W.	Bless The Lord, O My Soul
Peterson, John W.	Blessed Hope, The
Peterson, John W.	Born A King
Peterson, John W.	Born A King (Cantata)
Peterson, John W.	But Now Is Christ Risen
Peterson, John W.	Carol Of Christmas (No 5969
Peterson, John W.	Carol Of Christmas (No 5999
Peterson, John W.	Carol Of Christmas (No 6011
Peterson, John W.	Chariot Of Clouds
Peterson, John W.	Christ Is Born (No 4451)
Peterson, John W.	Christ Lives Through Me
Peterson, John W.	Christmas Cantata In Spanis
Peterson, John W.	Christmas Carols For Childr
Peterson, John W.	Come, Holy Spirit
Peterson, John W.	Declare His Glory
Peterson, John W.	Don't Let The Song Go Out O
Peterson, John W.	Doug Oldham Songbook (No 43
Peterson, John W.	Easter Alleluia, An
Peterson, John W.	Easter Cantata In Spanish
Peterson, John W.	Easter Song! (Cantata)
Peterson, John W.	Flag To Follow, A (W/Opt Br
Peterson, John W.	Folio Of Choir Favorites
Peterson, John W.	Folio Of Gospel Choir Favor
Peterson, John W.	God Knows All About Tomorro
Peterson, John W.	God Put His Hand On My Shou
Peterson, John W.	Good Life, The
Peterson, John W.	Great God Of Wonders
Peterson, John W.	Great Hymns Of The Faith
Peterson, John W.	Great Is The Glory Of The L
Peterson, John W.	Guitar Sing-A-Long (No 5540
Peterson, John W.	Hail To The King
Peterson, John W.	Hail, Glorious King (No 596
Peterson, John W.	Hail, Glorious King! (No 59
Peterson, John W.	Hail, Glorious King! (No 59
Peterson, John W.	Hail, Thou Once-Despised Je
Peterson, John W.	Hallelujah For The Cross (N
Peterson, John W.	Hallelujah For The Cross (N
Peterson, John W.	Hallelujah For The Cross (N
Peterson, John W.	Hallelujah! What A Savior!
Peterson, John W.	Hallelujah! What A Savior!
Peterson, John W.	Hallelujah! What A Savior!
Peterson, John W.	Hallelujah! What A Savior!
Peterson, John W.	Have Faith In God
Peterson, John W.	He Is Risen
Peterson, John W.	He Lovingly Guards Every Fo
Peterson, John W.	He Was Wounded For Our Tran
Peterson, John W.	He's Filling Up Heaven With
Peterson, John W.	Healing Love Of Jesus, The
Peterson, John W.	Higher Hands
Peterson, John W.	Hosanna
Peterson, John W.	How Long Will It Be?
Peterson, John W.	Hymn Of Worship
Peterson, John W.	Hymnal For Boys And Girls N
Peterson, John W.	I Am The Resurrection And T
Peterson, John W.	I Believe In Miracles
Peterson, John W.	I Want To Be There
Peterson, John W.	I'll Go Now
Peterson, John W.	In My Heart
Peterson, John W.	In Pleasant Places
Peterson, John W.	In This Old Troubled World
Peterson, John W.	It's A Wonderful, Wonderful
Peterson, John W.	Jesus Is A Precious Name

COMPOSER` INDEX

Composer	Title
Peterson, John W.	Jesus Is Coming (Musical)
Peterson, John W.	Jesus Is Coming (Theme Ii)
Peterson, John W.	Jesus Is The Friend Of Sinn
Peterson, John W.	Jesus The King Passes By
Peterson, John W.	Joy Of Heaven, The
Peterson, John W.	Joy To The World (No 5944)
Peterson, John W.	Joy To The World (No 5945)
Peterson, John W.	Joy To The World (No 6012)
Peterson, John W.	King Of Kings (No 4294)
Peterson, John W.	Lead Me, O Lead Me
Peterson, John W.	Lengthen The Cords And Stre
Peterson, John W.	Let Every Heart Rejoice
Peterson, John W.	Let The Whole World Know
Peterson, John W.	Living Praise
Peterson, John W.	Lost In The Night
Peterson, John W.	Love Transcending (No 5954)
Peterson, John W.	Love Transcending (No 5974)
Peterson, John W.	Love Transcending (No 5975)
Peterson, John W.	Miracle Melodies No 1
Peterson, John W.	Miracle Melodies No 2 (No 5
Peterson, John W.	Miracle Melodies No 3 (No 5
Peterson, John W.	Miracle Melodies No 4 (No 5
Peterson, John W.	Miracle Melodies No 5 (No 5
Peterson, John W.	Miracle Melodies No 6 (No 5
Peterson, John W.	Miracle Melodies No 7 (No 5
Peterson, John W.	Miracle Melodies No 8 (No 5
Peterson, John W.	Miracle Melodies No 9 (No 5
Peterson, John W.	Never In A Million Years
Peterson, John W.	Night Of Miracles (No 5976)
Peterson, John W.	Night Of Miracles Spanish E
Peterson, John W.	Night Of Miracles-Dramatiza
Peterson, John W.	No Greater Love (No 5977)
Peterson, John W.	No Greater Love (No 5984)
Peterson, John W.	No Greater Love (No 5992)
Peterson, John W.	No More Death
Peterson, John W.	No One Understands Like Jes
Peterson, John W.	Not To The Hills
Peterson, John W.	Now Sing, All Saints
Peterson, John W.	O Glorious Love
Peterson, John W.	O Glorious Resurrection Day
Peterson, John W.	Over The Sunset Mountains
Peterson, John W.	Praise Him Now
Peterson, John W.	Qonswe Od Qonswea
Peterson, John W.	Quartet Favorites No 1 (No
Peterson, John W.	Quartet Favorites No 2 (No
Peterson, John W.	Really Live
Peterson, John W.	Rise Up And Sing Praise
Peterson, John W.	Send Thy Holy Breath
Peterson, John W.	Shepherd Of Love
Peterson, John W.	Shepherd Of Love
Peterson, John W.	Show A Little Bit Of Love A
Peterson, John W.	Since We All Believe In Jes
Peterson, John W.	Singing Men (Male Quartets
Peterson, John W.	Singing Youth
Peterson, John W.	So Send I You (With Brass)
Peterson, John W.	Solid Rock, The
Peterson, John W.	Solos For Christmas No 1
Peterson, John W.	Solos For Christmas No 2
Peterson, John W.	Solos For Easter
Peterson, John W.	Something New For Christmas
Peterson, John W.	Song Favorites For Low Voic
Peterson, John W.	Song Favorites For Trios
Peterson, John W.	Stand Up And Bless The Lord
Peterson, John W.	Steal Away
Peterson, John W.	Take My Life And Let It Be
Peterson, John W.	Take Time To Pray
Peterson, John W.	Take Up Your Cross And Foll
Peterson, John W.	Teach Me To Love
Peterson, John W.	Tell The Good News
Peterson, John W.	The Christmas Choir No 1 (N
Peterson, John W.	The Country-Western Choir N
Peterson, John W.	The Glory Of Easter (No 596
Peterson, John W.	The Glory Of Easter (No 598
Peterson, John W.	The Glory Of Easter (No 599
Peterson, John W.	The Good Life (Musical)
Peterson, John W.	The Night The Angels Sang (
Peterson, John W.	The Sound Of Singing (No 59
Peterson, John W.	The Sound Of Singing (No 59
Peterson, John W.	The Story Of Christmas (No
Peterson, John W.	The Story Of Christmas (No
Peterson, John W.	The Story Of Christmas (No
Peterson, John W.	The Three Part Christmas Ch
Peterson, John W.	The Wonder Of Christmas (No
Peterson, John W.	The Wonder Of Christmas (No
Peterson, John W.	The Wonder Of Christmas (No
Peterson, John W.	Then The Lord Stood By Me
Peterson, John W.	There Is No Room
Peterson, John W.	There's A New Song In My He
Peterson, John W.	Think On These Things
Peterson, John W.	This Is The Day The Lord Ha
Peterson, John W.	Three Part Choir No 1 (No 5
Peterson, John W.	Three Part Choir No 2 (No 5
Peterson, John W.	Three Part Choir No 3 (No 5
Peterson, John W.	Three Part Choir No 4 (No 4
Peterson, John W.	Top Songs For High Voice (N
Peterson, John W.	Top Songs For Men (No 5831)
Peterson, John W.	Top Songs For Soloists No 1
Peterson, John W.	Top Songs For Soloists No 2
Peterson, John W.	Top Songs For Trios (No 577
Peterson, John W.	We Magnify Our Father God
Peterson, John W.	Where Is He?
Peterson, John W.	Who's Goin To Walk That Roa
Peterson, John W.	Wise Men Still Seek Him
Peterson, John W.	With A Holy Hush
Peterson, John W.	Wonderful Is Jesus
Peterson, John W.	Youth Favorites
Petrich, Roger T.	Choral Var On "Ah Holy Jesu
Petrich, Roger T.	O Wondrous Type
Pettis, Audrey E.	I Have A Friend
Pettis, Audrey E.	The Right Choice
Petty Doug	When I Climb Them Golden St
Petty Doug	Where Was Jesus
Petzold	And Lo, The Star
Petzold	More Than Raiment
Petzold	Rejoice Greatly
Pfautsch, Lloyd	A Canticle Of Commemoration
Pfautsch, Lloyd	A Canticle Of Thanksgiving
Pfautsch, Lloyd	Abraham And Isaac
Pfautsch, Lloyd	Carol For Children, A
Pfautsch, Lloyd	Christ Is Arisen!
Pfautsch, Lloyd	Christian Dost Thou See The
Pfautsch, Lloyd	Commitment (Flute Optional)
Pfautsch, Lloyd	Coverdale's Carol
Pfautsch, Lloyd	Easter Bell Carol
Pfautsch, Lloyd	Festival Prelude
Pfautsch, Lloyd	Festival Prelude On I'll Pr
Pfautsch, Lloyd	God Is My Strong Salvation
Pfautsch, Lloyd	God Is My Strong Salvation
Pfautsch, Lloyd	God Of Might, We Praise Thy
Pfautsch, Lloyd	God With Us (Opt Brs)
Pfautsch, Lloyd	Guiding Christ Our Shepherd
Pfautsch, Lloyd	I Will Lift Up Mine Eyes
Pfautsch, Lloyd	I'll Praise My Maker (Opt B
Pfautsch, Lloyd	Joseph Dearest, Joseph Mine
Pfautsch, Lloyd	Knight Without A Sword
Pfautsch, Lloyd	Lord Is My Light, The
Pfautsch, Lloyd	Mary, Mary
Pfautsch, Lloyd	New Is Old, The
Pfautsch, Lloyd	Puer Nobis
Pfautsch, Lloyd	Reconciliation
Pfautsch, Lloyd	Seven Words Of Love
Pfautsch, Lloyd	Six Anthems For Junior Choi
Pfautsch, Lloyd	Temptation Of Christ, The
Pfautsch, Lloyd	The Lord Is In This Place (
Pfautsch, Lloyd	Three Organ Preludes On Hym
Pflueger	How Long Wilt Thou Forget M
Philips, Peter 1	Ascendit, Deus (Md)
Phillip	Vigil Peter & Paul Psalm (I
Phillips, David	It Must Be The Season Of Th
Phillips, J. Gerald	The Lord's Prayer
Piae Cantiones, Silvia	Christ Our Leader (4-Part A
Picca, Angelo Della	All The Ends Of The Earth (
Picca, Angelo Della	Alleluia (Icet)
Picca, Angelo Della	Be Merciful O Lord (Icet)
Picca, Angelo Della	Be With Me Lord (Icet)
Picca, Angelo Della	Christmas Vigil Psalm (Icet
Picca, Angelo Della	Common Of Saints (Icet)
Picca, Angelo Della	Common Responses (Icet)
Picca, Angelo Della	Dead, Mass Of, (Icet) Respo
Picca, Angelo Della	Glory And Praise To You (Ic
Picca, Angelo Della	Glory To God (Icet)(Mass Of
Picca, Angelo Della	Glory To You, Word Of God(I
Picca, Angelo Della	God Mounts His Throne (Icet
Picca, Angelo Della	His Love Is Everlasting (Ic
Picca, Angelo Della	Holy, Holy, Holy (Icet)
Picca, Angelo Della	If Today You Hear His Voice
Picca, Angelo Della	Lamb Of God (Icet) (Me)
Picca, Angelo Della	Let Us Go Rejoicing (Icet)
Picca, Angelo Della	Lord Every Nation (Icet)
Picca, Angelo Della	Lord Have Mercy (Icet)
Picca, Angelo Della	Lord Let Us See Your Kindne
Picca, Angelo Della	Lord Send Out Your Spirit (
Picca, Angelo Della	Lord You Have The Word (Ice
Picca, Angelo Della	Lord's Prayer 1
Picca, Angelo Della	Lord's Prayer 2
Picca, Angelo Della	Marriage (Response)
Picca, Angelo Della	Mass Volume Ii
Picca, Angelo Della	My God, My God (Icet)
Picca, Angelo Della	My Soul Is Thirsting For Yo
Picca, Angelo Della	Praise And Honor To You (Ic
Picca, Angelo Della	Praise To You Lord Jesus Ch
Picca, Angelo Della	Responses 75-86 Psalms (Ice
Picca, Angelo Della	Responses 87-88 Gospel Accl
Picca, Angelo Della	Responsorial Psalms Ritual
Picca, Angelo Della	Springs Of Water (Icet)
Picca, Angelo Della	Taste And See (Icet)
Picca, Angelo Della	This Is The Day The Lord Ha
Picca, Angelo Della	To You, O Lord (Icet)
Picca, Angelo Della	Vigil Pentecost Alleluia (V
Picca, Angelo Della	Vigil Pentecost Psalm (Icet
Picca, Angelo Della	We Are His People (Icet)
Picca, Angelo Della	With The Lord There Is Merc
Pice	O God, Our Help In Ages Pas
Pickell	Christ Child Is Born (Opt O
Pickell	Christmas Morn (Spiritual)
Pickell	Littlest Christmas Tree
Pickell	Through The Eyes Of A Child
Pickell, Ed	Mary Had A Baby Boy (E)
Pickell, Ed	O Dove Of Peace (Not H.Sp.)
Pierluigi, Giovanni	O Blessed Jesus
Pieters,Jenny&Delores	The Magic Touch
Pinelli, G B	Magnificat (Long)
Pinkham	Easter Cantata (W/Brass, Pe
Pinkham	St. Mark Passion (W/Soli)
Pinkham	Stabat Mater (W/Sop Solo)
Pisk, Paul A.	Psalm 30
Pitoni-Douglas (Arr)	Give Praise Unto The Lord (
Pitoni/Wiley (Arr)	Laudate Dominum (Ps 150) A
Pitoni, G/Ed Lee	Cantate Domino
Pitoni, Giuseppe	Cantate Domino
Pitoni, Giuseppe O	Cantate Domino
Pitts,W./Carmichael	The Church In The Wildwood
Plettner	Chorale Prelude On O Trinit
Plettner	Improvisation On Father
Pohlmann	Ave Maria (Lat & Eng)
Pohlmann	Bells At Christmas (A Cap)
Pohlmann (Durocher)	Message Of The Bells
Polin, Claire	De Spei
Polin, Claire	Infinito
Polin, Claire	Rosa Mundi
Polin, Claire	Te Deum
Polistina/Hebble	And Rejoice!
Pont, Kenneth (Arr)	The Lords Prayer (Spiritual
Pool, Kenneth	I Will Lift Up Mine Eyes
Pooler, Marie	A Child Is Born In Bethlehe
Pooler, Marie	All My Heart This Night Rej
Pooler, Marie	Angels From The Realms Of G
Pooler, Marie	As Lately We Watched
Pooler, Marie	Away In A Manger
Pooler, Marie	Be Thou My Vision
Pooler, Marie	Calvary's Mountain
Pooler, Marie	Children Of The Heavenly Fa
Pooler, Marie	Children Of The Heavenly Fa
Pooler, Marie	Come, Thou Long-Expected Je
Pooler, Marie	Good Shepherd, The
Pooler, Marie	Hosanna
Pooler, Marie	How Far Is It To Bethlehem?
Pooler, Marie	Let Our Gladness Know No En
Pooler, Marie	Lord God, We Worship Thee
Pooler, Marie	Man Of Sorrows
Pooler, Marie	My Shepherd Will Supply My
Pooler, Marie	Now It Is Christmas Time
Pooler, Marie	O Come Let Us Adore Him (Ch
Pooler, Marie	Ride On In Majesty
Pooler, Marie	That Easter Day With Joy Wa
Pooler, Marie	The Little King Of The Worl
Pooler, Marie	Thou Art Worthy
Pooler, Marie	Wondrous Love
Pooler, Marie	Ye Lands To The Lord
Porta, Costanzo	Vobis Datum Est
Porta, Costanzo	You Are Given To Know
Porter	Silence Of God, The
Porter	Tidings Of Comfort And Joy
Postel, C M	I Hold The Kingdom
Powell	A Meditation Upon The Passi
Powell	Anointed Of God
Powell	Chorale Prelude On Angelus
Powell	Chorale-Prelude On "Bedford
Powell	Drop, Drop, Slow Tears
Powell	Elegy For Organ
Powell	Fantasy On Victimae Paschal
Powell	Four Preludes On Early Amer
Powell	Four Psalm Preludes
Powell	Four Psalm Preludes Set Ii
Powell	I Call With My Own Heart
Powell	I Will Sing Of The Mercies
Powell	In All The World
Powell	Introduction And Passacagli
Powell	Jesus, My Lord, My God, My
Powell	Let Thy Love Flow Down
Powell	O Give Thanks
Powell	Our Lord Is Risen
Powell	Psalm 13
Powell	Sacred Harp Suite
Powell	Sing A Song Of Joy
Powell	Sing We
Powell	Six Easter Preludes
Powell	Six Easter Preludes (Hymn-T
Powell	Surely The Lord Is In This
Powell	Three Miniatures For Organ
Powell	Two Christmas Preludes (Mod
Powell, Rick (Arr)	Praise Song (Collection)
Powell, Robert J.	Chorale Prelude On Bedford
Powell, Robert J.	Christ The Lord, Is Risen A
Powell, Robert J.	Festival Anthems For Sab
Powell, Robert J.	From The Rising Of The Sun
Powell, Robert J.	Glory To God
Powell, Robert J.	If Ye Then Be Risen (Opt Ac
Powell, Robert J.	Jesus! Name Of Wondrous Lov
Powell, Robert J.	Let Saints On Earth
Powell, Robert J.	Lo, Round The Throne A Glor
Powell, Robert J.	Now Glad Of Heart
Powell, Robert J.	O Newborn Child
Powell, Robert J.	O Thou To Whose All-Searchi
Powell, Robert J.	O Trinity Of Blessed Light
Powell, Robert J.	Seven Words From The Cross
Powell, Robert J.	Three Christmas Anthems For
Powell, Robert J.	Three Treble Choir Anthems
Powell, Robert J.	Today In Bethlehem
Powell, Robert J.	Trumpeters And Singers Were

COMPOSER INDEX

Powell, Robert J.	Unfold, Unfold! Take In His
Power, Leonel	Gloria (D)
Power, Leonel	Sanctus
Powers James	Will I Have To Pay
Powers, Chet	Let's Get Together
Powers, George	Christ Our Passover (Md)
Powers, George	Create In Me
Praetorius	O God The Father, Eternal O
Praetorius	To Us Is Born (W/Bells)
Praetorius-Bliss	Now Sing We, Now Rejoice
Praetorius-Schalk	Christ Our Lord, Who Died T
Praetorius/Christiansn	Lo, How A Rose
Praetorius/Tortolano	Make A Joyful Sound (5 Voic
Praetorius/Vulpius	Lo, How A Rose (4 Voices)
Praetorius, M	From Heaven On High
Praetorius, M	God's Infant Son
Praetorius, M	Lo, How A Rose E'er Bloomin
Praetorius, M	Praise God, Ye Christians
Praetorius, M	Praise The Lord
Praetorius, M	Rejoice, Ye Christian Breth
Praetorius, M	Sing We All Now With One Ac
Praetorius, M	The Morning Star
Praetorius, M	To Us Is Born Immanuel
Praetorius, M	While Shepherds Watched The
Praetorius, M.	All Glory Be To God On High
Praetorius, M. (Cain)	Lo, How A Rose E'er Bloomin
Praetorius, M.-Overby	Lo, How A Rose Ere Blooming
Praetorius,M./Ruening	Thirteen Amens & Alleluias
Prather, Lillian	For God So Loved The World
Predmore, G	O Faithful Cross
Prendergast, Richard	To Christ The King
Pressel, Juliet	Song Of My People
Preston, Simon	Jubilate Deo (D)
Preston, Simon	Missa Brevis (Md)
Preus	Love Came Down At Christmas
Preuss, Arthur	Now Proclaim His Birth In S
Price	Alleluia!
Price	Breathe On Me, Breath Of Go
Price	Can't You Hear?
Price	Garden Hymn, The
Price	God Of Grace And God Of Glo
Price	I Sing Of God
Price	I Sing The Mighty Power Of
Price	I Will Extol Thee
Price	King Is Riding By, The
Price	Show Me The Way
Price	Soldiers Of Christ, Arise
Price	Surely God Is In This Place
Price	Tis So Sweet To Trust In Je
Price	Twas On One Sunday Morning
Price	We Thank Thee, O Lord
Price (Arr)	This Is Jesus
Price/Johnson	I'll Trust And Never Be Afr
Price, Benton	Take Up Thy Cross
Price, Benton	This Is My Father's World
Price, Flo	I Like The Sound Of America
Price, William	Dayenu
Price, William	Singers, Sing
Price, William (Text)	Come, Live In Us
Price, William (Text)	O Christ Our King
Prichard/Decou	Alleluia Alleluia
Prichard/Johnson	I Will Sing The Wondrous St
Prichard, R H	Love Divine
Proskinisomen, D	Come Let Us Worship
Proskinisomen, D	Let All Mortal Flesh Keep S
Pross, Daniel J.	Alleluias (Accompaniment)
Pross, Daniel J.	Gospel Acclamation Verses A
Pross, Daniel J.	Mass Of Praise (Icet)
Proulx, R.,Gelineau	This Is The Day (W/ Perc,Be
Proulx, Richard	A Festival Eucharist (Icet)
Proulx, Richard	Advent Anthem
Proulx, Richard	Alleluia And Psalm For East
Proulx, Richard	And The Best Is Love
Proulx, Richard	Behold Now, The House Of Go
Proulx, Richard	Beloved, Let Us Love (Solo)
Proulx, Richard	Christ The Lord Is Risen Ag
Proulx, Richard	Christmas Processional
Proulx, Richard	Festival Anthem On Crown Hi
Proulx, Richard	Gaudeamus
Proulx, Richard	Glory To God (Angelic Hymn)
Proulx, Richard	Gospel Acclamations, Holy O
Proulx, Richard	Happy The Man
Proulx, Richard	Holy, Holy, Holy
Proulx, Richard	How Blest Are They
Proulx, Richard	I Bind My Heart
Proulx, Richard	Jesus, Lead The Way
Proulx, Richard	Lamb Of God
Proulx, Richard	Look For Me In Lowly Men
Proulx, Richard	Lord Have Mercy
Proulx, Richard	Lord, You Have The Words
Proulx, Richard	Mass Of The Redeemer (Cath,
Proulx, Richard	My Heart Is Full Today
Proulx, Richard	My Soul Give Thanks
Proulx, Richard	Nuptial Blessing
Proulx, Richard	Of The Kindness Of The Lord
Proulx, Richard	Once In Royal David's City
Proulx, Richard	Praise Ye The Lord, Ye Chil
Proulx, Richard	Processional Psalm
Proulx, Richard	Processional Psalm For Lent
Proulx, Richard	Psalm 134, Behold Now, Bles
Proulx, Richard	Psalm 84 (How Lovely)
Proulx, Richard	Psalm 98
Proulx, Richard	Sing We Merrily (W/Brass, O
Proulx, Richard	Song Of The Three Young Men
Proulx, Richard	The Just Man Shall Flourish
Proulx, Richard	The Lord's Prayer
Proulx, Richard	This Is The Day The Lord Ha
Proulx, Richard	This World My God (Evening)
Proulx, Richard	To Deum Laudamus
Proulx, Richard	Ubi Caritas Et Amor (Eng &
Pugh	Shepherds' Carol, The
Pulkingham, Betty C.	Ask, And It Shall Be Given
Pulkingham, Betty C.	Bless Thou The Lord (Ps 103
Pulkingham, Betty C.	Christ Our Passover (Crg,Gu
Pulkingham, Betty C.	Gloria (Mass For King Of Gl
Pulkingham, Betty C.	Ho! Everyone That Thirsteth
Pulkingham, Betty C.	Knock, Knock
Pulkingham, Betty C.	Kyrie (3fold) Mass For King
Pulkingham, Betty C.	Kyrie (6fold) Mass For King
Pulkingham, Betty C.	Kyrie (9fold) Mass For King
Pulkingham, Betty C.	Melchizedek Mass For The Ki
Pulkingham, Betty C.	Our Father (Organ + Guitar)
Pulkingham, Betty C.	Preface, Sanctus, Benedictu
Pulkingham, Betty C.	Psalm 84 (O How Amiable)
Pulkingham, Betty C.	Rain Song
Pulkingham, Betty C.	Sam Vel
Pulkingham, Betty C.	Sorsum Corda (English)
Pulkingham, Betty C.	Te Deum Laudamus (Eng,Org,G
Pulkingham, Betty C.	The Acclamations (Christ Ha
Pulkingham, Betty C.	The Body Song
Pulkingham, Betty C.	The Song Of Moses (Ex 15)
Pulkingham, Betty C.	There's A River Of Life (Vv
Pulkingham, Wes&Betty	Allelujah Today
Pulkingham,B.C.(Arr)	My Soul Doth Magnify
Pulsifer, Thomas	Psalm 67
Purcell, H. -Kleinsasser	Magnificat
Purcell, H. (Ratcliffe	Music From "King Arthur"
Purcell, Henry	Benedicite (Md)
Purcell, Henry	Do You Know?
Purcell, Henry	Early, O Lord, My Fainting
Purcell, Henry	Five Sacred Choruses
Purcell, Henry	Hear Me, O Lord, The Great
Purcell, Henry	How Blest Are They (M)
Purcell, Henry	Hymn For Ascensiontide (E)
Purcell, Henry	Lord, I Can Suffer
Purcell, Henry	Magnificat And Nunc Dimitti
Purcell, Henry	O Give Thanks
Purcell, Henry	O God, The King Of Glory
Purcell, Henry	O Happy Man
Purcell, Henry	Psalm 150
Purcell, Henry	Rejoice In The Lord Always
Purcell, Henry	Sing, O Sing To The Lord
Purcell, Henry	Te Deum In D
Purcell, Henry	Thou Knowest, Lord, The Sec
Purcell, Henry	Ye Tuneful Muses
Purcell, Henry (Arr)	Evening Hymn
Purcell, Henry (Ehret)	Sound The Trumpet (2 Pt Acc
Purday/Johnson	God Of Our Life
Purdie, Hunter	The Donkey
Purifoy, John	Come To Me All Who Labor
Purifoy, John	Someday My Lord Will Come
Purifoy, John	Walkin' In The Light Of His
Purri, Ralph	Acclamation
Purzycki, Krzysztof Z.	Walk In Peace United
Pyle, Francis	Father, We Praise Thee
Pyle, Francis J.	Full Stature
Quinlan, Paul	A Little Further On The Way
Quinlan, Paul	Blest Be The Name Of The Lo
Quinlan, Paul	Canticle Of Judith
Quinlan, Paul	Clap Your Hands
Quinlan, Paul	Father, Bless This Work
Quinlan, Paul	From The Depths
Quinlan, Paul	Glory Bound (From Psalm 29)
Quinlan, Paul	Glory Hallelujah
Quinlan, Paul	Glory To God
Quinlan, Paul	Glory To God (Folk Mass No.
Quinlan, Paul	Glory To The Father
Quinlan, Paul	God Arises
Quinlan, Paul	Halay, When To God I Send A
Quinlan, Paul	Halleujah
Quinlan, Paul	Help Me Know The Way
Quinlan, Paul	Holy, Holy Is The Lord
Quinlan, Paul	Holy, Holy, Holy (Folk Mass
Quinlan, Paul	How Can You Really Care? (P
Quinlan, Paul	How I Rejoiced
Quinlan, Paul	How Long O Lord
Quinlan, Paul	I Look To God
Quinlan, Paul	It's A Brand New Day
Quinlan, Paul	It's A Brand New Day
Quinlan, Paul	Lamb Of God (Folk Mass No.4
Quinlan, Paul	Like A Deer In Winter (Ps.
Quinlan, Paul	Look To The Mountains
Quinlan, Paul	Lord Have Mercy (Kyrie)(Fo
Quinlan, Paul	Lord, You See Me
Quinlan, Paul	Magnificat (Luke), The
Quinlan, Paul	My Soul Thirsts For The Lor
Quinlan, Paul	Not To Us Lord
Quinlan, Paul	O Lord How Great Is Your Na
Quinlan, Paul	O Lord Of Hosts
Quinlan, Paul	O, Praise The Lord
Quinlan, Paul	Praise God, Praise Him Here
Quinlan, Paul	Praise The Lord
Quinlan, Paul	Praise The Lord In Many Voi
Quinlan, Paul	Praise Ye, The Lord
Quinlan, Paul	Praise, The Holy Of Holies
Quinlan, Paul	Psalm 100 The Lord Be With
Quinlan, Paul	Psalm 11 Run Like A Deer
Quinlan, Paul	Psalm 113 Blest Be The Name
Quinlan, Paul	Psalm 114 Israel Went Out
Quinlan, Paul	Psalm 130 From The Depths
Quinlan, Paul	Psalm 136 Praise God, Prais
Quinlan, Paul	Psalm 23 The Lord Is My She
Quinlan, Paul	Psalm 34 I Looked To God
Quinlan, Paul	Psalm 39 When My Heart Was
Quinlan, Paul	Psalm 47 Clap Your Hands
Quinlan, Paul	Psalm 47 Sing Halleluia, Pr
Quinlan, Paul	Psalm 51 Have Mercy, Lord
Quinlan, Paul	Psalm 84 O Lord Of Hosts
Quinlan, Paul	Psalm 92 Glory To The Fathe
Quinlan, Paul	Psalm 96 Sing To God A Joyo
Quinlan, Paul	Psalm 99 Holy, Holy Is The
Quinlan, Paul	Save Me
Quinlan, Paul	Sermon On The Mount
Quinlan, Paul	Sing Hosanna, Sing (Ps. 92)
Quinlan, Paul	Sing To God
Quinlan, Paul	Sing To God A Brand New Can
Quinlan, Paul	Sing To God A Joyous Song
Quinlan, Paul	Song Of Thanks
Quinlan, Paul	The Lord Be With You
Quinlan, Paul	The Lord Is My Shepherd
Quinlan, Paul	The Lord Is My Shepherd
Quinlan, Paul	Tremble, Tremble Little Ear
Quinlan, Paul	We Are All Held In His Hand
Quinlan, Paul	Who Will Dwell On God's Mou
Quinn, M.	Behold The Royal Cross On H
Quinn, M.	Redeemer Of The Nations
Quinn, M.	Sing My Tongue The Ageless
Quinn, M.	With These Our Lenten Praye
Radice, John	Come To The Lord
Radice, John	In The Lord We Will Live
Radice, John	This Is What We Bring
Rado/Ragni/Macdermot	The Flesh Failures
Rains, Dorothy Best	A Child's Message Of Easter
Rains, Dorothy Best	Shadow Scenes Of The Saviou
Rameau(Nelson)	Come, Thou Long-Expected Je
Rameau-Nelson	Wake, O Shepherds (W/Violin
Ramey, Troy	Great Change
Ramey, Troy	I'm On My Way To Heaven Any
Ramey, Troy	Mother Take Your Rest
Ramey, Troy	Move To A Better Home
Ramey, Troy	Prayer Is A Part Of Man
Ramey, Troy	Run On
Ramey, Troy	Stay With Me Jesus
Ramey, Troy	The Train Is Gone
Ramey, Troy	You're Gonna Need Somebody
Ramseth	God Is Love
Ramseth, B.	From The Beginning
Ramseth, B.	Spirit Boundless
Ramsfield (Arr)	March Of The Three Kings
Randegger, A	Praise The Lord
Randegger, A	Praise Ye The Lord
Raph, Alan	Christmas Night
Rasley	Beneath The Cross Of Jesus
Rasley	Bread Of Heaven
Rasley	Canticle Of Praise, A
Rasley	Carol For Eastertide, A
Rasley	Carol For The Christ-Child,
Rasley	Children's Hymn Of Praise,
Rasley	Choral Fanfare On "Holy, Ho
Rasley	Come And Adore Him
Rasley	Come, Ye Children, Sweetly
Rasley	Crown Him Lord Of All!
Rasley	Easter Carol
Rasley	Hand In Hand With God
Rasley	He's My Friend
Rasley	Holy, Holy, Holy
Rasley	Jesus, I Come
Rasley	Lead On, O King Eternal
Rasley	Miracle Of Bethlehem, The
Rasley	O Happy Home
Rasley	Onward, Christian Soldiers
Rasley	Song Of God, The
Rasley	Surely God Is In This Place
Rasley	What A Friend
Rasley	What Can I Give Him?
Rasley	What Think Ye Of Christ?
Rasley/Cross	Now Is Christ Risen Cantata
Rasley, John M.	A Heritage Of Folk Anthems
Rasley, John M.	Beholding Thee, Lord Jesus
Rasley, John M.	Carol Of Praise, A
Rasley, John M.	Easter Hymn
Rasley, John M.	From All That Dwell Below T
Rasley, John M.	God Doth Not Slumber Nor Sl
Rasley, John M.	Gospel Favorites For The Sm
Rasley, John M.	Jesus, The Very Thought Of
Rasley, John M.	Lo, God Is Here
Rasley, John M.	My Jesus, I Love Thee
Rasley, John M.	My Lord, My God, My All
Rasley, John M.	Paean Of Praise (Church Ann
Rasley, John M.	Ring The Bells (No 5040)

COMPOSER INDEX

Rasley, John M.	Song Of Praise
Rasley, John M.	The Christmas Choir No 2 (N
Rasley, John M.	The Easter Choir (No 5330)
Rasley, John M.	There'll Always Be A Christ
Ratzlaff, Paul	Lift Up Your Heads, O Ye Ga
Ravenscroft, Thomas	Two Sacred Pieces (Md)
Rawls	Hosanna Be The Children's S
Rawls, Kathryn	Christmas Is A Beautiful Wo
Raymond, Joseph	Great Is Thy Reward
Read	Quiet Music For Organ
Read, D	Sherburne
Read, Daniel	Hamshire, (Good Friday) W/V
Read, Daniel	Mortality
Read, Daniel	Newport (From Four Plain-Tu
Read, Daniel	Sherburne
Read, Daniel	While Shepherds Watch'd The
Read, Gardner	Though I Speak With The Ton
Read, Gardner	Vital Spark Of Heav'nly Fla
Read, Holden & Law	An Early American Christmas
Reading, John	Preces And Responses (M)
Ream	Day Of Dawning Brotherhood
Ream	Lambs Also Love Thee, The
Ream	So Lowly Doth The Savior Ri
Ream, Albert	A Holy Stillness
Ream, Albert	Ye Folk Afar
Ream, Albert W.	Morning Prayer
Red, Buryl	Let The People Praise
Redd/Hubbard/Merriw.	New Way Of Life, A
Redd/Hubbard/Merriwea	Christians Tribulation
Redd, Gene C.	A Soldier's Prayer
Redd,G.C./H. Hubbard	I Wish That I Had Been Ther
Redd,Gc/Bid Causey	Ain't Never Seen So Much Ra
Redd,Gc/H.Hubbard	Jesus Will Move Every
Redd,Gc/H.Hubbard	Think Of The Goodness Of Go
Redd,Gc/H.Hubbard	Where Were You Going
Redd,Gc/H.Hubbard	Yes I'll Know Him
Redd,Gc/R.Merriw.	He Said He Would Deliver Me
Redner/Decou	O Little Town Of Bethlehem
Redner/Hess	O Little Town Of Bethlehem
Reed, Alfred	Chorale Prelude In E Minor
Rees	Winds Through The Olive Tre
Rees/Morgan	Breathe On Me, Breath Of Go
Reese, Jim	Crusade Choir (No Zd-5474)
Reeve	Good Folk On Earth Below
Regan, Joe	Glory And Praise To You
Regan, Joe	Lenten Holy
Reilly, Cyril A.	Agnus Dei (Thomas More Mass
Reilly, Cyril A.	Brother Jesus, I Am Small
Reilly, Cyril A.	Dearest Father, You Are Goo
Reilly, Cyril A.	Father, We Thank You
Reilly, Cyril A.	Gloria (Thomas More Mass)
Reilly, Cyril A.	Kyrie (Thomas More Mass)
Reilly, Cyril A.	Sanctus (Thomas More Mass)
Reilly, Cyril A.	This Is The Day
Reilly, Cyril A.	We Long For You, O Lord
Reilly, Cyril A.	Where Two Or Three
Reilly, Cyril A.	You Are Shepherd
Reissiger-Christiansen	Lord Of Spirits
Remondi/Andrews	How Sacred A Feast
Remondi/Lee	We Adore You, O Lord Jesus
Render, Jan	O Come, All Ye Children
Repp, Ray	Allelu
Repp, Ray	And I Will Follow (Psalm 23
Repp, Ray	Angelic Song (First Mass)
Repp, Ray	Angelic Song (Second Mass)
Repp, Ray	Clap Your Hands
Repp, Ray	Come Away
Repp, Ray	Come, Children, Hear Me
Repp, Ray	Come, My Brothers
Repp, Ray	Forevermore
Repp, Ray	Glory To God On High
Repp, Ray	God The Father
Repp, Ray	Hear Them Cryin'
Repp, Ray	Hear, O Lord
Repp, Ray	Here We Are
Repp, Ray	How Long, O Lord
Repp, Ray	Hymn Of Praise (First Mass)
Repp, Ray	Hymn Of Praise (Second Mass
Repp, Ray	I Am The Resurrection
Repp, Ray	I Lift Up My Eyes
Repp, Ray	I'm Not Afraid
Repp, Ray	In The Month Of December
Repp, Ray	Into Your Hands
Repp, Ray	It's A Sign Of Love
Repp, Ray	Look Out Your Window
Repp, Ray	Of My Hands
Repp, Ray	Peace, My Friends
Repp, Ray	Prayer For Mercy (First Mas
Repp, Ray	Prayer For Mercy (Second Ma
Repp, Ray	Shout From The Highest Moun
Repp, Ray	Sing Hosanna, Halleluia
Repp, Ray	Sing Out, My Soul, To The L
Repp, Ray	So Lonely
Repp, Ray	Song To The Lamb Of God (Fi
Repp, Ray	Song To The Lamb Of God (Se
Repp, Ray	The Easter Song
Repp, Ray	The Lord's Prayer (First Ma
Repp, Ray	The Lord's Prayer (Second M
Repp, Ray	The Love Of Christ
Repp, Ray	This Is The Day
Repp, Ray	This Is The Day That The Lo
Repp, Ray	Till All My People Are One
Repp, Ray	To Be Alive
Repp, Ray	To Cry Is To Die
Repp, Ray	Wake Up, My People
Repp, Ray	We Need Time
Repp, Ray	What A Great Thing It Is
Repp, Ray	Why, Oh Why
Reske	Dedication
Reske	Lamb Of Calvary
Reske	Prayer, A
Rettino, Ernest W.	Christ In Me
Rettino, Ernest W.	Doer Of The Lord
Rettino, Ernest W.	I'll Never Leave You
Rettino, Ernest W.	Let Me See
Rettino, Ernest W.	Matthew 19:17
Rettino, Ernest W.	Root-Toot-To
Rettino, Ernest W.	Seek And Ye Shall Find
Rettino, Ernest W.	The Eyes Of The Lord
Rettino, Ernest W.	The Lord Thy God In The Mid
Rettino, Ernest W.	Written In The Word
Reutter, Johann	Hail, Dear Virgin (W/Organ)
Reutter, Johann	Jesu, Jesu, Dulcissime
Reutter, Johann Georg	Veni, Virgo Sacrata
Rhea, Raymond	America, Your Torch Burns Y
Rhea, Raymond	O God, Thou Art My God
Rheinberger	Star Of Bethlehem, Op 164 E
Rheinberger, J. G.	Mass In C, Op 169
Rhoads, William	Christmas Cameos Suite
Rhodes	Responses
Rhodes	They Shall See The Glory Of
Rhodes, Harold	Fight The Good Fight (E)
Richo	Come Let Us Join In Prayer
Richolson	Christ Is Born
Richolson	Song Of Thanksgiving, A
Richter, Willy	Be Thou Faithful Unto Death
Rickard	Gloria (A Cappella, Long)
Rickard	Rejoice In The Lord
Rickard, Jeffrey H.	Lord, Speak To Me
Rickard, Jeffrey H.	Prayer Of St Augustine
Ridout, Alan	Communion Service (Alt Seri
Riedel	Four Canons
Riedel	Nine Easy Canons
Riedel	The Angels And The Shepherd
Riegel, Bob	Our Father
Riese	New Life, The
Rigby, John	Reign, Master Jesus
Rimbault/Decou	O Happy Day
Rimsky-Korsakoff(Kirk)	Christ The King Now Is Born
Rimsky-Korsakoff/Amend	Glory
Rios, David	Romans 8:14,15
Ripellino, D. & Schaef	Psalm 97 (98)
Ripper, Theodore W.	Now Quit Your Care
Risewick, Jack	Guide Us
Risewick, Jack M.	A Peace For All Mankind
Risewick, Jack M.	Prepare For The Coming
Risewick, Jack M.	Shout Praises To The Lord
Ritter	Go To Dark Gethsemane
Ritter	Seven Last Words, The
Ritter,P./Carmichael	Sun Of My Soul (A Cap,
Rivers, Clarence	Bless The Lord
Rivers, Clarence Jos.	Glory To God
Rivers, Clarence Jos.	God Is Love
Rivers, Clarence Jos.	There Is None Like Him
Robbins/Hampton	Most High Omnipotent God
Robers	Hosanna! Hosanna!
Roberton, Hugh S	Let All The World In Every
Roberts	Seek Ye The Lord
Roberts	Seek Ye The Lord
Roberts	Seek Ye The Lord (Ten Solo)
Roberts, J V	Peace I Leave With You
Roberts, J V	Seek Ye The Lord
Roberts, Ricky	Come Unto Me
Robin, Bob	Abba, Father (Rom 8:15-16)
Robinson, C C	Let All On Earth Their Voic
Robinson, Eddie	Only God
Robinson, G W	A Very Merry Christmas
Robinson,E./Brown,C.	I Give My All To Thee (W/Pi
Robison	Communion From Four Folk-Hy
Robison	Fioucia From Three Folk Hym
Rocherolle, Eugenie	Joyous Alleluia
Rockwood, Gay Hylander	Processional & Alleluia(Xma
Rodgers, David	By The Manger
Rodney	Calvary
Rodney, Paul	Calvary
Roesch	I'm Gonna Let My Love Shine
Roesch	We've Got A Lot To Live For
Roff, J/Bobak, J	Receive Ye The Body Of Chri
Roff, J/Bobak, J	Virgin Mother
Roff, Joseph	All My Heart This Night Rej
Roff, Joseph	All You Peoples, Clap Your
Roff, Joseph	Almighty And Everlasting Go
Roff, Joseph	Bless, O Lord, These Rings
Roff, Joseph	Chorale Prelude On Jesu Du,
Roff, Joseph	Christ Was Born On Christma
Roff, Joseph	Christ, Our Paschal Lamb
Roff, Joseph	Come, Let Us Praise The Lor
Roff, Joseph	Father, We Gather Here To P
Roff, Joseph	Give Thanks To The Lord
Roff, Joseph	God Is Not Dead
Roff, Joseph	God's Plan
Roff, Joseph	Great King Of Peace
Roff, Joseph	Hail Mary
Roff, Joseph	Hail, True Virginity
Roff, Joseph	Have Faith In God
Roff, Joseph	He Who Follows Me
Roff, Joseph	He Will Receive The Blessin
Roff, Joseph	Here Is A Great Priest
Roff, Joseph	Holy Spirit, Hear Us
Roff, Joseph	I Am The Bread Of Life
Roff, Joseph	I Am With You
Roff, Joseph	If Anyone Wishes To Come Af
Roff, Joseph	It Is You, O Lord
Roff, Joseph	Let The Heavens Be Glad
Roff, Joseph	Let The Light Of Thy Counte
Roff, Joseph	Let The Peace Of God
Roff, Joseph	Let Thy Mercy, O Lord, Be U
Roff, Joseph	Lighten Mine Eyes
Roff, Joseph	Listen Christian (Soc. Gosp
Roff, Joseph	Mass For Congregations (Ice
Roff, Joseph	Mass For Two Voices (Icet)
Roff, Joseph	Mass In Honor Of St Joseph
Roff, Joseph	Memorial Acclamations I-Iv
Roff, Joseph	My Soul Wait Thou Only Upon
Roff, Joseph	No Longer Will I Call You S
Roff, Joseph	O God Of All Beauty
Roff, Joseph	People's Mass (Icet)
Roff, Joseph	Priest And Bishop
Roff, Joseph	Seasonal Responsorial Psalm
Roff, Joseph	Selected Music For Funerals
Roff, Joseph	Service Suite For Organ
Roff, Joseph	Simon The Cyrenean Speaks
Roff, Joseph	Sing Joyfully To The Lord
Roff, Joseph	Six Service Pieces For Orga
Roff, Joseph	Soul Of My Savior
Roff, Joseph	Strengthen, O God
Roff, Joseph	Surely He Hath Borne Our Gr
Roff, Joseph	Taken Up In Glory
Roff, Joseph	The Earth Feared And Was Si
Roff, Joseph	The Earth Shall Be Filled
Roff, Joseph	The Lord Has Sworn
Roff, Joseph	The Lord Is My Portion
Roff, Joseph	Triptych
Roff, Joseph	Upon Easter Day
Roff, Joseph	What Return Shall I Make To
Roff, Joseph	Where Charity And Love Are
Roff, Joseph	With An Everlasting Love
Roff, Joseph	Yours Are The Heavens
Roff, Joseph (Ed)	The Divine Liturgy
Rogers	Balm In Gilead
Rogers	Carol Of The Bells
Rogers	Christ The Lord Is Risen To
Rogers	Fellowship Divine
Rogers	Glory To God
Rogers	Happy Birthday, Gentle Savi
Rogers	I'm Not Afraid Anymore
Rogers	Joy Dawned Again On Easter
Rogers	Let Us Break Bread Together
Rogers	O Love, How Deep
Rogers	Prayer For Our Country, A
Rogers	Savior, Like A Shepherd Lea
Rogers	Treasure Of Heaven, The
Rogers/Harper	Joy Of A Sinner Set Free, T
Rogers/White	Let All With Sweet Accord
Rogers, Benjamin	Evening Service In 'a Re' M
Rogers, Bernard	Psalm 68
Rogers, Bernard	The Prophet Isaiah
Rogers, J H	Be Ye Therefore Followers O
Rogers, J H	Doth Not Wisdom Cry
Rogers, J H	Fear Not, O Land
Rogers, J H	Great Peace Have They
Rogers, J H	I Will Lift Up Mine Eyes
Rogers, J H	Lord, For Thy Tender Mercie
Rogers, J H	May The Words Of My Mouth
Rogers, J H	Now If Christ Be Preached
Rogers, J H	O Taste And See
Rogers, J H	Thus Saith The Lord Of Host
Rogers, Lee	Land Of Our Loyalty
Rogers, Lee (Arr.)	Holy Manna
Roh, Johann	Come You Faithful (4-Part A
Rohlig	Fantasy On O Come All Ye Fa
Rohlig	Fifteen Preludes
Rohlig	Fifty-Five Hymn Intonations
Rohlig	Good Christian Men Rejoice
Rohlig	Hymn Intonations (55)
Rohlig	Now Thank We All Our God (M
Rohlig	O Clap Your Hands
Rohlig	Prelude On Christ Is Arisen
Rohlig	Sonata I For Organ
Rohlig	Ten Pieces For Organ
Rohlig	Thirty New Settings Of Fami
Rohlig, Harald	Good Christian Men, Rejoice
Rohlig, Harald	Now Thank We All Our God
Rohlig, Harald	We Come Unto Our Fathers' G
Romfh, Paul	Memorial Acclamation
Root-Harris (Arr)	O Come, Let Us Sing
Rorem	Christ The Lord Is Ris'n (A
Rorem, Ned	An Angel Speaks To The Shep
Rorem, Ned	Cycle Of Holy Songs
Rorem, Ned	Requiem

COMPOSER INDEX

Rorem, Ned	The Resurrection
Rorem, Ned	Two Holy Songs (Ps. 134, Ps
Rose Lon	Lord Watch Over Mother
Rose, Michael	Sing To The Lord A Joyful S
Rosenmuller, Johann	A Prayer For Today
Rossello(Ar Beveridge)	Adoramus Te (We Adore Thee)
Rossello, Francesco	Adoramus Te
Rossetti Young	Love Came Down At Christmas
Rossini, G.A. (D1868)	Stabat Mater
Rossini, Gioacchino	O Salutaris Hostia
Rossini, Gioacchino	Thou Whose Redeeming Sacrif
Roth/Landon	In My Heart There Rings A M
Rovison/Turner	Water Of Time
Rowe, D.	Centurion's Song
Rowe, D.	Pave The Way
Rowe, D.	We Come And Go
Rowley, Alec	Praise (Me)
Rozsa, Miklos	Twenty-Third Psalm, The
Rramon/Decou	Just A Wayward Lamb
Rubinstein	Hear Our Prayer
Ruby, Lyndal	God's Been Good To Me
Rudcki, Stanley	Glory To God (Chardin Mass)
Rudcki, Stanley	Holy, Holy, Holy (Chardin M
Rudcki, Stanley	Lamb Of God (Chardin Mass)
Rudcki, Stanley	The Nicene Creed(Credo)(Cha
Rudcki, Stanly	Lord Have Mercy (Kyrie)(Ch
Rudski, Stanley	Mass In Honor Of Chicago
Ruggles	What Child Is This?
Runyan/Landon	Great Is Thy Faithfulness
Rush, John	O Lord My God
Russ, Bob	Song Of Mary
Russel, Carlton	Magnificat
Russell	Bread Of Life
Russell (Arr)	Adoration, The
Russell-Sellers	Wonderful Wonderful Jesus
Russell, Leslie	O Brother Man (E)
Russell, Olive (Arr)	The Lord Into His Garden (M
Russo, Robert	Alleluia God Is Love
Russo, Robert	King Of Kings (Glory Glory)
Rusthoi	Tenderly
Rusthoi/Mickelson	When We See Christ
Rutter, John	Christ The Lord Is Risen Ag
Rutter, John	Communion Service, Series 3
Rutter, John	Gloria
Rutter, John	God Be In My Head (E)
Rutter, John	O Clap Your Hands (Ps 47)
Rutter, John	Praise Ye The Lord (Ps 150)
Rutter, John	Psalm 121 (I Will Lift Up M
Rutter, John	The Falcon
Rutter, John	Two Hymns Of Praise
Ryder, Noah F	See That Babe In The Lowly
Ryder, Noah F	What You Gonna Call Yo Pret
Sabatini, Leo	The Rest Of Our Lives
Sacco, John	The Bells Ring Out For Chri
Sacco, John	The Spelling Of Christmas
Sadler, Rebecca	I Belong To Jesus
Saint-Saens, Camille	Ave Verum
Saint-Saens, Camille	Bring Costly Offerings
Saint-Saens, Camille	Christmas Oratorio
Saint-Saens, Camille	Give Praise All Earthly Men
Saint-Saens, Camille	Glory To The Father
Saint-Saens, Camille	Grant Unto Me
Saint-Saens, Camille	Jesu, Gentlest Saviour
Saint-Saens, Camille	Lift Up Your Songs Of Prais
Saint-Saens, Camille	Mass For 4 Voices, Solo & C
Saint-Saens, Camille	My Soul Doth Magnify The Lo
Saint-Saens, Camille	Praise Ye The Lord
Salathiel, L	Did Not Our Heart Burn With
Salathiel, L	Surely He Hath Borne Our Gr
Salem	Early American Tune
Salisbury	Psalm 19
Salisbury Jr, Wallace	Live With The Lord
Salisbury Jr, Wallace	You Can't Buy A Savior
Salisbury, Sonny	Here Comes Jesus
Salisbury, Wallace	Lord, Have Mercy; Save My S
Salsbury, Sonny	Backpacker's Suite(Youth Mu
Salsbury, Sonny	Love Came Down(Musical)
Salter, S	Mary's Manger Song
Sanders, Robert	Beautiful Valley, The
Sanders, Robert	Jesus Calls Us
Sanders, Robert L	Death Of Absalom, The
Sanford	Good News In The Kingdom
Sanford	Hear The Lambs
Sanford	Jesus, Son Of God
Sankey/Bunzel	Trusting Jesus
Santa Cruz, Domingo	Alabanzas Del Adviento
Santa Cruz, Domingo	Cantares De Pascua
Sapaugh, C/Austin, B	Try A Little Kindness
Sargent, Malcolm	Carol Of Beauty (Md)
Sarner, Richard	Christmas Eve Is Here
Sartori (Beveridge)	Christus Factus Est(Lat,Eng
Sartori, Baldasaro	Christus Factus Est
Sateren, Leland B.	A Great And Mighty Wonder
Sateren, Leland B.	Alternate Responses And Te
Sateren, Leland B.	As Men Of Old Their First F
Sateren, Leland B.	Be Ye Joyful
Sateren, Leland B.	Breath Of God
Sateren, Leland B.	Christ The Sure Foundation
Sateren, Leland B.	Come, Holy Ghost, In Love
Sateren, Leland B.	Come, Thou Long-Expected Je
Sateren, Leland B.	Day Of Pentecost
Sateren, Leland B.	Deep Were His Wounds
Sateren, Leland B.	God Is God
Sateren, Leland B.	Hosanna, Son Of David
Sateren, Leland B.	I Come, O Lord, Unto Thee
Sateren, Leland B.	I Love The Church
Sateren, Leland B.	In His Care
Sateren, Leland B.	Jerusalem, My Happy Home
Sateren, Leland B.	Jesus, In Thy Dying Woes
Sateren, Leland B.	Jesus, Let Our Souls Be Fed
Sateren, Leland B.	Let Us Break Bread Together
Sateren, Leland B.	Lord Is Thy Keeper, The
Sateren, Leland B.	Love Walks The World In Fle
Sateren, Leland B.	My Heart Is Longing To Prai
Sateren, Leland B.	O God, The Rock Of Ages
Sateren, Leland B.	O Lord, Thou Art My God And
Sateren, Leland B.	On The Wood His Arms Are St
Sateren, Leland B.	Once I Sang
Sateren, Leland B.	Sing Alleluia, Jesus Lives
Sateren, Leland B.	So Dost Thou Give
Sateren, Leland B.	Sorrowful Road, The
Sateren, Leland B.	The Present Hour
Sateren, Leland B.	They Follow Me
Sateren, Leland B.	Tis Finished! So The Savior
Sateren, Leland B.	To Know Thou Art
Sateren, Leland B.	Turn Not Thy Face
Sateren, Leland B.	We Three Are One
Savage, Bob (Ed)	Cantos De Evangelismo
Savage, Bob (Ed)	Cofre De Canticos
Savage, Bob (Ed)	Fifty Latin American Favori
Savage, Robert (Ed)	Dias Especiales (No 5374)
Savals/Mattei/Blunt	I Wonder Why
Sawyers	Hold My Hand, Dear Lord
Saxe, Serge	Wedded Souls
Scarlatti-Coggin	Alleluia, Praise God
Scarlatti, Alessandro	Exultate Deo
Scarlatti, Alessandro	Prepare Now Your Finest Cha
Scarlatti, Alessandro	Sanctus
Scarlatti, D.	Credo
Schaefer, T. & Ripelli	Be Filled With The Spirit
Schaffer, Jeanne E.	Words From The Cross, The
Schaffer, Joe	Thanks Be To God
Schalk	A Child Is Born In Bethlehe
Schaffer, Robert J.	Accept O Lord
Schaffer, Robert J.	Born Again
Schaffer, Robert J.	Common Of Doctors (Icet) Ps
Schaffer, Robert J.	Common Of Doctors Alleluia
Schaffer, Robert J.	Common Of Martyrs Psalm (Ic
Schaffer, Robert J.	Father, I Put My Life In Yo
Schaffer, Robert J.	Gift Of Wheat From Thy Teem
Schaffer, Robert J.	Glory To God (Bcl)
Schaffer, Robert J.	Holy, Holy, Holy (Icet)
Schaffer, Robert J.	In Love We Gather
Schaffer, Robert J.	Joyous Coming Of Our Lord
Schaffer, Robert J.	Lamb Of God (Icet)
Schaffer, Robert J.	Lord Have Mercy (Icet)
Schaffer, Robert J.	O My Lord
Schaffer, Robert J.	O Son Of Man
Schaffer, Robert J.	Preparing Now
Schaffer, Robert J.	These Two
Schaffer, Robert J.	To Rise Again
Schaffer, Robert J.	Vigil Assumption-Psalm (Ice
Schaffer, Robert J.	Vigil Assumption-Alleluia
Schaffer, Robert J.	We Go Into The House Of The
Schalk, Carl (Ed)	Psalms For The Church Year
Scheidt-Ehret	Now Thank We All Our God
Scheidt-Nelson	Good Christians, Now Rejoic
Scheidt/Tortolano Ed	The Lord Said You Are My So
Scheidt, S	Sic Deus Dilexit Mundum
Scheidt,S./Tortolano	The Right Hand Of The Lord
Schein, Johann H	Maria Magdalene Et Altera M
Schein, Johann H	O Blessed Lord
Schein, Johann H	O Domine
Schein, Johann H	When Mary Magdalene
Schiavone, J	I Am The Bread Of Life
Schiavone, John	Mass In Honor Of All Saints
Schiavone, John	Mass In Praise Of Holy Spir
Schiavone, John	Mass In Praise Of Jesus Chr
Schilling, F	Jubilate
Schirmer, Rudolph	The Gift Of Christmas
Schmal, Desmond	Father Almighty
Schmidt	Behold, I Stand At The Door
Schmidt	Fantasienne And Fughetta
Schmidt	In The Hollow Of Your Hand
Schmidt/Heflin	I Walk Along With Jesus
Schmidt, Jackie	Psalm 41
Schmutz	Ein Gebet
Schmutz	His Mercy Endureth Forever
Schmutz, Albert	O Lord, Our God
Schmutz, Albert C.	Bread Of The World
Schneider, Kent E.	All That Has Life Praise Go
Schneider, Kent E.	Bread Of Presence
Schneider, Kent E.	Burst Of Christ
Schneider, Kent E.	Can't Take It With You
Schneider, Kent E.	Child, The
Schneider, Kent E.	Church Within Us
Schneider, Kent E.	Create In Me
Schneider, Kent E.	Faithful Gather, The
Schneider, Kent E.	Glory To God
Schneider, Kent E.	God's For Real Man
Schneider, Kent E.	Gospel Rappings
Schneider, Kent E.	Greet A New Day
Schneider, Kent E.	Greet The Dawn
Schneider, Kent E.	Holy, Holy, Holy
Schneider, Kent E.	I Believe In One God (Creed
Schneider, Kent E.	Keep In Mind
Schneider, Kent E.	Lamb Of God
Schneider, Kent E.	Life Is A Circle
Schneider, Kent E.	Lord Have Mercy
Schneider, Kent E.	Lord, Inspire Our Worship
Schneider, Kent E.	Lord's Prayer
Schneider, Kent E.	Lovers Are Special People
Schneider, Kent E.	Mary's Song
Schneider, Kent E.	Mourning's Glory
Schneider, Kent E.	Nothin' Left To Fear
Schneider, Kent E.	Only In The Midst Of The Wo
Schneider, Kent E.	Praise Ye, The Lord
Schneider, Kent E.	Projection 29
Schneider, Kent E.	Psalm 98
Schneider, Kent E.	Silent Night
Schneider, Kent E.	Song Of Love
Schneider, Kent E.	Song Of Thankfulness
Schneider, Kent E.	Soon A New Dawn
Schneider, Kent E.	Soundings For New Beginning
Schneider, Kent E.	Travelin' 40 Days
Schneider, Kent E.	Woodlawn Walk
Schneider, Kent E.	You're In The Right Place
Schneider,Kent E.(Arr)	Let Us Break Bread
Schneider,Kent E.(Arr)	Mighty Fortress, A
Schneider,Kent E.(Arr)	We Three Kings
Schoen, Douglas E.	Hymns For Brass Quartet (No
Schoen, F	May God Have Pity On Us
Schoen, Frank (Rev.)	Blessing Over Water
Schoenbachler, Tim	Baptism Prayer
Schoenbachler, Tim	Lamentations
Schoenbachler, Tim	Lord Is My Hope, The
Schoenbachler, Tim	Make Known Your Way
Schoenbachler, Tim	People Of God
Schoenbachler, Tim	Rise Up, Jerusalem
Schoenbachler, Tim	Simeon's Canticle
Schoenbachler, Tim	Song For The Masses, A
Schoenbachler, Tim	Yes, Lord, Amen
Schoenfeld, William	Secret, The
Schoenfeld, William C.	Presence, The
Schoenfeld, William C.	Steward's Prayer, The
Scholfield/Carmichael	Saved, Saved
Scholtes/Krogstad	They'll Know We Are Christi
Scholtes, Peter	Choose Life
Scholtes, Peter	Glory Be To Israel
Scholtes, Peter	Glory To God (Missa Bossa N
Scholtes, Peter	Holy, Holy, Holy (Missa Bos
Scholtes, Peter	Holy, Holy, Holy (67th Stre
Scholtes, Peter	Lamb Of God (Missa Bossa No
Scholtes, Peter	Lamb Of God (67th Street Ma
Scholtes, Peter	Lord Have Mercy (Kyrie)
Scholtes, Peter	Lord Have Mercy (Kyrie)
Scholtes, Peter	Shout And Clap Your Hands
Scholtes, Peter	The Lord Bless You
Scholtes, Peter	The Lord's Prayer (Missa Bo
Scholtes, Peter	They'll Know We Are Christi
Scholtes, Peter	We Gather Together
Schop-Pooler, M.	Jesus, Name All Names Above
Schrader, Jack	Choral Stylings (No Zd-5473
Schroeder, John	Father Lead Me Day By Day
Schroth	Holy Night!
Schroth, G	A Litany Of Thanksgiving
Schroth, G	All From Saba Shall Come
Schroth, G	Come Down, O Love Divine
Schroth, G	For The People Of God
Schroth, G	He Has Borne Our Woes
Schroth, G	He Shall Rule From Sea To S
Schroth, G	Let Us Stand In Prayer
Schroth, G	This Is The Day
Schroth, G	Yours Is Princely Power
Schubert	Holy Is The Lord
Schubert, F(Arr Hines)	O Lord God Of My Salvation
Schubert, Franz J.	Ave Maria
Schubert, Franz J.	Chorus Of Angels
Schubert, Franz J.	Come Unto Me
Schubert, Franz J.	God Is My Guide
Schubert, Franz J.	Great Is Jehovah
Schubert, Franz J.	Kyrie
Schubert, Franz J.	Mass #1 In F
Schubert, Franz J.	Mass In Ab And Eb
Schubert, Franz J.	Mass In C Major
Schubert, Franz J.	Mass In G (In Bb)
Schubert, Franz J.	Mass In G Major No. 2
Schubert, Franz J.	Mass No. 2 In G Major
Schubert, Franz J.	Miriam's Song Of Triumph
Schubert, Franz J.	Offertorium, Salve Regina
Schubert, Franz J.	Sound The Trumpet, Strike T
Schubert, Franz J.	Stabat Mater
Schubert, Franz J.	Tantum Ergo
Schubert, Franz J.	The Lord Is My Shepherd
Schubert, Franz J.	The Lord Is My Shepherd (Ps
Schubert, Franz J.	The Omnipotence
Schubert, Franz J.	They Sang That Night In Bet
Schubert, Franz J.	Turn Your Thoughts To Those
Schuetky/Howorth	Emitte Spiritum Tuum (Lat,
Schuetky, Fr Jos	Send Forth Thy Spirit

COMPOSER INDEX

Schultz	I'll Live For Jesus
Schultz, Heinrich	Glory To God
Schuman, William	Te Deum
Schumann-Christiansen	How Fair The Church
Schumann-Christiansen	How Great Are Thy Wonders
Schumann-Christiansen	Yea, Though I Wander
Schumann, Robert	Advent Song Op 84
Schumann, Robert	Mass Opus 147
Schutte, Dan	Like Cedars They Shall Stan
Schutte, Dan & Murray	All My Days
Schutte, Dan, S. J.	Blessed Are You
Schutte, Dan, S. J.	Come To Me All Who Are Wear
Schutte, Dan, S. J.	Come With Me Into The Field
Schutte, Dan, S. J.	Glory To God
Schutte, Dan, S. J.	Happy Is The Man
Schutte, Dan, S. J.	Holy
Schutte, Dan, S. J.	If The Lord Does Not Build
Schutte, Dan, S. J.	Lord Have Mercy
Schutte, Dan, S. J.	May The Angels
Schutte, Dan, S. J.	Mountains And Hills
Schutte, Dan, S. J.	Psalm 150
Schutte, Dan, S. J.	Servant Song
Schutte, Dan, S. J.	Sing A New Song
Schutte, Dan, S. J.	Though The Mountains May Fa
Schutte, Dan, S. J.	Valleys Of Green
Schutte, Dan, S. J.	What You Hear In The Dark
Schutte, Dan, S. J.	With Merry Dancing
Schutte, Dan, S. J.	Yahweh, The Faithful One
Schutte, Dan, S. J.	You Are My Sons
Schutte, Dan, S. J.	You Are Near
Schutte, Dan, S.J.	In The Morning
Schutz/Ehret	Our Lord Did Suffer Death
Schutz/Hardwicke	Thrice Holy Lord
Schutz/Heinrich	Help Us, Jesus Christ, God'
Schutz, Heinrich	A Child To Us Is Born
Schutz, Heinrich	Behold This Child Is Set Fo
Schutz, Heinrich	Blessed The Faithful
Schutz, Heinrich	Cantate Domino
Schutz, Heinrich	Cantate, Domini Canticum No
Schutz, Heinrich	Cantiones Sacrea: Heu Mihi
Schutz, Heinrich	Cantiones Sacrea: In Te Dom
Schutz, Heinrich	Chorus Of The Angels
Schutz, Heinrich	Christ, Be Thine The Glory
Schutz, Heinrich	Christ, Our Blessed Savior
Schutz, Heinrich	Christmas Oratorio
Schutz, Heinrich	Deus, Misereatur Nostri
Schutz, Heinrich	Domine, Non Est Exaltum Cor
Schutz, Heinrich	Dulcissime Et Benignissime
Schutz, Heinrich	German Magnificat
Schutz, Heinrich	Great Is The Lord
Schutz, Heinrich	He Who With Weeping Soweth
Schutz, Heinrich	Hear Me, O Lord
Schutz, Heinrich	Heute Ist Christus Der Herr
Schutz, Heinrich	I Am The Resurrection And T
Schutz, Heinrich	I Know That My Redeemer Liv
Schutz, Heinrich	I Waited For The Lord (Ps 4
Schutz, Heinrich	I Will Praise The Lord
Schutz, Heinrich	If God Be For Us, Who Shall
Schutz, Heinrich	In Te Domine Speravi
Schutz, Heinrich	In Te, Domine, Speravi
Schutz, Heinrich	Ist Nicht Ephraim Mein Teur
Schutz, Heinrich	Lift Up Your Heads, O Ye Ga
Schutz, Heinrich	Lo, I Am The Voice Of One C
Schutz, Heinrich	Lo, The Angel Said To The S
Schutz, Heinrich	Lobt Gott Mit Schall
Schutz, Heinrich	Lord Jesus On The Cross Was
Schutz, Heinrich	Lord, Create In Me A Clean
Schutz, Heinrich	Lord, If I But Thee May Hav
Schutz, Heinrich	Lord, My Hope Is In Thee
Schutz, Heinrich	Lord, Redeemer Of All Who K
Schutz, Heinrich	Many Shall Come From The Ea
Schutz, Heinrich	O Jesus, Thou Son Of God
Schutz, Heinrich	One Thing I Ask Of The Lord
Schutz, Heinrich	Our Father
Schutz, Heinrich	Out Of The Depths We Cry, L
Schutz, Heinrich	Praise God With Sound (Psal
Schutz, Heinrich	Praise To The Lord God
Schutz, Heinrich	Praise Ye The Lord
Schutz, Heinrich	Psalm 121
Schutz, Heinrich	Purge Ut Therefore The Old
Schutz, Heinrich	Quoniam Ad Te Clamabo, Domi
Schutz, Heinrich	Responsorium
Schutz, Heinrich	Saul. Sacred Concerto(Ger)
Schutz, Heinrich	Selections From Canciones S
Schutz, Heinrich	Seven Last Words
Schutz, Heinrich	Sing To The Lord
Schutz, Heinrich	Song Of Praise
Schutz, Heinrich	Spes Mea, Christe, Deus
Schutz, Heinrich	Symphonia Sacra: Mein Sohn,
Schutz, Heinrich	The Birth Of Our Lord And S
Schutz, Heinrich	The Heavens Declare The Glo
Schutz, Heinrich	The Passion According To St
Schutz, Heinrich	The Passion According To St
Schutz, Heinrich	The Passion According To St
Schutz, Heinrich	The Pharisee And The Public
Schutz, Heinrich	The Seven Last Words From T
Schutz, Heinrich	Thou Art Jesus, Savior And
Schutz, Heinrich	Thy Love Brings Joy
Schutz, Heinrich	Troset Troset Mein Volk
Schutz, Heinrich	Vaterunser, Das
Schutz, Heinrich	Verleih Uns Frieden Genadig
Schutz, Heinrich	What Pain Our Master Did's't
Schutz, Heinrich	Wondrous Is The Life In Hea
Schutz,H./Ed Reuning	Psalm 102 (Becker Psalter)
Schutz,H./Ed Reuning	Psalm 130 (Becker Psalter)
Schutz,H./Ed Reuning	Psalm 143 (Becker Psalter)
Schutz,H./Ed Reuning	Psalm 32 (Becker Psalter)En
Schutz,H./Ed Reuning	Psalm 38 (Becker Psalter)En
Schutz,H./Ed Reuning	Psalm 51 (Becker Psalter)En
Schutz,H./Ed Reuning	Psalm 6 (Becker Psalter) En
Schwadron	Keep Not Thy Silence
Schwadron, A A	Sh'ma Yisroeyl
Schwadron, A A	The Lamb
Schwartz, Paul	It Is A Good Thing To Give
Schwartz, Stephen	All Good Gifts
Schwartz, Stephen	Day By Day
Schwartz, Stephen	Light Of The World
Schwartz, Stephen	O Bless The Lord, My Soul
Schwartz, Stephen	On The Willows
Schwartz, Stephen	Prepare Ye The Way Of The L
Schwartz, Stephen	Save The People
Schwartz, Stephen	Turn Back, O Man
Schwartz, Stephen	We Beseech Thee
Scott/Johnston	Open My Eyes
Scott, J P	Come, Ye Blessed
Scott, J P	Consider The Lilies
Scott, Sarah	Three Introits For Festival
Scott, T. (Arr)	Praise And Elation
Sculthorpe, Peter	Morning-Song For The Christ
Seagard	Epiphany Adoration (Solo)
Seagard	The Shepherds' Adoration
Searle, Humphrey	A Little Hymn To Mary
Sedores, Sil	Oh, Lord, Make Me An Instru
Seeger, P/Hays, L.	The Hammer Song
Seeger, Pete	Turn, Turn, Turn
Seeger, Pete	Where Have All The Flowers
Selner, J	Favorite Christmas Carols
Senfl/Guettler	Fecit Potentium
Senfl, Ludwig	The Bells At Speyer
Sergisson, Carol	His Name Is Love
Serly, Tibor	A Little Christmas Cantata
Serly, Tibor	Hymn Of Nativity
Severson, Roland	Lord Is King, The
Sevitzky, Fabien	Christmas Bells
Sewell Homer	If The Good Lord's Willing
Sewell Homer	Is This America
Sewell Homer	Looking Reaching For My Lor
Sewell Homer	When This World Ends
Sewell Homer/Jones O.	Fathers Table Grace
Shafer, William	God Forbid That I Should Bo
Shafer, William	Reproaches, The
Shafer, William	Right Hand Of The Lord, The
Shafer, William	Run, Christian, Run
Shaltz, Gregory	All The World Acclaims Your
Shaltz, Gregory	Christ's Body, Given Up For
Shaltz, Gregory	I Call You Friends
Shaltz, Gregory	Let Us Make Music For God
Shaltz, Gregory	Lord Be Not Far From Me
Shaltz, Gregory	My Gift For You
Shaltz, Gregory	Oh Lord, I Long To See Your
Shaltz, Gregory	You Have Made Us
Shapero, Harold	Hebrew Cantata
Shapero, Harold	Two Psalms (Ps. 146, Ps. 11
Shaw	All Creatures Of Our God An
Shaw-Parker	Carol Of The Birds
Shaw, Jim	Bring A Little Sunshine
Shaw, Jim	Coming Together
Shaw, Jim	Free From Fear
Shaw, Jim	Open Your Eyes
Shaw, Jim	Our Father
Shaw, Jim	Save The Mission
Shaw, Jim	So Close To You And Me
Shaw, Jim	We Are Hungry
Shaw, Martin	Go Forth With God! (Me)
Shaw, Martin	O Christ Who Holds The Open
Shaw, Martin	O Light From Age To Age The
Shaw, Martin	The Easter Anthems
Shaw, Robert Arr	Calvary
Shaw, Watkins (Ed)	Four Settings Of Preces & R
Shea	I Am Not Alone Today
Shea	Where Have You Gone, My Lon
Shea	Who Knows The Answer?
Shea (Arr)	Alleluia! Sing To Jesus
Shea, George Beverly	George Beverly Shea Gospel
Shea, George Beverly	George Beverly Shea Solos
Sheehan, Ann Marie	Healing Of The Nations
Shelley	King Of Love My Shepherd Is
Shelley	Still, Still With Thee
Shelley, H R	Breast The Wave, Christian
Shelley, H R	Christian, The Morn Breaks
Shelley, H R	God Is Love
Shelley, H R	Hark, Hark, My Soul!
Shelley, H R	Now Abideth Faith, Hope And
Shelley, H R	Saviour, When Night In olve
Shelley, H R	Star Of The Orient
Shelley, H R	The King Of Love My Shepher
Shelley, H R	The Resurrection
Shelley, Tim	We Offer Bread And Wine
Shelley, Tom	All Of Creation
Shelley, Tom	Christ Loves Us
Shelley, Tom	Come, Sing, Praise The Lord
Shelley, Tom	Come, Spirit, Come
Shelley, Tom	Glory To God
Shelley, Tom	Hear Mr. Lord, I'm Callin'
Shelley, Tom	Hear Us, Oh Lord
Shelley, Tom	How Can This Be
Shelley, Tom	In The Mornin'
Shelley, Tom	Jesus In The Mornin'
Shelley, Tom	Look All Around You
Shelley, Tom	Lord, I Am Not Worthy
Shelley, Tom	Mary, Your Child Is God
Shelley, Tom	Our Father
Shelley, Tom	Our Father, The Lords Praye
Shelley, Tom	Praise The Father
Shelley, Tom	Reach Out
Shelley, Tom	Sing Out Hosannah
Shelley, Tom	Some Other Man
Shelley, Tom	The Baptism Song
Shelley, Tom	The Drums Beat On
Shelley, Tom	The Road Of Christ
Shelley, Tom	The Spirit Came One Morn'
Shelley, Tom	The Wedding Feast
Shelley, Tom	The World Around Us
Shelley, Tom	To Your Table
Shelley, Tom	Where Two Or Three Are Gath
Shelley, Tom	With Jesus, Our Brother
Shelley, Tom	With These Rings
Shelley, Tom	Yahweh Rejoices
Shelley, Tom	Yahweh, Our God
Shenk	Shepherd's Nativity Song, T
Shepard, T G	O Jesus, Thou Are Standing
Shephard	Benedicite, Omnia Opera Dom
Shepherd, John	Haste Thee, O God (Me)
Sheppard/Hess	This Is My Father's World
Sheppard, J Stanley	Benedicite, Omnia Opera
Sheppard, J Stanley	Remember, O Thou Man
Sherberg/Shippy/Bolte	Can't Find The Time
Sherberg, Jon	Love Will Bring Us Back
Sherman, P	Exit
Shields	Beside The Still Waters
Shimmons, C	Jesus Pleases
Shimmons, C	The Sabbath Of God
Shipp, Clifford M.	My Soul Thirsts For God (Ps
Shipp, Clifford M.	O God Our Help In Ages Past
Showalter/Drevits	Leaning On The Everlasting
Showalter/Hess	Leaning On The Everlasting
Shrubsole (Arr Cartfor	All Hail The Power
Shure	Star, A Shepherd, A Lamb, A
Sibelius	Before The Dawn
Sibelius/Decou	Be Still, My Soul
Sibelius, J	A Morning Prayer
Sibelius, J	Song Of Peace, A
Sibelius, J	Trust
Sibelius, Jean	Hymn To The Earth
Sibelius, Jean	This Is My Song
Silk, R. J.	Sing And Rejoice (Md)
Silson	Christ Is Risen, Alleluia!
Silva	Beside The Still Waters
Silva	Show A Little Love
Silver	Out Of The Depths
Silvia, Helen	Abba, Father(4-Part Arrange
Silvia, Helen	All Our Hope Of Salvation (
Silvia, Helen	Amen! (4-Part Arrangement)
Silvia, Helen	An Age Had Passed
Silvia, Helen	An Angel Came To Nazareth
Silvia, Helen	Angels We Have Heard On Hig
Silvia, Helen	At That First Eucharist (4p
Silvia, Helen	Ave Maria (4-Part Arr.)
Silvia, Helen	Battle Hymn Of The Republic
Silvia, Helen	Bring To The Lord (4-Part A
Silvia, Helen	Child Was Born, A
Silvia, Helen	Christ Our Lord And Brother
Silvia, Helen	Come By Here
Silvia, Helen	Come To The Running River
Silvia, Helen	Come, Holy Spirit
Silvia, Helen	Come, Rich And Poor
Silvia, Helen	Come, Shake The Mountains
Silvia, Helen	Dayenu
Silvia, Helen	First Noel, The
Silvia, Helen	Give Thanks To God The Fath
Silvia, Helen	Give The King Your Final Ju
Silvia, Helen	Glory Hosanna
Silvia, Helen	Go Tell Your People (4-Part
Silvia, Helen	Great Amen (4-Partrarr)
Silvia, Helen	Greet The Risen Lord With J
Silvia, Helen	He's Got The Whole World In
Silvia, Helen	Holy God
Silvia, Helen	Holy, Holy, Holy (4-Part Ar
Silvia, Helen	How Blessed Are They Who He
Silvia, Helen	I Am The Way (4-Part Arr)
Silvia, Helen	In The Lord We Will Live (4
Silvia, Helen	In Your Holy Place (4-Part
Silvia, Helen	Joy To The World
Silvia, Helen	Let All Mortal Flesh Keep S
Silvia, Helen	Let Us Break Bread Together
Silvia, Helen	Live In The Light (4-Part A
Silvia, Helen	Lord Has Risen In Glory, Th
Silvia, Helen	Marana-Tha
Silvia, Helen	Mary, Filled With Grace
Silvia, Helen	My God Is A Rock

COMPOSER INDEX

Composer	Title	Composer	Title	Composer	Title
Silvia, Helen	Noel	Smith	Lily Of The Valley, The	Snogren/Johnson	Ring, Bells, O Ring
Silvia, Helen	Now Hear What God Will Give	Smith	Make A Joyful Noise	Snow, Robert J.	Hail Mary Full Of Grace
Silvia, Helen	Now Thank We All Our God	Smith	Men For The Crisis Hour	Snyder	This Christmastide
Silvia, Helen	O Christ Our King (4-Part A	Smith	Moment By Moment	Soechtig	Song That The Angels Sang
Silvia, Helen	O Come, O Come Emmanuel	Smith	My Lord Is Like A Shepherd	Soler, Joseph	Two Songs (From Saint Paul)
Silvia, Helen	O God Our Help	Smith	O Come, All Ye Faithful	Somary, J	How Lovely Is Thy Dwelling
Silvia, Helen	Praise The Lord (4-Part Arr	Smith	O Little Town Of Bethlehem	Somary, Johannes	Music For Eucharistic Praye
Silvia, Helen	Prayer Of The Faithful For	Smith	O Love, How Deep	Somerville, S. 1	Psalm 100 (99)
Silvia, Helen	Prayer Of The Faithful For	Smith	O Sing Unto The Lord A New	Soriano, F. (Ed Lee)	Ave Regina Coelorum (E & L)
Silvia, Helen	Prayer Of The Faithful For		Old Jordan	Southbridge	All Good Gifts Around Us
Silvia, Helen	Prayer Of The Faithful For	Smith	On Jordan's Stormy Banks	Southbridge	I Have Been To The Mountain
Silvia, Helen	Redeemer King	Smith	Promised One, The	Southbridge	O Lord And Master Of Us All
Silvia, Helen.	Rise Up	Smith	Risen Christ, The	Southbridge	Ride On King Jesus!
Silvia, Helen	Run, Christian, Run (4-Part	Smith	Search Me, O God	Southbridge	We Welcome Glad Easter
Silvia, Helen	Salem City	Smith	Spirit Of God	Southbridge, James	Seek Ye The Lord
Silvia, Helen	Shalom	Smith	Take It To Jesus	Souther, Billy	Evangelism Arrangements No
Silvia, Helen	Sing Of Mary	Smith	Take Time To Be Holy	Souther, Billy	Evangelism Arrangements No
Silvia, Helen	Singers, Sing	Smith	To Zion Jesus Came	Souther, Billy	Sing! Make A Joyful Sound N
Silvia, Helen	Son Of God	Smith	Under His Wings	Souther, Billy	Sing! Make A Joyful Sound N
Silvia, Helen	Song Of Daniel	Smith	With All Who Love Thy Name,	Souther, Billy	Sing! Make A Joyful Sound N
Silvia, Helen	Song Of The City	Smith	Worship The Lord In The Bea	Souther, Billy	Sing! Make A Joyful Sound N
Silvia, Helen	Spirit Of Strength	Smith Charles N.	Think On Me	Sowerby, Leo	Come, Holy Ghost, Draw Near
Silvia, Helen	That Easter Day	Smith-Childs	He Will Heal	Sowerby, Leo	I Will Lift Up My Eyes
Silvia, Helen	This Day A Rose Of Judah	Smith-Harper	Back To The Prairies	Sowerby, Leo	Jesus, Bright And Morning S
Silvia, Helen	Tis A Gift To Be Simple (4-	Smith/Ackley	Wedding Prayer, A	Sowerby, Leo	The Lord Ascendeth Up On Hi
Silvia, Helen	To Jesus Christ Our Soverei	Smith/Bolks	Deeper And Deeper	Spannaus/Kraehenbuehl	Lord Of All Nations
Silvia, Helen	Today The World Is Filled	Smith/Childs	I'll Sing	Sparks	Brother John
Silvia, Helen	What Love Have We Denied To	Smith/Childs	O Wondrous Life	Speaks, Oley	Come, Spirit Of The Living
Silvia, Helen	What You Gave Us	Smith/Harper	Always Remembered	Speaks, Oley	In The End Of The Sabbath
Silvia, Helen	Where Love Is Living	Smith/Harper	Come With Your Heartache	Speaks, Oley	Let Not Your Heart Be Troub
Silvia, Helen	Who Is He That Stands Trium	Smith/Harper	He Changed My Life	Speaks, Oley	More Love To Thee, O Christ
Silvia, Helen	You Are The Light Of The Wo	Smith/Harper	I'm Singing For My Lord	Speaks, Oley	O Master, Let Me Walk With
Silvia, Helen	You Christians All	Smith/Harper	Jesus Cares	Speaks, Oley	The Lord Is My Light
Silvia, Helen Trad Rus	Bless The Lord (4-Part Arra	Smith/Harper	My Heart Would Sing Of Jesu	Speaks, Oley	The Prayer Perfect
Silvia, Ray	I Sing Your Song	Smith/Harper	Sometimes	Speaks, Oley	There's A Song In The Air
Silvia, Ray	Lullaby Of The Spirit	Smith/Huntley	When I've Changed My Addres	Speaks, Oley	Thou Wilt Keep Him In Perfe
Simeone/Davis/Onorati	The Little Drummer Boy	Smith/Williams	Jesus, I Love Thee	Speaks, Oley	Twilight And Dawn
Simper	Break Forth Into Joy	Smith, G Riley, R	We Come To Praise His Name	Specner, Tim	We've Got A Great Big Wonde
Simper	He Shall Reign Forever	Smith, Gloria Jean	God's Love Is Such A Beauti	Spedding, Frank	Lord, When The Wise Men Cam
Simper, C	Break Forth Into Joy	Smith, Gloria Jean	Lonely	Speehand/Johnson	This Is My Father's World
Simper, C	Break Forth Into Joy	Smith, Gregg	Ave Maria	Spencer, Glenn	Song Of The Prodigal
Simper, C	King Of Kings	Smith, Gregg	Babel	Spencer, Glenn	Surely I Can Believe
Simutis, Leonard	Mass For Parishes	Smith, Gregg	Set Me As A Seal	Spencer, Hal	Colored Christmas Lights
Sinclair, Jerry	Alleluia (8x)	Smith, Gregg	The Lord Bless Thee And Kee	Spencer, Hal	Devil, Devil Go Away
Singenberger, Otto	In Christ The Prince Of Pea	Smith, Harold	O Come And Mourn	Spencer, Hal	Hallelujah, Praise The Lord
Sinzheimer	Song Of Mary (W/Insts)	Smith, Harold	O Savior, Precious Savior	Spencer, Hal	Merry Merry Christmas
Sinzheimer	The Song Of Mary	Smith, Harold	Two Introits	Spencer, Hal	Soon I'll See His Face
Sisler, Hampson	Every Good & Perfect Gift	Smith, Henry C	Hear Us As We Pray	Spencer, Hal	What A Wonderful Way To Go
Sisler, Hampson	Let Us Exalt Him (W/Opt Tpt	Smith, Herb	Praise Ye The Lord!	Spicker, M	Fear Not, O Israel
Sisler, Hampson	Who Is This That Cometh (Is	Smith, I/Caldwell, W	God Is So Wonderful	Spicker, M	Holy, Holy, Holy
Sittler	The Spirit Of The Lord (W/G	Smith, John Z.	Come Rest A Little While	Spilman	Away In A Manger
Sizemore, G./ Hall, T	Wrinkled And Old	Smith, John Z.	Give God A Chance And Be Ma	Spiritual	I Know The Lord's Laid His
Sizemore, G/Hall, T	I'm Gonna Ride That Train T	Smith, John Z.	God's Love Is The Love For	Spiritual	I Want Jesus To Walk With M
Sizemore, G/Sizemore.	I'll Be Fightin' Old Satan	Smith, John Z.	I Thank God For Amazing Gra	Spiritual/Artman	Seeking To Become
Skoog/Johnson	Glory To God We Sing	Smith, John Z.	Jesus Will Fix It After Awh	Spiritual/Decou	Were You There?
Slack, Roy	I Was Glad (Ps 122)	Smith, John Z.	Lord Keep Me In The Holy Ba	Spiritual/Decou	Yes, He Did
Slater	Easter Introit, An	Smith, John Z.	There Is No Need To Walk Al	Spiritual/Drevits	Joshua Fit The Battle Of Je
Slater	Mighty Fortress, A	Smith, Lani	A Service Of Shadows	Spiritual/Johnson	Hold Out Your Light
Slater	With Broken Heart And Contr	Smith, Lani	Breathe On Me Breath Of God	Spiritual/Lundberg, J.	Rise-Shine
Slater, Richard	Praise The Lord Through Eve	Smith, Lani	Come, Ye That Love The Lord	Spohr, L	As Pants The Hart
Slater, Richard W.	A Song Of Mary & Jesus (W/F	Smith, Lani	How Firm A Foundation	Spong	American Hymns And Carols O
Slater, Richard W.	O Lord, Thou Hast Searched	Smith, Lani	I Am Trusting Thee. Lord Je	Spong	Early American Compositions
Slater, Richard W.	O Praise The Lord (W/Brass,	Smith, Lani	I've Got Jesus	Spong	Organ Rarities, Volume I
Slates, Philip	I Wait For The Lord	Smith, Lani	It's All About Love.	Sprague, Richard L	Gloria In Excelsis
Slates, Philip M.	Peace Of Lord	Smith, Lani	It's The Lord's Thing.	Spratlen, Abbye	Go On My Child
Slauson, Lloyd N.	Stand Up For Jesus(W/Opt Tr	Smith, Lani	Jubilation!	Sprouse, W	Since I Met Jesus
Slauson, Loyal	Great Jehovah Hear Thy Chil	Smith, Lani	Little Lord Jesus	Sr M. M. Keane/Wesley	O Joseph, Mighty Patron
Slauson, Loyal	Marching To Zion	Smith, Lani	Lord Jesus, Think On Me	Sr. Margarita	Jesus Christ Our Lord & God
Sleeth	Long Time Ago	Smith, Lani	My Jesus, I Love Thee	St. Benedict's Farm	Bid Me Come
Sleeth, Natalie	Jubilate Deo (W/Brs)	Smith, Lani	No Greater Love	St. Benedict's Farm	Canticle Of Mary, Magnifica
Sluss, Robert	Nunc Dimittis	Smith, Lani	O Give Thanks Unto The Lord	St. Benedict's Farm	Come Alive
Smart/Decou	Angels, From The Realms Of	Smith, Lani	O Love Of God, Most Full	St. Benedict's Farm	Glory To God
Smart/Rasley	Lead On, O King Eternal	Smith, Lani	One Small Child	St. Benedict's Farm	He Cried
Smart, H	Lead On, O King Eternal	Smith, Lani	Something For Jesus	St. Benedict's Farm	Holy, Holy, Holy
Smit, Leo	Christmas Carol	Smith, Lani	The Lily Of The Valley	St. Benedict's Farm	I Do Believe
Smit, Leo	Psalm	Smith, Lani	The Visitor	St. Benedict's Farm	If I Wanted To Hide
Smith	Alleluia Verse (Christmas V	Smith, Lani	Wings Of Prayer	St. Benedict's Farm	Lamb Of God
Smith	Amazing Grace	Smith, Lani	Ye Servants Of God	St. Benedict's Farm	Lord Have Mercy
Smith	Child Of Hope, A	Smith, P.	Psalm 34	St. Benedict's Farm	O My Achin Rib(Adams Compla
Smith	Christ The Lord Is Born	Smith, Randy	Kingdom Of Children	St. Benedict's Farm	Our Father
Smith	Common Of Pastors (Icet) Ps	Smith, Roger	Alleluia! Alleluia! Allelui	St. Benedict's Farm	Remember Me
Smith	Day By Day	Smith, Roger	Holy, Holy (Angelic Song)	St. Benedict's Farm	Safe Under His Wing
Smith	Day Of Brotherhood, The	Smith, Roger	Hosanna For Joy	St. Benedict's Farm	Samson (Novelty Song)
Smith	Emmaus Road	Smith, Roger	Lord Have Mercy	St. Benedict's Farm	Sing, Christians, Sing
Smith	Even For One	Smith, Roger	Penitential Response	St. Benedict's Farm	Sparrows
Smith	Father, We Praise Thee	Smith, Roger	Roger's Alleluia (Gospel Ac	St. Benedict's Farm	Sweet Wine
Smith	Guide Me, O Thou Great Jeho	Smith, Roger	World Within, A	St. Benedict's Farm	The Lord Is Here
Smith	Hark! The Herald Angels Sin	Smith, Roger	Yahweh Is A Saving Lord (Ps	St. Benedict's Farm	The Lord Is My Light
Smith	Have Thine Own Way, Lord	Smith, Roger (Adpt.)	Christ Our Lord Has Died (A	St. Benedict's Farm	The Man Next Door
Smith	He Never Said A Mumblin' Wo	Smith, Roger & Regan,	You Are A Priest Forever	St. Benedict's Farm	The Name Of Jesus
Smith	Hey, Manger Child	Smith, T.	Tedd Smith's Hymn Transcrip	St. Benedict's Farm	Yesterday
Smith	Hosanna, Loud Hosanna	Smith, T.	Tedd Smith's Piano Solo Arr	St. Clair, Wendell	Tell Me Why
Smith	Hymn Of Praise	Smith, Tedd	Piano Duets At One Keyboard	Stacey, Helen; Kent, R	I'll Wear A New White Robe
Smith	I Sing Of The Glory Of The	Smith, William	Psalm 85 (Md)	Stacy M. Laney E.C.	In The Autograph Of God
Smith	Is There Anybody Here?	Smith,I Mccarter,W	When The Lord Laid His Hand	Stadler, M	Behold The Great Priest
Smith	Jesus, Lover Of My Soul	Smoldon, W. L. Ed	Planctus Mariae (Latin & En	Stadler, Maximilian	Credidi Propter
Smith	Just As I Am	Smoldon, W. L. Ed	Sponsus (The Bridegroom)Act	Stahl, D	The Son In My Life
Smith	Let All Together Praise Our	Smoldon, W. L. Ed	Visitatio Sepulchri (Acting	Stahl, Denny	Jesus Is The Morning
		Smoldon, W.L. (Ed)	Peregrinus (Acting Version)	Stahl, Denny	Let Me Walk
		Snell	Praise God With Loud Songs	Stainer, Sir John	Adoration

COMPOSER INDEX

Stainer, Sir John	Fling Wide The Gates
Stainer, Sir John	Fling Wide The Gates
Stainer, Sir John	God So Loved The World
Stainer, Sir John	God So Loved The World
Stainer, Sir John	God So Loved The World
Stainer, Sir John	God So Loved The World
Stainer, Sir John	Grieve Not The Holy Spirit
Stainer, Sir John	I Am Alpha And Omega
Stainer, Sir John	Jesus Said Unto The People
Stainer, Sir John	O Lamb Of God
Stainer, Sir John	Sabbath Bells
Stainer, Sir John	Sing Noel, Merry Noel
Stainer, Sir John	The Appeal Of The Crucified
Stainer, Sir John	The Crucifixion (No 5808)
Stainer, Sir John	The Sevenfold Amen
Stainer, Sir John	They Have Taken Away My Lor
Stainer, Sir John	What Are These That Are Arr
Staley, F. Broadus	God Be Merciful Unto Us
Stamps, Robert J.	God And Man At Table
Stamps, Robert J.	Litany For The Lord's Comin
Stanford, C V	Jubilate
Stanphill	There's Room At The Cross F
Stanphill/Decou	He Knows What He's Doin All
Stanphill/Decou	Jesus And Me
Stanphill/Decou	Room At The Cross For You
Stanphill/Ferrin	Drifting
Stanphill/Ferrin	I'm A-Goin To Glory
Stanphill/Johnson	Mansion Over The Hilltop
Stanphill/Johnson	We'll Talk It Over
Stanphill/Johnson	Yesterday's Gone
Stanphill/Johnson	You Can Have A Song In Your
Stanphill, Ira	Ira Stanphill Favorites No
Stanphill, Ira	Ira Stanphill Favorites No
Stanphill, Ira	Ira Stanphill Favorites No
Stanphill, Ira	The Sinner And The Song (Mu
Stanphill, Ira F.	Happiness Is The Lord
Stanton, W. K.	Alleluia! Hearts To Heaven
Stanton, W. K.	Christ Is The World's True
Starer, Robert	Give Thanks Unto The Lord
Starer, Robert	Have Mercy Upon Me, O Lord
Starks	Christmas Introit
Stassen, Linda	Sing Hallelujah
Statham, Heathcote	Communion Service In D (Me)
Statham, Heathcote	Drop Down, Ye Heaven (Is 45
Staton	Midnight, Sleeping Bethlehe
Staton	There's A Wideness In God's
Staton, Kenneth	With Happy Voices Ringing
Ste. Marie, Patricia	As A Child Before The Lord
Ste. Marie, Patricia	Come To Jerusalem
Ste. Marie, Patricia	God Has Made Us One In His
Ste. Marie, Patricia	How Lovely Is Your Dwelling
Ste. Marie, Patricia	I Will Sing And Make Music
Ste. Marie, Patricia	Jesus Christ, King Of Kings
Ste. Marie, Patricia	Lord Make Me Know Your Ways
Ste. Marie, Patricia	Sing Unto The Lamb
Ste. Marie, Patricia	The Kingdom Of God
Stearnman, Dave	Capernaum Comes Alive
Stearns, P.	Sixty Pieces For The Manual
Stearns, Peter Pindar	Twenty Hymn Preludes For Or
Stebbins/Landon	Have Thine Own Way, Lord
Steel, A. (Arr.)	How Firm A Foundation
Steel, Christopher	Thou, O God, Art Praised In
Steffe-Wilson	Battle Hymn Of The Republic
Steinke, Greg	Twenty-Third Psalm
Stern	Sing Unto The Lord A New So
Stevens	Everything Is Beautiful
Stevens (Arr)	Go Tell It On The Mountain
Stevens (Arr)	God Rest You Merry Gentleme
Stevens, Halsey	Four Carols
Stevens, Halsey	Psalm 98
Stevens, Marsha J.	Can I Show You
Stevens, Marsha J.	Face In The Crowd
Stevens, Marsha J.	For Those Tears I Died
Stevens, Marsha J.	Russ's Song
Stevens, Marsha J.	The Search
Stevens, Marsha J.	Tried In The Fire
Stevens, Marsha J.	Where Else Would I Go
Stevens, Russ	You're A Gift
Stevens, Sammy	Savior Of The World
Stevens, Sammy	The Star
Stewart, C H And H G	God Will Answer Prayer
Stewart, C. Hylton	Evening Service In C: Magni
Stewart, Curtis	Lord, Build Me A Cabin In G
Stewart, H J	Holy, Holy, Holy Lord God A
Stewart, Malcolm	Jerusalem
Stewart, Malcolm	Peter And John
Stickles, William	Faithful Shepherd, Guide Me
Stickles, William	To Come, O Lord, To Thee
Still, William Grant	Christmas In The Western Wo
Stiltz, E.	Smile
Stipe, T R & Butler, C	Two Roads
Stipe, Thomas	Goin' Home To The Master
Stipe, Thomas	Life In Jesus
Stipe, Thomas	Old Gray Ford
Stipe, Thomas Richard	Big City Blues
Stipe, Thomas Richard	Come Quickly Jesus
Stockton/Rasley	Only Trust Him
Stone (Arr)	Angels We Have Heard On Hig
Stone (Arr)	Bring A Torch, Jeannette
Stone (Arr)	Coventry Carol
Stone, Robert	The Lord's Prayer (E)
Stone, Walter C.	No One Can Ever Be Equal To
Stooky/Yarrow Et Al	The Song Is Love
Storrs/Decou	Have I Done My Best For Jes
Strahan-Cross, R.	Enter O People Of God
Stralsund Gesangbuch	Praise To The Lord (4-Part
Strange, J D	Tear Down The Walls
Strange, Joy Deanne	More Than Words
Strange, Joy Deanne	On Your Own
Stravinsky, Igor	Symphony Of Psalms
Street, Tilson	Come, Holy Spirit
Street, Tilson	Leave, Then, Thy Foolish Ra
Street, Tilson	Nearer, Any God, To Thee
Strickland, Lily	Saviour, Hear Us When We Pr
Strickler, David	Hymn Anthems
Strickler, David	Now The Green Blade Riseth
Strickler, David	O Where Are Kings And Empir
Strickler, David	Save Me, O God
Strickling	Sing We All Noel
Strickling, George F.	Carols For Christmas (Ssa)
Strickling, George F.	Father, O Hear Me
Stroh, Virginia	Praise Ye The Lord, Allelui
Stromberg, V.	I Hear Music
Stuntz	Thanks Be To Thee, O God
Suitor, Lee	I Bind Unto Myself Today
Sullivan	It Came Upon The Midnight C
Sullivan	Lord, Open Thou Our Eyes
Sullivan	Nature's Anthem Of Praise
Sullivan-Handley	Golden Harps Are Sounding
Sullivan/Decou	Onward,Christian Soldiers
Sullivan/Denton	Christmas Meditation
Sullivan/Wilson	Onward, Christian Soldiers
Sullivan, Arthur	God Shall Wipe Away All Tea
Sullivan,Sr.Mary Hope	Walk On
Summerlin,E.,Miller,W.	Gift Of Joy
Summerlin,E.,Miller,W.	Liturgy Of The Holy Spirit
Summerlin,E.,Miller,W.	The Coming Of Christ (3 Pts
Summers, George	Where The Children Run Free
Sumner/Yungton	Child Of The King, A
Suriano, Francisco	Hail, Queen Of Heaven, Be J
Surovchak	Master, What Shall I Do?
Susanni	Traditional German Carol
Swanson/Drevits	Christmas Long Ago
Swanson, Darlene J.	If My People
Sweelinck	Born Today
Sweelinck, J. P.	Arise, O Ye Servants
Sweeney	Beauty Is
Sweeney	Forever
Sweeney	God Is Alive
Sweeney	I'm Living, I'm Living
Sweeney	It's Mine, It's Mine
Sweeney	What Have You Given
Sweney/Mayfield	Sunshine In My Soul
Sweney/Mclellan	Beulah Land
Sydeman, William	Thanksgiving Song
Sydow	Hosanna! Blessed Is He!
Sydow	Promised One, The
Sykes/Decou	Thank You, Lord
Sylvester, Erich	Alleluia
Sylvester, Erich	Amen
Sylvester, Erich	Best Is Yet To Come, The
Sylvester, Erich	Blessed Be God Forever
Sylvester, Erich	Christ Will Come Again
Sylvester, Erich	Come Life, Shaker Life
Sylvester, Erich	Dying You Destroyed Our Dea
Sylvester, Erich	Glory To God
Sylvester, Erich	Good News
Sylvester, Erich	Holy
Sylvester, Erich	Lamb Of God
Sylvester, Erich	Lord Have Mercy
Sylvester, Erich	Lord's Prayer, The
Sylvester, Erich	Peaceful Pastures
Sylvester, Erich	Stay With Me
Sylvester, Erich	This Is A Holy Day
Sylvester, Erich	Today Is The Crown Of Creat
Sylvester, Erich	Your Song That I Sing
Sylvester, Erich (Arr)	Amazing Grace
Sylvester, Erich (Arr.	Evening Prayer
Sylvester, Erich (Arr.	Simple Gifts
Symons, Christopher	Sing We Merrily (Ps 81)
Takacs, Jeno	Shepherd, Hark
Tallis, T.(Arr Lynn)	O Nata Lux De Lumine (Lat &
Tallis, Thomas	All Praise To Thee
Tallis, Thomas	All Praise To Thee (Canon)
Tallis, Thomas	Almighty Word (As By R.V. W
Tallis, Thomas	Audivi, Media Nocte (Md)
Tallis, Thomas	Festal Responses (E)
Tallis, Thomas	Glory To Thee My God This N
Tallis, Thomas	I Ieiunio Et Fletu (M)
Tallis, Thomas	I Will Give You A New Comma
Tallis, Thomas	If Ye Love Me (Me)
Tallis, Thomas	If Ye Love Me, Keep My Comm
Tallis, Thomas	Mass For Four Voices
Tallis, Thomas	Mihi Autem Nimis (Blessed B
Tallis, Thomas	Nineteen Anthems In Four Vo
Tallis, Thomas	O Lord, Give Thy Holy Spiri
Tallis, Thomas	O Nata Lux De Lumine
Tallis, Thomas	O Nata Lux De Lumine (Me)
Tallis, Thomas	O Sacrum Convivium (Md)
Tallis, Thomas	Purge Me, O Lord (Me)
Tallis, Thomas	Rise, God! Judge Thou The E
Tallis, Thomas	Salvator Mundi (Md)
Tallis, Thomas	Short Evening Service (Dori
Tallis, Thomas	Spem In Alium Nunquam Habui
Tallis, Thomas	Te Deum (Md)
Tallis, Thomas	That Virgin's Child
Tallis, Thomas	The Lamentations Of Jeremia
Tallis, Thomas	This Is My Commandment
Tallis, Thomas	Verily, Verily, I Say Unto
Tallis, Thomas(D1585)	Mass Salve Intemerata
Tallis,T./Tortolano	Tallis Canon (4 Voices)
Talmadge	Christmas Bells, The
Talmadge, C. L.	Lord Of All Power And Might
Talmadge, C. L.	Thou Art The Way
Talmadge, C. L.	We Love The Place, O God
Talmadge, Charles	Lord Jesus Think On Me
Taranto	Rejoice!For We Are Saved
Tarner	Seek And Ye Shall Find
Tarner	Show Me A Window
Tarner	Teach Me To Love Thee More
Tashlin/Kenner	Spread The Word
Taverner, John	Christe Jesu, Gaude Plurimu
Taverner, John	Christe Jesu, Pastor Bone
Taverner, John	Dum Transisset Sabatum
Taverner, John	Five Anthems
Taverner, John	Mass Corona Spinea
Taverner, John	Mass Gloria Tibi Trinitas
Taverner, John	Mass Mater Christi
Taverner, John	Mass O Michaeli
Taverner, John	Mass Plain Song
Taverner, John	Mass Sine Nomine
Taverner, John	Mass Small Devotion
Taverner, John	The "Leroy" Kyrie
Taverner, John	Three Magnificats
Taverner, John(D1545)	Mass The Western Wynde
Taylor/Dallas	I Wish I Knew How It Would
Taylor, R.	Daddy, Sing For Jesus
Taylor, R.	Love Like The Springtime
Taylor, R.	That's How Real God Can Be
Taylor,W./Hendrix,J.	God Supplies What I Need
Tchaikovsky, P. I.	A Legend
Tchaikovsky, P. I.	Hymn Of Praise
Tchaikovsky, P. I.	Our Father
Tcherepnin, A.	Mass In English (A Cap)
Tcherepnin, A.	Processional And Recessiona
Telemann	Come, All Ye Saints
Telemann	Didst Thou Suffer Shame?
Telemann	I Will Sing Praises
Telemann-Nelson	O Come, Holy Spirit(W/Conti
Telemann-Nelson	O Not To Us, Good Lord (Opt
Telemann, G.P.(D1767)	Psalm 117
Telemann, Georg P	I Will Praise The Lord
Telemann,G./Tortolano	Sing To The Lord (3 Voices)
Telemann,G./Tortolano	The Heavens Are Telling (3
Temple	Hail Mary
Temple, S./Hershberg,S	Great Day In Bethlehem (Can
Temple, Sebastian	Abraham Sent Them Away
Temple, Sebastian	All That I Am
Temple, Sebastian	And Abraham Cried
Temple, Sebastian	And Rachel Loved Him
Temple, Sebastian	And The Waters Keep On Runn
Temple, Sebastian	Babble Babel
Temple, Sebastian	Blessed Sacrament, The
Temple, Sebastian	Blessing Of St. Francis
Temple, Sebastian	Brothers All
Temple, Sebastian	By Their Fruit Shall Ye Kno
Temple, Sebastian	Canticle Of The Sun
Temple, Sebastian	Church Is Where Men Are, Th
Temple, Sebastian	Come Holy Spirit Come (Fire
Temple, Sebastian	Cosmic Christ (You Are The
Temple, Sebastian	Do You Know?
Temple, Sebastian	Dream, Pharoah, Dream
Temple, Sebastian	Eastward In Eden
Temple, Sebastian	Faith, Hope And Charity
Temple, Sebastian	Famine Came Upon The Land
Temple, Sebastian	Fifty Just Men
Temple, Sebastian	Follow Christ
Temple, Sebastian	Forbidden Fruit
Temple, Sebastian	Glorious God
Temple, Sebastian	Go In Peace And Love (W/Gui
Temple, Sebastian	God Is A Fire Of Love
Temple, Sebastian	Good Lady Poverty
Temple, Sebastian	Here At The Table Of The Lo
Temple, Sebastian	Holy Spirit Of The Living G
Temple, Sebastian	Holy, Holy, Holy Lord (Hymn
Temple, Sebastian	How Good It Is
Temple, Sebastian	How Great Is Your Name
Temple, Sebastian	I Sing A Song Of Teilhard
Temple, Sebastian	I'll Fashion Me A People
Temple, Sebastian	I'll Raise You Up (Calypso)
Temple, Sebastian	In Sodom Town
Temple, Sebastian	In This Bread (We Share The
Temple, Sebastian	It Is They
Temple, Sebastian	Jacob's Ladder
Temple, Sebastian	Jacob's Lament
Temple, Sebastian	Jesus Christ Is Lord
Temple, Sebastian	Jesus Christ, Our King
Temple, Sebastian	Jesus We're Waiting For You
Temple, Sebastian	Lamp Unto My Feet (W/Guitar
Temple, Sebastian	Leave It In The Hands Of Th

Composer	Title
Temple, Sebastian	Let's Make Peace
Temple, Sebastian	Living God, The
Temple, Sebastian	Look At Jesus
Temple, Sebastian	Make Me A Channel Of Your P
Temple, Sebastian	Make Me Your Own (I Give Yo
Temple, Sebastian	Mass Is Ended, The
Temple, Sebastian	My Sons Abel And Cain
Temple, Sebastian	One Gentle, One Wild
Temple, Sebastian	Patter, Patter
Temple, Sebastian	Prayer For Peace
Temple, Sebastian	Prayer Of St. Francis
Temple, Sebastian	Quick, Quick
Temple, Sebastian	Red, Yellow, Purple And Gre
Temple, Sebastian	Restore My Church
Temple, Sebastian	Said The Lord
Temple, Sebastian	Sing The Praise Of Jesus
Temple, Sebastian	Song Of Sarah
Temple, Sebastian	Sons Of Jacob
Temple, Sebastian	Strangest Dream, The
Temple, Sebastian	Take My Hands
Temple, Sebastian	Teilhard's Offering
Temple, Sebastian	Teilhard's Vision
Temple, Sebastian	The Fire Of Love
Temple, Sebastian	The Last Day (We're A Pilgr
Temple, Sebastian	The Lord Of Evolution
Temple, Sebastian	The Universe Is Singing
Temple, Sebastian	The Word (Though The Rivers
Temple, Sebastian	Tomorrow And Tomorrow
Temple, Sebastian	Walls (You Have Made A Fiel
Temple, Sebastian	We Are One
Temple, Sebastian	We Thank You (In Sunshine &
Temple, Sebastian	Welcome, Lord (W/Guitar)
Temple, Sebastian	Where Two Or Three Are Gath
Temple, Sebastian	Wondrous Is Your Presence
Temple, Sebastian	Wrestlers, The
Temple, Sebastian	Yes, Lord (I Heard You Call
Temple, Sebastian	You Are The Answer
Temple, Sebastian	Your Will Be Done
Tenney, Mildred	Thy Way, Not Mine, O Lord
Terry, Richard,Silvia,	Alleluia! Let The Song Of G
Teschner/Decou	All Glory, Laud, And Honor
Thackray, Roy	Pleasure It Is
Theobald, James	Alleluia-Amen
Theophane, Sr. M	O Holy Banquet
Theophane, Sr. M	Psalm 22
Theophane, Sr. M	Psalm 33
Theophane, Sr. M	The Lord Has Chosen Him
Thiem, James	A Sky Without Sunlight
Thiem, James	An Appointed Time
Thiem, James	Freedom Song
Thiem, James	Jubilee
Thiem, James	Lamentations
Thiem, James	Parousia Song
Thiem, James	Shout
Thiem, James	Sons Of God
Thiem, James	The Dirge Of David
Thiem, James	The Four Seasons
Thiem, James	The Tree Of Life
Thiem, James	Waiting
Thiem, James	Wonderful World
Thiman, Eric H.	A Seasonal Thanksgiving
Thiman, Eric H.	All That's Good And Great A
Thiman, Eric H.	Christ Who Knows All His Sh
Thiman, Eric H.	Christ, Whose Glory Fills T
Thiman, Eric H.	Hark The Glad Sound
Thiman, Eric H.	How Beauteous Are Their Fee
Thiman, Eric H.	Love Came Down At Christmas
Thiman, Eric H.	Mary's Nowell
Thiman, Eric H.	O Thou, To Whom In Ancient
Thiman, Eric H.	Praise The Lord, His Glorie
Thiman, Eric H.	Round Me Falls The Night
Thiman, Eric H.	The Book Of Stories
Thomas/Decou	Hallelujah! We Shall Rise
Thomas, Daniel B.	So Great A Gift (No 5985) C
Thomas, Paul	Head That Once Was Crowned
Thomerson, Kathleen	I Want To Walk As A Child
Thomerson, Kathleen	Jesus, I Love You
Thomerson, Kathleen	Psalm 136 (O Give Thanks)
Thompson	All Hail The Power Of Jesus
Thompson	Am I A Soldier Of The Cross
Thompson	Canticle Of Love, A
Thompson	Come, Ye Thankful People
Thompson	Deer Is Panting For The Str
Thompson	Echo Carol, The
Thompson	Garden Hymn, The
Thompson	Glory To The King Of Kings
Thompson	Go Ye And Teach All Nations
Thompson	God Is Love
Thompson	God Of Love My Shepherd Is,
Thompson	How Firm A Foundation
Thompson	Hymn To The Godhead
Thompson	Hymn To The Trinity
Thompson	I Have Quieted My Soul
Thompson	I Heard The Voice Of Jesus
Thompson	Lead On, O King Eternal
Thompson	More Love To Thee
Thompson	O For A Thousand Tongues
Thompson	O God, Our Help In Ages Pas
Thompson	O Gracious King
Thompson	O Lord, Our Lord
Thompson	O Love Of God
Thompson	Onward, Christian Soldiers
Thompson	Praise God In His Holiness
Thompson	Praise The Lord Of Heaven
Thompson	Praise To The Lord, The Alm
Thompson	Praised Be My Lord
Thompson	Psalm Of Thanksgiving, A
Thompson	Rose Of Christmas, The
Thompson	Sing And Give Praise
Thompson	Song Of The Angels, The
Thompson	Stand Up For Jesus
Thompson	These Are Thy Glorious Work
Thompson	Thou Hope Of Every Contrite
Thompson	When Love Came Down
Thompson	When Love Was Born
Thompson, Robert B.	Lift Up Your Heads, O Ye Ga
Thompson, V. D.	Dear Lord, Who Once Upon Th
Thompson, V. D.	Mercy And Truth
Thomson, Virgil	Consider, Lord
Thomson, Virgil	My Master Hath A Garden
Thomson, Virgil	The Bell Doth Toll
Thomson, Virgil	The Holly And The Ivy
Thygerson	Consider The Lilies
Thygerson	Crown Him Lord Of All
Thygerson	Crown Him With Many Crowns
Thygerson	Gloria To God On High
Thygerson	Hallelujah, Praise The Lord
Thygerson	Hush, My Babe
Thygerson	Long Ago In Bethlehem
Thygerson	Make A Joyful Noise
Thygerson	No Room In The Inn
Thygerson	Praise God In His Sanctuary
Thygerson	Right On With Number One!
Thygerson	Sing A New Song Unto The Lo
Thygerson	Sing And Rejoice
Thygerson	Teach All Nations
Thygerson, Robert W	Born In A Stable
Thygerson, Robert W	Wasn't That A Mighty Day!
Thygerson, Robert W.	How Many Miles Must We Go?
Tiffault	Oh Jerusalem
Tigner, Marcy	Sing With Marcy (No 5455)
Till, Lee Roy	Sing His Praises No 1 (No 5
Till, Lee Roy	Sing His Praises No 2 (No 5
Tindley/Shepard	Nothing Between
Titcomb, Everett	Christ The Lord Is Risen (W
Titcomb, Everett	Herald Of Good Tiding (W/Tp
Titcomb, Everett	O For A Closer Walk With Go
Titcomb, Everett	Spirit Of The Lord, The (Un
Titcomb, Everett	Wedding Processional (Mod E
Tlucek, Tim	Hey Brothers!
Tolosko/Wiskirchen	Brass Sounds Of Christmas
Tolosko/Wiskirchen	Hymns Of Praise And Glory
Tombelle, F De La	Gabriel Angelus
Tomblings, Philip	All From The Sun's Uprise
Tomblings, Philip	Come, My Way, My Truth, My
Tomblings, Philip	Seek The Lord (E)
Tompkins, Thomas	Absalom
Tompkins, Thomas	Have Mercy On Me
Tompkins, Thomas	Have Mercy Upon Me, O God
Tompkins, Thomas	Magnificat And Nunc Dimitti
Tompkins, Thomas	O Give Thanks Unto The Lord
Tompkins, Thomas	O God, Wonderful Art Thou
Tompkins, Thomas	O How Amiable (Ps 84) (Md)
Tompkins, Thomas	O Praise The Lord All Ye He
Tompkins, Thomas	O Pray For The Peace Of Jer
Tompkins, Thomas	O Pray For The Peace Of Jer
Tompkins, Thomas	Praise The Lord, O My Soul
Tompkins, Thomas	Psalm 104 (103)
Tompkins, Thomas	When David Heard That Absal
Toney/Toney, B.	I Believe What The Bible Sa
Toolan, Sr Suzanne	Acclamation
Toolan, Sr Suzanne	Advent Glad Song (Heartily
Toolan, Sr Suzanne	Behold I Stand At The Door
Toolan, Sr Suzanne	Ephesians Hymn (Blessed Be)
Toolan, Sr Suzanne	Ephesians Hymn Ii (May Chri
Toolan, Sr Suzanne	Friendship Hymn (I Shall No
Toolan, Sr Suzanne	Gradual And Alleluia
Toolan, Sr Suzanne	Hymn Of Joy (Let Us Live In
Toolan, Sr Suzanne	Hymn Of Unity (The Glory Yo
Toolan, Sr Suzanne	I Am The Bread Of Life
Toolan, Sr Suzanne	Let Us All Rejoice
Toolan, Sr Suzanne	Living Spirit
Toolan, Sr Suzanne	Living Spirit (Blessed Be T
Toolan, Sr Suzanne	Living Waters (Scriptural C
Toolan, Sr Suzanne	May The Roads Rise Up
Toolan, Sr Suzanne	My Lord Is Alive
Toolan, Sr Suzanne	Peace Hymn (Truly I Assure
Toolan, Sr Suzanne	Praise To The Lord
Toolan, Sr Suzanne	Psalm 23
Toolan, Sr Suzanne	Psalm 84 (How Lovely)
Toolan, Sr Suzanne	Sing Joyfully To The Lord
Toolan, Sr Suzanne	Song Of Covenant
Toolan, Sr Suzanne	Stilled & Quiet Is My Soul
Toolan, Sr Suzanne	The Word (In The Beginning)
Toolan, Sr Suzanne	This Is The Day
Toolan, Sr Suzanne	Tree Of Life
Toolan, Sr Suzanne	Walk In Light (God Is Light
Toolan, Sr Suzanne	Yes I Will Arise
Toolan,S.&O'sullivan R	Tell It Out (All Creation H
Toolan,S.&O'sullivan R	The Call (How Brightly Deep
Tortolano/Folk Tune	My Shepherd Will Supply My
Tortolano, W	Nineteen Liturgical Rounds
Tourjee/Johnson	There's A Wideness In God's
Tours, B.	In Thee, O Lord, Have I Put
Tours, B.	O Be Joyful In The Lord
Tours, B.	Sing, O Heavens
Tower, A Wesley	We Three Kings
Towner/Peterson	At Calvary
Townsend	Forgive Me (E)
Track, G/ Burke, H C	To The Lord I Cry
Track, Gerhard	A Star
Track, Gerhard	All Men Seek God
Track, Gerhard	Evening Shadows Gently Fall
Track, Gerhard	Glory To God In The Highest
Track, Gerhard	Let All Mortal Flesh Keep S
Track, Gerhard	Let Us All With Gladsome Vo
Track, Gerhard	Mass In C Minor
Track, Gerhard	Missa Brevis
Track, Gerhard	Missa Brevis (Salzburg Mass
Track, Gerhard	O Come, Let Us Sing To The
Track, Gerhard	O Give Thanks To The Lord
Track, Gerhard	O Lord Most High, With All
Track, Gerhard	Out Of The Depths (A Cap)
Track, Gerhard	Psalm 150: Praise Ye The Lo
Track, Gerhard	Rejoice, O Blessed Creation
Track, Gerhard	Still, Still (Arr)
Track, Gerhard	The Bagpiper's Carol (Arr)
Track, Gerhard	The Icy December (Arr)
Track, Gerhard	There Is A God
Track, Gerhard	This Most Glorious Day
Track, Gerhard	Thy Little Ones Dear Lord A
Track, Gerhard	To You I Lift My Soul
Track, Gerhard	Whence Art Thou My Maiden?
Track, Gerhard	Ye Sons And Daughters
Tracy, Shawn (Rev.)	Blessed Are You
Tracy, Shawn (Rev.)	Come To Me, I've Come To Yo
Tracy, Shawn (Rev.)	Come To The Table Of The Lo
Tracy, Shawn (Rev.)	He Came
Tracy, Shawn (Rev.)	Long Song, The
Tracy, Shawn (Rev.)	Peace I Give To You
Tracy, Shawn (Rev.)	Revelation (I Want You Shou
Tracy, Shawn (Rev.)	We Are The People Of The Lo
Trad.-Gaither/Gaither	Sweeter Than The Day Before
Trad/Tortolano	Amazing Grace (In 19 Rounds
Trad/Tortolano Ed	The Lord Is My Shepherd 2 V
Traditional Byzantine	Trisagion
Traditional English	First Noel, The
Traditional Hebrew	Shalom
Traditional/Decou	Amazing Grace
Traditional/Decou	Angels And Shepherds
Traditional/Decou	Arise, My Soul, Arise!
Traditional/Decou	Christ The Lord Is Risen To
Traditional/Decou	Come, Christians, Join To S
Traditional/Decou	Go Tell It On The Mountain
Traditional/Decou	God Rest You Merry Gentleme
Traditional/Decou	How Firm A Foundation
Traditional/Decou	I Have Decided To Follow Je
Traditional/Decou	I Know That My Redeemer Liv
Traditional/Decou	Immortal, Invisible
Traditional/Decou	O Day Of Rest And Gladness
Traditional/Decou	Resurrection Alleluia
Traditional/Decou	Wondrous Love
Traditional/Engel	O Come, Let Us Sing
Traditional/Johnson	Ain't Dat Good News
Traditional/Johnson	Be Thou My Vision
Traditional/Johnson	Brethren, We Have Met To Wo
Traditional/Johnson	Children Of The Heavenly Fa
Traditional/Johnson	Every Time I Feel The Spiri
Traditional/Johnson	Hail To The Lord's Anointed
Traditional/Johnson	Holy God, We Praise Thy Nam
Traditional/Johnson	In Christ There Is No East
Traditional/Johnson	Lord Is King, The
Traditional/Johnson	No Room In The Inn
Traditional/Johnson	O Come, O Come Immanuel
Traditional/Johnson	Prepare The Way O Zion
Traditional/Johnson	Ride On, King Jesus
Traditional/Johnson	Sing Praise To God!
Traditional/Johnson	Wayfaring Stranger, The
Traditional/Johnson	What Child Is This?
Traditional/Johnson	What Star Is This?
Traditional/Johnson	While By Our Sheep
Traditional/Johnson	Who Is On The Lord's Side?
Traditional/Krogstad	My Country, Tis Of Thee
Traditional/Lundberg	I Sing The Mighty Power Of
Traditional/Mayfield	Here Comes Jesus
Traditional/Mayfield	Kum Ba Yah
Traditional/Mickelson	Alleluia!
Traditional/Mickelson	Amazing Grace
Traditional/Mickelson	He's Got The Whole World In
Traditional/Mickelson	I Will Arise And Go To Jesu
Traditional/Mickelson	Yes I'll Sing The Wondrous
Traditional/Nichols	Praise Ye The Lord, The Alm
Traditional/Peterson	Angels We Have Heard On Hig
Traditional/Peterson	Christ The Lord Is Risen To
Traditional/Peterson	How Firm A Foundation
Traditional/Peterson	When His Salvation Bringing
Traditional/Rasley	Bound For Canaan
Traditional/Rasley	Carol Of The Bagpipers
Traditional/Rasley	Come Ye Faithful, Raise The
Traditional/Rasley	Deep Was The Silence

COMPOSER INDEX

Traditional/Rasley	Fairest Lord Jesus
Traditional/Rasley	Holy Art Thou, O God!
Traditional/Rasley	Just A Closer Walk With The
Traditional/Rasley	Let All Mortal Flesh Keep S
Traditional/Rasley	Merrily On High
Traditional/Rasley	My God, How Wonderful Thou
Traditional/Rasley	My Shepherd Will Supply My
Traditional/Rasley	O How I Love Jesus
Traditional/Rasley	O Thou, In Whose Presence
Traditional/Rasley	Sleep, My Savior, Sleep
Traditional/Rasley	When Love Was Born
Traditional/Shepard	Old-Time Religion, The
Traditional/Shepard	We Praise Thee, O God, Our
Traditional/Wyrtzen	Alleluia!
Traditional/Wyrtzen	I Know Where I'm Going
Traditional/Wyrtzen	I Love Thee
Traditional/Wyrtzen	O Holy Savior
Traditional/Wyrtzen	Praise Him In The Morning
Traditional/Wyrtzen	Rolled Away (Revisited)
Tricamo/Pallardy	My God Is Standing Over Me
Tricamo/Pallardy	What Would I Do
Triplett	O God, Thou Faithful God
Triplett, Robert F.	Two Psalms For High Voice
Trombley, Richard	Blessed Is The Man
Trued	This Is My Commandment
Trued, Clarence	Eternal Trinity
Trued, S. Clarence	Give Ear, O Lord
Trued, S. Clarence	O God Of Love
Trued, S. Clarence	Save Me, O Lord!
Trusler, Ivan	Angel And The Shepherds, Th
Tschaikowsky/Douglas	Sing Praises To God A Cap
Tschaikowsky, P.	Legende
Tschesnokoff-Cain	Cherubim Song (A Cap)
Tschesnokoff-Cain	Nunc Dimittis And Gloria (A
Tschesnokoff, P.	Salvation Is Created
Tucciarone, Angel	Be Aware
Tucciarone, Angel	Celebrate Life
Tucciarone, Angel	From Despair To Hope
Tucciarone, Angel	He Is Here Among Us
Tucciarone, Angel	Hosanna In The Highest
Tucciarone, Angel	I Will Give Thanks
Tucciarone, Angel	If We Saw Him
Tucciarone, Angel	O Lord
Tucciarone, Angel	Peace To All
Tucciarone, Angel	Prayer To Our Father
Tucciarone, Angel	Promise Of Salvation
Tucciarone, Angel	Somethin' Happened Today
Tucciarone, Angel	Unites Us All Together As O
Tucciarone, Angel	When We Eat This Bread
Turner C. Kenneth	Stand Up And Bless The Lord
Turner, Robert	Prophetic Song
Turner, Roy	God Is Moving On
Turner, Roy	Hallelujah, I Want To Sing
Turner, Roy	The Dancing Heart
Turton, William, Alt.	At That First Eucharist
Tweedy/Warrack	Eternal God, Whose Power Up
Twomey/Wise/Weisman	A Family That Prays Togethe
Twynham, R. F.	Alleluia (Icet)
Twynham, R. F.	Antiphons For Holy Week
Twynham, R. F.	Come, Thou Holy Spirit, Com
Twynham, R. F.	It Is Good To Give Thanks
Twynham, R. F.	O Come, Good Spirit
Twynham, R. F.	See Your People (Ministry)
Ty, C	He Fed Them With Most Preci
Tyacke Louis	Dear God In Heaven
Tye, Christopher	Christ Rising Again (M)
Tye, Christopher	Deliver Us, Good Lord (Me)
Tye, Christopher	Evening Service; Magnificat
Tye, Christopher	Give Alms Of Thy Goods (Me)
Tye, Christopher	I Will Exalt Thee & Sing Un
Tye, Christopher	O God Be Merciful
Tye, Christopher	Praise Ye The Lord, Ye Chil
Tyler, Don	Come, Thou Long Expected Je
Udulutsch, Irvin	Memorial Acclamation 1
Ufford/Mickelson	Throw Out The Lifeline
Ugartechea, Michael	God Is Love
Ugartechea, Michael	Hosanna
Ugartechea, Ruth	God Don't Care Who You Are
Uhl, Pat	Song Of Daniel
Uhl,Pat&Gilligan,M.	Canticle Of The Gift(Versio
Uhl,Pat&Gilligan,M.	Canticle Of The Gift(Versio
Uhl,Pat&Gilligan,M.	Canticle Of The Three Young
Uhl,Pat&Gilligan,M.	Canticle Of The Three Young
Ulrich, Lorraine	God Reveals Himself To Me
Ultan, Lloyd	Alleluia
Urquhart, Dan	Psalm 149
Vaet, Jacobus	Six Motets
Vail	I Will Magnify Thee
Vail	King All-Glorious
Vail	Lord Is Risen Today, The
Vail/Mickelson	Close To Thee
Van	I Wonder As I Wander
Van Camp, L.	Rounds For Church And Sunda
Van Der Puy/Ferrin	I'll Trust And Never Be Afr
Van Dyke, Paul C.	Away In A Manger
Van Dyke, Paul C.	Dost Thou In A Manger Lie?
Van Dyke, Paul C.	God Of All Grace
Van Dyke, Paul C.	I Saw Three Ships
Van Dyke, Paul C.	Prayer For God's Blessing
Van Dyke, Paul C.	Sing, This Blessed Morn.
Van Horn	Newborn Baby
Van Horn/Decou	God's Word Shall Stand
Van Iderstine, A. P.	Garden Hymn (A Cap)
Van Iderstine, A. P.	Wondrous Love (A Cap)
Van Koert, Han	Sing To The Lord (4-Part Ar
Van Woert	Resurrection Morn
Vandall/Decou	My Sins Are Gone
Vanderhoek, Bert	Love Divine (Me)
Vanderhoek, Bert	My God, And Is Thy Table Sp
Vanderslice, Ellen	If My People
Vandre	Hymns For Brass Quartet
Vanhorn, Charles	All-Time Favorites For The
Vanhorn, Charles	All-Time Favorites For The
Vanhorn, Charles	All-Time Favorites For The
Vann, Stanley	Behold How Good And Joyful
Vaughan, Rodger	Psalm 100 (M)
Vdorak/Hughes	Come To Me
Verdi, Giuseppe	Laudate Alla Virgine (Femal
Verdi, Giuseppe	Pater Noster
Verdi, Giuseppe	Prayer Canon From Aroldo
Verdi, Giuseppe	Requiem
Verdi, Giuseppe	Stabat Mater 1
Verdi, Giuseppe	Te Deum
Verdi, Ralph C.	God's Place
Verdi, Ralph C.	Psalm 121: Let Us Go To God
Verdi, Ralph C.	Wedding Song
Verdi, Ralph C. (Rev.)	Psalm 100
Verdonck, C. Ed Herter	Ave Maria (Lat) A Cap
Vermulst, Jan	Glory To God (People's Mass
Vermulst, Jan	Holy, Holy, Holy (Icet)
Vermulst, Jan	Lamb Of God (Icet)
Vermulst, Jan	Lord Have Mercy (Icet)
Vermulst, Jan	Peoples Mass (Icet)
Vermulst, Jan	Psalm 150 (Alleluia)
Vermulst, Jan	We Come To You With Longing
Vernon, Knight	Swords Into Plowshares
Vernon, Sr. M	Hymn Of Praise
Verrall, John Ed	Carols And Songs For Christ
Verrees, Leon	I Do Not Ask, O Lord
Viadana, L	Exsultate Justi
Viadana, L. (D1627)	Missa Sine Nomine
Viadana, Lodovico	Hail, O Hail True Body
Vibbert-Eastman/Estman	All Things Work Together Fo
Vick	All That's Good And Great A
Vick	Jesus Shall Reign
Vick	Jesus, Thy Boundless Love T
Vick	O Blessed Day Of Motherhood
Vick, B.	Tell The Blessed Tidings
Vick, Beryl Jr	My God, Accept My Heart
Vick, Beryl Jr	O God, Whose Presence Glows
Vick, Beryl Jr. (Arr)	Beautiful Savior (Jr Choir
Vickers, Wendy	Come To My Table
Vickers, Wendy	Get On Board
Vickers, Wendy	Glory To God
Vickers, Wendy	Go In Peace
Vickers, Wendy	High Time
Vickers, Wendy	Holy, Holy
Vickers, Wendy	Keep The Faith On Movin'
Vickers, Wendy	Let Me Do It With Love
Vickers, Wendy	Lord Gave Me A Song To Sing
Vickers, Wendy	Sow A Seed
Vickers, Wendy (Arr.)	Were You There?
Victoria/Krone	Ave Maria
Victoria, Tomas Luis	Agnus Dei
Victoria, Tomas Luis	Hail, Virgin Mary
Victoria, Tomas Luis	Jesu Dulcis Memoria
Victoria, Tomas Luis	O Crux Ave
Victoria, Tomas Luis	O Hail Sacred Cross
Victoria, Tomas Luis	Victimae Paschali Laudes
Vidal, Paul	Chanson Des Anges
Viger, Cathy	God Did!
Villa-Lobos, Hector	Filhas De Maria
Vincent, Chas.	There Were Shepherds
Vissing, Sr. Rosalie	Abba, Father
Vissing, Sr. Rosalie	Come Lord Jesus
Vissing, Sr. Rosalie	His Praise Is Higher Than T
Vissing, Sr. Rosalie	Jesus Is Lord
Vissing, Sr. Rosalie	My Heart Stands Ready
Vissing, Sr. Rosalie	O Living Water
Vissing, Sr. Rosalie	Remain In Me
Vissing, Sr. Rosalie	Thanksgiving Song
Vittoria-Sateren, L.	Of The Glorious Body Tellin
Vittoria, Ludovico De	Missa Pro Defunctis
Vittoria, Ludovico De	Missa Simile Est Regnum
Vittoria, Ludovico De	O Quam Gloriosum Est Regnum
Vittoria, T L	Ave Maria
Vittoria, T L	Ecce Sacerdos Magnus
Vittoria, T L	Gaudent In Coelis
Vittoria, T L	Tantum Ergo
Vittoria, T L Da	Verbum Caro In A Minor
Vittoria, T L Da	Verbum Caro In G
Vittoria, T. L. Da	Domine Non Sum Dignus (E &
Vittoria, T.L./Klein	Is It Nothing (O Vos Omnes)
Vittoria, Tomas L. De	Darkness Was Over All
Vivaldi	Come, Thou Spirit Everlasti
Vivaldi, A.	Credo
Vivaldi, A.	Gloria
Vivaldi, A.	Magnificat
Vivaldi, A. Arr Ehret	Crucifixus
Vivaldi, Antonio	Gloria In Excelsis
Von Kreisler, Alex	Psalm 117 (Opt Brass Quarte
Von Kreisler, Alex	Whither Shall I Go
Voss, Herman	Herman Voss Presents Organ
Voss, Herman	Herman Voss Presents Organ
Vulpius, Melchior	Praise Ye The Lord
Wade/Peterson	O Come, All Ye Faithful
Wade, John F.	O Come, All Ye Faithful (4
Wade, Walter	A Christmas Fantasy
Wade, Walter	Eye Hath Not Seen (A Cap)
Wade, Walter	Four American Folk Hymns
Wade, Walter	Three Anthems Of Praise
Wade, Walter	What Wondrous Love
Wadely, F. W.	That God Doth Love The Worl
Wagner, Lavern J.	A Mass For All Occasions
Wagner, Lavern J.	A Mass For Lent
Wagner, Lavern J.	Gentle Hands
Wagner, Lavern J.	Glory To Jesus
Wagner, Lavern J.	Now You Will Feel No Rain
Wagner, Lavern J.	Praise God
Wagner, Lavern J.	Praise The Lord Who Lives A
Wagner, Lavern J.	Prayer Of St. Francis
Wagner, Lavern J.	Rejoice, O Church, Exalt In
Wagner, Lavern J.	The Beatitudes
Wagner, Lavern J.	We Say Thank You, Lord
Wagner, Lavern J.	Without Love
Wagner, R.	All Praise To God, In Light
Wagner, R. (Arr Mayer)	Enter With The Blest (Tannh
Walker, Jack	Wise Men From The East (Gui
Walker, Mary Lou	Butterfly Song
Walker, Mary Lou	Put On Love
Walker, Mary Lou	Wind Song
Wallace, George	Grant Us Thy Spirit
Wallace, George	In A World That Needs Thy L
Walter	Child Of Bethlehem, The
Walter	Christ The Lord Is Born
Walter	Good Tidings Of Joy
Walter	Jerusalem, My Happy Home
Walter	Nine Compositions For Organ
Walter	O Thou In All Thy Might So
Walter	Six Hymn-Tune Preludes
Walter	Thou Hidden Love Of God
Walter	Transcriptions For Organ
Walter, Samuel	Blessed Are The Pure In Hea
Walter, Samuel	Christ Is The World's True
Walter, Samuel	Hearts To Heaven And Voices
Walter, Samuel	Holy, Holy, Holy
Walter, Samuel	How Firm A Foundation
Walter, Samuel	Lord Reigneth, The
Walter, Samuel	Lord, Have Mercy Upon Us
Walter, Samuel	O Lamb Of God
Walter, Samuel	O Most Loving Father (Unacc
Walter, Samuel	Peace Be Unto You
Walter, Samuel	There's A Light Upon The Mo
Walther, J	Come Holy Ghost
Walton, William	A Litany (M)
Walton, William	Belshazzar's Feast (Oratori
Walton, William	Coronation Te Deum
Walton, William	Gloria
Walton, William	Jubilate Deo (Md)
Walton, William	Missa Brevis (Md)
Walton, William	O Let Me Tread In The Right
Walton, William	Set Me As A Seal Upon Thine
Walton, William	The Twelve (For Apostles)
Walton, William	Where Does The Uttered Musi
Walworth, Clarence	Holy God
Wapen, Francis A	Come, Let Us Bow Down
Ward	O For A Thousand Tongues
Ward/Decou	America The Beautiful
Ward/Johnson	America The Beautiful
Warkentin	Sleep Celestial Infant (Mex
Warland	Be Joyful, O Earth
Warland, Dale	Thee We Adore (A Cap)
Warner	Psalm 98
Warner/Gotrich	Higher Road, The
Warner, Richard	Soldiers Of Christ, Arise!
Warren/Johnson	God Of Our Fathers
Warren, George	God Of Our Fathers (4-Part
Warren, William	Prepare Ye The Way
Warren, William	The Glory Of The Lord (Md)
Wasner	The Babe
Wasner, Franz	Children's Blessing
Wasner, Franz	The Christmas Nightingale
Wasner, Franz	When Jesus In The Garden
Waterman	Creation, The
Waterman	David (Unison)
Waterman, Frances	He Has Made A Special Place
Waters, James	Psalm 31
Watson, M.	Praise The Lord, O My Soul
Watts, Isaac	Joy To The World
Watts, Isaac	O God Our Help
Watts, Isaac	When My Weak Eyes Can See T
Wayne, Millie	My Guiding Star
Weaver	One Star
Webbe/Decou	Come, Ye Disconsolate
Webber/Rice	Hosanna
Webber/Rice	I Don't Know How To Love Hi
Webber, Lloyd	O Thou That Art The Light E
Weber/Elbert	You Gave Us Lord Your Sacre
Weber, Dennis	Christ The Lord Is Risen To
Weber, R/Bradbury, W.	Thanks Be To Christ (Your B

COMPOSER INDEX

Weber, R/Sibelius, J.	Waters Of Love (God's Power
Weber, Richard F	Agnus Dei (Missa Brevis)
Wedish/Decou	O Mighty God, When I Behold
Weeden/Decou	Sunlight
Weelkes, Thomas	All People Clap Your Hands
Weelkes, Thomas	Alleluia, I Heard A Voice
Weelkes, Thomas	Gloria In Excelsis (Md)
Weelkes, Thomas	Hosanna To The Son Of David
Weelkes, Thomas	Lord To Thee I Make My Moan
Weelkes, Thomas	Magnificat And Nunc Dimitti
Weelkes, Thomas	O How Amiable (Ps 84)
Wehr, David A.	Anthems For Special Occasio
Wehr, David A.	Dear Jesus Boy
Wehr, David A.	I Want Jesus To Walk With M
Wehr, David A.	Nearer, My God, To Thee
Wehr, David A.	Put Forth, O God, Thy Spiri
Wehr, David A.	Thy Kingdom Come, O Lord
Wehr, David A.	We Thank You
Weinandt	Ancient Of Days
Weisberg/Sommers	Pickin' The Sun Down
Welch, James	O My Saints
Welch, James	Well Done, Good And Faithfu
Welch, Phil	Sweet Sweet Sound
Welch, Ray	Be Still, My Soul, And List
Weldon, J (Coggin)	O How Great Is The Lord Of
Weller (Ed)	We Sing To God (In 3 Volume
Wellesz, Egon	In Resurrectione Domini
Wells	With My Hand In Thine
Wells-Williamson	Joyous Carol (Divided Parts
Wells, Dana	Four Modern Anthems
Wells, Dana F.	Anthem For Springtime
Wells, Dana F.	Let Us Now Praise Famous Me
Wells, Dana F.	Three Sacred Solos For Medi
Wells, Tony	It's A Gift To Be Simple
Welz, Joey	By The Grace Of God
Welz, Joey	Touch Them With Love
Welz, Joey-Wray, Link	Goin' Home
Welz, Joey-Wray, Link	Jesus, Be My Friend
Welz, Joey-Wray, Link	Listen To The Voices, That
Wendy Fremin	Be Ye Still
Wennerberg/Douglas	Let Us Now Our Voices Raise
Wescott	Gift Of Light
Wesley/Rasley	Church's One Foundation, Th
Wesley, C. (Stone)	Brightest And Best
Wesley, S. S.	Lead Me, Lord
West, J. E.	O, How Amiable
West, J. E.	The Lord Is Exalted
West, J. E.	The Woods And Every Sweet-S
Westbrook, Francis B.	Swing Low, Sweet Chariot
Westendorf	Sing To Mary, Mother Most M
Westendorf/Hern	These Forty Days Of Lent
Westendorf/Parker	Psalm 96 (95)
Westendorf/Picca	Members Of One Mystic Body
Westendorf/Picca	Psalm 127 (126)
Westendorf/Picca	Psalm 42 (41)
Westendorf/Picca	Psalm 45(44)
Westendorf/Takass	Psalm 136 (135)
Westendorf/Takass	Psalm 51 (50)
Westendorf/Takass	Psalm 63 (62)
Westendorf/Vermulst	Psalm 150 (W/Triple Allelui
Westendorf/Vermulst	Psalm 84 (83)
Westendorf, Omer	All Men On Earth
Westendorf, Omer	Francis, Friend Of All Thin
Westendorf, Omer	God's Blessing Sends Us For
Westendorf, Omer	God's Holy Mountain We Asce
Westendorf, Omer	Great Shepherd Of A Loyal F
Westendorf, Omer	Hail Blessed Lady
Westendorf, Omer	Hail Christ, Our Royal Prie
Westendorf, Omer	Hail Maiden Mary
Westendorf, Omer	Lord We Gather At Your Alta
Westendorf, Omer	Now Joined By God
Westendorf, Omer	O God All Knowing & All Jus
Westendorf, Omer	O Lord You Know Our Weaknes
Westendorf, Omer	Psalm 128 (127)
Westendorf, Omer	Psalm 23 (22)
Westendorf, Omer	Psalm 4
Westendorf, Omer	Sent Forth By God's Blessin
Westendorf, Omer	Shepherd Of Souls In Love C
Westendorf, Omer	St. Joseph Was A Just Man
Westendorf, Omer	This Day God Made
Westendorf, Omer	We Gather Together
Westendorf, Omer	Where Charity And Love Prev
Wetherill	Blessed Are They
Wetherill	Carol Of The Trees
Wetherill	I Will Lift Up Mine Eyes
Wetherill	Prayer Of Humble Access, A
Wetzler, Robert	A Son Is Born Of Mary
Wetzler, Robert	Ah, Dearest Jesu, Holy Chil
Wetzler, Robert	All Poor Men And Humble
Wetzler, Robert	Bless Us, God Of Loving (So
Wetzler, Robert	Christmas Down
Wetzler, Robert	Come Take My Yoke
Wetzler, Robert	Crown Him Lord Of All
Wetzler, Robert	Doxology (Hurrah To God)
Wetzler, Robert	Easter Dawning
Wetzler, Robert	Go Ye Into All The World
Wetzler, Robert	God, Hurrah (Mezzo Sop/Eng
Wetzler, Robert	Good Tidings
Wetzler, Robert	Hail Thee, Spirit, Lord Ete
Wetzler, Robert	Hark A Thrilling Voice Is S
Wetzler, Robert	He Is Born
Wetzler, Robert	Introits (For Various Seaso
Wetzler, Robert	Look Ye Saints, The Sight I
Wetzler, Robert	Lord, Make Me An Instrument
Lord, Remember Us	Wetzler, Rob
Wetzler, Robert	Lord, Surround Us With Holy
Wetzler, Robert	Lord, We Are Glad For Those
Wetzler, Robert	Lord, We Praise You For The
Wetzler, Robert	Love Came Down At Christmas
Wetzler, Robert	Mary (Optional Instruments)
Wetzler, Robert	Meditation On Woodworth
Wetzler, Robert	O Jesus, King Most Wonderfu
Wetzler, Robert	On Calvary's Hill
Wetzler, Robert	Onward Ye Saints
Wetzler, Robert	Psalm 128
Wetzler, Robert	Shepherds Come A-Running
Wetzler, Robert	Still, Still, Still
Wetzler, Robert	The Snow Lay On The Ground
Wetzler, Robert	This Little Babe (W/Guitar)
Wetzler, Robert	Thy Little Ones, Dear Lord,
Wetzler, Robert	Trilogy Of Praise
Wetzler, Robert	Two Lenten Meditations
Wetzler, Robert	What Shall I Render
Wetzler, Robert	Winds Thru The Olive Trees
Whettam, Graham	Then Spake Solomon
Whikehart, Lewis E.	The Love Of God
White	I Got My Religion In Time
White	Omnes Gentes, Plaudite
White	Power
White	Triumph
White	Two Junior Choir Anthems
White/Johnson	His Love Is Wonderful To Me
White/Rasley	Jesus, Wonderful Lord
White/Watkins	Morning Trumpet, The
White/Wood	Morning Trumpet
White, Edward L	Glory To God In The Highest
White, Jack Noble	Our Father In Heaven
White, Jack Noble	We're Goin' On A Picnic
White, L. J.	A Prayer Of St. Richard Of
White, L. J.	Communion Service
White, Louie	Jubilate Deo
White, Matthew	O Praise God In His Holines
White, Michael	Goin' Home On A Cloud
White, Michael	Oh, Little Child Of Bethleh
White, Michael	Sleep, Little Lord
White, Michael	The Magic Morning
White, Michael	The Silver Bells
White, Richard	Three Psalms
White, Robert	Christe, Qui Lux Es Et Dies
White, Robert	O Praise God In His Holines
White, Robert (1574)	Lamentations For 5 & 6 Voic
White, Robert (1574)	Magnificat
Whitecotton	Call, The
Whitehead, Alfred	When Morning Gilds The Sky
Whitemore, Joan M.	I Will Live To Sing Your Pr
Whitemore, Joan M.	Shout Joyfully To God
Whitemore, Joan M.	You Are With Me
Whitford/Decou	On A Rugged Hill
Whitlock, Percy	Jesu, Grant Me This I Pray
Whitlock, Percy	Sing Praise To God Who Reig
Whitlock, Percy	Three Introits
Whitney	Twelve Responses And Senten
Whitol/Peterson	My God And I
Whittier/Englert, E.	O Brother Man
Wiant, Bliss	Great Commission, The
Wichmann, Russell	Bell Carol (Jr + Sr Choirs)
Wickens, Dennis	Jubilate Deo (Md)
Wickens, Dennis	O Vos Omnes (Lam 1, V. 12)
Wickham, J & Angle, D	You're Caught In A World
Wickham, J M	The Days Of Noah
Wihtol, A. A.	Come And Gather, Little Chi
Wihtol, A. A.	Halleluyah, Christ Is Risen
Wihtol, A. A.	Night So Dark And Hour So L
Wilbye, John(Ed Brown)	Homo Natus De Muliere
Wiley	Glad Tidings Of Great Joy
Wiley	Praise The Lord With Gladne
Wiley (Arr)	Sing To The Lord (A Cap)
Wilhelm	Allelu! Rejoice And Sing!
Wilhelm	Bethlehem Star, The
Wilhelm	God Gave Him Life Again!
Wilhelm, Patricia	Peace I Leave With You
Wilhousky (Arr)	Carol-Noel (A Capella)
Wilkes, Jon	By Their Fruits Ye Shall Kn
Wilkes, R. W.	Incline Your Ear
Wilkes, T. & Stevenson	What Color Is God's Skin?
Wilkey, Terrence	Handful Of Clay
Wilkey, Terrence	I Thank You, Lord
Wilkey, Terrence	Word Of Light
Willan	O Sing Unto The Lord A New
Willan, Healey	Blessed Art Thou, O Lord (M
Willan, Healey	Communion Service
Willan, Healey	Great Is The Lord (Md)
Willan, Healey	Liturgical Motets
Willan, Healey	Magnificat And Nunc Dimitti
Willan, Healey	O Be Joyful In The Lord (Ps
Willan, Healey	Ten Faux Bourdons On Well-K
Willan, Healey	The Three Kings
Willan, Healey	What Is This Lovely Fragran
Williams	Alleluia
Williams	Christ The Lord Is Risen Ag
Williams	Great Is The Mystery
Williams	Have You Any Room For Jesus
Williams	I Am The Resurrection And T
Williams	Love Must Rule In Man's Hea
Williams	O Taste And See
Williams	Ring, Ye Bells
Williams	Shout The Glad Tidings
Williams/Decou	Come, We That Love The Lord
Williams/Johnson	At The Name Of Jesus
Williams/Johnson	Christ Is Risen
Williams/Peterson	I Love Thy Kingdom, Lord
Williams, C. L.	Thou Wilt Keep Him In Perfe
Williams, Charles	Change It
Williams, David	Hallowed And Gracious Is Th
Williams, David	I Know Not Where The Road M
Williams, David	O For A Thousand Tongues To
Williams, David	Shepherds Went Their Hasty
Williams, David H.	Who Passes Yonder Through T
Williams, G.	What A Friend We Have In Je
Williams, Grace	Ave Maris Stella
Williams, J.	Children Gather Round
Williams, J.	Hell
Williams, J.	Holy Spirit
Williams, J.	I Am
Williams, J.	People Everywhere Are Gathe
Williams, J.	The Judgement Day
Williams, J.	The Mark Of Time
Williams, J.	The Morning Sun
Williams, Ralph V.	Crown Him The King Of Kings
Williams, Vaughan	For All The Saints
Williams, Vaughan R.	A Choral Flourish (From Ps
Williams, Vaughan R.	A Song Of Thanksgiving
Williams, Vaughan R.	All Hail The Power (Tune "M
Williams, Vaughan R.	At The Name Of Jesus
Williams, Vaughan R.	Benedicite (Eng)
Williams, Vaughan R.	Communion Service In D Mino
Williams, Vaughan R.	Dona Nobis Pacem
Williams, Vaughan R.	Fantasia On The Old 104th P
Williams, Vaughan R.	Festival Te Deum (On Trad.
Williams, Vaughan R. N	For All The Saints
Williams, Vaughan R.	For All The Saints (M)
Williams, Vaughan R.	He That Is Down Need Fear N
Williams, Vaughan R.	Magnificat
Williams, Vaughan R.	Morning Service In D Minor
Williams, Vaughan R.	My Soul, Praise The Lord (M
Williams, Vaughan R.	O How Amiable (Me)
Williams, Vaughan R.	O Taste And See (Ps 34)
Williams, Vaughan R.	Pilgrim's Journey (Cantata)
Williams, Vaughan R.	Te Deum And Benedictus
Williams, Vaughan R.	Te Deum In G (Md)
Williams, Vaughan R.	The Old Hundredth Psalm Tun
Williams, Vaughan R.	The Souls Of The Righteous
Williams, Vaughan R.	The Twenty-Third Psalm
Williams, Vaughan R.,	Valiant-For-Truth (Md)
Williams, Vaughan R.	Vision Of Aeroplanes (Ezek
Williams, Willie Jr.	Don't Cry
Williamson, Malcolm	Come, Ye Thankful People, C
Williamson, Malcolm	Easter Carol
Williamson, Malcolm	Mass Of Saint Andrew
Williamson, Malcolm	Procession Of Palms
Williamson, Malcolm	Six Christmas Songs
Williamson, Malcolm	Six Evening Hymns
Williamson, Malcolm	Sonnet (On Hearing The Dies
Williamson, Malcolm	The Morning Of The Day Of D
Willis	Unto Thee, O Lord
Wills, Arthur	Evening Service
Wills, Arthur	Give Us Faith For Today
Wills, Arthur	Let God Arise
Wills, Arthur	Popular Psalm Settings
Wilson	All Glory, Laud, And Honor
Wilson	All Hail The Power Of Jesus
Wilson	All Shall Be Well
Wilson	Are Ye Able-Said The Master
Wilson	At Calvery
Wilson	Battle Hymn Of The Republic
Wilson	Bells On Christmas Day, The
Wilson	Beneath The Cross Of Jesus
Wilson	Birth (From He Lived The G
Wilson	Blessed Assurance, Jesus Is
Wilson	Blessed Redeemer
Wilson	Carol Ye
Wilson	Child Of Heaven
Wilson	Choral Service For Thanksgi
Wilson	Choral Service For Watch Ni
Wilson	Christ Is Born!
Wilson	Christ The Lord Is Risen To
Wilson	Crusade
Wilson	Crusader's Hymn
Wilson	Desert Shall Rejoice, The
Wilson	Did Jesus Weep For Me?
Wilson	Does Jesus Care?
Wilson	Festival Of Christmas
Wilson	Festival Of Lessons And Car
Wilson	Follow Me
Wilson	God Of Our Fathers
Wilson	Hallelujah! What A Savior!
Wilson	He Leadeth Me
Wilson	He Shall Feed His Flock
Wilson	His Love Is All Around
Wilson	I Will Sing

Composer	Title	Composer	Title	Composer	Title
Wilson	If The Christ Should Come T	Winter, Miriam T.	He Comes	Wise, Joe	Sing Praise To The Lord
Wilson	Immortal, Invisible	Winter, Miriam T.	Hear My Call	Wise, Joe	Song For Martin (Moses)
Wilson	Jacob's Ladder	Winter, Miriam T.	Help My Unbelief	Wise, Joe	Song Of Blessing
Wilson	Jesus Calls Us	Winter, Miriam T.	Holy, Holy, Holy (1964 Text	Wise, Joe	Song Of The Wounded
Wilson	Jesus, Lover Of My Soul	Winter, Miriam T.	How I Have Longed	Wise, Joe	Take Our Bread
Wilson	Just For You	Winter, Miriam T.	Howl My Soul	Wise, Joe	The Lord Said To Me (Ccd)
Wilson	King Of Love, The	Winter, Miriam T.	I Built A Garden	Wise, Joe	This Is My Gift
Wilson	Last Trip To Jerusalem	Winter, Miriam T.	I Know The Secret	Wise, Joe	Time To Die
Wilson	Lead Me, Savior	Winter, Miriam T.	In The Beginning	Wise, Joe	To Be Your Body
Wilson	Let Earth Receive Her King	Winter, Miriam T.	It's A Long Road To Freedom	Wise, Joe	Until
Wilson	Lonesome Valley	Winter, Miriam T.	John	Wise, Joe	Visit, The
Wilson	Lord Is My Shepherd, The	Winter, Miriam T.	Joy Is Like The Rain	Wise, Joe	Watch With Me
Wilson	Mighty Fortress, A	Winter, Miriam T.	Knock, Knock	Wise, Joe	We All Stand At Your Table
Wilson	More Holiness Give Me	Winter, Miriam T.	Lamb Of God (1964 Text)	Wise, Joe	We Are Your Bread
Wilson	My Lord, What A Morning	Winter, Miriam T.	Let There Be Peace	Wise, Joe	We Will Hear Your Word
Wilson	My Shepherd Will Supply My	Winter, Miriam T.	Lift Up Your Hearts	Wise, Joe	Welcome In
Wilson	Nativity, The	Winter, Miriam T.	Lord Have Mercy (1964 Text)	Wise, Joe	When We Eat This Bread
Wilson	O Brother Man	Winter, Miriam T.	Love Your Brother	Wise, Joe	Yes To You, My Lord
Wilson	O God, Thy Hands The Heaven	Winter, Miriam T.	Loved By The Lord	Wise, Joe	Yes To You, My Lord
Wilson	O Sleep, My Fairest One	Winter, Miriam T.	Night	Wise, Joe	You Are The Way
Wilson	Praise To The Lord, The Alm	Winter, Miriam T.	No Longer Alone	Wise, Joe	You Fill The Day
Wilson	Rejoice, The Lord Is King	Winter, Miriam T.	O What A Happening	Wise, Joe	Yours Is Princely Power K
Wilson	Sing We Now Of Christmas	Winter, Miriam T.	Our Father	Wise, Judah L.	God Of The World
Wilson	Somebody's Knocking At Your	Winter, Miriam T.	Our Father	Wise, Judah L.	Hallelujah (Psalm 150)
Wilson	Song Of The Holy Night	Winter, Miriam T.	Peace Upon Earth	Wise, Judah L.	Our God Is King (Notre Diev
Wilson	Spirit Of The Lord, The	Winter, Miriam T.	Peter	Wise, Judah L.	Peace Be Unto You
Wilson	Sweet Music	Winter, Miriam T.	Pilgrim Song	Wise, Michael	Magnificat And Nunc Dimitti
Wilson	Take Up Thy Cross	Winter, Miriam T.	Praise God	Withrow	Twelve Hymn Accompaniments
Wilson	Teach Me Thy Way	Winter, Miriam T.	Praise The Lord	Withrow	Variations On Mit Freuden Z
Wilson	The Resurrection (W/Insts)	Winter, Miriam T.	Runnin'	Witt, Christian F.	Give The King Your Final Ju
Wilson	Though Your Sins Be As Scar	Winter, Miriam T.	Seek First The Kingdom	Wittig, Evan	Happy The Man (Ps 1) W/Guit
Wilson	To God All Praise And Glory	Winter, Miriam T.	Seven Times	Wojcik, Richard J.	All Our Hope Of Salvation
Wilson	Upper Room, The	Winter, Miriam T.	Shout The Good News	Wojcik, Richard J.	Christ Has Died
Wilson	Westminster Carol	Winter, Miriam T.	Silent The Night	Wojcik, Richard J.	Ecumenical Hymn To God Our
Wilson	What Child Is This?	Winter, Miriam T.	Sing Of Birth	Wojcik, Richard J.	Father Almighty (4–Part Arr
Wilson	Why Should He Love Me So?	Winter, Miriam T.	So Full Of Song	Wojcik, Richard J.	God Of Our Fathers
Wilson	Within The Silence	Winter, Miriam T.	Song For The Sun	Wojcik, Richard J.	God Of Our Fathers (4–Part
Wilson (Arr)	All Is Well	Winter, Miriam T.	Song Of Glory	Wojcik, Richard J.	Grant Us Peace (4–Part Arr)
Wilson (Arr)	Norwegian Christmas Carol,	Winter, Miriam T.	Song Of Loveliness	Wojcik, Richard J.	I Lift My Soul (4–Part Arr)
Wilson, Al	John Mckay Sings Al Wilson	Winter, Miriam T.	Speak To Me, Wind	Wojcik, Richard J.	In Christ The Prince Of Pea
Wilson, I	Alone In The Garden	Winter, Miriam T.	Spirit Of God	Wojcik, Richard J.	In Heaven Give Glory
Wilson, I	And There Were Shepherds	Winter, Miriam T.	Spirit Of The Lord	Wojcik, Richard J.	My God Is A Rock
Wilson, I	Christmas Song Of Songs The	Winter, Miriam T.	Take Courage	Wojtowicz, Elaine	Joy, Joy, Joy
Wilson, I	Mother's Prayer, A	Winter, Miriam T.	Ten Lepers	Wolf	Blessed Assurance
Wilson, I	Music Of Christmas, The	Winter, Miriam T.	Thank You For Today	Wolf, Hugo	Christmas Night
Wilson, I	Night Of Holy Memories	Winter, Miriam T.	Thank You, Jesus	Wolf, S.D.	Adeste Fideles (W/Tpts,Org,
Wilson, I	O Night Of Holy Memory	Winter, Miriam T.	The Sower	Wolfe, Jacques	British Children's Prayer
Wilson, I	Thou Art The Living Christ	Winter, Miriam T.	The Visit	Wolff, S. Drummond	Christians, Sing Out With E
Wilson, I	Yuletide Memories	Winter, Miriam T.	The Wedding Banquet (I Cann	Wolff, S. Drummond	Rejoice, The Lord Is King
Wilson, James R.	Give Unto The Lord	Winter, Miriam T.	Three Tents "One For Moses"	Wood	A Hymn Of Youth
Wilson, James R.	How Excellent Is Thy Name	Winter, Miriam T.	Wonderful	Wood	Austrian Shepherd's Carol
Wilson, James R.	Lord Hear My Voice	Winter, Miriam T.	Yet I Believe	Wood	Come Gracious Spirit
Wilson, Janet	No Help	Winter, Miriam T.	Zaccheus (There Was A Man)	Wood	I Am So Glad Each Christmas
Wilson, R C	Forty Days To Easter	Wise, Joe	A New Commandment	Wood	I Am The Good Shepherd
Wilson, Roger C	A Christmas Concert	Wise, Joe	All I Am, I Give To You	Wood	Jubilate Deo (Ps 100 W/Inst
Wilson, Roger C	Close To Thee	Wise, Joe	Alleluia	Wood	O Fear The Lord, Ye His Sai
Wilson, Roger C	I Met My Master	Wise, Joe	Amen	Wood	Song Of Peace, A
Wilson, Roger C	Shepherd Of Souls	Wise, Joe	And Then It Dawns On Me	Wood	That Easter Day With Joy Wa
Wilson, Roger C.	Amen	Wise, Joe	Be A New Man	Wood	The Glory Of Our King
Wilson, Roger C.	Hark, The Glad Sound	Wise, Joe	Be Consoled, I Am Near	Wood	Traveler, The
Wilson, Roger C.	The Lord Is My Shepherd	Wise, Joe	Blessed Are Those	Wood, Abraham	Brevity
Wilt, Roberta	Don't Let Them Have Their W	Wise, Joe	Bread You Have Given Us	Wood, Abraham	Walpole (From Two Plain–Tun
Wilt, Roberta	Don't Wait	Wise, Joe	Christ Has Died (Icet) Asca	Wood, Charles	Summer Ended
Winberry, M/Roff, J	How Lovely Are Your Works	Wise, Joe	Close Your Eyes	Wood, Dale	Arise My Soul, Arise!
Winberry, Mary	Christ Is The Spring	Wise, Joe	Come To Me	Wood, Dale	Lamb, The
Winberry, Mary	Sing Alleluia	Wise, Joe	Die With Us	Wood, Dale	Slumber, O Holy Jesu
Winberry, Mary	Sing Out, My Soul	Wise, Joe	Doxology––Amen	Wood, Dale	Slumber, O Holy Jesu (Chris
Winberry, Mary & Malat	Our Time Is Now	Wise, Joe	Dying You Destroyed Our Dea	Wood, Mike	Acclamation
Winberry, Mary & Malat	Pentecost Day	Wise, Joe	Eye Hasn't Seen	Wood, Mike	Alleluia
Winberry, Mary & Malat	Pilgrimage	Wise, Joe	Fill It With Sunshine	Wood, Mike	Amy's Song
Winberry,Mary & Malate	How Wonderful And Great	Wise, Joe	For Tommy: Thanɴs For The C	Wood, Mike	Because We Are One
Winberry,Mary & Malate	Know That I Am God	Wise, Joe	Gentle Love Song, A	Wood, Mike	Celebration (Timmy's Song)
Winberry,Mary & Malate	Litany Of The Spirit	Wise, Joe	Glory	Wood, Mike	Glory
Winkworth, Catherine	Now Thank We All Our God	Wise, Joe	Go Now In Peace	Wood, Mike	God Gives Freely
Winston, Colleen, Osb	He Came	Wise, Joe	God Is My Life	Wood, Mike	I Am My Brother's Brother
Winston, Colleen, Osb	Song Of Tears And Triumph	Wise, Joe	Gonna Sing My Lord	Wood, Mike	Lamb Of God
Winter, John	Magnificat And Nunc Dimitti	Wise, Joe	Here Is My Life	Wood, Mike	Love Is Like A Circle
Winter, Miriam T.	A Virgin	Wise, Joe	Holy, Holy I	Wood, Mike	On The Road
Winter, Miriam T.	Ballad Of The Prodigal Son	Wise, Joe	Holy, Holy, Holy	Wood, Mike	Pilgrim's Road
Winter, Miriam T.	Ballad Of The Seasons	Wise, Joe	I Believe In You	Wood, Mike	Pilgrim's Song
Winter, Miriam T.	Ballad Of The Women	Wise, Joe	I Went To Cincinnati	Wood, Mike	Praise And Honor
Winter, Miriam T.	Beatitudes	Wise, Joe	I'll Be There	Wood, Mike	The Earth Is Filled
Winter, Miriam T.	Child Of Morning	Wise, Joe	Jesus You Are Here	Wood, Mike	Together Again(Scotty's Son
Winter, Miriam T.	Children Of The Lord	Wise, Joe	Jesus, In Our Hands	Wood, Mike	We Reach Out For Love
Winter, Miriam T.	Christ Is King	Wise, Joe	Lamb Of God	Wood, Mike/Randall,Win	Daily Bread
Winter, Miriam T.	Christ Is My Rock	Wise, Joe	Let The Heavens Be Glad (Cc	Wood, Mike/Zettler, M.	Lonely Days
Winter, Miriam T.	Christmas Ballad	Wise, Joe	Lift Your Voice	Woodham, Steven Ross	Psalm 42
Winter, Miriam T.	Come Down, Lord	Wise, Joe	Lord By Your Cross	Woodman, R. H.	A Thanksgiving Day Ode
Winter, Miriam T.	Come To The Springs Of Livi	Wise, Joe	Lord Give Me A Heart Of Fle	Woodman, R. H.	The Lord Is My Rock
Winter, Miriam T.	Come, Lord Jesus (The Night	Wise, Joe	Lord Have Mercy (Icet)	Woodman, R. H.	The Love Of God
Winter, Miriam T.	Creed (1964 Text)	Wise, Joe	Lord Teach Us To Pray	Woodward, George R.	Lord Is Drawing Near, The
Winter, Miriam T.	Don't Be Afraid	Wise, Joe	Maleita's Song	Woodward, H. H.	Rejoice Greatly
Winter, Miriam T.	Don't Worry (About Food)	Wise, Joe	My Lord Will Come Again	Woodward, H. H.	The Radiant Morn Hath Passe
Winter, Miriam T.	Easter Song	Wise, Joe	My People	Woodward, H. H.	The Sun Shall Be No More Th
Winter, Miriam T.	Father, Thy Will Be Done	Wise, Joe	Noise Song, The	Work (Arr)	All I Want
Winter, Miriam T.	Glory To God (1964 Text)	Wise, Joe	Our Father	Wortley, Howard S.	From Whom All Blessings Flo
Winter, Miriam T.	God Gives His People Streng	Wise, Joe	Peace, Joy, Happiness	Wortley, Howard S.	I Will Go To The Mountain
Winter, Miriam T.	God Loves A Cheerful Giver	Wise, Joe	Re–Member Me	Wortley, Howard S.	I'm Gonna Put My Shoes On
Winter, Miriam T.	God Speaks	Wise, Joe	Reginas Song	Wortley, Howard S.	Joyous Celebration
Winter, Miriam T.	He Bought The Whole Field	Wise, Joe	Seed, The	Wortley, Howard S.	Lights Of Hanukkah

COMPOSER INDEX

Wortley, Howard S.	Squattin' Little Squillit
Wright	Mount Calvery
Wright, Alberta C.	Walk In Sunlight (Cantata)
Wright, Bob	Let The People Praise Thee
Wright, Bob	O For A Thousand Tongues To
Wright, E/Strickling,	Wings Over America
Wright, Russell	Someone Watches Over Me
Wrightman, N.	Chapel In The Hollow
Wrightman, N.	You Got To Have Jesus In Yo
Wrynn, Paul	They Gathered At The River
Wsyrtzen/Walvoord	Now Sounds (No 4500)
Wurttemberg	Give Thanks To The Lord (4-
Wurttemberg Gesangbuch	Proclaim To The World (4-Pa
Wyatt	Let Us Sing The New Song
Wyatt (Arr)	Carol Of The Angels (Sop So
Wyatt (Arr)	Thou Wilt Keep Him (A Cap)
Wyatt 1	Lord's My Shepherd (Ps 23)O
Wyatt, Van	All Praise To Our Redeeming
Wyatt, Van	Come Let Us Tune Our Loftie
Wyeth/Decou	Come, Thou Fount
Wynne, Mike	I Am The Way
Wyrtzen-Johnson	Hymnal For Contemporary Chr
Wyrtzen/Krogstad	Fifty Folk Favorites (No 50
Wyrtzen/Krogstad	Listen He's Here (No 4721)
Wyrtzen/Walvoord	Travelin' Road (Cantata)
Wyrtzen, Don	Breakthrough (Musical) (No
Wyrtzen, Don	Celebrate
Wyrtzen, Don	Celebration Songs (No 4360)
Wyrtzen, Don	Celebration Songs For Choir
Wyrtzen, Don	Come, Let Us Sing To The Lo
Wyrtzen, Don	Dark/Light
Wyrtzen, Don	Dimensions In Music (No 567
Wyrtzen, Don	Discovery
Wyrtzen, Don	Divine Priority, The
Wyrtzen, Don	Favorite Prophetic Songs Fo
Wyrtzen, Don	For By Grace
Wyrtzen, Don	God That Was Real
Wyrtzen, Don	God/Man (Satb) (No 4520) Ca
Wyrtzen, Don	Hallelujah, Yes, Praise The
Wyrtzen, Don	He Loves You, My Friend
Wyrtzen, Don	He'll Break Through The Blu
Wyrtzen, Don	Heart Of Love, A
Wyrtzen, Don	I Wonder If It's Happened Y
Wyrtzen, Don	I'll Never Be The Same Agai
Wyrtzen, Don	Jesus-My Joy
Wyrtzen, Don	Let's Celebrate Easter
Wyrtzen, Don	Look Up And See Jesus
Wyrtzen, Don	Look! See My God!
Wyrtzen, Don	Lord Is My Shepherd, The
Wyrtzen, Don	Love Was When
Wyrtzen, Don	Master's Tough, The
Wyrtzen, Don	My Soapbox (No 5617)
Wyrtzen, Don	No Lonely Day (No 4504)
Wyrtzen, Don	No Time
Wyrtzen, Don	O Give Me A Soapbox
Wyrtzen, Don	On Belief
Wyrtzen, Don	Our Sacrifice Of Praise
Wyrtzen, Don	Praise Him
Wyrtzen, Don	Really Live (No 4351)
Wyrtzen, Don	Rock On The Head
Wyrtzen, Don	Sandals
Wyrtzen, Don	Seasons Of Rapture
Wyrtzen, Don	Seek Ye The Lord
Wyrtzen, Don	So Let Me Live
Wyrtzen, Don	Sounds Of Celebration No 1
Wyrtzen, Don	The Times And The Seasons
Wyrtzen, Don	This World Outside
Wyrtzen, Don	Till He Comes
Wyrtzen, Don	To Be What You Want Me To B
Wyrtzen, Don	Unbounded Grace
Wyrtzen, Don	Why Do I Sing?
Wyrtzen, Don	Why Not Now?
Wyrtzen, Don	Windows Of The Mind
Wyrtzen, Don	Worthy Is The Lamb
Wyrtzen, Don	Yesterday,Today And Tomorro
Wyton	Fanfare-Improvisation On Az
Wyton	Psalm 130
Yantis, David	A Lenten Folk Song
Yantis, David	A Little Each Day
Yantis, David	A Prayer Song
Yantis, David	A Time Of Joy
Yantis, David	A Tool In The Hands Of God
Yantis, David	All
Yantis, David	All The Roads Lead Home
Yantis, David	Amen
Yantis, David	Believing
Yantis, David	Beyond A Dream
Yantis, David	Blessed Be These Moments
Yantis, David	Christ The King
Yantis, David	Come As A Child
Yantis, David	Come Together
Yantis, David	Complete Love
Yantis, David	Create In Me A Clean Heart
Yantis, David	Do It With Your Love
Yantis, David	Ebb And Flow
Yantis, David	Fill Me, Holy Spirit
Yantis, David	For His Loving Kindness
Yantis, David	Free Me
Yantis, David	Glory
Yantis, David	Glory To God
Yantis, David	Go Forth
Yantis, David	Go In Peace
Yantis, David	Goin' Easy
Yantis, David	Holy, Holy, Holy
Yantis, David	Holy, Holy, Holy (Celebrati
Yantis, David	I've Been Touched By His Ha
Yantis, David	It's But A Road
Yantis, David	Jesus Has Something For You
Yantis, David	Joy In Christ, Alleluia
Yantis, David	Let Me Sow Love
Yantis, David	Look Within
Yantis, David	Lord Have Mercy
Yantis, David	Now And Forever
Yantis, David	O Lamb Of God
Yantis, David	Of Your Love
Yantis, David	Our Father
Yantis, David	Pass My Love Around
Yantis, David	Praise God
Yantis, David	Praise God From Whom All
Yantis, David	Reaching Out
Yantis, David	Rejoice
Yantis, David	Sing Alleluia To The King
Yantis, David	Smile Song
Yantis, David	Song Of Love, Hope & Good C
Yantis, David	The Apostle's Creed
Yantis, David	The Body Of Christ
Yantis, David	The Door You Try To Open
Yantis, David	The Joy Song
Yantis, David	The Lord's Prayer
Yantis, David	The New Amen Song
Yantis, David	The Nicene Creed
Yantis, David	The Peace Of Christ Be With
Yantis, David	The Spirit Of The Lord
Yantis, David	There Is A New Wind Blowin'
Yantis, David	This Is Real
Yantis, David	Turn It Over To Jesus
Yantis, David	Unconditional Love
Yantis, David	We Come Praising God
Yantis, David	What Then Of Your Soul?
Yantis, David	When I Witness
Yantis, David	Where Do I See God?
Yantis, David	Why Limit God?
Yantis, David (Ed)	The Contemporary Hymn Book
Yarrow	Day Is Done
Yarrow	Early In The Morning
Yarrow/Stookey	The Very Last Day
Yarrow/Yardley	If I Had Wings
Yeaman, W. Holladay	Praise The Lord, O My Soul
Yes, Huai-Deh	This Glorious Christmas Nig
Ylvisaker, J & A.	John The Baptizer
Ylvisaker, J & A.	Nicodemus
Ylvisaker, J & A.	Song Of The Stable Boy
Ylvisaker, J & A.	The Birth
Ylvisaker, J. (Arr)	Wade In The Water
Ylvisaker, J. & A.	Follow Me
Ylvisaker, J. & A.	Judas Iscariot
Ylvisaker, J. & A.	Peter & The Angel
Ylvisaker, J. & A.	The Rich Young Ruler
Ylvisaker, J. & A.	The Victory Dance
Ylvisaker, J. & A.	Thomas
Ylvisaker, J. & A.	Water Of Life
Ylvisaker, John	Palm Sunday
York/Decou	This Is Why I Want To Go
Young	Awake, Psaltry And Harp
Young	Eight Compositions For Orga
Young	Gonna Ride That Heavenly Tr
Young	Let The Whole Creation Cry
Young	Prelude On A Southern Folk
Young	Recessional
Young	Sing We Noel
Young	Sing Ye Joyfully To The Lor
Young, C & Strange, J	In Jesus Name
Young, C.	Hearts And Voices Raise (W
Young, C.	What Child Is This? (W/Perc
Young, Carlton R.	Bread Of Life, The
Young, Carlton R.	Let All The World In Every
Young, Carolyn K.	Mary's Lullaby
Young, Carolyn K.	Since I Found My Life In Hi
Young, Gordon	All Ye Servants Of The Lord
Young, Gordon	Alleluia
Young, Gordon	Almighty And Everlasting Go
Young, Gordon	American's Creed, The
Young, Gordon	As The Heart Panteth
Young, Gordon	Bless The Lord, O My Soul
Young, Gordon	Canticle For Easter, A
Young, Gordon	Come, Ye Sinners, Poor And
Young, Gordon	Come, Ye That Love The Lord
Young, Gordon	Echo Alleluia
Young, Gordon	Fanfare For A Holy Day
Young, Gordon	Glorious Is Thy Holy Name
Young, Gordon	Gracious Spirit, Love Divin
Young, Gordon	Grant Us Thy Peace
Young, Gordon	Great Is The Lord
Young, Gordon	I Am The Way, The Truth, An
Young, Gordon	I Believe
Young, Gordon	I Give Myself Unto Prayer
Young, Gordon	I Love Thy Kingdom, Lord
Young, Gordon	In My Garden
Young, Gordon	In The Year That King Uzzia
Young, Gordon	Jesu, Our Blessed Hope Of H
Young, Gordon	Jesus, Our Lord, Is Risen T
Young, Gordon	Jesus, Thou Blessed Name Of
Young, Gordon	Litany For Easter (A Cap)
Young, Gordon	Lord Of The Worlds Above
Young, Gordon	Lord's My Shepherd, The
Young, Gordon	Moist With One Drop Of Thy
Young, Gordon	Now Praise We Great And Fam
Young, Gordon	Now Sing We All Noel
Young, Gordon	O Clap Your Hands (Ps 47)
Young, Gordon	O God, Our Help In Ages Pas
Young, Gordon	O Lord Support Us All The D
Young, Gordon	O Love, How Deep
Young, Gordon	Peace Within Thy Walls
Young, Gordon	Praise Ye The Lord (Ps 113)
Young, Gordon	Sing To The Lord With Cheer
Young, Gordon	Stand Up, Stand Up For Jesu
Young, Gordon	Sublime Alleluia, A
Young, Gordon	Three Anthems Of Commitment
Young, Gordon	Venite Adoremus
Young, Gordon	Who Is This That Comes In G
Young, P	God Of The Earth
Young, R. Otha	Lord Give Me Wings
Young, R. Otha	Stand By Me, Jesus
Young, Robert H.	Children Of The King
Young, Robert H.	Surely, God Is In This Holy
Young, Robert H.	Thou Dost Keep Him In Perfe
Youse	Gates Of Heaven Are Open
Zachau-Pasquet, J.	Come Holy Spirit, God And L
Zaumeyer	Alleluia
Zaumeyer, John	Lord's Prayer
Zaumeyer, John	Psalm 25
Zawacki, Cathy	Isaiah 43
Zgodava	Carol Of Joy (Aleria)
Zgodava	Noel Nouvelet
Zielenski, Mikolaj	Vox In Rama (E & L) (M)
Zimmerman	Psalm 23 (W/Org & Str. Bass
Zimmerman, James	Rejoice! Rejoice!
Zimmermann	A Mighty Fortress Is Our Go
Zimmermann	Crucifixion (Long)
Zimmermann	I Am Glad
Zimmermann	In That Great Gettin' Up Mo
Zimmermann	Psalm 100
Zingarelli, N	Be Not Far From Me
Zsigray, Joe	Alleluia
Zsigray, Joe	Amen, Alleluia!
Zsigray, Joe	Anamnesis
Zsigray, Joe	Arise, Come Sing In The Mor
Zsigray, Joe	Ave Maria
Zsigray, Joe	Blessed Be God
Zsigray, Joe	Christ Died For Our Sins
Zsigray, Joe	Christ Has Died (Acclamatio
Zsigray, Joe	Christ Our Light
Zsigray, Joe	Come Thou Holy Spirit Come
Zsigray, Joe	Coming Of Our Lord, The
Zsigray, Joe	Concluding Rite
Zsigray, Joe	Doxology And "Amen"
Zsigray, Joe	Doxology And Great Amen
Zsigray, Joe	Dying You Destroyed Our Dea
Zsigray, Joe	Earth Is Full Of The Goodne
Zsigray, Joe	Forever I Will Sing
Zsigray, Joe	Gloria
Zsigray, Joe	Gloria
Zsigray, Joe	Glory And Praise Forever
Zsigray, Joe	Happy Are They Who Hope In
Zsigray, Joe	Heavenly Father Hear Us
Zsigray, Joe	Holy, Holy
Zsigray, Joe	Hosanna!
Zsigray, Joe	If We Have One Another
Zsigray, Joe	In Him Everything Was Creat
Zsigray, Joe	Introductory Rite
Zsigray, Joe	Kyrie
Zsigray, Joe	Lamb Of God
Zsigray, Joe	Lamb Of God
Zsigray, Joe	Lord Be With Us
Zsigray, Joe	Lord By Your Cross
Zsigray, Joe	Lord Is Compassionate, The
Zsigray, Joe	Lord Is My Light And My Sal
Zsigray, Joe	Lord Is My Shepherd, The
Zsigray, Joe	Lord It Is Good To Give Tha
Zsigray, Joe	Lord You Are My Refuge
Zsigray, Joe	Lord, By Your Cross And Res
Zsigray, Joe	Many Are We Yet One We Are
Zsigray, Joe	May The Angels
Zsigray, Joe	O Bless The Lord My Soul
Zsigray, Joe	Our Father
Zsigray, Joe	Palm Sunday Processional
Zsigray, Joe	Proclaim His Marvelous Deed
Zsigray, Joe	Sanctus
Zsigray, Joe	Searching For The Lord
Zsigray, Joe	Sing A Song Of Love
Zsigray, Joe	Sing To The Mountains
Zsigray, Joe	Song For Pauline
Zsigray, Joe	Song Of Thanksgiving
Zsigray, Joe	Stay With Your People, Lord
Zsigray, Joe	We Will Celebrate
Zsigray, Joe	When We Eat This Bread
Zsigray, Joe	When We Eat This Bread
Zsigray, Joe	Words Of Institution
Zsigray, Joe	You Will Show Me The Path T
Zsigray, Joe	Your Name O Lord

COMPOSER INDEX

Zsigray, Joe	Your Word Is A Lamp To My F
Zunic, Sr. Mary Grace	Glory Of Joy
Zunic, Sr. Mary Grace	Psalm 30 I Praise You, O Lo
Zur, Menachem	Two Shabbat Songs

PUBLISHERS OF RELIGIOUS MUSIC

The publishers shown here are known to have one title or more which is religious in theme, or is otherwise useful for worship. The three letter code identified with each publisher appears next to each title listed in the categorized listing, and also in the alphabetized listing. Readers interested in individual songs may write to the appropriate publisher for copies or for more information.

For a variety of good reasons, this edition of THE MUSIC LOCATOR does not list every title published by every publisher listed below. Some publishers are listed below even though none of their titles are in this book.

Because of the free style naming conventions used among music publishers, each publisher is listed twice below. The first listing is in exact alphabetical order – by the three letter code. The second listing is in approximate alphabetical order – by the publisher name.

One final note: There are more than 2,000 known publishers of music in the USA alone. Most of them do not produce religious music or music for worship, so they are not included here. If a reader wishes to locate a publisher not listed, a more general index of publishers should be consulted. Your library may have the current "Billboard International Buyer's Guide", which contains a good list.

Publishers Alphabetically by Code

Abingdon Music	201 Eighth Ave	S Nashville	Tn 37202	Abi
Ann Ben Music	Box 2388	Toluca Lake	Ca 91602	Abm
Acta Foundation	4848 N Clark	Chicago	Il 60640	Acf
American Catholic Press	1223 Rossell Ave	Oak Park	Il 60302	Acp
Ahab Music	1707 Grand Ave	Nashville	Tn 37212	Aha
Alba House		Canfield	Oh 44406	Ahc
Almanac Music/T.R.O.	10 Columbus Circle	New York	Ny 10019	Alm
Mrs Ann Marie Sheehan	Bedord R R	Millcove, Pei,	Ca Nada	Ams
Tommy Arceneaux	150 Ravan Ave	Harahan	La 70123	Arc
Asaph Productions	P O Box 7972	Fresno	Ca 93727	Asa
Astronette Publ Co	2037 Alvarado Dr Ne	Albuquerque	Nm87110	Ast
Augsburg Publishing Co	426 South Fifth St	Minneapolis	Mn 55415	Aug
Avant-Garde Records	250 W 57th St	New York,	Ny 10019	Avg
Barnegat Music	720 Seventh Ave	New York,	Ny 10036	Bar
Broude Bros Ltd	56 West 45th St	New York,	Ny 10036	Bbl
Beechwood Music	1750 Vine	Hollywood	Ca 90028	Bch
Beckenhorst Press	3841 North High St	Columbus	Oh 43214	Bec
Belwin-Mills Publishing Corp	16 W 61 St	New York	Ny 10023	Bel
Bethany Fellowship Inc	6820 Auto Club Rd	Minneapolis	Mn 55438	Bfi
Boston Music Company	116 Boylston St	Boston	Ma 02116	Bos
Briarmeade Music Unltd	P O Box 11387	St Louis	Mo 63105	Bri
Bula Publishing Co	Route 1	Crossville	Il 62827	Bul
Cameron Bros Revivals	46 King St, Peterhead	Aberdeenshire	Sc Otlnd	Cam
Carmelite Fathers Guild	Pineland R D 1	New Florence	Pa 19544	Car
Cedarwood Publishing Co	815 16th Ave South	Nashville	Tn 37203	Ced
Composer's Forum (Cfcw)	P O Box 8554	Sugar Creek	Mo 64054	Cfc
C F Peters Corp	373 Park Ave South	New York	Ny 10016	Cfp
Carl Fischer Inc	56-62 Cooper Square	New York	Ny 10003	Cfs
Children Of The Day	506 Traverse	Costa Mesa	Ca 92606	Chd
Christ House		Lafayette,	Nj 07848	Chh
Creation House Inc		Carol Stream	Il 60187	Chi
Ctr For Contemporary Celebrtn.	P O Box 3024	West Lafayette	In 47906	Ccc
Church Of The Messiah	231 E Grand Blvd	Detroit	Mi 48207	Chm
Chappell Music Co.	810 Seventh Ave	New York	Ny 10019	Chp
Coke Music	680 Beach St	San Francisco	Ca 94109	Cke
Cherry Lane Music	560 Sylvan Ave	Englewood Cliffs	Nj 07632	Clm
Coburn Press	P O Box 72	Sherman	Ct 06784	Cob
Cokesbury	2101 Woodward Ave	Detroit	Mi 48201	Cok
Colgems Music/Screen Gems	711 5th Ave	New York	Ny 10022	Col
Concordia Publ House	3558 S Jefferson Ave	St Louis	Mo 63118	Con
Corda Music Inc	3398 Nahatan Way	Las Vegas	Nv 89109	Cor
Catalpa Publ Co	2609 Nw 36th St	Oklahoma City	Ok 73112	Cpc
Country Star Music	439 Wiley Ave	Franklin	Pa 16323	Csm
Gary Cusimano	2838 Palmer Ave	New Orleans	La 70118	Cus
Dino Productions Inc	1717 N Highland 606	Hollywood	Ca 90028	Din
District Music Company	9224 Rosslyn Station	Arlington	Va 22209	Dis
Dove Publications		Pecos	Nm87552	Dov
Duane Music, Inc	382 Clarence Ave	Sunnyvale	Ca 94086	Dua
E C Schirmer Music Co	112 South St	Boston	Ma 02111	Ecs
Elkan-Vogel Inc	Presser Pl.	Bryn Mawr	Pa 19010	Elv
Wm B Eerdman Publ Co	255 Jefferson Ave Se	Grand Rapids	Mi 49502	Erd
Essex Music Intl Inc/T.R.O	10 Columbus Circle	New York	Ny 10019	Esx
Franciscan Communications Ctr.	1229 S Santee St	Los Angeles	Ca 90015	Fcc
F E L Publications	1925 Pontius Ave	Los Angeles	Ca 90025	Fel
The Fishermen Inc	P O Box 903	Woodland Park	Co 80836	Fis
Faith And Life Press	724 Main St Box 347	Newton	Ks 67114	Flp
Fall River/Sanga Music	250 W 57th St #2017	New York	Ny 10019	Frm
Freshwater/Ufo Music Inc	7720 Sunset Blvd	Los Angeles	Ca 90046	Frs
Galaxy Music Corp	2121 Broadway	New York	Ny 10023	Gal
Gomut Company	1100 Bwy P O Box 329	San Antonio	Tx 78292	Gam
Rev Enrico Garzilli	North American College	Vatican City	Eu Rope	Gar
G I A Publications Inc	7404 S Mason Ave	Chicago	Il 60638	Gia
Gaither Music Co	P O Box 300	Alexandria	In 46001	Gmc
Gospel Music Library	625 Nf 78th Ave	Portland	Or 97213	Gml
Growick Music Publishers	P O Box 90639	Nashville	Tn 37209	Gmp
Gospel Publishing House	1445 Boonville Ave	Springfield	Mo 65802	Gph
General Recording & A/V	434 Sandalwood	San Antonio	Tx 78216	Gra
Giving Room Mus/Segel&Goldman	9200 Sunset Blvd #1000	Los Angeles	Ca 90069	Grm
G Schirmer Inc	866 Third Ave	New York	Ny 10022	Gsc
Hal Leonard Publ Co	8112 West Bluemound Rd	Milwaukee	Wi 53213	Hal
Hamblen Music Co Inc	P O Box 8118	Universal City	Ca 91608	Ham
Hargail Music Press	28 W 38 St	New York	Ny 10018	Har
Heritage Music Press	501 E Third St	Dayton	Oh 45401	Her
Henry Oakes	1103 Neff Ave South	West Covina	Ca 91790	Hhh
Raymond A Hoffman Co	1500 Blk E. Douglas	Wichita	Ks 67214	Hof
Holub & Associates	432 Park Ave S	New York	Ny 10016	Hol
Hope Publishing Co	380 S Main St	Carol Stream	Il 60187	Hop
H W Gray Publ	16 W. 61st St	New York	Ny 10023	Hwg
The Composer's Press	177 East 87th St	New York	Ny 10028	Icp
Irving Music	1416 N Labrea	Hollywood	Ca 90028	Irv
Ivan Mogul Music Corp	40 East 49th St	New York	Ny 10017	Ivm
Fr. Willard Jabusch	St Mary Of Lake Sem	Mundelein	Il 60060	Jab
Jan-Lee Music	260 El Camino Dr	Beverly Hills	Ca 90212	Jan
J Albert & Son Pt Ltd	139 King St, Sidney, Nsw	Australia	2000	Jas
James E Byrne	12242 Mallory Dr	Largo	Fl 33540	Jeb
J Fischer & Bro	16 W. 61st St	New York	Ny 10023	Jfs
James Hendrix Ent	P O Box 1368	Nashville	Tn 37202	Jhe
Jim Hall Music	301 S 4th St Box 975	Norfolk	Nb 68701	Jhm
J S Paluch Co Inc	1800 W Winnemac Ave	Chicago	Il 60640	Jsp
John T Benson Company	1625 Broadway	Nashville	Tn 37202	Jtb
Edwin F Kalmus	P O Box 1007	Opa-Locka	Fl 33054	Kal
Karen Barrie	4643 N Central Park	Chicago	Il 60625	Kbr
Kelly Music Publ	439 Wiley Ave	Franklin	Pa 16323	Kmp
Jacob Krieger	9 Winship St (Rear) #3	Brighton	Ma 02135	Krg
Leeds Music/Mca Music	445 Park Ave	New York	Ny 10022	Lds
Lexicon Music Inc	P O Box 1790	Waco	Tx 76703	Lex
Liturgical Conference	1330 Massachusetts Av Nw	Washington	Dc 20005	Lit
The Lockman Foundation		La Habra	Ca 90631	Loc
Logos International	185 North Ave	Plainfield	Nj 07060	Log
Lorenz Publishing Co	501 E Third St	Dayton	Oh 45401	Lor
Lea Pocket Scores	P O Box 138 Audubon St	New York	Ny 10032	Lps
Lyresong Music	1227 Spring St Nw	Atlanta	Ga 30309	Lym
Mcafee Music Corp	501 E Third St	Dayton	Oh 45401	Maf
Mid America Music	Box B 155 First St	Carlisle	Ia 50047	Mam
Manna Music Inc	2111 Kenmere Ave	Burbank	Ca 91504	Man
Maranatha Music	P O Box 4669	Irvine	Ca 92664	Mar
Moody Press	820 North Lasalle St	Chicago	Il 60610	Mbi
Music Corp Of America	445 Park Ave	New York	Ny 10022	Mca
Marianist Comm Cntr	P O Box 3830	St Louis	Mo 63122	Mcc
Maclen Music/Atv	1370 Av Of The Americas	New York	Ny 10019	Mcl
Ludlow Music, Inc/T.R.O.	10 Columbus Circle	New York	Ny 10019	Mcl
Mi-Da-Mark Music	P O Box 2388	Toluca Lake	Ca 91602	Mdm
Meadows Music	1727 Roanoke Ave	Sacramento	Ca 95838	Med
Melody Trails/T.R.O.	10 Columbus Circle	New York	Ny 10019	Mel
Memnon Ltd	P O Box 84	Glen Cove Li	Ny 11542	Mem
Mayhew-Mccrimmon Ltd	10 High St, Sgrt Wakering	Essex, England		Mhw
Miller Music/United Artists	6920 Sunset Blvd.	Los Angeles	Ca 90028	Mil
Minstral Publications Inc	4314 3rd N W	Seattle	Wa 98107	Min
Maryknoll Sisters		Maryknoll	Ny 10545	Mkn
Marylhurst Music	Box 281	Marylhurst	Or 97036	Mlh
Metropolitan Music Co	4225 University Blvd	Houston	Tx 77005	Mmc
Morehouse – Barlow	14 E. 41st St.	New York	Ny 10017	Mob
Main Stave Music	P O Box 3763	Hollywood	Ca 90028	Msm
Music Press	P O Box 1052	Tuskegee	Al 36088	Mus
N A L R	2110 W Peoria Ave	Phoenix	Az 85029	Nal
Northern Music/Mca Music	445 Park Ave	New York	Ny 10022	Nor
Novello Publications	P O Box 1811	Trenton	Nj 08610	Nov
New York Times Music	655 Madison Ave	New York	Ny 10021	Nyt
Oakridge Music	829 North Sylvania	Fort Worth	Tx 76111	Oak
Oxford University Press	200 Madison Ave	New York	Ny 10016	Oxf
Paydirt Music	1227 Spring St Nw	Atlanta	Ga 30309	Pdm
Pepamar Music Corp	112 South St	Boston	Ma 02111	Pep
Peer Intl Corp	1740 Broadway	New York	Ny 10019	Pic
Process Music Publ	439 Wiley Ave	Franklin	Pa 16323	Pmp
Paulist Neman Press	1865 Broadway	New York	Ny?10023	Pnp
Proclamation Productions	Orange Square	Port Jervis	Ny 12771	Prc
Pro Art Publ Inc	Box 234	Westbury	Ny 11590	Pro
Resource Publications	P O Box 444	Saratoga	Ca 95070	Rpb
Raven Music	4107 Woodland Pk N	Seattle	Wa 98103	Rav
Rongwen Music Inc	56 West 45th St	New York	Ny 10036	Ron
Sacred Music Press	501 E Third St	Dayton	Oh 45401	Sac
Saul Avenue Publishing Co	1632 Central Parkway	Cincinnati	Oh 45210	Sav
St Benedict's Farm	Box 366	Waelder	Tx 78959	Sbf
Schumann Music Co	136 West 52nd St	New York	Ny 10019	Sch
Seesaw Music Corp	177 East 87th St	New York	Ny 10028	See
Seyah Music	1227 Spring St Nw	Atlanta	Ga 30309	Scm
Shalom Community	1504 Polk	Wichita Falls	Tx 76309	Sha
Schmitt, Hall And Mccreary	110 N Fifth St	Minneapolis	Mn 55403	Shm
Silhouette Music	P O Box 41	Johnsonville	Sc 29555	Sil
Siquomb/Segel&Goldman, Inc	9200 Sunset Blvd #1000	Los Angeles	Ca 90069	Siq
Southern Music Company	1100 Bwy/Po Box 329	San Antonio	Tx 78292	Smc
Sunday Missal Service	1012 Vermont St	Quincy	Il 62301	Sms
St Nathanson Music	50 Brighton First Rd	Brooklyn	Ny 11235	Snm
Southern Music Publ	1740 Broadway	New York	Ny 10019	Som
Rev Robert J Stamps	7777 S Lewis	Tulsa	Ok 74105	Sta
Sterling Music Co	9165 Sunset Blvd St 300	Los Angeles	Ca 90069	Ste
Stimuli Inc	P O Box 20066	Cincinnati	Oh 45220	Sti
Stormking Music/Sanga Music	250 W 57th St #2017	New York	Ny 10019	Stk
Startime Music	6313 Peach Ave	Van Nuys	Ca 91411	Stm
Stonebess Music Co	163 Orizaba Ave	San Francisco	Ca 94132	Sto
String & Reed Music	622 State St	New Orleans	La 70118	Str
Tall Corn Publ Co	Box B 155 First Str	Carlisle	Ia 50047	Tal
Twentieth Century Music Corp	8255 Sunset Blvd	Los Angeles	Ca 90046	Twe
United Artists Music	10 Columbus Circle	New York	Ny 10019	Uam
The Composer's Press	177 E 87th St	New York	Ny 10028	Tcp
Ursula Music Co	Box 544	Annapolis	Md 21404	Urs
United Church Press	1505 Race St.	Philadelphia	Pa 19102	Ucp
Valando Music Inc	1700 Broadway	New York	Ny 10019	Val
Vanguard Music Corp	250 W 57th St	New York	Ny 10019	Van
Vernacular Hymns Publ	4805 Northwest Blvd	Spokane	Wa 99205	Vrn
Mr Wm Booth-Clibborn	2006 Ne Weidler St No 12	Portland	Or 97232	Wbc
Warner Bros Music	9200 Sunset Blvd	Los Angeles	Ca 90069	Wbp
Weston Priory Prod		Weston	Vt 05161	Wes

PUBLISHERS OF RELIGIOUS MUSIC

Word Of God Music	P O Box 87	Ann Arbor	Mi 48107 Wgm
World Library Publications	2145 Central Parkway	Cincinnati	Oh 45214 Wlp
Word Inc	P O Box 1790	Waco	Tx 76703 Wrd
David Yantis Music Ministry	Box "N"	Bonita	Ca 92202 Yan
Ybarra Music	Box 665	Lemon Grove	Ca 92045 Yba
Zondervan Music Pubs	1415 Lake Drive Se	Grand Rapids	Mi 49506 Zon

Publishers Alphabetically by Name

Abingdon Music	201 Eighth Ave	S Nashville	Tn 37202 Abi
Acta Foundation	4848 N Clark	Chicago	Il 60640 Acf
Ahab Music	1707 Grand Ave	Nashville	Tn 37212 Aha
Alba House		Canfield	Oh 44406 Ahc
J Albert & Son Pt Ltd	139 King St, Sidney, Nsw	Australia	2000 Jas
Almanac Music/T.R.O.	10 Columbus Circle	New York	Ny 10019 Alm
American Catholic Press	1223 Rossell Ave	Oak Park	Il 60302 Acp
Ann Ben Music	Box 2388	Toluca Lake	Ca 91602 Abm
Tommy Arceneaux	150 Ravan Ave	Harahan	La 70123 Arc
Asaph Productions	P O Box 7972	Fresno	Ca 93727 Asa
Astronette Publ Co	2037 Alvarado Dr Ne	Albuquerque	Nm 87110 Ast
Augsburg Publishing Co	426 South Fifth St	Minneapolis	Mn 55415 Aug
Avant-Garde Records	250 W 57th St	New York,	Ny 10019 Avg
Barnegat Music	720 Seventh Ave	New York,	Ny 10036 Bar
Karen Barrie	4643 N Central Park	Chicago	Il 60625 Kbr
Beckenhorst Press	3841 North High St	Columbus	Oh 43214 Bec
Beechwood Music	1750 Vine	Hollywood	Ca 90028 Bch
Belwin-Mills Publishing Corp	16 W 61 St	New York	Ny 10023 Bel
John T Benson Company	1625 Broadway	Nashville	Tn 37202 Jtb
Bethany Fellowship Inc	6820 Auto Club Rd	Minneapolis	Mn 55438 Bfi
Mr Wm Booth-Clibborn	2006 Ne Weidler St No 12	Portland	Or 97232 Wbc
Boston Music Company	116 Boylston St	Boston	Ma 02116 Bos
Briarmeade Music Unltd	P O Box 11387	St Louis	Mo 63105 Bri
Broude Bros Ltd	56 West 45th St	New York,	Ny 10036 Bbl
Bula Publishing Co	Route 1	Crossville	Il 62827 Bul
James E Byrne	12242 Mallory Dr	Largo	Fl 33540 Jeb
Cameron Bros Revivals	46 King St, Peterhead	Aberdeenshire	Sc Otlnd Cam
Carmelite Fathers Guild	Pineland R D 1	New Florence	Pa 19544 Car
Catalpa Publ Co	2609 Nw 36th St	Oklahoma City	Ok 73112 Cpc
Cedarwood Publishing Co	815 16th Ave South	Nashville	Tn 37203 Ced
Ctr For Contemporary Celebrtn.	P O Box 3024	West Lafayette	In 47906 Ccc
Cherry Lane Music	560 Sylvan Ave	Englewood Cliffs	Nj 07632 Clm
Children Of The Day	506 Traverse	Costa Mesa	Ca 92606 Chd
Christ House		Lafayette,	Nj 07848 Chh
Chappell Music Co.	810 Seventh Ave	New York	Ny 10019 Chp
Church Of The Messiah	231 E Grand Blvd	Detroit	Mi 48207 Chm
Coburn Press	P O Box 72	Sherman	Ct 06784 Cob
Coke Music	680 Beach St	San Francisco	Ca 94109 Cke
Cokesbury	2101 Woodward Ave	Detroit	Mi 48201 Cok
Colgems Music/Screen Gems	711 5th Ave	New York	Ny 10022 Col
Composer's Forum (Cfcw)	P O Box 8554	Sugar Creek	Mo 64054 Cfc
The Composer's Press	177 East 87th St	New York	Ny 10028 Icp
Concordia Publ House	3558 S Jefferson Ave	St Louis	Mo 63118 Con
Corda Music Inc	3398 Nahatan Way	Las Vegas	Nv 89109 Cor
Country Star Music	439 Wiley Ave	Franklin	Pa 16323 Csm
Creation House Inc		Carol Stream	Il 60187 Chi
Gary Cusimano	2838 Palmer Ave	New Orleans	La 70118 Cus
Dino Productions Inc	1717 N Highland 606	Hollywood	Ca 90028 Din
District Music Company	9224 Rosslyn Station	Arlington	Va 22209 Dis
Dove Publications		Pecos	Nm 87552 Dov
Duane Music, Inc	382 Clarence Ave	Sunnyvale	Ca 94086 Dua
Wm B Eerdman Publ Co	255 Jefferson Ave Se	Grand Rapids	Mi 49502 Erd
Elkan-Vogel Inc	Presser Pl.	Bryn Mawr	Pa 19010 Elv
Essex Music Intl Inc/T.R.O	10 Columbus Circle	New York	Ny 10019 Esx
Faith And Life Press	724 Main St Box 347	Newton	Ks 67114 Flp
Fall River/Sanga Music	250 W 57th St #2017	New York	Ny 10019 Frm
F E L Publications	1925 Pontius Ave	Los Angeles	Ca 90025 Fel
Carl Fischer Inc	56-62 Cooper Square	New York	Ny 10003 Cfs
J Fischer & Bro	16 W. 61st St	New York	Ny 10023 Jfs
The Fishermen Inc	P O Box 903	Woodland Park	Co 80836 Fis
Franciscan Communications Ctr.	1229 S Santee St	Los Angeles	Ca 90015 Fcc
Freshwater/Ufo Music Inc	7720 Sunset Blvd	Los Angeles	Ca 90046 Frs
Gaither Music Co	P O Box 300	Alexandria	In 46001 Gmc
Galaxy Music Corp	2121 Broadway	New York	Ny 10023 Gal
Gamut Company	1100 Bwy P O Box 329	San Antonio	Tx 78292 Gam
Rev Enrico Garzilli	North American College	Vatican City	Eu Rope Gar
General Recording & A/V	434 Sandalwood	San Antonio	Tx 78216 Gra
G I A Publications Inc	7404 S Mason Ave	Chicago	Il 60638 Gia
Giving Room Mus/Segel&Goldman	9200 Sunset Blvd #1000	Los Angeles	Ca 90069 Grm
Gospel Music Library	625 Nf 78th Ave	Portland	Or 97213 Gml
Gospel Publishing House	1445 Boonville Ave	Springfield	Mo 65802 Gph
Grawick Music Publishers	P O Box 90639	Nashville	Tn 37209 Gmp
H W Gray Publ	16 W. 61st St	New York	Ny 10023 Hwg
Jim Hall Music	301 S 4th St Box 975	Norfolk	Nb 68701 Jhm
Hamblen Music Co Inc	P O Box 8118	Universal City	Ca 91608 Ham
Hargail Music Press	28 W 38 St	New York	Ny 10018 Har
James Hendrix Ent	P O Box 1368	Nashville	Tn 37202 Jhe
Heritage Music Press	501 E Third St	Dayton	Oh 45401 Her
Raymond A Hoffman Co	1500 Blk E. Douglas	Wichita	Ks 67214 Hof
Holub & Associates	432 Park Ave S	New York	Ny 10016 Hol
Hope Publishing Co	380 S Main St	Carol Stream	Il 60187 Hop
Irving Music	1416 N Labrea	Hollywood	Ca 90028 Irv
Ivan Mogul Music Corp	40 East 49th St	New York	Ny 10017 Ivm
Fr. Willard Jabusch	St Mary Of Lake Sem	Mundelein	Il 60060 Jab
Jan-Lee Music	260 El Camino Dr	Beverly Hills	Ca 90212 Jan
Edwin F Kalmus	P O Box 1007	Opa-Locka	Fl 33054 Kal
Kama-Sutra Music	810 Seventh Ave	New York	Ny 10017 Kam
Kelly Music Publ	439 Wiley Ave	Franklin	Pa 16323 Kmp
Jacob Krieger	9 Winship St (Rear) #3	Brighton	Ma 02135 Krg
Lea Pocket Scores	P O Box 138 Audubon St	New York	Ny 10032 Lps
Leeds Music/Mca Music	445 Park Ave	New York	Ny 10022 Lds
Hal Leonard Publ Co	8112 West Bluemound Rd	Milwaukee	Wi 53213 Hal
Lexicon Music Inc	P O Box 1790	Waco	Tx 76703 Lex
Liturgical Conference	1330 Massachusetts Av Nw	Washington	Dc 20005 Lit
The Lockman Foundation		La Habra	Ca 90631 Loc
Logos International	185 North Ave	Plainfield	Nj 07060 Log
Lorenz Publishing Co	501 E Third St	Dayton	Oh 45401 Lor
Ludlow Music, Inc/T.R.O.	10 Columbus Circle	New York	Ny 10019 Mcl
Lyresong Music	1227 Spring St Nw	Atlanta	Ga 30309 Lym
Maclen Music/Atv	1370 Av Of The Americas	New York	Ny 10019 Mcl
Main Stave Music	P O Box 3763	Hollywood	Ca 90028 Msm
Manna Music Inc	2111 Kenmere Ave	Burbank	Ca 91504 Man
Maranatha Music	P O Box 4669	Irvine	Ca 92664 Mar
Marianist Comm Cntr	P O Box 3830	St Louis	Mo 63122 Mcc
Maryknoll Sisters		Maryknoll	Ny 10545 Mkn
Marylhurst Music	Box 281	Marylhurst	Or 97036 Mlh
Mayhew-Mccrimmon Ltd	10 High St, Sgrt Wakering	Essex, England	Mhw
Mcafee Music Corp	501 E Third St	Dayton	Oh 45401 Maf
Meadows Music	1727 Roanoke Ave	Sacramento	Ca 95838 Med
Melody Trails/T.R.O.	10 Columbus Circle	New York	Ny 10019 Mel
Memnon Ltd	P O Box 84	Glen Cove Li	Ny 11542 Mem
Metropolitan Music Co	4225 University Blvd	Houston	Tx 77005 Mmc
Mi-Da-Mark Music	P O Box 2388	Toluca Lake	Ca 91602 Mdm
Mid America Music	Box B 155 First St	Carlisle	Ia 50047 Mam
Miller Music/United Artists	6920 Sunset Blvd.	Los Angeles	Ca 90028 Mil
Minstral Publications Inc	4314 3rd N W	Seattle	Wa 98107 Min
Moody Press	820 North Lasalle St	Chicago	Il 60610 Mbi
Morehouse - Barlow	14 E.41st St.	New York	Ny 10017 Mob
Music Corp Of America	445 Park Ave	New York	Ny 10022 Mca
Music Press	P O Box 1052	Tuskegee	Al 36088 Mus
N A L R	2110 W Peoria Ave	Phoenix	Az 85029 Nal
New York Times Music	655 Madison Ave	New York	Ny 10021 Nyt
Northern Music/Mca Music	445 Park Ave	New York	Ny 10022 Nor
Novello Publications	P O Box 1811	Trenton	Nj 08610 Nov
Henry Oakes	1103 Neff Ave South	West Covina	Ca 91790 Hhh
Oakridge Music	829 North Sylvania	Fort Worth	Tx 76111 Oak
Oxford University Press	200 Madison Ave	New York	Ny 10016 Oxf
J S Paluch Co Inc	1800 W Winnemac Ave	Chicago	Il 60640 Jsp
Paulist Neman Press	1865 Broadway	New York	Ny 10023 Pnp
Paydirt Music	1227 Spring St Nw	Atlanta	Ga 30309 Pdm
Peer Intl Corp	1740 Broadway	New York	Ny 10019 Pic
Pepamar Music Corp	112 South St	Boston	Ma 02111 Pep
C F Peters Corp	373 Park Ave South	New York	Ny 10016 Cfp
Pro Art Publ Inc	Box 234	Westbury	Ny 11590 Pro
Process Music Publ	439 Wiley Ave	Franklin	Pa 16323 Pmp
Proclamation Productions	Orange Square	Port Jervis	Ny 12771 Prc
Raven Music	4107 Woodland Pk N	Seattle	Wa 98103 Rav
Resource Publications	P O Box 444	Saratoga	Ca 95070 Rpb
Rongwen Music Inc	56 West 45th St	New York	Ny 10036 Ron
Sacred Music Press	501 E Third St	Dayton	Oh 45401 Sac
St Benedict's Farm	Box 366	Waelder	Tx 78959 Sbf
St Nathanson Music	50 Brighton First Rd	Brooklyn	Ny 11235 Snm
Saul Avenue Publishing Co	1632 Central Parkway	Cincinnati	Oh 45210 Sav
G Schirmer Inc	866 Third Ave	New York	Ny 10022 Gsc
E C Schirmer Music Co	112 South St	Boston	Ma 02111 Ecs
Schmitt, Hall And Mccreary	110 N Fifth St	Minneapolis	Mn 55403 Shm
Schumann Music Co	136 West 52nd St	New York	Ny 10019 Sch
Seesaw Music Corp	177 East 87th St	New York	Ny 10028 See
Seyah Music	1227 Spring St Nw	Atlanta	Ga 30309 Sem
Shalom Community	1504 Polk	Wichita Falls	Tx 76309 Sha
Mrs Ann Marie Sheehan	Bedord R R	Millcove, Pei,	Ca Nada Ams
Silhouette Music	P O Box 41	Johnsonville	Sc 29555 Sil
Siquomb/Segel&Goldman, Inc	9200 Sunset Blvd #1000	Los Angeles	Ca 90069 Siq
Southern Music Company	1100 Bwy/Po Box 329	San Antonio	Tx 78292 Smc
Southern Music Publ	1740 Broadway	New York	Ny 10019 Som
Rev Robert J Stamps	7777 S Lewis	Tulsa	Ok 74105 Sta
Startime Music	6313 Peach Ave	Van Nuys	Ca 91411 Stm
Sterling Music Co	9165 Sunset Blvd St 300	Los Angeles	Ca 90069 Ste
Stimuli Inc	P O Box 20066	Cincinnati	Oh 45220 Sti
Stonebess Music Co	163 Orizaba Ave	San Francisco	Ca 94132 Sto
String & Reed Music	622 State St	New Orleans	La 70118 Str
Stormking Music/Sanga Music	250 W 57th St #2017	New York	Ny 10019 Stk
Sunday Missal Service	1012 Vermont St	Quincy	Il 62301 Sms
Tall Corn Publ Co	Box B 155 First Str	Carlisle	Ia 50047 Tal
The Composer's Press	177 E 87th St	New York	Ny 10028 Tcp
Twentieth Century Music Corp	8255 Sunset Blvd	Los Angeles	Ca 90046 Twe
United Artists Music	10 Columbus Circle	New York	Ny 10019 Uam
United Church Press	1505 Race St.	Philadelphia	Pa 19102 Ucp
Ursula Music Co	Box 544	Annapolis	Md 21404 Urs
Valando Music Inc	1700 Broadway	New York	Ny 10019 Val
Vanguard Music Corp	250 W 57th St	New York	Ny 10019 Van
Vernacular Hymns Publ	4805 Northwest Blvd	Spokane	Wa 99205 Vrn
Warner Bros Music	9200 Sunset Blvd	Los Angeles	Ca 90069 Wbp
Weston Priory Prod		Weston	Vt 05161 Wes
Word Inc	P O Box 1790	Waco	Tx 76703 Wrd
Word Of God Music	P O Box 87	Ann Arbor	Mi 48107 Wgm
World Library Publications	2145 Central Parkway	Cincinnati	Oh 45214 Wlp
David Yantis Music Ministry	Box "N"	Bonita	Ca 92202 Yan
Ybarra Music	Box 665	Lemon Grove	Ca 92045 Yba
Zondervan Music Pubs	1415 Lake Drive Se	Grand Rapids	Mi 49506 Zon

MODERN LITURGY is the leading creative resource journal for good liturgy.

MODERN LITURGY — is a unique periodical. It provides a continuing source of fresh ideas, informed feature articles, and practical helps for parish "Liturgists". Each issue is focused on a special theme and offers five kinds of unique practical helps.

Liturgical Art Forms are our particular speciality. No other resource periodical offers such an array of visual arts, original music, poetry and other art forms. These arts are presented in their entirety and in a usable form. Each issue brings songs to play and sing, and poetry for meditation or for planning word services. Other liturgical art forms, such as mimies, dramas, stories, and sacred dances are often presented in example liturgies on the theme of the issue. Finally, each feature is accompanied by our award-winning illustrations. These are easily adapted for banners, bulletins, posters, programs, and slides.

Feature Articles develop the theme of each issue on practical, cultural, theological, and historical levels. Intended as aids in building and maintaining a strong liturgical background, some articles explore contemporary questions in liturgical theology. Other articles concentrate on the practical implementation of the theme in a parish or classroom situation.

Ideas and Suggestions for planning; these come in several forms. In addition to the articles and art forms, each issue carries a group of brief workshop columns which treat both technical and aesthetic topics of interest to our readers. Here you will find practical input from experts in many liturgical specialties, such as use of symbols, lectoring, musicianship, presidential style, and several others. This is the kind of assistance which is usually available only at expensive conferences or through time-consuming academic course work. Such aids are sure to stimulate your planning sessions.

Reviews, Critiques, and Surveys of good materials from many different sources are presented in each issue. Tom Simons' popular survey column suggests books, periodicals, cassettes, audio/visual programs, films, and other special resources. Frequently, formal reviews are presented which discuss books, records, or other special efforts in detail. Each issue also contains a handy guide to additional related articles, songs, and ideas for full exploitation of the theme of the issue.

Sharings of good liturgies, successful techniques, valuable experiences, and other practical helps form our other major kind of assistance. Each issue carries at least one full example for practical use or adaptation. Still other ideas are shared by our readers. Their ideas often act as a catalyst in the creative process.

Subscription Plans

Four unique plans tailored for four common situations:

Full Community Subscription — This program provides maximum resources for your parish or prayer community. It includes one year (eight issues) of MODERN LITURGY, four accompanying cassette or 8-track recordings, and an annual license to print, perform, and otherwise use during your subscription year the good music, arts, and example services from each issue (and all previous issues) in your parish or prayer community.

Community Subscription — This program includes eight issues of MODERN LITURGY and an annual license to print, perform, and otherwise use during your subscription year the good music, arts, and example services from each issue (and all previous issues) in your parish or prayer community.

Full Individual Subscription — This subscription includes eight issues of MODERN LITURGY and four accompanying stereo recordings in cassette or 8-track form. The recordings shorten the time required to learn or evaluate each song.

Individual Subscription — This subscription includes eight issues of MODERN LITURGY mailed to a residential address.

RESOURCE PUBLICATIONS
PO BOX 444
SARATOGA, CA 95070

Ask a tew professional liturgists about **MODERN LITURGY.** Chances are that you will find that they concur with comments like the following from our mailbag:

This is a fine piece of work. Keep it coming. I'm adding it to a resource list for my course in resources for educational ministry.

Professor Eugene C. Kreider
Northwestern Lutheran Theological
Seminary
St. Paul, Minnesota

For a long time now I have watched with interest the growing pains of your magazine and I can only congratulate you on the progress and quality of the publication ... You certainly have made it into a very respectable publication which no one in church music and liturgy can afford to ignore. That is an Accomplishment! Please keep it up!

Reverend Ralph Verdi, CPPS
Composer in Residence
St. Joseph's College
Rensselaer, Indiana

isw
Institute for Spirituality and Worship

Unique programs of Theological Renewal for the Contemporary Church:

Liturgical Leadership
Initial religious Formation
Ongoing Spiritual Renewal
Prayer Apostolate
Spiritual Ministry with the Laity
Charismatic Spirituality

The Nine month program consists of:

regular course work
faculty-organized seminars
on-going student reflection groups
specific workshops and lectures
participation in the social, liturgical
and communitarian life of the ISW

The program in Liturgical Leadership offers the students an area of concentration in preparation for work in various liturgical situations:

the parish
liturgical commissions
religious communities
youth work
campus ministry
retreat work
religious education

The Seminar in liturgical leadership will be concerned with liturgical planning, the liturgical environment, ecumenical liturgical spirituality, liturgy and drama, liturgical dance, mime in the liturgy and liturgical music.

Students who are concentrating in the area of liturgical leadership may participate in the other programs of the ISW to the degree that this is feasible.

A sampling of the courses suggested for those majoring in liturgy includes:

Liturgical Theology
Christian Sacramentality
Liturgy: Presidential Style
Pastoral Communication
Theology and Mass Media
Historical and Theological Basis
for Contemporary Liturgy
The Foundation of Jewish Liturgy

Historical Dimensions of the
Christian Liturgy
The Eucharistic Prayer
Ritual and Psychology of
Religious Experience
The Christian Year
Introduction to Hymnody
Pastoral and Liturgical Theology
of the Sacraments

The minimum academic requirement for admittance is a bachelor's degree or its equivalent. The institute awards the Certificate of Theological Studies (C.T.S.), the Master of Theology degree (Th.M.) and the Master of Sacred Theology (S.T.M.). An M.A. degree can be obtained in conjunction with the Graduate Theological Union.

For further information or for necessary application forms, write:

Institute for Spirituality and Worship
Jesuit School of Theology at Berkeley
1735 LeRoy Avenue
Berkeley CA 94709
(415) 841-8804

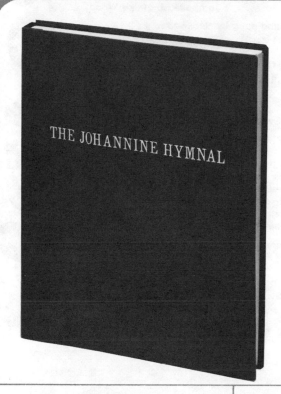

Gather 'Round

Songs for Celebration

Songs for Celebration

with melody line and guitar chords, and with keyboard and/or flute arrangements on selected compositions.

Edited by Paul F. Page

Announcing a collection of 88 liturgical compositions especially appropriate for congregational use.

More than a songbook, this work combines contemporary music from 28 composers with handy thematic and seasonal indexes, plus a music planning chart to further assist parish musicians.

Here is a most *usable* collection of liturgical music. From Advent through Pentecost, for Sunday liturgy or special thematic services, you will find *Gather 'Round* to consist of musically good, singable selections, in a variety of musical styles.

These 88 compositions, which appeared serially in the first thirteen issues of *Modern Liturgy* are now available in a handsome book with a practical "open flat" plastic binding.

Suggested arrangements and performance demonstrations of each composition are available in a set of seven inexpensive stereo recordings (cassettes or 8-track cartridge only). A complete listing of all available recordings is given on the next page.

Features:

- original-new-music
- proven from pages of MODERN LITURGY magazine.
- Demonstration recordings available at low cost.
- Clear, large, easy to read type.
- Cross indexes to facilitate planning for special liturgies.

Gather 'Round - Book ...... **$ 9.00**
Set of seven recordings **$29.25**

Send the order form to:
Resource Publications
PO Box 444
Saratoga, CA 95070

Index of Accompanying Stereo Recordings

The music in *Gather 'Round* is available on seven stereo recordings as shown below. The recordings are available in the form of cassettes or in the form of 8-track cartridges. The recordings have been prepared as an inexpensive teaching device to help groups and classes learn the music. (Set of 7 recordings: $29.25)

Recording 1111
Mass For The People
   Lord Have Mercy
   Response To First Reading
   Alleluia
   Holy Holy Holy
   Acclamation
   Great Amen
   Our Father
   Lamb of God
Psalm 150
Simple Gifts
Take Heart

Recording 1213
Show Forth The Glory
Joy Joy Joy
Miriam's Song
Peace
Evening Song
Holy Holy Holy
Come To The Water
Antiphons
Gather 'Round
Go Out To The Whole World
Psalm 103
Go Forth, People of God

Recording 1415
Memorial Acclamation
Alleluia
Give It Life
I In Them
This Is The Day
You Will Be My People
Be Like The Sun
Lord Have Mercy
Brotherhood
Our Father
As The Hills Are 'Round
   About Jerusalem
Every Day
As A Family

Recording 1617
Acclamation
Believe
Alleluia
Acclamation
Be Glad, Be Happy
Memorial Acclamation
Glory of Joy
Red Balloon
Give Thanks
God Dwells In The Hearts
God Is Love
Lord Have Mercy
Praise

Recording 1821
Quietly He Came
Prepare! The Lord Is Near
To The Living God
O Antiphons
Christmas Acclamation
From Despair To Hope
Many Times I Have Turned
Jesus Loves Me As I Am
Acclamation
Restore Us

Recording 2223
A Prayer For Eastertide
Blessed Be God
Everybody Sing Alleluia
Alleluia
Acclamation
Blessed Be The Name
   Of The Lord
You Have Put On Christ
Abba, Father
Each Man's Joy
How Good Is God
Psalm Tone I
Psalm Tone II
I've Got A Light
May The Roads Rise Up
The Truth Will Make
   You Free

Recording 2425
Song of Covenant
Blessing
Beatitudes
We Have All Been To The Water
What Great Marvels
Let Us All Rejoice
Sing A New Song
The Ballad of Paul
Come, My Friend
Green Growing Plants
God Did
Praise Him

Order Form

Enclosed is my check, money order, or authorized purchase order in the amount of $_____. Please rush the following items to the address below:

Quantity	Description	Amount
	Copies of Gather 'Round, plastic comb bound, at $9.00 each.	
	Set(s) of seven accompanying recordings at $29.25 for each set of seven. Specify: ☐ cassettes or ☐ 8-track cartridges.	
	Individual recordings at $4.50 each. Circle: 1111, 1213, 1415, 1617, 1821, 2223, 2425. Specify: ☐ cassettes or ☐ 8-track cartridge.	
	California residents add 6% state sales tax.	
	Uniform postage and handling: Book - $.75 One or more recordings - $.75 Both book and tapes - $1.20	
	Total Amount Due	

Name_____

Street_____

City/State/Zip_____

Gift of:_____
(gifts prepaid only - a card will be sent.)

Practical, Singable, Seasonal, Thematic

The music in Gather 'Round is especially useful for congregational participation. Most of the melodies can be handled by any congregation, and recordings are available to help teach the more difficult pieces. The hymn texts have been carefully reviewed for theological content by our noted liturgy editor, Rev. James L. Empereur, SJ, Ph.D.

This is new music: the fresh touch of contemporary song, submitted by twenty eight active composers from almost as many states.

Gather 'Round offers a large number of choices for every liturgical situation. There are thirty four pieces which can be effectively used for one or more of the liturgical seasons: Advent, Christmas, Lent, Easter, and Pentecost. Or, choose from indexed selections for Baptism, Confirmation, Reconciliation, and/or Marriage.

Several other songs can be used in structuring services on more general themes such as family prayer, faith, peace, praise, and thanksgiving. Included are twelve new songs specifically written for children's liturgy, plus settings of psalms, responses, acclamations, and other parts of the liturgy. To get a taste of fresh but fully tested music, fill in the order form and return it with your payment to:

Resource Publications, PO Box 444, Saratoga, CA 95070

Ideas for Planning

Listed below are unique source books. Each one deals with a specific liturgical theme. Each is filled with practical ideas, songs, visual arts, examples, and theological/historical background material to help you develop thematic services for worship. Surprise! They are published issues of MODERN LITURGY, available while they last for only $2.00 each. Write for a current list of available issues, or order from this list. To get your copies, xerox this page, mark the ones you wish, enclose your check for the total amount and send it to the address below.

_____ 1:1 Introduction/Christmas
_____ 1:2 Lent/Visual Ideas
_____ 1:4 Pentecost
_____ 1:5 Family Prayer
_____ 1:6 Planning Liturgy
_____ 1:8 Christmas
_____ 2:1 Reconciliation
_____ 2:2 Easter
_____ 2:3 Prayer
_____ 2:4 Wedding Liturgy
_____ 2:5 Liturgical Drama
_____ 2:6 School and CCD Liturgy
_____ 2:7 Death and Funerals
_____ 2:8 Sexism in Liturgy
_____ 3:1 Bicentennial Liturgy
_____ 3:2 Good Friday
_____ 3:3 Initiation Liturgy
_____ 3:4 Jewish Roots of Worship
_____ 3:5 The Environment for Worship
_____ 3:6 Music Ministry
_____ 3:7 Liturgy and Culture
_____ 3:8 Storytelling in Liturgy

MODERN LITURGY
P.O. Box 444
Saratoga, CA 95070

PICTURE THE DAWNING

songs of hope for prayer and reflection
by Paul F. Page

Here is a truly varied collection of original music, which stands as an integrated work of art, reflecting in music and in symbol the great mysteries of life. Taken individually, the songs are appropriate for use in worship or for listening and reflection. Their colorful arrangements and instrumentation make them especially useful as mood setting music.

Picture The Dawning — Stereo LP Album ($7.00)
Picture the Dawning (4:18)
Come, Lord (4:05)
Peace (2:20)
Spread Your Love (2:55)
Let Me, Lord (2:38)
Sometimes, O Lord (4:10)
Remember us (2:02)
My Peace, My Joy, My Love (2:37)
Sing Praise (2:43)
Be Strong For Me (4:31)
Offering (2:14)
Reproaches (3:16)
King Of Love (2:03)

Picture The Dawning — Songbook ($4.95)
With complete melody, guitar chords, full keyboard accompaniment, plus optional arrangements and part scores for flute, cello, bass, clarinet, and trumpet.

"What a pleasure to listen to a recording which expresses simple, warm, loving, and sensitive feelings toward the Lord and His People. The lyrics are sincere, easy to understand, and are very inspiring. All the selections would be appropriate for church and religious occasions, and I feel some of the numbers would appeal to every vocal group."

Vicki Wyant
Music Director
Saratoga Music and Fine Arts Center
Saratoga, California

"Picture The Dawning presents imaginative creativity at the service of the Gospel, stating the familiar themes in a fresh way, for listening and reflecting. Paul Page's characteristic lilting piano accompaniments are a rippling-stream undercurrent that gives sparkling life and movement to these fine pieces. His sensitive singing endows the words with a conviction that sets one thinking. . ."

Rev. John H. Olivier, SS
Pastor/Music Director
St. Peter's Parish
Pacifica, California

Other good things
from
Resource Publications

For prices, further information, or a free descriptive brochure on these resource aids, write: Resource Publications, P.O.Box 444, Saratoga, CA 95070.

MODERN LITURGY magazine is a practical and creative resource journal for anyone involved with worship. This magazine covers all the liturgical arts and presents concrete examples of songs, poems, and visual art forms in every issue. Other content includes articles and features which give theological, historical, and practical educational background on themes from the field of liturgy.

Now MODERN LITURGY offers four different subscription plans, to meet the needs of the individuals, parishes, prayer communities, planning committees, and other groups which form its readership.

Full Community. This subscription provides maximum resources for your liturgy program. It includes one year (eight issues) of MODERN LITURGY, four accompanying stereo cassette recordings, and an annual license to print, perform, and otherwise use the good music, arts, and example services from each issue (and all previous issues) in your parish or prayer community.

Community. A community subscription includes eight issues of MODERN LITURGY and an annual license to print, perform, and otherwise use the good music, arts, and example services from each issue (and all previous issues) in your parish or prayer community.

Full Individual. This subscription plan includes eight issues of MODERN LITURGY and four accompanying stereo cassette recordings of the original music carried in each issue. For people on the move, these recordings can shorten the time required to learn or evaluate each piece.

Individual. This is a conventional subscription which brings eight issues of MODERN LITURGY to your residential address. If your parish has a community subscription, and you wish your own set of copies, this is for you.

THEMATIC IDEA BOOKS on a growing number of topics in liturgy. The ideas, songs, visual arts, and informative articles can help in planning liturgies for special occasions. These are published issues of MODERN LITURGY which focus on a specific liturgical theme.

CASSETTE RECORDINGS of contemporary original music for worship. These recordings provide a continuous supply of fresh musical ideas for a wide variety of worship situations. They may be purchased separately, or they may be subscribed to in the form of a "full" subscription to MODERN LITURGY.

THE MODERN LITURGY HANDBOOK is a good reference and study guide for planners of worship. It is composed of articles edited from early issues of MODERN LITURGY, plus original material by Rev. James L. Empereur, SJ. This and other resources for worship are available through our MODERN LITURGY BOOKSTORE — a "shop by mail" resource service.

GATHER 'ROUND is a collection of eighty-eight contemporary songs for worship, edited by Paul F. Page. It includes the work of twenty-eight composers and provides fresh hymns for virtually all liturgical situations. You will want other sources of new music too, but *Gather 'Round* can make a solid contribution to your repertoire. Each song is demonstrated, with a suggested arrangement in an inexpensive set of seven accompanying recordings (optional).

PILGRIM'S ROAD: a collection of fresh music for worship. Some of these songs are reflective. Some are strictly liturgical. Several are appropriate for such milestones in life as baptisms, weddings, funerals, and eucharist. And yet in each one, the statement of deep faith made by the music brings a sense of joy to those who hear each song. Mike Wood's music gives us a sensitive interpretation of life in the 1970's which will reflect the faith and hope of every member of the family.

PICTURE THE DAWNING is an album of contemporary liturgical music by Paul F. Page. The album is a unified work of art, which revolves around the great mysteries of life. The mystery of creation, of a loving God, of the Passion, and the Resurrection are traced on one level. The cyclic wonder and mystery of human life is traced on another level. An accompanying songbook provides full keyboard accompaniment, as well as melody line, guitar chords, plus optional part scores for flute, clarinet, trumpet, cello, and bass.